1994

MW00714520

Mobil
Travel
Guide®

California and the West

Arizona

California

Nevada

Utah

Prentice Hall Travel

This series of regional guides is published by Prentice Hall Travel in collaboration with Mobil Corporation, which has sponsored the books since 1958. The aim of the *Mobil Travel Guide* is to provide the most comprehensive, up-to-date, and useful regional guides at the lowest possible price. All properties listed are inspected by trained, experienced field representatives. There is no charge to any establishment for inclusion in these guides, and only establishments that meet *Mobil Travel Guide* criteria are listed.

Every effort has been made to select a variety of all types of lodging and dining establishments available in a given locale. However, space limitations make it impossible to include every fine establishment, and the fact that some omissions occur does not imply adverse criticism or inferiority to listed establishments.

Information in the *Mobil Travel Guide* is revised and updated yearly. Ratings are reviewed annually on the basis of reports from our field representatives, opinions of many local and regional consultants and careful analysis of all available relevant material, including more than 100,000 opinions from users of the *Mobil Travel Guide*. All ratings are impartial and every effort is made to rate fairly and consistently.

At the time of inspection, all establishments were clean, well-managed and met *Mobil Travel Guide* standards. Occasionally an establishment may go out of business or change ownership after date of publication. By calling ahead readers can avoid the disappointment of a closed or changed establishment.

By revising our listings yearly, we hope to make a contribution to maintaining and raising the standards of restaurants and accommodations available to travelers across the country. We are most interested in hearing from our readers about their experiences at the establishments we list, as well as any other comments about the quality and usefulness of *Mobil Travel Guide*. Every communication from our readers is carefully studied with the object of making the *Mobil Travel Guide* better. Please address suggestions or comments about attractions, accommodations, or restaurants to *Mobil Travel Guide*, Prentice Hall Travel, 108 Wilmot Road, Suite 450, Deerfield, IL 60015.

THE EDITORS

Guide Staff

Managing Director and Editor-in-Chief
Alice M. Wisel

Editorial Manager
Janet Y. Arthur

Inspection Manager
Denni Hosch

Production Coordinator
Diane E. Connolly

Staff Assistant
Margaret Bolton

Editors

Thomas Grant   Ann Mendes   Peter Uremovic
Michael Warnecke

Acknowledgements

We gratefully acknowledge the help of our 100 field representatives for their efficient and perceptive inspection of every hotel, motel, motor hotel, inn, resort and restaurant listed; the proprietors of these establishments for their cooperation in showing their facilities and providing information about them; our many friends and users of previous editions of *Mobil Travel Guide;* and the thousands of Chambers of Commerce, Convention and Visitors' Bureaus, city, state and provincial tourism offices and government agencies for their time and information.

Mobil

Published in 1994 by Prentice Hall General Reference and Travel A Division of Simon & Schuster Inc.
15 Columbus Circle
New York, NY 10023

ISBN 0-671-874497
ISSN 0076-9843

Manufactured in the United States of America
10 9 8 7 6 5 4 3 2 1

MAP SYMBOLS

ROAD CLASSIFICATIONS

CONTROLLED ACCESS HIGHWAYS (Entrance and Exit only at Interchanges)	Interchanges
TOLL HIGHWAYS	
OTHER DIVIDED HIGHWAYS	
PRINCIPAL THROUGH HIGHWAYS	Paved Gravel
OTHER THROUGH HIGHWAYS	Paved Gravel Dirt
CONNECTING HIGHWAYS	Paved Gravel Dirt

HIGHWAY MARKERS

INTERSTATE (80)   UNITED STATES (40)   STATE AND PROVINCIAL (34)
TRANS-CANADA (1)   QUEBEC AUTOROUTE (15)   MEXICO FEDERAL (2)

SPECIAL SYMBOLS

STATE AND PROVINCIAL PARKS
With Campsites ▲   Without Campsites ◇

RECREATION AREAS
With Campsites ▲   Without Campsites △

POINTS OF INTEREST ■

SCHEDULED AIRLINE STOPS ✈

MILITARY AIRPORTS ✈

PORTS OF ENTRY ∗
Open 24 Hours ⍟   Inquire Locally ⍟

MILEAGES

TIME ZONE BOUNDARIES ·······

MOUNTAIN PASSES
Usually closed in Winter)(
Usually open in Winter)(

SPECIAL FEATURES

NATIONAL PARKS, MONUMENTS AND RECREATION AREAS

NATIONAL FORESTS

INDIAN RESERVATIONS

MILITARY RESERVATIONS

POPULATION SYMBOLS

◉ Capital Cities   ⊙ 10,000 to 25,000   ▢ 100,000 to 500,000
○ Under 5,000   ⊙ 25,000 to 50,000
⊙ 5,000 to 10,000   ⊙ 50,000 to 100,000   ▣ 500,000 and over

*All persons (American citizens and aliens) are required under penalty of law to report for customs inspection when entering the United States. All persons departing from the United States are advised to contact customs officials regarding re-entry.

Contents

California and the West

Introduction

Maps

A map of each state covered in this volume precedes the introduction. Larger, more detailed maps are available in the *Mobil Road Atlas* in bookstores and at many Mobil service stations.

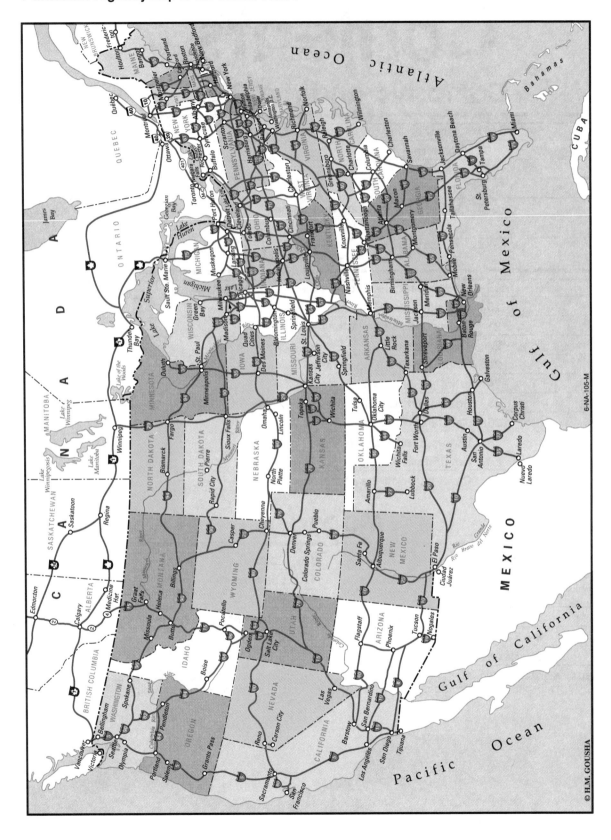

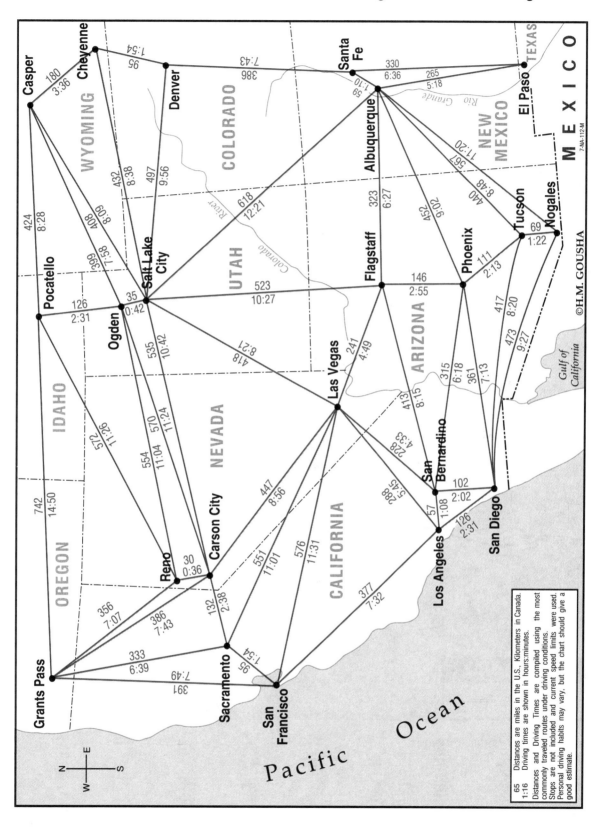

7-NA-112-M

65
1:16
Distances are miles in the U.S., Kilometers in Canada.
Driving times are shown in hours:minutes.

Distances and Driving Times are compiled using the most commonly traveled routes under driving conditions. Stops are not included and current speed limits were used. Personal driving habits may vary, but the chart should give a good estimate.

ARIZONA

MILES 0 10 20 30 50 70
KILOMETERS 0 10 30 50 70 113

© H.M. GOUSHA

M 12-UH-1081-5

PHOENIX AND VICINITY

MILES
KILOMETERS

N
W—E
S

FORT MC DOWELL INDIAN RESERVATION

MC DOWELL MOUNTAINS

SALT RIVER INDIAN RESERVATION

SCOTTSDALE

TOWN OF PARADISE VALLEY

PHOENIX MOUNTAIN PRESERVE

PHOENIX

GLENDALE

PEORIA

EL MIRAGE

Youngtown

AVONDALE

Tolleson

MESA

TEMPE

GUADALUPE

GILBERT

PHOENIX SOUTH MOUNTAIN PARK

GILA RIVER INDIAN RESERVATION

© H.M. GOUSHA

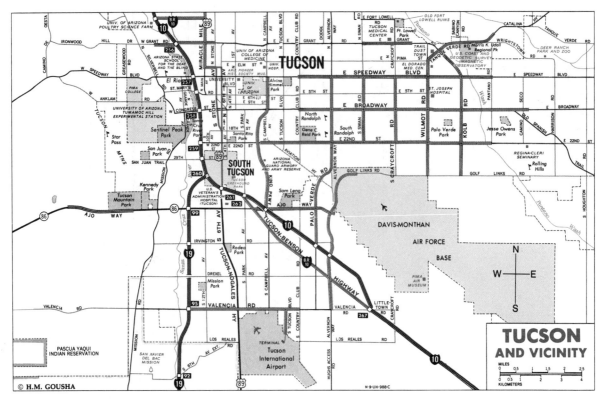

TUCSON
AND VICINITY

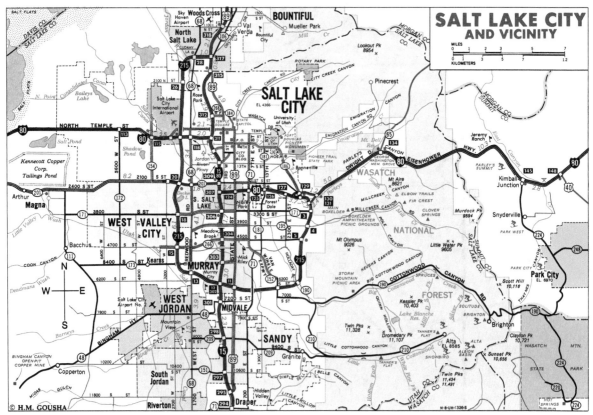

SALT LAKE CITY
AND VICINITY

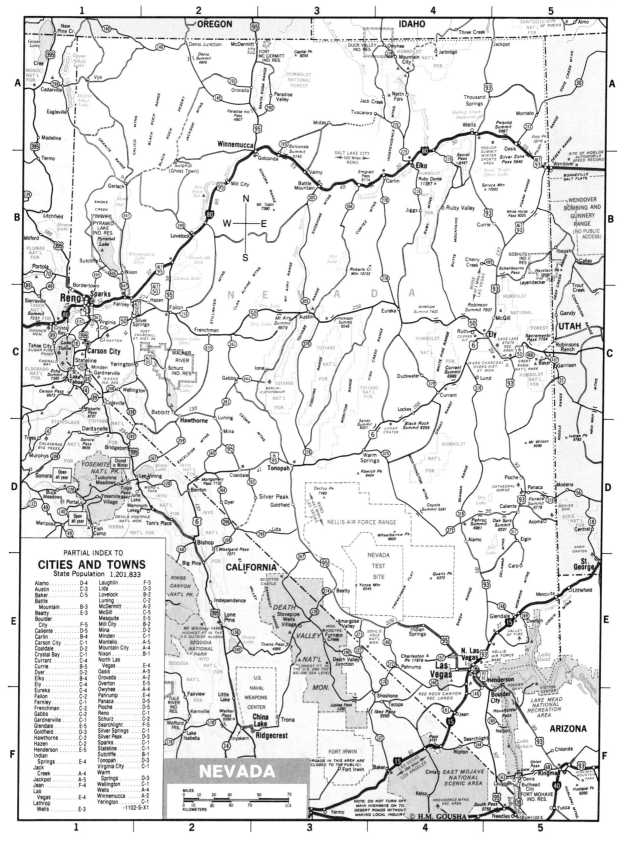

NEVADA

MILES
0 10 20 30   50   70
0 10   30   50   113
KILOMETERS

NOTE: DO NOT TURN OFF
MAIN HIGHWAYS ON TO
DESERT ROADS WITHOUT
MAKING LOCAL INQUIRY.

© H.M. GOUSHA

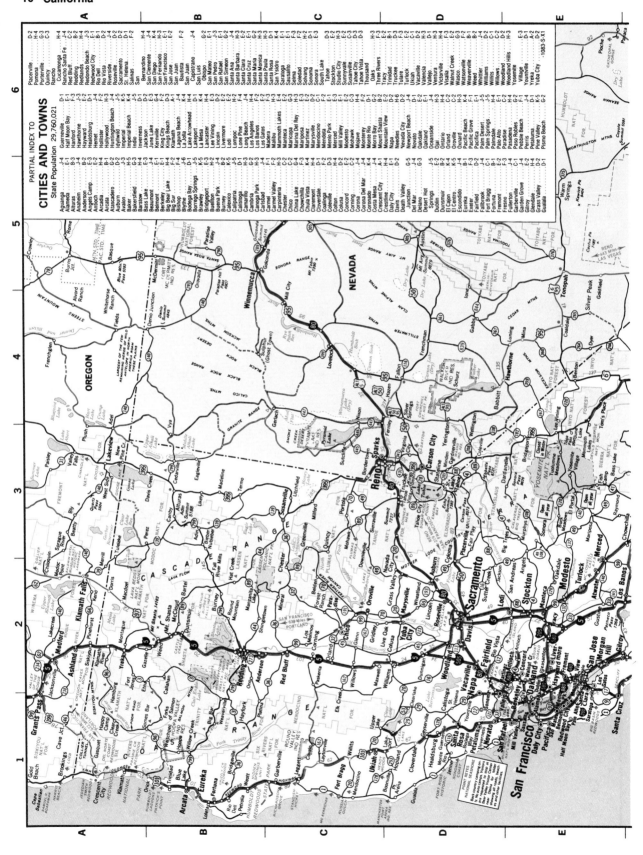

CALIFORNIA

PACIFIC OCEAN

MEXICO

ARIZONA

SONORA

BAJA CALIF

© H.M. GOUSHA

MILES
KILOMETERS

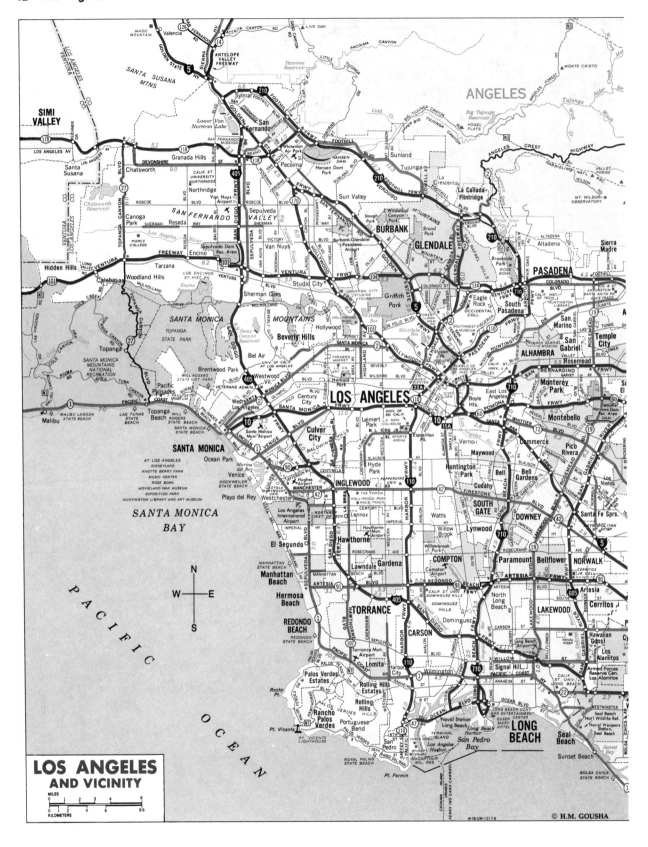

LOS ANGELES
AND VICINITY

MILES
0 1 2 3 4 5 6
KILOMETERS
0 2 4 6 8 9.6

© H.M. GOUSHA

M-12-UH-1217-5

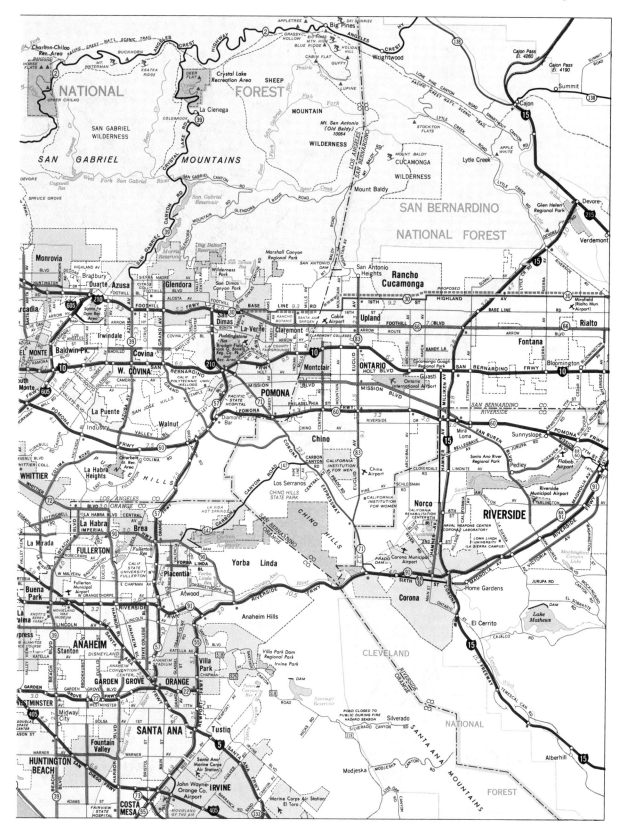

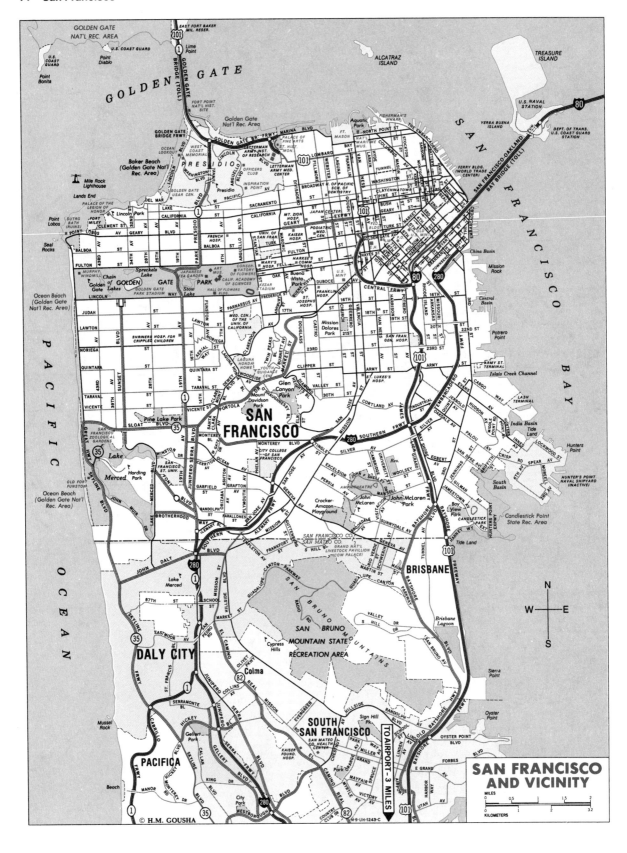

SAN FRANCISCO
AND VICINITY

© H.M. GOUSHA

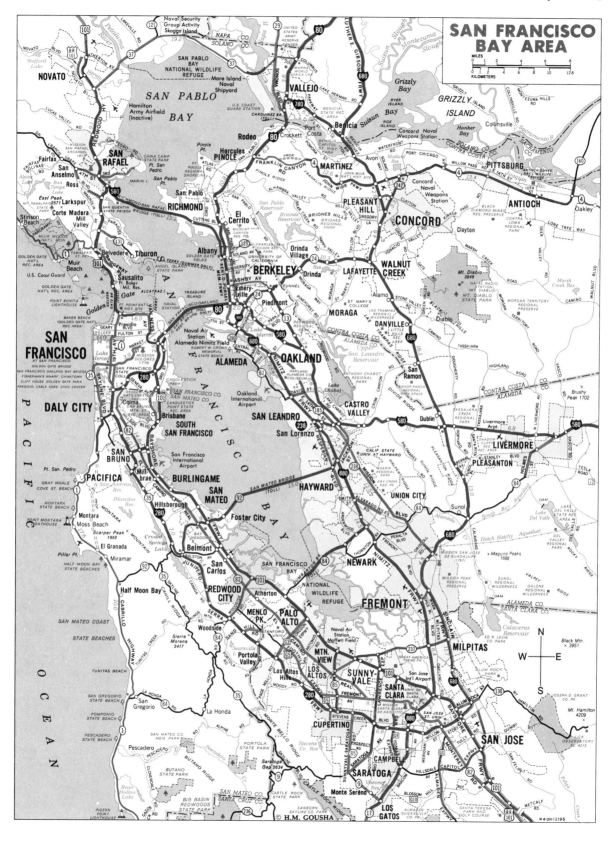

SAN FRANCISCO
BAY AREA

©H.M. GOUSHA

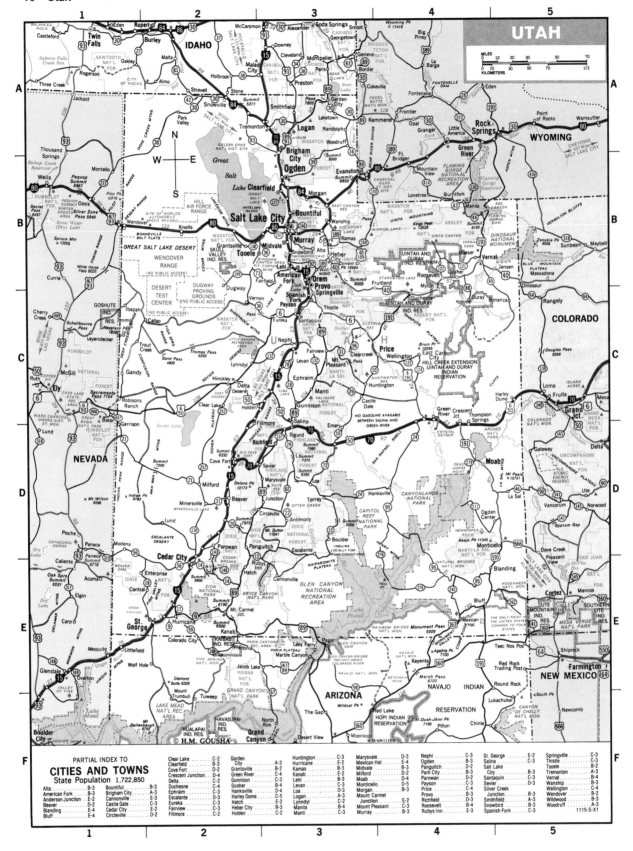

UTAH

© H.M. GOUSHA
1115-S-X1

YOU CAN HELP MAKE *MOBIL TRAVEL GUIDE* MORE ACCURATE AND USEFUL

ALL INFORMATION WILL BE KEPT CONFIDENTIAL

Your Name _____
(Please Print)

Street _____

City, State _____

Were Children with you on trip? ☐ Yes ☐ No

No. people in your party _____

Your occupation _____

1.

Establishment name _____

Hotel ☐   Resort ☐   Cafeteria ☐
Motel ☐   Inn ☐   Restaurant ☐

Street _____ City _____ State _____

Do you agree with our description? ☐ Yes ☐ No If not, give reason _____

Please give us your opinion of the following:

ROOM DECOR	CLEANLINESS	SERVICE	FOOD
☐ Excellent	☐ Spotless	☐ Excellent	☐ Excellent
☐ Good	☐ Clean	☐ Good	☐ Good
☐ Fair	☐ Unclean	☐ Fair	☐ Fair
☐ Poor	☐ Dirty	☐ Poor	☐ Poor

1994 *GUIDE* RATING _____ ★
CHECK YOUR SUGGESTED RATING BELOW:
☐ ★ good, satisfactory   ☐ ★★★★ outstanding
☐ ★★ very good   ☐ ★★★★★ one of best
☐ ★★★ excellent   in country
☐ ✓ unusually good value

Comments: _____

Date of visit _____   First visit ☐ Yes ☐ No

2.

Establishment name _____

Hotel ☐   Resort ☐   Cafeteria ☐
Motel ☐   Inn ☐   Restaurant ☐

Street _____ City _____ State _____

Do you agree with our description? ☐ Yes ☐ No If not, give reason _____

Please give us your opinion of the following:

ROOM DECOR	CLEANLINESS	SERVICE	FOOD
☐ Excellent	☐ Spotless	☐ Excellent	☐ Excellent
☐ Good	☐ Clean	☐ Good	☐ Good
☐ Fair	☐ Unclean	☐ Fair	☐ Fair
☐ Poor	☐ Dirty	☐ Poor	☐ Poor

1994 *GUIDE* RATING _____ ★
CHECK YOUR SUGGESTED RATING BELOW:
☐ ★ good, satisfactory   ☐ ★★★★ outstanding
☐ ★★ very good   ☐ ★★★★★ one of best
☐ ★★★ excellent   in country
☐ ✓ unusually good value

Comments: _____

Date of visit _____   First visit ☐ Yes ☐ No

1994 WHAT TO SEE AND DO—ATTRACTIONS/EVENTS

3.

Name of Attraction/Event _____

Listed in _____ Date of visit _____
     City   State

Do you agree with our description? _____ Yes _____ No

Please give your opinion of the attraction/event:

_____ Excellent _____ Good _____ Fair _____ Poor

Comments: _____

FOLD IN THIRDS AND TAPE (OR SEAL) FOR MAILING—DO NOT STAPLE

CUT ALONG DOTTED LINE

Revised editions are now being prepared for publication next year:

Northeastern States: Connecticut, Maine, Massachusetts, New Hampshire, New York, Rhode Island, Vermont, Eastern Canada.

Middle Atlantic States: Delaware, District of Columbia, Maryland, New Jersey, North Carolina, Pennsylvania, South Carolina, Virginia, West Virginia.

Southeastern States: Alabama, Florida, Georgia, Kentucky, Mississippi, Tennessee.

Great Lakes States: Illinois, Indiana, Michigan, Ohio, Wisconsin; Ontario, Canada.

Northwestern States: Idaho, Iowa, Minnesota, Montana, Nebraska, North Dakota, Oregon, South Dakota, Washington, Wyoming; Western Canada.

Southwestern States: Arkansas, Colorado, Kansas, Louisiana, Missouri, New Mexico, Oklahoma, Texas.

Frequent Travelers' Guide to Major Cities: Detailed coverage of 46 Major Cities, plus airport and street maps.

Mobil Travel Guides are available at Mobil Service Stations, bookstores, or by mail from Mobil Travel Guides, P.O. Box 493, Mt. Morris, IL 61054.

HOW CAN WE IMPROVE *MOBIL TRAVEL GUIDE?*

Mobil Travel Guide is constantly revising and improving. All attractions are updated and all listings are revised and evaluated annually. You can contribute to the accuracy and usefulness of the *Guide* by sending us your reactions to the places you have visited. Your suggestions for improvement of the *Guide* are also welcome. Just complete this prepaid mailing form or address letters to: *Mobil Travel Guide,* Prentice Hall Press, Suite 450, 108 Wilmot Road, Deerfield, IL 60015. The editors of the *Mobil Travel Guide* appreciate your useful comments.

Have you sent us one of these forms before?   ☐ Yes   ☐ No

Please make any general comment here. Thanks! _____

_____

_____

_____

Introduction

The *Mobil Travel Guide* offers complete travel planning information for recreational and business travelers alike. Whether you are planning an extended trip, getting away for the weekend or dining close to home, you will find the current detailed information you need to know in this *Guide*. By selecting and confirming your destination in advance and driving the most direct route, you can save time and money. Use your *Guide* to plan activities in advance so that when you arrive you won't waste valuable time deciding what to do.

An outstanding feature of the *Mobil Travel Guide* is its valuable quality ratings and information on more than 20,000 lodgings and restaurants. **There is no charge to an establishment for inclusion in *Mobil Travel Guide* publications.**

During the inspection of establishments, field representatives identify fire protection equipment in lodgings. The inspection does not extend to every room nor does it determine whether the equipment is working properly. The ⓢ symbol appearing at the end of a lodging listing indicates the presence of smoke detectors and/or sprinkler systems. This symbol does not appear in our restaurant listings because the presence of this equipment is assumed. Travelers wishing to gain more information on fire protection systems at properties should contact the establishment directly to verify the installation and working condition of their systems.

The Ⅾ symbol appearing at the end of a lodging or restaurant listing indicates compliance with the *Mobil Travel Guide* Disabled Criteria. Details on the standards required for a property to receive this symbol are given in the section entitled "Disabled Traveler Information" in this Introduction.

The *Mobil Travel Guide* Disabled Criteria are unique to our publication and were designed to meet the standards developed by our editorial staff. Please do not confuse them with the universal handicap symbol requirements. Travelers wishing to gain more information on facilities and services for the disabled should contact the establishments directly.

The 7 regional editions of the *Mobil Travel Guide* cover the 48 contiguous states and selected cities in 8 Canadian provinces. In each book the information is organized in the same easy-to-follow format. The states are arranged alphabetically and begin with a general introduction covering vital statistics, historical and geographical data, hunting, fishing, and seat belt regulations, visitor centers, and listings of state recreational areas, national forests, National Park Service Areas, interstate highways and ski areas (where applicable).

Cities are arranged alphabetically within each state. Next to city names are map coordinates, for example Boston (B-4), that refer to the appropriate color state map in the front of the *Guide*. Under the bold rule you will find population figures taken from the most recent census of the Bureau of Census, Department of Commerce. The text of larger cities also includes street maps and airport maps. Following city names are brief descriptions of the city, a "What To See and Do" section and listings of annual and seasonal events. Some 16,000 attractions and more than 5,500 events are highlighted. A mailing address and phone number for the local chamber of commerce or office of tourism is given whenever possible, as are cross-references, for example (See Havana, Petersburg), to nearby towns and cities with either additional things to see and do or with accommodations and/or restaurants. The Quality-Rated listings of lodgings and restaurants follow this information.

This Introduction section explains the features of the *Guide* in more detail and provides useful travel advice.

Discount Coupons

The *Mobil Travel Guide* is pleased to offer discounts from major companies for products and services. These coupons can be found at the back of this book.

The *Mobil Travel Guide* and Prentice Hall may not be held responsible for the failure of any participating company to honor these discounts.

Rating System

🐎 Pegasus, the Flying Red Horse, is a trademark of Mobil Oil Corporation. This symbol next to a town name indicates the presence of one or more Mobil service stations in the area.

The star symbols and check marks are used in rating hotels, motor hotels, lodges, motels, inns, resorts, and restaurants:

★	**Good, better than average**
★★	**Very good**
★★★	**Excellent**
★★★★	**Outstanding—worth a special trip**
★★★★★	**One of the best in the country**
✔	**In addition, an unusually good value, relatively inexpensive**

Listing Symbols

Ⅾ	Disabled facilities available
🐾	Pets allowed
🎣	Fishing on property
🐎	Horseback riding on premises

⛷ Snow skiing nearby

🏌 Golf, 9-hole minimum on premises or privileges within 10 miles

🎾 Tennis court(s) on premises or privileges within 5 miles

🏊 Swimming on premises

🏋 Exercise equipment or room on premises

🏃 Jogging on premises

✈ Airport access within 2 miles of premises

🚭 Nonsmoking rooms

🔥 Smoke detector and/or sprinkler system

SC Senior Citizen rates

Attraction Symbols

Each attraction has a fee code that translates as follows:

Free	=	no charge
¢	=	up to $2
¢¢	=	$2.01 to $5
¢¢¢	=	$5.01 to $10
¢¢¢¢	=	$10.01 to $15
¢¢¢¢¢	=	over $15

Credit Cards

The major credit cards honored by each establishment are indicated by initials at the end of the listing. When credit cards are not accepted, the listing will indicate this information. Please remember that Mobil Corporation credit cards cannot be used for payment of meals and room charges. Be sure the credit cards you plan to use in your travels are current and will not expire before your trip is over. If you should lose one, report the loss immediately

The following letters indicate credit cards that are accepted by the listed establishments:

A-American Express
C-Carte Blanche
D-Diners Club
DS-Discover
ER-En Route
MC-MasterCard
V-Visa
JCB-Japanese Credit Bureau

How to Read the Lodging & Restaurant Listings

Each listing of a motel, lodge, motor hotel, hotel, inn and resort gives the quality rating, name, address, directions (when there is no street address), phone number (local and 800), room rates, seasons open (if not year-round) and number and type of rooms available. Facsimile (FAX) numbers appear immediately following an establishment's phone number for properties offering this service to all of their guests. Major cities listings, lodgings and restaurants, include the neighborhood and/or directions from downtown as an aid to finding your way around the city. Maps showing these neighborhoods can be found immediately following the city map. Geographic descriptions of the neighborhoods are given under the "City Neighborhoods" heading, followed by a table of restaurants arranged by neighborhood, in alphabetical order. The listings also include information on recreational and dining facilities on or adjacent to the establishment and credit card information. Some hotels and motor hotels offer **LUXURY LEVELS,** and you will find specific information on these special accommodations within the listing.

Restaurant listings give the quality rating, name, address, directions (when there is no street address), phone number, hours and days of operation, price range for each meal served and cuisine specialties. Additionally, special features such as chef ownership, ambience, entertainment, and credit card information are noted.

When a listing is located in a town that does not have its own city heading, it will appear under the city nearest to its location. In these cases, the address and town appear in parenthesis immediately following the name of the establishment.

When looking for a specific establishment, use the index located at the back of this *Guide.* You will find the establishment name, city and state under which it is listed, as well as the page number.

The ✈ symbol at the end of a lodging listing indicates that the establishment is within two miles of access to a major, commercial airport. Listings located within 5 miles of major, commercial airports appear under the "Airport" heading, following the city listings.

The 🐾 symbol at the end of a lodging listing indicates pets allowed. Further information on restrictions and fees can be found in the listing or by contacting the lodging directly.

You will find that many lodgings and restaurants have a check mark (✔) before the quality rating. This denotes "an unusually good value, relatively inexpensive." The criteria for this designation are found in the section entitled "Explaining the Ratings," under the heading "Good Value Check Mark."

Mobil Travel Guide makes every effort to select a variety of lodging and dining establishments in a given locale. Occasionally, an establishment may go out of business or change ownership just after our publication deadline. By calling ahead for reservations you can avoid the disappointment of discovering a closed or changed establishment. Space limitations necessitate the omission of many fine places; however, no adverse criticism is implied or should be inferred.

Neither Prentice Hall nor Mobil Corporation can be held responsible for changes in prices, name, management or deterioration in services. There is no contractual agreement between management and the *Mobil Travel Guide* to guarantee prices or services. **There is no charge to an establishment for inclusion in *Mobil Travel Guide* publications.**

Motels and Lodges

Motels and lodges provide accommodations in low-rise structures with rooms easily accessible to parking areas. They have outdoor room entry and small, functional lobbies. Shops and businesses will be found only in the higher-rated properties.

Service is often limited and dining may not be offered in lower-rated motels and lodges. However, higher-rated properties will offer such services as bellmen, room service and restaurants serving three meals daily.

Lodges differ from motels primarily in their emphasis on outdoor recreational activities and in location. They are often found in resort and rural areas rather than major cities and along highways.

Motor Hotels

Motor hotels offer the convenience of motels as well as many of the services of hotels. They range from low-rise structures offering limited services to multi-storied buildings with a wide range of services and facilities. Dual building entry, elevators, inside hallways and parking areas near access doors are some of the features of a motor hotel.

Lobbies offer sitting areas, 24 hour desk and switchboard services. Often bellman and valet services are found in motor hotels as well as restaurants serving three meals a day. Expanded recreational facilities and more than one restaurant will be available in higher-rated properties. Because the following features and services apply to most establishments, they are not shown in the listing of motels and motor hotels:

- Year-round operation with a single rate structure
- European plan (meals not included in room rate)
- Bathroom with tub and/or shower in each room
- Air-conditioned/heated, often with individual room control
- Cots
- Daily maid service
- Free parking
- Phones in rooms
- Elevators

The distinction between motor hotels and hotels in metropolitan areas is minor.

Hotels

To be categorized as a hotel, the establishment must have most of the following facilities and services: multiple floors, a restaurant and/or coffee shop, elevators, room service, bellhops, valet services, spacious lobby and some recreational facilities.

A hotel offers its guests a broad spectrum of lodging experiences. Because the following features and services apply to most establishments, they are not shown in the listing:

- Year-round operation with a single rate structure
- European plan (meals not included in room rate)
- Bathroom with tub and/or shower in each room
- Air-conditioned/heated, often with individual room control
- Daily maid service
- Valet service (one-day laundry/cleaning service)
- Room service during hours restaurant is open
- Elevator
- Phones in rooms
- Bellhops
- Oversize beds available

LUXURY LEVEL: Many hotels offer their guests increased luxury accommodations on floors or towers that operate as a separate unit from the main establishment.

A boldface title, *LUXURY LEVEL(S)*, follows the principal hotel listing with information pertinent to that level. There is no separate rating for this listing; the rating given applies to the overall hotel.

The criteria used to determine the qualifications for this distinctive listing are:

1. A minimum of one entire floor of the total structure must be devoted to the luxury level.

2. Management must provide no less than three of these four services:

- Separate check-in and check-out services
- Concierge services
- Private lounge
- Private elevator service (key access)

Complimentary breakfast and snacks are commonly offered on these floors as well as upscale amenities and services.

Resorts

Resorts are establishments specializing in stays of three days or more. They usually offer American Plan and/or housekeeping accommodations, with an emphasis on recreational facilities, often providing the services of a social director.

Food services are of primary importance at a resort. Guests must be able to obtain three meals a day on the premises or be provided with grocery stores to enable them to obtain food for meal preparation without leaving the premises.

When horseback riding is indicated, phone ahead to inquire about English saddle availability; Western style is assumed.

Inns

Frequently thought of as a small hotel, an inn is a place of homelike comfort and warm hospitality. It is often a structure of historic significance, located in an equally interesting environmental setting.

Meals are at a special time at an inn, and frequently tea and sherry are served in the late afternoon. Rooms are usually individually decorated, featuring antiques or furnishings representative of the locale. Phones and bathrooms may not be available in every room.

Guest Ranches

Like resorts, guest ranches specialize in stays of three days or more. Guest ranches also offer meal plans and extensive outdoor activities such as horseback riding. Stables and trails exist on the ranch; daily, expert instruction is part of the program. Ranging from casual to rustic, many guest ranches are working ranches, and guests are encouraged to participate in various aspects of ranch life. Eating is often family style and may also include cookouts as part of morning, midday or evening trail rides. Phone ahead to inquire about English saddle availability; Western style is assumed.

Cottage Colonies

Cottage colonies are housekeeping cottages and cabins that are usually found in recreational areas. When dining or recreational facilities are available on the premises, you will find it noted in the listing.

Restaurants

Unless otherwise specified, restaurants listed:

- Are open daily, year-round
- Offer chiefly American cooking

An *a la carte* menu provides entree prices covering the main dish only. *Semi-a la carte* indicates vegetable, salad, soup, appetizer or other accompaniments to the main dish. *Table d'hôte* means a full meal for a stated price, with no *a la carte* selections available. *Prix fixe* indicates a fixed price for any meal on the menu.

Since restaurant listings include detailed information, by carefully reading the listing and comparing prices you can easily determine whether the restaurant is formal and elegant or informal and comfortable for families. When children's meals are offered you will find it noted in the listing.

Unrated Dining Spots

Chosen for their unique atmosphere, specialized menu and local flavor, restaurants listed under the Unrated Dining Spots category appear without a *Mobil Travel Guide* rating. However, they have been inspected by our team of field representatives and meet our high standards of cleanliness and maintenance.

These establishments feature a wide range of dining, from pizza, ice cream, sandwiches and health food to cafeterias and English tea service in fine hotels. They often offer extraordinary values, quick service and regional flavor and are worth a visit when traveling to a city offering these special listings.

Unrated Dining Spots can be found after restaurant listings in many cities.

Prices and Taxes

All prices quoted in *Mobil Travel Guide* publications are expected to be in effect at the time of publication and during the entire year; however, prices cannot be guaranteed.

In some localities there may be short-term price variations because of special events or holidays. Whenever possible, these price changes are noted. Certain resorts have complicated rate structures that vary with the time of year; it's a good idea to contact the management to confirm specific rates.

State and city sales taxes as well as special room taxes can bring your room rates up as high as 25% per day. We are unable to bring this specific information into the listings, but strongly urge that you ask about these taxes when placing reservations with establishments. Another charge that is often overlooked by travelers is that of telephone usage. Frequently, hotels charge a service fee for unanswered phone calls and credit card calls as well as long distance calls. It is advised that you read the information offered by the establishment before placing phone calls from your room. It is not unusual for a hotel to send bills for telephone calls to your home after you have checked out. Be certain to take the time to read your bill carefully before checking out. You will not be expected to pay for charges that were not explained in the printed matter given to you at the time of check-in. The use of public telephones in hotel lobbies should not be overlooked since the financial benefits may outweigh the inconvenience.

Explaining the Ratings

The *Mobil Travel Guide* has been rating motels, lodges, motor hotels, hotels, inns, resorts and restaurants since the first edition was published in 1958. For years it was the only guidebook to provide such ratings on a national basis, and *Mobil Travel Guide* remains one of the few guidebooks to rate restaurants across the country.

The rating categories, ★ through ★★★★★, apply nationally. The principal areas of evaluation are quality of physical structure, furnishings, maintenance, housekeeping, overall service and food service. Climate, historic, cultural and artistic variations representative of regional differences are major factors in each rating. No rating is ever final and, since each is subject to annual review, each establishment must continue to earn its rating and has a chance to improve it as well.

Every establishment listed in *Mobil Travel Guide* publications is inspected by experienced field representatives who submit detailed reports to the editorial offices. From these reports, the editors extract information for listings and acertain that establishments to be recommended are clean, well-maintained, well-managed and above average.

Ratings are based upon the inspection reports, written evaluations of staff members who stay and dine anonymously at establishments throughout the year, and an extensive review of guest comments received by the *Mobil Travel Guide*.

Every effort is made to assure that ratings are fair and accurate; the designated ratings are published to serve as an aid to travelers and should not be used for any other purpose.

A further rating designation exists and that is Unrated. When major changes have occurred during the one-year period prior to publication, there will be no star rating. These changes may be in management, ownership, general manager and master chef. If an establishment is undergoing major renovation/refurbishment or has been in operation less than one year, it will also appear unrated. The decision to list an establishment "unrated" is the responsibility of the Rating Committee.

The rating for each establishment—motel, lodge, motor hotel, hotel, inn, resort, guest ranch, or restaurant—is measured against others of the same type. The criteria for rating accommodations are related to the number and quality of facilities, guest services, luxury of appointments and attitude and professionalism of staff and management. Restaurant evaluations emphasize quality of food, preparation, presentation, freshness of ingredients, quality of service, attitude and professionalism of staff/management. Because each type of establishment is viewed also in terms of its own style, unique characteristics, decor and ambience, these additional qualities are also considered in determining a rating.

Good Value Check Mark

The check mark (✔) designation appearing in front of the star rating of an establishment listing indicates "an unusually good value, relatively inexpensive." It will appear with the listing in the following manner:

✔★PRENTICE MOTOR INN

Lodging establishments rated with a good value check mark have been determined to be clean and well-maintained, offering some appointments such as room phones, free television, pools and breakfast on or adjacent to the premises, at economical prices. Restaurant establishments rated with a good value check mark have been determined to be clean and well-maintained, offering good food at economical prices.

Due to the fact that prevailing rates vary regionally, we are able to be more selective in our good value rated establishments in some areas than in others. However, you will find a wide range of these properties to visit in all locales.

In major cities and resort areas prices tend to be higher than in outlying areas, therefore the criteria for the good value check mark have two distinct variations. The following price range has been used to determine those properties awarded the good value check mark:

Major City and Resort Area Listings

Lodging—single, average $75-$85 per night
         double, average $85-$100 per night

Restaurants—lunch, average $17, complete meal
        dinner, exclusive of beverages and gratuities, average $25, complete meal

Local Area Listing

Lodging—single, average $45-$50 per night
        double, average $55-$65 per night

Restaurants—lunch, average $9, complete meal
        dinner, exclusive of beverages and gratuities, average $17, complete meal

Terms and Abbreviations

The following terms and abbreviations are used consistently throughout the listings.

AP Indicates American plan (lodging plus all meals)

Bar Liquor, wine and beer are served at a bar or in a cocktail lounge and usually with meals unless otherwise indicated (e.g., "wine, beer")

Ck-in; ck-out Check-in time; check-out time

Coin lndry Self-service laundry

Complete meal Indicates soup and/or salad, entree, dessert and non-alcoholic beverage

Continental bkfst Usually coffee and a roll or doughnut

Cover "Cover" is a sum in addition to the actual cost of food and drink in restaurants

D Followed by a price; indicates room rate for two persons in one room (one or two beds; charge may be higher if two double beds are offered)

Each addl Extra charge for each additional person beyond the stated number of persons for a given price

Early In referring to season openings or closings, approximately the first third of a month (May 1 to May 10); check with management for exact date

Early-bird dinner A meal served at specified hours, at a reduced price

EP Indicates European plan (lodging only)

Exc Except

Exercise equipt Two or more pieces of exercise equipment on the premises

Exercise rm When an instructor is on the premises, this term is used to indicate both exercise equipment and room

FAX Facsimile machines available to all guests

Golf privileges Privileges at a course within 10 miles

Hols Holidays

In-rm movies Video cassette player available for use with video tapes

Kit. or kits. A kitchen or kitchenette with stove or microwave, sink, and refrigerator that is either part of the room or a separate room. If the kitchen is not fully equipped, the listing will indicate "no equipt" or "some equipt"

Late In referring to season openings or closings, approximately the last third of a month (May 21 to May 31); check with management for exact date

MAP Indicates modified American plan (lodging plus two meals)

Mid In referring to season openings or closings, approximately the middle third of a month (May 11 to May 20); check with management for exact date

No elvtr In a hotel with more than two stories, it is assumed there is an elevator, so it is not noted; only its absence is noted

No phones Only the absence of phones is noted

Parking Indicates that there is a parking lot on the premises

Private club A cocktail lounge or bar available to members and their guests (in Motels and Hotels where these clubs exist, registered guests can usually use the club as guests of the management; frequently the same is true of restaurants)

Prix fixe A full meal for a stated price; usually one price quoted

Res Reservations

S Followed by a price; indicates room rate for one person

Serv bar Where drinks are prepared for dining patrons only

Serv charge Service charge is the amount added to restaurant check in lieu of tip

Snow skiing downhill/x-country Downhill and/or cross-country skiing within 20 miles of property

Table d'hôte A full meal for a stated price dependent upon entree selection

Tennis privileges Privileges at tennis courts within 5 miles

TV Indicates color television; B/W indicates black-and-white television

Under 18 free Children under a specific age not charged if staying in room with one or both parents

Valet parking Indicates that an attendant is available to park and retrieve a car

Disabled Traveler Information

The *Mobil Travel Guide* disabled symbol ⬛D shown in accommodations and restaurants is intended to serve travelers with limited handicaps, temporary impairments or the semi-ambulatory. In attractions, facilities providing for the needs of the disabled are noted in the description of the attraction.

The *Mobil Travel Guide* Disabled Criteria are unique to our publication and were designed to meet the standards developed by our editorial staff. Please do not confuse them with the universal handicap symbol requirements. Travelers wishing to gain more information on facilities and services for the disabled should contact the establishments directly.

When the ⬛D symbol appears following a listing, the establishment is equipped with facilities to accommodate persons in wheelchairs, on crutches or the aged in need of easy access to doorways and restroom facilities. Severely handicapped persons, as well as the hearing and visually impaired, should not assume establishments bearing our symbol will offer facilities to meet their needs. We suggest these persons phone an establishment before their visit to ascertain if their particular needs will be met.

The following facilities must be available at all lodging properties bearing our disabled symbol:

Public Areas

- Handicapped parking near access ramps
- Ramps at entryways to buildings
- Swinging entryway doors minimum 3'-0"
- Restrooms on main level with room to operate a wheelchair; handrails at commode areas
- Elevators equipped with grab bars; lowered control buttons
- Restaurants, easy-access doorways; restrooms with room to operate wheelchair; handrails at commode areas

Rooms

- Minimum 3'-0" width entryway to rooms
- Low-pile carpet
- Telephone at bedside and in bathroom
- Bed placed at wheelchair height
- Minimum 3'-0" width doorway to bathroom
- Bath, open sink—no cabinet; room to operate wheelchair
- Handrails at commode areas; tub handrails
- "Peep" hole in room entry door, wheelchair accessible
- Closet rods and shelves, wheelchair accessible

Restaurants

The following facilities must be available at all free-standing restaurants bearing our disabled symbol:

- Handicapped parking beside access ramps
- Ramps at entryways to building (front entry)
- Tables to accommodate wheelchairs
- Main-floor restrooms; minimum 3'-0" width entryway
- Restrooms with room to operate wheelchair; handrails at commode areas

Tips for Travel

The passage of the Americans with Disabilities Act (ADA) of 1990 means that all hotels and motels in the US have to make their facilities and services accessible to all guests. Although this law went into effect early in 1992, it will take some time for the more than 40,000 hotels and motels to implement the renovation programs to make their facilities totally accessible to every guest.

Any facility opened after January 26, 1993, must be designed and built totally in accordance with ADA Accessibility Guidelines. This means that a certain percentage of the rooms must be accessible to guests who have mobility, vision, hearing or speech impairments. In addition, all public spaces must be accessible to all guests to use and enjoy.

While all existing hotels and motels will not be totally accessible, you can expect all properties to be aware of the

ADA and to make efforts to accommodate the special needs of any guest who has a physical disability.

To get the kind of service you need and have a right to expect, do not hesitate when making a reservation to:

- ask about the availability of accessbile rooms, parking, entrance, restaurant, lounge or any other facilities that are important to you.
- inquire about any special accommodations, transportation, hearing impaired equipment or services you may need.
- ask about the accessibility of the room. For example, do both the room entry and bathroom doors have 32″ of clear width? Is there a 5′ diameter turning space in the bedroom and bathroom?

When your stay is over, fill out the guest comment card and let the management know about the facilities, equipment and services that worked for you and those that need to be improved.

Additional Publications

The most complete listing of published material on traveling with disabilities is readily available from *The Disability Bookshop,* Twin Peaks Press, PO Box 129, Vancouver, Washington 98666; phone 206/694-2462 or 800/638-2256.

Access America Series, an Atlas & Guide to the National Parks for Visitors with Disabilities is published by Northern Cartographic, Inc., PO Box 133, Burlington, Vermont 05402, $8.95, and is subdivided into regional publications. Contact *The Disability Bookshop* for current regional titles and costs. A smaller, but still comprehensive, guidebook to the national parks is a 1992 publication, *Easy Access to National Parks: the Sierra Club Guide for People with Disabilities;* Sierra Club, distributed by Random, May 1992, $16 (paperback). Local public libraries should have relevant books on travel for people with disabilities. Individuals should contact the reference librarian at their public library for assistance.

The Reference Section of the National Library Service for the Blind and Physically Handicapped (NLS), Library of Congress, provides information and resources on blindness and physical disabilities, as well as information about the NLS talking-book program. For further information contact: Reference Section, National Library Service for the Blind and Physically Handicapped, Library of Congress, Washington, DC 20542; phone 202/707-9275 or 202/707-5100.

Travel Tips

Lodging

Many hotels in major metropolitan areas have special weekend package plans. These plans offer considerable savings on rooms and often include breakfast, cocktails and some meal discounts as well. Information on specific pricing for these specials is not available because prices change frequently throughout the year. We suggest you phone to obtain such information prior to your trip.

LUXURY LEVEL accommodations, which appear within some hotel and motor hotel listings, frequently offer a good value because many of them provide breakfast, cocktails, newspapers and upgraded amenities which are included in the price of the room.

Dining

Reservations are important at most major city restaurants. Many restaurants will ask you to confirm your reservation by calling back the day you are to dine. Should you fail to do so, your reservation will not be held for you.

In fine restaurants the pace is leisurely, the service is very professional and the prices are above average. Most of the dishes are cooked to order, and patrons' requests for special preparation are handled graciously.

Four-Star and Five-Star establishments are usually quite expensive because they offer higher food quality, superior service and distinctive decor. Read the listing and see if they are open for lunch. While the lunch prices are considerably higher than those at other restaurants, you may still enjoy the ambience, service and cuisine of a famous establishment for about half the cost of a dinner.

''Early bird'' dinners are popular in many parts of the country, and they offer considerable savings on dinner prices. Information on the availability of these dinners has been given to us by restaurant management, but we suggest you phone ahead and ask if they still offer this special plan.

Tipping

Lodgings: Doormen in major city hotels are usually given $1 for getting you into a cab. Bellmen expect $1 per bag, but never less than a $2 tip if you have only one bag. Concierges are tipped according to the service they perform. Suggestions on sightseeing or restaurants, as well as making reservations for dining, are standard services often requiring no tip. However, when reservations are obtained at restaurants known to be difficult to get into, a gratuity of $5 should be considered. If theater or sporting event tickets are obtained, a tip is expected, often $5 to $10. Maids, often overlooked by guests, may be tipped $1 to $2 per each day of your stay.

Restaurants: Coffee shop and counter service wait staff are usually given 8 to 10 percent of the bill. In full service restaurants, 15 percent of the bill, before sales tax, is suggested. In fine dining restaurants, where the staff is large and share the gratuity, 18 to 20 percent is recommended. The number of restaurants adding service charges to the bill is increasing. Carefully review your bill to make certain an automatic gratuity was not charged.

Airports: Curbside luggage handlers expect $1 per bag. Car rental shuttle drivers who help with your luggage appreciate a $1 or $2 tip. **Remember, tipping is an expression of**

appreciation for good service. **You need not tip if service is poor—tipping is discretionary.**

10 Tips for Worry-Free Travel

1. Be sure to notify local police and leave a phone number where you can be contacted in case of emergency.

2. Lock doors and windows, but leave shades up and lights on (or on an automatic timer).

3. Stop newspaper deliveries and discontinue garbage pickups.

4. Remove food and defrost refrigerator; store valuables in a safe place; disconnect electrical appliances; turn off gas jets, including hot water heater; turn off water faucets and drain pipes in severe weather.

5. Remember to pack personal medicines and duplicate prescriptions; spare eyeglasses or the prescription; sunglasses; suntan lotion; First Aid kit; insect spray; towels and tissues; writing materials.

6. Make sure that proof of car insurance is in your glove compartment; also take along your driver's license and those of other passengers (check expiration dates); car registration; copies of birth certificates (if driving outside U.S.); traveler's checks. Be sure you have a duplicate set of car keys.

7. Check to see that you have a jack, spare tire, repair kit, emergency tools, flashlights, tire chains, spare fan belt, windshield scraper, auto fuses, lug wrench and work gloves. A pre-trip tune-up won't hurt—and, of course, be sure to "fill up" before you start out.

8. Also check vehicle's battery, oil and air filters, cooling system, brakes and lights.

9. Remember "extras" like hunting/fishing licenses and equipment; camera and film; bathing suits, beach accessories, sports equipment; portable radio and/or TV; picnic accessories.

10. Buckle up your seat belt, and have a nice trip!

Maps and Map Coordinates

There is a map of each state and selected cities in the front of the *Mobil Travel Guide*. As you read through the *Guide*, you will find a map coordinate following each town heading. There is a corresponding coordinate on the appropriate state map.

Street and airport maps are included in the text of selected larger cities.

What To See and Do

This section appears at the beginning of each city and town listing and provides concise descriptions of notable attractions

in the area—museums, art galleries, amusement parks, universities, historic sites and houses, plantations, churches, state parks, ski areas and so on. Municipal parks, tennis courts, swimming pools, golf courses, and small educational institutions are generally excluded, since these are common to most towns. *Mobil Travel Guide* editors strive for a balance of recreational, athletic, cultural, historical and educational interests.

Every effort has been made to ensure that the information in this publication was accurate at the time it was printed. Neither Prentice Hall nor Mobil Corporation can be held responsible for changes that occurred after publication. We regret any inconvenience you may incur due to improper information being listed.

Following the name of the attraction is the street address or location. Directions are given from the center of the town under which the attraction is listed; please note that this may not be the town in which the attraction is located. For instance, directions for an attraction listed under Springfield may state "225 W Hawthorne, 12 mi N off US 42 in Zionsville." Area codes are not provided for each attraction if the code is the same as that shown in the city statistics. Similarly, zip codes are given only if they differ from the one listed in the city statistics. Next comes a brief description of the attraction, the months and days it is open, handicapped facilities (if any) and phone number. Each attraction has a fee code that translates as follows:

Free	=	no charge
¢	=	up to $2
¢¢	=	$2.01 to $5
¢¢¢	=	$5.01 to $10
¢¢¢¢	=	$10.01 to $15
¢¢¢¢¢	=	over $15

Events

Immediately following the "What To See and Do" section is the name, address and phone number of the local chamber of commerce or tourist bureau you may contact for further information. Following this are listings of annual, seasonal, and special events. An annual event is one that is held every year for a period of usually no longer than a week to 10 days. A seasonal event is one that may or may not be annual and that is held for a number of weeks or months in the year, such as horse racing, summer theater, concert or opera seasons, professional sports. Special event listings occur infrequently and mark a certain date or event, such as a centennial or commemorative celebration.

Additional Visitor Information

For larger cities, this is where you will find the chamber of commerce name, address and phone number. In addition, you are given the names of magazines or guides to the city, location of visitor centers, information on public transportation, and other helpful information.

Special Travel Features

Federal Recreation Areas

While many national parks and recreation areas may be entered and used free of charge, others require an entrance fee (ranging from $1 to $4/person to $3 to $10/carload) and/or a "use fee" for special services and facilities. Those travelers who plan to make several visits to federal recreation areas will be dollars ahead if they investigate several money-saving programs coordinated by the National Park Service, US Department of the Interior.

Park Pass. An annual entrance permit to a specific park, monument, historic site or recreation area in the National Park System that charges entrance fees, the Park Pass costs $10 or $15, depending upon the area, and is neither refundable nor transferable.

The Pass admits the permit holder and any accompanying passengers in a private noncommercial vehicle or, in the case of walk-in facilities, the holder's spouse, children and parents. It is valid for entrance fees only and does not cover use fees, such as those for cave tours, camping or parking.

A Park Pass may be purchased in person or by mail from the National Park Sevice unit at which the pass will be honored.

Golden Eagle Passport. Issued to persons 17 to 61 years of age is good for one calendar year and costs $25. The Golden Eagle Passport entitles the purchaser and up to 6 people accompanying him or her in a private noncommercial vehicle to enter any federal outdoor recreation area that charges an entrance fee. These include national parks, monuments, historic and memorial parks and seashores. The passport will also admit the purchaser and family to most walk-in admission fee areas such as historical houses, buildings and museums in federal areas. However, it does not cover "use fees," such as fees for camping, boat-launching equipment, parking, or cave tours.

The Golden Eagle Passport may be purchased in person or by mail from: the National Park Service, Office of Public Inquiries, Room 1013, US Department of the Interior, 18th and C Streets NW, Washington, DC 20240, or phone 202/208-4747; at any of the 10 regional offices throughout the country; and at any area of the National Park System. The Golden Eagle Passport is not transferable, nor is the $25 refundable if the passport is not used, stolen or lost.

Golden Age Passport. Issued to citizens and permanent residents of the United States 62 years or older, this passport is a free lifetime entrance permit to fee-charging recreation areas. The fee exemption extends to those accompanying the permit holder in a private noncommercial vehicle or, in the case of walk-in facilities, to the holder's spouse and children. The passport entitles the holder to a 50% discount on "use fees" charged in park areas, but not to fees charged by concessionaires.

Golden Age Passports must be obtained in person; mail requests will not be honored. The applicant must show proof of age, i.e., a driver's license, a birth certificate or a signed affidavit attesting to one's age (Medicare cards are not acceptable proof). Passports are available at most federally operated recreation areas where they are used. They may be obtained at the National Park Service Headquarters in Washington, DC (see preceding Golden Eagle Passport section), at any of the park system's regional offices, at National Forest Supervisors' offices and at most Ranger Station offices (for location see NATIONAL PARK SERVICE AREAS AND NATIONAL FORESTS in the state introductory section of the *Guide*).

Golden Access Passport. Issued to citizens and permanent residents of the United States who are physically disabled or visually impaired, this passport is a free lifetime entrance permit to fee-charging federal recreation areas. The fee exception extends to those accompanying the permit holder in a private noncommercial vehicle or, in the case of walk-in facilities, to the holder's spouse, children and parents. The passport entitles the holder to a 50% discount on "use fees" charged in park areas, but not to fees charged by concessionaires.

Golden Access Passports must be obtained in person; mail requests will not be honored. Proof of eligbility to receive federal benefits is required (under programs such as Disability Retirement, Compensation for Military Service-Connnected Disability, Coal Mine Safety and Health Act, etc.), or an affidavit must be signed attesting to eligibility. These passports are available at the same outlets as Golden Age Passports.

Savings for Seniors

Mobil Travel Guide publications note senior citizen rates in lodgings, restaurants and attractions. Always call ahead to confirm that the discount is being offered. Carry proof of age, such as a passport, birth certificate or driver's license. Medicare cards are often accepted as proof. Contact the following organizations for additional information:

1. American Association of Retired Persons (AARP)
   Special Services Dept
   601 E Street NW
   Washington, DC 20049
   Phone 202/434-2277

2. National Council of Senior Citizens
   1331 F Street NW
   Washington, DC 20004
   Phone 202/347-8800

The mature traveler on a limited budget should look for the senior citizen discount symbol in Lodging and Restaurant listings. Also, pay special attention to all listings in the Guide highlighted by a check mark (✔). (See Federal Recreation Areas for Golden Age Passport information.)

Border Crossing Regulations (Canada)

Citizens of the United States do not need visas to enter Canada, but proof of citizenship is required. Proof of citizenship includes a passport, birth certificate or voter's registration card. A driver's license is not acceptable. Naturalized citizens should carry their naturalization certificates or their US passport, as these documents will be necessary for a return to the United States. Young people under 18 years of age who are traveling on their own should carry a letter from parents or guardian giving them permission to travel in Canada.

Travelers entering Canada in automobiles licensed in the United States may tour the provinces for up to three months without fee. Any necessary permits are issued at port of entry. Drivers are advised to carry their motor vehicle registration card and, if the car is not registered in the driver's name, a letter from the registered owner authorizing use of the vehicle.

If the car is rented, carry a copy of the rental contract stipulating use in Canada. For your protection, ask your car insurer for a Canadian Non-resident Interprovince Motor Vehicle Liability Insurance Card. This card ensures that your insurance company observes the minimum of financial responsibility in Canada.

The use of seat belts by drivers and passengers is compulsory in some provinces. For additional information, see individual provinces. A permit is required for the use of citizens' band radios. Rabies vaccination certificates are required for dogs or cats.

No handguns may be brought into Canada. If you plan to hunt, sporting rifles and shotguns, plus 200 rounds of ammunition per person, will be admitted duty-free. Hunting and fishing licenses must be obtained from the appropriate province. Each province has its own regulations concerning the transportation of firearms.

The Canadian dollar's rate of exchange with the US dollar varies. For specific information on rate of exchange, contact the nearest bank. Since customs regulations can change, the *Guide* recommends that you contact the Canadian consulate or embassy in your area. Offices are located in Atlanta, Boston, Buffalo, Chicago, Cleveland, Dallas, Detroit, Los Angeles, Minneapolis, New York City, Philadelphia, San Francisco, Seattle and Washington, DC. For the most current and detailed listing of regulations and sources, ask for the annually revised brochure "Canada: Travel Information," which is available upon request.

Border Crossing Regulations (Mexico)

Proof of citizenship is required for travel into Mexico; a passport or certified birth certificate are acceptable. Aliens must carry their alien registration cards. Naturalized citizens should carry their certificates. If you take your car, you may find it more convenient to unload all baggage before crossing than to go through a thorough customs inspection upon your return. Your automobile insurance is not valid in Mexico; get a one-day policy before crossing. US currency is accepted in all border cities.

You will not be permitted to bring any plants, fruits or vegetables into the United States.

Federal regulations permit each US citizen, 21 years of age or older, to bring back one quart of alcoholic beverage, duty-free. However, state regulations vary and may be more strict; check locally before entering Mexico. New regulations may be issued at any time, so be sure to check further if you have any questions. Mexico does not observe Daylight Saving Time.

If you are planning to stay more than 24 hours or if you are a naturalized citizen or resident alien, get a copy of current border regulations from the nearest Mexican consulate or Tourism Office before crossing and make sure you understand them. A helpful booklet, "Know Before You Go," may be obtained free of charge from the nearest office of the US Customs Service.

Car Care

Familiarize yourself with the owner's manual for your car. It provides valuable advice for service and maintenance. Get a lubrication and oil change, an inspection of tires, fan belts and cooling system, and a check of engine performance, lights and brakes. Any other regular services recommended by the car manufacturer should be performed as well.

Once your car is ready for the road, make certain your insurance is paid up—and don't forget your registration certificate, insurance information, driver's license and an extra set of keys.

Keep your seat belt and harness fastened. Watch your instrument panel closely—your panel gauges or indicators will alert you to potential problems. If a problem arises, get to a service station as soon as possible.

A world of convenience is yours with a Mobil credit card. Mobil's gasoline, oil and tires, as well as many other products and services may be charged at Mobil dealers in the U.S. as well as at certain other dealers throughout Canada.

Road Emergencies

The best insurance against an emergency is proper maintenance of your car. Despite care, however, the unexpected can happen. Here are a few tips for handling emergencies:

Accidents. If you should have an accident, observe the following:

- Do not leave accident scene
- Help the injured but don't move them unless necessary
- Call police—ask for medical help if needed
- Get names, addresses, license numbers and insurance company of persons involved
- Get names and addresses of at least two witnesses

- Get description and registration number of cars involved
- Report accident to your insurance company
- Diagram the accident showing cars involved

Breakdowns. If your car breaks down, get out of traffic as soon as possible, pulling off the road if you can. Turn on your emergency flashers and raise the hood. If you have no flashers, tie a white cloth to the roadside door handle or antenna. Stay near your car but off the road. Carry and use flares or reflectors to keep your car from being hit.

Blowout. Do not overreact if you have a tire blowout. Hold the wheel steady—do not jerk it. Gradually let up on the gas pedal, steer straight and coast to a stop. If you have to brake, do so very gently.

Collision. "If a collision is imminent, you will need to make these split-second decisions," advises the National Safety Council's Defensive Driving Course. "Drive right, away from the oncoming vehicle. Drive with control, don't skid off the road. If you are forced to drive off the road, look for either something soft, like bushes or small trees, or something fixed, like a break-away pole or a fence to break your impact. A fixed object has no momentum, and the crash will be less intense than if you had hit the oncoming vehicle. If you are unable to ride off the road, try to collide with the oncoming vehicle at an angle. A glancing blow is less dangerous than hitting a vehicle head on."

Flat tire. Drive off the road, even if you risk ruining your tire. Set the parking brake firmly, but remember it may not hold if a rear wheel is off the ground. Put wooden blocks, bricks or stones tightly against the front and rear of the tire diagonally opposite the flat. After removing the hubcap, loosen each wheel nut about one-half turn. Position the jack exactly as the instruc-

tions indicate, then raise the car an inch or two to determine how the jack fits. (If it appears to be about to slip, stop and wait for help.)

Jack the car until the flat is about three inches off the ground, remove the wheel nuts and put them in the hubcap. Keep your body away from the car. Handle the tire from the sides; never put your hand above or underneath the tire.

Slide the spare tire into place, using the wrench as a lever. You may have to raise the jack a little farther. Screw the nuts on firmly, and jack the car down, standing at the side, not in front of the car. Finally, fully tighten the wheel nuts and leave the hubcap off as a reminder to have the flat fixed.

Skids. When your car skids, let up on the gas gently, keeping some power going to the wheels. Steer into the direction of the skid, and brake only after you have the car under complete control.

Stuck wheels. If you get stuck in the mud or snow, don't spin the wheels. Rock the car by gently accelerating ahead and back in rhythm with the car's natural tendency.

Equipment. The following checklist describes the necessary equipment to carry at all times:

- ☐ Spare tire; tool kit; first aid kit; flashlight
- ☐ Road flares; jumper cables; gloves
- ☐ Container of motor oil; a can opener
- ☐ Empty one-gallon container (Note: Check local laws governing type of container to use for gasoline.)
- ☐ Spare parts, fan belt and fuses
- ☐ In winter: chains, ice scraper, de-icer in spray can, shovel, "liquid chain" or a bag of sand
- ☐ Major credit card and auto club identification

HOW TO SURVIVE A HOTEL FIRE

The chances are quite slim that you will ever encounter a hotel or motel fire. In addition, should you hear an alarm or see smoke, the danger is almost always less than you think it to be. But in the event you do encounter a fire, **ENSURE YOUR SURVIVAL WITH BASIC PREPARATION AND CALM ACTION.**

PREPARATION IS QUICK AND EASY

WHEN YOU CHECK INTO YOUR ROOM, DO THE FOLLOWING SAFETY CHECK:
- *Where are the fire exits?* Walk to at least two, counting the doors along the way in case you need to find the exit in the dark.
- *Where are the fire extinguishers and alarms?* Walk to them quickly.
- *Where is the "off switch" on your room's air conditioner?* In case of fire, turn off the air conditioner to prevent smoke from being sucked into your room.
- *Where is your room key?* Keep your key with you so you may reenter your room.

IF THERE'S A FIRE . . . STAY CALM

Keep in mind that smoke, poisonous gases, and panic are the greatest threats. The fresh air you need to breathe is at or near the floor. Get on your hands and knees; stay low, keep calm and react as follows:

If you find a fire,
- pull the nearest fire alarm;
- then use a fire extinguisher *if the fire is small;*
- leave the building through the fire exit.

Never enter an elevator when fire is threatening.

If you hear an alarm from your room,
- take your room key;
- check the door for heat, but *do not open a hot door;*
- crack the door open if it is cool;
- use the fire exit if the hall is clear of thick smoke, but *slam the door shut if the hall is smoky.*

If your exit is blocked,
- try another exit;
- or if all exits are smoky, go back to your room—it's the safest place;
- and if you cannot get to your room, go to the roof.

If you must stay in your room because thick smoke blocks the fire exits,
- turn off the air conditioner;
- stuff wet towels under the door and in air vents to keep smoke out;
- fill your bathtub with water and keep wastebaskets or ice buckets nearby to remoisten the cloths or toss water on heating walls;
- phone your location to the front desk or directly to the fire department;
- *stay low, below smoke and poisonous gases, and await assistance.*
- A wet towel tied around your nose and mouth is an effective filter.

Hotel/Motel Toll-Free '800' Numbers

This selected list is a handy guide for hotel/motel toll-free reservation numbers. You can save time and money by using them in the continental United States and Canada; Alaska and Hawaii are not included. Although these '800' numbers were in effect at press time, the *Mobil Travel Guide* cannot be responsible should any of them change. Many establishments do not have toll-free reservation numbers. Consult your local telephone directory for regional listings. The toll-free numbers designated 'TDD' are answered by a telecommunications service for the deaf. *Don't forget to dial "1" before each number.*

Best Western International, Inc.
800-528-1234 Cont'l USA & Canada
800-528-2222 TDD

Budgetel Inns
800-4-BUDGET Cont'l USA

Budget Host
800-BUD-HOST

Canadian Pacific/Doubletree Hotels
800-258-0444 Cont'l USA

Clarion Hotels
800-CLARION

Comfort Inns
800-228-5150 Cont'l USA

Courtyard by Marriott
800-321-2211 Cont'l USA

Days Inn
800-325-2525 Cont'l USA

Drury Inns
800-325-8300 Cont'l USA

Econo Lodges of America
800-446-6900 Cont'l USA & Canada

Embassy Suites
800-362-2779 Cont'l USA

Exel Inns of America
800-356-8013 Cont'l USA

Fairfield Inn by Marriott
800-228-2800

Fairmont Hotels
800-527-4727 Cont'l USA

Four Seasons Hotels
800-332-3442 Cont'l USA & Canada

Friendship Inns of America Int'l
800-453-4511 Cont'l USA

Guest Quarters
800-424-2900 Cont'l USA
800-PICKETT

Hampton Inn
800-HAMPTON Cont'l USA

Hilton Hotels Corp
800-HILTONS Cont'l USA
800-368-1133 TDD

Holiday Inns
800-HOLIDAY Cont'l USA & Canada
800-238-5544 TDD

Howard Johnson
800-654-2000 Cont'l USA & Canada
800-654-8442 TDD

Hyatt Corp
800-228-9000 Cont'l USA & Canada

Inns of America
800-826-0778 USA

Inter-Continental Hotels
800-327-0200 Cont'l USA, HI & Canada

La Quinta Motor Inns, Inc.
800-531-5900 Cont'l USA
800-426-3101 TDD

Loews Hotels
800-223-0888 Cont'l USA exc NY

Marriott Hotels
800-228-9290 Cont'l USA

Master Hosts Inns (Hospitality)
800-251-1962 Cont'l USA & Canada

Omni Hotels
800-843-6664 Cont'l USA & Canada

Park Inns Int'l
800-437-PARK

Quality Inns
800-228-5151 Cont'l USA & Canada

Radisson Hotel Corp
800-333-3333 Cont'l USA & Canada

Ramada Inns
800-2-RAMADA Cont'l USA
800-228-3232 TDD

Red Carpet/Scottish Inns (Hospitality)
800-251-1962 Cont'l USA & Canada

Red Lion-Thunderbird
800-547-8010 Cont'l USA & Canada

Red Roof Inns
800-843-7663 Cont'l USA & Canada

Residence Inn By Marriott
800-331-3131

Ritz-Carlton
800-241-3333 Cont'l USA

Rodeway Inns International
800-228-2000 Cont'l USA

Sheraton Hotels & Inns
800-325-3535 Cont'l USA & Canada

Shilo Inns
800-222-2244

Signature Inns
800-822-5252

Stouffer Hotels and Resorts
800-HOTELS-1 Cont'l USA & Canada

Super 8 Motels
800-843-1991 Cont'l USA & Canada
800-800-8000 Cont'l USA & Canada

Susse Chalet Motor Lodges & Inns
800-258-1980 Cont'l USA & Canada

Travelodge International Inc./Viscount Hotels
800-255-3050 Cont'l USA & Canada

Trusthouse Forte Hotels
800-225-5843 Cont'l USA & Canada

Vagabond Hotels Inc.
800-522-1555 Cont'l USA
800-468-2251 Canada

Westin Hotels
800-228-3000 Cont'l USA & Canada

Wyndham Hotels
800-822-4200

Car Rental Toll-Free '800' Numbers

Advantage Rent A Car
800-777-5500 Cont'l USA

Agency Rent-A-Car
800-321-1972 Cont'l USA

Airways Rent A Car
800-952-9200

Alamo Rent-A-Car
800-327-9633 Cont'l USA,
Canada

Allstate Rent-A-Car
800-634-6186 Cont'l USA

Avis-Reservations Center
800-331-1212 Cont'l USA,
Canada

Budget Rent-A-Car
800-527-0700 Cont'l USA,
Canada

Dollar Rent-A-Car
800-800-4000 Cont'l USA,
Canada

Enterprise Rent-A-Car
800-325-8007 Cont'l USA

Hertz Corporation
800-654-3131 Cont'l USA
800-654-3001 Canada

National Car Rental
800-CAR-RENT Cont'l USA,
Canada

Payless Rent-A-Car Inc
800-237-2804 Cont'l USA

Sears Rent-A-Car
800-527-0770 Cont'l USA

Thrifty Rent-A-Car
800-367-2277 Cont'l USA,
Canada

USA Rent-A-Car System, Inc.
800-USA-CARS

U-Save Auto Rental of America
800-272-USAV

Value Rent-A-Car
800-327-2501 Cont'l USA,
Canada

Airline Toll-Free '800' Numbers

American Airlines, Inc. (AA)
800-433-7300

Canadian Airlines Intl, LTD
800-426-7000

Continental Airlines (CO)
800-525-0280

Delta Air Lines, Inc. (DL)
800-221-1212

Northwest Airlines, Inc. (NW)
800-225-2525

Southwest Airlines (WN)
800-435-9792

Trans World Airlines, Inc. (TW)
800-221-2000

United Air Lines, Inc. (UA)
800-241-6522

USAir (US)
800-428-4322

Arizona

Population: 3,665,228
Land area: 113,510 square miles
Elevation: 70–12,633 feet
Highest point: Humphreys Peak (Coconino County)
Entered Union: February 14, 1912 (48th state)
Capital: Phoenix
Motto: God enriches
Nickname: Grand Canyon State
State flower: Saguaro (sah-WAH-ro) cactus blossom
State bird: Cactus wren
State tree: Palo Verde
State fair: Mid-October, 1994, in Phoenix
Time zone: Mountain

This rapidly growing state has more than tripled its population since 1940. Its irrigated farms grow citrus fruits, cotton, vegetables and grain on lush green lands that contrast sharply with the surrounding desert. It also produces 60 percent of the nation's copper.

As a vacation state, its progress has been spectacular. In winter, the areas around Phoenix, Tucson and Yuma offer sunshine, relaxation and informal Western living. Air conditioning and swimming pools make year-round living pleasant. In summer, the northern mountains, cool forests, spectacular canyons, trout streams and lakes offer a variety of vacation activities, including hunting and fishing camps, ghost and mining towns, meadows filled with wildflowers, intriguing ancient Native American villages, cliff dwellings and dude ranches.

Francisco Vasquez de Coronado crossed the area in 1540 on his ill-fated search for the nonexistent gold of Cibola. Grizzled prospectors panned for gold in mountain streams and hit pay dirt. The missions built by Father Kino and his successors date back as far as 1692. Irrigation ditches, built by Hohokam Indians hundreds of years earlier, have been incorporated into modern systems.

The state has 23 reservations and one of the largest Native American populations in the United States. More than half of the Native American population is Navajo. Craft specialties include basketry, pottery, weaving, jewelry and kachina dolls.

Arizona is a state of contrasts. It has modern and prehistoric civilizations; mountains, deserts and modern agriculture. Arizona offers fascinating adventures for everyone.

National Park Service Areas

Arizona has two national parks, Grand Canyon and Petrified Forest (see both); 14 national monuments: Canyon de Chelly, Casa Grande Ruins, Chiricahua, Montezuma Castle, Navajo, Organ Pipe Cactus, Pipe Spring, Saguaro, Sunset Crater Volcano, Wupatki (see all), Tonto, Tuzigoot (see COTTONWOOD), Walnut Canyon (see FLAGSTAFF) and Hohokam Pima (not open to the public); one national memorial, Coronado (see SIERRA VISTA); two national recreation areas, Glen Canyon (see PAGE) and Lake Mead (see NEVADA); two national historic sites, Hubbell Trading Post (see GANADO) and Fort Bowie (see WILLCOX); and one national historical park, Tumacacori (see).

National Forests

The following is an alphabetical listing of National Forests and towns they are listed under.

Apache-Sitgreaves National Forest (see SHOW LOW and SPRINGERVILLE): Forest Supervisor in Springerville; Ranger offices in Alpine*, Clifton, Heber*, Lakeside*, Springerville.

Coconino National Forest (see FLAGSTAFF): Forest Supervisor in Flagstaff; Ranger offices in Flagstaff, Long Valley*, Mormon Lake*, Sedona.

Coronado National Forest (see TUCSON): Forest Supervisor in Tucson; Ranger offices in Douglas, Nogales, Safford, Sierra Vista, Tucson.

Kaibab National Forest (see WILLIAMS): Forest Supervisor in Williams; Ranger offices in Fredonia*, Tusayan*, Williams.

Prescott National Forest (see PRESCOTT): Forest Supervisor in Prescott; Ranger offices in Camp Verde*, Chino Valley*, Prescott.

Tonto National Forest (see PAYSON): Forest Supervisor in Phoenix; Ranger offices in Carefree, Globe, Mesa, Payson, Roosevelt*, Young*.

*Not described in text

State Recreation Areas

The following towns list state recreation areas in their vicinity under What to See and Do; refer to the individual town for directions and park information.

Listed under **Cottonwood:** see Dead Horse Ranch State Park.

Listed under **Lake Havasu City:** see Lake Havasu State Park (Cattail Cove and Windsor Beach units).

Listed under **Mesa:** see Lost Dutchman State Park.

Listed under **Parker:** see Buckskin Mountain State Park.

Listed under **Patagonia:** see Patagonia Lake State Park.

Listed under **Safford:** see Roper Lake State Park.

Listed under **Sedona:** see Slide Rock State Park.

Listed under **Springerville:** see Lyman Lake State Park.

Listed under **Tucson:** see Catalina State Park.

Water-related activities, hiking, riding, various other sports, picnicking, camping and visitor centers are available in many of these areas. There is a $3–$5/car day-use fee at state parks; $40 annual day-use permit is available. Camping $7–$15/day. Arizona also has seven state historic parks ($3; guided tours addl fee) and the Boyce Thompson Arboretum (see GLOBE). For further information on recreational areas contact Arizona State Parks, 800 W Washington, Suite 415, Phoenix 85007; 602/542-4174.

Fishing & Hunting

Both are excellent in a number of sections of the state. Nonresident fishing licenses: 1-day (exc Colorado River), $8; 5-day, $18.50; 9-day, all species, $27.50; general, $38; Colorado River, all species, $32.50; trout stamp, $40. Urban fishing (for 14 lakes in 7 cities), $12.00. Inquire for fees to fish on Indian reservations. Nonresident hunting licenses: 3-day small game, $38; general, $85.50. Tags cost from $50.50 for turkey to $3,753 for buffalo. Permits for most big-game species available by drawing only. Combination nonresident licenses (fishing and hunting), $137.50 (incl trout stamp). Fees subject to change. For updated information contact the Arizona Game & Fish Department, 2221 W Greenway Rd, Phoenix 85023; 602/942-3000, ext 210.

Skiing

The following towns list ski areas in their vicinity under What to See and Do; refer to the individual town for directions and park information.

Listed under **Flagstaff:** see Arizona Snowbowl ‡ and Mormon Lake Ski Center ‡‡.

Listed under **Mc Nary:** see Sunrise Park Resort.

Listed under **Tucson:** see Mt Lemmon Ski Valley.

Listed under **Williams:** see Williams Ski Area ‡.

‡Also cross-country trails
‡‡Only cross-country trails

Safety Belt Information

Safety belts are mandatory for all persons in front seat of vehicle. Children under 4 years or under 40 pounds in weight must be in an approved safety seat anywhere in vehicle. For further information phone 602/223-2000.

Interstate Highway System

The following alphabetical listing of Arizona towns in *Mobil Travel Guide* shows that these cities are within 10 miles of the indicated Interstate highway. A highway map should, however, be checked for the nearest exit.

INTERSTATE 8: Casa Grande, Gila Bend, Yuma.

INTERSTATE 10: Casa Grande, Chandler, Glendale, Litchfield Park, Mesa, Phoenix, Scottsdale, Tempe, Tucson, Willcox.

INTERSTATE 17: Cottonwood, Flagstaff, Glendale, Mesa, Phoenix, Scottsdale, Sedona, Tempe.

INTERSTATE 19: Nogales, Tucson.

INTERSTATE 40: Flagstaff, Holbrook, Kingman, Seligman, Williams, Winslow.

Additional Visitor Information

Arizona Highways is an excellent monthly magazine; contact 2039 W Lewis Ave, Phoenix 85009. Several informative booklets may be obtained from the Arizona Office of Tourism, 1100 W Washington, Phoenix 85007; 602/542-TOUR or 800/842-8257.

Bisbee (F-4)

Founded: 1880 **Pop:** 6,288 **Elev:** 5,400 ft **Area code:** 602 **Zip:** 85603

Bisbee once was a tough mining town known as "Queen of the Copper Camps." Sprawled along the sides of two narrow canyons, the town's streets are too steep even for mail carriers, making Bisbee the largest nonsuburban town in the United States without home mail delivery service.

What to See and Do

1. **Mule Pass Tunnel.** US 80 passes through this 6,042-foot-high, 1,400-foot-long tunnel, Arizona's longest.
2. **Bisbee Mining and Historical Museum.** 5 Copper Queen Plaza. Housed in the 1897 office building of the Copper Queen Consolidated Mining Co. Depicts early development of this urban center through displays on mining, minerals, social history and period offices; historical photographs. Shattuck Research Library. (Daily; closed Jan 1, Dec 25) Also operates **Muheim Heritage House** (early 1900s). 207B Youngblood Hill. (Thurs only) Phone 432-7071 or -7848. ¢¢
3. **Bisbee Restoration Association & Historical Museum.** 37 Main St. Local historical and pioneer artifacts; Native American relics. (Daily exc Sun; closed major hols) Donation. Phone 432-4106 or -2386.
4. **Copper mine tours.**

   Lavender Pit. On US 80. A 340-acre open-pit copper mine, now inactive. Approx 1-hr van tour of surface mine and historic district (daily; closed Thanksgiving, Dec 25). Lavender Viewpoint (daily; free). Phone 432-2071. ¢¢¢

   Queen Mine. US 80 near Old Bisbee. Approx 1-hr guided tour on mine train; takes visitor 1,800 feet into mine tunnel. Mine temperature 47°F–49°F; jacket recommended. (Daily; closed Thanksgiving, Dec 25) Phone 432-2071. ¢¢¢

(For further information contact the Greater Bisbee Chamber of Commerce, #7 Naco Rd, Box BA; 432-5421.)

(See Douglas, Sierra Vista, Tombstone)

Hotel

★ ★**COPPER QUEEN.** *(PO Drawer CQ) 11 Howell Ave.* 602/432-2216; res: 800/247-5829. 45 rms, 4 story. S, D $65–$100; each addl $5. Crib $5. TV; cable. Heated pool. Restaurant 7 am–2:30 pm, 5:30–9 pm; Sat 7 am–10 pm; Sun to 9 pm. Bar 11–1 am; entertainment Fri–Sat.

Ck-out 11 am. Meeting rm. Built 1902; rich in historic charm. Cr cds: A, DS, MC, V.

Inns

★ ★BISBEE GRAND HOTEL. *(PO Box 825) 61 Main St. 602/ 432-5900; res: 800/421-1909.* 8 air-cooled rms, 4 with bath, 2 story, 3 suites. No rm phones. S, D $50–$75; suites $95. Complimentary full bkfst. Restaurant nearby. Bar. Ck-out 11 am, ck-in 2 pm. In restored turn-of-the-century hotel (1908); all guest rms are on the 2nd floor. Elegant Victorian atmosphere; antiques. Totally nonsmoking. Cr cds: A, DS, MC, V.

✔ ★ ★BISBEE INN. *(Box 1855) 45 OK St. 602/432-5131.* 18 rms, no private baths, 2 story. S $29; D $39; each addl $6; wkly rates. Crib $6. Pet accepted, some restrictions. TV in sitting rm; cable. Complimentary full bkfst 8:15–10 am. Ck-out 11 am, ck-in after 3 pm. Coin lndry. Restored 1917 hotel. Totally nonsmoking. Cr cds: DS, MC, V.

★ ★ ★THE GREENWAY HOUSE. *401 Cole Ave. 602/432-7170; res: 800/253-3325.* 8 kit. units, 2 story. S, D $75–$125; each addl $15; 2-night min. Complimentary continental bkfst in rms. Restaurant nearby. Outdoor bar. Ck-out 11 am, ck-in 1–6 pm. Game rm. Grills. Historic house (1906); antique furnishings. Totally nonsmoking. Cr cds: A, MC, V.

★ ★PARK PLACE. *200 E Vista. 602/432-3054; res: 800/388-4388; FAX 602/459-7603.* 4 units, 3 A/C, 2 with bath, 2 story, 2 suites. No rm phones. S, D $40; suites $60. TV in sitting rm. Complimentary full bkfst, tea, sherry. Restaurant nearby. Ck-out, ck-in varies. Free local airport, bus depot transportation. Balconies. Mediterranean-style home (1910) with terraces overlooking park. Traditional decor; some antiques. Totally nonsmoking. Cr cds: MC, V.

Restaurant

✔ ★THE WINE GALLERY BISTRO. *41 Main St. 602/432-3447.* Hrs: 11:30 am–2:30 pm, 5:30–9 pm; Sat from 5:30 pm. Closed Tues & Wed; some major hols. Italian menu. Wine, beer. Semi-a la carte: lunch $3.75–$5.95, dinner $8.95–$16.95. Child's meals. Specializes in gulf shrimp, pasta dishes. No cr cds accepted.

Bullhead City (B-1)

Founded: 1946 **Pop:** 21,951 (Bullhead City-Riviera) **Elev:** 540 ft **Area code:** 602 **Zip:** 86430

Bullhead City was established in 1945 as a construction camp for Davis Dam, a reclamation facility located three miles to the north. The name is derived from its proximity to Bullhead Rock, now largely concealed by the waters of Lake Mojave. Bullhead City is across the Colorado River from Laughlin, NV (see) and its casinos.

What to See and Do

1. **Davis Dam and Power Plant.** 4 mi N on Colorado River. Dam (200 ft high, 1,600 ft long) impounds Lake Mohave, which has a surface area of 28,500 acres and reaches 67 river miles upstream to Hoover Dam. Self-guided tour through power plant (daily). Phone 754-3628. **Free.**

2. **Fishing, camping.** Trout, bass, bluegill, crappie and catfish. Campsites, picnic grounds at Katherine, 5 miles N, a part of the Lake Mead National Recreation Area (see NEVADA). Standard fees.

(For further information contact the Chamber of Commerce, PO Box 66; 754-4121.)

(See Kingman; also see Needles, CA, and Laughlin, NV)

Motels

★BEST WESTERN-GRAND VISTA. *1817 Arcadia Plaza (86442), off AZ 95. 602/763-3300; FAX 602/763-4447.* 80 rms, 3 story. S, D $39–$95; wkly rates. Crib free. TV; cable. Pool; whirlpool. Complimentary coffee in lobby. Restaurant nearby. Ck-out noon. Meeting rm. Cr cds: A, C, D, DS, MC, V.

✔ ★ECONO LODGE-RIVERSIDE. *1717 AZ 95 (86442). 602/ 758-8080; FAX 602/758-8283.* 64 rms, 2 story, 13 suites. S $32–$65; D $45–$78; each addl $6; suites $55–$95; under 12 free; wkly rates. Crib $6. TV; cable. Pool. Complimentary continental bkfst, coffee. Restaurant nearby. Ck-out 11 am. Some refrigerators. On river. Cr cds: A, D, DS, MC, V.

★LAKE MOHAVE RESORT & MARINA. *Katherine Landing, 6 mi NE, 3½ mi N of AZ 68, N of Davis Dam. 602/754-3245; res: 800/752-9669.* 51 rms, 1–2 story, 14 kits. S, D $60; each addl $6; kit. units $83; under 5 free. Crib $6. Pet accepted, some restrictions. Restaurant 7 am–9 pm mid-Apr-Nov. Bar 4–10 pm. Ck-out 11 am. Free airport transportation. Water sports; houseboats, boat moorings, boat rental, fishing supplies. Private patios, balconies. Spacious grounds. View of lake. Cr cds: MC, V.

★ ★TRAVELODGE. *(PO Box 3037) 2360 4th St. 602/754-3000; FAX 602/754-5234.* 90 rms, 2 story. S, D $45–$75; higher rates special events. Crib free. Pet accepted; $5. TV; cable. Pool; whirlpool. Complimentary continental bkfst, coffee. Restaurant nearby. Ck-out noon. Refrigerators. Cr cds: A, C, MC, V.

Restaurants

★EL ENCANTO. *125 Lone St, at the River Queen Resort. 602/754-5100.* Hrs: 11 am–11 pm. Closed some major hols. Res accepted. Mexican, Amer menu. Bar. Semi-a la carte: lunch $3–$5.25, dinner $5.60–$10. Child's meals. Parking. Outdoor dining. Mexican decor. Cr cds: MC, V.

✔ ★GERARD'S. *1670 AZ 95, at the Silver Creek Inn. 602/763-8400.* Hrs: 7 am–2 pm; wkends from 8 am. Closed Mon. Res accepted. Bar. Semi-a la carte: bkfst $2.95–$4, lunch $3.50–$5.95. Parking. Cr cds: A, C, D, DS, MC, V.

Canyon de Chelly National Monument (B-5)

(In NE corner of state at Chinle)

The smooth red sandstone walls of the canyon extend straight up as much as a thousand feet from the nearly flat sand bottom. When William of Normandy defeated the English at the Battle of Hastings in 1066, the Pueblo had already built apartment houses in these walls. Many ruins are still here.

The Navajo came long after the original tenants had abandoned these structures. In 1864, Kit Carson's men drove nearly all the Navajo out of the area, marching them on foot 300 miles to the Bosque Redondo in eastern New Mexico. Since 1868, Navajo have returned to farming, cultivating the orchards and grazing their sheep in the canyon. In 1931, Canyon de Chelly (pronounced "de-SHAY") and its tributaries, Canyon del Muerto and Monument Canyon, were designated a national monument.

There are more than 60 major ruins, some dating from circa A.D. 300, in these canyons. White House, Antelope House and Mummy Cave are among the most picturesque. Most ruins are inaccessible, but can be seen from either the canyon bottom or from the road along the top of the precipitous walls. The 2 spectacular, 16-mile rim drives can be made by car in any season. Lookout points, sometimes a short distance from the road, are clearly marked. The only self-guided trail (2½-mi round trip) leads to the canyon floor and White House ruin from White House Overlook. Other hikes can only be made with a National Park Service permit and an authorized Navajo guide (fee); also ranger-guided hikes (Memorial Day–Labor Day). Only four-wheel drive vehicles are allowed in the canyons; each vehicle must be accompanied by an authorized Navajo guide and requires a National Park Service permit obtainable from a ranger at the visitor center (fee).

The visitor center has an archaeological museum, administrative offices and rest rooms. (Daily; free) Rim drive guides and White House Trail guides at visitor center. Picnic areas and campgrounds (free).

What to See and Do

Canyon Tours. Thunderbird Lodge (see MOTELS). Lodge personnel conduct special jeep tours into the canyons; half-day (daily) and full-day (Apr–Oct; daily) trips. Phone 674-5841 or -5842. ¢¢¢¢¢

(For further information contact the Superintendent, Box 588, Chinle 86503; 602/674-5500 or -5501.)

(See Ganado)

Motels

★ ★ **CANYON DE CHELLY.** *(Box 295, Chinle 86503) 3 blks E of AZ 191.* 602/674-5875; res: 800/327-0354; FAX 602/674-3715. 102 rms. Early May–Oct: S $94; D $96; each addl $4; lower rates rest of yr. Crib free. TV; cable. Indoor pool. Complimentary coffee in rms. Restaurant 6:30 am–10 pm. Ck-out 11 am. Gift shop. Picnic tables. Navajo decor. Cr cds: A, D, MC, V.

⚊ 🚫 ⊙ SC

★ ★ **THUNDERBIRD LODGE.** *(Box 548, Chinle 86503) 3 mi SE of AZ 191 at entrance to monument.* 602/674-5841. 72 rms in motel, lodge. Mar–Oct: S $80–$83; D $82–$88; each addl $4; lower rates rest of yr. Crib $4. TV; cable. Restaurant 6:30 am–9 pm; winter hrs vary. Ck-out 11 am. Meeting rm. Free airport transportation. Canyon tours avail. Cr cds: A, C, D, DS, MC, V.

D 🚫 ⊙

Carefree (D-3)

Pop: 1,666 **Elev:** 2,389 ft **Area code:** 602 **Zip:** 85377

The immense Tonto National Forest (see PAYSON) stretches to the north and east; the Ranger District office for the forest's Cave Creek District is located here. Located in the center of town is the largest and most accurate sundial in the Western Hemisphere.

(For information about this area contact the Carefree/Cave Creek Chamber of Commerce, 748 Easy St, Marywood Plaza, Box 734; 488-3381.)

Annual Event

Fiesta Days. PRCA rodeo, parade. Usually 1st wkend Apr.

(See Chandler, Mesa, Phoenix, Scottsdale, Tempe)

Resort

★ ★ ★ **BOULDERS RESORT & CLUB.** *(Box 2090) 34631 N Tom Darlington Dr.* 602/488-9009; res: 800/553-1717; FAX 602/488-4118. 136 casitas, 1–2 story; also patio homes. MAP, late Jan–mid-May: S $450; D $525; each addl $80; under 13 free; EP avail; golf, tennis rates; lower rates mid-May–mid-June & early Sept–mid-Jan. Serv charge $15 per rm per day. Closed July 5–early Sept. Crib free. Pet accepted, some restrictions; $50 non-refundable. TV; cable. 2 heated pools; poolside serv. Dining rm (public by res) 7–10:30 am, noon–2:30 pm, 6–9:30 pm (also see LATILLA). Box lunches. Snack bar. Rm serv. Bar 11–1 am. Ck-out noon, ck-in 4 pm. Grocery, coin lndry, package store 2 mi. Meeting rms. Gift shop. Airport transportation. Tennis, pro. 36-hole golf, greens fee $105, pro, putting green, driving range. Entertainment; dancing. Exercise rm; instructor, weights, bicycles, whirlpool, sauna, steam rm. Massage. Refrigerators, fireplaces. Private patios. Built in the land of giant boulders, mountain-rimmed landscapes; designed to complement terrain. Handcrafted Native American art; natural flagstone floors. Decorated in desert tones. Cr cds: A, C, D, MC, V.

D 🏊 🛥 🌮 🏖 ⛵ 🏃 🏃 🚫 ⊙ 🕎

Restaurants

✔ ★ **CANTINA DEL PEDREGAL.** *(34505 N Scottsdale Rd, at el Pedregal, Scottsdale) E on Carefee Hwy.* 602/488-0715. Hrs: 11:30 am–3 pm, 5–10 pm; June–Sept 5–10 pm only. Closed Thanksgiving, Dec 25; also Tues June–Sept. Res accepted. Mexican menu. Bar. Semi-a la carte: lunch $4.95–$10.95, dinner $7.95–$12.95. Child's meals. Specialties: Mexican Gulf shrimp, fajitas, chili rellenos. Guitarist, vocalist Fri or Sat. Parking. Patio dining. Colorful decor. Totally nonsmoking. Cr cds: A, C, D, MC, V.

D

★ ★ **IANUZZI RISTORANTE.** *(34505 N Scottsdale Rd, el Pedregal at the Boulders, Scottsdale) S on I-17.* 602/488-4141. Hrs: 11:30 am–3 pm, 5–10 pm; Fri, Sat to 10:30 pm; Sun noon–10 pm. Closed Thanksgiving, Dec 25. Res accepted. Contemporary Italian menu. Bar. Semi-a la carte: lunch $6.95–$10.95, dinner $10.95–$20. Specialties: fettucine meravigliose con vodka, fegato alla Veneziana con polenta, osso buco Milanese. Parking. Outdoor dining. Spectacular views of city lights and sunset. Cr cds: A, C, D, MC, V.

D

★ ★ ★ **LATILLA.** *(See Boulders Resort & Club Resort)* 602/488-9009. Hrs: 7–10:30 am, 6–9:30 pm; Sun brunch 11:30 am–2 pm. Closed July–Aug. Bar 11–1 am. A la carte entrees: bkfst $3.75–$15, dinner $20–$28. Sun brunch $28. Specializes in rack of lamb, Pacific salmon, grilled sea scallops. Own baking. Entertainment. Outdoor dining in season. Southwestern decor, artwork; scenic view of desert landscape. Jacket. Cr cds: A, C, D, MC, V.

D

Casa Grande (D-3)

Pop: 19,082 **Elev:** 1,405 ft **Area code:** 602 **Zip:** 85222

Named for the Hohokam ruins northeast of town (see #3), Casa Grande is situated in an agricultural and industrial area.

What to See and Do

1. **Casa Grande Valley Historical Society & Museum.** 110 W Florence Blvd. Exhibits tracing Casa Grande Valley growth from prehistoric times to present with emphasis on farm, ranch, mining and domestic life. Gift shop. (Mid-Sept–mid-June, daily exc Mon; closed major hols) Phone 836-2223. ¢

2. **Picacho Peak State Park.** 24 mi SE off I-10, Picacho Peak exit. This 3,400-acre park includes a sheer-sided peak rising 1,500 feet above the desert floor that was a landmark for early travelers. The only Civil War battle in Arizona was fought near here. Colorful spring wildflowers; desert nature study. Hiking. Picnicking (shelter). Interpretive center programs (seasonal). Standard fees. Phone 466-3183.

3. **Casa Grande Ruins National Monument** (see). Approx 14 mi E on AZ 84, 287, then 9 mi N on AZ 87.

(For further information contact the Chamber of Commerce, 575 N Marshall St; 836-2125.)

Annual Event

O'Odham Tash–Casa Grande's Indian Days. Rodeo, parades, ceremonial dances, arts & crafts, chicken scratch dance & bands; Native American foods, barbecue. Advance reservations advised. Phone 836-4723. Mid-Feb.

(See Florence, Gila Bend, Phoenix)

Motor Hotel

★★**HOLIDAY INN.** 777 N Pinal Ave. 602/426-3500; FAX 602/836-4728. 175 rms, 4 story. Jan–Apr: S $65; D $71; each addl $6; suites $100; under 18 free; lower rates rest of yr. Crib free. Pet accepted. TV; cable. Heated pool; whirlpool. Restaurant 6 am–10 pm. Rm serv. Bar 11–1 am; entertainment, dancing wkends. Ck-out noon. Coin lndry. Meeting rms. Sundries. Gift shop. Free bus depot transportation. Refrigerator, wet bar in suites. Cr cds: A, C, D, DS, ER, MC, V, JCB.

Resort

★★★**FRANCISCO GRANDE RESORT & GOLF CLUB.** 26000 Gila Bend Hwy, 4 mi W via AZ 84. 602/836-6444; res: 800/237-4238 (AZ). 112 units, 8 story. Jan–Apr: S, D $56–$106; each addl $15; suites $126–$196; kits. $196; under 18 free; lower rates rest of yr. TV. Heated pool; wading pool, poolside serv. Dining rm 6:30 am–10 pm. Box lunches. Snack bar. Picnics. Bar 10–1 am, Sun from noon. Ck-out noon, ck-in 3 pm. Convention facilities. Valet serv. Airport, bus depot transportation. Tennis. 18-hole golf, greens fee $35, pro, putting green, driving range. Health club privileges. Exercise equipt; treadmill, rowing machine. Lawn games. Entertainment, dancing. Balconies. Cr cds: A, C, D, MC, V.

Restaurant

✔★★**MI AMIGO RICARDO.** 821 E Florence Blvd. 602/836-3858. Hrs: 11 am–9 pm. Closed some hols. Res accepted. Mexican menu. Wine, beer. Semi-a la carte: lunch, dinner $5–$7. Specializes in enchiladas, chimichangas, flautas. Own tortillas. Parking. Mexican decorations. Cr cds: MC, V.

D

Casa Grande Ruins National Monument (D-3)

(33 mi SE of Chandler on AZ 87, 1 mi N of Coolidge)

The Hohokam people existed in the Salt and Gila river valleys for hundreds of years before abandoning the region sometime before 1450. They built irrigation canals in order to grow beans, corn, squash, and cotton. Casa Grande (Big House) was built during the 14th century.

Casa Grande was constructed of *caliche*-bearing soil (a crust of calcium carbonate on stony soil) and is four stories high (although the first story was filled in with dirt). The top story probably provided an excellent view of the surrounding country and may have been used for astronomical observations.

After being occupied for some 100 years, Casa Grande was abandoned. Father Kino, the Jesuit missionary and explorer, sighted and named it Big House in 1694.

Casa Grande is the only structure of its type and size in southern Arizona. It is covered by a large protective roof. There is a museum with archaeological exhibits (daily); ranger talks, self-guided tours. For further information contact Park Archaeologist, 1100 Ruins Dr, Coolidge 85228; 602/723-3172. ¢

(For accommodations see Casa Grande, Chandler, Phoenix, also see Florence)

Chandler (D-3)

Pop: 90,533 **Elev:** 1,213 ft **Area code:** 602

Cotton, citrus fruits, pecans and sugar beets are grown in the surrounding area. A growing number of high-technology companies have facilities here. Williams Air Force Base is 10 miles east of town.

What to See and Do

1. **Gila River Arts & Crafts Center.** 15 mi S via AZ 93 at jct I-10 (exit 175), on Gila River Indian Reservation. Gallery featuring the works of outstanding Native American artists and artisans from more than 30 tribes. Restaurant features Native American food. Museum (free) preserves cultural heritage of Pima and Maricopa tribes. Gila Heritage Park features five Native American villages. (Daily; closed major hols) Phone 963-3981.   **Free.**

2. **Casa Grande Ruins National Monument** (see). 33 mi SE on AZ 87.

(For further information contact the Chamber of Commerce, 218 N Arizona Ave, 85224; 963-4571.)

Seasonal Event

Baseball Spring Training. Compadre Stadium, Ocotillo & Alma School Rd. Milwaukee Brewers. Phone 895-1200. Mar.

(See Mesa, Phoenix, Scottsdale, Tempe)

Motel

✔★**ALOHA.** 445 N Arizona Ave (85224). 602/963-3403. 26 rms, 19 kits. Mid-Dec–mid-Apr: S $40–$54; D, kits. $40–$60; each addl $8; lower rates rest of yr. Crib $2. TV. Heated pool. Restaurant adj 5 am–10 pm. Ck-out 11 am. Picnic tables, grills. Cr cds: A, MC, V.

Motor Hotel

★★**WYNDHAM GARDEN HOTEL.** *7475 W Chandler Blvd (85226).* 602/961-4444; FAX 602/940-0269. 159 rms, 4 story, 16 suites. Mid-Jan–mid-May: S, D $109–$129; each addl $10; suites $119–$139; under 18 free; lower rates rest of yr. TV; cable. Heated pool; poolside serv. Restaurant 6:30 am–10 pm. Rm serv. Bar 4–11 pm. Ck-out noon. Meeting rms. Valet serv. Free airport transportation. Exercise equipt; weight machines, bicycles, whirlpool. Cr cds: A, C, D, DS, ER, MC, V, JCB.

D ⊠ ♣ ⊛ ⊘ SC

Resort

★★★**SHERATON SAN MARCOS.** *1 San Marcos Pl (85224).* 602/963-6655; FAX 602/899-5441. 296 units, 4 story. Jan–May: S $180–$195; D $195–$210; each addl $10; suites $240–$575; under 18 free; wkly rates; golf, tennis, honeymoon plans; lower rates rest of yr. Crib free. TV; cable. 2 heated pools; poolside serv. Restaurant 6 am–10 pm. Rm serv 24 hrs. Bar 11–1 am; entertainment, dancing. Ck-out noon, ck-in 3 pm. Convention facilities. Bellhops. Valet serv. Concierge. Gift shop. Airport, RR station, bus depot transportation. Lighted tennis, pro. 18-hole golf, greens fee $62, pro, putting green, driving range. Exercise equipt; weight machine, bicycles, whirlpool. Balconies. Historic resort; mission-revival architecture. Cr cds: A, C, D, DS, MC, V.

D ⊿ ⊿ ⊠ ⊼ ⊼ ⊘ ⊛ SC

Chiricahua National Monument (E-5)

(32 mi SE of Willcox on AZ 186, then 4 mi E on AZ 181)

This national monument features 20 square miles of picturesque natural rock sculptures and deep twisting canyons.

The Chiricahua (Cheer-a-CAH-wah) Apaches hunted in the Chiricahua Mountain range. Cochise, Geronimo, "Big Foot" Massai and other well-known Apaches undoubtedly found their way into this region during the 1870s and 1880s. A visitor center, near the entrance, has botanical, zoological and historical displays. (Daily) Per person (no car) ¢; Per car ¢¢

At Massai Point Overlook, geologic exhibits explain the volcanic origin of the monument. The road up Bonita Canyon leads to a number of other outlook points; there are also 20 miles of excellent day-use trails to points of special interest.

Picnicking and camping sites are located within the national monument. Campground (fee); 26-foot limit on trailers. For further information contact Superintendent, Dos Cabezas Route, Box 6500, Willcox 85643; 602/824-3560.

(For accommodations see Willcox)

Clifton (D-5)

Settled: 1872 **Pop:** 2,840 **Elev:** 3,468 ft **Area code:** 602 **Zip:** 85533

The scenic Coronado Trail (US 666) begins here and continues north 90 miles to Alpine. The Apache National Forest (see SHOW LOW) stretches north and east of Clifton; the Clifton Ranger District office of the Apache-Sitgreaves National Forest is located here.

What to See and Do

1. **Morenci Open Pit Copper Mine.** 5 mi NW via US 191 near Morenci. Operated by Phelps Dodge Morenci, Inc., the pit is one of the largest copper mines in the world. Tours; reservations advised. (Mon–Fri; closed major hols) Phone 865-4521, ext. 435.   **Free.**
2. **Old Jail & Locomotive.** S Coronado Blvd. Jail blasted out of mountainside; first occupied by the man who built it.

(For accommodations see Safford)

Cottonwood (C-3)

Pop: 5,918 **Elev:** 3,314 ft **Area code:** 602 **Zip:** 86326

This town is in the beautiful Verde Valley, an area offering many opportunities for exploration.

What to See and Do

1. **Jerome.** 8 mi W on US 89A, 3,200–5,200 ft almost straight up. A historic old copper-mining town with cobblestone streets and renovated structures now housing gift, jewelry, antique and pottery shops, art galleries, restaurants and hotels. Views of Verde Valley and the Mogollon Rim. For information phone the Chamber of Commerce, 634-2900. Also in Jerome is

   Jerome State Historic Park. Off US 89A. Douglas Memorial Mining Museum depicts history of Jerome, mining in Arizona; housed in former house of "Rawhide" Jimmy Douglas (fee). Picnicking. No overnight facilities. (Daily; closed Dec 25) Standard fees. Phone 634-5381.
2. **Tuzigoot National Monument.** 2 mi NW via N Main St, follow signs. Excavated pueblo occupied from A.D. 1000–1450. Visitor center, museum with artifacts of Sinagua culture. (Daily) Phone 634-5564. ¢
3. **Fort Verde State Historic Park.** 15 mi SE on AZ 279/260 in town of Camp Verde. Four original buildings of US Army fort, a major base during the campaigns of 1865–90; museum; two furnished officers' quarters; post doctor's quarters; military artifacts. Picnicking. (Daily; closed Dec 25) Phone 567-3275. ¢
4. **Montezuma Castle National Monument** (see). 20 mi SE on AZ 260, then N and E off I-17.
5. **Dead Horse Ranch State Park.** At Verde River, N of town on 5th St. This 320-acre park offers fishing. Nature trails, hiking. Picnicking (shelter). Camping (dump station). Visitor center. Standard fees. Phone 634-5283.

   (For further information contact the Cottonwood/Verde Valley Chamber of Commerce, 1010 S Main St; 634-7593.)

Annual Events

Verde Valley Fair. Fairgrounds. 4th wkend Apr.

Paseo de Casas. In Jerome (see #1). Tour of unique old homes. 3rd wkend May.

Fort Verde Days. In Camp Verde (see #3). Parade, dancing, barbecue, reenactments. 2nd wkend Oct.

(See Flagstaff, Prescott, Sedona)

Motels

★**BEST WESTERN COTTONWOOD INN.** *993 S Main.* 602/634-5575; FAX 602/255-0259. 64 rms, 2 story. Mid-Apr–mid-Sept: S $62–$67; D $65–$70; each addl $6; suites $100; under 12 free; lower rates rest of yr. Crib free. TV; cable. Heated pool; whirlpool. Restaurant

6 am–10 pm. Rm serv. Ck-out 11 am. Coin lndry. Meeting rms. Some refrigerators. Cr cds: A, C, D, DS, ER, MC, V.

★**QUALITY INN.** *302 W US 89A. 602/634-4207; FAX 602/634-5764.* 51 rms, 2 story. May–mid-Sept: S $59; D $68; each addl $10; under 18 free; lower rates rest of yr. Crib free. TV; cable. Heated pool; whirlpool. Restaurant 6 am–9 pm; Fri, Sat to 10 pm. Bar noon–10 pm; Sun 2–10 pm. Ck-out noon. Meeting rms. Cr cds: A, C, D, DS, MC, V.

Douglas (F-5)

Founded: 1901 **Pop:** 12,822 **Elev:** 4,004 ft **Area code:** 602 **Zip:** 85607

Located on the Mexican border, this diversified manufacturing town is a warm, sunny place abounding in Western hospitality. A Ranger District office of the Coronado National Forest (see TUCSON) is located here.

What to See and Do

Agua Prieta, Sonora, Mexico, is just across the border. (For border crossing regulations, see INTRODUCTION) It is a pleasant place with shops, a historical museum of the days of Pancho Villa, restaurants and cabarets.

(For further information contact the Chamber of Commerce, 1125 Pan American; 364-2477.)

Annual Events

Horse races. Cochise County Fairgrounds, N on Leslie Canyon Rd. Mid-Apr.

Cinco de Mayo. Mexican independence festival. Early May.

Douglas Fiestas. Mid-Sept.

Cochise County Fair & College Rodeo. Cochise County Fairgrounds. 3rd wkend Sept.

(See Bisbee)

Flagstaff (B-3)

Settled: 1876 **Pop:** 45,857 **Elev:** 6,910 ft **Area code:** 602

In 1876, a group of army scouts helped Thomas F. McMillan build the first shack here. They stripped a tall pine tree of its branches, tied an American flag to it and gave the town its present name. In 1882, Flagstaff became a railroad town when the Atlantic and Pacific Railroad (now the Santa Fe) was built.

Flagstaff, home of Northern Arizona University (1899), is an educational and cultural center. Tourism is Flagstaff's main industry; the city is a good place to see the Navajo country, Oak Creek Canyon (see #8), the Grand Canyon (see) and Humphreys Peak (12,633 ft), the tallest mountain in Arizona, 14 miles northwest. Tall pine forests of great beauty abound in the surrounding area. A Ranger District Office of the Coconino National Forest (see #5) is located here.

What to See and Do

1. **Lowell Observatory.** 1 mi W on Mars Hill Rd, off Santa Fe Ave. Established by Percival Lowell in 1894; the planet Pluto was discovered here in 1930. Guided tours; slide presentations; telescope viewing. Museum, gift shop. Telescope domes are unheated; appropriate clothing advised. For hours phone 774-2096.

2. **Museum of Northern Arizona.** 3 mi NW on US 180 (Fort Valley Rd). Exhibits on the archaeology, geology, biology, paleontology and fine arts of the Colorado Plateau; displays on contemporary Native American cultures of Northern Arizona. Arts and crafts shop; bookstore. Research center. (Daily; closed Jan 1, Thanksgiving, Dec 25) Phone 774-5211. ¢¢

3. **Arizona Historical Society Pioneer Museum.** 2½ mi NW on Fort Valley Rd (US 180). History of northern Arizona. (Daily exc Sun; closed hols) Phone 774-6272. **Free.**

4. **Riordan State Historic Park.** W on I-40, exit Flagstaff/Grand Canyon, then N on Milton Rd. Turn right at sign past 2nd light. Features a mansion built in 1904 by Michael and Timothy Riordan. The brothers played a significant role in the development of Flagstaff and northern Arizona. Original artifacts, hand-crafted furniture, mementos. Picnic area; no overnight facilities. Guided tours. (Daily; closed Dec 25) Phone 779-4395. ¢¢

5. **Coconino National Forest.** Surrounds city of Flagstaff and the community of Sedona (see). Outstanding scenic areas include Humphreys Peak, Arizona's highest point; parts of the Mogollon Rim and the Verde River Valley; the red rock country of Sedona and Oak Creek Canyon (see #8), where Zane Grey wrote *Call of the Canyon;* the San Francisco Peaks; seven wilderness areas; the eastern portions of Sycamore Canyon and Kendrick wilderness areas and the northern portion of Mazatzal Wilderness area; extinct volcanoes; high country lakes. Fishing, hunting on almost 2 million acres. Winter sports (see #6). Picnicking. Camping (fee). Standard fees. Phone 527-3600.

6. **Arizona Snowbowl Ski & Summer Resort.** 7 mi NW off US 180 at Snowbowl Rd in Coconino National Forest. Resort has 2 triple, 2 double chairlifts; patrol, school, rentals; restaurants, lounge; 2 day lodges. 32 trails, longest run over 2 miles; vertical drop 2,300 feet. (Mid-Dec–Mar, daily) Skyride (Memorial Day–Labor Day; fee) takes riders to 11,500-foot elevation. Phone 779-1951. ¢¢¢¢¢

7. **Walnut Canyon National Monument.** 7 mi E on I-40 (US 66), 3 mi off exit 204. A spectacular, rugged 400-foot-deep canyon with some 300 small cliff dwellings dating back to around A.D. 1100. The dwellings are well-preserved because they are under protective ledges in the canyon's limestone walls. There are two self-guided trails and an educational museum in the visitor center. Picnic grounds. (Daily; closed Dec 25) Nature trail accessible to wheelchairs. Phone 526-3367 or -0571. Per person ¢; Per vehicle ¢¢

8. **Oak Creek Canyon.** 14 mi S on US 89A. This spectacular gorge may look familiar to you. It's a favorite location for western movies. From the northern end the road starts with a lookout point atop the walls and descends nearly 2,000 feet to the stream bed. The creek has excellent trout fishing. At the southern mouth of the canyon is Sedona (see), a resort town.

9. **Mormon Lake Ski Center.** 28 mi SE off Lake Mary Rd on Mormon Lake Rd. Terrain includes snowy meadows, huge stands of pine, oak and aspen, old logging roads and turn-of-the-century railroad grades. School. Has 19 miles of marked, groomed trails; restaurant, bar; motel, cabins. Rentals. Guided tours. Phone 354-2240. ¢¢¢

10. **Wupatki National Monument** (see). 30 mi N on US 89.

(For further information contact the Chamber & Visitor's Center, 101 W Santa Fe, 86001-5598; 774-9541 or 800/842-7293.)

Annual Events

Winter Festival. Features art contest and exhibit; theater performances; workshops; sled dog and other races, games; Winterfaire, with arts and crafts; entertainment. Mid-Feb.

Zuni Artists' Exhibition. The Museum of Northern Arizona (see #2). Five days beginning Sat prior to Memorial Day.

Hopi Artists' Exhibition. The Museum of Northern Arizona (see #2). Late June–early July.

Indian Powwow. Downtown. Last wkend June.

Navajo Artists' Exhibition. The Museum of Northern Arizona (see #2). Last wkend July–1st wkend Aug.

Flagstaff Festival of the Arts. Northern Arizona University campus, SW edge of city. Symphonic/pops concerts, chamber music; theater; dance; art exhibits; poetry; film classics. Phone 774-7750 or 800/266-7740. July–early Aug.

Coconino County Fair. Labor Day wkend.

(See Cottonwood, Sedona, Williams, Winslow)

Motels

(Rates higher Indian Powwow)

★**ARIZONA MOUNTAIN INN.** *685 Lake Mary Rd (86001), near Pulliam Field Airport.* 602/774-8959. 18 units, 1–4 story, 15 kit. cottages, 3 suites. No A/C. No elvtr. No rm phones. S, D $60–$90; each addl $10; suites $70–$100; under 3 free; wkly rates. Pet accepted, some restrictions. Playground. Ck-out 11 am. Coin lndry. Free airport, RR station, bus depot transportation avail. Downhill/x-country ski 14 mi. Balconies. Picnic tables, grills. Rustic atmosphere. Cr cds: DS, MC, V.

🄳 🄿 👤 ✕ 🚫 🄌

✔ ★★**BEST WESTERN PONY SOLDIER.** *3030 US 66 (86004).* 602/526-2388; FAX 602/527-8329. 90 rms, 2 story. Apr–Oct: S $55–$65; D $65–$75; each addl $5; suites $85–$95; under 12 free; lower rates rest of yr. Crib $5. TV; cable. Indoor pool. Complimentary continental bkfst. Restaurant 6 am–10 pm; Fri, Sat to 11 pm. Rm serv from 5 pm. Bar from 11 am. Ck-out 11 am. Meeting rms. Gift shop. Downhill ski 15 mi. Cr cds: A, C, D, DS, MC, V, JCB.

👤 🚬 🚫 🄌 SC

★★**COMFORT INN.** *914 S Milton Rd (86001), 1 mi N of I-40 exit 195B.* 602/774-7326. 67 rms, 2 story. June–Oct: S $62–$76; D $65–$76; each addl $5; under 18 free; lower rates rest of yr. Crib $2. Pet accepted. TV; cable. Heated pool (in season). Restaurant nearby. Ck-out 11 am. Downhill ski 15 mi. Cr cds: A, C, D, DS, ER, MC, V, JCB.

🄳 🄿 👤 🚬 🚫 🄌 SC

✔ ★**ECONO LODGE EAST.** *3601 E Lockitt Rd (86004).* 602/527-1477; FAX 602/527-0228. 50 rms, 3 story. Mid-Mar–Oct: S, D $60–$99; under 18 free; higher rates: hols, special events; lower rates rest of yr. Crib $5. TV; cable. Complimentary coffee in lobby. Restaurant adj 6 am–11 pm. Ck-out 11 am. Coin lndry. Some refrigerators. Cr cds: A, C, D, DS, MC, V.

🄳 🚫 🄌 SC

★★**FAIRFIELD INN BY MARRIOTT.** *2005 S Milton Rd (86001).* 602/773-1300. 135 rms, 3 story. Mid-May–Oct: S, D $65.95–$87.95; each addl $7; under 18 free; lower rates rest of yr. Crib free. TV; cable. Pool. Complimentary continental bkfst, coffee. Restaurant opp open 24 hrs. Ck-out noon. Meeting rm. Downhill/x-country ski 15 mi. Cr cds: A, D, DS, MC, V.

🄳 👤 🚬 🚫 🄌 SC

★★**QUALITY INN.** *2000 S Milton Rd (86001).* 602/774-8771; FAX 602/774-0216. 96 rms, 2 story. May–Sept: S $75–$91; D $84–$100; each addl $5; under 18 free; lower rates rest of yr. Crib free. Pet accepted. TV; cable. Heated pool. Complimentary continental bkfst. Restaurant adj open 24 hrs. Ck-out 11 am. Downhill ski 15 mi. Cr cds: A, C, D, DS, ER, MC, V, JCB.

🄿 👤 🚬 🚫 🄌 SC

✔ ★**SUPER 8.** *3725 Kasper Ave (86004), US 66, 89 at Business Rte 40.* 602/526-0818; FAX 602/526-8786. 86 rms, 2 story. Apr–Sept: S $42.88–$48.88; D $55.88–$66.88; each addl $5; lower rates rest of yr. Crib free. TV; cable. Restaurant adj 6 am–midnight. Ck-out 11 am. Whirlpool, sauna. Downhill ski 15 mi. Cr cds: A, C, D, DS, MC, V.

🄳 👤 🚫 🄌 SC

★★**TRAVELODGE SUITES.** *2755 Woodland Village Blvd (86001).* 602/773-1111; FAX 602/774-1449. 89 suites, 2 story. May–Sept: S, D $69–$110; under 17 free; lower rates rest of yr. Crib free. Pet accepted; $25 refundable. TV; cable. Heated pool. Complimentary continental bkfst, coffee. Restaurant opp 6 am–10 pm. Ck-out 11 am. Coin lndry. Meeting rms. Sundries. Gift shop. Free airport, RR station, bus depot transportation. Exercise equipt; weight machine, bicycles, whirlpool, sauna. Refrigerators. Cr cds: A, C, D, DS, ER, MC, V.

🄳 🄿 👤 🚬 👤 🚫 🄌 SC

Motor Hotels

★★**HOLIDAY INN.** *2320 Lucky Lane (86004).* 602/526-1150; FAX 602/779-2610. 157 rms, 5 story. Mid-Apr–mid-Oct: S, D $69–$119; each addl $10; under 18 free; lower rates rest of yr. Crib free. Pet accepted; $20 refundable. TV; cable. Heated pool; whirlpool. Restaurant 6–10 am, 5–10 pm. Rm serv. Bar 4 pm–1 am. Ck-out noon. Coin lndry. Meeting rms. Bellhops. Valet serv. Free airport, RR station, bus depot transportation. Downhill ski 11 mi. Cr cds: A, C, D, DS, ER, MC, V, JCB.

🄳 🄿 👤 🚬 👤 🚫 🄌 SC

★★★**LITTLE AMERICA HOTEL.** *(Box 3900, 86003) 2515 E Butler Ave.* 602/779-2741; res: 800/352-4386; FAX 602/779-7983. 248 rms, 2 story. May–Oct: S, D $89–$99; each addl $10; suites $110–$185; under 12 free; lower rates rest of yr. Crib free. TV; cable. Heated pool (in season); lifeguard. Restaurant open 24 hrs. Rm serv 6 am–midnight. Bar 11–1 am, Sun from noon; entertainment, dancing. Ck-out 1 pm. Meeting rms. Bellhops. Valet serv. Concierge. Gift shop. Sundries. Free airport, RR station, bus depot transportation. Tennis privileges. Golf privileges. Downhill ski 7 mi. Health club privileges. Lawn games. Bathrm phones; many refrigerators; some fireplaces. Cr cds: A, C, D, DS, MC, V.

🄳 👤 🎾 🚬 👤 🚫 🄌

★★**QUALITY SUITES.** *706 S Milton Rd (86001).* 602/774-4333; FAX 602/774-0216. 102 suites, 3 story. Early June–mid-Sept: suites $92–$173; lower rates rest of yr. TV; cable. Heated pool; whirlpool. Complimentary full bkfst. Restaurant adj 11 am–11 pm. Ck-out noon. Meeting rm. Gift shop. Downhill ski 12 mi. Refrigerators, minibars. Cr cds: A, C, D, DS, ER, MC, V, JCB.

🄳 👤 🚬 🚫 🄌 SC

Restaurants

(A city ordinance bans smoking in all restaurants within the city limits of Flagstaff.)

★**BUSTER'S.** *1800 S Milton Rd.* 602/774-5155. Hrs: 11:30 am–10 pm; Fri, Sat to 11 pm; Sun brunch 11:30 am–2 pm. Closed Thanksgiving, Dec 25. Res accepted. Bar to 1 am. Semi-a la carte: lunch $5.25–$8.25, dinner $8.95–$17.95. Sun brunch $5.25–$17.95. Child's meals. Specializes in prime rib, fresh fish, mesquite-grilled steak. Oyster bar. Parking. Casual dining. Cr cds: A, C, D, DS, MC, V.

🄳

★★★**CHEZ MARC BISTRO.** *503 Humphreys St.* 602/774-1343. Hrs: 11:30 am–2:30 pm, 5:30–9 pm; Fri, Sat to 9:30 pm. Closed Dec 25. Res accepted. French menu. Bar. Wine list. Semi-a la carte: lunch $4.50–$11.25, dinner $12.95–$19.95. Specializes in rack of lamb, sterling salmon, trilogy of squab, lamb sirloin & duck confit. Parking. Outdoor dining. Country French bistro atmosphere. Cr cds: A, D, DS, MC, V.

🄳

★★**COTTAGE PLACE.** *126 W Cottage Ave.* 602/774-8431. Hrs: 5–9:30 pm. Closed Mon; Thanksgiving, Dec 25. Res accepted. No A/C. Continental menu. Wine, beer. Semi-a la carte: dinner $13–$19. Child's meals. Specialties: veal Regina, fresh salmon, roast duckling.

Own desserts. Parking. Intimate dining in 1908 cottage. Former residence of town mayor. Cr cds: A, MC, V.

★**FIDDLER'S.** *702 Milton Rd. 602/774-6689.* Hrs: 11:30 am–10 pm. Closed some major hols. Res accepted. Bar. Semi-a la carte: lunch $5.95–$10.95, dinner $6.95–$28. Child's meals. Specializes in prime rib, seafood, pasta. Parking. Cr cds: A, D, MC, V.

✔ ★**KACHINA DOWNTOWN.** *522 E AZ 66. 602/779-1944.* Hrs: 10 am–9 pm; Fri, Sat to 10 pm; Sun 3–8 pm. Closed some major hols. Res accepted. Mexican menu. Bar. Semi-a la carte: lunch $5.25–$14.50. Specializes in chimichangas, Mexican-style chicken-fried steak, chile relleno. Parking. Cantina decor. Cr cds: A, C, D, DS, MC, V.

✔ ★**MAMMA LUISA ITALIAN.** *2710 N Steves Blvd. 602/526-6809.* Hrs: 11:30 am–2 pm, 5–10 pm; Sat & Sun from 5 pm. Closed some major hols. Res accepted. Italian menu. Serv bar. Semi-a la carte: lunch $4.25–$7.50, dinner $5.25–$15.50. Child's meals. Specialties: chicken rollantini, veal saltimbocca. Parking. Cr cds: A, DS, MC, V.

Florence (D-3)

Pop: 7,510 **Elev:** 1,490 ft **Area code:** 602 **Zip:** 85232

Set in the desert amid multicolored mountains, the seat of Pinal County is the fifth oldest pioneer settlement in the state. Florence has many early houses still standing, making the town something of a living relic of pioneer days.

What to See and Do

1. **Pinal County Historical Society Museum.** 715 S Main St. Exhibits depict early life in the area. (Wed–Sun; closed some major hols; also mid-July–Aug) Donation. Phone 868-4382.
2. **McFarland State Historic Park** (1878). Ruggles Ave & Main St. First of four courthouses built here; restored adobe building with interpretive center, displays of early Arizona and US legal history, and the personal collections of Governor Ernest McFarland, also a US Senator and state supreme court justice. (Thurs–Mon; closed Dec 25) Phone 868-5216. ¢
3. **Casa Grande Ruins National Monument** (see). 10 mi W via AZ 287, then S on AZ 87.

(For further information contact the Chamber of Commerce, Box 929, phone 868-9433; or the Pinal County Visitor Center, Mon–Fri, located in the historic Jacob Suter house, 912 N Pinal St, PO Box 967, phone 868-4331.)

Annual Event

Junior Parada. Three-day celebration features parade and rodeo. Sat of Thanksgiving wkend.

(For accommodations see Casa Grande)

Ganado (B-5)

Pop: 1,257 **Elev:** 6,386 ft **Area code:** 602 **Zip:** 86505

What to See and Do

Hubbell Trading Post National Historic Site. 1 mi W on AZ 264. The oldest continuously operating trading post (1878) on the Navajo Reservation; named for founder, John Lorenzo Hubbell, who began trading with the Navajo in 1876. Construction of the present-day post began in 1883. The visitor center houses exhibits; Navajo weavers and a silversmith can be observed at work; tours of the Hubbell house, containing paintings, Navajo rugs and Native American arts & crafts; self-guided tour of the grounds (ranger-conducted programs in summer). (Daily; closed Jan 1, Thanksgiving, Dec 25) Phone 755-3475 or -3477. **Free.**

(For accommodations see Canyon de Chelly National Monument, also see Window Rock)

Gila Bend (D-2)

Pop: 1,747 **Elev:** 736 ft **Area code:** 602 **Zip:** 85337

Located on a desert plain near a sharp bend in the Gila River, Gila Bend was home to a flourishing Native American community prior to the arrival of Spanish explorers in the 17th century.

(See Casa Grande)

Motel

★★**BEST WESTERN SPACE AGE LODGE.** *(Box C) 401 E Pima. 602/683-2273.* 41 rms. Jan–Apr: S $46–$60; D $50–$68; each addl $5; under 17 free; lower rates rest of yr. Crib free. Pet accepted. TV; cable. Pool; whirlpool. Restaurant open 24 hrs. Ck-out noon. Some refrigerators. Cr cds: A, C, D, DS, MC, V, JCB.

Glendale (D-3)

Founded: 1892 **Pop:** 148,134 **Elev:** 1,150 ft **Area code:** 602

Located just west of Phoenix in the beautiful and scenic Valley of the Sun, Glendale shares all of the urban advantages of the area. Luke AFB is located nearby.

(For information about this area contact the Glendale Chamber of Commerce, 7105 N 59th Ave, Box 249, 85311; 937-4754.)

Annual Event

Thunderbird Balloon Classic–100 Hot-Air Balloon Race & Air Show. Glendale Airport, 6767 N Glen Harbor Blvd. Phone 978-7208. 1st wk Nov.

(See Litchfield Park, Mesa, Phoenix, Scottsdale, Tempe)

Motel

✔ ★★**BEST WESTERN SAGE INN.** *5940 NW Grand Ave (85301). 602/939-9431; FAX 602/939-9431, ext 146.* 83 rms, 2 story. Jan–Apr: S, D $55–$66; each addl $4; under 12 free; lower rates rest of yr. Crib $3. Pet accepted. TV; cable. 2 pools. Complimentary continental bkfst. Restaurant adj 6 am–9 pm. Ck-out 11 am. Coin lndry. Meeting rm. Refrigerators. Cr cds: A, C, D, DS, MC, V, JCB.

Globe (D-4)

Settled: 1876 **Pop:** 6,062 **Elev:** 3,509 ft **Area code:** 602 **Zip:** 85501

A silver strike settled Globe, but copper made the town what it is today. One of the original copper mines, Old Dominion, is no longer worked; however, other mines are still in operation. Cattle ranching also contributes to the economy. A Ranger District office for the Tonto National Forest (see PAYSON) is located here.

What to See and Do

1. **Gila County Historical Museum.** 1 mi N on US 60. Exhibit of artifacts of Gila County, including those of the Apache. (Mon–Fri; closed hols) Donation. Phone 425-7385.

2. **Besh-Ba-Gowah Indian Ruins.** From end of S Broad St turn right across bridge, continue on Jess Hayes Rd. Ruins of a village inhabited by the Salado from 1225 to 1400. More than 200 rooms. Visitor center, museum. (Daily; closed Jan 1, Thanksgiving, Dec 25) Phone 425-0320. ¢

3. **Boyce Thompson Southwestern Arboretum.** 28 mi W on US 60; 3 mi W of Superior. Large collection of plants from arid parts of world added to native flora in high Sonoran Desert setting at foot of Picket Post Mt; labeled plants in 39-acre garden. Picnicking. Visitor center features biological and historical displays. (Daily; closed Dec 25) Phone 689-2811. ¢¢

(For further information contact the Greater Globe-Miami Chamber of Commerce, 1360 N Broad St, Box 2539, 85502; 425-4495.)

Annual Events

Old-time Fiddlers Contest. 3rd wkend July.

Gila County Fair. 4 days mid-Sept.

Apache Days. 4th wkend Oct.

(See San Carlos)

Motels

★ ★**BEST WESTERN COPPER HILLS INN.** *(Rte 1, Box 506, Miami 85539)* 3½ mi W on US 60, 70. 602/425-7151; FAX 602/425-2504. 68 rms, 2 story. S, D $49–$59; each addl $4; suites $75–$85; under 12 free. Crib $5. Pet accepted, some restrictions. TV; cable. Pool. Restaurant 5 am–9 pm; dining rm 11:45 am–2 pm, 5–9 pm. Bar 10–1 am, Sun to 9 pm. Ck-out noon. Gift shop. Refrigerators, bathrm phones. Cr cds: A, C, D, DS, MC, V.

★ ★**CLOUD NINE.** *(PO Box 1043)* At jct US 60 & 70. 602/425-5741; res: 800/432-6655. 61 rms, 2 story. S $47–$59; D $50–$69; each addl $7; under 14 free. Crib $5. Pet accepted, some restrictions. TV; cable. Heated pool; whirlpool. Restaurant 6 am–10 pm. Ck-out noon. Refrigerators. Picnic tables. Cr cds: A, C, D, DS, ER, MC, V, JCB.

Grand Canyon National Park (B-3)

Area code: 602

Every minute of the day, the light changes the colors and form of this magnificent spectacle. Sunrises and sunsets are particularly superb.

In 1540, Spanish explorer de Cardenas became the first European to see this canyon of the Colorado River, but he and his party were unable to cross and soon left. In 1857, American Lieutenant Joseph Ives said the region was " altogether valueless. . . . Ours has been the first and will doubtless be the last party of whites to visit this profitless locality."

As much as 18 miles wide and about a mile deep, the canyon has wildlife that includes at least 220 different species of birds, 67 species of mammals, 27 species of reptiles and 5 species of amphibians.

The South Rim (see), open all year, has the greatest number of services and is the most popular to visit. The North Rim (see), blocked by heavy snows in winter, is open from approximately mid-May–late October. One rim can be reached from the other by a 215-mile drive. The South Rim has an altitude of about 7,000 feet; the North Rim is about 8,100 feet. The river is some 4,600 feet below the South Rim. It is seven miles via the South Kaibab Trail and nine miles via the Bright Angel Trail from the South Rim to the bottom of the canyon.

The park now encompasses more than one million acres. Of the Grand Canyon's roughly 275-mile length, the first 50 or so miles along the Colorado River comprise what is known as Marble Canyon, where 3,000-foot, near-vertical walls of sandstone and limestone may be seen. US 89A crosses the Navajo Bridge 467 feet above the Colorado River.

Pets must be on a leash and are excluded from certain areas. For further information contact the Superintendent, PO Box 129, Grand Canyon 86023; 638-7888. Per car ¢¢¢

(See Flagstaff, Williams)

North Rim (Grand Canyon National Park) (B-3)

(215 mi NW of Flagstaff: 116 mi N via US 89, 55 mi W via Alt US 89, then 44 mi S via AZ 67) **Zip:** 86052

(SUMMER ONLY)

What to See and Do

1. **Drive to Cape Royal.** About 23 mi from Bright Angel Point over paved road. Several good viewpoints along way. Many think the view from here is better than from the South Rim. Archaeology and geology talks in summer & fall.

2. **Muleback trips** into canyon (daytime only). Also horseback trips (along rim only, not into canyon). Phone Canyon Trail Rides 602/638-2292 (summer) or 801/679-8665 (winter).

3. **Programs** by naturalists; occasionally other events. Consult information board at Grand Canyon Lodge for schedule.   **Free.**

4. **Camping.** Campsites, trailer parking space at North Rim Campground (7-day limit; no hookups). For camping reservations phone Mistix at 800/365-2267. ¢¢¢   For lodging information at the North Rim phone TW Recreational Services, Inc. at 801/586-7686.

5. **Hiking.** Six trails (¼ mi–10 mi); some are self-guided.

Motel

(Air conditioning is rarely necessary at this elevation)

(This lodge in the park is under concession from the Dept of the Interior. For reservations contact TW Recreational Services, Inc, Box 400, Cedar City, UT 84720; 801/586-7686.)

✔ ★ ★**GRAND CANYON LODGE.** *(Mailing address: Box 400, Cedar City, UT 84720)* At canyon rim, S on AZ 67. 602/638-2611; res: 801/586-7686. 201 units; 161 cabins, 40 motel rms. May–Oct: S, D $45–$69; each addl $5; under 13 free. Closed rest of yr. Crib $5. Restaurant 6:30–10 am, 11:30 am–2:30 pm, 5–9:30 pm. Bar 11:30 am–10:30 pm. Ck-out 11 am. Bellhops. Sundries. Gift shop. Game rm. Some fireplaces. View of canyon. Cr cds: A, C, D, MC, V.

South Rim (Grand Canyon National Park) (B-3)

(Approx 80 mi NW of Flagstaff via US 180) **Zip:** 86023

(OPEN ALL YEAR)

What to See and Do

1. **Visitor Center.** National Park Service. Grand Canyon Village. Has information, maps, pamphlets and exhibits. (Daily)   **Free.**

2. **Drives to viewpoints.** There are West Rim and East Rim drives out from Grand Canyon Village; each is rewarding. Grandview Point and Desert View on the East Rim Drive are especially magnificent. West Rim Drive closed to private vehicles late May–late Sept. Free shuttle buses serve West Rim & Village area during this period.

3. **Yavapai Museum.** On rim, 1 mi E of Grand Canyon village. Scenic views, exhibits, information. (Daily)   **Free.**

4. **Tusayan Museum.** East Rim Drive, 20 mi E of Grand Canyon village. Exhibits on prehistoric man in the Southwest. Excavated pueblo ruin (ca 1185) nearby. (Daily, weather permitting)   **Free.**

5. **Guided river trips.** Reservations should be made well in advance.

   Multi-day trips within the park. Phone Grand Canyon National Park at 602/638-7888 (touch tone 1-3-7-1) for a written list of commercial outfitters.

   One-day trips available from Page to Lees Ferry, in Glen Canyon National Recreation Area; phone ARA-Wilderness River Adventures at 602/645-3279.

6. **Evening programs** every night all year by Park Service ranger-naturalist in outdoor amphitheater; inside Shrine of the Ages Building during the colder months; daytime talks given all year at Yavapai Museum (see #3) and at Visitor Center (see #1).   **Free.**

7. **Hiking down into canyon.** Not recommended except for those in good physical condition, because heat and 4,500-foot climb back are exhausting. Consult Back Country Office staff before attempting this. (**Caution:** always carry sufficient water and food; neither is available along trails.) Reservations required for camping below the rim; by mail from Back Country Reservation Office, PO Box 129, Grand Canyon 86023, or in person at Back Country Reservation Office, located at Camper Service.

8. **Mule trip into canyon.** Easier than walking and quite safe; a number of trips are scheduled, all with guides. There are some limitations. Trips take one, two or three days. Reservations should be made several months in advance (preferably one year prior). For information phone Fred Harvey, Inc at 602/638-2401.

9. **Camping.** Sites (no hookups) at Mather Campground (fee); reservations can be made through Mistix by phone at 800/365-2267. Adj is Trailer Village, with trailer sites (hookups; fee); for reservations phone 602/638-2401. ¢¢¢¢–¢¢¢¢¢

10. **Kaibab National Forest.** Adj to both North and South Rims are units of this 1.5 million-acre forest (see WILLIAMS). The Ranger District office for the Tusayan District is located in Tusayan, several miles south of the park.

11. **Grand Canyon IMAX Theatre.** AZ 64/US 180, 1 mi S of park entrance. Large screen film (35-min) highlighting features of Grand Canyon. (Daily) For schedule information phone 602/638-2203. ¢¢¢

12. **Scenic flights over Grand Canyon.** Many operators offer air tours of the Canyon. Flights out of many different airports. For a partial list of companies contact the Grand Canyon Chamber of Commerce, PO Box 3007, Grand Canyon, 86023.

Motels

★★**BEST WESTERN GRAND CANYON SQUIRE INN.** (Box 130) 7 mi S on US 180 (AZ 64), just S of park entrance. 602/638-2681; FAX 602/638-2782. 250 rms, 3 story. Apr–Oct: S, D $100–$120; each addl $5; under 12 free; lower rates rest of yr. Crib avail. TV; cable. Heated pool; poolside serv. Playground. Restaurant 6:30 am–10 pm. Bar 10–1 am. Ck-out noon. Coin lndry. Meeting rms. Bellhops. Concierge. Sundries. Gift shop. Airport transportation. Tennis. Exercise equipt; weight machine, treadmill, whirlpool, sauna. Game rm. Rec rm. Six lane bowling alley on premises. Cr cds: A, C, D, DS, MC, V, JCB.

✔★**BRIGHT ANGEL LODGE.** W Rim Dr, 2 mi W on US 180 (AZ 64). 602/638-2631; res: 602/638-2401; FAX 602/638-9247. 89 rms: 39 in hotel, 15 with bath; 50 cabins. No A/C. S, D $50–$102; each addl $7; suite $202. Crib free. TV in some rms. Restaurant 6:30 am–10 pm. Bar 11–1 am, Sun from noon; entertainment exc Mon. Ck-out 11 am. Bellhops. Sundries. Gift shop. Barber, beauty shop. Fireplace in some cabins. Some canyon-side rms. Canyon tour serv. Kennel. Cr cds: A, C, D, DS, MC, V, JCB.

★**KACHINA LODGE.** 3 mi W on US 180 (AZ 64); register at El Tovar Hotel (see). 602/638-2631; res: 602/638-2401; FAX 602/638-9247. 48 air-cooled rms, 2 story. S, D $89–$99; each addl $9. Crib free. TV; cable. Restaurant adj 6:30 am–2 pm, 5–10 pm. Ck-out 11 am. Meeting rms. Bellhops. Canyon tour serv. Kennel. Cr cds: A, C, D, DS, MC, V, JCB.

★**MASWIK NORTH.** 2½ mi W on US 180 (AZ 64). 602/638-2631; res: 602/638-2401; FAX 602/638-9247. 160 rms, 2 story. S, D $88–$98; each addl $8; under 16 free. Crib free. TV; cable. Restaurant 6 am–10 pm. Bar 11–1 am. Ck-out 11 am. Bellhops. Sundries. Gift shop. Some private patios, balconies. Canyon tour serv. Kennel. Cr cds: A, C, D, DS, MC, V, JCB.

★★**QUALITY INN GRAND CANYON.** (Box 520) AZ 64, near Grand Canyon IMAX Theatre. 602/638-2673; FAX 602/638-9537. 176 rms, 3 story. Apr–Oct: S, D $103–$118; each addl $6; under 2 free; lower rates rest of yr. Crib $6. TV; cable. Pool; whirlpool. Restaurant nearby. Ck-out 11 am. Gift shop. Some minibars. Balconies. Cr cds: A, C, D, DS, ER, MC, V, JCB.

★**RED FEATHER LODGE.** (Box 1460) AZ 64 & US 180. 602/638-2414; res: 800/538-2345; FAX 602/638-9216. 106 rms, 2 story. May–Oct: S, D $110; each addl $5; lower rates rest of yr. Crib $6. TV; cable. Restaurant 7 am–10 pm. Ck-out 11 am. Gift shop. Free airport transportation. Downhill ski 8 mi; x-country ski 1 mi. Balconies. Cr cds: A, C, D, MC, V.

★**THUNDERBIRD LODGE.** Village Loop Dr, 2 mi W on US 180 (AZ 64); register at Bright Angel Lodge Motel (see). 602/638-2631; res: 602/638-2401; FAX 602/638-9247. 55 air-cooled rms, 2 story. S, D $89–$99; each addl $9. Crib free. TV; cable. Restaurant adj 6:30 am–10 pm. Ck-out 11 am. Meeting rms. Bellhops. Some canyon-side rms. Canyon tour serv. Kennel. Cr cds: A, C, D, DS, MC, V, JCB.

✔★**YAVAPAI LODGE.** Mather Center, 1 mi W of AZ 64, opp visitor center. 602/638-2631; res: 602/638-2401; FAX 602/638-9247. 358 rms, 2 story. No A/C. Mid-Mar–Oct: S, D $69–$88; each addl $9. Closed rest of yr exc wk of Thanksgiving & Dec 25. Crib free. TV. Restaurant 6 am–10 pm; snack bar 11:30 am–midnight. Ck-out 11 am. Bellhops. Sundries. Canyon tour serv. Kennel. Cr cds: A, C, D, DS, MC, V, JCB.

Hotel

★ ★ ★ **EL TOVAR.** *(Box 699) 3 mi W of entrance on US 180 (AZ 64). 602/638-2631; res: 602/638-2401; FAX 602/638-9247.* 78 rms, 3 story. S, D $102–$164; each addl $11; suites $167–$252. Crib free. TV; cable. Restaurant (see EL TOVAR DINING ROOM). Bar 11–1 am, Sun from noon; entertainment exc Sun, Mon. Ck-out 11 am. Concierge. Gift shop. Built 1905. Some suites with balcony overlooking canyon. Kennels. Cr cds: A, C, D, DS, MC, V, JCB.

Restaurants

★ ★ ★ **EL TOVAR DINING ROOM.** *(See El Tovar Hotel) 602/638-2631.* Hrs: 6:30 am–2 pm, 5–10 pm. Res required. Bar. Wine cellar. Semi-a la carte: bkfst $1.95–$11.65, lunch $2.50–$15.10, dinner $13–$24. Child's meals. Specialty: 3-course vegetarian meal. Parking. Stone fireplaces. Native American murals. Overlooks Grand Canyon. Totally nonsmoking. Cr cds: A, C, D, DS, MC, V, JCB.

★ **STEAKHOUSE AT GRAND CANYON.** *AZ 64 & US 180, across from IMAX theater. 602/638-2780.* Hrs: 5–10 pm. Closed Dec–Feb. Bar. Semi-a la carte: dinner $6.95–$19.95. Child's meals. Specialty: choice Colorado beef cooked on open oak wood fire. Own biscuits. Hayrides, stage coach rides Mar–Oct. Parking. Old West decor; brick fireplace. Covered wagon in front yard. No cr cds accepted.

Greer (C-5)

Pop: 125 (est) **Elev:** 8,380 ft **Area code:** 602 **Zip:** 85927

Within the Apache-Sitgreaves National Forest, this town is 18 miles southwest of Springerville (see) on AZ 273. Cross-country and downhill skiing are available nearby from December to March; fishing, hunting, backpacking, bicycling and camping are popular at other times of year.

(See McNary, Pinetop, Springerville)

Lodge

★ ★ **GREER LODGE.** *(PO Box 244) ½ mi S of post office on AZ 373. 602/735-7515.* 10 rms in main lodge, 3 story, 6 kit. cabins (1–2 bedrms), little lodge with kit. (4 bedrms, 3 baths), 2 story. No A/C. No elvtr. No rm phones. S $90–$100; D $120–$130; each addl $20–$30; kit. units $95–$105; each addl (after 2nd person) $15–$25; little lodge $280–$300; each addl (after 8th person) $15–$25; fly-fishing school package. Crib avail. TV in lobby. Complimentary full bkfst (exc kit. units). Restaurant (public by res) 7–10 am, 11:30 am–3 pm, 5–9 pm. Bar 10 am–10 pm. Ck-out 11 am. Meeting rm. X-country ski 1 mi. Ice-skating. Sleigh rides. Stocked trout pond. Picnic tables, grills. Sun deck. Fireplace, piano in living room. On 17 acres; overlooks Little Colorado River. Cr cds: MC, V.

Restaurant

★ **MOLLY BUTLER.** *100 Main St, Butler's Lodge. 602/735-7226.* Hrs: 5–9 pm. Res accepted. No A/C. Bar 8–1 am. Semi-a la carte: dinner $6.95–$32.50. Specializes in prime rib, steak, seafood. Parking. Old West atmosphere; 2 dining areas; rustic decor. Scenic view of valley meadows, mountains. Cr cds: MC, V.

Holbrook (C-4)

Pop: 4,686 **Elev:** 5,083 ft **Area code:** 602 **Zip:** 86025

What to See and Do

1. **Navajo County Historical Museum.** 100 E Arizona, in Old County Courthouse. Exhibits on Navajo, Apache, Hopi and Hispanic culture; petrified forest; local history; dinosaurs. (May–Sept, daily exc Sun; rest of yr, Mon–Fri; closed major hols) Donation. Phone 524-6558.

2. **Petrified Forest National Park** (see). North entrance, 26 mi E on US 66/I-40; south entrance, 19 mi E on US 180.

3. **Apache-Sitgreaves National Forests.** 46 mi S on AZ 77 to Show Low (see).

(For further information contact the Chamber of Commerce, 100 E Arizona St; 524-6558.)

Annual Events

Old West Days. 1st wk of June.

Navajo County Fair. Late Aug.

Navajo County Horse Races. 2nd & 3rd wkends Sept.

(See Hopi and Navajo Indian Reservations, Winslow)

Motels

✔ ★ **BEST WESTERN ADOBE INN.** *615 W Hopi Dr. 602/524-3948.* 54 rms, 2 story. May–Sept: S $48–$56; D $54–$62; each addl $2; lower rates rest of yr. Crib $2. Pet accepted, some restrictions. TV; cable. Heated pool. Complimentary continental bkfst. Restaurant adj 4–10 pm. Ck-out 11 am. Cr cds: A, C, D, DS, MC, V.

★ ★ **BEST WESTERN ARIZONIAN INN.** *2508 E Navajo Blvd. 602/524-2611.* 70 rms, 2 story. May–Aug: S $48–$60; D $56–$68; each addl $4; lower rates rest of yr. Crib $5. Pet accepted, some restrictions. TV; cable. Heated pool. Complimentary coffee in lobby. Restaurant adj open 24 hrs. Ck-out 11 am. Cr cds: A, C, D, DS, MC, V.

Hopi Indian Reservation (B-4)

Completely surrounded by the Navajo Indian Reservation (see) is the 1.5 million-acre Hopi Indian Reservation. The Hopi are pueblo Indians of Shoshonean ancestry who have lived here for more than 1,000 years. The Hopi have a complex religious system. Excellent farmers, they also herd sheep, as well as craft pottery, silver jewelry, kachina dolls and baskets. They live in some of the most intriguing towns on the North American continent.

Both the Navajo and Hopi are singers and dancers—each in their own style. The Hopi are most famous for their Snake Dance, which may not be viewed by visitors. But there are dozens of other beautiful ceremonies that visitors are allowed to watch. However, the photographing, recording or sketching of any events on the reservation is prohibited. For event information phone 602/734-6648.

All major roads leading into and across the Navajo and Hopi Reservations are paved. Do not venture off the main highways.

The Hopi towns are located, for the most part, on three mesas. On the first mesa is Walpi, founded around 1680, one of the most beautiful Hopi pueblos. It is built on the tip of a narrow, steep-walled mesa, along with its companion villages, Sichomovi and Hano, which are inhabited by the Tewa and Hano Indians. Hanoans speak a Tewa language as well as Hopi. You can drive to Sichomovi and walk along a narrow connecting mesa to Walpi. Only passenger cars are allowed on the mesa; no RVs or trailers. Individuals of Walpi and First Mesa Villages offer Hopi pottery and kachina dolls for sale; inquire locally.

The second mesa has three towns: Mishongnovi, Shipaulovi and Shongopovi, each fascinating in its own way. The Hopi Cultural Center, located on the second mesa, includes a museum and craft shops (daily); a restaurant serving both Hopi and American food and a motel; reservations (phone 602/734-2421) for May–Aug should be made at least three months in advance. Near the Cultural Center is a primitive campground (free). The third mesa has Oraibi, the oldest Hopi town, and its three offshoots, Bacabi, Kyakotsmovi and Hotevilla, a town of considerable interest. A restaurant, a small motel and tent & trailer sites can be found at Keams Canyon. There are not many places to stay, so plan your trip carefully.

(For accommodations see Canyon de Chelly National Monument, Holbrook, Kayenta, Page)

Kayenta (A-4)

Pop: 4,372 **Elev:** 5,641 ft **Area code:** 602 **Zip:** 86033

Located in the spectacular Monument Valley, Kayenta's (Kay-en-TAY) surrounding area offers some of the most memorable sightseeing in the state; the great tinted monoliths are spectacular.

What to See and Do

1. **Navajo National Monument** (see). 20 mi SW on US 160, then 9 mi N on AZ 564.
2. **Monument Valley Navajo Tribal Park.** 25 mi NE off US 163. Self-guided tours of the valley (road conditions vary, inquire locally); for guided tours, inquire at Tribal Visitor Center or lodge (see GOULDING'S MONUMENT VALLEY LODGE MOTEL). Camping (at Park Headquarters only; fee). (Daily; closed Jan 1, Dec 25) Sr citizen rate. Admission to park ¢¢
3. **Crawley's Monument Valley Tours, Inc.** Guided tours in back-country vehicles to Monument Valley, Mystery Valley and Hunt's Mesa. (Daily) Phone 697-3734 or -3463. ¢¢¢¢¢

(See Hopi and Navajo Indian Reservations)

Motels

★★**GOULDING'S MONUMENT VALLEY LODGE.** *(Box 360001, Monument Valley, UT 84536) 21 mi N, then 1½ mi W via US 163. 801/727-3231.* 19 rms in lodge, 41 rms in 2-story motel; 2 cabins. S, D $92; each addl $6; cabins $100. Pet accepted. TV; in-rm movies avail. Indoor pool. Restaurant 7 am–10 pm; closed Jan–mid-Mar. Ck-out 11 am. Coin lndry. Sundries. Gift shop. Private patios, balconies. Guided jeep tours. 1 bldg is old trading post; now museum. John Wayne movie filmed here. Navajo Tribal Park 5 mi. Cr cds: A, C, D, DS, ER, MC, V, JCB.

★★**HOLIDAY INN.** *(Box 307) Jct US 160, 163. 602/697-3221; FAX 602/697-3349.* 160 rms, 2 story. Apr–Nov: S, D $90–$105; each addl $5; suites $100–$115; under 18 free; lower rates rest of yr. Crib free. TV; cable. Pool; wading pool. Restaurant 6 am–10 pm. Rm serv. Ck-out noon. Coin lndry. Sundries. Gift shop. Cr cds: A, C, D, DS, ER, MC, V, JCB.

Kingman (B-1)

Pop: 12,722 **Elev:** 3,341 ft **Area code:** 602 **Zip:** 86401

Kingman is the seat of Mohave County. It lies at the junction of two transcontinental highways, I-40 reaching from the East to the West coast, and US 93 from Fairbanks, Alaska, to Guatemala, Mexico. It is a convenient stop on the way to the Grand Canyon, Las Vegas or Los Angeles. Nearby are Lakes Mead, Mohave and Havasu, with year-round swimming, waterskiing, fishing and boating. To the south are the beautiful Hualapai Mountains. This once was a rich silver and gold mining area; several ghost towns are nearby.

What to See and Do

1. **Mohave Museum of History & Art.** 400 W Beale St, ¼ mi E of I-40, Beale St/Las Vegas exit. Exhibits trace local and state history; portrait collection of US presidents and first ladies; Andy Devine display; turquoise display; rebuilt 1926 pipe organ; Native American displays. Local artists' gallery. (Daily; closed major hols) Phone 753-3195. ¢
2. **Bonelli House** (1894). 430 E Spring St. One of the earliest permanent structures in the city. Restored and furnished with many original pieces. (Thurs–Mon afternoons; closed hols) Phone 753-1413 or -3195. **Free.**
3. **Oatman.** 28 mi SW, located on old US 66. In the 1930s, this was the last stop in Arizona before entering the Mojave Desert in California. Created in 1906 as a tent camp, it flourished as a gold mining center until 1942, when Congress declared that gold mining was no longer essential to the war effort. The ghost town has been kept as authentic as possible; several motion pictures have been filmed here. Wild burros abound, many roaming streets that are lined with historic buildings, former mine sites, old town jail, old & modern hotel, museum, turquoise & antique shops. Gunfights staged on wkends. Contact the Oatman Chamber of Commerce, 768-7400.

(For further information contact the Kingman Chamber of Commerce, Box 1150, 86402; 753-6106.)

Annual Events

Mohave County Fair. 1st wkend after Labor Day.

Andy Devine Days & PRCA Rodeo. Sports tournaments, parade, other events. 3 days late Sept.

(See Bullhead City, Lake Havasu City)

Motels

★★**BEST WESTERN A WAYFARER'S INN.** *2815 E Andy Devine Ave. 602/753-6271; res: 800/548-5695; FAX 602/753-9608.* 100 rms, 2 story. May–Sept: S $50; D $47–$57; each addl $5; suites $73; under 12 free; lower rates rest of yr. Crib $5. TV; cable. Heated pool. Restaurant adj 6 am–9 pm. Ck-out noon. Coin lndry. Refrigerators. Cr cds: A, C, D, DS, MC, V, JCB.

★**DAYS INN.** *3023 Andy Devine Ave. 602/753-7500.* 60 rms, 2 story, 40 kit. units. May–Sept: S, D $55–$75; kit. units $60; higher rates hols; lower rates rest of yr. Crib free. Pet accepted; $3. TV. Heated pool; whirlpool. Coffee in lobby. Restaurant opp 6 am–11 pm. Coin lndry. Cr cds: A, C, D, DS, ER, MC, V, JCB.

✔★**HILL TOP.** *1901 E Andy Devine Ave. 602/753-2198.* 29 rms. May–Sept: S $24–$30; D $28–$45; each addl $5; higher rates hol wkends; lower rates rest of yr. Crib $5. TV; cable. Heated pool. Restaurant nearby. Ck-out 11 am. Coin Indry. Refrigerators avail. Cr cds: DS, MC, V.

★**HOLIDAY INN.** *3100 E Andy Devine Ave. 602/753-6262; FAX 602/753-7137.* 116 rms, 2 story. S, D $49–$69; each addl $5; under 12 free. Crib free. Pet accepted, some restrictions. TV; cable. Pool. Restaurant 6 am–10 pm. Rm serv 7 am–9 pm. Bar 5 pm–1 am. Ck-out noon. Coin Indry. Meeting rms. Valet serv. Sundries. Health club privileges. Cr cds: A, C, D, DS, ER, MC, V, JCB.

★**QUALITY INN.** *1400 E Andy Devine Ave. 602/753-4747.* 98 rms, 1–2 story. June–Aug: S $44–$49; D, kit. units $49–$54; each addl $5; under 18 free; lower rates rest of yr. Crib free. Pet accepted, some restrictions. TV; cable. Pool. Complimentary continental bkfst. Complimentary coffee in rms. Ck-out noon. Meeting rm. Beauty shop. Free airport transportation. Exercise equipt; treadmill, bicycle, whirlpool, sauna. Cr cds: A, C, D, DS, ER, MC, V, JCB.

Restaurant

✔ ★**HOUSE OF CHAN.** *960 W Beale St. 602/753-3232.* Hrs: 11 am–10 pm. Closed Sun; Jan 1. Res accepted. Chinese, Amer menu. Bar. Semi-a la carte: lunch $3.25–$5.25, dinner $6.95–$12.95. Specializes in Cantonese cuisine, prime rib, seafood. Parking. Oriental decor. Cr cds: A, MC, V.

Lake Havasu City (C-1)

Founded: 1964 **Pop:** 24,363 **Elev:** 600 ft **Area code:** 602 **Zip:** 86403

This is the center of a year-round resort area on the shores of 45-mile-long Lake Havasu. London Bridge, imported from England and reassembled here as part of a recreational area, was designed by John Rennie and built in 1824–31; it spanned the Thames River in London until 1968. It now connects the mainland city with a three-square-mile island that has a marina, golf course, tennis courts, campgrounds and other recreational facilities.

What to See and Do

1. **London Bridge English Village.** 1550 London Bridge Rd. English-style village on 21 acres; home of the world-famous London Bridge. Specialty shops, restaurants; boat rides; 9-hole golf course; accommodations (see MOTOR HOTELS). Village (daily). Phone 855-0888 or -0880. Admission ¢

2. **Sightseeing.** One-hour trolley tour, phone 453-7112. Lake Havasu Boat Tours, phone 855-7979. ¢¢¢

3. **Lake Havasu State Park.** There are 13,000 acres along 23 miles of shoreline. **Windsor Beach Unit,** 2 mi N on old US 95 (London Bridge Rd), has swimming; fishing; boating (ramps). Hiking. Ramadas. Camping (dump station). Phone 855-2784. **Cattail Cove Unit,** 15 mi S, ½ mi W of US 95, has swimming; fishing; boating (ramps). Camping (incl some water-access sites; fee). Standard fees. Phone 855-1223.

4. **Topock Gorge.** 10 mi N on lake (accessible only by boat). S boundary of Havasu National Wildlife Refuge. Scenic steep volcanic banks along Colorado River. Migratory birds winter here; herons, cormorants and egrets nest (Apr–May). Fishing. Picnicking. Phone 619/326-3853. **Free.**

(For further information contact the Lake Havasu Area Visitor & Convention Bureau, 1930 Mesquite Ave, Suite 3; 855-4115 or 800/242-8278.)

(See Kingman, Parker; also see Needles, CA)

Motor Hotels

★**HOLIDAY INN.** *245 London Bridge Rd. 602/855-4071; FAX 602/855-2379.* 162 rms, 4 story. Feb–Nov: S $45–$78; D $53–$86; each addl $8; suites $97–$135; under 18 free; wkly rates; golf plan; higher rates: hols, special events; lower rates rest of yr. Crib free. Pet accepted, some restrictions. TV; cable. Heated pool. Restaurant 6 am–10 pm. Rm serv. Bar 11–1 am; Sun from noon; entertainment, dancing exc Sun. Ck-out noon. Coin Indry. Meeting rms. Free airport transportation. Game rm. Some refrigerators. Balconies. On lake; state park adj. Cr cds: A, C, D, DS, ER, MC, V, JCB.

★★**RAMADA LONDON BRIDGE RESORT.** *1477 Queens Bay Rd, near Municipal Airport. 602/855-0888; FAX 602/855-9209.* 137 rms, 3 story. S, D $75–$150; suites $125–$250; under 12 free. Pet accepted, some restrictions. $10 per day. TV. 3 heated pools; whirlpool. Restaurants 7 am–2 pm, 5–9 pm. Bar 11–1 am. Meeting rms. Shopping arcade. Beauty shop. Airport transportation. Lighted tennis. Lighted 9-hole golf, pro, putting green. Exercise equipt; weights, bicycles, whirlpool. Some bathrm phones, refrigerators. Private patios, balconies. Picnic tables. On lake. Cr cds: A, C, D, DS, MC, V.

Restaurant

★★**SHUGRUE'S.** *1425 McCulloch Blvd. 602/453-1400.* Hrs: 11 am–10 pm. Closed Dec 25. Res accepted. Bar to 1 am. Semi-a la carte: lunch $4.25–$7.95, dinner $9.95–$32.95. Child's meals. Specializes in fresh seafood, steak, chicken. Parking. Multi-level dining. Nautical atmosphere. Overlooks London Bridge. Cr cds: A, MC, V.

Lake Mead National Recreation Area

(see Nevada)

Litchfield Park (D-3)

Pop: 3,303 **Elev:** 1,027 ft **Area code:** 602 **Zip:** 85340

In 1916, the Goodyear Tire and Rubber Company purchased and leased two tracts of land to grow Egyptian cotton. One tract was west of the Agua Fria River and was, for a short time, referred to as the Agua Fria Ranch. In 1926, the name was changed to Litchfield in honor of Paul W. Litchfield, vice president of the company.

What to See and Do

Wildlife World Zoo. 3 mi W on Northern Ave. Houses a family of dromedaries (single-humped camels); exotic bird aviary; three species of rare antelope; monkeys; kangaroos; wallabies; leopards; tigers; all five species of the world's flightless birds. Petting zoo; concession. (Daily) Phone 935-WILD. ¢¢¢

(For further information contact the Tri-City West Chamber of Commerce, 501 W Van Buren, Suite K, Avondale 85323; 932-2260.)

Annual Events

Estrella Rodeo. In Goodyear. Includes entertainment, family games, dance. Late Feb.

Billy Moore Days. Held in Avondale and Goodyear. Carnival, entertainment, parade, other events. Mid-Oct.

(See Glendale, Mesa, Phoenix, Scottsdale, Tempe)

Resort

★ ★ ★ ★ ★ **THE WIGWAM.** *(PO Box 278) Litchfield & Indian School Rds, 2½ mi N of I-10 Litchfield Rd exit. 602/935-3811; FAX 602/935-3737.* 331 rms & suites in 1–2 story casitas. EP, Jan–Apr: S, D $230–$250; each addl $25; suites $335–$425; under 18 free; golf rates; AP on request; family rates avail hol seasons; lower rates rest of yr. Crib free. TV; cable, in-rm movies. 2 heated pools; poolside serv. Playground. Supervised child's activities. Dining rm (public by res) 6:30–10:30 am, 11:30 am–2:30 pm, 5–10 pm (also see THE ARIZONA KITCHEN). Rm serv 24 hrs. Box lunches, bkfst rides, steak fries. Bar 11–1 am. Ck-out 1 pm, ck-in 4 pm. Meeting rms. Valet serv. Gift shop. Barber, beauty shop. Airport transportation $20/person. Lighted tennis, pro. 54-hole golf, greens fee $80–$90 (incl cart), putting greens. Stagecoach, hayrides. Bicycles. Skeet, trapshooting. Indoor, outdoor games. Soc dir; entertainment, dancing; special hol programs for families. Exercise equipt; weights, bicycles, whirlpool, sauna, steam rm. Masseuse. Refrigerators; some fireplaces, wet bars, minibars. Library. Private patios. Luxurious resort on 75 beautifully landscaped acres. Cr cds: A, C, D, DS, ER, MC, V, JCB.

Restaurants

★ ★ ★ **THE ARIZONA KITCHEN.** *(See The Wigwam Resort) 602/935-3811.* Hrs: 6–11 pm. Closed Sun. Res accepted. Southwestern menu. Bar 4–11 pm. Wine list. A la carte entrees: dinner $11.95–$24. Specialties: smoked corn chowder, jalapeño honey mustard glazed duck, southwestern cuisine. Guitarist (classical music). Open display kitchen; brick floor, fireplace; Southwestern artifacts. Cr cds: A, C, D, DS, ER, MC, V, JCB.

★ ★ **LE GOURMAND.** *12345 W Indian School Rd. 602/935-1515.* Hrs: 5:30–9 pm; winter from 4:30 pm. Closed Mon. Res accepted. French, continental menu. Serv bar. Complete meals: dinner $15–$20. Child's meals. Specializes in seafood, rack of lamb. Parking. Cr cds: A, MC, V.

Marble Canyon (A-3)

Pop: 150 (est) **Elev:** 3,580 ft **Area code:** 602 **Zip:** 86036

What to See and Do

1. **River-running trips.** Multi-day trips on the Colorado River. For a list of commercial operators contact Grand Canyon National Park, PO Box 129, Grand Canyon 86023; 638-7888.

2. **Marble Canyon.** Part of Grand Canyon National Park (see).

(See Page)

Motels

★ **CLIFF DWELLERS LODGE.** *(Box HC 67-30) 10 mi W of Marble Canyon on US 89A. 602/355-2228; res: 800/433-2543.* 20 rms. Apr–Nov: S, D $50–$65; each addl $4; lower rates rest of yr. Restaurant 6 am–2 pm, 5–9 pm (winter hrs may vary). Ck-out 11 am. Trading post. Hiking, fishing; river raft trips. 3,500-ft airstrip. Cr cds: DS, MC, V.

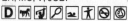

 ★ **MARBLE CANYON LODGE.** *(Box 1) At Navajo Bridge on US 89A. 602/355-2225; res: 800/726-1789.* 58 rms, some kits. May–Aug: S $40; D $45–$55; each addl $5; suites $80–$90; kit. units $40–$50; under 12 free; some lower rates rest of yr. Crib free. Pet accepted. Complimentary coffee in rms. Restaurant 6:30 am–9 pm; Dec–Mar 7 am–8 pm. Bar 6 am–9 pm. Ck-out 11 am. Coin lndry. Meeting rms. Sundries. Hiking. 4,500-ft paved landing strip. Shuttle serv for river rafting. Cr cds: MC, V.

McNary (C-5)

Pop: 355 **Elev:** 7,316 ft **Area code:** 602 **Zip:** 85930

McNary is in the northeastern section of the Fort Apache Indian Reservation. "Hon-dah" is Apache for "be my guest," and visitors find a warm welcome here. The White Mountain Apaches have a number of recreation areas on their reservation. Trout fishing, exploring and camping are available. For further information contact White Mountain Recreation Enterprise, Game & Fish Dept, Box 220, Whiteriver 85941; 338-4385.

What to See and Do

Sunrise Park Resort. 20 mi E on AZ 260, then S on AZ 273, on Fort Apache Indian Reservation. Resort has 2 quad, 4 triple, 2 double chairlifts, 3 rope tows; patrol, school, rentals; cafeteria, restaurants, bars. 62 runs. Also snowboarding. (Nov–mid-Apr, daily) Summer activities include swimming; fishing; canoeing. Hiking, horseback riding; tennis. Camping. Phone 735-7669 or 800/55-HOTEL. ¢¢¢¢¢

(For accommodations see Greer, Pinetop, Show Low, Springerville)

Mesa (D-3)

Founded: 1878 **Pop:** 288,091 **Elev:** 1,241 ft **Area code:** 602

Mesa, Spanish for "tabletop," sits atop a plateau overlooking the Valley of the Sun and is one of the state's largest and fastest-growing cities. Mesa offers year-round golf, tennis, hiking and water sports. It also provides easy access to other Arizona and Southwest attractions.

What to See and Do

1. **Arizona Mormon Temple Visitors' Center.** 525 E Main St. Murals; 10-foot replica of Thorvaldsen's *Christus* statue; history of prehistoric irrigation; films; dioramas; information. Temple gardens (site of concert series) have large variety of trees, cacti and shrubs collected from all over the world; extensive light display during Christmas season. The Church of Jesus Christ of Latter-Day Saints (Mormon) Arizona Temple is located just south of visitor center (not open to the public). Tours of the visitor center (daily). Phone 964-7164. **Free.**

2. **Mesa Southwest Museum.** 53 N MacDonald. Displays trace Mesa history from dinosaurs to Space Age and emphasize Arizona history and archaeology. Participatory exhibits include panning for gold, "legendarium" and 1890s territorial jail cells. Changing exhibits; animated dinosaurs; Native American & pioneer celebrations; adobe schoolhouse. (Daily exc Mon) Sr citizen rate. Phone 644-2230. **¢¢**

3. **Arizona Museum for Youth.** 35 N Robson. Fine arts museum with changing hands-on exhibits for children. (Daily exc Mon; closed major hols) Phone 644-2467. **¢**

4. **Champlin Fighter Museum.** Falcon Field, 4636 Fighter Aces Dr. Large vintage fighter aircraft collection of WW I and WW II planes;

also art gallery with paintings of aircraft in combat; display of automatic weapons; extensive collection of photos of fighter aces from WW I to Vietnam; fighter library. (Daily) Phone 830-4540. ¢¢¢

5. **Lost Dutchman State Park.** 14 mi E via US 60/89 to Apache Junction, then 5 mi NE via AZ 88 (Apache Trail Hwy). A 300-acre park in the Superstition Mts area. Hiking. Picnicking (shelter). Improved camping (dump station). Interpretive trails and access to nearby forest service wilderness area. (Daily; closed Dec 25) Standard fees. Nature trail for physically impaired. Phone 982-4485.

6. **River tubing. Salt River Recreation Inc.** 15 mi NE in Tonto National Forest (see PAYSON): E on US 60 to Power Rd, then N to jct Usery Pass Hwy. (Mid-Apr–Sept) Fee includes tube rental and shuttle bus service to various points on the Salt River. Phone 984-3305. ¢¢¢

7. **Arizona Steamboat Cruises.** Narrated tours and twilight dinner cruises of Canyon Lake, following the original path of the Salt River. For schedule and information phone 827-9144. ¢¢¢¢–¢¢¢¢¢

(For further information contact the Convention & Visitors Bureau, 120 N Center, 85201; 969-1307.)

Annual Events

Mesa Territorial Days. Rockin R Ranch. Arizona's birthday party celebrated in Old West style. Western arts and crafts, music, food; rodeo. 3rd wkend Feb.

Arizona Renaissance Festival. Phone 472-2700. Wkends mid-Feb–mid-Mar.

Seasonal Event

Baseball Spring Training. Ho Ho Kam Park. Chicago Cubs. Phone 964-4467. Mar.

(See Casa Grande, Chandler, Phoenix, Scottsdale, Tempe)

Motels

★★**BEST WESTERN DOBSON RANCH INN & RESORT.** *1666 S Dobson Rd (85202).* 602/831-7000; FAX 602/831-7000, ext 513. 212 rms, 2 story. Jan–Apr: S $88–$94; D $106–$113; each addl $7; suites $125; under 12 free; some wkend rates; lower rates rest of yr. Crib $3. TV; cable. Heated pool. Restaurant 6:30 am–10 pm. Rm serv. Bar 10–1 am. Ck-out noon. Meeting rms. Valet serv. Sundries. Tennis privileges. Golf privileges. Exercise equipt; weights, bicycles, whirlpool. Refrigerators avail. Cr cds: A, C, D, DS, ER, MC, V, JCB.

D 🏋 🏌 ⊠ 👤 🛇 ⊙ SC

★★**COURTYARD BY MARRIOTT.** *1221 S Westwood St (85210).* 602/461-3000; FAX 602/461-0179. 148 units, 3 story. Jan–mid-Apr: S $76–$112; D $86–$124; each addl (after 4th person) $10; suites $100–$130; wkend, wkly rates; lower rates rest of yr. TV; cable. Heated pool. Complimentary coffee in rms. Restaurant 6:30–11 am. Bar 4–11 pm. Ck-out 1 pm. Coin lndry. Meeting rms. Valet serv. Sundries. Exercise equipt; weight machine, bicycles, whirlpool. Refrigerator in suites. Many balconies. Cr cds: A, C, D, DS, MC, V.

D ⊠ 👤 🛇 ⊙ SC

★★**DAYS INN.** *333 W Juanita Ave (85210).* 602/844-8900; FAX 602/844-8900, ext 401. 124 units, 3 story. Jan–Apr: S, D $69–$79; each addl $5; suites $125; studio rms $95; under 12 free; lower rates rest of yr. Crib free. TV; cable. Heated pool. Complimentary continental bkfst. Ck-out noon. Coin lndry. Meeting rms. Valet serv. Exercise equipt; stair machine, bicycle, whirlpool, sauna. Refrigerators. Cr cds: A, C, D, DS, MC, V.

D 🏌 ⊠ 👤 🛇 ⊙ SC

★★**HAMPTON INN.** *1563 S Gilbert Rd (85204).* 602/926-3600; FAX 602/926-4892. 116 rms, 4 story. Mid-Dec–mid-Apr: S $64–$77; D $80–$90; under 18 free; lower rates rest of yr. Crib free. TV; cable. Heated pool; whirlpool. Complimentary continental bkfst. Ck-out noon. Coin lndry. Meeting rms. Refrigerators. Cr cds: A, C, D, DS, MC, V.

D ⊠ 🛇 ⊙ SC

✔ ★★**LEXINGTON HOTEL SUITES.** *1410 S Country Club Dr (85210).* 602/964-2897; FAX 602/833-0536. 120 kit. units, 2 story. Jan–Apr: S, D $49–$139; studio rms $79; under 16 free; wkly rates; lower rates rest of yr. Crib free. Pet accepted, some restrictions. TV; cable. Heated pool; whirlpool. Complimentary continental bkfst. Restaurant opp 11 am–7 pm. Ck-out noon. Coin lndry. Meeting rms. Cr cds: A, C, D, MC, V.

D 🐾 ⊠ 🛇 ⊙ SC

★★**QUALITY INN-ROYAL MESA.** *951 W Main St (85201).* 602/833-1231; FAX 602/833-1231, ext 200. 100 rms, 2 story, 25 kit. units. Mid-Jan–mid-Apr: S $59–$85; D $65–$95; each addl $6; kit. units $69–$92; under 18 free; some wkend, wkly rates; golf plans; higher rates Fiesta Bowl; lower rates rest of yr. Crib $2. Pet accepted, some restrictions; $4. TV; cable. Heated pool. Restaurant (hrs vary with season). Bar (hrs vary with season). Ck-out noon. Meeting rm. Valet serv. Exercise equipt; weights, bicycles, whirlpool, sauna. Some refrigerators, bathrm phones. Private patios, balconies. Cr cds: A, C, D, DS, ER, MC, V, JCB.

D 🐾 ⊠ 🏌 👤 🛇 ⊙ SC

✔ ★★**REGIS INN.** *5531 E Main St (85205).* 602/981-8111; res: 800/527-3447. 61 rms, 2 story. Mid-Dec–mid-Apr: S $59; D $65–$72; suites $72–$75; under 12 free; lower rates rest of yr. Crib $5. TV; cable. Heated pool; whirlpool. Complimentary continental bkfst 6–9 am. Complimentary coffee. Restaurant nearby. Ck-out 11 am. Refrigerator in suites. Cr cds: A, D, MC, V.

D ⊠ 🛇 ⊙ SC

Hotels

★★★**HILTON PAVILION.** *1011 W Holmes Ave (85210).* 602/833-5555; FAX 602/649-1886. 262 rms, 8 story, 62 suites. Jan–Apr: S $85–$135; D $95–$145; each addl $10; suites $115–$300; under 18 free; some wkend rates; lower rates rest of yr. Crib free. TV; cable. Heated pool; poolside serv (in season). Restaurant 6:30 am–10 pm. Bar 11 am–midnight; entertainment Tues–Sat. Ck-out noon. Convention facilities. Gift shop. Beauty shop. Tennis privileges. Golf privileges. Exercise equipt; weight machine, bicycles, whirlpool. Some bathrm phones; refrigerator, wet bar in suites. *LUXURY LEVEL:* PAVILION CLUB LEVEL. 73 rms, 9 suites. S $95–$135; D $105–$145; suites $115–$300. Concierge. Private lounge. Complimentary continental bkfst, refreshments. Cr cds: A, C, D, DS, MC, V.

D 🏋 🏌 🐾 ⊠ 🏌 👤 🛇 ⊙ SC

★★**SHERATON.** *200 N Centennial Way (85201).* 602/898-8300; FAX 602/964-9279. 271 rms, 12 story. Jan–mid-May: S $90–$110; D $100–$120; each addl $10; suites $115–$150; under 18 free; lower rates rest of yr. Crib $10. TV; cable. Heated pool; poolside bar serv. Restaurant 6 am–2 pm, 4:30–10 pm. Bar 11–1 am. Ck-out noon. Meeting rms. 18-hole golf privileges, putting green, driving range. Exercise equipt; weight machine, bicycle, whirlpool. Refrigerators, minibars. Balconies. Elaborate landscaping with palm trees, fountain. *LUXURY LEVEL:* EXECUTIVE LEVEL. 57 rms, 2 floors, 9 suites. Jan–mid-May: S $130–$140; D $140–$150; suites $115–$150; lower rates rest of yr. Private lounge. Wet bar in suites. Complimentary continental bkfst, refreshments. Cr cds: A, D, DS, MC, V.

D 🏋 ⊠ 👤 🏌 🛇 ⊙

Resorts

★★★**ARIZONA GOLF RESORT & CONFERENCE CENTER.** *425 S Power Rd (85206),* 1 mi N of Superstition Fwy. 602/832-3202; res:

800/528-8282 (US); FAX 602/981-0151. 162 kit. units, 1–2 story. Jan–Apr: S, D $105–$155; each addl $15–$25; suites $145–$280; under 12 free; golf package; lower rates rest of yr. Crib free. Pet accepted. TV; cable. Heated pool. Dining rm 6 am–9 pm. Bar 10 am–midnight; entertainment, dancing Wed–Sat. Ck-out noon, ck-in 3 pm. Coin lndry. Convention facilities. Valet serv. Lighted tennis. 18-hole golf, pro, putting green, driving range. Private patios, balconies. Picnic tables, grill. Cr cds: A, C, D, DS, ER, MC, V.

★★★**GOLD CANYON RANCH.** *(6100 S Kings Ranch Rd, Apache Junction 85219)* 7 mi E on US 60. 602/982-9090; res: 800/624-6445; FAX 602/830-5211. 57 units, some kits. Jan–mid-May: S, D $130–$210; each addl $10; under 18 free; lower rates rest of yr. TV; cable. Heated pool; whirlpool, poolside serv. Dining rm (public by res) 7 am–10 pm. Rm serv. Box lunches, cookouts, bkfst trail rides. Bar 10:30–1 am. Ck-out 11 am, ck-in 4 pm. Meeting rms. Valet serv. Lighted tennis. 18-hole golf, greens fee $75 (incl cart), pro, driving range, putting green. Bicycle rentals. Refrigerators, fireplaces; many whirlpools. Private patios. In foothills of Superstition Mountains on 3,300 acres. Cr cds: A, D, MC, V.

Restaurants

★★**AMERICAN GRILL.** *1233 S Alma School Rd.* 602/844-1918. Hrs: 11 am–3 pm, 4:30–10 pm; Fri to 11 pm; Sat 11:30 am–2:30 pm, 4:30–11 pm; Sun 4:30–9 pm; Sun brunch 11 am–2:30 pm. Closed Dec 25. Res accepted. Bar. Semi-a la carte: lunch $5.95–$8.50, dinner $10.95–$18.95. Sun brunch $12.95. Child's meals. Specializes in fresh fish, steak. Pianist Wed–Sat. Garage parking. Outdoor dining. Art deco motif. Cr cds: A, D, MC, V.

★**BAVARIAN POINT.** *4815 E Main St.* 602/830-0999. Hrs: 11 am–10 pm. Closed July 4. German, continental menu. Bar to midnight. Semi-a la carte: lunch $5.50–$11.95, dinner $9.95–$19.95. Specialties: kalbsfilet, sauerbraten. Salad bar. Entertainment Fri, Sat. Parking. Cr cds: MC, V.

★**BRUNELLO.** *1954 S Dobson.* 602/897-0140. Hrs: 11:30 am–3 pm, 5–10 pm; Fri to 11 pm; Sat 5–11 pm; Sun 4:30–10 pm. Closed Thanksgiving, Dec 25. Res accepted. Italian menu. Bar. Semi-a la carte: lunch $5.50–$9.95, dinner $8.95–$17.95. Specialties: shrimp Michelangelo, chicken Scarpariella, filet mignon. Parking. Outdoor dining. Cr cds: A, D, MC, V.

✔★★**CHINA GATE.** *2050 W Guadalupe.* 602/897-0607. Hrs: 11:30 am–2 pm, 5–10 pm; Fri, Sat to 10:30 pm; Sun noon–3 pm, 4:30–9:30 pm. Closed Thanksgiving. Res accepted. Chinese menu. Bar. Semi-a la carte: lunch $3.95–$5.25, dinner $5.50–$14.95. Specialties: Empress shrimp, volcano beef, twice-cooked chicken. Entertainment Fri, Sat. Parking. Cr cds: A, D, DS, MC, V.

✔★★**LANDMARK.** *809 W Main St.* 602/962-4652. Hrs: 11:30 am–2 pm, 4–9 pm; Sat from 4 pm; Sun noon–7 pm. Closed July 4, Thanksgiving, Dec 25. Serv bar. Semi-a la carte: lunch $4.75–$8.95, dinner $8.45–$13.45. Child's meals. Specializes in seafood, beef, chicken. Salad bar. Parking. Former Mormon church (ca 1905). Antiques, original artwork. Cr cds: A, C, D, DS, MC, V.

✔★**MATTA'S.** *932 E Main St.* 602/964-7881. Hrs: 11 am–10 pm; Sun–Tues to 9 pm. Closed major hols. Res accepted. Mexican, Amer menu. Bar. Semi-a la carte: lunch $2.50–$4.95, dinner $5.25–$7.95. Child's meals. Specializes in tacos, chimichangas, meat-stuffed chile rellenos. Parking. Mariachi band Fri, Sat. Cr cds: A, C, D, DS, MC, V.

★★**RAFFAELE'S.** *2909 S Dobson Rd.* 602/838-0090. Hrs: 11 am–3 pm, 5–10 pm; Sat 5–11 pm; Sun 3–10 pm. Closed Thanksgiving,

Dec 25. Res accepted. Italian menu. Bar. Semi-a la carte: lunch $6.50–$8.95, dinner $7.95–$19.95. Specialties: chicken Vesuvio, vitello alla boscaiola, homemade pasta, cioppino. Parking. Cr cds: A, C, D, MC, V.

Unrated Dining Spots

HARRY & STEVE'S CHICAGO GRILL. *161 N Centennial Way.* 602/844-8448. Hrs: 11 am–10 pm; Sun to 8 pm. Bar. Semi-a la carte: lunch $4.25–$5.95, dinner $7.50–$9.95. Specializes in hamburgers, grilled chicken. Outdoor dining. Sports memorabilia. Cr cds: D, MC, V.

ORGAN STOP PIZZA. *2250 W Southern Ave.* 602/834-5325. Hrs: 5–9:30 pm; Fri, Sat to 10:30 pm. Closed Thanksgiving, Dec 25. Wine. Beer. A la carte entrees: dinner $4.50–$6.50. Specializes in pizza, pasta. Salad bar. Entertainment. Parking. No cr cds accepted.

Montezuma Castle National Monument (C-3)

(20 mi SE of Cottonwood on AZ 260, then N and E off I-17)

This 5-story, 20-room structure was built by Native Americans more than 800 years ago and is one of the most remarkable cliff dwellings in the United States. Perched under a protective cliff, which rises 150 feet, the dwelling is 70 feet straight up from the talus.

Visitors are not permitted to enter the castle, but there is a self-guided trail offering a good view of the structure and of other ruins in the immediate area. Castle "A," a second ruin, is nearby. Montezuma Well, about 11 miles northeast, is a 470-foot-wide limestone sinkhole, with a lake 55 feet deep. Around the rim are well-preserved cliff dwellings. An irrigation system built by the inhabitants about 800 years ago leads from the spring. Limited picnicking; no camping. The Castle Visitor Center and a self-guided trail are both accessible to wheelchairs. (Daily) Senior citizen rate (US citizens only). For further information contact the Chief Ranger, Box 219, Camp Verde 86322; 602/567-3322. ¢

(For accommodations see Cottonwood, Flagstaff)

Navajo Indian Reservation (A/B-4/5)

The Navajo Nation is both the largest Native American tribe and reservation in the United States. The reservation covers more than 25,000 square miles within three states: the larger portion in northeast Arizona and the rest in New Mexico and Utah.

More than 400 years ago, the Navajo people (the Dineh) moved into the arid southwestern region of the United States and carved out a way of life that was in harmony with the natural beauty of present-day Arizona, New Mexico and Utah. In the 1800s, this harmonious life was interrupted by westward-moving settlers and the marauding cavalry. For the Navajo, this conflict resulted in their forced removal from their ancestral land and the "Long Walk" to Fort Sumner, New Mexico. This forced removal of the Navajo was judged a failure; in 1868, they were allowed to return to their homeland.

Coal, oil and uranium have been discovered on the reservation. The income from these, which is handled democratically by the tribe, has helped to improve its economic and educational situation.

The Navajo continue to practice many of their ancient ceremonies, including the Navajo Fire Dance and the Yei-bi-chei (winter) and Enemy Way Dances (summer). Many ceremonies are associated with curing the sick and are primarily religious in nature. Visitors must obtain permission to view these events; photography, recording and sketching are prohibited.

Most of the traders on the reservation are friendly and helpful. Do not hesitate to ask them when and where the dances take place. Navajo Tribal rangers, who patrol tribal parks, also are extremely helpful and can answer almost any question that may arise.

There are a number of paved roads across the Navajo and Hopi Reservations (see)—as well as some unpaved gravel and dirt roads. During the rainy season (mostly Aug–Sept), the unpaved roads are difficult or impassable; it is best to stay off them.

Some of the most spectacular areas in Navajoland are Canyon de Chelly National Monument (see); Navajo National Monument (see); Monument Valley Navajo Tribal Park, north of Kayenta (see); Four Corners Monument; and Rainbow Bridge National Monument (see UT). Hubbell Trading Post National Historic Site is in Ganado (see).

Accommodations on the reservation are limited; reservations are needed months in advance. For information contact the Navajoland Tourism Dept, Box 663; 871-6659.

(For accommodations see Holbrook, Kayenta, Page, Winslow)

Navajo National Monument (A-4)

(20 mi SW of Kayenta on US 160, then 9 mi N on paved road AZ 564 to Visitors Center)

This monument is comprised of 3 scattered areas totaling 600 acres and is surrounded by the Navajo Reservation. Each area is the location of a large and remarkable prehistoric cliff dwelling. Two of the ruins are accessible by guided tour.

Headquarters for the monument and the visitor center are near Betatakin, the most accessible of the three cliff dwellings. Guided tours, limited to 24 people, are arranged on a first-come, first-served basis (May–Sept; tours sometimes possible earlier in spring and late in fall; phone for schedule). Hiking distance is five miles round trip over a steep trail and takes five to six hours. Because of hot temperatures, high elevations and rugged terrain, this tour is recommended only for those in good physical condition. Betatakin may also be viewed from the Sandal Trail overlook—a half-mile, one-way, self-guided trail. (Daily; weather permitting)

The largest and best preserved area, Keet Seel (Memorial Day–Labor Day, phone for schedule), is eight miles one-way by foot or horseback from headquarters. A permit is required either way, and reservations can be made up to 2 months in advance. Primitive campground available for overnight hikers. The horseback trip takes all day; horses should be reserved several weeks ahead of time (fee for horses & for guide; no children under 12 unless previous riding experience).

The visitor center has a museum and film program. There are picnic tables, campgrounds (May–mid-Oct) and a craft shop at the headquarters area. (Daily; closed Jan 1, Thanksgiving, Dec 25) Contact the Superintendent, HC-71, Box 3, Tonalea 86044-9704; 602/672-2366 or -2367. **Free.**

(For accommodations see Kayenta)

Nogales (F-4)

Founded: 1880 **Pop:** 19,489 **Elev:** 3,869 ft **Area code:** 602 **Zip:** 85621

This is a pleasant city and port of entry directly across the border from Nogales, Mexico. (For border crossing regulations, see INTRODUCTION.) A Ranger District office of the Coronado National Forest (see TUCSON) is located here.

What to See and Do

1. **Pimeria Alta Historical Society Museum.** 136 N Grand Ave, in former City Hall. History of southern Arizona and northern Sonora, from A.D. 1000 to the present. Photo collection; library; archives; self-guided walking tours. (Daily; closed most major hols) Phone 287-4621. **Free.**

2. **Peña Blanca Lake and Recreation Area.** 8 mi N on I-19 (US 89), then 9 mi W on AZ 289, Ruby Rd, in Coronado National Forest (see TUCSON). Fishing; boating. Picnicking, restaurant, lodge. Cabins. Phone 281-2800. For camping information phone 281-2296.

3. **Tumacacori National Historical Park** (see). 18 mi N on I-19 (US 89).

4. **Tubac Presidio State Historic Park.** 20 mi N off I-19. Arizona's first European settlement, where a presidio (military post) was built in 1752. Spanish colonial and territorial ruins. Picnicking, ramadas. Museum with exhibits and underground view of the remains of the presidio's main building. (Daily; closed Dec 25) Phone 398-2252. ¢

(For further information contact the Nogales-Santa Cruz County Chamber of Commerce, Kino Park; 287-3685.)

(See Patagonia, Tucson)

Motels

★ ★ **AMERICANA.** 639 N Grand Ave. 602/287-7211; res: 800/874-8079; FAX 602/287-5188. 97 rms, 2 story. Nov–May: S $45–$55; D $55–$70; each addl $5; under 12 free; lower rates rest of yr. Crib $5. Pet accepted, some restrictions; $5 non-refundable. TV; cable. Pool; poolside serv. Restaurant 6:30 am–10 pm. Rm serv. Bar 11–1 am, Sun from noon. Ck-out noon. Meeting rms. Valet serv. Barber, beauty shop. Some refrigerators. Cr cds: A, C, D, MC, V.

🐾 ⚂ 🚫 ⏱ SC

✔ ★ ★ **SUPER 8.** 547 W Mariposa Rd, at I-19 exit 4. 602/281-2242; FAX 602/281-2242, ext 400. 116 rms, 3 story. No elvtr. S $41.88; D $44.88–$47.88; under 12 free. Crib $2. Pet accepted, some restrictions; $5 non-refundable. TV; cable. Pool; whirlpool. Restaurant 6 am–9 pm. Bar 11 am–11 pm, closed Sun. Ck-out noon. Coin lndry. Meeting rms. Valet serv. Refrigerators. Cr cds: A, C, D, DS, MC, V.

D ⚂ 🚫 ⏱ SC

Resort

★ ★ **RIO RICO.** 1064 Camino Caralampi, 12 mi N on I-19, exit 17. 602/281-1901; res: 800/288-4746; FAX 602/281-7132. 175 rms, 2–3 story. No elvtr. S, D $70–$80; each addl $10; suites $175–$300; under 12 free; golf, tennis, horseback riding plans; some lower rates mid-Apr–Sept. Crib $10. TV; cable. Heated pool; poolside serv. Dining rm 6 am–2 pm, 5–10 pm. Box lunches, picnics. Rm serv. Bar 11–1 am; entertainment wkends, dancing. Ck-out noon, ck-in 4 pm. Convention facilities. Grocery ½ mi. Coin lndry. Meeting rms. Valet serv. Gift shop. Beauty shop. Airport, local transportation. Lighted tennis. 18-hole golf privileges, pro, putting green, driving range. Stables. Exercise equipt; weights, bicycles, whirlpool, sauna. Lawn games. Private patios, balconies. Western cook-outs. On mesa top with scenic view. Cr cds: A, C, D, DS, MC, V.

Restaurant

★ ★MR C'S. *282 W View Point Dr, I-19 exit 4. 602/281-9000.*
Hrs: 11–1 am. Closed Jan 1, Thanksgiving, Dec 25; also Sun June–Oct.
Res accepted. Bar. Semi-a la carte: lunch $5–$15, dinner $7.95–$30.
Child's meals. Specializes in guaymas shrimp, fresh fish & steak. Salad
bar. Entertainment. Parking. Hilltop location; supper club atmosphere.
Cr cds: D, DS, MC, V.

Oak Creek Canyon

(see Flagstaff)

Organ Pipe Cactus National Monument (E-2)

(16 mi S of Ajo on AZ 85)

This 516-square-mile Sonoran desert area on the Mexican border is
Arizona's largest national monument. The organ pipe cactus grows as
high as 20 feet and has 30 or more arms, which resemble organ pipes.
The plant blooms in May and June. Blossoms, usually at branch tips, are
white with pink or lavender touches. Depending on the rainfall, during
February and March, parts of the area may be covered with Mexican
goldpoppy, magenta owlclover, blue lupine and bright orange mallow.
Mesquite, saguaro, several species of cholla, barrel cacti, paloverde
trees, creosote bush, ocotillo and other desert plants thrive here.

There are two graded scenic drives, which are self-guided: the 53-
mile Puerto Blanco and the 21-mile Ajo Mountain drives. There is a 208-
site campground near headquarters (May–mid-Jan, 30-day limit; mid-
Jan–Apr, 14-day limit; 35-ft RV limit; fee), no reservations; groceries (5
miles). Information service and exhibits are at the visitor center (daily).
Standard fees. For further information contact the Superintendent, Rte
1, Box 100, Ajo 85321; 602/387-6849.

Motel

★GRINGO PASS. *(Box 266, Lukeville 85341) 5 mi S of
Monument on AZ 85. 602/254-9284 or 257-0887.* 12 rms. S $42; D $58;
kit. unit $50–$65; apts. $76; wkly, monthly rates. Crib free. TV. Pool.
Complimentary coffee in rms. Restaurant nearby. Ck-out 11 am. Picnic
tables. Trailer parking. Cr cds: MC, V.

Inns

★ ★GUEST HOUSE INN. *(3 Guest House Rd, Ajo 85321) 20
mi N on AZ 85. 602/387-6133.* 4 rms. Sept–May: S $59; D $69; each addl
$10; lower rates rest of yr. TV in sitting rm; cable. Complimentary full
bkfst. Restaurant nearby. Ck-out 11 am, ck-in 2 pm. Former
executive guest house (1925) built by Phelps Dodge Corporation for visiting company officials; stately dining rm. Cr cds: D, MC, V.

★ ★MINE MANAGER'S HOUSE. *(1 Greenway Dr, Ajo 85321)
15 mi N on US 85. 602/387-6505; FAX 602/387-6508.* 5 rms. Mid-
Oct–mid-Apr: D $65–$99; each addl $5–$10; lower rates rest of yr. TV in
sitting rm. Pool privileges. Complimentary full bkfst, coffee. Ck-out 10
am, ck-in 2 pm. Coin lndry. Gift shop. Private parking. Lighted tennis. 9-
hole golf privileges. Whirlpool. Library; sitting rm. Antiques. Cr cds: MC,
V.

Page (A-3)

Pop: 6,598 Elev: 4,000 ft Area code: 602 Zip: 86040

Page is at the east end of the Glen Canyon Dam, on the Colorado River.
The dam, 710 feet high, forms Lake Powell, a part of the Glen Canyon
National Recreation Area. The lake, 186 miles long with 1,900 miles of
shoreline, is the second largest man-made lake in the United States.

The dam was built for the Bureau of Reclamation for water storage
and the generation of electric power. The lake is named for John Wesley
Powell, the intrepid and brilliant geologist who lost an arm at the Battle
of Shiloh, led an expedition down the Colorado in 1869 and was later
director of the US Geological Survey.

What to See and Do

1. **Glen Canyon National Recreation Area.** More than one million
   acres including Lake Powell. Ranger station, 7 mi N of dam at
   Wahweap. Campfire program (Memorial Day–Labor Day). Swimming, waterskiing; fishing, boating (ramps, marina). Hiking. Picnicking, restaurants, lodge. Camping. Developed areas in Utah
   include Bullfrog, Hite, Halls Crossing, Dangling Rope (accessible
   by boat only); many of these have ranger stations, marinas, boat
   rentals & trips, supplies, camping and lodging. Lees Ferry on
   Colorado River (approx 15 mi downstream from dam, but a 45-mi
   drive SW from Page) has a launch ramp and camping. Visitor
   center on canyon rim, adj to Glen Canyon Bridge on US 89, has
   historical exhibits. (Daily; closed Jan 1, Dec 25) Guided tours
   (summer). Phone 645-2511. Camping ¢¢¢
2. **Boat trips on Lake Powell.** 6 mi N on US 89 at Wahweap Lodge &
   Marina. One-hour to one-day trips, some including Rainbow Bridge
   National Monument. Houseboat and powerboat rentals. Advance
   reservations advised. Phone 278-8888 or 800/528-6154.
3. **Wilderness River Adventures.** Half-day smoothwater trip on the
   Colorado River in Glen Canyon in raftlike neoprene boats.
   (Feb–Nov) Phone 800/528-6154. ¢¢¢¢¢
4. **Scenic flights over area.** Page Airport, ½ mi NE on US 89. Trips vary
   from 30 minutes to more than 2 hours. (Daily; closed Jan 1,
   Thanksgiving, Dec 25) For fee information contact Lake Powell Air
   Service, Box 1385; 645-2494.
5. **John Wesley Powell Memorial Museum.** 6 N Lake Powell Blvd.
   Fluorescent rock collection, Native American artifacts; books,
   videos; replica of Powell's boat. (Schedule varies with season)
   Phone 645-9496. **Free.**
6. **Rainbow Bridge National Monument** (see under UTAH). Approx 60
   mi NE in Utah, NW of Navajo Mountain.

(For further information contact the Page/Lake Powell Chamber of
Commerce, 638 Elm St, Box 727; 645-2741.)

(See Marble Canyon, Navajo Indian Reservation)

Motels

✔ ★BEST WESTERN-WESTON'S INN. *(Box 1746) 207 N
Lake Powell Blvd. 602/645-2451; FAX 602/645-9552.* 91 rms, 1–3 story.
S $53–$58; D $63–$81; each addl $5; under 12 free. Crib $3. TV; cable.
Heated pool. Complimentary continental bkfst. Restaurant adj 5:30
am–10 pm. Ck-out noon. Free local airport transportation 8 am–10 pm.
Some balconies. Cr cds: A, C, D, DS, MC, V.

✔ ★EMPIRE HOUSE. *(Box 1747) 107 S Lake Powell Blvd.
602/645-2406.* 69 rms, 2 story. Apr–Oct: S $50; D $62; each addl $5;
under 12 free with 2 adults; some lower rates rest of yr. Crib $2. Pet
accepted. TV; cable. Pool. Restaurant 5:30 am–9 pm. Bar 3 pm–1 am,

closed Dec–Mar. Ck-out 11 am. Gift shop. Free airport transportation. Balconies. Cr cds: MC, V.

★ ★ ★ INN AT LAKE POWELL. *(PO Box C) 716 Rimview Dr. 602/645-2466; res: 800/826-2718; FAX 602/645-2466, ext 501.* 103 units, 3 story. Apr–Oct: S $62–$82; D $69–$92; each addl $10; suites $125; under 18 free; lower rates rest of yr. Crib free. Pet accepted. TV; cable. Pool; whirlpool. Restaurant 6 am–10 pm. Bar. Ck-out noon. Meeting rm. Airport transportation. Overlooking Glen Canyon Dam & Lake Powell. Cr cds: A, C, D, DS, MC, V.

★ LAKE POWELL. *(Box 1597) 4 mi NW of Glen Canyon Dam on US 89 at Wahweap jct. 602/645-2477; res: 800/528-6154 (exc AZ).* 24 rms, 2 story. May–Oct: S $54.50; D $59.75–$65.50; each addl $5.25; under 12 free; lower rates rest of yr. Crib $5.25. TV. Pool privileges. Ck-out 11 am. Free airport transportation. View of canyon, cliffs, Lake Powell. Cr cds: A, C, D, DS, MC, V.

Motor Hotels

★ ★ HOLIDAY INN PAGE. *(Box 1867) 287 N Lake Powell Blvd. 602/645-8851; FAX 602/645-2523.* 130 rms, 3 story. Mid-Apr–Oct: S, D $85–$99; each addl $7; under 18 free; lower rates rest of yr. Crib free. TV; cable. Heated pool. Restaurant 6 am–10 pm. Rm serv from 7 am. Bar 4 pm–1 am in summer. Ck-out 11 am. Coin lndry. Meeting rms. Bellhops. Valet serv. Sundries. Gift shop. Free airport transportation in summer. Private patios, balconies. Picnic tables, grills. Cr cds: A, C, D, DS, MC, V, JCB.

★ ★ ★ WAHWEAP LODGE & MARINA. *(Box 1597) 5 mi NW of Dam at Glen Canyon Recreation Area, 2½ mi SE of US 89. 602/645-2433.* 350 rms in 3 bldgs, 2 story. May–Oct: S $82.95–$91.45; D $91.45–$99.95; each addl $9; suites $165.25; under 12 free; lower rates rest of yr. Crib $6. TV; cable. 2 heated pools; whirlpool, poolside serv. Restaurants 6 am–10 pm. Bar 11–1 am, Sun from noon; entertainment, dancing exc Sun (in season). Ck-out 11 am. Coin lndry. Meeting rms. Bellhops. Valet serv. Concierge. Sundries. Gift shop. Free local airport transportation. Free shuttle serv to town. Golf privileges. Some wet bars. Private patios, balconies. On lake. Boats, motorboats, scenic boat trips. Host for national bass fishing tounaments. Cr cds: A, C, D, DS, MC, V.

Restaurants

★ ★ BELLA NAPOLI. *810 N Navajo Dr. 602/645-2706.* Hrs: 5–9 pm. Closed Nov–Feb. Italian menu. Semi-a la carte: dinner $7–$16. Specializes in scampi. Cr cds: DS, MC, V.

★ KEN'S OLD WEST. *718 Vista. 602/645-5160.* Hrs: 4–11 pm. Closed Jan 1, Thanksgiving, Dec 25. Bar to 1 am. Semi-a la carte: dinner $6.95–$18.95. Child's meals. Specializes in prime rib, steak, barbecued ribs. Salad bar. Country band exc Sun. Parking. Patio dining. Cr cds: A, DS, MC, V.

Parker (C-1)

Founded: 1908 **Pop:** 2,897 **Elev:** 413 ft **Area code:** 602 **Zip:** 85344

Parker is located on the east bank of the Colorado River, about 16 miles south of Parker Dam (320 ft high, 856 ft long), which forms Lake Havasu. Popular recreational activities in the area include fishing, frogging, boating, jet and water skiing, hunting, golfing, rock hunting and camping. The town has become the trade center for surrounding communities and the Colorado Indian Reservation.

What to See and Do

1. **Colorado River Indian Tribes Museum and Library.** 2nd Ave at Mohave Rd. Exhibits interpret the history of the four Colorado River Tribes: Mohave, Chemehuevi, Navajo & Hopi. Authentic Native American arts & crafts for sale. Operated by the Colorado River Indian Tribes. (Mon–Fri; closed hols) Phone 669-9211. **Free.** The museum is part of the

   Colorado River Indian Tribes Reservation. More than 278,000 acres in Arizona and California. Fishing, hunting (tribal permit required); boating, waterskiing. Camping (fee).

2. **Parker Dam & Power Plant.** 17 mi N via AZ 95, Riverside Dr exit. One of the deepest dams in the world, 65 percent of its structural height of 320 feet is below the riverbed. Only 85 feet of the dam is visible while another 62 feet of its superstructure rises above the roadway, across the top of the dam. Self-guided tours of the dam; recorded lectures, illustrated maps and close-up views of major features of the power plant. (Daily) **Free.**

3. **Buckskin Mountain State Park.** 11 mi NE on AZ 95. 1,676 acres. Scenic bluffs overlooking the Colorado River. Swimming; fishing; boating (ramp, marina). Nature trails, hiking. Picnicking (shelter), concession. Camping (electric hookups, dump station), riverside cabanas (fee). Phone 667-3231. **River Island Unit,** ½ mi N of main unit, has boating (ramp). Picnicking (shelter). Camping. (Daily) Standard fees. Phone 667-3386 or -3231.

4. **La Paz County Park.** 8½ mi N on AZ 95. A 540-acre park with 4,000 feet of Colorado River beach frontage. Swimming, waterskiing; fishing; boating (ramps). Tennis court, golf course, driving range. Picnicking (shelter), playground. Camping (electric hookups, dump station). Fee for some activities. Phone 667-2069.

(For further information contact the Chamber of Commerce, 1217 California Ave, PO Box 627; 669-2174.)

Annual Events

Parker-Score 400 Off Road Race. Three Arizona loops–400 miles of desert racing. Phone 669-2174. Late Jan.

La Paz County Fair. Carnival, livestock auction, farm olympics, entertainment. Mid-Mar.

Holiday Lighted Boat Parade. Decorated boats parade on the 11-mile strip to selected site for trophy presentation; viewing from both sides of the river. Dec.

(See Lake Havasu City; also see Blythe, CA)

Motel

★ KOFA INN. *(Box 1069) 1700 California Ave. 602/669-2101.* 41 rms, 1–2 story. S, D $31–$36; each addl $4. Crib $4. TV; cable. Pool. Restaurant adj open 24 hrs. Ck-out noon. Sundries. Cr cds: A, C, D, MC, V.

Restaurant

★ LOS ARCOS. *1100 California Ave. 602/669-2375.* Hrs: 11 am–9 pm; wkends to 10 pm. Closed Sun; some major hols. Res accepted. Mexican menu. Bar from 11 am. Semi-a la carte: lunch $3.95, dinner $4.95–$13. Specializes in dishes prepared with green and red chili peppers. Mexican decor. No cr cds accepted.

Patagonia (E-4)

Pop: 888 **Elev:** 4,057 ft **Area code:** 602 **Zip:** 85624

A small cattle town with a distinct mining flavor, Patagonia is surrounded by beautiful mountains and Hollywood-style Western scenery.

What to See and Do

1. **Patagonia-Sonoita Creek Preserve.** Along AZ 82; watch for directional signs to the entrance. The 312 acres extend downstream along Sonoita Creek for more than 1 mile. Bordered by willows, cottonwoods and ash, it provides a perfect sanctuary for more than 250 species of birds. For schedule and fee information phone 394-2400.

2. **Patagonia Lake State Park.** 8 mi S on AZ 82, then 4 mi N on Patagonia Lake Rd. A 265-acre park with a lake. Swimming beach; fishing; boating (ramp, rentals, marina). Hiking. Picnicking, concession, ramadas. Camping (dump station). Standard fees. Phone 287-6965.

(For further information contact the Town of Patagonia, Town Hall, Box 767; 394-2958.)

(See Nogales, Sierra Vista)

Motel

★ ★**STAGE STOP INN.** *(Box 777) 301 N McKeown, 1 blk S of AZ 82. 602/394-2211.* 43 rms, 2 story, 11 kits. S $39.95; D $49.95; each addl $10; suites, kit. units $59–$95; under 6 free; golf plan. Crib $7.50. TV; cable. Heated pool. Restaurant 7 am–10 pm. Ck-out noon. Meeting rms. Some balconies. Sun deck. Frontier atmosphere. Tours. Cr cds: A, MC, V.

Payson (C-3)

Founded: 1882 **Pop:** 8,377 **Elev:** 4,887 ft **Area code:** 602 **Zip:** 85541

Payson, in the heart of the Tonto National Forest, provides many outdoor recreational activities in a mild climate.

What to See and Do

Tonto National Forest. This area includes almost three million acres of desert and mountain landscape. Six lakes along the Salt and Verde rivers provide opportunities for fishing, boating, hiking and camping. Seven wilderness areas are located within the forest's boundaries, providing hiking and bridle trails. The forest also features Tonto Natural Bridge, the largest natural travertine bridge in the world. Scenic attractions include the Apache Trail, Four Peaks, the Mogollon Rim and Sonoran Desert country. Phone 225-5200.

(For further information contact the Chamber of Commerce, Box 1380, 85547; 800/552-3068.)

Annual Events

Country Music Festival. June.

Sawdust Festival, Loggers' Competition. Mid-July.

World's Oldest Continuous PRCA Rodeo. Mid-Aug.

Old-Time Fiddler's Contest & Festival. Late Sept.

(See Phoenix)

Motel

★ ★**SWISS VILLAGE LODGE.** *(PO Box 399) 801 N Beeline Hwy (AZ 87), ¼ mi N of AZ 260. 602/474-3241; res: 800/247-9477.* 99

rms, 2 story, 65 kits. (no equipt). Apr–Nov: S, D $49–$89; each addl $10; kit. units $59–$89; apt (2-bedrm) $109; under 17 free; lower rates rest of yr. Crib $10. Pet accepted; $10 per day. TV; cable. Heated pool (summer). Complimentary coffee in rms. Restaurant 6 am–9 pm. Bar. Ck-out 11 am. Refrigerators; some fireplaces. Private patios. Cr cds: A, MC, V.

Restaurants

✔ ★**AUNT ALICE'S.** *512 N Beeline Hwy (AZ 87). 602/474-4720.* Hrs: 6:30 am–8 pm; Fri, Sat to 9 pm. Closed Dec 25. Semi-a la carte: bkfst $2–$6.95, lunch $4–$7, dinner $5–$10. Child's meals. Specializes in steak, country cooking. Parking. Cr cds: MC, V.

★**LA CASA PEQUEÑA.** *911 S Beeline Hwy (AZ 87). 602/474-6329.* Hrs: 11 am–10 pm. Closed Thanksgiving, Dec 25. Mexican, Amer menu. Bar to 1 am. Semi-a la carte: lunch $4.25–$7.95, dinner $5.50–$13.95. Specialties: la casa chimichanga, chicken Acapulco. Entertainment Fri-Sat. Parking. Mexican decor; large collection of wheeled decanters. Cr cds: MC, V.

✔ ★**MARIO'S VILLA.** *600 E AZ 260. 602/474-5429.* Hrs: 11 am–9 pm; Fri, Sat to 10 pm. Closed some major hols. Italian, Amer menu. Bar. Semi-a la carte: lunch $4–$7, dinner $4.25–$12.95. Child's meals. Specializes in pasta, steak, seafood. Parking. Dining rm features multi-colored glass lamps, oil paintings. Cr cds: A, C, D, DS, MC, V.

Petrified Forest National Park (C-5)

(North entrance: 26 mi E of Holbrook on I-40. South entrance: 19 mi E of Holbrook on US 180)

These 93,532 acres include the most spectacular display of petrified wood in the world. The trees of the original forest may have grown in upland areas and then washed into ponds by streams. Subsequently, the trees were buried under sediment and volcanic ash, causing the wood to be filled gradually with mineral compounds. The grain, now multicolored by the compounds, is still visible in some specimens.

The visitor center is located at the entrance from I-40. The Rainbow Forest Museum (off US 180) depicts the process in detail; polished sections, fossils and crystals are on display. (Daily; closed Jan 1, Dec 25) Service stations and cafeteria at the north entrance; snacks only at south entrance. Prehistoric Pueblo inhabitants left countless petroglyphs of animals, figures and symbols carved on sandstone throughout the park.

The park contains a portion of the Painted Desert, a colorful area extending 200 miles along the north bank of the Little Colorado River. This highly eroded area of mesas, pinnacles, washes and canyons is part of the Chinle formation, a soft shale, clay, marl and sandstone stratum of Triassic age. The sunlight and clouds passing over this spectacular scenery create an effect of constant, kaleidoscopic change. There are very good viewpoints along the park road.

Picnicking facilities at Rainbow Forest and at Chinde Point on the rim of the Painted Desert; no campgrounds. **Important:** It is forbidden to take even the smallest piece of petrified wood or any other object from this area. Nearby curio shops sell wood taken from areas outside the park. (Daily; closed Jan 1, Dec 25) Standard fees. Contact the Superintendent, Petrified Forest National Park, Box 2217, 86028; 602/524-6228.

(For accommodations see Holbrook)

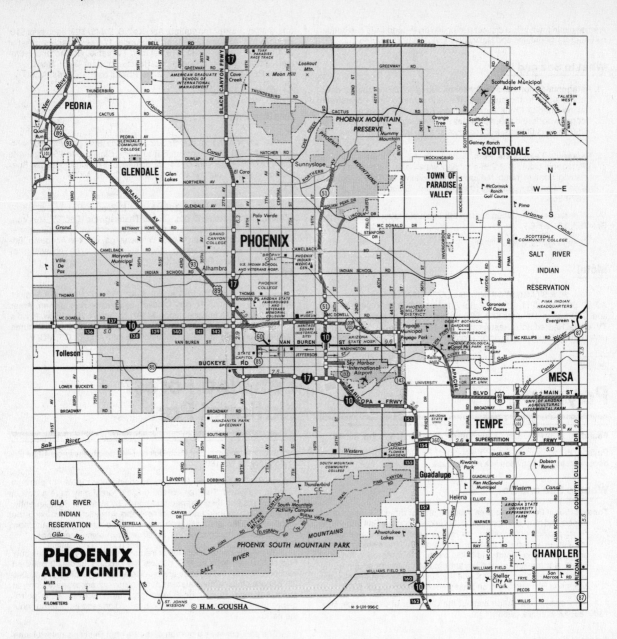

Phoenix (D-3)

Settled: 1864 **Pop:** 983,403 **Elev:** 1,090 ft **Area code:** 602

The capital of Arizona lies on flat desert, surrounded by mountains and green irrigated fields of cotton, lettuce, melons and alfalfa and groves of oranges, grapefruit, lemons and olives. It is a resort area, as well as an industrial area. It is also the home of Grand Canyon University (1949). The sun shines practically every day. Most rain falls in December, with some precipitation in summer. There is swimming, fishing, boating, horseback riding, golf and tennis. Phoenix, like Tucson, is a health center, known for its warm temperatures and low humidity. As a vacation spot, it is both sophisticated and informal.

Transportation

Car Rental Agencies: See toll-free numbers under Introduction.

Public Transportation: Buses (City of Phoenix Transit System), phone 253-5000.

Rail Passenger Service: Amtrak 800/872-7245.

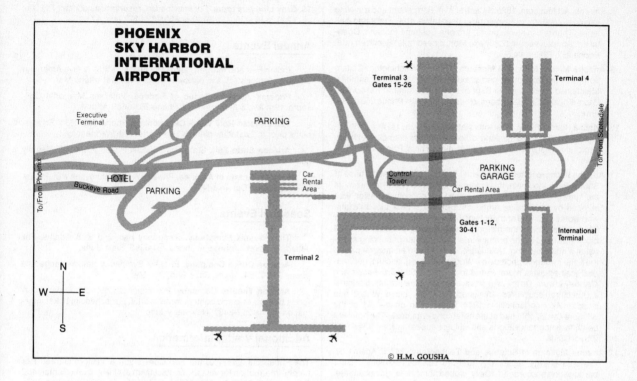

PHOENIX SKY HARBOR INTERNATIONAL AIRPORT

Executive Terminal

PARKING

Terminal 3
Gates 15-26

Terminal 4

To/From Scottsdale

To/From Phoenix

HOTEL

PARKING

Buckeye Road

Car Rental Area

Control Tower

PARKING GARAGE

Car Rental Area

Gates 1-12, 30-41

International Terminal

Terminal 2

N W E S

© H.M. GOUSHA

Airport Information

Phoenix Sky Harbor Intl Airport: Information 273-3300; lost and found 273-3307; weather 265-5550; cash machines, Terminals 2–4; Ambassadors Club (TWA), Terminal 2; Crown Room (Delta), Terminal 3, North Concourse; Ambassadors Club (TWA), Terminal 2; USAir Club (US Air), Terminal 2; WorldClub (Northwest), Terminal 3, North Concourse; Phoenix Club (America West), Terminal 4.

Terminals: Terminal 2: Alaska, TWA, United, USAir, USAir Express; Terminal 3: American, Continental, Delta, Northwest; Terminal 4: Aeromexico, Aero California, America West, Southwest, International Concourse

(Airlines and their terminal locations may change. Before leaving for the airport, you should phone the airline to confirm terminal location for your flight.)

What to See and Do

1. **Arizona State Capitol Museum.** W Washington St & 17th Ave. Built of native stone with a landscaped area including a large variety of native trees, shrubs and cacti. Four-story restored Capitol Museum exhibits include re-creation of the original 1912 governor's office and the early House and Senate chambers and galleries. (Mon–Fri; closed hols) To arrange tours phone 542-4581 or -4675. **Free.**

2. **Phoenix Museum of History.** 1002 W Van Buren St. More than 2,000 years of Arizona history; changing exhibits. (Wed–Sun; closed major hols) Phone 253-2734. **Free.**

3. **The Heard Museum.** 22 E Monte Vista Rd. The arts and lifestyles of Southwest Native American culture, prehistoric to contemporary

representation. Changing exhibits include primitive art from throughout the world and Native American art. Also features Goldwater kachina doll collection; artist demonstrations. (Daily; closed hols) Sr citizen rate. Phone 252-8848. **¢¢**

4. **Arizona Hall of Fame Museum.** 1101 W Washington; located in the restored Carnegie Library (1908). Changing exhibits focus on people who have made significant contributions to Arizona. Guided tours (by appt). (Mon–Fri; closed hols) Phone 255-2110 or 542-4581 (tours). **Free.**

5. **Desert Botanical Garden.** Galvin Pkwy, in Papago Park. Includes 150 acres of plants from the world's deserts; self-guided nature walk; public lectures; Cactus Show (Mar). (Daily) Sr citizen rate. Phone 941-1217. **¢¢**

6. **Phoenix Zoo.** 455 N Galvin Pkwy, in Papago Park. A 125-acre zoo; home to more than 1,300 mammals, birds and reptiles, most in naturalistic exhibits. Features rare Sumatran tigers; Tropical Flights aviary; African savannah; Arizona Trail exhibit, with native animals; children's zoo; safari train tours; refreshment centers. (Daily) Phone 273-1341. **¢¢¢** Opp zoo is

Hall of Flame Firefighting Museum. 6101 E Van Buren St. The nation's largest collection of antique fire equipment, hand- and horse-drawn (from 1725) and motorized (1906–1961); fire communications, firemarks, artwork, models and memorabilia. (Daily exc Sun; closed Jan 1, Thanksgiving, Dec 25) Sr citizen rate. Phone 275-3473. **¢¢**

7. **Pueblo Grande Museum and Cultural Park.** 4619 E Washington St, approx 1 mile NE of Sky Harbor Airport. A Hohokam archaeological site and ruin, thought to have been occupied between A.D. 500–1450. Museum features permanent and changing exhibits. (Daily; closed hols) Phone 495-0900. **¢**

8. **Phoenix Art Museum.** 1625 N Central Ave. Permanent and traveling exhibits; Western, contemporary, decorative arts, European galleries; Thorne miniature rooms; Arizona Costume Institute; Oriental art; sculpture court. (Daily exc Mon; closed hols) Sr citizen rate. Phone 257-1222. ¢¢

9. **Arizona Mining & Mineral Museum.** 1502 W Washington. Collections of minerals, ores, gems; petrified wood; mining exhibits. Maintained by the Arizona Dept of Mines and Mineral Resources. (Mon–Fri, also Sat afternoons; closed state hols) Phone 255-3791. **Free.**

10. **Arizona History Room.** First Interstate Bank Plaza, 1st Ave & Washington St. Territorial banking office of 1800s; changing exhibits depict life in early Arizona. (Mon–Fri; closed hols) Phone 229-4624. **Free.**

11. **Arizona Biltmore Hotel.** 24th St and Missouri. Located at the base of Squaw Peak Mountain, this landmark structure (1929) is known as the ''Jewel of the Desert.'' The resort's architectural design was inspired by the famous American architect, Frank Lloyd Wright, who worked with the architect and builder, Albert Chase McArthur. For the first time in the history of architecture, pre-cast concrete block was used as the primary interior and exterior building material of a major building. Unique pieces of art are an integral part of the hotel's interiors, including a Wright-designed, back-lit, geometrical stained-glass mural in the foyer, titled *Saguaro Forms and Cactus Flowers.* On the grounds are the *Biltmore Sprites,* 6 original architectural sculptures, designed by Frank Lloyd Wright and sculptor Alfonso Iannelli in 1914. Information on the art of the Biltmore can be obtained at the hotel concierge desk. The hotel will be undergoing renovations and will not appear in the 1994 *Mobil Travel Guide.*

12. **Arizona Museum of Science and Technology.** 147 E Adams St. Features energy, technology and life sciences exhibits. Visitor participation encouraged. (Daily; closed some hols) Sr citizen rate. Phone 256-9388. ¢¢

13. **Heritage Square.** 7th St & Monroe. Historical city park has eight turn-of-the-century houses, including restored 1895 Victorian Rosson House (Wed–Sun; fee) and Arizona Doll & Toy Museum. Also open-air Lath House Pavilion. (Daily exc Mon) Sr citizen rate. Phone 262-5029. **Free.**

14. **Phoenix Mountains Preserve.** Located in both the northern and southern parts of the city, the parks offer more than 23,500 acres of unique desert mountain recreational activities. Hiking, riding and picnicking. Phone 262-6861. **Free.**

    Squaw Peak Park. 2701 E Squaw Peak Dr (22nd St and Lincoln Dr). Hiking trail (1¼ mi) offers panoramic view of city; park also offers access to other mountain trails. Picnicking (shelter). Phone 262-7901.

    Echo Canyon (Camelback Mountain). E McDonald & Tatum Blvd. Hiking trails, including trail to top of Camelback Mountain. Phone 256-3220.

    South Mountain. 10919 S Central. Offers 16,000 acres in a rugged mountain range. Hiking trails, park drives to scenic overlooks. Picnicking (shelter). Phone 262-6111 or 495-0222.

    North Mountain Recreation Area. 10600 N 7th St. Hiking on mountain trails Picnicking (shelter). Phone 262-7901.

15. **Tonto National Forest.** 20 mi NE on AZ 87. (See PAYSON)

16. **Mystery Castle.** 7 mi S via Central Ave, E on Baseline Rd, S on 7th St, then E on Mineral Rd. Unique stone and sand castle built by one man, over a period of 18 years, for his daughter. The castle features 18 furnished rooms, 13 fireplaces, a cantilevered stairway and a chapel. (Oct–early July, daily exc Mon) Phone 268-1581. ¢¢

17. **Thoroughbred Horse Racing.** Turf Paradise, 19th Ave & Bell Rd, 10 mi N on I-17 to Bell Rd exit. (Early Oct–May, Wed–Sun; closed some hols) Phone 942-1101.

18. **Dog racing.** Greyhound Park, 40th & E Washington Sts. (Daily exc Mon) Phone 273-7181.

19. **Gray Line bus tours.** For information, reservations contact PO Box 21126, 85036; 495-9100 or 800/732-0327 (exc AZ).

Annual Events

Indian Fair and Market. Heard Museum (see #3). Native American artisans, demonstrations, dances, native foods. 1st wkend Mar.

Phoenix Jaycees Rodeo of Rodeos. Veterans Memorial Coliseum, 19th Ave & McDowell Rd. Phone 263-5689. Mid-Mar.

Yaqui Indian Holy Week Ceremonials. Phone 883-2838. Fri evenings prior to Easter, beginning 1st Fri after Ash Wednesday.

Arizona State Fair. State Fairgrounds. Phone 252-6771. Usually mid-Oct.

Cowboy Artists of America. Phoenix Art Museum (see #8). Phone 257-1222. Late Oct–mid-Nov.

Seasonal Events

The Phoenix Symphony. Symphony Hall, 2nd St & Adams. For schedule, ticket information phone 264-6363. Sept–June.

Arizona Opera Company. Phoenix Symphony Hall. For schedule phone 266-7464. Thurs, Sat & Sun. Oct–Mar.

Arizona Theatre Company. Professional regional company performs both classic and contemporary works. For schedule, ticket information phone 252-8497. Nov–early June.

Additional Visitor Information

The Phoenix & Valley of the Sun Convention & Visitors Bureau has helpful information for visitors; contact them at One Arizona Center, 400 E Van Buren St, Suite 600, 85004; 254-6500; visitor information, 252-5588.

Phoenix Metro Magazine, available at newsstands, has up-to-date information on cultural events and articles of interest to visitors.

Phoenix Area Suburbs

The following suburbs in the Phoenix area are included in the *Mobil Travel Guide.* For information on any one of them, see the individual alphabetical listing. Glendale, Mesa, Scottsdale, Tempe.

Motels

    ✔ ★**COMFORT INN-NORTH.** 1711 W Bell Rd (85023). 602/866-2089; FAX 602/789-7669. 154 rms, 3 story, 24 suites. Jan–Apr: S $59–$69; D $64–$74; each addl $5; suites $79–$89; under 18 free; lower rates rest of yr. Crib free. Pet accepted, some restrictions; $10. TV; cable. Heated pool; whirlpool. Complimentary continental bkfst, coffee. Restaurant nearby. Ck-out noon. Coin lndry. Valet serv. Refrigerator, wet bar in suites. Suites have balconies. Cr cds: A, C, D, DS, ER, MC, V, JCB.

D 🐾 ⚲ 🚫 🪙 SC

    ★ ★**COURTYARD BY MARRIOTT.** 2621 S 47th St (85034), near Sky Harbor Intl Airport. 602/966-4300; FAX 602/966-0198. 145 units, 4 story. Jan–late Apr: S $109–$126; D $120–$137; each addl $10; suites $126–$137; wkend, wkly rates; some lower rates rest of yr. Crib free. TV; cable. Heated pool. Complimentary coffee in rms. Restaurant 6:30 am–2 pm, 5–10 pm; wkends from 7 am. Bar 4–11 pm. Ck-out 1 pm. Coin lndry. Meeting rms. Valet serv. Free airport transportation. Exercise equipt; weight machine, bicycles, whirlpool. Refrigerator in suites. Many balconies. Cr cds: A, C, D, DS, MC, V.

D ⚲ 🏋 ✖ 🚫 ⊚

    ★ ★**COURTYARD BY MARRIOTT.** 2101 E Camelback Rd (85016). 602/955-5200; FAX 602/955-1101. 155 rms, 4 story. Jan–Apr: S

$115–$125; D $125–$135; suites $135–$155; wkend, wkly, hol rates; lower rates rest of yr. Crib free. TV; cable. Heated pool. Complimentary coffee in rms. Restaurant 6:30–11 am; wkends 7 am–1 pm. Rm serv. Bar. Ck-out 1 pm. Coin lndry. Meeting rms. Valet serv. Exercise equipt; weight machine, bicycles, whirlpool. Refrigerator in suites. Balconies. Cr cds: A, C, D, DS, MC, V.

★★HAMPTON INN. 8101 N Black Canyon Hwy (85021), I-17 exit Northern Ave. 602/864-6233; FAX 602/995-7503. 149 rms, 3 story. Jan–mid-Apr: S $75; D $80 under 18 free; lower rates rest of yr. Crib free. Pet accepted, some restrictions. TV; cable. Heated pool; whirlpool. Complimentary continental bkfst. Ck-out noon. Meeting rm. Cr cds: A, C, D, DS, MC, V.

★★LA QUINTA-COLISEUM WEST. 2725 N Black Canyon Hwy (85009), I-17 exit Thomas Rd. 602/258-6271; FAX 602/340-9255. 139 rms, 2 story. Jan–Apr: S $61; D $71; each addl $8; under 18 free; lower rates rest of yr. Crib free. Pet accepted, some restrictions. TV; cable. Heated pool. Complimentary continental bkfst in lobby. Restaurant adj open 24 hrs. Ck-out noon. Coin lndry. Valet serv. Cr cds: A, C, D, DS, MC, V.

✓★PREMIER INN. 10402 N Black Canyon Hwy (85051), at I-17 Peoria Ave exit. 602/943-2371; res: 800/786-6835; FAX 602/943-5847. 253 rms, 2 story. Jan–Apr: S $49.95–$59.95; D $53.95–$62.95; suites $66.95–$99.95; lower rates rest of yr. Crib $3. Pet accepted, some restrictions. TV; cable. 2 pools, 1 heated; wading pool. Bar 11–2 am. Ck-out noon. Coin lndry. Meeting rms. Tennis. Bathrm phone in suites. Some private patios. Cr cds: A, D, DS, MC, V.

✓★TRAVELODGE METROCENTER. 8617 N Black Canyon Hwy (85021). 602/995-9500; FAX 602/995-0150. 175 rms, 2 story. Mid-Jan–mid-Apr: S $50–$56; D $59–$65; each addl $7; under 18 free; wkly rates; lower rates rest of yr. Crib free. Pet accepted, some restrictions; $50 refundable and $5 per day. TV; cable. Heated pool; whirlpool. Complimentary continental bkfst, coffee. Restaurant nearby. Ck-out noon. Coin lndry. Meeting rms. Airport, RR station, bus depot transportation. Health club privileges. Picnic tables. Cr cds: A, C, D, DS, ER, MC, V, JCB.

Motor Hotels

★★★BEST WESTERN GRACE INN AHWATUKEE. 10831 S 51st St (85044), just S of I-10 Elliott Rd exit. 602/893-3000; FAX 602/496-8303. 160 rms, 6 story. Jan–mid-Apr: S, D $100–$130; each addl $10; suites $125–$175; under 17 free; lower rates rest of yr. Crib free. Pet accepted, some restrictions; $50 ($25 refundable). TV; cable. Heated pool; poolside serv. Restaurant 6 am–9 pm. Rm serv. Bar 11:30–1 am, Sun from noon; entertainment, dancing exc Sun. Ck-out noon. Meeting rms. Bellhops. Valet serv. Sundries. Barber, beauty shop. Free airport transportation. Lighted tennis. 18-hole golf privileges. Exercise rm; instructor, weights, bicycles, whirlpool. Lawn games. Refrigerators. Balconies. *LUXURY LEVEL: CONCIERGE LEVEL.* 26 rms. S $125; D $135. Private lounge. Complimentary continental bkfst 6:30–8:30 am, refreshments.
Cr cds: A, C, D, DS, MC, V.

★★BEST WESTERN INNSUITES AT SQUAW PEAK. 1615 E Northern Ave (85020). 602/997-6285; FAX 602/943-1407. 122 rms, 2 story, 4 kits. Jan–mid-Apr: S $72–$78; D $78–$87; kit. suites $85–$132; under 19 free; wkend rates; lower rates rest of yr. Crib free. Pet accepted; $25 refundable. TV; cable. Heated pool. Complimentary continental bkfst. Complimentary coffee & juice in rms. Ck-out noon. Meeting

rms. Exercise equipt; weights, bicycle, whirlpool. Refrigerators. Picnic tables, grills. Cr cds: A, C, D, DS, MC, V.

✓★★DAYS INN CAMELBACK. 502 W Camelback Rd (85013). 602/264-9290; FAX 602/264-3068. 166 rms, 4 story. Jan–Apr: S $59–$78; D $64–$83; each addl $10; suites $130–$160; lower rates rest of yr. Crib free. Pet accepted; $10 per day. TV; cable. Heated pool; whirlpool, poolside serv. Restaurant 6:30 am–2 pm, 5–9:30 pm. Rm serv. Bar 5 pm–1 am. Ck-out noon. Meeting rms. Valet serv. Some refrigerators. Cr cds: A, C, D, DS, MC, V.

★★★FOUNTAIN SUITES. 2577 W Greenway Rd (85023). 602/375-1777; res: 800/527-7715 (exc AZ); FAX 602/375-1777, ext 5555. 314 suites, 2–3 story. Jan–mid-May: S, D $89–$155; under 18 free; lower rates rest of yr. Pet accepted, some restrictions; $100 non-refundable. TV; cable. Heated pool; whirlpool, sauna, poolside serv. Restaurant 6 am–10 pm. Rm serv. Bar 11–1 am; entertainment, dancing. Ck-out noon. Coin lndry. Meeting rms. Bellhops. Valet serv. Lighted tennis. Golf privileges. Refrigerators, minibars. Stucco and red-tile roofed building reminiscent of traditional resort hotels. Cr cds: A, C, D, DS, ER, MC, V, JCB.

★★LA QUINTA (formerly Sheraton Greenway Inn). 2510 W Greenway Rd (85023). 602/993-0800; FAX 602/789-9172. 149 rms, 2 story. Jan–mid-Apr: S $75; D $109; each addl $10; suites $135; under 18 free; wkend rates; lower rates rest of yr. Crib free. Pet accepted; $25. TV; cable. Heated pool; wading pool, sauna, poolside serv. Complimentary bkfst. Restaurant 6:30 am–2:30 pm, 5–10 pm. Rm serv. Bar 4 pm–1 am, Sun 10 am–10 pm. Ck-out noon. Meeting rms. Lighted tennis. Golf privileges, driving range. Some refrigerators, honor bars. Cr cds: A, C, D, DS, ER, MC, V.

★★PHOENIX AIRPORT HILTON. 2435 S 47th St (85034), near Sky Harbor Intl Airport. 602/894-1600; FAX 602/894-0326. 255 units, 4 story. Jan–Apr: S $124–$189; D $139–$204; each addl $15; suites $185–$275; under 18 free; lower rates rest of yr. Crib avail. TV; cable. Pool; poolside serv. Restaurant 6 am–10 pm. Rm serv to midnight. Bar 11 am–midnight; entertainment exc Sun. Ck-out noon. Convention facilities. Bellhops. Valet serv. Concierge. Sundries. Gift shop. Free airport transportation. Exercise equipt; weight machines, bicycles, whirlpool. Minibars. Many balconies. *LUXURY LEVEL: TOWERS.* 62 rms, 4 suites. S $144–$209; D $159–$224. Private lounge. Complimentary continental bkfst, refreshments.
Cr cds: A, C, D, DS, ER, MC, V, JCB.

✓★★QUALITY INN SOUTHMOUNTAIN. 5121 E La Puente Ave (85044). 602/893-3900; FAX 602/496-0815. 193 rms, 4 story. Jan–Apr: S $59–$69; D $69–$79; suites $105–$125; under 17 free; lower rates rest of yr. Crib free. Pet accepted; $25 refundable. TV; cable. Heated pool; whirlpool. Restaurant 6:30–11 am, 5–9 pm. Rm serv. Ck-out 11 am. Coin lndry. Meeting rms. Valet serv. Cr cds: A, C, D, DS, ER, MC, V, JCB.

✓★★RAMADA INN METROCENTER. 12027 N 28th Dr (85029). 602/866-7000; FAX 602/942-7512. 167 rms, 4 story. Jan–Apr: S $65–$80; D $75–$90; each addl $6; suites $85–$110; under 18 free; lower rates rest of yr. Crib free. Pet accepted. TV; cable. Heated pool; whirlpool, poolside serv. Restaurant 6 am–2 pm, 4–10 pm. Rm serv. Bar 4 pm–midnight. Ck-out noon. Meeting rms. Valet serv. Gift shop. Cr cds: A, C, D, DS, ER, MC, V, JCB.

★★WYNDHAM GARDEN HOTEL. 2641 W Union Hills Dr (85027), at I-17. 602/978-2222; FAX 602/978-9139. 166 rms, 2 story. Jan–Apr: S $99; D $109; each addl $10; suites $119; under 18 free; lower rates rest of yr. Pet accepted, some restrictions; $25 non-refundable. TV; cable. Heated pool; whirlpool, poolside serv. Restaurant 6:30 am–10 pm. Rm serv 5–10 pm. Bar 4:30–11 pm. Ck-out noon. Coin lndry.

Meeting rms. Valet serv. Sundries. Some bathrm phones. Private patios. Cr cds: A, C, D, DS, ER, MC, V, JCB.

[icons]

★★ **WYNDHAM GARDEN HOTEL.** *427 N 44th St (85008), near Sky Harbor Intl Airport. 602/220-4400; FAX 602/231-8703.* 214 rms, 7 story, 24 suites. Jan–Apr: S $109–$119; D $119–$129; each addl $10; suites $129–$139; under 18 free; lower rates rest of yr. Crib free. TV; cable. Heated pool; poolside serv. Restaurant 6:30 am–2 pm, 5–10 pm. Rm serv. Bar 3–11 pm. Ck-out noon. Meeting rms. Valet serv. Sundries. Free airport transportation. Exercise equipt; weight machine, bicycles, whirlpool. Some bathrm phones. Cr cds: A, C, D, DS, ER, MC, V, JCB.

[icons]

Hotels

★★★ **BEST WESTERN EXECUTIVE PARK** (formerly Westcoast Executive Park). *1100 N Central Ave (85004). 602/252-2100; FAX 602/340-1989.* 107 rms, 8 story. Jan–Apr: S $84–$94; D $94–$104; each addl $10; under 13 free; wkend rates; lower rates rest of yr. Crib free. TV; cable. Heated pool; poolside serv. Coffee in rms. Restaurant 6:30 am–10 pm. Bar 11 am–11 pm, Sun from noon. Ck-out noon. Meeting rms. Free airport transportation. Exercise equipt; weight machine, bicycles, whirlpool, sauna. Some bathrm phones, refrigerators, wet bars. Balconies. Panoramic mountain views. Cr cds: A, C, D, DS, ER, MC, V.

[icons]

★★★ **CRESCENT.** *2620 W Dunlap Ave (85021), at I-17. 602/943-8200; res: 800/423-4126; FAX 602/371-2857.* 342 rms, 8 story. Early Jan–mid-May: S $119–$159; D $130–$179; each addl $15; suites $250–$500; some wkend rates; lower rates rest of yr. Crib free. Pet accepted, some restrictions; $100 ($75 refundable). TV; cable. Heated pool; poolside serv. Restaurant 6 am–11 pm. Bar 11–1 am; entertainment. Ck-out noon. Convention facilities. Gift shop. Free covered parking. Lighted tennis. Exercise rm; instructor, weights, bicycles, whirlpool, sauna, steam rm. Lawn games. Refrigerators, minibars. Balconies. Some fireplaces. Some suites with panoramic view of north mountain range. Elaborate information & business center just off lobby. *LUXURY LEVEL:* CONCIERGE LEVEL. 78 rms, 2 floors, 12 suites. S $139–$179; D $149–$189; suites $250–$500. Concierge. Private lounge. Complimentary continental bkfst, refreshments.
Cr cds: A, C, D, DS, ER, MC, V, JCB.

[icons]

★★★ **CROWN STERLING SUITES–BILTMORE.** *2630 E Camelback Rd (85016). 602/955-3992; res: 800/433-4600; FAX 602/955-6479.* 232 kit. suites, 5 story. Jan–Apr: S $160–$180; D $172–$192; each addl $10; under 13 free; lower rates rest of yr. Crib free. TV; cable. Heated pool; whirlpool, poolside serv. Complimentary full bkfst. Restaurant 11 am–10 pm. Bar to midnight; entertainment Tues–Sat. Ck-out 1 pm. Meeting rms. Gift shop. Tennis, golf privileges. Private patios, balconies. Atrium with lush garden & fish pond. Cr cds: A, C, D, DS, ER, MC, V.

[icons]

★★★ **DOUBLETREE SUITES–PHOENIX GATEWAY CENTER.** *320 N 44th St (85008), near Sky Harbor Intl Airport. 602/225-0500; FAX 602/225-0957.* 242 suites, 6 story. Jan–Apr: S, D $89–$149; each addl $10; under 17 free; wkend rates; lower rates rest of yr. Crib free. Pet accepted, some restrictions. TV; cable. Heated pool; whirlpool, sauna, poolside serv. Complimentary full bkfst. Restaurant 6:30 am–10 pm. Bar 11–1 am. Ck-out noon. Meeting rms. Gift shop. Free airport transportation. Tennis. Health club privileges. Refrigerators, minibars. Central atrium with 2 banks of glass elevators. Cr cds: A, C, D, DS, MC, V.

[icons]

★★ **EMBASSY SUITES–CAMELHEAD.** *1515 N 44th St (85008), near Sky Harbor Intl Airport. 602/244-8800; FAX 602/244-8800, ext 7534.* 229 suites, 4 story. Jan–Apr: S, D $135–$145; each addl $10; under 12 free; lower rates rest of yr. Crib free. TV; cable. Heated pool; whirlpool, poolside serv. Complimentary full bkfst. Restaurant 11:30

am–2 pm, 5–11 pm. Bar 11:30–1 am. Ck-out noon. Coin lndry. Meeting rms. Gift shop. Free airport transportation. Health club privileges. Balconies. Grills. Glass-enclosed elvtr overlooks courtyard. Cr cds: A, C, D, DS, MC, V, JCB.

[icons]

★★★ **HOTEL WESTCOURT.** *10220 N Metro Pkwy E (85051), at Metrocenter Shopping Ctr, I-17 Peoria exit. 602/997-5900; res: 800/858-1033; FAX 602/943-1056.* 284 rms, 5 story. Jan–May: S $95–$152; D $105–$162; each addl $10; suites $150–$250; under 12 free; wkend rates; lower rates rest of yr. Crib free. TV; cable. Heated pool; poolside serv. Restaurant 6:30 am–11 pm. Bar, Sun from 10 am; entertainment. Ck-out noon. Concierge. Shopping arcade. Lighted tennis. Golf privileges. Exercise equipt; weights, bicycles, whirlpool, sauna. Heliport. *LUXURY LEVEL:* PLAZA COURT. 38 rms. S $115–$152; D $125–$152. Private lounge, honor bar. Library, meeting rms. Complimentary continental bkfst, refreshments.
Cr cds: A, C, D, DS, ER, MC, V, JCB.

[icons]

★★★ **HYATT REGENCY PHOENIX AT CIVIC PLAZA.** *122 N 2nd St (85004). 602/252-1234; FAX 602/254-9472.* 712 rms, 24 story. Jan–May: S $165; D $190; suites $250–$700; under 18 free; wkend rates; lower rates rest of yr. Crib free. Valet, garage $7/day. TV; cable. Heated pool; whirlpool, poolside serv. Restaurant 6 am–midnight (also see COMPASS). Bar 11–1 am. Ck-out noon. Meeting rms. Concierge. Shopping arcade. Tennis privileges. Golf privileges. Wet bar in some suites. Some balconies. Cr cds: A, C, D, DS, ER, MC, V, JCB.

[icons]

★★ **LEXINGTON HOTEL & CITY SQUARE SPORTS CLUB.** *100 W Clarendon Ave (85013). 602/279-9811; FAX 602/631-9358.* 167 rms, 7 story. Oct–Apr: S $75–$100; D $85–$110; each addl $10; under 18 free; wkend rates; lower rates rest of yr. Crib free. Pet accepted, some restrictions; $25 refundable. TV; cable. Heated pool; poolside serv. Coffee in rms. Restaurant 6:30 am–10 pm. Bar 11 am–10 pm, Sun from noon. Ck-out noon. Shopping arcade. Valet parking. Free transportation from airport. Exercise rm; instructor, weights, bicycles, whirlpool, steam rm, sauna. Many refrigerators. Some balconies. Cr cds: A, C, D, DS, ER, MC, V.

[icons]

★★ **RADISSON-MIDTOWN.** *401 W Clarendon Ave (85013), between Indian School Rd & Osborn Ave. 602/234-2464; FAX 602/277-2602.* 106 rms, 4 story, 88 kits. Jan–May: S, D $112–$138; each addl $10; suites $105–$135; under 18 free; wkend rates; lower rates rest of yr. Crib free. TV; cable. Heated pool; whirlpool, poolside serv. Complimentary continental bkfst. Restaurant 6 am–10 pm. Bar 11:30–1 am. Ck-out noon. Meeting rms. Free airport transportation. Some refrigerators. Courtyard. Cr cds: A, C, D, DS, ER, MC, V, JCB.

[icons]

★★★★ **THE RITZ-CARLTON, PHOENIX.** *2401 E Camelback Rd (85016), in the Camelback Esplanade. 602/468-0700; res: 800/241-3333; FAX 602/957-6076.* 281 rms, 11 story, 14 suites. Jan–May: S, D $150–$230; suites $275–$375; under 12 free; lower rates rest of yr. Crib avail. TV; cable. Heated pool; poolside serv. Restaurant (see THE GRILL). Rm serv 24 hrs. Bar 11–1 am; entertainment Tues–Sat. Ck-out noon. Convention facilities. Concierge. Gift shop. Covered parking. Airport, RR station, bus depot transportation; free transportation to golf courses. Lighted tennis. Golf privileges. Exercise rm; instructor, weight machines, treadmill, whirlpool, sauna. Massage. Bicycle rentals. Bathrm phones, minibars. Old World elegance in a cosmopolitan setting. *LUXURY LEVEL:* RITZ-CARLTON CLUB. 16 rms, 5 suites. S, D $230; suites $350–$550. Concierge. Private lounge, honor bar. Complimentary continental bkfst, refreshments.
Cr cds: A, C, D, DS, ER, MC, V, JCB.

[icons]

★★ **SAN CARLOS.** *202 N Central Ave (85004). 602/253-4121; res: 800/528-5446; FAX 602/253-4121, ext 209.* 120 rms, 7 story. Jan–Apr: S $89; D $99; each addl $10; suites $129–$159; under 12 free. Crib free. TV; cable. Heated pool. Complimentary continental bkfst 7–10 am. Restaurant 7 am–8 pm. Ck-out noon. Meeting rms. Refrigerators avail. Cr cds: A, C, D, DS, MC, V.

Inn

★ ★ ★ **MARICOPA MANOR.** *15 W Pasadena Ave (85013).* 602/274-6302; FAX 602/263-9695. 5 rms, 1 kit. Sept–May: S, D, kit. unit $129; each addl $15; under 10 free; lower rates rest of yr. TV; cable. Complimentary continental bkfst in rms. Restaurant nearby. Ck-out 11 am, ck-in 4–6 pm. Picnic tables. Totally nonsmoking. Restored Spanish mission-style mansion (1928); antiques, library/sitting rm. Cr cds: MC, V.

Resorts

★ ★ ★ **POINTE HILTON ON SOUTH MOUNTAIN.** *7777 South Pointe Pkwy (85044).* 602/438-9000; FAX 602/431-6535. 638 suites, 2–4 story. Jan–mid-May: S, D $215–$235; each addl $10; suites $275–$450; under 18 free; lower rates rest of yr. TV; cable. 6 heated pools; wading pool, poolside serv. Supervised child's activities. Dining rm (public by res) 6 am–midnight. Rm serv. Bar 11–1 am. Ck-out noon, ck-in 4 pm. Coin lndry. Convention facilities. Airport, RR station, bus depot transportation. Sports dir. Lighted tennis, pro. 18-hole golf, greens fee $80 (incl cart), pro, putting green. Bicycles. Game rm. Rec rm. Exercise rm; instructor, weights, bicycles, whirlpool, sauna, steam rm. Refrigerators; some fireplaces. Private patios, balconies. Cr cds: A, C, D, DS, ER, MC, V.

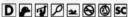

★ ★ **ROYAL PALMS INN.** *5200 E Camelback Rd (85018).* 602/840-3610; res: 800/672-6011 (exc AZ), 800/548-1202 (CAN); FAX 602/840-0233. 120 rms, 1–2 story, 34 kits. Mid-Jan–late Apr: S $100–$150; D $140–$220; each addl $10; suites, kit. units $165–$220; under 5 free; some wkend rates; lower rates rest of yr. Crib $10. Pet accepted. TV; cable. 2 heated pools; poolside serv. Dining rm 7 am–2 pm, 6–10 pm. Box lunches. Bar 11 am–midnight. Ck-out noon. Coin lndry. Meeting rms. Valet serv. Airport, RR station, bus depot transportation. Tennis, pro. 9- & 36-hole golf, putting green. Entertainment, dancing. Some balconies. Spanish architecture; antiques; tile walks in date & citrus orchard. Cr cds: A, C, D, DS, ER, MC, V.

Restaurants

★ ★ ★ **AVANTI'S OF PHOENIX.** *2728 E Thomas Rd.* 602/956-0900. Hrs: 11:30 am–3 pm, 5:30–11 pm; Sat, Sun from 5:30 pm. Closed Dec 25. Res required. Continental, Northern Italian menu. Bar. Wine list. Semi-a la carte: lunch $4.75–$15.50, dinner $8.75–$25.50. Specializes in veal, fresh pasta, fresh mussels. Own pastries, pasta. Entertainment Tues–Sat. Valet parking. Cr cds: A, C, D, MC, V.

★ **AYAKO OF TOKYO.** *2564 E Camelback Rd.* 602/955-7007. Hrs: 11:30 am–2:30 pm, 5:30–10 pm; Fri, Sat to 10:30 pm; Sun 5–9:30 pm. Closed some major hols. Res accepted. Japanese menu. Bar. Semi-a la carte: lunch $4.25–$12, dinner $10.50–$30. Specialties: Imperial dinner, sushi. Teppanyaki cooking. Parking. Cr cds: A, D, MC, V, JCB.

D

✔ ★ **BAXTER'S.** *4514 E Cactus Rd.* 602/953-9200. Hrs: 11:30 am–10 pm; Fri to 11 pm; Sat 9 am–11 pm; Sun 9 am–10 pm. Closed Dec 25. Res accepted. Bar. Semi-a la carte: bkfst $4.95–$8.95, lunch $4.95–$8.95, dinner $4.95–$15.95. Child's meals. Specializes in barbecued ribs, chicken, steak. DJ (evenings). Parking. Western ranch atmosphere. Cr cds: A, C, D, DS, MC, V.

D

✔ ★ **BIG WONG.** *616 W Indian School Rd.* 602/277-2870. Hrs: 11 am–11 pm; wkends to 1:30 am. Res accepted. Chinese menu. Semi-a la carte: lunch $4.25–$5.35, dinner $4.25–$13.50. Specializes in King Dao spare ribs, black pepper steak, seafood. Parking. Cr cds: MC, V.

D

✔ ★ **CHIANTI RISTORANTE.** *3943 E Camelback Rd.* 602/957-9840. Hrs: 11:30 am–10 pm; Sat, Sun from 5 pm. Closed Thanksgiving, Dec 25. Res accepted. Italian menu. Serv bar. Semi-a la carte: lunch $5.95–$8.95, dinner $6.95–$12.95. Child's meals. Specializes in pasta, pizza, chicken. Parking. Cr cds: A, MC, V.

D

★ ★ ★ **CHRISTOPHER'S.** *2398 E Camelback Rd, in Biltmore Financial Center.* 602/957-3214. Hrs: 6–10 pm; Fri & Sat to 11 pm. Closed Jan 1, Memorial Day, Labor Day; also Mon & Tues in summer. Res accepted. Classical French cuisine. Bar. Extensive wine cellar, one of the largest in the state. Semi-a la carte: dinner $22–$28. Prix fixe: dinner $70–$110. Child's meals. Specialties: crêpe foie gras, house-smoked salmon. Own baking. Valet parking. Glass-encased wine cellar focal point of well-appointed, cherrywood-trimmed dining room. Chef-owned. Jacket. Cr cds: A, C, D, MC, V.

D

★ ★ **CHRISTOPHER'S BISTRO.** *2398 E Camelback Rd, in Biltmore Financial Center.* 602/957-3214. Hrs: 11 am–midnight; Sun from 5 pm. Closed some major hols. Res accepted. French/Amer bistro menu. Bar. Wine cellar. A la carte entrees: lunch $6–$16, dinner $8–$21. Specializes in rotisserie chicken, braised lamb shank, rack of lamb. Valet parking. Outdoor dining. Bistro-style dining room. Cr cds: A, C, D, MC, V.

D

★ **CHUBB'S.** *6522 N 16th St.* 602/279-3459. Hrs: 11 am–3 pm, 5–10 pm; Fri & Sat to 11 pm; early-bird dinner 5–7 pm Sun–Thurs. Closed Thanksgiving, Dec 25. Res accepted. Bar. Semi-a la carte: lunch $4.25–$7.95, dinner $8.95–$19.95. Specializes in onion soup, prime rib, steak. Parking. English pub atmosphere. Cr cds: A, MC, V.

D

★ ★ **COMPASS.** *(See Hyatt Regency Phoenix at Civic Plaza Hotel)* 602/440-3166. Hrs: 11 am–2:30 pm, 5:30–10 pm; Sun brunch 10 am–2:30 pm. Res accepted. Southwestern menu. Bar 11–12:30 am. Semi-a la carte: lunch $6.50–$9, dinner $16–$19.75. Sun brunch $21.50. Child's meals. Specializes in prime rib, stuffed chicken with jalapeño cornbread. Own baking. Valet parking. Revolving dining area on 24th floor; panoramic view of city. Cr cds: A, C, D, DS, ER, MC, V, JCB.

D

★ ★ **COPPER CREEK STEAKHOUSE & GRILLE.** *455 N 3rd St, at the Arizona Center.* 602/253-7100. Hrs: 4–10:30 pm; Fri & Sat to 11:30 pm. Closed Thanksgiving, Dec 25. Res accepted. Bar. Semi-a la carte: dinner $13–$18. Specializes in steak; fire-roasted chicken, ribs & chops. Parking. Blue sky mural. Overlooks Arizona Center gardens. Cr cds: A, MC, V.

D

★ ★ ★ **DIFFERENT POINTE OF VIEW.** *11111 N 7th St, at The Pointe Hilton At Tapatio Cliffs Resort.* 602/863-0912. Hrs: 6–10 pm. Res accepted. International American fusion cuisine. Bar 5 pm–1 am. Award-winning wine cellar. A la carte entrees: dinner $21–$28. Prix fixe: dinner (June–Sept) $17.95. Sun brunch (Oct–Father's Day) $18.95. Child's meals. Specializes in seafood, regional dishes, vegetarian dishes, wild game. Own baking. Entertainment Tues–Sat. Valet parking. On mountaintop, beautiful view. Cr cds: A, C, D, DS, MC, V.

D

★ ★ **FISH MARKET.** *1720 E Camelback Rd.* 602/277-3474. Hrs: 11 am–9:30 pm; Fri, Sat to 10 pm; Sun noon–9:30 pm; early-bird dinner 3–6 pm. Closed Thanksgiving, Dec 25. Res accepted. Bar. Semi-a la carte: lunch $6–$18, dinner $8–$20. Child's meals. Specializes in fresh fish, live shellfish, smoked fish. Oyster bar. Parking. Outdoor dining. Nautical decor. Retail fish market. Cr cds: A, D, DS, MC, V.

D

★★**GREEKFEST.** *1940 E Camelback Rd. 602/265-2990.* Hrs: 11 am–2:30 pm, 5–10 pm; Fri, Sat to 11 pm; Sun 5–9 pm. Closed some major hols. Res accepted. Greek menu. Wine, beer. Semi-a la carte: lunch $4.95–$12, dinner $6.95–$18. Child's meals. Specializes in lamb exohiko, fresh fish "chios," souvlaki. Parking. Greek taverna-style decor; festive atmosphere. Cr cds: D, MC, V.

D

★★★**THE GRILL.** *(See The Ritz-Carlton, Phoenix Hotel) 602/468-0700.* Hrs: 5–10:30 pm; Sept–mid-May also 11:30 am–2:30 pm (Mon–Fri). Res accepted. Bar 11:30–1 am. Wine cellar. Semi-a la carte: lunch $7–$12.50, dinner $19–$25. Child's meals. Specialties: sautéed veal medallions, free range chicken breast, seafood mixed grill. Own baking. Pianist and saxophonist. Valet parking. Dining rm features brass chandeliers. Cr cds: A, C, D, DS, ER, MC, V, JCB.

D

✔★**HOUSTON'S.** *2425 E Camelback Rd, #110. 602/957-9700.* Hrs: 11 am–11 pm; Fri, Sat to midnight; Sun to 10 pm. Closed Thanksgiving, Dec 25. Bar. Semi-a la carte: lunch, dinner $6.25–$15. Specializes in baby back ribs, fresh grilled fish, thin-crust pizza. Parking. Outdoor dining. Cr cds: A, MC, V.

D

✔★**INDIAN DELHI PALACE.** *5050 E McDowell Rd. 602/244-8181.* Hrs: 11:30 am–2:30 pm, 5–10 pm; Sat & Sun 11:30 am–10 pm. Res accepted. Indian menu. Bar. Lunch buffet (11:30 am–2:30 pm; Sat & Sun to 4:30 pm): $5.99. A la carte entrees: dinner $10–$15. Specialties: tandoori chicken, lamb Pasanda Newabi, tandoori shrimp masala. Parking. Cr cds: A, MC, V.

★★★**LA FONTANELLA.** *4231 E Indian School Rd. 602/955-1213.* Hrs: 11 am–2 pm, 4:30–9:30 pm; Sat, Sun from 4:30 pm. Closed Dec 25; also Mon May–Sept. Res accepted. Italian menu. Bar. Semi-a la carte: lunch $4.50–$6.50, dinner $6.50–$17.75. Child's meals. Specialties: rack of lamb, osso bucco, pasta with seafood. Own desserts. Parking. Cr cds: A, MC, V.

★★**LE RHONE.** *(9401 W Thunderbird Rd, Peoria) NW on US 89/60. 602/933-0151.* Hrs: 5:30–8:30 pm. Closed Mon; Jan 1. Res accepted. Swiss, continental menu. Bar. Semi-a la carte: dinner $16.90–$23.75. Specialties: châteaubriand, jumbo gulf shrimp provençale, rack of lamb. Pianist. Parking. Cr cds: A, D, DS, MC, V.

D

★★**LOMBARDI'S AT THE ARIZONA CENTER.** *455 N 3rd St, at the Arizona Center. 602/257-8323.* Hrs: 11 am–11 pm; Fri & Sat to midnight; Sun to 10 pm; Sun brunch 11 am–2 pm. Closed Dec 25. Res accepted. Italian menu. Bar. A la carte entrees: lunch $6–$12, dinner $8–$15. Sun brunch $6–$12. Specialties: cioppino Livornese, tagliolini al frutti di mare, capelli d'angelo al pomodoro e basilico. Valet parking. Patio dining. Open kitchen. Cr cds: A, C, D, MC, V.

✔★**LONG LIFE.** *7575 N 16th St. 602/997-8785.* Hrs: 11:30 am–2:30 pm, 4:30–9:30 pm; Sun from 4:30 pm. Closed July 4, Thanksgiving. Res accepted. Chinese menu. Bar. Semi-a la carte: lunch $3.95–$4.95, dinner $6.75–$10.95. Specialties: Yui-shan spicy shrimp, Hunan beef. Parking. Cr cds: A, D, MC, V.

D

✔★**MARILYN'S.** *12631 N Tatum Blvd. 602/953-2121.* Hrs: 11 am–10 pm; Fri, Sat to 10:30 pm. Closed Thanksgiving, Dec 25. Mexican menu. Bar. Semi-a la carte: lunch $4.50–$6.50, dinner $7–$11. Child's meals. Specialties: fajitas, chimichangas, pollo fundido. Parking. Southwestern decor; fiesta atmosphere. Cr cds: A, MC, V.

D

★**MR. LOUIE'S MILANO'S.** *1044 E Camelback Rd. 602/241-1044.* Hrs: 11 am–3 pm, 5–10 pm; Sat from 5 pm. Closed Sun; some major hols. Res accepted. Italian menu. Bar. Semi-a la carte: lunch $5.95–$8.95, dinner $7.95–$14.95. Child's meals. Specializes in lamb shanks, eggplant Parmesan, fresh seafood. Parking. Italian country cottage decor. Fireplace. Cr cds: A, C, D, MC, V.

D

★★**OSCAR TAYLOR.** *2420 E Camelback Rd, at 24th St, in Biltmore Fashion Park. 602/956-5705.* Hrs: 11 am–10 pm; early-bird dinner 4–6 pm; Sun brunch to 2:30 pm. Closed Dec 25. Res accepted. Bar 11 am–midnight, Sun to 10 pm. Semi-a la carte: lunch $6–$10, dinner $10–$20. Sun brunch $13.95. Child's meals. Specializes in barbecued ribs, prime steak. Parking. Outdoor dining. Bakery, deli on premises. Cr cds: A, D, DS, MC, V.

D

★**PASTA SEGIO'S.** *1904 E Camelback Rd. 602/277-2782.* Hrs: 11:30 am–2:30 pm, 5–10 pm; Fri to 11 pm; Sat 5–11 pm; Sun 4:30–9 pm. Closed major hols. Res accepted. Italian menu. Serv bar. Semi-a la carte: lunch $5.80–$7.80, dinner $7.95–$15. Child's meals. Specialties: pastas, osso buco, chocolate mousse. Parking. Cr cds: A, C, D, DS, ER, MC, V, JCB.

D

★★**RAFFAELE'S.** *2999 N 44th St. 602/952-0063.* Hrs: 11:30 am–3 pm, 5–10 pm; Fri to 11 pm; Sat 5–11 pm; Sun 5–10 pm. Closed Thanksgiving, Dec 25. Res accepted. Italian menu. Bar. Semi-a la carte: lunch $5.95–$8.95, dinner $6.95–$21.95. Specialties: spaghetti al cartoccio, vitello saltimbocca. Valet parking (Mon–Sat). Outdoor dining. Contemporary decor; view of fountain, courtyard. Cr cds: A, D, MC, V.

D

★★**ROXSAND.** *2594 E Camelback Rd, Biltmore Fashion Park. 602/381-0444.* Hrs: 11 am–11 pm; Sun noon–9:30 pm. Closed most major hols. Res accepted. Contemporary continental cuisine. Bar. Semi-a la carte: lunch $6.95–$9.95, dinner $10.95–$23. Child's meals. Specializes in air-dried duck, roasted rack of lamb, seafood. Valet parking. Outdoor dining. Offers over 15 daily selections of pastries/desserts. Cr cds: A, C, D, MC, V.

D

★★**STEAMERS GENUINE SEAFOOD.** *2576 E Camelback Rd. 602/956-3631.* Hrs: 11:30 am–11 pm; Sun 5–10 pm; early-bird dinner 5–6:30 pm. Closed Thanksgiving, Dec 25. Res accepted. Bar to midnight. Semi-a la carte: lunch $4.50–$9.95, dinner $11.50–$22.50. Child's meals. Specialties: Maryland crab cakes, live Maine lobster. Oyster bar. Valet parking. Outdoor dining. Bright and colorful, spacious dining area. Cr cds: A, C, D, DS, MC, V.

D

★★**STOCKYARDS.** *5001 E Washington St. 602/273-7378.* Hrs: 11 am–2 pm, 5–10 pm; Sat from 5 pm; Sun 4:30–9 pm. Closed Memorial Day, July 4, Thanksgiving, Dec 25. Res accepted. Bar. Semi-a la carte: lunch $3.95–$12, dinner $9–$27.95. Specializes in prime rib, fresh fish. Parking. Located in landmark Stock Exchange Bldg. 3 restored dining rms; fireplace. Old West cattlemen's club atmosphere. Cr cds: A, C, D, MC, V.

★**T-BONE STEAKHOUSE.** *10037 S 19th Ave, 11 mi S in South Mountain area. 602/276-0945.* Hrs: 5–10 pm. Closed Thanksgiving, Dec 24 & 25. Bar. Semi-a la carte: dinner $7.95–$19.95. Child's meals. Specializes in steak. Salad bar. Vocalist Fri, Sat. Parking. Outdoor dining. Rustic, old Western steakhouse in foothills of the mountains; scenic view of valley and downtown Phoenix. All cooking is done over mesquite coals and much of it is done outside. Cr cds: A, MC, V.

★★**TAPAS PAPA FRITA.** *3213 E Camelback Rd. 602/381-0474.* Hrs: 11:30 am–midnight; Fri to 1 am; Sat 5:30 pm–1 am; Sun 5:30 pm–midnight. Closed most major hols. Res accepted. Spanish menu. Bar. Semi-a la carte: lunch $3.50–$6.95, dinner $9.95–$15.95. Specialties: grouper with clams, asparagus and egg, fresh seafood. Flamenco guitarist nightly; flamenco dancers Tues–Sat. Parking. Spanish atmosphere; colorful decor. Cr cds: A, C, D, MC, V.

D

★★TIMOTHY'S. 6335 N 16th St. 602/277-7634. Hrs: 5 pm–1 am. Closed Labor Day, Dec 24–25. Res accepted. Bar. Semi-a la carte: dinner $15.95–$19.95. Jazz musicians. Valet parking. Art deco, jazz theme. Cr cds: A, C, D, DS, MC, V.

D

★★★VINCENT GUERITHAULT ON CAMELBACK. 3930 E Camelback Rd. 602/224-0225. Hrs: 11:30 am–2:30 pm, 6–10:30 pm; Sat from 5:30 pm. Closed major hols; also Sun May–Sept. Res accepted. Southwestern, French menu. Bar. Wine list. A la carte entrees: lunch $5.50–$8.95, dinner $18.50–$22. Specializes in mesquite-grilled beef, chicken & seafood, homemade ice cream. Own baking. Valet parking. Country French decor. Cr cds: A, D, MC, V.

D

Unrated Dining Spots

CHOMPIE'S. 3202 E Greenway Rd, Greenway Park Plaza. 602/971-8010. Hrs: 6 am–9 pm; Mon to 3 pm; Sat 7 am–9 pm; Sun 7 am–8 pm. Res accepted. Kosher style deli menu. Wine, beer. Semi-a la carte: bkfst $2.50–$6, lunch $3.50–$7, dinner $5.95–$10.95. Child's meals. Own baking. Parking. Family-owned New York kosher style deli, bakery & bagel factory. Cr cds: MC, V.

D

DUCK AND DECANTER. 1651 E Camelback Rd. 602/274-5429. Hrs: 9 am–7 pm; Thurs, Fri to 9 pm; Sun from 10 am. Closed some major hols. Bar. A la carte entrees: lunch, dinner $2.50–$5.50. Child's meals. Specializes in albacore tuna sandwich. Guitarist Thurs–Sun evenings. Parking. Outdoor dining. Gourmet, wine shop. Totally nonsmoking. Cr cds: A, MC, V.

D

ED DEBEVIC'S. 2102 E Highland Ave, in Town & Country Shopping Ctr. 602/956-2760. Hrs: 11 am–10 pm; Fri, Sat to 11 pm. Closed Thanksgiving, Dec 25. Bar. A la carte entrees: lunch, dinner $2.75–$5.95. Child's meals. Specializes in hamburgers, malts, french fries. Salad bar. 50s-style diner; jukebox. Cr cds: MC, V.

D

EDDIE'S GRILLE. 4747 N 7th St. 602/241-1188. Hrs: 11:30 am–2:30 pm. Contemporary Amer menu. Bar. Semi-a la carte: lunch $5–$12.95. Specializes in steak, seafood, lamb. Outdoor dining. Patio with pool and fountain. Cr cds: A, MC, V.

D

FURRS CAFETERIA. 8114 N Black Canyon Hwy. 602/995-1588. Hrs: 11 am–8 pm. Closed Dec 25. Avg ck: lunch, dinner $5–$5.50. Specialties: chicken-fried steak, millionaire pie. Parking. Cr cds: A, MC, V.

D

Pinetop (C-4)

Pop: 2,422 **Elev:** 6,959 ft **Area code:** 602 **Zip:** 85935

Trout fishing, horseback riding, hiking, biking and golfing are popular summer activities here; skiing and snowmobiling draw many winter visitors.

(For information about this area contact the Pinetop/Lakeside Chamber of Commerce, PO Box 266; 367-4290.)

(See McNary, Show Low)

Motels

★BEST WESTERN. (Box 1006) 404 White Mountain Blvd, on AZ 260. 602/367-6667; FAX 602/367-6672. 41 rms, 2 story. May–mid-Sept & mid-Oct–mid-Apr: S $54; D $65; each addl $5; under 12 free; higher rates hols; lower rates rest of yr. Crib $5. Pet accepted, some restrictions; $5 per day. TV; cable, in-rm movies. Complimentary coffee, tea in lobby. Ck-out 11 am. Sundries. Whirlpool. Cr cds: A, D, DS, MC, V.

D 🏕 🚭 ⊘ SC

★LAKESIDE INN. (Box 1130-D) 1637 Hwy 260, on AZ 260. 602/368-6600; res: 800/843-4792. 56 rms, 2 story. May–Oct, Dec–Mar: S, D $60–$85; each addl $8; under 12 free; golf packages; higher rates hol wkends; lower rates rest of yr. TV; cable, in-rm movies avail. Complimentary continental bkfst, coffee. Ck-out 11 am. Whirlpool. Refrigerators. Cr cds: A, C, D, DS, ER, MC, V.

D 🚭 ⊘ SC

Restaurant

★★CHARLIE CLARK'S STEAK HOUSE. On AZ 260. 602/367-4900. Hrs: 5–10 pm. Closed Mon in Apr. Res accepted. Bar. Semi-a la carte: dinner $8.95–$19.95. Child's meals. Specializes in prime rib, barbecued ribs, mesquite-cooked steak. Parking. Cr cds: MC, V.

D

Pipe Spring National Monument (A-2)

(14 mi W of Fredonia on spur off AZ 389)

Located on the Kaibab-Paiute Indian Reservation, the focal point of this monument is a beautifully built sandstone Mormon fort, dating back to 1870. Several years earlier, Brigham Young had ordered the exploration of this region north of the Grand Canyon. According to legend, rifleman William "Gunlock Bill" Hamblin gave the place its name by shooting the bottom out of a smoking pipe at 50 paces.

The fort, actually a fortified ranchhouse, was built under the direction of Bishop Anson P. Winsor to protect the families caring for the church's cattle. Cattle drives, headed for the railroad in Cedar City, Utah, began here.

Guide service (daily); living history demonstrations (June–Aug). Kaibab Paiute Campground (fee), one-half mile N of access road to visitor center. Area closed Jan 1, Thanksgiving, Dec 25. Contact the Superintendent, HC 65, Box 5, Fredonia 86022; 602/643-7105. ¢

(For accommodations see Kanab, UT)

Prescott (C-3)

Founded: 1864 **Pop:** 26,455 **Elev:** 5,368 ft **Area code:** 602

When President Lincoln established the territory of Arizona, Prescott became the capital. In 1867, the capital was moved to Tucson and then back to Prescott in 1877. After much wrangling, it was finally moved to Phoenix in 1889.

Tourism and manufacturing are now Prescott's principal occupations. The climate is mild during summer and winter. The Prescott National Forest surrounds the city; its headquarters are located here.

What to See and Do

1. **Sharlot Hall Museum.** 415 W Gurley St. Period houses include the Territorial Governor's Mansion (1864), restored in 1929 by poet-historian Sharlot Hall; Fort Misery (1864); William Bashford house (1877); and John C. Frémont house (1875). Period furnishings. Museum, library & archives. Also on grounds are grave of Pauline Weaver; rose and herb garden; pioneer schoolhouse. All buildings (daily exc Mon; also open Memorial Day & Labor Day; closed Jan 1, Thanksgiving, Dec 25). Phone 445-3122. ¢

2. **Smoki Museum.** 126 N Arizona St. Native American artifacts, ancient and modern. (May–Sept, Mon–Tues & Thurs–Sat, also Sun afternoons) Phone 445-1230. ¢

3. **Prescott National Forest.** 20 mi NE on US 89A or 1 mi SW on US 89. Minerals and varied vegetation abound in this forest (more than 1 million acres). Within the forest are Juniper Mesa, Apache Creek, Granite Mountain, Castle Creek, Woodchute and Cedar Bench wilderness areas, and parts of Sycamore Canyon and Pine Mt wilderness areas. Fishing (Granite Basin, Lynx lakes), hunting. Picnicking. Camping. Phone 445-1762.

4. **Arcosanti.** 36 mi SE on AZ 69 to Cordes Junction, then 2 mi E on unnumbered road (follow signs or inquire locally for directions). Architectural project by Paolo Soleri and the Cosanti Foundation. This prototype town is being constructed as a functioning example of "arcology," a fusion of architecture and ecology. Guided tours. (Daily; closed major hols) Sr citizen rate. Phone 632-7135. ¢¢

(For further information contact the Chamber of Commerce, 117 W Goodwin St, PO Box 1147, 86302; 445-2000.)

Annual Events

George Phippen Memorial Western Art Show. Dozens of artists. Memorial Day wknd.

Territorial Prescott Days. Courthouse Plaza, and throughout city. Art show, craft demonstrations, old-fashioned contests, home tours. Early June.

Prescott Frontier Days Rodeo. Fairgrounds on Miller Valley Rd. Also parade & fireworks. July 4 wknd.

Bluegrass Festival. 3rd wkend July

Smoki Native American Festival. Dedicated to the preservation of Native American lore. Phone 445-1230. 2nd wkend Aug.

Yavapai County Fair. Mid–late Sept.

(See Cottonwood)

Motels

★**BEST WESTERN PRESCOTTONIAN.** *1317 E Gurley St (86301), at jct US 89, AZ 69. 602/445-3096; FAX 602/778-2976.* 121 rms, 2–3 story. No elvtr. Apr–Sept: S $49–$69; D $70–$85; each addl $7; suites $100–$160; higher rates special events; lower rates rest of yr. Crib free. Pet accepted. TV; cable. Pool; whirlpool. Restaurant 6 am–11 pm. Bar noon–10 pm. Ck-out noon. Coin lndry. Some refrigerators. Some private patios, balconies. Cr cds: A, C, D, DS, ER, MC, V.

✔★**COMFORT INN.** *1290 White Spar Rd (86303), US 89S, 1½ mi S from courthouse. 602/778-5770.* 61 rms, 2 story, 11 kit. units. Apr–Oct: S $45–$75; D $51–$75; each addl $7; kit. units $65–$75; under 6 free; higher rates wkends and some hols; lower rates rest of yr. Crib free. TV; cable. Complimentary coffee. Restaurant nearby. Ck-out 11 am. Whirlpool. Some refrigerators. Cr cds: A, C, D, DS, MC, V.

★★**HOTEL VENDOME.** *230 S Cortez St (86303). 602/776-0900.* 21 rms, 2 story, 4 suites. No A/C. May–Nov: S, D $60–$70; suites $90–$100; under 18 free; higher rates July 4; lower rates rest of yr. Crib free. TV; cable. Complimentary continental bkfst, coffee. Restaurant adj

11 am–9 pm. Bar 11 am–11 pm. Ck-out noon. Restored 1917 lodging house. Cr cds: A, C, D, DS, MC, V.

Hotels

★★**HASSAYAMPA INN.** *122 E Gurley St (86301). 602/778-9434; FAX 602/778-9434, ext 109.* 67 rms, 4 story. May–Oct: S, D $90–$104; each addl $10; suites $130–$160; under 6 free; lower rates rest of yr. Crib free. TV; cable. Complimentary full bkfst. Restaurant 7 am–2 pm, 5–9 pm. Bar 11 am–2:30 pm, 5–10 pm; Fri, Sat to 11 pm. Ck-out noon. Meeting rms. Maintained vintage hotel (1927); original wall stenciling, decorative tiles. Cr cds: A, C, D, DS, MC, V.

★★★**SHERATON RESORT & CONFERENCE CENTER.** *1500 AZ 69 (86301). 602/776-1666; FAX 602/776-8544.* 161 rms, 5 story, 80 suites. Apr–Oct: S $95–$130; D $105–$140; suites $115–$160; under 15 free; golf plans; lower rates rest of yr. Crib free. Pet accepted; $50 refundable. TV; cable. Indoor/outdoor pool; poolside serv. Restaurant 6 am–10 pm. Bar 11–12:30 am; entertainment, dancing Tues–Sat. Ck-out noon. Meeting rms. Gift shop. Barber, beauty shop. Free local airport, bus depot transportation. Lighted tennis, pro. 36-hole golf privileges, pro. Exercise equipt; weight machines, bicycles, whirlpool, sauna. Bathrm phones, refrigerators. Balconies. Casino. On hill overlooking city. Cr cds: A, C, D, DS, MC, V.

Inns

★★**MARK'S HOUSE.** *203 E Union St, 1 blk S of Gurley St, 1 blk E of courthouse. 602/778-4632.* 4 suites. No A/C. No rm phones. Suites $75–$135; wkly rates. Complimentary full bkfst, coffee, tea, sherry. Restaurant nearby. Ck-out 10 am, ck-in 4 pm. Victorian inn (1894). Elegant antique furnishings create a turn-of-the-century mood. Panoramic view from the veranda. Totally nonsmoking. Cr cds: MC, V.

★**PRESCOTT COUNTRY INN.** *503 S Montezuma St (86303), on US 89. 602/445-7991.* 12 kit. cottages. S, D $59–$125; under 6 free; each addl $10. Crib $5. TV; cable. Pool privileges. Complimentary continental bkfst in cottages. Restaurant nearby. Ck-out 11 am, ck-in 3 pm. Lighted tennis privileges. Health club privileges. Grills. Individually decorated rms; handmade quilts. Cr cds: MC, V.

Restaurants

✔★**GURLEY STREET GRILL.** *230 Gurley St. 602/445-3388.* Hrs: 11–1 am. Closed Dec 25. Bar. Semi-a la carte: lunch $4.25–$7.25, dinner $5.95–$12.95. Child's meals. Specializes in fresh pasta, hamburgers, gourmet pizza. Patio dining. Pub-style atmosphere. Open kitchen. Cr cds: A, DS, MC, V.

★★**MURPHY'S.** *201 N Cortez. 602/445-4044.* Hrs: Summer: 11 am–11 pm; rest of yr: 11 am–10 pm, Fri & Sat to 11 pm; early-bird dinner Sun–Thurs 4:30–6 pm; Sun brunch to 3 pm. Closed day after Labor Day, Dec 25. Bar to 1 am. Semi-a la carte: lunch $5.25–$9.95, dinner $10.95–$16.95. Child's meals. Specialties: mesquite-broiled fresh fish, hand-cut steak, prime rib. Own bread. Memorabilia from turn-of-the-century on display. Restored mercantile building is one of oldest in Southwest. Cr cds: A, DS, MC, V.

✔★**PINE CONE INN.** *1245 White Spar Rd. 602/445-2970.* Hrs: 8 am–10:30 pm; Mon from 11 am; early-bird dinner 4–6 pm. Closed Dec 24–26. Res accepted. Bar to 11 pm. Semi-a la carte: bkfst $2.50–$4.95, lunch $4–$8.25, dinner $6.50–$13.50. Specializes in steak, seafood. Entertainment Wed–Sun. Parking. Family-owned. Cr cds: A, MC, V.

★★PRESCOTT MINING COMPANY. *155 Plaza Dr. 602/445-1991.* Hrs: 11 am–10 pm; early-bird dinner 4–6 pm. Res accepted. Bar to midnight. Semi-a la carte: lunch $4.95–$8.95, dinner $9.95–$18.95. Child's meals. Specializes in fresh seafood, prime rib. Pianist Wed–Sun. Parking. Outdoor dining. Old mining camp decor; mining equipment displayed. Overlooks waterfall. Cr cds: A, D, DS, MC, V.

Safford (D-5)

Founded: 1874 **Pop:** 7,359 **Elev:** 2,920 ft **Area code:** 602 **Zip:** 85546

Safford is a marketplace for cotton, alfalfa, grain, vegetables and fruit produced on 35,000 acres irrigated by waters from the Gila River. It is the trade center for a wide area. Nearby is Aravaipa Canyon, a designated primitive area. A Ranger District office for the Coronado National Forest (see TUCSON) is located here.

What to See and Do

1. **The Swift Trail** snakes its way 36 mi SW from Safford to the high elevations of the Pinaleño Mountains in Coronado National Forest; splendid view from the top. There are five developed campgrounds (mid-Apr–mid-Nov, weather permitting); trout fishing at Riggs Flat Lake and in the streams. The upper elevations of AZ 366 are closed from mid-Nov–mid-Apr. Phone 428-4150. Camping ¢¢¢
2. **Roper Lake State Park.** 6 mi S, ½ mi E of US 666. This 320-acre park includes a small man-made lake, a swimming beach and natural hot springs with tubs for public use; fishing (dock); boat launch (no gas-powered motors). Nature trails, hiking. Picnicking (shelter). Camping, tent & trailer sites (hook-ups, dump station). Fishing dock accessible to the disabled. **Dankworth Unit,** 6 mi S, is a day-use area with fishing and picnicking. Standard fees. Phone 428-6760.

(For further information contact the Graham County Chamber of Commerce, 1111 Thatcher Blvd; 428-2511.)

Annual Events

Fiesta de Mayo. Mexican-American commemoration of *Cinco de Mayo* (May 5th), date of Mexican independence from Europe. 1st wkend May.

Pioneer Days. Commemorates Mormon settlement. Late July.

Graham County Fair. Mid-Oct.

(See Willcox)

Motels

★★BEST WESTERN DESERT INN. *1391 Thatcher Blvd. 602/428-0521; FAX 602/428-7653.* 70 rms, 2 story. S $57–$80; D $62–$80; each addl $6; under 12 free. Crib $3. TV; cable. Heated pool. Coffee in rms. Restaurant adj 6 am–9:30 pm. Bar 11 am–10 pm, Sun from noon. Ck-out noon. Coin lndry. Free local airport, bus depot transportation. Refrigerators. Cr cds: A, C, D, DS, MC, V.

✔★★COMFORT INN. *1578 W Thatcher Blvd. 602/428-5851; FAX 602/428-4968.* 44 rms, 2 story. S $41; D $44–$49; each addl $5; under 18 free; golf plans. Crib $3. TV; cable. Heated pool. Complimentary continental bkfst. Ck-out 11 am. Cr cds: A, C, D, DS, ER, MC, V.

Restaurant

★CASA MAÑANA. *502 1st Ave. 602/428-3170.* Hrs: 11 am–9 pm; Fri, Sat to 10 pm. Closed Sun; Jan 1, Thanksgiving, Dec 25. Res accepted. Mexican, Amer menu. Beer. A la carte entrees: lunch, dinner $3.50–$14. Specializes in green chili chimichangas, fajitas, fried ice cream. Parking. Spanish decor. Cr cds: MC, V.

Saguaro National Monument (E-3 – E-4)

(Rincon Mt District: 17 mi E of Tucson via Broadway and Old Spanish Trail. Tucson Mt District: 16 mi W of Tucson via Speedway and Gates Pass Rd)

The saguaro (sah-WAH-ro) cactus may grow as high as 50 feet and may live to be 200 years old. The fluted columns, spined with sharp, tough needles, may branch into fantastic shapes. During the rainy season, large saguaros can absorb enough water to sustain themselves during the dry season.

The suguaro's waxy, white blossoms (Arizona's state flower), which open at night and close the following afternoon, bloom in May and June; the red fruit ripens in July. The Tohono O'odham eat this fruit fresh and dried; they also use it to make jellies, jams and wines.

Wildlife is abundant. Gila woodpeckers and gilded flickers drill nest holes in the saguaro trunks. Once vacated, these holes become home to many other species of birds, including the tiny elf owl. Peccaries (piglike mammals), coyotes, mule deer and other animals are often seen. Yuccas, agaves, prickly pears, mesquite, paloverde trees and many other desert plants grow here.

The Rincon Mountain District offers nature trails, guided nature walks (winter), eight-mile self-guided drive, mountain hiking, bridle trails. Picnicking (no water). Back country camping. Visitor center with museum and orientation film. Per car ¢¢

The Tucson Mt District offers nature trails, a six-mile self-guided drive and hiking and bridle trails. Five picnic areas (no water). Information center (daily). For further information contact the Superintendent, 3693 S Old Spanish Trail, Tucson 85730; 602/670-6680. **Free.**

(For accommodations see Tucson)

San Carlos (D-4)

Pop: 2,918 **Elev:** 2,635 ft **Area code:** 602 **Zip:** 85550

The San Carlos Apache Indian Reservation covers almost 2 million acres ranging from desert to pine forests. Many lakes, rivers and ponds offer fishing (fee) year-round for trout, bass and catfish. Camping (fee). Apache guides may be hired to lead visitors into the wilderness portions of the reservation. Sunrise ceremonial dances are held from time to time.

(For information about this area contact the San Carlos Recreation & Wildlife Dept, PO Box 97; 475-2343.)

(For accommodations see Globe)

Scottsdale (D-3)

Pop: 130,069 **Elev:** 1,250 ft **Area code:** 602

This prosperous, residential suburb of Phoenix (see) is a popular resort destination. There is a reconstructed old Western town, with false fronts, hitching rails and a frontier atmosphere (see #4). There also is excellent shopping and dining at a wide variety of specialty stores and restaurants.

What to See and Do

1. **Corporate Jets Grand Canyon Air Tours.** Scottsdale Municipal Airport. Half-day flights over northern Arizona and a close-up view of the Grand Canyon from above the rim. (Daily, weather permitting) (See GRAND CANYON NATIONAL PARK) For reservations and information phone 948-2400.

2. **Cosanti Foundation.** 6433 Doubletree Ranch Rd. Earth-formed concrete structures and studios by Italian architect Paolo Soleri; constructed by Soleri's students. Soleri windbells made in crafts areas. (Daily; closed major hols) Phone 948-6145. ¢

3. **Taliesin West.** At Cactus Rd & 108th St. Winter house of Frank Lloyd Wright; now campus of the Taliesin Foundation; historic landmark of notable design. Tours; bookstore. (Daily; closed major hols) Phone 860-2700 or -8810 (recording). ¢¢¢¢

4. **Rawhide 1880's Western Town.** 23023 N Scottsdale Rd. Town recreated in the image of the Old West; steakhouse and saloon; museum; 20 shops; displays; rodeos; cowboy gunfights; stagecoach ride; petting ranch. (Daily; closed Dec 25) Fee for some attractions. Phone 563-1880.

5. **Scottsdale Center for the Arts.** 7383 Scottsdale Mall. Offers theater, dance; classical, jazz and popular music; lectures; outdoor festivals and concerts. Sculpture garden; art exhibits (gallery: daily; closed major hols). Phone 994-2787 or -2301.

6. **McCormick Railroad Park.** 7301 E Indian Bend Road. This 30-acre city park was created by civic support and volunteer labor. Displays include a full-size Baldwin steam engine, baggage car, and the Roald Amundsen Pullman car; exhibits by model railroad clubs; railroad hobby and artifact shops. Train rides aboard the steam-powered, nearly half-size *Paradise and Pacific* on 1 mile of 15-inch gauge track (fee). Museum, playground with 1929 carousel, picnic areas, desert arboretum; park office. (Daily; closed Thanksgiving, Dec 25) Phone 994-2312. Train rides ¢

7. **Wild West Jeep Tours.** Four-hour guided desert tour. Includes opportunity to shoot a pistol; see working gold mine and Native American petroglyphs; explore an ancient ruin. (Daily) Phone 941-8355. ¢¢¢¢¢

8. **Gray Line sightseeing tours.** Contact PO Box 21126, Phoenix 85036; 495-9100.

(For further information contact the Chamber of Commerce, 7343 Scottsdale Mall, 85251; 945-8481.)

Annual Events

Parada del Sol & Rodeo. Parade, late Jan; rodeo, early Feb.

Arabian Horse Show. Westworld, 16601 N Pima Rd. Phone 951-1180. One wk, mid-Feb.

The Tradition at Desert Mt. Senior PGA Tour golf tournament. Cochise Golf Course at Desert Mt, 10333 Rockaway Hills. Phone 443-1597. Early Apr.

Seasonal Event

Baseball Spring Training. Scottsdale Stadium. San Francisco Giants. Mar.

(See Chandler, Glendale, Mesa, Phoenix, Tempe)

Motels

✔ ★ ★ **BEST WESTERN PAPAGO INN.** 7017 E McDowell Rd (85257). 602/947-7335; FAX 602/994-0692. 58 rms, 2 story. Mid-Jan–mid-Apr: S, D $88–$110; each addl $5; under 12 free; lower rates rest of yr. Crib $5. TV; cable. Heated pool; poolside serv. Coffee in rms.

Restaurant 7 am–2 pm, 5–9 pm. Rm serv. Bar 11–1 am. Ck-out noon. Coin lndry. Valet serv. Free airport transportation. Exercise equipt; weights, bicycles, whirlpool, sauna. Bathrm phones, refrigerators. Shopping mall adj. Cr cds: A, C, D, DS, ER, MC, V, JCB.

D ⊷ ⫴ ⊗ ⓞ SC

★ ★ ★ **COURTYARD BY MARRIOTT.** 13444 E Shea Blvd (85259), near Mayo Clinic. 602/860-4000; FAX 602/860-4308. 124 rms, 2 story, 12 suites. Jan–mid-May: S, D $100–$115; suites $125; 12 suites rest of yr. Crib free. TV; cable. Heated pool; whirlpool. Complimentary coffee in rms. Restaurant 6:30 am–9 pm; Sat, Sun 7 am–2 pm, 5–9 pm. Bar 4–11 pm. Ck-out 1 pm. Coin lndry. Meeting rms. Valet serv. Free Mayo Clinic transportation. Airport, RR station, bus depot transportation. Refrigerator in suites. Many balconies. Cr cds: A, C, D, DS, MC, V.

D ⫰ ⊗ ⓞ

✔ ★ ★ **FAIRFIELD INN BY MARRIOTT.** 13440 N Scottsdale Rd (85254). 602/483-0042; FAX 602/483-0042, ext 709. 133 rms, 3 story. Jan–Apr: S, D $84.95–$94.95; under 18 free; lower rates rest of yr. TV; cable. Heated pool; whirlpool. Complimentary continental bkfst, coffee in lobby. Restaurant nearby. Ck-out noon. Meeting rm. Valet serv. Picnic table. Cr cds: A, C, D, DS, MC, V.

D ⫰ ⊗ ⓞ SC

★ ★ **HOSPITALITY SUITE RESORT.** 409 N Scottsdale Rd (85257). 602/949-5115; res: 800/445-5115; FAX 602/941-8014. 209 kit. suites (1–2 rm), 2–3 story. Mid-Jan–Mar: S $99–$109; D $124–$134; each addl $10; under 13 free; lower rates rest of yr. Crib $10. Pet accepted, some restrictions; $100. TV; cable, in-rm movies. 3 heated pools; whirlpool, poolside serv. Complimentary full bkfst. Restaurant 6:30 am–10 pm. Rm serv. Bar 11–1 am; entertainment, dancing Thurs–Sat. Ck-out 11 am. Coin lndry. Meeting rms. Bellhops. Valet serv. Free airport transportation. Lighted tennis. Lawn games. Refrigerators. Grills. Cr cds: A, C, D, DS, ER, MC, V.

D ⫰ ⫲ ⊗ ⓞ SC

★ ★ **RESIDENCE INN BY MARRIOTT.** 6040 N Scottsdale Rd (85253). 602/948-8666; FAX 602/443-4869. 122 kit. suites, 2 story. Feb–Apr: S $129–$160; D $175–$214; each addl $10; under 12 free; golf plans; lower rates rest of yr. Crib free. Pet accepted, some restrictions; $50 and $6 per day (after 6th day). TV; cable. Heated pool. Complimentary continental bkfst. Complimentary coffee in rms. Restaurant opp 6 am–10 pm. Ck-out noon. Coin lndry. Meeting rm. Valet serv. Airport, RR station, bus depot transportation. Lighted tennis privileges. 36-hole golf privileges, pro, putting green, driving range. Exercise equipt; weight machine, bicycles, whirlpool. Health club privileges. Grills. Cr cds: A, C, D, DS, MC, V, JCB.

D ⫰ ⫴ ⊗ ⓞ SC

✔ ★ **RODEWAY INN.** 7110 E Indian School Rd (85251). 602/946-3456; FAX 602/946-4248. 64 rms, 2 story. Mid-Jan–mid-Apr: S $84–$91; D $92–$99; each addl $8; suites $117–$126; under 19 free; wkly rates; lower rates rest of yr. Crib $6. TV; cable. Heated pool; whirlpool. Complimentary continental bkfst, coffee. Restaurant opp 6 am–11 pm. Ck-out noon. Cr cds: A, C, D, DS, ER, MC, V, JCB.

⫰ ⊗ ⓞ SC

★ ★ **SAFARI RESORT.** 4611 N Scottsdale Rd (85251). 602/945-0721; FAX 602/946-4703. 188 rms, 2 story, 64 kits. Jan–Apr: S $92–$130; D $102–$140; each addl $10; suites $135–$145; kit. units $130–$140; under 18 free; lower rates rest of yr. Crib free. Pet accepted; $50 refundable. TV; cable; in-rm movies. 2 heated pools; whirlpool. Complimentary continental bkfst. Restaurant 11 am–11 pm. Rm serv 7 am–10 pm. Bar 11–1 am. Ck-out noon. Meeting rms. Coin lndry. Bellhops. Gift shop. Health club privileges. Lawn games. Many private patios, balconies. Cr cds: A, C, D, DS, MC, V.

D ⫰ ⊗ ⓞ SC

✔ ★ ★ **SCOTTSDALE INN AT ELDORADO PARK.** 7707 E McDowell Rd (85257). 602/941-1202; res: 800/238-8851; FAX 602/990-7873. 120 rms, 2 story. Jan–Apr: S $75; D $80; under 18 free; lower rates rest of yr. Crib free. Pet accepted, some restrictions. TV; cable. Heated pool; whirlpool. Complimentary continental bkfst 7–10 am. Restaurant adj 7 am–10 pm; closed Sun. Ck-out noon. Coin lndry. Meeting rms. Refrigerators. Picnic tables, grills. Cr cds: A, C, D, DS, MC, V.

Motor Hotels

★★**BEST WESTERN THUNDERBIRD SUITES.** *7515 E Butherus Dr (85260).* 602/951-4000; FAX 602/483-9046. 120 suites, 4 story. Mid-Jan–mid-Apr: S, D $130–$140; under 14 free; wkly, monthly rates; golf plans; lower rates rest of yr. Crib free. TV; cable. Heated pool; whirlpool, poolside serv. Continental bkfst. Restaurant 6:30 am–10 pm. Rm serv. Bar noon–1 am. Ck-out noon. Coin lndry. Meeting rms. Valet serv. Airport transportation. Refrigerators. Balconies. Cr cds: A, C, D, DS, ER, MC, V.

★★★**HILTON RESORT & SPA.** *6333 N Scottsdale Rd (85250).* 602/948-7750; FAX 602/948-2232. 187 rms, 2–3 story, 45 villas. Jan–Apr: S $105–$165; D $115–$175; each addl $15; suites $165–$375; under 18 free; lower rates rest of yr. Crib $5. TV; cable. Heated pool; wading pool, poolside serv. Restaurant 6:30 am–10 pm. Rm serv to 11 pm. Bar 11–1 am; entertainment, dancing Wed–Sat. Ck-out 1 pm. Meeting rms. Bellhops. Valet serv. Gift shop. Beauty shop. Lighted tennis, pro, shop. Golf privileges. Exercise rm; instructor, weights, bicycles, whirlpool, sauna, steam rm. Refrigerator in villas. Cr cds: A, C, D, DS, ER, MC, V, JCB.

★★★**RED LION'S LA POSADA.** *4949 E Lincoln Dr (85253).* 602/952-0420; FAX 602/840-8576. 264 rms. Jan–mid-May: S, D $175–$250; each addl $10; suites $750–$1,050; under 18 free; golf plan; lower rates rest of yr. Crib free. Pet accepted, some restrictions. TV; cable. 2 heated pools; poolside serv. Supervised child's activities (summer). Restaurant 6 am–10 pm. Rm serv. Bar noon–1 am; dancing Wed–Sat. Ck-out noon. Convention facilities. Bellhops. Valet serv. Sundries. Gift shop. Barber, beauty shop. Free airport transportation. Lighted tennis, pro, shop. Golf privileges, 2 putting greens. Exercise rm; instructor, weights, bicycles, whirlpool, sauna. Some refrigerators, honor bars. Private patios. Multiple casacading waterfalls; lagoon-like pool. At foot of Camelback Mountain. Cr cds: A, C, D, DS, ER, MC, V, JCB.

★★★**RESORT SUITES.** *7677 E Princess Blvd (85255).* 602/585-1234; res: 800/541-5203; FAX 602/585-1457. 297 units (1–4 bedrm), 2 story. Jan–mid-Apr: S, D $170–$200; suites $300–$590; under 16 free; lower rates rest of yr. Crib free. TV; cable. Heated pool; poolside serv. Complimentary coffee in rms. Restaurant 6–1 am. Rm serv. Bar 6 pm–1 am. Ck-out 10 am. Coin lndry. Convention facilities. Bellhops. Concierge. Exercise equipt; weight machine, bicycles, whirlpool. Balconies. Cr cds: A, MC, V.

★★**SUNBURST HOTEL & CONFERENCE CENTER.** *4925 N Scottsdale Rd (85251).* 602/945-7666; res: 800/528-7867 (exc AZ); FAX 602/946-4056. 208 rms, 2 story. Jan–Apr: S $135–$175; D $150–$180; each addl $15; suites $190–$300; under 18 free; wkend rates; golf plans; lower rates rest of yr. TV; cable. Heated pool; whirlpool, poolside serv. Complimentary continental bkfst. Complimentary coffee in rms. Restaurant 7 am–10 pm; Fri & Sat to 11 pm. Rm serv. Bar 5 pm–1 am; entertainment, dancing. Ck-out noon. Meeting rms. Bellhops. Concierge. Gift shop. Airport transportation. Tennis privileges. Golf privileges. Health club privileges. Lawn games. Refrigerators. Private patios, balconies. Cr cds: A, C, D, DS, MC, V.

★★★**WYNDHAM PARADISE VALLEY RESORT.** *5401 N Scottsdale Rd (85250).* 602/947-5400; FAX 602/946-1524. 387 rms, 2 story. Jan–mid-June: S $180–$225; D $195–$240; each addl $15; suites $350–$1,400; under 18 free; wkend rates; golf plans; lower rates rest of yr. Crib free. TV; cable. 2 heated pools; poolside serv. Restaurants 6:30 am–11 pm. Rm serv. Bar 11–1 am. Ck-out noon. Convention facilities.

Concierge. Gift shop. Barber, beauty shop. 6 tennis courts, 2 indoor. Golf privileges. Exercise rm; instructor, weights, bicycles, whirlpool, steam rm, sauna. Bathrm phones, minibars. Private patios, balconies. Grill. Unique building design; extensive grounds elaborately landscaped; patio area overlooks courtyard. Cr cds: A, C, D, DS, ER, MC, V, JCB.

Hotels

★★**EMBASSY SUITES.** *5001 N Scottsdale Rd (85250).* 602/949-1414; FAX 602/947-2675. 311 suites, 4 story. Jan–Apr: S $145; D $155; each addl $10; under 12 free; lower rates rest of yr. Crib free. TV; cable. 2 heated pools; poolside serv. Complimentary full bkfst. Complimentary coffee in rms. Restaurants 11 am–10 pm; Fri, Sat to 11 pm. Bars to 1 am. Ck-out noon. Coin lndry. Meeting rms. Concierge. Gift shop. Free airport, RR station, bus depot transportation. Lighted tennis, pro. Golf privileges. Exercise equipt; weights, bicycles, whirlpool. Rec rm. Refrigerators; some bathrm phones. Balconies. Grills. Cr cds: A, C, D, DS, MC, V.

★★★**MARRIOTT SUITES.** *7325 E 3rd Ave (85251).* 602/945-1550; FAX 602/945-2005. 251 suites, 8 story. Jan–Apr: S, D $169; lower rates rest of yr. Crib free. TV; cable. Heated pool; poolside serv. Complimentary continental bkfst. Restaurant 6:30 am–10 pm. Bar 5–11 pm. Ck-out noon. Coin lndry. Meeting rms. Valet; covered parking. Tennis, golf privileges. Exercise equipt; weight machines, bicycles, whirlpool, sauna. Refrigerators. Many private patios, balconies. Cr cds: A, C, D, DS, ER, MC, V, JCB.

Inn

★★★**INN AT THE CITADEL.** *8700 E Pinnacle Peak Rd (85255), at Inn at the Citadel Complex.* 602/585-6133; res: 800/927-8367; FAX 602/585-3436. 11 suites, 2 story. Mid-Jan–May: S, D $195–$265; each addl (after 4th person) $20; under 12 free; lower rates rest of yr. Crib free. TV; cable. Complimentary continental bkfst. Dining rm 7 am–10 pm. Rm serv. Ck-out noon, ck-in 3 pm. Golf privileges. Some balconies. Southwestern decor; each rm individually decorated with antiques, artwork. View of Sonoran Desert. Cr cds: A, D, MC, V.

Resorts

★**CAMELVIEW.** *7601 E Indian Bend Rd (85250).* 602/991-2400; res: 800/852-5205; FAX 602/998-2261. 200 rms, 3 story. Jan–Apr: S $110; D $120; each addl $10; under 12 free; AP, MAP avail; package plans; lower rates rest of yr. TV; cable. Heated pool; poolside serv. Coffee in rms. Dining rm 6:30 am–10 pm. Box lunches. Rm serv. Bar 11–1 am. Ck-out noon, ck-in 3 pm. Convention facilities. Valet serv. Gift shop. Free airport transportation. 36-hole golf privileges, pro. Lawn games. Some refrigerators. Some private patios. Cr cds: A, C, D, DS, ER, MC, V.

★★★★**HYATT REGENCY SCOTTSDALE.** *7500 E Doubletree Ranch Rd (85258), ½ mi E of Scottsdale Rd.* 602/991-3388; FAX 602/483-5550. 475 units in main bldg, 4 story, 7 casitas on lake, 1–4 bedrm. EP, Jan–mid-May: S, D $285–$375; suites $400–$2,500; under 19 free; golf & romance packages; lower rates rest of yr. Crib free. TV; cable. 10 heated pools; wading pool, poolside serv; clock tower with water slide. Playground. Supervised child's activities. Dining rm (public by res) 6:30 am–10 pm (also see GOLDEN SWAN). Rm serv 24 hrs. Bar noon–1 am. Ck-out noon, ck-in 4 pm. Meeting rms. Concierge. Airport transportation. Complimentary valet parking. Rec dir. 8 tennis courts, 4 lighted, pro. 27-hole golf, greens fee $90, pro, putting green, driving range. Manmade beach. Gondolas. Bicycles. Lawn games. Exercise rm; instructor,

weights, bicycles, sauna, steam rm. Massage. Minibars. Balconies. Fireplace, wet bar in casitas. Resort located on 640-acre Gainey Ranch. Elaborate landscaping; 28 fountains, 47 waterfalls, 300 palm trees. Atrium lobby with 3-story sculpture. *LUXURY LEVEL:* REGENCY CLUB. 44 rms. S, D $375. Concierge. Private lounge. Complimentary European bkfst, refreshments.
Cr cds: A, C, D, DS, ER, MC, V, JCB.

★★★★ **MARRIOTT'S CAMELBACK INN RESORT GOLF CLUB & SPA.** *5402 E Lincoln Dr (85253), Paradise Valley, northeast of downtown. 602/948-1700; res: 800/24-CAMEL; FAX 602/951-8469.* 423 rms in 1–2 story casitas. Jan–May: S, D $235–$285; each addl $10; suites $375–$1,550; AP addl $58 per person; MAP addl $44 per person; Camelback plan (bkfst, lunch) addl $29 per person; under 18 free; wkend rates; golf, tennis, spa, honeymoon and family packages avail; lower rates rest of yr. Crib free. Pet accepted. TV; cable. 3 pools, heated; whirlpool, sauna, steam rm, poolside buffet, poolside serv, lifeguards. Supervised child's activities (wkends; also school vacation wks Easter, Thanksgiving, Christmas). Dining rm 6:30 am–10 pm (also see CHAPARRAL DINING ROOM). Rm serv to midnight. Box lunches. Bars 11–1 am. Ck-out noon, ck-in 4 pm. Coin lndry. Valet serv. Concierge. Barber, beauty shop. Gift & sport shops. Airport transportation. Lighted tennis, pro. 36-hole golf, greens fee $75–$85, electric cart free, teaching pros, putting greens, driving range, golf school. Bicycles. Lawn games. Soc dir; entertainment; movies winter & spring hols. Full service European health spa offers state-of-the-art equipment and training; includes extensive fitness and exercise facilities, body and beauty treatments, specially designed spa cuisine. Refrigerators, minibars. Wet bar, fireplace, private pool in some suites. Private patios; many balconies. On 125 acres; beautifully landscaped grounds. Luxurious; an oasis in the desert. Cr cds: A, C, D, DS, ER, MC, V, JCB.

★★ **MARRIOTT'S MOUNTAIN SHADOWS.** *5641 E Lincoln Dr (85253). 602/948-7111; FAX 602/951-5430.* 338 rms, 1–2 story. Jan–mid-May: S, D $199–$235; each addl $10; suites $300–$750; under 18 free; lower rates rest of yr. Crib free. Pet accepted, some restrictions. TV; cable. 3 heated pools; lifeguards. Supervised child's activities. Dining rms 6:30 am–11 pm. Rm serv. Box lunches. Snack bar. Bars 11–1 am. Ck-out noon, ck-in 4 pm. Convention facilities. Valet serv. Gift shop. Barber, beauty shop. Airport transportation avail. Lighted tennis, pro. 54-hole golf, greens fee $44 (incl cart), pro, putting greens, driving range. Lawn games. Soc dir; entertainment, dancing; movies on hols. Exercise rm; instructor, weights, bicycles, whirlpool, sauna. Minibars; many bathrm phones. Wet bar in suites; presidential suites have 2 baths. Private patios, balconies. On 70 acres; 3 acres of gardens. Cr cds: A, C, D, DS, MC, V, JCB.

★★★ **ORANGE TREE GOLF & CONFERENCE RESORT.** *10601 N 56th St (85254). 602/948-6100; res: 800/228-0386; FAX 602/483-6074.* 160 suites, 2 story. Jan–May: S, D $200–$250; under 18 free; wkly rates; golf plan; lower rates rest of yr. Crib free. Pet accepted, some restrictions; $100 refundable. TV; in-rm movies. Heated pool; wading pool, whirlpool, poolside serv. Supervised child's activities (in season). Coffee in rms. Dining rm 6 am–10 pm. Box lunches. Snack bar. Picnics. Rm serv. Bar 10–1 am; entertainment, dancing. Ck-out noon, ck-in 3 pm. Grocery 1 mi. Coin lndry 5 mi. Package store 1 mi. Meeting rms. Bellhops. Valet serv. Concierge. Gift shop. Airport transportation. Sports dir. Tennis privileges. 18-hole golf, greens fee $75 (incl cart), pro. Health club privileges. Bathrm phones, refrigerators, minibars. Private patios, balconies. Golf resort with country club atmosphere. Cr cds: A, D, DS, MC, V, JCB.

★★★★ **THE PHOENICIAN.** *6000 E Camelback Rd (85251), at 60th St. 602/941-8200; res: 800/888-8234; FAX 602/947-4311.* 580 rms: 473 rms in main bldg, 4–6 story, 107 casitas. EP, late Aug–late June: S, D, casitas $290–$425; each addl $50; suites $850–$4,400; under 12 free; golf plans; spa & holiday packages; lower rates rest of yr. Crib free. TV; cable, in-rm movies avail. 5 heated pools; 2 wading pools, poolside serv. Supervised child's activities. Dining rms (public by res) 6 am–10

pm (also see MARY ELAINE'S). Rm serv 24 hrs. Bar 11–1 am; entertainment. Ck-out noon, ck-in 4 pm. Lndry facilities. Convention facilities. Bellhops. Valet serv. Concierge. Shopping arcade. Barber, beauty shop. Airport transportation. Sports dir. 11 lighted tennis courts, pro. 18-hole golf, greens fee $95, pro, putting green, driving range. Hiking. Bicycle rentals. Lawn games. Exercise rm; instructor, weight machine, bicycles, whirlpool, sauna, steam rm. Massage. Complete spa center. Bathrm phones, minibars; some refrigerators, wet bars. Balconies. Picnic tables. Located on 130 acres, at the base of Camelback Mountain. World-class resort features a masterly blend of nature, landscaping, architecture and fine art. Handcrafted furnishings. Some casitas with hand-carved marble fireplace. Cr cds: A, C, D, DS, MC, V, JCB.

★★ **REGAL McCORMICK RANCH.** *7401 N Scottsdale Rd (85253). 602/948-5050; res: 800/243-1332; FAX 602/948-9113.* 125 rms, 3 story, 51 kit. villas (2–3 bedrm). Jan–Apr: S $150–$240; D $160–$240; each addl $10; suites $265–$600; villas $340–$495; under 18 free; golf, tennis plans; lower rates rest of yr. Crib $10. TV; cable. Heated pool; whirlpool, poolside serv. Dining rm 6:30 am–10 pm. Rm serv. Bar 11–1 am; entertainment. Ck-out noon, ck-in 3 pm. Convention facilities. Valet serv. Concierge. Gift shop. Airport, bus depot transportation. Lighted tennis, pro. Golf privileges, pro, putting green, driving range. Dock; sailboats, paddleboats. Sightseeing, desert trips. Lawn games. Soc dir. Refrigerators, minibars. Wet bar, fireplace in villas. Private patios, balconies. 10 acres on Camelback Lake; view of McDowell Mountains. Cr cds: A, C, D, DS, MC, V.

★★★ **THE REGISTRY.** *7171 N Scottsdale Rd (85253). 602/991-3800; res: 800/247-9810; FAX 602/948-1381.* 318 rms, 2 story, 45 suites (31 bi-level), 10 parlor and 4 luxury suites. Early Jan–mid-May: S, D $190–$290; each addl $25; suites $325–$1,700; under 18 free; lower rates rest of yr. Crib free. TV; cable. 3 heated pools; poolside serv, lifeguard. Snack bar. Dining rms 6:30 am–10 pm. Rm serv 24 hrs. Bar 11–1 am. Ck-out noon, ck-in 4 pm. Coin lndry. Convention facilities. Valet serv. Concierge. Gift shop. Barber, beauty shop. Lighted tennis, pro. 36-hole golf privileges. Exercise equipt; weight machine, bicycles, whirlpool, sauna. Lawn games. Entertainment, dancing Thurs–Sat. Many refrigerators; some wet bars, fireplaces. Private patios, balconies. On 76 acres. Cr cds: A, C, D, DS, ER, MC, V.

★★★ **SCOTTSDALE CONFERENCE RESORT.** *7700 E McCormick Pkwy (85258). 602/991-9000; res: 800/528-0293; FAX 602/596-7422.* 326 rms, 3 story, 21 suites, 12 casitas. Jan–Mar: S $250; D $330; suites $515–$835; casitas $560; under 16 free; lower rates rest of yr. TV; cable. 2 heated pools; poolside serv. Dining rm 7 am–11 pm. Bar 11–1 am. Ck-out 1 pm, ck-in 3 pm. Convention facilities. Gift shop. Lighted tennis, pro. 36-hole golf, greens fee $75, pro, putting green, driving range. Exercise rm; instructor, weight machines, bicycles, whirlpool, sauna, steam rm. Game rm. Bathrm phones, refrigerators. Private patios, balconies. Spanish-colonial architecture; lush landscaping. Cr cds: A, C, D, DS, MC, V.

★★★ **SCOTTSDALE PLAZA.** *7200 N Scottsdale Rd (85253). 602/948-5000; res: 800/832-2025; FAX 602/998-5971.* 404 rms, 2 story, 180 suites. Jan–Apr: S, D $210–$225; each addl $10; suites $300–$2,500; under 17 free; wkend rates; AP, MAP avail; lower rates rest of yr. Crib free. Pet accepted, some restrictions; $100 ($50 refundable). TV; cable. 5 heated pools; poolside serv. Supervised child's activities (Jan–Apr, mid-Sept–Dec). Dining rm 6 am–11 pm (also see REMINGTON). Rm serv. Bar 11–1 am; entertainment, dancing. Ck-out noon, ck-in 3 pm. Valet serv. Convention facilities. Concierge. Sundries. Gift shop. Beauty shop. Airport transportation. Lighted tennis, pro. Racquetball. Golf privileges. Bike rentals. Lawn games. Exercise equipt; weights, bicycles, sauna. Refrigerators, minibars; many wet bars. Spanish colonial-style buildings; exceptional pool with waterfall. Cr cds: A, C, D, DS, ER, MC, V, JCB.

★★★ **SCOTTSDALE PRINCESS.** *7575 E Princess Dr (85255), off Scottsdale Rd just N of Bell Rd.* 602/585-4848; res: 800/223-1818; FAX 602/585-0086. 600 rms, 3–4 story, 86 suites, 75 casitas. Jan–May: S, D $260–$350; each addl $30; suites $480–$2,200; casitas $320–$630; under 12 free; golf & tennis plans; spa & hol packages; lower rates rest of yr. TV; cable. 3 heated pools; poolside serv. Supervised child's activities (Memorial Day–Labor Day & hols). Dining rms 6:30 am–11 pm (also see LA HACIENDA). Rm serv 24 hrs. 7 bars 11–1 am; entertainment, dancing. Ck-out noon, ck-in 4 pm. Convention facilities. Concierge. Shopping arcade. Barber, beauty shop. Valet parking. Airport, RR station, bus depot transportation. Lighted tennis, pro. 36-hole golf, greens fee $35–$92, pro, putting green, driving range. Croquet, badminton. Racquetball, squash, basketball. Exercise rm; instructor, weight machines, bicycles, whirlpool, sauna, steam rm. Massage. Stocked lagoons; fishing rods and tackle box avail for guests. Bathrm phones, refrigerators, minibars. Some fireplaces. Private patios, balconies. Picnic tables. 450 acres; elaborate landscaping; waterways; central courtyard with waterfall. Cr cds: A, C, D, DS, MC, V, JCB.

★★ **STOUFFER COTTONWOODS RESORT.** *6160 N Scottsdale Rd (85253).* 602/991-1414; FAX 602/951-3350. 107 suites, 64 rms. Jan–mid-May: S, D $205; each addl $10; suites $235–$275; kit. units $275–$295; under 18 free; package plans; lower rates rest of yr. Crib free. Pet accepted, some restrictions; $50 refundable. TV; cable. 3 heated pools; whirlpools, poolside serv. Complimentary continental bkfst in rms. Restaurant 6 am–10:30 pm. Rm serv 24 hrs. Bar noon–1 am. Ck-out noon. Meeting rms. Bellhops. Valet serv. Airport transportation. Lighted tennis, pro. Golf privileges. Bicycle rentals. Refrigerators, minibars; some bathrm phones, fireplaces. Whirlpool on patios. Adj to Borgata shopping complex. Cr cds: A, C, D, DS, ER, MC, V, JCB.

Restaurants

★ **ALDO BALDO.** *7014 E Camelback Rd, in Fashion Square.* 602/994-0062. Hrs: 11 am–10 pm; Fri, Sat to 11 pm. Closed Thanksgiving, Dec 25. Res accepted. Italian menu. Bar. Semi-a la carte: lunch $5–$9, dinner $8–$18. Child's meals. Specialties: linguini con salmone, penne quattro formaggi, pasta dishes, espresso. Parking. Outdoor dining. Open kitchen. Cr cds: A, C, D, MC, V.

★ **AMERICAN GRILL.** *6113 N Scottsdale Rd.* 602/948-9907. Hrs: 11:30 am–10 pm; Fri, Sat to 11 pm; Sun 4:30–10 pm; early-bird dinner 4:30–6 pm. Closed Dec 25. Res accepted. Bar to 11 pm; Fri, Sat to midnight. Semi-a la carte: lunch $4.95–$10.50, dinner $13.95–$21.95. Specializes in mustard raspberry shrimp, blackened rockfish, barbecued ribs. Entertainment Tues–Sat. Parking. Outdoor dining. Cr cds: A, D, MC, V.

★★ **AVANTI'S OF SCOTTSDALE.** *3102 N Scottsdale Rd.* 602/949-8333. Hrs: 5:30–10:30 pm; Fri, Sat to 11 pm. Res accepted. Italian, continental menu. Bar 5:30 pm–1 am. Wine list. Semi-a la carte: dinner $14.50–$23.50. Specializes in seafood, veal. Own pasta. Pianist Tues–Sat. Valet parking. Black & white decor. Cr cds: A, D, MC, V.

★★★ **BISTRO LA CHAUMIERE.** *6910 Main St.* 602/946-5115. Hrs: 5–11 pm. Closed Sun; most major hols; also July & Aug. Res accepted. French bistro menu. Bar. Extensive wine list. Semi-a la carte: dinner $11–$18. Specialties: steak au poivre vert, salmon baked with strawberry balsamic vinegar, Dover sole. Own pastries. Parking. Outdoor dining among pecan and citrus trees. Many antiques; massive stone hearth; vaulted ceiling. Family-owned. Cr cds: A, D, MC, V.

★★★ **CHAPARRAL DINING ROOM.** *(See Marriott's Camelback Inn Resort)* 602/948-1700. Hrs: 6–10 pm; Fri, Sat to 11 pm. Res accepted. Continental menu. Bar to 1 am. Wine cellar. A la carte entrees: dinner $25–$35. Specialties: lobster bisque, Dover sole, rack of lamb.

Own baking. Classical guitarist (in season). Valet parking. Outside entrance apart from hotel. View of mountain. Jacket (in season). Cr cds: A, C, D, DS, ER, MC, V, JCB.

★★ **DON & CHARLIE'S AMERICAN RIB & CHOP HOUSE.** *7501 E Camelback Rd.* 602/990-0900. Hrs: 5–10 pm; Fri, Sat to 10:30 pm; Sun 4:30–9 pm. Closed Thanksgiving. Res accepted. Bar. Semi-a la carte: dinner $9.95–$21.95. Child's meals. Specializes in barbecued ribs, prime center cut steak. Own pies, cakes. Parking. Photos of celebrities, sports memorabilia on walls. Cr cds: A, C, D, DS, MC, V.

✔ **EDDIE CHAN'S.** *9699 N Hayden Rd.* 602/998-8188. Hrs: 11:30 am–10 pm; Sat from noon; Sun from 4:30 pm; early-bird dinner 4:30–6:30 pm. Closed July 4, Thanksgiving, Dec 25. Res accepted. Chinese menu. Serv bar. Semi-a la carte: lunch $3.50–$4.95, dinner $5.25–$14. Specialties: lemon chicken, black pepper chicken, Mongolian beef. Parking. Artwork. Cr cds: A, C, D, MC, V.

★★★ **8700.** *8700 E Pinnacle Peak Rd, at the Citadel Complex.* 602/994-8700. Hrs: 6–10 pm. Res accepted. Southwestern menu. Bar 5 pm–midnight. Wine list. Semi-a la carte: dinner $11.95–$32. Specializes in beef, chicken, seafood. Own baking. Outdoor dining. Parking. Many original oil paintings. Cr cds: A, D, MC, V.

✔★★ **EL CHORRO LODGE.** *5550 E Lincoln Dr.* 602/948-5170. Hrs: 11 am–3 pm, 5:30–11 pm; Sat, Sun from 9 am. Res accepted. Bar. Semi-a la carte: bkfst (Sat, Sun) $3.95–$13.95, lunch $5.95–$13.95, dinner $13.95–$39. Sun brunch $6–$14.50. Specializes in châteaubriand, rack of lamb, prime beef. Valet parking. Outdoor dining. Western decor, paintings. Fireplaces. Family-owned. Cr cds: A, C, D, MC, V.

✔★★ **EL TORITO.** *6200 N Scottsdale Rd, in Lincoln Plaza.* 602/948-8376. Hrs: 11 am–10 pm; Fri, Sat to 11 pm; Sun brunch 10 am–2 pm. Closed Thanksgiving, Dec 25. Res accepted. Mexican menu. Bar to 1 am. Semi-a la carte: lunch $4.95–$7, dinner $6.95–$12. Sun brunch $8.95. Child's meals. Specializes in sizzling fajitas, seafood. Parking. Cr cds: A, C, D, DS, MC, V.

★ **FAMOUS PACIFIC FISH COMPANY & CROW'S NEST.** *4321 N Scottsdale Rd, between Camelback & Indian School Rds, in multi-level structure at Galleria Shopping Mall.* 602/941-0602. Hrs: 11 am–10 pm; Fri & Sat to 11 pm; Sun noon–10 pm; early-bird dinner 4–6 pm. Closed Thanksgiving, Dec 25. Res accepted. Bar. Semi-a la carte: lunch $4.95–$10.95, dinner $8.95–$22.95. Child's meals. Specialties: mesquite-broiled fish in Southwestern sauces, exotic soups & salads. Outdoor dining. **Crow's Nest,** 11 am–midnight; Fri & Sat to 1 am; Sun noon–10 pm. Famous Pacific Fish Company dining on first 2 floors; nautical decor, memorabilia; open kitchen. Crow's Nest features more than 200 American and international beers, extensive wine list; located on 3rd floor and opens into Galleria Shopping Mall. Cr cds: A, C, D, DS, MC, V.

★★ **GLASS DOOR.** *6939 Main St.* 602/994-5303. Hrs: 11:30 am–10 pm. Closed Sun; major hols. Res accepted. Continental menu. Bar. Semi-a la carte: lunch $6.50–$10.50, dinner $13–$26.50. Specializes in fresh seafood, beef, lamb. Valet parking. Patio dining. Dinner theater on wkends. Cr cds: A, D, MC, V.

★★ **GOLDEN SWAN.** *(See Hyatt Regency Scottsdale Resort)* 602/991-3388. Hrs: 6–10 pm; Sun brunch 10 am–2 pm. Res accepted. Regional American cuisine. Bar. Extensive wine list. A la carte entrees: dinner $16.75–$24. Sun brunch $21.95. Child's meals. Specialties: ranch chicken baked in red rock clay, Sonoma veal chop with peach and basil chutney. Own pastries. Valet parking. Formal room with ebony columns; outdoor dining in pavilion beside lagoon with swans. Sunday brunch buffet in kitchen. Braille menu. Cr cds: A, C, D, DS, ER, MC, V, JCB.

Ⓓ

★★**IMPECCABLE PIG.** *7042 E Indian School Rd. 602/941-1141.* Hrs: 11 am–3 pm, 5–9 pm; Mon to 3 pm; early-bird dinner Tues–Sat 5–6:45 pm. Closed Sun; major hols. Res accepted. Serv bar. Semi-a la carte: lunch $6.95–$8.95, dinner $13.95–$19.95. Own soups. Parking. Glass-enclosed patio dining. Blackboard menu, changes daily. Period decor; antiques. Cr cds: A, D, MC, V.

Ⓓ

★★**JEAN CLAUDE'S PETIT CAFE.** *7340 E Shoeman Ln. 602/947-5288.* Hrs: 11:30 am–2:30 pm, 6–10 pm; Sat from 6 pm. Closed Sun; Jan 1, Dec 25. Res accepted. French menu. Bar. A la carte entrees: lunch $5.50–$10.50, dinner $12.95–$18.95. Child's meals. Specialties: duck with raspberry vinegar sauce, fresh grilled salmon with tarragon sauce, raspberry on chocolate soufflé. Contemporary decor. Cr cds: A, C, D, MC, V.

✔★**JULIO'S.** *7243 E Camelback Rd. 602/423-0058.* Hrs: 11 am–10 pm; Fri, Sat to 11 pm. Closed Easter, Thanksgiving, Dec 25. Mexican menu. Bar. Semi-a la carte: lunch, dinner $5.75–$12.95. Child's meals. Specializes in fajitas, pollo magnifico. Art deco, cantina-style decor; colorful neon lighting. Cr cds: A, C, D, MC, V.

Ⓓ

✔★**KYOTO.** *7170 Stetson Dr. 602/990-9374.* Hrs: 11 am–2 pm, 5:30–11 pm. Closed most major hols. Res accepted. Japanese menu. Bar. Semi-a la carte: lunch $3.50–$5, dinner $11–$16. Specialties: sushi, teriyaki chicken. Salad bar. Parking. Tableside cooking. Cr cds: A, C, D, DS, MC, V.

★★★**L'ECOLE.** *8100 E Camelback Rd. 602/990-7639.* Hrs: 11:30 am–1:30 pm, 6:30–8 pm. Closed Sat, Sun; major hols. Res required. Continental menu. Bar. Wine list. Complete meals: lunch $7.50–$11.50, dinner $13.50–$18. Specializes in fish, chicken, steak. Own baking. Menu changes wkly. Parking. Primarily staffed by students of the Scottsdale Culinary Institute. Cr cds: DS, MC, V.

Ⓓ

★★**LA BRUSCHETTA.** *4515 N Scottsdale Rd. 602/946-7236.* Hrs: 5:30 pm–midnight. Closed Sun; some major hols. Res accepted. Italian menu. Bar. A la carte entrees: dinner $10.50–$23. Child's meals. Specializes in northern Italian cuisine. Parking. Cr cds: A, MC, V.

Ⓓ

★★★★**LA HACIENDA.** *(See Scottsdale Princess Resort) 602/585-4848.* Hrs: 6–11 pm. Closed Mon (seasonal). Res accepted. Mexican menu. Bar. Wine list. A la carte entrees: dinner $14.25–$22.95. Child's meals. Specialties: filete al chipotle (char-broiled beef tenderloin), rack of lamb, suckling pig. Own baking. Entertainment. Valet parking. Outdoor dining. Authentic Mexican cuisine served in a traditional hacienda-style setting; semi-formal, 2 fireplaces. Continental service. Cr cds: A, C, D, DS, MC, V, JCB.

Ⓓ

✔★**LOS OLIVOS.** *7328 E 2nd St. 602/946-2256.* Hrs: 11 am–10:30 pm; Fri, Sat to 1 am. Closed most major hols. Res accepted. Mexican menu. Bar. Semi-a la carte: lunch, dinner $4.50–$13.50. Child's meals. Specialties: sour cream enchiladas, chimichanga supreme, fajitas. Band Fri, Sat. Parking. Family-owned. Cr cds: A, C, D, DS, MC, V.

Ⓓ

★★**MANCUSO'S.** *6166 N Scottsdale Rd, at the Borgata. 602/948-9988.* Hrs: 5–10:30 pm. Closed Thanksgiving, Dec 25. Res accepted. Northern Italian, continental menu. Complete meals: dinner $12.95–$24.95. Specializes in veal, pasta, seafood. Piano lounge. Valet parking. Cr cds: A, C, D, DS, MC, V.

Ⓓ

★★**MARIA'S WHEN IN NAPLES.** *7000 E Shea Blvd. 602/991-6887.* Hrs: 11:30 am–2:30 pm, 5–10 pm; Sat & Sun from 5 pm. Closed Jan 1, Thanksgiving, Dec 25. Res accepted. Italian menu. Bar.

Semi-a la carte: lunch $6.95–$10.95, dinner $8.95–$17.95. Specializes in pasta dishes, veal, antipasto. Own desserts. Parking. Outdoor dining. Open kitchen. Multi-tiered dining. Cr cds: A, C, D, DS, MC, V.

Ⓓ

✔★**MARKET AT THE CITADEL.** *8700 E Pinnacle Peak Rd, at Inn at the Citadel Complex. 602/585-0635.* Hrs: 7 am–10 pm. Res accepted. Bar. Semi-a la carte: bkfst $2.95–$7.95, lunch & dinner $4.95–$15.95. Specializes in chicken & dumplings, meat loaf, slow-roasted chicken. Parking. Outdoor, cantina-style dining. Southwestern decor. Totally nonsmoking. Cr cds: A, C, D, MC, V.

★★★**MARY ELAINE'S.** *(See The Phoenician Resort) 602/423-2530.* Hrs: 6–10 pm. Closed Sun. Res accepted. Contemporary cuisine. Bar. Wine cellar. A la carte entrees: dinner $29. Complete meals: dinner $65. Child's meals. Specializes in fresh seafood from around the world, rack of lamb, veal. Entertainment. Valet parking. Intimate dining in elegant atmosphere. Overlooks valley. Jacket. Cr cds: A, C, D, DS, MC, V, JCB.

Ⓓ

✔★★**MR C'S.** *4302 N Scottsdale Rd, opp the Galleria. 602/941-4460.* Hrs: 11 am–2:30 pm, 5–10 pm; Fri, Sat to 11 pm. Closed Thanksgiving, Dec 25. Res accepted. Chinese menu. Bar. Semi-a la carte: lunch $5.95–$7.50, dinner $7.50–$13.50. Specialties: macadamia chicken, jade lobster, Royal mandarin and Cantonese cooking. Elegant decor; Chinese paintings, ceramics, artwork. Cr cds: A, D, DS, MC, V.

Ⓓ

★**PISCHKE'S PARADISE.** *7217 E 1st St. 602/481-0067.* Hrs: 7 am–midnight. Closed Sun; most major hols. Bar. Semi-a la carte: bkfst $3–$7, lunch $4–$8, dinner $4–$16. Specialties: Cajun chicken, shrimp paradise, Cajun Caesar salad. Outdoor dining. Colorful prints; photos above bar. Cr cds: A, DS, MC, V.

Ⓓ

★★**THE QUILTED BEAR.** *6316 N Scottsdale Rd. 602/948-7760.* Hrs: 7 am–10 pm; Sun from 8 am. Res accepted. Semi-a la carte: bkfst $1.99–$7.95, lunch $4.95–$8.50, dinner $5.95–$18.95. Child's meals. Specializes in seafood, prime rib. Salad bar. Own soups. Parking. Outdoor dining. Colorful decor; stained-glass windows. Cr cds: A, C, D, DS, MC, V.

★★★**REMINGTON.** *(See Scottsdale Plaza Resort) 602/951-5101.* Hrs: 11:30 am–2:30 pm, 5–10 pm; Sat, Sun from 5 pm; early-bird dinner (exc hols) 5–6:30 pm; Sun brunch 11 am–2:30 pm. Res accepted. Continental menu. Bar 4:30 pm–midnight. Wine cellar. A la carte entrees: lunch $5.95–$12.50, dinner $16.95–$23.95. Sun brunch $18.95. Specializes in seafood, rack of lamb, mesquite-grilled steak. Jazz. Valet parking. Outdoor dining. Elegant Southwestern decor; columns, vaulted dome ceiling with sky mural. Cr cds: A, D, DS, MC, V.

Ⓓ

★★★**RUTH'S CHRIS STEAK HOUSE.** *7001 N Scottsdale Rd. 602/991-5988.* Hrs: 5–10 pm; Fri & Sat to 10:30 pm. Closed Thanksgiving, Dec 25. Res accepted. Bar. A la carte entrees: dinner $16–$34. Specializes in USDA prime-aged, corn-fed Midwestern beef; fresh seafood. Parking. Outdoor dining. Casual dining in traditional steakhouse. Cr cds: A, D, MC, V.

Ⓓ

★★**SALT CELLAR.** *550 N Hayden Rd. 602/947-1963.* Hrs: 5–11 pm; Fri, Sat to midnight. Closed Dec 25. Res accepted. Bar 4 pm–1 am. A la carte entrees: dinner $13.95–$27.95. Child's meals. Specializes in Yakimono ahi, king crab legs, live Maine lobster, variety of seafood. Parking. Restaurant located underground, in former salt cellar. Rustic decor. Cr cds: A, MC, V.

★★**TRAPPER'S.** *3815 N Scottsdale Rd. 602/990-9256.* Hrs: 5–9:30 pm; wkends to 10 pm. Closed some major hols. Res accepted. Bar from 4 pm. Semi-a la carte: dinner $9.95–$17.95. Specializes in

Norwegian salmon, prime rib, burnt creme custard. Parking. Casual dining. Cr cds: A, D, MC, V.

★★**THE VISTAS AT OAXACA.** *8711 E Pinnacle Peak Rd. 602/998-2222.* Hrs: 5:30–9:30 pm. Closed major hols. Res accepted. Bar from 5 pm. Semi-a la carte: dinner $12.95–$27.95. Child's meals. Specializes in prime rib, seafood. Parking. Outdoor dining. Mexican courtyard architecture with bell tower; antiques, art work. View of desert gardens. Cr cds: A, C, D, DS, MC, V.

★★★**VOLTAIRE.** *8340 E McDonald Dr. 602/948-1005.* Hrs: 5:30–10 pm. Closed Sun, Mon; some major hols; also June–Sept. Res required. French, continental menu. Bar. Wine list. Semi-a la carte: dinner $16–$20.50. Specializes in rack of lamb, sandabs with white grapes, sweetbreads. Parking. Jacket. Cr cds: A, MC, V.

★**YAMAKASA.** *9301 E Shea Blvd. 602/860-5605.* Hrs: 11:30 am–2 pm, 5:30–10 pm; Sun 4–9 pm. Closed major hols. Res required. Japanese menu. Bar. Semi-a la carte: lunch $3.95–$12.95, dinner $5.95–$18.95. Specializes in sushi, sashimi. Tableside preparation. Traditional Japanese seating. Cr cds: A, C, D, MC, V.

Unrated Dining Spot

HARRY & STEVE'S CHICAGO GRILL. *7295 E Stetson, 2 blks E of Scottsdale Rd. 602/990-2827.* Hrs: 11:30–1 am. Closed Dec 25. Bar. Semi-a la carte: lunch $4–$10, dinner $4–$12. Specializes in pork tenderloin, steak, hamburgers. Parking. Bi-level dining. Cr cds: A, D, MC, V.

Sedona (C-3)

Founded: 1902 **Pop:** 7,720 **Elev:** 4,400 ft **Area code:** 602 **Zip:** 86336

Originally a pioneer settlement, Sedona has grown considerably. This is a resort area with many beautiful houses. In town is Tlaquepaque (T-lock-ay-POCK-ay), a four-and-one-half-acre area of gardens, courtyards, fountains, a chapel and assorted shops and restaurants incorporating architectural forms of Old Mexico. There is good trout fishing in Oak Creek. A Ranger District office for the Coconino National Forest is here.

What to See and Do

1. **Chapel of the Holy Cross.** 2½ mi S on AZ 179. Chapel perched between two pinnacles of uniquely colored red sandstone. Open to all for prayer and meditation. (Daily) Phone 282-4069.

2. **Tlaquepaque.** On AZ 179. Consists of 40 art galleries and stores set in a Spanish-style courtyard; cafes. (Daily exc hols) Phone 282-4838. (See ANNUAL EVENTS)

3. **Jeep tours.** Two-hour back country trips. (Daily) Other tours also avail. For details contact Pink Jeep Tours, 282-5000; Time Expeditions, 282-2137; Red Rock Jeep Tours, 282-6826.

4. **Oak Creek Canyon.** A beautiful drive along a spectacular fishing stream, N toward Flagstaff (see). In the canyon is

   Slide Rock State Park. 7 mi N on US 89A. A 43-acre day-use park on Oak Creek. Swimming, natural sandstone waterslide; fishing. Hiking. Picnicking. Standard fees. Phone 282-3034.

   (For further information contact the Sedona-Oak Creek Canyon Chamber of Commerce, PO Box 478, 86339; 282-7722.)

Annual Events

Sedona Jazz on the Rocks. Late Sept.

Fiesta del Tlaquepaque. (See #2). Mexican carnival, food, music. 1st Sat Oct.

Festival of Lights at Tlaquepaque. (See #2). Christmas candle-light procession. 2nd wkend Dec.

(See Cottonwood, Flagstaff)

Motels

✔★★**BELL ROCK INN.** *6246 AZ 179. 602/282-4161.* 47 rms, 1–2 story. Mid-Feb–Nov: S $55–$95; D $80–$95; lower rates rest of yr. TV. Heated pool; whirlpool. Restaurant 7:30 am–2 pm, 5–9 pm. Bar 11 am–11 pm; entertainment Thurs–Sat. Ck-out 11 am. Meeting rm. Tennis. Golf privileges. Cr cds: A, MC, V.

✔★**CANYON PORTAL.** *280 N US 89A. 602/282-7125; res: 800/542-8484; FAX 602/282-1825.* 29 rms, 2 story. Mar–Nov: S, D $59–$89; each addl $5; house (2-bedrm) $100; under 6 free; wkly rates; lower rates rest of yr. Crib $5. TV; cable. Heated pool. Complimentary coffee in lobby. Restaurant opp 6:30 am–10 pm. Ck-out 11 am. Some private patios, balconies. Cr cds: MC, V.

★**QUALITY INN-KINGS RANSOM.** *(Box 180) 1 mi S at jct US 89A & AZ 179. 602/282-7151.* 65 rms, 2 story. Feb–Nov: S $65–$105; D $77–$107; each addl $10; suites $135–$175; under 18 free; lower rates rest of yr. Crib free. Pet accepted, some restrictions. TV; cable. Heated pool; whirlpool. Restaurant 7 am–10 pm. Ck-out 11 am. Lawn games. Some refrigerators. Some private patios, balconies. Set among red rocks of Sedona. Cr cds: A, C, D, DS, ER, MC, V, JCB.

Motor Hotel

★★**BEST WESTERN ARROYO ROBLE.** *(Box NN) 400 N US 89A. 602/282-4001.* 52 rms, 5 story. Mar–Nov: S $110–$125; D $115–$130; each addl $5; studio rms $125–$135; under 12 free; lower rates rest of yr. Crib free. TV; cable. Heated pool; whirlpool. Complimentary coffee in rms. Restaurant opp 8 am–9 pm. Ck-out 11 am. Coin lndry. Tennis privileges. Health club privileges. Some private patios, balconies. Views of red sandstone buttes. Cr cds: A, D, DS, MC, V.

Inns

★★★★**CANYON VILLA BED & BREAKFAST.** *125 Canyon Circle Dr. 602/284-1226; res: 800/453-1166; FAX 602/284-2114.* 11 rms, 2 story. S, D $85–$155; each addl $25. Prefer children over 10 yrs. TV; cable. Heated pool. Complimentary full bkfst, tea; afternoon refreshments, evening snacks. Restaurant nearby. Ck-out 11 am, ck-in 4–6 pm. Tennis privileges. 18-hole golf privileges, greens fee $45–$55. Health club privileges. Patios, balconies. Southwestern decor with Old World influences; each rm individually decorated. Cr cds: MC, V.

CASA SEDONA BED & BREAKFAST. *(Too new to be rated) 55 Hozoni Dr. 602/282-2938; res: 800/525-3756.* 11 rms, 2 story. No rm phones. S $85–$140; D $95–$150; each addl $25; golf plans. TV in sitting rm; cable. Complimentary full bkfst. Complimentary coffee in library. Ck-out 11 am, ck-in 3–6 pm. Tennis privileges. Golf privileges. Health club privileges. Refrigerators. Balconies. Picnic tables. Each rm with view of red rocks. Totally nonsmoking. Cr cds: DS, MC, V.

★★★**THE GRAHAM BED AND BREAKFAST INN.** *150 Canyon Circle Dr, 6½ mi S via AZ 179, turn off onto Bell Rock Blvd. 602/284-1425; res: 800/228-1425.* 6 rms, 2 story. S $83–$175; D $98–$190; each addl $20. TV in sitting rm. Pool; whirlpool. Complimentary full bkfst, afternoon refreshments. Ck-out 11 am, ck-in 4–6 pm. Gift shop. Balconies. Each rm individually decorated; some antiques. Scenic view from all rms. Fireplace, whirlpool in some rms. Guest library. Bicycles avail. Totally nonsmoking. Cr cds: DS, MC, V.

Resorts

★ ★ ★ENCHANTMENT RESORT. *525 Boynton Canyon Rd, 3 mi SW on US 89A to Dry Creek Rd, then 5 mi N in Boynton Canyon. 602/282-2900; res: 800/826-4180; FAX 601/282-9249.* 162 rms, 56 kit. casitas (2-bedrm). Mar–July & mid-Sept–Dec 1: S, D $185–$200; suites $260–$285; casitas (to 4 persons) $460–$505; under 12 yrs free; other packages avail; lower rates rest of yr. Crib free. TV; cable. 6 heated pools. Supervised child's activities. Dining rm (see YAVAPAI ROOM); pianist Fri–Sat; Sun brunch 11 am–2:30 pm. Box lunches. Picnics. Rm serv 6 am–midnight. Bar 11 am–midnight; Sun from 10 am. Ck-out noon, ck-in 4 pm. Meeting rms. Valet serv. Gift shop. Airport transportation. Tennis, pro. 6-hole pitch and putt. Croquet. Game rm. Hiking. Exercise rm; instructor, weights, bicycles, whirlpools, saunas, steam rms. Many refrigerators, fireplaces. Private patios, balconies. Many grills. 2 casitas with private pool. 70 acres, located in Boynton Canyon in a dramatic setting of the Red Rock country of Sedona. Cr cds: A, DS, MC, V.

★ ★LOS ABRIGADOS. *160 Portal Lane. 602/282-1777; res: 800/521-3131; FAX 602/282-2614.* 175 suites (1 & 2 bedrms), 1–2 story. S, D $215–$375; each addl $15; under 16 free. Crib free. TV; cable. Pool; poolside serv. Supervised child's activities (Memorial Day–Labor Day). Dining rm (see THE CANYON ROSE). Box lunches; steak-fry area on Oak Creek. Rm serv. Bar 11–1 am; entertainment, dancing. Ck-out noon, ck-in 4 pm. Meeting rms. Valet serv. Concierge. Gift shop. Beauty shop. Free Sedona airport, bus depot, golf transportation. Sports dir. Tennis. Golf privileges. Sand volleyball court. Exercise rm; instructor, weights, bicycles, whirlpool, sauna, steam rm. Fishing in Oak Creek. Refrigerators; some fireplaces. Private patios, balconies. Spanish-style stucco & tile-roofed buildings set among buttes of Oak Creek Canyon. Former ranch site & early movie location. Cr cds: A, C, D, DS, MC, V, JCB.

★ ★POCO DIABLO. *(Box 1709) 2 mi S on AZ 179. 602/282-7333; res: 800/528-4275; FAX 602/282-2090.* 109 rms, 2 story. Mid-Mar–mid-Nov: S, D $115–$170; each addl $10; suites $250–$350; under 12 free; lower rates rest of yr. Crib free. TV; cable. 2 heated pools; whirlpools, poolside serv. Dining rm (public by res) 7 am–9 pm. Rm serv. Bar 11–1 am. Ck-out noon, ck-in 3 pm. Meeting rms. Sundries. Gift shop. Free airport, bus depot transportation. Lighted tennis, par 3 golf, greens fee $7. Masseuse. Refrigerators; some in-rm spas, fireplaces. Some private patios, balconies. Views of red sandstone mountains. Cr cds: A, C, D, DS, MC, V.

Restaurants

★ ★ ★THE CANYON ROSE. *(See Los Abrigados Resort) 602/282-7673.* Hrs: 7 am–2 pm, 5–10 pm; early-bird dinner 5–6:30 pm; Sun brunch 9 am–2 pm. Res accepted. Continental menu. Bar. Wine cellar. Semi-a la carte: bkfst $3–$7.95, lunch $3.75–$9.50, dinner $12–$26. Sun brunch $22. Child's meals. Specialties: pan-seared veal sirloin steak, vodka-poached salmon, blue corn meal gnocchi. Pianist Fri & Sat; jazz trio Sun brunch. Parking. Outdoor dining. Multi-tiered dining; panoramic view of Sedona. Cr cds: A, C, D, DS, ER, MC, V, JCB.

✔ ★EL RINCON. *AZ 179, Tlaquepaque Village, on the banks of Oak Creek. 602/282-4648.* Hrs: 11 am–9 pm; Sun noon–5 pm; Nov–Jan 11 am–8 pm. Closed Mon; Jan 1, Thanksgiving, Dec 25; also Feb. Res accepted. Mexican menu. Bar. A la carte entrees: lunch, dinner $2.95–$12.95. Child's meals. Specialties: chimichangas, Navajo pizzas. Outdoor dining. Cr cds: MC, V.

★ ★HEARTLINE CAFE. *1610 W US 89A. 602/282-0785.* Hrs: 11 am–3 pm, 5–9:30 pm; Fri & Sat to 10 pm; Sun 5–9 pm. Res accepted. Continental menu. Bar. Semi-a la carte: lunch $5.95–$10.95, dinner $9.25–$18.95. Child's meals. Patio dining. Cottage surrounded by English garden. Cr cds: A, DS, MC, V, JCB.

✔ ★HIDEAWAY. *179 Country Square. 602/282-4204.* Hrs: 11 am–10 pm. Closed some major hols. Italian menu. Bar. Semi-a la carte: lunch $4–$7, dinner $5–$13. Child's meals. Specializes in pizza, antipasto salad, fettucine. Guitarist Wed–Sun. Parking. Outdoor dining overlooking Oak Creek & Red Rock Mountains. Dining rm features stained-glass windows. Cr cds: DS, MC, V.

★ ★RENÉ AT TLAQUEPAQUE. *On AZ 179 in Tlaquepaque Arts and Crafts Village. 602/282-9225.* Hrs: 11:30 am–2:30 pm, 5:30–9:30 pm. Closed Thanksgiving, Dec 25. Res accepted. Continental menu. Bar. Semi-a la carte: lunch $5.75–$9. A la carte entrees: dinner $16.75–$24.75. Specialties: French onion soup, rack of lamb, poached salmon. Outdoor dining. Collection of Western art. Cr cds: A, MC, V.

★ ★ROSEBUDS. *320 US 89A. 602/282-3022.* Hrs: 11 am–9:30 pm; Fri & Sat to 10 pm. Closed Dec 25. Res accepted. Bar to midnight. Semi-a la carte: lunch $5.95–$8.95, dinner $8.95–$17.95. Specializes in Angus prime rib, seafood, steak. Parking. Panoramic view of Sedona's red rocks. Cr cds: MC, V.

★ ★ ★SEDONA SWISS RESTAURANT & CAFE. *350 Jordan Rd. 602/282-7959.* Hrs: 7 am–9:30 pm. Closed Sun. Res accepted. Wine list. Complete meals: bkfst $3.25–$6.50. Buffet: lunch $1.95–$6.50. Semi-a la carte: dinner $8.50–$23.95. Child's meals. Specialties: veal eminé Zurichoise, carré d'agneau provençale, coquilles St.-Jacques. Entertainment Wed & Sat. Parking. Outdoor dining. Open kitchen. Stucco walls; fireplace. Original art on display. Cr cds: MC, V.

★ ★SHUGRUE'S. *2250 W US 89A, 2 mi W on US 89A. 602/282-2943.* Hrs: 8 am–3 pm, 5–9 pm; Fri, Sat to 10 pm; Mon from 11 am. Closed Dec 25. Res accepted; required wkends. Bar 8–1 am. Semi-a la carte: bkfst $2.95–$9.25, lunch $5.95–$10.95, dinner $8.95–$18.95. Child's meals. Specializes in fresh seafood, steak, creative bkfsts. Entertainment wkends. Parking. Dining rm overlooks garden. Cr cds: A, MC, V.

★ ★SHUGRUE'S HILLSIDE GRILL. *671 AZ 179. 602/282-5300.* Hrs: 11:30 am–3:30 pm, 5:30–9:30 pm. Closed Dec 25. Res accepted. Continental menu. Bar. Semi-a la carte: lunch $6.25–$11.50, dinner $10.95–$22.95. Child's meals. Specializes in steak, seafood, rack of lamb. Jazz Fri–Sun. Parking. Outdoor dining. Located high upon a hill; commanding view of rock formations. Cr cds: A, MC, V.

★ ★ ★YAVAPAI ROOM. *(See Enchantment Resort) 602/282-2900.* Hrs: 7 am–2 pm, 6–9:30 pm; Sun brunch 11:30 am–2 pm. Res accepted. Southwest regional menu. Bar 11 am–midnight. Wine cellar. Semi-a la carte: bkfst $3.25–$10.50. A la carte entrees: lunch $7.50–$11.95, dinner $17–$24. Sun brunch $17.95. Specializes in wild game, Southwest regional cuisine. Pianist Fri & Sat evenings; jazz duo Sun brunch. Parking. Outdoor dining. Original art, antiques, artifacts displayed. Scenic view of Boynton Canyon. Cr cds: A, D, DS, MC, V.

Seligman (B-2)

Pop: 950 (est) **Elev:** 5,242 ft **Area code:** 602 **Zip:** 86337

What to See and Do

Grand Canyon Caverns. 25 mi NW on AZ 66. Includes the 18,000-square-foot "Chapel of Ages" and other rooms and tunnels; three-quarter mile trail; temperature 56°F. Elevator takes visitors 210 feet underground; guided tours. Motel, restaurant; western-style cookouts (May–Sept). (Daily; closed Dec 25) Golden Age Passport accepted. Phone 422-3223. ¢¢¢

(For accommodations see Flagstaff, Williams)

Sells (E-3)

Pop: 2,750 **Elev:** 2,360 ft **Area code:** 602 **Zip:** 85634

This is the headquarters of the Tohono O'Odham Indian Reservation (almost 3 million acres). The Papagos, of Piman stock, farm, raise cattle and craft pottery and baskets. The main road (AZ 86) passes through the reservation, and side roads lead to other villages. The older houses are made of saguaro ribs plastered with mud. More recently, burnt adobe (mud brick) construction and conventional housing have been adopted.

What to See and Do

Kitt Peak National Observatory (National Optical Astronomy Observatories). Approx 36 mi NE on AZ 86, then 12 mi S on AZ 386, in the Quinlan Mountains of the Sonoran Desert (elevation 6,882 ft). Site of world's largest collection of ground-based optical telescopes; 36-, 50-, 84- and 158-inch stellar telescopes; world's largest solar telescope (60 in). Museum with exhibits. Tours. Observatory (daily; closed major hols). Phone 325-9200 or -3426. ¢

(For further information contact the Tohono O'Odham Nation Executive Office, Box 837; 383-2221.)

(For accommodations see Tucson)

Show Low (C-4)

Pop: 5,019 **Elev:** 6,347 ft **Area code:** 602 **Zip:** 85901

This town in the Apache-Sitgreaves National Forest is a good stop for the hunter, fisherman, photographer or nature lover.

What to See and Do

1. **Hunting.** Elk, deer, turkey, bear, mountain lion, and antelope.
2. **Fishing. Rainbow Lake.** 8 mi SE on AZ 260. **Show Low Lake.** 4 mi SE off AZ 260. **Fool Hollow Lake.** 3 mi NW. Many others in area. Boat rentals at some lakes.
3. **Apache-Sitgreaves National Forests.** Combined into one administrative unit, these two forests (see SPRINGERVILLE) encompass more than two million acres of diverse terrain. The Sitgreaves Forest (AZ 260) is named for Captain Lorenzo Sitgreaves, conductor of the first scientific expedition across the state in the 1850s; part of the General George Cook military trail is here. Fishing, hunting. Self-guided nature hikes. Picnicking. Camping (dump sta-

tion; fee). Sat evening programs in summer. For camping reservations phone 800/283-2267. For other information phone 333-4301.

(For further information contact the Chamber of Commerce, Box 1083; 537-2326 or -2800.)

(See McNary, Pinetop)

Motels

✔ ★DAYS INN. *(Box 2437) US 60W. 602/537-4356.* 122 rms, 2 story. Mid-May–mid-Sept: S $45–$65; D $53–$69; each addl $4; higher rates special events; lower rates rest of yr. Crib $5. Pet accepted, some restrictions; $50 refundable. TV; cable. Heated pool. Restaurant 6 am–midnight. Ck-out noon. Meeting rms. Beauty shop. Cr cds: A, C, D, DS, MC, V.

★SUPER 8. *1941 E Deuce of Clubs. 602/537-7694.* 42 rms, 2 story. S $31.50–$38.50; D $36.50–$46.50; each addl $5; under 13 free; higher rates special events; wkly rates. Crib $3. Pet accepted, some restrictions; $25 refundable. TV; cable. Restaurant adj 5:30 am–9 pm. Ck-out 11 am. Cr cds: A, C, D, DS, MC, V.

Lodge

★ ★BEST WESTERN PAINT PONY LODGE. *581 W Deuce of Clubs, near Show Low Municipal Airport. 602/537-5773; FAX 602/537-5766.* 32 rms, 2 story. Mid-May–mid-Sept: S $65–$72; D $66–$74; each addl $10; higher rates hols; lower rates rest of yr. Crib $5. TV; cable. Complimentary coffee in lobby. Restaurant 11 am–2 pm, 5–10 pm; wkend hrs vary. Rm serv. Bar; entertainment, dancing Fri. Ck-out 11 am. Meeting rms. Sundries. Free airport transportation. X-country ski 13 mi. Some refrigerators. Cr cds: A, C, D, DS, MC, V.

Restaurant

★BRANDING IRON STEAK HOUSE. *1231 E Deuce of Clubs. 602/537-5151.* Hrs: 11 am–2 pm, 5–10 pm; early-bird dinner Sun–Fri 5–7 pm. Closed Dec 25. Res accepted. Bar. Semi-a la carte: lunch $4–$8, dinner $8–$24. Child's meals. Specializes in steak, prime rib, seafood. Salad bar. Parking. Cr cds: C, D, DS, MC, V.

Sierra Vista (E-4)

Pop: 32,983 **Elev:** 4,623 ft **Area code:** 602 **Zip:** 85635

What to See and Do

1. **Fort Huachuca.** Founded by the US Army in 1877 to protect settlers and travelers from hostile Apache raids, the fort is now the home of the US Army Intelligence Center, the Information Systems Command and the Electronic Proving Ground. A historical museum is on the "Old Post," Boyd & Grierson Aves (daily; closed hols). The historic Old Post area (1885–1895) is typical of frontier post construction and is home to the post's ceremonial cavalry unit; open to public. Directions and visitor's pass at main gate, just W of Sierra Vista. Bronze statue of buffalo soldier. Phone 533-2714. **Free.**
2. **Coronado National Memorial.** 16 mi S via AZ 92 to Coronado Memorial Rd then W on Montezuma Canyon Rd. Commanding view of part of Coronado's route through the Southwest in 1540–42. Hiking trails. Picnic grounds. Visitor center (daily; closed most hols). Phone 366-5515. **Free.**

3. **Coronado National Forest** (see TUCSON). One of the larger sections of the forest lies to the south and west of Fort Huachuca Military Reservation. Picnicking, camping (fee). Parker Canyon Lake offers boating, fishing and camping. A Ranger District office is located in Sierra Vista. Phone 378-0311.

(For further information contact the Chamber of Commerce, 77 Calle Portal, Suite A140; 458-6940.)

(See Patagonia)

Motels

★★**SIERRA SUITES.** *391 E Fry Blvd. 602/459-4221; FAX 602/459-8449.* 100 rms, 2 story. S, D $44–$70; suites $70; under 18 free; golf plans. Crib free. Pet accepted, some restrictions; $50 refundable. TV; cable. Heated pool; whirlpool. Complimentary continental bkfst. Bar 4–9 pm. Ck-out 11 am. Meeting rms. Health club privileges. Refrigerators. Cr cds: A, D, DS, MC, V.

✔★**SUPER 8.** *100 Fab Ave. 602/459-5380; FAX 602/459-6052.* 52 rms, 2 story. S $39.88; D $45.88–$46.88; each addl $3; under 13 free; golf plans. Crib free. Pet accepted, some restrictions; $80 refundable. TV; cable. Pool. Complimentary continental bkfst. Restaurant nearby. Ck-out 11 am. Refrigerators; many wet bars. Cr cds: A, C, D, DS, MC, V.

Motor Hotel

★★**RAMADA INN.** *2047 S AZ 92. 602/459-5900; FAX 602/458-1347.* 148 rms, 3 story. S, D $52–$78; each addl $8; suites $95–$115; under 16 free; golf plans. Crib $8. Pet accepted, some restrictions; $50 refundable. TV; cable. Heated pool; whirlpool. Coffee in rms. Restaurant 6 am–9 pm. Rm serv. Bar 4–11 pm, Fri & Sat to 1 am; entertainment. Ck-out 11 am. Coin lndry. Meeting rms. Valet serv. Free local airport transportation. Health club privileges. Refrigerators, microwaves avail. Cr cds: A, C, D, DS, ER, MC, V, JCB.

Inn

★★**RAMSEY CANYON.** *(31 Ramsey Canyon, Hereford 85615)* 6 mi S of Fry Blvd on AZ 92, then 3½ mi on Ramsey Canyon Rd, adj to Nature Conservancy's Mile Hi/Ramsey Canyon Preserve. 602/378-3010. 9 units: 6 rms in house, 2 cottages. No A/C. No rm phones. S, D $75–$85; each addl $10. Children over 12 yrs only. Complimentary full bkfst (exc cottages), refreshments. Ck-in 4–6 pm, ck-out 10 am. Situated on a winding mountain stream, in a wooded canyon, this is a hummingbird haven; peak season is Mar–Oct. More than 10 species visit the Inn's feeders during the year. Charming country inn with antiques throughout; bounded on 2 sides by Coronado National Forest. Totally nonsmoking. No cr cds accepted.

Restaurants

★★**GOLDEN CHINA.** *325 W Fry Blvd, 2 blks from main gate of Ft Huachuca. 602/458-8588.* Hrs: 11 am–2 pm, 4–9:30 pm; Sat, Sun from noon. Closed Easter, Thanksgiving, Dec 25. Res accepted. Chinese menu. Bar. Complete meals: lunch $3.55–$5.50. Buffet: lunch $5. Semi-a la carte: dinner $5–$22. Child's meals. Specialties: Szechwan, Mandarin, Cantoneese and Hunan dishes. Parking. Oriental gold-relief mural on rear wall; carved teakwood ceiling fixtures; black lacquered screens. Cr cds: C, D, DS, MC, V.

★★**THE MESQUITE TREE.** *Jct AZ 92S & Carr Canyon Rd. 602/378-2758.* Hrs: 11 am–2:30 pm, 5–9 pm; Sun 5–8 pm. Closed Mon; Jan 1, Thanksgiving, Dec 25. Res accepted. Bar. Semi-a la carte: lunch $3.95–$6.50, dinner $6.50–$17. Child's meals. Specializes in prime rib, seafood. Parking. Outdoor dining. Antique collection displayed in main dining rm; electric model train travels on an elevated platform along the walls of a glass-enclosed dining area. Cr cds: A, DS, MC, V.

Springerville (C-5)

Pop: 1,802 **Elev:** 6,968 ft **Area code:** 602 **Zip:** 85938

The headquarters for the Apache-Sitgreaves National Forests is located here.

What to See and Do

1. **Madonna of the Trail.** Main St. Erected in 1927, the statue is one of twelve identical monuments placed in states along the National Old Trails Highway to commemorate pioneer women who trekked west.

2. **Apache-Sitgreaves National Forests.** Combined into one administrative unit, these two forests (see SHOW LOW) encompass more than two million acres of diverse terrain. The Apache Forest (on US 180/666) features the Mt Baldy, Escudilla and Bear Wallow wilderness areas and Blue Range Primitive Area, which are accessible only by foot or horseback, and the Coronado Trail (US 666), the route followed by the explorer in 1540. Lake and stream fishing, big-game hunting. Picnicking. Camping (fee charged in some campgrounds); for reservations phone 800/283-CAMP. For information phone 333-4301.

3. **Lyman Lake State Park.** 18 mi N on US 180/666. There are 1,180 acres bordering on a 1,500-acre reservoir near headwaters of the Little Colorado River; high desert, juniper country. Swimming, waterskiing; fishing (walleye, trout, channel & blue catfish); boating (ramps). Hiking. Picnicking (shelter). Tent & trailer sites (dump station). Standard fees. Phone 337-4441.

(For further information contact the Round Valley Chamber of Commerce, 418 E Main St, PO Box 31; 333-2123.)

(See Greer, McNary)

Motel

★**EL-JO MOTOR INN.** *(Box 175) 425 E Main St. 602/333-4314; res: 800/638-6114.* 36 rms, 2 story. S, D $24–$32. Crib $2. Pet accepted. TV; cable. Restaurant 5 am–9:30 pm. Bar 11–1 am. Ck-out 11 am. City park opp. Cr cds: A, C, D, DS, MC, V.

Sunset Crater Volcano National Monument (B-3)

(15 mi N of Flagstaff on US 89, then 2 mi E on Sunset Crater/Wupatki Loop Road)

Between the growing seasons of 1064 and 1065, violent volcanic eruptions built a large cone-shaped mountain of cinders and ash called a cinder cone volcano. Around the base of the cinder cone, lava flowed from cracks, creating the Bonito Lava Flow on the west side of the cone and the Kana'a Lava Flow on the east side. The approximate date of the initial eruption was determined by examining tree rings of timber found in the remains of Indian pueblos at Wupatki National Monument (see).

This cinder cone, now called Sunset Crater, stands about 1,000 feet above the surrounding terrain. Mineral deposits around the rim stained the cinders, giving the summit a perpetual sunset hue, thus the name Sunset Crater. Along the Lava Flow Trail at the base of the cone, visitors will find ''squeeze-ups'' and other geologic features related to lava flows.

Park rangers are on duty all year. Do not attempt to drive off the roads; the cinders are soft, and the surrounding landscape is very fragile. The US Forest Service maintains a campground (Mid-May–mid-Sept; fee) opposite the visitor center. Guided tours and naturalist activities are offered during the summer. Visitor center (daily; closed Dec 25). A 20-mile paved road leads to Wupatki National Monument (see). Phone 602/556-7042.

(For accommodations see Flagstaff)

Tempe (D-3)

Founded: 1871 **Pop:** 141,865 **Elev:** 1,160 ft **Area code:** 602

Founded as a trading post by the father of former Senator Carl Hayden, this city is now the site of Arizona State University, the state's oldest institution of higher learning.

What to See and Do

1. **Arizona State University** (1885). (42,000 students) In town center on US 60/80/89. Divided into 12 colleges. Included on the 700-acre main campus are several museums and collections featuring meteorites; anthropology and geology exhibits; the Charles Trumbull Hayden Library and the Daniel Noble Science and Engineering Library. For campus tour information phone 965-4980. Also on campus are

     Nelson Fine Arts Center and **Matthews Center.** Exhibits of American paintings and sculpture; Latin American art; comprehensive print collection; American crockery and ceramics. Tours available. (Matthews: Tues–Fri; Nelson: daily exc Mon; closed hols) Phone 965-ARTS.   **Free.**

     Grady Gammage Memorial Auditorium. (1964). Last major work designed by Frank Lloyd Wright. Guided tours (daily exc Sun). Phone 965-3434 (box office) or -4050 (tours).

2. **Tempe Historical Museum.** 809 E Southern. Exhibits relating the history of Tempe from the prehistoric Hohokam to the present; artifacts, videos, interactive exhibits. Research library. Gift shop. (Daily exc Fri; closed major hols) Sr citizen rate. Phone 350-5100. ¢¢

3. **Niels Petersen House Museum.** 1414 W Southern Ave. Built in 1892 and remodeled in the 1930s. Restoration retains characteristics of both the Victorian era and the 1930s. Half-hour, docent-guided tours are available. (Tues–Thurs, Sat) Phone 350-5151.   **Free.**

4. **Big Surf.** 1500 N McClintock Dr. Water park with water slides; ocean swimming; boogie board riding, body surfing on raft; rafting in freshwater lagoon with controlled three–five-foot waves; children's shallow water area; bathhouses, rentals, concessions. (Memorial Day–Labor Day, daily) Phone 947-SURF.   ¢¢¢¢

(For further information contact the Chamber of Commerce, 60 E 5th St, Suite #3, 85281; 967-7891.)

Annual Events

Fiesta Bowl. ASU Sun Devil Stadium. College football. Jan 1.

Spring Festival of the Arts. Last wkend Mar.

Fiesta Bowl Block Party. Includes games, rides, entertainment, pep rally, fireworks, food. Dec 31.

Seasonal Event

Professional sports. Sun Devil Stadium. Phoenix Cardinals (NFL Football). Phone 379-0101. Sept–Dec. Tempe Diablo Stadium. California Angels (baseball) spring training. Phone 438-8900. Early Mar–early Apr.

(See Chandler, Glendale, Mesa, Phoenix, Scottsdale)

Motels

✓ ★ **COMFORT INN.** *5300 S Priest Dr (85283). 602/820-7500.* 160 rms, 4 story. Jan–Apr: S $40–$55; D $55–$75; each addl $5; under 18 free; lower rates rest of yr. Crib free. Pet accepted. TV; cable. Heated pool; whirlpool. Complimentary continental bkfst. Ck-out noon. Meeting rms. Free airport transportation. Cr cds: A, C, D, DS, ER, MC, V, JCB.

★ **COUNTRY SUITES BY CARLSON.** *1660 W Elliot Rd (85283). 602/345-8585; FAX 602/345-7461.* 139 kit. suites, 3 story. Mid-Jan–Apr: kit. suites $72–$92, each addl $6; under 16 free; wkly rates; golf plans; lower rates rest of yr. Crib free. Pet accepted, some restrictions; $75 non-refundable. TV; cable. Pool; wading pool; whirlpool. Complimentary continental bkfst. Complimentary coffee in rms. Restaurant nearby. Ck-out noon. Coin lndry. Meeting rms. Valet serv. Free airport transportation. Lighted tennis privileges. Health club privileges. Cr cds: A, C, D, DS, ER, MC, V, JCB.

★ **LA QUINTA.** *911 S 48th St (85281), near Sky Harbor Intl Airport. 602/967-4465; FAX 602/921-9172.* 129 rms, 3 story. Jan–early Apr: S, D $69–$76; each addl $5; suites $92; under 18 free; lower rates rest of yr. Crib free. Pet accepted, some restrictions. TV; cable. Heated pool. Complimentary continental bkfst. Restaurant adj open 24 hrs. Ck-out noon. Meeting rm. Free airport transportation. Putting green. Cr cds: A, D, DS, MC, V.

★ ★ **RODEWAY AIRPORT EAST.** *1550 S 52nd St (85281), near Sky Harbor Intl Airport. 602/967-3000; FAX 602/966-9568.* 100 rms, 2 story. Jan–Apr: S $55–$65; D $60–$70; each addl $6; under 18 free; higher rates Fiesta Bowl; lower rates rest of yr. TV; cable. Heated pool; whirlpool. Complimentary continental bkfst. Complimentary coffee in rms. Restaurant adj 6 am–10 pm. Ck-out noon. Meeting rms. Sundries. Free airport transportation. Health club privileges. Refrigerators avail. Cr cds: A, C, D, DS, ER, MC, V, JCB.

✓ ★ **TRAVELODGE-TEMPE/UNIVERSITY.** *1005 E Apache Blvd (85281). 602/968-7871; FAX 602/968-3991.* 56 rms, 2 story. Jan–Apr: S $42–$54; D $48–$62; each addl $4; under 12 free; lower rates rest of yr. Crib free. Pet accepted, some restrictions; $4 per day. TV; cable. Pool. Complimentary continental bkfst. Complimentary coffee in rms. Restaurant nearby. Ck-out noon. Coin lndry. Airport, RR station, bus depot transportation. Golf privileges. Refrigerators avail. Cr cds: A, C, D, DS, ER, MC, V, JCB.

Motor Hotels

★ ★ ★ **FIESTA INN.** *2100 S Priest Dr (85282). 602/967-1441; res: 800/528-6481 (exc AZ), 800/528-6482 (AZ); FAX 602/967-0224.* 270 rms, 3 story. Jan–mid-Apr: S $75–$110; D $77–$120; each addl $8; suites $135–$175; under 14 free; lower rates rest of yr. Crib free. TV; cable. Heated pool; poolside serv. Coffee in rms. Restaurant 6:30 am–10 pm. Rm serv. Bar 11–1 am. Ck-out 1 pm. Meeting rms. Bellhops. Valet serv. Concierge. Sundries. Complimentary airport transportation. Lighted tennis. 18-hole golf privileges, putting green, driving range. Exercise equipt; weights, bicycles, whirlpool, sauna. Refrigerators. Mexican antiques. Cr cds: A, C, D, DS, MC, V.

★★HOLIDAY INN. *915 E Apache Blvd (85281). 602/968-3451; FAX 602/968-6262.* 190 rms, 4 story. Jan–Apr: S $81; D $91; suites, studio rms $91–$109; under 19 free; lower rates rest of yr. Crib free. Pet accepted. TV; cable. Heated pool; whirlpool, poolside serv. Restaurant 6 am–10 pm. Rm serv. Bar noon–1 am. Ck-out 1 pm. Free lndry facilities. Meeting rms. Bellhops. Valet serv. Gift shop. Free airport transportation. Tennis & golf privileges. Refrigerators, minibars. Some private patios, balconies. Cr cds: A, C, D, DS, MC, V, JCB.

D ⊠ 🐾 🗐 🖉 ≥ 🚫 🕐 SC

✔★HOWARD JOHNSON. *225 E Apache Blvd (85281), opp Arizona State University. 602/967-9431; FAX 602/967-9431, ext 299.* 138 rms, 7 story. Jan–mid-May: S $62–$69; D $72–$79; each addl $7; under 18 free; higher rates Fiesta Bowl; lower rates rest of yr. Crib free. Pet accepted, some restrictions; $50 refundable. TV; cable. Heated pool. Restaurant 6 am–11 pm. Ck-out noon. Coin lndry. Meeting rms. Bellhops. Free airport transportation. Exercise equipt; weight machine, bicycles. Balconies. Cr cds: A, C, D, DS, ER, MC, V, JCB.

D ⊠ 🐾 ≥ 🕴 🚫 🕐 SC

★★INNSUITES. *1651 W Baseline Rd (85283), at I-10. 602/897-7900; res: 800/842-4242; FAX 602/491-1008.* 170 rms, 2–3 story, 81 kits. Jan–Apr: S, D $69–$89; suites, kit. units $82–$89; under 18 free; lower rates rest of yr. Crib free. Pet accepted; $25 refundable. TV; cable. Heated pool; whirlpool. Playground. Complimentary continental bkfst. Complimentary coffee in rms. Restaurant 6–10:30 am, 4:30–6 pm; Oct–Apr 6 am–10 pm. Ck-out noon. Coin lndry. Meeting rms. Valet serv. Free airport transportation. Lighted tennis. Exercise equipt; weight machine, rowing machine. Refrigerators. Some private patios, balconies. Grills. Cr cds: A, C, D, DS, MC, V.

D ⊠ 🐾 🖉 ≥ 🕴 🚫 🕐 SC

★★★RAMADA HOTEL SKY HARBOR. *1600 S 52nd St (85281), at Sky Harbor Intl Airport. 602/967-6600; FAX 602/829-9427.* 212 rms, 4 story. Jan–Apr: S $90–$100; D $95–$105; each addl $10; suites $180; under 18 free; wknd rates; lower rates rest of yr. Crib free. TV; cable. Indoor/outdoor pool; whirlpool, poolside serv. Restaurant 6 am–10 pm. Rm serv. Bar 11–1 am; entertainment, dancing exc Sun. Ck-out noon. Meeting rms. Bellhops. Valet serv. Sundries. Free airport transportation. Bathrm phones. Private patios, balconies. Cr cds: A, C, D, DS, MC, V.

D ≥ ✈ 🚫 🕐 SC

Hotels

★★★THE BUTTES. *2000 Westcourt Way (85282), 1 mi S of I-10, exit 48th St from W, or Broadway from E. 602/225-9000; res: 800/843-1986; FAX 602/438-8622.* 350 rms, 4–5 story. Jan–May: S, D $195–$225; each addl $15; suites $375–$1,500; under 18 free; lower rates rest of yr. Crib free. Pet accepted, some restrictions. TV; cable. 2 heated pools (1 with waterslide); poolside serv. Restaurants 6 am–11 pm. Rm serv 24 hrs. Bar 4 pm–1 am. Ck-out noon. Meeting rms. Concierge. Gift shop. Airport transportation. Lighted tennis. Golf privileges, pro. Exercise equipt; weights, bicycles, sauna. Minibars. Some private patios. Large resort built into mountainside. Heliport. *LUXURY LEVEL:* CONCIERGE LEVEL. 42 rms. S, D $225. Private lounge. Complimentary continental bkfst, refreshments.
Cr cds: A, C, D, DS, ER, MC, V, JCB.

D ⊠ 🐾 🗐 🖉 🕴 ≥ 🕴 🕴 🚫 🕐

★★EMBASSY SUITES-TEMPE/ASU. *4400 S Rural Rd (85282). 602/897-7444; FAX 602/897-6112.* 224 suites, 1–3 story. Jan–May: suites for 2, $139–$159; each addl $10; under 12 free; wknd packages; higher rates Fiesta Bowl; lower rates rest of yr. Crib free. TV; cable. Heated pool; poolside serv. Complimentary bkfst. Restaurant 11 am–10 pm. Bar 11–1 am. Ck-out 1 pm. Meeting rms. Free airport transportation. Exercise equipt; weight machine, treadmill, whirlpool, sauna. Game rm. Refrigerators. Private patios, balconies. Picnic tables, grill. Cr cds: A, C, D, DS, MC, V, JCB.

D ≥ 🕴 🚫 🕐

★★RADISSON-TEMPE MISSION PALMS (formerly Sheraton). *60 E 5th St (85281). 602/894-1400; FAX 602/968-7677.* 303 rms, 4 story. Jan–Apr: S $99–$130; D $109–$140; each addl $10; suites $135–$250; under 18 free; higher rates: Fiesta Bowl, art festival; lower rates rest of yr. Crib free. TV; cable. Heated pool; whirlpool, poolside serv. Restaurant 6:30 am–9:30 pm. Bar 11–1 am. Ck-out noon. Convention facilities. Shopping arcade. Free airport transportation. Lighted tennis. Golf privileges. Refrigerator in suites. Cr cds: A, C, D, DS, ER, MC, V.

D ⊠ 🐾 🖉 ≥ 🚫 🕐 SC

Restaurants

✔★★HOUSE OF TRICKS. *114 E 7th St. 602/968-1114.* Hrs: 11 am–9 pm; Sat from 5 pm. Closed Sun; most major hols; also 2 wks in summer. Res accepted. Contemporary Amer menu. A la carte entrees: lunch $1.50–$6.95, dinner $8.75–$13.75. Specializes in soups. Parking. Outdoor dining. Restored cottage (1918); hardwood and tile floors, stone fireplace. Cr cds: A, C, D, DS, MC, V.

D

★HUNGRY HUNTER. *4455 S Rural Rd. 602/838-8388.* Hrs: 11:30 am–2 pm, 5–10 pm; Sun 4–9 pm. Closed July 4, Dec 25. Res accepted. Bar. Semi-a la carte: lunch $5–$8, dinner $12.95–$17.95. Child's meals. Specializes in steak, prime rib, fresh seafood. Parking. Cr cds: A, C, D, DS, MC, V.

D

✔★MACAYO'S DEPOT CANTINA. *300 S Ash Ave. 602/966-6677.* Hrs: 11 am–11 pm; Fri, Sat to midnight. Closed Thanksgiving, Dec 25. Res accepted. Mexican menu. Bar. Semi-a la carte: lunch $3.95–$8.95, dinner $5.95–$10.95. Child's meals. Specialties: pork carnitas, chicken or steak fajitas. Entertainment Fri, Sat. Parking. Outdoor dining. Old Mexican-style cantina, located in a converted train station. Cr cds: A, C, D, DS, MC, V.

D

Tombstone (E-4)

Founded: 1879 **Pop:** 1,220 **Elev:** 4,540 ft **Area code:** 602 **Zip:** 85638

Shortly after Ed Schieffelin discovered silver, Tombstone became a rough-and-tumble town with saloons, bawdyhouses and lots of gunfighting. Tombstone's most famous battle was that of the O.K. Corral, between the Earps and the Clantons in 1881. Later, water rose in the mines and could not be pumped out; fires and other catastrophes occurred, but Tombstone was "the town too tough to die." Now a health and winter resort, it is also a museum of Arizona frontier life. In 1962, the town was designated a National Historic Landmark by the US Department of the Interior.

What to See and Do

1. **Office of the Tombstone** *Epitaph.* 5th St, near Allen St. The oldest continuously published newspaper in Arizona, founded in 1880; it is now a monthly journal of Western history. Office houses collection of early printing equipment. (Daily) Phone 457-2211. **Free.**

2. **Bird Cage Theatre.** Allen & 6th Sts. Formerly a frontier cabaret (1880s), this famous landmark has seen many of the West's most famous characters. In its heyday it was known as "the wildest and wickedest nightspot between Basin St and the Barbary Coast." The upstairs "cages," where feathered girls plied their trade, inspired the refrain, "only a bird in a gilded cage." Original fixtures, furnishings. (Daily) Phone 457-3421. ¢¢

3. **Boothill Graveyard.** NW on US 80W. About 250 marked graves, some with unusual epitaphs, many of famous characters.

4. **O.K. Corral.** Allen St, between 3rd & 4th Sts. Restored stagecoach office and buildings surrounding gunfight site; life-size figures;

Fly's Photography Gallery (adj) has early photos. (Daily; closed Dec 25) ¢

5. **Rose Tree Inn Museum.** Toughnut & 4th Sts. Largest rose bush in the world, spreading over 8,000 square feet; blooms in Apr. Museum in 1880 house (oldest in town); original furniture, documents. (Daily; closed Dec 25) Phone 457-3326. ¢

6. **Tombstone Courthouse State Historic Park** (1882). Toughnut & 3rd Sts. off US 80. Victorian building (1882) houses exhibits recalling Tombstone in the turbulent 1880s. Tombstone and Cochise County history. (Daily; closed Dec 25) Phone 457-3311. ¢

7. **St Paul's Episcopal Church** (1882). N 3rd & Safford Sts. Oldest Protestant church still in use in state; original fixtures.

8. **Tombstone Historama.** Adj O.K. Corral (see #4). Electronic diorama & film narrated by Vincent Price tell story of Tombstone. (Daily; hrly showings; closed Dec 25) ¢

9. **Crystal Palace Saloon.** 5th & Allen Sts. Restored. Dancing Fri–Sun evenings. (Daily)

(For further information contact the Tourism Assoc, Box 917; 457-2211.)

Annual Events

Territorial Days. Commemorates formal founding of the town. Fire-hose cart races and other events typical of a celebration in Arizona's early days. 1st wkend Mar.

Wyatt Earp Days. Also fiddlers' contests. Memorial Day wkend.

Wild West Days and Rendezvous of Gunfighters. Labor Day wkend.

"Helldorado." Three days of reenactments of Tombstone events of the 1880s. 3rd Fri–Sun Oct.

(See Bisbee)

Motel

 ✔ ★ ★ **BEST WESTERN LOOKOUT LODGE.** *(Box 787)* ½ mi NW on US 80. 602/457-2223; FAX 602/457-3870. 40 rms, 2 story. S $45–$55; D $55–$65; each addl $5; under 12 free; higher rates special events. Crib free. Pet accepted, some restrictions; $50 and $5 per day. TV; cable. Heated pool. Complimentary continental bkfst, coffee. Restaurant nearby. Ck-out 11 am. Cr cds: A, C, D, DS, ER, MC, V.

Restaurant

★ **NELLIE CASHMAN.** *5th & Toughnut.* 602/457-2212. Hrs: 7 am–9 pm. No A/C. Semi-a la carte: bkfst $1.95–$4.55, lunch $3.10–$6, dinner $5.95–$16.95. Child's meals. Specializes in chicken, pork, steak. Outdoor dining. In historic adobe building (1879); established in 1882 by Nellie Cashman, "the angel of Tombstone," at height of silver boom; antique furnishings. Cr cds: MC, V.

Tucson (E-4)

Founded: 1775 **Pop:** 405,390 **Elev:** 2,386 ft **Area code:** 602

Tucson (TOO-sahn) offers a rare combination of delightful Western living, colorful desert and mountain scenery and cosmopolitan culture.

It is one of several US cities that developed under four flags. The Spanish standard flew first over the Presidio of Tucson, built to withstand Apache attacks in 1776. Later, Tucson flew under the flags of Mexico, the Confederate States and, finally, the United States.

Today, Tucson is a resort area, an educational and copper center, a cotton and cattle market, headquarters for the Coronado National

Forest and a place of business for several large industries. Health-seekers, under proper medical advice, nearly always find relief. The city's shops, restaurants, resorts and points of interest are varied and numerous.

What to See and Do

1. **University of Arizona** (1885). (35,000 students) N Park Ave & E University Blvd. The 343-acre campus is beautifully landscaped, with handsome buildings. Visitor Center, located at University Blvd & Cherry Ave, has campus maps and information on attractions and activities. Tours (daily exc Sun). Phone 621-5130. On campus are

   Arizona State Museum. N Park Ave & E University Blvd. Exhibits on the Native American cultures of Arizona and the Southwest from 10,000 years ago to the present. (Mon–Sat; also Sun afternoons; closed major hols) Phone 621-6302. **Free.**

   Museum of Art and Faculty of Fine Arts. N Park Ave & E Speedway Blvd. Art museum (free) with extensive collection, including Renaissance, baroque and contemporary art; changing exhibits. (Mon–Fri, also Sun afternoons; summer hrs vary; closed major hols) Music building and theater, in which plays are produced by students. Inquire locally for programs. Phone 621-7567.

   Mineralogical Museum. Second Street, in Geology Bldg. Rocks, minerals, gemstones and cuttings; paleontological materials. Meteorite exhibit. (Mon–Fri; closed major hols) Phone 621-4227. **Free.**

   Flandrau Science Center & Planetarium. N Cherry Ave & E University Blvd. Interactive, hands-on science exhibits (daily; closed major hols; free); planetarium shows (limited hrs). Nightly telescope viewing (Tues–Sat). Laser light shows (Wed–Sat; fee). Phone 621-7827. ¢¢

   Center for Creative Photography. S of pedestrian underpass on E Speedway Blvd, 1 blk E of N Park Ave. Archives library, including archives of Ansel Adams and Richard Avedon, collection of works by more than 100 major photographers; changing exhibits. (Mon–Fri & Sun afternoons; summer hrs vary; closed hols) Phone 621-7968. **Free.**

2. **Biosphere 2.** 35 mi N on US 89 to AZ 77 milepost 96, then ½ mi N to Biosphere 2 Rd. An ambitious attempt to learn more about our planet's ecosystems began in September of 1991 with the first of a series of missions in this 3½-acre, glass-enclosed, self-sustaining model of Earth. Isolated from the outside, a rotating crew of researchers rely entirely on the air, water and food generated and recycled within the structure. It contains over 3,500 species of plants and animals in multiple ecosystems, including a tropical rain forest with an 85-ft high mountain. Although visitors are not permitted within the experimental portions of the enclosure, they may view the interior from outside as well as enjoy many other exhibits located throughout the campus. Because of variance in research schedule, the biospherian crew may not always be present. Walking tours (wear comfortable shoes) include multimedia introduction to Biosphere 2. Visitor center. Gift shop. Restaurant. (Daily; closed Dec 25) Sr citizen rate. Phone 825-6200. ¢¢¢¢

3. **Arizona Historical Society Museum, Library and Archives.** 949 E 2nd St at Park Ave. Exhibits depicting state history from the Spanish colonial period to present; costume room; Arizona mining hall; photography gallery; gift shop. Research library contains collections on Western history; manuscripts. (Museum: daily. Library: daily exc Sun. Both closed Jan 1, Thanksgiving, Dec 25) Phone 628-5774. **Free.**

4. **Arizona Historical Society Frémont House Museum** (ca 1880). 151 S Granada Ave, in the Tucson Community Center Complex, downtown. Adobe house restored and furnished in period style. Once occupied by John C. Frémont's daughter, Elizabeth, when he was territorial governor (1878–81). Special programs all year, including slide shows on Arizona history (Sat; free) and walking tours of historic sites (Nov–Apr, Sat; fee; registration in advance). Museum (Wed–Sat). Phone 622-0956. **Free.**

5. **Tucson Museum of Art.** 140 N Main Ave. Housed in six buildings within the boundaries of El Presidio Historic District (ca 1800). Pre-

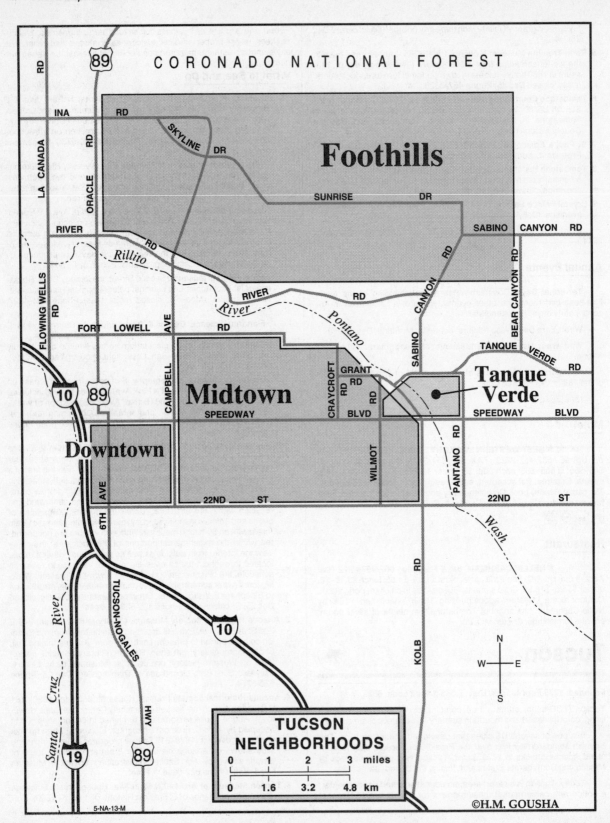

CORONADO NATIONAL FOREST

Foothills

Midtown

Tanque Verde

Downtown

RD

89

INA

LA CANADA

ORACLE RD

SKYLINE DR

SUNRISE DR

RIVER

RD

Rillito

River

RIVER RD

RD

Pontano

SABINO CANYON RD

BEAR CANYON RD

TANQUE VERDE RD

FLOWING WELLS RD

FORT LOWELL RD

CAMPBELL AVE

CRAYCROFT RD

GRANT RD

RD

BLVD

SABINO CANYON RD

SPEEDWAY BLVD

10

89

SPEEDWAY

WILMOT RD

PANTANO RD

6TH AVE

22ND ST

22ND ST

KOLB RD

Wash

Santa Cruz River

TUCSON-NOGALES HWY

10

19

89

N
W E
S

TUCSON NEIGHBORHOODS

0	1	2	3	miles
0	1.6	3.2	4.8	km

5-NA-13-M

©H.M. GOUSHA

Columbian, Spanish colonial and Western artifacts; decorative arts and paintings; art of the Americas; contemporary art and crafts; changing exhibits. Mexican heritage museum; historic presidio room; 6,000-volume art resource library; art school. (Daily; closed hols) Phone 624-2333. ¢

6. **Arizona Historical Society Fort Lowell Museum.** 2900 N Craycroft Rd; in Fort Lowell County Park, N end of Craycroft Rd. Reconstruction of commanding officer's quarters. Exhibits, period furniture. (Wed–Sat; closed hols) Phone 885-3832. **Free.**

7. **Pima Air & Space Museum.** 6000 E Valencia Rd; I-10 to exit 267 (Valencia Rd), then E. Aviation history exhibits with an outstanding collection of more than 180 aircraft, both military & civilian. (Daily; closed Dec 25) Sr citizen rate. Phone 574-9658. ¢¢

8. **Titan Missile Museum.** Located in Green Valley, approx 20 mi S via I-19, exit 69 (Duval Mine Rd), then W, past La Canada, turn right & follow signs. Deactivated Titan II missile on display; memorabilia, models, rocket engine that powered the missile, support vehicles, UH1F helicopter, various exhibits. A one-hour guided tour begins with a briefing and includes visit down into the missile silo (may be strenuous; no high heeled shoes permitted in the missile silo). The silo may also be viewed from a glass observation area located at the museum level. (Nov–Apr, daily; rest of yr, Wed–Sun) Sr citizen rate. For information and tour schedule phone 625-7736. ¢¢

9. **Old Town Artisans.** 186 N Meyer Ave. Restored adobe building (ca 1850s) in the historic El Presidio neighborhood is a marketplace for handcrafted Southwestern and Latin American art. Courtyard cafe. (Daily; closed most major hols) Phone 623-5787.

10. **Tucson Botanical Gardens.** 2150 N Alvernon Way. Gardens include Mediterranean and landscaping plants; native wildflowers; tropical greenhouse; xeriscape/solar demonstration garden. Tours, botanical classes; special events. (Daily; closed major hols) Sr citizen rate. Phone 326-9255. ¢¢

11. **International Wildlife Museum.** 4800 W Gates Pass Rd, on Speedway 5 mi W of I-10. Includes hundreds of wildlife exhibits from around the world; hands-on, interactive computer displays; videos; cafe. (Daily; closed Jan 1, Thanksgiving, Dec 25) Sr citizen rate. Phone 624-4024. ¢¢

12. **Tohono Chul Park.** Ina & Oracle Rds, entrance at 7366 N Paseo del Norte. A 37-acre preserve with more than 400 species of arid climate plants; nature trails; demonstration garden; geology wall; recirculating stream; ethnobotanical garden. Many varieties of wild birds visit the park. Exhibits, galleries, tea room and gift shops in restored adobe house (daily; closed July 4). (Daily) Phone 575-8468. **Free.**

13. **Reid Park.** 22nd & Country Club Rd. Fishing; picnicking; zoo; rose garden; outdoor performance center. (Daily exc Dec 25) Sr citizen rate. Phone 791-4873 or -3204 (zoo). Zoo ¢¢

14. **Tucson Mountain Park.** 12 mi W, via AZ 86 (Ajo Wai) about 6 mi to Kinney Rd, turn right. More than 18,000 acres of saguaro cactus and mountain scenery. Picnic facilities. Gilbert Ray Campground (electric hookups, dump station; fee). Phone 883-4200 or 740-2690. Also here are

Arizona-Sonora Desert Museum. Live desert creatures: mountain lions, beavers, bighorn sheep, birds, tarantulas, prairie dogs, snakes, otters and many others. Nature trails through labeled desert botanical gardens. Underground earth sciences center with limestone caves; geological, mineral and mining exhibits. Orientation room provides information on natural history of deserts. (Daily) Phone 883-2702. ¢¢¢

Old Tucson Studios. 201 S Kinney Rd. A replica of Tucson in the 1860s. Originally built for the movie *Arizona* and still being used as a location for television and movie films. It is also an Old West attraction, with daily gunfights and stunt shows as well as Iron Door Mine, narrow-gauge train and stagecoach rides. Movies, saloon, entertainment, soundstage special effects show; petting corral; shops, restaurants. (Daily; closed Thanksgiving, Dec 25) Phone 883-0100. ¢¢¢¢

15. **Coronado National Forest.** NE, E and S of city. Mt Lemmon Recreation Area, part of this forest (almost two million acres), offers fishing, bird-watching. Hiking, horseback riding. Picnicking. Skiing. Camping (fee). Madera Canyon offers recreation facilities, lodge. Peña Blanca Lake and Recreation Area (see NOGALES) and the Chiricahua Wilderness area in the SE corner of the state are part of the 12 areas that make up the forest. The Santa Catalina Ranger District, located in Tucson (phone 749-8700), has its headquarters at Sabino Canyon, 12 mi NE on Sabino Canyon Rd; a quarter-mile nature trail begins at the headquarters, as does a shuttle ride almost four miles into Sabino Canyon (fee). Phone 670-4552.

16. **Catalina State Park.** 9 mi N on US 77. A 5,500-acre desert park with vast array of plants and wildlife; bird area (nearly 170 species). Nature & horseback riding trails, hiking, trail access to adj Coronado National Forest. Picnicking. Camping (dump station). Standard fees. Phone 628-5798.

17. **Picacho Peak State Park.** 35 mi NW on I-10, Picacho Peak exit. (See CASA GRANDE)

18. **Kitt Peak National Observatory.** 44 mi SW on AZ 86, then 12 mi S on AZ 386. (See SELLS)

19. **Colossal Cave.** 19 mi SE on I-10 to Vail, then 7 mi N on Colossal Cave Rd. Fossilized marine life provides evidence of ocean that once covered Arizona desert. 72°F year round. 45-min guided tour. (Daily) Phone 647-7275. ¢¢¢

20. **Mt Lemmon Ski Valley.** 35 mi NE via Mt Lemmon Hwy. Double chairlift, 2 tows; patrol, school, rentals; snack bar, restaurant. 15 runs, longest run 1 mile; vertical drop 900 feet. (Late Dec–mid-Apr, daily) Chairlift operates rest of year (daily; fee). Nature trails. Phone 576-1400. ¢¢¢¢¢

21. **Greyhound racing.** Tucson Greyhound Park, S 4th Ave at 36th St. Parimutuel wagering. Sr citizens free all matinees. For schedule information phone 884-7576. ¢–¢¢

22. **Gray Line bus tours.** Contact PO Box 1991, 85702; 622-8811.

(For further information contact the Metropolitan Tucson Convention & Visitors Bureau, 130 S Scott Ave, 85701; 624-1817.)

Annual Events

Northern Telecom Open. Starr Pass & Tucson National Golf Courses. $1.1 million tournament featuring top pros. 2nd wk Jan.

Gem & Mineral Show. Tucson Convention Center. Displays of minerals; jewelry; lapidary skills; Smithsonian Institution collection. Feb.

Tucson Festival. Throughout the city. Commemorates Tucson's cultural and historic heritage with a torchlight pageant, Native American dances, children's parade, Mexican fiesta, frontier encampment and other events. Late Mar–Apr. Also included are

Fiesta del Presidio. Tucson Museum of Art Plaza. Low-rider car show, dancing, Mexican fiesta events, costumes, food.

San Xavier Pageant & Fiesta. At San Xavier del Bac Mission. Mission Rd, S of city. Impressive celebration of this mission's founding with torchlight procession, bonfires, fireworks, Native American dances.

Seasonal Events

Baseball. Hi Corbett Field, Reid City Park. Colorado Rockies spring training. Mar. Phone 791-4266; AAA Houston Astros' minor league team, Tucson Toros. Apr–Sept. Phone 325-2621.

Tucson Symphony Orchestra. Convention Center Music Hall. Phone 882-8585. Sept–May.

Arizona Theatre Company. The Temple of Music & Art. The State Theatre of Arizona performs both classic and contemporary works. Evening performances Tues–Sun; matinees Wed, Sat & Sun. Phone 622-2823. Sept–May.

Arizona Opera. Convention Center Music Hall. Thurs & Sat. Phone 293-4336. Oct–Mar.

City Neighborhoods

Many of the restaurants, unrated dining establishments and some lodgings listed under Tucson include neighborhoods as well as exact street addresses. A map showing these neighborhoods can be found on the preceding page. Geographic descriptions of these areas are given, followed by a table of restaurants arranged by neighborhood.

Downtown: South of Speedway Blvd, west of Campbell Ave, north of 22nd St and east of US 10. **North of Downtown:** North of Speedway Blvd. **East of Downtown:** East of Kolb Rd. **West of Downtown:** West of US 10.

Foothills: South of Coronado National Forest, west of Bear Canyon Rd, north of River Rd and east of Oracle Rd.

Midtown: South of Ft Lowell Rd, west of Kolb Rd, north of 26th St and east of Campbell Ave.

Tanque Verde: South of Tanque Verde Rd, west of Pantano Rd, north of Speedway Blvd and east of Wilmot Rd.

(See Nogales)

TUCSON RESTAURANTS
BY NEIGHBORHOOD AREAS

(For full description, see alphabetical listings under Restaurants)

DOWNTOWN

Delectables. 533 N 4th Ave

El Adobe. 40 W Broadway

El Charro. 311 N Court Ave

Janos. 150 N Main

NORTH OF DOWNTOWN

Cafe Terra Cotta. 4310 N Campbell Ave

Capriccio. 4825 N 1st Ave

Daniel's Trattoria. 4340 N Campbell Ave

Mekong. 6462 N Oracle Rd

Tohono Chul Tea Room. 7366 N Paseo del Norte

EAST OF DOWNTOWN

Japanese Kitchen. 8424 Old Spanish Trail

Saguaro Corners. 3750 S Old Spanish Trail

Szechuan's. 8898 E Tanque Verde Rd

WEST OF DOWNTOWN

Daisy Mae's Steak House. 2735 W Anklam

Scordato's. 4405 W Speedway Blvd

FOOTHILLS

Anthony's in the Catalinas. 6440 N Campbell Ave

El Corral. 2201 E River Rd

La Villa (The Westin La Paloma Resort). 3800 E Sunrise Dr

Landmark Cafe. 7117 N Oracle Rd

The Tack Room. 2800 N Sabino Canyon Rd

Ventana Room (Loews Ventana Canyon Resort). 7000 N Resort Dr

MIDTOWN

Blue Willow. 2616 N Campbell Ave

Buddy's Grill. 4821 E Grant Rd

Charles. 6400 E El Dorado Circle

Da Vinci. 3535 E Fort Lowell

Furrs Cafeteria. 5910 E Broadway

The Good Earth. 6366 E Broadway

Great Wall China. 2445 S Craycroft

Ilsa's Konditorei & Cafe. 2960 N Swan Rd

La Placita Cafe. 2950 N Swan Rd

Le Bistro. 2574 N Campbell Ave

Le Rendez-Vous. 3844 E Fort Lowell

Lotus Garden. 5975 E Speedway Blvd

Palomino. 2959 N Swan Rd

TANQUE VERDE

The Eclectic Cafe. 7053 E Tanque Verde Rd

Jerome's. 6958 E Tanque Verde Rd

Millie's West Pancake Haus. 6530 E Tanque Verde Rd

Olive Tree. 7000 E Tanque Verde Rd

Pinnacle Peak. 6541 E Tanque Verde Rd

Ristorante San Remo. 2210 N Indian Ruins

Note: When a listing is located in a town that does not have its own city heading, it will appear under the city nearest to its location. In these cases, the address and town appear in parenthesis immediately following the name of the establishment.

Motels

★ ★ ★**BEST WESTERN-A ROYAL SUN INN & SUITES.** *1015 N Stone (85705), I-10 exit 257, downtown.* 602/622-8871; FAX 602/623-2267. 59 rms, 2 story, 20 suites. Feb–mid-Apr: S $85–$120; D $99–$120; each addl $10; suites $110–$160; higher rates gem show; lower rates rest of yr. Crib free. TV; cable, in-rm movies. Heated pool; poolside serv. Restaurant 6 am–11 pm. Rm serv. Bar 10–1 am; dancing. Meeting rms. Bellhops. Valet serv. Airport transportation. Exercise equipt; weight machine, bicycles, whirlpool, sauna. Bathrm phones, refrigerators; some wet bars. Balconies. Cr cds: A, C, D, DS, ER, MC, V, JCB.

★ ★**BEST WESTERN INNSUITES-CATALINA FOOTHILLS.** *6201 N Oracle Rd (85704), in Foothills.* 602/297-8111; FAX 602/297-2935. 159 rms, 2 story, 74 kit. suites. Jan–Apr: S, D $79–$99; 2-rm suites $89–$150; under 19 free; wknd, wkly rates; lower rates rest of yr. Crib free. Pet accepted, some restrictions; $25 refundable. TV; cable. Heated pool. Complimentary buffet bkfst. Restaurant adj 6–2 am. Ck-out noon. Coin lndry. Meeting rms. Valet serv. Lighted tennis. Exercise equipt; weight machine, bicycles, whirlpool. Refrigerators; some in-rm whirlpools. Some private patios, balconies. Grills. Cr cds: A, C, D, DS, MC, V.

★ ★ ★**CLARION HOTEL-AIRPORT.** *6801 S Tucson Blvd (85706), near Intl Airport, south of downtown.* 602/746-3932; FAX 602/889-9934. 191 rms, 2 story. Sept–Apr: S $49.95–$99.95; D $59.95–$109.95; each addl $10; suites $79.95–$149.95; under 18 free; wknd rates; lower rates rest of yr. Crib free. Pet accepted, some restrictions; $30. TV; cable. Heated pool; whirlpool; poolside serv. Complimentary full bkfst. Restaurant 6 am–10 pm. Rm serv. Bar. Ck-out noon. Coin lndry. Meeting rms. Bellhops. Valet serv. Sundries. Free airport transportation. 18-hole golf privileges. Health club privileges. Refrigerators. Private patios. Picnic tables, grills. "Raid the Fridge" 10 pm–midnight; guests offered sandwiches and snacks in lobby. Cr cds: A, C, D, DS, ER, MC, V, JCB.

⬛🅳 🌊 🍴 ⬛ ✕ ⊘ ◎ **SC**

★★**COUNTRY SUITES BY CARLSON.** *7411 N Oracle Rd (85704), in Foothills.* 602/575-9255; res: 800/456-4000; FAX 602/575-8671. 155 kit. suites, 3 story. Jan–Apr: S, D $75–$156; under 16 free; wkly rates; lower rates rest of yr. Crib free. TV; cable. Heated pool; whirlpool. Continental bkfst. Restaurant opp 6–1 am. Ck-out noon. Coin lndry. Meeting rm. Valet serv. Free airport, RR station, bus depot transportation. Tennis, golf privileges, putting green. Health club privileges. Cr cds: A, C, D, DS, MC, V.

🍴 🌊 ⊘ ◎ **SC**

★★**COURTYARD BY MARRIOTT.** *2505 E Executive Dr (85706), near Intl Airport, south of downtown.* 602/573-0000; FAX 602/573-0470. 149 units, 3 story. Jan–Apr: S $80–$95; D $90–$102; each addl $10; suites $95–$110; under 12 free; wkly rates; lower rates rest of yr. Crib free. TV; cable. Heated pool. Complimentary coffee in rms. Restaurant 6:30 am–2 pm, 5–10 pm; wknds 7 am–2 pm. Bar 4–11 pm. Ck-out 1 pm. Coin lndry. Meeting rms. Valet serv. Free airport transportation. Exercise equipt; weight machine, bicycles, whirlpool. Refrigerator in suites. Some balconies, some patios. Cr cds: A, C, D, DS, MC, V.

⬛🅳 🌊 ✈ ✕ ⊘ ◎ **SC**

✔ ★★**HAMPTON INN-AIRPORT.** *6971 S Tucson Blvd (85706), near Intl Airport, south of downtown.* 602/889-5789; FAX 602/889-4002. 125 units, 4 story. Jan–Apr: S $65; D $69; suites $75–$79; under 18 free; higher rates special events; lower rates rest of yr. Crib free. Pet accepted, some restrictions. TV; cable. Heated pool; whirlpool. Complimentary continental bkfst. Restaurant nearby. Ck-out noon. Coin lndry. Meeting rms. Bellhops. Valet serv. Free airport transportation. Health club privileges. Some refrigerators. Private patios, balconies. Cr cds: A, C, D, DS, ER, MC, V.

⬛🅳 🐾 🌊 ✕ ⊘ ◎ **SC**

★★**LA QUINTA.** *6404 E Broadway (85710), in Midtown.* 602/747-1414; FAX 602/745-6903. 140 rms, 2 story. Jan–Apr: S $71; D $80; each addl $6; under 18 free; lower rates rest of yr. Crib free. TV; cable. Heated pool; whirlpool. Complimentary continental bkfst. Restaurant adj open 24 hrs. Ck-out noon. Coin lndry. Meeting rms. Health club privileges. Some private patios, balconies. Cr cds: A, C, D, DS, MC, V.

⬛🅳 🌊 ⊘ ◎ **SC**

★★**THE LODGE ON THE DESERT.** *(Box 42500, 85733) 306 N Alvernon Way, in Midtown.* 602/325-3366; res: 800/456-5634; FAX 602/327-5834. 40 rms, 1–2 story, 8 kits, 9 villas. Nov–May: S $76–$101; D $86–$113; each addl $10; AP, MAP avail; lower rates rest of yr. Crib $6. TV. Heated pool; poolside serv. Complimentary continental bkfst in rms. Restaurant 7–9:30 am, noon–1:30 pm, 6–8:30 pm; Sat, Sun from 7:30 am. Rm serv. Bar 11:30 am–2 pm, 5–9 pm. Ck-out noon. Valet serv. Airport transportation. Golf privileges, greens fee, pro. Lawn games. Some refrigerators, fireplaces. Cr cds: A, C, D, DS, MC, V, JCB.

🍴 🌊 ◎

✔ ★**PARK INN INTERNATIONAL.** *2803 E Valencia (85706), near Intl Airport, south of downtown.* 602/294-2500; FAX 602/741-0851. 95 rms, 3 story. Dec–mid-Apr: S $48–$80; D $53–$90; suites $80–$115; under 12 free; wkly rates; golf plan; lower rates rest of yr. Crib free. TV; cable. Heated pool; whirlpool, poolside serv. Restaurant 6 am–10 pm. Rm serv. Bar 4 pm–1 am; Sun from noon. Ck-out noon. Meeting rms. Valet serv. Free airport transportation. Refrigerator in suites. Cr cds: A, C, D, DS, ER, MC, V, JCB.

⬛🅳 🌊 ✕ ⊘ ◎ **SC**

✔ ★**QUALITY INN-UNIVERSITY.** *1601 N Oracle Rd (85705), downtown.* 602/623-6666; FAX 602/884-7422. 184 rms, 2 story. Jan–Apr: S, D $44–$56; each addl $5; kit. units $106; under 18 free; lower rates rest of yr. Crib $5. Pet accepted; $15 non-refundable. TV. Heated pool. Restaurant 6:30–11 am, 5:30–9 pm; Fri & Sat to 10 pm. Rm serv. Bar 2 pm–1 am. Ck-out 11 am. Coin lndry. Meeting rms. Valet serv.

Gift shop. Lawn games. Refrigerators. Some private patios, balconies. Cr cds: A, C, D, DS, ER, MC, V, JCB.

🐾 🌊 ⊘ ◎ **SC**

★★**RAMADA INN FOOTHILLS.** *6944 E Tanque Verde Rd (85715), in Tanque Verde.* 602/886-9595; FAX 602/721-8466. 113 units, 2 story. Jan–Apr: S $60–$80; D $70–$90; each addl $8; suites $70–$99; under 18 free; lower rates rest of yr. Crib free. Pet accepted, some restrictions; $10 non-refundable. TV; cable. Heated pool; whirlpool, sauna. Continental bkfst. Restaurant adj 6 am–11 pm. Ck-out noon. Coin lndry. Meeting rms. Some refrigerators. Cr cds: A, C, D, DS, ER, MC, V, JCB.

🐾 🌊 ⊘ ◎ **SC**

★★**RESIDENCE INN BY MARRIOTT.** *6477 E Speedway Blvd (85710), in Midtown.* 602/721-0991; FAX 602/290-8323. 128 kit. suites, 2 story. Jan–Apr: S, D $130–$155; under 13 free; wkend, wkly, monthly rates; lower rates rest of yr. Crib free. Pet accepted; $150 ($50–$75 non-refundable). TV; cable, in-rm movies. Pool. Complimentary buffet bkfst. Restaurant adj open 24 hrs. Ck-out noon. Coin lndry. Meeting rms. Valet serv. Free airport transportation. Tennis privileges. Health club privileges. Lawn games. Fireplaces. Private patios, balconies. Picnic tables, grills. Cr cds: A, C, D, DS, MC, V, JCB.

⬛🅳 🐾 🌿 🌊 ⊘ ◎ **SC**

✔ ★★**RODEWAY INN-NORTH.** *1365 W Grant Rd (85745), north of downtown.* 602/622-7791; FAX 602/629-0201. 146 rms, 2 story. S, D $48–$68; each addl $6; studio rms $55–$70; under 19 free; summer rates. Crib free. TV; cable. Heated pool. Complimentary continental bkfst. Restaurant 6 am–9 pm. Rm serv. Bar 2 pm–midnight. Ck-out noon. Coin lndry. Meeting rms. Bellhops. Valet serv. Free airport transportation. Cr cds: A, C, D, DS, MC, V.

🌊 ⊘ ◎ **SC**

✔ ★★**SMUGGLER'S INN.** *6350 E Speedway Blvd (85710), in Midtown.* 602/296-3292; res: 800/525-8852; FAX 602/722-3713. 150 rms, 2 story, 28 kits. S $49–$89; D $56–$99; each addl $10; suites, kit. units $78–$115; under 15 free. Crib free. TV; cable. Heated pool; whirlpool. Restaurant 6:30 am–10 pm. Rm serv. Bar 11:30–1 am, Sun from noon; dancing. Ck-out 1 pm. Coin lndry. Meeting rms. Valet serv. Airport transportation. Lighted tennis privileges, pro. 18-hole golf privileges, putting green. Health club privileges. Bathrm phones. Private patios, balconies. Cr cds: A, C, D, DS, ER, MC, V, JCB.

🍴 🌿 🌊 ⊘ ◎ **SC**

★★**TANQUE VERDE INN.** *7007 E Tanque Verde Rd (85715), in Tanque Verde.* 602/298-2300; res: 800/882-6756. 90 rms, 2 story, 60 kits. Jan–Apr: S $72; D $90; suites $90; kit. units $70–$100; under 16 free; wkly rates; lower rates rest of yr. Crib free. Pet accepted, some restrictions. TV; cable. Heated pool; whirlpool. Complimentary continental bkfst. Restaurant adj 7 am–9 pm. Ck-out noon. Coin lndry. Meeting rm. Bellhops. Valet serv. Health club privileges. Bathrm phones; some refrigerators. Private patios, balconies. Rms overlook fountains in courtyards. Cr cds: A, C, D, DS, MC, V.

⬛🅳 🐾 🌊 ⊘ ◎ **SC**

✔ ★**WAYWARD WINDS LODGE.** *707 W Miracle Mile (85705), north of downtown.* 602/791-7526. 41 rms, 19 kits. Dec–Apr: S, D $54–$59; each addl $5; suites $64–$75; kit. units $69–$75; under 18 free; lower rates rest of yr. Closed Aug. Crib free. TV. Heated pool. Complimentary continental bkfst in season, coffee. Restaurant nearby. Ck-out noon. Coin lndry. Rec rm. Lawn games. Picnic tables, grill. Spacious grounds. Cr cds: C, D, DS, MC, V, JCB.

🌊 ◎ **SC**

Motor Hotels

★★★**DOUBLETREE.** *445 S Alvernon Way (85711), in Midtown.* 602/881-4200; FAX 602/323-5225. 295 rms, 2–9 story. Jan–Mar: S $110–$145; D $120–$155; each addl $10; suites $190–$375; under 17 free; lower rates rest of yr. Crib free. TV; cable. Heated pool; poolside serv, lifeguard. Restaurant 6 am–11 pm. Rm serv. Bars 11–1 am, Sun

from noon; entertainment, dancing. Ck-out noon. Meeting rms. Bellhops. Valet serv. Gift shop. Beauty shop. Lighted tennis, pro. 18-hole
golf privileges. Exercise equipt; weight machine, bicycles, whirlpool.
Minibars. Private patios. Cr cds: A, C, D, DS, ER, MC, V, JCB.

[D] [🏊] [🐾] [🛥] [🏃] [Ⓢ] [◎] [SC]

★ ★ **EMBASSY SUITES BROADWAY.** *5335 E Broadway
(85711), in Midtown.* 602/745-2700; FAX 602/790-9232. 142 suites, 3
story. No elvtr. Jan–Apr: S $84–$149; D $94–$159; each addl $10; under
12 free; lower rates rest of yr. Crib free. Pet accepted, some restrictions;
$25. TV; cable. Heated pool; whirlpool, sauna. Complimentary full bkfst.
Restaurant adj 8 am–10 pm. Ck-out 1 pm. Coin lndry. Meeting rms.
Bellhops. Valet serv. Sundries. Free airport transportation. Health club
privileges. Game rm. Grills. Cr cds: A, C, D, DS, MC, V, JCB.

[D] [🐾] [🛥] [Ⓢ] [◎] [SC]

★ ★ **HOLIDAY INN PALO VERDE.** *4550 S Palo Verde Blvd
(85714), south of downtown.* 602/746-1161; FAX 602/741-1170. 299
rms, 6 story. Jan–mid-Apr: S $75–$85; D $83–$93; each addl $8; suites
$93–$130; under 19 free; lower rates rest of yr. Crib free. Pet accepted,
some restrictions. TV; cable. Heated pool; poolside serv. Restaurant 6
am–2:30 pm; dining rm 5–10 pm. Rm serv. Bar 11–1 am, Sun from noon.
Ck-out noon. Coin lndry. Meeting rms. Bellhops. Valet serv. Gift shop.
Free airport transportation. Lighted tennis. Exercise equipt; weights,
bicycles, whirlpool, sauna. Some refrigerators. On 8 acres. Cr cds: A, C,
D, DS, MC, V, JCB.

[D] [🐾] [🛥] [🏃] [Ⓢ] [◎] [SC]

★ ★ **PLAZA.** *1900 E Speedway Blvd (85719), I-10 exit Speedway Blvd E, in Midtown.* 602/327-7341; res: 800/843-8052 (exc AZ),
800/654-3010 (AZ); FAX 602/327-0276. 150 rms, 7 story. Jan–May: S
$71–$81; D $79–$99; each addl $10; under 15 free; lower rates rest of yr.
Crib free. TV; cable. Heated pool; whirlpool, poolside serv. Restaurant
6:30 am–10 pm. Rm serv. Bar 11–1 am; Sun from 11 am. Ck-out noon.
Meeting rms. Bellhops. Valet serv. Concierge. Airport transportation.
Some refrigerators. Balconies. Cr cds: A, C, D, MC, V.

[🛥] [Ⓢ] [◎] [SC]

★ ★ ★ **VISCOUNT SUITE HOTEL.** *4855 E Broadway (85711), in
Midtown.* 602/745-6500; FAX 602/790-5114. 215 suites, 4 story.
Jan–Apr: S $132; D $142; each addl $10; under 12 free; wkly rates; lower
rates rest of yr. TV; cable. Heated pool; poolside serv. Complimentary
full bkfst. Restaurant 6 am–9:30 pm; Sat & Sun 7 am–10 pm. Rm serv.
Bar 11–1 am. Ck-out noon. Meeting rms. Bellhops. Sundries. Airport
transportation. Tennis privileges. Golf privileges. Exercise equipt;
weights, bicycles, whirlpool, sauna. Health club privileges. Some refrigerators. Cr cds: A, C, D, DS, ER, MC, V.

[D] [🐾] [🛥] [🏃] [Ⓢ] [◎] [SC]

★ ★ **WINDMILL INN AT ST PHILIP'S PLAZA.** *4250 N Campbell Ave (85718), in Foothills.* 602/577-0007; res: 800/547-4747; FAX
602/577-0045. 122 suites, 3 story. Jan–late Apr: suites $92–$100; each
addl $6; under 18 free; lower rates rest of yr. Pet accepted, some
restrictions. TV; cable. Heated pool; whirlpool. Complimentary continental bkfst in rms. Complimentary coffee in lobby. Restaurant adj 10
am–11 pm. Ck-out 11 am. Coin lndry. Meeting rms. Bellhops. Valet serv.
Bathrm phones, refrigerators, wet bars. Library featuring best sellers.
Cr cds: A, C, D, DS, MC, V.

[D] [🐾] [🛥] [Ⓢ] [◎] [SC]

Hotels

★ ★ ★ **EMBASSY SUITES HOTEL & CONFERENCE CENTER.**
7051 S Tucson Blvd (85706), near Intl Airport, south of downtown. 602/
573-0700; FAX 602/741-9645. 204 kit. suites, 3 story. Jan–mid-May: S
$104; D $119; each addl $10; under 12 free; wkend rates; lower rates
rest of yr. Crib free. Pet accepted, some restrictions; $35. TV; cable.
Heated pool; poolside serv. Complimentary full bkfst. Restaurant 11
am–10 pm; Fri, Sat to 11 pm. Bar 11–1 am; Sun from noon. Ck-out 1 pm.
Coin lndry. Meeting rms. Gift shop. Free airport transportation. Exercise

equipt; weight machines, bicycles, whirlpool. Grills. Cr cds: A, C, D, DS,
ER, MC, V.

[D] [🐾] [🛥] [🏃] [✕] [Ⓢ] [◎] [SC]

★ ★ ★ **HILTON.** *7600 E Broadway (85710), east of downtown.*
602/721-5600; FAX 602/721-5696. 225 rms, 7 story. Jan–mid-May, mid-
Sept–Dec: S $89–$139; D $102–$152; each addl $13; suites $130–$307;
under 18 free; some wkend rates; lower rates rest of yr. Crib free. Pet
accepted, some restrictions. TV; cable, in-rm movies. Heated pool;
poolside serv. Complimentary coffee in rms. Restaurant 6 am–10 pm.
Bar 11–1 am, Sun from 10 am. Ck-out 1 pm. Convention facilities.
Concierge. Gift shop. Tennis privileges. Golf privileges, greens fee
$15–$30. Health club privileges. Minibars; some bathrm phones. ***LUX-
URY LEVEL.*** 38 units. S $121–$145; D $141–$169; suites $151–$307.
Private lounge. Complimentary bkfst, refreshments.
Cr cds: A, C, D, DS, ER, MC, V.

[D] [🐾] [🛥] [🐾] [🛥] [Ⓢ] [◎] [SC]

✔ ★ **HOLIDAY INN-CITY CENTER.** *181 W Broadway (85701),
downtown.* 602/624-8711; FAX 602/623-8121. 309 rms, 14 story.
Jan–Mar: S $50–$85; D $60–$95; each addl $10; suites $110–$250;
under 19 free; golf package plans; lower rates rest of yr. Crib free. Pet
accepted, some restrictions; $25 refundable. TV; cable. Heated pool;
poolside serv. Restaurant 6 am–2 pm, 5–10 pm. Bar. Ck-out noon.
Convention facilities. Gift shop. Free garage parking. Airport transportation. Health club privileges. Adj to Tucson Convention Center, music
hall, theater, government offices. Cr cds: A, D, DS, ER, MC, V, JCB.

[🐾] [🛥] [Ⓢ] [◎] [SC]

★ ★ ★ **HOTEL PARK TUCSON.** *5151 E Grant Rd (85712), in
Midtown.* 602/323-6262; res: 800/257-7275; FAX 602/325-2989. 216
rms, 4 story. Mid-Jan–May: S, D $105–$155; under 15 free; wkend
rates; lower rates rest of yr. Crib $5. TV; cable. Heated pool; poolside
serv. Complimentary full bkfst. Restaurant 6:30–9:30 am, 11:30 am–2
pm; wkends 7 am–10 pm. Bar 11–1 am; entertainment. Ck-out 1 pm.
Coin lndry. Meeting rms. Gift shop. Tennis privileges. Golf privileges.
Health club privileges. Refrigerators. Glass-enclosed elevators. Cr cds:
A, C, D, MC, V.

[D] [🛥] [🐾] [🛥] [Ⓢ] [◎] [SC]

★ ★ **RADISSON SUITE.** *6555 E Speedway Blvd (85710), in
Midtown.* 602/721-7100; FAX 602/721-1991. 304 suites, 5 story.
Jan–Apr: suites $125–$135; under 17 free; honeymoon wkend rates;
lower rates rest of yr. Crib free. Pet accepted, some restrictions; $25.
TV; cable. Heated pool; poolside serv. Complimentary full bkfst. Restau-
rant 6 am–11 pm. Rm serv 24 hrs. Bar. Ck-out noon. Coin lndry.
Convention facilities. Gift shop. Lighted & indoor tennis privileges. Golf
privileges. Exercise equipt; weights, bicycles, whirlpool. Health club
privileges. Refrigerators; minibars avail. Balconies. Picnic tables, grills.
Cr cds: A, C, D, DS, MC, V, JCB.

[D] [🐾] [🛥] [🐾] [🛥] [🏃] [Ⓢ] [◎] [SC]

Inns

★ ★ **CASA ALEGRE.** *316 E Speedway, west of downtown.*
602/628-1800; FAX 602/792-1880. 4 rms, 2 rms with shower only. No rm
phones. Sept–May: S $65–$75; D $70–$80; under 12 free; wkly rates;
lower rates rest of yr. TV in sitting rm. Pool. Complimentary full bkfst,
tea/sherry. Complimentary coffee in library. Restaurant nearby. Ck-out
noon, ck-in 3 pm. Parking. Built 1915; Native American artifacts, mining-
era antiques. Totally nonsmoking. Cr cds: MC, V.

[🛥] [Ⓢ] [◎] [SC]

★ ★ ★ **EL PRESIDIO BED & BREAKFAST INN.** *297 N Main Ave
(85701), downtown.* 602/623-6151. 4 suites, 2 kit. suites. Sept–May: S,
D $70–$105; wkly, monthly rates; lower rates rest of yr. TV. Complimentary full bkfst, refreshments. Restaurant adj 11 am–10 pm. Ck-out 11:30
am, ck-in late afternoon. Street parking. Health club privileges. Square,
hipped-roof adobe house (1874) with balustrade & veranda; antiques.

Courtyard, period landscaping. Totally nonsmoking. No cr cds accepted.

🚫 Ⓟ

★ ★ ★ LA POSADA DEL VALLE. *1640 N Campbell Ave (85719), in Midtown. 602/795-3840.* 5 rms. 2 rm phones. Sept–May: D $90–$125; lower rates rest of yr. Some TV; also in lobby. Complimentary continental bkfst; full bkfst wkends, tea. Restaurant nearby. Ck-out 11 am, ck-in 2 pm. Adobe house (1929) with patios, enclosed sun porch; antiques. Totally nonsmoking. Cr cds: MC, V.

🚫 Ⓟ SC

Resorts

★ ★ ★ LOEWS VENTANA CANYON RESORT. *7000 N Resort Dr (85715), in Foothills. 602/299-2020; res: 800/234-5117; FAX 602/299-6832.* 398 rms, 4 story. Mid-Jan–late May: S, D $265–$345; each addl $20; suites $400–$1,400; under 18 free; lower rates rest of yr. Crib free. TV; cable, in-rm movies. Heated pool; poolside serv. High tea service. 4 dining rms (also see VENTANA ROOM). Rm serv 24 hrs. Bar 11–1 am, Sun from 10 am; entertainment, dancing exc Mon. Ck-out noon, ck-in 3 pm. Meeting rms. Concierge. Shopping arcade. Airport transportation. Lighted tennis. 18-hole golf, greens fee $50–$95, par 4, putting green, driving range. Pro shop. Lawn games. Rec rm. Game rm. Exercise rm; instructor, weight machines, bicycles, whirlpool, sauna, steam rm. Massage. Bathrm phones, refrigerators. Private patios, balconies. Picnic tables. The resort overlooks an 80-ft waterfall with waters coursing through the property, feeding a 1½-acre lake. Property is at an elevation of 3,013 ft, affording views of mountains & city of Tucson. Cr cds: A, C, D, DS, MC, V, JCB.

D 🍴 🚲 Ⓟ ⛱ 🚶 🏃 🚫 Ⓟ

★ ★ SHERATON EL CONQUISTADOR GOLF & TENNIS RESORT. *10000 N Oracle Rd (85737), in Foothills. 602/544-5000; res: 800/325-7832; FAX 602/544-1224.* 440 rms. Jan–May: S, D $180–$280; suites, studio rms $230–$570; under 17 free; wknd, golf, tennis plans; varied lower rates rest of yr. Crib free. Pet accepted, some restrictions. TV; cable, in-rm movies avail. Heated pools; poolside serv. Free supervised child's activities. 6 dining rms 6 am–11 pm. Rm serv 24 hrs. Bar 11:30–1 am, Sun from 10:30 am; entertainment. Ck-out noon, ck-in 4 pm. Convention facilities. Bellhops. Valet serv. Concierge. Shopping arcade. Beauty shop. Pro shop. Sports dir. Lighted tennis, pro. 45-hole golf, greens fee (incl cart) $95 ($45 in summer), pro, putting green, driving range. Bicycles. Bkfst & evening rides; hayrides. Exercise rm; instructor, weights, bicycles, whirlpools, sauna. Minibars; some bathrm phones, wet bars. Private patios, balconies. Cr cds: A, C, D, DS, ER, MC, V, JCB.

D 🐴 🍴 Ⓟ ⛱ 🚶 🏃 🚫 Ⓟ

★ ★ ★ TUCSON NATIONAL GOLF AND CONFERENCE RESORT. *2727 W Club Dr (85741), north of downtown. 602/297-2271; res: 800/528-4856; FAX 602/742-2452.* 116 units, 2 story. Jan–Apr: S, D $250–$295; each addl $10; suites $325–$375; under 12 free; golf plans; AP avail; lower rates rest of yr. TV; cable. Heated pool; poolside serv. Dining rm 6:30 am–10 pm. Rm serv to midnight. Box lunches, snack bar. Bars 10–1 am; Sun from noon. Ck-out noon, ck-in 3 pm. Convention facilities. Concierge. Gift shop. Barber, beauty shop. Airport transportation avail. Sports dir. Lighted tennis, pro. 27-hole championship golf, greens fee $50–$90, pro, golf cart (mandatory) $15, putting green, driving ranges. Soc dir. Entertainment, dancing. Exercise rm; instructor, weights, bicycles, sauna, steam rm. Massage. Full service spa. Wet bars, refrigerators; many fireplaces. Private patios, balconies. On 650 acres with 11 lakes; attractively landscaped. View of Santa Catalina Mountains. Cr cds: A, C, D, MC, V.

D 🍴 Ⓟ ⛱ 🚶 🏃 🚫 Ⓟ SC

★ ★ VENTANA CANYON GOLF & RACQUET CLUB. *6200 N Clubhouse Lane (85715), in Foothills. 602/577-1400; res: 800/828-5701; FAX 602/299-0256.* 48 kit. units, 2 story. Mid-Jan–mid-Apr: 1-bedrm $265–$360; 2-bedrm $370–$410; each addl $35; under 17 free; wkly rates; lower rates rest of yr. Crib $5. TV; cable. Heated pool; wading pool, poolside serv. Dining rm 11 am–2 pm, 6–10 pm. Rm serv. Bar 11

am–midnight. Ck-out noon, ck-in 3 pm. Valet serv. Free lndry facilities. Package store 4 mi. Meeting rms. Beauty shop. Airport transportation. Sports dir. 12 lighted tennis courts, pro. 36-hole golf, greens fee $40–$90, pro, driving range, putting green, pro shop. Soc dir. Exercise rm; instructor, weight machines, bicycles, whirlpool, sauna, steam rm. Private patios, balconies. Cr cds: A, MC, V.

🍴 Ⓟ ⛱ 🚶 🏃 🚫 Ⓟ

★ ★ ★ ★ THE WESTIN LA PALOMA. *3800 E Sunrise Dr (85718), foothills of Catalina Mountains, in Foothills. 602/742-6000; res: 800/876-3683; FAX 602/577-5878.* 487 units, 3 story. Jan–May: S, D $275–$315; each addl $20; suites from $425; under 18 free; AP, MAP, golf, tennis plans; wknd rates; lower rates rest of yr. Crib free. TV; cable. Heated pool; poolside serv. Supervised child's activities. Dining rm (public by res) 6:30 am–10 pm (also see LA VILLA). Box lunches, snack bar, picnics. Rm serv 24 hrs. Bar 11–1 am. Ck-out noon, ck-in 4 pm. Package store 2 mi. Convention facilities. Bellhops. Valet serv. Concierge. Shopping arcade. Valet parking. Airport transportation; mall shuttle. Sports dir. 12 lighted tennis courts (4 clay), pro. 27-hole golf (Jack Nicklaus Signature Design), greens fee $85, pro, putting green, driving range. Bicycles. Lawn games. Horseback privileges 15 mi. Soc dir; entertainment, movies. Game rm. Rec rm. Exercise rm; instructor, weight machines, bicycles, whirlpool, steam rm. Massage. Some fireplaces; whirlpool, sauna or weight rm in suites. Extensive grounds, elaborately landscaped. Southwestern elegance; antiques, artwork. Cr cds: A, C, D, DS, ER, MC, V, JCB.

D 🍴 Ⓟ ⛱ 🚶 🏃 🚫 Ⓟ SC

★ ★ ★ WESTWARD LOOK. *245 E Ina Rd (85704), in Foothills. 602/297-1151; res: 800/722-2500; FAX 602/297-9023.* 244 rms, 1–2 story. Jan–Apr: S, D $120; suites from $240; AP, MAP avail; lower rates rest of yr. Crib free. Pet accepted, some restrictions; $50 refundable. TV; cable. 3 heated pools; poolside serv. Complimentary coffee in rms. Dining rm 7 am–10 pm. Rm serv. Bar 11–1 am; Sun from 10 am. Ck-out noon, ck-in 3 pm. Meeting rms. Valet serv. Gift shop. Lighted tennis, pro. 18-hole golf privileges. Entertainment, dancing exc Mon. Aerobic classes. Exercise equipt; weight machines, bicycles, whirlpool. Fitness trails. Lawn games. Refrigerators, minibars. Private patios, balconies. Picnic tables, grills. On 74 acres in foothills of Catalina Mountains; elaborately landscaped. Cr cds: A, C, D, DS, MC, V.

D 🐴 🍴 Ⓟ ⛱ 🚶 🏃 🚫 Ⓟ

Guest Ranches

★ ★ LAZY K BAR RANCH. *8401 N Scenic Dr (85743), in Foothills. 602/744-3050; res: 800/321-7018.* 23 rms in 8 buildings. AP (inclusive), Sept–mid-June: S $110–$165; D $170–$270; each addl $75; 6–17, $40; under 6, $20. Closed rest of yr. TV in lounge. Heated pool; whirlpool. Playground. Family-style meals 8–9 am, 12:30–1:30 pm, 6:30–7:30 pm. Box lunches, picnics, cookouts. Private club open 24 hrs, setups. Ck-out noon, ck-in 1 pm. Coin lndry. Meeting rms. Grocery, package store 8 mi. Free airport, RR station transportation. 2 lighted tennis courts. Trap-shooting. Lawn games. Hayrides, rodeos. Entertainment, dancing, movies. Rec rm. Some fireplaces. Picnic tables. Some private patios. Library. Golf nearby. Adobe main house (1933). On 160 acres; beautiful desert and mountain trails. Cr cds: A, DS, MC, V, JCB.

🐴 Ⓟ ⛱ Ⓟ

★ ★ ★ TANQUE VERDE GUEST RANCH. *14301 E Speedway Blvd (85748), 18 mi E via Speedway Blvd, in Foothills. 602/296-6275; res: 800/234-DUDE; FAX 602/721-9426.* 58 rms in casitas. AP (inclusive), mid-Dec–Apr: S $215–$260; D $240–$340; each addl $65–$80; serv charge 15%; lower rates rest of yr. Crib $15. B/W & color TV avail; color in living rm. 2 heated pools, 1 indoor; wading pool. Playground. Supervised child's activities (mid-Nov–Apr). Dining rm (public by res) 8–9 am, noon–1:30 pm, 6–7 pm. Box lunches, picnics, cookouts. Ck-out noon, ck-in 2 pm. Coin lndry. Package store. Meeting rms. Gift shop. Free airport, RR station, bus depot transportation (4-night min). Sports dir. Tennis, pro in season. 18-hole golf privileges. Indoor, outdoor games. Soc dir; entertainment, dancing. Rec rm. Exercise equipt; weight machine, bicycles. Sightseeing trips; overnight trail rides avail; rodeos. Full-time naturalist, bird-banding program (2 hikes/day). Refrigerators; many fireplaces. Private patios. Historic ranch dates from 1868. Picturesque atmosphere; bronze sculpture of owner at entrance. Small lake on property. Cr cds: A, DS, MC, V.

D [icons]

★★★**WHITE STALLION RANCH.** *9251 W Twin Peaks Rd (85743), in Foothills.* 602/297-0252; res: 800/782-5546; FAX 602/744-2786. 29 rms in cottages & lodge. AP (inclusive); mid-Dec–Apr: S $129; D $105–$117/person; 3rd person $79; suites $124–$144/person; wkly rates; slightly lower rates Oct–mid-Dec. Closed rest of yr. Crib free. Heated pool; hot tub. Family-style meals (public by res). Box lunches, cookouts. Bar. Ck-out 11 am, ck-in 2 pm. Coin lndry. Meeting rms. Gift shop. Free airport, RR station, bus depot transportation. Tennis. Golf privileges. Trap & target shooting. Lawn games. Bkfst rides, hayrides, rodeos, bonfires with entertainment. Rec rm. Some refrigerators. Library. Informal ranch on 3,000 acres. Petting zoo. No cr cds accepted.

[icons]

Restaurants

★★★**ANTHONY'S IN THE CATALINAS.** *6440 N Campbell Ave, in Foothills.* 602/299-1771. Hrs: 11:30 am–2:30 pm, 5:30–10 pm; Sun from 5:30 pm. Closed Jan 1, Dec 25. Res accepted. Continental menu. Bar from noon. Wine cellar. A la carte entrees: lunch $5.50–$9.95, dinner $11.95–$24.50. Child's meals. Specializes in lamb, fresh fish, veal. Own baking. Pianist evenings. Valet parking. Outdoor dining. View of city, mountains. Cr cds: A, C, D, MC, V.

D

✔★★**BUDDY'S GRILL.** *4821 E Grant Rd, in Crossroads Festival Shopping Center, in Midtown.* 602/795-2226. Hrs: 11 am–10:30 pm; Fri, Sat to 11 pm. Res accepted. Bar to 1 am. A la carte entrees: lunch $2.95–$11.95, dinner $2.95–$12.95. Specialties: mesquite-grilled fresh fish, Black Angus beef steak. Parking. Exhibition kitchen; soda fountain. Cr cds: A, C, D, DS, MC, V.

D

★★★**CAFE TERRA COTTA.** *4310 N Campbell Ave, north of downtown.* 602/577-8100. Hrs: 11 am–10 pm; Fri, Sat to 11 pm; Sun from 10 am. Closed Thanksgiving, Dec 25. Res accepted. Wine list. A la carte entrees: lunch $6.95–$12.95, dinner $12–$20.50. Specialties: prawns stuffed with goat cheese, black bean chili with sirloin, contemporary Southwestern cuisine. Own desserts. Parking. Patio dining. Airy, light Southwestern atmosphere. Cr cds: A, D, DS, MC, V.

D

★★★**CAPRICCIO.** *4825 N 1st Ave, north of downtown.* 602/887-2333. Hrs: 6–9:30 pm. Closed Sun; major hols; also July. Res accepted. Italian menu. Serv bar. Wine list. Semi-a la carte: dinner $11.95–$18.95 Specialties: roast duckling with green peppercorn sauce, veal porterhouse with zingarella sauce. Own pastries. Parking. European decor. Cr cds: A, MC, V.

★★★**CHARLES.** *6400 E El Dorado Circle, in Midtown.* 602/296-7173. Hrs: 5 pm–closing; early-bird dinner 5–6:45 pm. Closed Sun. Res accepted. Continental menu. Bar to 1 am. Wine list. Semi-a la carte: dinner $9.95–$34.95. Child's meals. Specialties: shrimp & scallops à la Greque, veal el Dorado. Pianist Fri, Sat. Valet parking. Stately stone mansion; antiques. Cr cds: A, C, D, DS, MC, V.

D

★★**DA VINCI.** *3535 E Fort Lowell, in Midtown.* 602/881-0947. Hrs: 4–10 pm. Closed Sun; major hols. Italian menu. Bar. Semi-a la carte: dinner $7.95–$14. Child's meals. Specialties: scampi portofino, pasta. Parking. Italian sculpture, stained glass. Cr cds: A, MC, V.

D

★**DAISY MAE'S STEAK HOUSE.** *2735 W Anklam, west of downtown.* 602/792-8888. Hrs: 5–10 pm; Fri, Sat to 11 pm. Closed Thanksgiving, Dec 25. Res accepted. Semi-a la carte: dinner $7.95–$18.95. Child's meals. Specializes in Angus beef, mesquite-bar-

becued steak. Parking. Outdoor dining. Western memorabilia; rustic decor. Cr cds: A, DS, MC, V.

★★★**DANIEL'S TRATTORIA.** *4340 N Campbell, in St Phillip's Plaza, north of downtown.* 602/742-3200. Hrs: 5–9 pm; Fri, Sat to 10 pm. Closed Thanksgiving, Dec 25. Res accepted; required Fri, Sat. Contemporary Northern Italian menu. Bar. Wine list. A la carte entrees: dinner $12.95–$24.95. Specializes in veal, seafood. Own baking. Parking. Outdoor dining. Overlooks plaza. Cr cds: A, C, D, MC, V.

D

✔★★**DELECTABLES.** *533 N 4th Ave, downtown.* 602/884-9289. Hrs: 11 am–11 pm; Sun to 5 pm. Closed some major hols. Res accepted. Wine, beer. Semi-a la carte: lunch, dinner $3.50–$10.95. Specializes in homemade soups, salads, sandwiches. Parking. Outdoor dining. Cr cds: MC, V, JCB.

D

★**THE ECLECTIC CAFE.** *7053 E Tanque Verde Rd, in Tanque Verde.* 602/885-2842. Hrs: 11 am–9 pm; Sat, Sun from 8 am. Closed Thanksgiving, Dec 25. Mexican, continental menu. Wine, beer. Semi-a la carte: bkfst $3.75–$7.75, lunch, dinner $3.25–$9.95. Child's meals. Specializes in Mexican soup, salad, desserts. Parking. Totally nonsmoking. Cr cds: MC, V.

D

✔★**EL ADOBE.** *40 W Broadway, downtown.* 602/791-7458. Hrs: 11 am–9 pm; Fri, Sat to 10 pm. Closed Sun; Jan 1, Thanksgiving, Dec 25. Res accepted. Mexican menu. Serv bar. Semi-a la carte: lunch $3.85–$8.95, dinner $7.95–$10.95. Child's meals. Specializes in tacos, chimichangas. Outdoor dining. Historic adobe house (1868). Cr cds: A, D, DS, MC, V, JCB.

D

★★**EL CHARRO.** *311 N Court Ave, downtown.* 602/622-5465. Hrs: 11 am–9 pm; Fri, Sat to 10 pm; Sat, Sun brunch to 2 pm. Closed most major hols. Res accepted. Mexican menu. Bar. Semi-a la carte: lunch $3–$7, dinner $4–$15.50. Sat, Sun brunch $4–$6. Child's meals. Specialties: carne seca, topopo. Own desserts. Patio dining. Colorful Mexican decor. In historic house (1896); stained-glass windows; antiques. Braille menu. Family-owned. Cr cds: A, D, MC, V.

✔★★**EL CORRAL.** *2201 E River Rd, just E of Campbell, in Foothills.* 602/299-6092. Hrs: 5–10 pm. Closed Thanksgiving, Dec 25. Bar. Semi-a la carte: dinner $6.95–$11.25. Child's meals. Specializes in prime rib, steak, barbecue ribs. Parking. Located in a rustic adobe, ranch-style building; 6 dining rms, each with its own individual character and decor; fireplace in most dining rms. Inlaid Mexican tile, Indian & Western paintings, ocotillo rib and/or beamed ceilings. Cr cds: D, DS, MC, V.

D

✔★★**THE GOOD EARTH.** *6366 E Broadway, in Midtown.* 602/745-6600. Hrs: 7 am–10 pm; Fri, Sat to 11 pm; Sun from 9 am. Closed day after Labor Day, Thanksgiving, Dec 25. Wine, beer. Semi-a la carte: bkfst $2.35–$5.90, lunch $3.95–$6.95, dinner $6.95–$9.95. Child's meals. Specializes in fresh fish, pasta, vegetarian dishes. Parking. No cr cds accepted.

D SC

★★**GREAT WALL CHINA.** *2445 S Craycroft, in Midtown.* 602/747-4049. Hrs: 11 am–10:30 pm; Fri to 10:30 pm; Sat 11:30 am–10:30 pm; Sun 11:30 am–10 pm. Closed Thanksgiving, Dec 25. Chinese menu. Bar. Complete meals: lunch $4.50–$5.50. Semi-a la carte: dinner $6.50–$22.50. Specialties: Peking duck, volcano beef. Parking. Outside resembles segment of Great Wall; waterfall, stream & wooden bridge at entrance. Antique, hand-painted furniture. Cr cds: A, MC, V.

D

✔★**ILSA'S KONDITOREI & CAFE.** *2960 N Swan Rd, at Plaza Palomino, in Midtown.* 602/795-8050. Hrs: 8 am–6 pm; Thurs to 9 pm. Closed Sun; some major hols; also Mon after Easter. German menu. A la carte entrees: bkfst $2.50–$5.25, lunch $3–$8. Prix fixe: dinner $13.50.

Specialties: Ilsa's salat platte, Birnen toast. Own baking. Outdoor dining. Old world country decor. Cr cds: MC, V.

★ ★ ★ **JANOS.** *150 N Main, Tucson Museum of Art Plaza, El Presidio Historic District, downtown. 602/884-9426.* Hrs: 5:30 pm until closing. Closed Sun; Jan 1, Dec 25; also Mon during mid-May–Sept. Res accepted. French-inspired Southwest regional cuisine. Bar. Wine cellar. Semi-a la carte: dinner $16.50–$28. Summer Samplers menu (May–Sept, Tues–Fri) $12.95. Pre-performance menu (during theater season) $22.50. Specialties: Asian-style lamb noissettes, eggplant au gratin with minted port sauce, grilled Norwegian salmon beurre rouge with asparagus flan & wild mushrooms. Fresh ingredients; grow own herbs. Own baking, pastas, brioche. Parking. Outdoor dining. Adobe building built 1865, saguaro rib ceiling; antiques. Chef-owned. Cr cds: A, D, MC, V.

[D]

★ ★ **JAPANESE KITCHEN.** *8424 Old Spanish Trail, east of downtown. 602/886-4131.* Hrs: 11:30 am–2 pm, 5–9:30 pm; Fri to 10:30 pm; Sat 5–10:30 pm; Sun 5–9:30 pm. Res accepted. Japanese menu. Bar. Semi-a la carte: lunch $4.95–$10.95, dinner $10.95–$25.95. Child's meals. Specializes in steak, seafood, chicken. Sushi bar. Teppanyaki preparation. Parking. Japanese decor. Cr cds: A, MC, V.

[D]

★ ★ ★ **JEROME'S.** *6958 E Tanque Verde Rd, in Tanque Verde. 602/721-0311.* Hrs: 11:30 am–2 pm, 5–10 pm; Fri to 10:30 pm; Sat 5–10:30 pm; Sun 5–10 pm; early-bird dinner 5–7 pm; Sun brunch 11 am–2 pm. Closed Jan 1, Thanksgiving, Dec 25. Res accepted. Creole, Cajun, Amer menu. Bar. Wine list. Semi-a la carte: lunch $4.95–$10.95, dinner $10–$17.95. Sun champagne brunch $15.95. Child's meals. Specialties: sweetwater barbecued duck, blackened fish of the day, wild game. Own baking, desserts. Parking. Country decor; wood beams, brick fireplace. Cr cds: A, C, D, DS, MC, V.

[D]

★ ★ **LA PLACITA CAFE.** *2950 N Swan Rd, at the Plaza Palomino, in Midtown. 602/881-1150.* Hrs: 11:30 am–2:30 pm, 5–9:30 pm; Sun from 5 pm. Closed Jan 1, Thanksgiving, Dec 25. Res accepted. Mexican menu. Serv bar. Semi-a la carte: lunch $4.50–$6.95, dinner $5.95–$14.95. Specialties: bistec Mexicana al minuto, pescado cabrilla (estilo hermosillo), chiles rellenos. Own tortillas. Outdoor dining. Sonoran decor; turn-of-the-century Tucson prints, raised-hearth tile fireplace, serape drapes. Cr cds: A, MC, V.

★ ★ ★ **LA VILLA.** *(See The Westin La Paloma Resort) 602/577-5806.* Hrs: 5–10:30 pm. Res accepted. Wine cellar. Semi-a la carte: dinner $15.50–$22.50. Child's meals. Specializes in seafood featuring Pacific Rim specialties, Norwegian salmon, shrimp with cilantro, prime meats, pasta. Own pastries. Parking. Outdoor dining. Arches, beamed ceiling. Cr cds: A, C, D, DS, ER, MC, V, JCB.

[D]

★ ★ **LANDMARK CAFE.** *7117 N Oracle Rd, in Foothills. 602/575-9277.* Hrs: 10 am–10 pm; wkends from 8 am. Closed Dec 25; also wk of July 4. Res accepted. Continental menu. Serv bar. Semi-a la carte: lunch $4.95–$8.95, dinner $9.95–$23.95. Specialties: game mixed grill, Norwegian salmon. Parking. Patio dining under vine-draped trellis. Cr cds: A, D, DS, MC, V.

★ ★ ★ **LE BISTRO.** *2574 N Campbell Ave, in Midtown. 602/327-3086.* Hrs: 11 am–9:30 pm; Fri to 11 pm; Sat 5–11 pm; Sun from 5 pm. Closed Thanksgiving, Dec 25. Res accepted. Serv bar. A la carte entrees: lunch $5.95–$9.95, dinner $8.25–$15.95. Specialties: blackened scallops, duck liver pâté & cornichons, salmon with ginger crust. Parking. Cr cds: DS, MC, V.

★ ★ ★ **LE RENDEZ-VOUS.** *3844 E Fort Lowell, in Midtown. 602/323-7373.* Hrs: 11:30 am–2:00 pm, 6–10 pm; Fri to 11 pm; Sat 6–11 pm; Sun from 6 pm. Closed Mon; Jan 1, Dec 25. Res accepted; required wkends. French menu. Serv bar. Semi-a la carte: lunch $4.50–$9.95, dinner $15.95–$21.95. Child's meals. Specialties: beef Wellington, salmon Talousie, steak au poivre. Parking. Enclosed patio dining. Cr cds: A, C, D, MC, V.

[D]

★ ★ **LOTUS GARDEN.** *5975 E Speedway Blvd, in Midtown. 602/298-3351.* Hrs: 11:30 am–11 pm; Fri, Sat to midnight. Closed Thanksgiving, Dec 25. Res accepted. Chinese menu. Serv bar. Semi-a la carte: lunch $3.95–$6.50, dinner $8.50–$20. Specialties: sautéed spicy lobster, Mongolian beef, moo shu vegetables. Parking. Patio dining with unique Oriental fountain, stream and bridge. Etched-glass panels separate dining areas. Family-owned. Cr cds: A, C, D, MC, V.

[D]

★ **MEKONG.** *6462 N Oracle Rd, in Plaza del Oro shopping center, north of downtown. 602/575-9402.* Hrs: 11 am–9:30 pm; Sun 4–9 pm. Serv bar. A la carte entrees: lunch, dinner $3.65–$18.95. Specialties: aromatic beef, five spices roasted chicken. Cr cds: DS, MC, V.

[D]

★ ★ ★ **OLIVE TREE.** *7000 E Tanque Verde Rd, in Tanque Verde. 602/298-1845.* Hrs: 11:30 am–10 pm; Sun 5–9 pm. Closed some major hols. Res accepted. Greek, continental menu. Bar. Wine list. Semi-a la carte: lunch $5.95–$8.50, dinner $11.95–$17.95. Child's meals. Specializes in lamb, pasta, fish. Parking. Outdoor dining near fountain. Intimate indoor dining. Cr cds: A, MC, V.

[D]

★ ★ ★ **PALOMINO.** *2959 N Swan Rd, in Midtown. 602/795-5561.* Hrs: 11:30 am–2 pm, 5–10 pm; Mon from 5 pm. Closed Sun; major hols; also 2 wks Aug. Res accepted. Continental menu. Bar to midnight. Wine list. Semi-a la carte: lunch $5–$10, dinner $11–$19. Child's meals. Specializes in bouillabaisse, fresh fish, sweetbreads. Own pastries. Greek night Wed. Pianist Fri–Sat. Parking. Spanish mediterranean decor. Family-owned. Cr cds: A, C, D, DS, MC, V.

✔ ★ ★ **PINNACLE PEAK.** *6541 E Tanque Verde Rd, in Tanque Verde. 602/296-0911.* Hrs: 5–10 pm. Closed Thanksgiving, Dec 25. Bar. Semi-a la carte: dinner $3.95–$11.95. Child's meals. Specializes in steak, ribs. Open mesquite broiler. Parking. Old West atmosphere. Family-owned. Cr cds: D, DS, MC, V.

[D]

★ ★ **RISTORANTE SAN REMO.** *2210 N Indian Ruins, in Tanque Verde. 602/296-9378.* Hrs: 6–10 pm. Closed Mon; major hols. Res accepted. Continental menu. Serv bar. Semi-a la carte: dinner $12.50–$21.50. Specialties: coquilles Frangelique, rack of lamb. Parking. Cr cds: A, D, DS, MC, V.

[D]

★ **SAGUARO CORNERS.** *3750 S Old Spanish Trail, ¼ mi S of east section of Saguaro Natl Monument, east of downtown. 602/886-5424.* Hrs: noon–2:30 pm, 5–9:30 pm. Closed Mon; Thanksgiving, Dec 25; also Aug. Res accepted. Bar. Semi-a la carte: lunch $4.25–$10.50, dinner $7–$17.50. Child's meals. Parking. View of desert wildlife. Family-owned. Cr cds: A, MC, V.

★ ★ ★ **SCORDATO'S.** *4405 W Speedway Blvd, west of downtown. 602/792-3055.* Hrs: 5–10 pm; Sun 4–9 pm. Closed Mon; July 4, Thanksgiving, Dec 25. Res accepted. Italian, continental menu. Bar. Wine cellar. Semi-a la carte: dinner $13.95–$22.95. Child's meals. Specializes in veal stresa, fresh seafood, steak. Own pastries. Parking. Outdoor dining. Desert & mountain view. Cr cds: A, C, D, DS, MC, V.

✔ ★ **SZECHUAN'S.** *8898 E Tanque Verde Rd, east of downtown. 602/749-2300.* Hrs: 11 am–9:30 pm; Fri–Sun from 11:30 am. Closed Thanksgiving. Res accepted. Chinese menu. Serv bar. Semi-a la carte: lunch $3.65–$3.99, dinner $6.25–$8.95. Specializes in dragon Phoenix, shrimp, sesame chicken. Parking. Chinese artifacts. Cr cds: MC, V.

[D]

★ ★ ★ ★ **THE TACK ROOM.** *2800 N Sabino Canyon Rd, in Foothills. 602/722-2800.* Hrs: from 6 pm. Closed Mon off-season; also 1st two wks July. Res suggested. Southwestern, Amer cuisine. Bar 5:30

pm–1 am. Wine cellar. A la carte entrees: dinner $24.50–$32.50. Child's meals. Specialties: rack of lamb with mesquite honey & lime, slow-roasted duckling with Merlot wine sauce, Arizona four-pepper steak, live Maine lobster. Own baking. Valet parking. White adobe hacienda; Spanish decor with fireplaces; window views of mesquite grove and mountains. Unique backdrop for elegant dining and continental service. Gourmet cuisine since 1946. Family-owned. Cr cds: A, C, D, DS, MC, V, JCB.

★★★**VENTANA ROOM.** *(See Loews Ventana Canyon Resort)* *602/299-2020.* Hrs: 6–10:30 pm. Res accepted. Bar. Wine cellar. A la carte entrees: dinner $18–$26. Specialties: mesquite-broiled salmon with ginger cream sauce, duckling breast with cactus pear sauce. Own pastries. Harpist. Valet parking. Elegant dining; panoramic view. Cr cds: A, C, D, DS, MC, V, JCB.

Unrated Dining Spots

BLUE WILLOW. *2616 N Campbell Ave, in Midtown.* *602/795-8736.* Hrs: 7 am–11 pm; Thur, Fri to midnight; Sat 8 am–midnight; Sun 8 am–11 pm. Closed Thanksgiving, Dec 25. Air-cooled. Wine, beer. Semi-a la carte: bkfst $2.75–$6.25, lunch $2.75–$6.95, dinner $2.75–$7.95. Specializes in omelettes, desserts. Parking. Outdoor dining. Cr cds: MC, V.

FURRS CAFETERIA. *5910 E Broadway, in Park Mall Shopping Ctr, in Midtown.* *602/747-7881.* Hrs: 11 am–8 pm. Closed Dec 24 evening. Avg ck: lunch, dinner $4.50. Specializes in roast beef, fried chicken. No cr cds accepted.

MILLIE'S WEST PANCAKE HAUS. *6530 E Tanque Verde Rd, in Tanque Verde.* *602/298-4250.* Hrs: 6:30 am–3 pm. Closed Mon; Jan 1, Thanksgiving, Dec 25. Res accepted. Semi-a la carte: bkfst $3.50–$5.50, lunch $4–$8. Child's meals. Specialties: pancakes, chicken salad. Country inn atmosphere; 2 dining rms. Fireplace; collection of plates & prints displayed. No cr cds accepted.

TOHONO CHUL TEA ROOM. *7366 N Paseo del Norte, in Tohono Chul Park, north of downtown.* *602/797-1711.* Hrs: 8 am–5 pm; Sun brunch to 2 pm. Closed Jan 1, July 4, Thanksgiving, Dec 25. Serv bar. Semi-a la carte: bkfst $1.75–$6.25, lunch $4.95–$9.95. Sun brunch $4.95–$9.95. Child's meals. Specializes in scones, salads, homemade soups. Parking. Outdoor dining. Adobe house in park dedicated to arid flora and landscape. Gift shop. Cr cds: A, MC, V.

Tumacacori National Historical Park (E-3)

(Exit 29 on I-19, 48 mi S of Tucson, 18 mi N of Nogales)

Father Kino, a Jesuit missionary, visited the Pima Indian town of Tumacacori in 1691. Work began on the historic mission church in 1800, but was abandoned in 1848.

There is a beautiful patio garden and a museum with fine dioramas (daily; closed Thanksgiving, Dec 25). Self-guided trail; guided tours with advance notice. There is a fiesta held on the first Sunday in December with entertainment, music and food. Contact the Superintendent, PO Box 67, Tumacacori 85640; 602/398-2341. ¢

(See Nogales, Patagonia, Tucson)

Motel

★★★**TUBAC GOLF RESORT.** *(Box 1297, Tubac 85646)* On I-19, exit 40, 2 mi S on E Frontage Rd. 602/398-2211; res: 800/848-7893. 32 rms, 9 kits. Mid-Dec–mid-Apr: D $103–$130; each addl $10; lower rates rest of yr. Crib free. Pet accepted, some restrictions. TV. Heated pool. Complimentary coffee in rms. Restaurant 7 am–9 pm. Bar to 10 pm, Sun from 10 am. Ck-out 11 am. Coin lndry. Meeting rm. Tennis. 18-hole golf, greens fee $36 (incl cart), putting green, pro. Pro shop. Refrigerators avail. Many fireplaces. Many private patios. Mexican decor. Pool area has mountain view. Cr cds: A, MC, V.

Walnut Canyon National Monument

(see Flagstaff)

Wickenburg (C-2)

Founded: 1863 **Pop:** 4,515 **Elev:** 2,070 ft **Area code:** 602 **Zip:** 85358

Wickenburg was first settled by early Hispanic families who established ranches in the area and traded with the local Native Americans. The town was relatively unpopulated until a Prussian named Henry Wickenburg picked up a rock to throw at a stubborn burro and stumbled onto the richest gold find in Arizona, the Vulture Mine. His find began a $30 million boom and the birth of a town. Today Wickenburg has turned to dude ranching and the winter resort business. Rockhounding is very popular here.

What to See and Do

1. **The Jail Tree.** Tegner & Wickenburg Way. This tree was used from 1863 to 1890 (until the first jail was built) to chain rowdy prisoners. Friends and relatives visited the prisoners and brought picnic lunches. Escapes were unknown.
2. **Frontier Street.** Preserved in early 1900s style. Train depot (houses Chamber of Commerce), brick Hassayampa building (former hotel) and many other historic buildings.
3. **Little Red Schoolhouse.** 4 blks N of Wickenburg Way on Tegner. Pioneer schoolhouse.
4. **Old 761 Santa Fe Steam Locomotive.** At Apache and Tegner, behind Town Hall. This engine and tender ran the track between Chicago and the West.
5. **Desert Caballeros Western Museum.** 21 N Frontier St. Western art gallery; diorama room; street scene (ca 1915); period rooms; mineral display; Native American exhibit. (Daily; closed major hols) Sr citizen rate. Phone 684-2272. ¢¢

(The Chamber of Commerce, PO Drawer CC, and the visitors center at Santa Fe Depot, 216 Frontier St, have an informative booklet. Phone 684-5479.)

Annual Events

Gold Rush Days. Bonanza days revived, with chance to pan for gold and keep all you find. Rodeo; parade. 2nd wknd Feb.

Bluegrass Music Festival. Four-Corner States Championship. 2nd wknd Nov.

(See Phoenix)

Motels

★★**AMERICINN.** *850 E Wickenburg Way. 602/684-5461; res: 800/634-3444; FAX 602/684-5461, ext 118.* 29 rms, 2 story. Nov–May: S $51–$65; D $55–$71; each addl $6; under 16 free; lower rates rest of yr. Crib free. TV. Heated pool; whirlpool. Restaurant 7 am–1:30 pm, 5–8:30 pm. Rm serv. Bar. Ck-out noon. Private patios, balconies. Cr cds: A, C, D, DS, MC, V.

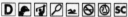

✔★★**BEST WESTERN RANCHO GRANDE.** *(Box 1328) 293 E Wickenburg Way. 602/684-5445; FAX 602/684-7380.* 80 rms, 1–2 story. 24 kits. Nov–Apr: S $50–$64; D $54–$76; each addl $3; suites $72–$80; lower rates rest of yr. Crib $3. Pet accepted. TV; cable. Heated pool; whirlpool. Playground. Complimentary coffee in rms. Restaurant nearby. Ck-out noon. Meeting rms. Bellhops. Valet serv. Free local airport transportation. Tennis. Golf privileges. Some bathrm phones. Private patios, balconies. Cr cds: A, C, D, DS, ER, MC, V, JCB.

Guest Ranches

★★★**FLYING E RANCH.** *(Box EEE) 2801 W Wickenburg Way, 4 mi W on AZ 60W. 602/684-2690; FAX 602/684-5304.* 16 units. AP (2-day min), Nov–May: S $120–$140; D $185–$225; each addl $75; family rates. Closed rest of yr. TV. Heated pool. Family-style meals. Bkfst cookouts, chuckwagon dinners. Setups. Ck-out noon, ck-in varies. Trail rides (fee); hay rides. Tennis. Golf privileges. Shuffleboard. Exercise equipt; weight machine, stair machine, sauna. Occasional entertainment; square dancing. Refrigerators. On 20,000-acre working cattle ranch in shadow of Vulture Peak. No cr cds accepted.

★★**WICKENBURG INN TENNIS & GUEST RANCH.** *(Box P) 8 mi NW on US 89. 602/684-7811; res: 800/528-4227; FAX 602/684-2981.* 6 rms in lodge, 41 casitas. Jan–May, AP: S $165–$250; D $255–$340; each addl $50; family rates; lower rates rest of yr. Serv charge 15%. Crib free. TV. Heated pool; whirlpool. Playground. Supervised child's activities (major hols). Dining rm (public by res) 7–9 am, noon–2 pm, 6–8:30 pm. Served & buffet meals in lodge dining rm. Box lunches, picnics, cookouts. Bar 11 am–11 pm. Ck-out noon, ck-in 3 pm. Free lndry facilities. Meeting rms. Phoenix airport transportation (fee). Tennis, pros, shop. Golf privileges at a 9- and an 18-hole courses, greens fee $40–$80. 3 trail rides. Occasional entertainment; square dancing. Nature program; movies. Crafts center, instruction. Fireplace, wet bar in casitas. Private patios, balconies; some sun decks. Many antiques, handcrafted furnishings. 4,700-acre wildlife refuge. Cr cds: A, DS, MC, V.

Restaurant

★**GOLD NUGGET.** *222 E Wickenburg Way. 602/684-2858.* Hrs: 6 am–10 pm. Res accepted. Bar from 10 am. Semi-a la carte: bkfst $3.75–$7.95, lunch $3.75–$10.95, dinner $8.75–$14.50. Child's meals. Specializes in steak, prime rib. Parking. Turn-of-the-century decor; red rose motif. Family-owned. Cr cds: MC, V.

D

Willcox (E-5)

Pop: 3,122 **Elev:** 4,200 ft **Area code:** 602 **Zip:** 85643

What to See and Do

1. **Chiricahua National Monument** (see). 32 mi SE on AZ 186, then 4 mi E on AZ 181.
2. **Fort Bowie National Historic Site.** 22 mi SE on AZ 186, then 6 mi NE on graded road leading E into Apache Pass and 2 mi to trailhead, then walk 1½ mi on foot trail to the fort ruins. Visitors pass ruins of Butterfield Stage Station, post cemetery, Apache Spring and the first Fort Bowie on the way to ruins of the second Fort Bowie. Visitor center. Carry water in summer, beware of flash floods and rattlesnakes. Do not climb on ruins or disturb any of the site's features. Phone 847-2500.   **Free.**
3. **Cochise Information Center & Museum of the Southwest.** 1 mi N via Circle I Road just off Ft Grant Rd, exit from I-10. Chiricahua Apache exhibits; mineral collection; photographic display of Southwestern historic sites; Willcox Cowboy Hall of Fame; Heritage Park; art exhibits; observation deck. (Daily; closed Jan 1, Thanksgiving, Dec 25) Phone 384-2272.   **Free.**
4. **Amerind Foundation.** Approx 25 mi SW via I-10, exit 318 on Dragoon Rd in Dragoon. Amerind (short for American Indian) Museum contains one of the finest collections of archaeological and ethnological artifacts in the country. Displayed in art gallery are paintings by Anglo and Native American artists. Picnic area, museum shop. (Sept–May, daily; rest of yr, Wed–Sun; closed major hols) Sr citizen rate. Phone 586-3666.   ¢¢

(For further information contact the Chamber of Commerce, Cochise Information Center, 1500 N Circle I Road; 384-3606 or -2272.)

Annual Event

Rex Allen Days. PRCA Rodeo, concert by Rex Allen, Jr, parade, barbecue, country fair, Western dances, carnival, art show. 1st wkend Oct.

(See Safford)

Motels

★★**BEST WESTERN PLAZA INN.** *1100 W Rex Allen Dr, I-10, exit 340. 602/384-3556; FAX 602/384-2679.* 92 rms, 2 story. S, D $45–$80; each addl $5; suites $80; under 12 free; wkend rates. Crib free. Pet accepted, some restrictions. TV; cable. Heated pool; whirlpool. Complimentary full bkfst. Coffee in rms. Restaurant 6 am–10 pm. Rm serv. Bar 11–1 am; Sat, Sun from noon. Ck-out noon. Coin lndry. Meeting rms. Gift shop. Beauty shop. Many refrigerators. Cr cds: A, C, D, DS, MC, V.

✔★★**ECONO LODGE.** *724 N Bisbee Ave. 602/384-4222; FAX 602/384-3785.* 73 rms, 2 story. June–Aug & Nov–Feb: S $38–$48; D $46–$56; each addl $5; under 18 free; higher rates Rex Allen Days; lower rates rest of yr. Crib free. Pet accepted, some restrictions. TV; cable. Heated pool. Complimentary coffee. Restaurant opp open 24 hrs. Ck-out noon. Coin lndry. Cr cds: A, C, D, DS, ER, MC, V, JCB.

Williams (Coconino Co) (B-3)

Settled: 1880 **Pop:** 2,532 **Elev:** 6,750 ft **Area code:** 602 **Zip:** 86046

This town lies at the foot of Bill Williams Mountain (named for an early trapper and guide) and is the principal entrance to the Grand Canyon (see). It is a resort town in the midst of Kaibab National Forest, which has its headquarters here. There are seven small fishing lakes in the surrounding area.

What to See and Do

1. **Grand Canyon National Park** (see). Approx 50 mi N on US 180 (AZ 64) to South Rim.
2. **Kaibab National Forest.** More than 1.5 million acres; one area surrounds Williams and includes Sycamore Canyon and Kendrick Mt wilderness areas and part of National Historic Rte 66; a second area is 42 mi N on US 180 (AZ 64) near South Rim of Grand Canyon; a third area lies N of Grand Canyon (outstanding views of the canyon from seldom visited vista points in this area) and includes Kanab Creek and Saddle Mountain wilderness areas, the Kaibab Plateau and the North Rim Parkway National Scenic Byway. The forest is home for a variety of wildlife unique to this area, including mule deer and the Kaibab squirrel. Fishing (trout), hunting. Picnicking. Camping (fee). Phone 635-2681. Also in forest is

    Williams Ski Area. 4 mi S of town, on the north slopes of Bill Williams Mt. Pomalift, rope tow; patrol, school, rentals; snack bar. (Mid-Dec–Easter, daily exc Wed) Sledding slopes and cross-country trails nearby. Phone 635-9330. ¢¢¢¢¢
3. **Grand Canyon Railway.** First operated by Santa Fe Railroad in 1901 as an alternative to the stagecoach, this restored line carries passengers northward aboard authentically refurbished steam locomotives and coaches. Full-day round trips include 3½-hr layover at canyon. At Williams depot, there is a museum of railroad history. Railway (June–Sept, daily; Mar–May, Wed–Sun; Feb–Nov, Fri–Sun; Dec, Sat & Sun; also Dec 25–Jan 1, daily). For reservations, phone 800/843-8724. Railway ¢¢¢¢¢

(For further information contact the Williams-Grand Canyon Chamber of Commerce, 820 W Bill Williams Ave, PO Box 235; 635-4061.)

Annual Events

Bill Williams Rendezvous Days. Black powder shoot, carnival, helicopter and hot air balloon rides, parade, barbecue, pioneer arts & crafts, stage shows. Memorial Day wkend.

Cowpunchers' Reunion and Old-Timers' Rodeo. Williams Rodeo Grounds. Working cowboys compete in events. 1st wk Aug.

(See Flagstaff, Seligman)

Motels

★EL RANCHO. *617 E Bill Williams Ave. 602/635-2552; res: 800/228-2370; FAX 602/635-4173.* 25 rms, 2 story, 2 suites. Mid-May–Sept: S $52–$85; D $57–$85; each addl $5; suites $70–$100; under 12 free; lower rates rest of yr. Crib $3. Pet accepted; $5 per day. TV; cable. Heated pool. Complimentary coffee in lobby. Restaurant opp 6 am–10 pm. Ck-out 11 am. Free airport, RR station transportation. Downhill ski 4 mi. Some refrigerators. Cr cds: A, DS, MC, V.

[icons]

✔★NORRIS. *1001 W Bill Williams Ave. 602/635-2202; FAX 602/635-9202.* 34 rms. May–Sept: S, D $54–$64; each addl $5; under 3 free; ski plans; lower rates rest of yr. Crib $7. TV; cable. Complimentary coffee in lobby. Restaurant nearby. Ck-out 11 am. Free airport, RR station transportation. Downhill ski 4 mi. Whirlpool. Many refrigerators. Grills. Cr cds: A, DS, MC, V.

[icons]

★RAMADA LIMITED. *710 W Bill Williams Ave. 602/635-4464; FAX 602/635-4814.* 48 rms, 2 story, 7 suites. May–Sept: S, D $95–$125; each addl $10; suites $115–$185; under 18 free; lower rates rest of yr. Crib free. TV; cable. Complimentary continental bkfst. Complimentary coffee in lobby. Restaurant nearby. Ck-out noon. Downhill ski 4 mi. Refrigerators avail. Minibar in suites. Cr cds: A, D, DS, MC, V.

[icons]

Restaurant

★ROD'S STEAK HOUSE. *301 E Bill Williams Ave. 602/635-2671.* Hrs: 11 am–10 pm. Closed Thanksgiving, Dec 24, 25. Res accepted. Bar. Semi-a la carte: lunch $3.50–$7.50, dinner $7–$23. Child's meals. Specializes in mesquite-broiled steak. Parking. Paintings of the Old West. Cr cds: DS, MC, V.

Window Rock (B-5)

Pop: 3,306 **Elev:** 6,880 ft **Area code:** 602 **Zip:** 86515

This is the headquarters of the Navajo Nation. The 88-member tribal council, democratically elected, meets in an octagonal council building; tribal officials conduct tribal business from Window Rock.

Behind the town is a natural bridge that looks like a window. It is in the midst of a colorful group of sandstone formation called "The Window Rock."

What to See and Do

1. **Navajo Nation Museum.** At Tse Bonito Park, E of jct AZ 264 and Indian Rte 12, on AZ 264 in Navajo Arts & Crafts Enterprise Center. Established in 1961 to preserve Navajo history, art, culture and natural history; permanent and temporary exhibits. Literature and Navajo information available. (Apr–Sept, daily exc Sun; rest of yr, Mon–Fri; closed tribal & other hols) Donation. Phone 871-6673.
2. **Navajo Nation Zoological and Botanical Park.** Tse Bonito Park, E of jct AZ 264 and Indian Rte 12, on AZ 264. Features a representative collection of animals and plants of historical or cultural importance to the Navajo people. (Daily; closed Jan 1, Dec 25) Phone 871-6573. **Free.**
3. **St Michaels.** 3 mi W. Catholic mission, established in 1898, that has done much for the education and health of the tribe. Original mission building now serves as a museum depicting history of the area. Gift shop. (Memorial Day–Labor Day, daily) Donation. Phone 871-4172.
4. **Canyon de Chelly National Monument** (see).

(For further information contact the Navajoland Tourism Department, PO Box 663; 871-6659 or -7371.)

Annual Events

Powwow and PRCA Rodeo. July 4.

Navajo Nation Fair. Navajo Nation Fairgrounds. Navajo traditional song & dance; Inter-tribal powwow; All-Indian Rodeo; parade; concerts; exhibits. Contact PO Drawer U; 871-6478. Five days beginning Wed after Labor Day.

Winslow (C-4)

Founded: 1880 **Pop:** 8,190 **Elev:** 4,880 ft **Area code:** 602 **Zip:** 86047

A railroad town, Winslow is also a trade center and convenient stopping point in the midst of a colorful and intriguing area; a miniature painted desert lies to the northwest. The Apache-Sitgreaves National Forest, with the world's largest stand of ponderosa pine, lies about 25 miles to the south.

What to See and Do

1. **Meteor Crater.** 20 mi W on I-40, then 5 mi S on Meteor Crater Rd. Crater is 4,150 feet from rim to rim and 560 feet deep. The world's best preserved meteorite crater is used as training site for astronauts. Museum, lecture; Astronaut Hall of Fame; telescope on highest point of the crater's rim offers excellent view of surrounding area. (Daily) Sr citizen rate. Phone 289-2362 or 774-8350. ¢¢¢

2. **Old Trails Museum.** 212 N Kinsley Ave. Operated by the Navajo County Historical Society; exhibits and displays of local history, Native American artifacts and early Americana. (Apr–Oct, Tues–Sat; rest of yr, Tues, Thurs & Sat; closed hols) Phone 289-5861. **Free.**

3. **Homolovi Ruins State Park.** 3 mi E on I-40, then 1 mi N on AZ 87. This park contains six major Anasazi ruins dating from 1250 to 1450. Arizona State Museum conducts occasional excavations (June, July). Trails. Visitor center, museum; interpretive programs. Standard fees. (Daily; closed Dec 25) Phone 289-4106.

(For further information contact the Chamber of Commerce, 300 W North Rd, PO Box 460; 289-2434.)

(See Holbrook, Hopi & Navajo Indian Reservations)

Motels

⭐⭐⭐**BEST WESTERN ADOBE INN.** *1701 N Park Dr. 602/289-4638.* 72 rms, 2 story. June–Aug: S $48–$53; D $58–$65; suites $67–$75; under 12 free; lower rates rest of yr. Crib $2. Pet accepted, some restrictions. TV; cable, in-rm movies. Indoor pool; whirlpool. Restaurant 6 am–2 pm, 4–10 pm; Sun to 9 pm. Rm serv. Bar 4–11 pm. Ckout 11 am. Coin lndry. Meeting rms. Free airport, RR station, bus depot transportation. Cr cds: A, C, D, DS, ER, MC, V.

✔⭐**ECONO LODGE.** *N Park Dr & I-40 exit 253. 602/289-4687; FAX 602/289-9377.* 72 rms, 2 story. Late May–Sept: S $42; D $47; each addl $5; under 18 free; lower rates rest of yr. Pet accepted; $2 per day. TV; cable. Restaurant opp 6 am–11 pm. Ck-out 11 am. Cr cds: A, C, D, DS, MC, V.

Restaurants

⭐**ENTRÉ.** *W I-40, 1½ mi W on I-40 Business (AZ 66W). 602/289-2141.* Hrs: 11 am–9:30 pm; wkends to 10 pm. Chinese, Amer menu. Bar. Semi-a la carte: lunch, dinner $4.25–$16.95. Lunch buffet (Mon–Fri) $4.75. Chinese decor. Cr cds: A, DS, MC, V.

✔⭐**FALCON.** *1113 3rd St. 602/289-2342.* Hrs: 5:30 am–9 pm. Closed Thanksgiving, Dec 25. Bar. Semi-a la carte: bkfst $3.60–$6.50, lunch $3.95–$4.75, dinner $5.50–$11.50. Child's meals. Specialties: chicken-fried steak, N.Y. steak sandwich, roast turkey. Parking. Family-owned. Cr cds: A, MC, V.

Wupatki National Monument (B-3)

(30 mi N of Flagstaff on US 89)

The nearly 2,700 masonry ruins of the Sinagua and Anasazi cultures were occupied between 1100 and 1250. The largest of them, Wupatki, was 3 stories high, with about 100 rooms. The eruption of nearby Sunset Crater (see) spread volcanic ash over the area and for a time made this an active farming center.

The ruins trail is self-guided; books are available at its starting point. The visitor center and main ruin are open daily (closed Dec 25). Rangers on duty. An 18-mile paved road leads to Sunset Crater Volcano National Monument (see). Nearest camping at Bonito Campground (phone 602/526-0866). Contact the Superintendent, HC 33, Box 444A, Flagstaff 86004; 602/527-7040. Per vehicle ¢¢

(For accommodations see Flagstaff)

Yuma (D-1)

Founded: 1849 **Pop:** 54,923 **Elev:** 138 ft **Area code:** 602

Hernando de Alarcón, working with the Coronado Expedition, passed this point on the Colorado River in 1540. Father Kino came into the area in 1699. Padre Francisco Tomas Garces established a mission in 1780 that was destroyed a year later. The Yuma Crossing, where the Colorado River narrows between the Yuma Territorial Prison and Fort Yuma (one of Arizona's oldest military posts), was made a historic landmark in recognition of its long service as a river crossing for many peoples.

Yuma's air-conditioned stopping places are a great comfort to motorists crossing the desert. If you think you have seen some of this scenery before, you are probably right; movie producers have used the dunes and desert for location shots.

Irrigation from the Colorado River makes it profitable to raise cattle, alfalfa, cotton, melons, lettuce, citrus fruits and other crops here. A Marine Corps Air Station and an army proving grounds are adjacent to the town.

What to See and Do

1. **Yuma Territorial Prison State Historic Park.** Off I-8, Giss Pkwy exit. Remains of 1876 prison; museum, original cell blocks. Southwest artifacts and prison relics. (Daily; closed Dec 25) Phone 783-4771. ¢¢ Nearby is

   Yuma Quartermaster Depot. 2nd Ave & Colorado River, behind City Hall. Established in 1864, the depot served as a supply distribution point for troops stationed at military outposts in the Arizona Territory. Tours. At Yuma Crossing of the Colorado River. (Daily; closed Dec 25) Sr citizen rate. Phone 329-0404. ¢¢

2. **Arizona Historical Society Century House Museum and Gardens.** 240 Madison Ave. Home of the late E.F. Sanquinetti, pioneer merchant; now a division of the Arizona Historical Society. Artifacts from Arizona Territory, including documents, photographs, furniture and clothing. Gardens and exotic birds surround museum. Historical library open by appt. (Tues–Sat; closed hols) Phone 782-1841. **Free.**

3. **Quechan Museum.** Fort Yuma. Part of one of the oldest military posts (1855) associated with the Arizona Territory; offered protection to settlers and secured the Yuma Crossing. Fort Yuma is headquarters for the Quechan Tribe. Museum houses tribal relics of southwestern Colorado River Yuman groups. (Mon–Fri; closed hols) Phone 619/572-0661. ¢

4. **Yuma River Tours.** 1920 Arizona Ave. Narrated historical tours on the Colorado River; half- and full-day trips. Sunset dinner cruise. Also jeep tours to sand dunes. (Daily) Phone 783-4400.

5. **Yuma Valley Railway.** Levee at 8th St. Tracks run 12 miles through fields along the Colorado River levee and Morelos Dam. Two-hour trip; dinner trips. (Fri–Sun) Sr citizen rate. Phone 783-3456. ¢¢¢

6. **Imperial National Wildlife Refuge.** 40 mi N via US 95. Bird-watching; photography. Fishing, hunting. Hiking. Interpretive center-office (Mon–Fri). Phone 783-3371. **Free.**

7. Greyhound and horse racing. Greyhound Park. 4000 S 4th Ave, 3 mi S. Horse racing (Wed–Sun; also Sat–Sun matinees) Greyhound racing (Tues–Sun; also Tues matinees). Phone 726-4655. **¢**

(For further information contact the Yuma County Chamber of Commerce, 377 Main St, PO Box 230, 85366; 782-2567.)

Annual Events

Yuma County Fair. 5 days early Apr.

Thoroughbred & Quarter Horse Racing. Fairgrounds track. Pari-mutuel betting. 1 wkend late Oct.

Motels

✔ ★**AIRPORTER STARDUST INN.** 711 E 32nd St (85365), near Intl Airport. 602/726-4721; FAX 602/344-0452. 80 rms, 2 story. Jan–Apr: S $55–$60; D $60–$70; each addl $5; under 17 free; lower rates rest of yr. Crib free. TV; cable. Heated pool. Restaurant 6–10 pm. Bar 4 pm–1 am. Ck-out noon. Coin lndry. Meeting rms. Lighted tennis privileges. Some refrigerators. Cr cds: A, C, D, DS, MC, V.

$\boxed{D} \; \boxed{\oslash} \; \boxed{\approx} \; \boxed{\times} \; \boxed{\ominus} \; \boxed{\circledcirc} \; \boxed{SC}$

★★**BEST WESTERN.** 1450 Castle Dome Ave (85365). 602/783-8341; FAX 602/783-1349. 166 rms. Jan–Apr: S $58–$89; D $68–$94; 2-rm suites $72–$94; under 20 free; higher rates opening wk dove season; lower rates rest of yr. Crib free. Pet accepted. TV; cable. Heated pool. Complimentary continental bkfst. Complimentary coffee in rms. Ck-out noon. Coin lndry. Valet serv. Lighted tennis. Exercise equipt; weights, bicycles, whirlpool. Refrigerators. Cr cds: A, C, D, DS, MC, V, JCB.

$\boxed{D} \; \boxed{\oslash} \; \boxed{\oslash} \; \boxed{\approx} \; \boxed{\dagger} \; \boxed{\ominus} \; \boxed{\circledcirc} \; \boxed{SC}$

★★**HOLIDAY INN EXPRESS.** 3181 S 4th Ave (85364). 602/344-1420; FAX 602/341-0158. 120 rms, 2 story. Jan–mid-Apr: S $63–$73; D $69–$79; each addl $6; under 19 free; lower rates rest of yr. Crib free. Pet accepted. TV; cable, in-rm movies. Heated pool; whirlpool. Continental bkfst 6–9 am. Coffee in rms. Ck-out noon. Coin lndry. Valet serv. Free airport transportation. Health club privileges. Refrigerators. Cr cds: A, C, D, DS, MC, V, JCB.

$\boxed{D} \; \boxed{\oslash} \; \boxed{\approx} \; \boxed{\ominus} \; \boxed{\circledcirc} \; \boxed{SC}$

★★**LA FUENTE INN.** 1513 E 16th St (85365). 602/329-1814; res: 800/841-1814; FAX 602/343-2671. 50 rms, 2 story, 46 suites. Jan–May: S $66–$70; D $70–$76; each addl $5; suites $80–$90; under 12 free; higher rates special events; lower rates rest of yr. Crib free. TV; cable. Heated pool. Complimentary continental bkfst. Coffee in rms. Restaurant adj open 24 hrs. Ck-out noon. Coin lndry. Free airport, RR station, bus depot transportation. Exercise equipt; weights, bicycles, whirlpool. Health club privileges. Refrigerators; many wet bars. Near Yuma Airport. Cr cds: A, C, D, DS, MC, V.

$\boxed{D} \; \boxed{\approx} \; \boxed{\dagger} \; \boxed{\ominus} \; \boxed{SC}$

★★**PARK INN INTERNATIONAL.** 2600 S 4th Ave (85364). 602/726-4830; FAX 602/341-0551. 164 suites, 3 story. Oct–Apr: S $86; D $96; each addl $10; under 16 free; lower rates rest of yr. Crib free. TV; cable. Heated pool; whirlpool. Complimentary continental bkfst. Res-

taurant adj open 24 hrs. Ck-out noon. Meeting rms. Bellhops. Valet serv. Airport, RR station, bus depot transportation. Health club privileges. Refrigerators, wet bars. Cr cds: A, C, D, ER, MC, V.

$\boxed{D} \; \boxed{\approx} \; \boxed{\ominus} \; \boxed{\circledcirc} \; \boxed{SC}$

✔ ★**TORCH LITE LODGE.** 2501 S 4th Ave (85364). 602/344-1600. 40 rms, 2 story, 6 kits. Jan–Mar: S, D $27–$89; each addl $5; kit. units $10 addl; higher rates dove season, certain winter wkends; lower rates rest of yr. TV; cable. Heated pool. Complimentary coffee. Restaurant adj 5 am–10 pm. Ck-out noon. Cr cds: A, C, D, MC, V.

$\boxed{\approx} \; \boxed{\ominus} \; \boxed{\circledcirc}$

Motor Hotel

★★★**SHILO INN.** 1550 S Castle Dome Rd (85365), off I-8 exit 16th St. 602/782-9511; FAX 602/783-1538. 135 rms, 4 story, 14 kits. S, D $79–$95; each addl $10; kit. units $102–$105; patio-side rms $105–$110; under 12 free; monthly rates; higher rates Padre & dove seasons. Crib $6. TV; cable, in-rm movies avail. Heated pool; poolside serv. Restaurant 6 am–10 pm. Rm serv. Bar to 1 am. Ck-out noon. Coin lndry. Meeting rms. Valet serv. Gift shop. Free airport, RR station, bus depot transportation. Exercise equipt; weight machines, bicycles, whirlpool, sauna, steam bath. Bathrm phones, refrigerators. Private patios, balconies. Cr cds: A, D, DS, MC, V.

$\boxed{D} \; \boxed{\approx} \; \boxed{\dagger} \; \boxed{\ominus} \; \boxed{\circledcirc} \; \boxed{SC}$

Restaurants

★**THE CROSSING.** 2690 S 4th Ave. 602/726-5551. Hrs: 11 am–9 pm; Fri, Sat to 10 pm. Res accepted. Italian, Amer menu. Wine, beer. Semi-a la carte: lunch, dinner $3.95–$14.95. Child's meals. Specializes in prime rib, catfish, buffalo wings. Parking. Cr cds: A, C, D, DS, ER, MC, V.

★★**HUNGRY HUNTER.** 2355 S 4th Ave. 602/782-3637. Hrs: 11 am–2:30 pm, 5–10 pm; Sat, Sun from 5 pm. Closed Dec 25. Res accepted. Bar to 11 pm. Semi-a la carte: lunch $4–$8, dinner $9.95–$35. Child's meals. Specializes in prime rib, steak, fresh seafood. Parking. Cr cds: A, D, DS, MC, V.

$\boxed{D}$

✔ ★★**MANDARIN PALACE.** 350 E 32nd St. 602/344-2805. Hrs: 11 am–10 pm; Fri, Sat to 11 pm. Res accepted. Chinese, Amer menu. Bar. A la carte entrees: lunch $4.95–$5.95, dinner $8–$13. Specialties: crispy beef a la Szechwan, rainbow shrimp, smoked tea duck. Parking. Elegant Oriental decor. Cr cds: A, D, MC, V.

Unrated Dining Spot

GARDEN CAFE & SPICE COMPANY. 250 S Madison. 602/783-1491. Hrs: 10 am–3 pm; Sat, Sun from 10 am. Closed Easter, Thanksgiving, Dec 25; also July–Sept. Mexican, continental menu. Semi-a la carte: bkfst $2.50–$5.95, lunch $5–$7. Specializes in espresso, capuccino, Swedish oatmeal pancakes. Parking. Outdoor dining with garden; country store. In 1887 house. Cr cds: A, MC, V.

California

Population: 29,760,020	
Land area: 156,297 square miles	
Elevation: 282 feet below sea level–14,494 feet	
Highest point: Mount Whitney (Between Inyo, Tulare Counties)	
Entered Union: September 9, 1850 (31st state)	
Capital: Sacramento	
Motto: *Eureka* (I have found it)	
Nickname: Golden State	
State flower: Golden Poppy	
State bird: California Valley Quail	
State tree: Redwood	
State fair: Late August–early September, 1994, in Sacramento	
Time zone: Pacific	

California has the largest population of any state in the United States. Within it, only 80 miles apart, are the lowest and highest points in the contiguous US—Death Valley and Mount Whitney. It has ski areas and blistering deserts, mountains and beaches, giant redwoods and giant missiles, Spanish missions and skyscrapers. The oldest living things on earth grow here—a stand of bristlecone pine said to be 4,600 years old. San Francisco, key city of northern California, is cosmopolitan, beautiful, proud, Old-Worldly. Los Angeles, in southern California, is bright and brazen, growing, modern. California, 780 miles long, up to 350 miles wide, does things in a big way.

Almost every crop of the US grows here. Prunes, huge oranges, bales of cotton and tons of vegetables roll out from the factory farms in the fertile valleys. California leads the nation in the production of more than 35 fruits and vegetables including grapes, peaches, apricots, olives, figs, lemons, avocados, walnuts, almonds, sugar beets, rice, plums, prunes, dates and nectarines. It also leads in the production of dried, canned and frozen fruits and vegetables, wine as well as eggs, turkeys, safflower, beeswax and honey. Homegrown industries include Hollywood movies, television, electronics, aircraft and missiles.

Spaniards, Mexicans, English, Russians and others helped write the history of the state. The first explorer to venture into the waters of California was Portuguese—Juan Rodriguez Cabrillo, in 1542. In 1579, Sir Francis Drake explored the coastal waters and is believed to have landed just northwest of what is now San Francisco. Beginning in 1769, Spanish colonial policy sprinkled a trail of missions around which the first towns developed. The Mexican flag flew over California after Mexico won independence from Spain in 1821. American settlers later wrenched the colony from Mexico and organized the short-lived Bear Flag Republic. On July 7, 1846, Commodore John D. Sloat raised the US flag at Monterey. Under the Treaty of Guadalupe Hidalgo, California became part of what was to be the coastal boundary of the United States in 1848.

Perhaps the most important event in its history was the discovery of gold in January of 1848, setting off a sudden mass migration that transformed the drowsy, placid countryside and accelerated the opening of the Far West by several decades. The 49ers who came for gold found greater riches in the fertile soil of the valleys and the markets of the young cities.

During and after World War II, California grew at an astounding pace in both industry and population. Jet travel across the Pacific makes the state a gateway to the Orient.

National Park Service Areas

California has seven national monuments: Cabrillo (see SAN DIEGO), Death Valley, Devils Postpile, Joshua Tree, Lava Beds, Muir Woods and Pinnacles (see all) and six national parks: Channel Islands, Lassen Volcanic, Sequoia and Kings Canyon, Yosemite (see all) and Redwood (see CRESCENT CITY). There are also Point Reyes National Seashore (see INVERNESS), Whiskeytown-Shasta-Trinity National Recreation Area (see REDDING), Golden Gate National Recreation Area (see SAN FRANCISCO), John Muir National Historic Site (see MARTINEZ), Eugene O'Neill National Historic Site (see PLEASANTON) and Fort Point National Historic Site (see SAN FRANCISCO). For information on camping, weather and road conditions for 17 parks within the California National Park System, phone 415/556-0560 or write Western Region Information Office, National Park Service, Fort Mason, Building 201, San Francisco, CA 94123.

National Forests

The following is an alphabetical listing of National Forests and towns they are listed under.

Angeles National Forest (see PASADENA): Forest Supervisor in Arcadia; Ranger offices in Flintridge*, Glendora*, Pearblossom*, San Fernando, Saugus*.

Cleveland National Forest (see PINE VALLEY): Forest Supervisor in San Diego; Ranger offices in Alpine*, Corona, Escondido.

Eldorado National Forest (see PLACERVILLE): Forest Supervisor in Placerville; Ranger offices in Camino*, Georgetown*, Jackson, Pioneer*, Placerville, Pollock Pines*.

Inyo National Forest (see INYO NATIONAL FOREST): Forest Supervisor in Bishop; Ranger offices in Bishop, Lee Vining, Lone Pine, Mammoth Lakes.

Klamath National Forest (see YREKA): Forest Supervisor in Yreka; Ranger offices in Etna*, Fort Jones*, Happy Camp*, Klamath River*, Macdoel*, Orleans*, Sawyers Bar*.

Lassen National Forest (see SUSANVILLE): Forest Supervisor in Susanville; Ranger offices in Chester, Fall River Mills*, Susanville.

Los Padres National Forest (see KING CITY and SANTA BARBARA): Forest Supervisor in Goleta*; Ranger offices in Frazier Park*, King City, Ojai, Santa Barbara, Santa Maria.

Mendocino National Forest (see WILLOWS): Forest Supervisor in Willows; Ranger offices in Corning*, Covelo*, Stonyford*, Upper Lake*.

Modoc National Forest (see ALTURAS): Forest Supervisor in Alturas; Ranger offices in Adin*, Canby*, Cedarville*, Tulelake*.

Plumas National Forest (see QUINCY): Forest Supervisor in Quincy; Ranger offices in Blairsden*, Challenge*, Greenville*, Milford*, Oroville, Quincy.

San Bernardino National Forest (see SAN BERNARDINO): Forest Supervisor in San Bernardino; Ranger offices in Fawnskin*, Fontana*, Idyllwild, Mentone*, Rimforest*.

Sequoia National Forest (see PORTERVILLE): Forest Supervisor in Porterville; Ranger offices in Bakersfield, California Hot Springs*, Dunlap*, Kernville, Porterville.

Shasta-Trinity National Forests (see REDDING): Forest Supervisor in Redding; Ranger offices in Big Bar*, Hayfork*, McCloud*, Mt Shasta, Platina*, Redding, Weaverville.

Sierra National Forest (see FRESNO): Forest Supervisor in Fresno; Ranger offices in Mariposa*, North Fork*, Oakhurst*, Sanger*, Shaver Lake*.

Six Rivers National Forest (see EUREKA): Forest Supervisor in Eureka; Ranger offices in Bridgeville*, Gasquet*, McKinleyville*, Orleans*, Salyer*, Willow Creek*, Zenia*.

Stanislaus National Forest (see SONORA): Forest Supervisor in Sonora; Ranger offices in Groveland*, Hathaway Pines*, Mi-wuk Village*, Sonora.

Tahoe National Forest*: Ranger offices in Camptonville*, Foresthill*, Grass Valley, Nevada City, Sierraville*, Truckee.

Toiyabe National Forest (see RENO, NV): Forest Supervisor in Sparks, NV; Ranger office in Bridgeport.

*Not described in text

For general information about national forests within California, contact USDA, Forest Service, 630 Sansome St, San Francisco 94111, phone 415/705-2874. For camping reservations only, phone 800/283-CAMP or phone the supervisor of any particular forest directly.

State Recreation Areas

The following towns list state recreation areas in their vicinity under What to See and Do; refer to the individual town for directions and park information.

Listed under **Anza-Borrego Desert State Park:** see Anza-Borrego Desert State Park.

Listed under **Auburn:** see Folsom Lake State Recreation Area.

Listed under **Big Basin Redwoods State Park:** see Big Basin Redwoods State Park.

Listed under **Big Sur:** see Pfeiffer-Big Sur State Park.

Listed under **Burney:** see McArthur-Burney Falls Memorial State Park.

Listed under **Carlsbad:** see South Carlsbad State Beach.

Listed under **Clear Lake Area:** see Clear Lake State Park.

Listed under **Crescent City:** see Del Norte Coast Redwoods, Jedediah Smith Redwoods and Prairie Creek Redwoods state parks.

Listed under **Crestline:** see Silverwood Lake State Recreation Area.

Listed under **Dunsmuir:** see Castle Crags State Park.

Listed under **Fort Bragg:** see MacKerricher State Park.

Listed under **Fort Ross State Historic Park:** see Salt Point State Park and Sonoma Coast State Beach.

Listed under **Fresno:** see Millerton Lake State Recreation Area.

Listed under **Gilroy:** see Henry W. Coe State Park.

Listed under **Guerneville:** see Armstrong Redwoods State Reserve.

Listed under **Humboldt Redwoods State Park:** see Humboldt Redwoods State Park.

Listed under **Idyllwild:** see Mt San Jacinto State Park.

Listed under **Inverness:** see Samuel P. Taylor and Tomales Bay state parks.

Listed under **Jackson:** see Indian Grinding Rock State Historic Park.

Listed under **Lake Tahoe Area:** see D.L. Bliss, Emerald Bay, Grover Hot Springs, Sugar Pine Point state parks and Tahoe State Recreation Area.

Listed under **Los Angeles:** see Will Rogers State Historic Park.

Listed under **Mendocino:** see Mendocino Headlands, Russian Gulch and Van Damme state parks.

Listed under **Mill Valley:** see Mt Tamalpais State Park.

Listed under **Modesto:** see Caswell Memorial State Park and Turlock Lake State Recreation Area.

Listed under **Morro Bay:** see Morro Bay State Park.

Listed under **Mt Diablo State Park:** see Mt Diablo State Park.

Listed under **Needles:** see Providence Mountains State Recreation Area.

Listed under **Nevada City:** see Malakoff Diggins State Historic Park.

Listed under **Oroville:** see Lake Oroville State Recreation Area.

Listed under **Placerville:** see Marshall Gold Discovery State Historic Park.

Listed under **Redwood Hwy:** see Grizzly Creek Redwoods State Park.

Listed under **Richardson Grove State Park:** see Richardson Grove State Park.

Listed under **Salton Sea State Recreation Area:** see Salton Sea State Recreation Area.

Listed under **San Clemente:** see San Clemente State Beach.

Listed under **Santa Barbara:** see Carpinteria State Beach.

Listed under **Santa Cruz:** see Forest of Nisene Marks State Park, Henry Cowell Redwoods State Park, Natural Bridges Beach and Seacliff Beach.

Listed under **Trinidad:** see Patrick's Point State Park.

Listed under **Truckee:** see Donner Memorial State Park.

Listed under **Ventura:** see Emma Wood, McGrath and San Buenaventura state beaches.

Water-related activities, hiking, riding, various other sports, picnicking, nature trails, and visitor centers, as well as camping, are available in many of these areas. Some parks limit camping to a maximum consecutive period of 7–30 days, depending on season and popularity of area. Campsite charges are $12–$25/night/vehicle; trailer hookups $9–$25. For campsite reservations phone 800/444-7275 from anywhere in the continental United States; out of country phone customer service at 800/695-CAN-X. Day-use fee is $2–$6/vehicle; car with boat $11; annual pass for $75 includes unlimited day-use, $125 with boat; boat launching $3–$5. Fees may vary in some areas. There are also small fees for some activities at some areas. Pets on leash only, permitted in campground and day-use areas only, $1/night (camping), $1 (day-use). Reservations for Hearst San Simeon State Historical Monument (see) can be made by phone, 800/444-4445. For map folder listing and describing state parks ($2), contact the Publications Section, Department of Parks and Recreation, PO Box 942896, Sacramento 94296-0001; 916/653-4000. For general park information phone 916/653-6995.

Fishing & Hunting

Streams, rivers, canals and lakes provide a great variety of freshwater fish. Salmon and steelhead trout run in great numbers in major coastal rivers north of San Francisco. Everything from barracuda to smelt may be found along or off the shore.

Hunting for deer, bear and other big game is available in most national forests, other public lands and some private lands (by permission) except in national and state parks, where firearms are prohibited. Waterfowl, quail and dove shooting can be arranged at public management areas and in private shooting preserves. Tidepool collecting is illegal without special permit.

A fishing license is required for all persons 16 and older to fish in either inland or ocean waters. Some public piers in ocean waters allow fishing without a license (list available on request). A hunting license is required to hunt any animal. For information contact the California Department of Fish and Game, 1416 9th St, Sacramento 95814. For general information phone 916/653-7664; for license information phone 916/227-2244.

Skiing

The following towns list ski areas in their vicinity under What to See and Do; refer to the individual town for directions and information.

Listed under **Big Bear Lake:** see Bear Mt and Snow Summit ski areas.

Listed under **Fresno:** see Sierra Summit Ski Area.

Listed under **June Lake:** see June Mt Ski Area.

Listed under **Lake Arrowhead:** see Snow Valley Ski Area.

Listed under **Lake Tahoe Area:** see Alpine Meadows, Heavenly ‡, Kirkwood ‡, Sierra Ski Ranch and Squaw Valley USA ‡ ski areas.

Listed under **Lassen Volcanic National Park:** see Lassen Volcanic National Park Winter Sports Area ‡.

Listed under **Mammoth Lakes:** see Mammoth Mountain Ski Area.

Listed under **Mt Shasta:** see Mt Shasta Ski Park.

Listed under **San Bernardino:** see Mountain High Ski Area.

Listed under **Sonora:** see Bear Valley ‡ and Dodge Ridge ski areas.

Listed under **Truckee:** see Boreal, Donner Ski Ranch, Northstar ‡, Royal Gorge Cross-Country ‡‡, Soda Springs, Sugar Bowl and Tahoe Donner ‡ ski areas.

Listed under **Yosemite National Park:** see Badger Pass Ski Area ‡.

‡ Also cross-country trails
‡‡ Only cross-country trails

For skiing information contact the California Ski Industry Assn, 340 Townsend St, San Francisco 94107; 415/543-7036.

Safety Belt Information

Safety belts are mandatory for all persons anywhere in vehicle. Children under 4 years or under 40 pounds in weight must be in an approved safety seat anywhere in vehicle. For further information phone 916/657-7202.

Interstate Highway System

The following alphabetical listing of California towns in *Mobil Travel Guide* shows that these cities are within 10 miles of the indicated Interstate highways. A highway map should, however, be checked for the nearest exit.

INTERSTATE 5: Anaheim, Buena Park, Carlsbad, Costa Mesa, Del Mar, Dunsmuir, Fullerton, Garden Grove, Irvine, Lodi, Los Angeles Area, Mount Shasta, Oceanside, Orange, Rancho Santa Fe, Red Bluff, Redding, Sacramento, San Clemente, San Diego, San Fernando Valley Area, San Juan Capistrano, Santa Ana, Stockton, Valencia, Willows, Yreka.

INTERSTATE 8: Calexico, El Cajon, El Centro, Pine Valley, San Diego.

INTERSTATE 10: Beaumont, Blythe, Claremont, Desert Hot Springs, Indio, Los Angeles Area, Ontario, Palm Desert, Palm Springs, Pomona, Redlands, San Bernardino, Santa Monica, West Covina.

INTERSTATE 15: Barstow, Corona, Escondido, Redlands, Riverside, San Bernardino, San Diego, Temecula, Victorville.

INTERSTATE 40: Barstow, Needles.

INTERSTATE 80: Auburn, Berkeley, Davis, Fairfield, Oakland, Sacramento, San Francisco, Truckee, Vacaville, Vallejo.

INTERSTATE 110: Arcadia, Beverly Hills, Burbank, Culver City, Glendale, Long Beach, Los Angeles, Los Angeles Intl Airport Area, Marina Del Rey, Pasadena, Redondo Beach, San Gabriel, San Marino, San Pedro, Torrance, Westwood Village.

Additional Visitor Information

For material on northern California, contact the San Francisco Convention & Visitors Bureau, 201 3rd St, Suite 900, San Francisco 94103, phone 415/974-6900 or the Redwood Empire Assn, 785 Market St, 15th Floor, San Francisco 94103, phone 415/543-8334 (will send 48-page *Visitors Guide* to Northern Coast/Redwood area; enclose $3 for postage and handling). For southern California, contact the Greater Los Angeles Visitors and Convention Bureau, 515 S Figueroa St, 11th floor, Los Angeles 90071, phone 213/624-7300; the San Diego Convention and Visitors Bureau, 11 Horton Plaza, 1st & F Sts, San Diego 92101, phone 619/236-1212, is also helpful. Serious hikers should consult *Sierra North* or *Sierra South*, available from the Wilderness Press, 2440 Bancroft Way, Berkeley 94704 or phone 800/443-7227. For general information contact the California Office of Tourism, Dept of Commerce, 801 K St, Suite 1600, Sacramento 95814, phone 800/862-2543. The monthly magazine *Sunset* gives special attention to West Coast travel and life. Sunset Publishing Corp also publishes the Sunset Travel Books, among which are: *Northern California* and *Southern California*.

Contact Sunset Publishing Corp, 80 Willow Rd, Menlo Park 94025-3691; phone 800/227-7346 outside California or 800/321-0372 in California.

Alturas (B-3)

Pop: 3,231 Elev: 4,366 ft Area code: 916 Zip: 96101

What to See and Do

1. **Modoc County Historical Museum.** 600 S Main St. More than 4,000 Native American artifacts, including arrowheads and spear points and many other items; exhibits of local history, including antique gun collection. (May–Oct, schedule varies; phone ahead) Phone 233-6328. ¢

2. **Modoc National Wildlife Refuge.** 2 mi S on County 115. Nesting habitat for the Great Basin Canada goose; also ducks, sandhill cranes, other interesting birds. (Daily, daylight hrs; Dorris Reservoir Recreation Area closed during waterfowl hunting season; inquire about fees. Refuge closed to public fishing except Dorris Reservoir Recreation Area.) Phone 233-3572.   **Free.**

3. **Modoc National Forest.** Sections surrounding Alturas reached via US 395 and CA 139/299. Scene of the Modoc Indian Wars, this forest of nearly 2 million acres is famous for its scenic trails through the South Warner Wilderness. In Medicine Lake Highlands Area there is a spectacular flow of jumbled black lava surrounding islands of timber; craters, cinder cones and lava tube caves. For wildlife watchers, the Modoc National Forest is home to more than 300 species of wildlife; the Pacific Flyway for migratory waterfowl crosses directly over the forest, making this area a bird watcher's paradise. Swimming, stream and lake fishing, hunting. Winter sports area. Picnicking. Camping. Contact the Forest Supervisor, 441 N Main St; phone 233-5811.

(For further information contact the Chamber of Commerce, 522 S Main St; 233-2819.)

Annual Events

Fandango Celebration. Early July.

Modoc-The Last Frontier Fair. In Cedarville. Phone 279-2315. 4 days, wkend before Labor Day.

Motels

★★**BEST WESTERN TRAILSIDE INN.** 343 N Main St. 916/233-4111. 39 rms, 2 story, 4 kits. May–Oct: S $42; D $46–$48; each addl $5; kit. units $5 addl; lower rates rest of yr. Crib $5. Pet accepted, some restrictions. TV; cable, in-rm movies. Pool. Complimentary coffee. Restaurant nearby. Ck-out 11 am. Free local airport transportation. Downhill/x-country ski 10 mi. Cr cds: A, C, D, DS, MC, V.

🅿️ 🐾 ⚓ 🚫 ◎ SC

✔★**HACIENDA.** 201 E 12th St. 916/233-3459. 20 rms, 2 kits. S $27; D $29–$45; each addl $3; kit. units $5 addl; under 8 free. Crib free. Pet accepted. TV; cable. Complimentary coffee in rms. Restaurant nearby. Ck-out 11:30 am. Free local airport, bus depot transportation. Downhill/x-country ski 10 mi. Refrigerators. Cr cds: A, C, D, DS, MC, V.

🅿️ 🐾 ⚓ 🚫 ◎ SC

Restaurants

✔★**BRASS RAIL.** US 395N, 1 mi N. 916/233-2906. Hrs: 11:30 am–2 pm, 5:30–10 pm. Closed Mon; Thanksgiving, Dec 25; also Jan. Basque menu. Bar to 2 am. Complete meals: lunch $7, dinner $14. Child's meals. Specializes in Basque lamb, own wine. Parking. Former whiskey distillery. Cr cds: MC, V.

★★**NILES HOTEL & SALOON.** 304 S Main St. 916/233-3261. Hrs: 11:30 am–2 pm, 5:30–10 pm; Sat & Sun from 5:30 pm. Closed Memorial Day, Labor Day, Dec 25. Res accepted. Bar. Semi-a la carte: lunch $3.95–$9.50, dinner $10.95–$16.95. Specializes in prime rib, fresh sturgeon. Entertainment twice each month. Restored turn-of-the-century Victorian hotel. Cr cds: MC, V.

Anaheim (J-4)

Founded: 1857 Pop: 266,406 Elev: 160 ft Area code: 714

Once part of a Spanish land grant, "Anaheim" was bought and settled by German colonists who came to this land to grow grapes and produce wine. The town takes its name from the Santa Ana River and the German word for "home." Today Anaheim is known as the home of Disneyland.

What to See and Do

1. **Disneyland** (see). On Harbor Blvd, off Santa Ana Frwy.

2. **Pacific Coast Sightseeing.** For information contact 1213 E Howell Ave, 92805; 978-8855.

(For further information contact the Anaheim Area Visitor & Convention Bureau, 800 W Katella Ave, PO Box 4270, 92803; 999-8999.)

Seasonal Event

Professional sports. California Angels (baseball, Apr–Sept), Los Angeles Rams (football, Sept–Dec), Anaheim Stadium, 2000 Gene Autry Way. For tickets phone 634-2000 (Angels) or 937-6767 (Rams).

(See Buena Park, Corona, Los Angeles, Santa Ana)

Motels

★★**BEST WESTERN STOVALL'S INN.** 1110 W Katella Ave (92802), 1 blk S & 1 blk W of Disneyland. 714/778-1880; FAX 714/778-3805. 290 rms, 3 story. S $50–$75; D $55–$80; suites $110–$150; under 18 free. Crib free. TV; in-rm movies avail. 2 pools, 1 heated; wading pool, whirlpools. Complimentary coffee, tea in rms. Restaurant adj open 24 hrs. Bar 4 pm–midnight; closed Sun. Ck-out noon. Coin lndry. Gift shop. Free Disneyland transportation. Refrigerator in suites. Picnic area. Topiary garden. Cr cds: A, C, D, DS, ER, MC, V.

D ⚓ 🚫 ◎ SC

★★**CAROUSEL INN & SUITES.** 1530 S Harbor Blvd (92802), opp Disneyland. 714/758-0444; res: 800/854-6767 (US), 800/621-0032 (Canada); FAX 714/772-9965. 130 rms, 2–5 story, 26 suites. S, D $45–$69; suites $59–$119; under 18 free. Crib $5. TV; cable, in-rm movies. Heated pool. Complimentary continental bkfst. Restaurant nearby. Ck-out 11 am. Coin lndry. RR station, bus depot, Disneyland transportation. Refrigerators. Cr cds: A, DS, MC, V.

D ⚓ 🚫 ◎ SC

✔★**COMFORT INN.** 2200 S Harbor Blvd (92802), 1 mi S of Disneyland. 714/750-5211; FAX 714/750-2226. 66 rms, 2 story. S $39–$69; D $42–$79; each addl $5; under 18 free; package plans. TV; in-rm movies. Heated pool; whirlpool. Complimentary continental bkfst. Coffee in lobby. Restaurant nearby. Ck-out 11 am. Coin lndry. Valet serv. Cr cds: A, C, D, DS, ER, MC, V, JCB.

D ⚓ 🚫 ◎ SC

★**COMFORT PARK SUITES.** 2141 S Harbor Blvd (92802), 3 blks S of Disneyland. 714/971-3553; FAX 714/971-4609. 94 suites, 4 story. S, D $68–$115; under 18 free; wkly rates. Crib $5. TV; cable. Indoor pool; whirlpool. Complimentary continental bkfst, coffee. Restaurant nearby. Ck-out 11 am. Coin lndry. Meeting rm. Refrigerators. Cr cds: A, C, D, DS, ER, MC, V, JCB.

D ⚓ 🚫 ◎ SC

★★**COMFORT SUITES.** 201 N Via Cortez (92807), CA 91 Imperial Hwy exit, S to Santa Ana Canyon, E to Via Cortez. 714/921-1100; FAX 714/637-8790. 161 rms, 4 story. S, D $64–$90; under 18 free. Crib $5. TV; cable, in-rm movies avail. Heated pool. Complimentary continental bkfst, coffee. Restaurant adj 7–2 am. Ck-out noon. Coin lndry. Meeting rms. Exercise equipt; weight machine, bicycles, whirlpool, sauna. Refrigerators. Cr cds: A, C, D, DS, ER, MC, V, JCB.

D ⚓ 🍴 ⊘ ◔ SC

★**DAYS INN ANAHEIM/DISNEYLAND.** 1030 W Ball Rd (92802), near jct I-5 & Harbor Blvd. 714/520-0101; FAX 714/758-9406. 45 rms, 3 story. June–Aug: S $56–$68; D $66–$78; each addl $6; under 12 free; higher rates hols; lower rates rest of yr. Crib free. TV; in-rm movies. Heated pool; whirlpool. Complimentary continental bkfst. Coffee in rms. Restaurant nearby. Ck-out 11 am. Coin lndry. Airport, RR station transportation. Free Disneyland transportation. Some refrigerators, wet bars. Cr cds: A, C, D, DS, MC, V, JCB.

D ⚓ ⊘ ◔ SC

★★**GRANADA INN.** 2375 W Lincoln Ave (92801), I-5 Brookhurst St exit, S to Lincoln Ave then ½ mi W. 714/774-7370; res: 800/648-8685; FAX 714/774-8068. 80 kit. units, 3 story. June–Aug: S $60; D $70; each addl $8; under 16 free (limit 2); wkly rates in winter; lower rates rest of yr. Crib free. TV; cable. Heated pool. Complimentary continental bkfst. Restaurant 6:30 am–9:30 pm. Bar. Ck-out noon. Beauty shop. Free Disneyland, Knott's Berry Farm transportation. Sightseeing tours. Golf nearby. Private patios, balconies. Cr cds: A, C, D, DS, MC, V.

⚓ ⊘ ◔ SC

★★**HAMPTON INN.** 300 E Katella Way (92802), 1 mi E of Disneyland, at jct Katella Ave & Katella Way. 714/772-8713; FAX 714/778-1235. 136 rms, 5 story. S $54–$64; D $64–$74; under 18 free. Crib free. Pet accepted, some restrictions. TV; cable. Heated pool. Complimentary continental bkfst, coffee. Ck-out noon. Meeting rm. Free Disneyland transportation. Cr cds: A, C, D, DS, MC, V.

D 🏊 ⚓ ⊘ ◔ SC

✔ ★**MARCO POLO INN.** 1604 S Harbor Blvd (92802), opp Disneyland. 714/635-3630; res: 800/624-3940; FAX 714/520-3290. 58 units, 2 story, 8 suites. S $40–$68; D $44–$75; each addl $4; suites $75–$120; under 12 free. Crib $5. TV; cable. Heated pool; whirlpool. Complimentary continental bkfst. Coffee in rms. Restaurant adj open 24 hrs. Ck-out 11 am. Coin lndry. Refrigerators. Cr cds: A, C, D, DS, MC, V, JCB.

D ⚓ ⊘ ◔ SC

✔ ★**PARK VUE INN.** 1570 S Harbor Blvd (92802), opp Disneyland. 714/772-5721; res: 800/854-0199; FAX 714/635-0964. 90 units, 2 story, 15 suites, 4 kits. S $38–$60; D $42–$68; each addl $4; suites $75–$120; kits. $65–$105; under 12 free. Crib $4. TV; cable. Heated pool; wading pool. Complimentary continental bkfst. Coffee in rms. Restaurant adj open 24 hrs. Ck-out 11 am. Coin lndry. Free Disneyland transportation. Refrigerators. Cr cds: A, C, D, DS, ER, MC, V.

⚓ ⊘ ◔ SC

✔ ★**PENNY SLEEPER INN.** 1441 S Manchester Ave (92802), 1 blk E of Disneyland. 714/991-8100; res: 800/854-6118; FAX 714/533-6430. 202 rms, 2 story. S $37–$45; D $41–$56; under 18 free. Crib free. TV; cable. Heated pool. Complimentary continental bkfst. Restaurant nearby. Ck-out noon. Coin lndry. Valet serv. Gift shop. Free RR station, bus depot, Disneyland transportation. Cr cds: A, DS, ER, MC, V.

D ⚓ ⊘ ◔ SC

★**RODEWAY INN.** 800 S Beach Blvd (92804), CA 91 Beach Blvd exit, 3 mi S. 714/995-5700. 74 units, 3 story, 6 kits. July–Aug: S $44–$58; D $48–$68; each addl $6; kit. units $50–$64; under 17 free; wkly rates; lower rates rest of yr. Crib free. Pet accepted, some restrictions. TV; cable. Heated pool. Complimentary coffee in lobby. Restaurant nearby. Ck-out 11 am. Coin lndry. Meeting rms. Some refrigerators, minibars. Cr cds: A, C, D, DS, ER, MC, V.

D 🏊 ⚓ ⊘ ◔ SC

★**SAGA INN.** 1650 S Harbor Blvd (92802), opp Disneyland. 714/772-0440; res: 800/854-6097 (exc CA), 800/442-4402 (CA); FAX 714/991-8219. 186 rms, 2–4 story. S $50–$60; D $56–$74; each addl $5; suites $76–$120; under 17 free. Crib $5. TV. Heated pool; whirlpool. Restaurant adj 11 am–10 pm. Ck-out 11 am. Coin lndry. Valet serv. Gift shop. Free Disneyland transportation. Some refrigerators, wet bars. Cr cds: A, C, D, DS, ER, MC, V, JCB.

D ⚓ ⊘ ◔ SC

✔ ★**SUPER 8-ANAHEIM PARK.** 915 S West St (92802), near jct I-5 & Harbor Blvd. 714/778-0350; FAX 714/778-3878. 113 rms, 3 story. May–Sept: S $39–$49; D $42–$60; each addl $6; under 12 free; lower rates rest of yr. TV; cable. Heated pool; whirlpool. Complimentary continental bkfst. Restaurant adj 6 am–11 pm. Ck-out 11 am. Coin lndry. Free Disneyland transportation. Cr cds: A, C, D, DS, ER, MC, V.

D ⚓ ⊘ ◔ SC

★**TRAVELODGE MAINGATE.** 1717 S Harbor Blvd (92802), adj Disneyland main entrance. 714/635-6550; FAX 714/635-1502. 254 rms, 2 story. June–Aug & late Dec–early Jan: S, D $65–$70; suites, kit. units $85; under 18 free; lower rates rest of yr. Crib free. TV; cable. 2 heated pools; wading pool, whirlpool, sauna. Complimentary coffee in rms. Restaurant adj 7 am–10 pm. Ck-out noon. Coin lndry. Meeting rm. Valet serv. Gift shop. Airport transportation; free Disneyland transportation. Some refrigerators. Cr cds: A, C, D, DS, ER, MC, V, JCB.

⚓ ⊘ ◔ SC

Motor Hotels

★★**CONESTOGA.** 1240 S Walnut St (92802), near jct I-5 & Harbor Blvd. 714/535-0300; res: 800/321-3531 (exc CA), 800/321-3530 (CA); FAX 714/491-8953. 252 rms, 6 story. S $89–$99; D $99–$109; each addl $8; suites, studio rms $145–$225; under 16 free; package plans. Crib free. TV; cable, in-rm movies. Heated pool; whirlpool. poolside serv. Complimentary coffee in rms. Restaurant 6:30 am–10 pm. Rm serv 24 hrs. Bar 11–1:30 am. Ck-out noon. Meeting rms. Bellhops. Valet serv. Gift shop. Free Disneyland transportation. Game rm. Refrigerator, wet bar in suites. Disneyland ¼ mi. Cr cds: A, C, D, DS, ER, MC, V, JCB.

D ⚓ ⊘ ◔ SC

★★★**HOLIDAY INN ANAHEIM CENTER.** 1221 S Harbor Blvd (92805), near jct I-5. 714/758-0900; FAX 714/533-1804. 254 rms, 5 story. May–Aug: S, D $75–$90; each addl $10; under 18 free; lower rates rest of yr. Pet accepted, some restrictions; $10 per visit. TV; cable. Heated pool; poolside serv. Restaurant 6:30 am–10 pm. Rm serv. Bar 5 pm–midnight. Ck-out noon. Meeting rms. Bellhops. Valet serv. Gift shop. Free Disneyland and Buena Park transportation. Game rm. Refrigerators avail. Cr cds: A, C, D, DS, ER, MC, V, JCB.

D 🏊 ⚓ ⊘ ◔ SC

★★**HOLIDAY INN MAINGATE.** 1850 S Harbor Blvd (92802), Anaheim Convention Center 1 blk; 1 blk S of Disneyland. 714/750-2801; FAX 714/971-4754. 312 rms, 5–8 story. S, D $89–$99; each addl $10; suites $175–$250; under 19 free. Crib free. TV; cable. Heated pool; wading pool. Restaurant 6 am–10 pm. Rm serv. Bar noon–midnight; entertainment. Ck-out noon. Coin lndry. Convention facilities. Valet serv. Concierge. Gift shop. Free Disneyland, Knott's Berry Farm transportation. Game rm. Some refrigerators. Cr cds: A, C, D, DS, MC, V, JCB.

D ⚓ ⊘ ◔ SC

★★★**HOWARD JOHNSON.** 1380 S Harbor Blvd (92802), opp Disneyland. 714/776-6120; FAX 714/533-3578. 320 rms in 6 bldgs, 2, 4 & 7 story. S $59–$70; D $65–$85; each addl $7; suites $145; under 18 free; package plans. Crib free. TV; cable, in-rm movies. 2 heated pools; wading pool, whirlpool, poolside serv. Coffee in rms. Restaurant 6 am–midnight. Rm serv to 10 pm. Ck-out noon. Coin lndry. Meeting rm. Bellhops. Valet serv. Gift shop. Free Disneyland transportation. Game rm. Some refrigerators. Private patios, balconies. Cr cds: A, C, D, DS, ER, MC, V, JCB.

D ⚓ ⊘ ◔ SC

★ ★JOLLY ROGER HOTEL. *640 W Katella Ave (92802), 1 blk S of Disneyland.* 714/772-7621; res: 800/446-1555; FAX 714/772-2308. 235 rms, 2–4 story. S, D $65–$95; each addl $10; suites $185–$200; under 17 free. Crib free. TV; cable, in-rm movies. 2 heated pools; whirlpools. Restaurant 6:30 am–11 am. Rm serv. Bar 10:30–2 am; entertainment. Ck-out 11 am. Meeting rms. Valet serv. Sundries. Gift shop. Barber, beauty shop. Free Disneyland transportation. Some refrigerators. Bathrm phone, wet bar in suites. Balconies. Cr cds: A, C, D, DS, MC, V.

D ⅊ ⌲ ⊘ ◎ SC

✔ ★ ★QUALITY HOTEL MAINGATE. *616 Convention Way (92802), Anaheim Convention Center adj; 2 blks S of Disneyland.* 714/750-3131; FAX 714/750-9027. 284 rms, 9 story. S $55–$95; D $65–$95; each addl $10; suites $90–$250; under 18 free. Crib free. Pet accepted. TV. Heated pool; poolside serv. Restaurant 6:30 am–5 pm; dining rm 5–10 pm. Rm serv. Bar 4 pm–midnight; entertainment, dancing. Ck-out noon. Convention facilities. Bellhops. Gift shop. Beauty shop. Disneyland, bus depot transportation. Game rm. Balconies. Cr cds: A, C, D, DS, ER, MC, V, JCB.

D ⅊ ⌲ ⊘ ◎ SC

★RAMADA MAINGATE. *1460 S Harbor Blvd (92802), opp Disneyland.* 714/772-6777; FAX 714/999-1727. 465 rms, 9 story. S $79–$89; D $89–$99; each addl (after 4th person) $10; suites $110; under 18 free; package plans. Crib free. TV; cable. Heated pool; whirlpool. Complimentary coffee in rms. Restaurant adj 6 am–midnight. Ck-out noon. Coin lndry. Meeting rms. Bellhops. Valet serv. Sundries. Gift shop. Game rm. Some refrigerators. Cr cds: A, C, D, DS, ER, MC, V, JCB.

D ⌲ ⊘ ◎ SC

★ ★ ★SHERATON ANAHEIM HOTEL. *1015 W Ball Rd (92802), near jct I-5 & Harbor Blvd.* 714/778-1700; FAX 714/535-3889. 491 units, 3 & 4 story. May–Sept: S $115; D $130; each addl $15; suites $265; under 18 free; lower rates rest of yr. Crib free. TV; cable, in-rm movies. Heated pool. Restaurant 6 am–11 pm. Bar. Ck-out noon. Coin lndry. Convention facilities. Bellhops. Valet serv. Gift shop. Airport transportation; free Disneyland transportation. Game rm. Wet bars. Disneyland 2 blks. Cr cds: A, C, D, DS, ER, MC, V, JCB.

D ⌲ ⊘ ◎ SC

Hotels

★ ★ ★CROWN STERLING SUITES. *3100 E Frontera St (92806), CA 91, Glassell St exit, S to Frontera St then 1 blk E.* 714/632-1221; res: 800/433-4600; FAX 714/632-9963. 222 suites, 7 story. S $129–$139; D $139–$149; each addl $10; under 12 free. Pet accepted, some restrictions; $5 per day. TV; cable, in-rm movies. Indoor pool; whirlpool, sauna, steam rm. Complimentary full bkfst. Coffee in rms. Restaurants 11 am–11 pm. Bar to 1 am; entertainment, dancing. Ck-out noon. Meeting rms. Gift shop. Free Disneyland, Knott's Berry Farm and Convention Center transportation. Refrigerators. Private patios, decks. 7-story atrium courtyard with fountains, koi ponds, ducks, waterfalls. Cr cds: A, C, D, DS, ER, MC, V.

D ⅊ ⌲ ⊘ ◎ SC

★ ★ ★DISNEYLAND HOTEL. *1150 W Cerritos Ave (92802), opp Disneyland.* 714/778-6600; FAX 714/956-6582. 1,131 rms, 11–14 story. S, D $150–$185; each addl $15; suites from $400; under 18 free. Crib free. Parking $10. TV; cable. 3 heated pools. Playground. Restaurants 6:30 am–midnight. Bars 11–2 am. Ck-out 11 am. Convention facilities. Concierge. Shopping arcade. Airport, bus depot, Disneyland transportation (monorail & tram). Lighted tennis. Exercise rm; instructor, weight machine, bicycles. Game rm. Minibars. Private patios, balconies. On 60 acres. Tropical gardens, waterfalls, fish ponds. Amphitheater; fantasy water shows. Beach, marina, pedalboats. *LUXURY LEVEL:* CONCIERGE LEVEL. 69 rms, 10 suites, 3 floors. S, D $210–$230; suites $300–$2,000. Concierge. Private lounge, honor bar. Complimentary continental bkfst, refreshments. Cr cds: A, C, D, MC, V, JCB.

D ⅊ ⌲ 𝍠 ⊘ ◎ SC

★GRAND. *1 Hotel Way (92802), opp Disneyland.* 714/772-7777; res: 800/421-6662; FAX 714/774-7281. 242 units, 9 story. S $85–$110; D $95–$120; each addl $10; suites $125–$235; under 18 free. Crib free. Pet accepted, some restrictions. TV; cable, in-rm movies. Pool; poolside serv. Playground. Restaurant 6 am–11 pm. Bar 11:30–2 am. Ck-out noon. Convention facilities. Gift shop. Airport transportation. Exercise equipt; weight machines, bicycle, whirlpool. Game rm. Refrigerator in some suites; wet bar in luxury suites. Balconies. Cr cds: A, C, D, DS, ER, MC, V, JCB.

D ⅊ ⌲ 𝍠 ⊘ ◎ SC

★ ★HILTON HOTEL & TOWERS. *777 Convention Way (92802), 2 blks S of Disneyland.* 714/750-4321; FAX 714/740-4460. 1,600 units, 14 story. S $160–$220; D $180–$245; each addl $20; suites $550–$1,050; family rates. Crib free. Covered parking: valet $8, garage in/out $6. TV; cable. 2 heated pools, 1 indoor; poolside serv. Free supervised child's activities (Memorial Day–Labor Day). 4 restaurants 6–2 am. 3 bars from 11 am; entertainment, dancing. Ck-out noon. Convention facilities. Concierge. Shopping arcade. Barber, beauty shop. Free Disneyland, bus depot transportation. Exercise rm; instructor, weights, bicycles, whirlpool, sauna, steam rm. Some refrigerators. Some private patios, balconies. *LUXURY LEVEL:* THE TOWERS. 135 rms, 9 suites. S $235; D $255; suites $700–$1,400. Private lounge. Full wet bar in suites. In-rm movies. Complimentary continental bkfst, refreshments, newspaper.
Cr cds: A, C, D, DS, ER, MC, V, JCB.

D ⌲ 𝍠 ⊘ ◎ SC

★ ★ ★HYATT REGENCY ALICANTE. *100 Plaza Alicante (92803), jct Harbor & Chapman Blvds, 1 mi S of Disneyland.* 714/750-1234; FAX 714/740-0465. 396 rms, 17 story. S $79–$129; D $89–$149; each addl $25; suites $225–$895; under 17 free; Disneyland & Knott's Berry Farm packages. Valet parking $6. TV; cable, in-rm movies. Heated pool; poolside serv. Supervised child's activities (Fri, Sat evenings). Restaurant 6 am–midnight. Bar 11–2 am. Ck-out noon. Convention facilities. Concierge. Shopping arcade. Airport, RR station, bus depot, Disneyland transportation. Tennis. Exercise equipt; weights, bicycles, whirlpool. Game rm. Some bathrm phones. Some balconies. 17-story atrium with 60-ft palm trees provides tropical atmosphere. Cr cds: A, C, D, DS, ER, MC, V, JCB.

D ⅊ ⌲ 𝍠 ⊘ ◎ SC

★ ★ ★MARRIOTT. *700 W Convention Way (92802), adj to Anaheim Convention Center; Disneyland 2 blks.* 714/750-8000; FAX 714/750-9100. 1,033 rms, 19 story. S $119–$169; D $139–$199; each addl $10; suites $150–$900; parlor rms $160; under 18 free. Crib free. Garage parking $5; valet $12. TV; cable. 2 heated pools, 1 indoor/outdoor; poolside serv. Continental bkfst in lobby. Restaurant 6:30 am–11 pm; Fri, Sat to midnight. Bar 11–2 am. Ck-out noon. Coin lndry. Convention facilities. Concierge. Shopping arcade. Barber, beauty shop. Airport transportation. Free Disneyland transportation. Exercise equipt; weights, bicycles, 2 whirlpools, sauna. Game rm. Bathrm phone, refrigerator in some rms. Some balconies. *LUXURY LEVEL:* CONCIERGE LEVEL. 69 rms, 2 floors. S $169; D $180. Ck-out 4 pm. Concierge. Private lounge, honor bar. Complimentary continental bkfst, refreshments, newspaper.
Cr cds: A, C, D, DS, MC, V, JCB.

D ⌲ 𝍠 ⊘ ◎ SC

★ ★PAN PACIFIC. *1717 S West St (92802), opp Disneyland.* 714/999-0990; res: 800/821-8976 (exc CA), 800/321-8976 (CA); FAX 714/999-0745. 502 rms, 15 story. S, D $125–$175; each addl $10; suites $350–$750; under 18 free; seasonal packages. Garage parking $6, valet $10. TV; cable. Heated pool; whirlpool. Restaurant 6:30 am–11 pm. Bar 11–2 am. Ck-out noon. Convention facilities. Concierge. Health club privileges. Some refrigerators. Some private patios. Central atrium with skylight; observation elevator. Cr cds: A, C, D, MC, V, JCB.

D ⌲ ⊘ ◎ SC

Restaurants

★★**BESSIE WALLS.** *1074 N Tustin Ave, CA 91 Tustin Ave exit, 1 blk N.* 714/630-2812. Hrs: 11 am–2:30 pm, 5–9 pm; Sat from 5 pm; Sun brunch 10 am–2:30 pm. Closed Dec 25. Res accepted. Bar. Semi-a la carte: lunch $5.95–$9.95, dinner $7.95–$19.95. Sun brunch $14.95. Child's meals. Specializes in early California dishes. Piano bar Fri, Sat. Parking. In Spanish-styled mansion. Panoramic view of nearby hills and lake. Cr cds: A, DS, MC, V.

D

★★**THE CATCH.** *1929 S State College Blvd, opp Anaheim Stadium.* 714/634-1829. Hrs: 11:30 am–2:30 pm, 5–9:30 pm; Fri to 10:30 pm; Sat 5–10:30 pm. Closed Sun (exc LA Angels games). Res accepted. Bar. Semi-a la carte: lunch $7.95–$11.95, dinner $9.50–$19.95. Child's meals. Specializes in fresh seafood, pasta, prime rib. Valet parking. Outdoor dining. Cr cds: A, C, D, MC, V.

D SC

★★**CATTLEMAN'S WHARF.** *1160 W Ball Rd, near jct I-5 & Harbor Blvd.* 714/535-1622. Hrs: 5–10 pm; Fri, Sat to 11 pm; Sun from 4 pm; Sun brunch 10 am–2 pm. Res accepted. Bar. Semi-a la carte: dinner $9.95–$32.95. Sun brunch $11.95. Child's meals. Specializes in steak, seafood. Entertainment. Valet parking. 5 dining rms: Shogun, Garden, Tara, Ben Franklin, Paulette's. Different design in each rm. Cr cds: A, C, D, DS, MC, V.

D

★★**FOXFIRE.** *5717 Santa Ana Canyon Rd, CA 91 Imperial Hwy exit S.* 714/974-5400. Hrs: 11 am–10 pm; Sat from 5 pm; Sun 10 am–2 pm, 4:30–9 pm; early-bird dinner 5–6:30 pm; Sun brunch 10 am–2 pm. Closed most major hols. Res accepted. Continental menu. Bar to 1:30 am Tues–Sat. Semi-a la carte: lunch $6.75–$13.95, dinner $7.95–$22.95. Sun brunch $15.95. Child's meals. Specializes in pasta, prime rib, seafood. Band Tues–Sat. Parking. Family-owned. Cr cds: A, C, D, MC, V.

D SC

✔★**HANSA HOUSE SMORGASBORD.** *1840 S Harbor Blvd, 1 blk S of Disneyland.* 714/750-2411. Hrs: 7–11 am, noon–3 pm, 4:30–9 pm. Scandinavian menu. Bar. Buffet: bkfst $5.25, lunch $6.25, dinner $9.95. Sun brunch buffet $7.50. Child's meals. Specialty: Swedish-American smorgasbord. Salad bar. Parking. Scandinavian decor. Family-owned. Cr cds: A, DS, MC, V.

✔★**THE KETTLE.** *1776 W Lincoln Ave, I-5 Euclid St exit, S to Lincoln Ave then ¼ mi W.* 714/774-5557. Hrs: 11 am–10 pm; Sat, Sun from 4 pm; early-bird dinner 4–6:30 pm. Closed Mon. Res accepted. Continental menu. Bar. Semi-a la carte: lunch $4.95–$7.95, dinner $9.95–$14.95. Child's meals. Specializes in steak, seafood. Entertainment. Parking. Early Amer decor; 2 fireplaces. Cr cds: A, C, D, MC, V.

★★★**MR. STOX.** *1105 E Katella Ave, CA 57 Katella Ave exit, 1 mi W.* 714/634-2994. Hrs: 11:30 am–11 pm; Sat, Sun from 5:30 pm. Closed Jan 1, July 4, Dec 25. Res accepted. Bar. Wine cellar. A la carte entrees: lunch $7.25–$13.95, dinner $7.95–$29.95. Specializes in fresh seafood, pasta. Own baking, herbs, desserts. Pianist, harpist. Valet parking. Cr cds: A, C, D, DS, MC, V.

★★**THEE WHITE HOUSE.** *887 S Anaheim Blvd, near jct I-5 & Harbor Blvd.* 714/772-1381. Hrs: 11:30 am–2:30 pm, 5:30–10 pm; Sat, Sun from 5:30 pm. Closed major hols. Res accepted. Northern Italian menu. Bar. A la carte entrees: lunch $6.75–$12.50, dinner $16–$25. Specializes in veal, pasta, fresh fish. Parking. Built 1909; restored estate fashioned after the White House. Cr cds: A, C, D, MC, V.

D

Antioch (E-2)

Pop: 62,195 **Elev:** 25 ft **Area code:** 510 **Zip:** 94509

What to See and Do

1. **Contra Loma Regional Park.** From CA 4, S on Lone Tree Way to Golf Course Rd then right on Frederickson Lane to park entrance. Approx 775 acres. Lake swimming (summer, daily), sand beach; fishing; boating. Hiking, bicycling. Picnicking, concession. (Daily) Phone 757-0404. Per vehicle ¢¢

2. **Black Diamond Mines Regional Preserve.** From CA 4, S on Somersville Rd. These 3,650 acres on flanks of Mt Diablo (see MT DIABLO STATE PARK) contain coal, silica sand mines and the Rose Hill Cemetery. Hiking, bicycle and bridle trails. Picnicking. Naturalist programs. Preserve (daily). Phone 757-2620.

(For further information contact the Chamber of Commerce, 608 W 2nd St; 757-1800.)

Annual Event

Contra Costa County Fair. Fairgrounds, 10th & L Sts. Phone 757-4400. Late July.

(See Concord, Martinez, Oakland, Vallejo)

Motels

★★**BEST WESTERN HERITAGE INN.** *3210 Delta Fair Blvd.* 510/778-2000; FAX 510/778-2000, ext 200. 75 units, 3 story. S $67–$77; D $73–$82; each addl $5; suites, kits. $95–$150; under 12 free. Crib free. TV; cable. Pool; whirlpool. Complimentary continental bkfst. Restaurant adj open 24 hrs. Meeting rms. Some refrigerators. Cr cds: A, C, D, DS, MC, V.

D ⇌ ⊛ ⊚ SC

✔★★**RAMADA.** *2436 Mahogany Way.* 510/754-6600; FAX 510/754-6828. 116 rms, 3 story. S $58–$66; D $63–$71; each addl $8; suites $77–$150; under 16 free. Crib free. TV; cable. Heated pool; whirlpool. Complimentary continental bkfst. Coffee in rms. Restaurant nearby. Coin lndry. Meeting rms. Sundries. Refrigerators. Cr cds: A, C, D, DS, MC, V, JCB.

D ⇌ ⊛ ⊚ SC

Restaurant

★**RIVERVIEW LODGE.** *Foot of I Street.* 510/757-2272 or -2273. Hrs: 11 am–midnight. Closed Dec 25. Res accepted. Bar to 2 am. A la carte entrees: lunch, dinner $4.25–$16. Specializes in seafood, prime rib. Parking. Overlooks San Joaquin River; some dockage. Family-owned. Cr cds: A, C, D, MC, V.

Anza-Borrego Desert State Park (J-5 – K-5)

Approximately 600,000 acres of desert wilderness are preserved here, relieved by an occasional spring-fed oasis and colorful canyons. CA 78 bisects the park, with Borrego Springs (see), park headquarters and the visitor center to the north. Other improved roads are County S-2, S-3 and S-22. Anyone who wants to explore seriously must use a 4-wheel drive vehicle; road condition information is available at the visitor center. Driving across sand can be rough on vehicles and passengers. The best time to visit is November–mid-May. Six hundred species of flowering plants in the park soften the somewhat austere landscape during the spring months. Elephant trees reach the northernmost limits of their range in Anza-Borrego Park; rare smoke trees and fan palms grow here around natural seeps and springs. The park provides a refuge for wildlife, including roadrunners, rare Bighorn sheep and kit foxes. There are nature, hiking and bridle trails and picnic grounds. Improved campsites (trailer hookups in Borrego Springs) are scattered in the park; primitive camping is allowed throughout the park and there is a horse campground. Naturalist programs, tours, campfire programs are offered weekends, November–May. A self-guided auto tour brochure is available at the visitor center (Oct–May, daily; rest of yr, wkends), west of Borrego Springs (see). Standard fees. Phone 619/767-5311.

Arcadia (H-4)

Pop: 48,290 **Elev:** 485 ft **Area code:** 818

Arcadia is known as the home of Santa Anita Park racetrack.

What to See and Do

1. **Los Angeles State and County Arboretum.** 301 N Baldwin Ave, 6 mi N of San Bernardino Frwy and just S of Foothill Frwy. More than 200 peacocks roam 127 acres; plants from many parts of the world. Water conservation garden; aquatic gardens and waterfalls. Historical area with Hugo Reid Adobe (1839), Queen Anne Cottage (1885). Greenhouses, library, demonstration home gardens. Tram tours. Sr citizen rate. (Daily) Phone 821-3222. ¢¢

2. **Santa Anita Park.** 285 W Huntington Dr. Thoroughbred racing. (Early Oct–early Nov & Dec 26–late Apr, Wed–Sun; closed some major hols) Phone 574-7223.

(For further information contact the Chamber of Commerce, 388 W Huntington Dr, 91007; 447-2159.)

(See Los Angeles, Pasadena)

Motels

 ★★**HAMPTON INN.** *311 E Huntington Dr (91006).* 818/574-5600; FAX 818/446-2748. 131 rms, 4 story. S $55–$63; D $65–$73; under 18 free; higher rates Rose Bowl. Crib free. Pet accepted. TV; cable. Heated pool. Complimentary continental bkfst, coffee. Restaurant adj 11–1 am. Ck-out noon. Cr cds: A, C, D, DS, MC, V.

★★**RESIDENCE INN BY MARRIOTT.** *321 E Huntington Dr (91006).* 818/446-6500; FAX 818/446-5824. 120 kit. suites, 2 story. Kit. suites $112–$142; higher rates Rose Bowl (4-night min). Crib free. Pet accepted; $50–$75 per visit. TV. Heated pool; whirlpool. Complimentary continental bkfst. Complimentary coffee in rms. Restaurant nearby. Ck-out noon. Coin lndry. Meeting rms. Valet serv. Free airport transportation. Cr cds: A, C, D, DS, MC, V, JCB.

Hotel

★★★**EMBASSY SUITES.** *211 E Huntington Dr (91006).* 818/445-8525; FAX 818/445-8548. 194 suites, 7 story. S $119–$155; D $134–$170; each addl $15; under 12 free; wkend rates. Crib free. Pet accepted, some restrictions; $5 per day. TV; cable. Indoor pool; whirlpool, sauna, steam rm. Complimentary full bkfst. Restaurant 11 am–3 pm, 5–10 pm. Ck-out 1 pm. Lndry facilities. Gift shop. Free airport transportation. Refrigerators. Cr cds: A, C, D, DS, MC, V.

Restaurants

★★★**CHEZ SATEAU.** *850 S Baldwin Ave.* 818/446-8806. Hrs: 11:30 am–2:30 pm, 5:30–9 pm; Fri, Sat to 10 pm; early-bird dinner 5:30–6:30 pm; Sun brunch 10:30 am–2:30 pm. Closed Mon; Jan 1. Res accepted. Continental menu. Bar. Wine list. Semi-a la carte: lunch $9–$12.50, dinner $13–$20. *Prix fixe:* dinner (5:30–6:30 pm) $17.25. Sun brunch $14.75. Specializes in fish & seasonal dishes. Own pastries. Valet parking. Country French decor. Cr cds: A, C, D, MC, V, JCB.

D

★★**THE DERBY.** *233 E Huntington Dr.* 818/447-8173. Hrs: 11 am–midnight; Sat 4 pm–midnight; Sun 5–11 pm. Closed Dec 25. Res accepted. Semi-a la carte: lunch $5.95–$15.95, dinner $10.95–$24.95. Child's meals. Specializes in steak, seafood, pasta, cappuccino. Own cheesecakes. Entertainment Wed–Sat. Valet parking. Beamed ceiling, fireplaces. Portraits of famous Thoroughbreds & jockeys. Family-owned. Cr cds: A, C, D, DS, MC, V.

★★★**LA PARISIENNE.** *(1101 E Huntington Dr, Monrovia) I-210 Mountain Ave exit, N to Huntington then E 2 blks.* 818/357-3359. Hrs: 11:30 am–2 pm, 5:30–9:30 pm; Sat 5–10 pm. Closed Sun; most major hols. Res accepted. French menu. Bar. Wine list. Semi-a la carte: lunch $9.95–$14.95, dinner $14.95–$21.95. Specialties: bouillabaisse, duck with orange sauce, veal Normande. Own pastries. French country atmosphere. Cr cds: A, C, MC, V.

D

Atascadero (G-2)

Founded: 1913 **Pop:** 23,138 **Elev:** 855 ft **Area code:** 805 **Zip:** 93422

In the foothills of the Santa Lucia Mountains, Atascadero was founded by St Louis publisher E.G. Lewis, who also founded University City, Missouri. Lewis developed the town to be a self-sustaining community or colony. However, as with his Missouri venture, Lewis was forced into bankruptcy after ten years and the community failed to achieve its objective.

What to See and Do

1. **Atascadero Historical Society Museum.** 6500 Palma Ave. E.G. Lewis' original Atascadero Colony Administration Building (1918); Italian-Renaissance architecture. Houses displays on local history and Lewis' projects. (Daily exc Sun; closed hols) Fee for some special events. Phone 466-8341. **Free.**

2. **Atascadero Lake.** 2 mi W of US 101 on CA 41. Fishing. Picnicking, playground. Phone 461-5085. On premises is

   Paddock Zoo. Assortment of domestic, native and exotic animals. (Daily; closed Jan 1, Thanksgiving, Dec 25) Phone 461-5080. ¢

3. **Pesenti Winery.** 2900 Vineyard Dr, N via US 101, exit CA 46W in Templeton. Wine tasting, gifts, glassware, self-guided tours. (Daily; closed Dec 25) Phone 434-1030. **Free.**

(For further information and a list of wineries contact the Chamber of Commerce, 6550 El Camino Real; 466-2044.)

Annual Event

Colony Days. Parade, activities, arts & crafts, displays, food booths. 3rd Sat Oct.

(For accommodations see Morro Bay, Paso Robles, San Luis Obispo)

Auburn (D-2)

Settled: 1848 **Pop:** 10,592 **Elev:** 1,297 ft **Area code:** 916 **Zip:** 95603

Here is a town with a split personality: the restored "old town" retains its gold rush boomtown flavor; the other Auburn, built on a hilltop, is a modern city. In 1848 a mining camp called North Fork Dry Diggins was renamed for Auburn, New York. It developed as a center for gold rush camps and survived when the railroad came through and orchards were planted after the gold gave out.

What to See and Do

1. **Old Town.** Walk along Lincoln Way, Sacramento, Commercial & Court Sts. Restored area. Chamber of Commerce has information.
2. **Gold Country Museum.** 1273 High St, at the Gold Country Fairgrounds. Exhibits depicting early days of Placer County; history of gold mining and lifestyle of gold miners. (Daily exc Mon; closed hols) Phone 889-6500. ¢ Admission includes

    Bernhard Museum Complex. 291 Auburn-Folsom Rd. Restored 14-room house (1851), winery (1874) and art gallery. Living history programs. Guided tours (daily exc Mon; closed hols). Phone 889-6500.
3. **Folsom Lake State Recreation Area.** Off Folsom-Auburn Rd, near the town of Folsom. This 17,545-acre area offers swimming, water-skiing; fishing; boating (rentals, marina). Bicycle, hiking and bridle trails. Historic Folsom Powerhouse (Wed–Sun). Picnicking, concession; camping (dump station). Standard fees. Phone 988-0205.

(For further information contact the Auburn Area Chamber of Commerce, 601 Lincoln Way; 885-5616.)

Annual Events

Wild West Stampede. Gold Country Fairgrounds. 3rd wkend Apr.

Placer County Fair. 2 mi N off I-80, on Washington Blvd in Roseville. Phone 786-2023. Mid-July.

Gold Country Fair. Thurs–Sun, wkend after Labor Day wkend.

(See Grass Valley, Placerville, Sacramento)

Motels

★★**AUBURN INN.** *1875 Auburn Ravine Rd, CA 49 at Foresthill exit.* 916/885-1800; res: 800/272-1444; FAX 916/888-6424. 81 rms, 2 story. S $52–$58; D $58–$64; each addl $6; suites $100–$120; under 12 free. Crib $4. TV; cable. Heated pool (seasonal); whirlpool. Complimentary continental bkfst. Restaurant opp open 24 hrs. Ck-out noon. Coin lndry. Meeting rms. Cr cds: A, C, D, MC, V.

✔★**BEST WESTERN GOLDEN KEY.** *13450 Lincoln Way, CA 49 at Foresthill exit.* 916/885-8611; FAX 916/888-0319. 68 rms, 2 story. S $50–$55; D $56–$58; each addl $6; wkly rates. Crib $4. Pet accepted, some restrictions. TV. Heated pool. Complimentary continental bkfst. Coffee in rms. Restaurant nearby. Ck-out noon. Coin lndry. Meeting rm. Some refrigerators. Cr cds: A, C, D, DS, ER, MC, V, JCB.

Restaurants

★★**HEADQUARTER HOUSE.** *47500 Musso Rd, NE off I-80 Bell exit.* 916/878-1906. Hrs: 11:30 am–2:30 pm, 5–10 pm; Sun 4:30–9:30 pm; Sun brunch 10 am–2 pm. Closed Mon, Tues; some hols. Res accepted. Continental menu. Bar. Semi-a la carte: lunch $8.95–$11.75, dinner $18–$23. Sun brunch $8.50–$12.95. Specialties: salmon sauté, prime rib. Own desserts, mission bread. Pianist evenings and Sun brunch. Parking. Totally nonsmoking. Cr cds: A, C, DS, MC, V.

D

✔★**LOU LA BONTE'S.** *13460 Lincoln Way, CA 49 at Foresthill exit.* 916/885-9193. Hrs: 6:30 am–10 pm; Fri, Sat to 10:30 pm. Continental menu. Bar. Semi-a la carte: bkfst $3.95–$8.95, lunch $5–$9.50, dinner $6.95–$16.95. Brunch $6.95–$10.95. Child's meals.

Specializes in steak, seafood, prime rib. Piano bar. Dinner theater. Parking. Cr cds: A, C, D, MC, V.

Avalon (Catalina Island) (J-3)

Pop: 2,918 **Elev:** 20 ft **Area code:** 310 **Zip:** 90704

Avalon is the sportfishing and resort capital of 22-mile-long, 8-mile-wide Santa Catalina Island. The peaks of the island rise from the Pacific, 29 miles southwest of Los Angeles harbor. The waters abound with tuna, swordfish, sea bass, barracuda and mackerel. Scuba diving, golf, tennis, riding, swimming and hunting are popular.

Discovered in 1542 by Juan Rodriguez Cabrillo, the Portuguese navigator, it was named by the Spanish explorer Sebastian Viscaino in 1602. Later, Russians and Aleuts used the island as a base to hunt sea otter. The town experienced a brief miniature gold rush in 1863. In 1919, William Wrigley, Jr, chewing gum magnate and owner of the Chicago Cubs major league baseball team, bought controlling interest in the Santa Catalina Island Company from the Banning brothers, who had incorporated the island. Wrigley established a program of conservation that still applies; today, 86% of Catalina Island is protected by the Santa Catalina Island Conservancy. Tourism is the island's only industry and source of revenue today.

Daily air or boat service to the island is available all year from Long Beach (see) and San Pedro; boat service only from Newport Beach and San Diego.

What to See and Do

1. **Wrigley Memorial and Botanical Garden.** 1400 Avalon Canyon Rd. Native trees, cactus, succulent plants and flowering shrubs on 38 acres surround memorial to a man who contributed much to Catalina Island. (Daily). Tram may run here from Island Plaza (summer only; fee). Phone 510-2288. ¢
2. **Catalina tours and trips.** Santa Catalina Island Company Discovery Tours offer boat and bus tours to several points of interest. Contact Box 737, phone 510-2500 or 800/4-AVALON (CA). Catalina Adventure Tours offers boat and bus tours. Contact Box 1314; 510-2888.
3. **Catalina Island Museum.** Casino Building. Permanent exhibits on history of island; natural history and archaeology displays. (Daily) Phone 510-2414. ¢

(For further information and a free booklet listing many annual events, contact the Catalina Island Chamber of Commerce & Visitors Bureau, PO Box 217; 510-1520.)

(See Laguna Beach, Long Beach, Newport Beach, San Pedro)

Motels

★**EL TERADO TERRACE.** *230 Marilla Ave.* 310/510-0831. 18 rms, 2 story, 2 suites. No A/C. No rm phones. May–Oct: S, D $75–$120; each addl $10; suites $170; lower rates rest of yr. TV. Complimentary coffee in rms. Restaurant nearby. Ck-out 11 am. Free shuttle to boat dock. Whirlpool. Some refrigerators. Cr cds: A, DS, MC, V.

★**SEAPORT VILLAGE INN.** *(Box 2411) 119 Maiden Lane.* 310/510-0344; res: 800/222-8254. 28 rms, 4 story, 11 kits. No rm phones. May–Sept: S, D $99–$199; each addl $15; suites, kit. units (1–4 people) $169–$199; package plans; lower rates rest of yr. Crib free. TV.

Complimentary coffee. Ck-out 10 am. Whirlpool. Some refrigerators. Balconies. Picnic tables, grills. Harbor view. Cr cds: A, MC, V.

★★VILLA PORTOFINO. *(Box 127) 111 Crescent Ave. 310/510-0555.* 34 rms, 3 story. No A/C. No elvtr. No rm phones. June–Sept & wkends: S, D $86–$110; each addl $10; suites $145–$250; lower rates rest of yr. Crib $10. TV; cable. Complimentary continental bkfst. Restaurant 5–10 pm. Bar 5–1 am. Ck-out 11 am. Bellhops. Sun deck. Some rms overlook bay. Cr cds: A, C, D, DS, MC, V.

★★★VISTA DEL MAR. *(Box 1979) 417 Crescent Ave. 310/510-1452; FAX 310/510-2917.* 13 rms, 2 suites. All rms on 3rd floor. May–Oct: S, D $95–$275; lower rates rest of yr. Crib free. TV; cable, in-rm movies. Complimentary continental bkfst. Coffee in rms. Ck-out 11 am. Refrigerators, fireplaces. Some in-rm whirlpools. Swimming beach. Atrium courtyard. Cr cds: A, DS, MC, V.

Motor Hotel

★★★HOTEL ST LAUREN. *(Box 497) Metropole & Beacon. 310/510-2299.* 42 rms, 6 story. May–mid-Oct: S, D $85–$200; each addl $25; package plans avail; lower rates rest of yr. Crib free. TV; cable. Restaurant nearby. Ck-out 11 am. Victorian-style architecture. Ocean 1 blk. Cr cds: MC, V.

Hotels

★GLENMORE PLAZA. *(Box 155) 120 Sumner Ave. 310/510-0017; res: 800/422-8254; FAX 310/510-2833.* 50 rms, 4 story, 4 suites. No elvtr. Apr–Nov: S, D $85–$225; suites $210–$400; under 12 free; higher rates wkends (2-night min); lower rates rest of yr. Crib avail. TV; cable. Complimentary continental bkfst. No rm serv. Ck-out 10:30 am. Free boat dock transportation. Built 1891. Bay ½ blk. Cr cds: A, DS, MC, V.

★HOTEL CATALINA. *(Box 365) 129 Whittley Ave. 310/510-0027.* 34 rms, 3 story. No A/C. No elvtr. No rm phones. Mid-May–Oct: S, D $85–$110; each addl $10; summer wkends 2-night min, hols 3-day min. TV. Restaurant nearby. Ck-out 10 am. Free shuttle to boat dock. Whirlpool. Picnic tables, grills. Harbor view. Restored hotel built 1892. Cr cds: A, DS, MC, V.

★★★HOTEL METROPOLE. *(Box 1900) 205 Crescent Ave, in Metropole Marketplace. 310/510-1884; res: 800/300-8528; FAX 310/510-2534.* 48 rms, 3 story. May–Oct: S, D $110–$275; each addl $15; 2-bedrm suite $675; under 12 free; off-season packages; lower rates rest of yr. Crib $15. TV; cable. Complimentary continental bkfst. No rm serv. Ck-out 11 am. Coin lndry. Meeting rms. Shopping arcade. Roof-top whirlpool & sun deck. Minibars; many in-rm whirlpools, fireplaces. Balconies. Ocean view. Totally nonsmoking. Cr cds: A, MC, V.

Inn

★★★★INN ON MT. ADA. *(PO Box 2560) 398 Wrigley Rd. 310/510-2030.* 6 rms, 2 story. AP, June–Oct & wkends: D $320–$590; each addl $100; lower wkday rates rest of yr. TV in library. Full bkfst 8:30–10 am, light deli lunch, full dinner; refreshments, wine. Ck-out 11 am, ck-in 2 pm. Complimentary transportation to and from boats and helicopter. Many fireplaces. Balconies. Historic Georgian-colonial home, former Wrigley mansion; antiques. Terrace; spectacular view of ocean, harbor,

mountains. Use of golf cart during stay. Totally nonsmoking. Cr cds: A, DS, MC, V.

Restaurants

★ANTONIO'S PIZZERIA & CATALINA CABARET. *230 Crescent Ave. 310/510-0008.* Hrs: 8 am–11 pm; Fri & Sat to midnight. Italian, Amer menu. Bar. A la carte entrees: bkfst $3.95–$6.95. Semi-a la carte: lunch $5–$8, dinner $5–$20. Specialties: Catalina calzone, pizza, pasta. Entertainment Thurs–Sun. Outdoor dining. Early 1950s decor. 1955 Seeberg juke box at each table. Overlooks harbor. Cr cds: MC, V.

★★ARMSTRONG'S FISH MARKET & SEAFOOD. *306 Crescent Ave, at harbor. 310/510-0113.* Hrs: 11 am–9 pm; Sat & Sun to 10 pm. Closed Thanksgiving, Dec 25. Bar. Semi-a la carte: lunch $5.95–$10.95, dinner $8.95–$24.95. Specializes in seafood cooked over mesquite wood, abalone, lobster. Outdoor dining. Deck overlooks harbor. Cr cds: A, DS, MC, V.

✔★★BLUE PARROTT. *205 Crescent Ave, in Metropole Marketplace. 310/510-2465.* Hrs: 11 am–midnight; Fri & Sat to 2 am. No A/C. Bar. A la carte entrees: lunch $5–$9, dinner $7–$15. Child's meals. Specializes in steak, seafood, Caribbean dishes. Polynesian decor. Harbor view. Cr cds: A, D, DS, MC, V.

★★CHANNEL HOUSE. *205 Crescent Ave, in Metropole Marketplace. 310/510-1617.* Hrs: 11 am–2 pm, 5–10 pm. Closed Jan & Feb. Res accepted. Continental menu. Bar. Semi-a la carte: lunch $5–$8, dinner $15–$29. Child's meals. Specializes in seafood, duckling à la orange, pepper steak, rack of lamb. Pianist Fri & Sat. Outdoor dining. Antique wooden bar. Cr cds: A, DS, MC, V.

Bakersfield (G-3)

Founded: 1869 **Pop:** 174,820 **Elev:** 408 ft **Area code:** 805

Surrounded by oil wells and fields of cotton and grain, Bakersfield is an important trading center—the hub of a network of highways that carry its produce and products to major cities. Founded by Colonel Thomas Baker, the town awakened in 1885 when gold was discovered in the Kern River Canyon. Overnight it changed from a placid farm town to a wild mining community, complete with gunfights and gambling halls. A fire in 1889 destroyed most of the old town and resulted in considerable modernization. The discovery of oil in 1899 rekindled the gold rush hysterics. Unlike gold, oil has remained an important part of the city's economy. Bakersfield is the seat of Kern County (8,064 square miles; third largest county in the state). Nearby vineyards produce 25 percent of California wine, and surrounding fields provide a colorful flower display in spring. A Ranger District office of the Sequoia National Forest (see PORTERVILLE) is located here.

What to See and Do

1. **Kern County Museum.** 3801 Chester Ave, 3 mi E of CA 99 & Pierce Rd interchange. Complete 16-acre outdoor museum of 60 restored or representational buildings including Queen Anne style mansion (1891), log cabin, wooden jail, hotel, drugstore; 1898 locomotive, oil-drilling rig and horse-drawn vehicles. Main museum building contains changing exhibits on natural and cultural history of the area. (Daily; closed Jan 1, Thanksgiving, Dec 24, 25 & 31) Tickets available through ticket office; phone for hrs. Sr citizen rate. Phone 32-EVENT or 861-2132. ¢¢

2. **California Living Museum.** 14000 Alfred Harrell Hwy, 12 mi NE via CA 178. Botanical garden and zoo house plants and animals native to California; natural history museum; interpretive tours. (Daily exc

Mon; closed Thanksgiving, Dec 25) Sr citizen rate. Phone 872-2256. ¢¢

3. Scenic drive. Go E on CA 178 and follow the Kern River through a rock-dotted canyon. Many fine places for picnicking, camping and fishing along the road.

4. Tule Elk State Reserve. 20 mi W via Stockdale Hwy, then S on Morris Rd to Station Rd, then ¼ mi W. This 969-acre reserve is home for a small herd of elk native only to California. Picnic shelters. Phone 765-5004. Per vehicle ¢¢

(For further information contact the Chamber of Commerce, 1033 Truxtun Ave, PO Box 1947, 93303; 327-4421.)

Annual Event

Kern County Fair. Late Sept.

Motels

★★**BEST WESTERN HILL HOUSE.** 700 Truxtun (93301), near civic center. 805/327-4064; FAX 805/327-1247. 99 rms, 2 story. S $50–$60; D $55–$65; each addl $10; suite $95; under 18 free; New Year's plans. Crib free. Pet accepted; $3. TV; cable. Pool. Complimentary continental bkfst. Restaurant 6 am–2 pm, 5–10 pm. Bar. Ck-out noon. Meeting rms. Exercise equipt; weight machine, bicycles. Refrigerators. Balconies. Cr cds: A, C, D, DS, MC, V.

D ✉ 🛬 ⓧ 🅢 Ⓒ SC

✔ ★★**CALIFORNIA INN.** 3400 Chester Lane (93309). 805/328-1100; FAX 805/328-0433. 74 units, 3 story. S $37–$41; D $39–$45; each addl $4; suites $85; under 18 free. Crib $4. TV; cable. Pool; whirlpool, sauna. Complimentary continental bkfst. Complimentary coffee in rms. Restaurant adj 6 am–11 pm. Ck-out noon. Coin lndry. Refrigerators. Cr cds: A, C, D, DS, MC, V.

D ✉ 🅢 Ⓒ SC

★★**COURTYARD BY MARRIOTT.** 3601 Marriott Dr (93308). 805/324-6660; FAX 805/324-1185. 146 rms, 3 story. S $71; D $81; suites $85–$95; wkly, wkend rates. Crib free. TV. Heated pool. Restaurant 6:30 am–2 pm, 5–10:30 pm. Serv bar 3–11 pm. Ck-out 1 pm. Coin lndry. Meeting rms. Valet serv. Exercise equipt; weight machine, bicycles, whirlpool. Some balconies. Cr cds: A, C, D, DS, MC, V.

D ✉ 🛬 ⓧ 🅢 Ⓒ SC

✔ ★**ECONOMY INNS OF AMERICA.** 6100 Knudsen Dr (93308). 805/392-1800. 156 rms, 2 story. S $22.90; D $29.90–$33.90; up to 4, $38.90. Pet accepted. TV; cable. Heated pool. Restaurant opp open 24 hrs. Ck-out 11 am. Cr cds: A, MC, V.

D ✉ 🅢 Ⓒ SC

★**LA QUINTA.** 3232 Riverside Dr (93308). 805/325-7400; FAX 805/324-6032. 129 rms, 3 story. S $52–$60; D $57–$65; each addl $5; suites $64–$69; under 18 free. Crib free. Pet accepted. TV. Heated pool. Complimentary coffee in lobby. Restaurant adj 5:30 am–10 pm. Ck-out noon. Meeting rms. Cr cds: A, C, D, DS, MC, V.

D ✉ 🅢 Ⓒ SC

★**QUALITY INN.** 1011 Oak St (93304). 805/325-0772; res: 800/221-6382 (CA); FAX 805/325-4646. 90 units, 2 story. S $42–$60; D $50–$60; each addl $5; suites from $56; under 10 free. Crib free. TV; cable, in-rm movies avail. Pool; whirlpool, sauna. Complimentary continental bkfst. Restaurant adj 6 am–11 pm. Ck-out noon. Coin lndry. Valet serv. Some private patios, balconies. Cr cds: A, C, D, DS, ER, MC, V, JCB.

D ✉ 🅢 Ⓒ SC

★★**RAMADA INN.** 3535 Rosedale Hwy (93308). 805/327-0681; FAX 805/327-0681, ext 432. 197 rms, 2 story. S $54–$62; D $67; each addl $5; under 18 free; wkend rates. Crib free. TV; cable. Pool; whirlpool. Restaurant 6:30 am–10 pm. Rm serv 7 am–9 pm. Bar 11 am–midnight; wkends 5 pm–1 am. Ck-out noon. Coin lndry. Meeting

rms. Valet serv. Free airport transportation. Patios, balconies. Cr cds: A, C, D, DS, MC, V.

D 🛬 Ⓒ SC

✔ ★★**RIO MIRADA.** 4500 Pierce Rd (93308). 805/324-5555; res: 800/822-3050 (CA); FAX 805/325-0106. 208 rms, 3 story. S $39–$46; D $46–$58; each addl $5; suites, kit. units $56–$64; under 12 free. Pet accepted; $10. TV; cable. Pool; sauna. Restaurant adj 6–10 pm. Bar. Ck-out noon. Coin lndry. Meeting rms. Valet serv. Sundries. Free airport, RR station, bus depot transportation. Refrigerator in suites. Some balconies. Grill. Cr cds: A, C, D, DS, ER, MC, V, JCB.

D ✉ 🛬 ⓧ 🅢 Ⓒ SC

★★★**SHERATON INN.** 5101 California Ave (93309). 805/325-9700; FAX 805/323-3508. 198 rms, 2 story. S $75–$110; D $85–$115; each addl $10; suites $125–$300; under 17 free. Crib free. TV; cable, in-rm movies avail. Heated pool. Complimentary continental bkfst. Coffee, tea in rms. Restaurant 6:30 am–11 pm. Rm serv. Bar 5 pm–2 am. Ck-out 1 pm. Meeting rms. Bellhops. Valet serv. Gift shop. Airport, RR station, bus depot transportation. Exercise equipt; weights, bicycles, whirlpool. Some refrigerators. Private patios. Tropical decor; atrium. Extensive grounds. Cr cds: A, C, D, DS, MC, V, JCB.

D ✉ 🛬 ⓧ 🅢 Ⓒ SC

★**SUPER 8.** 901 Real Rd (93309). 805/322-1012; FAX 805/322-7636. 90 rms, 3 story. S $42–$50; D $50–$58; each addl $3; under 12 free. Crib free. TV; cable. Pool. Complimentary continental bkfst, coffee 24 hrs. Restaurant nearby. Ck-out 11 am. Cr cds: A, C, D, DS, MC, V.

D ✉ 🅢 Ⓒ SC

Motor Hotel

★★**DAYS INN.** 3540 Rosedale Hwy (93308). 805/326-1111; FAX 805/326-1513. 122 rms, 5 story. S $55–$65; D $65–$75; each addl $10; under 18 free. Crib free. TV; cable. Heated pool; whirlpool. Restaurant 6 am–10 pm. Rm serv. Bar 5 pm–midnight. Ck-out noon. Meeting rms. Valet serv. Airport, RR station, bus depot transportation. Health club privileges. Cr cds: A, C, D, DS, MC, V.

D ✉ 🅢 Ⓒ SC

Resort

★★**RIO BRAVO.** 11200 Lake Ming Rd (93306). 805/872-5000; res: 800/282-5000; FAX 805/872-6546. 109 units, 2 story. S $68; D $78; studio rms $68–$78; each addl $10; suites $156–$234; under 12 free; golf & tennis packages. Crib free. TV; cable, in-rm movies avail. 2 pools; lifeguard (summer). Dining rm 6 am–2:30 pm, 5:30–10:30 pm. Box lunches. Bar 11 am–midnight. Ck-out noon, ck-in 2 pm. Coin lndry. Grocery, package store 5 blks. Meeting rms. Free airport, RR station, bus depot transportation. Lighted tennis, pro. Golf privileges, greens fee $45, pro, putting green, driving range. Whitewater rafting (May–Sept). Soc dir. Exercise rm; instructor, weights, bicycles, whirlpool, sauna, steam rm. Some refrigerators, fireplaces. Private patios, balconies. Cr cds: A, C, D, DS, MC, V, JCB.

D 🛟 ⛳ 🎾 ✉ 🚶 🅢 Ⓒ SC

Guest Ranch

★★**QUARTER CIRCLE U RANKIN RANCH.** (Box 36, Caliente 93518) E on CA 58 to approx 3 mi E of Caliente where road forks; either 9½ mi on left branch on steep, narrow road over mountains, or 20 mi on right branch around mountains via scenic road. 805/867-2511. 12 rms, 6 cabins. No rm phones. AP: S $135/person; D $125/person; children $80; wkly rates; lower rates Apr–May & Sept–Oct. Closed last Sun Sept–wk before Easter. Crib avail. Heated pool. Playground. Free supervised child's activities. Complimentary coffee in rms. Dining rm, 3 sittings: 7:30–9 am, 12:30 pm & 6:30 pm. Box lunches. Ck-out 1 pm, ck-in 3:30 pm. Grocery 5 mi. Meeting rms. Gift shop. Tennis. Boating. Hiking. Hay wagon rides. Lawn games. Soc dir. Square dancing. Rec rm. 31,000-acre working ranch (founded 1863) in Tehachapi Mountains. Cr cds: A, MC, V.

Restaurants

★★**MAMA TOSCA'S.** *6631 Ming Ave, in Laurelglen Plaza.* 805/831-1242. Hrs: 11:30 am–2 pm, 5:30–10 pm; Sat from 5:30 pm. Closed Sun; major hols. Res accepted. Italian, Amer menu. Bar. Semi-a la carte: lunch $6.95–$19.95, dinner $9.95–$30. Specialties: veal scaloppini, eggplant Parmesan, rack of lamb. Vocalist, band Fri & Sat. Parking. Cr cds: A, C, MC, V.

✔★**ROSA'S.** *2400 Columbus.* 805/872-1606. Hrs: 11 am–2 pm, 4–9:30 pm; Fri to 10 pm; Sat 4–10 pm; Sun 4–9:30 pm. Closed Easter, Thanksgiving, Dec 25. Res accepted. Italian, Amer menu. Wine, beer. Semi-a la carte: lunch $3.50–$5.95, dinner $7.50–$12.95. Specialties: linguine with clams, fettucine Alfredo, lasagne. Parking. Patio dining. Italian village atmosphere. Family-owned. Cr cds: MC, V.

★**WOOL GROWERS.** *620 E 19th St.* 805/327-9584. Hrs: 11:30 am–2 pm, 6–9:30 pm. Closed Sun; Thanksgiving, Dec 25. Res accepted. Basque menu. Bar 9 am–11:30 pm. Complete meals: lunch $5.50–$11.50, dinner $10.50–$15.50. Child's meals. Specializes in French Basque dishes. Parking. Family-owned. Cr cds: MC, V.

Barstow (H-4)

Founded: 1880 **Pop:** 21,472 **Elev:** 2,106 ft **Area code:** 619 **Zip:** 92311

In the heart of the beautiful high desert country, Barstow is a former frontier town that has become one of the fastest-growing cities in San Bernardino County. Once a desert junction for overland wagon trains and an outfitting station for Death Valley expeditions, Barstow thrives on nearby military installations and a $15 million tourist trade. It is the hub of three major highways that carry tourists into the Mojave Desert.

What to See and Do

1. **Calico Ghost Town Regional Park.** 10 mi E via I-15, then 4 mi N on Ghost Town Rd. Restored 1880s mining town. For six decades a dust-shrouded ghost town; privately restored in 1954. General store, old schoolhouse, the Maggie Mine, collection of paintings in "Lil's Saloon," print, pottery, basket and leather shops; tramway; railroad, mine tours; shooting gallery. (See ANNUAL EVENTS) Nearby are the Calico Mountains, which yielded $86 million in silver in 15 years. Camping (some hookups; fee). (Daily; closed Dec 25) Parking (fee); special events higher. Phone 254-2122. Parking per car ¢¢¢ E of Calico is

   Odessa Canyon. Rock-studded landscape created by volcanic action. Erosion has etched striking rock formations. No cars.

2. **Mojave River Valley Museum.** 270 E Virginia Way. Rock and mineral displays; photographs; archaeology and railroad displays; Native American exhibits. (Daily; closed major hols) Donation. Phone 256-5452.

3. **Calico Early Man Site.** 18 mi E via I-15, Minneola Rd exit, then 2¾ mi on graded dirt road. Archaeological digs; stone tool artifacts fashioned by early man approx 200,000 yrs ago are still visible in the walls of the excavations. Oldest evidence of human activity in the Western Hemisphere. Only New World site ever worked by Louis S. B. Leakey, who served as project director until his death. Two master pits open for viewing; small museum. (Thurs–Sun; closed hols) Guided tours. For further information contact Bureau of Land Management, Barstow Resource Area, 150 Coolwater Lane; 256-8313. **Free.**

4. **Rainbow Basin.** 10 mi N on Fort Irwin Rd. Panorama of rocks deeply etched with vivid colors. Owl Canyon is 1½ miles north. Strip of sharp towering rocks and balanced rocks.

5. **Afton Canyon.** 40 mi E on I-15. Created in prehistoric times when Lake Mojave broke through, chiseling a gorge through layers of multicolored rock.

6. **Mule Canyon and Fiery Gulch.** 14 mi NE. Cathedral-like rocks, S-shaped formations, crimson walls, natural arches. No cars.

(For further information contact the Desert Information Center, 831 Barstow Rd; 256-8313.)

Annual Events

Calico Hullabaloo. Calico Ghost Town (see #1). World tobacco spitting championships, old miner's stew cook-off, flapjack races, horseshoe pitching championships. Palm Sunday wknd.

Calico Spring Festival. Calico Ghost Town (see #1). Fiddle and banjo contests, bluegrass music, gunfights, 1880s games, clogging hoedown. Mother's Day wknd.

Calico Days. Calico Ghost Town (see #1). Country music, Wild West parade, national gunfight stunt championship, burro race, 1880s games. Columbus Day wknd.

Calico Fine Arts Festival. Calico Ghost Town (see #1). Native American dance and works of art by many of the west's foremost artists displayed along Main St. 1st wknd Nov.

(See Victorville)

Motels

★★**BEST WESTERN DESERT VILLA.** *1984 E Main St.* 619/256-1781; FAX 619/256-9265. 95 rms, 2 story, 8 kit. units. S $62–$76; D $64–$78; each addl $2; kit. units $67–$70; under 12 free. Crib free. TV; cable, in-rm movies avail. Pool; whirlpool. Complimentary continental bkfst 6–10 am. Coffee in rms. Restaurant 5–10 pm. Ck-out noon. Coin lndry. Some refrigerators. Cr cds: A, C, D, DS, ER, MC, V, JCB.

★**HOWARD JOHNSON.** *1431 E Main St.* 619/256-0661; FAX 619/256-8392. 63 rms, 2 story. S $45–$65; D $47–$75; each addl $8; under 18 free. Crib free. TV; cable. Pool; wading pool. Coffee in lobby. Restaurant adj open 24 hrs. Ck-out noon. Meeting rm. Coin lndry. Private patios, balconies. Cr cds: A, C, D, DS, ER, MC, V, JCB.

✔★**SLEEP INN.** *1861 W Main St.* 619/256-1300; res: 800/627-5337; FAX 619/256-6825. 65 rms, 3 story. No elvtr. S $32.95–$38.95; D $43.95–$48.95; under 18 free. Crib $6. TV; in-rm movies. Heated pool. Complimentary coffee in lobby 6–9 am. Restaurant opp 6 am–11 pm. Ck-out 11 am. Cr cds: A, D, DS, ER, MC, V, JCB.

Restaurant

★★**IDLE SPURS STEAK HOUSE.** *29557 W CA 58.* 619/256-8888. Hrs: 11 am–9:30 pm; Fri, Sat to 10 pm; Sun to 9 pm. Closed Jan 1, Thanksgiving, Dec 24–25. Res accepted. Bar to midnight. Semi-a la carte: lunch $6.50–$9.95, dinner $10.95–$24.95. Specializes in prime rib. Parking. Patio dining. Western decor. Cr cds: A, MC, V.

Beaumont (J-4)

Pop: 9,685 **Elev:** 2,573 ft **Area code:** 909 **Zip:** 92223

What to See and Do

Edward-Dean Museum of Decorative Arts. 9401 Oak Glen Rd, in Cherry Valley. 17th- and 19th-century European and Asian furniture, bronzes, porcelains, rugs, paintings. (Daily exc Mon; closed hols; also Aug) Phone 845-2626. ¢

(For further information contact the Chamber of Commerce, 450 E 4th St, Box 291; 845-9541.)

(See Hemet, Palm Springs, Redlands, Riverside, San Bernardino)

Motel

✔ ★ ★ **BEST WESTERN EL RANCHO.** *550 Beaumont Ave, I-10 Beaumont Ave exit, 1 blk N.* 909/845-2176. 52 rms, 2 story. S $40–$46; D $43–$49; each addl $3; suites $43–$65. Crib $3. TV; cable. Heated pool. Restaurant 6 am–9:30 pm. Bar 9:30–1:30 am. Ck-out noon. Meeting rm. Cr cds: A, C, D, DS, MC, V.

Resort

★ ★ **HIGHLAND SPRINGS.** *(Box 218) 3 mi N of I-10, Highland Springs Ave exit.* 909/845-1151; res: 800/735-2948; FAX 909/845-8090. 94 cottages, 1 & 2 story. MAP: S $120–$170; D $140–$195; suites $180–$245; family rates. TV. Heated pool; poolside serv (summer). Free supervised child's activities (school vacations, hols). Dining rm (public by res) 9–11 am, 1–2:30 pm, 6–7:30 pm. Bar 5 pm–2 am. Ck-out noon, ck-in 3 pm. Meeting rms. Lighted tennis. Golf privileges. Exercise equipt; weight machine, bicycles, whirlpool, sauna. Hayrides. Bicycles. Lawn games. Entertainment, dancing wkends. Rec rm. Game rm. Refrigerators. Picnic tables. On 900 acres in foothills of Mt San Gorgonio. Established 1884. Cr cds: DS, MC, V.

Berkeley (E-1)

Settled: 1841 **Pop:** 102,724 **Elev:** 152 ft **Area code:** 510

Berkeley is the home of the principal campus of the University of California and more than 300 industries. With an average monthly high temperature of 64°F, Berkeley regards itself as "one of America's most refreshing cities."

Named for George Berkeley, Bishop of Cloyne, an 18th-century Irish philosopher, the area was once a part of the vast Rancho San Antonio. Shortly after a group of developers bought the townsite, the College of California was founded—later to become the University of California.

The town's population was increased by refugees from the San Francisco earthquake and fire of 1906. In September of 1923, one-quarter of Berkeley was destroyed by fire. Quickly rebuilt, the city government instituted one of the most efficient fire-prevention systems in the country.

What to See and Do

1. **University of California** (1873). (30,370 students) 2 mi E of Eastshore Frwy, I-80, at E end of University Ave. Covers more than 1,200 acres in the foothills of the E shore of San Francisco Bay. Instruction in fields of learning from agriculture to zoology. The oldest of nine campuses, its white granite buildings are surrounded by groves of oak trees; its 307-ft campanile can be seen from a great distance (elevator, fee). Phone 642-5215 for visitor information. On or near the campus are

   Phoebe Apperson Hearst Museum of Anthropology. On Bancroft Way, at end of College Ave. In Kroeber Hall. Changing exhibits on ancient and modern lands and people (daily exc Mon; closed major hols). Sr citizen rate. Phone 643-7648. ¢

   Worth Ryder Art Gallery. 116 Kroeber Hall. Changing exhibits. (Sept–May, Tues–Thurs) Hrs subject to change. Phone 642-2582. **Free.**

   Art Museum. 2626 Bancroft Way. Includes Hans Hofmann paintings, outdoor sculpture garden, Pacific Film Archive film program; 11 exhibition galleries. (Wed–Sun) Sr citizen rate. Phone 642-1207. ¢¢

   Earth Sciences Building. N Gate entrance from Hearst Ave. Museum of Paleontology seismograph; fossil (several dinosaurs, including a baby), rock and mineral collections and exhibits. (Daily; closed major hols) Phone 642-1821. **Free.**

   International House. Bancroft Way & Piedmont Ave. This is a fine example of Mission-revival architecture. The dome is visible for miles. Built in 1930, this was the second such institution in the world. It serves as home and program center for 600 foreign and American students.

   The Greek Theatre. At E Gate. Gift of William Randolph Hearst; an amphitheater where leading pop and jazz artists perform.

   Botanical Garden. On Centennial Drive in Strawberry Canyon. Many unusual plants, including native, Asian, Australian and South American collections and a redwood grove; visitor center. (Daily; closed Dec 25) Tours (Sat & Sun). Phone 642-3343. **Free.**

   Lawrence Hall of Science. Centennial Dr, S of Grizzly Peak Blvd. Hands-on exhibits and activities for all ages. Classes, films, planetarium shows, discovery labs, special events and programs on a variety of scientific topics. (Daily; closed university hols) Sr citizen rate. Phone 642-5132. ¢¢

2. **Bade Institute of Biblical Archaeology.** Pacific School of Religion, 1798 Scenic Ave. Devoted to archaeology of Palestine from 3200 B.C.–A.D. 600. Bible collection has documents from 5th–18th centuries. Museum (Mon–Fri; closed hols). Phone 848-0528, ext 211. **Free.**

3. **Judah L. Magnes Museum.** 2911 Russell St, one blk N of Pine & Ashby. Artistic, historical and literary materials, including ceremonial objects and textiles, trace Jewish life and culture throughout the world; Western Jewish History Center houses documentation of Jewish contributions to the history of the American West; research library of rare and illustrated Jewish books and manuscripts; permanent collection and changing exhibits of traditional and contemporary Jewish artists and themes. (Sun–Thurs; closed Jewish and legal hols) Guided tours (Sun & Wed; also by appt). Phone 549-6950. **Free.**

4. **Municipal Rose Garden.** Euclid Ave & Eunice St. Collection of 4,000 roses; 200 varieties. (Daily; best blooms mid-May–Sept) Phone 644-6371. **Free.**

5. **Grizzly Peak Blvd.** A winding drive along the crest of hills behind the city; it offers views of most of San Francisco Bay and the surrounding cities.

6. **Charles Lee Tilden Regional Park.** E on CA 24 to Fish Ranch Rd exit, then W to Grizzly Peak Blvd, right to park. The park's 2,078 recreational acres include swimming (fee), swimming beach, bathhouse; fishing at Lake Anza. Nature, hiking, bicycle, bridle trails. 18-hole golf (fee). Picnicking, concessions. Environmental Education Center, Little Farm, Jewel Lake. Merry-go-round, pony and steam train rides (fee); botanical garden of native California plants. Park connects with East Bay Skyline National Trail at Inspiration Point. (Daily) Phone 525-2233. **Free.**

7. **Wildcat Canyon Regional Park.** N of Tilden Regional Park, access from Tilden Nature Area. On 2,421 acres. Hiking, jogging, bicycle and bridle trails. Picnicking. Interpretive programs. Bird watching. (Daily) **Free.**

8. **Berkeley Marina.** 201 University Ave, ½ mi W of Eastshore Frwy, I-80, at W end of University Ave, on San Francisco Bay. Public fishing pier (free); bait and tackle shop; sportfishing boat; 950

berths, 25 visitor berths; phone 644-6376. Protected sailing basin; 4-lane boat ramp (fee). Motel, restaurants.

(For further information contact the Chamber of Commerce, 1834 University Ave, 94703; 549-7000 or -7003.)

(See Oakland, San Francisco, San Rafael, Sausalito)

Motel

✔ ★CAMPUS. *1619 University Ave (94703). 510/841-3844; FAX 510/841-8134.* 23 rms, 2 story, 1 kit. No A/C. S $45–$50; D $50–$60; suites $80–$95; kit. unit $80. Crib $10. TV. Complimentary coffee in rms. Restaurant nearby. Ck-out 11 am. Univ of CA 5 blks. Cr cds: A, C, DS, MC, V.

Motor Hotel

★ ★MARRIOTT BERKELEY MARINA. *200 Marina Blvd (94710). 510/548-7920; FAX 510/548-7944.* 375 rms, 4 story. S, D $129–$139; each addl $15; suites $250–$875; under 12 free. Crib free. TV; cable. 2 indoor pools; poolside serv. Restaurant 6 am–11 pm. Rm serv. Bar 11–2 am; Sun to midnight. Ck-out noon. Meeting rms. Gift shop. Exercise equipt; weights, bicycles, whirlpool, sauna. Dockage. Game rm. Rec rm. Wet bar in suites. Some balconies, private patios. *LUXURY LEVEL:* CONCIERGE LEVEL. 30 rms, 1 suite. S, D $139; suite $700. Concierge. Private lounge. Complimentary bkfst, refreshments wkdays.
Cr cds: A, C, D, DS, MC, V, JCB.

Hotels

★ ★DURANT. *2600 Durant Ave (94704). 510/845-8981; res: 800/238-7268; FAX 510/486-8336.* 140 rms, 6 story. No A/C. S $85–$140; D $95–$140; each addl $10; suites $180–$240; under 12 free. Crib free. Limited covered valet parking $5/day. TV. Complimentary continental bkfst. Restaurant 11 am–10 pm. Rm serv to 9 pm. Bar. Ck-out noon. Meeting rms. Airport transportation. Some refrigerators, wet bars. City landmark (1928). Cr cds: A, D, ER, MC, V.

★ ★SHATTUCK. *2086 Allston Way (94704). 510/845-7300; res: 800/237-5359 (exc CA), 800/742-8825 (CA); FAX 510/644-2088.* 175 rms, 6 story. No A/C. S $78–$85; D $92–$100; each addl $15; suites from $99; under 12 free. Crib $5. TV. Complimentary continental bkfst. Restaurant 7–10 am, 11:30 am–2:30 pm, 5:30–11 pm. Bar 11–1:30 am. Ck-out noon. Meeting rms. Health club adj. City landmark (1910). Cr cds: A, C, D, DS, MC, V.

Inn

★ ★ ★GRAMMA'S ROSE GARDEN INN. *2740 Telegraph Ave (94705). 510/549-2145; FAX 510/549-1085.* 40 rms. No A/C. S, D $85–$175. Free coffee, tea. Free full bkfst 7–9 am, Sat & Sun 7:30–9:30 am; refreshments 5–8 pm. Ck-out noon, ck-in 2 pm. Many fireplaces. Some private patios. Some rms in 2 restored Victorian mansions; antiques; fireplace in some rms. Some private decks; English country garden. Also Victorian-style cottage with fireplace. Cr cds: A, C, D, MC, V, JCB.

Restaurants

✔ ★CASA DE EVA. *2826 Telegraph Ave. 510/548-1505.* Hrs: 11 am–9:30 pm; Sat from 2 pm. Closed Sun. Res accepted. Mexican menu. Wine, beer. Semi-a la carte: lunch $3.50–$7, dinner $5–$9.95.

Child's meals. Specialties: chalupas, enchiladas Veracruzanas, flautas. Mexican decor. Art collection. Family-owned. Cr cds: A, MC, V.

★ ★ ★CHEZ PANISSE RESTAURANT & CAFE. *1517 Shattuck Ave. 510/548-5525.* Hrs: Cafe (upper level) 11:30 am–11:30 pm; Restaurant dining rm (main floor) 6–9:15 pm. Closed Sun; Dec 25. Res accepted in cafe; required in dining rm. Continental menu. Beer. Wine list. A la carte entrees: lunch $18–$22, dinner $18–$27. *Prix fixe*: dinner $35–$65. Own baking. Cr cds: A, DS, MC, V.

✔ ★FOURTH STREET GRILL. *1820 4th St. 510/849-0526.* Hrs: 11:30 am–2:30 pm, 5:30–9:30 pm; Thurs to 10 pm; Fri, Sat to 10:30 pm; Sun 5–9:30 pm. Closed Mon; Jan 1, Easter, Dec 24, 25. Res accepted. No A/C. Bar. A la carte entrees: lunch $5.50–$12, dinner $11–$18. Specializes in seafood, pasta. Rotating menu. Cr cds: A, C, D, MC, V.

★ ★ ★RESTAURANT METROPOLE. *2271 Shattuck Ave. 510/848-3080.* Hrs: 11:30 am–3 pm, 5–10 pm; Fri, Sat to 10:30 pm. Closed some major hols. Res accepted. Country French menu. Bar 5 pm–1 am; Fri, Sat to 1:30 am. Wine list. A la carte entrees: lunch $7–$14, dinner $14–$31. Child's meals. Specializes in wild game, fresh seafood, aged Black Angus beef. Own pastries. Entertainment. Country French decor. City landmark (1926). Cr cds: A, MC, V.

★ ★ ★SANTA FE BAR & GRILL. *1310 University Ave. 510/841-4740.* Hrs: 11:30 am–3 pm, 5–11 pm; Fri, Sat to midnight. Res accepted. Bar to 2 am. A la carte entrees: lunch $3.95–$12.95, dinner $9.95–$17.95. Own baking. Pianist. Parking. In turn-of-the-century Santa Fe Railroad depot; historic landmark. Cr cds: A, C, D, MC, V.

★ ★ ★SKATES ON THE BAY. *100 Seawall Dr. 510/549-1900.* Hrs: 11:15 am–10 pm; Fri, Sat to 10:30 pm; Sun 10:15 am–10 pm; Sun brunch to 3 pm. Closed July 4, Thanksgiving, Dec 25. Res accepted. Bar. Semi-a la carte: lunch $5.95–$13.95, dinner $6.95–$16.95. Sun brunch $6.95–$15.95. Child's meals. Specializes in mesquite-grilled meats, fresh seafood, pasta. Parking. Pier leads to entrance. View of Golden Gate Bridge. Cr cds: A, MC, V.

✔ ★ ★VOLGA. *2128 Oxford St. 510/843-3323.* Hrs: 11 am–2:30 pm, 5–10 pm. Closed Thanksgiving, Dec 25. Res accepted. Russian menu. Wine, beer. Semi-a la carte: lunch $4.95–$6.95, dinner $7.95–$13.95. Specialties: beef Stroganoff, chicken Kiev, kabab. Classical pianist Mon–Thurs. Parking. Outdoor dining. Totally nonsmoking. Cr cds: A, MC, V.

Beverly Hills *

Pop: 31,971 **Elev:** 225 ft **Area code:** 310
6 mi W of US 101 (Hollywood Frwy) on CA 2 (Santa Monica Blvd), 10 mi W of Downtown Los Angeles (H-4).

Beverly Hills, an independent community 5.6 square miles in area, is entirely surrounded by the City of Los Angeles. It is famous for its exclusive residential districts, home to many movie and TV personalities. It boasts an international shopping area with the celebrated Rodeo Drive as its hub.

(For further information contact the Visitors Bureau, 239 S Beverly Dr, 90212; 271-8174 or 800/345-2210.)

(See Hollywood, Los Angeles)

Motor Hotels

✔ ★ ★ ★BEVERLY HILLS RITZ HOTEL. *10300 Wilshire Blvd (90024). 310/275-5575; res: 800/800-1234; FAX 310/278-3325.* 116

suites, 5 story. S, D $105–$310. Crib avail. TV; cable, in-rm movies. Heated pool; poolside serv. Restaurant 7 am–10 pm. Rm serv. Bar. Ck-out noon. Meeting rm. Bellhops. Exercise equipt; weight machine, treadmill, whirlpool. Refrigerators, minibars. Many balconies. Garden; tropical plants. Cr cds: A, C, D, DS, MC, V, JCB.

★★**RADISSON BEVERLY PAVILION.** *9360 Wilshire Blvd (90212). 310/273-1400; res: 800/421-0545 (exc CA), 800/441-5050 (CA); FAX 310/859-8551.* 110 rms, 8 story. S $140–$175; D $160–$195; each addl $20; suites $265–$415. Crib free. TV. Bellhops. Rooftop pool; poolside serv. Restaurant 7 am–10 pm. Rm serv. Bar 10 am–midnight. Ck-out noon. Meeting rms. Valet serv. Gift shop. Free local transportation. Bathrm phones, refrigerators. Cr cds: A, C, D, MC, V, JCB.

Hotels

★★★**BEVERLY HILTON.** *9876 Wilshire Blvd (90210) at jct Santa Monica Blvd (CA 2). 310/274-7777; FAX 310/285-1313.* 581 rms, 8 story. S $180–$220; D $200–$245; each addl $25; suites $400–$1,200; family rates. Crib free. Garage, valet parking $14. TV; cable. Heated pool; wading pool, poolside serv. Restaurant 6:45–10 am, 11:30 am–2:30 pm, 5:30–10 pm; dining rm 5 pm–midnight (also see L'ESCOFFIER). Rm serv 24 hrs. Bars 11:30–2 am. Ck-out noon. Meeting rms. Concierge. Shopping arcade. Barber, beauty shop. Complimentary transportation to nearby shopping. Exercise equipt; weight machines, bicycles. Some bathrm phones, refrigerators. Patio; balconies. Lanai rms around pool. Cr cds: A, C, D, DS, ER, MC, V, JCB.

★★★**BEVERLY RODEO.** *360 N Rodeo Dr (90210). 310/273-0300; res: 800/356-7575; FAX 310/859-8730.* 86 rms, 4 story. S $160–$180; D $190–$210; each addl $2; suites $280–$390; under 12 free. Crib free. Parking $9. TV. Restaurant 6:30 am–10:30 pm. Bar 10 am–10:30 pm. Ck-out noon. Concierge. Bathrm phones. Some private patios, balconies. Cr cds: A, C, D, MC, V, JCB.

★★★**HOTEL NIKKO AT BEVERLY HILLS.** *(465 S La Cienega Blvd, Los Angeles 90048) N of Wilshire Blvd, La Cienega at Burton Way. 310/247-0400; res: 800/645-5687; FAX 310/247-0315.* 304 rms, 7 story, 51 suites. S $220–$285; D $245–$310; each addl $25; suites $325–$1,200; under 12 free; wkend rates. Crib free. TV; cable. Complimentary coffee in rms. Restaurants 6:30 am–11 pm. Rm serv 24 hrs. Lobby bar 11:30–1 am; entertainment. Ck-out 1 pm. Concierge. Gift shop. Free garage parking. Tennis privileges. Golf privileges. Exercise rm; instructor, weight machine, bicycles. Masseuse. Complete health club. Bathrm phones. Japanese soaking tubs. Stocked minibars. Balconies. Blend of bold American architecture and traditional Japanese simplicity. Cr cds: A, C, D, DS, MC, V, JCB.

★★★★**THE PENINSULA, BEVERLY HILLS.** *9882 Little Santa Monica Blvd (90212), at Wilshire Blvd. 310/273-4888; res: 800/462-7899; FAX 310/858-6663.* 200 units, 4 story, 32 suites, 16 villas (2 story, 1–2 bedrm). S, D $280–$325; each addl $35; suites & villas $400–$2,500; under 12 free; wkend rates. Crib free. Valet parking $15. TV; cable, in-rm movies. Heated rooftop pool; poolside serv. Complimentary tea, newspaper on arrival. Restaurant 6:30 am–11 pm. Rm serv 24 hrs. Bar from 11:30 am; pianist. Ck-out 1 pm. Meeting rms. Concierge. Gift shop. Clothing & jewelery stores. Airport transportation; Rolls-Royce limos avail. Tennis privileges. 18-hole golf privileges, pro, putting green, driving range. Exercise rm; instructor, weight machine, treadmill, whirlpool, sauna. Massage. Aerobics classes. Bathrm phones, stocked minibars; many wet bars. Balconies. Landscaped gardens with fountains. Luxurious residential setting. Cr cds: A, C, D, DS, ER, MC, V, JCB.

★★★**REGENT BEVERLY WILSHIRE.** *9500 Wilshire Blvd (90212). 310/275-5200; res: 800/545-4000; FAX 310/274-2851.* 300 rms, 10 & 12 story, 36 suites. S, D $255–$395; suites $425–$4,000; under 18

free. Covered parking, valet $15. Heated pool; poolside serv. Restaurant (see THE DINING ROOM). Rm serv 24 hrs. Bar 11–2 am; entertainment. Ck-out noon. Convention facilities. Concierge. Gift shop. Beauty shop. Golf privileges. Exercise equipt; weights, bicycles, 2 whirlpools, sauna, steam rm. Bathrm phones, refrigerators. Some balconies. Cr cds: A, C, D, DS, ER, MC, V, JCB.

Inn

✔★★★**CARLYLE.** *(1119 S Robertson Blvd, Los Angeles 90035) W on Wilshire Blvd to Robertson Blvd, then S; between Olympic & Pico Blvds. 310/275-4445; res: 800-3-CARLYLE; FAX 310/859-0496.* 32 rms, 5 story. S $105; D $115 each addl $10; suites $120; under 12 free; wkly rates, package plans. Crib free. TV; cable. Complimentary full bkfst, tea, sherry. Complimentary coffee in rms. Dining rm 7–10:30 am, 4–6 pm (tea). Also restaurant nearby. Ck-out 1 pm, ck-in 4 pm. Bellhops. Valet serv. Concierge. Private parking. Airport transportation avail. Exercise equipt; bicycles, treadmill. Health club privileges. Rms are on 4 levels of circular terraces overlooking a lush courtyard, terrace and spa. Offers European hospitality and service in a contemporary setting. Cr cds: A, C, D, MC, V.

Restaurants

★★**BEVERLY HILLS BAR & GRILL.** *9474 Little Santa Monica Blvd. 310/274-8926.* Hrs: 11:30–2 am; Sat from 5 pm. Closed Sun; major hols. Res accepted. Bar. Wine cellar. Semi-a la carte: lunch $8–$18, dinner $8–$29. Specializes in aged rib steak, veal chops, grilled tuna & swordfish. Valet parking. Cr cds: A, C, D, MC, V.

✔★★**BEVERLY HILLS R. J.'S-THE RIB JOINT.** *252 N Beverly Dr. 310/274-7427.* Hrs: 11:30 am–10 pm; Fri & Sat to 11 pm; Sun from 10:30 am. Bar. Complete meals: lunch $5.95–$12.95, dinner $8.95–$29.95. Sun brunch $21.95. Specializes in barbecued ribs, chicken, steak, mile-high chocolate cake. Salad bar. Pianist. Magician. Valet parking. Old-time atmosphere; sawdust on floor, ceiling fans, old photos, stained glass. Cr cds: A, C, D, MC, V, JCB.

★★★**BISTRO GARDEN.** *176 N Canon Dr. 310/550-3900.* Hrs: 11:30 am–11:30 pm. Closed major hols. Res required. Continental menu. Bar. Semi-a la carte: lunch $15–$25, dinner $25–$40. Specialties: Swiss bratwurst, canelloni. Pianist. Valet parking. French country garden atmosphere. Outdoor dining. Cr cds: A, C, D, MC, V.

★★**CAFE GALE.** *8400 Wilshire Blvd, at corner of Gale Dr. 213/655-2494.* Hrs: 11:30 am–10 pm; Fri & Sat 10 am–3 pm, 5–11 pm; early-bird dinner Mon–Fri 5:30–6:30 pm. Res accepted. Eclectic menu. Bar. A la carte entrees: lunch $3–$12, dinner $7–$18. Specializes in pastas, chicken, fish, steak. Valet parking. Hi-tech interior; ceilings with exposed metallic ducts, 2 interior walls of glass-brick style, display cases with collection of antique model trucks dating from 1920s & 1930s. Cr cds: A, MC, V.

✔★★**CARROLL O'CONNOR'S PLACE.** *369 N Bedford Dr. 310/273-7585.* Hrs: 11:30 am–10:30 pm; Mon to 10 pm; wkends to 11 pm. Closed Jan 1, Dec 25. Res accepted. Continental menu. Bar. A la carte entrees: lunch $8–$16, dinner $10–$18. Specializes in seafood, meatloaf, bread & rice puddings. Homemade chocolate chip cookies. Pianist. Valet parking. Outdoor dining. Photo collection of Carroll O'Connor's shows and movies on display. Cr cds: A, C, D, MC, V.

★★**DA VINCI.** *9737 Santa Monica Blvd, downtown. 310/273-0960.* Hrs: 11:30 am–2:30 pm, 5:30–10:30 pm; Sat & Sun from 5:30 pm. Res accepted. Italian menu. Bar. A la carte entrees: lunch $12–$25, dinner $25–$30. Complete meals: dinner $27.95. Specialties: osso buco Milanese, fresh homemade pasta, fresh fish. Own desserts. Valet parking. Jacket. Cr cds: A, C, D, MC, V, JCB.

★ ★ ★DAVID SLAY'S LA VERANDA. *225 S Beverly Dr. 310/274-7246.* Hrs: 11:30 am–2:30 pm, 6–10 pm; Sat 6–11 pm; Sun 5–9:30 pm. Closed most major hols. California cuisine. Bar. Wine list. A la carte entrees: lunch $11.75–$25, dinner $25–$75. Specialties: pan-roasted scallops, salmon quesadilla, fried spinach. Valet parking. Casual atmosphere; contemporary dining. Cr cds: A, D, MC, V.

★ ★ ★THE DINING ROOM. *(See Regent Beverly Wilshire Hotel)* *310/275-5200.* Hrs: 7 am–2 pm, 6–11 pm; Sun 10:30 am–2 pm, 6–11 pm; Sun brunch 10 am–2:30 pm. Res accepted. Continental menu. Bar 11–2 am; pianist. Wine cellar. A la carte entrees: bkfst $6–$20, lunch $12–$26, dinner $16–$30. Sun brunch $18.50–$30. Specializes in mesquite-grilled meats and fish. Own baking. Valet parking. Seasonal menu with daily specials. Display kitchen. Decor in Grand European style. Jacket. Cr cds: A, C, D, DS, ER, MC, V, JCB.

D

★ ★THE GRILL. *9560 Dayton Way. 310/276-0615.* Hrs: 11:30 am–midnight. Closed Sun; major hols. Res required. Bar. A la carte entrees: lunch $12–$20, dinner $15–$30. Specializes in fresh seafood, steak, chops. Valet parking. Turn-of-the-century decor. Cr cds: A, D, MC, V.

D

★ ★ ★IL CIELO. *9018 Burton Way. 310/276-9990.* Hrs: 11:30 am–3 pm, 6–10:30 pm; Fri to 11 pm; Sat 6–11 pm. Closed most major hols. Res accepted. Italian menu. Beer. Wine list. A la carte entrees: lunch $8–$13, dinner $13–$20. Specializes in fresh seafood, homemade pasta, veal. Own pastries. Violinist. Valet parking. Outdoor dining. Gardens, fountains. Cr cds: A, C, D, DS, MC, V, JCB.

★ ★ ★JIMMY'S. *201 Moreno Dr. 213/879-2394.* Hrs: 11:30 am–3 pm, 5:30 pm–midnight. Closed Sun; major hols. French menu. Bar 11:30–2 am. Wine cellar. A la carte entrees: lunch from $15, dinner from $25. Specialties: peppered salmon, crème brulée Napoleon, Maryland crab cakes. Own pastries. Elegant French decor with a California touch. Cr cds: A, C, D, MC, V.

D

✔ ★ ★KIPPAN. *260 N Beverly Dr. 310/858-0535.* Hrs: 11:30 am–2:30 pm, 5:30–10:30 pm; Fri & Sat to 11 pm; Sun to 10 pm. Closed major hols. Res accepted. Japanese menu. Wine, beer. A la carte entrees: lunch from $5.80, dinner from $8.80. Specialty: sushi bar. Contemporary Japanese decor. Cr cds: A, D, MC, V.

D

★ ★ ★L'ESCOFFIER. *(See Beverly Hilton Hotel) 310/274-7777.* Hrs: 6:30–10:30 pm; Fri & Sat to 11:30 pm. Closed Sun, Mon. Res accepted. California, French menu. Bar. A la carte entrees: dinner $26–$32. Complete meals: dinner $47.50. Specializes in veal dishes, steak Diane flambé. Own baking. Entertainment. Valet parking. Rooftop dining. View of city. Cr cds: A, C, D, DS, ER, MC, V.

★ ★LA FAMIGLIA. *453 N Canon Dr. 310/276-6208.* Hrs: 5:30 pm–closing. Closed major hols. Res accepted. Italian menu. Bar. A la carte entrees: dinner $12.75–$24. Specializes in fresh fish, homemade pasta, veal, poultry. Valet parking. Cr cds: A, C, D, MC, V.

★ ★ ★LA SCALA. *410 N Canon Dr. 310/275-0579 or 550-8288.* Hrs: 11:30 am–10:30 pm. Closed Sun; major hols. Res required. Northern Italian menu. Bar. A la carte entrees: lunch $7.50–$18, dinner $13.95–$27.95. Specializes in homemade pasta, veal. Valet parking. Family-owned. Cr cds: A, C, D, DS, MC, V, JCB.

★ ★LAWRY'S THE PRIME RIB. *100 N La Cienega Blvd, at Wilshire Blvd. 310/652-2827.* Hrs: 5–10:30 pm; Fri to midnight; Sat 4:30 pm–midnight; Sun 3–10 pm. Closed Dec 25. Res accepted. Bar. Semi-a la carte: dinner $17.95–$24.95. Limited menu. Specializes in prime rib, fish, spinning salad bowl, Yorkshire pudding. Own desserts. Valet parking. Cr cds: A, C, D, DS, MC, V, JCB.

D

★ ★ ★THE MANDARIN. *430 N Camden Dr. 213/272-0267.* Hrs: 11:30 am–10 pm; Fri & Sat to 10:30 pm; Sun 5–10 pm. Closed Jan 1, July 4, Thanksgiving, Dec 25. Res accepted. Mandarin Chinese menu. Bar. A la carte entrees: lunch $15–$20, dinner $25–$30. Specialties: Peking duck, beggar's chicken. 24-hr advance notice for mandarin specialties. Valet parking. Exhibition kitchen. Chinese decor. Cr cds: A, C, D, MC, V.

D

★ ★MAPLE DRIVE. *345 N Maple Dr. 310/274-9800.* Hrs: 11:30 am–2:30 pm, 6–10 pm; Fri to 11 pm; Sat 6–11 pm. Closed Sun; Jan 1, Dec 25. Res required. California, Mediterranean menu. Bar. A la carte entrees: lunch $10–$17, dinner $15–$26. Specialties: fried calamari, tuna tartar, grilled swordfish, chili. Pianist. Valet parking (dinner). Outdoor dining. Exhibition kitchen. Changing display of artwork. Cr cds: A, MC, V.

★MATSUHISA. *129 N La Cienega Blvd. 310/659-9639.* Hrs: 11:45 am–2:15 pm, 5:45–10:15 pm; Sat & Sun from 5:45 pm. Closed most major hols. Res accepted. Wine, beer. Semi-a la carte: lunch $10–$15, dinner $40–$60. Omakase dishes from $60. Specializes in gourmet seafood, sushi. Tempura bar. Valet parking. Lobster tank. Totally nonsmoking. Cr cds: A, D, MC, V.

★ ★PREGO. *362 N Camden Dr. 310/277-7346.* Hrs: 11:30 am–midnight; Sun from 5 pm. Closed Thanksgiving, Dec 25. Res accepted. Northern Italian menu. Bar. A la carte entrees: lunch $8–$18, dinner $15–$28. Specializes in homemade pasta, fresh fish. Valet parking evenings. Oak-burning pizza oven & mesquite grill. Cr cds: A, C, D, MC, V.

D

★ ★ ★ROBATA. *250 N Robertson Blvd. 310/274-5533.* Hrs: noon–2:30 pm, 5:30–10:30 pm. Closed most major hols. Res accepted. Japanese menu. Bar. Wine list. A la carte entrees: lunch $7–$20, dinner $40–$60. Specializes in sushi, tempura, sashimi. Contemporary Japanese atmosphere; dramatic lighting, antiques, hand-painted screens. Cr cds: A, C, D, MC, V, JCB.

D

★ ★ ★TATOU RESTAURANT & SUPPER CLUB. *233 N Beverly Dr. 310/274-9955.* Hrs: 6 pm–4 am. Closed Sun; some major hols. Res required. Bar. Extensive wine list. Complete meals: dinner from $20. Specialties: wood-fire grilled free range chicken, deviled crabcakes, oven-roasted honey mustard salmon. Entertainment. Atmosphere reminiscent of 1940s Hollywood-style supper club. Theatrical setting with ornately draped ceiling, faux palm trees; stage at one end of dining rm. Jacket. Cr cds: A, DS, MC, V.

D

★ ★ ★TRIBECA. *242 N Beverly Dr. 310/271-1595.* Hrs: noon–4 pm, 6 pm–midnight; Fri & Sat 6 pm–1 am. Closed Memorial Day, July 4, Dec 25. Res accepted; required wkends. Bar to 2 am. A la carte entrees: lunch $8–$16, dinner $15–$30. Specializes in seafood, meats, pasta, salads. Valet parking (evenings). Turn-of-the-century decor. Cr cds: A, C, D, DS, MC, V.

Unrated Dining Spot

ED DEBEVIC'S. *134 N La Cienega Blvd. 310/659-1952.* Hrs: 11:30 am–11 pm; Fri & Sat to 1 am. Closed Thanksgiving, Dec 25. Res accepted. Bar. Semi-a la carte: lunch, dinner $4.50–$7.50. Child's meals. Specialties: meatloaf, hamburgers, chicken. Own desserts. Salad bar. Valet parking. 1950s-style diner; memorabilia of the era. Staff provides entertainment: singing, dancing. Cr cds: A, MC, V.

Big Basin Redwoods State Park (E-1)

(23 mi N of Santa Cruz via CA 9, 236)

This 20,000-acre park is one of the most popular parks in California. The area was set aside as the state's first redwood preserve in 1902. Its redwood groves include trees 300 feet high. There are about 50 miles of hiking and riding trails, plus numerous picnic sites and campgrounds with full facilities (limit 8 persons per site; reservations required in summer). Ranger-conducted nature program, held in the summer, includes campfire programs and guided hikes. Flora and fauna of the park are on display in exhibits at the nature lodge. Supplies are available at a concession and a store. Standard fees. Phone 408/338-6132.

(For accommodations see Santa Cruz)

Big Bear Lake (H-4)

Pop: 5,351 **Elev:** 6,754 ft **Area code:** 909 **Zip:** 92315

This is a growing, year-round recreation area in the San Bernardino National Forest (see SAN BERNARDINO). Fishing, riding, golf, bicycling, picnicking, hiking and camping are available in summer; skiing and other winter sports are also popular in season.

What to See and Do

1. Skiing.

Snow Summit. ½ mi S off CA 18. 2 quad, 3 triple and 6 double chairlifts; patrol, school, rentals; snowmaking; cafeteria, 3 restaurants, bar; day care. Longest run 1¼ mi; vertical drop 1,200 ft. (Mid-Nov–Apr, daily) Night skiing, snowboarding. Chairlift also operates in summer (June–early Oct). Phone 866-5766; for snow conditions phone 866-4621. ¢¢¢¢

Bear Mt. 2 mi S off CA 18. 1 quad, 1 high-speed quad, 3 triple, 4 double chairlifts, 2 Pomalifts; patrol, school, rentals; snowmaking; cafe, 3 restaurants, bar. Longest run 2½ mi; vertical drop 1,700 ft. (Thanksgiving–Easter, daily) Hiking, golf, zoo (May–mid-Oct, daily). Phone 585-2519. ¢¢¢¢

2. Alpine Slide & Recreation Area. Approx ¼ mi W on CA 18. Includes Alpine bobsled-type ride (all yr), water slide (summer) and inner tubing (winter). (Daily) Phone 866-4626.

(For further information contact the Chamber of Commerce, 41647 Big Bear Blvd, Box 2860; 866-4608 or -7000.)

(See Lake Arrowhead, Redlands, Riverside, San Bernardino)

Motels

★★★**BIG BEAR INN.** *(PO Box 1814) 42200 Moonridge Rd. 909/866-3471; res: 800/232-7466.* 80 rms, 2 story. S, D $75–$225; each addl $20; suites $235–$500. TV. Heated pool; whirlpool. Restaurant hrs vary (seasonal). Rm serv. Bar; entertainment, dancing wknds. Ck-out noon. Meeting rms. Bellhops. Downhill ski 1 mi. Fireplaces. European chateau-style decor. Cr cds: A, MC, V.

★**BIG BEAR LAKE INN CIENEGA.** *(PO Box 1665) 39471 Big Bear Blvd. 909/866-3477; res: 800/843-0103.* 52 rms, 2 story, 8 kit. units. S, D $51–$95; kit. units $64–$106; under 12 free; higher rates hols (2-night min). TV; cable. Pool; whirlpool. Complimentary continental

bkfst, coffee. Restaurant nearby. Ck-out 11 am. Meeting rm. Downhill/x-country ski 3½ mi. Refrigerators. Cr cds: A, MC, V.

★★**ESCAPE FOR ALL SEASONS.** *(PO Box 1909) 41935 Switzerland Dr, at base of Snow Summit Ski Area. 909/866-7504; res: 800/722-4366 (CA, OR); FAX 909/866-7507.* 60 kit. suites, 2 story. Nov–Mar: kit. suites $120–$300; wkly, monthly rates; lower rates rest of yr. Crib avail. TV; cable, in-rm movies avail. Restaurant opp 6:30 am–10 pm. Ck-out 10 am. Tennis. Downhill/x-country ski adj. Fireplaces. Some balconies. Cr cds: MC, V.

✔★**GOLDMINE LODGE.** *(PO Box 198) 42268 Moonridge Rd. 909/866-8786; res: 800/487-3168; FAX 909/866-1592.* 11 units, 2 story, 6 kit. suites. S, D $49–$89; each addl $10; kit. suites $65–$115; under 18 free; ski plans. Crib free. TV; cable. Playground. Complimentary continental bkfst. Coffee in rms. Restaurant nearby. Ck-out 11 am. Downhill/x-country ski 1 mi. Whirlpool. Lawn games. Fireplace in suites. Picnic tables, grills. Set amid pine forest in San Bernardino Mountains. Cr cds: A, C, D, DS, MC, V.

★★**MARINA RIVIERA RESORT.** *(PO Box 979) 40770 Lakeview Dr. 909/866-7545; FAX 909/866-6705.* 42 rms, 3 story. S, D $75–$125; kit. units $135–$175. Crib $6. TV. Pool; whirlpool. Complimentary continental bkfst. Restaurant opp 4 pm–2 am. Ck-out 11 am. Downhill/x-country ski 1 mi. Refrigerators. Balconies. Picnic tables, grills. Rms overlook lake. Lawn games. Private beach. Cr cds: A, C, D, MC, V.

★**ROBINHOOD INN.** *(PO Box 1801) 40797 Lakeview Dr, in village. 909/866-4643; res: 800/544-7454.* 21 rms, 2 story. S, D $32–$149; each addl $10; under 12 free. TV. Complimentary continental bkfst. Restaurant adj 11 am–10 pm. Ck-out 11 am. Downhill/x-country ski ½ mi. Whirlpool. Some fireplaces. Sun deck. Cr cds: A, C, D, DS, MC, V.

✔★**SMOKETREE LODGE.** *(PO Box 2801) 40210 Big Bear Blvd (CA 18). 909/866-2415; res: 800/352-8581.* 5 rms in main bldg, 2 story, 13 kit. cottages. S, D $49–$80; kit. cottages $69–$170; family rates; higher rates hols; lower rates wkdays. Crib free. TV. Heated pool; whirlpool. Playground. Complimentary coffee in rms. Restaurant adj 7 am–3 pm. Ck-out 11 am. Downhill/x-country ski 3 mi. Fireplaces. Lawn games. Picnic tables, grills. Cr cds: A, C, D, DS, MC, V.

Inns

★★★**EAGLE'S NEST.** *(PO Box 1003) 41675 Big Bear Blvd. 909/866-6465.* 5 rms, 2 story, 5 cottages. S, D $70–$140; wkly rates. Pet accepted, some restrictions. TV avail. Continental bkfst. Ck-out 11 am, ck-in 2 pm. Ski area transportation. Downhill/x-country ski ¼ mi. Complimentary bicycles avail. Some fireplaces. Western decor; antiques. Horse & carriage rides avail (fee). Main building totally nonsmoking. Cr cds: MC, V.

★★**KNICKERBOCKER MANSION.** *(PO Box 3661) 869 S Knickerbocker Rd. 909/866-8221.* 6 rms in main bldg, 2 share baths, 4 story; 4 rms in lodge, 2 story. S, D $95–$165; each addl $10; 2-day min wkends. TV. Complimentary full bkfst. Ck-out noon, ck-in 2 pm. Meeting rms. X-country ski on site. Whirlpool. Lawn games. Balconies. Historic log mansion (early 1920s) on 2½ acres of heavily wooded forest. Antiques; turn-of-the-century furnishings; double-sided stone fireplace. Sun deck. Swimming lake 8 blks. Totally nonsmoking. Cr cds: MC, V.

★★**WAINWRIGHT.** *(PO Box 130406) 43113 Moonridge Rd. 909/585-6914.* 4 rms, 2 with bath, 4 story. No rm phones. S, D $85–$145;

suite $120–$140; ski, golf, mountain bike and boating package plans. Adults preferred. TV in sitting rm; cable. Complimentary full bkfst, tea, sherry. Coffee in rms. Ck-out 11 am, ck-in 2 pm. Ski resort transportation. Downhill/x-country ski ½ mi. English Tudor-style inn; leaded glass windows, English country manor decor. Set amid pine forest in San Bernardino Mountains. Totally nonsmoking. Cr cds: A, C, D, MC, V, JCB.

Restaurant

✔ ★★BLUE WHALE LAKESIDE. *350 Alden Rd, off Big Bear Blvd. 909/866-5771.* Hrs: 4–10 pm; Fri to 11 pm; Sat noon–midnight; Sun 10 am–10 pm; Sun brunch 10 am–3 pm. Res accepted. Bar. Semi-a la carte: lunch $4.95–$6.95, dinner $7.95–$21.95. Sun brunch $8.95. Child's meals. Specializes in fresh seafood, prime rib, "California grill" items. Oyster bar (summer). Salad bar. Pianist wkends. Parking. Outdoor dining. Late 19th-century building. Boat dock; view of lake. Cr cds: A, DS, MC, V.

Big Sur (F-2)

Pop: 1,000 (est) **Elev:** 155 ft **Area code:** 408 **Zip:** 93920

Big Sur is 30 miles south of Monterey on CA 1, with the Santa Lucia Range on the east and the Pacific Ocean on the west. **Pfeiffer-Big Sur State Park** contains a coast redwood forest. Recreational opportunities include swimming, fishing and hiking. Picnicking and camping facilities are available. There is also a lodge, gift shop and store. Naturalist programs are offered. Standard fees. Day use, per vehicle ¢¢¢

(For further information contact Pfeiffer-Big Sur State Park #1; 667-2315.)

(See Carmel, Carmel Valley, Monterey, Pacific Grove)

Lodge

★★POST RANCH INN. *(PO Box 291) 28 mi S on CA 1. 408/667-2200; res: 800/527-2000; FAX 408/667-2419.* 30 cabins. D $255–$495; under 10 free; spa plans; higher rates wkends & hols (2–3 night min). Crib free. 2 heated pools (1 soaking pool adj to restaurant and 1 lap pool located in the meadow below the inn). Complimentary continental bkfst. Complimentary coffee in rms. Dining rm noon–2:30 pm, 5:30–10 pm. Rm serv. Ck-out 1 pm, ck-in 4 pm. Concierge. Bellhop. Refrigerators, minibars. Balconies. Free wine tasting Sat. Situated on 98 acres overlooking the Pacific Ocean. Each guest unit has wood-burning fireplace, hot tub and offers spectacular ocean or mountain view. Cr cds: A, MC, V.

Inn

★★★★VENTANA. *On CA 1. 408/667-2331; res: 800/628-6500 (CA).* 59 rms, 1–2 story. S, D $165–$360; each addl $50; suites $310–$440. TV; cable, in-rm movies. 2 heated pools; sauna, Japanese hot baths, poolside beverage serv. Continental bkfst. Complimentary wine & cheese 4–5:30 pm. Dining rm (see VENTANA). Bar 11 am–midnight. Ck-out 1 pm, ck-in 4:30 pm. Bellhops. Wet bars; many fireplaces; some hot tubs. Balconies. Sun deck. Secluded hideaway on Big Sur coastline; spectacular views. Cr cds: A, C, D, DS, MC, V.

Restaurants

✔ ★★GLEN OAKS. *15 mi S on CA 1. 408/667-2623.* Hrs: 6–9:30 pm. Closed Dec 25. Res accepted. Wine, beer. Semi-a la carte:

dinner $7–$17.95. Specializes in fresh salmon, pasta, vegetarian dishes. Own desserts. Parking. French country atmosphere. Cr cds: MC, V.

★NEPENTHE. *On CA 1. 408/667-2345.* Hrs: 11:30 am–10 pm. No A/C. Bar. Semi-a la carte: lunch $7–$11.50, dinner $9.25–$23.50. Specializes in roast chicken, quiche, fresh fish. Parking. Outdoor dining. 40-mile view of Pacific coastline. Family-owned. Cr cds: A, MC, V.

★★★★VENTANA. *(See Ventana Inn) 408/667-2331.* Hrs: noon–3 pm, 6–10 pm; winter to 9 pm; Sat, Sun & hols from 11 am. Res accepted. Bar to midnight. A la carte entrees: lunch $9.50–$15, dinner $16.50–$25. Specializes in oak-grilled meats and fresh fish, California cuisine with continental influence. Own baking. Parking. Outdoor dining (lunch). Views of ocean, mountains and 50 miles of coastline. Cr cds: A, D, MC, V.

Bishop (F-4)

Pop: 3,475 **Elev:** 4,147 ft **Area code:** 619 **Zip:** 93514

What to See and Do

1. **Laws Railroad Museum & Historical Site.** 5 mi NE on US 6, then ½ mi E on Silver Canyon Rd. Laws Post Office with old-fashioned equipment, 1883 depot, narrow-gauge locomotive, restored station agent's five-room house; hand-operated gallows-type turntable used 1883–1960, when Laws was the northern terminus of the Laws-Keeler Branch of the Southern Pacific Railroad; water tower, pumphouse; mining exhibits; library and arts building; Western building; pioneer building; firehouse; bottle house; doctor's office; country store; Native American exhibit. (Daily, weather permitting; closed Jan 1, Thanksgiving, Dec 25) Donation. Phone 873-5950.

2. **Ancient Bristlecone Pine Forest.** In the White and Inyo Mountains of the Inyo National Forest (see). CA 168 E from Big Pine to White Mountain Rd to Schulman Grove & Patriarch Grove. These trees are estimated to be more than 4,600 years old, making them the oldest known living things on earth. Naturalist programs. White Mt Rd District Visitor Center (July 4–Labor Day, daily). Contact visitor center, 798 N Main St, phone 873-2500; or Supervisor, 873 N Main St, phone 873-2400.

(For further information contact the Chamber of Commerce, 690 N Main St; 873-8405.)

Annual Events

Mule Days. Mule show and sale; barbecue. Memorial Day wkend.

Tri-County Fair, Wild West Rodeo. Early Sept.

Motels

★★BEST WESTERN HOLIDAY SPA LODGE. *1025 N Main St. 619/873-3543.* 89 rms, 1–2 story. May–Oct: S $54–$70; D $64–$77; each addl $5; higher rates hols; lower rates rest of yr. Crib $10. Pet accepted, some restrictions. TV; cable. Pool; whirlpool. Complimentary coffee in rms. Ck-out 11 am. Coin lndry. X-country ski 20 mi. Fish cleaning, freezer facilities. Refrigerators. Cr cds: A, C, D, DS, MC, V, JCB.

✔ ★BISHOP INN. *805 N Main St. 619/873-4284; res: 800/576-4080.* 52 rms, 2 story. S $47–$53; D $54–$62; each addl $5; suites $62–$76; higher rates hols. Crib $5. Pet accepted. TV; cable. Heated pool; whirlpool. Complimentary coffee in rms. Restaurant nearby. Ck-out 11 am. Coin lndry. Fish cleaning, freezer facilities. Refrigerators; some wet bars. Picnic tables, grill. Cr cds: A, C, D, MC, V.

★ ★**NATIONAL 9 HIGH SIERRA LODGE.** *1005 N Main St. 619/873-8426; res: 800/662-1162 (CA).* 52 units, 2 story, 2 kits. S $44–$46; D $54–$56; each addl $5; kit. units $6 addl. Crib $3. TV; cable. Heated pool; whirlpool. Complimentary coffee in rms. Restaurant opp open 24 hrs. Ck-out noon. Fish clean & store. Refrigerators. Cr cds: A, C, D, DS, ER, MC, V.

★**THUNDERBIRD.** *190 W Pine St. 619/873-4215; res: 800/82-T-BIRD.* 23 rms, 2 story. S $34–$44; D $40–$60; each addl $4. Crib $2. Pet accepted, some restrictions. TV; cable. Coffee in rms. Restaurant nearby. Ck-out 11 am. X-country ski 20 mi. Refrigerators. Cr cds: A, MC, V.

Inn

★ ★**CHALFANT HOUSE.** *213 Academy St. 619/872-1790.* 7 rms, 2 story. S $50; D $60; each addl $15; suite $75. TV in sitting rm. Complimentary full bkfst, refreshments. Restaurant nearby. Ck-out 11 am, ck-in 3 pm. Built 1898 by publisher of first area newspaper; furnished with antiques. Totally nonsmoking. Cr cd: A.

Restaurants

✔ ★ ★**FIREHOUSE GRILL.** *2206 N Sierra Hwy. 619/873-4888.* Hrs: 4:30–10 pm; early-bird dinner 4:30–6 pm. Res accepted. Bar. Semi-a la carte: dinner $8–$18. Specializes in prime rib, fresh seafood, teriyaki chicken, fettucine. Parking. Cr cds: A, C, D, DS, MC, V.

★**INYO COUNTRY STORE & RESTAURANT.** *177 Academy St. 619/872-2552.* Hrs: 8 am–5 pm; Thurs-Sat to 9 pm. Closed Sun; Dec 25. Res accepted. Italian, Amer menu. A la carte entrees: bkfst $2.95–$8.95, lunch $3.15–$5.25, dinner $3.95–$6.95. Semi-a la carte: dinner $7.95–$19.95. Specializes in lamb, steak, Northern Italian cuisine. Gift shop; deli. Totally nonsmoking. No cr cds accepted.

★**WHISKEY CREEK.** *524 N Main St. 619/873-7174.* Hrs: 7 am–9 pm; June–Sept to 10 pm. Closed Dec 25. Res accepted. Bar. Semi-a la carte: bkfst $2.25–$9.95, lunch $4.50–$15.95, dinner $8.95–$18.95. Child's meals. Specializes in barbecue, prime rib, seafood. Parking. Outdoor dining. Country decor; indoor gazebo. Gift shop; small bakery (limited items). Cr cds: A, C, D, DS, MC, V.

Blythe (J-6)

Settled: 1910 **Pop:** 8,428 **Elev:** 270 ft **Area code:** 619 **Zip:** 92225

Thomas Blythe, an Englishman, came here with an idea of turning this portion of the Colorado River valley into another Nile River valley. The techniques of modern irrigation have allowed that dream to come true as a series of dams has converted the desert into rich farmland and a vast recreational area. There is still some mining in the Palo Verde Valley and rockhounding is good in some nearby areas.

What to See and Do

1. **Riverside camping.** There are 30 camps for sports enthusiasts along the banks of the Colorado, Mayflower Park among them. Approx 30,000–50,000 people visit here each winter to hunt deer,

duck, pheasant, quail, doves and geese and to fish for bass, crappie, bluegill and catfish.

2. **Palo Verde Lagoon.** 20 mi S on CA 78. A natural lake with fishing, picnicking and camping facilities.

3. **Indian Lore Monument.** 15 mi N. Giant intaglio pictographs.

4. **Cibola National Wildlife Refuge.** 20 mi S of I-10, on Colorado River near Cibola, AZ. Large flocks of Canada geese, ducks, sandhill cranes and wintering passerine birds. Swimming; fishing, hunting; boating. Picnicking. Visitor center (daily; closed hols) Contact PO Box AP; phone 602/857-3253.

5. **Canoe trips.** 1–5-day self-guided trips on lower Colorado River. Fishing, boating, waterskiing, camping. Canoe rentals; delivery and pickup. For schedule and fee information contact Desert Canoe Rentals, 12400 14th Ave; phone 922-8753.

(For further information contact the Chamber of Commerce, 201 S Broadway; phone 922-8166 or 800/445-0541 in CA, 800/443-5513 outside CA.)

Annual Events

Colorado River Country Music Festival. Late Jan.

Colorado River Country Fair. Mid-Apr.

Colorado River Cruise. From Blythe to Martinez Lake Resort. A 75-mile round-trip sightseeing cruise for families draws about 125 boats from all over the western US. 2 days May.

Motels

(Rates may be higher for dove-hunting season in early Sept; res necessary, 3-day min.)

★ ★**BEST WESTERN SAHARA.** *825 W Hobsonway. 619/922-7105; FAX 619/922-5836.* 47 rms. S $49–$66; D $54–$70; each addl $5; under 12 free; higher rates special events. Crib free. TV; cable, in-rm movies avail. Pool; whirlpool. Complimentary continental bkfst. Complimentary coffee in rms. Restaurant opp 6 am–10:30 pm. Ck-out noon. Refrigerators. Cr cds: A, C, D, DS, ER, MC, V.

✔ ★**COMFORT INN.** *903 W Hobsonway. 619/922-4146; FAX 619/922-7629.* 48 rms, 2 story. S $48–$58; D $52–$60; each addl $5; under 18 free; higher rates special events. Crib free. TV; cable. Pool. Complimentary coffee in lobby. Restaurant opp 5 am–11 pm. Ck-out noon. Refrigerators. Cr cds: A, C, D, DS, ER, MC, V, JCB.

Bodega Bay (D-1)

Settled: 1835 **Pop:** 1,127 **Elev:** 120 ft **Area code:** 707 **Zip:** 94923

(See Inverness, Santa Rosa)

Motels

★ ★ ★**BEST WESTERN BODEGA BAY LODGE.** *103 Coast Hwy 1, ½ mi S on CA 1. 707/875-3525; FAX 707/875-2428.* 78 rms, 2 story. No A/C. S, D $130–$210; each addl $10; under 12 free. Crib free. TV; cable. Heated pool. Continental bkfst. Complimentary coffee in rms. Restaurant 6–9 pm. Rm serv. Ck-out 11:30 am. Meeting rms. Exercise equipt; weights, bicycles, whirlpool, sauna. Refrigerators, fireplaces; some wet bars. Private patios, balconies. Golf adj. Overlooks bay, beach. Cr cds: A, C, D, DS, MC, V.

★ ★**BODEGA COAST INN.** *(PO Box 55) 521 Coast Hwy. 707/875-2217; res: 800/346-6999 (CA); FAX 707/875-2964.* 45 rms, 3 story.

Apr–Nov: S, D $84–$180; each addl $10; under 12 free; lower rates rest of yr. Crib free. TV; cable, in-rm movies. Complimentary coffee in rms. Restaurant 8 am–9 pm. Ck-out noon. Meeting rm. Whirlpool. Refrigerators. Balconies. Bay view. Cr cds: A, C, D, DS, MC, V.

Motor Hotel

★ ★ ★ **INN AT THE TIDES.** *(Box 640) 800 Coast Hwy. 707/875-2751; res: 800/541-7788; FAX 707/875-3023.* 86 rms, 2 story. No A/C. S, D $110–$160; each addl $10; suites $185–$210; under 12 free; mid-wk rates; golf plan. Crib free. TV; cable. Indoor/outdoor pool; whirlpool, sauna. Complimentary continental bkfst. Restaurant 5–10 pm; closed Mon & Tues. Rm serv 8–11 am, 5–10 pm. Bar from 5 pm; closed Mon & Tues. Ck-out noon. Meeting rms. Refrigerators. Some private patios. Opp ocean. Cr cds: A, MC, V, JCB.

Inns

★ ★ **BAY HILL MANSION.** *(PO Box 567) 3919 Bay Hill Rd. 707/875-3577; res: 800/526-5927.* 5 rms, 3 with bath, 2 story. No A/C. Rm phones avail. June–Sept: S $80–$100; D $95–$160; each addl $20; under 4 free; lower rates rest of yr. Crib free. TV in sitting rm. Complimentary full bkfst, coffee, tea, wine. Restaurant adj 9 am–10 pm; closed Mon. Ck-out 11 am, ck-in 4 pm. Whirlpool. Decks with view of Bodega Bay and ocean. Totally nonsmoking. Cr cds: MC, V.

✔ ★ **SCHOOLHOUSE INN.** *(PO Box 136, Bodega 94922, 17110 Bodega Lane) 4 mi E on Bay Hwy. 707/876-3257.* 4 rms, 2 story. No A/C. No rm phones. D $75–$90; each addl $15; higher rates hols (2-night min). Closed Dec 25. Children over 10 yrs only. TV in sitting rm. Complimentary full bkfst, coffee, tea. Ck-out 11 am, ck-in 4–7 pm. Built in 1873 as schoolhouse; appeared in the Alfred Hitchcock film *The Birds.* Guest rms on 1st floor; 2nd floor used as sitting/dining area. Totally nonsmoking. Cr cds: MC, V.

Borrego Springs *(J-5)*

Pop: 2,244 **Elev:** 700 ft **Area code:** 619 **Zip:** 92004

Artifacts from the area show that nomadic Indians lived here at least 5,000 years ago. Although prospectors and cattle ranchers had driven through the desert in the late 19th century, it wasn't until 1906 that the first permanent white settler arrived.

In the winter and spring, wildflowers transform the desert's valleys, canyons and washes into a rainbow of colors, creating an oasis in the midst of the desert.

What to See and Do

Anza-Borrego Desert State Park (see). Approximately 600,000 acres surrounding Borrego Springs. Hiking, nature and bridle trails. Picnicking. Camping. Standard fees. Visitor center with underground desert museum. Phone 767-5311.

(For further information contact the Chamber of Commerce, PO Box 66; 767-5555.)

Motel

✔ ★ **PALM CANYON RESORT.** *(Box 956) 221 Palm Canyon Dr. 619/767-5341; res: 800/242-0044 (CA); FAX 619/767-4073.* 44 rms, 2 story. Mid-Nov–mid-May: S, D $75–$135; each addl $10; under 13 free; lower rates rest of yr. TV; cable. Heated pool; whirlpool. Compli-

mentary coffee in rms. Restaurant 7 am–10 pm; off-season 11 am–9 pm. Ck-out noon. Coin lndry. Meeting rms. Sundries. Gift shop. Free airport transportation. Tennis privileges. Cr cds: A, C, D, DS, MC, V.

Resort

★ ★ ★ **LA CASA DEL ZORRO.** *3845 Yaqui Pass Rd, at Borrego Springs Rd, 5 mi SE of Christmas Circle. 619/767-5323; res: 800/824-1884; FAX 619/767-5963.* 77 units, 19 kit. cottages. Nov–May: S, D $95–$450; suites $125–$350; kit. cottages $150–$500; under 8 free; lower rates rest of yr. Crib free. TV; cable. Heated pools; whirlpools. Restaurant (see LA CASA DEL ZORRO). Rm serv 7 am–11 pm. Bar 11–2 am; entertainment Wed–Sun. Ck-out noon, ck-in 4 pm. Meeting rm. Bellhops. Concierge. Gift shop. Beauty shop. Free airport transportation. Lighted tennis, pro. Bicycles. Minibar in suites. Some fireplaces. Golf adj. Desert resort surrounded by Anza Borrego State Park. Cr cds: A, C, D, DS, MC, V.

Restaurants

★ ★ ★ **LA CASA DEL ZORRO.** *(See La Casa Del Zorro Resort) 619/767-5323.* Hrs: 7 am–10 pm; Fri & Sat to 11 pm; early-bird dinner 4–6 pm. Res accepted. Bar 10 am–midnight; Fri & Sat to 2 am. Wine list. Semi-a la carte: bkfst $3.50–$12, lunch $5–$15, dinner $12–$40. Child's meals. Specializes in steak, fresh seafood. Parking. Outdoor dining. Original oil paintings. Overlooks rose garden. Family-owned. Cr cds: A, C, D, DS, MC, V.

★ ★ ★ **LE PAVILLION AT RAMS HILL.** *1881 Rams Hill Rd, at Rams Hill Country Club. 619/767-5000.* Hrs: noon–2 pm, 6–8:30 pm; Sun brunch 8 am–2 pm. Closed Mon–Thurs (June–Sept). Res accepted. Continental menu. Bar 11 am–9 pm. Wine list. A la carte entrees: lunch $6.50–$11.50. Semi-a la carte: dinner $16–$24. Sun brunch $10. Specializes in roasted rack of lamb, medallions of veal. Parking. Casual dining; scenic desert and golf course setting. Cr cds: A, MC, V.

Bridgeport *(E-3)*

Pop: 500 (est) **Elev:** 6,473 ft **Area code:** 619 **Zip:** 93517

A Ranger District office of the Toiyabe National Forest (see RENO, NV) is located here.

What to See and Do

1. **Bodie State Historic Park.** 7 mi S on US 395, then 13 mi E on partially unpaved road; not cleared in winter. Unrestored ghost town of the late 1800s. Between 1879 and 1881 more than 10,000 people lived here. Fires in 1892 and 1932 took their toll and now only about five percent of the town remains. A self-guiding brochure takes you through the main part of town; church (ca 1880), jail, two-room school, Miners Union Hall (now a museum), hillside cemetery with monument to James A. Garfield. Picnicking. Phone 647-6445. Day use, per car ¢¢

2. **Yosemite National Park** (see). Approx 20 mi S via US 395, then 8 mi W via CA 120.

(See Coleville, Lee Vining)

Motels

✔ ★ **SILVER MAPLE.** *(Box 327) 20 Main St. 619/932-7383.* 20 rms. No A/C. No rm phones. S $50–$55; D $55–$65; each addl $10. Pet accepted. TV. Complimentary coffee in rms. Restaurant opp 6 am–10 pm. Ck-out 11 am. Lawn games. Picnic tables. Grills. Cr cds: A, C, D, DS, MC, V.

★ ★WALKER RIVER LODGE. (Box 695) On US 395. 619/932-7021. 34 rms, 1–2 story. Mid-Apr–Oct: S $65–$90; D $70–$115; each addl $10; kit. units $95–$180; lower rates rest of yr. Crib free. Pet accepted. TV; cable. Heated pool; whirlpool. Complimentary coffee in rms. Restaurant opp 6 am–2 pm. Ck-out 11 am. Gift shop. Some refrigerators. Some balconies. Picnic tables, grills. Fish freezer. Cr cds: A, C, D, DS, MC, V.

Inn

★ ★ ★CAIN HOUSE. (Box 454) 11 Main St. 619/932-7040; res: 800/433-CAIN. 6 rms, 2 story. No A/C. S, D $80–$135; each addl $20. TV; cable. Complimentary full bkfst, wine & cheese. Complimentary coffee in rms. Restaurant nearby. Ck-out 11 am, ck-in 3 pm. Lawn games. Grills. Former residence of prominent local family. Totally non-smoking. Cr cds: A, C, D, DS, MC, V.

Buena Park (J-4)

Pop: 68,784 **Elev:** 74 ft **Area code:** 714

What to See and Do

1. **Knott's Berry Farm.** 8039 Beach Blvd, 2 mi S of Santa Ana Frwy (US 101, I-5) on CA 39. Re-created town of gold rush days; focus on the history, heritage and culture of the West. Family entertainment park situated on 150 acres; includes exciting rides, live entertainment, shops, food. This is the official home of Snoopy and the Peanuts characters. Farm is also noted for its berry preserves. (Daily; closed Dec 25) Sr citizen rate. Phone 220-5200 (recording). ¢¢¢¢¢

2. **Movieland Wax Museum.** 7711 Beach Blvd. Museum houses more than 280 wax figures of Hollywood's greatest stars in more than 160 realistic movie sets; covers 70 years of movie history. Shop for favorite movie souvenirs and visit Chamber of Horrors. (Daily) Sr citizen rate. Phone 522-1154. Combination ticket ¢¢¢¢¢; Includes admission to

    Ripley's Believe It or Not Museum. Opp Movieland. Houses a collection of oddities and anthropological artifacts that allow visitors to experience first hand that truth is indeed stranger than fiction. (Daily) Sr citizen rate. Phone 522-7045.

    (For further information contact the Convention & Visitors Office, 6280 Manchester Blvd, Suite 103, 90621; 994-1511 or 800/541-3953.)

    (See Anaheim, La Habra, Long Beach, Whittier)

Motels

✔ ★ ★BEST WESTERN BUENA PARK INN. 8580 Stanton Ave (90620), CA 91 Beach Blvd exit, S to Crescent Ave, E to Stanton Ave, then 2 blks S. 714/828-5211; res: 800/654-2889 (CA). 63 rms, 2 story. S $38–$48; D $42–$56; each addl $5–$8; suites $70–$89; under 12 free; higher rates summer hols. Crib $5. Pet accepted, some restrictions; $10. TV. Heated pool. Continental bkfst. Coffee in rms. Restaurant adj 7 am–midnight. Ck-out 11 am. Coin lndry. Some refrigerators. Cr cds: A, C, D, DS, MC, V.

★ ★COURTYARD BY MARRIOTT. 7621 Beach Blvd (90620), CA 91 Beach Blvd exit, 2 blks S. 714/670-6600; FAX 714/670-0360. 145

rms, 2 story. S $72–$82; D $82–$92; suites $99–$109; under 18 free; wkly, wkend rates. Crib free. TV; cable. Heated pool. Complimentary coffee in rms. Restaurant 6:30–10 am. Bar 5–10:30 pm. Ck-out 1 pm. Coin lndry. Meeting rms. Valet serv. Sundries. Exercise equipt; weights, bicycle, whirlpool. Some refrigerators. Balconies. Cr cds: A, C, D, DS, MC, V.

✔ ★ ★FAIRFIELD INN BY MARRIOTT. 7032 Orangethorpe Ave (90621), CA 91 Knott Ave exit, N to Orangethorpe Ave then E 1 blk. 714/523-1488. 135 rms, 3 story. S $36.95–$45.95; D $42.95–$54.95; each addl $3; under 18 free. Crib free. TV; cable. Heated pool. Complimentary continental bkfst, coffee in lobby. Restaurant opp 6 am–midnight; Fri, Sat to 2 am. Ck-out noon. Meeting rm. Sundries. Cr cds: A, C, D, DS, MC, V.

★ ★HAMPTON INN. 7828 Orangethorpe Ave (90620), CA 91 Beach Blvd exit, N to Orangethorpe Ave, 1 blk E. 714/670-7200; FAX 714/522-3319. 176 units, 7 story. S $49–$62; D $52–$62; under 18 free. Crib free. TV; cable. Heated pool; whirlpool. Complimentary continental bkfst. Ck-out noon. Coin lndry. Meeting rms. Valet serv. Disneyland, Knott's Berry Farm transportation. Cr cds: A, C, D, DS, MC, V.

★TRAVELER'S INN. 7121 Beach Blvd (90620), CA 91 Beach Blvd exit, 1 blk N. 714/670-9000; res: 800/633-8300; FAX 714/522-7280. 128 units, 4 story. S $35; D $41; each addl $4; suites $56–$71; under 12 free. Crib free. TV; cable. Heated pool; whirlpool. Restaurant nearby. Ck-out noon. Meeting rms. Valet serv. Free local attractions transportation. Cr cds: A, C, D, DS, MC, V.

Motor Hotel

★ ★ ★EMBASSY SUITES. 7762 Beach Blvd (90620), I-5 Beach Blvd exit, 5 blks S. 714/739-5600; FAX 714/521-9650. 202 kit. suites, 4 story. S $99–$154; D $94–$159; each addl $15; under 12 free. Crib free. TV; cable. Heated pool. Complimentary full bkfst. Restaurant 11:30 am–1:30 pm, 5–10 pm. Rm serv 11 am–10 pm. Bar. Ck-out 1 pm. Coin lndry. Meeting rms. Valet serv. Gift shop. Free Disneyland transportation. Health club privileges. Game rm. Refrigerators. Balconies. Grills. Knott's Berry Farm 1 blk. Cr cds: A, C, D, DS, MC, V.

Hotels

★ ★BUENA PARK HOTEL & CONVENTION CENTER. 7675 Crescent Ave (90620), CA 91 Beach Blvd exit, N to Crescent Ave then 1 blk W. 714/995-1111; res: 800/854-8792 (exc CA), 800/422-4444 (CA); FAX 714/828-8590. 350 rms, 9 story. S $75; D $85; suites $175–$500; under 13 free. Crib free. TV. Heated pool; whirlpool, poolside serv. Restaurant 5:30 am–midnight. Bar 11–2 am. Ck-out noon. Convention facilities. Concierge. Airport transportation. Health club privileges. Some refrigerators. Cr cds: A, C, D, DS, MC, V, JCB.

★ ★SHERATON CERRITOS AT TOWNE CENTER. (12725 Center Court Dr, Cerritos 90701) 4 mi W on CA 91, Bloomfield Ave exit S. 310/809-1500; FAX 310/403-2080. 203 rms, 8 story. S, D $79–$135; each addl $15; suites $160–$300; under 18 free. Crib free. TV; cable. Heated pool; poolside serv. Restaurant 6:30 am–10 pm. Bar noon–1 am. Ck-out noon. Convention facilities. Concierge. Gift shop. Free Disneyland transportation. Exercise equipt; weight machine, bicycles, whirlpool. Minibars; some bathrm phones. Atrium. Cr cds: A, C, D, DS, ER, MC, V, JCB.

★ ★ ★SHERATON NORWALK METRO-CENTRE. (13111 Sycamore Dr, Norwalk 90650) N via I-5, Norwalk Blvd. exit. 310/863-6666; FAX 310/868-4486. 175 rms, 8 story, 27 suites. S $95–$115; D

$105–$125; each addl $10; suites $125–$299; under 17 free; wkend rates. Crib free. TV; cable. Heated pool; whirlpool, poolside serv. Complimentary continental bkfst. Complimentary coffee in rms. Restaurant 6 am–10 pm. Bar. Ck-out noon. Meeting rms. Concierge. Airport transportation. Refrigerators, minibars. Cr cds: A, C, D, DS, ER, MC, V, JCB.

Unrated Dining Spot

MEDIEVAL TIMES. *7662 Beach Blvd. 714/521-4740.* Hrs: show at 7 pm; Sat at 4 pm, 6:30 pm & 8:45 pm; Sun at 1 pm, 4 pm & 7 pm. Res required. Bar. Complete meals: adults $28.95–$34.95, children $18.95–$20.95. Medieval tournament competitions include ring piercing, javelin throwing, sword fighting, jousting. Reproduction of 11th-century castle; medieval decor. Hall of Banners and Flags. Museum of Torture. Parking. Cr cds: A, DS, MC, V.

D SC

Burbank *

Pop: 93,643 **Elev:** 598 ft **Area code:** 818
*9 mi N of Downtown Los Angeles (H-4) on I-5 (Golden State Frwy).

(For general information and attractions see Los Angeles)

Motel

✔ ★**SAFARI.** *1911 W Olive Ave (91506), I-5 Olive Ave exit SW approx 1 mi.* 818/845-8586; res: 800/782-4373; FAX 818/845-0054. 110 rms, 2–3 story. S $48–$70; D $58–$80; each addl $10; kit. units $371–$546/wk; higher rates Dec 29–Jan 2 (2-day min). Crib $6. TV. Heated pool; whirlpool. Restaurant 6:30 am–10 pm; wkends from 7 am. Rm serv. Bar. Ck-out noon. Airport transportation. Refrigerators. Cr cds: A, C, D, MC, V.

Hotel

★★**HILTON-BURBANK AIRPORT.** *2500 Hollywood Way (91505), I-5 Hollywood Way exit S 1½ mi, opp Burbank Airport.* 818/843-6000; FAX 818/842-9720. 500 rms, 8–9 story. S $116–$156; D $131–$171; each addl $15; suites $156–$275; family, wkend rates. Crib free. Pet accepted. TV; cable, in-rm movies. 2 heated pools; poolside serv. Restaurant 6 am–11 pm. Rm serv 24 hrs. Bar 10–2 am; entertainment, dancing. Ck-out noon. Coin lndry. Convention facilities. Concierge. Gift shop. Free local airport transportation. Exercise equipt; weight machine, bicycles, whirlpool, sauna. Refrigerator in suites. Cr cds: A, C, D, DS, ER, MC, V.

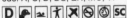

Burlingame

(see San Francisco Airport Area)

Burney (B-2)

Pop: 3,423 **Elev:** 3,173 ft **Area code:** 916 **Zip:** 96013

All the attractions of outdoor living are in the area surrounding Shasta Lake, Mt Shasta (see) and Lassen Volcanic National Park (see).

What to See and Do

1. **Lassen National Forest.** (see SUSANVILLE). S & E of town. In the forest is

   Hat Creek Recreation Area. 17 mi SE on CA 89. Fishing, picnicking, camping. Geological sites include Subway Cave, a lava tube, and Spattercone, a guided volcanic nature trail. Camping and fishing facilities for the disabled. Phone 336-5521.

2. **McArthur-Burney Falls Memorial State Park.** 5 mi E on CA 299, then 6 mi N on CA 89. These 853 acres encompass Burney Falls (in season, water bubbles from underground springs, flows a half-mile, then drops over a precipice in 129-foot twin falls). Swimming; fishing, boat launching. Nature and hiking trails. Picnicking, concession. Camping. Naturalist program. Standard fees. Phone 335-2777.

(For further information contact the Chamber of Commerce, PO Box 36; 335-2111.)

(For accommodations see Mt Shasta, Redding)

Calexico (K-5)

Founded: 1900 **Pop:** 18,633 **Elev:** 2 ft **Area code:** 619 **Zip:** 92231

Once a tent town of the Imperial Land Company, this community at the south end of the Imperial Valley is separated from its much larger sister city, Mexicali, Mexico, by only a fence. The town represents the marriage of two diverse cultures. It serves as a port of entry to the US. (For Border Crossing Regulations see INTRODUCTION.)

(For further information contact the Chamber of Commerce, PO Box 948; phone 357-1166.)

(See El Centro)

Motor Hotel

✔★★**HOLLIE'S FIESTA HOTEL.** *801 Imperial Ave.* 619/357-3571; FAX 619/357-7975. 60 rms, 2 story. S, D $42–$63; each addl $5; suites $77; kit. units $55–$75; under 16 free. Crib free. TV; cable. Heated pool. Restaurant 6 am–6 pm. Rm serv. Ck-out noon. Free covered parking. Some refrigerators. Cr cds: A, C, D, MC, V.

Calistoga (D-1)

Founded: 1859 **Pop:** 4,468 **Elev:** 362 ft **Area code:** 707 **Zip:** 94515

Samuel Brannan, a wealthy San Francisco entrepreneur, came here in 1859 and recognized that the natural hot-water geysers, mineral springs and mineralized mud baths would support a resort community. Brannan considered the new resort the Saratoga of California; thus Calistoga. He was also among those who cultivated grape vines on the surrounding hillsides. As a result, Calistoga is a thriving resort town and center of an important wine-producing area.

What to See and Do

1. **Mount St Helena** (4,344 ft). 8 mi N on CA 29. Extinct volcano where Robert Louis Stevenson honeymooned in 1880 and wrote "The Silverado Squatters." Robert Louis Stevenson State Park, on Mount St Helena, has monument (a statue of the author holding an open book) located near the site of the Silverado mine; three-quarter-mile hiking trail from parking lot.

2. **Petrified Forest.** 8 mi W on Petrified Forest Rd. Contains redwoods buried more than 3 million years ago by the eruption of Mt St

Helena. The trees were knocked down by a volcanic explosion and then buried in volcanic ash. Discovered around 1860, some trees are as large as 80 ft long and 12 ft in diameter, with details excellently preserved. Picnic area. (Daily) Phone 942-6667. **¢¢**

3. **Old Faithful Geyser of California.** 1299 Tubbs Lane. Approx 60-foot-high geyser is one of few, other than Yellowstone's Old Faithful, that erupts at regular intervals. Picnic area; snack bar; gift shop. (Daily; yearly average eruption approx every 40 min) Sr citizen rate. Phone 942-6463. **¢¢**

4. **Sterling Vineyards.** 1111 Dunaweal Lane. Access to winery by aerial tramway; self-guided tour; shop; wine tasting. Tour includes a considerable amount of walking. Under 16 must be accompanied by adult. Roof-top terrace picnic area. (Daily; closed Jan 1, Thanksgiving, Dec 25) Phone 942-3344. Tramway **¢¢¢**

5. **Sharpsteen Museum and Sam Brannan Cottage.** 1311 Washington St. History of Calistoga in diorama and shadow box form; changing exhibits include hardware, hand mirrors, clothing, dolls, furniture. Restored cottage (1860) contains furniture of the period. (Daily; closed Thanksgiving, Dec 25) Phone 942-5911.   **Free.**

(For further information contact the Chamber of Commerce, 1458 Lincoln Ave; 942-6333.)

Annual Event

Napa County Fair. Fairgrounds, Oak St. Oct.

(See Napa, Petaluma, St Helena, Santa Rosa, Sonoma)

Motel

✔ ★★**DR WILKINSON'S HOT SPRINGS.** 1507 Lincoln Ave. 707/942-4102; FAX 707/226-1171. 42 units, 2 story, 16 kits. S $49–$84; D $54–$100; each addl $8; kit. units $59–$90; special package plans. Crib free. TV; cable. 3 heated pools, 1 indoor; whirlpool, steam rm. Complimentary coffee in rms. Restaurant nearby. Ck-out noon. Meeting rm. Mud & mineral baths; massage. Many refrigerators. Victorian house (1877). Cr cds: A, MC, V.

Hotel

★★**MOUNT VIEW.** 1457 Lincoln Ave. 707/942-6877; FAX 707/942-6904. 22 rms, 8 suites, 3 cottages. S, D $90–$125; each addl $15; suites, cottages $125–$175. Crib free. TV; cable. Pool; whirlpool, poolside serv (summer). Restaurant 8 am–3 pm, 5:30–10 pm. Bar 10:30–2 am; entertainment wkends. Ck-out noon. Meeting rm. Some in-rm whirlpools. Some suites with balcony. Restored hotel (1917); National Historic Monument. Old World decor. Original furniture; antiques. Cr cds: A, MC, V.

Inns

✔ ★**CALISTOGA.** 1250 Lincoln Ave. 707/942-4101. 18 rms, all share bath, 2 story. No A/C. No rm phones. S, D $50–$55. Closed Dec 25. Complimentary continental bkfst, refreshments. Restaurant (see CALISTOGA INN). Ck-out 11 am, ck-in 3 pm. Street parking. Balconies. Built 1900. On-site brewery in old watertower. Beer garden. Cr cds: MC, V.

★★★**CHRISTOPHER'S INN.** 1010 Foothill Blvd. 707/942-5755. 10 rms, 4 with shower only, 2 story. No rm phones. Apr–Nov: S, D $105–$170; suite $145; higher rates wkends & hols (2-night min); lower rates rest of yr. TV in some rms; cable. Complimentary continental bkfst; coffee in library on request. Restaurant nearby. Ck-out 11 am, ck-in 2 pm. Concierge. Bellhop. Picnic tables. Built 1918; renovated to include

modern amenities. English country decor; many antiques. Fireplaces. Totally nonsmoking. Cr cds: A, MC, V.

★**CULVER'S.** 1805 Foothill Blvd. 707/942-4535. 6 rms, all share bath, 3 story. No rm phones. May–Nov: S, D $95–$115; each addl $25; wkday rates; lower rates rest of yr. Closed Dec 24, 25. Children over 16 yrs only. Pool (summer); whirlpool, sauna. Complimentary full bkfst, tea, afternoon sherry & refreshments. Ck-out 11 am, ck-in 3–6 pm. Antiques. Built 1875. Totally nonsmoking. No cr cds accepted.

★★★**FOOTHILL HOUSE.** 3037 Foothill Blvd. 707/942-6933; res: 800/942-6933; FAX 707/942-5692. 2 rms, 1 cottage. Rm phones on request. S, D $120–$230; each addl $15. TV; cable. Bkfst 8–9:30 am. Complimentary wine. Complimentary coffee in rms. Ck-out 11 am, ck-in 3:30 pm. Lndry facilities avail. Refrigerators. Some in-rm whirlpools. Some private patios. Remodeled turn-of-the-century farmhouse. Individually decorated rms with country antiques. Audio cassette library in rms. Fireplaces. Sun deck. Fish pond. Totally nonsmoking. Cr cds: A, MC, V.

★**MEADOWLARK COUNTRY HOUSE.** 601 Petrified Forest Rd. 707/942-5651. 4 rms, 2 story. S, D $110–$145. TV in sitting rm; cable. Pool. Complimentary full bkfst, coffee. Ck-out 11:30 am, ck-in 3:30 pm. Picnic tables. English antiques. English country pine antiques. Totally nonsmoking. Cr cds: MC, V.

★**THE PINK MANSION.** 1415 Foothill Blvd. 707/942-0558. 6 rms, 2 story. Phone in suite. Mid-Apr–mid-Nov: S, D $105–$160; each addl $15; wkend rates; lower rates rest of yr. Crib free. TV in some rms. Complimentary full bkfst, wine & cheese. Restaurant nearby. Ck-out 11 am, ck-in 3 pm. Rec rm. Balconies. Antiques. Library/sitting rm. Built 1875. Country garden. Totally nonsmoking. Cr cds: MC, V.

★★★**SILVER ROSE.** 351 Rosedale Rd. 707/942-9581; res: 800/995-9381 (CA); FAX 707/942-0841. 9 rms, 2 story. No rm phones. S, D $115–$195. Pool; whirlpool. Complimentary continental bkfst, afternoon refreshments. Ck-out noon, ck-in 3–7 pm. Whirlpool in suite. Balconies. Picnic tables. Antiques. Library/sitting rm. Totally nonsmoking. Cr cds: A, DS, MC, V.

Restaurants

★**ALEX'S.** 1437 Lincoln Ave. 707/942-6868. Hrs: 4–10 pm; Sun 2–9 pm; early-bird dinner Tues–Fri 4–6 pm. Closed Mon; Jan 1; also Dec. Res accepted. Bar from 2 pm. Semi-a la carte: dinner $6.50–$16.95. Child's meals. Specializes in prime rib, seafood. Large mural of California wine country landmarks. Family-owned. Cr cds: A, MC, V.

✔ ★**CAFE PACIFICO.** 1237 Lincoln Ave. 707/942-4400. Hrs: 11 am–10 pm; Sat & Sun from 10 am; Sat & Sun brunch to 3 pm. Closed Thanksgiving, Dec 25. Mexican menu. Bar to 11 pm. Semi-a la carte: lunch $2.75–$9.25, dinner $5.95–$13.95. Sat, Sun brunch $2.75–$8.95. Child's meals. Specializes in authentic Mexican dishes. Cr cds: MC, V.

★**CALISTOGA INN.** (See Calistoga Inn) 707/942-4101. Hrs: 9–11 am, 11:30 am–3 pm, 5:30 pm–closing. Closed Dec 25. Wine, beer. A la carte entrees: lunch $5–$12, dinner $12–$18. Semi-a la carte: bkfst $7.50. Specializes in fresh seafood. Entertainment Wed, Fri & Sat. Outdoor dining. Cr cds: MC, V.

Camarillo (H-3)

Pop: 52,303 **Elev:** 160 ft **Area code:** 805 **Zip:** 93010

What to See and Do

Channel Islands Aviation. Offers trips to Santa Rosa Island, in the Channel Islands National Park; 1-day scenic trips and flights for camping avail. For information phone 987-1301.

(For further information contact the Chamber of Commerce, 632 Las Posas Rd; 484-4383.)

(See Oxnard, Thousand Oaks, Ventura)

Motels

✔ ★ ★ **BEST WESTERN CAMARILLO INN.** *295 Daily Dr. 805/987-4991; FAX 805/388-3679.* 58 rms, 2 story. S $50; D $55–$60; each addl $5; under 13 free. Crib $5. TV; in-rm movies avail. Heated pool; whirlpool. Complimentary continental bkfst. Restaurant adj 6–2 am. Ck-out 11 am. Meeting rms. Valet serv. Cr cds: A, C, D, DS, ER, MC, V, JCB.

★ ★ ★ **COUNTRY INN.** *1405 Del Norte Rd. 805/983-7171; res: 800/447-3529; FAX 805/983-1838.* 100 rms, 3 story. S $74–$84; D $84–$90; each addl $10; suites $110–$145; under 12 free. TV; in-rm movies. Heated pool; whirlpool. Complimentary full bkfst. Ck-out noon. Lndry facilities. Health club privileges. Refrigerators. Cr cds: A, C, D, DS, MC, V, JCB.

Motor Hotel

★ ★ **DEL NORTE INN.** *4444 Central Ave. 805/485-3999; res: 800/447-3529.* 111 rms, 3 story, 24 kit. units. S $69–$74; D $79–$84; each addl $10; kit. units $90–$100; under 12 free. Crib free. TV; in-rm movies. Heated pool; whirlpool. Complimentary continental bkfst, coffee. Restaurant adj 8 am–10 pm. Ck-out noon. Coin lndry. Meeting rms. Valet serv. Refrigerators. Balconies. Grill. Cr cds: A, C, D, DS, MC, V, JCB.

Restaurant

★ ★ **CRAB HOUSE.** *350 N Lantana. 805/987-4979.* Hrs: 11 am–9 pm; Fri to 10 pm; Sat 4–10 pm; Sun 1–9 pm. Closed Dec 25. Res accepted. Bar 11 am–11 pm, Fri-Sat to midnight. Semi-a la carte: lunch $3.50–$9.95, dinner $7.95–$26.95. Child's meals. Specializes in live Maine lobster, seafood, steak. Parking. Outdoor dining. Contemporary tavern decor; oak paneling, black and white checkered floor, etched-glass rm dividers depicting seascape. Exhibition kitchen. Cr cds: A, MC, V.

Ⓓ

Cambria (G-2)

Pop: 5,382 **Elev:** 65 ft **Area code:** 805 **Zip:** 93428

Cambria's early commerce centered on lumbering, ranching, mining and shipping. However, the town's shipping and whaling volume declined as trade relied on the railroad extending to San Luis Obispo. Today Cambria is known as an artists' colony on California's central coast.

What to See and Do

1. **Hearst-San Simeon State Historical Monument** (see). Approximately 7 mi N on CA 1.
2. **Beach recreation.** Beachcoming for jade, agate and quartz; rock and surf fishing at Moonstone Beach. Whale watching late

Dec–early Feb. The large rocks at Piedras Blancas are a prime refuge for sea lions and sea otters.

(For further information contact the Chamber of Commerce, 767 Main St; 927-3624.)

(See Morro Bay, San Simeon)

Motels

★ ★ **BEST WESTERN MARINERS INN.** *6180 Moonstone Beach Dr. 805/927-4624; FAX 805/927-3425.* 26 rms. No A/C. Mid-June–mid-Sept: S $79–$85; D $89–$95; each addl $10; lower rates rest of yr. Crib avail. Pet accepted, some restrictions. TV; cable, in-rm movies. Complimentary continental bkfst. Complimentary coffee in rms. Restaurant adj 6–9 pm. Ck-out 11 am. Whirlpool. Some refrigerators, fireplaces. Whale-watching deck. On ocean. Cr cds: A, C, D, DS, MC, V.

★ **CAMBRIA SHORES.** *6276 Moonstone Beach Dr. 805/927-8644; res: 800/433-9179 (CA).* 24 rms. No A/C. Mid-May–mid-Sept, wkends, hols: S, D $75–$105; each addl $5; lower rates rest of yr. Crib $5. TV; cable. Complimentary continental bkfst. Complimentary coffee in rms. Ck-out 11 am. Refrigerators. Ocean view; beach opp. Hearst Castle 6 mi. Cr cds: A, C, D, DS, MC, V.

✔ ★ ★ **CASTLE INN.** *6620 Moonstone Beach Dr. 805/927-8605; FAX 805/927-3179.* 31 rms. May–Oct: S $55–$95; D $65–$100; each addl $5; lower rates rest of yr. Crib $5. TV; cable. Heated pool; whirlpool. Complimentary continental bkfst. Ck-out 11 am. Many refrigerators. Ocean view; beach opp. Cr cds: DS, MC, V.

Inns

★ ★ ★ **BLUE DOLPHIN.** *6470 Moonstone Beach Dr. 805/927-3300.* 18 rms, 2 story. No A/C. Apr–Oct: S, D $95–$185; each addl $5; lower rates rest of yr. Crib $5. TV; cable, in-rm movies avail. Complimentary continental bkfst, coffee, tea in tea room. Restaurant nearby. Ck-out 11 am, ck-in 3 pm. Refrigerators. Some wet bars. Some patios. On beach; most rms with ocean view. Fireplaces. Some canopy beds. Combines modern conveniences with ambience of an elegant European countryside inn. Rms uniquely designed, with English country fabrics and wall coverings. Cr cds: A, C, D, MC, V.

★ ★ ★ **BLUE WHALE.** *6736 Moonstone Beach Dr. 805/927-4647.* 6 rms. No A/C. S, D $135–$170; higher rates wkends & hols (2-night min); some lower rates Dec & Jan. TV; cable. Complimentary full bkfst, afternoon wine & cheese. Restaurant nearby. Ck-out 11 am, ck-in 2 pm. Gift shop. Refrigerators. Country-style inn situated on bluffs overlooking the Pacific Ocean. Each rm individually decorated; canopy beds, fireplaces. All rms with ocean view. Totally nonsmoking. Cr cds: MC, V.

★ ★ **J. PATRICK HOUSE.** *2990 Burton Dr, above East Village area just off CA 1. 805/927-3812.* 8 rms, 2 story. No A/C. No rm phones. S, D $100–$120. Children over 16 yrs only. Complimentary continental bkfst, wine & cheese. Ck-out 11 am, ck-in 2 pm. Fireplaces. Each rm individually decorated; antiques, homemade quilts. Early American-style log house; garden with arbor; extensive grounds & landscaping. Totally nonsmoking. Cr cds: MC, V.

★ ★ **MOONSTONE.** *5860 Moonstone Beach Dr. 805/927-4815.* 7 rms, 1–2 story. No A/C. S, D $90–$135; each addl $10. TV; cable, in-rm movies. Complimentary continental bkfst, wine & cheese. Complimentary coffee in rms. Restaurant nearby. Ck-out 11 am, ck-in 3 pm.

Whirlpool. Refrigerators, fireplaces. Antiques; crystal chandelier in lobby. On ocean; all rms with ocean view. Cr cds: A, C, D, DS, MC, V.

★ ★ ★**SAND PEBBLES.** *6252 Moonstone Beach Dr. 805/927-5600.* 23 rms, 1–2 story. No A/C. May–Oct: S, D $85–$185; each addl $5; lower rates rest of yr. Crib $5. TV; cable, in-rm movies. Complimentary continental bkfst, tea, coffee. Restaurant nearby. Ck-out 11 am, ck-in 3 pm. Refrigerators; some in-rm whirlpools. Each rm individually decorated; canopy beds, fireplaces. Inn overlooks ocean; most rms have panoramic view. Cr cds: A, D, MC, V.

Restaurants

✔ ★ ★**BRAMBLES.** *4005 Burton Dr. 805/927-4716.* Hrs: 4–9:30 pm; Sat to 10 pm; early-bird dinner Sun–Fri 4–6 pm, Sat 4–5:30 pm; Sun brunch 9:30 am–2 pm. Res accepted. No A/C. Bar. Semi-a la carte: dinner from $7.95. Sun brunch $8.95–$12.95. Child's meals. Specialties: prime rib with Yorkshire pudding, oak-broiled fresh salmon. Parking. Victorian decor; antiques. Cr cds: A, D, DS, MC, V.

★ ★**IAN'S.** *2150 Center St. 805/927-8649.* Hrs: 6–9:30 pm; Fri & Sat also 11:30 am–2:30 pm; Sun brunch 10 am–2:30 pm. Closed Dec 25. Res accepted. Bar. Semi-a la carte: lunch $5–$6, dinner $7.50–$25. Sun brunch $5.25–$6. Specialties: planked salmon filet with sweet mustard sauce, grilled rack of lamb with mint cilantro sauce. Seasonal menu. Multi-level dining. Totally nonsmoking. Cr cds: A, MC, V.

★ ★**MOONRAKER.** *6550 Moonstone Beach Dr. 805/927-3859.* Hrs: 11 am–2:30 pm, 5–9:30 pm; June–Aug from 8 am; wkend hrs vary Sept–May; early-bird dinner 4:30–6 pm. Closed Thanksgiving; also Jan and Wed from Labor Day–Memorial Day. Cajun menu. Bar. Semi-a la carte: bkfst $2–$5.95, lunch $4–$9.25, dinner $5.50–$33.95. Sun brunch $9.95. Child's meals. Specializes in seafood, steak. Entertainment wkends. Parking. Outdoor dining. Cr cds: A, MC, V.

★ ★**ROBIN'S.** *4095 Burton Dr, at Center St. 805/927-5007.* Hrs: 11 am–9 pm; Sun from 5 pm. Closed Thanksgiving, Dec 25. Res accepted. No A/C. Varied menu. Wine, beer. A la carte entrees: lunch $3.95–$9.95, dinner $4.95–$14.95. Specializes in vegetarian dishes with local organically grown produce. Salad deli. Parking. Outdoor dining. Garden. Totally nonsmoking. Cr cds: A, MC, V.

Carlsbad (J-4)

Pop: 63,126 **Elev:** 39 ft **Area code:** 619

Named for Karlsbad, Czechoslovakia (now Bohemia), a famous European spa, this beach-oriented community is a playground for golfers, tennis players, waterskiers and fishermen.

What to See and Do

South Carlsbad State Beach. 3 mi S on Carlsbad Blvd. Swimming, surfing; fishing. Improved camping (dump station). Standard fees. Phone 438-3143 or 800/444-PARK.

(For further information contact the Convention & Visitors Bureau, PO Box 1246, 92018; 434-6093 or 800/227-5722.)

Annual Events

Tournament of Champions. Golf. Contact Tournament Director, La Costa Resort and Spa; phone 438-9111, ext 4612. Early Jan.

Carlsbad Village Fair. More than 800 art, craft and antique vendors; food, entertainment. 1st Sun May & 1st Sun Nov.

(See Escondido, La Jolla, Oceanside, San Diego, San Juan Capistrano)

Motels

★ ★**BEST WESTERN ANDERSEN'S INN.** *850 Palomar Airport Rd (92008). 619/438-7880; FAX 619/931-0499.* 145 rms, 2 story. Mid-May–Sept: S, D $70–$98; under 12 free; lower rates rest of yr. Crib free. TV; cable. Heated pool; whirlpool. Restaurant 6:30 am–9 pm. Bar 11 am–midnight, Fri & Sat to 2 am; entertainment, dancing Tues–Sat. Ck-out 11 am. Coin lndry. Meeting rms. Valet serv. Private patios, balconies. Cr cds: A, D, MC, V.

★ ★**CARLSBAD INN BEACH RESORT.** *3075 Carlsbad Blvd (92008). 619/434-7020; res: 800/235-3939; FAX 619/431-4594.* 62 rms, 3 story, 27 kit. units. S $105–$125; D $115–$135; each addl $10; suites $175; kit. units $105–$125; under 12 free. Crib $10. TV; cable, in-rm movies. Heated pool. Playground. Supervised child's activities (seasonal). Complimentary coffee in rms. Restaurant adj 7 am–11 pm. Ck-out 11 am. Coin lndry. Meeting rms. Exercise equipt; weights, bicycles, whirlpools, sauna. Lawn games. Bathrm phone in suites. Picnic tables. Near beach. Cr cds: A, C, D, DS, ER, MC, V, JCB.

✔ ★**ECONOMY INNS OF AMERICA.** *751 Raintree Dr (92009), W of I-5, Poinsettia Ln exit. 619/931-1185.* 126 rms, 3 story. June–mid-Sept: S $39.90; D $49.90–$54.90; lower rates rest of yr. Pet accepted. TV; cable. Heated pool. Complimentary continental bkfst. Ck-out 11 am. Ocean 2 blks. Cr cds: A, MC, V.

★ ★**OCEAN MANOR.** *2950 Ocean St (92008). 619/729-2493; res: 800/624-7263.* 48 rms, 2 story, 26 kit. suites. Mid-June–mid-Sept: S, D $69–$125; wkly rates; lower rates rest of yr. Crib $5. TV; cable. Heated pool. Restaurant adj 7 am–10 pm. Ck-out 11 am. Coin lndry. Picnic tables, grills. Opp beach. Cr cds: A, C, D, DS, MC, V.

★ ★**RAMADA INN SUITES.** *751 Macadamia Dr (92009). 619/438-2285; FAX 619/438-4547.* 121 kit. suites, 3 story. June–Aug: kit. suites $69–$109; under 16 free; lower rates rest of yr. Crib free. TV; cable. Heated pool; whirlpool. Complimentary continental bkfst. Complimentary coffee in rms. Restaurant adj 11 am–2:30 pm, 5–10 pm. Ck-out noon. Coin lndry. Meeting rms. Valet serv. Opp ocean. Cr cds: A, C, D, DS, MC, V, JCB.

Resort

★ ★ ★**LA COSTA RESORT & SPA.** *Costa Del Mar Rd (92009), 2 mi E of I-5 La Costa Ave exit. 619/438-9111; res: 800/854-5000; FAX 619/438-3758.* 480 rms in hotel, 2–3 story, 2–3 bedrm houses. AP: S, D $215–$325; suites $375–$2,000; golf, tennis, spa package plans; MAP avail. Crib free. TV; cable, in-rm movies. 2 heated pools; poolside serv. Supervised child's activities. Restaurant 6:30 am–11 pm; also 4 dining rms. Rm serv to 1 am. Snack bar. Bar. Ck-out noon, ck-in 4 pm. Meeting rms. Valet serv. Concierge. Shopping arcade. Airport transportation. Lighted tennis courts including clay, composition & grass, pro. 36-hole golf, putting green, driving range. Bicycles. Soc dir. Exercise rm; instructor, weights, bicycles, whirlpool, steam rm, sauna. Full service health spa. Minibars; wet bar in some suites. Some private patios. Cr cds: A, C, D, DS, ER, MC, V, JCB.

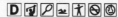

Restaurants

★★**HENRY'S.** *264 Carlsbad Village Dr. 619/729-9244.* Hrs: 11:30 am–2:30 pm, 4:30–9:30 pm; Fri & Sat 5:30–10:30 pm; Sun 4:30–9:30 pm. Closed some major hols. Res accepted. Continental menu. Bar. Semi-a la carte: lunch $3.95–$8.95, dinner $9.95–$18.95. Child's meals. Specializes in veal, seafood. Entertainment. Parking. Cr cds: A, C, D, DS, MC, V.

★★**TUSCANY.** *6981 El Camino Real. 619/929-8111.* Hrs: 11:30 am–11 pm; Sat from 4 pm. Closed Thanksgiving. Res accepted. Italian menu. Bar. Semi-a la carte: lunch $3.95–$14.95, dinner $8.95–$17.95. Specializes in pasta, seafood, Northern Italian dishes. Parking. Italian villa-style decor. Cr cds: A, MC, V.

Carmel (F-1)

Founded: early 1600s **Pop:** 4,239 **Elev:** 220 ft **Area code:** 408

On a curving beach at the foot of rolling hills, Carmel sits at one of the loveliest spots along the California coast. A center for artists and writers since the turn of the century, Carmel fiercely protects its individuality. The architecture is a mixture of every style and whim of the literary and artistic populace. The area attracts a lively tourist trade. Spanish settlers named the spot for the Carmelite Friars who accompanied them.

What to See and Do

1. **Mission San Carlos Borromeo del Rio Carmelo.** 1 mi S off CA 1, then W to 3080 Rio Rd. Basilica founded by Fray Junipero Serra in 1770; his burial place. Headquarters for the California missions. (Daily; closed Thanksgiving, Dec 25) Phone 624-3600. **¢**

2. **Biblical Garden.** Church of the Wayfarer, Lincoln St & 7th Ave. Oldest church in Carmel, founded in 1904. Stained-glass windows in the sanctuary depict Biblical and local scenes. A Gaza St Galy mosaic, sundial on a granite boulder, mosaic cross in the garden. A 32-rank pipe organ provides quarterly concerts. Garden contains trees and plants mentioned in the Bible and indigenous to the Holy Land. (Daily) Phone 624-3550. **Free.**

3. **Point Lobos State Reserve.** 3 mi S on CA 1. Sea Lion Rocks, Bird Island just offshore. Natural grove of Monterey cypress. Picnic area (no fires or stoves), naturalist programs. No dogs. (Day use only) Sr citizen rate. Phone 624-4909. Per vehicle **¢¢¢**

4. **Art Galleries.** There are a large number of galleries displaying a wide variety of art in the Carmel area. A brochure, *The Guide To Carmel,* containing a list of galleries may be obtained from the Carmel Business Assn, PO Box 4444, 93921. Phone 624-2522.

5. **Seventeen-Mile Drive** from Carmel to Monterey (see MONTEREY).

6. **Rancho Cañada Golf Club.** Carmel Valley Rd, 1 mi E of CA 1. Two 18-hole championship courses; driving range. (Daily) Phone 624-0111.

7. **The Barnyard.** CA 1, Carmel Valley Rd exit, then take 1st right and enter Barnyard from 26400 Carmel Rancho Blvd. Shopping area with 1½ acres of terraced flower gardens around rustic, old style California barns housing a number of shops, galleries and restaurants.

(For further information and scenic tours contact the Carmel Business Assn, San Carlos between 5th and 6th Sts, PO Box 4444, 93921; 624-2522.)

Annual Events

Wine Festival. Usually Mar.

Carmel Outdoor Art Festival. Sunset Center. Phone 659-6547. Late June.

Carmel Bach Festival. Sunset Center, San Carlos & 9th Sts. Concerts, recitals, lectures, special events. Contact PO Box 575, 93921; phone 624-1521. Late July–early Aug.

(See Carmel Valley, Monterey, Pacific Grove, Pebble Beach)

Motels

(Higher rates on holidays and during special events)

★★★**ADOBE INN.** *(Box 4115, 93921) Dolores St & 8th Ave. 408/624-3933; res: 800/388-3933; FAX 408/624-8636.* 20 rms, 2 story, 4 suites. No A/C. S, D $120–$190; suites $225–$285; under 12 free. TV. Heated pool; sauna. Complimentary continental bkfst. Complimentary coffee in rms. Restaurant adj 11:30 am–10 pm. Ck-out noon. Meeting rm. Free covered parking. Minibars. Balconies. Cr cds: A, MC, V.

✔★**BEST WESTERN TOWN HOUSE LODGE.** *(PO Box 3574, 93921) 5th Ave & San Carlos St. 408/624-1261.* 28 rms. Apr–Oct: S, D $84–$94; each addl $6; lower rates rest of yr. TV. Pool. Restaurant nearby. Ck-out 11 am. Sun deck. Cr cds: A, C, D, DS, MC, V.

★★**CANDLE LIGHT INN.** *(Box 1900, 93921) San Carlos St, between 4th & 5th Aves. 408/624-6451; res: 800/433-4732.* 19 rms, 2 story, 7 kit. units. No A/C. June–Oct, wkends: S, D $125–$145; each addl $15; kit. units $145; under 12 free; 2-day min wkends; lower rates rest of yr. TV; cable. Heated pool. Complimentary continental bkfst. Ck-out noon. Refrigerators; some fireplaces. Cr cds: A, C, D, DS, ER, MC, V, JCB.

✔★**CARMEL RIVER INN.** *(Box 221609, 93922) 1 mi S on CA 1, at bridge. 408/624-1575; res: 800/882-8142.* 19 rms, 2 story, 24 cottages, 13 kits. No A/C. S, D $85–$90; each addl $5; cottages $70–$125. TV; cable. Heated pool. Coffee in rms. Restaurant nearby. Ck-out 11 am. Fireplace in some cottages. Private patios, balconies. Cr cds: MC, V.

★**CARMEL TORRES INN.** *(Box XX, 93921) Ocean Ave & Torres St. 408/624-3387.* 17 rms, 2 story. No A/C. No rm phones. May–Oct: S, D $90–$180; lower rates rest of yr. TV; cable. Continental bkfst. Complimentary coffee in rms. Ck-out 11 am. Each rm individually decorated. Cr cds: A, C, D, DS, MC, V.

✔★**COMFORT INN.** *(Box 2266, 93921) Carpenter St & Second Ave. 408/624-3113; FAX 408/624-5456.* 25 cottages, 2 kits. No A/C. May–Oct: S, D $89–$175; each addl $10; kits. $125–$175; lower rates rest of yr. Crib $5. TV; cable. Complimentary continental bkfst. Coffee in rms. Ck-out 11 am. Whirlpool, sauna. Some refrigerators. Fireplaces. Cr cds: A, C, D, DS, MC, V, JCB.

★★**DOLPHIN INN.** *(Box 1900, 93921) San Carlos St & 4th Ave. 408/624-5356; res: 800/433-4732.* 26 rms, 2 story. No A/C. June–Oct, wkends: S, D $99–$139; each addl $15; suites $185–$200; under 12 free; 2-day min wkends; lower rates rest of yr. TV; cable. Heated pool. Complimentary continental bkfst in rms. Restaurant 7 am–10 pm. Ck-out noon. Refrigerators. Some fireplaces. Cr cds: A, C, D, DS, ER, MC, V, JCB.

★★**HORIZON INN.** *(Box 1693, 93921) Junipero & 3rd Aves. 408/624-5327; res: 800/350-7723; FAX 408/626-8253.* 20 rms, 1–2 story, 4 kits. (oven in 1); 6 suites (1 bedrm) in bldg opp. No A/C. S, D $95–$155; each addl $15; kit. units $15–$25 addl, 1-bedrm suites $140–$175. TV; cable. Heated pool. Complimentary continental bkfst in rms. Restaurant nearby. Ck-out 11 am. Refrigerators, fireplaces. Some private patios, balconies. Some rms with ocean view. Cr cds: A, MC, V.

★★**LOBOS LODGE.** *(Drawer L-1, 93921) Monte Verde St at Ocean Ave.* 408/624-3874. 30 rms, 1–3 story. S, D $90–$115; each addl $20; suites $135–$165. TV. Continental bkfst served in rms 8–9:30 am. Ck-out noon. Refrigerators, fireplaces. Private patios, balconies. Beach 4 blks. Cr cds: A, MC, V.

★★★**MISSION RANCH.** *26270 Dolores St (92923), behind Carmel Mission.* 408/624-6436; res: 800/538-8221; FAX 408/626-4163. 29 rms, 6 in farmhouse. No A/C. June–Oct: S, D $95–$225; each addl $15; bunkhouse suite (1 bdrm) $195; under 13 free; lower rates rest of yr. Crib free. TV. Complimentary continental bkfst. Restaurant 4:30–11 pm; Sat & Sun from 11 am. Bar; entertainment. Ck-out noon. Meeting rms. Tennis, pro. Exercise equipt; weight machine, bicycles. Balconies. Stone fireplaces. Country decor; ranch atmosphere. Swimming beach 2 blks. Totally nonsmoking. Cr cds: A, D, MC, V.

★★**SVENDSGAARD'S INN.** *(Box 1900, 93921) 4th Ave & San Carlos St.* 408/624-1511; res: 800/433-4732. 34 rms, 1–2 story, 12 kits. (no ovens). No A/C. June–Oct, wkends: S, D $99–$145; each addl $15; suites $175–$190; under 12 free; 2-day min wkends; lower rates rest of yr. TV; cable. Heated pool. Complimentary continental bkfst in rms. Restaurant nearby. Ck-out noon. Refrigerators; some fireplaces. Country decor. Cr cds: A, C, D, DS, ER, MC, V, JCB.

★★**TALLY HO INN.** *(Box 3726, 93921) 6th Ave & Monte Verde St.* 408/624-2232; FAX 408/624-2661. 14 rms, 1–2 story. No A/C. Some rm phones. S, D $105–$225; 2-day min wkends. TV; cable. Complimentary continental bkfst. Restaurant opp from 8:30 am. Ck-out noon. Some fireplaces. Some private patios. Landscaped gardens. Cr cds: A, MC, V.

★★★**TICKLE PINK INN AT CARMEL HIGHLANDS.** *155 Highlands Dr (93923).* 408/624-1244; res: 800/635-4774; FAX 408/626-9516. 34 rms in 2 bldgs, 2 & 3 story. No A/C. No elvtr. S, D $129–$199; each addl $25; suites $189–$259; cottage $229–$279; 2-day min wkends, 3-day min special events. TV; cable. Continental bkfst. Complimentary refreshments, afternoon wine & cheese. Restaurant adj 7 am–11 pm. Ck-out noon. Sundries. Refrigerators; some wet bars, fireplaces. Many balconies. Scenic view of coast. Cr cds: A, MC, V.

✔★**WAYFARER INN.** *(Box 1896, 93921) 4th Ave & Mission St.* 408/624-2711; res: 800/533-2711. 17 rms, 2 story. No A/C. S, D $57.50–$137; each addl $10. Crib avail. TV; cable; in-rm movies. Complimentary continental bkfst. Restaurant nearby. Ck-out noon. Many fireplaces. Cr cds: A, D, DS, MC, V.

★★**WAYSIDE INN.** *(Box 1900, 93921) 7th Ave & Mission St.* 408/624-5336; res: 800/433-4732. 21 rms, 2 story, 10 kits. No A/C. Mid-June–mid-Oct & wkends: S, D $99–$145; each addl $15; suites $195–$235; kit. units $145–$235; 2-day min wkends; lower rates rest of yr. TV; cable. Complimentary continental bkfst in rms. Restaurant nearby. Ck-out noon. Some balconies. Colonial Williamsburg decor. Cr cds: A, C, D, DS, ER, MC, V.

Lodges

★★★**HIGHLANDS INN.** *(Box 1700, 93921) 4 mi S of Carmel on CA 1.* 408/624-3801; res: 800/538-9525 (exc CA), 800/682-4811 (CA); FAX 408/626-1574. 142 rms, 1–2 story, 100 spa suites. S, D $225–$275; each addl $25; spa suites $325–$400; 2-bedrm suites $550–$650; under 16 free. Crib free. TV; cable, in-rm movies. Heated pool; poolside serv.

Restaurant 7 am–11 pm (also see PACIFIC'S EDGE). Rm serv. Bar 11:30–2 am; entertainment. Ck-out noon. Meeting rms. Bellhops. Valet serv. Concierge. Gift shop. Gourmet market. Bicycles. Minibars; whirlpool, woodburning fireplace in most rms; full kit. in suites. Private patios, balconies. On 12 wooded acres; views of Pacific Ocean and Big Sur coast. Cr cds: A, C, D, DS, MC, V, JCB.

★★★★★**QUAIL LODGE RESORT & GOLF CLUB.** *8205 Valley Greens Dr (93923), Golf Club at Quail Lodge.* 408/624-1581; res: 800/538-9516 (exc CA), 800/682-9303 (CA); FAX 408/624-3726. 100 units. S, D $195–$245; each addl $25; suites $285–$515; children free; golf plan exc wkends. TV; cable. 2 heated pools; poolside serv. Complimentary coffee, newspaper in rms, afternoon tea 3–5 pm. Restaurant (see THE COVEY). Rm serv 7 am–11 pm. 2 bars: 11 am–7 pm & 5 pm–1 am; entertainment Tues–Sun. Ck-out 1 pm. Meeting rms. Bellhops. Concierge. Tennis $10/day, pro. 18-hole golf greens fee $85, putting greens, driving range. Hot tub. Bicycles avail. Lawn games. Some fireplaces, wet bars. Private patios, balconies. Magnificent setting. Spacious grounds; duck ponds; miles of nature trails. Cr cds: A, C, D, DS, MC, V, JCB.

Hotel

★★★**LA PLAYA.** *(Box 900, 93921) Camino Real at 8th Ave.* 408/624-6476; res: 800/582-8900 (CA); FAX 408/624-7966. 75 rms, 3–4 story. S, D $110–$210; each addl $15; suites $300–$425; kit. cottages $210–$495; under 12 free. Crib free. TV; cable. Heated pool; poolside serv. Restaurant 7 am–10 pm. Bar 11 am–midnight. Ck-out noon. Meeting rms. Concierge. Valet parking. Minibars. Private patios. Renovated Mediterranean-style villa (1904). Rms have views of gardens, ocean, Point Lobos Reserve, Pebble Beach or Carmel. Cr cds: A, D, MC, V.

Inns

✔★★**CARMEL GARDEN COURT.** *(PO Box 6226, 93921) 4th Ave & Torres St.* 408/624-6926; FAX 408/624-4935. 9 rms. No A/C. 1 rm phone. June–Aug: S, D $90–$185; suite $250–$385; higher rates: wkends (2-night min), special events; lower rates rest of yr. Adults preferred. TV; cable, in-rm movies. Complimentary continental bkfst, tea, sherry. Complimentary coffee in rms. Restaurant nearby. Ck-out 11 am, ck-in 2 pm. Refrigerators. Garden. Beach 10 blks. Totally nonsmoking. Cr cds: A, MC, V.

★★★**CARRIAGE HOUSE.** *(Box 1900, 93921) Junipero Ave between 7th & 8th Aves.* 408/625-2585; res: 800/433-4732. 13 rms, 2 story. No A/C. S, D $165–$225; each addl $15; under 12 free; 2-day min wkends. TV; cable. Complimentary continental bkfst in rms. Complimentary wine. Restaurant nearby. Ck-out noon, ck-in 3 pm. Refrigerators, wet bars, fireplaces; many sunken baths; whirlpool in some rms. Antique furnishings. Cr cds: A, C, D, DS, ER, MC, V, JCB.

★★**COBBLESTONE INN.** *(Box 3185, 93921) Junipero & 8th Aves.* 408/625-5222. 24 rms, 2 story. S, D $95–$175; each addl $15; suites $160–$175. TV. Complimentary full bkfst, refreshments. Ck-out noon, ck-in 2 pm. Refrigerators, fireplaces. New England country decor; cobblestone courtyard. Cr cds: A, D, MC, V.

★★**CYPRESS.** *(Box Y, 93921) Lincoln St & 7th Ave.* 408/624-3871; res: 800/443-7443; FAX 408/624-8216. 33 rms, 2 story. D $94–$198; each addl $15; lower rates Dec–Jan. Pet accepted; $15. TV; cable. Continental bkfst. Ck-out noon, ck-in 3 pm. Bellhops. Valet serv. Some refrigerators. Some verandas. Mediterranean facade; set in heart of Carmel Village. Cr cds: A, MC, V, JCB.

★★HAPPY LANDING. *(Box 2619, 93921) Monte Verde St,
between 5th & 6th Aves.* 408/624-7917. 5 rms, 2 suites. No A/C. No rm
phones. S, D $95–$115; each addl $15; suites $150. Children over 12 yrs
only. TV. Complimentary continental bkfst, coffee, tea, sherry. Restaurant nearby. Ck-out 11:30 am, ck-in 2 pm. Some street parking. Cathedral ceilings; antiques. Garden; gazebo; fish pond. Cr cds: MC, V.

★★NORMANDY INN. *(Box 1706, 93921) Ocean Ave & Monte
Verde St.* 408/624-3825; res: 800/343-3825. 45 rms, 2 story, 4 suites, 3
kit. cottages. Apr–Oct: S, D $98–$145; each addl $10; suites $175–$185;
kit. cottages $300–$350; lower rates rest of yr. TV. Heated pool. Complimentary continental bkfst. Ck-out 11 am, ck-in 2 pm. Some refrigerators. Fireplace in cottages. French country garden atmosphere. Cr cds:
A, MC, V.

★★SANDPIPER INN. *2408 Bay View Ave (93923).* 408/624-
6433. 16 rms, 2 story. No A/C. No rm phones. S, D $90–$170; each addl
$20; 3-day min hols & special events. TV in sitting rm, some rms; cable.
Complimentary continental bkfst buffet, sherry. Ck-out noon, ck-in after
2 pm. Concierge. Some fireplaces. Some rms with ocean view. Antiques. Cr cds: A, MC, V.

★STONEHOUSE INN. *(Box 2517, 93921) 8th Ave & Monte
Verde St.* 408/624-4569. 6 rms, share bath, 2 story. No A/C. No rm
phones. S, D $90–$135; 2-day minimum wkends. Children over 12 yrs
only. Complimentary continental bkfst buffet 8:30–11 am, evening refreshments. Ck-out noon, ck-in 3 pm. Built 1906. Antiques. Garden. Cr
cds: MC, V.

✔★★VAGABOND'S HOUSE INN. *(Box 2747, 93921) 4th Ave &
Dolores St.* 408/624-7738. 11 rms, 1–2 story. No A/C. S, D $79–$145;
each addl $20. Children over 12 yrs only. TV; cable. Complimentary
continental bkfst. Ck-out noon, ck-in 3 pm. Concierge. Fireplaces. Antiques. Courtyard garden. Cr cds: A, MC, V.

Restaurants

★★★ANTON & MICHEL'S. *Mission St, ½ blk S of Ocean Ave.*
408/624-2406. Hrs: 11:30 am–3 pm, 5:30–9:30 pm. Res accepted. Continental menu. Bar 11 am–midnight. A la carte entrees: lunch
$6.25–$11.50, dinner $14.50–$32.50. Specialties: rack of lamb, fresh
abalone, chicken Jerusalem. Garden view from main dining room. Cr
cds: A, C, D, MC, V, JCB.

✔★BIRGIT & DAGMAR. *Dolores St between 7th & Ocean
Aves.* 408/624-3723. Hrs: 8 am–8 pm; Oct–May to 3 pm. No A/C.
Scandinavian menu. Wine, beer. Semi-a la carte: bkfst, lunch
$3.95–$5.95, dinner $10–$14.95. Specialties: Swedish pancakes,
crêpes, homemade bread, meatballs. Own desserts. Colorful Swedish
decor. No cr cds accepted.

★★★CASANOVA. *5th Ave between San Carlos & Mission Sts.*
408/625-0501. Hrs: 8–11 am, 11:30 am–3 pm, 5:30–10:30 pm; Sun
brunch 9 am–3 pm. Closed Dec 25. Res accepted. No A/C. Extensive
wine cellar. French, Italian menu. Semi-a la carte: bkfst $4.50–$6, lunch
$7.75–$11.75, dinner $19–$27. Sun brunch $5.50–$12.50. Specializes
in southern French & northern Italian cuisine. Own baking, pasta. Outdoor dining. Cr cds: MC, V.

★★CLAM BOX. *Mission St & 5th Ave.* 408/624-8597. Hrs:
4:30–9 pm. Closed Mon; Thanksgiving. Res accepted. No A/C. Continental menu. Bar 4–10 pm. Complete meals: dinner $11.50–$15.75.
Child's meals. Specializes in seafood, chicken. Own desserts. Outdoor
dining. Cr cds: A, MC, V.

★★THE COVEY. *(See Quail Lodge Resort & Golf Club)* 408/
624-1581. Hrs: 6:30–11 pm. Res accepted. No A/C. European menu.
Bar 5 pm–1 am. Wine list; many wines from local vineyards. A la carte
entrees: dinner $17–$37. Specializes in veal, fresh seafood, abalone.

Own pastries. Entertainment. Parking. Overlooks lake. Jacket. Cr cds:
A, C, D, MC, V, JCB.

D

★★★CRÈME CARMEL. *San Carlos St & 7th Ave, in Carmel
Square.* 408/624-0444. Hrs: 5:30–10 pm. Closed Thanksgiving; also wk
of Dec 25. Res accepted. French, California menu. Wine list. A la carte
entrees: dinner $17–$24. Specialties: duck, tasting menu, fresh fish,
goat cheese tart. Own pastries. Cr cds: MC, V.

★★FLAHERTY'S SEAFOOD GRILL & OYSTER BAR. *6th Ave
& Dolores St.* 408/625-1500. Hrs: 11:30 am–9:30 pm; early-bird dinner
Mon–Thurs 5–6:30 pm. Closed Dec 25. Res accepted. A la carte entrees: lunch $4.50–$10.95, dinner $12.99–$29.95. Specializes in fresh
seasonal seafood, shellfish. Own desserts. Cr cds: MC, V.

D

✔★★FLYING FISH GRILL. *7th Ave & Mission St.* 408/625-
2828. Hrs: 5–10 pm. Res accepted. Japanese menu. Semi-a la carte:
dinner $8–$16. Specialties: paper-wrapped catfish, ying yang salmon,
seafood clay pot. Pacific Rim decor; flying fish motif includes fish-
themed artwork & papier mâché flying fish decorations. Cr cds: MC, V,
JCB.

★★★FRENCH POODLE. *Junipero Ave at 5th Ave.* 408/624-
8643. Hrs: 5:30–9:30 pm. Closed Wed, Sun; Dec 25; also June. Res
accepted. No A/C. French menu. Semi-a la carte: dinner $14–$35.
Extensive wine list. Specialties: le magret de canard au vieux porto, les
noisettes d'agneau au thym et à la moutarde de Dijon, abalone
meunière. Own desserts. Intimate dining. Cr cds: A, D, MC, V.

★★★GIULIANO'S. *Mission St & 5th Ave.* 408/625-5231. Hrs:
11:30 am–2:30 pm, 6–9:30 pm; Fri & Sat to 10 pm; Sun & Mon from 6 pm.
Closed Thanksgiving, Dec 25. Res accepted. Northern Italian menu.
Beer. Wine list. A la carte entrees: lunch $5–$10, dinner $10–$26.
Specialties: carpaccio, profiterole al Giuliano, agnolotti pasta. Own
baking, pasta. Braille menu. Cr cds: A, MC, V.

D

★GREEK TAVERNA. *Delores St, just S of Ocean Ave.* 408/
624-9394. Hrs: 11 am–9 pm; wkends to 10 pm. Closed Wed; Dec 25. Res
accepted. No A/C. Greek menu. Wine, beer. Complete meals: lunch
$5.75–$8.95. A la carte entrees: dinner $8.95–$16.95. Platter for two:
$26.95. Child's meals. Specialties: moussaka, pastichio, Greek salad.
Casual dining; display of Greek plates and artifacts. Cr cds: MC, V.

D

★KATY'S PLACE. *Mission St, between 5th and 6th.* 408/
624-0199. Hrs: 7 am–2 pm. Closed Thanksgiving, Dec 25. No A/C. Wine,
beer. A la carte entrees: bkfst, lunch $3.95–$9.95. Specialties: eggs
Benedict, French toast, fresh berry pancakes, omelets. Outdoor dining.
Casual dining; country-style decor and atmosphere. No cr cds accepted.

★★L'ESCARGOT. *Mission St & 4th Ave.* 408/624-4914. Hrs:
5:30–9:30 pm. Closed Sun; some major hols. Res accepted. French
menu. Serv bar. Wine cellar. A la carte entrees: dinner $16–$23. Specializes in duck, fresh seafood, poulet à la crème, homemade desserts.
European decor. Cr cds: A, MC, V.

✔★★LA BOHÊME. *Delores St, between Ocean Ave & 7th Ave.*
408/624-7500. Hrs: 5:30–10 pm. Closed Easter, Thanksgiving, Dec 25.
No A/C. European/country menu. Wine, beer. Complete meals: dinner
$17.75. Specialties change nightly. European village atmosphere. Cr
cds: MC, V.

D

★★LA BRASSERIE Q POINT. *Ocean Ave, between Dolores
& Lincoln Sts.* 408/624-2569. Hrs: 5:30–10 pm. Closed Dec 25. Res
accepted. French, Japanese menu. Bar. Semi-a la carte: dinner
$12.95–$19.95. Specializes in fresh seafood, grilled meats, pasta. Fireplace, paintings. Cr cds: A, C, D, DS, MC, V, JCB.

D

★★PACIFIC'S EDGE. *(See Highlands Inn Lodge)* 408/624-
3801. Hrs: 11:30 am–2:30 pm, 6–10 pm; Fri & Sat to 10:30 pm; Sun

brunch 10 am–2:30 pm. Res accepted. Contemporary regional cuisine. Bar 11–2 am. Wine cellar. A la carte entrees: lunch $8–$15, dinner $25–$40. Complete meals: dinner $38; with wine, $58. Sun brunch $24. Specialties: Monterey Bay salmon, filet of beef on black pepper ravioli, classic crème brulée. Entertainment evenings. Valet parking. Understated elegance; spectacular ocean view. Cr cds: A, C, D, DS, MC, V, JCB.

✔ ★ ★PATISSERIE BOISSIERE. *Mission St, between Ocean & 7th.* *408/624-5008.* Hrs: 9 am–9:30 pm; Mon & Tues to 5 pm. Closed Thanksgiving, Dec 25. Res accepted. Continental menu. Wine, beer. A la carte entrees: bkfst $4.50–$7.50. Semi-a la carte: lunch $6–$11.95, dinner $7.50–$15.50. Specialties: French onion soup, coquille Saint-Jaques, salmon baked in parchment paper. Louis XV dining room. Cr cds: A, MC, V.

★ ★ ★RAFFAELLO. *Mission St, between Ocean & 7th Aves.* *408/624-1541.* Hrs: 6–10 pm. Closed Tues; also first 3 wks Jan. Res accepted. Northern Italian menu. Beer. Wine cellar. Semi-a la carte: dinner $13.50–$20.50. Specialties: cannelloni alla Raffaello, fettucine alla Romana, sogliola parigina, vitella alla Piemontese. Own desserts. Paintings; fireplace. Family-owned. Cr cds: A, MC, V.

★ ★ ★RIO GRILL. *CA 1 & Rio Rd, in Crossroads Shopping Ctr.* *408/625-5436.* Hrs: 11:30 am–11 pm. Closed Thanksgiving, Dec 25. Res accepted. Bar to midnight. Wine cellar. A la carte entrees: lunch $6–$12, dinner $6–$15. Specializes in oakwood grilled chicken, fish, meat. Own pastries, ice cream. Outdoor dining. Southwestern adobe decor. Cr cds: A, MC, V.

★ ★ROBATA GRILL & SAKE BAR. *3658 The Barnyard, at CA 1.* *408/624-2643.* Hrs: 5–11 pm. Closed Thanksgiving, Dec 24 & 25. Japanese menu. Bar. Semi-a la carte: dinner $9.95–$25.95. Specializes in robata, sushi. Parking. Japanese farmhouse decor. Cr cds: A, MC, V.

★ ★SANS SOUCI. *Lincoln St, between 5th & 6th Aves.* *408/624-6220.* Hrs: 6–10 pm. Closed Wed. Res accepted. No A/C. French menu. Bar. Wine list. Semi-a la carte: dinner $18–$30. Specializes in duck, veal, fresh seafood. French decor; fireplace. Family-owned. Cr cds: A, MC, V.

✔ ★ ★SILVER JONES. *3690 The Barnyard, in Barnyard Shopping Center.* *408/624-5200.* Hrs: 11:30 am–3 pm, 5:30–9:30 pm; Sun brunch 11 am–3 pm. Closed Dec 25. Res accepted. Mediterranean, Southwestern menu. Wine, beer. Semi-a la carte: lunch $5.95–$8.50, dinner $8–$14. Sun brunch $5.95–$8.50. Specializes in organic salads, grilled local seafood, homemade pasta & pizza. Outdoor dining. Cr cds: A, D, MC, V.

Unrated Dining Spot

THUNDERBIRD BOOKSHOP. *3600 Barnyard Plaza.* *408/624-1803 or -9414.* Hrs: 11 am–3:30 pm, 5–8:30 pm; Mon to 3:30 pm. Closed some hols. No A/C. Wine, beer. Semi-a la carte: lunch from $2.25, dinner $6.95–$15.95. Specializes in roast beef, fish, popovers. Outdoor dining. Glass-enclosed garden rm. Cr cds: MC, V.

Carmel Valley (F-2)

Pop: 4,407 **Elev:** 400 ft **Area code:** 408 **Zip:** 93924

(See Carmel, Monterey)

Motel

★ ★ROBLES DEL RIO LODGE. *200 Punta del Monte.* *408/659-3705.* 33 rms, 2 story, 5 kit. cottages. S, D $80–$120; cottages $150–$160; off-season rates avail. TV; cable. Pool; whirlpool, sauna. Complimentary bkfst. Restaurant 11:30 am–2 pm, 5:30–9 pm. Bar from 10:30 am. Ck-out noon. Meeting rms. Tennis. Lawn games. Some refrigerators. Fireplace in cottages. Cr cds: MC, V.

Inn

★ ★ ★VALLEY LODGE. *(Box 93)* *Carmel Valley Rd at Ford Rd.* *408/659-2261.* 31 rms, 1–2 story, 8 kits. No A/C. S, D $95–$115; each addl $10; studios $135; kit. units, cottages $155–$235; higher rates: hols & special events. Crib free. TV; cable. Heated pool. Complimentary continental bkfst. Complimentary coffee in rms. Ck-out noon, ck-in after 2 pm. Meeting rm. Exercise equipt; weights, bicycles, whirlpool, sauna. Lawn games. Fireplace in suites & cottages; some wet bars. Private patios, balconies. Cr cds: A, MC, V.

Resort

CARMEL VALLEY RANCH (4-Star 1993; New owner, therefore not rated). *(1 Old Ranch Rd, Carmel 93923)* *408/625-9500; res: 800/4-CARMEL.* 100 suites. D $235–$700; each addl $20; under 12 free. Crib free. TV; cable. 2 heated pools; whirlpool, sauna, poolside serv. Restaurants 7 am–2 pm; dining rm 6–10 pm. Box lunches, snack bar. Rm serv 24 hrs. Bar 11 am–midnight. Ck-out noon, ck-in 4 pm. Meeting rms. Concierge. Gift shop. Free airport transportation. Tennis, pro. 18-hole golf, greens fee $80, pro, putting green, driving range, pro shop. Entertainment. Refrigerators, fireplaces. Private decks, balconies. Contemporary California ranch-style suites. Original art collection in lobby; rotates tri-annually. Elaborate landscaping. Private guard gate; exclusive hideaway resort on 1,700 acres in the Santa Lucia Mountains. Cr cds: A, C, D, MC, V, JCB.

Restaurant

★WILL'S FARGO. *Carmel Valley Rd, in village.* *408/659-2774.* Hrs: 5:30–10 pm; Sun from 5 pm. Closed Jan 1, Thanksgiving, Dec 25. Res accepted. No A/C. Bar from 5 pm. Semi-a la carte: dinner $14.95–$24.95. Specializes in steak, abalone. Own dressings. Parking. Butcher shop. 1850s decor; old Western bar, fireplace. Family-owned. Cr cds: A, C, D, MC, V.

Catalina Island

(see Avalon)

Channel Islands National Park (H2, H3, J3)

(Off the coast of southern California)

Eight islands, extending over a range of 150 miles in the Pacific Ocean, make up this chain of which five have been set aside by the government as Channel Islands National Park. Visitors can reach the National Park by commercial boat (see VENTURA). Anacapa Island, 14 miles south of Ventura, is actually a slender chain of 3 islands, 5 miles long with average width of one-half mile; Santa Barbara Island, 38 miles west of San Pedro, is roughly triangular with its greatest dimension being

1¼ miles. Santa Rosa Island (40 miles offshore) and San Miguel Island (45 miles offshore) are also part of the park and may be reached by commercial flights (see CAMARILLO).

On Anacapa Island in early spring there is a spectacular display of wildflowers; a yellow table of the giant coreopsis, with its large flowers, is visible from a great distance. Sea mammals, including the California sea lion and harbor seal, are observed around the island's rocky shores. From January through March the annual migration of gray whales passes close to Anacapa. The island also has a self-guided nature trail and a museum. Ranger-guided tours available all year. Scuba and skin diving are popular sports, since the islands are noted for their variety of marine life.

Santa Barbara Island is a marine terrace with steep cliffs, some rising to more than 500 feet. Numerous caves, coves, offshore pillars and blowholes are also found. Since Santa Barbara is so isolated that sea mammals, including the huge elephant seal, are occasional visitors. Bird watching is excellent on this island and numerous species may be observed, including Xantus' murrelet, American kestrel, brown pelican, black oystercatcher, orange-crowned warbler and others. Self-guided trails and ranger-conducted walking tours are available. Camping is permitted on Anacapa, Santa Barbara, Santa Rosa and San Miguel Islands. Permits are issued in advance and may be obtained by calling the park visitor center; 805/658-5700. No pets are permitted on the islands.

San Miguel Island (14 square miles) contains an outstanding number of natural features, including "caliche" or "fossil forests," which give the island landscape an eerie, almost alien appearance. It is the only island where six pinniped (seals and sea lions) species are found, more than are found in any other single location in the world. In order to land on the island a permit must be acquired from park headquarters prior to your visit.

Santa Rosa Island (53 square miles) is now owned by Channel Islands National Park. Visitors to the island must be accompanied by a park ranger. For camping, a permit is required; a landing permit is required only for ranger-led walks & hikes (arranged by appt). Santa Cruz Island, although legislatively part of the Channel Islands National Park, remains in joint ownership; the east end of Santa Cruz is jointly owned by the National Park Service and private individuals. Information about public access to this island may be obtained from the Santa Cruz Island Preserve, 213 Stearns Wharf, Santa Barbara 93101, phone 805/964-7839. A visitor center (open all year) at 1901 Spinnaker Dr in Ventura offers information, exhibits and audiovisual programs; phone 805/658-5730. For further information contact Park Superintendent, 1901 Spinnaker Dr, Ventura 93001; phone 805/658-5700.

Chester (C-2)

Pop: 2,082 **Elev:** 4,528 ft **Area code:** 916 **Zip:** 96020

The Lake Almanor area offers both summer and winter sports. Mt Lassen is 30 miles north and west. Fishing is good in the lake and surrounding streams served by many boat landings and ramps. Deer, bear, waterfowl and birds are plentiful in season. There are many resorts, tent & trailer sites and two scenic golf courses around the lake and a number of improved campsites within 5 miles of Chester, at Almanor and at Greenville. Chester is also the home of the Collins Pine Sawmill, one of the largest in the state. A Ranger District office of the Lassen National Forest (see SUSANVILLE) is also located here.

(For further information contact the Chester/Lake Almanor Chamber of Commerce, 529 Main St, PO Box 1198; 258-2426.)

(For accommodations see Quincy, Susanville)

Chico (C-2)

Settled: 1843 **Pop:** 40,079 **Elev:** 200 ft **Area code:** 916

Chico was originally settled in 1843 as Rancho Del Arroyo by General John Bidwell, a leading agriculturist of the 19th century as well as a gold-miner, statesman and a US congressman. Chico is now a city of diversified business, industry and agriculture in an area that is said to produce 20 percent of the world's almonds.

What to See and Do

1. **Chico Museum.** 141 Salem St, at Second St. History museum housed in 1904 Carnegie Library; permanent and changing exhibits include local history artifacts and photos, Chinese Temple. Programs, activities. (Wed–Sun afternoons) Donation. Phone 891-4336.
2. **California State University, Chico** (1887). (15,000 students) W 1st St. On 115 tree-shaded acres; art galleries (daily exc Sat); "anthromuseum"; campus tour. Nearby is a 1,000-acre college farm. Phone 898-6116 or -5307.
3. **Bidwell Park.** ½ mi E on E 4th St. 10-mi-long, 2,250-acre city park with stream; site of location shots for many movies, including *The Adventures of Robin Hood*. Swimming pools; picnicking; 18-hole golf, NE end of park; bridle, foot and nature trails; kiddie playland. Phone 895-4972.
4. **Bidwell Mansion State Historic Park** (1868). 525 Esplanade. This is the 26-room Victorian house of the founder of Chico (candidate for US president in 1892); 1st, 2nd and 3rd floors restored. (Daily; closed Jan 1, Thanksgiving, Dec 25). Phone 895-6144. ¢

(For further information contact the Chamber of Commerce, 500 Main St, PO Box 3038, 95927; 891-5556 or 800/852-8570.)

Annual Events

Bidwell Classic Marathon. 1st Sat Mar.

Silver Dollar Fair. Phone 895-4666. 5 days late May.

Chico Expo. Phone 891-5556. 1st wkend Oct.

(See Oroville)

Motels

★★**BEST WESTERN HERITAGE INN.** *25 Heritage Lane (95926), on CA 99.* 916/894-8600; FAX 916/894-8600, ext 142. 101 rms, 3 story. S $58–$66; D $62–$72; each addl $7; under 12 free; higher rates: university graduation wknd, auto races. Crib free. TV. Pool. Complimentary continental bkfst, coffee. Ck-out 11 am. Meeting rms. Exercise equipt; bicycles, stair machine, whirlpool. Some refrigerators, wet bars. Cr cds: A, C, D, DS, MC, V, JCB.

✔★**ECONO LODGE.** *630 Main St (95928).* 916/895-1323; FAX 916/343-2719. 43 rms, 2 story. S $34–$40; D $34–$50; each addl $5; kit. units $8 addl; under 16 free. Crib free. Pet accepted. TV; cable, in-rm movies. Pool. Complimentary coffee in rms. Restaurant adj open 24 hrs. Ck-out 11 am. Cr cds: A, C, D, DS, MC, V.

✔★**MOTEL ORLEANS.** *655 Manzanita Court (95926), just off CA 99 Cohasset exit.* 916/345-2533; res: 800/626-1900. 53 rms, 3 story. S $32; D $36; suites $48; under 12 free; wkly rates. Crib $4. Pet accepted; $25. TV; cable. Pool. Complimentary morning coffee in lobby. Restaurant adj. Ck-out 11 am. Some refrigerators. Cr cds: A, C, D, DS, MC, V.

Motor Hotel

★★★**HOLIDAY INN.** *685 Manzanita Ct (95926).* 916/345-2491; FAX 916/893-3040. 174 rms, 5 story. S $65–$76; D $68–$84; each addl $6; suites $100–$130; under 18 free. Crib free. Pet accepted. TV; cable, in-rm movies. Pool; whirlpool. Complimentary morning coffee. Restaurant 6 am–10 pm. Rm serv. Bar from 5 pm; entertainment. Ck-out noon. Coin lndry. Meeting rms. Bellhops. Valet serv. Free airport, bus depot transportation. Refrigerator in suites. Cr cds: A, C, D, DS, MC, V, JCB.

Chula Vista (K-4)

Pop: 135,163 **Elev:** 75 ft **Area code:** 619

The name Chula Vista is Spanish for "beautiful view." Set between the mountains and the sea, the city lives up to its name.

(For general information and attractions see San Diego.)

Motels

★ ★ **BEST WESTERN OTAY VALLEY INN.** *4450 Otay Valley Rd (91911).* 619/422-2600; FAX 619/425-4605. 120 rms, 3 story. May–Sept: S $50–$57; D $60–$75; each addl $10; suites $90–$100; under 18 free; lower rates rest of yr. Crib free. TV; cable. Heated pool; whirlpool. Complimentary continental bkfst. Restaurant adj 6:30 am–10:30 pm. Ck-out noon. Coin lndry. Meeting rms. Valet serv. Free airport, RR station, bus depot, border transportation. Refrigerators avail. Cr cds: A, C, D, DS, ER, MC, V, JCB.

✔ ★ ★ **DAYS INN.** *225 Bay Blvd (91910), I-5 E Street exit.* 619/425-8200; FAX 619/426-7411. 118 rms, 2 story. Mid-May–mid-Sept: S, D $45–$50; each addl $5; under 12 free; lower rates rest of yr. Crib free. Pet accepted; $25. TV; cable. Heated pool; poolside serv. Restaurant 5:30 am–8 pm. Ck-out noon. Valet serv. Sundries. Some refrigerators. Cr cds: A, C, D, DS, MC, V.

★ ★ **RAMADA INN.** *91 Bonita Rd (91910).* 619/425-9999; FAX 619/425-8934. 97 rms, 4 story. June–Sept: S $59–$67; D $67–$77; each addl $8; suites $69–$77; under 18 free; lower rates rest of yr. Crib free. TV; cable. Heated pool; whirlpool. Restaurant adj 6:30 am–11 pm. Ck-out noon. Meeting rm. Cr cds: A, C, D, DS, ER, MC, V, JCB.

✔ ★ **RODEWAY INN.** *778 Broadway (91910).* 619/476-9555. 49 rms, 3 story. S $40–$50; D $45–$55; each addl $5; under 18 free; wkly rates. Crib $5. Pool; whirlpool. Complimentary coffee in lobby. Restaurant nearby. Ck-out 11:30 am. Meeting rm. Refrigerators avail. Cr cds: A, C, D, DS, ER, MC, V, JCB.

Restaurants

★ ★ **BUTCHER SHOP.** *556 Broadway.* 619/420-9440. Hrs: 11–1 am; Sun 2–10 pm. Closed Thanksgiving, Dec 25. Bar to 2 am. Semi-a la carte: lunch $5.95–$12.95, dinner $6.95–$26.95. Specializes in prime rib, steak. Parking. Family-owned. Cr cds: A, C, D, DS, MC, V.

✔ ★ **LA FONDA ROBERTO'S.** *300 3rd Ave, at F Street.* 619/585-3017. Hrs: 11 am–10 pm; early-bird dinner Mon–Fri 4–6 pm; Sun brunch 11 am–3 pm. Res accepted. Mexican menu. Wine, beer. Semi-a la carte: lunch $3.95–$6.50, dinner $5.95–$9.95. Buffet: lunch $4.95. Sun brunch $6.95. Child's meals. Specialties: mole poblano, cochinita pibil de Yucatan. Cr cds: A, C, DS, MC, V.

Claremont (H-4)

Pop: 32,503 **Elev:** 1,169 ft **Area code:** 909 **Zip:** 91711

What to See and Do

The Claremont Colleges. College Ave between 1st St & Foothill Blvd (CA 66). A distinguished group of institutions comprised of Pomona College (1887) (1,400 students), Claremont Graduate School (1925) (1,800 students), Scripps College (1926) (550 students), Claremont McKenna College (1946) (850 students), Harvey Mudd College (1955) (620 students) and Pitzer College (1963) (700 students). Phone 621-8000. On campus are

Montgomery Art Gallery and **Lang Art Gallery.** Exhibits. (Daily; closed school hols & June–Aug) Phone 621-8283. **Free.**

Graduate School Art Building. Exhibits. (Daily, wkends by appt) Phone 621-8071. **Free.**

Rancho Santa Ana Botanic Garden. 1500 N College Ave, N of Foothill Blvd. Native plants. (Daily; closed Jan 1, July 4, Thanksgiving, Dec 25) Phone 625-8767. **Free.**

(For further information contact the Chamber of Commerce, 205 N Yale Ave; 624-1681.)

(See Ontario, Pasadena, Pomona, Riverside)

Motel

✔ ★ ★ **RAMADA INN & TENNIS CLUB.** *840 S Indian Hill Blvd, I-10 Indian Hill Blvd exit, 1 blk S.* 909/621-4831; FAX 909/626-8452. 126 rms, 2 story. S $54; D $58; each addl $8; under 12 free; higher rates special events. Crib free. Pet accepted; $7 per day. TV; cable. Heated pool; wading pool; whirlpool. Restaurant 11:30 am–2 pm, 5–10 pm. Rm serv. Bar. Ck-out noon. Coin lndry. Meeting rms. Valet serv. Free airport transportation. Lighted tennis. Refrigerators. Cr cds: A, C, D, DS, MC, V.

Hotel

★ ★ **GRISWOLD'S INN.** *555 W Foothill Blvd, I-10 Indian Hill Blvd exit N.* 909/626-2411; res: 800/854-5733 (exc CA), 800/821-0341 (CA); FAX 909/624-0756. 273 units, 3 story. S $69; D $79; each addl $10; suites $125–$195; under 12 free. Crib free. TV; cable, in-rm movies. Heated pool; poolside serv. Restaurant 6 am–10 pm. Bar 11–1:30 am, Sun to midnight; entertainment. Ck-out noon. Convention facilities. Shopping arcade. Free airport transportation. Tennis privileges. Health club privileges. Wet bar in suites. Patio with fountain. Candlelight dinner theater. Cr cds: A, C, D, DS, MC, V.

Restaurants

★ ★ **MIYAKO GARDENS.** *860 S Indian Hill Blvd, I-10 Indian Hill Blvd exit, 1 blk S.* 909/621-6087. Hrs: 11:30 am–2 pm, 5–10 pm; Sat from 5 pm. Closed Sun; some major hols. Res accepted. Japanese, Amer menu. Bar. Semi-a la carte: lunch $5–$8.50, dinner $11.75–$25. Child's meals. Specializes in hibachi cooking, steak. Parking. Glass-enclosed Japanese garden. Cr cds: A, C, D, DS, MC, V.

★ ★ **YIANNIS.** *238 Yale Ave, I-10 Indian Hill Blvd exit, 1½ mi N to Claremont "Village."* 909/621-2413. Hrs: 11 am–10 pm. Closed Mon; major hols; also 2 wks Dec & 2 wks Aug. Greek menu. Bar. A la carte entrees: lunch $6.35–$7.55, dinner $9.95–$12.95. Sun brunch $6.75. Specializes in moussaka, souvlakia. Own bread, baklava. Greek artifacts; colorful lamps. Family-owned. Cr cds: A, MC, V.

Clear Lake Area (Lake Co) (D-1)

Area code: 707

This is a popular recreation area for fishing, hunting, swimming, boating, golf and other sports.

What to See and Do

Clear Lake State Park. 3 mi NE of Kelseyville on Soda Bay Rd. Pomo Indians once occupied this area. Swimming, waterskiing; fishing; boating (ramp). Nature, hiking trails. Picnicking. Camping (no hook-ups, dump station). Visitor center with wildlife dioramas, aquarium; nature films. Standard fees. Phone 279-4293. Day use per vehicle ¢¢

(For further information and auto tours contact the Lake County Chamber of Commerce, 290 S Main St, PO Box 295, Lakeport 95453; 263-5092.)

Annual Events

Lake County Rodeo. Lake County Fairgrounds, Lakeport. July.

Lake County Fair and Horse Show. Lake County Fairgrounds. Phone 263-6182. Labor Day wkend.

(See Healdsburg, Ukiah)

Motel

✔ ★ **ANCHORAGE INN.** (950 N Main St, Lakeport 95453) 707/263-5417. 34 rms, 2 story, 20 kits. S $37; D $45; 1–2 bedrm suites & kit. units from $65. TV; cable. Pool; whirlpool, sauna. Complimentary coffee in rms. Restaurant opp 6 am–9 pm. Ck-out 11 am. Coin lndry. Private patios; some balconies. Picnic tables, grills. Dockage. On Clear Lake. Cr cds: A, D, MC, V.

Motor Hotel

★ ★ ★ **BEST WESTERN EL GRANDE INN.** (Box 4598, 15135 Lakeshore Dr, Clearlake 95422) 707/994-2000; FAX 707/994-2042. 68 rms, 4 story. S $67; D $73; each addl $6; suites $70–$90. Crib free. TV; cable. Indoor pool; whirlpool. Complimentary coffee in rms. Restaurant 7 am–10 pm. Bar noon–midnight. Ck-out 11 am. Meeting rms. Refrigerator in suites. Spanish-style lobby. All rms open to atrium. Cr cds: A, C, D, DS, MC, V.

Resort

★ ★ **KONOCTI HARBOR INN.** (8727 Soda Bay Rd, Kelseyville 95451) 707/279-4281; res: 800/862-4930; FAX 707/279-9205. 251 units, apts & cottages, 1–3 story, 98 kits. No elvtr. S $55–$75; D $65–$85; each addl $10; apts (to 4 persons) $165–$185; under 12 free; sports package plans; off-season rates. TV; cable. 2 heated pools; wading pool, life-guard in summer. Playground. Supervised child's activities. Dining rms 7 am–10 pm; Fri, Sat to 11 pm. Box lunches, snack bar. Bar 10–2 am. Ck-out 11 am, ck-in 4 pm. Coin lndry. Meeting rms. Gift shop. Beauty shop. Local airport transportation. Sports dir. Lighted tennis, pro. Golf privileges. Miniature golf. Launching ramp; dockage; waterskiing, boat rides; paddleboat cruises; jet skiing. Protected lake swimming. Lawn games. Rec rm. Sun deck. Exercise rm; instructor, weights, bicycles, whirlpool, sauna. Massage therapy. Refrigerators. Private patios, bal-

conies. Picnic tables, grills. On Clear Lake. Cr cds: A, C, D, DS, MC, V, JCB.

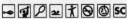

Coleville (D-3)

Pop: 60 (est) **Elev:** 5,400 ft **Area code:** 916 **Zip:** 96107

(See Bridgeport)

Motel

✔ ★ **ANDRUSS.** (Walker Rte, Box 64) 5 mi S on US 395. 916/495-2216. 12 air-cooled rms, 4 kits. No rm phones. S $36; D, kit. units $42–$52; each addl $4. Crib free. Pet accepted. TV; cable. Heated pool. Playground. Complimentary coffee in rms. Restaurant opp 6 am–10 pm. Ck-out 11 am. Lawn games. Picnic tables, grill. Fish cleaning, freezing facilities. Cr cds: MC, V.

Coloma

(see Placerville)

Concord (E-2)

Pop: 111,348 **Elev:** 70 ft **Area code:** 510

What to See and Do

Concord Pavilion. 2000 Kirker Pass Rd. Roofed, open-air performance and assembly facility, with lawn and reserved pavilion seating for 8,500; popular entertainment performances, sports and special events (Apr–Oct). Phone 762-2277.

(For further information contact the Convention & Visitors Bureau, 2151 Salvio St, 94520; 685-1184.)

(See Martinez, Oakland, Vallejo)

Motels

★ **BEST WESTERN HERITAGE INN.** 4600 Clayton Rd (94521). 510/686-4466; FAX 510/825-0581. 126 rms, 2 story. S, D $65–$70; each addl $5; kit. units $67–$71; under 18 free. Crib free. Pet accepted; $50. TV; cable. Pool; whirlpool, sauna. Complimentary continental bkfst. Restaurant 6 am–midnight. Ck-out 11 am. Meeting rms. Valet serv. Sundries. Refrigerators; some wet bars. Cr cds: A, C, D, DS, MC, V, JCB.

✔ ★ **COMFORT INN.** 1370 Monument Blvd (94520). 510/827-8998; FAX 510/798-3374. 42 kit. units, 3 story. S, D $54–$79; each addl $5; suites $64–$74; wkly, monthly rates. Pet accepted, some restrictions. TV; cable, in-rm movies. Pool. Complimentary continental bkfst, coffee in lobby. Restaurant nearby. Ck-out noon. Coin lndry. Patios, balconies. Cr cds: A, D, DS, MC, V, JCB.

Motor Hotel

★ ★ ★ **SHERATON HOTEL & CONFERENCE CENTER.** 45 John Glenn Dr (94520), adj to Buchanan Airport. 510/825-7700; FAX 510/674-9567. 325 rms, 3 story. S $80–$110; D $90–$120; each addl $15; suites

$135–$325; under 17 free. Crib free. Pet accepted. Heated pool. TV; cable, in-rm movies. Restaurant 6 am–2 pm, 5–10:30 pm. Rm serv. Bar 11–2 am; entertainment. Ck-out noon. Meeting rms. Bellhops. Valet serv. Sundries. Gift shop. Free airport transportation. Indoor putting green. Exercise equipt; weights, bicycles, whirlpool. Cr cds: A, C, D, DS, ER, MC, V.

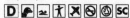

Hotel

★★★HILTON CONCORD. *1970 Diamond Blvd (94520). 510/827-2000; FAX 510/671-0984.* 330 rms, 11 story. S $99–$129; D $109–$139; each addl $10; suites $375–$475; family, wkend rates. Crib free. TV; cable, in-rm movies. Heated pool. Complimentary full bkfst 6:30–9:30 am, Sat, Sun & hols 7–10 am. Restaurant 6:30 am–10 pm, wkends from 7 am. Bar 11 am–midnight; entertainment Mon–Fri. Ck-out noon. Convention facilities. Exercise equipt; weight machine, bicycles, whirlpool. Cr cds: A, C, D, DS, ER, MC, V.

Corona (J-4)

Established: 1896 **Pop:** 76,095 **Elev:** 678 ft **Area code:** 909

A Ranger District office of the Cleveland National Forest (see PINE VALLEY) is located in Corona.

What to See and Do

1. **Prado Basin County Park.** 4½ mi N on River Rd. 1,837-acre wildlife refuge area along the Santa Ana River has nature trail and picnicking. (Wkends only) For general park information, phone 275-4310. Per vehicle ¢¢

2. **Glen Ivy Hot Springs.** 25000 Glen Ivy Rd, 8 mi S via I-15 at Temescal Canyon Rd exit. Natural hot mineral spa. Swimming, 15 outdoor mineral baths, massage, sauna, clay bath, outdoor poolside dining. (Daily; closed Thanksgiving, Dec 25) Sr citizen rate. Phone 277-3529. ¢¢¢¢

(For further information contact the Chamber of Commerce, 904 E 6th St, 91719; 737-3350.)

(See Ontario, Riverside)

Motels

★★BEST WESTERN KINGS INN. *1084 Pomona Rd (91720), CA 91 Lincoln Ave exit, then 1 blk N. 909/734-4241; FAX 909/279-5371.* 88 rms, 2 story. S, D $49–$57; each addl $5. Crib free. TV; cable. Heated pool; whirlpool. Complimentary continental bkfst. Restaurant adj 6 am–10 pm. Ck-out noon. Meeting rm. Some refrigerators. Cr cds: A, C, D, DS, MC, V, JCB.

✔★EXECUTIVE INN & SUITES. *1805 W 6th St (91720), CA 91 Maple St exit to 6th St, then 2 blks E. 909/371-7185; res: 800/523-9321; FAX 909/371-8339.* 56 rms, 2 story. S $44; D $48; each addl $6; suites $46–$50; kits. $50; under 12 free. TV; cable, in-rm movies. Heated pool; whirlpool. Complimentary coffee in lobby. Restaurant adj open 24 hrs. Ck-out 11 am. Meeting rm. Some refrigerators. Cr cds: A, C, D, DS, MC, V.

Motor Hotel

★★COUNTRY SIDE INN. *2260 Griffin Way (91719), CA 91 McKinley St exit N. 909/734-2140; res: 800/448-8810; FAX 909/734-*

4056. 100 rms, 2 story. S $59; D $69; each addl $10; under 12 free. Crib free. TV; cable. Heated pool; whirlpool. Complimentary full bkfst; coffee in lobby. Restaurant opp 7 am–11 pm. Ck-out noon. Meeting rms. Valet serv. Airport transportation. Refrigerators. Cr cds: A, C, D, DS, MC, V.

Corona Del Mar (J-4)

Elev: 75 ft **Area code:** 714 **Zip:** 92625

This community is part of Newport Beach (see).

Restaurants

★★★FIVE CROWNS. *3801 E Pacific Coast Hwy. 714/760-0331.* Hrs: 5–10:30 pm; Sun 4–10 pm; Sun brunch 10:30 am–3 pm. Closed July 4, Dec 25. Res accepted. Bar. Wine list. A la carte entrees: dinner $16–$27. Sun brunch $10–$17. Specializes in prime rib, rack of lamb, fresh fish. Valet parking. Patio, greenhouse dining. English-style inn, fireplaces. Cr cds: A, C, D, DS, MC, V, JCB.

★★MATTEO'S. *2325 E Pacific Coast Hwy. 714/673-8267.* Hrs: 5–10 pm; Fri–Sun to 11 pm. Closed Mon; major hols. Res accepted. Italian menu. Bar. Semi-a la carte: dinner $11–$22.50. Child's meals. Specializes in pasta, veal, whitefish, steak. Valet parking. Family-owned. Cr cds: A, C, D, MC, V.

★QUIET WOMAN. *3224 E Pacific Coast Hwy, at jct CA 1/73. 714/640-7440.* Hrs: 11 am–3 pm, 5–10 pm; Fri to 11 pm; Sat 5–11 pm; Sun 5–10 pm. Closed major hols. Bar to 1:30 am. Semi-a la carte: lunch $5.95–$14.95, dinner $8.95–$25.95. Specializes in rack of lamb, fresh swordfish. Entertainment Wed–Sat. English pub decor. Cr cds: A, MC, V.

Coronado (K-4)

Pop: 26,540 **Elev:** 25 ft **Area code:** 619 **Zip:** 92118

Known as the Crown City, Coronado lies across the bay from San Diego and is connected to the mainland by a long, narrow sandbar called the Silver Strand and by the beautiful Coronado Bridge. It is the site of the famous Hotel del Coronado (1888).

(For general information and attractions see San Diego.)

Motels

✔★★EL CORDOVA. *1351 Orange Ave. 619/435-4131; FAX 619/435-0632.* 40 units, 2 story. 28 kits. No A/C. Mid-June–mid-Sept: S, D $70–$90; suites $100–$155; studio rms $85–$105; wkly, monthly rates off-season; lower rates rest of yr. Crib free. Pet accepted, some restrictions; $50. TV; cable. Heated pool. Restaurant 11 am–10 pm. Bar adj. Ck-out noon. Picnic tables, grills. Historic mansion (1902). Cr cds: A, C, D, DS, MC, V.

★★★GLORIETTA BAY INN. *1630 Glorietta Blvd. 619/435-3101; res: 800/283-9383; FAX 619/435-6182.* 98 units, 2 story, 33 kits. S $84–$115; D $94–$130; each addl $10; suites, kit. units $129–$179. Crib $10. TV; cable. Heated pool. Continental bkfst in lobby. Ck-out noon. Coin lndry. Meeting rm. Bicycles. Refrigerators. Many private patios, balconies. Some rms overlook Glorietta Bay. Historic house (1908), part of Speckels mansion. Cr cds: A, C, D, DS, MC, V.

Hotel

LE MERIDIEN SAN DIEGO AT CORONADO. (4-Star 1993; New general manager, therefore not rated) *2000 2nd St. 619/435-3000; res: 800/543-4300; FAX 619/435-3032.* 300 rms, 3 story, 7 suites, 28 villas. S, D $165–$255; each addl $20; suites, villas $375–$650; under 12 free. Crib free. Covered parking $7; valet. TV; cable. 3 heated pools; poolside serv. Restaurant 6:30 am–10 pm (also see MARUIS). Rm serv 24 hrs. Bar 4 pm–1 am; entertainment. Ck-out noon. Convention facilities. Concierge. Shops. Lighted tennis, pro, shop, tennis clinic. Exercise rm; instructor, weight machines, bicycles, whirlpool, sauna. Massage. Minibars. Private patios. On bay; scuba, snorkeling, windsurfing classes on request. Bike rental with guide; floral & wildlife tour. European health spa facilities. Located on 16 acres with koi-stocked streams, lush lagoons and exotic birds. Pier; 2 slips. Luxury resort hotel; interior of the hotel reflects its French heritage and California setting. Cr cds: A, C, D, DS, ER, MC, V, JCB.

D ⊘ ⇙ ✕ ⊘ ⌾

Inn

★★**CORONADO VICTORIAN HOUSE.** *1000 8th St. 619/435-2200.* 7 air-cooled rms, 3 story. S, D $175–$375; each addl $50. Crib free. Complimentary full bkfst. Dinner served on request. Restaurant 1 blk open 24 hrs. Ck-out 11 am, ck-in 4 pm. Some balconies. Historic inn (1894), elegantly restored. Each rm individually decorated; many antiques. Large dance studio for fitness & dance instruction. Ocean, beach 3 blks. Cr cds: A, DS, MC, V.

D ⊘ ⌾

Resorts

★★★★**HOTEL DEL CORONADO.** *1500 Orange Ave. 619/435-6611; res: 800/HOTEL-DEL; FAX 619/522-8238 or 619/522-8262.* 691 rms, 311 A/C. S, D from $149; each addl $25; suites from $399; under 15 free. Crib free. Parking $10; valet $3. TV; cable. 2 heated pools; poolside serv. Supervised child's activities. Dining rm open 24 hrs (also see CROWN ROOM). Rm serv 24 hrs. Bar 7–2 am; entertainment, dancing 9 pm–1:30 am. Ck-out noon, ck-in 3 pm. Convention facilities. Concierge. Shopping arcade. Barber, beauty shop. Lighted tennis, pro. Game rm. Exercise rm; instructor, weights, bicycles, whirlpool, steam rm. Massage. Minibars; many bathrm phones. Many private patios, balconies. Beautiful Victorian building (1888), historic landmark; antiques; gardens; elaborately landscaped. On swimming beach; sail and power boat rentals avail at hotel docks. Public golf nearby. Cr cds: A, C, D, DS, MC, V, JCB.

D ⊘ ⇙ ✕ ⊘ ⌾

★★★★**LOEWS CORONADO BAY RESORT.** *4000 Coronado Bay Rd. 619/424-4000; res: 800/235-6397; FAX 619/424-4400.* 440 rms, 3 story. S, D $165–$245; each addl $20; suites $325–$1,400; under 18 free; tennis & other package plans avail. Crib free. TV; cable. 3 pools, heated; poolside serv. Supervised child's activities. Restaurant (see AZZURA POINT). Box lunches. Rm serv 24 hrs. Bar 11–2 am; entertainment, dancing. Ck-out noon, ck-in 3 pm. Grocery. Complimentary guest lndry. Package store. Convention facilities. Bellhops. Valet serv. Concierge. Gift shop. Barber, beauty shop. Sports dir. 5 lighted tennis courts, pro. Beach, boats, water skiing, swimming. Bicycles (rentals). Lawn games. Game rm. Exercise equipt; weight machine, treadmill, whirlpools, sauna. Massage. Bathrm phones, minibars; some wet bars. Complimentary refrigerator on request. Balconies. On 15-acre peninsula; full service, 80-slip marina, docking. New England seaside ambiance. Sweeping view of ocean and skyline. Cr cds: A, C, D, DS, MC, V, JCB.

D ⊘ ⇙ ✕ ✖ ⊘ ⌾

Restaurants

★★★**AZZURA POINT.** *(See Loews Coronado Bay Resort) 619/424-4000.* Hrs: 6–10 pm; Fri & Sat to 10:30 pm; Sun 5:30–10 pm. Res accepted. American Pacific Rim menu. Bar. Extensive wine list. Semi-a la carte: dinner $16.50–$22.95. Child's meals. Specializes in seafood. Valet parking. Panoramic view of the bay, ocean and city skyline. Cr cds: A, C, D, DS, MC, V, JCB.

★★**BRIGANTINE.** *1333 Orange Ave. 619/435-4166.* Hrs: 11:30 am–2:30 pm, 5–10:30 pm; Fri to 11:30 pm; Sat 5–11:30 pm; Sun 5–10:30 pm; early-bird dinner Sun–Thurs 5–7 pm. Res accepted. Bar to 2 am. Semi-a la carte: lunch $6.50–$11, dinner $6.50–$25. Child's meals. Specializes in fresh seafood, steak. Parking. Nautical decor. Family-owned. Cr cds: A, C, D, MC, V.

D

★★★**CHEZ LOMA.** *1132 Loma Ave. 619/435-0661.* Hrs: 11:30 am–2 pm, 5:30–10 pm; Sat & Sun from 5:30 pm; early-bird dinner 5:30–6:30 pm; Sun brunch 10 am–2 pm. Closed Mon; Jan 1, July 4, Dec 25. Res accepted; required Fri & Sat. Provincial European menu. Beer. Wine cellar. Semi-a la carte: lunch $3.95–$9.95, dinner $13.95–$20.95. Sun brunch $9.95. Specializes in duck, seafood. Own desserts. Historic landmark house (1889). Cr cds: A, C, D, MC, V.

★★★**CROWN ROOM.** *(See Hotel del Coronado Resort) 619/435-6611.* Hrs: 7 am–9:30 pm; early-bird dinner Mon–Sat 5–6:30 pm. Res accepted. Country French cuisine. Serv bar. Wine cellar. Semi-a la carte: bkfst from $6.95, lunch from $8.50, dinner $13.95–$20. *Prix fixe:* dinner $27.50. Buffet: Sun dinner $29.95. Child's meals. Specializes in lamb, fresh fish. Own baking. Pianist Fri, Sat. Valet parking. Rotating menu. Historic 1888 structure; hand-tooled dome ceiling. Cr cds: A, C, D, DS, MC, V, JCB.

D SC

★★★**MARUIS.** *(See Le Meridien San Diego at Coronado Hotel) 619/435-3000.* Hrs: 6–10 pm. Closed Sun & Mon. Res accepted. French Provençale menu. Serv bar. Wine list. A la carte entrees: dinner $20–$30. *Prix fixe:* dinner $49 & $69. Specializes in southern French cuisine. Own pastries. Valet parking. Mediterranean atmosphere. Cr cds: A, C, D, DS, ER, MC, V, JCB.

D

✔★★**MEXICAN VILLAGE RESTAURANTE.** *120 Orange Ave. 619/435-1822.* Hrs: 11 am–10 pm; Fri & Sat to 11 pm; Sun brunch 8 am–1 pm. Mexican, Amer menu. Bar to 11 pm; Fri & Sat to 2 am. Semi-a la carte: lunch $4.55–$7.25, dinner $5.95–$14.95. Sun brunch $4.25–$6. Child's meals. Specializes in Mexican pizza, romaine salad. Entertainment. Local landmark; opened 1945. Several dining rms; Mexican decor and artifacts. Cr cds: A, D, DS, MC, V.

D SC

★★**PEOHE'S.** *1201 1st St. 619/437-4474.* Hrs: 11:30 am–2:30 pm, 5:30–10 pm; Sat 5–11 pm; Sun brunch 10:30 am–2 pm. Res accepted. Varied menu. Bar; pianist. Semi-a la carte: lunch $7.95–$13.95, dinner $15–$25. Sun brunch $13–$18. Child's meals. Specialties: coconut crunchy shrimp, fresh Hawaiian fish. Parking. Outdoor dining. Tropical atmosphere with waterfalls and running streams; lush plants; ponds stocked with tropical fish; lobster tank. View of San Diego Harbor and skyline. Cr cds: A, D, DS, MC, V.

D

Corte Madera *

Pop: 8,272 **Elev:** 27 ft **Area code:** 415 **Zip:** 94925
3 mi S of San Rafael (E-1) off US 101 (Redwood Hwy).

(See San Francisco, San Rafael)

Motel

★★★**BEST WESTERN CORTE MADERA INN.** *1815 Redwood Hwy, at Madera Blvd.* 415/924-1502; FAX 415/924-5419. 110 rms, 2 story. S $80–$88; D $88–$98; each addl $8; suites $120–$145; under 12 free. Crib free. TV; cable. Heated pool; wading pool, lifeguard. Playground. Free continental bkfst in rms. Restaurant 6:30 am–midnight, Fri & Sat to 2 am. Ck-out noon. Coin lndry. Meeting rms. Bellhops. Valet serv. Sundries. Gift shop. Airport transportation. Exercise equipt; weights, bicycles, whirlpools. Game rm. Some bathrm phones, refrigerators. Private patios, balconies. Picnic tables. Cr cds: A, C, D, DS, ER, MC, V, JCB.

Restaurants

★★★**LARK CREEK INN.** *(234 Magnolia Ave, Larkspur) 2 mi N on US 101, Tamalpais Dr exit, 1 mi W to Magnolia Ave.* 415/924-7766. Hrs: 11:30 am–2:30 pm, 5:30–10 pm; Fri to 10:30 pm; Sat 5–10:30 pm; Sun 5–10 pm; Sun brunch 10 am–1:30 pm. Res accepted. No A/C. Regional Amer cuisine. Bar. Wine list. A la carte entrees: lunch $7–$14, dinner $12–$19. Sun brunch $8–$14. Specializes in fresh fish, brick oven roasted meats. Own pastries. Parking. Outdoor dining. Victorian house surrounded by redwood trees; bordered by creek. Totally non-smoking. Cr cds: A, D, MC, V.

★★**SAVANNAH GRILL.** *55 Tamal Vista Blvd.* 415/924-6774. Hrs: 11:30 am–4:30 pm, 5:30–10 pm; Fri, Sat to 10:30 pm; Sun noon–9 pm. Closed Thanksgiving, Dec 25. Res accepted. Bar to 11 pm; Fri & Sat to midnight. Semi-a la carte: lunch $7.95–$15.95, dinner $7.95–$18.95. Parking. Outdoor dining. View of Mt Tamalpais. Cr cds: A, MC, V.

Costa Mesa (J-4)

Pop: 96,357 Elev: 101 ft Area code: 714

(For information about this area contact the Chamber of Commerce, 1835 Newport Blvd, Ste E270, 92627; 574-8780.)

Annual Events

Taste of Costa Mesa. Town Center Park, near South Coast Plaza. A 3-day outdoor event features various types of foods, beverages; entertainment. Phone 574-8780. One wkend May.

Highland Gathering and Games. Orange County Fairgrounds. Scottish games, dancing; soccer, rugby; piping, drumming competition. Memorial Day wkend.

Orange County Fair. Orange County Fairgrounds. Rodeo, livestock, exhibits, home arts, contests, photography, nightly entertainment, floriculture display, wine show, carnival, motorcycle races. Phone 751-3247. July.

(See Huntington Beach, Irvine, Newport Beach, Santa Ana)

Motels

★**ANA MESA SUITES.** *3597 Harbor Blvd (92626).* 714/662-3500; res: 800/767-2519; FAX 714/549-7126. 50 units, 3 story, 35 suites, 25 kits. S, D $51; suites $59–$77; kits. $64–$77; under 18 free; wkly rates. Crib $5. Pet accepted. TV; cable, in-rm movies. Pool. Complimentary continental bkfst. Restaurant nearby. Ck-out 11 am. Coin lndry. Meeting rms. Free airport transportation. Refrigerators, in-rm whirlpools. Cr cds: A, C, D, DS, ER, MC, V, JCB.

★★★**BEST WESTERN NEWPORT MESA INN.** *2642 Newport Blvd (92627).* 714/650-3020; FAX 714/642-1220. 97 rms, 3 story. S $54–$66; D $58–$72; each addl $6–$8; suites $99; under 12 free; package plans. Crib $6. TV. Heated pool. Complimentary coffee in rms. Restaurant 11:30 am–10:30 pm. Rm serv. Ck-out noon. Coin lndry. Meeting rms. Free airport transportation. Bathrm phones; some in-rm whirlpools. Refrigerators avail. Cr cds: A, C, D, DS, MC, V.

✔★**COZY INN.** *325 W Bay St (92627).* 714/650-2055. 29 rms, 2 story, 11 kits. June–mid-Sept: S $40–$42; D $44–$48; each addl $4; kit. units $10 addl; under 8 free; wkly rates; lower rates rest of yr. TV. Pool. Ck-out 11 am. Some refrigerators. Cr cds: A, C, D, DS, MC, V.

✔★**VAGABOND INN.** *3205 Harbor Blvd (92626).* 714/557-8360; FAX 714/662-7596. 127 rms, 2 story. May–Sept: S $35–$50; D $45–$69; each addl $5; suites $69–$79; under 19 free; higher rates special events; lower rates rest of yr. TV; cable. Pool. Restaurant adj 6 am–10 pm. Ck-out noon. Meeting rms. Valet serv. Local airport transportation. Exercise equipt; weights, bicycles, whirlpool. Mission-style building. Cr cds: A, C, D, DS, MC, V.

Motor Hotels

★★★**COUNTRY SIDE INN AND SUITES.** *325 Bristol St (92626), I-405 Bristol South exit, near John Wayne Airport.* 714/549-0300; res: 800/322-9992; FAX 714/662-0828. 290 units in 2 bldgs, 3 & 4 story, 135 suites. S $85–$95; D, suites $95–$140; under 13 free; wkly, seasonal rates; lower rates some wkends. Crib free. TV. 2 heated pools. Complimentary full bkfst. Restaurant 6:30 am–10 pm. Rm serv. Bar 11:30 am–11 pm. Ck-out noon. Coin lndry. Meeting rms. Bellhops. Valet serv. Concierge. Gift shop. Free airport transportation. Exercise equipt; weight machine, bicycles, whirlpools. Refrigerators. Fireplace in lobby, many antiques; open air courtyard with imported tile fountain. Cr cds: A, C, D, DS, MC, V.

★★★**RED LION HOTEL-ORANGE COUNTY AIRPORT.** *3050 Bristol St (92626), near John Wayne Airport.* 714/540-7000; FAX 714/540-9176. 484 rms, 7 story. S $99–$129; D $129–$165; each addl $15; suites $450–$650; under 18 free. Crib $10. TV; in-rm movies. Heated pool; poolside serv. Restaurant 6 am–10 pm. Rm serv. Bar 11–2 am; entertainment, dancing. Ck-out 1 pm. Convention facilities. Concierge. Gift shop. Barber, beauty shop. Covered valet parking. Free local airport, South Coast Plaza transportation. Tennis & golf privileges. Exercise equipt; weights, bicycles, whirlpool, sauna. Masseur. Game rm. Minibars. Many private patios, balconies. Solarium lobby. *LUXURY LEVEL:* EXECUTIVE LEVEL. 73 rms. S $134–$165; D $144–$185. Private lounge. Coffee in rms. Complimentary continental bkfst. Cr cds: A, C, D, DS, ER, MC, V, JCB.

Hotels

★★★**MARRIOTT SUITES.** *500 Anton Blvd (92626), off I-405 Bristol Ave exit.* 714/957-1100; FAX 714/966-8495. 253 suites, 11 story. S $119–$139; D $119–$159; each addl $20; under 18 free; wkend rates. Crib free. TV; cable. Heated pool; poolside serv. Complimentary continental bkfst. Complimentary coffee in rms. Restaurant 6:30 am–10 pm. Bar 11 am–11 pm. Ck-out noon. Free lndry facilities. Meeting rms. Gift shop. Free garage parking. Free airport transportation. Exercise equipt; weight machine, bicycles, whirlpool. Refrigerators. Balconies. Cr cds: A, C, D, DS, ER, MC, V, JCB.

★★★★**THE WESTIN SOUTH COAST PLAZA.** *686 Anton Blvd (92626).* 714/540-2500; FAX 714/754-7996. 390 rms, 16 story. S, D $139–$164; each addl $20; suites $200–$915; under 18 free; wkend package plans. Crib free. Valet parking $6. TV; cable. Heated pool;

poolside serv. Restaurant 6:30 am–10 pm; wkends from 7 am. Rm serv 24 hrs. Bar noon–1 am; entertainment Tues–Sat. Ck-out 1 pm. Convention facilities. Gift shop. Free local airport transportation. Disneyland transportation avail. Lighted tennis. Exercise equipt; weight machine, bicycles. Game deck: volleyball. Refrigerators, minibars; wet bar in some suites. South Coast Plaza Retail Center & Village adj. *LUXURY LEVEL:* **EXECUTIVE LEVEL.** 50 rms, 5 suites, 2 floors. S, D $164. Concierge. Private lounge, honor bar. In-rm movies. Complimentary continental bkfst, refreshments, newspaper, shoeshine.
Cr cds: A, C, D, DS, ER, MC, V, JCB.

★ ★**WYNDHAM GARDENS** (formerly Beverly Heritage). *3350 Ave of the Arts (92626).* 714/751-5100; FAX 714/751-0129. 238 rms, 6 story. S, D $99–$139; each addl $10; suites $109–$180; under 12 free; wkly, wkend rates; higher rates special events. TV; cable. Pool; poolside serv. Coffee in rms. Restaurant 7 am–10 pm. Bar 4 pm–midnight. Ck-out noon. Meeting rms. Valet parking. Free local airport transportation. Exercise equipt; weights, bicycles, whirlpool. Refrigerators avail. Private patios, balconies. Fireplace in lobby; marble floors. Pool area overlooks park. Cr cds: A, C, D, DS, MC, V.

Restaurants

★**EL TORITO GRILL.** *633 Anton Blvd.* 714/662-2672. Hrs: 11:30 am–10 pm; Fri & Sat to 11 pm; Sun brunch 10 am–2:30 pm. Closed Thanksgiving, Dec 25. Res accepted. Mexican, Southwestern menu. Bar to 1 am. A la carte entrees: lunch $5.25–$9.95, dinner $5.50–$12.95. Sun brunch $10.95. Specializes in grilled fresh fish, enchiladas, fajitas. Own tortillas. Valet parking. Southwestern decor. Cr cds: A, C, D, DS, MC, V.

Ⓓ

✔ ★**TRATTORIA SPIGA.** *3333 Bear St, in Chrystal Court shopping mall.* 714/540-3365. Hrs: 11 am–10 pm; Sun to 7 pm. Closed Jan 1, Easter, Dec 25. Res accepted. Italian menu. Bar. A la carte entrees: lunch, dinner $3.95–$12.95. Specialties: assaggini, rotelle dello chef, Italian-style thin crust pizza. Trattoria-style dining in inner courtyard of mall. Cr cds: A, C, D, DS, MC, V.

Ⓓ

Unrated Dining Spot

TEA & SYMPATHY. *369 E 17th St, at jct Tustin Ave.* 714/645-4860. Hrs: 11 am–6 pm; Sun brunch to 4 pm. Closed Dec 25. British menu. Wine, beer. Semi-a la carte: lunch $2.75–$9.50. Sun brunch $6.95–$11.95. Parking. Traditional English tea room. Cr cds: MC, V.

Crescent City (A-1)

Founded: 1852 **Pop:** 4,380 **Elev:** 44 ft **Area code:** 707 **Zip:** 95531

The crescent-shaped beach that gives the city its name outlines a busy harbor. A party of treasure seekers discovered the harbor, and the city was laid out a year later.

What to See and Do

1. **Point St George.** N of beach. The *Brother Jonathan,* a side-wheeler, was wrecked here in 1865. Of 232 persons aboard, 203 died; they are buried in Brother Jonathan Cemetery, Pebble Beach Dr & 9th St.

2. **Battery Point Lighthouse** (1856). On Battery Point, at the end of A St; accessible only at low tide; museum. (Apr–Sept, Wed–Sun) Phone 464-3089. ¢

3. **Del Norte County Historical Society Main Museum.** 577 H Street. Research center for local history; 2-story lighthouse lens (1892), Native American and pioneer exhibits housed in former county jail. (May–Sept, Mon–Fri) Phone 464-3922. ¢

4. **Redwood National Park.** S of town. Stretching 46 miles north and south, including 30 miles of coastline, and about 7 miles wide at its greatest width. Headquarters at 2nd & K Streets has exhibits, information. Established in 1968; the 113,200-acre park, home of what is said to be the world's tallest tree, offers hiking trails; picnic areas; scenic drives; shuttle bus (summer); interpretive programs. Contact 1111 2nd St; 464-6101 for details. Exhibits and information at Ranger Station 10 miles east or at Redwood Information Center, 2 miles south of Orick. **Free.** The three state parks located within the national park boundaries are

   Jedediah Smith Redwoods State Park. 9 mi NE off US 101 on US 199. Stout Memorial Grove, at the center of Mill Creek Flat, is about 4 mi from park entrance. Swimming; fishing. Nature, hiking trails. Picnicking. Camping (dump station). Standard fees. Phone 464-9533. Day use ¢¢

   Del Norte Coast Redwoods State Park. 7 mi S on US 101. Redwood trees grow on steep slopes just above the surf. Rhododendrons blanket the slopes, blooming in May and June. Nature, hiking trails. Picnicking. Camping (dump station). Standard fees. Phone 464-9533. Day use ¢¢

   Prairie Creek Redwoods State Park. 33 mi S on US 101. These 14,000 acres are adorned by magnificent groves of coast redwoods. Gold Bluffs Beach was worked for gold in 1851, but most of it remained hopelessly mixed in vast amounts of sand and rock. Lush ferns cover the 50-foot walls of Fern Canyon and moss carpets the fallen tree trunks. Fishing. Hiking on 75 miles of nature trails. Picnicking. Educational displays in visitor center. Frequent campfire programs and ranger-conducted hikes in summer. Two campgrounds: **Elk Prairie,** tent & trailer (reservations recommended; **Gold Bluffs Beach,** approx 3½ mi S via US 101 to Davison Rd (unpaved road; vehicle size and weight restriction). Standard fees. Information phone 488-2171; reservations phone 800/444-7275.

5. **Rellim Redwood Company Demonstration Forest.** 4 mi S on US 101. Guided tour (summer) or self-guided tour (winter) through industrial redwood forest managed for continuous production of timber. Picnic tables, play area, overlooks. (Daylight hrs) Phone 464-3144. **Free.**

(For maps and further information contact the Chamber of Commerce, Visitor Information Center, 1001 Front St; 464-3174 or 800/343-8300.)

Annual Events

World Championship Crab Races & Crab Feed. Washington's Birthday wkend.

Easter in July Lily Festival. Lily Float contest, crafts, food. July.

(See Redwood Highway)

Motels

★**AMERICAN BEST.** *685 US 101S.* 707/464-4111; res: 800/622-9923. 49 rms, 2 story. No A/C. June–Sept: S, D $57.50–$67.50; family rates; lower rates rest of yr. Crib free. TV; cable. Complimentary coffee in lobby. Restaurant adj 6:30 am–9 pm. Ck-out 11 am. Free airport transportation. Balconies. Ocean opp. Cr cds: A, D, DS, MC, V.

Ⓓ

★ ★**CURLY REDWOOD LODGE.** *701 Redwood Hwy S.* 707/464-2137. 36 rms, 1–2 story. No A/C. June–Sept: S, D $52–$59; each addl $5; suites $78; lower rates rest of yr. Crib $5. TV; cable. Complimentary morning coffee. Restaurant opp 7 am–10 pm. Ck-out 11 am.

Entire building constructed of wood from a single Curly Redwood tree. Harbor opp. Cr cds: A, C, D, MC, V.

✔ ★ ★ **PACIFIC.** (Box 595) ¾ mi N on US 101. 707/464-4141; res: 800/323-7917; FAX 707/465-3274. 62 rms, 2 story. No A/C. May–Sept: S $45; D $53–$60; each addl $5; suites $78; lower rates rest of yr. Crib $5. TV; cable. Complimentary morning coffee. Restaurant 6 am–9 pm. Bar 3 pm–2 am. Ck-out noon. Meeting rms. Sundries. Free airport transportation. Whirlpool, sauna. Cr cds: A, C, D, MC, V.

Restaurant

★ ★ **HARBOR VIEW GROTTO.** 155 Citizen's Dock, 1 mi S of US 101. 707/464-3815. Hrs: 4–10 pm; winter to 9 pm. Closed Jan 1, Thanksgiving, Dec 24, 25. Bar. Semi-a la carte: dinner $8.25–$24.95. Child's meals. Specializes in clam chowder, seafood, steak. Parking. On 2nd & 3rd floors; view of harbor. Cr cds: MC, V.

SC

Crestline (H-4)

Pop: 8,594 **Elev:** 5,000 ft **Area code:** 909 **Zip:** 92325

What to See and Do

1. **Lake Gregory Regional Park.** Lake Dr & Gregory Rd, E of town. Swimming beach (Memorial Day wkend–Labor Day wkend); fishing, rowboats (rentals); picnicking, snack bars. Park (last wkend Apr–3rd wkend Oct). Phone 338-2233. Swimming (per person) ¢¢

2. **Silverwood Lake State Recreation Area.** 12 mi E off I-15 on CA 138. Swimming; fishing; boating (rentals). Nature, bicycle trails. Picnicking, concession. Camping (dump station). Visitor center. Standard fees. Phone 389-2303 or -2281.

(For further information contact the Chamber of Commerce, PO Box 926; 338-2706.)

(For accommodations see Lake Arrowhead)

Cucamonga
(see Rancho Cucamonga)

Culver City *

Pop: 38,793 **Elev:** 94 ft **Area codes:** 213 or 310
*Just S of I-10 (Santa Monica Frwy), 7 mi W of Downtown Los Angeles (H-4).

(For general information and attractions see Los Angeles.)

Hotels

★ **RAMADA.** 6333 Bristol Pkwy (90230). 310/670-3200; FAX 310/641-8925. 260 rms, 12 story. S $85–$105; D $95–$115; each addl $10; suites $175–$250; under 18 free; wkend rates. Crib free. Pet accepted. TV. Heated pool; poolside serv. Restaurant 6 am–11 pm. Bar 11–1 am. Ck-out noon. Meeting rms. Shopping arcade. Airport transportation. Exercise equipt; weights, bicycles, whirlpool. Wet bar, refrigerator in suites. Cr cds: A, C, D, DS, MC, V.

★ ★ ★ **RED LION HOTEL-LOS ANGELES AIRPORT** (formerly Pacifica Hotel & Conference Center). 6161 Centinela Ave. 310/649-1776; FAX 310/649-4411. 368 rms, 12 story. S $95–$120; D $105–$135; each addl $10; suites $175–$425; under 18 free. Crib free. TV. Heated pool. Restaurant 6 am–11 pm. Bar 11–2 am; entertainment, dancing Fri & Sat. Ck-out noon. Convention facilities. Gift shop. Free airport, shopping transportation. Exercise equipt; weights, bicycles, whirlpool. Cr cds: A, C, D, DS, MC, V.

Dana Point
(see Laguna Beach)

Davis (D-2)

Settled: 1868 **Pop:** 46,209 **Elev:** 50 ft **Area code:** 916 **Zip:** 95616

The pioneer settler Jerome C. Davis planted 400 acres of wheat, barley, orchards and vineyards and pastured great herds of livestock here. Since then, Davis has remained the center of a rich agricultural area. The city is also known for its energy conservation programs and projects. A prime example is Village Homes Solar Village. Obtain a self-guided tour brochure at City Hall, 23 Russell Blvd.

What to See and Do

Davis Campus of the University of California (1905). (23,000 students) On CA 113, I-80. Nearly 5,200 acres with College of Agricultural and Environmental Sciences, College of Engineering, College of Letters and Science, School of Veterinary Medicine, School of Law, Graduate School of Management and School of Medicine. Art exhibits displayed in the Nelson and Union Memorial galleries and in the C.N. Gorman Museum. Tours. Phone 752-8111.

(For further information contact the Davis Area Chamber of Commerce, 228 B Street; 756-5160.)

Annual Event

Picnic Day. Sponsored by Associated Students of Univ of California at Davis. Includes parade, floats, exhibits, aquacade, dachshund races, concerts, horse show, rodeo, sheepdog trials. Phone 752-1990. Mid-Apr.

(See Napa, Sacramento, Vacaville)

Motels

✔ ★ **BEST WESTERN UNIVERSITY LODGE.** 123 B Street. 916/756-7890; FAX 916/756-0245. 54 rms, 2 story, some kits. S $52–$60; D $55–$65; each addl $5. Crib $5. TV. Complimentary coffee in rms. Restaurant opp 6 am–11 pm. Ck-out noon. Exercise equipt; bicycle, weight machines, whirlpool. Refrigerators. Univ of CA 1 blk. Cr cds: A, C, D, DS, MC, V.

★ **RAMADA INN.** 110 F Street. 916/753-3600; FAX 916/758-8623. 134 rms, 2–3 story. S $58; D $73; each addl $10; suites $85; under 12 free; higher rates: graduation & picnic wkends. Crib free. TV. Heated pool. Complimentary coffee in lobby. Restaurant adj open 24 hrs. Ck-out noon. Meeting rms. Valet serv. Some refrigerators. Balconies. Cr cds: A, D, DS, MC, V.

Restaurants

✔ ★ **MR. B'S BAR AND GRILL.** *217 E Street. 916/756-3757.* Hrs: 11 am–3 pm, 5–9 pm; Sat, Sun brunch 9 am–1 pm. Closed Jan 1, Thanksgiving, Dec 25. Res accepted; required hols. Bar to 2 am. Semi-a la carte: lunch $3.25–$7.95, dinner $4.50–$14. Sun brunch $3.25–$6.95. Child's meals. Specializes in fresh seafood, champagne chicken, salads. Disc jockey Wed–Sat. Outdoor dining. Totally nonsmoking. Cr cds: A, DS, MC, V.

★ ★ **SOGA'S.** *222 D Street. 916/757-1733.* Hrs: 11:30 am–2:30 pm, 5–9 pm; Fri & Sat to 10 pm. Closed Sun, Mon; most major hols. Res accepted; required wkends. Wine, beer. Semi-a la carte: lunch $6–$9, dinner $12–$18. Specializes in seafood, pasta. Outdoor dining. Reminiscent of a 1930s home; fireplace. Cr cds: A, MC, V.

Death Valley National Monument (F4, G5)

(70 mi E of Lone Pine on CA 190)

Here, approximately 300 miles northeast of Los Angeles, are more than 3,000 square miles of rugged desert, peaks and depressions—an unusual and colorful geography. The monument is one vast geological museum, revealing secrets of ages gone by. Millions of years ago, this was part of the Pacific Ocean; then violent uplifts of the earth occurred, creating mountain ranges and draining water to the west. Today, 200 square miles of the valley are at or below sea level; the lowest point on the continent (282 feet below sea level) is here; Telescope Peak (11,049 feet) towers directly above it. The valley itself is about 140 miles long and 4 to 16 miles wide. The average rainfall is less than 2 inches a year. From October until May the climate is very pleasant. In summer it is extremely hot; a maximum temperature of 134°F in the shade has been recorded. If considered altogether, this is the lowest, hottest, driest area in the world.

Death Valley was named in 1849 when a party of gold hunters took a short cut here and were stranded for several weeks awaiting help. The discovery and subsequent mining of borax, hauled out by the famous 20-mule teams, led to development of the valley as a tourist attraction.

The visitor center at Furnace Creek is open daily. Guided walks, evening programs and talks (Nov–Apr). Golden Age, Golden Eagle, Golden Access passports (see INTRODUCTION). Phone 619/786-2331. Per car ¢¢

What to See and Do

1. **Visitor Center.** At Furnace Creek. It is recommended that visitors stop here before continuing on for an orientation film, day-trip suggestions, help in organizing sightseeing routes and important information on camping areas and road conditions. Phone 619/786-2331.

2. **Zabriskie Point.** View of Death Valley and the Panamint Range from the rugged badlands of the Black Mountains.

3. **20-Mule-Team Canyon.** Viewed from a twisting road; RVs and trailers are not allowed on this road. (This is an unpaved, one-way road; watch carefully for the entrance sign.)

4. **Dante's View** (5,475 ft). View of Death Valley with a steep drop to 279 feet below sea level at Badwater.

5. **Golden Canyon.** Offers a display of color ranging from deep purple to rich gold. Mushroom Rock, an odd-shaped outcropping, is south of the canyon.

6. **Artist's Palette.** A particularly scenic auto drive (9 miles one way), with spectacular colors. Because of difficult roads, RVs and trailers are advised not to drive here.

7. **Devil's Golf Course.** Vast beds of rugged salt crystals.

8. **Natural Bridge.** A bridge spanning a colorful canyon in the Black Mountains; 1-mile walking trail.

9. **Badwater.** At 279 feet below sea level, near the lowest spot on the North American continent; look for sea level sign.

10. **Sand dunes.** Sand blown by the wind into dunes 5 to 80 feet high.

11. **Scotty's Castle.** A desert mansion (ca 1922–1931), designed and built to be viewed as a work of art, as well as a house. The furnishings are typical of the period; many were especially designed and hand-crafted for this house. Living history tours are led by costumed interpreters. ¢¢

12. **Rhyolite Ghost Town.** This was the largest town in the mining history of Death Valley in the early 1900s; 5,000–10,000 people lived here then. The town bloomed from 1905–1910; by 1911 it was a ghost town. One structure still left standing from that era is the "bottle house," constructed of 12,000–50,000 beer and liquor bottles (depending on who does the estimating).

13. **Ubehebe Crater.** Crater left by a volcanic steam explosion.

14. **Charcoal kilns.** Beehive-shaped stone structures, formerly used to make charcoal for nearby mines. **Note:** The last mile of the access road is unpaved.

15. **Telescope Peak.** Highest point in the Panamint Range (11,049 ft). (Although there is a 14-mile round-trip hiking trail, it is inaccessible in the winter months.)

16. **Camping.** Developed and primitive camping in area; limited hookups. It is suggested that campers check with the visitors center for important information on camping facilities and road conditions.

NOTE: It can be very dangerous to venture off paved roads in this area in the summer months. Carefully obey all National Park Service signs and regulations. Make sure you have plenty of gas and oil. Carry water when you explore this monument, especially in hot weather. For further information contact Superintendent, Death Valley National Monument, Death Valley 92328; phone 619/786-2331.

Annual Event

Resurrection of Rhyolite Ghost Town. Costumed participants, through the use of vignettes, turn back the clock to the time when Rhyolite was a dynamic mining community. Usually mid-Mar.

Motel

✔ ★ **STOVE PIPE WELLS VILLAGE.** *CA 190 (92328). 619/786-2387; FAX 619/786-2389.* 83 rms, 5 buildings. No rm phones. S, D $53–$69; each addl $10; under 12 free. Crib $5. Pet accepted, some restrictions; $10–$25 refundable. Heated pool. Restaurant 7–10 am, 11:30 am–2 pm, 5:30–9 pm. Bar 4–11 pm; occasional entertainment, dancing. Ck-out 11 am. Sundries. Tennis privileges. Landing strip. Panoramic view of mountains, desert, dunes. Cr cds: MC, V.

Motor Hotel

★ ★ ★ **FURNACE CREEK INN.** *(Box 1, 92328) ¾ mi S on CA 190. 619/786-2361; FAX 619/786-2307 or -2514.* 68 units, 4 story. Oct–May: S $175; D $235–$243; each addl $14; suites $275–$325; under 5 free. Closed rest of yr. TV. Natural thermal spring water pool; poolside serv. Complimentary continental bkfst. Restaurant 7:30–10 am, noon–1 pm, 6–8 pm (also see INN DINING ROOM and L'OTTIMOS). Rm serv. Bar; entertainment, dancing exc Mon. Ck-out noon. Bellhops. Concierge. Gift shop. Lighted tennis, pro. Golf privileges, greens fee $28, driving range. Exercise equipt; weight machine, bicycles, sauna. Lawn games. Library. Refrigerators. Private patios, balconies. Free newspaper Mon–Sat. 1920s–30s decor; native stone in many areas. Cr cds: A, C, D, DS, MC, V.

Guest Ranch

★★**FURNACE CREEK RANCH.** *(Box 1, 92328) On CA 190, near monument headquarters. 619/786-2345; res: 800/528-6367; FAX 619/786-2307.* 224 rms, 1–2 story. S, D $70–$120; each addl $14; under 18 free. TV in most rms; cable. Natural thermal spring water pool. Playground. Dining rms 5:30 am–10 pm. Ck-out noon, ck-in 4 pm. Grocery. Coin lndry. Package store. Gift shop. Sports dir. Lighted tennis. Golf, greens fee $28, pro, driving range. Lawn games. Museum. Guided tours. Some refrigerators. Cr cds: A, C, D, DS, MC, V, JCB.

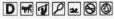

Restaurants

★★★**INN DINING ROOM.** *(See Furnace Creek Inn Motor Hotel) 619/786-2361.* Hrs: 7–10 am, 6–8 pm; Sun brunch 11 am–2 pm. Closed mid-May–mid-Oct. Res accepted. Continental menu. Bar 11–2 am. Wine list. A la carte entrees: bkfst $7–$15, dinner $14.95–$29.95. Sun brunch $15. Specializes in lamb, veal, prime rib. Own baking. Pianist Wed–Sun. Valet parking. 1930s decor; beam ceilings. Jacket. Totally nonsmoking. Cr cds: A, C, D, DS, MC, V.

★★**L'OTTIMOS.** *(See Furnace Creek Inn Motor Hotel) 619/786-2361.* Hrs: 5–10 pm. Closed mid-May–mid-Oct. Res accepted. Bar 11–2 am. Wine list. Semi-a la carte: dinner $11–$24. Specializes in Italian cuisine. Own baking, pastries. Entertainment Tues–Sun. Parking. Native stone walls, hand-hewn wood trim. Cr cds: A, C, D, DS, MC, V.

Del Mar (J-4)

Pop: 4,860 **Elev:** 100 ft **Area code:** 619 **Zip:** 92014

This village-by-the sea community offers attractive white beaches, brilliant sunsets and lazy fishing from the shore. It is also an attractive area for year-round ballooning. Contact Chamber of Commerce.

(For information about this area contact the Greater Del Mar Chamber of Commerce, 1442 Camino Del Mar, Suite 214; 755-4844.)

Annual Event

Del Mar Fair. Fairgrounds. Name entertainment, carnival; livestock, trade, hobby and flower exhibits. Phone 755-1161. 16 days mid-June–early July.

Seasonal Event

Del Mar Thoroughbred Club. County Fairgrounds. Thoroughbred horse racing. For prices, schedule and information phone 755-1141; for ticket reservations phone 481-1207. Late July–mid-Sept.

(See Carlsbad, La Jolla, San Diego)

Motels

★★★**CLARION CARRIAGE HOUSE INN.** *720 Camino del Mar. 619/755-9765; res: 800/451-4515 (exc CA), 800/453-4411 (CA); FAX 619/792-8196.* 80 rms, 3 story, 22 kits. No A/C. June–Sept: S $80–$99; D $85–$99; lower rates rest of yr. Crib free. TV; cable. Heated pool; whirlpool. Complimentary continental bkfst in rms. Ck-out 11 am. Coin

lndry. Meeting rm. Bellhops. Many balconies. Cr cds: A, C, D, DS, ER, MC, V, JCB.

✔★★**COUNTRY SIDE INN.** *(1661 Villa Cardiff, Cardiff-by-the-Sea 92007) N via I-5, 1 blk E of Birmingham exit. 619/944-0427; res: 800/322-9993; FAX 619/944-7708.* 102 rms, 2 story. S $59–$95; D $65–$115; each addl $8; under 12 free. Crib free. TV; cable. Heated pool; whirlpool. Complimentary full bkfst, coffee. Ck-out noon. Meeting rms. Refrigerators. Country French decor. Ocean, swimming beach 1 mi. Cr cds: A, C, D, MC, V.

Hotel

★★★**HILTON.** *15575 Jimmy Durante Blvd. 619/792-5200; FAX 619/792-9538.* 245 units, 3 story, 15 suites. S $75–$155; D $90–$165; each addl $15; suites $225–$650; family rates; special package plans. Crib free. TV; cable. Pool; whirlpool, poolside serv. Restaurant 6 am–11 pm. Bar 5 pm–1 am; entertainment, dancing. Ck-out noon. Convention facilities. Concierge. Gift shop. Beach transportation. Tennis privileges. Health club privileges. Some refrigerators, minibars. Beach 4 blks. Cr cds: A, C, D, DS, ER, MC, V.

Resort

★★★**L'AUBERGE DEL MAR RESORT & SPA.** (4-Star 1993; New general manager, therefore not rated) *(PO Box 2889) 1540 Camino del Mar. 619/259-1515; res: 800/553-1336; FAX 619/755-4940.* 123 rms, 3 story, 8 suites. S, D $165–$250; each addl $25; suites $325–$750; tennis, golf, special package plans. Crib avail. Valet, underground parking (fee). TV; cable. 2 heated pools; poolside serv. Restaurant (see TOURLAS RESTAURANT & TERRACE). Afternoon tea 3–5 pm. Bar 11 am–midnight; entertainment Fri, Sat. Ck-out noon, ck-in 4 pm. Concierge. Shopping arcade. Lighted tennis. 18-hole golf privileges. Exercise rm; instructor, weights, stair machine, sauna, steam rm. Massage. Full service European spa. Minibars. Overlooking the Pacific Ocean, in the village of Del Mar. Ocean 1 blk; some rms with ocean view. Cr cds: A, C, D, DS, MC, V.

Restaurants

★★**CILANTROS.** *3702 Via de la Valle. 619/259-8777.* Hrs: 11:30 am–10 pm; Fri & Sat to 11 pm; Sun to 9:30 pm. Closed Thanksgiving, Dec 24, 25. Res accepted. Southwestern menu. Bar to midnight. A la carte entrees: lunch $3.25–$8.95, dinner $3.25–$17.75. Specialties: fajitas, spit-roasted chicken. Own tortillas. Parking. Patio dining. Southwestern decor. Totally nonsmoking. Cr cds: A, MC, V.

★★**EPAZOTE.** *1555 Camino del Mar, in Del Mar Plaza. 619/259-9966.* Hrs: 11:30 am–10 pm; wkends 11 am–11 pm. Closed Thanksgiving, Dec 24, 25. Res accepted. Mexican menu. Bar. A la carte entrees: lunch $6–$10, dinner $8.95–$18.95. Specialties: spit-roasted chicken, Swiss chard enchiladas. Valet parking. Outdoor dining. View of ocean. Cr cds: A, MC, V.

★★**IL FORNAIO.** *1555 Camino del Mar, in Del Mar Plaza. 619/755-8876.* Hrs: 11:30 am–11 pm; Fri to midnight; Sat & Sun 9 am–11 pm. Closed Thanksgiving, Dec 25. Res accepted. Italian menu. Bar. A la carte entrees: lunch $8–$16, dinner $8–$18. Specializes in northern Italian dishes. Valet parking $3. Outdoor dining. View of ocean. Cr cds: A, C, D, MC, V.

✔★★**JAKE'S DEL MAR.** *1660 Coast Blvd. 619/755-2002.* Hrs: 11:15 am–2:30 pm, 5–10 pm; Sun & Mon from 5 pm; Fri to 10:30 pm; Sat

5–10:30 pm; Sun brunch 10 am–2:30 pm. Closed Thanksgiving, Dec 25. Res accepted. No A/C. Continental menu. Bar to midnight. Semi-a la carte: lunch $7.95–$9.95, dinner $13.95–$18.95. Sun brunch $8.95. Specializes in fresh seafood, rack of lamb. Own desserts. Valet parking. Patio dining. Ocean view. Cr cds: A, MC, V.

★ ★ ★PACIFICA DEL MAR. *1555 Camino del Mar, in Del Mar Plaza.* 619/792-0476. Hrs: 11 am–10 pm; Fri & Sat to 10:30 pm; Sun 9 am–1 pm, 4–10 pm; early-bird dinner 4–6:30 pm. Res accepted. Bar. A la carte entrees: bkfst (Sun only) $5.95–$9.95, lunch $6.50–$13, dinner $10–$20. Specializes in fresh California coastal cuisine. Valet parking. Patio dining. View of ocean. Cr cds: A, C, D, DS, MC, V.

D

★ ★TOURLAS RESTAURANT & TERRACE. *(See L'Auberge Del Mar Resort & Spa)* 619/259-1515 ext 460. Hrs: 6:30 am–2:30 pm, 6–10 pm; Sun brunch 10 am–2 pm. Res acepted. Bar 11 am–midnight. Semi-a la carte: bkfst $4.95–$8.95. A la carte entrees: lunch $5.75–$12.95, dinner $9.95–$19.95. Sun brunch $19.95. Specialties: tortilla soup with chicken and avocado, grilled swordfish with cashews and snow peas, American dishes with Southwest flair. Valet parking. Outdoor dining. Country French chateau decor; skylights. View of waterfall & gardens. Cr cds: A, C, D, DS, MC, V.

D

★ ★VILLA D'ESTE. *2282 Carmel Valley Rd.* 619/259-2006. Hrs: 11:30 am–2:30 pm, 5:30–10 pm; Sat & Sun from 5:30 pm. Closed Jan 1, Labor Day, Dec 25. Res accepted. Italian menu. Bar. Semi-a la carte: lunch $7.50–$12.50. A la carte entrees: dinner $10–$23. Complete meals: dinner $15.95. Specialties: costoletta, halibut Livornese. Own pasta. Parking. Patio dining. Old World Italian decor. Cr cds: A, C, D, DS, ER, MC, V, JCB.

D

Desert Hot Springs (J-5)

Pop: 11,668 **Elev:** 1,070 ft **Area code:** 619 **Zip:** 92240

What to See and Do

Cabot's Old Indian Pueblo and Museum. 67616 E Desert View. 35-room Hopi-style mansion contains exhibits of Coachella Valley history, Indian and Eskimo artifacts, Pueblo Art Gallery, trading post, rock shop and artists' studio. Also 43-foot redwood carving of an Indian head. 45-min tours (Wed–Sun). Sr citizen rate. Phone 329-7610. ¢¢

(For further information contact the Chamber of Commerce, 11711 West Dr; 329-6403 or 800/346-3347.)

(See Idyllwild, Indio, Palm Desert, Palm Springs)

Motel

★ ★DESERT HOT SPRINGS SPA & HOTEL. *10805 Palm Dr.* 619/329-6495; res: 800/843-6053 (CA); FAX 619/329-6915. 50 rms, 2 story. Mid-Dec–May: S, D $79–$99; each addl $10; suites $99–$119; lower rates rest of yr. Crib $5. TV. 8 natural hot mineral pools (open to public); wading pool, poolside serv. Restaurant 7 am–11 pm. Bar 10–2 am; entertainment. Ck-out noon. Sundries. Gift shop. Tennis privileges. 18-hole golf privileges. 6 whirlpools, sauna; natural mineral hot water in all pools. Refrigerators avail. Private patios, balconies. Cr cds: A, C, D, DS, MC, V.

Inn

✔ ★ ★TRAVELLERS REPOSE BED & BREAKFAST. *(PO Box 655)* 66920 First St. 619/329-9584. 3 rms, 2 story. No rm phones.

Sept–June: S $50–$67.50; D $55–$75; wkly rates. Closed rest of yr. Children over 12 yrs only. Heated pool; whirlpool. Complimentary continental bkfst, tea. Restaurant nearby. Ck-out 11 am, ck-in 2 pm. Free airport, bus depot transportation. Parlor. Each rm individually decorated. Totally nonsmoking. No cr cds accepted.

Devils Postpile National Monument (E-3)

(56 mi NW of Bishop, off US 395)

Just southeast of Yosemite National Park (see) and surrounded by Inyo National Forest (see) is Devils Postpile National Monument. The monument is among the finest examples of columnar basalt in the world, formed approximately 100,000 years ago when basalt lava erupted in the area. These columns, standing 40 to 60 feet high, are protected by the National Park Service. The formation is a half-mile hike from the ranger station. A short, steep trail leads to the top of the formation for a view of the ends of the columns, which have been polished by glaciers and resemble tile-like inlays. Pumice, a porous lava, and a nearby bubbling soda spring are evidence of recent volcanic activity.

Rainbow Falls is approximately two miles down the river trail from the Postpile. Here the San Joaquin River drops 101 feet—the foam-white water starkly contrasting with the dark cliffs. Its name was suggested by the rainbows that play across the falls in the afternoon. Fishing is permitted with license; hunting is prohibited. Picnic area on grounds. A campground is maintained in the northeast section. Park (July–mid-Oct, daily; closed rest of year). Ranger station (daily; hours may vary). Campfire programs and guides walks available; call for schedule. For further information contact PO Box 501, Mammoth Lakes 93546; phone 619/934-2289 (mid-June–Oct; rest of yr, phone 209/565-3134.) Camping per day ¢¢¢

(For accommodations see Mammoth Lakes)

Disneyland (J-4)

(26 mi S of Los Angeles on Harbor Blvd, off Santa Ana Frwy in Anaheim)

The Walt Disney Company has sprinkled magic over 80 beautifully landscaped acres in Anaheim to create a fantasy that tantalizes adults as well as children. Park guests meet Mickey Mouse and the Disney characters and experience real-life adventures. Transportation ranges from horse-drawn streetcars to monorails; restaurant fare varies from pancakes to continental cuisine. Summer schedule includes name entertainment daily, dancing, fireworks and parades. You'll need a minimum of eight hours to see Disneyland. Plan to rest up the next day.

What to See and Do

The eight main sections of Disneyland are

1. **Fantasyland.** Favorite Disney classics come to life in exciting adventures. Major attractions include It's a Small World, Pinocchio, Snow White, Dumbo, Peter Pan and Alice in Wonderland.

2. **Main St, U.S.A.** Revives turn-of-the-century nostalgia with steam-powered Disneyland railroad, old-time cinema, Market House, 1900 emporium; an inspiring Audio-Animatronics presentation, "The Walt Disney Story," featuring "Great Moments with Mr. Lincoln."

3. **Tomorrowland.** This land of the future explores inner and outer space; features include Space Mountain rollercoaster, Autopia, a skyway, Submarine Voyage, a 2½-mi monorail; People Mover, rocket ride; *American Journeys* and *Wonders of China* are presented in the Circle-Vision 360 Theatre; Magic Eye Theatre features *Captain EO;* Star Tours is an exciting out-of-this-world trip through the galaxy.

4. **Adventureland.** Take a "Jungle Cruise" through tropical rivers of the world, with lifelike alligators, hippos, gorillas, monkeys, water buffalo and Indian elephants; Swiss Family Tree House; Enchanted Tiki Room shows musical fantasy with Audio-Animatronics: birds, flowers, talking and singing Tiki gods.

5. **Frontierland.** Relive the Old West and capture the pioneer spirit with the *Mark Twain* sternwheel riverboat, keel boats, the Golden Horseshoe Jamboree and Big Thunder Mountain Railroad. FANTASMIC! is a special effects and character presentation (nightly anytime Disneyland is open after dark) on the Rivers of America, which flow between Frontierland and Tom Sawyer Island.

6. **New Orleans Square.** Shops, cafes, nostalgic courtyards, a "Pirates of the Caribbean" cruise and the Haunted Mansion.

7. **Critter Country.** Home of "Splash Mountain" log flume ride, Country Bear Playhouse, a 15-min country & western revue featuring musical Audio-Animatronic bears and Davy Crockett explorer canoes.

8. **Mickey's Toontown.** A three-dimensional cartoon environment where guests can visit the homes of Mickey Mouse and his friends, including Goofy's Bounce House and Chip 'n Dale's Tree Slide and Acorn Crawl. Other attractions include The Jolly Trolley, Gadget's Go Coaster and Roger Rabbit's Car Toon Spin.

Disneyland Attractions are open daily (extended hrs during major hols). Passport to Disneyland good for unlimited use of rides and attractions (except arcades). Guided tours. Facilities for the disabled include wheelchair rentals, ramps; tape cassettes for the visually impaired. Contact 1313 Harbor Blvd, PO Box 3232, Anaheim 92803; 714/999-4565. Passport (individual) $28.75; children ages 3–11 $23; under 3 yrs free.

(For accommodations see Anaheim, Buena Park, Los Angeles, Orange)

Dunsmuir (B-2)

Pop: 2,129 **Elev:** 2,289 ft **Area code:** 916 **Zip:** 96025

What to See and Do

Castle Crags State Park. 6 mi S off I-5. On 4,250 acres. Named for nearby granite peaks up to 6,600 feet high. Fishing (exc in the Sacramento River and its tributaries). Picnicking. Camping. Standard fees. Phone 235-2684. Day use per vehicle ¢¢

(For further information contact the Chamber of Commerce, PO Box 17; 235-2177.)

Annual Event

Railroad Days. 3rd or 4th wkend June.

(See Mt Shasta)

Motels

✔ ★**CEDAR LODGE.** *4201 Dunsmuir Ave. 916/235-4331.* 13 rms, 3 kits. S $28–$32; D $36–$50; each addl $4; kit. units $10 addl; family rates. Crib $4. Pet accepted. TV; cable, in-rm movies avail. Complimentary coffee in rms. Restaurant nearby. Ck-out 11 am. Down-

hill/x-country ski 16 mi. Private patios. Picnic tables, grill. Large exotic bird aviary. Near Sacramento River. Cr cds: A, MC, V.

★★**RAILROAD PARK RESORT.** *100 Railroad Park Rd. 916/235-4440.* 28 rms, 4 cabins. Mid-May–Sept: S $60; D $65; each addl $5; cabins $60–$65; golf plans; lower rates rest of yr. TV; cable. Pool; whirlpool. Restaurant 5–9 pm; closed Tues. Bar 4–11 pm. Ck-out 11 am. Coin lndry. Meeting rms. Sundries. Gift shop. Game rm. Lawn games. Some refrigerators. Picnic tables, grills. RV hookups. Rooms in authentic railroad cars; ¼ mi from Sacramento River. Cr cds: A, DS, MC, V.

El Cajon (K-4)

Pop: 88,693 **Elev:** 435 ft **Area code:** 619

(For general information and attractions see San Diego.)

Motels

★★**BEST WESTERN CONTINENTAL INN.** *650 N Mollison Ave (92021). 619/442-0601; FAX 619/442-0152.* 97 rms, 2–3 story, 12 suites, 12 kits. Mid-June–mid-Sept: S $48–$65; D $55–$65; each addl $5; suites $56–$120; kits. $65; under 12 free; lower rates rest of yr. Crib free. TV; cable. Heated pool; whirlpool. Complimentary continental bkfst, coffee. Restaurant opp open 24 hrs. Ck-out 11 am. Coin lndry. Meeting rms. Many refrigerators; some minibars. Many balconies. Cr cds: A, C, D, DS, MC, V.

★**DAYS INN-LA MESA.** *1250 El Cajon Blvd (92020). 619/588-8808; FAX 619/588-8482.* 110 rms, 4 story. June–Labor Day: S $43–$63; D $49–$69; each addl $6; under 12 free; wkly rates; lower rates rest of yr. Crib free. TV; cable, in-rm movies avail. Heated pool; whirlpool. Complimentary continental bkfst, coffee. Restaurant nearby. Ck-out 11 am. Coin lndry. Meeting rms. Cr cds: A, C, D, DS, ER, MC, V, JCB.

✔ ★**PLAZA INTERNATIONAL INN.** *683 N Mollison Ave (92021). 619/442-0973; res: 800/652-3030 (CA, AZ).* 60 rms, 2 story. S $29–$32; D $35–$39; kit. units $195/wk; wkly rates. Crib free. TV; cable. Pool; whirlpool, sauna. Complimentary coffee in rms. Restaurant adj open 24 hrs. Bar 6–2 am. Ck-out 11 am. Refrigerators. Cr cds: A, C, D, DS, MC, V.

★★**SINGING HILLS LODGE.** *3007 Dehesa Rd (92019). 619/442-3425; res: 800/457-5568; FAX 619/442-9574.* 102 rms, 1–2 story. S, D $74–$135; each addl $14; suites $94–$208; under 10 free. Crib $8. TV. 2 heated pools; whirlpool. Complimentary coffee in rms. Restaurant 6 am–4 pm; dining rm 5:30–10 pm. Bar 10–2 am; entertainment Tues–Sat. Ck-out 1:30 pm. Coin lndry. Meeting rms. Lighted tennis, pro. Three 18-hole golf courses, greens fee $8–$30. Refrigerators. Wet bar in suites. Private patios, balconies. View of mountains, valley and golf course. Cr cds: A, DS, MC, V.

El Centro (K-5)

Settled: 1901 **Pop:** 31,384 **Elev:** 40 ft below sea level **Area code:** 619 **Zip:** 92243

This busy marketplace in the center of the Imperial Valley is the largest town entirely below sea level in the US. Water from the All-American Canal and Hoover Dam has turned arid desert into lush farmland, which produces great crops of sugar beets, melons and lettuce. The Imperial Valley was once part of the Gulf of California; mountains east of El Centro are ringed with coral reefs. Other points of geological interest are Fossil Canyon, north of town, and Painted Gorge, northwest off I-8.

(For further information contact the Chamber of Commerce, 1100 Main St; 352-3681.)

(See Calexico)

Motels

★ ★ ★**BARBARA WORTH COUNTRY CLUB & INN.** *(2050 Country Club Dr, Holtville 92250) 8 mi E on CA 80. 619/356-2806; res: 800/356-3806; FAX 619/356-GOLF.* 103 rms, 2 story. S $48–$58; D $54–$64; each addl $6; kit. suites $160–$232; under 13 free; wkly rates; golf plans. Crib $6. TV; cable. 2 heated pools; whirlpool. Restaurant 6 am–10 pm. Rm serv. Bar 9–2 am. Ck-out noon. Meeting rms. 18-hole golf, greens fee $20–$35, putting green, driving range. Some refrigerators. Private balconies. Cr cds: A, C, D, DS, MC, V.

✓ ★**DEL CORONADO CROWN.** *330 N Imperial Ave. 619/353-0030; res: 800/653-3226; FAX 619/353-0415.* 50 rms, 2 story. S, D $38–$44; each addl $6; kit. unit $58; under 12 free; wkly rates. Crib free. Pet accepted; $6. TV; cable. Heated pool. Complimentary continental bkfst, coffee. Restaurant adj 5 am–10 pm. Ck-out noon. Refrigerators. Cr cds: A, C, D, DS, MC, V, JCB.

✓ ★**EXECUTIVE INN.** *725 State St. 619/352-8500.* 42 rms, 2 story, 5 kits. S, D $27–$31; kit. units $35–$45; each addl $5; suites $45–$55. Crib $5. TV; cable. Heated pool. Complimentary continental bkfst. Restaurant nearby. Ck-out 11 am. Coin lndry. Some free covered parking. Some refrigerators. Grills. Cr cds: MC, V.

★ ★**RAMADA INN.** *1455 Ocotillo Dr, I-8 & Imperial Ave. 619/352-5152; FAX 619/337-1567.* 150 rms, 2 story. S $46–$65; D $52–$75; each addl $6; suites $65–$70; under 19 free. Crib free. Pet accepted. TV; cable. Heated pool. Restaurant open 24 hrs. Rm serv 6 am–2 pm, 5–10 pm. Bar 11–1 am; dancing wknds. Ck-out noon. Coin lndry. Meeting rms. Free airport, bus depot transportation. Cr cds: A, C, D, DS, MC, V, JCB.

★ ★**VACATION INN.** *2000 Cottonwood Circle. 619/352-9523; res: 800/328-6289; FAX 619/353-7620.* 188 rms, 2 story. S $46–$55; D $53–$60; suites $65–$95; under 17 free; higher rates special events. Crib free. Pet accepted; $25. TV; cable. Heated pool; whirlpool, poolside serv. Restaurant 6 am–10 pm. Bar from 11 am. Ck-out noon. Coin lndry. Meeting rms. Some refrigerators. 31-space RV park adj. Cr cds: A, C, D, DS, MC, V.

Encino
(see Los Angeles)

Ensenada, Baja California, Mexico (K-4)

Pop: 175,000 (est) **Elev:** 10 ft

Located on Todos Santos Bay, some 65 miles south of the border, Ensenada charms northern visitors with its good fishing, mild climate

throughout the year and simple way of life. It is a favored vacation spot as well as the sports capital of Mexico. (For Border Crossing Regulations, see INTRODUCTION.)

What to See and Do

1. **Swimming.** 5-mi beach along the bay.
2. **Fishing.** Giant white sea bass, yellow-tail, barracuda, bonita and other game fish in summer; bass in winter. Permit required for fishing and boating. Contact the Mexican Fish Commission in San Diego; 619/233-6956.
3. **Hunting.** Ducks, geese, quail, deer. Best S of town in mountains and plains region. Permit required. Contact the Mexican Consulate in San Diego; 619/231-8414.

(For further information contact the Tourism & Convention Bureau, 7860 Mission Center Court, Suite 202, San Diego 92108; 619/299-8518, 298-4105, 800/225-2786 outside CA or 800/522-1516 in CA.)

Motels

(Tap water may be unfit for drinking)

★ ★**ESTERO BEACH RESORT.** *(Box 86) 6 mi S on MEX 1, on Estero Bay. Phone 011-52-617/6-62-30.* 110 rms, 1–2 story, 10 kit. cottages. Sept-Apr: S, D $68–$94; each addl $9; suites (no children) $94–$220; kit. cottages $68–$82; under 5 free; lower rates rest of yr. Restaurant 7:30 am–10:30 pm. Bar. Ck-out noon. Meeting rms. Shopping arcade. Tennis. Private patios, balconies. RV parking; hookups. Extensive grounds. Swimming beach. Cr cds: MC, V.

✓ ★ ★**HOTEL PARAISO LAS PALMAS.** *(Mailing address: 445 W San Ysidro Blvd, Ste 2507, San Ysidro, CA 92173) 206 Blvd Sanginez. Phone 011-52-617/7-17-01-08.* 66 rms, 3 story, 13 suites. No A/C. No elvtr. S, D $45–$55; each addl $5; suites $65–$125; under 12 free. Crib free. TV; cable. Pool; whirlpool. Restaurant 7 am–midnight. Rm serv. Bar. Ck-out 1 pm. Bellhops. Some minibars. Cr cds: A, MC, V.

★ ★**PUNTA MORRO.** *(Mailing address: PO Box 434263, San Diego, CA 92143) 2 mi N on MEX 1D. Phone 011-52-617/8-35-07; res: 800/526-6676.* 24 rms, 3 story, 21 kit. suites. No A/C. No elvtr. S, D $75–$80; kit. suites $80–$190. TV; cable. Pool; whirlpool. Restaurant (see PUNTA MORRO). Ck-out noon. Bellhops. Refrigerators. Balconies. Ocean view. Cr cds: A, MC, V.

★ ★**SAN NICOLAS RESORT.** *(Mailing address: PO Box 437060, San Ysidro, CA 92143) Ave Lopez Mateos, at Ave Guadalupe, 2 blks from convention center. Phone 011-52-667/6-19-01; FAX 011-52-617/6-49-30.* 150 rms, 3 story. S, D $48–$88; each addl $15; suites $130–$265; under 12 free. TV; cable. 2 heated pools; whirlpool, poolside serv. Complimentary coffee in rms. Restaurant 7 am–11 pm. Rm serv 7 am–11 pm. Bar 11–2:30 am, Sun from 9 am; entertainment, dancing. Ck-out noon. Meeting rms. Bellhops. Valet serv. Sundries. Barber, beauty shop. Refrigerators avail. Private patios, balconies. Cr cds: A, MC, V.

✓ ★**TRAVELODGE.** *(PO Box 1467) 130 Ave Blancarte. Phone 011-52-617/8-16-01; res: 800/578-7878; FAX 011-52-617/4-00-05.* 52 rms, 3 story. Apr–Sept: S, D $55–$60; each addl $8; suites $80–$150; family, wkly rates; lower rates rest of yr. Crib free. TV; cable. Heated pool; whirlpool. Complimentary coffee in rms. Restaurant 7:30 am–10:30 pm. Rm serv. Bar 10 am–11 pm; entertainment Fri & Sat. Ck-out noon. Meeting rms. Valet serv. Minibars. Balconies. Cr cds: A, MC, V.

Hotels

★★**CORONA.** (Mailing address: 482 W San Ysidro Blvd, Ste 303, San Ysidro, CA 92173) 1442 Blvd Costero, S of cruise boat terminal. Phone 011-52-617/6-09-01. 93 rms, 4 story. Apr–Aug: S, D $55–$95; each addl $8; suites $185–$200; under 12 free; higher rates Baja 1000 & 500 races; lower rates rest of yr. TV; cable. Heated pool. Complimentary coffee in lobby. Restaurant adj open 24 hrs. Bar noon–3 am; entertainment Tues–Sat. Ck-out noon. Balconies. Ocean view. On beach. Cr cds: A, MC, V.

★★★**LAS ROSAS BY THE SEA.** (Box 316) 2 mi N on MEX 1 D. Phone 011-52-617/4-43-10/20; FAX 011-52-617/4-45-95. 31 rms, 4 story, 6 suites. No A/C. S, D $101–$139; each addl $22; suites $128–$139; under 12, $16. Heated pool; poolside serv. Restaurant 7 am–11 pm. Bar; entertainment Fri–Sun. Ck-out noon. Shopping arcade. Exercise equipt; weights, bicycles, whirlpool, sauna. Massage avail. Balconies. Overlooks ocean. Cr cds: MC, V.

✔★★**VILLA MARINA.** (Mailing address: PO Box 727, Bonita, CA 91108) Jct Blancarte & Calle Lopez Mateo. Phone 011-52-617/8-33-21. 130 rms, 10 story. May–Sept: S, D $50–$75; suites $120–$200; lower rates rest of yr. TV; cable. Heated pool; poolside serv. Restaurant 7 am–9 pm. Bar 10–2 am. Ck-out 1 pm. Meeting rms. Shopping arcade. Covered parking. Balconies. Ocean 2 blks. Cr cds: MC, V.

Restaurants

★★**CASAMAR.** 987 Blvd Lazaro Cardenas. Phone 011-52-617/4-04-17. Hrs: noon–11 pm. Res accepted. Continental menu. Bar to 3 am. Semi-a la carte: lunch, dinner $5–$25. Specialties: mariscada (mixed seafood), abalone Casamar. Parking. Overlooks port. Cr cds: MC, V.

★★★**EL REY SOL.** Ave López Mateos & Blancarte 1000. Phone 011-52-617/8-17-33. Hrs: 7:30 am–11 pm. Res accepted. French, continental menu. Semi-a la carte: bkfst $5–$8, lunch, dinner $12–$25. Specializes in French gourmet dishes. Pianist (lunch & dinner). French provincial atmosphere. Family-owned. Cr cds: A, MC, V.

★★**HALIOTIS.** 179 Calle Delante, at Sangines. Phone 011-52-617/6-37-20. Hrs: 1–10 pm. Closed Tues; Jan 1, May 1, Dec 25; also Oct 1–15. Bar. Semi-a la carte: lunch, dinner $7–$19. Specializes in abalone, lobster, seafood. Parking. Nautical decor. Cr cds: MC, V.

★★**PUNTA MORRO.** (See Punta Morro Motel) Phone 011-52-617/8-35-07. Hrs: 1–10 pm; Fri–Sun 8 am–11 pm. No A/C. Continental menu. Bar. Semi-a la carte: bkfst $5–$12, lunch, dinner $10–$25. Specializes in swordfish, steak. Parking. Glass-enclosed oceanside dining rm; scenic view. Cr cds: A, MC, V.

Escondido (J-4)

Pop: 108,635 **Elev:** 684 ft **Area code:** 619

A Ranger District office of the Cleveland National Forest (see PINE VALLEY) is located here.

What to See and Do

1. **Escondido Heritage Walk.** 321 N Broadway. Escondido Historical Society history museum. Artifacts, books, preservation displays. Victorian ranch house; working blacksmith shop, early 1900s barn and windmill, 1888 Santa Fe railroad depot, railroad car with model train replica of the Oceanside to Escondido run (ca 1920). (Thurs–Sat; closed major hols exc July 4) Donation. Phone 743-8207.

2. **Palomar Observatory.** 35 mi NE on County S6. Here are a 200-inch Hale telescope (2nd largest in the US) and 48-inch and 60-inch telescopes. There is a visitors' gallery in the dome of the Hale telescope; Greenway Museum has photography from telescopes, exhibits explaining equipment. Self-guided tours. (Daily; closed Dec 24, 25) Phone 742-2119 (recording). **Free.**

3. **Lawrence Welk Resort Theatre-Museum.** At the Lawrence Welk Resort (see RESORT). Music Center houses memorabilia marking the milestones of Mr. Welk's career. (Daily) Theater and dance performances (fee). Phone 749-3448 or -3000. Museum **free.**

4. **Wineries.**

   Deer Park. 8 mi N, at 29013 Champagne Blvd. Grape vineyard, winery, Napa Valley wine tasting room (free) and deli; picnic areas. Also car museum with approximately 90 antique convertibles and other vintage vehicles on display. (Daily; closed Thanksgiving, Dec 25) Phone 749-1666. Museum **¢¢**

   Ferrara Winery. 1120 W 15th Ave. Producers of wine and grape juice. Self-guided tours, wine tasting. (Daily; closed Jan 1, Easter, Thanksgiving, Dec 25) Phone 745-7632. **Free.**

   Thomas Jaeger Winery. 13455 San Pasqual Rd. Guided and self-guided tours, wine tasting room; picnic area beneath grape arbor overlooks the vineyards and San Pasqual Valley. (Daily; closed Jan 1, Thanksgiving, Dec 25) Phone 738-6500. **Free.**

5. **San Pasqual Battlefield State Historic Park.** 8 mi E on CA 78. Interpretive displays of the Battle of San Pasqual, fought in December, 1846, during the Mexican War. Fifty acres within deeply weathered granite foothills; self-guided native plant trail; hiking. Picnicking. (Thurs–Mon; closed Jan 1, Thanksgiving, Dec 25) Phone 238-3380 or 489-0076. **Free.**

(For further information contact the Convention and Visitors Bureau, 720 N Broadway, 92025; 745-4741 or 800/848-3336.)

(See Carlsbad, La Jolla, San Diego)

Motels

★★★**QUAILS INN.** (1025 La Bonita Dr, San Marcos 92069) W on CA 78 to San Marcos. 619/744-0120; res: 800/447-6556; FAX 619/744-0748. 140 rms, 2 story. S, D $85–$115; each addl $10; suites, kit. cottages $165–$220; under 12 free; golf packages. Crib $10. Pet accepted, some restrictions; $10. TV; cable. 2 heated pools. Restaurant adj 6:30 am–10 pm. Bar 11–2 am. Ck-out noon. Meeting rms. Tennis privileges. 18-hole par 3 golf. Exercise equipt; weight machines, bicycle, whirlpool. Boat rental. Many private patios, balconies. On Lake San Marcos. Extensive grounds. Cr cds: A, D, DS, MC, V.

✔★★**SHERIDAN INN.** 1341 N Escondido Blvd (92026). 619/743-8338; FAX 619/743-0840. 58 rms, 2 story, 29 suites. S, D, suites $51–$57; wkly rates. Crib free. Pet accepted. TV; cable. Heated pool; whirlpool. Complimentary continental bkfst, coffee. Restaurant opp 7 am–9 pm. Ck-out noon. Health club privileges. Some refrigerators. Cr cds: A, C, D, DS, MC, V.

Resort

★★★**LAWRENCE WELK RESORT.** 8860 Lawrence Welk Dr (92026). 619/749-3000; res: 800/932-9355; FAX 619/749-6182. 418 rms, 2–3 story. S, D $90–$120; each addl $10; villas (2 night min) $200–$260; golf & theater packages. Pet accepted. TV; cable. 2 heated pools; 3 whirlpools. Dining rm 7 am–9 pm. Bar 11 am–midnight. Ck-out noon. Meeting rms. Concierge. Shopping arcade. Beauty shop. 3 lighted tennis courts. 3 18-hole golf courses, putting green. Dinner theater. Semi-private patios, balconies. Cr cds: A, C, D, MC, V.

Restaurant

★CAJUN CONNECTION. *(740 Nordhal Rd, San Marcos) W on CA 78, at jct Nordhal Rd.* 619/741-5680. Hrs: 11:30 am–9:30 pm; wkends from 7 am; early-bird dinner Mon–Thurs 5–6 pm. Closed Mon; Jan 1, Dec 25. Cajun menu. Wine, beer. Semi-a la carte: lunch $4.95–$15.95, dinner $8.95–$21.95. Child's meals. Specialties: crawfish etoufee, blackened fish. Parking. Colorful murals, Mardi Gras motif. Cr cds: A, DS, MC, V.

Unrated Dining Spot

T-BIRD DINER. *601 N Broadway.* 619/480-7855. Hrs: 8 am–9 pm; Fri, Sat to 11 pm. Closed Thanksgiving, Dec 25. Bar. Semi-a la carte: bkfst $2.49–$5.95; lunch, dinner $3.95–$8.50. Child's meals. Specializes in hamburgers, spaghetti. Disc jockey. Parking. Outdoor dining. 1950s-style diner with soda fountains. Thunderbird automobile on display in center of room. Cr cds: DS, MC, V.

Eureka (B-1)

Founded: 1850 **Pop:** 27,025 **Elev:** 44 ft **Area code:** 707 **Zip:** 95501

The largest fishing fleet north of San Francisco Bay makes the city of Eureka its main port. Lumbering is the city's major industry.

What to See and Do

1. **Fort Humboldt State Historic Park.** 3431 Fort Ave. Ulysses S. Grant was stationed at Fort Humboldt in 1854. Logging and military exhibits. Tours. Picnicking. (Daily; closed Jan 1, Thanksgiving, Dec 25) Phone 445-6567.   **Free.**

2. **Sequoia Park Zoo.** Glatt & W Sts. Area surrounded by 46 acres of redwoods; duck pond, gardens, picnic facilities, snack bar, children's playground. (Daily exc Mon) Phone 442-6552 or 443-8691. **Free.**

3. **Clarke Memorial Museum.** Third & E St. Regional history, collection of Karuk, Hupa, Wiyot and Yurok Indian basketry and ceremonial regalia; firearms, Victorian furniture and decorative art. Guided tours by appt. (Tues–Sat afternoons & July 4; closed some hols; also Jan) Donation. Phone 443-1947.

4. **Romano Gabriel Wooden Sculpture Garden.** 315 2nd St, in Old Town section (see #8). A colorful collection of folk art, constructed of wood in the mid-1900s. (Daily)   **Free.**

5. **Humboldt Bay Maritime Museum.** 1410 Second St. Pacific and northcoast maritime heritage displays; marine artifacts. (Daily, limited hrs; closed some hols) Donation. Phone 444-9440.

6. **Ferndale Museum.** 12 mi S on US 101, then 5 mi W in Ferndale, 3rd & Shaw Sts. Local history displays of "Cream City." (June–Sept, daily exc Mon; rest of yr, Wed–Sun; closed major hols, also Jan) Phone 786-4466.   ¢

7. **Fortuna Depot Museum.** 18 mi S on US 101 in Fortuna, Rohner Park. Train memorabilia, barbed wire collection, fishing and logging displays. In 1893 train depot. (June–Aug, daily afternoons; rest of yr, Sat–Wed afternoons; closed Dec 25) Phone 725-2495.   **Free.**

8. **Old Town.** 1st, 2nd & 3rd Sts, C to G Streets. Designated a National Historic District, this section of town has original buildings of early Eureka. Also here is a gazebo, cascading water fountain, sculptured benches, commercial and residential Victorian buildings; antique and specialty shops; horse & buggey rides (fee), trolley (fee); restaurants. All situated on waterfront of Humboldt Bay. Cruises of the bay are available (see #11).

9. **Six Rivers National Forest.** Reached via US 101, 199, CA 36, 96, 299. On 1,111,726 acres. The Klamath, Eel, Trinity, Van Duzen and Mad rivers provide excellent fishing. Hunting, camping, picnicking. Resorts and lodges located in and near forest. Standard fees.

Contact Forest Supervisor's Office, 1330 Bay Shore Way; 442-1721. Located within the Six Rivers National Forest is

Smith River National Recreation Area. (305,337 acres) This is the heart of one of the largest wild and scenic river systems (315 mi) in the US. Offers whitewater rafting, wilderness hiking, bird watching, nature study, world-class steelhead fishing, hunting and camping. For information contact Gasquet Ranger Station, Box 228 10600, Hwy 199, N Gasquet, 95543-0228; 457-3131.

10. **Woodley Island Marina.** 1 mi W via US 101, Samoa Bridge exit (CA 255). Mooring for commercial fishing boats and recreational craft; cafe and shops; site of *The Fisherman* memorial statue and Table Bluff Lighthouse.

11. **Humboldt Bay Harbor Cruise.** Foot of C Street. 1¼-hr trips. (June–Sept, 3 departures daily: 2 in the afternoon and 1 in the evening) Special charter rest of yr. Sr citizen rate. Phone 444-9440. ¢¢¢

12. **Arcata Architectural Tour.** City of Arcata, 8 mi N on US 101. Walking or driving tour to many Victorian structures, covering 35 city blocks. Obtain city map at Arcata Chamber of Commerce, 1062 G Street, 95521; phone 822-3619.

(For further information contact the Chamber of Commerce, 2112 Broadway; 442-3738 or 800/356-6381.)

Annual Events

Jazz Festival. Various locations in town. Last wkend Mar.

Rhododendron Festival. Varied events throughout Humboldt County include parades, races, art exhibits, contests, entertainment. Usually last wkend Apr–1st wk May.

Cross-Country Kinetic Sculpture Race. A 3-day, 35-mile cross-country race over land, water, beaches and highways. Participants race on their self-powered, artistically sculptured vehicles. Memorial Day wkend.

(See Trinidad)

Motels

★★★BEST WESTERN THUNDERBIRD INN. *232 W 5th St.* 707/443-2234; FAX 707/443-3489. 115 rms, some A/C, 2 story. Mid-May–mid-Oct: S $70–$80; D $74–$84; each addl $5; suites $90–$140; lower rates rest of yr. Crib free. TV; cable. Heated pool; whirlpool. Coffee in rms. Restaurant 6 am–1 pm. Rm serv. Wine, beer. Ck-out noon. Coin lndry. Meeting rms. Sundries. Free bus depot transportation. Game rm. Some refrigerators. Cr cds: A, C, D, DS, ER, MC, V.

D ☒ ⊘ ⊚

★★CARSON HOUSE INN. *1209 4th St.* 707/443-1601; res: 800/772-1622; FAX 707/444-8365. 60 rms, 2 story. No A/C. June–mid-Oct: S, D $60–$95; each addl $10; suites $90–$115; lower rates rest of yr. Crib $5. TV; cable. Heated pool; wading pool; whirlpool, sauna. Complimentary coffee in rms. Restaurant opp 7 am–11 pm. Ck-out noon. Cr cds: A, C, D, DS, MC, V.

D ☒ ⊘ ⊚

✔★TRAVELODGE. *4 Fourth St.* 707/443-6345. 46 rms, 2 story. No A/C. S $29–$55; D $38–$73; each addl $7; under 18 free. Crib free. TV; cable. Heated pool. Coffee in rms. Restaurant nearby. Ck-out noon. Sundries. Cr cds: A, C, D, DS, ER, MC, V, JCB.

☒ ⊘ ⊚ SC

Motor Hotel

★★★RED LION INN. *1929 4th St.* 707/445-0844; FAX 707/445-2752. 178 rms, 3 story. S $80–$110; D $80–$125; each addl $10; suites $125–$175; under 18 free; wkend rates. Crib free. Pet accepted. TV; cable. Heated pool; whirlpool. Restaurant 6 am–10 pm. Rm serv. Bar; entertainment, dancing Fri, Sat. Ck-out noon. Meeting rms. Bellhops.

Valet serv. Sundries. Free airport transportation. Balconies. Cr cds: A, C, D, DS, ER, MC, V, JCB.

Hotel

★ ★ ★**EUREKA INN.** *518 7th St. 707/442-6441; res: 800/862-4906; FAX 707/442-0637.* 105 rms, 4 story. No A/C. S $85–$115; D $95–$145; each addl $10; suites $165–$275; under 16 free. Crib free. Pet accepted. TV; cable. Heated pool; whirlpool, saunas. Restaurant 6:30 am–11 pm; Sat, Sun from 7 am. Bar 11–2 am; entertainment. Ck-out 2 pm. Meeting rms. Free airport, bus depot transportation. Some bathrm phones. Fireplace in lobby. Historic Tudor-style building (1922). Cr cds: A, C, D, DS, MC, V.

Inns

★ ★ ★**AN ELEGANT VICTORIAN MANSION.** *1406 C Street. 707/444-3144.* 4 rms, 2 share bath, 2 story. No A/C. No rm phones. June–Sept: S $70–$95; D $95–$115; each addl $20; suite $90–$135; higher rates: hols, special events; lower rates rest of yr. Children over 15 yrs only. TV in sitting rm; cable. Complimentary full bkfst, morning coffee. Restaurant nearby. Ck-out 11 am, ck-in 3–6 pm. Free RR station, bus depot transportation. Sauna. Bicycles avail. Game rm. Lawn games. Picnic tables, grills. Victorian flower garden. Historic landmark (1888); restored; many antiques. Queen Anne-influenced Eastlake Victorian mansion located on a rise, overlooking the city, Humboldt Bay and the Samoa Peninsula. Totally nonsmoking. Cr cds: MC, V.

★ ★ ★**CARTER HOUSE.** *1033 3rd St. 707/445-1390.* 5 rms, 4 story. S, D $105–$145; suites $165–$275. Children over 10 yrs only. Complimentary full bkfst. Ck-out 11 am, ck-in 3–6 pm. Valet serv. Game rm. Suite with whirlpool, fireplace. Re-created 1884 San Francisco Victorian house. Antiques, Oriental rugs; marble fireplaces. Totally nonsmoking. Cr cds: A, MC, V.

★ ★ ★**GINGERBREAD MANSION.** *(PO Box 40, 400 Berding St, Ferndale 95536) 20 mi S via US 101, 1 blk E of Main St. 707/786-4000.* 9 rms, 2 story. No A/C. May–Oct: S $90–$170; D $110–$185; each addl $20; suites $140–$185; 2-day min hols; lower rates Sun–Thurs, Nov–Apr. Children over 10 yrs only. Complimentary full bkfst 9–9:30 am, tea 4–6 pm. Ck-out 11 am, ck-in 3–6 pm. Bicycles. Restored Victorian house (ca 1900); English gardens; in "Victorian Village" community setting. Elaborate bathrms; 4 parlors with 2 fireplaces; formal dining rm. Totally nonsmoking. Cr cds: A, MC, V.

★ ★ ★**HOTEL CARTER.** *301 L Street. 707/444-8062.* 25 rms, 3 story. S $79–$89; D $95–$165; suites $165–$225. Crib free. TV; cable. Complimentary bkfst, refreshments. Dining rm 7:30–10 am; Thurs–Mon 6–9 pm. Ck-out 11 am, ck-in 3–6 pm. Meeting rms. Valet serv. Some in-rm whirlpools; fireplace in suites. White pine antiques. Totally nonsmoking. Cr cds: A, D, DS, MC, V.

✔ ★ ★**OLD TOWN BED & BREAKFAST.** *1521 Third St, at edge of Old Town District. 707/445-3951; res: 800/331-5098.* 7 rms, 2 share bath, 2 story. No A/C. Some rm phones avail. S $55–$120; D $75–$150; each addl $20; lower rates winter. Children over 10 yrs only. TV in sitting rm. Complimentary full bkfst, morning coffee, tea, wine. Ck-out 11 am, ck-in 4–6 pm. Airport, RR station, bus depot transportation. Picnic tables, grills. Built 1871, oldest lodging in town; Greek-revival Victorian home with antique furnishings. Garden. Bay 1½ blks. Totally nonsmoking. Cr cds: A, C, D, DS, MC, V.

Restaurant

★ ★**LAZIO'S.** *327 2nd St, between D & E Streets. 707/443-9717.* Hrs: 11 am–9 pm; summer to 10 pm. Closed some major hols. Res accepted. Bar. Semi-a la carte: lunch $4.95–$10.50, dinner $9.95–$24.95. Child's meals. Specialties: Humboldt Bay shore plate, shrimp fettucine. Tri-level dining. Family-owned since 1944. Cr cds: DS, MC, V.

Fairfield (D-2)

Pop: 77,211 **Elev:** 15 ft **Area code:** 707 **Zip:** 94533

This is the home of Travis Air Force Base and the seat of Solano County.

What to See and Do

Western Railway Museum. 12 mi E on CA 12. Take a two-mile ride on electric streetcars and interurbans, with occasional steam and diesel operation. Museum collection includes 100 vintage railroad cars and trains operating on demonstration railroad; bookstore; picnic area. (July–Labor Day, Wed–Sun; Sept–June, Sat, Sun & most hols; closed Jan 1, Thanksgiving, Dec 25) Museum admission includes unlimited rides. Phone 374-2978. ¢¢

(See Vacaville, Vallejo)

Motels

★**BEST WESTERN CORDELIA INN.** *4373 Central Place, I-80 Suisun Valley Rd exit. 707/864-2029; FAX 707/864-5834.* 59 rms, 2 story. S $45–$48; D $54–$66; each addl $6; under 12 free; Marine World plans. Crib avail. Pet accepted, some restrictions. TV; cable. Pool; whirlpool. Complimentary continental bkfst. Complimentary coffee in rms. Restaurant nearby. Ck-out noon. Coin lndry. Valet serv. Refrigerators avail. Cr cds: A, C, D, DS, MC, V.

★ ★**HAMPTON INN.** *4441 Central Place. 707/864-1446; FAX 707/864-4288.* 54 rms, 3 suites, 3 story. S, D $52–$62; suites $105; higher rates summer wkends. Crib free. TV; cable. Heated pool (seasonal). Complimentary continental bkfst, coffee. Restaurant adj open 24 hrs. Ck-out noon. Meeting rms. Exercise equipt; rowers, stair machine. Refrigerator in suites. Cr cds: A, C, D, DS, MC, V.

Motor Hotel

★ ★**HOLIDAY INN.** *1350 Holiday Lane. 707/422-4111; FAX 707/428-3452.* 142 rms, 4 story. S, D $62–$89; each addl $7; under 20 free. Crib free. Pet accepted, some restrictions; $50. TV; cable. Pool; wading pool. Restaurant 6 am–2 pm, 5–10 pm. Rm serv to 10:30 pm. Bar noon–midnight. Ck-out noon. Meeting rms. Coin lndry. Bellhops. Valet serv. Health club privileges. Some private patios, balconies. Cr cds: A, C, D, DS, MC, V, JCB.

Restaurants

✔ ★**THE OLD SAN FRANCISCO EXPRESS PASTA RESTAURANT.** *4560 Central Way, I-80 Suisan Valley Rd exit. 707/425-5518.* Hrs: 11 am–9 pm; Fri & Sat to 10 pm. Res accepted. Bar. Complete meals: lunch, dinner $5.95–$12.95. Child's meals. Specializes in pastas, seafood, prime rib. Parking. Comprised of 11 railroad cars connected

together to form 2 large dining areas; some cars form private dining rms. Cr cds: MC, V.

★★SUNDANCE GRILLE. 2470 Martin Rd. 707/428-1100. Hrs: 11:30 am–3 pm, 5–10 pm; Sat from 5 pm; Sun from 4:30 pm; Sun brunch 11 am–3 pm. Bar. A la carte entrees: dinner $8.25–$24.85. Specializes in steak, prime rib, seafood. Entertainment: band Thurs 9 pm, comedy Wed 8 pm, Country-Western dance lessons ($5 per person) Sun, Mon & Thurs 7:30–9 pm. Parking. Southwestern decor, stone fireplaces. Totally nonsmoking. Cr cds: A, MC, V.

D

Fallbrook (J-4)

Settled: 1880s Pop: 22,095 Elev: 685 ft Area code: 619 Zip: 92028

(See Temecula)

Motels

★BEST WESTERN FRANCISCAN INN. 1635 S Mission Rd. 619/728-6174; FAX 619/731-6404. 51 rms, 1–2 story, 15 kits. S $45–$60; D $55–$70; each addl $5; kit. units $55–$75; under 12 free; wkly rates. Crib $5. TV; cable. Heated pool; whirlpool. Complimentary coffee. Ck-out 11 am. Cr cds: A, C, D, DS, MC, V.

✔★TRAVELODGE. 1608 S Mission Rd. 619/723-1127; FAX 619/723-2917. 36 units, 2 story, 6 kits. S $45; D $50; each addl $5; kits. $55–$60; under 17 free; wkly rates. Crib $5. TV; cable. Complimentary coffee in lobby. Restaurant opp 9 am–9 pm. Ck-out 11 am. Whirlpool. Balconies. Cr cds: A, C, D, DS, MC, V, JCB.

Resort

★★★PALA MESA. 2001 Old Hwy 395. 619/728-5881; res: 800/722-4700; FAX 619/723-8292. 133 rms, 1–2 story. S, D $120–$150; each addl $20; suites $150–$175; under 18 free; golf, tennis plans. Crib free. TV; cable. Heated pool. Dining rm 6 am–10 pm. Rm serv to 11 pm. Bar 11–2 am; entertainment, dancing Fri & Sat. Ck-out noon, ck-in 4 pm. Meeting rms. Valet serv (Mon–Fri). Gift shop. Airport transportation. Lighted tennis, pro. 18-hole golf, pro, putting green, driving range. Exercise equipt; weights, bicycle, whirlpool. Cr cds: A, C, D, DS, ER, MC, V.

Restaurants

★★PACKING HOUSE. 125 S Main St. 619/728-5458. Hrs: 11–2 am; early-bird dinner 4–6 pm; Sun brunch 10 am–2 pm. Closed major hols. Bar. Semi-a la carte: lunch $3–$7.95, dinner $7–$18. Sun brunch $6.95. Child's meals. Specializes in fresh seafood, veal, prime rib. Salad bar. Many antiques. Cr cds: MC, V.

✔★SAU-HY'S. 909 S Main St. 619/728-1000. Hrs: 11:30 am–10 pm. Closed July 4, Thanksgiving, Dec 25. Chinese menu. Wine, beer. A la carte entrees: lunch $4–$6, dinner $7–$10. Child's meals. Parking. Chinese decor, antiques. Cr cds: A, C, D, DS, MC, V.

Felton

(see Santa Cruz)

Fort Bragg (C-1)

Founded: 1884 Pop: 6,078 Elev: 75 ft Area code: 707 Zip: 95437

The town is a lumber, agricultural, recreational and fishing center that stands on the edge of the rocky coastline where the military post of Fort Bragg was set up in 1857. When the fort was abandoned in 1867, the land was opened for purchase and a lumber town sprang up. It was rebuilt after the earthquake of 1906. Driftwood and shell hunting are popular on nearby beaches.

What to See and Do

1. **Mendocino Coast Botanical Gardens.** 2 mi S on CA 1. Approx 47 acres of rhododendrons, heathers, perennials, fuchsias, coastal pine forest and ocean bluffs. Cafe; nursery; picnic areas; self-guided tours. (Daily) Sr citizen rate. Phone 964-4352. ¢¢

2. **The "Skunk Train."** Foot of Laurel St. Originally a logging railroad, the California Western Railroad train, affectionately known as "the Skunk," runs 40 miles through redwoods along the Noyo River and over the Coastal Range to Willits (see). Full-day round trips available aboard either diesel-powered motor cars or a diesel-pulled train (all yr). Half-day round trips are available from Fort Bragg (Mar–Nov, daily; rest of yr, wkends). Half-day and full-day trips are available from Willits (2nd Sat June–2nd Sat Sept; inquire for schedule). Contact California Western Railroad, Box 907; 964-6371. Round trip ¢¢¢¢

3. **Forest Tree Nursery.** Georgia-Pacific Corp, foot of Walnut St. Miniature forest with 3 million redwood and Douglas fir seedlings for reforestation on local timberland. Nature trail. Picnic tables. Visitor center (Mon–Fri; closed major hols). Phone 964-5651. **Free.**

4. **MacKerricher State Park.** 3 mi N on CA 1. Approx 10 mi of beach and ocean access. Fishing (nonmotorized boat launching). Nature, hiking trails. Picnicking. Camping (dump station; fee). Phone 937-5804. Day use **free;** Camping ¢¢¢

5. **Noyo.** 2 mi S on CA 1 at mouth of Noyo River. Fishing village with picturesque harbor; public boat launching; charter boats avail.

6. **Jughandle Ecological Staircase.** 5 mi S. Nature trail climbs from sea level to pygmy forest; 500,000 years of geological history. For information phone 937-5804.

(For further information contact the Fort Bragg-Mendocino Coast Chamber of Commerce, 322 N Main St, PO Box 1141; 961-6300 or 800/726-2780.)

Annual Events

Whale Festival. Whale watch tours & cruises, history walks, arts & crafts; chowder tasting. 3rd Sat Mar.

Rhododendron Show. More varieties of rhododendrons are grown here than anywhere else in the world. Late Apr or early May.

Salmon Barbecue. S Noyo harbor. Early July.

Paul Bunyan Days. Logging competition, gem and mineral show; parade (Mon); fuchsia show, arts & crafts. Labor Day wkend.

Winesong. More than 20 vintners pour for wine tasting, food tasting, music, wine auction. Sat after Labor Day.

Seasonal Event

Whale Watch. Dec–Apr.

(See Mendocino, Ukiah, Willits)

Motels

✔ ★ ★**HARBOR LITE LODGE.** *120 N Harbor Dr. 707/964-0221; res: 800/643-2700 (CA).* 79 rms, 2–3 story, 9 suites. No A/C. May–Oct, hols, wkends: S $53–$72; D $61–$72; each addl $6; suites $82–$94; lower rates rest of yr. Crib $6. TV; cable. Complimentary morning coffee. Restaurant nearby. Ck-out noon. Meeting rms. Sauna. Refrigerator in suites. Balconies. Footpath to beach. Most rms with harbor view. Cr cds: A, C, D, DS, MC, V.

D 🖭 🐾 ⊛

★ ★**PINE BEACH INN.** *(Box 1173) 4½ mi S on CA 1. 707/964-5603.* 51 rms, 1–2 story. No A/C. Apr–Oct: S, D $70–$90; suites $90–$145; lower rates rest of yr. Crib free. TV; cable. Restaurant 7–11:30 am, 5:30–9:30 pm; closed Jan–Mar. Bar from 5 pm. Ck-out noon. Meeting rms. Tennis. Private beach. Private patios, balconies. Some rms with ocean view. Cr cds: A, MC, V.

⊷ 🔎 ⊛ **SC**

✔ ★**SURF.** *(Box 488) 1220 S Main St. 707/964-5361; res: 800/339-5361 (exc CA).* 54 rms, 2 kit. units. No A/C. Mid-May–late Sept: S $65; D $69–$79; each addl $6; kit. units from $94; lower rates rest of yr. Crib $6. TV; cable. Coffee in rms. Restaurant nearby. Ck-out 11 am. Lawn games. Refrigerators avail. Picnic tables, grill. Some rms have ocean view. Cr cds: A, C, D, DS, MC, V.

🐾 ⊛ **SC**

Inns

★ ★**CLEONE LODGE.** *24600 N CA 1, 2½ mi N. 707/964-2788.* 10 rms, 1–2 story, 5 kits., 1 cottage. No A/C. Some rm phones. S, D $72–$102; each addl $8–$12; kit. cottage $94. TV; cable. Morning coffee/tea in office. Ck-out 11 am, ck-in 1:30 pm. Whirlpool. Walking trails. Many refrigerators, fireplaces. Antiques. Private patios, balconies. Picnic tables, grills. On 9½ acres; gazebo. Near beach. Cr cds: DS, MC, V.

🐾 ⊛

★ ★**GREY WHALE.** *615 N Main St. 707/964-0640; res: 800/382-7244.* 14 rms, 4 story. No A/C. S $60–$140; D $80–$160; each addl $22; suites $115–$160; 3-night min most major hols, 2-night min wkends. TV in some rms & in entertainment rm. Complimentary buffet bkfst 7:30–10 am, tea. Restaurant nearby. Ck-in, ck-out noon. Meeting rm. Game rm. Rec rm. Some fireplaces. Some private patios, balconies. Library. Antiques. Some rms with ocean view. Mendocino coast landmark since 1915; hand-carved whale sculpture on front lawn. 6 blks from ocean; 2 blks from Skunk Train Depot. Totally nonsmoking. Cr cds: DS, ER, MC, V.

D 🖭 ⊛

★ ★ ★**NOYO RIVER LODGE.** *500 Casa Del Noyo Dr. 707/964-8045; res: 800/628-1126; FAX 707/964-5354.* 16 rms, 1–2 story, 8 suites. No A/C. No rm phones. S, D $80–$115; suites $130–$140; mid-wk rates in winter. TV in suites; cable. Complimentary continental bkfst. Ck-out 11 am, ck-in 2 pm. Balconies. Picnic tables. Library/sitting rm; antiques. Built 1868; located on 2½ acres overlooking Noyo River, Noyo Harbor Fishing Village. Totally nonsmoking. Cr cds: DS, MC, V.

⊷ 🖭 ⊛

★ ★ ★**PUDDING CREEK INN.** *700 N Main St. 707/964-9529; res: 800/227-9529; FAX 707/961-0282.* 10 rms, 1–2 story. No A/C. No rm phones. May–Oct: S, D $65–$115; each addl $15; 2-day min wkends; 3-day min hol wkends; lower rates rest of yr. Closed Jan. Children over 9 yrs only. TV in rec rm. Complimentary full bkfst. Restaurant opp 8 am–9 pm. Ck-out 11 am, ck-in 2 pm. Parking. Picnic tables. 1884 Victorian house; enclosed garden courtyard. Ocean 2 blks. Totally nonsmoking. Cr cds: A, MC, V.

🐾 ⊛

Restaurants

★ ★ ★**THE RESTAURANT.** *418 N Main St, opp Skunk Railroad. 707/964-9800.* Hrs: 5–9 pm; Thurs & Fri 11:30 am–2 pm, 5–9 pm; Sun brunch 9 am–1 pm. Closed Wed; Thanksgiving, Dec 25; also 2–3 wks Mar. Res accepted. No A/C. Continental menu. Beer. Wine list. Semi-a la carte: lunch $5.75–$8.50, dinner $9.25–$17.25. Sun brunch $4.50–$6.75. Child's meals. Specializes in seasonal dishes, fresh salmon. Own baking. Jazz Fri, Sat evenings & Sun brunch. Parking. Totally nonsmoking. Cr cds: MC, V.

★ ★**THE WHARF.** *780 N Harbor Dr, at mouth of Noyo River Fishing Village. 707/964-4283.* Hrs: 11 am–10 pm. Res accepted. Bar to 2 am. Semi-a la carte: lunch $3.25–$8.95, dinner $9.25–$23. Child's meals. Specializes in fresh seafood, prime rib, steak. Parking. View of harbor, fishing boats. Cr cds: DS, MC, V.

 SC

Fort Ross State Historic Park (D-1)

(12 mi N of Jenner on CA 1)

This was once an outpost of the Russian empire. For nearly three decades the post and fort set up by the Russian-American Company of Alaska was an important center for the Russian sea otter trade. The entire ''Colony Ross of California'' was purchased by Captain John A. Sutter in 1841.

Here are reconstructions of the Russian Orthodox chapel (ca 1825), the original seven-sided and eight-sided blockhouses, the Commandant's house, officer's barracks and stockade walls. Interpretive exhibits. (Daily; closed Jan 1, Thanksgiving, Dec 25) Standard fees. Phone 707/865-2391 or 707/847-3286.

What to See and Do

1. **Salt Point State Park.** 18 mi N of Jenner. Located here are Pygmy forest, Gerstle Cove marine reserve. Hiking, riding trails. Picnicking. Camping. Standard fees. Nearby is

    Kruse Rhododendron State Reserve. Here are 317 acres of coastal vegetation. Trails.

2. **Sonoma Coast State Beach.** 12 mi S, between Jenner and Bodega Bay. On 4,200 acres along coastline. Sandy beaches, rocky headlands, sand dunes. Diving; fishing. Hiking. Picnicking. Camping. Standard fees. Phone 707/865-2391.

(See Bodega Bay, Guerneville, Healdsburg)

Motel

✔ ★ ★**SALT POINT LODGE AT OCEAN COVE.** *(23255 Coast Hwy 1, Jenner 95450) 6 mi N of Fort Ross on CA 1. 707/847-3234.* 16 rms, 2 story. No A/C. S, D $45–$125; each addl $10. Crib free. TV. Restaurant 9 am–9 pm, wkends 8 am–10 pm; Dec–Apr reduced hrs. Bar. Ck-out 11 am. Whirlpool, sauna. Sun deck. Some fireplaces. Balconies. Ocean view. Skin diving. Whale watching in season. Cr cds: DS, MC, V.

Inn

★ ★ ★ ★**TIMBERHILL RANCH.** *(35755 Hauser Bridge Rd, Cazadero 95421) 19 mi N of Jenner on Meyers Grade Rd to Hauser Bridge Rd. 707/847-3258; FAX 707/847-3342.* 15 cottages. No rm phones. MAP: S $275; D $296–$350; each addl $164–$175; wkly, winter rates; higher rates: Jan 1, Thanksgiving, Dec 25. Pool; whirlpool, poolside serv. Complimentary continental bkfst. Complimentary coffee in rms. Dining rm (public by res) noon–1 pm, 7–9 pm. Rm serv (bkfst delivered to cottages). Wine, beer. Ck-out noon, ck-in 4 pm. Meeting rms. Bellhops. Concierge. Gift shop. Tennis. 9-hole golf 15 mi. Hiking. Lawn games. Game rm. Refrigerators, minibars, fireplaces. Balconies. Unique hideaway, on 80 wooded acres, provides an atmosphere of tranquility and seclusion. Cedar guest cottages are positioned for maximum privacy. Electric carts provide transportation about grounds. Cr cds: A, MC, V.

Fremont (E-2)

Pop: 173,339 **Elev:** 53 ft **Area code:** 510

Lying at the southeast end of San Francisco Bay, this young town was created in 1956 from five Alameda County communities whose origin goes back to the days of the Ohlone Indians.

What to See and Do

1. **Mission San Jose** (1797). 43300 Mission Blvd. The reconstructed adobe church was originally built in 1809 and destroyed by an earthquake in 1868. A portion of the padres' living quarters that survived holds a museum. Original baptismal font, historic vestments and mission-era artifacts. (Daily; closed Jan 1, Easter, Thanksgiving, Dec 25) Donation. Phone 657-1797.

2. **Regional parks.**

   Ardenwood Regional Preserve and Historic Farm. I-880, CA 84 Decoto exit, right on Ardenwood Blvd to park entrance. A 208-acre 1890s working farm. Patterson House (tours). Horse-drawn wagon, haywagon rides, farming demonstrations and rail car tour. Picnic area. Sr citizen rate. (Apr–Nov, Thurs–Sun & Mon hols) Phone 796-0663. ¢¢¢

   Coyote Hills. 8000 Patterson Ranch Rd. Wetlands preserved on 966 acres. Hiking and bicycle trails. Picnicking. Guided tours of 2,000-yr-old Indian shell mounds (Sun); freshwater marsh; nature programs; access to Alameda Creek Trail, San Francisco Bay National Wildlife Refuge. (Daily). Phone 795-9385. Per car ¢¢

   Sunol Regional Wilderness. NE on I-680 to Calaveras Rd, then S to Geary Rd. Hiking trails. Picnicking. Camping (fee). Nature center and program; backpack area by reservation. Rugged terrain includes Maguire Peaks (1,688 ft), Flag Hill (1,360 ft). Connects with Ohlone Wilderness Trail (permit required). Phone 862-2244. Per car ¢¢

   For further information concerning the parks contact East Bay Regional Park District, 2950 Peralta Oaks Court, PO Box 5381, Oakland 94605-5369, phone 635-0135.

   (For further information contact the Chamber of Commerce, 2201 Walnut Ave, 94538; 795-2244.)

   (See Livermore, Oakland, San Jose, Santa Clara)

Motels

✔ ★ ★ **BEST WESTERN THUNDERBIRD INN.** 5400 Mowry Ave (94538). 510/792-4300; FAX 510/792-2643. 125 rms, 2–3 story. S $65; D $75; each addl $10; under 12 free. Crib free. Pet accepted, some restrictions; $50. TV; cable, in-rm movies. Heated pool; whirlpool, sauna. Complimentary continental bkfst. Restaurant adj. Ck-out noon. Meeting rms. Valet serv. Health club privileges. Some private patios, balconies. Cr cds: A, C, D, DS, MC, V, JCB.

★ ★ **COURTYARD BY MARRIOTT.** 47000 Lakeview Blvd (94538). 510/656-1800; FAX 510/656-2441. 146 rms, 3 story. S, D $81–$91; each addl $10; suites $96; under 12 free. Crib avail. TV; cable. Indoor pool. Complimentary coffee in rms. Restaurant 6:30 am–2 pm, 5–10 pm. Bar 4–11 pm. Ck-out 1 pm. Coin lndry. Meeting rms. Sundries. Exercise equipt; weight machine, bicycles, whirlpool. Some refrigerators. Balconies. Cr cds: A, C, D, DS, MC, V.

★ ★ **RESIDENCE INN BY MARRIOTT.** 5400 Farwell Place (94536), E of I-880, Mowry Ave exit. 510/794-5900; FAX 510/793-6587. 80 kit. suites, 2 story. Kit. suites $109–$129; wkly, monthly rates. Pet accepted, some restrictions; $75. TV; cable, in-rm movies avail. Pool; whirlpool. Complimentary continental bkfst. Restaurant adj 6 am–midnight. Ck-out noon. Coin lndry. Meeting rms. Valet serv. Airport transportation avail. Health club privileges. Private patios, balconies. Picnic tables, grills. Cr cds: A, C, D, DS, MC, V, JCB.

Hotel

★ ★ ★ **HILTON NEWARK-FREMONT.** (39900 Balentine Dr, Newark 94560) On I-880, at Stevenson Blvd exit. 510/490-8390; FAX 510/651-7828. 320 rms, 7 story. S $79–$104; D $94–$119; each addl $15; suites $135–$495; family rates; wkend rates. Crib free. TV; cable. Heated pool; poolside serv. Restaurant 6 am–10 pm. Bar 11–2 am; entertainment, dancing Fri & Sat. Ck-out noon. Meeting rms. Gift shop. Free local transp, RR station transportation. Exercise equipt; weights, bicycles, sauna. Some refrigerators. Some private patios, balconies. Cr cds: A, C, D, DS, ER, MC, V, JCB.

Inn

✔ ★ ★ **LORD BRADLEY'S INN.** 43344 Mission Blvd (94539), adj to Mission San Jose. 510/490-0520. 8 rms, 2 story. No A/C. No rm phones. S $65; D $75. Complimentary continental bkfst, coffee, tea. Restaurant nearby. Ck-out noon, ck-in 3 pm. Free lndry facilities. Some street parking. Built in 1868 as Solon Washington Hotel; survived earthquakes and fires that destroyed much of Mission San Jose; antique furnishings. Cr cds: C, D, MC, V, JCB.

Fresno (F-3)

Founded: 1874 **Pop:** 354,202 **Elev:** 296 ft **Area code:** 209

Fresno was founded when the population of Millerton moved in a body from that town to the railroad line. In the geographic center of the state and heart of the San Joaquin Valley—the great central California "Garden of the Sun"—Fresno and Fresno County are enjoying tremendous growth. The county claims the greatest annual agricultural production of any in the United States, handling more than $3 billion annually. One of the largest wineries in America (Guild) and the world's largest dried fruit packing plant (Sun Maid) are here.

What to See and Do

1. **Fresno Metropolitan Museum of Art, History and Science.** 1555 Van Ness. Displays on the heritage and culture of the San Joaquin Valley; hands-on science exhibits; touring exhibits. (Wed–Sun; closed hols) Sr citizen rate. Phone 441-1444. ¢¢

2. **The Discovery Center.** 1944 N Winery Ave. Participatory natural and physical science exhibits for families; outdoor exhibits, cactus garden; picnicking, Indian room. (Daily exc Mon) Sr citizen rate. Phone 251-5531 (recording) or -5533. ¢

3. **Kearney Mansion Museum** (1900–1903). 7160 W Kearney Blvd, 7 mi W via CA 99, exit Fresno St, entrance is ½ mi on the right; located in 225-acre Kearney Park. Historic mansion has been restored; contains many original furnishings, including European wallpapers

and art nouveau light fixtures. Servant's quarters adj houses ranch kitchen and museum gift shop. Narrated 45-min tour of mansion. (Fri–Sun afternoons; closed Jan 1, Easter, Dec 25) Phone 441-0862. Park **free** with admission to mansion tour. ¢¢

4. Roeding Park. W Belmont Ave & CA 99. Variety of trees and shrubs on 157 acres ranging from high mountain to tropical species. Boating (rentals). Tennis. Camellia garden, picnic areas; children's storyland (fee); playland (fee/ride); amphitheater. (Daily) In the park are

Chaffee Zoological Gardens. At the S end of the park, near Belmont Ave. This 18-acre zoo has more than 650 animals representing 200 species. Includes reptile house, elephant exhibit, humming bird and butterfly exhibits; also tropical rain forest exhibit containing plants and animal species found primarily in South American regions. (Daily) Sr citizen discount. Phone 498-2671. ¢¢

5. Woodward Park. Audubon Dr & CA 41. Approx 300 acres. Authentic Japanese garden (wkends only; summer wkday evenings, fee); fishing ponds for children under 16; jogging course; picnic area; bird sanctuary. (Daily)

6. Sierra National Forest. Sections NE & E reached via CA 41, 99, 168. Nearly 1.3 million acres ranging from rolling foothills to rugged, snow-capped mountains, 2 groves of giant sequoias, hundreds of natural lakes, 11 major reservoirs and unique geological formations. The topography can be rough and precipitous in higher elevations, with deep canyons and many beautiful meadows along streams and lakes; 5 wilderness areas. Rafting; boating, sailing; fishing, hunting. Downhill and cross-country skiing. Picnicking. Camping. Standard fees. Contact Forest Supervisor, 1600 Tollhouse, Clovis 93612; phone 487-5155.

7. Millerton Lake State Recreation Area. 21 mi NE via CA 41, Friant Rd. 14,107 acres. Swimming, waterskiing (lifeguards); fishing; boat launching. Hiking, riding trails. Picnicking, concession, store nearby. Camping (dump station). Standard fees. Phone 822-2332. Day use ¢¢¢

8. Kingsburg. 18 mi S via CA 99. Settled by Swedes, their colorful influence remains in this town. Swedish architectural design on buildings; dala horses and flags decorate streets. **Historical Society Museum** at 2321 Sierra St. Contact Kingsburg Chamber of Commerce, PO Box 515, Kingsburg 93631; phone 897-2925.

9. California State University, Fresno (1911). (19,000 students) Cedar and Shaw Aves, 9 mi NE of CA 99. Farm, arboretum, California wildlife habitat exhibits; tours. Phone 278-2795.

10. Sequoia and Kings Canyon National Parks (see). Approx 55 mi E on CA 180.

11. Yosemite National Park (see). 97 mi NE on CA 41.

12. Sierra Summit Ski Area. 65 mi NE on CA 168, in Sierra National Forest. 2 triple, 3 double chairlifts, 4 surface lifts; patrol, school, rentals; snowmaking; snack bar, cafeteria, restaurant, bar; lodge. (Mid-Nov–mid-Apr, daily) 25 runs; longest run 2¼ mi; vertical drop 1,600 ft. Half-day rates (wkends & hols). Phone 233-2500; for ski report phone 443-6111. ¢¢¢¢¢

13. CCInc Auto Tape Tours. These 90-minute cassettes offer mile-by-mile self-guided tours to Los Angeles (193 mi): historical and scenic points of interest through San Joaquin Valley, Bakersfield and Fort Tejon; to Mariposa (139 mi) with information on a unique 5-acre underground estate in Fresno (closed to the public), major scenic points in Yosemite National Park; to Monterey (142 mi) with a tour of San Luis reservoir, old stagecoach route to San Juan Bautista, historical account of the area. Fourteen different tour tapes of California are available. Tapes may be purchased directly from CCInc Auto Tape Tours, PO Box 227, 2 Elbrook Dr, Allendale, NJ 07401; 201/236-1666.

(For further information contact the Visitors Bureau, 808 M Street, 93721; 233-0836 or 800/788-0836.)

Annual Events

Clovis Rodeo. In Clovis, NE corner of Fresno. Parade. Phone 299-8838. Late Apr.

Swedish Festival. In Kingsburg (see #8). Parade, pancake bkfst, smörgasbord, entertainment, arts & crafts, carnival, Maypole, folk dancing. 3rd wkend May.

The Big Fresno Fair. Phone 453-3247. Oct.

Seasonal Event

Fresno County Blossom Trail. This 67-mi self-guided driving tour features the beauty of California agriculture during peak season (weather permitting). Highlights of the trail are fruit orchards, citrus groves, vineyards and historical points of interest. The Visitors Bureau has maps, information. Peak season late Feb–late Mar.

Motels

★★★**BEST WESTERN VILLAGE INN.** *3110 N Blackstone Ave (93703).* 209/226-2110; FAX 209/226-0539. 153 rms, 2 story. S $50–$54; D $54–$58; each addl $4; under 12 free. Crib $6. TV; in-rm movies. Pool; whirlpool. Complimentary continental bkfst 6:30–9:30 am. Complimentary coffee in rms. Restaurant adj open 24 hrs. Ck-out noon. Valet serv. Cr cds: A, C, D, DS, MC, V, JCB.

✔★★**CHATEAU BY PICCADILLY INNS.** *5113 E McKinley (93727),* near Fresno Air Terminal Airport. 209/456-1418; res: 800/445-2428 (CA); FAX 209/456-1418, ext 200. 78 rms, 2 story. S $39–$64; D $45–$70; each addl $6; under 12 free. Crib free. TV; cable, in-rm movies. Pool. Complimentary coffee in rms. Restaurant adj 6 am–10 pm. Ck-out 1 pm. Free airport, RR station, bus depot transportation. Bathrm phones; some refrigerators. Cr cds: A, C, D, DS, MC, V.

★★★**COURTYARD BY MARRIOTT.** *140 E Shaw Ave (93710).* 209/221-6000; FAX 209/221-0368. 146 rms, 3 story. S $79; D $89; under 13 free; wkend rates. Crib free. TV; cable. Heated pool. Complimentary coffee in rms. Restaurant 6:30 am–1:30 pm, 5–10 pm. Bar. Ck-out 1 pm. Coin lndry. Meeting rms. Sundries. Exercise equipt; weight machine, bicycles, whirlpool. Refrigerator in suites. Cr cds: A, C, D, DS, MC, V.

✔★**ECONOMY INNS OF AMERICA.** *2570 S East St (93706).* 209/486-1188. 121 rms, 2 story. S $25.90; D $32.30; each addl $5. Pet accepted. TV; cable. Heated pool. Restaurant nearby. Ck-out 11 am. Cr cds: A, MC, V.

★★★**PICCADILLY INN UNIVERSITY.** *4961 N Cedar Ave (93726).* 209/224-4200; res: 800/468-3587 (exc CA), 800/468-3522 (CA); FAX 209/227-2382. 190 rms, 3 story. S $94; D $104; each addl $10; suites $185–$195; under 12 free. TV. Pool. Coffee in rms. Restaurant nearby. Bar 5–8 pm. Ck-out 1 pm. Coin lndry. Meeting rms. Bellhops. Valet serv. Airport, RR station, bus depot transportation. Exercise equipt; weights, bicycles, whirlpool. Bathrm phones; some refrigerators. Private patios. Cr cds: A, C, D, DS, ER, MC, V.

★★★**SAN JOAQUIN.** *1309 W Shaw Ave (93711).* 209/225-1309; res: 800/775-1309; FAX 209/225-6021. 68 suites, 3 story. Suites $85–$175; under 5 free; wkly, monthly rates. Crib free. TV; cable, in-rm movies avail. Pool; whirlpool. Complimentary full bkfst. Complimentary coffee in rms. Restaurant nearby. Ck-out noon. Coin lndry. Meeting rms. Bellhops. Concierge. Free covered parking. Free airport, RR station transportation. Refrigerators. Balconies. Cr cds: A, C, D, DS, MC, V.

Motor Hotels

★ ★ ★HOLIDAY INN-AIRPORT. *5090 E Clinton Ave (93727), adj Fresno Air Terminal Airport.* 209/252-3611; FAX 209/456-8243. 210 rms, 2 story. S $74–$110; D $80–$110; each addl $8; under 18 free; wkend rates. Crib free. Pet accepted, some restrictions. TV. Indoor/outdoor pool; whirlpool, poolside serv. Restaurant 6 am–2 pm, 5–10:30 pm. Rm serv. Bar 11–2 am; dancing. Ck-out noon. Coin lndry. Meeting rms. Bellhops. Valet serv. Sundries. Airport transportation. Holidome. Game rm. Rec rm. Cr cds: A, C, D, DS, MC, V, JCB.

★ ★ ★PICCADILLY INN-AIRPORT. *5115 E McKinley Ave (93727), near Fresno Air Terminal Airport.* 209/251-6000; res: 800/468-3587 (exc CA), 800/468-3522 (CA); FAX 209/251-6956. 185 rms, 2 story. S $94; D $104; each addl $10; suites $185; under 12 free; wkend rates. Crib free. TV; in-rm movies. Pool; poolside serv. Complimentary coffee in rms. Restaurant 6 am–5 pm; dining rm 11 am–2 pm, 5–10 pm; Sat from 5 pm; Sun 5–9 pm. Rm serv. Bar 5–11 pm; Sat & Sun from 4 pm. Ck-out 1 pm. Coin lndry. Meeting rms. Bellhops. Valet serv. Sundries. Free airport transportation. Exercise equipt; weights, bicycles, whirlpool. Bathrm phones; some refrigerators. Private patios, balconies. Cr cds: A, C, D, DS, ER, MC, V.

★ ★RAMADA INN. *324 E Shaw Ave (93710).* 209/224-4040; FAX 209/222-4017. 167 rms, 2 story. S $64; D $70; each addl $6; suites $90; under 18 free; wkend rates. Crib free. TV; cable. Pool; whirlpool, poolside serv. Restaurant 6:30 am–1:30 pm, 5–10 pm. Rm serv. Bar 4 pm–midnight, Sun to 9 pm. Ck-out noon. Meeting rms. Bellhops. Valet serv. Free airport transportation. Cr cds: A, C, D, DS, ER, MC, V, JCB.

★ ★ ★SHERATON SMUGGLER'S INN. *3737 N Blackstone Ave (93726).* 209/226-2200; FAX 209/222-7147. 204 rms, 2 story. S $72–$85; D $75–$95; each addl $3; suites $160; under 17 free. Crib $3. TV; cable. Heated pool; poolside serv. Complimentary coffee in rms. Restaurant 6:30 am–10 pm. Rm serv to 9:30 pm. Bar 10–1 am; dancing Wed–Sat. Ck-out 1 pm. Meeting rms. Bellhops. Valet serv. Free airport, RR station, bus depot transportation. Exercise equipt; weights, bicycles, whirlpool. Bathrm phones. Private patios. Cr cds: A, C, D, DS, MC, V.

Hotels

★ ★ ★HILTON. *1055 Van Ness (93721).* 209/485-9000; FAX 209/485-7666. 192 rms, 9 story. S $74–$109; D $79–$119; each addl $10; suites $179–$525; under 18 free; wkend rates. Crib free. Pet accepted, some restrictions. TV; cable. Heated pool; whirlpool, poolside serv. Restaurant 6 am–11 pm. Rm serv 24 hrs. Bar. Ck-out noon. Meeting rms. Gift shop. Free airport transportation. Health club privileges. Cr cds: A, C, D, DS, MC, V.

★ ★HOLIDAY INN FRESNO CENTRE PLAZA. *2233 Ventura St (93721), opp Selland Arena.* 209/268-1000; FAX 209/486-6625. 317 rms, 8 story. S $72–$87; D $78–$97; each addl $8; suites $89–$195; under 18 free. Crib free. TV. 2 pools, 1 indoor; poolside serv. Restaurant 6:30 am–11 pm. Bar 5 pm–2 am; dancing. Ck-out noon. Convention facilities. Gift shop. Beauty shop. Free airport, RR station transportation. Exercise equipt; weight machine, treadmills, whirlpool. Holidome. 8-story atrium lobby. Cr cds: A, C, D, DS, ER, MC, V, JCB.

Restaurants

✔ ★GEORGE'S. *2405 Capitol St, inside Galleria Shopping Mall.* 209/264-9433. Hrs: 6 am–3 pm; Sat from 7 am. Closed Sun; major hols. Armenian menu. Wine, beer. Semi-a la carte: bkfst $2.75–$7.50,

lunch $3.50–$7.50. Specialties: lamb shank, shish kebab. No cr cds accepted.

★ ★ ★NICOLA'S. *3075 N Maroa Ave.* 209/224-1660. Hrs: 11:30 am–4 pm, 5–10 pm; Sat 5–11 pm; Sun 4–10 pm. Closed some major hols. Res accepted. Italian, Amer menu. Bar to 11:30 pm. Wine list. Semi-a la carte: lunch $4.95–$10.95, dinner $9.95–$18.95. Child's meals. Specializes in steak, salmon. Parking. Old World atmosphere. Cr cds: A, C, D, DS, MC, V.

★ ★RIPE TOMATO. *5064 N Palm Ave, in Fig Garden Mall.* 209/225-1850. Hrs: 11:30 am–2:30 pm, 6–10 pm. Closed Sun, Mon; major hols. Res accepted. French provincial menu. Bar. Semi-a la carte: lunch $8.95–$12.95, dinner $16.95–$24.95. Specializes in roast duck, salmon. Outdoor dining. Cr cds: MC, V.

Fullerton (J-4)

Pop: 114,144 **Elev:** 155 ft **Area code:** 714

(See Anaheim, Buena Park)

Motor Hotels

✔ ★ ★DAYS INN. *1500 S Raymond Ave (92631), CA 91 Raymond Ave exit, 1 blk N.* 714/635-9000; FAX 714/520-5831. 250 rms, 3–6 story. S, D $59–$89; suites $130–$270; under 17 free. Crib free. TV; cable, in-rm movies. Heated pool; poolside serv. Restaurant 6:30 am–10 pm. Rm serv. Bar 11–2 am. Ck-out noon. Coin lndry. Convention facilities. Bellhops. Valet serv. Gift shop. Free Disneyland, Knott's Berry Farm transportation. Exercise equipt; weights, bicycles, whirlpool. Game rm. Cr cds: A, C, D, DS, MC, V.

★ ★HOLIDAY INN. *222 W Houston Ave (92632), CA 91 Harbor Blvd exit, 1 blk N.* 714/992-1700; FAX 714/992-4843. 289 rms, 4 & 7 story. S $80–$90; D $90–$100; suites $125; under 12 free. Crib free. TV; cable, in-rm movies. Heated pool; wading pool, poolside serv. Coffee in rms. Restaurant 6 am–10 pm. Rm serv. Bar 11 am–midnight. Ck-out noon. Meeting rms. Bellhops. Free RR station, Disneyland, Knott's Berry Farm transportation. Exercise equipt; weight machine, bicycle. Game rm. Cr cds: A, C, D, DS, MC, V, JCB.

Hotels

★ ★ ★MARRIOTT AT CALIFORNIA STATE UNIVERSITY. *2701 E Nutwood Ave (92631), CA 57 Nutwood Ave exit, 1 blk W.* 714/738-7800; FAX 714/738-0288. 225 rms, 6 story. S $109; D $119; suites $250; under 12 free. Crib avail. Pet accepted. TV; cable, in-rm movies. Heated pool; poolside serv. Restaurant 6:30 am–10 pm. Bar 11 am–midnight. Ck-out noon. Convention facilities. Gift shop. Exercise equipt; weight machine, bicycles. whirlpool, sauna. Bathrm phone, refrigerator in suites. Cr cds: A, C, D, DS, MC, V, JCB.

★ ★RADISSON SUITES. *2932 E Nutwood Ave (92631), CA 57 Nutwood Ave exit, 1 blk E.* 714/579-7400; FAX 714/528-7945. 96 suites, 5 story. S, D $89; each addl $10; under 12 free. Crib free. TV; cable, in-rm movies. Heated pool. Complimentary continental bkfst. Complimentary coffee in rms. Restaurant adj open 24 hrs. Ck-out noon. Coin lndry. Meeting rms. Exercise equipt; weight machine, rowing machine. Bathrm phones, minibars, in-rm whirlpools. Some balconies. Cr cds: A, C, D, DS, ER, MC, V.

Restaurants

★★**AURORA.** *1341 S Euclid St, CA 91 Euclid St exit, 1 blk N.* *714/738-0272.* Hrs: 11:30 am–2 pm, 5–10 pm; Sat from 5 pm. Closed Sun; most major hols. Res accepted. Northern Italian, continental menu. Bar. A la carte entrees: lunch $5.95–$14.95, dinner $9.95–$26. Specializes in exotic wild game, fresh seafood. Parking. European decor. Extensive wine list. Cr cds: A, C, D, DS, MC, V.

★★★**THE CELLAR.** *305 N Harbor Blvd, CA 91 Harbor Blvd exit, 1½ mi N. 714/525-5682.* Hrs: from 6 pm. Closed Sun, Mon; major hols. Res accepted. French menu. Bar. Wine cellar. A la carte entrees: dinner $15–$25. Specializes in lamb, breast of pheasant, fresh seafood. Own baking. Parking. French decor. In cellar of former hotel (1922). Jacket. Cr cds: A, C, D, DS, ER, MC, V, JCB.

✔★★**MULBERRY STREET.** *114 W Wilshire Ave, CA 91 Harbor Blvd exit, 1½ mi N to Wilshire Ave then 1 blk W. 714/525-1056.* Hrs: 11:30–2 am; Sat 11:30 am–2:30 pm, 5 pm–2 am; Sun 5 pm–1 am. Closed Easter, Thanksgiving, Dec 25. Res accepted. Italian menu. Bar. Semi-a la carte: lunch $3.95–$9.95, dinner $6.25–$16.95. Child's meals. Specializes in fresh seafood. Own pasta. Parking. Cr cds: A, D, MC, V.

Garberville (C-1)

Pop: 900 (est) Elev: 533 ft Area code: 707 Zip: 95440

What to See and Do

1. **Richardson Grove State Park** (see). 8 mi S on US 101.
2. **King Range National Conservation Area.** 15 mi W off US 101. Approx 60,000 acres on the coast including King's Peak (4,087 ft). Saltwater and inland stream fishing; hunting. Hiking. Picnicking. Primitive camping (fee/car/night). Phone 822-7648 or 462-3873.
3. **Humboldt Redwoods State Park** (see). Approx 15 mi N via US 101.

Motels

★★**BEST WESTERN HUMBOLDT HOUSE.** *701 Redwood Dr. 707/923-2771; FAX 707/923-4259.* 75 rms, 2 story. June–Oct: S $58–$68; D $68–$78; each addl $5; family rates; lower rates rest of yr. Crib $5. TV; cable. Heated pool; whirlpool. Complimentary continental bkfst. Ck-out 11 am. Coin lndry. Meeting rms. Some refrigerators. Private patios, balconies. Fish cleaning & freezing facilities. Cr cds: A, C, D, DS, ER, MC, V, JCB.

✔★**GARBERVILLE.** *948 Redwood Dr. 707/923-2422.* 30 rms. Mid-May–mid-Oct: S $45–$55; D $50–$60; each addl $6; lower rates rest of yr. Crib $5. TV; cable. Complimentary coffee in rms. Restaurant 6 am–9:30 pm. Ck-out 11 am. Fish freezing facilities. Eel River 1 mi. Cr cds: A, C, D, DS, MC, V.

✔★**RANCHO.** *987 Redwood Dr. 707/923-2451.* 22 rms, 1–2 story. S, D $34–$70; each addl $4–$6. TV; cable. Heated pool. Complimentary coffee in rms. Restaurant nearby. Ck-out 11 am. Cr cds: A, C, D, MC, V.

★★**SHERWOOD FOREST.** *814 Redwood Dr. 707/923-2721; FAX 707/923-3677.* 33 rms. May–Oct: S $50; D $54–$58; each addl $5; suites, kit. units $80–$88; lower rates rest of yr. Crib $6. Pet accepted. TV; cable. Heated pool; whirlpool, sauna. Coffee in rms. Restaurant opp 6 am–3 pm. Ck-out 11 am. Coin lndry. Meeting rms. Free airport transportation. Some refrigerators. Picnic tables, grills. Fish cleaning & storage facilities. Cr cds: A, MC, V.

Inn

★★★**BENBOW.** *445 Lake Benbow Dr. 707/923-2124.* 55 rms, 2–4 story. S, D $98–$119; each addl $15; deluxe rms $125–$145; suites $180–$190; cottage $250–$260. Closed Jan 2–Apr 15 & Dec 1–18. TV in some rms; cable, in-rm movies. Complimentary afternoon tea & scones, early evening refreshments. Coffee & sherry in rms. Restaurant (see BENBOW INN). Bar 10:30 am–midnight (seasonal); entertainment. Ck-out noon, ck-in 2 pm. Bellhops. Free airport, bus depot transportation. 9-hole golf, greens fee $8.50–$10, putting green. Boats. Lawn games. Classic vintage movies nightly. Some refrigerators, fireplaces. On lake; private beach. Woodland setting. Tudor mansion resort hotel (1926); antiques. Cr cds: MC, V.

Restaurant

★★★**BENBOW INN.** *(See Benbow Inn) 707/923-2125.* Hrs: 8–11 am, noon–1:30 pm (seasonal), 6–9 pm; Sun to 1 pm. Closed Jan–mid-Apr; also 1st 3 wks Dec. Res required. Wine cellar. A la carte entrees: bkfst $3.75–$7.50, lunch $6.50–$10, dinner $11.95–$22. Child's meals. Specialties: filet mignon, fresh pasta, fresh fish, lamb. Own pastries, desserts. Pianist. Parking. Patio dining. Tudor decor; antiques. Totally nonsmoking. Cr cds: MC, V.

Garden Grove (J-4)

Pop: 143,050 Elev: 90 ft Area code: 714

What to See and Do

Crystal Cathedral. 12141 Lewis St. The all-glass church resembles a four-pointed crystal star. Designed by Philip Johnson; set on 36 acres of landscaped grounds. Guided tours (Mon–Sat, hrs may vary; closed hols). Phone 971-4013 or -4000. ¢

(See Anaheim, Orange, Santa Ana)

Motel

✔★★**BEST WESTERN PLAZA INTERNATIONAL INN.** *7912 Garden Grove Blvd (92641), CA 22 Beach Blvd exit, 1 blk N. 714/894-7568; FAX 714/894-6308.* 100 rms. Late May–early Sept: S $40–$49; D $44–$53; each addl $5; higher rates hols; lower rates rest of yr. Crib free. TV; cable. Heated pool; sauna. Coffee in rms. Restaurant adj 6 am–11 pm; wkends to midnight. Ck-out 11 am. Some refrigerators. Cr cds: A, C, D, DS, ER, MC, V, JCB.

Gilroy (E-2)

Pop: 31,487 Elev: 200 ft Area code: 408 Zip: 95020

What to See and Do

1. **Fortino Winery.** 5 mi W via CA 152, at 4525 Hecker Pass Highway. Small family winery. Tours, wine tasting room, picnic area, deli. (Daily; closed Easter, Thanksgiving, Dec 25) Phone 842-3305. **Free.**

2. **Henry W. Coe State Park.** 9 mi N on US 101, then 13 mi E of Morgan Hill on E Dunne Ave. Approx 68,000 acres. Highlights include unusually large manzanita shrubs and a botanical island formed of ponderosa pines. Hiking, backpacking, horseback riding, and mountain biking. Primitive drive-in campsites (no electric). Pine Ridge Museum displays ranch life in the late 1880s (Sat, Sun). Guided walks and evening programs (Mar–June, wkends). Standard fees. Phone 779-2728.

Annual Event

Gilroy Garlic Festival. Features Gourmet Alley, a giant open-air kitchen; cooking demonstrations and contests; food & beverage booths; arts & crafts; entertainment. Phone 842-1625. Last full wkend July.

(For accommodations see Salinas, San Jose)

Glendale (H-4)

Pop: 180,038 **Elev:** 571 ft **Area code:** 818

(For general information and attractions see Los Angeles.)

Motels

★★**BEST WESTERN EAGLE ROCK INN.** *(2911 Colorado Blvd, Los Angeles 90041)* At jct CA 2 & Colorado Blvd. 213/256-7711; FAX 213/255-6750. 50 rms, 3 story. S $55–$65; D $65–$75; each addl $5; under 18 free; higher rates Rose Bowl activities. Crib free. TV; cable. Heated pool; whirlpool. Complimentary continental bkfst, coffee. Restaurant adj 11 am–10 pm. Ck-out noon. Refrigerators. Cr cds: A, C, D, DS, MC, V.

★**VAGABOND INN.** *120 W Colorado St (91204),* 1 mi S of CA 134. 818/240-1700; FAX 818/548-8428. 52 rms, 3 story. S $58–$65; D $65–$70; each addl $5; under 19 free; higher rates: special events, Rose Bowl (3-day min). Crib free. Pet accepted. $3 per day. TV. Pool. Complimentary continental bkfst, coffee. Restaurant adj. Ck-out noon. Refrigerators avail. Cr cds: A, C, D, DS, ER, MC, V.

Restaurant

★★**FAR NIENTE RISTORANTE.** *204½ N Brand Blvd, ½ mi S of CA 134.* 818/242-3835. Hrs: 11:30 am–2:30 pm, 5:30–10 pm; Fri, Sat from 5:30 pm; Sun 5–9 pm. Closed major hols. Res accepted. Northern Italian menu. Bar. Semi-a la carte: lunch $8–$15, dinner $10–$17. Specialties: penne Far Niente, ravioli, fresh fish. Own pasta. Far niente, meaning "without a care," describes the atmosphere; relaxed and carefree. Cr cds: A, C, D, MC, V.

Ⓓ

Glendora

(see West Covina)

Grass Valley (D-2)

Settled: 1849 **Pop:** 9,048 **Elev:** 2,411 ft **Area code:** 916

Immigrants followed their half-starved cattle to this spot, little dreaming that under the thick grass were rich quartz deposits that were to make the Grass Valley area the richest gold mining region in California—the

Mother Lode country. The stamp mills, cyanide tanks and shafts are no longer in operation. Located on the edge of the Tahoe National Forest, Grass Valley has become a recreation center and retirement haven.

A Ranger District office of the Tahoe National Forest is located here.

What to See and Do

1. **Lola Montez House.** 248 Mill St. Facsimile of 1851 Grass Valley house once owned by Lola Montez; singer, dancer and *paramour* of the rich and famous. Now houses Grass Valley/Nevada County Chamber of Commerce. Museum on premises. (Daily exc Sun; closed hols) Phone 273-4667. **Free.**

2. **"Rough and Ready" Town.** 4 mi W on CA 20. Gold strike named after General Zachary Taylor, "Old Rough and Ready." At one time the miners tried to secede from the Union and form the independent Republic of Rough and Ready.

3. **Mining Museum-North Star Powerhouse.** Allison Ranch Rd. Hard rock mining display and artifacts; 30-foot Pelton water wheel; stamp mill; largest operational Cornish pump in the US. (May–Oct, daily) Phone 273-4255. **Free.**

4. **Empire Mine State Historic Park.** 10791 E Empire St. At one time, this historic hardrock gold mine was the largest and richest in California. Baronial cottage with formal gardens among 784 acres. Hiking. Picnicking. Visitor center, mining exhibits. Tours (Mar–Nov, daily; rest of yr, wkends by appt). Standard fees. Phone 273-8522.

(For further information contact the Chamber of Commerce, 248 Mill St, 95945; 273-4667 or 800/655-4667.)

Annual Events

Blue Grass Festival. Fairgrounds, McCourtney Rd. 3rd wkend June.

Nevada County Fair. Fairgrounds, McCourtney Rd. Rodeo, horse show, livestock, loggers Olympics. 4 days mid-Aug.

Cornish Christmas. In Old Town. Street fair. Cornish treats, musicians, entertainment, vendors. Late Nov–early Dec.

(See Nevada City)

Motel

✔★**HOLIDAY LODGE.** *1221 E Main St (95945).* 916/273-4406; res: 800/742-7125 (CA). 36 rms, 1–2 story. Mid-Apr-mid-Oct: S $38; D $46–$50; each addl $6; gold panning, hol rates; lower rates rest of yr. Crib $6. Pet accepted, some restrictions; $10. TV; cable. Pool. Continental bkfst. Restaurant nearby. Ck-out 11 am. Meeting rm. Some balconies. Cr cds: A, C, D, DS, MC, V.

Restaurants

★★★**SCHEIDEL'S.** *10100 Alta Sierra Dr,* off CA 49 at Alta Sierra exit. 916/273-5553. Hrs: 5:30–9:30 pm; Sun 4–9 pm. Closed Mon, Tues; Dec 24; also Jan. German, Amer menu. Bar. Semi-a la carte: dinner $8–$15.95. Child's meals. Specialties: veal Oscar, Wienerschnitzel, German marinated sauerbraten. Parking. Bavarian decor. Family-owned. Cr cds: MC, V.

Ⓓ SC

★★**THE STEWART HOUSE.** *124 Bank St.* 916/477-6368. Hrs: 11:30 am–2 pm, 5:30–9 pm; wkend to 10 pm; Sun brunch 10:30 am–2 pm. Closed Mon. Res accepted. Wine, beer. Semi-a la carte: lunch $2.50–$8.25, dinner $6.95–$15.95. Sun brunch $13.95. Specializes in fresh seafood, prime rib. Salad bar. Classical guitarist Fri–Sun. Parking. Outdoor dining. Historic house built 1888; 3 dining rms. Cr cds: A, MC, V.

Gualala (D-1)

Pop: 1,200 (est) **Elev:** 67 ft **Area code:** 707 **Zip:** 95445

Because of its relative isolation and quiet atmosphere, the area attracts many visitors. Favorite local activities include steelhead, abalone and silver salmon fishing, canoeing and swimming in the Gualala River and camping. A debate on the origin of the name "Gualala" has persisted for more than 100 years. Some say it derived from the native Pomo word *qhawala-li*, meaning "water coming down place," while others maintain that it is a Spanish rendering of Valhalla. ¢

What to See and Do

Point Arena Lighthouse and Museum. 15 mi N on CA 1. This 115-foot-tall lighthouse (1908) and Fog Signal Building (1869) houses historical artifacts and photographs. Viewing at top of lighthouse through a 2-ton lens. (Daily; closed Thanksgiving, Dec 25; also wkdays in Dec) Phone 882-2777. ¢

(For further information contact the Fort Bragg-Mendocino Coast Chamber of Commerce, 322 N Main St, PO Box 1141, Fort Bragg 95437; 961-6300.)

Motel

★★**SEA RANCH LODGE.** *(Box 44, The Sea Ranch 95497)* 10 mi S off CA 1. 707/785-2371; res: 800/732-7262; FAX 707/785-2243. 20 rms, 2 story. No A/C. No rm phones. S, D $125–$180; each addl $15; under 6 free; wkly rates; golf plans; mid-wk packages. Crib $5. 2 heated pools; sauna. Playground. Coffee in rms. Restaurant 8–10:30 am, 11:30 am–2:30 pm, 6–9 pm. Bar 11 am–midnight. Ck-out noon. Meeting rms. Tennis. 9-hole golf, greens fee $18–$35, pro, putting green, driving range. Some fireplaces. Picnic tables, grills. On bluff overlooking ocean; 5,500 acres in historic Sea Ranch. Cr cds: A, MC, V.

Inns

✔★★**GUALALA HOTEL.** *(Box 675)* S on CA 1. 707/884-3441. 18 rms, 5 with bath, 2 story. No rm phones. Mid-May–mid-Nov: S $39–$50; D $44–$55; suites $60; golf rates; lower rates rest of yr. TV in sitting rm. Dining rm 7 am–2 pm, 5–9:30 pm. Bar 11 am–11 pm, Fri–Sun 10–1 am. Ck-out noon, ck-in 2 pm. Local airport transportation. 9-hole golf privileges. Game rm. Picnic tables. Wine shop. Restored 1903 hotel; much original furniture; library. Opp beach. Cr cds: A, DS, MC, V.

★★**NORTH COAST COUNTRY INN.** 34591 S CA 1. 707/884-4537; res: 800/959-4537. 4 kit. units. No A/C. S, D $135; 2-night min wkends; 3-night min on 3-day hol wkends. Children over 12 yrs only. Free full bkfst. Ck-out 11 am, ck-in 2 pm. Gift shop. Free local airport transportation. Hot tub. Refrigerators, fireplaces. Private decks. Antiques, handmade quilts. Forested setting overlooking Mendocino coast. Totally nonsmoking. Cr cds: A, MC, V.

★★★**ST ORRES.** *(Box 523)* 2½ mi N on CA 1. 707/884-3303. 8 rms, 3 baths, 11 cottages. No A/C. No rm phones. S, D $60–$75; cottages $85–$180. Complimentary bkfst. Restaurant (see ST ORRES). Ck-out noon, ck-in 3 pm. Whirlpool, sauna in cottages. Balconies. Fireplace in most cottages. Built by local craftsmen with local materials. The house is similar to Russian dacha, with onion-domed towers; stained glass, beautiful woodwork. Most rms with ocean view. Beach opp. Cr cds: MC, V.

★★★**WHALE WATCH.** 35100 CA 1. 707/884-3667; res: 800/942-5342; FAX 707/884-4815. 18 rms, 1–2 story, 5 kits. No A/C. No rm

phones. S, D $160–$275. Adults only. Complimentary bkfst. Ck-out 11 am, ck-in 3 pm. Many in-rm whirlpools, fireplaces. Private patios. 2 acres on ocean bluff. Totally nonsmoking. Cr cds: A, MC, V.

Restaurant

★★★**ST ORRES.** *(See St Orres Inn)* 707/884-3335. Hrs: 6–9 pm; Sat 5:15–10 pm. Closed Wed Oct–May. No A/C. Res accepted; required wkends. Wine, beer. *Prix fixe:* dinner $28. Specializes in rack of lamb, fresh fish. Own baking. Parking. Natural wood, stained glass. Totally nonsmoking. No cr cds accepted.

Guerneville (D-1)

Pop: 1,966 **Elev:** 56 ft **Area code:** 707 **Zip:** 95446

This scenic area is popular for recreational vacations, with swimming, golf, fishing, canoeing and hiking nearby.

What to See and Do

1. **Armstrong Redwoods State Reserve.** 2 mi N off CA 116. Named for Colonel James Boydston Armstrong of Ohio, who settled here with his family in 1874. Nature, hiking, riding trails. Picnicking. Standard fees. Phone 865-2391 or 869-2015. Per vehicle ¢¢

2. **Korbel Champagne Cellars.** 13250 River Rd. Produces wine, champagne and brandy. Guided tours; century-old cellars; champagne, wine tasting; garden tours in summer (1 in morning and 1 in afternoon). (Daily; closed Jan 1, Easter, Thanksgiving, Dec 25) Phone 887-2294. **Free.**

(For additional area information contact Russian River Region, 14034 Armstrong Woods Rd, PO Box 255; 869-9212 or 800/253-8800.)

Annual Event

Russian River Jazz Festival. Johnson's Beach. Wkend after Labor Day.

(See Bodega Bay, Healdsburg, Santa Rosa)

Motel

★**DAYS INN BROOKSIDE LODGE.** *(Box 382)* CA 116 *(River Rd)* and Brookside Lane. 707/869-2470. 28 rms, 18 kit. units, 6 cottages. No A/C. May–Sept: S, D $68–$140; each addl $10; kit. units $88–$112; cottages with kit. $92–$150; family, wkly rates; higher rates special events; lower rates rest of yr. TV; cable. Heated pool; whirlpool, sauna. Free supervised child's activities (summer). Coffee in rms. Restaurant adj 6 am–10 pm. Ck-out 11 am. Game rm. Rec rm. Lawn games. Many refrigerators. Private patios, balconies. Picnic tables, grills. Cr cds: A, MC, V.

Inns

★★★**APPLEWOOD.** 13555 CA 116. 707/869-9093. 10 rms, 3 story. No A/C. S, D $115–$185. TV; cable. Pool; whirlpool. Complimentary full bkfst; dinner avail Mon, Wed & Sat. Ck-out noon, ck-in 3 pm. Free local airport transportation. Library. Antiques. Private patios, balconies. Picnic tables. County historical landmark. Totally nonsmoking. Cr cds: A, DS, MC, V.

★★**HIGHLAND DELL INN.** *(PO Box 370, 21050 River Blvd, Monte Rio 95462)* S on Bohemian Hwy, cross river, then left on River

Blvd. 707/865-1759; res: 800/767-1759; FAX 707/865-2732. 10 units, 3 story, 2 suites. No A/C. May–Oct: S, D $65–$150; suites $140–$225; lower rates rest of yr. Adults only. Pet accepted, some restrictions; $100. TV in 2 rms; cable. Pool. Complimentary full bkfst, coffee, tea & cookies. Restaurant adj 6–10 pm. Ck-out noon, ck-in 4–8 pm. Grills. Built 1906, this was the first lodging in Sonoma County to have hot & cold running water. Overlooks Russian River. Stained-glass windows; fireplace in lobby; heirloom antiques and collection of historic local photos. Cr cds: A, DS, MC, V, JCB.

★★RIDENHOUR RANCH HOUSE. 12850 River Rd, 7 mi E. 707/887-1033. 6 rms, 3 story, 2 cottages. D $95–$120; cottages $130. Complimentary full bkfst. Ck-out 11 am, ck-in 3–9 pm. Swimming in river 200 yds. Dinner avail. Library. Antiques, handmade quilts. Balconies. Gardens. Picnic tables. Totally nonsmoking. Cr cds: MC, V.

Half Moon Bay (E-1)

Pop: 8,886 **Elev:** 69 ft **Area code:** 415 **Zip:** 94019

(See San Mateo)

Motel

✔★HOLIDAY INN EXPRESS. 230 Cabrillo Hwy. 415/726-3400; FAX 415/726-1256. 52 rms, 2 story. Apr–Oct: S $65–$85; D $75–$85; each addl $10; higher rates Pumpkin Festival (2–3 day min); lower rates rest of yr. Crib free. Pet accepted; $10. TV. Complimentary continental bkfst. Restaurant nearby. Ck-out noon. Cr cds: A, C, D, DS, MC, V, JCB.

Motor Hotel

★★★BEST WESTERN HALF MOON BAY LODGE. 2400 S Cabrillo Hwy, on CA 1, 2½ mi S of jct CA 1, 92. 415/726-9000; FAX 415/726-7951. 81 rms, 2 story. No A/C. S $92–$134; D $108–$144; each addl $10; suites $130–$160; under 13 free. Crib free. TV; cable. Heated pool. Complimentary coffee in rms. Restaurant adj 6 am–10 pm. Ck-out 11:30 am. Meeting rms. Exercise equipt; rower, bicycles, whirlpool. Some refrigerators, fireplaces; many wet bars. Balconies. Overlooks golf course. Cr cds: A, C, D, DS, MC, V.

Inns

★★★CYPRESS INN. 407 Mirada Rd, 2½ mi N via CA 1, then Medio W to Mirada, at Miramar Beach. 415/726-6002; res: 800-83-BEACH; FAX 415/712-0380. 8 rms, 3 story. S, D $150–$275; under 12 free. TV; cable. Complimentary full bkfst, coffee; afternoon tea, wine. Complimentary coffee in rms on request. Restaurant opp 11:30 am–10:30 pm. Ck-out 1 pm, ck-in 4 pm. Massage therapy avail. Balconies. Fireplaces. Colorful collection of folk art. Oceanfront location with 5 mi of sandy beach. All rms have ocean view. Totally nonsmoking. Cr cds: A, MC, V.

★★OLD THYME INN. 779 Main St. 415/726-1616. 7 rms, 2 story. No A/C. No rm phones. S $70–$215; D $75–$220; each addl $25. Complimentary full bkfst, refreshments. Restaurant nearby. Ck-out 11 am, ck-in after 3 pm. Some in-rm whirlpools, fireplaces. Picnic tables. Library/sitting rm. Herb garden. Built 1899. Totally nonsmoking. Cr cds: A, DS, MC, V.

★★RANCHO SAN GREGORIO INN. (Rte 1, Box 54, 5086 San Gregorio Rd, San Gregorio 94074) S via CA 1, then approx 5 mi W on San Gregorio Rd (CA 84). 415/747-0810; FAX 415/747-0184. 4 rms, 2 story. No A/C. No rm phones. S, D $80–$135; under 3 yrs free. Crib free. Complimentary full bkfst, coffee. Ck-out noon, ck-in 3 pm. Airport transportation. Game rm. Lawn games. Picnic tables, grills. Overlooks historic San Gregorio Valley. Spanish mission-style home located on 15 acres; cactus courtyard; gazebo. Approx 5 mi from ocean, swimming beach. Totally nonsmoking. Cr cds: A, DS, MC, V.

★★★★SEAL COVE INN. (221 Cypress Ave, Moss Beach 94038) From US 101 or I-280, W on CA 92 to jct CA 1, then 6 mi N on CA 1 and left (W) on Cypress Ave. 415/728-7325; FAX 415/728-4116. 10 rms, 2 story, 2 suites. No A/C. S $165–$250; each addl $25; suites $250; under 3 free; higher rates hols (2-night min). Crib free. TV; in-rm movies. Complimentary full bkfst, coffee in rms, tea, wine. Restaurant nearby. Ck-out 11 am, ck-in 3 pm. Airport transportation. Tennis privileges. 18-hole golf privileges, greens fee $65–$85. Refrigerators, minibars. Many balconies. Picnic tables. Individually decorated rms; country antiques, wood-burning fireplaces. A path through bordering grove of cypress trees leads to the ocean bluff. Nearby are protected tidal pools and marine area. Totally nonsmoking. Cr cds: A, D, MC, V.

✔★★ZABALLA HOUSE. 324 Main St. 415/726-9123. 9 rms, 2 story. No rm phones. S, D $65–$150; each addl $10; under 3 free. Pet accepted; $10. Complimentary full bkfst buffet, coffee & evening beverages. Complimentary coffee in rms. Restaurant nearby. Ck-out 11 am, ck-in 3–7 pm. Game rm. Oldest building in town still standing (1859); fireplaces; some antiques. Picnic tables. Totally nonsmoking. Cr cds: A, DS, MC, V.

Restaurant

★★SHORE BIRD. (390 Capistrano Rd, Princeton-by-the-Sea) 4 mi N on CA 1. 415/728-5541. Hrs: 11:30 am–9 pm; Sun brunch 10:30 am–2 pm. Closed Thanksgiving, Dec 24, 25. Bar. Semi-a la carte: lunch $7.95–$15, dinner $10.95–$18. Sun brunch $14.95. Specializes in clam chowder, seafood, prime rib. Patio dining. Cr cds: A, C, D, DS, MC, V.

Hanford (F-3)

Pop: 30,897 **Elev:** 246 ft **Area code:** 209 **Zip:** 93230

China Alley, the century-old Chinatown, has been saved by Chef Winy's family. Two outstanding restaurants were the reason that presidents Eisenhower and Truman and Mao Tse-tung and Chiang Kai-shek suggested to others to eat in this historic town. One of these restaurants remains open (see IMPERIAL DYNASTY).

(For information about this area, contact the Hanford Visitor Agency, 200 Santa Fe, Suite D; 582-0483 or for events 800/722-1114.)

(See Visalia)

Motel

★DOWN TOWN. 101 N Redington St. 209/582-9036. 29 rms, 2 story. S $30–$34; D $34–$38; each addl $2. TV; cable. Complimentary coffee. Restaurant nearby. Ck-out 11 am. Cr cds: A, C, D, DS, MC, V.

Motor Hotel

★★★ **INN AT HARRIS RANCH.** *(Rte 1, Box 777, Coalinga 93210) 32 mi E on CA 198.* 209/935-0717; res: 800/942-2333; FAX 209/935-5061. 123 rms, 3 story. S, D $77–$92; each addl $8; suites $92–$225; under 12 free. Crib free. TV; cable. Heated pool; whirlpools. Restaurant 6:30 am–11 pm. Rm serv. Bar 10 am–midnight. Ck-out noon. Coin lndry. Meeting rms. Bellhops. Private patios, balconies. Private 2,800-foot paved and lighted airstrip on site. Cr cds: A, C, D, DS, ER, MC, V.

Inn

★★ **THE VICTORIAN INN.** *522 N Irwin St.* 209/583-8791. 30 rms in 4 Victorian-style buildings, 2 story, 3 suites. S, D $69–$79; suites $99–$110; under 5 free. TV; cable. Pool; poolside serv. Continental bkfst. Dining rm 7 am–2 pm. Also restaurant nearby. Ck-out 11 am, ck-in 2 pm. Balconies. Historic buildings (late 1800s), restored; many antiques. Cr cds: A, C, D, MC, V.

Restaurant

★★★ **IMPERIAL DYNASTY.** *2 China Alley, 7th & Green Sts.* 209/582-0196 or -0087. Hrs: 4:30–10 pm. Closed Mon; Jan 1, Thanksgiving, Dec 25; also 1 wk in Feb. Res accepted. Continental menu. Bar. Wine cellar. Complete meals: dinner $9.95–$29.95, gourmet dinner (1 wk advance notice) $50. Specialties: tournedos of beef bordelaise, escargots à la Bourguignonne, rack of lamb. Parking. Gourmet societies meet here; special meals prepared. In historic Chinese community; many original Chinese works of art, artifacts. Family-owned. Cr cds: A, MC, V.

Hayward (E-2)

Pop: 111,498 **Elev:** 111 ft **Area code:** 510

What to See and Do

1. **McConaghy Estate** (1886). 18701 Hesperian Blvd. Twelve-room Victorian farm house with period furnishings; carriage house; tank house. During December farm house is decorated for Christmas in 1886. Picnic and play areas in adj Kennedy Park. (Thurs–Sun; closed hols & Jan) Sr citizen rate. Phone 276-3010. ¢¢

2. **Hayward Area Historical Society Museum.** 22701 Main St. Displays include fire engines, costumes, California and local artifacts. Changing exhibits. (Daily exc Sun; closed hols) Phone 581-0223. ¢

3. **Garin Regional Park.** S on CA 238 to Garin Ave E. Secluded 1,520 acres in the Hayward hills with vistas of south bay area. Birdwatching, fishing at Jordan Pond; hiking, riding trails. Picnicking. Interpretive programs at visitor center; historic farm equipment. Per car (wkends & hols) ¢¢ Adj is

   Dry Creek Pioneer Regional Park. Enter via Garin Regional Park. On 1,563 acres. Birdwatching; hiking, riding trails. Picnicking. Interpretive programs. Per car ¢¢

(See Fremont, Oakland, San Francisco Airport Area)

Motel

★★ **EXECUTIVE INN.** 20777 Hesperian Blvd (94541), 1½ mi E on I-880, A St exit. 510/732-6300; res: 800/553-5083; FAX 510/783-

2265. 145 rms, 3 story, 23 suites. S, D $72–$76; each addl $4; suites $84–$88; under 12 free; wkend rates. Pet accepted, some restrictions. TV; cable. Heated pool. Complimentary continental bkfst, coffee. Restaurant nearby. Ck-out noon. Coin lndry. Meeting rms. Valet serv. Sundries. Free airport transportation. Health club privileges. Bathrm phones. Refrigerator in suites. Balconies. Cr cds: A, D, DS, MC, V.

Restaurant

★★★ **RUE DE MAIN.** *22622 Main St.* 510/537-0812. Hrs: 11:30 am–2:15 pm, 5:30–10:30 pm; Sat from 5:30 pm. Closed Sun (exc Mother's Day), Mon; major hols. Res accepted. French menu. Wine cellar; sommelier. Semi-a la carte: lunch $7.50–$15. A la carte entrees: dinner $13–$22. Specialty: médaillons de veau Chef William. Own pastries. Contemporary French decor; murals of French city scenes. Cr cds: A, C, D, MC, V.

Ⓓ

Healdsburg (D-1)

Pop: 9,469 **Elev:** 106 ft **Area code:** 707 **Zip:** 95448

What to See and Do

1. **Canoe trips.** One-day to five-day trips on Russian River (Apr–Oct). Equipment and transportation provided. Contact Trowbridge Canoe Trips, 20 Healdsburg Ave, phone 433-7247 or 800/640-1386.

2. **Russian River Wine Road.** More than 50 wineries are located in the Russian River wine region in northern Sonoma County; most are open to the public for wine tasting. A free map listing the wineries and inns is available from Russian River Wine Road, PO Box 46; phone 433-6782. Among them are

   Simi Winery. 16275 Healdsburg Ave. Winery dates from the turn of the century. Guided tours; wine tasting. (Daily; closed Jan 1, Easter, Thanksgiving, Dec 25) Contact PO Box 698; 433-6981. **Free.**

   Chateau Souverain. 5 mi N on US 101, Independence Lane exit, in Geyserville. Wine tasting, restaurant (Thurs–Mon). Contact Box 528, Geyserville 95441; 433-8281. **Free.**

   Geyser Peak Winery. 8 mi N via US 101, Canyon Rd exit, in Geyserville. Established in 1880. Picnic grounds. Tasting room (daily; closed major hols). Phone 857-9400 or 800/255-WINE in CA. **Free.**

3. **Warm Springs Dam/Lake Sonoma.** 11 mi W via US 101, Canyon Rd exit on Dry Creek Rd. Earth-filled dam, anadromous fish hatchery operated by California Dept of Fish and Game and the Army Corps of Engineers; park overlook provides scenic views of lake and nearby wine country. Swimming, fishing; boating (marina). Hiking, bridle trails. Picnic facilities at marina, at Yorty Creek and near visitor center. Primitive and improved camping (fee). Visitor center. (Thurs–Mon; closed major hols) Contact Visitor Center, 3333 Skaggs Springs Rd, Geyserville 95441; 433-9483.

(For further information and photocopy of self-guided walking tour, contact the Chamber of Commerce, 217 Healdsburg Ave; 433-6935 or 800/648-9922 in CA.)

Annual Event

Russian River Wine Fest. Wine tasting in plaza; entertainment, food, arts & crafts. Mid-May.

(See Bodega Bay, Guerneville, Santa Rosa)

Motel

✔ ★**BEST WESTERN DRY CREEK INN.** *198 Dry Creek Rd. 707/433-0300; FAX 707/433-1129.* 102 rms, 3 story. Apr–Oct: S, D $69–$84; each addl $10; under 12 free; mid-wk rates; lower rates rest of yr. Crib free. TV; cable, in-rm movies. Heated pool; whirlpool. Complimentary continental bkfst, coffee. Restaurant adj. Ck-out noon. Free lndry facilities. Meeting rms. Cr cds: A, C, D, DS, ER, MC, V, JCB.

Inns

★ ★**BELLE DE JOUR.** *16276 Healdsburg Ave. 707/431-9777.* 4 cottages. No rm phones. S, D $115–$185. Complimentary full bkfst, coffee. Ck-out 11 am, ck-in 4–7 pm. Many refrigerators, in-rm whirlpools, fireplaces. Balconies. Picnic tables. Hilltop setting on 6 acres. Totally nonsmoking. Cr cds: MC, V.

★ ★**CAMELLIA.** *211 North St. 707/433-8182; res: 800/727-8182; FAX 707/433-8130.* 9 rms, 2 story. No A/C. S, D $70–$125. Crib free. Heated pool. Complimentary full bkfst. Early evening refreshments. Ck-out 11 am, ck-in 3–6 pm. Valet serv. Victorian house; antique furnishings. Town's first hospital. Totally nonsmoking. Cr cds: A, MC, V.

★ ★**GRAPE LEAF.** *539 Johnson St. 707/433-8140.* 7 rms, 2 story. No rm phones. S, D $90–$150; each addl $30. Complimentary full bkfst, coffee wine & cheese. Restaurant nearby. Ck-out 11 am, ck-in 4–6 pm. In-rm whirlpools. Picnic tables. Antiques. Sitting rm. Skylights. Victorian house (1900). Totally nonsmoking. Cr cds: DS, MC, V.

✔ ★**HAYDON HOUSE.** *321 Haydon St. 707/433-5228.* 8 rms, 4 with bath, 2 story. No rm phones. S $65–$135; D $75–$150; each addl $15. TV in sitting rm. Complimentary full bkfst, coffee, tea & refreshments. Restaurant nearby. Ck-out 11 am, ck-in 3:30 pm. Some in-rm whirlpools. Balconies. Picnic tables. Antiques. Sitting rm. Queen Anne/Victorian house (1912). Totally nonsmoking. Cr cds: MC, V.

★ ★**INN ON THE PLAZA.** *(Box 1196) 110 Matheson St. 707/433-6991.* 9 rms. Rm phones avail. S, D $85–$175; each addl $35. TV; cable. Complimentary full bkfst, refreshments. Ck-out 11 am, ck-in 4–8 pm. Fireplace in some rms. Former Wells Fargo Express Bldg, built 1901; antiques, artwork, stained glass. Enclosed solarium garden. Cr cds: MC, V.

★ ★ ★**MADRONA MANOR.** *1001 Westside Rd. 707/433-4231; res: 800/258-4003; FAX 707/433-0703.* 21 rms, 2–3 story, 3 suites. S $125–$175; D $135–$185; suites $185–$225; under 6 free; MAP avail. Crib $10. Pool. Complimentary full bkfst. Dining rm 6–9 pm. Ck-out 11 am, ck-in 3 pm. Bellhops. Concierge. Many fireplaces. Balconies. Picnic tables. Antiques. Sitting rm. Built 1881. Extensive gardens. Cr cds: A, D, MC, V.

Restaurants

✔ ★**SAMBA JAVA.** *109A Plaza. 707/433-5282.* Hrs: 9 am–2:30 pm; Thurs–Sat also 6:30–9:30 pm. Closed Mon; also Dec 24–Jan 6. Res accepted. Wine, beer. A la carte entrees: bkfst $3–$6, lunch $5–$7.50, dinner $10–$16. Specializes in chicken, beef, Sonoma County produce and wines. Eclectic decor with tropical touches; display of artwork by Carribean artist. Totally nonsmoking. Cr cds: A, DS, MC, V.

★**WESTERN BOOT STEAK HOUSE.** *9 Mitchell Lane. 707/433-6362.* Hrs: 11:30 am–9 pm; early-bird dinner Mon–Thurs 4–6 pm. Closed most major hols. Res accepted. Wine, beer. Semi-a la carte: lunch $4.75–$8.50, dinner $7.95–$18.95. Child's meals. Specializes in char-broiled steak, spare ribs, beef ribs, seafood, pasta. Parking. Cr cds: MC, V.

Hearst-San Simeon State Historical Monument (G-2)

(42 mi N of San Luis Obispo on CA 1)

Crowning La Cuesta Encantada—the Enchanted Hill—is a princely domain of castle, guest houses, theater, pools and tennis courts created by William Randolph Hearst as his home and retreat. After his death in 1951, the estate was given to the state as a memorial to the late publisher's mother, Phoebe Adderson Hearst. For years Hearst Castle could be glimpsed by the public only through a telescope at the nearby village of San Simeon, but today it is open to the public. A "carefully planned, deliberate attempt to create a shrine of beauty," it was begun in 1919 under the direction of noted architect Julia Morgan. An army of workmen built the castle with its twin towers and surrounded it with formal Mediterranean gardens; construction continued for 28 years. And, though 3 guest houses and 115 rooms of the main house were completed, there was still much more Hearst had hoped to build.

Items collected by Hearst can be viewed in the castle and on the grounds. Features of the castle itself are the Refectory, an unbelievable "long, high, noble room" with a hand-carved ceiling and life-size statues of saints, silk banners from Siena and 16th-century choir stalls from European monasteries; the Assembly Room, with priceless tapestries; and the lavish theater where the latest motion pictures were shown.

The estate includes three luxurious "guest houses"; the Neptune Pool, with a pillared colonnade leading to an ancient Roman temple and an array of marble statuary, an indoor pool, magnificent gardens, fountains, walkways and, of course, the main house of 115 rooms.

Visitors may explore an exhibit on the life and times of William Randolph Hearst inside the Visitor Center at the bottom of the hill; food and gift concessions are also located here. There is an area to observe artifact restoration in progress; entrance to the exhibit is free.

Parking is available in a lot near CA 1, where buses transport visitors to the castle. Access to the castle and grounds is by guided tour only. Tour 1 takes in the grounds, a guest house and the lower level of the main house; Tour 2 visits the upper levels of the main house, which include Hearst's private suite; Tour 3 covers the north wing and a guest house, and includes a video about the construction of the castle; Tour 4 (available Apr–Oct) is spent mostly outside in the gardens but also includes behind-the-scenes areas such as the wine cellar and 2 floors of the largest guest house. Evening tours are available for selected evenings in the spring and fall; evening tours take in the highlights of the estate and include a living history program developed to give visitors a glimpse of life at the "Castle" in the early 1930s. All tours include the outdoor and indoor pools.

Day tours take approximately 1¾ hours; evening tours take approximately 2¼ hours. No pets. Reservations are recommended and are available up to eight weeks in advance through Mistix outlets; phone 800/444-7275 or 800/444-4445. Tickets are also available at the ticket office in the visitor center or at any one of several Mistix outlets within 50 miles of the castle. Tours entail much walking and climbing; wheelchairs can be accommodated under certain conditions and with 10 days advance notice by calling 805/927-2020; strollers cannot be accommodated. (Daily; closed Jan 1, Thanksgiving, Dec 25) For tour and reservation information, phone Mistix, 800/444-7275 or 800/444-4445.

(For information about the area contact the San Simeon Chamber of Commerce, PO Box 1, San Simeon 93452; 805/927-3500)

(For accommodations see Cambria, San Simeon)

Hemet (J-4)

Founded: 1890 **Pop:** 36,094 **Elev:** 1,596 ft **Area code:** 909

Located in the beautiful San Jacinto Valley, Hemet was once the largest producer of alfalfa and herbs in the country. Today it is near the hub of an area that includes ocean, desert, mountains, lakes, health resorts and springs, along with neighboring historic Native American reservations and large cattle ranches, all within an hour's drive.

What to See and Do

San Jacinto Valley Museum. 181 E Main St, 3 mi N in San Jacinto. Permanent and temporary exhibits of genealogy, Indian archaeology and a variety of historical items of San Jacinto Valley. (Tues–Sun, afternoons; closed Jan 1, Thanksgiving, Dec 25) For information phone 654-4952 or -7710. **Free.**

Annual Events

Ramona Pageant. Ramona Bowl, a 6,662-seat outdoor amphitheater built into the side of a mountain. Beautiful setting among the rolling hills, where most of the action of Helen Hunt Jackson's story takes place. More than 350 persons participate in this romance of early California, presented annually since 1923. Contact Ramona Pageant Assn, 27400 Ramona Bowl Rd, 92544; phone 658-3111 or 800/645-4465. 3 wkends late Apr–early May.

Farmers Fair. Lake Perris Fairgrounds, 12 mi W on CA 74 in Perris. Competitions and exhibits, food, activities, entertainment. Phone 657-4221. Early–mid-Oct.

(See Palm Springs, Riverside)

Motels

✔ ★ ★ **BEST WESTERN.** 2625 W Florida Ave (92545), I-215 exit CA 74, E 13 mi. 909/925-6605; FAX 909/925-7095. 72 rms, 2 story, 29 kits. S $44; D $46–$50; each addl $4–$6; suites $75; kit. units $50–$56; wkly, monthly rates; higher rates Ramona Pageant. Crib $4. TV. Heated pool; whirlpool. Continental bkfst. Coffee in rms. Restaurant adj open 24 hrs. Ck-out 11 am. Coin lndry. Lawn games. Refrigerators. Grills. Cr cds: A, C, D, DS, ER, MC, V.

★ ★ **QUALITY INN.** 800 W Florida Ave (92543), I-215 exit CA 74, E 13 mi. 909/929-6366; FAX 909/925-3016. 65 rms, 2 story, 30 kits. Jan–Apr: S $42–$46; D $50–$60; each addl $6; kit. units $54–$58; under 18 free; wkly, monthly rates; lower rates rest of yr. Crib free. TV; cable. Heated pool. Complimentary continental bkfst. Complimentary coffee in rms. Restaurant adj 6 am–9 pm. Ck-out noon. Coin lndry. Meeting rm. Exercise equipt; bicycles, rowing machine, whirlpool. Cr cds: A, C, D, DS, ER, MC, V, JCB.

★ ★ **RAMADA INN.** 3885 W Florida Ave (92545), I-215 exit CA 74, E 13 mi. 909/929-8900; FAX 909/925-3716. 100 rms, 2 story, 14 kits. S, D $45–$70; each addl $5; suites $62–$75; kit. units $62–$70; under 17 free; wkly, monthly rates; higher rates Ramona Pageant. Crib avail. TV; cable, in-rm movies avail. Heated pool; whirlpool. Complimentary continental bkfst. Coffee in rms. Restaurant adj 7 am–11 pm. Rm serv. Ck-out

noon. Coin lndry. Meeting rms. Valet serv. Some refrigerators. Private patios, balconies. Cr cds: A, C, D, DS, MC, V.

Restaurant

★ ★ **GABRIEL'S.** 360 N San Jacinto St, I-215 exit CA 74, E 13 mi to San Jacinto St then N 2 blks. 909/925-8281. Hrs: 7 am–10 pm; Sat from 5 pm; Sun brunch 10 am–2 pm. Closed Mon; Jan 1, July 4. Res accepted. Continental menu. Bar. Semi-a la carte: bkfst $1.95–$5, lunch $5–$7.95, dinner $6.75–$27. Sun brunch $3.95–$8.95. Child's meals. Specialties: rack of lamb, prime rib, moussaka. Own desserts. Parking. Cr cds: MC, V.

Hollywood (L.A.) (H-3)

Elev: 385 ft **Area code:** 213

Once known as "the glamour capital of the world" and often thought of as a separate city, Hollywood is actually a neighborhood of Los Angeles.

What to See and Do

1. **Walk of Fame.** Two strips along Hollywood's main business and entertainment section, roughly conforming to the shape of a large cross extending nearly 2½ miles. Charcoal & coral-colored terrazzo sidewalk inset with bronze names of entertainment celebrities.

2. **Hollywood Memorial Park Cemetery Mortuary.** On the grounds at 6000 Santa Monica Blvd. Crypts of Tyrone Power, Cecil B. De Mille, Rudolph Valentino, Douglas Fairbanks, Sr, Nelson Eddy and Norma Talmadge, as well as other famous stars, statesmen and industrialists. (Daily) Phone 469-1181.

3. **Westwood Memorial Cemetery.** (See WESTWOOD VILLAGE)

4. **Hollywood & Vine.** One of the most famous intersections in the world.

5. **Hollywood Bowl.** 2301 N Highland Ave, just SW of Hollywood Frwy. Huge outdoor amphitheater, where 250,000 hear "Symphony Under the Stars" each summer (see ANNUAL and SEASONAL EVENTS).

6. **Hollywood Studio Museum.** 2100 N Highland Ave. Dedicated to preserving the history of Hollywood's silent film era. Site of Hollywood's first feature-length Western, *The Squaw Man*, in 1913. Costumes, props, photographs, early movie artifacts. Gift shop. (Sat & Sun, phone for addl summer hrs; closed hols) Sr citizen rate. Phone 874-2276. ¢¢

7. **Mann's Chinese Theatre.** 6925 Hollywood Blvd, between Highland and La Brea. Scene of spectacular opening nights. Look for stars' handprints and footprints in cement. Phone 464-8111.

8. **Hollywood Blvd.** "Main Street" of moviedom.

9. **Hollywood Wax Museum.** 6767 Hollywood Blvd. More than 170 famous people of the past & present re-created in wax. Presidents, movie stars, Western scenes; theater. (Daily) Sr citizen rate. For information phone 462-8860. ¢¢¢

10. **Max Factor Museum of Beauty.** 1666 N Highland Ave, at Hollywood Blvd. Displays and exhibits of the 80-year make-up industry. Wigs and cosmetics; Hollywood star portraits and autographs. (Daily exc Sun; closed hols) Phone 463-6668. **Free.**

11. **Barnsdall Art Park.** 4800 Hollywood Blvd. Named after socialite Aline Barnsdall, who commisioned Frank Lloyd Wright to build her home and later gave the property to the city of Los Angeles. Phone 485-8665. Within the park are

    Hollyhock House. Built by Wright from 1919–21, the house was given its name for Aline Barnsdall's favorite flower. Extensive outdoor courtyards and terraces were designed by Wright to extend living spaces to outdoors. Tours. (Daily exc Mon) Phone 662-7272. ¢

Municipal Art Gallery. Features work by regional and local artists. (Daily exc Mon) Phone 485-4581. ¢

(For further information contact the Chamber of Commerce, 7000 Hollywood Blvd, Suite 1, 90028, phone 469-8311; or the Hollywood Visitors Information Center, 6541 Hollywood Blvd, phone 461-4213.)

Annual Events

Easter Sunrise Services. Hollywood Bowl (see #5). Interdenominational service with music of select choral groups.

Hollywood Christmas Parade. Sun after Thanksgiving.

(See Los Angeles)

Motels

✔ ★**BEST WESTERN.** 6141 Franklin Ave (90028), US 101 Gower St exit to Franklin Ave, then 1 blk W. 213/464-5181; FAX 213/962-0536. 82 units, 3-4 story, 45 kits. S $50-$55; D $65-$75; each addl $10; kit. units $10 addl; under 12 free; wkly rates; higher rates Rose Bowl. Crib $5. Pet accepted, some restrictions. Heated pool. TV; cable. Restaurant 5:30 am-9 pm. Rm serv. Ck-out noon. Sundries. Refrigerators. Cr cds: A, C, D, DS, ER, MC, V, JCB.

✔ ★**HALLMARK HOTEL.** 7023 Sunset Blvd (90028), US 101 exit Sunset Blvd W. 213/464-8344; res: 800/346-7723; FAX 213/962-9748. 74 rms, 2 story, 13 suites. S $56-$60; D $60-$66; each addl $10; suites $80; kits. $80; under 17 free; wkly rates. Crib free. TV; cable. Heated pool. Complimentary continental bkfst. Restaurant opp open 24 hrs. Ck-out 11 am. Coin lndry. Free covered parking. Airport transportation. Cr cds: A, C, D, DS, MC, V, JCB.

Hotels

★★**HOLIDAY INN.** 1755 N Highland Ave (90028), US 101 exit Highland Ave S ½ mi. 213/462-7181; FAX 213/466-9072. 470 rms, 23 story. S, D $94-$134; each addl $15; suites $119-$195; under 18 free. Crib free. Pet accepted, some restrictions. TV; cable. Heated pool. Restaurant 6 am-10 pm; revolving rooftop dining rm 6:30-11 pm. Bars 11-2 am; entertainment, dancing Tues-Sat. Ck-out noon. Coin lndry. Meeting rms. Concierge. Gift shop. Refrigerators avail. Cr cds: A, C, D, DS, MC, V, JCB.

★★**LE MONTROSE SUITE HOTEL DE GRAN LUXE** (formerly Valadon Suite Hotel). (900 Hammond St, West Hollywood 90069) US 101 exit Sunset Blvd W to Hammond St. 310/855-1115; res: 800/776-0666; FAX 310/657-9192. 110 suites, 5 story. Suites $145-$195; under 12 free; wknd rates. Crib free. Covered parking $8, valet. Pet accepted. TV; cable, in-rm movies. Heated pool; poolside serv. Restaurant 7 am-10:45 pm. Ck-out noon. Meeting rm. Concierge. Lighted tennis. Exercise rm; instructor, weight machine, treadmill, whirlpool, sauna. Bathrm phones, refrigerators, minibars, fireplaces; many wet bars. Some balconies. Art nouveau decor. Cr cds: A, C, D, ER, MC, V, JCB.

★★★**RADISSON HOLLYWOOD ROOSEVELT.** 7000 Hollywood Blvd (90028), US 101 exit Highland Ave, S to Hollywood Blvd. 213/466-7000; FAX 213/462-8056. 335 rms, 2-12 story, 30 suites. S, D $115-$180; each addl $20; suites $275-$1,500; under 18 free. Crib free. Valet parking $8. TV; cable. Heated pool; poolside serv. Restaurant 6 am-midnight. Bar; entertainment, dancing. Concierge. Gift shop. Exercise equipt; weight machine, bicycles, whirlpool. Minibars; some bathrm phones. Refrigerators avail. Site of first Academy Awards presentation. Cr cds: A, C, D, DS, ER, MC, V, JCB.

★★**RAMADA-WEST HOLLYWOOD.** (8585 Santa Monica Blvd, West Hollywood 90069) US 101 exit Santa Monica Blvd, then 5 mi W. 310/652-6400; FAX 310/652-2135. 175 rms, 4 story, 26 suites. S, D $105-$115; each addl $15; suites $139-$350; under 18 free. Crib free. TV; cable, in-rm movies avail. Heated pool. Restaurant 7-11 am, 5-11 pm. Ck-out noon. Coin lndry. Shopping arcade. Airport transportation. Health club privileges. Bathrm phones; some refrigerators, minibars. Some balconies. Cr cds: A, C, D, DS, MC, V, JCB.

Restaurants

★★**ANTONIO'S.** 7472 Melrose Ave, US 101 Melrose Ave exit, W 3 mi. 213/655-0480. Hrs: noon-3 pm, 5-11 pm. Closed Mon; some major hols. Res accepted. Mexican menu. Bar. A la carte entrees: lunch $7-$10, dinner $10.75-$16.95. Specialty: gallina en pipan (chicken in almond sauce). Strolling musicians wkend evenings. Valet parking. Family-owned. Cr cds: A, MC, V.

★★**CA' BREA.** 346 S La Brea Ave, I-10 La Brea Ave exit, N 2 mi. 213/938-2863. Hrs: 11:30 am-2:30 pm, 5:30-11 pm; Sat from 5:30 pm. Closed Sun. Res accepted. Northern Italian menu. Bar. A la carte entrees: lunch, dinner $15-$30. Specializes in authentic Venetian dishes. Valet parking. Italian cafe decor. Cr cds: A, D, DS, MC, V.

✔ ★**CAIOTI.** 2100 Laurel Canyon Blvd, N of Sunset Blvd at jct Kirkwood Dr. 213/650-2988. Hrs: 11 am-11 pm. Closed some major hols. Res accepted. Italian, Amer menu. Wine, beer. Semi-a la carte: lunch $6-$10, dinner $6-$14. Specializes in pizza, pasta, salad, grilled entrees. Own breads. Outdoor dining. Rural setting. Cr cds: A, MC, V.

★★**CITRUS.** 6703 Melrose Ave, US 101 Melrose Ave exit, W 2 mi. 213/857-0034. Hrs: noon-2:30 pm, 6:30-10:30 pm; Fri to 11 pm; Sat 6-11 pm. Closed Sun; major hols. Res accepted. California, French cuisine. Bar. A la carte entrees: lunch $20-$25, dinner $35-$50. Complete meals: dinner $50-$70. Specializes in baby salmon, scallops. Valet parking. Open kitchen. Cr cds: A, D, MC, V, JCB.

★★★**EMILIO'S.** 6602 Melrose Ave, US 101 Melrose Ave exit, W 2 mi. 213/935-4922. Hrs: 5 pm-midnight; Thurs & Fri also 11:30 am-3 pm; Sun buffet 5-9:30 pm. Closed Thanksgiving, Dec 25. Res accepted. Italian menu. Bar. Wine cellar. A la carte entrees: lunch $8.50-$15, dinner $10-$20. Buffet: dinner (Sun) $22. Child's meals. Specialties: brodetto di mare, chitarra al pomodoro e basilico. Own pasta. Valet parking. Balcony overlooking illuminated fountain. Family-owned. Cr cds: A, C, D, ER, MC, V, JCB.

★★**FENNEL.** 755 N La Cienega. 310/657-8787. Hrs: noon-2:30 pm, 6-10 pm; Sun from 6 pm. Closed Mon; most major hols. Res accepted. Bar. A la carte entrees: lunch $5-$20, dinner $10-$30. Specialties: half smoked salmon with lentils, roasted goat cheese, duck confit, daily specials. Valet parking. Outdoor dining. French bistro atmosphere. Cr cds: A, D, MC, V.

★★★**L'ORANGERIE.** 903 N La Cienega Blvd, US 101 Santa Monica Blvd exit, W to La Cienega Blvd then S 2 blks. 310/652-9770. Hrs: noon-2 pm, 6:30-11 pm; Sat-Mon from 6:30 pm. Res required. Classic French menu. Bar. A la carte entrees: lunch $15-$25, dinner $24-$52. Specializes in fish flown from France. Own pastries. Valet parking. Courtyard terrace dining. Classic French chateau decor. Jacket. Cr cds: A, C, D, DS, MC, V, JCB.

★ ★ **LA TOQUE.** *8171 Sunset Blvd, CA 101 Sunset Blvd exit W.* 213/656-7515. Hrs: noon–2 pm, 6:30–10 pm; wkends 6–10:30 pm. Closed Sun; some major hols. Res accepted. French menu. Bar. A la carte entrees: lunch $13–$18, dinner $18–$55. Specializes in fresh fish, pasta. Valet parking. French country decor; antique mirror. Jacket. Cr cds: A, D, DS, MC, V.

D

✔ ★ **LE PETIT FOUR.** *8654 Sunset Blvd.* 310/652-4308. Hrs: 8 am–11 pm; Sun from 9 am; Sun brunch 9 am–6 pm. Closed Dec 25. Res accepted. French, Italian menu. Wine, beer. Semi-a la carte: bkfst $3–$10.50, lunch, dinner $4.25–$12.50. Sun brunch $3–$10.50. Specializes in fresh fish, pasta, salad. Parking. Outdoor dining. Photo collection of models who frequent the restaurant. Sidewalk dining area has bistro atmosphere; lots of "star" watching. Cr cds: A, D, MC, V.

★ ★ **THE PALM.** *(9001 Santa Monica Blvd, West Hollywood) I-405 exit Santa Monica Blvd, NE 3 mi.* 310/550-8811. Hrs: noon–10:30 pm; Sat from 5 pm; Sun 5–9:30 pm. Closed most major hols. Res accepted. Bar. A la carte entrees: lunch $9–$15, dinner $14–$30. Specializes in steak, lobster. Valet parking. Several dining areas. Informal, "speakeasy" atmosphere. Hollywood caricatures cover walls and ceiling. Cr cds: A, C, D, MC, V.

D

★ ★ ★ **PATINA.** *5955 Melrose Ave, US 101 Melrose Ave exit.* 213/467-1108. Hrs: 11:30 am–2:30 pm, 6–9:30 pm; Fri to 10:30 pm; Sat 5:30–10:30 pm; Sun, Mon 6–9:30 pm. Closed some major hols. Res accepted; required wkends. French, California menu. Bar. Wine list. A la carte entrees: lunch $18–$25, dinner $35–$45. Specialties: Santa Barbara shrimp, peppered tournedos of tuna. Valet parking. Casual elegance. Cr cds: A, D, DS, MC, V.

D

★ ★ **RED CAR GRILL.** *(8571 Santa Monica Blvd, West Hollywood) CA 101 Santa Monica Blvd exit, W 5 mi.* 310/652-9263. Hrs: 7–11 am, 5–11 pm; Sat & Sun 7 am–11 pm. Closed some major hols. Res accepted. Bar. A la carte entrees: bkfst $3.95–$9.95, lunch $5.95–$15.95, dinner $8.95–$20.95. Specializes in dry-aged NY steak, barbecued ribs, grilled foods. Valet parking. Turn-of-the-century railroad dining car motif. Open grill. Cr cds: A, C, D, MC, V.

D

★ ★ ★ **RISTORANTE CHIANTI & CUCINA.** *7383 Melrose Ave, US 101 Melrose Ave exit, W 3 mi.* 213/653-8333. Hrs: Cucina 11:30 am–midnight, Sun from 5 pm; Chianti 5:30–11:30 pm; Sun from 5 pm. Closed Jan 1, Thanksgiving, Dec 25. Res accepted. Northern Italian menu. Bar. A la carte entrees: lunch, dinner $6.50–$18. Specialties: fettucine Alfredo, lombata di vitello. Valet parking. Two distinct dining areas. Cr cds: A, C, D, MC, V.

D

★ ★ ★ **SPAGO.** *(1114 Horn Ave, West Hollywood) US 101 Sunset Blvd exit, W to Horn Ave.* 310/652-4025. Hrs: 5:30 pm–midnight. Closed some major hols. Res required. California menu. Bar. A la carte entrees: dinner $45–$50. Specializes in gourmet pizza, lobster ravioli, fresh fish. Own pasta. Valet parking. View of West Hollywood. Cr cds: A, C, D, DS, MC, V.

D

★ ★ **TUTTOBENE.** *945 N Fairfax, S via Highland Ave, right on Fountain, left on Fairfax, at jct Romaine.* 213/655-7051. Hrs: 11:30 am–2:30 pm, 5–11 pm; Sat from 5 pm; Sun 5–9 pm. Closed Jan 1, Thanksgiving, Dec 25. Res accepted. Italian menu. Bar. A la carte entrees: lunch $15–$20, dinner $35–$45. Specialties: risotto, osso buco, tiramisu. Valet parking. 3 intimate dining areas with individual decor. Cr cds: A, C, D, MC, V, JCB.

D

★ ★ **YAMASHIRO.** *1999 N Sycamore Ave, US 101 Highland Ave exit, S to Franklin Ave then W to Sycamore, in Hollywood Hills.* 213/466-5125. Hrs: 5:30–10 pm; Fri, Sat to 11 pm. Closed some major hols. Res accepted. Japanese, continental menu. Bar 4:30 pm–1 am. Semi-a la carte: dinner $16–$30. Specialties: Yamashiro feast, tornedos Impe-

rial. Valet parking. Outdoor garden dining. Japanese palace and garden setting. View of Hollywood. Cr cds: A, C, D, DS, MC, V, JCB.

Humboldt Redwoods State Park (B-1)

(45 mi S of Eureka via US 101)

Park encompasses more than 51,000 acres, including 17,000 acres of old growth coast redwoods. The park is bisected by US 101 from Miranda on the south to Pepperwood on the north. This highway is paralleled by a road through the park called Avenue of the Giants, site of redwoods 300 feet tall. The south fork of the Eel River follows the Avenue through the park. Recreation includes swimming, fishing; nature, hiking and bridle trails; camping with trailer sanitation station. Humboldt Redwoods State Park also has a visitor center. Park headquarters is at Burlington, 2 mi S of Weott on the Avenue. Campfire and nature programs are offered. Standard fees. Contact Park Headquarters, PO Box 100, Weott 95571; 707/946-2409. About 12 mi N of the state park on US 101, in the town of Scotia, is

Pacific Lumber Company. A cooperative agreement in the late 1920s between the Pacific Lumber Company and the Save-the-Redwoods League led to the establishment of Humboldt Redwoods State Park. A total of nearly 20,000 acres of magnificent groves once owned by Pacific Lumber are now permanently protected in parks. In Scotia, tour Pacific Lumber's mill, said to be the world's largest redwood operation (Mon–Fri); phone 707/764-2222 for tour schedule. A museum (open summer months) features historic photographs and memorabilia from days gone by. **Free.**

(For accommodations see Garberville; also see Redwood Highway)

Huntington Beach (J-4)

Pop: 181,519 **Elev:** 28 ft **Area code:** 714

(See Costa Mesa, Newport Beach)

Motels

★ ★ ★ **BEST WESTERN SUNSET BEACH INN.** *(17205 Pacific Coast Hwy, Sunset Beach 90742) N on Pacific Coast Hwy.* 310/592-2532; FAX 310/592-4093. 50 rms, 3 story. S, D $79–$129; each addl $10; suites $99; under 12 free; wkly rates. TV; cable. Complimentary bkfst, coffee. Ck-out 11 am. Valet serv. Sundries. Whirlpool. Health club privileges. Refrigerators. Private patios, balconies. Beach opp. Cr cds: A, C, D, DS, MC, V.

D ⊛ SC

✔ ★ **COMFORT SUITES.** *16301 Beach Blvd (92647).* 714/841-1812. 102 suites, 3 story. S $54–$84; D $59–$89; each addl $5; under 18 free. Crib free. TV; cable. Heated pool. Complimentary continental bkfst, coffee. Restaurant opp 6–2 am. Ck-out 11 am. Coin lndry. Meeting rm. Valet serv. Exercise equipt; weights, bicycles, whirlpool. Refrigerators. Balconies. Cr cds: A, C, D, DS, ER, MC, V, JCB.

D ⇌ ⚓ ⊛ SC

Hotels

★ ★ ★ **HILTON WATERFRONT BEACH RESORT.** *21100 Pacific Coast Hwy (92648).* 714/960-7873; FAX 714/960-3791. 293 rms, 12 story. 36 suites. S, D $125–$250; each addl $15; suites $250–$350; under 18 free; wkend rates. Crib free. Garage, valet parking $7. TV; cable, in-rm movies. Heated pool; poolside serv. Supervised child's activities (June 12–Labor Day). Restaurant 6:30 am–11 pm. Bar 11–1:30 am; entertainment exc Sun. Ck-out noon. Meeting rms. Concierge. Gift shop. Airport transportation. Lighted tennis. Golf privileges. Bicycle rentals. Exercise rm; instructor, weight machine, bicycles, whirlpool. Massage therapy. Minibars; bathrm phone in suites. Balconies. All rms with ocean view. *LUXURY LEVEL.* 50 rms, 6 suites, 2 floors. S, D $250; suites $350–$1,200. Ck-out 1 pm. Private lounge, honor bar. Complimentary continental bkfst, refreshments. Cr cds: A, C, D, DS, ER, MC, V, JCB.

[icons]

✔ ★ **HOLIDAY INN.** 7667 Center Ave (92647), off Beach Blvd. 714/891-0123; FAX 714/895-4591. 224 rms, 8 story. S, D $49–$99; each addl $10; suites $158; under 18 free; wkend rates. Crib $10. TV; cable. Indoor pool. Complimentary coffee in rms. Restaurant 6:30 am–2 pm, 5–10 pm. Bar 5–11 pm. Ck-out noon. Gift shop. Free airport transportation as available. Exercise equipt; weight machine, bicycles, whirlpool. Cr cds: A, C, D, DS, MC, V, JCB.

[icons]

Restaurants

✔ ★ **EL TORITO.** 16060 Beach Blvd. 714/842-2541. Hrs: 11 am–10 pm; Fri, Sat to 1 am; Sun 9 am–10 pm; Sun brunch to 2 pm. Closed Thanksgiving, Dec 25. Res accepted. Mexican menu. Bar. A la carte entrees: lunch $4.75–$8.95, dinner $5.95–$12.95. Sun brunch $8.95. Specializes in chimichangas, fajitas. Own sauces. Parking. Patio dining. Mexican decor. Cr cds: A, C, D, DS, MC, V.

[icon]

★ **MAXWELL'S.** 317 Pacific Coast Hwy, at Huntington Beach pier. 714/536-2555. Hrs: 8 am–midnight; Sun brunch 9 am–3 pm. Res accepted. Bar from 9 am. Semi-a la carte: bkfst $2.95–$8.95, lunch $4.95–$16.95, dinner $9.95–$35.95. Daily champagne brunch $8.95. Sun brunch $17.95. Specializes in fresh fish. Own popovers. Valet parking. Outdoor dining. On beach at base of pier; ocean view. Fish tanks along walls. Cr cds: A, D, DS, MC, V.

[icon]

Idyllwild (J-5)

Pop: 2,853 **Elev:** 5,500 ft **Area code:** 909 **Zip:** 92549

Idyllwild, located in the San Jacinto Mountains amidst pine and cedar forests with towering mountains providing the backdrop, is a small alpine village at the gateway to thousands of acres of national forest, state and county parks. This popular resort and vacation area provides fishing in backcountry streams and lakes, hiking, rock climbing and riding. A Ranger District office of the San Bernadino National Forest (see SAN BERNARDINO) is located here.

What to See and Do

1. **Riverside County Parks.** Phone 275-4343.

   Idyllwild. 1 mi W at end of County Park Rd. Camping (fee); reservation phone 275-4343. Picnicking (fee), play area; hiking. Pets on leash. Visitor center with museum.

   Hurkey Creek. 6 mi SE via CA 243, 74, near Lake Hemet. Camping (fee). Picnicking (fee), play area; hiking. Pets on leash.

2. **Mt San Jacinto State Park.** On CA 243. On 3,682 acres. Nature and hiking trails. Picnicking. Camping (reservations recommended in summer). Interpretive programs. Standard fees. Phone 659-2607.

   (For further information contact the Chamber of Commerce, Box 304; 659-3259.)

   (See Palm Desert, Palm Springs)

Motels

★ ★ **QUIET CREEK INN.** 26345 Delano Dr. 909/659-6110. 5 suites, 5 studio rms. No rm phones. Suites $85; studio rms $71. TV. Complimentary coffee. Restaurant nearby. Ck-out 11 am. Meeting rms. Game rm. Lawn games. Refrigerators, fireplaces. Private patios, balconies. Picnic tables, grills. Cr cds: MC, V.

[icons]

✔ ★ ★ **WOODLAND PARK MANOR.** (Box 86) 55350 S Circle Dr. 909/659-2657. 11 cottages, 6 with kit. No A/C. S, D $64; each addl $5; kit. units $84–$148; under 4 free; wkdays rates Oct–May. Crib free. TV; in-rm movies avail. Heated pool. Playground. Complimentary coffee in rms. Restaurant nearby. Ck-out 11 am. Lawn games. Fireplaces. Picnic tables, grill. Sun decks. Scenic, mountainous area. Cr cds: MC, V.

[icons]

Inns

✔ ★ ★ **FERN VALLEY INN.** (Box 116) 25240 Fern Valley Rd. 909/659-2205. 11 cottage rms, 5 with kit. No A/C. S, D, studio rm $63–$85; each addl $10; kit. units $75–$95; wkdays rates winter. TV; cable. Heated pool (summer). Complimentary coffee. Restaurant nearby. Ck-out 11 am, ck-in 2 pm. Game rm. Lawn games. Refrigerators, fireplaces. Private patios. Rms furnished with antiques, brass beds, handmade quilts. Cr cds: MC, V.

[icons]

★ ★ **STRAWBERRY CREEK INN.** (PO Box 1818) 26370 Banning-Idyllwild Hwy (CA 243). 909/659-3202; res: 800/262-8969. 9 rms, 5 in main house and 4 wrap around the courtyard at the rear of the inn, also 1 kit. cottage. No A/C. No rm phones. S, D $80–$95; kit. cottage for 2, $125; each addl (in cottage) $20; 2-night min wkends. TV in cottage. Complimentary full bkfst (inn); also wine and cheese. Complimentary coffee in main house sitting rm. Restaurant nearby. Ck-out 11 am, ck-in 2–6 pm. Large rambling home nestled in the mountains, surrounded by pine and oak trees; Strawberry Creek is at edge of property. Totally nonsmoking. Cr cds: MC, V.

[icons]

Restaurants

★ ★ **CHART HOUSE.** 59405 N Circle Dr, Fern Valley Corners. 909/659-4645. Hrs: 5–9 pm; Fri to 10 pm; Sat 4:30–10 pm; Sun brunch 11:30 am–2 pm. Closed Mon–Wed (mid-Sept–May). Bar. Semi-a la carte: dinner $8.95–$33. Sun brunch $12.95. Child's meals. Specializes in steak, seafood, prime rib. Salad bar. Fireplace. Deck overlooks Strawberry Creek. Cr cds: A, C, D, DS, MC, V.

[icon]

★ ★ **GASTROGNOME.** 54381 Ridgeview, adj to Bank of America. 909/659-5055. Hrs: 5–9 pm; Fri, Sat to 10 pm; Sun 4–9 pm. Res accepted. Bar. A la carte entrees: dinner $9.95–$26.95. Specializes in seafood, chicken, rack of lamb, steak. Parking. Outdoor dining. Cabin setting, fireplace, stained glass. Cr cds: MC, V.

Indio (J-5)

Founded: 1876 **Pop:** 36,793 **Elev:** 14 ft below sea level **Area code:** 619 **Zip:** 92201

Founded as a railroad construction camp, the town took its name from the large number of Indians nearby. Few settlers came until the All-American Canal and its 500 miles of pipeline turned the Coachella Valley into an area so fertile that it now produces 59 types of crops, including 95 percent of all American dates. The groves in the valley are the thickest in the Western Hemisphere. Today Indio is a marketing and transportation hub for this agricultural outpouring.

What to See and Do

1. All-American Canal. N, E & W of the city. Brings water 125 miles from Colorado River.

2. Salton Sea State Recreation Area (see). 24 mi S via CA 111 to nearest shoreline.

3. Joshua Tree National Monument (see). 25 mi E on I-10.

4. General George S. Patton Memorial Museum. 30 mi E on US 60, I-10, at Chiriaco Summit. Once the desert training headquarters on approximately 18,000 sq mi in the California, Arizona and Nevada deserts. Gen. Patton selected this site to prepare his soldiers for combat in North Africa. Patton memorabilia, artifacts; desert survival displays; natural science exhibits. (Daily; closed Thanksgiving, Dec 25) Sr citizen rate. Phone 227-3483. ¢¢

(For further information contact the Chamber of Commerce, 82-503 CA 111, PO Box TTT; 347-0676.)

Annual Event

National Date Festival. County Fairgrounds on CA 111 between Oasis & Arabia Sts. Fair and pageant done in Arabian Nights style. For schedule phone 863-8245. Mid–late Feb.

(See Desert Hot Springs, Idyllwild, Palm Desert, Palm Springs)

Motels

★★**BEST WESTERN DATE TREE.** *81-909 Indio Blvd. 619/347-3421.* 121 rms, 2 story. Jan–May: S $58–$70; D $64–$74; each addl $6; suites, kit. units $98–$128; studio rms $80–$110; under 12 free; wkly rates; higher rates special events; lower rates rest of yr. Crib $10. Pet accepted, some restrictions. TV; cable. Heated pool; whirlpool. Playground. Complimentary continental bkfst. Restaurant adj open 24 hrs. Ck-out noon. Coin lndry. Game rm. Lawn games. Refrigerators. Balconies. Picnic tables, grills. Surrounded by palm trees, cactus gardens. Cr cds: A, C, D, DS, ER, MC, V.

✔★**COMFORT INN.** *43-505 Monroe St. 619/347-4044; FAX 619/347-1287.* 63 rms, 2 story. Dec–May: S $49–$69; D $59–$80; under 12 free; higher rates: late Dec, Bob Hope Classic, Date Festival, Fri & Sat Dec–May; lower rates rest of yr. Crib $6. TV; cable. Heated pool; whirlpool. Restaurant adj open 24 hrs. Ck-out 11 am. Many refrigerators. Cr cds: A, C, D, DS, ER, MC, V, JCB.

Inverness (D-1)

Pop: 1,422 **Elev:** 20 ft **Area code:** 415 **Zip:** 94937

What to See and Do

1. Point Reyes National Seashore. HQ ½ mi W of Olema on Bear Valley Rd. More than 70,000 acres on Point Reyes peninsula. Shipwrecks and explorers, including Sir Francis Drake, who is believed to have landed here, brighten the history of this area; traders, whalers, fur hunters and ranchers followed. The weather is changeable—in winter, be prepared for rain in the inland areas; in summer, fog and brisk winds on the beaches. The area is especially beautiful during the spring flower season (Feb–July). Access is possible to most beaches; wading at Drakes Beach; surf fishing. There are more than 150 miles of trails to upland country. Picnic areas are scattered throughout the park. Four hike-in campgrounds with limited facilities (by reservation only); no pets exc at some Point Reyes beaches. Visitor center at Drakes Beach (Sat, Sun & hols); interpretive programs and information at Bear Valley HQ (daily). For tours of the Point Reyes Lighthouse, phone 669-

1534. Visitor area (Thurs–Mon). Park (daily). Guided tours. Contact Point Reyes National Seashore, Point Reyes 94956; 663-1092. **Free.**

2. Tomales Bay State Park. 3 mi NW on Sir Francis Drake Blvd, 2 mi N on Pierce Point Rd. Virgin groves of Bishop pine and more than 300 species of plants grow on 1,018 acres. Swimming, sand beach; fishing. Hiking. Picnicking. Standard fees. Phone 669-1140. Per vehicle day use ¢¢

3. Samuel P. Taylor State Park. 2 mi S on CA 1 to Olema, then 6 mi E on Sir Francis Drake Blvd. On 2,800 acres of wooded countryside with many groves of coastal redwoods. Historic paper mill site. Hiking and bridle trails. Picnicking. Camping (Mar–Oct, by reservation through Mistix only; rest of yr, first come, first served). Standard fees. Phone 488-9897. Per vehicle day use ¢¢

(See Bodega Bay, San Rafael)

Inns

★★**BLACKTHORNE.** *(Box 712) 266 Vallejo Ave, ¼ mi W off Sir Francis Drake Blvd. 415/663-8621.* 5 rms, 2 share bath, 4 story. S, D $105–$185. Children over 14 yrs only. Complimentary buffet bkfst. Ck-out 11 am, ck-in 4–7 pm. Whirlpool. Balconies. Rustic structure resembles tree house; decks on four levels; wooded canyon setting. Totally nonsmoking. Cr cds: MC, V.

★★**POINT REYES SEASHORE LODGE.** *(PO Box 39, Olema 94950, 10021 Coastal Hwy 1) 4 mi E on CA 1. 415/663-9000; res: 800/404-LODGE; FAX 415/663-9030.* 21 rms, 7 with shower only, 3 suites. No A/C. S, D $85–$130; each addl over 11 yrs $15; 5–12 yrs, $5; suites $160–$190; under 5 free. TV in sitting rm; cable. Complimentary continental bkfst, coffee. Restaurant adj 11:30 am–9 pm. Ck-out noon, ck-in 3–6 pm. Concierge. Bellhop. Rec rm. Many in-rm whirlpools, fireplaces. Some refrigerators, wet bars. Some balconies. Rustic; resembles turn-of-the-century lodge. Cr cds: A, DS, MC, V.

★★**TEN INVERNESS WAY.** *(Box 63) 10 Inverness Way. 415/669-1648.* 5 rms, 3 story. No rm phones. S $100–$120; D $110–$130; each addl $15; suite $150. Complimentary full bkfst, afternoon refreshments. Ck-out 11 am, ck-in noon–1 pm, 5–7 pm. Whirlpool. Refrigerator avail. Library. Antiques, handmade quilts. Tomales Bay 1 blk. Built 1904. Totally nonsmoking. Cr cds: MC, V.

Restaurants

★★**MANKA'S INVERNESS LODGE.** *30 Callendar Way, at Argyle St. 415/669-1034.* Hrs: 6–9 pm; Sun 5:30–8:30 pm. Closed Tues & Wed. Res accepted. Wine, beer. Semi-a la carte: dinner $15–$23. Child's meals. Specializes in fish, game, regional foods. Parking. Built as a hunting lodge (1917). Totally nonsmoking. Cr cds: MC, V.

★**STATION HOUSE CAFE.** *(11180 Main St, Point Reyes Station) Approx 4 mi E via CA 1. 415/663-1515.* Hrs: 8 am–9 pm; Fri & Sat to 10 pm. Closed Thanksgiving, Dec 25. Res accepted. Bar; Fri & Sat to 11 pm. A la carte entrees: bkfst $4–$7, lunch $6–$11. Semi-a la carte: dinner $9–$18. Entertainment Fri, Sat & hols. Patio dining. Roadhouse-style restaurant. Cr cds: MC, V.

Inyo National Forest (E-4 – F-4)

(Sections E and W of Bishop, via US 395)

In this 2,000,000-acre area are 6 wilderness areas: John Muir, Golden Trout, Ansel Adams, Boundry Peak, South Sierra and Hoover, with hundreds of lakes and streams. Impressive peaks include Mt Whitney (14,495 ft) and the famous Minarets, a series of jagged, uniquely weathered peaks in the Sierra Nevada. Devils Postpile National Monument (see) is also within the boundaries of the forest. The Ancient Bristlecone Pine Forest (4,600 years old), 600-million-year-old fossils, views of one of the world's great fault scarps (the eastern Sierra Nevada) and a unique high-elevation alpine desert (10,000–14,000 ft) are all east of US 395 in the White Mts. Palisade Glacier (the southernmost glacier in the US) is west of US 395 (west of the town of Big Pine), on the boundary of John Muir Wilderness Area and Kings Canyon National Park. There are 83 campgrounds; many of them are accessible to the disabled (inquire for details).

The Mammoth Lakes Area (see MAMMOTH LAKES) includes Mammoth Lakes Basin, Inyo Craters, Earthquake Fault, Hot Creek and many historic and archaeological features. Ranger naturalists conduct guided tours during the summer and offer ski tours during the winter; evening programs take place in the visitor center all year.

Deer, bear, tule elk, bighorn sheep, rainbow, brown and golden trout and a variety of birds abound in the forest. Swimming, fishing, hunting, boating, riding, picnicking, hiking, camping and pack trips are available. Winter sports include nordic skiing, snow play areas, snowmobiling and downhill skiing on Mammoth Mountain (see MAMMOTH LAKES) and June Mountain (see JUNE LAKE). For further information contact Forest Supervisor, 873 N Main St, Bishop 93514, phone 619/873-2400; or the White Mountain Ranger District Office, 798 N Main St, Bishop 93514, phone 619/873-2500.

(For accommodations see Bishop)

Irvine *

Pop: 110,330 **Elev:** 195 ft **Area code:** 714
3 mi SE of Costa Mesa (J-4) on I-405 (San Diego Frwy).

The land area the community of Irvine lies on was once the property of the Irvine Ranch. In the heart of Orange County, Irvine is a totally planned community.

What to See and Do

University of California, Irvine (1965). (17,000 students) 2 mi W of I-405, Culver Rd exit. Undergraduate, graduate and medical schools on 1,489-acre campus. Taped and guided tours of campus. Phone 856-5011. Tours of adj San Joaquin Freshwater Marsh by reservation; phone 856-5181.

(For further information contact the Chamber of Commerce, 17200 Jamboree Blvd, Ste A, 92714; 660-9112.)

(See Costa Mesa, Laguna Beach, Newport Beach, Santa Ana)

Motels

✔ ★★**BEST WESTERN IRVINE HOST.** *1717 E Dyer Rd (92705), off CA 55 E Dyer Rd exit. 714/261-1515; FAX 714/261-1265.* 150 rms, 2 story. S $58–$74; D $64–$84; each addl $8; suites $170–$255; under 12 free. Crib $5. TV; cable, in-rm movies. Pool; whirlpool. Restaurant 6 am–10 pm; Fri to 11 pm; Sat & Sun 7 am–10 pm. Bar 11:30 am–11 pm. Ck-out noon. Meeting rms. Bellhops. Sundries. Free airport, health club, South Coast Plaza transportation. Health club privileges. Private patios, balconies. Cr cds: A, C, D, DS, ER, MC, V, JCB.

★★**HOLIDAY INN.** *17941 Von Karman Ave (92714), I-405 MacArthur Blvd exit, near John Wayne Airport. 714/863-1999; FAX 714/474-7236.* 336 rms, 14 story. S, D $113–$128; each addl $14; suites $125–$250; family rates; lower rates wknds. Crib free. Pet accepted, some restrictions. TV; cable. Indoor pool; poolside serv. Restaurant 6

am–10 pm. Rm serv. Bar 11:30 am–midnight; entertainment Fri. Ck-out noon. Coin lndry. Convention facilities. Bellhops. Valet serv. Gift shop. Free airport transportation. Bicycle rentals. Exercise equipt; weight machine, treadmill, whirlpool, sauna. Health club privileges. Refrigerator in suites. Cr cds: A, C, D, DS, MC, V, JCB.

Motor Hotel

★★**AIRPORTER GARDEN HOTEL.** *18700 MacArthur Blvd (92715), ¼ mi S of I-405 MacArthur Blvd exit. 714/833-2770; res: 800/854-3012 (exc CA), 800/432-7018 (CA); FAX 714/757-1228.* 212 rms, 3 story. S, D $79–$109; suites $109–$250. Crib free. TV. Heated pool; poolside serv. Restaurant 6 am–midnight. Rm serv. Bar 10:30–2 am; entertainment, dancing. Ck-out noon. Meeting rms. Bellhops. Shopping arcade. Barber, beauty shop. Free airport transportation. Excercise rm; weight machines, weights. Wet bar in suites. Balconies. Cr cds: A, C, D, MC, V.

Hotels

★★★**EMBASSY SUITES.** *2120 Main St (92714), 1 blk NE of I-405 MacArthur Blvd exit. 714/553-8332; FAX 714/261-5301.* 293 suites, 10 story. S, D $119–$159; each addl $10; wkend rates. Crib free. TV; cable. Indoor pool; whirlpool. Complimentary full bkfst. Restaurant 11 am–2 pm, 5:30–10 pm. Bar to 11 pm. Ck-out 1 pm. Meeting rms. Gift shop. Free airport transportation. Refrigerators. Sun deck. Cr cds: A, C, D, DS, MC, V.

★★★**HYATT REGENCY IRVINE.** *17900 Jamboree Rd (92714), off I-405 Jamboree Rd exit, near John Wayne Airport. 714/975-1234; FAX 714/852-1574.* 536 rms, 14 story. S $119–$155; D $139–$180; each addl $25; suites $250–$5,000; family, wkend rates. Crib free. Pet accepted, some restrictions. TV; cable, in-rm movies. Heated pool; poolside serv. Restaurants 6 am–midnight. Rm serv 24 hrs. Bar 10:30–2 am; entertainment, dancing exc Sun. Ck-out 1 pm. Convention facilities. Concierge. Gift shop. Valet parking. Free airport transportation. Lighted tennis, pro. Golf privileges. Exercise equipt; weights, bicycles, whirlpool, sauna. Some refrigerators. Private patios, balconies. *LUXURY LEVEL:* REGENCY CLUB. 52 rms, 7 suites, 3 floors. S, D $155–$200. Private lounge. In-rm movies. Complimentary continental bkfst, refreshments.
Cr cds: A, C, D, DS, ER, MC, V, JCB.

★★★**MARRIOTT IRVINE.** *18000 Von Karman Ave (92715), off I-405 Jamboree Blvd exit, adj to Koll Center, near John Wayne Airport. 714/553-0100; FAX 714/261-7059.* 490 rms, 17 story. S, D $79–$160; suites $250–$650; under 18 free. Crib avail. Pet accepted, some restrictions. TV; cable. Indoor/outdoor pool; poolside serv. Restaurant 6 am–10 pm; Fri, Sat to 11 pm. Bars 11–2 am; entertainment, dancing. Ck-out noon. Convention facilities. Guest lndry. Gift shop. Barber. Valet parking. Free airport transportation. Lighted tennis. Golf privileges. Exercise equipt; weights, bicycles, whirlpool, sauna. Massage therapy. Refrigerators avail. Refrigerator in suites. Some private patios. *LUXURY LEVEL:* CONCIERGE LEVEL. 91 rms, 6 suites, 3 floors. S, D $149. Concierge. Private lounge. Bathrm phones. Complimentary continental bkfst, refreshments.
Cr cds: A, C, D, DS, ER, MC, V, JCB.

Restaurants

★★★**CHANTECLAIR.** *18912 MacArthur Blvd, ½ mi S of I-405, opp John Wayne Airport. 714/752-8001.* Hrs: 11:30 am–2:30 pm, 6–10 pm; Fri & Sat 6–11 pm; Sun 6–10 pm; Sun brunch 10:30 am–2:30 pm. Res accepted. French, continental cuisine. Bar. Wine list. A la carte entrees: lunch $7.95–$13.95, dinner $18–$36. *Prix fixe:* lunch $12. Sun champagne brunch $14.95–$22.95. Specialties: duck confit salad, veal chop with morels sauce, Belgian-chocolate-dipped strawberries. Own desserts. Pianist exc Wed. Valet parking. Outdoor dining (lunch). Wine tasting (Wed). French provincial decor. Several dining areas. Fireplaces; atrium; garden. Jacket (dinner). Cr cds: A, C, D, MC, V.

★★**GULLIVER'S.** *18482 MacArthur Blvd, off I-405 MacArthur Blvd exit, opp John Wayne Airport.* 714/833-8411. Hrs: 11:30 am–2:30 pm, 6–10 pm. Closed Dec 25. Res accepted. Bar. Semi-a la carte: lunch $6.25–$13.25, dinner $16.50–$25.50. Specializes in prime rib. Parking. English tavern atmosphere. Cr cds: A, D, DS, MC, V.

★★**McCORMICK & SCHMICK'S.** *2000 Main St, off I-405 MacArthur Blvd exit.* 714/756-0505. Hrs: 11:30 am–11 pm; Sat from 5 pm; Sun 5–10 pm. Res accepted. Bar. Semi-a la carte: lunch $4.95–$9.95, dinner $4.95–$19.95. Specializes in swordfish, salmon, halibut. Oyster bar. Entertainment exc Sun. Parking. Outdoor dining. Stained-glass windows; wildlife artwork. Cr cds: A, C, D, DS, MC, V.

Jackson (D-2)

Pop: 3,545 **Elev:** 1,235 ft **Area code:** 209 **Zip:** 95642

A Ranger District office of the Eldorado National Forest (see PLACERVILLE) is located in Jackson.

What to See and Do

1. **Amador County Museum.** 225 Church St. Exhibits pertaining to gold country displayed in 1859 house; tours of Kennedy Mine model exhibit (fee). (Wed–Sun; closed major hols) Phone 223-6386. **Free.**
2. **Indian Grinding Rock State Historic Park.** 11½ mi NE via CA 88, Pine Grove-Volcano Rd. Site of reconstructed Miwok village with Indian petroglyphs, bedrock mortars. Interpretive trail, picnicking; camping. Regional Indian museum. Standard fees. Phone 296-7488.

(See Lodi, Sacramento)

Motels

★★**BEST WESTERN AMADOR INN.** *(Box 758)* 200 S CA 49, SE of jct CA 49 & 88. 209/223-0211; FAX 209/223-4836. 118 rms, 2 story. S $48–$56; D $64–$74; each addl $8; kit. units $10 addl; under 12 free. Crib free. Pet accepted; $4. TV. Pool. Restaurant adj open 24 hrs. Bar 11–2 am. Ck-out noon. Meeting rms. Some refrigerators, fireplaces. Cr cds: A, C, D, DS, MC, V.

✔★**JACKSON HOLIDAY LODGE.** *(Box 1147)* 850 N CA 49. 209/223-0486. 36 rms, 2 story, 8 kits. S $40–$53; D $45–$58; each addl $5; kit. units $66. Crib $5. Pet accepted, some restrictions; $10. TV; cable. Pool. Complimentary continental bkfst. Complimentary coffee in rms. Ck-out noon. Cr cds: A, MC, V.

Inns

★★★**THE FOXES.** *(Box 159, 77 Main St, Sutter Creek 95685)* N on CA 49. 209/267-5882; FAX 209/267-0712. 6 rms, 1–2 story. No rm phones. S, D $95–$135; 2-night min wkends. TV avail. Complimentary full bkfst in rms or garden. Ck-out 11 am, ck-in 3–6 pm. Covered parking.

Former Brinn House, built during the Gold Rush (1857). Antique furnishings. Totally nonsmoking. Cr cds: DS, MC, V.

★★**GATE HOUSE.** *1330 Jackson Gate Rd.* 209/223-3500; res: 800/726-4667 (CA). 5 air-cooled rms, 1–2 story, 1 cottage. S, D $85–$120; suite $120; higher rates Fri & Sat. Children over 12 yrs only. Pool. Complimentary full bkfst. Restaurant adj. Ck-out 11 am, ck-in 2:30 pm. Some fireplaces. Victorian architecture and furnishings. Built 1903. Beautiful gardens. Totally nonsmoking. Cr cds: DS, MC, V.

★★★**GOLD QUARTZ.** *(15 Bryson Dr, Sutter Creek 95685)* N on CA 49. 209/267-9155; res: 800/752-8738; FAX 209/267-9170. 24 rms, 2 story. S, D $75–$125; each addl $25; suites $125; lower rates avail. TV; cable. Complimentary full bkfst, coffee & afternoon tea. Ck-out noon, ck-in 3 pm. Many balconies. Sitting rm; antiques. Victorian/Queen Anne-style inn. Totally nonsmoking. Cr cds: A, MC, V.

★★**HANFORD HOUSE.** *(Box 1450, 61 Hanford St, Sutter Creek 95685)* N on CA 49. 209/267-0747. 9 rms, 2 story. S, D $65–$110. Complimentary bkfst, refreshments. Restaurant adj. Ck-out 11 am, ck-in 2:30 pm. Rooftop deck; shaded patio. Totally nonsmoking. Cr cds: DS, MC, V.

★★**SUTTER CREEK.** *(Box 385, 75 Main St, Sutter Creek 95685)* 4 mi N on CA 49. 209/267-5606. 18 rms, 1–2 story. No rm phones. S, D $50–$135; each addl $25; 2-day min wkends Feb–Dec. Children over 14 yrs only. Complimentary full bkfst. Ck-out 11 am, ck-in 2:30 pm. Some fireplaces. 1859 house; many antiques. Landscaped grounds; gardens. No cr cds accepted.

★★★**WEDGEWOOD INN.** *11941 Narcissus Rd, 7 mi W of jct CA 88 & Clinton-Irishtown Rd; recommend phone for directions from Jackson.* 209/296-4300; res: 800/933-4393. 6 rms, 1–2 story. No rm phones. S $75–$110; D $85–$130. Children over 12 yrs only. Complimentary full bkfst, coffee, tea. Ck-out 11 am, ck-in 3–6 pm. Lawn games. Some balconies. Picnic tables. Extensively furnished with antiques. Landscaped gardens; gazebo. Victorian replica building in scenic Sierra foothills. Totally nonsmoking. Cr cds: MC, V.

Restaurant

✔★★**PELARGONIUM.** *(51 Hanford St, Sutter Creek 95685)* N on CA 49. 209/267-5008. Hrs: 5:30–9 pm. Closed Sun; Thanksgiving, Dec 25; also late Jan–1st 2 wks Feb. Res accepted; required Fri, Sat. Wine, beer. Semi-a la carte: dinner $13.95–$16.95. Child's meals. Specialties: roast leg of lamb, stuffed pork chops. In converted residence; antiques. Totally nonsmoking. No cr cds accepted.

Joshua Tree National Monument (J-5)

(Entrances: 25 mi E of Indio on I-10 or S of Joshua Tree, Yucca Valley and Twentynine Palms on CA 62)

Covering more than 870 square miles, this monument preserves a section of two deserts: the Mojave and the Colorado. Particularly notable is the variety and richness of desert vegetation. The monument shelters many species of desert plants. The Joshua tree, which gives the monument its name, was christened thus by the Mormons because of its upstretched "arms." A member of the agave family, this giant yucca attains heights of more than 30 feet. The area consists of a series of block mountains, ranging in altitude from 1,000 to 6,000 feet and separated by desert flats. The summer gets very hot, and the temperature drops below freezing in the winter. Water is available only at the Black Rock Canyon Visitor Center/Campground, Cottonwood Campground, the Indian Cove Ranger Station and the Twentynine Palms Visitor Center. Pets on leash only; pets are not permitted on trails. Guided tours and campfire programs (Feb–Apr & Oct–Dec). Picnicking permitted in designated areas and campgrounds, but no fires may be built outside the campgrounds (see #7). For additional information contact 74485 National Monument Dr, Twentynine Palms 92277; 619/367-7511.

What to See and Do

1. **Oasis Visitor Center.** Monument HQ, just N of monument at Twentynine Palms entrance. Exhibits; self-guided nature trail through the Oasis of Mara, discovered by a government survey party in 1855. (Daily; closed Dec 25)

2. **Fortynine Palms Canyon.** Trail head 6 miles west of Oasis Visitor Center on Canyon Rd. Reached by 1½-mile trail, this is another beautiful California fan palm oasis. Day use only. (Oct–May)

3. **Lost Palms Canyon.** Reached by 4-mile trail from Cottonwood Spring. Shelters largest group of palms (120) in monument. Day use only.

4. **Hidden Valley Nature Trail.** One-mile loop; access from picnic area across Hidden Valley Campground. Valley enclosed by wall of rocks.

5. **Keys View** (5,185 ft). Sweeping view of Coachella valley, desert and mountain. A foot trail leads off the main road.

6. **Stands of Joshua trees.** In Queen and Lost Horse valleys.

7. **Camping.** Restricted to eight campgrounds with limited facilities; bring own firewood and water. 30-day limit, July–Sept; 14-day limit rest of yr. Cottonwood and Black Rock Canyon Campgrounds (fee); other campgrounds free. Campgrounds are operated on a first come first served basis except for Black Rock Canyon; for reservations phone Mistix, 800/365-2267 (Joshua Tree Code 5674.)

(See Desert Hot Springs, Indio, Palm Desert)

Motels

★★**BEST WESTERN GARDENS.** *(71-487 Twentynine Palms Hwy, Twentynine Palms 92277) E on CA 62.* 619/367-9141. 72 rms, 2 story, 8 kit. suites. S $54–$62; D $58–$66; each addl $8; kit. suites $84–$100; under 12 free. Crib free. TV. Heated pool; whirlpool. Complimentary continental bkfst. Restaurant nearby. Ck-out noon. Meeting rms. Refrigerator in suites. Grills. Cr cds: A, C, D, DS, MC, V.

★★**CIRCLE C.** *(6340 El Rey Ave, Twentynine Palms 92277) E on CA 62.* 619/367-7615; res: 800/545-9696; FAX 619/361-0247. 11 kit. units. S $80; D $95; each addl $25. TV; in-rm movies. Heated pool; whirlpool. Continental bkfst. Restaurant nearby. Ck-out 11 am. Meeting rm. Refrigerators. Picnic tables, grills. Cr cds: A, C, D, MC, V.

✔★**DESERT VIEW.** *(57471 Primrose Dr, Yucca Valley 92284) W on CA 62.* 619/365-9706. 14 rms. S $36.50–$39.50; D $39.50–$45.50; each addl $5; under 12 free. Crib free. TV; cable. Pool. Complimentary coffee in rms. Restaurant nearby. Ck-out 11 am. Cr cds: A, DS, MC, V.

June Lake (E-3)

Pop: 425 (est) **Elev:** 7,600 ft **Area code:** 619 **Zip:** 93529

What to See and Do

June Mountain Ski Area. W of US 395. 5 double chairlifts; 2 detachable quad chairlifts, 1 high-speed tram; patrol, school, rentals; snow boarding; cafeteria, bar; day care center. (Mid-Nov–Apr, daily) Longest run 2½ mi; vertical drop 2,590 ft. Half-day rates avail. Phone 934-2224.

(See Lee Vining, Mammoth Lakes)

Motel

★**BOULDER LODGE.** *(Box 68) 2 mi W of US 395 on CA 158.* 619/648-7533; FAX 619/648-7330. 32 rms, 3 story, 8 suites, 16 kits., 10 cabins. No rm phones. No A/C. S, D $48–$75; each addl $8–$10; suites $85–$230; kit. units $75–$160; cabins $50–$102; 5-bedrm house $300; wkly rates; ski plans; wkday rates in winter; higher rates: Aug–Labor Day & hols. Crib $8. TV; cable. Indoor pool; whirlpool, sauna. Playground. Restaurant nearby. Ck-out 11 am. Tennis. Downhill/x-country ski 5 mi. Game rm. Fish cleaning & freezing facilities. On June Lake. Cr cds: A, DS, MC, V.

Restaurant

★★**SIERRA INN.** *2 mi W on US 395.* 619/648-7774. Hrs: 5–10 pm. Closed Halloween–Thanksgiving & Easter to opening day of fishing season. Res accepted. Bar 5 pm–midnight. Semi-a la carte: dinner $6.95–$18.95. Buffet: dinner (Sat) $13.95. Child's meals. Specializes in steak, fresh seafood. Salad bar. Parking. View of mountains, lake. Cr cds: A, DS, MC, V.

SC

Kernville (G-4)

Pop: 1,656 **Elev:** 2,650 ft **Area code:** 619 **Zip:** 93238

A Ranger District office of the Sequoia National Forest (see PORTERVILLE) is located in Kernville. Trout fishing is enjoyed in nearby Kern River.

What to See and Do

1. **Isabella Lake.** S of town. Swimming, waterskiing; fishing; boating (marinas). More than 700 improved campsites with showers, rest rms (fee/site/night). Camp 9 & Auxiliary (primitive) camp areas (free). For information contact Sequoia National Forest, Lake Isabella Visitors Center, PO Box 3810, Lake Isabella, 93240-3810; 379-5646 or 376-3781.

2. **Greenhorn Mountain Park.** 12 mi W via CA 155 in Sequoia National Forest. Park has 90 campsites with barbecue pits, 115 picnic tables, camping supplies. Camping limited to 21 days, no reservations; pets on leash only. Phone 805/861-2345. Camping ¢¢¢¢

(For further information contact the Chamber of Commerce, 11447 Kernville Rd, PO Box 397; 376-2629.)

Annual Events

Whiskey Flat Days. Gold Rush days celebration. Mid- or late Feb.

Kernville Rod Run. Show for pre-1949 cars. 1st full wknd Oct.

Kernville Stampede. Usually Oct.

Motels

★**HI-HO RESORT LODGE.** *(Rte 1, Box 21) 11901 Sierra Way, 1 mi S on Kern River.* 619/376-2671. 8 air-cooled kit. cottages. No rm phones. S, D $60–$90; each addl $5; kit. units $10 addl; wkly rates. Crib $5. TV; cable. Heated pool; whirlpool. Playground. Ck-out 11 am. Coin lndry. Downhill/x-country ski 15 mi. Rec rm. Fireplaces. Picnic tables, grills. Cr cds: MC, V.

★★**WHISPERING PINES LODGE.** *(Rte 1, Box 41) 13745 Sierra Way.* 619/376-3733; FAX 619/376-3735. 11 rms, 7 kit. units. S, D $69–$129; each addl $10; kit. units $95–$99. Crib free. TV; cable, in-rm movies. Pool. Bkfst 8–10 am. Complimentary coffee in rms. Ck-out 11 am. Sundries. Gift shop. Many fireplaces. Balconies. Picnic tables, grills. On river. Totally nonsmoking. Cr cds: A, D, MC, V.

Inn

★★**KERN RIVER INN.** *(PO Box 1725) 119 Kern River Dr, opp Riverside Park.* 619/376-6750. 6 rms, 2 story. No rm phones. Apr–Oct: S $69–$79; D $79–$89; lower rates rest of yr. TV in sitting rm; cable. Complimentary full bkfst, afternoon refreshments. Restaurant nearby. Ck-out 11 am, ck-in 3–6 pm. Downhill/x-country ski 15 mi. Reproduction of 1900s Victorian home; fireplace in some rms. Located on scenic Kern River. Totally nonsmoking. Cr cds: C, D, MC, V, JCB.

Restaurants

★**JOHNNY McNALLY'S FAIRVIEW LODGE.** *(Star Rte, Box 95) 15 mi N on Kern River.* 619/376-2430. Hrs: 5–10 pm; Sun from 4 pm. Closed wkdays Nov–Mar. Bar 4:30 pm–2 am. Semi-a la carte: dinner $7.50–$27.95. Child's meals. Specializes in steak. Parking. Western decor. Hamburger stand mid-Apr–Sept, lunch. Cr cds: MC, V.

★**McDOWALL'S COUNTRY GOURMET.** *9 Big Blue Rd, opp park.* 619/376-3324. Hrs: 7 am–5 pm; Fri, Sat to 10 pm. Closed Nov–Apr 15. Wine, beer. Semi-a la carte: bkfst $5.95–$6.95, lunch $4.95–$8.95, dinner $9.95–$21.95. Child's meals. Specializes in steak, chicken, seafood. Outdoor dining. In restored log cabin building (ca 1920); gift shop. Totally nonsmoking. Cr cds: MC, V.

King City (F-2)

Pop: 7,634 **Elev:** 330 ft **Area code:** 408 **Zip:** 93930

What to See and Do

1. **Mission San Antonio de Padua.** 24 mi SW on County G14 in Jolon. Founded in 1771 as the third in the chain of missions. Restoration includes gristmill, waterwheel, wine vat; tannery; museum; Padres Garden. (Daily) Phone 385-4478. ¢

2. **Los Padres National Forest.** W of town is the forest's northernmost section. Contains the Santa Lucia Mts, which feature the southernmost groves of coastal redwoods and the only natural stands of bristlecone fir. The 164,575-acre Ventana Wilderness was almost completely burned in a 1977 fire, but vegetation in the fire area reestablished itself and provides an excellent opportunity to witness the changing conditions. Fishing. Hiking. Camping. For further information contact the District Ranger Office, 406 S Mildred, phone 385-5434; or the Forest Supervisor, 6144 Calle Real, Goleta 93117, phone 805/683-6711. (See SANTA BARBARA) Campground ¢¢¢

Annual Event

Mission San Antonio de Padua Fiesta. (See #1) Special Mass and music, barbecue, dancing. 2nd Sun June.

Motels

★**COURTESY INN.** *4 Broadway Circle, off US 101 Broadway exit.* 408/385-4646; res: 800/350-5616; FAX 408/385-6024. 64 rms, 35 suites. S $48–$56; D $51–$64; each addl $6; suites $59–$94; under 16 free. Crib free. Pet accepted, some restrictions; $10. TV; in-rm movies. Pool; whirlpool. Complimentary continental bkfst. Coffee in rms. Restaurant adj open 24 hrs. Ck-out noon. Coin lndry. Meeting rm. Refrigerators; whirlpool in suites. Cr cds: A, D, DS, MC, V.

✔★**KEEFER'S INN.** *615 Canal St.* 408/385-4843. 48 rms, 2 story. S $45–$48; D $48–$53; each addl $5; under 16 free. Crib $5. TV; cable. Pool; whirlpool. Complimentary continental bkfst to 11 am. Restaurant 7 am–10 pm. Ck-out 11 am. Coin lndry. Refrigerators. Cr cds: A, D, MC, V.

Kings Canyon National Park

(see Sequoia & Kings Canyon National Parks)

Laguna Beach (J-4)

Pop: 23,170 **Elev:** 40 ft **Area code:** 714

Artists have contributed to the quaint charm of this seaside town. Curio, arts and crafts and antique shops make leisurely strolling a pleasure. There is swimming and surfing at beautiful beaches.

What to See and Do

Laguna Playhouse. 606 Laguna Canyon Rd. Theater company presents dramas, comedies, musicals, children's theater. (Sept–June, daily exc Mon; closed Jan 1, Dec 25) Phone 494-8021 (afternoons) for schedule.

(For further information contact the Chamber of Commerce, 357 Glenneyre St, PO Box 396, 92652; 494-1018.)

Annual Event

Winter Festival. Artisans' fair, art exhibits, other events. Phone 494-1018. Late Feb or early Mar.

Seasonal Events

Festival of Arts & Pageant of the Masters. 650 Laguna Canyon Rd. All pageant seats reserved. Exhibits by 160 artists; *tableaux vivants;* entertainment; restaurant. Grounds: daily. For information on ticket prices and reservations, contact festival box office, phone 800/487-FEST. July–Aug.

Sawdust Festival. 935 Laguna Canyon Rd. Nearly 200 Laguna Beach artists showcase their work. Phone 494-3030. Daily, July–Aug.

(See Costa Mesa, Irvine, Newport Beach, San Juan Capistrano)

Motels

★ ★ BEN BROWN'S ALISO CREEK INN. 31106 S Coast Hwy (92677) 2 blks E of Pacific Coast Hwy. 714/499-2271; res: 800/223-3309. 62 suites, 1–2 story. No A/C. July–Aug: S, D $108–$172; each addl $10; lower rates rest of yr. Crib $5. TV; cable. Heated pool; wading pool. Restaurant 8 am–10 pm. Bar to 2 am; entertainment, dancing Fri–Sat. Ck-out noon. Coin lndry. Meeting rms. 9-hole golf, pro, putting green. Private patios, balconies. In secluded area of Aliso Canyon. Near ocean; fishing pier. Cr cds: A, MC, V.

D 🐕 ⊉ 🕐 SC

★ ★ BEST WESTERN LAGUNA REEF INN. 30806 S Coast Hwy (92651). 714/499-2227 or -3775. 43 rms, 2 story, 21 kits. Early July–mid-Sept: S, D $84–$94; each addl $10; suites, kit. units $95; wkly rates; lower rates rest of yr. TV; cable, in-rm movies. Heated pool; whirlpool, sauna. Complimentary continental bkfst. Restaurant nearby. Ck-out noon. Meeting rm. Some refrigerators. Botanical garden. Cr cds: A, C, D, DS, ER, MC, V.

⊉ 🚫 🕐

✔ ★ LAGUNA RIVIERA BEACH RESORT & SPA. 825 S Coast Hwy (92651). 714/494-1196. 41 rms, 5 story, 20 kits. No elvtr. No A/C. Mid-June–mid-Sept: S, D $72–$170; each addl $10; suites $89–$170; studio rms, kit. units $81–$158; lower rates rest of yr. Crib $5. TV; cable. Indoor pool; whirlpool, sauna. Complimentary continental bkfst. Afternoon tea (winter). Restaurant nearby. Ck-out noon. Rec rm. Some fireplaces. Balconies. Picnic tables. Sun decks, terraces. Oceanfront. Cr cds: A, C, D, DS, MC, V.

⊉ 🕐

✔ ★ SEACLIFF. 1661 S Coast Hwy (92651). 714/494-9717. 25 rms, 2 story, 4 kits. Memorial Day wkend–mid-Sept: S, D $65–$130; each addl $10; kit. units $95–$165; lower rates rest of yr. Crib $2.50. TV. Heated pool. Complimentary continental bkfst. Ck-out noon. Some balconies. Sun deck. Ocean view. Ocean ¼ blk. Cr cds: A, C, D, DS, MC, V.

⊉ 🕐 SC

✔ ★ TRAVELODGE LAKE FOREST. (23150 Lake Center Dr, El Toro 92630) 1½ blks E of I-5, Lake Forest Rd exit. 714/830-1000; FAX 714/830-4447. 124 rms, 2–3 story. Mid-June–mid-Sept: S $50; D $60; each addl $6; under 17 free; lower rates rest of yr. Crib free. TV; cable, in-rm movies avail. Heated pool; whirlpool. Complimentary coffee in rms. Restaurant nearby. Ck-out noon. Meeting rms. Health club privileges. Game rm. Cr cds: A, C, D, DS, ER, MC, V, JCB.

D ⊉ 🚫 🕐 SC

Motor Hotels

✔ ★ ★ COURTYARD BY MARRIOTT. (23175 Avenida de la Carlota, Laguna Hills 92653) I-5, Lake Forest Dr exit to Carlota. 714/859-5500; FAX 714/454-2158. 137 rms, 5 story. S $49–$79; D $49–$89; suites $80–$107. Crib free. TV; cable. Heated pool; whirlpool. Playground. Complimentary coffee in rms. Restaurant 6:30–11 am. Rm serv. Bar. Ck-out 1 pm. Coin lndry. Meeting rms. Valet serv. Refrigerator in suites. Balconies. Cr cds: A, D, DS, MC, V.

D ⊉ 🚫 🕐

★ ★ HOLIDAY INN. (25205 La Paz Rd, Laguna Hills 92653) E of Laguna Beach; I-5 La Paz Rd exit. 714/586-5000; FAX 714/581-7410. 147 rms, 4 story. S $69–$99; D $79–$109; each addl $10; under 19 free. Crib free. TV. Pool; poolside serv. Restaurant 6 am–3 pm, 5–10 pm. Rm serv. Bar; entertainment Tues–Sat. Ck-out 1 pm. Meeting rms. Bellhops. Valet serv. Free airport transportation. Cr cds: A, C, D, DS, MC, V, JCB.

D ⊉ 🚫 🕐 SC

★ ★ HOTEL ST. MAARTEN. 696 S Coast Hwy (92651). 714/494-1001; res: 800/228-5691; FAX 714/497-7107. 55 rms, 3 story. No elvtr. June–Sept: S $89; D $99; each addl $10; suites $169; higher rates

special events; lower rates rest of yr. TV; in-rm movies avail. Heated pool; sauna. Complimentary continental bkfst. Restaurant nearby. Bar. Ck-out noon. Meeting rm. Private patios. Opp beach. Cr cds: A, C, D, DS, MC, V.

⊉ 🕐 SC

★ ★ ★ INN AT LAGUNA BEACH. 211 N Coast Hwy (92651). 714/497-9722; res: 800/544-4479; FAX 714/497-9972. 70 rms, 5 story. July–Labor Day: S, D $139–$299; each addl $20; under 16 free; wkday rates; lower rates rest of yr. Crib free. TV; cable, in-rm movies. Heated pool. Complimentary continental bkfst. Restaurant adj 8 am–10 pm. Ck-out noon. Meeting rms. Bellhops. Minibars. Some private balconies. On ocean; beach. Cr cds: A, C, D, MC, V.

D ⊉ 🕐 🕐 SC

★ ★ VACATION VILLAGE. (Box 66) 647 S Coast Hwy (92651). 714/494-8566; res: 800/843-6895; FAX 714/494-1386. 133 rms in 5 buildings, 3–5 story, 70 kits. July–Labor Day (2-day min): S, D $80–$195; each addl $10; suites $175–$285; kit. units $95–$205; family, wkly rates Oct–Memorial Day; winter wkends (2-day min); some lower rates rest of yr. Crib $10. Pet accepted, some restrictions; $10. TV; cable. 2 heated pools; whirlpool. Complimentary coffee in rms. Restaurant 8 am–10 pm. Bar. Ck-out 11 am. Meeting rm. Bellhops. Some covered parking. Game rm. Many refrigerators. Some balconies. Sun deck. On beach. Cr cds: A, C, D, DS, MC, V.

🐕 ⊉ 🕐 SC

Hotels

★ ★ HILTON DANA POINT. (34402 Pacific Coast Hwy, Dana Point 92629) Approx 5 mi S on Coast Hwy. 714/661-1100; FAX 714/489-0628. 200 suites, 4 story. S, D $99–$165; each addl $15; children free. Crib avail. Valet parking $3. TV; in-rm movies. Heated pool. Complimentary continental bkfst. Restaurant 7 am–11 pm. Bar 4 pm–1 am; entertainment Fri & Sat. Ck-out noon. Meeting rms. Concierge. Gift shop. Exercise rm; instructor, weight machine, bicycles, whirlpool, sauna. Game rm. Refrigerators, wet bars. Balconies. Resort atmosphere. Opp swimming beach. Cr cds: A, C, D, DS, ER, MC, V, JCB.

D ⊉ 🏋 🚫 🕐 SC

★ ★ HOTEL LAGUNA. 425 S Coast Hwy (92651). 714/494-1151; FAX 714/497-2163. 66 rms, 5 story. No A/C. June–Labor Day: S, D $80–$130; each addl $10; under 12 free; lower rates rest of yr. TV; in-rm movies avail. Complimentary continental bkfst. Restaurant 7 am–10 pm. Bar 10–2 am; entertainment, dancing. Ck-out noon. Meeting rms. Barber, beauty shop. On ocean; private beach. Cr cds: A, C, D, DS, MC, V.

⊉ 🕐

★ ★ ★ SURF & SAND. 1555 S Coast Hwy (92651). 714/497-4477; res: 800/524-8621; FAX 714/494-7653. 157 rms, 9 story. No A/C. Late May–Oct: S, D $200–$295; suites $475–$675; lower rates rest of yr. Crib avail. TV. Heated pool; poolside serv. Restaurant 7 am–10:30 pm. Bar 11–2 am; pianist. Ck-out noon. Meeting rms. Concierge. Shopping arcade. Beauty shop. Covered parking, valet. Refrigerators, minibars. Private patios; balcony rms overlook ocean. On beach. Cr cds: A, C, D, MC, V.

D ⊉ 🚫 🕐

Inns

★ ★ BLUE LANTERN INN. (34343 Street of the Blue Lantern, Dana Point 92629) S on Coast Hwy, Blue Lantern exit. 714/661-1304; FAX 714/496-1483. 29 units, 3 story, 3 suites. S, D $135–$200; each addl $15; suites $250–$350; under 5 free; package plans; some lower rates mid-wk. Crib free. TV; cable. Complimentary full gourmet bkfst, coffee, tea, wine. Restaurant opp 11 am–11 pm. Ck-out noon, ck-in 3 pm. Bellhops. Concierge. Exercise equipt; weight machine, treadmill. In-rm whirlpools. Antiques. Fireplaces. Many rms have sunken sitting areas and most have private sun decks. Picnic tables. Located on a bluff overlooking yacht harbor; some rms have view of the coast. Park adj. Totally nonsmoking. Cr cds: A, MC, V.

★**CASA LAGUNA INN.** *2510 S Coast Hwy (92651). 714/ 494-2996.* 21 rms, 3 story, 5 kit. suites. S, D $105–$120; each addl $20; suites $150–$225; under 14 free; mid-wk, wkly rates. Crib $15. TV; cable. Heated pool. Continental bkfst. Wine, tea, refreshments 4:30–6 pm. Ck-out 11 am, ck-in 2 pm. Concierge. Some refrigerators. Balconies. Elaborate grounds; garden. Spanish architecture, individually decorated rms. Panoramic ocean views. Cr cds: A, C, D, DS, MC, V.

★**EILER'S INN.** *741 S Coast Hwy (92651). 714/494-3004.* 11 rms, 2 story. No A/C. No rm phones. Memorial Day–Sept: S $100–$170; D $100–$175; each addl $20. Continental bkfst, wine & cheese. Ck-out noon, ck-in 2 pm. Limited parking. Entertainment Sat in courtyard. Library, den; antiques. Central courtyard with flowers, tiered fountain. Cr cds: A, MC, V.

Resorts

★★**DANA POINT.** *(25135 Park Lantern, Dana Point 92629) 3 mi S on Coast Hwy. 714/661-5000; res: 800/533-9748; FAX 714/661-5358.* 341 rms, 3 & 4 story. S $170–$280; D $190–$300; suites $300–$1,200; under 18 free; wkend, whale-watching packages. Crib free. TV; cable. 2 heated pools; poolside serv. Supervised child's activities. Restaurant 6 am–11 pm. Picnics. Rm serv to 2 am. Bar 11–2 am; entertainment, dancing Fri & Sat. Ck-out noon, ck-in 3 pm. Grocery, package store ¼ mi. Coin lndry ½ mi. Convention facilities. Bellhops. Valet serv. Concierge. Gift shop. Free transportation to marina area. Sports dir. Lighted tennis, pro. Golf privileges, greens fee $50–$95, pro, putting green, driving range. Bicycles (rentals). Lawn games. Soc dir. Exercise rm; instructor, weight machine, bicycles, whirlpool, sauna. Refrigerators, minibars; some wet bars. Balconies. Opp beach. City park and children's playground adj. Located on the cliffs above the bay, with 42 acres of lawn and parkland. Cr cds: A, C, D, DS, MC, V.

★★★★**THE RITZ-CARLTON, LAGUNA NIGUEL.** *(33533 Ritz Carlton Dr, Dana Point 92629) 5 mi SW of I-5 Crown Valley Pkwy exit, 1 mi S on CA 1. 714/240-2000; res: 800/241-3333; FAX 714/240-0829.* 393 rms, 4 story, 31 suites. S, D $195–$450; each addl $50; suites $700–$2,500; under 18 free. Crib free. Valet parking $15. TV; cable, in-rm movies. 2 pools, heated; poolside serv. Supervised child's activities (mid-June–Aug). Restaurant 6:30 am–midnight (also see THE DINING ROOM); afternoon tea in library 2:30–5 pm. Rm serv 24 hrs. Bars; entertainment, dancing. Ck-out noon, ck-in 3 pm. Convention facilities. Bellhops. Valet serv. Concierge. Shopping arcade. Barber, beauty shop. International currency exchange. Airport transportation. Tennis, pro. 18-hole golf, greens fee Mon–Thurs $85, wkends $100, pro, putting green. Swimming beach. Lawn games. 2-mi bicycle path. Exercise rm; instructor, weights, bicycles, sauna, steam rm. Massage. Bathrm phones, refrigerators, minibars; fireplace in some suites. Balconies. Mediterranean villa-style resort on a 200-ft bluff overlooking the Pacific Ocean. Shuttle serv down to 2-mi beach. *LUXURY LEVEL:* RITZ-CARLTON CLUB. 27 rms, 11 suites. S, D $295–$450; suites $800–$2,500. Private lounge, honor bar. Whirlpool in some suites. Complimentary continental bkfst, refreshments. Cr cds: A, C, D, DS, MC, V.

Restaurants

★**THE BEACH HOUSE.** *619 Sleepy Hollow Lane, adj to Vacation Village. 714/494-9707.* Hrs: 8 am–10:30 pm. Closed Thanksgiving, Dec 25. Res accepted. No A/C. Bar from 10 am. Semi-a la carte: bkfst $4.95–$9.95, lunch $5.95–$12.95, dinner $9.95–$23.95. Child's meals. Specializes in fresh fish, seafood, steak. Oyster bar. Outdoor dining. On beach; view of ocean. Cr cds: A, MC, V.

★**CEDAR CREEK INN.** *384 Forest Ave. 714/497-8696.* Hrs: 11–12:30 am; Sun brunch to 3 pm. Closed Jan 1, July 4, Thanksgiving, Dec 24 & 25. Res required. Bar. A la carte entrees: lunch $5.95–$9.95. Semi-a la carte: dinner $5.95–$21.95. Sun brunch $5.95–$8.95. Child's meals. Specializes in pasta, prime rib, fresh fish. Own desserts. Entertainment. Parking. Old World atmosphere; skylit ceilings, stained-glass windows, murals of ocean scenes, stone fireplace. Cr cds: A, MC, V.

★★★★**THE DINING ROOM.** *(See The Ritz-Carlton, Laguna Niguel Resort) 714/240-2000.* Hrs: 6–10 pm. Closed Sun & Mon. Res accepted. Contemporary Mediterranean cuisine. *Prix fixe* dinners: 2-course $35, 3-course $42, 4-course $45, 5-course $53, 5-course with wines $80. Valet parking. Elegant decor; oil paintings, antiques. Jacket. Cr cds: A, C, D, DS, MC, V.

★★**KACHINA.** *222 Forest Ave. 714/497-5546.* Hrs: 5:30–10 pm; Fri & Sat to 11 pm; Sun brunch 10:30 am–2:30 pm. Closed Thanksgiving, Dec 25. Res accepted. Southwestern menu. Wine, beer. A la carte entrees: dinner $14–$22. Sun brunch $14.95. Specialties: red corn & chicken taquitos, sweet corn & grilled shrimp tamale, filet of salmon grilled in corn husk. Outdoor dining. Southwestern decor; Native American artwork. Cr cds: A, C, D, MC, V.

★★**LAS BRISAS DE LAGUNA.** *361 Cliff Dr. 714/497-5434.* Hrs: 8 am–3:30 pm, 5–10 pm; Sun 4–10 pm; Sun brunch 9 am–3 pm. Closed Thanksgiving, Dec 25. Res accepted. Mexican, continental menu. Bar 11–1 am. Buffet: bkfst $6.95. Semi-a la carte: lunch $6.95–$11.95, dinner $8.95–$22. Sun brunch $16.75. Specialties: playa del sole, filete de calamar, fresh seafood. Valet parking. Overlooks ocean. Cr cds: A, C, D, DS, MC, V.

★★**PARTNERS BISTRO & TERRACE.** *448 S Coast Hwy. 714/497-4441.* Hrs: 11:30 am–3 pm, 6–10 pm; Fri & Sat to 11 pm; Sun brunch 10:30 am–3 pm. Res accepted. No A/C. California menu. Wine, beer. A la carte entrees: lunch $3.95–$10, dinner $6.95–$16.95. Sun brunch $3.95–$11. Child's meals. Specialties: scallops with angel hair pasta, fresh seafood baked in paper. Terrace dining. Cr cds: A, MC, V.

✔★**REUBEN'S.** *(24001 Avenida de la Carlota, Laguna Hills) Just W of I-5, El Toro Rd exit. 714/830-9010.* Hrs: 11:30 am–3 pm, 4–10 pm; Sun from 4 pm; Sun brunch 10 am–2 pm. Res accepted. Bar to midnight; Sun, Mon to 10 pm. Semi-a la carte: lunch $5.99–$10.99, dinner $10.99–$19.99. Sun brunch $13.99. Specializes in prime rib, fresh fish, steak. Parking. Cr cds: A, C, D, MC, V, JCB.

✔★**SAN SHI GO.** *1100 S Coast Hwy, 303. 714/494-1551.* Hrs: 11:30 am–2 pm, 5–10 pm; Fri & Sat to 11 pm; Sun 5–9:30 pm. Closed July 4, Dec 25. Res accepted. No A/C. Japanese menu. Wine, beer. A la carte entrees: lunch $4.75–$10.95, dinner $7.95–$16.95. Specializes in sushi. Parking. Ocean view. Cr cds: A, DS, MC, V.

★★**TAVERN BY THE SEA.** *2007 S Coast Hwy. 714/497-6568.* Hrs: 5–11 pm. Closed Dec 25. Res accepted. Bar to 1 am. A la carte entrees: dinner $9.95–$18.95. Specializes in seafood, pasta. Parking. English tavern atmosphere. View of ocean. Cr cds: A, D, MC, V.

La Habra *

Pop: 51,266 **Elev:** 298 ft **Area code:** 310 **Zip:** 90631
Just N of Fullerton (J-4) on CA 72 (Harbor Blvd).

(See Buena Park, Whittier)

Motel

✔★**LA HABRA INN.** *700 N Beach Blvd, I-5 Beach Blvd exit, 6 mi N. 310/694-1991; res: 800/541-0199; FAX 310/697-1485.* 70 rms, 2 story. S $45–$55; D $50–$65; each addl $5; under 12 free. TV; cable.

Heated pool. Complimentary continental bkfst, coffee. Ck-out noon. Coin Indry. Meeting rms. Cr cds: A, C, D, DS, MC, V.

Restaurant

★ ★ ★ **THE CAT AND THE CUSTARD CUP.** *800 E Whittier Blvd, I-5 Beach Blvd exit N to Whittier Blvd, then ½ mi W.* 310/694-3812. Hrs: 11:30 am–2:30 pm, 5:30–10 pm; Mon to 9 pm; Sat 5:30–10:30 pm; Sun 5–9 pm. Closed July 4, Dec 25. Res accepted. Continental menu. Bar. A la carte entrees: lunch $7.75–$14.50, dinner $9.75–$24. Child's meals. Specialties: roast tenderloin of beef with choron sauce, roast duckling, fresh seafood. Own pastries. Pianist Tues–Sat. Parking. Antiques. Cr cds: A, C, D, DS, MC, V.

La Jolla (San Diego) (K-4)

Area code: 619 **Zip:** 92037

This resort community is known as the jewel of San Diego. Sandstone bluffs laced with white sand and sparkling ocean suggest the look of the French Riviera. La Jolla is also a recognized center for scientific research.

What to See and Do

1. **University of California, San Diego** (1960). (18,000 students) On La Jolla Village Dr & N Torrey Pines Rd near I-5. Scattered around campus is an outdoor collection of contemporary sculpture. Campus tours. Phone 534-8273 (recording) or -4831 (tour information).

2. **Stephen Birch Aquarium-Museum.** 2300 Expedition Way (entrance at N Torrey Pines), at Scripps Institution of Oceanography, Univ of California, San Diego; situated on a hilltop, with a spectacular view of the ocean. Visitors will be able to explore the "blue planet," from the depths of the ocean to the far reaches of outer space, at this impressive interpretive center. This facility presents undersea creatures in realistic habitats, and allows visitors to experience the frontiers of marine science through interactive museum exhibits. Tidepool exhibit. Bookshop. Beach and picnic areas nearby. (Daily) Phone 534-3474. ¢¢¢

3. **Museum of Contemporary Art.** 700 Prospect St. Permanent collection and changing exhibits of contemporary painting, sculpture, design, photography and architecture. Sculpture garden; bookstore; films, lecture programs. (Daily exc Mon; closed Jan 1, Thanksgiving, Dec 25) Sr citizen rate. Phone 454-3541. ¢¢

4. **Scripps Park at La Jolla Cove.** Oceanfront landscaped park with swimming beach, scuba & skin diving areas, picnic areas. (Daily)

5. **Kellogg Park.** At La Jolla Shores Beach, foot of Avenida de la Playa. Swimming, skin diving, surfing; bathing beach; small boat landing; boardwalk, picnic areas. (Daily)

6. **Wind'n'sea Beach.** At foot of Palomar St. Surfing area; also bathing beach. (Daily)

(For further information contact the La Jolla Town Council, 1055 Wall St, Suite 110; 454-1444.)

(See San Diego)

Motels

★ ★ **ANDREA VILLA INN.** *2402 Torrey Pines Rd.* 619/459-3311; res: 800/367-6467; FAX 619/459-1320. 49 rms, 2 story, 22 kits. Mid-June–mid-Sept: S, D, kit. units $70–$80; each addl $5; monthly, wkly rates; lower rates rest of yr. Crib $5. TV; cable. Heated pool;

whirlpool. Complimentary continental bkfst. Ck-out noon. Coin Indry. Sun deck. Beach 4 blks. Cr cds: A, C, D, DS, MC, V, JCB.

✔ ★ ★ **INN AT LA JOLLA.** *5440 La Jolla Blvd.* 619/454-6121; res: 800/367-6467; FAX 619/459-1377. 44 air-cooled units, 1–2 story, 21 kit. suites. Mid-June–mid-Sept: S $53–$74; D $59–$99; each addl $5; kit. suites $74–$110; under 18 free; wkly rates; lower rates rest of yr. Crib free. TV; cable. Heated pool; whirlpool. Complimentary continental bkfst, coffee. Restaurant nearby. Ck-out noon. Putting green. Some refrigerators. Cr cds: A, C, D, DS, MC, V.

✔ ★ **LA JOLLA PALMS INN.** *6705 La Jolla Blvd.* 619/454-7101; res: 800/451-0358; FAX 619/454-6957. 59 rms, 3 story, 17 kits. June–Sept: S, D $59–$99; each addl $5; suites $81–$150; kit. units $66–$95; under 18 free; lower rates rest of yr. Crib $5. Pet accepted, some restrictions; $10. TV; cable. Heated pool; whirlpool. Complimentary continental bkfst. Restaurant adj 7 am–10 pm. Bar. Ck-out noon. Coin Indry. Refrigerators. Beach 1 blk. Cr cds: A, C, D, DS, MC, V.

★ **LA JOLLA SHORES INN.** *5390 La Jolla Blvd.* 619/454-0175; res: 800/367-6467; FAX 619/459-1377. 39 air-cooled rms, 2 story, 4 suites, 8 kits. Mid-June–Sept: S $55–$70; D $85–$97; each addl $5; suites $130; kit. units $88–$96; under 18 free; lower rates rest of yr. Crib free. TV; cable. Heated pool. Complimentary coffee. Restaurant nearby. Ck-out 11 am. Many refrigerators. Cr cds: A, C, D, DS, MC, V.

★ ★ **RESIDENCE INN BY MARRIOTT.** *8901 Gilman Dr.* 619/587-1770; FAX 619/552-0387. 287 kit. suites, 2 story. Kit. suites $89–$179; wkly rates. Crib free. Pet accepted; $50 non-refundable and $6 per day. TV; cable, in-rm movies. 2 heated pools; 5 whirlpools. Complimentary continental bkfst. Restaurant nearby. Rm serv 11:30 am–10:30 pm. Ck-out noon. Coin Indry. Meeting rms. Valet serv. Free airport transportation. Volleyball. Refrigerators. Many fireplaces. Grills. Cr cds: A, C, D, DS, MC, V, JCB.

✔ ★ **SANDS.** *5417 La Jolla Blvd.* 619/459-3336; res: 800/367-6467 or 800/643-0530. 39 rms, 3 story, 3 kit. suites. Mid-June–mid-Sept: S $64–$89; D $69–$95; each addl $5; kit. suites $89–$119; under 12 free; monthly, wkly rates; lower rates rest of yr. Pet accepted, some restrictions; $50. TV; cable. Heated pool. Complimentary coffee in rms. Ck-out noon. Refrigerators. Many balconies. Beach nearby. Cr cds: A, C, D, DS, MC, V, JCB.

★ **TRAVELODGE LA JOLLA COVE.** *1141 Silverado St.* 619/454-0791; FAX 619/459-8534. 30 rms, 23 with shower only, 3 story. July–Aug: S, D $79–$150; wkly rates; higher rates hols; lower rates rest of yr. Crib $10. TV; cable. Complimentary continental bkfst. Restaurant nearby. Ck-out noon. Refrigerators avail. Sun decks. Picnic tables. Ocean, beach 2 blks. Cr cds: A, C, D, DS, ER, MC, V, JCB.

Motor Hotels

★ ★ ★ **BEST WESTERN INN BY THE SEA.** *7830 Fay Ave at Prospect St.* 619/459-4461; FAX 619/456-2578. 132 rms, 5 story. July–Aug: S $85–$120; D $95–$130; each addl $10; suites from $230; under 12 free; lower rates rest of yr. Crib free. TV; cable. Heated pool. Restaurant 6 am–10 pm. Rm serv from 7 am. Ck-out noon. Meeting rms. Bellhops. Valet serv. Exercise equipt; weight machine, bicycles, whirlpool. Some refrigerators. Balconies. Ocean view from some rms. Cr cds: A, C, D, DS, ER, MC, V, JCB.

★ ★ **RADISSON HOTEL LA JOLLA** (formerly La Jolla Village Inn). *3299 Holiday Court.* 619/453-5500; res: 800/333-3333; FAX 619/453-5550. 200 rms in 4 buildings, 2 story. S $69–$139; D $79–$149;

each addl $10; under 18 free. TV; cable, in-rm movies. Heated pool; poolside serv. Coffee in rms. Restaurant 6:30 am–10 pm. Rm serv. Bar; entertainment exc Sun. Ck-out noon. Meeting rms. Bellhops. Valet serv. Free airport, RR station, bus depot transportation. Tennis. Exercise equipt; weights, bicycles, whirlpool. Cr cds: A, C, D, DS, MC, V.

★★★SEA LODGE. 8110 Camino del Oro. 619/459-8271; res: 800/237-5211; FAX 619/456-9346. 128 rms, 3 story, 19 kits. Mid-June–mid-Sept: S $140–$210; D $155–$225; each addl $15; suites $285–$390; kits. $170–$330; under 6 free; lower rates rest of yr. Crib $10. TV; cable. Heated pool; wading pool, whirlpool, sauna, poolside serv. Coffee in rms. Restaurant 7 am–10 pm. Rm serv. Bar 10–1 am. Ck-out 11 am. Coin lndry. Meeting rms. Bellhops. Covered parking. Free airport, RR station transportation. Tennis. Refrigerators. Private patios, balconies. On ocean. Cr cds: A, C, D, DS, MC, V.

Hotels

★★COLONIAL INN. 910 Prospect St. 619/454-2181; res: 800/832-5525 (exc CA), 800/826-1278 (CA); FAX 619/454-5679. 75 air-cooled rms, 4 story, 8 suites. S, D $150–$200; suites $200–$350. Crib free. TV; cable. Heated pool. Complimentary continental bkfst. Ck-out noon. Meeting rms. Refrigerators. Beach 1 blk. Established 1913. Cr cds: A, C, D, MC, V.

★★★EMBASSY SUITES. 4550 La Jolla Village Dr. 619/453-0400; FAX 619/453-4226. 335 suites, 12 story. Suites $119–$164; under 12 free. Crib free. TV; cable. Indoor pool. Complimentary full bkfst. Coffee in rms. Restaurant 11 am–11 pm. Bar to 1 am. Ck-out noon. Coin lndry. Meeting rms. Gift shop. Exercise equipt; weights, bicycles, whirlpool, sauna. Game rm. Refrigerators, wet bars. Cr cds: A, C, D, DS, MC, V.

★★★EMPRESS. 7766 Fay Ave. 619/454-3001; res: 800/525-6552; FAX 619/454-6387. 72 rms, 5 story. S, D $95–$130; kit. suites $200–$250; under 12 free. Crib free. Valet parking $5. TV; cable. Continental bkfst. Coffee in rms. Restaurant 11:30 am–2 pm, 5:30–10 pm. Bar 11:30–1:30 am. Ck-out noon. Meeting rms. Exercise equipt; weight machine, bicycle, whirlpool, sauna. Refrigerators. Sun deck. Ocean 2 blks. Cr cds: A, C, D, DS, MC, V.

★★★★HYATT REGENCY LA JOLLA AT AVENTINE. 3777 La Jolla Village Dr. 619/552-1234; res: 800/233-1234; FAX 619/552-6066. 400 rms, 16 story, 25 suites. S, D $135–$185; each addl $25; suites $225–$500; under 18 free. Crib avail. Garage parking $7, valet $11. TV; cable. Pool; whirlpool. Restaurant 7 am–11 pm. Rm serv 24 hrs. Bar 11:30–2 am. Ck-out noon. Convention facilities. Concierge. Gift shop. Tennis. Golf privileges. Health club privileges. Minibars. Hotel designed by renowned architect Michael Graves; a unique blending of neo-classic, post modern and Mediterranean elements. *LUXURY LEVEL:* RE-GENCY CLUB. 51 rms, 6 suites, 3 floors. S $180; D $200; suites $500–$1,500. Concierge. Private lounge, honor bar. Minibars. Whirlpool in suites. Complimentary continental bkfst, refreshments. Cr cds: A, C, D, DS, ER, MC, V, JCB.

★★★LA VALENCIA. 1132 Prospect St. 619/454-0771; res: 800/451-0772; FAX 619/456-3921. 100 rms, 7 story, 8 kits. S, D $145–$285; each addl $10; suites $300–$600. Crib $10. TV; cable. Heated pool; poolside serv. Coffee in rms. Restaurant 6:30 am–11 pm. Rm serv 24 hrs. Bar; entertainment exc Sun. Ck-out noon. Meeting rms. Airport transportation. Exercise equipt; weights, bicycles, sauna. Lawn games. Bathrm phones; many refrigerators, minibars. Some private patios, balconies. Gardens. Beach opp. Cr cds: A, C, D, MC, V, JCB.

★★★MARRIOTT. 4240 La Jolla Village Dr. 619/587-1414; FAX 619/546-8518. 360 rms, 15 story. S, D $149–$169; each addl $10; suites $275–$650; under 18 free; wkend rates. Crib free. Pet accepted. Covered parking $7/night, valet $10. TV; cable. Indoor/outdoor pool. Restaurant 6:30 am–10 pm; Fri, Sat to 11 pm. Bar; entertainment exc Sun, dancing. Ck-out noon. Coin lndry. Convention facilities. Exercise equipt; weights, rowing machine, whirlpool, sauna. Game rm. Refrigerators avail. Private patios, balconies. *LUXURY LEVEL:* CONCIERGE LEVEL. 32 rms. S, D $139–$179. Concierge. Some wet bars. Complimentary full bkfst, refreshments. Cr cds: A, C, D, DS, ER, MC, V, JCB.

★★★★SHERATON GRANDE TORREY PINES. 10950 N Torrey Pines Rd. 619/558-1500; res: 800/325-3535; FAX 619/450-4584. 400 rms, 4 story. July–Sept: S, D $175–$215; each addl $20; suites $400–$2,500; under 18 free; lower rates rest of yr. Crib free. Valet parking $12; in/out $8. TV; cable. Heated pool; poolside serv. Restaurant 6 am–11 pm. Rm serv 24 hrs. Bar 11–2 am; pianist. Ck-out noon. Convention facilities. Concierge. Butler service each floor. Gift shop. Complimentary limo service within 5-mi radius. Lighted tennis. Exercise rm; instructor, weight machine, bicycles, whirlpool, sauna, steam rm. Health club privileges. Bicycle rentals. Bathrm phones, minibars. Wet bar in suites. Balconies. Located on a bluff above La Jolla, on the 18th fairway of Torrey Pines golf course. All rms with view of golf course or ocean. Cr cds: A, C, D, DS, ER, MC, V, JCB.

★★SUMMER HOUSE INN. 7955 La Jolla Shores Dr, at Torrey Pines Rd. 619/459-0261; res: 800/666-0261; FAX 619/459-7649. 90 rms, 11 story, 36 kits. July–Aug: S, D $89–$125; each addl $10; suites $145–$325; kits. $94–$130; under 18 free; monthly, wkly rates; package plans; lower rates rest of yr. TV; cable. Heated pool; whirlpool, sauna, poolside serv. Restaurant 7 am–10:30 pm. Bar 10–2 am; entertainment. Ck-out noon. Coin lndry. Meeting rms. Barber, beauty shop. Valet parking. Free airport, RR station, bus depot transportation. Health club privileges. Bathrm phones, refrigerators. Balconies. Cr cds: A, C, D, DS, MC, V, JCB.

Inns

★★★THE BED & BREAKFAST INN AT LA JOLLA. 7753 Draper Ave. 619/456-2066; FAX 619/459-7284. 16 rms, 2 story. Rm phones avail. S, D $85–$225. TV in sitting rm & penthouse. Complimentary continental bkfst, sherry, wine & cheese. Ck-out noon, ck-in 2–5 pm. Some refrigerators. Beach nearby. Cubist-style house built 1913; gardens. Cr cds: MC, V.

★★PROSPECT PARK INN. 1110 Prospect St. 619/454-0133; res: 800/433-1609; FAX 619/454-2056. 25 units, 4 story, 6 kits. S $79–$95; D $89–$109; each addl $10; suites $199–$259; kit. units $109–$119; wkly, monthly rates off season. Crib free. TV; cable. Complimentary continental bkfst. Complimentary coffee in rms. Restaurant adj 7 am–11 pm. Ck-out 11 am, ck-in 3 pm. Library. Balconies. Most rms have ocean view. Totally nonsmoking. Cr cds: A, D, DS, ER, MC, V.

Restaurants

★★ANTHONY'S LA JOLLA. 4120 La Jolla Village Dr. 619/457-5008. Hrs: 11:30 am–9 pm; Fri & Sat to 10 pm. Res accepted. Closed major hols. Bar 11:30–1 am. Semi-a la carte: lunch $4.95–$12.95, dinner $7.95–$27.50. Child's meals. Specializes in fresh seafood. Oyster bar. Parking. Family-owned. Cr cds: A, C, D, DS, MC, V.

★ASHOKA CUISINE OF INDIA. 8008 Girard Ave, La Jolla Cove Plaza, 2nd floor. 619/454-6263. Hrs: 11:30 am–2:30 pm, 5–9:30 pm; Fri & Sat to 10:30 pm. Closed Thanksgiving, Dec 25. Res accepted.

Indian menu. Wine, beer. Buffet: lunch $7.95. A la carte entrees: dinner $8.95–$18.95. Specialties: tandoori dishes, curries. Authentic Indian cuisine. Dining rm overlooks La Jolla Cove. Cr cds: A, C, D, DS, MC, V.

★★★**AVANTI.** *875 Prospect St.* 619/454-4288. Hrs: 5:30 pm–midnight; early-bird dinner 5:30–7 pm. Res accepted. Northern Italian menu. Bar to 2 am; piano bar. A la carte entrees: dinner $11–$21. Specialties: osso buco Milanese, pastas. Entertainment. Patio dining. Overlooks courtyard, trees, plants. Cr cds: A, D, MC, V.

D

✔★**CHANG'S CUISINE OF CHINA.** *8670 Genesee Ave.* 619/558-2288. Hrs: 11:30 am–10 pm; Fri to 11 am; Sat & Sun noon–11 pm. Closed Thanksgiving. Res accepted. Chinese menu. Bar. A la carte entrees: lunch $6–$7, dinner $8–$12. Specialties: Cantonese and Szechwan dishes. Parking. Chinese art objects on display. Cr cds: A, MC, V.

D

★★★**CINDY BLACK'S.** *5721 La Jolla Blvd.* 619/456-6299. Hrs: 5:30–10 pm; Fri also 11:30 am–2pm; Sun 5–8 pm. Res accepted. French country menu. Bar. A la carte entrees: lunch $6–$13, dinner $10.95–$25.95. *Prix fixe*: Sun dinner $14.95. Specialties: whole Dover sole meuniere, rack of lamb, grilled duck. Parking. Original art. Cr cds: A, D, DS, MC, V.

D

★★**CRAB CATCHER.** *1298 Prospect St, in Coast Walk Mall.* 619/454-9587. Hrs: 11:30 am–3 pm, 5:30–10 pm; Fri & Sat to 10:30 pm; Sun brunch 10:30 am–3 pm. Res accepted. Bar 11:30 am–midnight. A la carte entrees: lunch $7–$12.95, dinner $9–$17.95. Sun brunch $7–$13. Child's meals. Specializes in fresh fish, shellfish, pastas. Parking. Outdoor dining. View of cove. Cr cds: A, D, MC, V.

★★**GEORGE'S AT THE COVE.** *1250 Prospect St, Prospect Place Mall.* 619/454-4244. Hrs: 11:30 am–10 pm; Fri to 11 pm; Sat 8 am–11 pm; Sun 8 am–10 pm. Res accepted. Semi-a la carte: bkfst $4–$8.95, lunch $7–$14.95, dinner $15–$26. Child's meals. Specializes in fresh seafood. Own baking. Valet parking. Outdoor dining. View of cove. Cr cds: A, C, D, DS, MC, V.

★★**KIVA GRILL.** *8970 University Centre Lane.* 619/558-8600. Hrs: 11:30 am–10 pm; Fri & Sat to midnight; early-bird dinner Mon–Thurs 4–6 pm; Sun brunch 10 am–2 pm. Closed Thanksgiving, Dec 25. Res accepted. Southwestern, Mexican menu. Bar to 1:30 am. Semi-a la carte: lunch $5.50–$10.95, dinner $9–$18. Sun brunch $9–$12. Specializes in mesquite-broiled seafood & meat. Entertainment Tues–Thurs & Sun brunch. Valet parking. Outdoor dining. Southwestern decor. Open kitchen. Cr cds: A, D, DS, MC, V.

D

★★★**MARINE ROOM.** *2000 Spindrift Dr.* 619/459-7222. Hrs: 11:30 am–2:30 pm, 6–10 pm; Sun 10:30 am–2:30 pm. Res accepted. Bar to midnight. Semi-a la carte: lunch $7–$15, dinner $16–$30. Sun brunch $9.95–$13.50. Child's meals. Specializes in fresh seafood. Entertainment Thurs–Sun. Parking. On beach; view of ocean, cliffs. Family-owned. Cr cds: A, C, D, DS, MC, V.

D

★★**MILLIGAN'S BAR & GRILL.** *5786 La Jolla Blvd.* 619/459-7311. Hrs: 11 am–10 pm; Sun brunch to 2:30 pm. Closed Dec 25. Res accepted. Bar to midnight. A la carte entrees: lunch $5.95–$11.95, dinner $10.50–$23.95. Sun brunch $7.50–$12.95. Child's meals. Specializes in southern pan-fried chicken, fresh seafood. Piano bar Mon–Wed evenings; jazz Thurs–Sat evenings. Valet parking. Outdoor dining. Main floor dining area has mirrored ceilings, artwork. Casual dining on 2nd floor; ocean view. Cr cds: A, MC, V.

D

✔★★**PIATTI RISTORANTE.** *2182 Avenida de la Playa.* 619/454-1589. Hrs: 11:30 am–10 pm; Fri & Sat 11 am–11 pm; Sat & Sun brunch 11 am–3 pm. Res accepted. Italian menu. Bar. A la carte entrees: lunch $6.95–$12, dinner $8.75–$14. Sat, Sun brunch $6.95–$8.75. Specialties: il pollo arrosto, pappardelle fantasia, cannelloni "Mamma Concetta." Outdoor dining. Patio area has fountain. Cr cds: MC, V.

★★★**TOP O' THE COVE.** *1216 Prospect St.* 619/454-7779. Hrs: 11:30 am–10:30 pm; Sun brunch 10:30 am–2:30 pm. Res accepted. No A/C. Continental menu. Bar. Wine cellar. A la carte entrees: lunch $5–$16, dinner $24–$29. Specializes in game, fresh seafood. Own pastries. Pianist Wed–Sun. Valet parking. Outdoor dining. In converted cottage (1896); rare Morton fig trees at front entrance. 2nd floor dining rm overlooks ocean. Cr cds: A, D, MC, V.

✔★★★**TRIANGLES.** *4370 La Jolla Village Dr.* 619/453-6650. Hrs: 11:30–1 am. Closed Jan 1, Thanksgiving, Dec 25. Res accepted. Continental, California menu. Bar. Wine list. Semi-a la carte: lunch, dinner $7–$15. Specialties: fresh seafood, meats & vegetables. Parking. Outdoor dining. Victorian decor. Cr cds: A, MC, V.

D

Unrated Dining Spot

FRENCH PASTRY SHOP. *5550 La Jolla Blvd.* 619/454-9094. Hrs: 7:30 am–11 pm; Fri, Sat to midnight. Closed Jan 1, Dec 25. Continental menu. Semi-a la carte: bkfst $3.25–$6.75, lunch $3.50–$11.95, dinner $6.75–$14.95. Own baking, pâté, chocolates. Outdoor dining. Cr cds: MC, V.

Lake Arrowhead (H-4)

Pop: 6,539 **Elev:** 5,191 ft **Area code:** 909 **Zip:** 92352

This area specializes in year-round sports with swimming, boating, fishing, water sports on the lake in the summer and snow skiing in the winter. The lake, which is 2½ miles long and about one mile wide, is slightly north of the breathtaking Rim of the World Highway (CA 18), which is a Scenic Byway, in the San Bernardino National Forest (see SAN BERNARDINO).

What to See and Do

1. **Swimming.** Beach; waterskiing school. (Memorial Day–Labor Day)
2. **Lake Arrowhead Children's Museum.** Lower Peninsula, Lake Arrowhead Village. Offers a hands-on interactive setting for children; learning through play and activities. (Daily; closed Thanksgiving & Dec 25; limited hrs winter) Sr citizen rate. Phone 336-1332 (recording) or 336-3093. ¢¢
3. *Arrowhead Queen.* On the waterfront at Lake Arrowhead Village. Enjoy a 50-minute narrated boat cruise on Lake Arrowhead, past architectural points of interest and historical sites. (Daily; hrly departures) Sr citizen rate. Phone 336-6992. ¢¢¢
4. **Snow Valley Ski Resort.** 14 mi SE on CA 18, 30; 5 mi E of Running Springs. 5 triple, 8 double chairlifts; patrol, school, rentals; snowmaking; cafeteria, restaurant, bar. 25 runs; longest run 1¼ mi; vertical drop 1,141 ft. (Mid-Nov–Apr) Snowboarding. Summer activities include hiking, mountain biking, backpacking; camping; outdoor concerts. For information phone 867-2751; snow conditions, 625-6511. ¢¢¢¢¢
5. **Santa's Village.** 2 mi E on CA 18 in Skyforest. Santa and Mrs. Claus; puppet show; rides; picnicking. (Mid-June–mid-Sept & mid-Nov–Dec, daily; rest of yr, wkends & hols only; closed Dec 25 & Mar–late May) Phone 337-2481 (recording) or 336-3661. ¢¢¢

(For further information contact the Chamber of Commerce, PO Box 219; 337-3715.)

(See Big Bear Lake)

Motel

✔★**TREE TOP LODGE.** *(Box 186) 27992 Rainbow Dr, at jct CA 173, near Lake Arrowhead Village.* 909/337-2311; res: 800/358-8733. 20 rms, 1–2 story, 6 kits. S, D $49–$98; each addl $10; suites, kit.

units $69–$135; fireplace units $59–$118. Crib free. TV; cable. Heated pool. Complimentary coffee in lobby. Ck-out 11 am. Some refrigerators. Picnic tables, grill. Cr cds: A, C, D, MC, V, JCB.

Motor Hotel

★ ★LAKE ARROWHEAD RESORT (formerly Hilton). *(PO Box 1699) 27984 CA 189, W of jct CA 173.* 909/336-1511; res: 800/800-6792; FAX 909/336-1378. 261 rms, 3 story. S, D $109–$249; suites $259–$399; kit. units $259–329; family rates; package plans. TV; cable, in-rm movies. Heated pool; poolside serv. Supervised child's activities (June–Aug daily, Sept–May Sat only). Restaurant 7 am–11 pm. Rm serv. Bar 11–2 am; entertainment, dancing Fri & Sat. Ck-out noon. Meeting rms. Bellhops. Concierge. Gift shop. Beauty shop. Valet parking. Airport transportation. 2 lighted tennis courts. Downhill/x-country ski 20 mi. Exercise rm; instructor, weights, bicycles, 2 whirlpools, sauna, steam rm. Boating, waterskiing; fishing equipt avail. Outdoor games. Bicycle rentals. Minibars; many refrigerators, some fireplaces. Some balconies. On lake with private beach. Cr cds: A, C, D, DS, MC, V, JCB.

Inns

★ ★CHATEAU DU LAC. *(PO Box 1098) 3 mi from village, on Hospital Rd.* 909/337-6488; FAX 909/337-6746. 6 rms, 3 story. S, D $95–$250. Children over 14 yrs only. TV; also in sitting rm. Complimentary full bkfst, tea, sherry. Ck-out 11 am, ck-in 1 pm. Downhill ski 12 mi; x-country ski 13 mi. Situated on bluff overlooking lake. Antiques; library. Each rm individually decorated. Totally nonsmoking. Cr cds: A, DS, MC, V.

★ ★LAKEVIEW LODGE. *(PO Box 128) W of jct CA 173 & 189.* 909/337-6633; res: 800/358-5253. 9 units, 2 story, 2 suites. No rm phones. Late June–early Jan: S, D $75–$165; suites $110–$200; lower rates rest of yr. Adults preferred. TV; cable, in-rm movies. Complimentary continental bkfst, coffee. Restaurant nearby. Ck-out 11 am, ck-in 2–9 pm. Downhill ski 12 mi; x-country ski 10 mi. Lake 2 blks; swimming. Reconstructed lodge was once a private home; antique furnishings; Victorian-style decor. Totally nonsmoking. Cr cds: A, MC, V.

Restaurant

★ ★THE ROYAL OAK. *(27187 CA 189, Blue Jay)* Blue Jay town center, 1½ mi SW of Lake Arrowhead Village. 909/337-6018. Hrs: 5–10 pm; Fri & Sat to 11 pm; Sun brunch 10:30 am–3 pm. Closed Easter, Thanksgiving, Dec 25. Res accepted. Bar to 11 pm; Fri & Sat to 1 am. Semi-a la carte: dinner $9.50–$29.95. Sun brunch $5.95–$13.50. Specializes in prime rib, seafood, veal. Own desserts. Pianist. Parking. English Tudor decor. Cr cds: A, MC, V.

Lake County

(see Clear Lake Area)

Lake Tahoe Area (D-3)

Area codes: 916 (CA), 702 (NV)

Lake Tahoe is one of the most magnificent mountain lakes in the world, with an area of about 200 square miles, an altitude approximately 6,230 feet and a maximum depth of more than 1,600 feet. Mostly in California, partly in Nevada, it is circled by paved highways edged with campgrounds, lodges, motels and resorts. The lake, with some fine beaches, is surrounded by forests of ponderosa, Jeffery and sugar pine, white fir, juniper, cedar, aspen, dogwood, cottonwood, many other trees and a splendid assortment of wildflowers.

The Sierra Nevada, here composed mostly of hard granite, is a range built by a series of roughly parallel block faults along its eastern side, which have tipped the mountainous area to the west, with the eastern side much steeper than the western. Lake Tahoe lies in a trough between the Sierra proper and the Carson Range, similarly formed and generally regarded as a part of the Sierra, to its east.

There are spectacular views of the lake from many points on the surrounding highways. Eagle Creek, one of the thousands of mountain streams that feed the lake, cascades 1,500 feet over Eagle Falls into Emerald Bay at the southwestern part of the lake. Smaller mountain lakes are scattered around the Tahoe area; accessibility varies. Tahoe and El Dorado National Forests stretch north and west of the lake, offering many recreational facilities.

Public and commercial swimming (there are 29 public beaches), boating and fishing facilities are plentiful. In winter the area is a mecca for skiers. There is legalized gambling on the Nevada side.

What to See and Do

1. **Skiing.**

Squaw Valley USA. 5 mi NW of Tahoe City off CA 89. 3 high-speed quads, 8 triple, 15 double chairlifts, aerial cable car, gondola, 5 surface lifts; patrol, school, rentals; snack bars, cafeterias, restaurants, bars. Longest run 3½ mi; vertical drop 2,850 ft. (Mid-Nov–mid-May, daily) Cross-country skiing (25 mi); rentals. (Mid-Nov–Apr, daily) Tram also operates late May–Oct (daily & evenings). Phone 916/583-6985; for 24-hr snow information, 916/583-6955. ¢¢¢¢¢

Alpine Meadows. 6 mi NW of Tahoe City off CA 89. Quad chairlift, 2 triple, 8 double chairlifts, 1 Pomalift; patrol, school, rentals; snowmaking; children's snow school; snack bar, cafeteria, restaurant, bars. Longest run 2½ mi; vertical drop 1,800 ft. (Mid-Nov–June, daily) Phone 916/583-4232; for snow information, 916/581-8374. ¢¢¢¢¢

Heavenly Ski Resort. 1 mi E of US 50 in South Lake Tahoe. Aerial Tramway to 8,250 feet. 2 detachable quad chairlifts, 7 triple, 10 double chairlifts, 6 surface lifts; patrol, school, rentals; snowmaking; snack bar, cafeteria, restaurant, bars; 6 lodges. Longest run 5½ mi; vertical drop 3,600 ft. (Mid-Nov–mid-Apr, daily) Cross-country trails nearby. Tramway also operates May–Sept. Observation platform, sun deck; hiking trail; picnic area; restaurant, bar. Phone 702/541-1330 or 702/586-7000; for 24-hr ski conditions, 702/541-7544. Summer ¢¢¢¢; Winter ¢¢¢¢¢

Sierra Ski Ranch. 12 mi W of South Lake Tahoe on US 50. 3 high-speed detachable quad chairlifts, 1 triple chairlift, 4 double chairlifts; patrol, school, rentals; cafeterias. Longest run 3½ mi; vertical drop 2,212 ft. (Nov–Apr, daily) Shuttle bus service. Phone 916/659-7453 or -7474; snow information 916/659-7475. ¢¢¢¢¢

Kirkwood. 30 mi S off CA 88. 4 triple, 6 double chairlifts, 1 Pomalift; patrol, school, rentals; cafeteria, 4 restaurants, 4 bars. Longest run 2½ mi; vertical drop 2,000 ft. (Mid-Nov–Apr, daily) Cross-country skiing; machine-groomed trails. (Nov–May; daily) Half-day rates. Phone 209/258-6000; for snow conditions, 209/258-3000. ¢¢¢¢¢

2. **Riding. Camp Richardson Corral.** 1 & 2-hr rides, breakfast, steak and pack rides (May–Oct, daily); sleigh rides (Dec–Mar). For further information contact PO Box 8335, South Lake Tahoe 96158; 916/541-3113. ¢¢¢¢

3. **Boat rides.**

Lake Tahoe Cruises. Foot of Ski Run Blvd in South Lake Tahoe. *Tahoe Queen,* paddlewheeler, cruise boat to Emerald Bay (all yr, 3 departures daily, reservations required). Phone 916/541-3364. ¢¢¢¢–¢¢¢¢¢

MS *Dixie* Cruises. Tours of Lake Tahoe and Emerald Bay aboard paddlewheeler; sightseeing, bkfst and dinner cruises avail. Leaves

Zephyr Cove marina, 4 miles northeast of Stateline, NV on US 50. (May–Oct) Reservations recommended. Phone 702/588-3508 or 702/882-0786. Sightseeing ¢¢¢¢

4. US Forest Service Visitor Center. On CA 89, 3 mi NW of South Lake Tahoe. Information, campfire programs, guided nature walks; self-guided trails and auto tape tours. Visitors look into Taylor Creek from the Stream Profile Chamber; exhibits explain life cycle of trout. (Late June–early Sept, daily; Stream Profile Chamber open after Memorial Day–Oct, days vary) Contact US Forest Service, 870 Emerald Bay Rd, Suite 1, South Lake Tahoe 96150; 916/573-2600. **Free.**

5. State parks/recreation areas. Tahoe State Recreation Area. Near Tahoe City on CA 28. Pier, picnicking, camping. Phone 916/583-3074 (general information). **Sugar Pine Point State Park.** 10 mi S of Tahoe City on CA 89. Cross-country skiing. Camping. Phone 916/525-7982. Pine Lodge is refurbished turn-of-century summer home (Ehrman Mansion), tours (July–Labor Day). Fee/vehicle day use. **D.L. Bliss State Park.** 17 mi S of Tahoe City on CA 89. Beach, camping. Phone 916/525-7277. **Grover Hot Springs State Park.** 29 mi S of South Lake Tahoe on CA 89. Hot mineral pool, swimming. Camping. Phone 916/694-2248. **Emerald Bay State Park.** 22 mi S of Tahoe City on CA 89. Swimming; fishing. Picnicking. Camping. Closed in winter. Phone 916/541-3030. Standard fees. In Emerald Bay State Park is

Vikingsholm. Steep 1 mi walk from parking lot (CA 89). Old Scandinavian architecture and furnishings. Tours (July–Labor Day, daily). ¢¢

6. Lake Tahoe Historical Society Museum. 3058 US 50. Displays of Lake Tahoe's Native American history, Frémont's discovery and development as a resort center. (Memorial Day–Labor Day, daily; rest of yr, wkends) Phone 916/541-5458. ¢

7. CCInc Auto Tape Tours. These 90-minute cassettes offer mile-by-mile self-guided tours to Reno, NV (68 mi) with colorful history of boomtown days of Virginia City and Carson City; to Sacramento (217 mi) with tour of magnificent Sierras, history of gold rush days and Donner Pass tragedy; to Mariposa (194 mi) with description of local history of frontier towns of Diamond Springs, Eldorado and Chinese Camp. Fourteen different tour tapes of California are available. Tapes may be purchased directly from CCInc Auto Tape Tours, PO Box 227, 2 Elbrook Dr, Allendale, NJ 07401; 201/236-1666. ¢¢¢¢

8. Ponderosa Ranch (see CRYSTAL BAY, NV).

(For further information contact the Lake Tahoe Visitors Authority, PO Box 16299, South Lake Tahoe 96151. Phone 800/AT-TAHOE; for reservations phone 800/288-2463.)

Annual Event

Opening day on Lake Tahoe. Opening of the boating season. Celebration includes decoration contest & parade. Usually Memorial Day wkend.

Note: Accommodations around Lake Tahoe are listed under South Lake Tahoe, Tahoe City and Tahoe Vista. See also, under Nevada: Crystal Bay, Stateline. In this area many motels have higher rates in summer and during special events and holidays. Reservations advised.

Lancaster (H-4)

Pop: 97,291 **Elev:** 2,355 ft **Area code:** 805

What to See and Do

Edwards Air Force Base. 10 mi N via CA 14 to Rosamont, then 10 mi E on Rosamont Blvd. Landing site for the NASA space shuttle program. Free 90-minute walking tours (2 departures daily); res re-

quired, phone 258-3460 or -3446. For general information phone 258-3449.

(For further information contact the Chamber of Commerce, 44335 Lowtree Ave, 93534; 948-4518.)

Annual Event

Antelope Valley Fair and Alfalfa Festival. Fairgrounds. 11 days. Usually late Aug–Labor Day.

Seasonal Event

Wildflower Season. Antelope County Poppy Reserve. 15101 W Lancaster Rd. Usually late Mar–Apr.

(See Palmdale)

Motel

★ ★**BEST WESTERN ANTELOPE VALLEY INN.** 44055 N Sierra Hwy (93534). 805/948-4651. 148 units, 1–3 story. S $63; D $69; each addl $6; suites $125; under 12 free. Crib free. TV; cable. Heated pool; poolside serv. Playground. Restaurant 5 am–11 pm. Rm serv 6 am–10 pm. Bar 5 pm–1:30 am; entertainment Thurs–Sat. Ck-out 1 pm. Meeting rms. Valet serv. Barber, beauty shop. Health club privileges. Lawn games. Cr cds: A, C, D, DS, MC, V.

Motor Hotel

✔ ★ ★**RIO MIRADA.** 1651 W Avenue K (93534). 805/949-3423; res: 800/522-3050; FAX 805/949-0896. 178 rms, 4 story, 77 kit. suites. S $49–$80; D $56–$80; each addl $5; kit. suites $62–$80; under 5 free. TV; cable, in-rm movies avail. Heated pool. Complimentary continental bkfst, coffee. Restaurant adj 7 am–11 pm. Ck-out noon. Coin lndry. Meeting rms. Sundries. Free airport transportation. Health club privileges. Grills. Cr cds: A, C, D, DS, MC, V.

Restaurants

✔ ★**CASA DE MIGUEL.** 44245 N Sierra Hwy. 805/948-0793. Hrs: 11 am–10 pm; Fri, Sat to 11 pm; Sun brunch 10 am–2 pm. Closed Thanksgiving, Dec 25. Mexican menu. Bar. A la carte entrees: lunch, dinner $3–$13.95. Complete meals: lunch, dinner $6.25–$13.95. Sun brunch $7.95. Specialties: fajitas, camerones Miguel. Mexican decor; artifacts, antiques. Hand-carved mahogany throughout. Cr cds: A, D, MC, V.

★**EL TAPATIO.** 1006 E Avenue J. 805/948-9673. Hrs: 11 am–10 pm; Sun brunch 10 am–2 pm. Closed Thanksgiving, Dec 25. Res accepted. Mexican, Amer menu. Serv bar. Semi-a la carte: lunch $1.95–$6.95, dinner $4.95–$12.95. Sun brunch $6.45. Child's meals. Specialties: fajitas, tamales, rellenos. Parking. Mexican decor. Cr cds: A, D, MC, V.

Lassen Volcanic National Park (B-2 – C-2)

(44 mi E of Redding on CA 44; 51 mi E of Red Bluff via CA 36, 89)

This 165-square-mile park was created to preserve Lassen Peak (10,457 feet), a volcano last active in 1921. Lassen Park, in the southern-most part of the Cascade Range, contains glacial lakes, virgin forests, mountain meadows and snow-fed streams. Hydrothermal features, the Devastated Area and Chaos Jumbles can be seen from Lassen Park Road. Boiling mud pots and solfataras (exuding sulfurous gases) can be seen a short distance off the road at Sulphur Works. At Butte Lake, colorful masses of lava and volcanic ash blend with the forests, meadows and streams. The peak is named for Peter Lassen, a Danish pioneer who used it as a landmark in guiding immigrant trains into the northern Sacramento Valley.

The Devastated Area, after being denuded in 1915 by a mudflow and a hot blast, is slowly being reclaimed by small trees and flowers. The Chaos Crags, a group of lava plugs, were formed some 1,100 years ago. Bumpass Hell, a colorful area of mud pots, boiling pools and steam vents, is a three-mile round-trip hike from Lassen Park Road. Clouds of steam and sulfurous gases pour from vents in the thermal areas. Nearby is Lake Helen, named for Helen Tanner Brodt, first white woman to climb Lassen Peak (1864). At the northwest entrance is a visitor center (late June–Labor Day, daily) where one may find information on the park's human, natural and geological history. There are guided walks during the summer; self-guided nature trails and evening talks at some camp-grounds. Camping (fee/site/night) at seven campgrounds; two-week limit except at Lost Creek and Summit Lake campgrounds (seven-day limit); check at the Ranger Stations for regulations.

Lassen Park Road is open mid-June to mid-October, weather permitting. Sulphur Works (south) and Manzanita Lake (northwest) entrances are open during winter months for winter sports. The winter sports area near the southwest entrance has beginner-to-expert slopes, cross-country trails, a 1,100-foot chairlift, a 400-foot rope tow, rentals and lunches. (Weekends and holiday periods)

Some facilities for the disabled (visitor center, comfort station & amphitheater at Manzanita Lake; visitor contact station in Sulpher Works; other areas in park). For information and descriptive folder contact the Superintendent, PO Box 100, Mineral 96063; 916/595-4444.

(For accommodations see Red Bluff, Redding, also see Chester)

Lava Beds National Monument (A-2)

(30 mi SW of Tulelake, off CA 139)

Seventy-two square miles of volcanic formations are preserved here in the extreme northeast part of the state. Centuries ago rivers of molten lava flowed here. In cooling, they formed a strange and fantastic region. Cinder cones dot the landscape—one rising 476 feet from its base. Winding trenches mark the collapsed roofs of lava tubes, an indicator of the 200 caves beneath the surface. Throughout the area are masses of lava hardened into weird shapes. Spatter cones may be seen where vents in the lava formed vertical tubelike channels, some only 3 feet in diameter but reaching downward 100 feet.

Outstanding caves include Sentinel Cave, named for a lava forma-tion in its passageway; Catacombs Cave, with passageways resembling Rome's catacombs; and Skull Cave, with a broad entry cavern reaching approximately 80 feet in diameter. (The name comes from the many skulls of mountain sheep that were found here.) The National Park Service provides ladders and trails in the 24 caves easily accessible to the public.

In this rugged, other-world setting one of the most costly Indian campaigns in history took place. The Modoc War of 1872–73 saw a small band of Indians revolt against reservation life and fight a series of battles with US troops. Although obliged to care for their families and live off the country, the Modocs held off an army more than 20 times their number for 5 months.

There is a campground at Indian Well (fee/site/night, mid-May–Labor Day) and picnic areas at Fleener Chimneys and Captain Jacks Stronghold (no water). Guided walks, audiovisual programs, cave trips and campfire programs are held daily, mid-June–Labor Day. Head-quarters has a visitor center (daily). Golden Eagle, Golden Age and Golden Access Passport accepted (see INTRODUCTION). For further information, contact PO Box 867, Tulelake 96134; 916/667-2282. No gasoline is available in the park—fill gas tank before entering.

Lee Vining (E-3)

Settled: 1923 **Pop:** 600 (est) **Elev:** 6,781 ft **Area code:** 619 **Zip:** 93541

A Ranger District office of the Inyo National Forest (see) is located here.

What to See and Do

1. **Mono Lake.** E of town. Lake access NW & SW. Located in the Mono Basin National Forest Scenic Area, Mono Lake is one of North America's oldest lakes. It contains 250 percent more salt than the ocean, and millions of migratory waterfowl feed on brine shrimp and brine flies. Stratified limestone rock formations, or tufa, sur-round the lake. Samuel Clemens wrote about the lake and its islands, volcanoes and gulls in *Roughing It.* For information con-tact the Mono Basin National Forest Scenic Area, PO Box 429; or Scenic Area Visitor Center, phone 647-6572; ranger station, phone 647-6525.
2. **Yosemite National Park** (see). W on CA 120.

(See Bridgeport, June Lake)

Motel

★**GATEWAY.** *(Box 250) On US 395.* 619/647-6467. 12 rms, 1–2 story. No A/C. May–Oct: S, D $69–$79; lower rates rest of yr. Crib $3. TV; cable. Restaurant opp 6 am–10 pm. Ck-out 10 am. Downhill ski 11 mi; x-country ski 4 mi. Picnic tables, grills. Sun deck. Fish freezer. View of Mono Lake. Cr cds: A, DS, MC, V.

Littleriver

(see Mendocino)

Livermore (E-2)

Pop: 56,741 **Elev:** 486 ft **Area code:** 510 **Zip:** 94550

What to See and Do

1. **Lawrence Livermore National Laboratory's Visitor Center.** 5 mi E via East Ave to Greenville Rd. Research center operated by Univer-sity of California for the United States Dept of Energy. Multimedia presentation of the laboratory's major programs. Interactive and audio displays and computers allow for hands-on activities. (Mon, Tues, Thurs & Fri, also Wed afternoons; closed major hols) Phone 422-9797. **Free.**
2. **Del Valle Regional Park.** From I-580, S on N Livermore, E on Tesla Rd, right on Mines Rd, S on Del Valle Rd to park entrance. Center-piece of these 3,997 acres is a 5-mile-long lake. Swimming, wind-surfing, lifeguards in summer; fishing; boating (launch, rentals; 10 mph limit). Nature trails. Picnicking. Camping (all yr, fee; 150 sites; dump station, showers, 20 water/sewage hookups). Visitor center. For reservations phone 652-CAMP. Per car ¢¢

3. Shadow Cliffs Regional Recreation Area. Between Livermore and Pleasanton; from I-580, S on Santa Rita Rd, left onto Valley Ave, then left onto Stanley Blvd to park entrance. Formerly a gravel quarry on 255 acres. Swimming, bathhouse; fishing; boating (rentals). Hiking, riding trails. Picnicking. Giant water slide (Apr–Labor Day; fee). Ramp access to lake for the disabled. Per car ¢¢

4. Wineries.

Concannon Vineyard (1883). 4590 Tesla Rd, 3 mi S of I-580 via N Livermore Ave. Picnic facilities. Tours; wine tasting. (Daily; closed Jan 1, Easter, Thanksgiving, Dec 25). Horse carriage tours avail; inquire for details. Phone 447-3760. **Free.**

Wente Bros Winery. 5565 Tesla Rd, 2½ mi SE via S Livermore Ave. Guided tours, tasting (daily; closed Jan 1, July 4, Thanksgiving, Dec 25). Picnic facilities by request. Phone 447-3603. A second location, at 5050 Arroyo Blvd, has restaurant (see), visitors center (daily) and guided tours on the hr. Phone 447-3694. **Free.**

(For further information on the area contact the Chamber of Commerce, 2157 First St; 447-1606.)

Annual Events

HoneyFest. Celebration focusing on honey and bees. Late Apr.

Rodeo. PRCA sanctioned. 2 wkend June.

Great Livermore Airshow. At Livermore Airport. Last wkend July.

Fall Festival of the Arts. Gardella Green. Art and photography shows, crafts, concessions, performing arts events. 1st wkend Oct.

(See Fremont, Oakland, Pleasanton, San Jose, Santa Clara)

Restaurant

★ ★ ★**WENTE BROS. SPARKLING WINE CELLARS.** 5050 Arroyo Rd. 510/447-3696. Hrs: 11:30 am–2:30 pm, 5:30–9:30 pm; Sun 10:30 am–2:30 pm, 5–9:30 pm; Sun brunch to 2:30 pm. Res accepted. Wine cellar. A la carte entrees: lunch $7.50–$16, dinner $16–$26. Sun brunch $7.50–$14. Child's meals. Specializes in local meat and produce. Valet parking. Outdoor dining with view of grounds. Spanish villa decor. Cr cds: A, D, MC, V.

Lodi (E-2)

Pop: 51,874 **Elev:** 51 ft **Area code:** 209

Located in the northernmost county in the San Joaquin Valley, Lodi is surrounded by vineyards and a rich agricultural area. Lodi is home to the flame Tokay grape and eleven wineries.

What to See and Do

1. Lodi Lake Park. 1 mi W of US 99 on Turner Rd. Major recreational facility for a wide area. Swimming beach; boating (rentals, ramp); nature area; discovery center; picnicking. (Daily) Phone 333-6742 or -6888. Per car ¢¢

2. Micke Grove Park & Zoo. 11793 N Micke Grove Rd, 5 mi S, just off CA 99, Armstrong Rd exit. Japanese garden, camellia and rose gardens; picnicking; historical museum. Zoo and park (daily; closed Dec 25). Sr citizen rate. Phone 953-8800 or 331-7400. Park per car ¢–¢¢; Zoo admission ¢

3. Camanche Recreation Area, South Shore. 24 mi E off CA 12. Swimming, waterskiing; fishing; boating (rentals, marina); tennis.

Picnic facilities, concession, groceries. Camping (fee; hookups); cottages. Phone 763-5178.

(For further information contact the Lodi District Chamber of Commerce, 1330 S Ham Lane, 95242; 367-7840.)

Annual Events

Lodi Spring Wine Show & Food Faire. Festival Grounds, 413 E Lockeford St. Wine and food tastings from California wineries and food establishments. Art & flower shows; cooking demonstrations. Phone 369-2771. Early Apr.

International Spring Festival. Micke Grove Park (see #2). Ethnic food and dancing; stage shows. May.

Lodi Grape Festival and Harvest Fair. Festival Grounds, 413 E Lockeford St. County fair with exhibits, entertainment, carnival. Phone 369-2771. 3rd wkend Sept.

(See Sacramento, Stockton)

Motels

★**BEST WESTERN ROYAL HOST INN.** 710 S Cherokee Lane (95240). 209/369-8484. 48 rms, 2 story. S $45–$52; D $50–$60; each addl $8; suites $68. Crib $6. TV; cable. Heated pool. Complimentary coffee in rms, lobby. Restaurant adj 8–2 am. Ck-out 11 am. Some refrigerators. Cr cds: A, C, D, DS, MC, V.

★ ★**LODI MOTOR INN.** 1140 S Cherokee Lane (95240). 209/334-6422; FAX 209/368-7967. 95 rms, 2 story. S, D $54–$67; each addl $6; under 12 free. Crib free. TV; in-rm movies avail. Heated pool. Complimentary continental bkfst. Restaurant nearby. Ck-out 11 am. Coin lndry. Meeting rms. Exercise equipt; bicycles, rowing machine, whirlpool, sauna. Cr cds: A, C, D, DS, MC, V.

Inn

★ ★ ★**WINE & ROSES.** 2505 W Turner Rd (95242), jct Lower Sacramento Rd. 209/334-6988; FAX 209/334-6570. 10 rms, 2 story. S $69–$99; D $79–$99; each addl $10; suite $125; under 4 free. Crib free. TV; in-rm movies avail. Complimentary bkfst, tea, sherry. Dining rm 11:30 am–1:30 pm, 6–9 pm; Tues to 1:30 pm; Sat 6–9 pm; Sun brunch 10:30 am–2:30 pm; closed Mon. Rm serv. Ck-out 11 am, ck-in 3 pm. Health club privileges. Lawn games. Balconies. Picnic tables. Historic inn, built 1902; individually decorated rms; fireplace in sitting rm. Situated on 5 acres, with shade trees and flower gardens. Approx 1 mi from lake; swimming. Totally nonsmoking. Cr cds: A, MC, V.

Lompoc (H-2)

Settled: 1874 **Pop:** 37,649 **Elev:** 104 ft **Area code:** 805 **Zip:** 93436

Lompoc is the flower seed capital of the world; more than three-quarters of the world's flower seeds come from here. From June through September, the city is bordered by acres of vivid zinnias, marigolds, sweet peas, petunias and other blossoms. Vandenberg AFB is ten miles west of here.

What to See and Do

1. Mural Walk. Giant murals, painted by world class artists, adorn the exterior walls of buildings in old downtown.

2. La Purísima Mission State Historic Park. 3 mi NE at jct Purisima Rd & Mission Gate Rd. The 11th in a chain of 21 Franciscan missions.

Founded in 1787, moved in 1812. Restored in original setting. Indian artifacts, mission relics. Guide map at museum. Craft demonstrations in summer. Picnicking. Living history tours summer and fall; write for schedule, fees. (Daily, mid-morning–mid-afternoon; closed Jan 1, Thanksgiving, Dec 25) For further information contact 2295 Purisima Rd; 733-3713. Per vehicle ¢¢

(For further information and a 19-mile self-guided flower field tour brochure, contact the Chamber of Commerce, 111 North H Street, 2nd floor, Suite H; 736-4567.)

Annual Events

Greenhouse Tour. Spectacular display of flowers by Bodger Seed Company. Phone 736-9144. 1 day, Apr.

Flower Festival. Floral parade, flower exhibits, arts and craft show, entertainment, bus tours of 1,600 acres of flower fields. June.

(See Santa Maria, Solvang)

Motel

✔ ★ ★ **THE INN OF LOMPOC.** *1122 North H Street. 805/735-7744; res: 800/548-8231; FAX 805/736-0421.* 90 rms, 2 story. S $46–$51; D $51–$57; each addl $6; under 12 free. Crib free. TV; cable. Indoor pool. Complimentary continental bkfst. Restaurant adj 5 am–midnight. Ck-out noon. Coin lndry. Meeting rms. Valet serv. Exercise equipt; weights, bicycles, whirlpool. Game rm. Refrigerators. Cr cds: A, C, D, DS, ER, MC, V.

Motor Hotel

★ ★ **QUALITY INN.** *1621 North H Street. 805/735-8555; FAX 805/735-8566.* 225 rms, 4 story, 93 kits. S, D $48–$58; suites $58–$75; each addl $5; under 18 free. Crib free. Pet accepted; $10. TV; cable. Heated pool; whirlpool. Complimentary continental bkfst, coffee in lobby. Restaurant adj. Ck-out noon. Coin lndry. Valet serv. Driving range. Health club privileges. Cr cds: A, C, D, DS, ER, MC, V, JCB.

Hotel

★ ★ **EMBASSY SUITES.** *1117 North H St. 805/735-8311; FAX 805/735-8459.* 155 suites, 3 story. Suites $69–$79; each addl $10; under 12 free. Crib free. TV. Heated pool. Complimentary full bkfst. Coffee in rms. Ck-out noon. Coin lndry. Meeting rms. Exercise equipt; weights, bicycles, whirlpool. Refrigerators. Balconies. Cr cds: A, C, D, DS, MC, V, JCB.

Lone Pine (F-4)

Pop: 1,818 **Elev:** 3,733 ft **Area code:** 619 **Zip:** 93545

Dating from the early 1860s, Lone Pine caters to tourists and outfits hiking trips to nearby Mt Whitney (14,495 ft, tallest peak in the contiguous US). A 13-mile drive due west to the base of Mt Whitney leads through the unusual Alabama Hills.

A Ranger District office of the Inyo National Forest (see) is located here.

What to See and Do

1. **Death Valley National Monument** (see). 70 mi E on CA 190.

2. **Eastern California Museum.** 16 mi N via US 395, W on Center St in Independence. Little Pine Village; Indian baskets & artifacts; pioneer artifacts, photographs; natural history. (Daily exc Tues; closed major hols) Donation. Phone 878-0364 or -0258.

3. **The Commander's House** (1872). 16 mi N on US 395, 303 N Edwards in Independence. Victorian house, built for commander of Camp Independence and moved to present location in 1889; eight rooms of antique furniture, some made by soldiers at camp. (Late May–early Sept, Sat & Sun or by appt) Donation. Phone 878-0364 or -0258.

4. **Alabama Hills Recreation Area.** 2 mi W via Whitney Portal Rd. Site of Indian Wars in the 1860s; named for Southern warship *Alabama*. These hills are a favorite film location for TV and movie companies because of the unique rock formations and Sierra backdrop. Contact Chamber of Commerce for details.

(For further information contact the Chamber of Commerce, 126 S Main, PO Box 749; 876-4444.)

Annual Event

Lone Pine Film Festival. Celebration of movies made on location in Lone Pine. Fri evening concert; bus tour of movie locations; films; movie memorabilia; arts & crafts. Phone 876-4444 or -4314. Columbus Day wkend.

Motel

✔ ★ ★ **DOW VILLA.** *310 S Main St. 619/876-5521; res: 800/824-9317 (CA); FAX 619/876-5643.* 39 rms, 2 story. S, D $56; each addl $4; suites $60; golf packages. Crib free. TV; cable. Heated pool; whirlpool. Complimentary coffee in rms. Restaurant open 24 hrs. Ck-out noon. Refrigerators. Motel for motion picture casts since the early 1920s. Cr cds: A, C, D, DS, MC, V.

Long Beach (J-4)

Founded: 1881 **Pop:** 429,433 **Elev:** 29 ft **Area code:** 310

A multibillion-dollar redevelopment program helped Long Beach become one of southern California's most diverse waterfront destinations, recapturing the charm it first attained as a premier California seaside resort in the early 1900s. Projects involving hotels and major attractions, along with shopping, commercial and residential area development, contributed to the revitalization of both the downtown and the waterfront. A 21.5-mile light rail system, the Metro Blue Line, connects Long Beach and Los Angeles.

Founded by British-born W.E. Willmore as the "American Colony" of Willmore City, the name change to Long Beach was prompted by a desire to advertise its 5½-mile-long, 500-foot-wide beach. Earlier in this century, prosperity came with the elegant hotels and summer houses of the wealthy, and, later, with the discovery of oil. Today, the state's largest beach city derives its economic security from the aerospace, harbor, oil and tourism industries. McDonnell-Douglas is its largest employer.

What to See and Do

1. ***Queen Mary Seaport.*** Located at the south end of the Long Beach Frwy (710), at 1126 Queens Highway. This historic ship, which made more than 1,000 transatlantic crossings, is permanently docked here. Now a 365-room hotel and tourist attraction, it is the centerpiece of a 55-acre site that includes the Queen's Playland,

with a carousel, train rides and games, and the Queen's Marketplace, with a number of eateries open for bkfst, lunch and dinner and opportunities for shopping. Guided and self-guided tours avail; reservations accepted for dining and guided tours (addl fee). (Daily) Phone 435-3511. Admission ¢¢; Parking ¢¢

2. **Shoreline Village.** Adj to the Downtown Shoreline Marina at the foot of Pine Ave, just S of the Convention Center. This seven-acre shopping, dining and entertainment complex recaptures the look and charm of a turn-of-the-century California seacoast village. Special features include a collection of unique shops, galleries and restaurants, a historic carousel and a complete marine center with daily harbor cruises and seasonal whale watch excursions. Alternative transportation to Shoreline Village is available via the free Promenade Tram from downtown Long Beach, the Runabout Shuttle (also from downtown Long Beach) and the Water Taxi that transports passengers between Shoreline Village and the downtown marina. Phone 590-8427. **Free.**

3. **Long Beach Museum of Art.** 2300 E Ocean Blvd. Changing contemporary exhibitions housed in 1912 mansion overlooking the Pacific Ocean. Permanent collection includes American art, German expressionists, video art. Facilities include contemporary sculpture garden; education gallery; Media Arts Center (located in Station/ Annex at 5373 E 2nd St, phone 439-0751; video production and post-production access). (Wed–Sun, mid-morning–mid-afternoon; extended hrs Fri; closed Jan 1, July 4, Thanksgiving, Dec 25) Phone 439-2119. ¢¢

4. **Municipal Beach.** S of Ocean Blvd from Alamitos Ave to city limits. Lifeguards at many areas in summer. (Daily)

5. **Marinas. Downtown Shoreline/Shoreline Harbor.** 450 E Shoreline Dr. Slips for 1,824 pleasure craft; guest docking (fee). Phone 437-0375. Shoreline Village has restaurants, shops; 70-space RV park, phone 435-4960. Fishing piers, five launching ramps, biking trails. **Alamitos Bay.** 205 Marina Dr. Slips for 2,005 pleasure craft; guest docking. On grounds is Seaport Village; restaurants, shops. Phone 594-0951 or 437-0375.

6. **Alamitos Bay.** 7 mi of inland waterways for swimming, sunning, windsurfing, boating.

7. **Queen's Wharf.** 555 Pico Ave, in port of Long Beach. Entertainment/ fishing complex with full range of sportfishing vessels for half-day, three-quarter-day, full-day and night fishing excursions; restaurants; fish market. Whale watching (Jan–Apr). Phone 432-8993.

8. **Long Beach Convention and Entertainment Center.** 300 E Ocean Blvd, by S terminus of Long Beach Freeway. *(Undergoing major expansion; scheduled for completion fall of 1994.)* A 111-acre multi-purpose complex houses major sporting arena, convention/ exhibition complex and two traditional performing theaters. Terrace Theater has proscenium stage and Center Theater. Resident companies include Long Beach Symphony, Opera, Civic Light Opera and Classical Ballet. Phone 436-3636.

9. **Rancho Los Alamitos.** 6400 Bixby Hill Rd. Ninety-minute guided tours of adobe ranch house (ca 1800) with antique furnishings; six barns and outbuildings, including a blacksmith shop; five acres of gardens. (Wed–Sun afternoons; closed hols) Phone 431-3541. **Free.**

10. **Rancho Los Cerritos** (1844). 4600 Virginia Rd. One of original California land grants that became Long Beach. Renovated Monterey colonial-style adobe building served as headquarters for sheep ranchers in 1870s; historic garden; orientation exhibit. (Wed–Sun afternoons; closed hols; guided tours on the hr, wkends) Phone 424-9423. **Free.**

11. **General Phineas Banning Residence Museum.** 401 E M St in Wilmington. Restored Greek-revival house (1864); exhibits tell of Banning's role in the development of Los Angeles. Guided tours (Tues–Thurs, Sat & Sun). Phone 548-7777. ¢

12. **California State University, Long Beach** (1949). (32,000 students) 1250 Bellflower Blvd. On the 320-acre campus are monumental sculptures created by artists, from here and abroad, who participated in the first International Sculpture Symposium held in the US

(1965); art museum with displays and exhibits; the Earl Burns Miller Japanese Garden. For campus tours phone 985-5358.

13. **El Dorado East Regional Park and Nature Center.** 7550 E Spring St, at I-605. A 450-acre park with four fishing lakes, boat rentals, archery range, nature and hiking trails, picnicking. Museum and visitors center (free). (Daily) Accessible to the disabled (museum ramp and ¼-mi paved nature trail). Phone 421-9431, ext 3415. Per vehicle ¢¢

14. **Sightseeing cruises.**

Catalina Island. Daily excursions via Catalina Cruises. Departs from 320 Golden Shore Blvd. For schedule and fare information phone 213/253-9800 or 800/228-2546. ¢¢¢¢

Catalina Channel Express. Departs from *Queen Mary* (see #1). For schedule and fare information phone 519-7957.

(For further information contact the Long Beach Area Convention & Visitors Council, One World Trade Center, #300, 90831, phone 436-3645 or 800/4-LB-STAY; or Visitor Center, 3387 Long Beach Blvd, phone 426-6773 or 800/COAST-FUN.)

Annual Events

Toyota Grand Prix. International race held on downtown streets. Phone 981-2600. Usually 3 days Apr.

Long Beach Blues Festival. Mid-Sept.

Boat Parades. Early Dec.

(See Anaheim, Buena Park, Los Angeles, Santa Ana)

Motels

★★**RAMADA INN LONG BEACH.** *5325 E Pacific Coast Hwy (90804).* 310/597-1341; FAX 310/597-1664. 143 rms, 2 story. S, D $79–$89; each addl $5; suites $95–$125; under 18 free; wkly rates; higher rates Grand Prix. Crib free. TV; cable, in-rm movies. Heated pool. Restaurant 7 am–10 pm. Rm serv. Ck-out noon. Coin lndry. Meeting rms. Valet serv. Free local airport transportation. In-rm whirlpools. Cr cds: A, C, D, DS, ER, MC, V, JCB.

✔★**VAGABOND INN.** *185 Atlantic Ave (90802),* at Broadway. 310/435-3791; FAX 310/436-7510. 48 rms, 2 story. S $40–$50; D $45–$60; each addl $5; suites $105–$150; under 19 free; higher rates Grand Prix. Crib free. TV. Heated pool; whirlpool. Complimentary continental bkfst, coffee, tea. Restaurant nearby. Ck-out noon. Balconies. Cr cds: A, C, D, DS, ER, MC, V, JCB.

Motor Hotels

★★**BEST WESTERN GOLDEN SAILS HOTEL.** *6285 E Pacific Coast Hwy (90803).* 310/596-1631; FAX 310/594-0623, ext 333. 175 rms, 4 story. S, D $69–$130; each addl $10; suites $175–$210; under 12 free; package plans; higher rates: Grand Prix, special events. Crib free. TV; cable. Pool; whirlpool, poolside serv. Restaurant 6 am–10 pm. Rm serv. Bar 10–2 am; entertainment, dancing. Ck-out noon. Coin lndry. Meeting rms. Valet serv. Gift shop. Barber, beauty shop. Free local airport transportation. Refrigerators; some in-rm whirlpools. Private patios, balconies. Marina adj. Cr cds: A, C, D, DS, MC, V.

★★**CLARION EDGEWATER.** *6400 E Pacific Coast Hwy (90803).* 310/434-8451; FAX 310/598-6028. 249 rms, 2 story. S $79–$89; D $89–$99; each addl $10; suites $115–$215; under 18 free. Crib free. TV; cable. Heated pool; whirlpool, poolside serv. Restaurant 6 am–10 pm. Rm serv. Bar 4:30 pm–midnight; entertainment, dancing Fri & Sat. Ck-out noon. Meeting rms. Bellhops. Valet serv. Sundries. Gift shop.

Private patios, balconies. Some rms overlook marina. Cr cds: A, C, D, DS, ER, MC, V, JCB.

D 🏊 🚭 ⌚

★HOLIDAY INN CONVENTION & WORLD TRADE CENTER. *500 E 1st St (90802).* 310/435-8511; FAX 310/435-1370. 216 rms, 9 story. Mid-May–mid-Oct: S $79; D $89; each addl $10; under 18 free; wkend rates; higher rates: Grand Prix, special events; lower rates rest of yr. Crib free. TV; cable. Heated pool; sauna, poolside serv. Restaurant 6:30 am–2 pm, 5–10 pm. Rm serv. Ck-out noon. Coin lndry. Meeting rms. Bellhops. Valet serv. Local airport transportation. Balconies. Near beach, convention center. Cr cds: A, C, D, DS, MC, V.

D 🏊 🚭 ⌚ SC

✔ ★ ★HOWARD JOHNSON PLAZA HOTEL. *1133 Atlantic Ave (90813).* 310/590-8858; FAX 310/983-1607. 135 rms, 4 story. Apr–Oct: S, D $45–$56; each addl $10; under 12 free; wkend rates; lower rates rest of yr. Crib avail. TV; cable, in-rm movies avail. Heated pool; whirlpool. Restaurant 6:30 am–9 pm. Rm serv. Bar 4 pm–midnight. Coin lndry. Meeting rms. Bellhops. Valet serv. Free garage parking. Free airport transportation. Refrigerators. Cr cds: A, C, D, DS, ER, MC, V, JCB.

🏊 🚭 ⌚ SC

★TRAVELODGE HOTEL. *700 Queensway Dr (90802).* 310/435-7676; FAX 310/437-0866. 192 rms, 5 story. S $79–$89; D $89–$99; each addl $10; under 14 free. Crib free. Pet accepted, some restrictions. TV; cable. Heated pool; poolside serv. Complimentary coffee & tea in rms. Restaurant 6:30 am–10 pm; Sat & Sun from 7 am. Bar 11 am–midnight. Ck-out noon. Meeting rms. Airport transportation. Lighted tennis. Lawn games. Private patios, balconies. Many rms overlook harbor. Cr cds: A, C, D, DS, ER, MC, V, JCB.

D 🖇 🏊 🚶 🚭 ⌚ SC

Hotels

★ ★ ★HILTON. *Two World Trade Center (90831), adj to World Trade Center.* 310/983-3400; FAX 310/983-1200. 398 rms, 15 story. S $120–$170; D $140–$190; each addl $20; suites $425–$1,400; family rates; higher rates Grand Prix. Crib free. Pet accepted, some restrictions. Garage: self-park $5, valet $7. TV; cable. Pool; wading pool. Restaurant 6 am–midnight. Bar 11–2 am; entertainment, dancing (Fri, Sat). Ck-out noon. Convention facilities. Concierge. Gift shop. Beauty shop. Free airport transportation. Exercise equipt; weight machine, bicycles, whirlpool. Minibars; some wet bars; refrigerators avail. Balconies. Opp ocean; most rms have ocean view. Cr cds: A, C, D, DS, ER, MC, V, JCB.

D 🖇 🏊 🚶 🚭 ⌚

★ ★HYATT REGENCY. *200 S Pine (90802), adj to Convention Center at Long Beach Marina.* 310/491-1234; FAX 310/432-1972. 521 rms, 16 story. S $79–$159; D $79–$179; each addl $20; suites $275–$800; under 18 free. Crib free. Covered, garage, valet parking $7; self-park $5. TV; cable. Heated pool; poolside serv. Supervised child's activities (Fri & Sat evenings). Restaurant 6 am–midnight. Bar 11–2 am. Ck-out noon. Convention facilities. Concierge. Exercise equipt; weights, bicycles, whirlpool. Some refrigerators. Tours. Opp harbor. *LUXURY LEVEL: REGENCY CLUB. 491-1234, ext 52.* 50 rms. S $99–$159; D $99–$179. Private lounge, honor bar 5–11 pm. Wet bars. Bathrm phones. Complimentary continental bkfst, refreshments. Cr cds: A, C, D, DS, ER, MC, V, JCB.

D 🏊 🚶 🚭 ⌚ SC

★ ★MARRIOTT. *4700 Airport Plaza Dr (90815), at Municipal Airport.* 310/425-5210; FAX 310/425-2744. 311 rms, 8 story. S, D $129–$174; each addl $15; suites $375; under 13 free; wkend rates. TV; cable. 2 pools, 1 indoor; poolside serv. Restaurant 6:30 am–11 pm. Bar noon–2 pm; entertainment, dancing. Ck-out noon. Convention facilities. Concierge. Gift shop. Airport transportation. 18-hole golf privileges opp. Exercise equipt; weights, bicycles, whirlpool. *LUXURY LEVEL: CONCI-*

ERGE LEVEL. 43 rms. S, D $139. Private lounge. Complimentary continental bkfst, refreshments. Cr cds: A, C, D, DS, MC, V, JCB.

D 🖇 🏊 🚶 ✕ 🚭 ⌚ SC

★ ★ ★RAMADA RENAISSANCE. *111 E Ocean Blvd (90802).* 310/437-5900; FAX 310/437-3813. 374 rms, 12 story. S $95–$150; D $110–$165; each addl $15; suites $400–$900; under 18 free; wkly rates; higher rates Grand Prix. Valet parking $8, garage $6. TV; cable. Heated pool; poolside serv. Restaurant 6:30–11 pm. Bar to 2 am. Ck-out noon. Convention facilities. Concierge. Drugstore. Local airport transportation. Golf privileges. Exercise equipt; weights, bicycles. Minibars. Balconies. *LUXURY LEVEL: RENAISSANCE CLUB.* 74 rms, 2 floors. S $140; D $155; suites $400–$900. Private lounge. Wet bar in suites. Complimentary continental bkfst, refreshments, newspaper. Cr cds: A, C, D, DS, ER, MC, V, JCB.

D 🖇 🏊 🚶 🚭 ⌚ SC

★ ★ ★SHERATON. *333 E Ocean Blvd (90802).* 310/436-3000; FAX 310/436-9176. 460 rms, 16 story. S $105–$125; D $115–$135; each addl $20; suites $195–$885; under 17 free; higher rates Grand Prix. Crib free. Garage $7. TV; cable. Heated pool; poolside serv. Complimentary coffee in rms. Restaurant 6:30–1 am. Rm serv 24 hrs. Bar 11–2 am; entertainment, dancing. Ck-out noon. Convention facilities. Concierge. Gift shop. Free airport transportation. Exercise equipt; weight machine, bicycles, whirlpool, sauna. Minibars; some bathrm phones. Opp ocean. Cr cds: A, C, D, DS, ER, MC, V, JCB.

D 🏊 🚶 🚭 ⌚ SC

Inns

★ ★LORD MAYOR'S INN. *435 Cedar Ave (90802), Long Beach Frwy, exit 6th St.* 310/436-0324. 5 rms, 2 story. No A/C. D $85–$95; mystery night plans. Complimentary full bkfst, coffee, tea. Restaurant nearby. Ck-out 11:30 am, ck-in 4–6 pm. Balconies. Picnic tables. Restored historic Edwardian house (1904); former home of Charles Windham, first mayor of Long Beach. Each rm individually decorated; many antiques. Totally nonsmoking. Cr cds: A, MC, V.

🚭 ⌚

★ ★ ★SEAL BEACH INN & GARDENS. *(212 5th St, Seal Beach 90740) At Central Ave, near downtown Seal Beach.* 310/493-2416; FAX 310/799-0483. 23 rms, 2 story, 15 kits. Some A/C. S, D $108–$195; each addl $10; studio rms $62; suites $155–$195; kit. cottages $108–$145; wkly rates in winter. Crib $5. TV. Pool. Complimentary full bkfst, wine & refreshments. Restaurant nearby. Ck-out 11 am, ck-in 4–9 pm. Meeting rms. Bicycles. In-rm whirlpools; some fireplaces. Balconies. Ocean 300 yds. Restored inn (1923). Totally nonsmoking. Cr cds: A, D, MC, V, JCB.

🏊 🚭 ⌚ SC

Restaurants

✔ ★ANNELIESE'S BAVARIAN INN. *5730 E 2nd St.* 310/439-4098. Hrs: 11 am–2 pm, 4–9 pm; Sun from 4 pm. Closed Tues; major hols. Res accepted. German menu. Wine, beer. Semi-a la carte: lunch $7.50–$10.75, dinner $10.50–$14.75. Specialties: sauerbraten, Wienerschnitzel, rouladen. Bavarian decor. Cr cds: MC, V.

★ ★CHART HOUSE. *215 Marina Dr.* 310/598-9411. Hrs: 5–10 pm; Fri & Sat to 11 pm. Res accepted. Bar. Complete meals: dinner $12.45–$29.95. Specializes in seafood, prime rib, steak. Sixty-item salad bar. Own desserts. Parking. Nautical decor. View of marina. Cr cds: A, C, D, DS, MC, V.

✔ ★ ★MUM'S. *144 Pine Ave.* 310/437-7700. Hrs: 11 am–10 pm; Fri & Sat to midnight. Closed some major hols. Res accepted. California cuisine with Northern Italian influence. Bar 11–1 am. A la carte entrees: lunch, dinner $7.95–$16.95. Specialties: jumbo scallops wrapped in sole with lobster, ravioli, pizzas, calzones. Own pasta. Jazz Fri & Sat. Valet parking. Patio dining. Cr cds: A, C, D, DS, MC, V.

★ ★**RUSTY PELICAN.** *6550 Marina Dr. 310/594-6551.* Hrs: 11:30 am–10 pm; Fri & Sat to 11 pm; Sun 10 am–2:30 pm, 4:30–10 pm; Sun brunch to 2:30 pm. Res accepted. Bar to 1:30 am. Semi-a la carte: lunch $2.50–$9.95, dinner $10.50–$20.50. Seafood bar $2.95–$8.95. Sun brunch $7.95–$12.95. Specializes in fresh fish. Entertainment. Cr cds: A, D, DS, MC, V.

Los Altos

(see Mountain View)

Los Angeles Area (H-3)

Occupying a land area of 463½ square miles, Los Angeles has spilled over from the plain into the canyons and foothills. Like an empire in miniature, it boasts mountains and deserts, canyons formed by sky-scrapers and by rock, a Mediterranean climate and working ranches. The city has spread out and around the independent communities of Beverly Hills, Santa Monica, Culver City, Universal City and Inglewood. The Los Angeles city limits are twisting and confusing. Get a street map at any Mobil service station.

Los Angeles Area Suburbs

The following suburbs and towns in the Los Angeles area are included in the *Mobil Travel Guide.* For information on any one of them, see the individual alphabetical listing. SURROUNDED BY LOS ANGELES: Beverly Hills, Culver City. NORTH OF LOS ANGELES: Burbank, Glendale, San Fernando. NORTHEAST OF LOS ANGELES: Arcadia, Pasadena, San Gabriel, San Marino. EAST OF LOS ANGELES: Fullerton, La Habra, Pomona, Whittier. SOUTHEAST OF LOS ANGELES: Anaheim, Buena Park, Corona Del Mar, Costa Mesa, Garden Grove, Huntington Beach, Irvine, Laguna Beach, Newport Beach, Orange, Santa Ana; also see Disneyland. SOUTH OF LOS ANGELES: Long Beach, Torrance. WEST OF LOS ANGELES: Malibu, Marina Del Rey, Redondo Beach, Santa Monica. NORTHWEST OF LOS ANGELES (San Fernando Valley): San Fernando, Studio City, Valencia, Van Nuys, Woodland Hills.

Los Angeles Neighborhoods

The following neighborhoods in the city of Los Angeles are included in the *Mobil Travel Guide.* For information on any one of them, see the individual alphabetical listing. Hollywood, North Hollywood, San Pedro, Studio City, Van Nuys, Westwood Village and Woodland Hills.

Los Angeles (H-4)

Founded: 1781 **Pop:** 3,485,398 **Elev:** 330 ft **Area codes:** 213, 310 or 818 (San Fernando Valley)

Imagine a sprawling formation made up of a thousand pieces from a thousand different jigsaw puzzles. Illuminate it with klieg lights and flashing neon signs, garnish it with rhinestones, oranges and oil wells—and you have Los Angeles.

The city has many faces: excitement, tranquility, tall buildings, cottages, ultramodern electronics plants, off-beat religious sects, health fads, sunshine, smog, movie stars and would-be stars, artists, writers, libraries, museums, art galleries, super highways and real estate booms.

Los Angeles presents a distilled, concentrated picture of the United States. People are drawn to its glamour, riches, excitement and sunshine—all of which have encouraged a general informality. Beneath the glitter and salesmanship there is a pioneer spirit. Although no further geographic frontiers exist, many writers, researchers, scientists and

artists have settled in this area to explore scientific and intellectual frontiers.

Los Angeles is a young city with ancient roots. Along with modern architecture, exuberant growth and a cultural thirst, it has retained a Spanish serenity and historical interest. On September 4, 1781, Don Felipe de Neve, Governor of California, marched to the site of the present city and with solemn ceremonies founded El Pueblo de Nuestra Señora La Reina de Los Angeles de Porciuncula "The Town of Our Lady the Queen of the Angels of Porciuncula"—now popularly shortened to "Los Angeles."

The little pueblo slumbered until 1846, when the seizure of California by the United States converted it into a vigorous frontier community. The gold rush of 1849 fanned its growth; for a time lawlessness became so prevalent that the city was referred to as Los Diablos—The Devils. The railroads reached it in 1885 and 1886 and, helped by a fare war, brought a tidal wave of new settlers. By 1890 a land boom developed and the population figure reached 50,000, with oil derricks appearing everywhere. The piping in of water from the Owens Valley in 1913 paved the way for expansion and doubling of the population in the 1920s. In the half century between 1890 and 1940, the city grew from 50,395 to 1,504,277—a gain of more than 2,000 percent. The war years added new industries and brought new waves of population which continued throughout the 1980s. Presently, the city's economic assets are invested in "growth" industries such as electronics, machinery, chemicals, oil, printing, publishing, tourism and entertainment.

The city's geographic scope makes it almost essential that visitors drive their own car, or rent one, for sightseeing in areas other than the downtown section and Westwood. Parking facilities are ample.

Transportation

Airport: See LOS ANGELES INTL AIRPORT AREA.

Car Rental Agencies: See toll-free numbers under Introduction.

Public Transportation: Buses (Rapid Transit), phone 213/626-4455.

Rail Passenger Service: Amtrak 800/872-7245.

What to See and Do

1. **"The Stack"** is a four-level junction of freeways. Motorists are likely to arrive in central Los Angeles on one of them. The high-speed six- and eight-lane roads cut across town: Hollywood Frwy to Hollywood and San Fernando Valley; Harbor Frwy to the south; Santa Ana Frwy to the southeast; San Bernardino Frwy to the east; Pasadena Frwy to Pasadena.

2. **Downtown.** Contains, among others, these facilities:

   City Hall. 200 N Spring St. First tall building constructed in southern California. Observation deck (27th floor) in the tower (closed for renovation). (Mon–Fri; closed hols) Phone 213/485-4423. **Free.**

   Hall of Justice. 211 W Temple St. County law enforcement headquarters.

   Music Center of Los Angeles County. 135 N Grand Ave, at First St. Performing arts center contains Dorothy Chandler Pavilion, Ahmanson Theatre, Mark Taper Forum. Daily performances by renowned music, dance and theater companies. (See SEASONAL EVENTS) Free guided tours. Phone 213/972-7211 for ticket information.

   ARCO Plaza. 505 S Flower St. Bi-level, subterranean shopping center; art shows, exhibits; restaurants, specialty & service shops.

   Los Angeles Children's Museum. 310 N Main St. "Hands-on" exhibits and programs designed to help children satisfy their curiosity about the world in which they live; includes "City Streets," where children drive a bus and ride a policeman's motorcycle, recording and TV studios and "H-2-O," a participatory look at how to use and conserve water. Phone 213/687-8800. **¢¢**

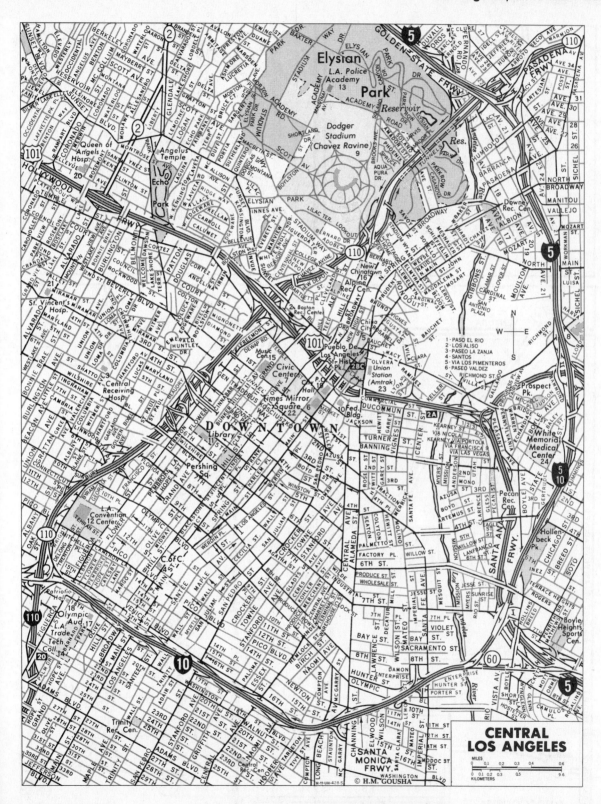

CENTRAL LOS ANGELES

1 - PASO EL RIO
2 - LOS ALISO
3 - PASEO LA ZANJA
4 - SANTOS
5 - VIA LOS PIMENTEROS
6 - PASEO VALDEZ

© H.M. GOUSHA

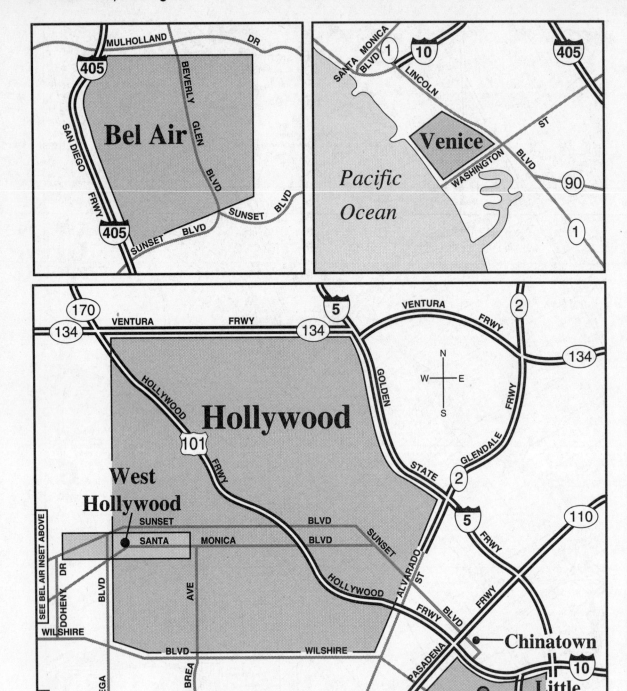

MULHOLLAND DR

405

BEVERLY GLEN BLVD

SAN DIEGO FRWY

Bel Air

405

SUNSET BLVD

SUNSET BLVD

SANTA MONICA BLVD

1

10

405

LINCOLN

ST

Venice

WASHINGTON BLVD

Pacific Ocean

90

1

170

134

VENTURA FRWY

5

134

VENTURA FRWY

2

134

HOLLYWOOD

101

Hollywood

GOLDEN STATE

N
W E
S

GLENDALE FRWY

2

5

110

West Hollywood

SUNSET BLVD

SANTA MONICA BLVD

SUNSET

FRWY

HOLLYWOOD

ALVARADO ST

5 FRWY

SEE BEL AIR INSET ABOVE

DOHENY DR

BLVD

AVE

WILSHIRE

BLVD

WILSHIRE

LA CIENEGA

LA BREA

SEE VENICE INSET ABOVE

10

LOS ANGELES NEIGHBORHOODS

0   1   2.0 miles

0   1.6   3.2 km

© H.M.GOUSHA

PASADENA FRWY

BLVD

Chinatown

10

Little Tokyo

Downtown

110

10

60

5

5-NA-10-M

Museum of Contemporary Art (MOCA). 250 S Grand Ave, at California Plaza. Seven-level museum devoted to art created since the early 1940s. The building, most of which is below street level, features 11 pyramidial skylight forms and a 53-ft barrel-vaulted structure housing the library and boardroom and serving as the entrance to the exhibits below. Paintings, photographs, drawings, sculptures, and "transmedia." (Daily exc Mon; closed Jan 1, Thanksgiving, Dec 25) Sr citizen rate. Phone 213/621-2766 or 626-6222. ¢¢

Wells Fargo History Museum. 333 S Grand Ave, Plaza Level. More than 140 years of Wells Fargo history depicted by displays and exhibits, including Dorsey gold collection, stagecoaches, treasure boxes, reward posters, 19th-century tools, archival documents, photographs, Western art objects and a reproduction of a Wells Fargo office (ca 1860); audiovisual presentations. (Mon–Fri; closed hols) Phone 213/253-7166 or -7169.   **Free.**

Los Angeles Mall. Spring St across from City Hall. Mall complex; shops, restaurants; triforium; music and light presentation.

World Trade Center. 350 S Figueroa St. Retail stores, restaurants, banks, golf driving ranges, tennis center, travel and tour services. Concourse mural depicts the history of world trade. Phone 213/489-3337.

Broadway Plaza. 7th & Hope Sts. Designed after an Italian Renaissance shopping galleria.

Little Tokyo. 1st St between Main & San Pedro Sts. Japanese restaurants, art and crafts shops, flower exhibits.

Chinatown. N Broadway near College St. Quaint shops and Chinese restaurants on "Street of the Golden Palace."

3. **El Pueblo de Los Angeles Historic Monument.** 845 N Alameda St. Marks area close to where original pueblo of Los Angeles was founded in 1781. Much of the park has been restored; additional building restorations are underway that will also reflect the history and atmosphere of old Los Angeles. Exhibit on "History of Water in Los Angeles." (Tues–Sat) For tour reservations phone 213/628-1274.   **Free.**   The park includes

Avila Adobe. The oldest existing house in Los Angeles (ca 1820), damaged by an earthquake in 1971, now restored as an example of 1840s lifestyle in honor of Los Angeles' Hispanic heritage. (Tues–Sat)   **Free.**

Old Plaza Firehouse. Built as Los Angeles' first firehouse in 1884; restored as a museum with photographs and fire-fighting equipment of 19th century. (Tues–Sat)   **Free.**

Nuestra Señora La Reina de Los Angeles (Our Lady Queen of the Angels) (1818–1822). The restored Old Plaza Catholic Church is still an active parish. Contains fine old statuary. (Daily)   **Free.**

Olvera Street. Preserved as a picturesque Mexican street market with stalls, shops and restaurants selling traditional food and merchandise. It has several annual celebrations, which include Blessing of the Animals (Sat before Easter), Cinco de Mayo (May 5), the city's birthday (Sept 4), Mexican Independence Day (Sept 15) and Los Posadas (Dec 16–24). (Daily)   **Free.**

Tribute to Christine Sterling. Honors woman who led movement to renovate and preserve area, and who created Olvera Street marketplace. (Tues–Sat)   **Free.**

Guided walking tours leave from the Docent Office, 130 Paseo de la Plaza, next to Old Plaza Firehouse (Tues–Sat). For reservations phone 213/628-1274.   **Free.**

Sepulveda House (1887). Partially restored Victorian business block; also houses **Visitors Center** (daily exc Sun). Offers 18-minute film on early history of Los Angeles and the park (Tues–Sat; free). Phone 213/628-1274.

4. **Griffith Park.** N end of Vermont Ave, bordered by Ventura Frwy on N, Golden State Frwy on E, Los Feliz Blvd entrances on S. (Daily) Some activities charge admission. More than 4,000 mountainous acres with swimming pool (fee); bridle paths; four golf courses (fee; phone 213/485-5515); tennis courts (fee), baseball fields and many picnic grounds. Also in park are merry-go-round, miniature railroad, refreshment stands and

Los Angeles Zoo. 5333 Zoo Dr, in center of park. On 113 landscaped acres; animals grouped by continental origin; reptile house, aviary, aquatic section; koala house; children's zoo; animal rides. Tram service. Picnic areas, concessions. (Daily; closed Dec 25) Sr citizen rate. Phone 213/666-4090. ¢¢¢

Griffith Observatory and Planetarium. 2800 E Observatory Rd. Includes Hall of Science (summer, daily; winter, daily exc Mon; closed Thanksgiving, Dec 24, 25; free). Planetarium has frequent shows (daily exc Mon in winter; under age 5 admitted only 1:30 pm shows and special children's shows; sr citizen discount all shows). Telescope (nightly exc Mon in winter). Laserium light concerts (phone 818/997-3624); bookshop. Phone 213/664-1191 (recording) for planetarium show schedule. ¢¢

Travel Town. Forest Lawn & Zoo Drs, S off Ventura Frwy. Transportation museum with antique trains, steam engines, planes, fire engines, cable cars. Picnic areas, concession. (Daily; closed Dec 25) Phone 213/662-5874.   **Free.**

Greek Theatre. Scene of summer season of musical events in open-air setting.

5. **UCLA Mildred Mathias Botanical Garden.** Hilgard & Le Conte Aves. Collection of plants, trees and shrubs. Parking (fee). (Daily; closed university & federal hols, also Jan 2 & the day after Thanksgiving & Dec 24) Guided tour of campus from visitors center (wkdays). Phone 310/206-8147.   **Free.**

6. **Elysian Park.** Near intersection of Pasadena & Golden State Frwys. Covers 575 acres with beautiful landscaping. Picnicking, playground, tennis courts and ballfields. Dodger Stadium, home of L.A. Dodgers baseball team, is located here. (See SEASONAL EVENTS) (Daily)   **Free.**

7. **Descanso Gardens.** 1418 Descanso Dr, just S of Foothill Blvd in La Cañada/Flintridge. On 165 acres with 10-acre native plant garden. Ornamental camellia gardens, more than 100,000 plants in bloom Dec–Mar, peaking in mid-Feb. Azalea and rhododendron display Mar–Apr; 5-acre rose garden in bloom May–Oct; iris and lilacs in spring; annuals in summer. (Daily exc Dec 25) Tram tours (daily). Hospitality House with changing artwork (daily). Oriental Pavilion with teahouse (daily exc Mon). Guided tours. Sr citizen rate. Phone 818/952-4400. ¢¢

8. **Los Angeles State and County Arboretum** (see ARCADIA).

9. **Exposition Park.** Figueroa St & Exposition Blvd. Park includes sunken rose garden, picnic grounds. Sports arena, Los Angeles Swimming Stadium. Park is also the setting for

Los Angeles Memorial Coliseum. 3911 S Figueroa St. Home field for USC and Raiders football teams. Also scene of soccer, concerts, track events and many others. Seating capacity of 92,516. Tours on request. Phone 213/747-7111, ext 211. Tour ¢

Natural History Museum of Los Angeles County. 900 Exposition Blvd. Permanent science exhibits feature mammal, bird, insect and marine life as well as dinosaurs, other prehistoric fossils and extinct creatures. Minerals and metals display includes extensive collection of cut gems. History gallery includes features on US history; 400 years of life in California; displays of pre-Columbian cultures. Cafeteria. (Daily exc Mon; closed Jan 1, Thanksgiving, Dec 25) Free admission 1st Tues of month. Phone 213/744-3414 or -3466 (recording). ¢¢¢

California Museum of Science and Industry. 700 State Dr, adj to the Coliseum. Hands-on exhibits on science, mathematics, economics, the urban environment, energy and health. Hall of Health; Aerospace Hall; earthquake simulator; IMAX theater offers films (fee). (Daily; closed Jan 1, Thanksgiving, Dec 25) Phone 213/744-7400.   **Free.**

10. **Lummis Home and Garden State Historical Monument.** 200 E Ave 43, adj to Pasadena Frwy (CA 110). Picturesque stone-faced house of Charles F. Lummis (1859–1928), author, historian, librarian and archaeologist; surrounded by model 2-acre water-conserving garden. Also headquarters for Historical Society of Southern California. (Fri–Sun afternoons; closed hols) Phone 213/222-0546. **Free.**

11. Beit Hashoah, Museum of Tolerance. 9760 W Pico Blvd, The Simon Wiesenthal Center. Unique museum focuses on two central themes: the Holocaust and the history of racism and prejudice in the American experience. For schedule and fee information phone 310/553-9036.

12. Southwest Museum. 234 Museum Dr, at Marmion Way, Pasadena Frwy Ave 43 exit. Prehistoric to contemporary American Indian art and artifacts; research library. (Daily exc Mon; closed major hols) Sr citizen rate. Phone 213/221-2163.   ¢¢

13. South Coast Botanic Garden. 26300 Crenshaw Blvd, 1 mi S of Pacific Coast Hwy in Palos Verdes Peninsula. Hillside and coastal plants on 87 acres of filled land. (Daily; closed Dec 25) Sr citizen rate. Phone 310/544-6815.   ¢

14. Mulholland Drive. Reached by Laurel Canyon Blvd, Hollywood Blvd, Coldwater Canyon Dr, Beverly Glen Blvd and other roads. Runs along crest of Santa Monica Mts. For a look at the Los Angeles hills and canyons and views of the city and San Fernando Valley, this drive is unsurpassed.

15. Farmers Market. Corner of 3rd & Fairfax Ave. Historic landmark with outdoor food stalls, restaurants and shops. (Daily; closed hols) Phone 213/933-9211.

16. State Historic Parks.

Los Encinos. 16756 Moorpark St, in Encino. Early California ranch; exhibits of ranch life contained in nine-room adobe. Blacksmith shop, spring and small lake. Picnicking. Afternoon tours (fee). Grounds (Wed–Sun). Phone 818/784-4849.   **Free.**

Will Rogers. 15 mi W, 1501 Will Rogers State Park Rd, in Pacific Palisades. Home contains Rogers memorabilia, western art, Native American artifacts; audio tour and film. Hiking and riding trails (horses not avail). Picnicking. (Daily; closed Jan 1, Thanksgiving, Dec 25) Polo games (Sat afternoons, Sun mornings weather permitting). Phone 310/454-8212. Per vehicle (per day) and tour   ¢¢

17. Los Angeles County Museum of Art. 5905 Wilshire Blvd, 2 blocks E of Fairfax Ave. This outstanding museum consists of five buildings. The Robert Anderson Bldg houses the 20th-century art collection and traveling exhibitions; the Ahmanson Bldg houses small changing exhibits and the museum's permanent collection, including paintings, sculptures, graphic arts, costumes, textiles and decorative arts of different cultures and periods, dating from prehistoric to modern times; the Hammer Bldg has major changing exhibits; the Leo S. Bing Center has music, film and theater programs; two cafes and educational services; and the Pavilion for Japanese Art displays Japanese paintings, sculpture, lacquerware, screens, scrolls and prints. (Daily exc Mon; closed Jan 1, Thanksgiving, Dec 25) Free admission 2nd Tues each month. Phone 213/857-6111; recorded message, 213/857-6000.   ¢¢

18. George C. Page Museum of La Brea Discoveries. 5801 Wilshire Blvd, in Hancock Park. Houses more than one million prehistoric specimens recovered from the La Brea asphalt deposits or "tar pits." More than 30 exhibits, including reconstructed skeletons; murals, theaters. (Daily exc Mon; closed Jan 1, Thanksgiving, Dec 25) Sr citizen rate. Free on 2nd Tues of each month. Phone 213/857-6311 or 213/936-2230 (recorded information).   ¢¢

19. TV production studios.

CBS Television City. 7800 Beverly Blvd, at Fairfax Ave, 90036. West Coast studios of CBS-Television and source of many of its network telecasts. Write for free tickets well in advance (specify dates and shows preferred) and enclose a stamped, self-addressed envelope. Tickets may also be picked up at Information Window (daily) on a first come, first served basis. Age limits for admittance vary and are specified on tickets; children under 12 not admitted to any broadcast; ages 12–15 with adult only. Phone 213/852-2624.

NBC Studios Tour. 3000 W Alameda Ave, Burbank 91523. Free tickets to a taping of one of NBC's TV shows; free parking. Age limits are specified on face of tickets. For tour information phone 818/840-3537 (24 hrs). For general information phone 818/840-4444. Tours (Mon–Fri)   ¢¢¢

20. Universal Studios Hollywood. 100 Universal Dr, ½ blk N of Hollywood Frwy in Universal City. Offers a full day of behind-the-scenes views of Hollywood's largest and busiest studio; 45-min tram ride through 420-acre production area where motion pictures and television films are made. Experience the excitement of *Backdraft* Live, fly with *E.T.*, face *King Kong*, and feel Earthquake, the Big One; also, take "the greatest ride in history" on *Back to the Future,* The Ride. Tours (daily; closed Thanksgiving, Dec 25). Sr citizen rate. Phone 818/508-9600 (recording) or 818/622-3750.   ¢¢¢¢¢

21. Paramount Film and Television Studios. 5555 Melrose Ave, between Van Ness Ave and Gower St. Two-hour walking tour of studios (Mon–Fri; no tours hols) and tapings of situation comedies and talk shows (seasonal; usually Tues or Fri evenings). closed major hols). Walking tour given 2 times daily. Minimum age 10 yrs for studio tour and 18 yrs for television tapings. For taping schedule write to Paramount Promotional Services, 5555 Melrose Ave. Tickets available in person only at 860 N Gower St, Hollywood. Phone 213/956-1777. Tour   ¢¢¢;   Tapings **free.**

22. Amateur Athletic Foundation. 2141 W Adams Blvd; 5 mi SW via Santa Monica Freeway, Western Ave exit. Sports museum contains more than 35,000 print and non-print volumes, multipurpose pavilion, audio and video exhibits, Olympic awards and memorabilia; Resource Center (by appt only). (Mon–Fri; closed hols) Phone 213/730-9600.   **Free.**

23. Watts Towers. 1765 E 107th St, S of Century Blvd, E of Harbor Frwy in Watts. Eight spires made of reinforced steel covered with cement, assembled without welding, nuts or bolts and encrusted with 70,000 bits of tile, crockery and bottles. Built solely by the late Simon Rodia over a 33-year period, described as "paramount achievement of 20th-century American folk art." Two of the towers rise 100 feet. Also art center (free) at 1727 E 107th St. Sr citizen rate. Phone 213/569-8181. Tower   ¢

24. Beach areas. There are miles of oceanfront in Los Angeles County within 35 miles of downtown Los Angeles. Beaches include Malibu, Santa Monica, Ocean Park, Venice, Manhattan, Redondo, Long Beach and others. Redondo Beach has a horseshoe pier and yacht harbor.

25. Universities.

University of Southern California (1880). (29,500 students) 3551 University Ave. Fisher Gallery (Sept–Apr, Tues–Sat; May–Aug, by appt) phone 213/740-4561; Hancock Memorial Museum (Mon–Fri by appt) phone 213/740-0433; Arnold Schoenberg Institute (Mon–Fri) phone 213/740-4090. For tour information, phone 213/740-1616 or -2300.

University of California, Los Angeles (UCLA) (1919). (34,000 students) 405 Hilgard Ave. Tours (Mon–Fri). Art gallery (see #26), botanical garden (see #5), Franklin D. Murphy Sculpture Garden. Parking (fee). Phone 213/206-8147. Also here is

Fowler Museum of Cultural History, UCLA. Located near the center of the campus. Changing exhibits on cultures around the world. (Wed–Sun afternoons, also Thurs evenings) Enter campus from Sunset Blvd, at the Westwood Plaza entrance, and inquire about parking availability at the information kiosk. For information phone 310/825-4361. Parking   ¢¢

26. Wight Art Gallery. 405 Hilgard Ave, at University of California, Los Angeles (see #25). Changing exhibitions of paintings, sculpture, design, architecture, prints and drawings; Grunwald Center for Graphic Arts; Franklin D. Murphy Sculpture Garden. (Daily exc Mon) Phone 310/825-9345.   **Free.**

27. Sightseeing tours.

Gray Line bus tours. Contact 6541 Hollywood Blvd, 90028; phone 213/856-5900.

CCInc Auto Tape Tours. These 90-minute cassettes offer mile-by-mile self-guided tours to Fresno (193 mi) with historical and scenic points of interest through San Joaquin Valley, Bakersfield and Fort Tejon; to San Luis Obispo (188 mi) with major points of interest in Hollywood, Santa Barbara, Solvang, historical account of California missions. Fourteen different tour tapes of California are available. Tapes may be purchased directly from CCInc, PO Box 227, 2 Elbrook Dr, Allendale, NJ 07401; 201/236-1666. **¢¢¢¢**

28. In the area are

Hollywood (see). Reached via Hollywood Frwy.

Disneyland (see). 26 mi SE via Santa Ana Frwy in Anaheim.

Six Flags Magic Mountain (see VALENCIA).

Cabrillo Marine Museum (see SAN PEDRO).

Los Angeles Maritime Museum (see SAN PEDRO).

Mission San Fernando Rey de España (see SAN FERNANDO).

Trips to Catalina Island (see LONG BEACH). Also from Los Angeles International Airport.

Knott's Berry Farm (see BUENA PARK).

Ports o'Call Village (see SAN PEDRO).

29. Industrial tour. San Antonio Winery. 737 Lamar St. Winery, gift shop, wine tasting; restaurant. Tours. (Daily; closed major hols) Phone 213/223-1401. **Free.**

Annual Events

Chinese New Year. Jan or Feb.

Hanamatsuri. Festival honoring Buddha's birthday at Japanese Village Plaza. Usually wkend Apr.

Cinco de Mayo Celebration. El Pueblo de Los Angeles Historic Monument (see #3). Arts and crafts, music and dancing. May 5.

Asian Cultural Festival. West Los Angeles Mall. Sat in mid-July.

Nisei Week. Little Tokyo. Japanese cultural exhibits. Aug.

Los Angeles County Fair. Fairplex, 1101 W McKinley Ave in Pomona (see). Largest in the nation. Mid-Sept–early Oct.

Seasonal Events

Horse racing.

Santa Anita Park (see ARCADIA).

Hollywood Park. Century Blvd & Prairie Ave in Inglewood. Phone 213/419-1500. Early Apr–late July & early Nov–late Dec.

Greek Theatre in Griffith Park (see #4). Musical events. Mid-June–late Sept.

Los Angeles Music Center Opera. Music Center of Los Angeles County, Dorothy Chandler Pavilion (see #2). Phone 213/972-7211. Early Sept–June.

Professional sports. Dodgers (baseball), Dodger Stadium, 1000 Elysian Park Ave, E of Sunset Blvd, in Elysian Park. Raiders (football), LA Coliseum (see #9). Rams (football), Angels (baseball), Anaheim Stadium in Anaheim (see). Clippers (basketball), Sports Arena at Exposition Park, 3911 S Figueroa St. Lakers (basketball), Kings (hockey), the Great Western Forum, 3900 W Manchester Ave, at Prairie Ave in Inglewood.

Special Event

World Cup 94. Los Angeles will be one of nine US cities to host games of the XV World Cup soccer tournament. This will be the first time the event is held in North America. The Rose Bowl in Pasadena (see) will be the site of eight matches and of the World Cup Final on July 17. Tickets avail through Ticketmaster. For further information phone World Cup Public Information, 310/277-9494. Mid-June–mid-July.

Additional Visitor Information

The Los Angeles Convention and Visitors Bureau, 633 W Fifth St, Suite 6000, 90071; 213/624-7300, handles written inquiries and has general information brochures available in English, French, German, Japanese and Spanish. Printed tourist guides are available at two visitor information centers: downtown at 685 S Figueroa St, phone 213/689-8822; and Hollywood, 6541 Hollywood Blvd, phone 213/689-8822. In addition, multilingual counselors are on staff at each information center to assist visitors.

Los Angeles Magazine, available at newsstands, has up-to-date information on cultural events and articles of interest to visitors.

Los Angeles Area Suburbs

For Los Angeles area suburbs listed in the *Mobil Travel Guide*, see LOS ANGELES AREA, which precedes LOS ANGELES.

Los Angeles Intl Airport Area

For additional accommodations, see LOS ANGELES INTL AIRPORT AREA, which follows LOS ANGELES.

City Neighborhoods

Many of the restaurants, unrated dining establishments and some lodgings listed under Los Angeles include neighborhoods as well as exact street addresses. A map showing these neighborhoods can be found immediately following the city map. Geographic descriptions of these areas are given, followed by a table of restaurants arranged by neighborhood.

Bel Air: West of Downtown; south of Mulholland Dr, west of Beverly Hills, north of the University of California Los Angeles (UCLA) campus and east of the San Diego Frwy (I-405).

Chinatown: Directly north of Downtown; south of Bernard St, west of N Broadway, north of College St and east of Hill St.

Downtown: South of the Hollywood Frwy (US 101), west of the Golden State Frwy (I-5), north of the Santa Monica Frwy (I-10) and east of the Pasadena Frwy (CA 110). **North of Downtown:** North of US 101. **South of Downtown:** South of I-10. **West of Downtown:** West of the Pasadena Frwy (CA 110).

Hollywood see: Area northwest of Downtown; south of Mulholland Dr, Universal City and the Ventura Frwy (CA 134), west of the Golden State Frwy (I-5) and Alvarado St (CA 2), north of Wilshire Blvd and east of La Cienega Blvd.

Little Tokyo: Area of Downtown south of 1st St, west of Central Ave, north of 3rd St and east of San Pedro St.

Venice: Oceanfront area south of Santa Monica, west of Lincoln Blvd (CA 1) and north of Washington St.

West Hollywood: Area south and north of Santa Monica Blvd, between Doheny Dr on the west and La Brea Ave on the east.

LOS ANGELES RESTAURANTS
BY NEIGHBORHOOD AREAS

(For full description, see alphabetical listings under Restaurants; also see restaurants listed under HOLLYWOOD.)

BEL AIR

Bel-Air Dining Room (Bel-Air Hotel). 701 Stone Canyon Rd

Four Oaks. 2181 N Beverly Glen

CHINATOWN

Little Joe's. 900 N Broadway

Ocean Seafood. 747 N Broadway

DOWNTOWN

Bernard's (Biltmore Hotel). 506 S Grand Ave

Pavilion. 165 N Grand Ave

Phillipe The Original. 1001 N Alameda St

Rex II Ristorante. 617 S Olive St

Sonora Cafe. 445 S Figueroa St

The Tower. 1150 S Olive St

NORTH OF DOWNTOWN

Les Freres Taix. 1911 Sunset Blvd

Tam-O-Shanter Inn. 2980 Los Feliz Blvd

SOUTH OF DOWNTOWN

Champagne Bis. 10506 Little Santa Monica Blvd

WEST OF DOWNTOWN

Campanile. 624 S La Brea Ave

Cassell's. 3266 W 6th St

City. 180 S La Brea Ave

Gardens (Four Seasons Hotel). 300 S Doheny Dr

Hard Rock Cafe. 8600 Beverly Blvd

J.W.'s (J.W. Marriott at Century City Hotel). 2151 Avenue of the Stars

La Chaumiere (Century Plaza Hotel & Tower). 2025 Avenue of the Stars

Locanda Veneta. 8638 W Third St

Madeo. 8897 Beverly Blvd

Orleans. 11705 National Blvd

Primi. 10543 W Pico Blvd

Sisley Italian Kitchen. 10800 W Pico Blvd

Note: When a listing is located in a town that does not have its own city heading, it will appear under the city nearest to its location. In these cases, the address and town appear in parenthesis immediately following the name of the establishment.

Motels

✔ ★**BEST WESTERN EXECUTIVE MOTOR INN MID-WIL-SHIRE.** 603 S New Hampshire Ave (90005), west of downtown. 213/385-4444. 90 rms, 5 story. July–Aug: S $58–$63; D $63–$68; each addl $3; under 12 free; wkend plans; lower rates rest of yr. Crib free. TV; cable. Indoor pool. Complimentary continental bkfst 7–9 am. Ck-out noon. Coin lndry. Valet serv. Sundries. Exercise equipt; treadmill, stair machine, whirlpool, sauna. Refrigerators. Cr cds: A, D, DS, MC, V, JCB.

▣ ⛵ ⊛ ⊜ SC

★★**RESIDENCE INN BY MARRIOTT.** (1700 N Sepulveda Blvd, Manhattan Beach 90266) CA 405 to Rosecrans exit. 310/546-7627. 176 kit. suites, 2 story. S $115–$150; D $150–$190; each addl $10; under 12 free; wkly, monthly rates. Crib free. Pet accepted, some restrictions. TV; cable, in-rm movies. Heated pool; whirlpool. Complimentary continental bkfst. Restaurant nearby. Ck-out noon. Meeting rm. Valet serv. Free airport transportation. Balconies. Cr cds: A, C, D, DS, MC, V, JCB.

▣ 🐾 ⚓ ⊛ ⊜ SC

Motor Hotels

★★**CENTURY CITY INN.** 10330 W Olympic Blvd (90064), west of downtown. 310/553-1000; res: 800/553-1005, 800/553-3253 (CAN); FAX 310/277-1633. 46 rms, 3 story, 14 suites. S $99–$129; D $114–$143; each addl $15; suites $119–$159; under 7 free; wkly rates. Crib free. Valet parking $5.50. TV; cable, in-rm movies. Complimentary continental bkfst. Ck-out noon. Bellhops. Valet serv. Lighted tennis privileges. Health club privileges. Refrigerators, bathrm phones, in-rm whirlpools. Cr cds: A, D, DS, MC, V.

▣ ⛵ ⚓ ⊛ SC

★★**COURTYARD BY MARRIOTT** (formerly Chesterfield Hotel Deluxe). 10320 W Olympic Blvd (90064), west of downtown. 310/556-2777; FAX 310/203-0563. 133 rms, 4 story. S $99–$119; D $109–$129; each addl $10; suites $125–$135; wkend rates. TV; cable. Coffee in rms. Restaurant 6–10:30 am. Bar 5 pm–midnight. Ck-out noon. Meeting rms. Bellhops. Valet serv. Free valet parking. Shuttle to Beverly Hills, Century City. Exercise equipt; weights, bicycles, whirlpool. Minibars. Balconies. Cr cds: A, D, DS, MC, V.

▣ 🏃 ⚓ ⊛ ⊜ SC

✔ ★**HOLIDAY INN DOWNTOWN.** 750 Garland Ave (90015), downtown. 213/628-5242; FAX 213/628-1201. 205 rms, 6 story. S, D $79–$119; under 18 free. Crib free. TV; cable. Pool. Restaurant 6 am–10 pm. Rm serv. Ck-out noon. Coin lndry. Meeting rms. Bellhops. Valet serv. Airport transportation. Cr cds: A, C, D, DS, MC, V, JCB.

⚓ ⊛ SC

✔ ★**HOWARD JOHNSON CENTRAL.** 1640 Marengo St (90033), north of downtown. 213/223-3841; FAX 213/222-4039. 122 rms, 7 story. S $56; D $62; each addl $8; 3-day min Rose Bowl. Crib free. TV; cable. Pool. Restaurant 6:30 am–2 pm, 5–10 pm; Sat, Sun 7 am–1 pm, 5–9 pm. Rm serv. Bar 11 am–midnight. Ck-out noon. Meeting rms. Bellhops. Valet serv. Sundries. Free downtown transportation. Cr cds: A, C, D, DS, MC, V, JCB.

⚓ ⊗ ⊛ SC

★★**MIYAKO INN & SPA.** 328 E 1st St (90012), in Little Tokyo. 213/617-2000; FAX 213/617-2700. 174 rms, 11 story. S $85–$97; D $95–$107; under 12 free. Covered parking $6. TV; cable. Restaurant 7 am–10 pm. Bar; entertainment. Ck-out noon. Meeting rms. Bellhops. Valet serv. Whirlpool, sauna, steam rm. Japanese-style massage. Refrigerators. In heart of Little Tokyo. Cr cds: A, C, D, DS, MC, V, JCB.

▣ ⊗ ⊛ SC

Hotels

★★**BARNABEY'S.** (3501 Sepulveda Blvd, Manhattan Beach 90266) S via I-405, Rosecrans exit. 310/545-8466; res: 800/552-5285 (US), 800/851-7678 (CAN); FAX 310/545-8621. 126 rms, 3 story. S $129–$144; D $144–$159; suites $149–$450; under 12 free; hol, wkend rates. Crib $15. Garage parking $4; valet. TV. Indoor/outdoor pool. Complimentary full bkfst. Complimentary coffee in rms. Restaurant 6:30 am–11 pm. Bar 11 am–midnight; entertainment Tues–Sat. Ck-out noon. Meeting rms. Gift shop. Free airport transportation. European-style decor; antiques. Cr cds: A, C, D, DS, MC, V.

⚓ ⊗ SC

★★★**BEL AGE.** 1020 N San Vicente (90069), in West Hollywood. 310/854-1111; FAX 310/854-0926. 200 suites, 8 story. S, D $195–$500; each addl $25; under 12 free; wkend rates. Valet parking $14. TV; in-rm movies avail. Heated pool; poolside serv. Restaurants 7 am–9 pm, Thurs–Sat to 1 am. Rm serv 24 hrs. Bar 11–2 am. Ck-out 1 pm. Convention facilities. Concierge. Shopping arcade. Barber, beauty shops. Bathrm phones, minibars, wet bars. Private patios, balconies. Complimentary fresh fruit, mineral water upon arrival. Complimentary shoeshine. Cr cds: A, C, D, MC, V, JCB.

▣ ⚓ ⊛

★★★★**BEL-AIR.** 701 Stone Canyon Rd (90077), in Bel Air. 310/472-1211; FAX 310/476-5890. 92 rms, some kits. S $235–$395; D $265–$435; suites $550–$2,000. TV; cable, in-rm movies avail. Heated pool; poolside serv, lifeguard. Restaurant (see BEL-AIR DINING ROOM). Rm serv 24 hrs. Bar 10–2 am; entertainment. Ck-out 1 pm. Meeting rms. Concierge. Valet parking. Airport transportation. Bathrm phones; some wood-burning fireplaces. Private patios. Vintage resort hotel; individually decorated rms. Lush gardens, serene atmosphere. Tea service on arrival. Cr cds: A, C, D, MC, V, JCB.

[symbols]

★ ★ ★ **BEVERLY PLAZA.** 8384 W 3rd St (90048), west of downtown. 213/658-6600; res: 800/624-6835 (exc CA); FAX 213/653-3464. 98 rms, 5 story. S $106–$158; D $116–$168; each addl $10; under 12 free. TV; cable, in-rm movies. Heated pool; poolside serv. Restaurant 7 am–10:30 pm. Rm serv 24 hrs. Bar 11 am–midnight; entertainment Thurs–Sun. Ck-out noon. Meeting rms. Concierge. Valet parking. Exercise equipt; weights, bicycles, sauna. Bathrm phones, minibars. Cr cds: A, C, D, DS, MC, V.

[symbols] SC

★ ★ ★ **BILTMORE.** 506 S Grand Ave (90071), downtown. 213/624-1011; res: 800/421-8000 (exc CA), 800/252-0175 (CA); FAX 213/612-1545. 700 rms, 12 story. S $140–$230; D $160–$245; each addl $30; suites $390–$1,800; under 12 free; wknd package plan. Garage $16. Heated pool. TV; cable. Restaurant 6 am–11 pm (also see BERNARD'S). Rm serv 24 hrs. Bars; entertainment. Ck-out noon. Convention facilities. Free shuttle service throughout downtown Los Angeles. Exercise equipt; weights, bicycles, sauna. Wet bar in most suites. Some bathrm phones. Historic landmark; opened 1923. Italian Renaissance architecture. *LUXURY LEVEL:* **CONCIERGE LEVEL.** 65 rms, 6 suites, 2 floors. S $230; D $245. Concierge. Private lounge, honor bar. Minibars. Complimentary continental bkfst, refreshments, newspaper. Cr cds: A, C, D, DS, ER, MC, V, JCB.

[symbols] SC

CENTURY PLAZA HOTEL & TOWER. (4-Star 1993; New general manager, therefore not rated) 2025 Ave of the Stars (90067), in Century City, west of downtown. 310/277-2000; FAX 310/551-3355. 1,072 rms, 19–30 story. S $150; D $175; each addl $25; suites $250–$1,100. Tower: S $210; D $235–$300; suites $900–$3,000; each addl $30; under 18 free. TV. Heated pool; poolside serv in summer. Restaurant 6–1 am (also see LA CHAUMIERE). Rm serv 24 hrs. 3 bars 11–2 am; entertainment. Ck-out 1 pm. Lndry facilities 24 hrs. Convention facilities. Concierge. Barber, beauty shop. Valet parking. Airport transportation avail. Exercise equipt; weight machine, bicycles, whirlpool. Tennis & health club privileges adj. Bathrm phones. Balconies. Modern hotel on 10 landscaped acres; Japanese garden. Cr cds: A, C, D, DS, ER, MC, V, JCB.

[symbols] SC

★ ★ **CHATEAU MARMONT.** 8221 Sunset Blvd (90046), in West Hollywood. 213/656-1010; FAX 213/655-5311. 63 rms, 7 story, 54 kits. S, D $150; suites $195–$270; cottages, kits. $210; monthly rates. Pet accepted. TV; cable, in-rm movies avail. Heated pool; poolside serv. Restaurant 6–2 am. Ck-out noon. Garage, free valet parking. Refrigerators. Private patios, balconies. Neo-Gothic chateau-style building; old Hollywood landmark. Cr cds: A, C, D, MC, V.

[symbols]

★ ★ ★ **CHECKERS HOTEL KEMPINSKI LOS ANGELES.** 535 S Grand Ave (90071), downtown. 213/624-0000; res: 800/426-3135; FAX 213/626-9906. 188 rms, 12 story, 15 suites. S, D $180–$190; each addl $35; suites $380–$950; under 18 free; wknd rates. Crib free. Valet parking $21. TV; cable, in-rm movies avail. Heated pool; poolside serv. Restaurant 6:30 am–10 pm. Rm serv 24 hrs. Bar 11:30–2 am. Meeting rms. Concierge. Airport transportation. Exercise rm; instructor, weight machine, bicycles, whirlpool, sauna, steam rm. Massage. Library. Bathrm phones, minibars. Residential-style luxury hotel; lobby features exquisite Oriental and contemporary works of art, antiques. Cr cds: A, C, D, DS, ER, MC, V, JCB.

[symbols] SC

★ ★ ★ ★ **FOUR SEASONS.** 300 S Doheny Dr (90048), west of downtown. 310/273-2222; FAX 310/859-3824. 285 rms, 16 story. S $235–$315; D $260–$340; suites $350–$2,000; family, wknd rates. TV; cable. Pool; poolside serv, lifeguard. Restaurant 6:30 am–11:30 pm (also see GARDENS). Traditional afternoon tea. Rm serv 24 hrs. Bar 11–1 am; pianist. Ck-out 1 pm. Convention facilities. Concierge 24 hrs. Gift

shop. Underground parking. Complimentary limo to Beverly Hills, Century City. Tennis privileges. 18-hole golf privileges. Exercise rm; instructor, weights, bicycles, whirlpool. Massage. Bathrm phones, refrigerators. Balconies. Distinctly Californian; understated elegance. Cr cds: A, C, D, ER, MC, V, JCB.

[symbols]

★ ★ ★ **HILTON & TOWERS.** 930 Wilshire Blvd (90017), downtown. 213/629-4321; FAX 213/488-9869. 900 rms, 16 story. S $139–$209; D $159–$229; each addl $20; suites $375–$575; family rates. Crib free. Garage $19. TV; cable. Heated pool; poolside serv. Restaurants 6 am–11 pm. Bar 10–2 am; pianist. Ck-out noon. Convention facilities. Concierge. Shopping arcade. Barber, beauty shop. Exercise equipt; weight machines, bicycles. Minibars. *LUXURY LEVEL:* **TOWERS.** 96 rms, 4 suites, 2 floors. S $179–$229; D $199–$249; suites $425–$610. Honor bar. Complimentary bkfst, refreshments. Cr cds: A, C, D, DS, ER, MC, V, JCB.

[symbols] SC

★ ★ ★ **HILTON & TOWERS, UNIVERSAL CITY.** (555 University Terrace Pkwy, Universal City 91608) N on US 101, Lankersham exit. 818/506-2500; FAX 818/509-2031. 449 units, 24 story, 26 suites. S, D $150–$180; each addl $20; suites $250–$1,395; children free with parent; monthly rates. Crib free. Pet accepted, some restrictions. Garage parking $9, valet $11.50. TV; cable. Heated pool; poolside serv. Restaurant 6:30 am–11 pm. Rm serv 24 hrs. Bar 11–1:30 am; entertainment, dancing Wed–Sun. Ck-out noon. Convention facilities. Concierge. Gift shop. Airport transportation avail. Exercise equipt; weight machine, bicycles, whirlpool, steam rm. Bathrm phones, minibars. Wet bar in suites. Some suites with vaulted, skylit ceiling; panoramic view of city. *LUXURY LEVEL:* **TOWERS.** 36 rms, 8 suites, 2 floors. S, D $150–$180; suites $250–$500. Concierge. Privage lounge, honor bar. Complimentary continental bkfst, refreshments. Cr cds: A, C, D, DS, ER, MC, V, JCB.

[symbols] SC

★ ★ **HOLIDAY INN.** 170 N Church Lane (90049), I-405 Sunset Blvd exit, west of downtown. 310/476-6411; FAX 310/472-1157. 211 rms, 17 story. S $104–$128; D $114–$138; each addl $10; suites $210; under 19 free; hol, wknd, wkly rates; higher rates special events; some lower rates in winter. Crib free. Pet accepted, some restrictions. TV; cable. Heated pool; poolside serv. Restaurant 6 am–11 pm. Bar. Ck-out noon. Coin lndry. Meeting rms. Concierge. Exercise equipt; weight machine, bicycles, whirlpool. Refrigerators avail. Balconies. Cr cds: A, C, D, DS, MC, V, JCB.

[symbols] SC

✔ ★ ★ **HOLIDAY INN CONVENTION CENTER.** 1020 S Figueroa St (90015), opp Convention Center, downtown. 213/748-1291; FAX 213/748-6028. 195 rms, 9 story. S, D $79–$135; each addl $15; suites $158–$210; under 18 free; wknd rates; higher rates: selected conventions, some special events. Crib free. Pet accepted, some restrictions. TV; cable. Heated pool; poolside serv. Complimentary coffee in rms. Restaurant 6 am–10 pm. Bar noon–midnight. Ck-out noon. Convention facilities. Coin lndry. Gift shop. Exercise equipt; bicycles, treadmill, sauna. Cr cds: A, C, D, DS, MC, V, JCB.

[symbols] SC

★ ★ ★ **HOTEL SOFITEL MA MAISON.** 8555 Beverly Blvd (90048), at La Cienega, west of downtown. 310/278-5444; res: 800/221-4542; FAX 310/657-2816. 311 rms, 10 story. S, D $190–$450; each addl $20; suites $200–$450; under 18 free; wknd rates. Crib free. Valet parking $14. TV; cable. Heated pool; poolside serv. Restaurant 6 am–midnight. Rm serv 24 hrs. Bar from 11 am; entertainment. Ck-out 1 pm. Convention facilities. Concierge. Shopping arcade. Barber, beauty shop. Tennis privileges. Exercise equipt; weight machines, bicycles. Bathrm phones, refrigerators, minibars, wet bars. Balconies. Contemporary Mediterranean-style hotel features a blend of French and Californian cultures. Cr cds: A, C, D, DS, ER, MC, V, JCB.

[symbols]

★ ★ ★ **HYATT REGENCY.** 711 S Hope St (90017), I-110 exit 6th St, downtown. 213/683-1234; FAX 213/629-3230. 485 rms, 24 story. S

$149–$195; D $174–$220; each addl $25; suites $225–$550; under 18 free; wkend, package plans. Crib free. Garage parking; valet $13.50. TV; cable. Restaurant 6:30 am–11 pm. Bar 11:30–1 am; entertainment. Ck-out noon. Convention facilities. Concierge. Shopping arcade. Barber, beauty shop. Airport transportation. Exercise equipt; weights, bicycles, whirlpool. Health club privileges. Some minibars. *LUXURY LEVEL:* RE-GENCY CLUB. 52 rms, 4 suites, 2 floors. S $195; D $220. Private lounge, honor bar. Complimentary continental bkfst, refreshments. Cr cds: A, C, D, DS, ER, MC, V, JCB.

D 🏋 🕆 ⊘ ⓒ SC

★ ★ ★ ★ J.W. MARRIOTT AT CENTURY CITY. *2151 Avenue of the Stars (90067), west of downtown. 310/277-2777; FAX 310/785-9240.* 367 rms, 17 story, 189 suites. S $209–$259; D $239–$289; suites $275–$2,500; under 18 free; wkend package plans. Valet parking $14. TV; cable. 2 heated pools, 1 indoor; poolside serv. Restaurant (see J.W.'S). Rm serv 24 hrs. Bar 11:30–1:30 am; pianist. Ck-out 1 pm. Meeting rms. Concierge. Shopping arcade. Courtesy limo 5-mi radius. Tennis & golf privileges. Exercise rm; instructor, weight machines, bicycles, whirlpool, sauna, steam rm. Massage. Bathrm phones, refrigerators, minibars. Private patios, balconies. Scenic view from all rms. French chateau decor. Cr cds: A, C, D, DS, ER, MC, V, JCB.

D 🏋 🚲 ⚓ 🕆 ⊘ ⓒ SC

★ ★ LE DUFY. *1000 Westmount Dr (90069), in West Hollywood. 310/657-7400; res: 800/253-7997; FAX 310/854-6744.* 103 suites, 4 story, 100 kits. S, D $149–$225; under 12 free; monthly rates. Crib free. Covered parking $8. TV; cable. Pool; poolside serv. Restaurant 7 am–11 pm. Ck-out noon. Coin lndry. Meeting rms. Concierge. Exercise equipt; bicycle, treadmill, whirlpool, sauna. Bathrm phones, refrigerators, fireplaces. Balconies. Original artwork. Cr cds: A, C, D, MC, V, JCB.

⚓ 🕆 ⊘ ⓒ

★ ★ LE PARC. *733 N West Knoll Dr (90069), in West Hollywood. 310/855-8888; FAX 310/659-7812.* 154 suites, 3 story. S, D $145–$215; each addl $30; under 12 free. Crib avail. TV; cable, in-rm movies. Heated pool; poolside serv. Restaurant 7 am–10:30 pm. Bar to midnight. Ck-out noon. Meeting rms. Concierge. Valet parking. Lighted tennis, pro. Exercise equipt; weights, bicycles, whirlpool, sauna. Refrigerators, fireplaces, minibars. Private patios, balconies. Cr cds: A, C, D, MC, V, JCB.

🚲 ⚓ 🕆 ⊘ ⓒ

★ ★ ★ MONDRIAN. *8440 Sunset Blvd (90069), at La Cienega Blvd in West Hollywood. 213/650-8999; FAX 213/654-5804.* 224 suites, 12 story. S, D $175–$475; under 12 free. TV; cable, in-rm movies avail. Heated pool; poolside serv. Restaurant 7 am–11 pm. Rm serv 24 hrs. Bar 11–2 am; pianist. Ck-out noon. Concierge. Covered valet parking. Exercise equipt; weights, bicycles, whirlpool, sauna. Bathrm phones, refrigerators, minibars, wet bars. Some balconies. Contemporary decor. Cr cds: A, C, D, ER, MC, V, JCB.

⚓ 🕆 ⊘ ⓒ

★ ★ ★ NEW OTANI HOTEL & GARDEN. *120 S Los Angeles St (90012), in Little Tokyo. 213/629-1200; FAX 213/622-0980.* 435 rms, 21 story. S $145–$205; D $170–$230; each addl $20; suites $400–$750; under 12 free. Covered parking $8.80/day; valet $13.30. TV. Restaurant 6 am–midnight. Bar 10–1 am; pianist. Ck-out noon. Meeting rms. Concierge. Shopping arcade. Barber, beauty shop. Japanese health spa. Bathrm phones, refrigerators. Japanese-style decor, gardens. Cr cds: A, C, D, MC, V, JCB.

D ⊘ ⓒ SC

✔ ★ ★ OXFORD PALACE. *745 S Oxford Ave (90005), I-10 exit Western Ave, west of downtown. 213/389-8000; res: 800/532-7887; FAX 213/389-8500.* 86 rms, 4 story, 9 suites. S $89–$122; D $99–$133; each addl $25; suites $100–$445; under 12 free. Crib $15. TV; cable. Restaurant 7–10 am, 11 am–3 pm, 6–11 pm. Rm serv 24 hrs. Bar. Ck-out noon. Meeting rms. Concierge. Shopping arcade. Gift shop. Garage parking. Refrigerators, minibars. Some balconies. Cr cds: A, C, D, DS, MC, V.

D ⊘ ⓒ SC

★ ★ RADISSON BEL-AIR. *11461 Sunset Blvd (90049), in Bel Air. 310/476-6571; FAX 310/471-6310.* 162 rms, 2 story. S $119–$159; D $129–$169; each addl $10; suites $189–$499; under 18 free; wkend rates. TV; in-rm movies. Heated pool; poolside serv. Restaurant 7 am–11 pm. Bar. Ck-out noon. Meeting rms. Gift shop. Barber, beauty shop. Valet parking. Free UCLA transportation. Tennis, pro. Bathrm phones, refrigerators, minibars. Private patios, balconies. Cr cds: A, C, D, MC, V.

D 🚲 ⚓ ⊘ ⓒ SC

★ ★ RADISSON WILSHIRE PLAZA HOTEL LOS ANGELES. *3515 Wilshire Blvd (90010), west of downtown. 213/381-7411; FAX 213/386-7379.* 396 rms, 12 story. S $109–$129; D $119–$139; each addl $15; suites $250–$500; under 18 free. Crib free. Garage parking: self-park $5.50, valet $7.70. TV; cable. Heated pool; poolside serv. Restaurant 6 am–11 pm. Bar; entertainment 4 pm–11 am. Ck-out noon. Convention facilities. Concierge. Barber. Putting green. Minibars. Refrigerator in suites. Cr cds: A, C, D, DS, MC, V, JCB.

D ⚓ ⊘ ⓒ SC

★ ★ ★ SHERATON GRANDE. *333 S Figueroa St (90071), downtown. 213/617-1133; FAX 213/617-6055.* 470 rms, 14 story. S $180–$200; D $200–$250; each addl $25; suites $475–$1,400; studio rms $275; under 18 free. Crib free. Valet parking $16.50. TV; cable. Heated pool; poolside serv. Complimentary coffee or tea. Restaurants 6:30 am–midnight. Rm serv 24 hrs. Bars; entertainment. Ck-out noon. Meeting rms. Concierge. Butler serv (all rms). Airport transportation; free transportation to Beverly Hills Music Center. Movie theaters. Bathrm phones, minibars. Cr cds: A, C, D, DS, ER, MC, V, JCB.

D ⚓ ⊘ ⓒ SC

★ ★ ★ SHERATON-UNIVERSAL. *(333 Universal Terrace Pkwy, Universal City 91608)* ¼ mi E on US 101 Lankershim Blvd exit; on lot of Universal Studios. *818/980-1212; FAX 818/985-4980.* 444 rms, 19 story. S, D $160–$220; each addl $20; suites $240–$745; under 18 free. Crib free. Garage $9; valet parking $12. TV; cable. Pool; poolside serv. Coffee in rms. Restaurant 6–1 am. Bar 11–2 am. Ck-out noon. Convention facilities. Concierge. Exercise equipt; stair machine, bicycles. Health club privileges. Game rm. Refrigerators, minibars. Private patios, balconies. Overlooks San Fernando Valley and Hollywood Hills. Cr cds: A, C, D, DS, ER, MC, V, JCB.

D ⚓ 🕆 ⊘ ⓒ SC

★ ★ ★ SUNSET MARQUIS. *1200 N Alta Loma Rd (90069), west of downtown. 310/657-1333; FAX 310/652-5300.* 118 suites, 19 with kit., 3 story, 12 villas. S, D suites, kit. units $215–$295; each addl $30; villas $450–$1,200. Crib free. TV; cable. 2 heated pools; poolside serv. Restaurant 7 am–midnight. Rm serv 24 hrs. Bar; entertainment. Ck-out 1 pm. Meeting rms. Concierge. Butler service avail. Free valet or self-parking. Airport transportation. Exercise equipt; weights, bicycles, whirlpool, sauna, steam rm. Massage. Refrigerators; steam bath in some rms; wet bar in suites; bathrm phones in villas. Private patios, balconies. Cr cds: A, C, D, MC, V.

D ⚓ 🕆 ⊘ ⓒ

★ ★ ★ WESTIN BONAVENTURE. *404 S Figueroa St (90071), downtown. 213/624-1000; FAX 213/612-4800.* 1,463 rms, 35 story. S $157–$182; D $175–$200; each addl $25; suites $325–$2,010; under 18 free. Crib free. Garage $18.15/day. TV; cable. Heated pool; poolside serv. Restaurants 6:30 am–midnight. Rm serv 24 hrs. Bar 11–2 am; entertainment Fri & Sat. Ck-out 1 pm. Convention facilities. Concierge. Shopping arcade. Health club privileges. Six-story atrium lobby. Cr cds: A, C, D, DS, ER, MC, V, JCB.

D ⚓ ⊘ ⓒ

Inns

✔ ★ ★ SALISBURY HOUSE. *2273 W 20th St (90018), west of downtown. 213/737-7817; res: 800/373-1778.* 5 rms, 2 share bath, 1 A/C, 3 story. Phones avail. S $70–$95; D $75–$100; each addl $10. TV avail. Complimentary full bkfst. Ck-out 11 am, ck-in 3–4 pm. Refrigerators. Classic example of California Craftsman bungalow (1909), it has been used as a location for several motion picture and TV productions; antiques, original leaded and stained glass. Cr cds: A, MC, V.

★★**VENICE BEACH HOUSE.** *15 30th Ave (90291), in Venice.* 310/823-1966; FAX 310/823-1842. 9 units, 5 baths, 2 share bath, 2 story. Shared bath $80–$90; private bath $110–$150. TV; cable. Complimentary continental bkfst. Afternoon refreshments. Ck-out 11 am, ck-in 3–9 pm. Some private patios, balconies. 1911 California Craftsman house. Venice beach ¼ blk. Totally nonsmoking. Cr cds: A, MC, V.

Restaurants

(At press time legislation was pending regarding a ban on smoking in Los Angeles restaurants)

★★★**BEL-AIR DINING ROOM.** *(See Bel-Air Hotel)* 310/472-1211. Hrs: 7–10:30 am, 11:30 am–2:30 pm, 6:30–10:30 pm; Sat & Sun brunch 11 am–2:30 pm. Res accepted. California menu. Bar. Complete meals: bkfst $8–$13. A la carte entrees: lunch $15–$26.50, dinner $28–$40. Specializes in seasonal dishes. Own pastries. Valet parking. Outdoor dining on bougainvillea-covered terrace, overlooking Swan Lake. Intimate dining; fireplace. Cr cds: A, C, D, MC, V, JCB.

★★★**BERNARD'S.** *(See Biltmore Hotel)* 213/612-1580. Hrs: 11:30 am–2 pm, 6–10 pm; Fri to 10:30 pm; Sat 6–10:30 pm. Closed Sun; major hols. Res accepted. Continental menu. Wine cellar. A la carte entrees: lunch $13–$21, dinner $22–$31. Specializes in seafood. Own baking. Harpist. Valet parking. Jacket (dinner). Cr cds: A, C, D, ER, MC, V, JCB.

★★**CAMPANILE.** *624 S La Brea Ave, west of downtown.* 213/938-1447. Hrs: 8 am–2 pm, 6–10 pm; Fri & Sat to 11 pm; Sun 8 am–1:30 pm. Closed Memorial Day, Thanksgiving, Dec 25. Res accepted. California-Italian menu. Bar. Semi-a la carte: bkfst $3–$15, lunch $10–$25, dinner $30–$40. Specialties: focaccia, risotto cake, prime rib. Valet parking. Charlie Chaplin's original studio. Mexican tile fountain; skylights. Cr cds: A, DS, MC, V.

★★★**CHAMPAGNE BIS.** *10506 Little Santa Monica Blvd, south of downtown.* 310/474-6619. Hrs: 11:30 am–2:30 pm, 6–10:30 pm; Sat & Sun from 6 pm. Closed Dec 24, 25. Res accepted. French menu. Wine cellar. Semi-a la carte: lunch $15–$20, dinner $14.75–$27. Complete meals: dinner $25 & $70. Specialties: country cassoulet, bouillabaisse, pan-fried salmon. Own pastries. Valet parking. Beamed ceiling; tapestry chairs; contemporary artwork. Jacket. Cr cds: A, C, D, MC, V, JCB.

★★★**CITY.** *180 S La Brea Ave, west of downtown.* 213/938-2155. Hrs: 7:30 am–11 pm; Fri & Sat to 11:45 pm; Sun to 10 pm. Closed major hols. Res accepted. Continental menu. Bar. A la carte entrees: bkfst $3.50–$7.50, lunch $5.50–$13, dinner $10.50–$19.75. Child's meals. Specializes in seafood, tandoori cooking. Own baking. Valet parking. Outdoor dining. Cr cds: A, MC, V.

★★★**FOUR OAKS.** *2181 N Beverly Glen, in Bel Air.* 310/470-2265. Hrs: 11:30 am–2 pm, 6–10 pm; Sun & Mon from 6 pm; Sun brunch 10:30 am–2:30 pm. Closed some major hols. Res accepted. French, California menu. Bar. A la carte entrees: lunch $20–$25, dinner $35–$50. Sun champagne brunch $27.50. Menu changes seasonally; emphasizes natural ingredients. Own desserts. Valet parking. Patio dining. Mediterranean decor. Built 1890. Cr cds: MC, V.

★★★**GARDENS.** *(See Four Seasons Hotel)* 310/273-2222. Hrs: 7 am–11 pm; Sun brunch 10 am–2:30 pm. Res accepted. Continental menu. Bar 11–1 am. Wine cellar. A la carte entrees: bkfst $5.95–$14, lunch $8.95–$18, dinner $18–$42. Sun brunch $36. Child's meals. Specializes in veal, rack of lamb, seafood. Own baking, ice cream. Valet

parking. Outdoor dining. European decor. Jacket. Cr cds: A, C, D, MC, V, JCB.

✔★★★**J.W.'S.** *(See J.W. Marriott At Century City Hotel)* 310/277-2777. Hrs: 6:30 am–10:30 pm; Sat & Sun from 7 am; afternoon tea 3:30–5 pm; Sun brunch 10:30 am–2 pm. Res accepted. Continental, California menu. Bar 11:30–1:30 am. Wine cellar. A la carte entrees: bkfst $8–$12.50, lunch $9.50–$15.50, dinner $13.50–$18. Sun brunch $21.95. Afternoon tea $2–$10.50. Seasonal menu; changes monthly. Own baking. Valet parking. Outdoor dining overlooking lush garden. Cr cds: A, C, D, DS, ER, MC, V, JCB.

★★★**LA CHAUMIERE.** *(See Century Plaza Hotel & Tower)* 310/277-2000. Hrs: 11:45 am–2:30 pm, 6–10:30 pm; Sat & Sun 6–10 pm. Res accepted. French menu. Bar; piano bar. Wine list. A la carte entrees: lunch $13.50–$20, dinner $22–$28. Menu changes seasonally. Own baking. Valet parking. French country decor; solarium. Original artwork. Jacket. Cr cds: A, C, D, DS, MC, V.

★**LES FRERES TAIX.** *1911 Sunset Blvd, north of downtown.* 213/484-1265. Hrs: 11 am–10 pm; Sun to 9 pm. Closed Dec 25. Res accepted. Country French menu. Bar. Complete meals: lunch $4.95–$14.95, dinner $4.95–$22.95. Child's meals. Specialties: escargots à la Bourguignonne, duck à l'orange. Own soups. Valet parking. Family-owned. Cr cds: A, C, D, DS, MC, V.

✔★**LITTLE JOE'S.** *900 N Broadway, in Chinatown.* 213/489-4900. Hrs: 11 am–9 pm. Closed Sun; major hols. Res accepted. Italian, Amer menu. Bar. A la carte entrees: lunch $5.50–$9.95, dinner $7–$18.50. Child's meals. Specializes in homemade ravioli, halibut. Valet parking. Near Dodger Stadium, Civic Center. Family-owned. Cr cds: A, C, D, DS, MC, V, JCB.

★★★**LOCANDA VENETA.** *8638 W Third St, opp Cedars Sinai Hospital, west of downtown.* 310/274-1893. Hrs: 11:30 am–2:30 pm, 5:30–10:30 pm; Fri to 11 pm; Sat 5:30–11 pm. Closed Sun. Res accepted. Italian menu. Beer. Wine list. A la carte entrees: lunch, dinner $15–$35. Specializes in seafood, pasta. Own baking, pasta. Valet parking. Windows open to street; open kitchen. Cr cds: A, MC, V.

★★**MADEO.** *8897 Beverly Blvd, west of downtown.* 310/859-4903. Hrs: noon–3 pm, 6:30–11 pm; Sat & Sun from 6:30 pm. Closed Dec 25. Res accepted. Italian menu. Bar. Wine cellar. A la carte entrees: lunch $10–$30, dinner $30–$50. Specialties: branzino, leg of veal. Own pastries. Pianist nightly. Valet parking. Wood-burning oven. Cr cds: A, C, D, MC, V.

✔★★**OCEAN SEAFOOD.** *747 N Broadway, on 2nd floor, in Chinatown.* 213/687-3088. Hrs: 8 am–10 pm. Res accepted. Chinese menu. Bar. A la carte entrees: bkfst, lunch $5–$10, dinner $10–$20. Specializes in deep-fried shrimp, pan-fried lobster, steamed fish, poultry. Cr cds: MC, V.

★★**ORLEANS.** *11705 National Blvd, at Barrington, west of downtown.* 310/479-4187. Hrs: 11:30 am–2 pm, 6–9:30 pm; Fri to 10:30 pm; Sat 6–10:30 pm; Sun 6–9:30 pm. Closed some major hols. Res accepted. Cajun, Creole menu. Bar. Semi-a la carte: lunch $8–$12, dinner $20–$35. Child's meals. Specialties: blackened prime rib, Cajun "popcorn" (crawfish & alligator). Valet parking. Interior reminiscent of Louisiana antebellum home; primitive paintings; fireplace. Cr cds: A, D, MC, V.

★★**PAVILION.** *165 N Grand Ave, in Los Angeles County Music Center, downtown.* 213/972-7333. Hrs: 11:30 am–2:30 pm, 5:30–8:30 pm; Sun brunch 11 am–2:30 pm. Closed Dec 25. Res accepted. Continental menu. A la carte entrees: lunch $8–$14. Buffet: lunch $13, dinner $17–$27. Sun brunch $21. Harpist. Valet parking. Top of Dorothy Chandler Pavilion. Cr cds: A, C, D, MC, V.

★★**PRIMI**. *10543 W Pico Blvd, west of downtown.* 310/475-9235. Hrs: 11:30 am–2:30 pm, 5:30–11 pm. Res accepted. Italian menu. Bar. A la carte entrees: lunch $10–$19, dinner $16–$22. Specializes in homemade pasta. Own breads, desserts. Valet parking. Outdoor dining. Cr cds: A, C, D, MC, V.

★★★**REX II RISTORANTE**. *617 S Olive St, downtown.* 213/627-2300. Hrs: 6–10 pm; Thurs & Fri also noon–2 pm. Closed Sun; hols. Res accepted. Italian menu. Bar. Wine list. Complete meals: lunch $35–$40 (3-course lunch $35), dinner $65–$80 (4-course dinner $55). Specializes in 6-course meals ($70). Own pastries. Pianist, dancing evenings. Valet parking. Landmark building (1928). Art deco. Jacket. Cr cds: A, C, D, MC, V.

✔★**SISLEY ITALIAN KITCHEN**. *10800 W Pico Blvd, in West-side Pavilion Shopping Center, west of downtown.* 310/446-3030. Hrs: 11:30 am–10 pm; Fri & Sat to 10:30 pm; Sun noon–9 pm. Res accepted. Italian, California menu. Bar. A la carte entrees: lunch $6.25–$10, dinner $7.50–$12. Specialties: cioppino, crab cakes, pasta. Valet parking. Outdoor dining. Italian cafe decor. Cr cds: A, MC, V.

★★**SONORA CAFE**. *445 S Figueroa St, in the Union Bank Building, downtown.* 213/624-1800. Hrs: 11 am–2:30 pm, 5:30–10 pm; Sun 5–9 pm; Mon 5:30–9 pm. Closed major hols. Res accepted. Southwestern menu. Bar. A la carte entrees: lunch $8–$14, dinner $12–$24. Specializes in fresh seafood, fajitas. Parking. Outdoor dining. Casual, Southwestern decor; stucco walls, woven murals, pottery. Open kitchen. Cr cds: A, D, MC, V.

★★**TAM-O-SHANTER INN**. *2980 Los Feliz Blvd, east of I-5, north of downtown.* 213/664-0228. Hrs: 11 am–3 pm, 5–10 pm; Fri & Sat to 11 pm; Sun 4–10 pm; Sun brunch 10:30 am–2:30 pm. Closed July 4, Dec 25. Continental, Amer menu. Bar. Semi-a la carte: lunch $7.95–$12.95, dinner $12.95–$22.95. Sun brunch $9.50–$15.50. Child's meals. Specializes in prime rib & Yorkshire pudding, creamed spinach. Sandwich bar. Valet parking. Piano bar. Fireplace. Scottish motif. Family-owned. Cr cds: A, C, D, DS, MC, V, JCB.

D **SC**

★★★**THE TOWER**. *1150 S Olive St, on top of Trans-America Center, downtown.* 213/746-1554. Hrs: 11:30 am–2 pm, 5:30–10 pm; Sat 5:30–11 pm; early-bird dinner 5:30–6:30 pm. Closed Sun; major hols. Res accepted. Continental menu. Bar. Wine cellar. A la carte entrees: lunch $15–$20, dinner $25–$35. Specialties: sautéed peppered salmon, Louisiana crabcakes. Harpist (lunch), pianist (dinner). Valet parking. 360° view of city from 32nd floor. Jacket. Cr cds: A, MC, V.

D

Unrated Dining Spots

CASSELL'S. *3266 W 6th St, west of downtown.* 213/480-8668. Hrs: 10:30 am–4 pm. Closed Sun; major hols. A la carte entrees: lunch $4.60–$5.80. Specializes in prime beef hamburgers. Old-style hamburger diner. No cr cds accepted.

D

HARD ROCK CAFE. *8600 Beverly Blvd, west of downtown.* 310/276-7605. Hrs: 11:30–12:30 am. Closed Labor Day, Thanksgiving, Dec 25. Bar. Semi-a la carte: lunch, dinner $5.95–$15. Child's meals. Specialties: lime barbecued chicken, grilled hamburgers. Valet parking. Extensive rock 'n roll memorabilia collection. Cr cds: MC, V.

D

PHILLIPE THE ORIGINAL. *1001 N Alameda St, downtown.* 213/628-3781. Hrs: 6 am–10 pm. Closed Thanksgiving, Dec 25. Wine, beer. A la carte entrees: bkfst $1–$4.50, lunch, dinner $3.25–$5. Specializes in French dip sandwiches, salads, baked apples. Own cin-namon rolls, muffins, donuts. Parking. Since 1908; old-style dining hall. No cr cds accepted.

D

UNCLE BILL'S PANCAKE HOUSE. *(1305 Highland Ave, Manhattan Beach)* S on Pacific Coast Hwy. 310/545-5177. Hrs: 6 am–3 pm; wkends, hols from 7 am. Closed Jan 1, Thanksgiving, Dec 25. Semi-a la carte: bkfst $3.25–$5.95, lunch $3.50–$6.50. Specializes in potatoes Stroganoff, strawberry waffles, homemade muffins. Parking. Small, cozy atmosphere. Converted 1908 house. No cr cds accepted.

Los Angeles Intl Airport Area *

15 mi SW of Los Angeles (B-4) via I-110 to CA 42.

Services and Information

Information: 310/646-5252.

Lost and Found: 310/417-0440.

Weather: 213/554-1212.

Club Lounges: Admirals Club (American), Terminal 4; Crown Room (Delta), Terminal 5; Red Carpet Club (United), Terminal 7; USAir Club (US Air), Terminal 1; WorldClub (Northwest), Terminal 2.

Terminals

Terminal 1: America West, Southwest, USAir, USAir Express

Terminal 2: Air Canada, Avianca, Hawaiian Air, LOT, Northwest, VASP

Terminal 3: Alaska Airlines, Midwest Express, TWA

Terminal 4: American, American Eagle

Terminal 5: Delta

Terminal 6: Continental, Skywest

Terminal 7: United, United Express, Virgin Atlantic (departures)

Imperial Terminal: Air LA (departures), Alpha, Grand Airways, MGM Grand Air, Pacific Coast

International Terminal: Aero California, Aerolines Argentinas, Aeromexico, Aeroquetzal, Air France, Air LA (arrivals), Air New Zeland, Alitalia, American Trans Air, ANA (All Nippon), Asiana, Aviateca, British Airways, Canadian Airlines Intl, Cathay Pacific, China Airlines, China Eastern, Ecuatoriana, Egypt Air, El Al, Garuda, Iberia, Japan Airlines, KLM, Korean Air, LACSA, Lan Chile, Lufthansa, MAC (Military), Malaysian, Mexicana, Philippine Airlines, QANTAS, SAS, Singapore, Swissair, TACA, Thai, UTA, Varig, Virgin Atlantic (arrivals)

Heliport: Helitrans, LA Helicopter

(Airlines and their terminal locations may change. Before leaving for the airport, you should phone the airline to confirm terminal location for your flight.)

(See Los Angeles, also see Los Angeles Area)

Motels

✔★★★**AIRPORT CENTURY INN**. *(5547 W Century Blvd, Los Angeles 90045)* ½ mi W on I-405, at Century Blvd & Aviation Blvd. 310/649-4000; res: 800/421-3939; FAX 310/649-0311. 147 rms, 2 story. S $62–$69; D $69–$82; each addl $8; under 18 free. Crib $4. TV; cable, in-rm movies. Pool; poolside serv. Restaurant open 24 hrs. Rm serv 6 am–10 pm. Bar 10–2 am. Ck-out noon. Coin lndry. Bellhops. Valet serv.

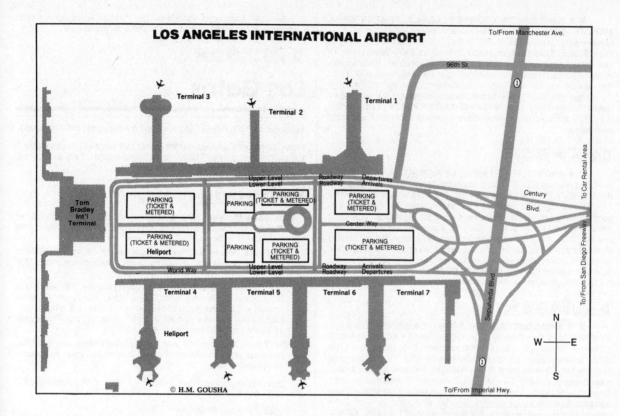

LOS ANGELES INTERNATIONAL AIRPORT

© H.M. GOUSHA

Gift shop. Free airport transportation. Some private patios, balconies. Cr cds: A, C, D, DS, ER, MC, V, JCB.

★★**HAMPTON INN.** *(10300 La Cienega Blvd, Inglewood 90304) ¾ mi E on Century Blvd, then S on La Cienega Blvd.* 310/337-1000; FAX 310/645-6925. 149 rms, 7 story. S $65–$75; D $78–$88; under 18 free. Crib free. Pet accepted, some restrictions. TV. Complimentary continental bkfst, coffee. Restaurant nearby. Ck-out noon. Meeting rms. Valet serv. Free airport transportation. Exercise equipt; weight machine, bicycles, sauna. Cr cds: A, C, D, DS, MC, V.

Hotels

★**AIRPORT MARINA.** *(8601 Lincoln Blvd, Los Angeles 90045) Jct Lincoln Blvd and Manchester Ave, NW edge of Intl Airport.* 310/670-8111; FAX 310/337-1883. 770 rms, 12 story. S, D $75–$125; each addl $10; suites $150–$375; under 18 free. Crib free. TV. Pool; poolside serv. Restaurants 5:30 am–10:30 pm. Bar 4 pm–2 am; entertainment, dancing. Ck-out 1 pm. Meeting rms. Barber, beauty shop. Free airport transportation. Some private patios, balconies. Tropical garden patio. Golf, tennis opp. *LUXURY LEVEL: GUEST OF HONOR.* 23 rms. S, D $125. Private lounge. Some wet bars. Complimentary continental bkfst.
Cr cds: A, C, D, MC, V.

★★**CROWN STERLING SUITES.** *(1440 E Imperial Ave, El Segundo 90245) ½ mi S on Sepulveda Blvd, then 1 blk W on Imperial Ave.* 310/640-3600; FAX 310/322-0954. 350 suites, 5 story. S, D $119–$169; each addl $15; under 12 free; wkend rates. Pet accepted,

some restrictions. TV; cable. Indoor pool; whirlpool. Complimentary full bkfst. Restaurant 11 am–10 pm. Bar 11–2 am. Ck-out 1 pm. Meeting rms. Gift shop. Free covered parking. Free airport transportation. Health club privileges. Refrigerators. Balconies. Sun deck. Spanish mission architecture. Near beach. Cr cds: A, C, D, DS, ER, MC, V.

★★**DOUBLETREE CLUB.** *(1985 E Grand Ave, El Segundo 90245) 1½ mi S of airport on Sepulveda Blvd, in business park.* 310/322-0999; FAX 310/322-4758. 215 rms, 7 story. S $99; D $109; each addl $10; suites $125; under 18 free. Crib $10. TV; cable. Heated pool. Complimentary full bkfst. Restaurant 6–10 am, 11 am–2 pm, 5–10 pm. Bar. Ck-out 1 pm. Meeting rms. Free airport transportation. Exercise equipt; weight machines, bicycles, whirlpool. Cr cds: A, C, D, DS, MC, V, JCB.

HILTON & TOWERS-LOS ANGELES AIRPORT. (Remodeling incomplete when inspected, therefore not rated) *(5711 W Century Blvd, Los Angeles 90045) ¾ mi E on Century Blvd.* 310/410-4000; FAX 310/410-6250. 1,279 rms, 17 story. S $135–$165; D $150–$180; each addl $15; suites $280–$600; family, wkend rates. Valet parking $13.50, garage $8.50. TV; cable. Heated pool; poolside serv (seasonal). Restaurants 6 am–midnight. Bar 11–2 am; entertainment, dancing. Ck-out 11 am. Convention facilities. Coin lndry. Drugstore. Airport transportation. Exercise rm; instructor, weights, bicycles, whirlpool, sauna. Game rm. Some bathrm phones; refrigerators avail. Some private patios. *LUXURY LEVEL: THE TOWERS.* 155 rms, 5 suites, 2 floors. S $165; D $180; suites $380–$600. Private lounge, honor bar. Bathrm phones. Complimentary continental bkfst, refreshments.
Cr cds: A, C, D, DS, ER, MC, V, JCB.

★ ★ ★HOLIDAY INN CROWNE PLAZA-L.A. INTERNATIONAL AIRPORT. *(5985 W Century Blvd, Los Angeles 90045) ¼ mi E on Century Blvd.* 310/642-7500; FAX 310/417-3608. 615 rms, 16 story. S $124–$139; D $139–$154; each addl $15; suites $300–$600; under 19 free; wkend rates. Crib free. Garage $6.60. Pet accepted, some restrictions. TV; cable. Heated pool; whirlpool, sauna. Restaurant 6 am–11 pm. Rm serv 24 hrs. Bar 11–2 am; entertainment, dancing. Ck-out noon. Concierge. Gift shop. Free airport, beach, shopping transportation. Health club privileges. *LUXURY LEVEL:* CROWN PLAZA CLUB. 46 rms. S $139; D $154. Private lounge. Complimentary continental bkfst, refreshments.
Cr cds: A, C, D, DS, MC, V.

D 🐾 ⚓ 🏋 ✕ 🔕 ⊙ **SC**

★ ★HYATT AT LOS ANGELES AIRPORT. *(6225 W Century Blvd, Los Angeles 90045) At entrance to Intl Airport.* 310/672-1234; FAX 310/641-6924. 597 rms, 12 story. S $125–$155; D $140–$170; each addl $15; suites $275–$550; under 18 free; wkend rates. TV; cable. Heated pool; poolside serv. Supervised child's activities. Restaurant 6:30–1:30 am; dining rms 11 am–10:30 pm. Bars 11–2 am; dancing, entertainment exc Sun. Ck-out 1 pm. Convention facilities. Concierge. Barber, beauty shop. Garage. Free airport transportation. Exercise rm; instructor, weights, bicycles, whirlpool. Bathrm phones, minibars; wet bar in suites. Sun deck. *LUXURY LEVEL:* REGENCY CLUB. 50 rms, 14 suites. S $165; D $180. Complimentary continental bkfst, refreshments.
Cr cds: A, C, D, DS, ER, MC, V, JCB.

D ⚓ 🏋 ✕ 🔕 ⊙ **SC**

★ ★ ★MARRIOTT AIRPORT. *(5855 W Century Blvd, Los Angeles 90045) ½ mi E on Century Blvd.* 310/641-5700; FAX 310/337-5358. 1,012 rms, 18 story. S, D $144–$154; each addl $10; suites from $189; family, wkend rates. Crib free. Valet parking $10. TV. Heated pool; poolside serv. 3 restaurants 6 am–midnight. Rm serv 24 hrs. 2 bars; entertainment, dancing. Ck-out 1 pm. Coin lndry. Convention facilities. Concierge. Shopping arcade. Barber, beauty shop. Free airport transportation. Exercise equipt; weights, bicycles, whirlpool. Game rm. Some bathrm phones, refrigerators. Balconies. *LUXURY LEVEL:* CONCIERGE FLOOR. *Ext 1614.* 73 rms. S $149; D $159. Honor bar. Complimentary continental bkfst, refreshments.
Cr cds: A, C, D, DS, MC, V, JCB.

D ⚓ 🏋 ✕ 🔕 ⊙ **SC**

✔ ★ ★QUALITY HOTEL-LOS ANGELES AIRPORT. *(5249 W Century Blvd, Los Angeles 90045) 1¼ mi E on Century Blvd.* 310/645-2200; FAX 310/641-8214. 277 rms, 10 story. S $49–$75; D $49–$85; each addl $10; under 16 free; wkend rates. TV. Pool; poolside serv. Restaurant 6 am–10 pm. Bar 5 pm–2 am; entertainment Thurs–Sat. Ck-out 1 pm. Convention facilities. Garage parking. Free airport transportation. Exercise equipt; weights, bicycles. Cr cds: A, C, D, DS, ER, MC, V, JCB.

D ⚓ 🏋 ✕ 🔕 ⊙ **SC**

★ ★SHERATON LOS ANGELES AIRPORT. *(6101 W Century Blvd, Los Angeles 90045) ¼ mi E on Century Blvd.* 310/642-1111; FAX 310/410-1267. 807 rms, 15 story. S $115–$175; D $120–$195; each addl $20; suites $180–$500; under 17 free; wkend rates. Crib free. TV; cable. Heated pool; poolside serv. Restaurant 6–1:30 am. Bar 11–2 am; entertainment, piano bar. Ck-out 1 pm. Convention facilities. Concierge. Valet parking. Free airport transportation. Exercise equipt; weights, bicycles, whirlpool. Minibars. Cr cds: A, C, D, DS, ER, MC, V, JCB.

D ⚓ 🏋 ✕ 🔕 ⊙ **SC**

★ ★ ★THE WESTIN-L.A. AIRPORT. *(5400 W Century Blvd, Los Angeles 90045) 1¼ mi E on Century Blvd.* 310/216-5858; FAX 310/645-8053. 740 rms, 12 story. S, D $139–$149; each addl $10; suites $275–$1,349; under 18 free; wkend plans. Covered parking $8. TV; cable. Heated pool. Complimentary coffee. Restaurant 6 am–midnight. Rm serv 24 hrs. Bar 10–2 am; entertainment. Ck-out 1 pm. Convention facilities. Gift shop. Free airport transportation. Exercise rm; instructor, weights, bicycles, whirlpool, sauna. Minibars; bathrm phones in suites. Balconies. *LUXURY LEVEL:* CLUB LEVEL. 105 rms, 9 suites, 2 floors. S,

D $154–$164. Concierge. Private lounge. Wet bar, whirlpool in suites. Complimentary continental bkfst, refreshments, newspaper.
Cr cds: A, C, D, DS, MC, V, JCB.

D ⚓ 🏋 ✕ 🔕 ⊙ **SC**

Los Gatos (E-2)

Founded: ca 1870 **Pop:** 27,357 **Elev:** 385 ft **Area code:** 408 **Zip:** 95030

Free roaming wildcats inspired the name "La Rinconada de Los Gatos," the corner of the cats. Today, two sculptured cats, Leo and Leona, guard the town entrance at Poets Canyon.

What to See and Do

1. **Los Gatos Museum.** Main & Tait Sts. Natural history exhibits; art displays, art history. In restored firehouse. (Wed–Sun; closed hols & Dec 24, 31) Phone 395-7375.   **Free.**
2. **Los Gatos Forbes Mill History Museum.** 75 Church St. Historic landmark; former grain mill. (Wed–Sun) For information phone 395-7375.
3. **Youth Science Institute-Vasona Discovery Center.** 296 Garden Hill Dr. Located in Vasona Lake County Park, this Junior Museum houses aquaria with local and native fish, reptiles and amphibians. Native plant trail. Museum (daily exc Mon); park (daily). Phone 356-4945. Parking fee (summer).   **Free.**
4. **Old Town.** 50 University Ave. Shops, restaurants, art galleries, flowered garden walkways, housed in what was once an elementary school (1921).

(For further information contact the Chamber of Commerce, PO Box 1820; 354-9300.)

(See San Jose, Saratoga)

Motels

★ ★GARDEN INN OF LOS GATOS. 46 E Main St. 408/354-6446; res: 800/888-8248; FAX 408/354-5911. 28 rms, 12 kits. Mid-May–mid-Sept: S, D $60–$75; suites $70–$135; kit. units $70–$85; lower rates rest of yr. Crib free. TV; cable. Pool. Complimentary continental bkfst. Restaurant opp 6 am–11 pm. Ck-out 11 am. Health club privileges. Refrigerators. Private patios. Hacienda decor, elaborate gardens. Cr cds: A, C, D, MC, V.

⚓ 🔕 ⊙ **SC**

★ ★LA HACIENDA INN. 18840 Saratoga-Los Gatos Rd. 408/354-9230; FAX 408/354-7590. 21 rms, 3 kits. S $78–$105; D $83–$110; each addl $10; suites, kit. units $85–$110; under 6 free. Crib free. TV. Pool; whirlpool. Complimentary continental bkfst. Restaurant (see LA HACIENDA). Rm serv 11 am–10 pm; Fri, Sat to 7 pm. Ck-out noon. Meeting rm. Refrigerators; some fireplaces. Private patios. Beautifully landscaped grounds. Cr cds: A, C, D, DS, MC, V.

⚓ ⊙ **SC**

★ ★ ★LODGE AT VILLA FELICE. 15350 Winchester Blvd. 408/395-6710; res: 800/662-9229; FAX 408/354-1826. 33 rms, 2 story. S, D $98–$119; each addl $10; suites $138–$220 under 16 free. Crib free. TV; cable, in-rm movies avail. Heated pool; whirlpool. Complimentary continental bkfst. Restaurant 11:30 am–10 pm. Rm serv. Bar 11:30–1 am; entertainment, dancing Fri, Sat. Ck-out noon. Meeting rms. Valet serv. Sundries. Some refrigerators, in-rm saunas. Private patios, balconies. On mountain; view of Lake Vasona. Cr cds: A, C, D, MC, V.

D ⚓ 🔕 ⊙ **SC**

✔ ★LOS GATOS MOTOR INN. 55 Saratoga Ave. 408/356-9191; res: 800/642-7889; FAX 408/356-7502. 60 rms, 2 story. S $60; D $65–$70; each addl $5. Crib $5. TV; cable. Heated pool. Complimentary continental bkfst. Restaurant opp 6:30 am–10 pm. Ck-out noon. Sundries. Cr cds: A, C, D, MC, V.

Motor Hotels

★ ★ **LOS GATOS LODGE.** *50 Saratoga Ave. 408/354-3300; res: 800/322-8811 (exc CA), 800/231-8676 (CA); FAX 408/354/5451.* 125 rms, 2 story, 8 kits. S, D $79–$85; each addl $10; suites, kit. units $85–$95; under 12 free; some lower rates off season. Crib free. Pet accepted. TV; cable. Heated pool; whirlpool. Restaurant 6:30 am–9:30 pm. Bar 11–2 am; entertainment, dancing Wed–Sat. Ck-out noon. Coin lndry. Meeting rms. Valet serv. Sundries. Free airport transportation. Putting green. Lawn games. All rms have private patio or deck. Cr cds: A, C, D, DS, MC, V.

★ ★ **TOLL HOUSE.** *140 S Santa Cruz Ave. 408/395-7070; res: 800/238-6111 (exc CA), 800/821-5518 (CA); FAX 408/395-3730.* 98 rms, 3 story. S $79; D $85; suites $125–$158; under 12 free; wkend rates. Crib free. Pet accepted, some restrictions; $50. TV; cable, in-rm movies avail. Complimentary continental bkfst Mon–Fri. Restaurant 6 am–10 pm; Fri & Sat to 11 pm. Rm serv 24 hrs. Bar; entertainment, dancing Fri & Sat. Ck-out noon. Meeting rms. Concierge. Airport transportation. Health club privileges. Some refrigerators. Private patios, balconies. Cr cds: A, C, D, DS, MC, V.

Restaurant

★ ★ **LA HACIENDA.** *(See La Hacienda Inn Motel) 408/354-6669.* Hrs: 11 am–11 pm; Sun 10 am–10 pm; Sun brunch to 2 pm. Closed Dec 25. Res accepted. Continental menu. Bar. A la carte entrees: lunch $6.95–$13.95. Complete meals: dinner $13.95–$44. Sun champagne brunch $7.95–$11.95. Child's meals. Specializes in Italian dishes. Own pasta. Parking. Country inn atmosphere; fireplace. Garden patio. Cr cds: A, C, D, DS, MC, V.

Madera (F-3)

Pop: 29,281 **Elev:** 270 ft **Area code:** 209 **Zip:** 93637

(See Fresno)

Motel

✔ ★ **ECONOMY INNS OF AMERICA.** *1855 W Cleveland Ave. 209/661-1131.* 80 rms, 2 story. S $26.90; D $34.90–$41.90. Pet accepted. TV. Heated pool. Restaurant adj 6 am–10 pm. Ck-out 11 am. Cr cds: A, MC, V.

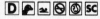

Motor Hotel

★ ★ **BEST WESTERN MADERA VALLEY INN.** *317 North G St. 209/673-5164; FAX 209/661-8426.* 95 rms, 5 story. S $52–$55; D $58–$64; each addl $4; suites $114; under 12 free. Crib free. TV; cable. Complimentary coffee in rms. Restaurant 6 am–9 pm. Rm serv. Bar 11:30–2 am. Ck-out noon. Meeting rms. Bellhops. Health club privileges. Free local airport transportation. Cr cds: A, C, D, DS, MC, V, JCB.

Restaurant

✔ ★ **FRUIT BASKET.** *117 S Gateway Dr. 209/674-2805.* Hrs: 6 am–9:30 pm. Closed some major hols. Wine. A la carte entrees: bkfst $2.35–$8.10. Complete meals: lunch $4.95–$5.25, dinner $6.40–$10.90. Child's meals. Specializes in pot roast, chicken-fried steak. Parking. Opp city park. Cr cds: MC, V.

Malibu (H-3)

Pop: 7,000 (est) **Elev:** 25 ft **Area code:** 310 **Zip:** 90265

What to See and Do

1. **J. Paul Getty Museum.** 17985 Pacific Coast Hwy. Extensive permanent collection of Greek and Roman antiquities, pre-20th-century Western European paintings, drawings, sculpture, illuminated manuscripts, decorative arts & 19th- and 20th-century European and American photographs; housed in a re-created 1st-century A.D. Roman country villa with interior and exterior gardens. Parking reservations required for car, van or charter bus; visitors may also arrive by bicycle, motorcycle, taxi, RTD bus #434 (with museum pass from bus driver) or drop off at gatehouse. No walk-in traffic. (Daily exc Mon) For reservations phone 458-2003. **Free.**

2. **Pepperdine University** (1937). (2,300 students) 24255 Pacific Coast Highway. School of Law as well as college of arts, sciences and letters, cultural arts center and Weisman Museum of Art located on 830-acre campus. Phone 456-4000.

(For general information and attractions see Los Angeles, Santa Monica.)

Motels

✔ ★ **CASA MALIBU INN ON THE BEACH.** *22752 Pacific Coast Hwy. 310/456-2219.* 21 rms, 1–2 story, 6 kits. No A/C. June–Nov: S, D $85–$140; each addl $10; kit. units $10 addl (3-day min); lower rates rest of yr. Crib $10. TV. Coffee in rms. Restaurant nearby. Ck-out noon. Refrigerators. Sun deck. Private beach. Cr cds: MC, V.

★ ★ **MALIBU COUNTRY INN.** *6506 Westward Beach Rd, off Pacific Coast Hwy, Kanan exit. 310/457-9622; FAX 310/457-1349.* 15 rms, 1–2 story. No A/C. June–Sept: S, D $125–$155; under 7 free; lower rates rest of yr. Crib $10. TV; cable. Heated pool. Complimentary coffee in rms. Restaurant 8 am–2:30 pm. Ck-out noon. Balconies. Some rms with ocean view. 1940s Cape Cod-style building with 3 acres of garden; located on a bluff overlooking Zuma Beach. Cr cds: A, MC, V.

Hotel

★ ★ **MALIBU BEACH INN.** *22878 Pacific Coast Hwy. 310/456-6444; res: 800/462-5428 (US), 800/255-1007 (CAN); FAX 310/456-1499.* 47 rms, 3 story. Apr–Sept: S, D $125–$265; each addl $15; suites $225–$290; 2-night min in season; lower rates rest of yr. TV; cable, in-rm movies. Complimentary continental bkfst. Complimentary coffee in rms. Restaurant nearby. Rm serv 24 hrs. Ck-out noon. Gift shop. Health club privileges. Minibars; fireplaces; some in-rm whirlpools. Balconies. Tile-roofed, Mediterranean-style hotel on beach. Cr cds: A, C, D, MC, V, JCB.

Restaurants

★ ★ **BEAU RIVAGE.** *26025 Pacific Coast Hwy. 310/456-5733.* Hrs: 5–11 pm; Sun 11 am–4 pm, 5–10 pm. Closed Jan 1, Dec 25. Res accepted. Mediterranean menu. Bar to midnight. Wine cellar. Semi-a la carte: lunch $10–$15, dinner $20–$35. Specializes in game dishes, fresh seafood, fresh pasta. Own baking. Pianist Mon–Thurs, guitarist, vocalist Fri & Sun. Parking. Outdoor dining. All herbs, flowers grown in garden. French country inn decor; ocean view. Cr cds: A, C, D, MC, V.

D

✔ ★ **COOGIE'S BEACH CAFE.** *23750 Pacific Coast Hwy.* 310/317-1444. Hrs: 7:30 am–9 pm; Fri & Sat to 10 pm. Wine, beer. A la carte entrees: bkfst $3–$6.95, lunch $4.50–$7.95, dinner $6.50–$14.50. Specializes in American favorites and original Malibu cuisine served in a tropical atmosphere. Totally nonsmoking. Cr cds: A, MC, V.

D

★ ★ **GEOFFREY'S.** *27400 Pacific Coast Hwy.* 310/457-1519. Hrs: noon–11 pm; Fri & Sat to midnight; Sun 10 am–10 pm. Res accepted. Bar. Wine list. A la carte entrees: lunch $10–$30, dinner $14–$34. Specializes in fresh seafood, pasta. Valet parking. Patio dining. Panoramic view of ocean. Cr cds: A, D, MC, V, JCB.

D

★ ★ **GRANITA.** *23725 W Malibu Rd, N on Pacific Coast Hwy.* 310/456-0488. Hrs: 11:30 am–2 pm, 6 pm to closing. Closed Jan 1, Thanksgiving, Dec 24 & 25. Res accepted; required wkends. California cuisine. Bar. Extensive wine list. A la carte entrees: lunch $6–$20, dinner $8–$45. Specialties: Mediterranean fish soup, crisp potato galette with gravlax, dill cream and fresh chives, lobster club sandwich. Parking. Outdoor dining. Unique interior with underwater ocean fantasy theme. Cr cds: MC, V.

D

★ **MOONSHADOWS.** *20356 Pacific Coast Hwy.* 310/456-3010. Hrs: 5–10:30 pm; Fri & Sat to midnight; Sun 3–10:30 pm; Sat & Sun brunch 10:30 am–2:30 pm. Closed Thanksgiving, Dec 25. Bar. Semi-a la carte: dinner $10.95–$35.95. Specializes in steak, lobster, fresh fish of the day. Salad bar. Valet parking. Overlooks ocean. Cr cds: A, C, D, DS, MC, V.

Mammoth Lakes (E-4)

Pop: 4,785 **Elev:** 7,800 ft **Area code:** 619 **Zip:** 93546

Spectacular scenery and a variety of recreational opportunities are found in this region of rugged peaks, numerous lakes, streams and waterfalls, alpine meadows and extensive forests. Much of the outstanding scenery was created by volcanos or carved by glaciers.

What to See and Do

1. **Mammoth Mountain Ski Area.** In Inyo National Forest. 5 quad, 7 triple, 14 double chairlifts, 2 gondolas, 1 Pomalift, T-bar; patrol, school, rentals; concession, cafeterias, restaurant. More than 150 runs; longest run 2½ mi; vertical drop 3,100 ft. (Nov–June, daily) Half-day rates. Gondola ride (daily). The racing department offers daily races and clinics. Phone 934-2571; snow conditions, 934-6166; also 213/935-8866 from Los Angeles, 714/955-0692 from Orange County, 231-7785 from San Diego. ¢¢¢¢¢

2. **Mammoth Mountain Bike Park.** In the summer, the ski mountain is transformed into a bike mountain. Ride the gondola to the top of the mountain and bike down on a variety of trails, suited to various skills and ages. Helmets are required within park boundaries. (July–Sept, daily, weather permitting) Fee for activities. Phone 934-2571.

3. **Mammoth Visitor Center Ranger Station.** At the edge of town, surrounded by Inyo National Forest. Visitor summer activities (July 4–Labor Day wkend) include interpretive tours, evening programs, and Jr-Ranger programs (6–12 yrs). Visitor center (yr-round). Phone 924-1094 for 24-hr recording, -5500 for details, -5531 (TDD). All family campgrounds (exc ½ of Sherwin Creek, which requires reservations) on first come, first served basis; group camping and

Sherwin Creek camping reservable through Mistix. Shady Rest campground open in winter (tent camping only). Self-registration for backpackers during non-quota season; wilderness permits required all yr. Quota season last wkend June–Sept 15; advance applications must be postmarked Mar 1 or later (fee; no phone reservations). Contact Mammoth Ranger District, Box 148; 924-5500.

4. **Pack trips** for wilderness camping.

Mammoth Lakes Pack Outfit. 4 mi SW on Lake Mary Rd near Lake Mary. Contact PO Box 61; 934-2434.

Red's Meadow Pack Station and Resort. 15 mi W on Minaret Hwy. Contact Box 395; phone 934-2345 (summer), 873-3928 (winter) or 800/292-7758.

McGee Creek Pack Station. 12 mi SW. Contact Rte 1, Box 162 M; 935-4324 (summer) or 878-2207.

5. **Fishing, boating, rentals. Crowley Lake** 6 mi S on US 395. **Sherwin Creek** (fishing, camping), 3 mi SE of ranger station. **Convict Lake**, 4 mi SE of Mammoth Junction, 2 mi W of US 395. SW on Lake Mary road are **Twin Lakes** (camping), **Lake Mary** (camping), **Coldwater** (camping), **Lake George** (camping), **Pine City** (camping). Fees charged at recreation sites. All campgrounds first come, first served basis (self-registration); Sherwin Creek reservable through Mistix. For further details and information on other areas contact the Mammoth Ranger District, Box 148; phone 924-5500.

6. **Devils Postpile National Monument** (see).

(For further information contact the Mammoth Lakes Visitor Bureau, PO Box 48; 934-8006 or 800/367-6572. The Visitor Center is located on Main Street.)

(See Bishop, June Lake)

Motels

(Wkend, holiday rates are usually higher in this area)

✔ ★ **ECONO LODGE WILDWOOD INN.** *(Box 568) ¼ mi W of Old Mammoth Rd on Main St (CA 203).* 619/934-6855; FAX 619/934-5165. 32 rms, 2 story. No A/C. Nov–Apr: S $49–$79; D $59–$99; ski plans; lower rates rest of yr. Pet accepted. TV; cable. Heated pool; whirlpool. Continental bkfst. Coffee in rms. Restaurant nearby. Ck-out 10 am. Downhill/x-country ski 3 mi. Some refrigerators. Mountain view from some rms. Cr cds: A, C, D, DS, MC, V.

🐾 🏊 ≈ ⊘ ⊙ **SC**

★ ★ **QUALITY INN.** *(Box 3507) 3537 Main St (CA 203).* 619/934-5114; FAX 619/934-5165. 61 rms, 2 story. No A/C. S $65–$89; D $69–$140; each addl $5–$10; under 18 free. Crib free. TV; cable. Complimentary continental bkfst. Complimentary coffee in rms. Restaurant nearby. Ck-out 10 am. Garage. Downhill/x-country ski 2 mi. Whirlpool. Cr cds: A, C, D, DS, MC, V, JCB.

D 🏊 ⊘ ⊙ **SC**

★ ★ **SHILO INN.** *(Box 2179) 2963 Main St (CA 203).* 619/934-4500; FAX 619/934-7594. 71 rms, 4 story. Mid-Nov–mid-Apr: S, D $90–$140; under 12 free; lower rates rest of yr. Crib free. Pet accepted, some restrictions; $6. TV. Indoor pool. Complimentary continental bkfst, coffee. Restaurant opp 5 am–10 pm. Ck-out noon. Coin lndry. Meeting rms. Garage parking. Free airport transportation. Downhill/x-country ski 5 mi. Exercise equipt; weight machine, bicycles, whirlpool, sauna. Bathrm phones, refrigerators. Cr cds: A, C, D, DS, ER, MC, V, JCB.

D 🐾 🏊 ≈ 🏃 ⊘ ⊙ **SC**

Lodges

★ ★ **JAGERHOF.** *(Box 1648) 663 Old Mammoth Rd, ½ mi S on Old Mammoth Rd.* 619/934-6162; FAX 619/924-2012. 24 rms, 2 story, 7 kits. No A/C. Nov–Apr: S, D $69–$85; kit. units $135; package plan avail; lower rates rest of yr. TV; cable. Complimentary continental bkfst, coffee, tea. Restaurant opp 6:30 am–10 pm. Ck-out 11 am. Coin lndry. Meeting rm. Downhill ski 1½ mi; x-country ski ¼ mi. Whirlpool, sauna. Hiking trails. Some balconies. Cr cds: MC, V.

★ ★ ★**MAMMOTH MOUNTAIN INN.** *(Box 353) 1 Minaret Rd. 619/934-2581; res: 800/228-4947; FAX 619/934-0700.* 214 rms, 3 story, 50 kit. apts. Nov–Apr: S, D $100–$190; suites $165–$200; family, mid-wk rates; ski plans; lower rates rest of yr. Crib free. TV; cable. Playground. Supervised child's activities. Restaurant 7 am–3 pm; dining rm 7 am–9:30 pm. Box lunches. Snack bar. Barbecues. Rm serv. Bar 11–1 am. Ck-out 11 am. Coin lndry. Meeting rms. Bellhops. Concierge. Covered parking. Free airport, bus depot transportation. Downhill/cross-country ski on site. Sleighing. Horseback riding. Haywagon rides. Bicycles. Soc dir. Entertainment. Whirlpools. Game rm. Fish/hike guides. Some balconies. Picnic tables. Cr cds: A, MC, V.

Motor Hotel

★**ALPINE LODGE.** *(PO Box 389) 6209 Minaret Rd. 619/934-8526; res: 800/526-0007; FAX 619/934-2226.* 66 rms, 3 story, 4 kit. cottages (showers only). No A/C. Nov–Mar: S $46–$49; D $66–$96; each addl $10; kit. cottages (2-night min) $140–$155; under 8 free; wkly rates; lower rates rest of yr. Deposit required. Crib $10. TV; cable. Complimentary coffee in rms. Restaurant nearby. Ck-out 10 am. Downhill/x-country ski 1 mi. Whirlpool, sauna. Fireplace in cottages. Totally nonsmoking. Cr cds: MC, V.

Inn

★**SNOW GOOSE.** *(Box 946) 57 Forest Trail. 619/934-2660; res: 800/874-7368 (CA); FAX 619/934-5655.* 18 rms, 2 story, 4 suites, 6 kits. No A/C. Nov–Apr, MAP: S, D $78–$168; each addl $10; suites $148–$168; ski plans; lower rates rest of yr. TV; cable. Complimentary full bkfst. Restaurant opp 7 am–midnight. Ck-out 10 am, ck-in 2 pm. Downhill/x-country ski 3 mi. Balconies. Library/sitting rm; antiques. Snow goose motif throughout. Cr cds: A, D, DS, MC, V.

Restaurants

✔ ★**GRINGO'S.** *On Main St, ½ blk W of Old Mammoth Rd. 619/934-8595.* Hrs: 4–10 pm. Mexican menu. Bar from 4 pm. A la carte entrees: dinner $6.45–$12.95. Semi-a la carte: dinner $6.45–$12.95. Specializes in fajitas, rotisserie-cooked chicken. Parking. Outdoor dining. Colorful Mexican decor. Cr cds: DS, MC, V.

★ ★**SELLINGER'S.** *On Old Mammoth Rd, at Sierra Center Mall. 619/934-6090.* Hrs: 11 am–9 pm; Sat to 11 pm; Sun buffet brunch 9:30 am–2:30 pm. Res accepted. Bar to midnight. Semi-a la carte: lunch $3.95–$7.95, dinner $9.95–$17.95. Sun brunch $8.95. Child's meals. Specializes in prime rib, fresh seafood, pasta, steak. Parking. Large skylight over dining area. View of mountain. Totally nonsmoking. Cr cds: A, MC, V.

Manhattan Beach

(see Los Angeles)

Marina Del Rey (H-3)

Pop: 7,431 **Elev:** 10 ft **Area code:** 310 **Zip:** 90292

With its name, could this community next to Venice be anything but boat oriented? The 6,000-slip facility attracts many boating and sportfishing enthusiasts. Sail and power boat rentals, ocean cruises and fishing expeditions are available. In addition, there are waterfront biking and jogging trails.

What to See and Do

Fisherman's Village. 13763 Fiji Way. Modeled after a turn-of-the-century New England fishing town and located on the main channel of the largest man-made small craft harbor in the country. Cobblestone walks complement the nautical atmosphere and provide a panoramic view of the marina; boat rentals, fishing charters, harbor cruises; shops, boutiques and restaurants. Entertainment throughout the yr (weather permitting), including free jazz concerts (Sun). (Daily) Phone 823-5411.

(For further information contact the Chamber of Commerce, 14014 Tahiti Way; 821-0555.)

(See Los Angeles, Santa Monica)

Motel

✔ ★**FOGHORN HARBOR INN.** *4140 Via Marina. 310/823-4626; res: 800/423-4940 (exc CA), 800/624-7351 (CA); FAX 310/578-1964.* 24 rms, 2 story. June–Aug: S, D $80–$110; each addl $10; under 10 free; wkly rates; lower rates rest of yr. Crib free. Pet accepted, some restrictions. TV. Restaurant adj 11:30 am–midnight. Ck-out 11:30 am. Free airport transportation. Refrigerators. Swimming beach. Cr cds: A, C, D, MC, V.

Motor Hotels

★ ★ ★**MARINA DEL REY.** *13534 Bali Way. 310/301-1000; res: 800/882-4000 (exc CA), 800/862-7462 (CA); FAX 310/301-8167.* 160 rms, 3 story. S $125–$190; D $145–$210; each addl $20; suites $350–$400; under 12 free. TV; cable. Heated pool; poolside serv. Restaurant 6 am–4 pm; Fri–Sun to 6 pm; dining rm 6–11 pm. Bar noon–1:30 am. Ck-out noon. Meeting rms. Gift shop. Free airport transportation. Putting green. Charter boats. Some bathrm phones. Private patios, balconies. On waterfront; view of marina. Cr cds: A, C, D, MC, V.

★ ★ ★**MARINA INTERNATIONAL.** *4200 Admiralty Way. 310/301-2000; res: 800/882-4000 (exc CA), 800/862-7462 (CA); FAX 310/301-6687.* 110 rms, 3 story, 25 bungalows. S $110–$160; D $120–$180; each addl $15; suites, bungalows $198–$288; under 12 free; wkend rates, package plans avail. TV; cable. Heated pool; whirlpool, poolside serv. Restaurant 6:30 am–2 pm. Bar 5–11 pm. Ck-out noon. Meeting rms. Bellhops. Garage parking. Free airport transportation. Cr cds: A, C, D, MC, V.

★ ★ ★**MARRIOTT MARINA DEL REY.** *13480 Maxella Ave. 310/822-8555; FAX 310/823-2996.* 283 rms, 5 story. S $139–$149; D $149–$159; each addl $10; parlor rms $134–$144; under 12 free; wkend rates. Crib free. TV; cable. Heated pool; whirlpool, poolside serv. Restaurant 6:30 am–10 pm; Fri & Sat to 10:30 pm. Rm serv. Bar 11–2 am; entertainment; dancing Wed–Sat. Ck-out noon. Meeting rms. Bellhops. Gift shop. Free airport transportation avail. Tennis opp. Minibars. Private patios, balconies. Shopping arcade adj. Cr cds: A, C, D, DS, MC, V, JCB.

Hotels

★ ★ ★**DOUBLETREE.** *4100 Admiralty Way. 310/301-3000; FAX 310/301-6890.* 370 rms, 9 story. S $125–$145; D $145–$175; suites

$165–$1,000; under 18 free; wkend packages. Valet parking $6. TV; cable. Pool; poolside serv. Restaurants 6 am–11 pm. Bar 10–1:30 am; entertainment. Ck-out noon. Convention facilities. Concierge. Gift shop. Free airport, shopping, beach transportation. Tennis privileges. Health club privileges. Bathrm phones, refrigerators. Balconies. Opp beach. *LUXURY LEVEL:* **SIGNATURE CLUB.** 42 rms. S $145; D $175. Private lounge. Complimentary continental bkfst, refreshments. Cr cds: A, C, D, DS, ER, MC, V, JCB.

★ ★ ★ ★ **THE RITZ-CARLTON, MARINA DEL REY.** *4375 Admiralty Way.* 310/823-1700. 306 rms, 12 story. S, D $185–$325; suites $495–$2,000; under 18 free; wkend rates. Crib free. Valet parking $15. Pool; poolside serv. Supervised children's activities (wkends). Restaurant 6 am–11 pm. Rm serv 24 hrs. Bar 11–1 am; pianist. Ck-out noon. Convention facilities. Concierge. Gift shop. Free airport transportation. Lighted tennis, pro. Golf privileges. Exercise rm; instructor, weights, bicycles, whirlpool. Masseuse. Bathrm phones, refrigerators, minibars. Balconies. Bicycle rentals. Overlooking marina; yachts for charter. *LUXURY LEVEL:* **RITZ-CARLTON CLUB.** 52 rms, 2 suites, 2 floors. S, D $295; suites $595–$2,000. Private lounge, honor bar. Complimentary continental bkfst, refreshments, food service 5 times daily, magazines. Cr cds: A, C, D, DS, ER, MC, V, JCB.

Restaurant

★ **CHARLEY BROWN'S.** *4445 Admiralty Way.* 310/823-4534. Hrs: 11:30 am–10 pm; Fri to 11 pm; Sat 4–11 pm; Sun 4–9:30 pm; Sun brunch 9:30 am–2 pm. Res accepted. Bar. Semi-a la carte: lunch $5.95–$9.95, dinner $9.95–$19.95. Sun brunch $13.95. Child's meals. Specializes in prime rib, steak, seafood. Parking. View of marina. Cr cds: A, C, D, DS, MC, V.

Martinez (E-2)

Pop: 31,808 **Elev:** 23 ft **Area code:** 510 **Zip:** 94553

What to See and Do

1. **John Muir National Historic Site.** 4202 Alhambra Ave. House built in 1882 was the home of the conservationist, author and advocate of the National Park system. Visitor center, film, self-guided tours (Wed–Sun; closed Jan 1, Thanksgiving, Dec 25). Martinez Adobe (1849) is also on the grounds. Sr citizen rate. Phone 228-8860. ¢

2. **Briones Regional Park.** N entrance 2 mi S of Arnold Industrial Hwy (CA 4) via Alhambra Valley Rd. Covers 5,484 acres of rolling hills and wooded ravines. John Muir Nature Area at north end. Hiking on many trails including two self-guided nature trails, horseback riding. Picnicking. Archery range. Connects with Briones to Mt Diablo Trail. Phone 635-0135. Per car (seasonal) ¢¢

(For accommodations see Concord, Oakland, Vallejo)

Marysville (D-2)

Settled: 1842 **Pop:** 12,324 **Elev:** 63 ft **Area code:** 916 **Zip:** 95901

Marysville is at the confluence of the Yuba and Feather rivers. The river town was once the third largest community in the state. Hydraulic mining has raised the Yuba River bed so that it is above, rather than below, the city. The river is contained by huge levees. Named for a survivor of the Donner Party, the town was the head of river navigation—the point where miners continued upriver by foot to the gold diggings.

What to See and Do

Bok Kai Temple. D St on the Levee. Chinese temple, built in 1879, honors Bok Kai, river god of good fortune. Caretaker will open temple for visitors; guided tours may be arranged by appt (daily). Donation. Contact Chamber of Commerce for information.

(For further information contact the Yuba-Sutter Chamber of Commerce, 429 10th St, PO Box 1429; 743-6501.)

Annual Events

Bok Kai Festival. Parade, street entertainment, Lion Dances; martial arts demonstrations; 1-mi run; climaxed by firing of the "Lucky Bombs." Feb or Mar.

Stampede Days. Riverfront Park. Stampede and rodeo sponsored by the Flying U Rodeo; parade, activities. Memorial Day wkend.

California Prune Festival. Yuba-Sutter Fairgrounds in Yuba City. Food, wine tasting, music, art displays, children's activities. Usually 2nd wkend Sept.

Beckwourth Frontier Days. In commeration of when James Beckwourth passed through here in the 1850s. Costumed participants re-create the life as it was then; events including muzzle loaders; wagon train. 1st wkend Oct.

(See Oroville)

Motels

★ ★ **BEST WESTERN BONANZA INN.** *(1001 Clark Ave, Yuba City 95991)* 1 blk N of CA 20, ½ mi E of CA 99. 916/674-8824; FAX 916/674-0563. 125 rms, 2–3 story. S $62–$66; D $66–$74; each addl $4; suites $85–$120. TV; cable. Pool; whirlpool. Restaurant 6 am–10 pm. Bar 4 pm–midnight. Ck-out noon. Meeting rms. Some refrigerators, in-rm whirlpools, fireplaces, balconies. Cr cds: A, C, D, DS, MC, V.

✔ ★ **VADA'S.** *(545 Colusa Ave, Yuba City 95991)* On CA 20 in Yuba City. 916/671-1151. 40 rms, 1–2 story, 7 kits. S $28–$33; D $34–$46; each addl $5; suites $40–$47; kit. units $3–$6 addl. Crib $3. TV; cable. Complimentary coffee in rms. Restaurant adj open 24 hrs. Ck-out 11 am. Airport transportation. Cr cds: A, D, DS, MC, V.

Mendocino (C-1)

Founded: 1852 **Pop:** 1,100 (est) **Elev:** 125 ft **Area code:** 707 **Zip:** 95460

Once a remote lumber port, Mendocino has evolved into an artists' colony and popular vacation spot. The town's 19th-century legacy is reflected in its Cape Cod/New England architecture.

What to See and Do

1. **Mendocino Art Center.** 45200 Little Lake St. Classes in ceramics, textiles, painting, drawing, printmaking and sculpture. Exhibition/sales gallery, art library, gardens; theatrical productions and arts and crafts fairs. (Daily; closed Jan 1, Dec 25) Phone 937-5818. Free.

2. **Kelley House Museum & Library** (1861). 45007 Albion St. Displays feature antique photographs, exhibits of local artifacts and private collections. (June–Sept, afternoons; also by appt) Phone 937-5791. ¢

3. **State parks.**

   Russian Gulch. 2 mi N via CA 1. Swimming beach; entry point for skin divers; fishing. Hiking, bicycle trails. Picnicking. Camping. Standard fees. (May be closed winter months) Phone 937-5804.

Van Damme. 3 mi S via CA 1. In the SE portion of this 2,190-acre park is Pygmy Forest, where poor soil conditions inhibit tree growth. Some trees, nearly 200 years old, have trunks only ¼ inch in diameter. Fishing; beach with access for divers & boaters. Nature, hiking trails. Picnicking. Camping, environmental camping. Phone 937-5804.

Mendocino Headlands. Surrounds town; on 347 acres. Includes 1850s building (Ford House Visitor Center) containing exhibits on town and local history; phone 937-5397. Bluff areas/headlands offer ocean view, sandy beach; fishing. Hiking. Phone 937-5804. **Free.**

(For further information contact the Fort Bragg-Mendocino Coast Chamber of Commerce, 332 N Main St, PO Box 1141, Fort Bragg 95437; 961-6300 or 800/726-2780.)

Annual Events

Whale Festival. 1st wkend Mar.

Mendocino Music Festival. Chamber, symphonic, choral, opera and jazz concerts. 10 days July.

Mendocino Christmas Festival. Tour of inns; events. First 2 wks Dec.

(See Fort Bragg, Ukiah, Willits)

Inns

★★★**ALBION RIVER INN.** *(Box 100, 3790 N CA 1, Albion 95410) 6 mi S on CA 1, at the mouth of the Albion River. 707/937-1919; res: 800/479-7944 (northern CA).* 20 rms. No A/C. S, D $110–$185. Complimentary full bkfst. Complimentary coffee in rms. Restaurant (see ALBION RIVER INN RESTAURANT). Ck-out noon, ck-in 3 pm. Many fireplaces; some whirlpools. Some balconies. 10 landscaped acres on cliff above ocean; flower gardens. Individually decorated rms; antiques. View of ocean. Cr cds: A, MC, V.

✔ ★★**BLACKBERRY.** *44951 Larkin Rd. 707/937-5281.* 13 rms, 2 kit. units. No A/C. No rm phones. S $65–$100; D $70–$120; each addl $5; kit. units $120; mid-wk rates in winter. TV; cable. Complimentary continental bkfst, tea. Coffee in rms. Ck-out 11 am, ck-in 1 pm. Lawn games. Many fireplaces; some refrigerators. Ocean view. Cr cds: MC, V.

★★★**ELK COVE.** *(Box 367, 6300 S CA 1, Elk 95432) 15 mi S on CA 1. 707/877-3321.* 8 rms. No A/C. No rm phones. D $98–$148; lower mid-wk rates. Children over 12 yrs only. Complimentary full bkfst. Ck-out 11 am, ck-in 3–6 pm. Free local airport, bus depot transportation. Library; sitting rm. Antiques. Some wood burning stoves. Picnic tables, grills. Gazebo. Former executive guest house (1883). Overlooks ocean; private beach. Totally nonsmoking. No cr cds accepted.

★★★**HARBOR HOUSE.** *(Box 369, 5600 S CA 1, Elk 95432) 14 mi S on CA 1. 707/877-3203.* 10 rms, 2 story, 4 cottages. No A/C. No rm phones. MAP: S $125–$205; D $160–$240; each addl $50; mid-wk rates Jan–Mar. Children over 12 yrs only. Full bkfst 8:30–9:30 am, dinner 7 pm. Ck-out noon, ck-in 2 pm. Lawn games. Many fireplaces. Library. Antiques, original artwork, piano. Private beach. Built in 1916 for lumber company executive. No cr cds accepted.

★★**HEADLANDS.** *(Box 132) Jct Howard & Albion Sts. 707/937-4431.* 5 rms, 3 story. No A/C. No rm phones. S, D $103–$172. Complimentary full bkfst, tea & snacks. Restaurant nearby. Ck-out 11 am, ck-in 3 pm. Street parking. Fireplaces. Sitting rms; antiques. Victorian house (1868) built as town barber shop overlooks English garden, ocean. Totally nonsmoking. No cr cds accepted.

★★★**HILL HOUSE.** *(Box 625) 10701 Palette Dr. 707/937-0554; res: 800/422-0554 (Northern CA); FAX 707/937-1123.* 44 rms, 2 story, 4 suites. No A/C. S, D $100–$150; suites $195. TV; cable. Complimentary coffee in rms. Dining rm 7–10 am, 11:30 am–2:30 pm, 6–9 pm. Bar. Ck-out 11:30 am, ck-in 3 pm. Meeting rms. Private patios, balconies. Picnic tables. Library. Victorian decor. Overlooks ocean. On 2½ acres. Cr cds: A, MC, V.

★★**JOSHUA GRINDLE.** *(Box 647) 44800 Little Lake Rd, at CA 1. 707/937-4143.* 10 rms, 1–2 story. No A/C. No rm phones. S, D $95–$135; 2-night min wkends. Complimentary full bkfst, tea/sherry. Ck-out 11 am, ck-in 1 pm. Free local airport transportation. Lawn games. Antiques. Many fireplaces. New England country atmosphere. 2 acre English-style garden. Antique pump organ. Built 1879 by local banker. Overlooks ocean. Totally nonsmoking. Cr cds: DS, MC, V.

✔ ★★★**MENDOCINO.** *(Box 587) 45080 Main St. 707/937-0511; res: 800/548-0513; FAX 707/937-0513.* 51 rms, 38 with bath, 1–3 story. S, D $50–$160; each addl $20; suites $185–$225; lower rates wkdays. TV in some rms; cable. Dining rm 8 am–9:30 pm. Rm serv. Bar. Ck-out noon, ck-in 4 pm. Meeting rms. Bellhops. Some fireplaces. Some balconies. Antiques. Built 1878. Some rms with ocean view. Cr cds: A, MC, V.

★★★**STANFORD INN BY THE SEA.** *(Box 487) S on CA 1. 707/937-5615; res: 800/331-8884; FAX 707/937-0305.* 25 rms, 2 story, 2 kits. No A/C. S, D $160–$176; kit. suites $190–$230. Crib $5. Pet accepted. TV; cable, in-rm movies. Indoor pool; whirlpool, sauna. Complimentary full bkfst, wine. Coffee in rms. Ck-out noon, ck-in 4 pm. Bellhops. Concierge. Free local airport transportation. Refrigerators, fireplaces. Private patios, balconies. Antiques. Big River llamas on grounds. Tropical greenhouse. Organic gardens, nursery. On 10 acres of meadow, forest overlooking ocean, river. Totally nonsmoking. Cr cds: A, C, D, DS, ER, MC, V, JCB.

Restaurants

★★★**ALBION RIVER INN.** *(See Albion River Inn) 707/937-1919.* Hrs: 5:30–9:30 pm; wkends 5–10 pm. Res accepted. No A/C. Coastal country menu. Bar 4:30 pm–midnight. A la carte entrees: dinner $9.50–$19.50. Specializes in seafood, pasta, local produce. Pianist Fri, Sat. Parking. Fine art photography. On ocean. Totally nonsmoking. Cr cds: A, MC, V.

★★★**CAFE BEAUJOLAIS.** *961 Ukiah St. 707/937-5614.* Hrs: 8:30 am–2:30 pm, 5:45–9:30 pm. Closed Tues, Wed; Thanksgiving, Dec 25. Res accepted. No A/C. French, California menu. Beer. Wine list. A la carte entrees: bkfst $4.50–$9.75, lunch $6.50–$14.75, dinner $10–$22. Specializes in waffles, coffee cake, fresh salmon. Own baking. Bakery. Outdoor dining. Victorian atmosphere. Totally nonsmoking. No cr cds accepted.

Menlo Park *(E-1)*

Founded: 1854 **Pop:** 28,040 **Elev:** 70 ft **Area code:** 415 **Zip:** 94025

What to See and Do

1. **Allied Arts Guild.** 75 Arbor Rd, at Cambridge. Unique complex of shops set on a portion of the once vast Rancho de las Pulgas. Original barn and sheep sheds were preserved and new buildings constructed in Colonial Spanish design; formal gardens, paths and courtyards. (Daily exc Sun; closed hols) Phone 325-3259; for lunch & tea reservations phone 324-2588.

2. **Filoli House and Gardens** (1917). N on El Camino Real to Woodside Rd (CA 84), then 4 mi W to Cañada Rd, then 5 mi N, in Woodside.

This 654-acre estate contains the Georgian-style residence built for William B. Bourn II and 16-acre formal gardens. The gardens are an Italian Renaissance-style of parterres, terraces, lawns and pools. The house was featured in the television series "Dynasty." House and garden: guided tours (mid-Feb–mid-Nov, Tues–Sat), res required exc Fri; self-guided tours (Fri, also 1st Sat & 2nd Sun of each month), no res required. Three-mile guided nature hike (daily exc Sun). Phone 364-2880 for reservations. Tour of house and garden ¢¢¢; Nature hike ¢¢

3. **Sunset Publishing Corporation and Gardens.** Willow & Middlefield Rds. Publishers of *Sunset* magazine and books. Tour of editorial facilities and gardens. (Mon–Fri; closed hols) Phone 324-5479 or -5481. **Free.**

4. **Stanford Linear Accelerator Center (SLAC).** 2575 Sand Hill Rd, E of I-280. This 426-acre national facility houses a two-mile-long linear accelerator that generates the highest energy electron beams in the world. Two-hour tour consists of orientation, slide show and bus tour. (Limited hrs; res required) Phone 926-2204. **Free.**

(See Palo Alto, Redwood City, San Francisco, Santa Clara, Saratoga)

Motor Hotel

★ ★ ★ **STANFORD PARK.** *100 El Camino Real. 415/322-1234; res: 800/368-2468; FAX 415/322-0975.* 162 rms, 3–4 story. S $165–$200; D $180–$290; each addl $15; suites $200–$290; under 12 free. Crib free. TV; cable. Heated pool; poolside serv. Complimentary coffee. Restaurant (see PALM CAFE). High tea 2–4:30 pm. Rm serv 24 hrs. Bar 11–2 am. Ck-out noon. Meeting rms. Bellhops. Complimentary valet parking. Complimentary transportation within 5 mi radius. Exercise equipt; weights, bicycles, whirlpool, sauna. Bathrm phones, minibars; some refrigerators, fireplaces. Balconies. French provincial furniture. Cr cds: A, C, D, DS, MC, V, JCB.

Restaurant

★ ★ ★ **PALM CAFE.** *(See Stanford Park Motor Hotel) 415/322-1234.* Hrs: 6:45 am–2 pm, 5:30–10 pm; Sun brunch 10 am–2 pm. Res accepted. Bar 11–2 am. Wine list. Semi-a la carte: bkfst $5–$10, lunch, dinner $7–$22. Sun brunch $16.95. Specializes in fresh seafood, pasta, American regional cuisine with Pacific Rim influence. Own baking. Piano bar. Valet parking. Mix of contemporary with French country antiques. Cr cds: A, C, D, DS, MC, V, JCB.

Ⓓ

Merced (E-3)

Pop: 56,216 **Elev:** 172 ft **Area code:** 209

The gateway to Yosemite National Park (see), Merced is the center of a rich agricultural area with dairy and beef production as well as peach, almond, tomato and alfalfa crops. Publishing, canneries, metal and plastic manufacturers and Castle Air Force Base contribute to its economic base.

What to See and Do

1. **Merced County Courthouse Museum.** Courthouse Park, between 20th & 21st Sts. Restored courthouse with collection of antique dolls, quilts, historical exhibits. (Wed–Sun afternoons) Phone 723-2401. **Free.**

2. **Yosemite Wildlife Museum.** 2040 Yosemite Parkway. Mounted birds and animals displayed. (Daily exc Sun; closed Jan 1, Thanksgiving, Dec 25) Sr citizen rate. Phone 383-1052. ¢¢

3. **Lake Yosemite Park.** 5714 N Lake Rd, 5 mi NE on G St, 2 mi E on Bellvue Rd, then ½ mi N on N Lake Rd to park entrance. Swimming, sailing, waterskiing; fishing; boating. Picnicking. (Daily for sightseeing and fishing; no overnight camping) Fee for group facility use & boat launching. Phone 385-7426. Per vehicle ¢¢

4. **Castle Air Museum.** 8 mi N, adj to Castle AFB at Sante Fe and Buhach Rd. Displays 42 vintage military aircraft; indoor military museum; inquire for guided tours. Restaurant. Museum (daily, mid-morning–mid-afternoon; closed Jan 1, Easter, Thanksgiving, Dec 25) Phone 723-2178. ¢¢

(For further information contact the Convention & Visitors Bureau, 690 W 16th St, 95340; 384-3333 or 800/446-5353.)

Annual Events

West Coast Antique Fly-in. 1st full wkend June.

Merced County Fair. County Fairgrounds. Mid-July.

Central California Band Review. 1st Sat Nov.

Motel

✔ ★ ★ **BEST WESTERN PINE CONE INN.** *1213 V Street (95340). 209/723-3711; FAX 209/722-8551.* 98 rms, 2 story. S $56; D $65; each addl $5. Crib $5. TV. Pool. Restaurant 6 am–11 pm. Bar noon–11 pm, wkends to midnight. Ck-out noon. Meeting rm. Cr cds: A, C, D, DS, MC, V.

Restaurant

★ ★ **EAGLES NEST.** *2000 E Childs Ave. 209/723-1041.* Hrs: 6 am–10 pm; Sun brunch 8:30 am–2 pm. Res accepted; required some hols. Bar 10 am–midnight. Semi-a la carte: bkfst $1.95–$7, lunch $4.75–$10.20, dinner $6.49–$24.95. Sun brunch $8.95. Child's meals. Specialties: veal scallopini, stuffed teriyaki chicken. Parking. Outdoor dining. Rustic decor; etched glass depicts nature scenes. Cr cds: A, D, DS, MC, V.

Ⓓ SC

Mexico

(see Ensenada, Tijuana)

Millbrae

(see San Francisco)

Mill Valley (E-1)

Pop: 13,038 **Elev:** 80 ft **Area code:** 415 **Zip:** 94941

What to See and Do

Mt Tamalpais State Park. 6 mi W on Panoramic Hwy. This park is one of the favorite retreats of San Franciscans. The mountain rises 2,571 feet above sea level and provides a spectacular view of the entire bay area. A winding road climbs to a spot near the summit. Trails and bridle paths wind through the woods to attractive picnic areas; hike-in camping (fee; no vehicles). Muir Woods National Monument (see) is at the foot of the mountain. The Mountain Theatre, located just north of the park, presents plays in a natural amphitheater

(May–June). Standard fees. Phone 388-2070. Day use fee per car
¢¢

(See San Francisco, San Rafael)

Motel

★ **HOWARD JOHNSON.** *160 Shoreline Hwy. 415/332-5700; FAX 415/331-1859.* 100 rms, 2 story. July–Oct: S $70–$100; D $80–$105; suites $110–$120; each addl $10; under 16 free; lower rates rest of yr. Crib free. TV; cable. Pool; wading pool. Continental bkfst. Restaurant 7 am–10 pm. Rm serv. Ck-out noon. Meeting rms. Valet serv. Private patios, balconies. Cr cds: A, C, D, DS, ER, MC, V, JCB.

Inn

★ ★ **MOUNTAIN HOME.** *810 Panoramic Hwy. 415/381-9000.* 10 rms, 3 story. No A/C. S, D $131–$215; each addl $15. Complimentary full bkfst 8–10 am. Dining rm 11:30 am–3:30 pm, 5:30–9:30 pm. Rm serv. Ck-out 11 am, ck-in 3 pm. Fireplaces. Private patios, balconies. Scenic view. On road to Mt Tamalpais. Cr cds: MC, V.

Restaurants

★ ★ **GIRAMONTI.** *655 Redwood Hwy, off US 101 at Seminary Dr exit. 415/383-3000.* Hrs: 11:30 am–2 pm, 5–10 pm; Sat & Sun from 5 pm. Closed Thanksgiving, Dec 25. Res accepted. Italian menu. Beer, wine. A la carte entrees: lunch $5–$11.95, dinner $8.50–$14. Child's meals. Specializes in pasta, veal, seafood. Own desserts. Parking. Italian provincial decor. Cr cds: A, D, MC, V, JCB.

✔ ★ **O'LEARY'S.** *106 Throckmorton Ave. 415/381-1770.* Hrs: 11:30 am–10 pm; Fri & Sat to 10:30 pm. Closed Thanksgiving, Dec 25. Res accepted. No A/C. Bar to 2 am. Semi-a la carte: lunch $5–$12, dinner $5–$17. Specializes in seafood. Bistro atmosphere with framed magazine covers and prints of celebrities on walls. Cr cds: MC, V.

Modesto (E-2)

Founded: 1870 **Pop:** 164,730 **Elev:** 87 ft **Area code:** 209

A processing, shipping and marketing center for the rich farmlands of the central San Joaquin Valley and Stanislaus County, Modesto was named for a San Francisco banker who was too modest to publicize his own name. Nearby Don Pedro Dam provides the irrigation and power that is the key to the area's prosperity. Modesto is a gateway to Yosemite National Park (see) and the Gold Country.

What to See and Do

1. **McHenry Museum.** 1402 I Street. Historical exhibits in period rooms; schoolroom, doctor's office, blacksmith shop. (Daily exc Mon) Phone 577-5366. **Free.** One blk NE is the

    McHenry Mansion (1883). 15th & I Streets. Restored Victorian mansion built for one of Modesto's first families. Period furnishings. (Tues–Thurs & Sun; closed hols) Phone 577-5367. **Free.**

2. **Great Valley Museum of Natural History.** 1100 Stoddard Ave. Exhibits of natural plant and animal habitats and complete ecosystems. Also children's discovery room. (Tues–Sat) Phone 575-6196. ¢

3. **Caswell Memorial State Park.** 15 mi N via CA 99, S on Austin Rd. On 274 acres. Swimming; fishing. Nature, hiking trails. Picnicking. Camping. Standard fees. Phone 599-3810 or 826-1196.

4. **Turlock Lake State Recreation Area.** 23 mi E on CA 132. On 3,000 acres. Swimming, waterskiing; fishing; boating. Picnicking. Camping. Standard fees. Phone 874-2008.

5. **Don Pedro Lake Recreation Area.** Approx 37 mi E, N of CA 132 (see SONORA).

6. **Merced River Development Project.** 45 mi E, S of CA 132. **Exchequer Dam.** Rises 490 feet to impound Lake McClure (82-mi shoreline). **McClure Point, Barrett Cove, Horseshoe Bend and Bagby Recreation Areas. McSwain Dam** stands 80 feet high; impounds Lake McSwain (12½-mi shoreline). All areas offer swimming, showers, rest rms, waterskiing; fishing; boating (launching facilities; fee), marinas. Picnicking, concessions. Camping (fee; electricity addl). Contact Merced Irrigation District, Parks Dept, 9090 Lake McClure Rd, Snelling 95369; phone 800/468-8889.

(For further information contact the Convention & Visitors Bureau, 1114 J Street, PO Box 844, 95353; 577-5757 or 800/226-4282.)

Annual Event

Riverbank Cheese & Wine Exposition. 6 mi E on CA 108 in Riverbank. Two-day street festival with food booths, arts & crafts, antiques, entertainment. Extensive tasting of local wines and cheeses. Phone 869-4541. 2nd wkend Oct.

(See Oakdale, Stockton)

Motels

★ ★ ★ **BEST WESTERN MALLARD INN.** *1720 Sisk Rd (95350), US 99 Briggsmore Ave exit (N). 209/577-3825; FAX 209/577-1717.* 126 units, 2 story, 11 suites. S $72–$89; D $78–$94; each addl $6; suites $99–$195; under 18 free. Crib $5. TV; cable. Heated pool; whirlpool, poolside serv. Complimentary coffee in rms. Restaurant 7:30–9:30 am, 6–10 pm. Rm serv. Ck-out noon. Meeting rms. Sundries. Free airport transportation. Some refrigerators. Wet bar in suites. Cr cds: A, C, D, DS, MC, V.

✔ ★ ★ **SUNDIAL LODGE.** *808 McHenry Ave (95350). 209/523-5642; FAX 209/521-2692.* 49 rms, 2 story. S $44–$48; D $48–$52. Crib free. TV; cable. Pool. Restaurant 5 am–10 pm. Rm serv. Bar 10–2 am. Ck-out noon. Meeting rms. Valet serv. Private patios, balconies. Cr cds: A, MC, V.

✔ ★ **VAGABOND INN.** *1525 McHenry Ave (95350). 209/521-6340; FAX 209/575-2015.* 99 rms, 2 story. S $42–$52; D $47–$52; each addl $5; under 18 free. Crib free. TV; cable. Heated pool. Complimentary continental bkfst, coffee. Restaurant adj open 24 hrs. Ck-out noon. Cr cds: A, C, D, DS, MC, V.

Motor Hotel

★ ★ ★ **HOLIDAY INN.** *1612 Sisk Rd (95350), US 99 Briggsmore Ave exit (N). 209/521-1612; FAX 209/527-5074.* 186 rms, 2 story. S, D $70–$90; suites $150; under 18 free. Crib free. TV; cable, in-rm movies avail. 2 pools, 1 indoor. Playground. Restaurant 6:30 am–2 pm, 5–10 pm. Rm serv. Bar 11–1:30 am; entertainment, dancing Fri & Sat. Ck-out noon. Coin lndry. Meeting rms. Lighted tennis, pro. Exercise equipt; bicycles, rowing machine. Holidome. Rec rm. Cr cds: A, C, D, DS, MC, V, JCB.

Hotel

★ ★ ★ **RED LION.** *1150 9th St (95354). 209/526-6000; FAX 209/526-6096.* 265 rms, 10 story. S $102–$127; D $117–$139; each addl $15; suites $200–$450; under 18 free; wkend rates. Crib free. Valet parking $5. Pet accepted. TV; cable. Heated pool; poolside serv. Restaurant 6 am–10 pm. Bar 11–2 am; entertainment Tues & Wed, dancing Thurs–Sat. Ck-out 1 pm. Convention facilities. Gift shop. Beauty shop. Free airport transportation. Exercise equipt; weights, bicycles, whirlpool, sauna. Bathrm phones. Refrigerators avail. Cr cds: A, C, D, DS, ER, MC, V, JCB.

Monterey (F-2)

Founded: 1770 **Pop:** 31,954 **Elev:** 40 ft **Area code:** 408 **Zip:** 93940

The calm harbor, red-roofed white stucco houses, white sand beach, Monterey cypress and Monterey pine all existed in the days when Monterey was the Spanish heart of California. A mélange of Mexican, New England, sea, mission and ranch makes Monterey uniquely Californian in its culture and history. The Spanish explorer Sebastian Vizcaino sailed into the bay in 1602 and named it for the Count of Monte-Rey, Viceroy of Mexico. The spot was rediscovered in 1770 when Fray Crespi, Fray Junipero Serra and Gaspar de Portola took possession, founding the Presidio and the Mission San Carlos Borromeo del Rio Carmelo (see CARMEL). The King of Spain recognized it as the capital of California in 1775, but in 1822 it became part of the Mexican Republic. Soon after, American whalers and traders began to arrive. Commodore Sloat raised the American flag in 1846, ending years of opposition to Mexican rule. Delegates to a constitutional convention in 1849 met in Monterey and drew up California's first constitution. The city became a whaling center; fisheries, canneries and specialized agriculture developed. The sardine fisheries and canneries, in particular, inspired the novels *Cannery Row* and *Sweet Thursday* by John Steinbeck. Now, with the sardines gone and the canneries silent, the row has been taken over by an aquarium, gourmet restaurants and art galleries while Fisherman's Wharf offers fishing and sightseeing trips and the bay's famous sea otters; nearby is the Maritime Museum of Monterey.

What to See and Do

1. **"Path of History" tour.** Leads to many old buildings of distinction. These are marked with a plaque explaining the history and architecture. Several buildings are open to the public. Some of these buildings and a number of others are part of the Monterey State Historic Park. Obtain map at the Monterey Peninsula Chamber of Commerce and Visitor & Convention Bureau, 380 Alvarado St, or at the Monterey Visitors Center, Camino El Estero & Franklin Sts.

2. **Royal Presidio Chapel.** San Carlos Cathedral, 550 Church St, between Camino El Estero & Figueroa St. Founded June 3, 1770, the only presidio chapel remaining in California; in continuous use since 1795. Façade is considered most ornate of all California missions.

3. **Monterey State Historic Park.** 525 Polk St. Day ticket valid in all historic buildings in state historic park. Single tickets also available. (Park and building hrs may vary, phone ahead for schedule information; closed Jan 1, Thanksgiving, Dec 25) Phone 649-7118. Day ticket good for 2 days ¢¢

   Robert Louis Stevenson House. 530 Houston St. Preserved as a state historic monument with large collection of Stevenson memorabilia. Stevenson lived here for four months while visiting his future wife. (Tues & Thurs–Sun) Guided tours (hrs vary, inquire for schedule). Admission included in 2-day ticket.

   Custom House (1827). Custom House Plaza. Old Mexican custom house exhibit re-creates a cargo of the 1840s. Commodore Sloat raised the American flag over this adobe building in 1846,

bringing 600,000 square miles into the Union. (Daily, inquire for hrs; closed major hols) **Free.**

   Larkin House (1830s). 510 Calle Principal, at Jefferson St. Consulate for Thomas Larkin, first and only US consul to Mexican California (1843–1846). Large collection of antiques. (Mon, Wed & Fri–Sun) Guided tours (inquire for schedule). Admission included in 2-day ticket.

   Cooper-Molera House (1827). Corner of Polk and Munras. Largest complex in the park. Built by John Rogers Cooper, half-brother of Thomas Larkin. (Tues & Thurs–Sun; inquire for hrs) Admission included in 2-day ticket.

   Boston Store (1845). Scott & Olivier Sts. Restored general store built by Thomas Larkin and operated by Joseph Boston & Co. Houses a general merchandise store operated by the Montery History and Art Assn. (Wed–Sun; closed Jan 1, Thanksgiving, Dec 25) **Free.**

   Casa Soberanes (1842). 336 Pacific St. Adobe house containing displays of Monterey history from 1840–1970. Excellent example of adobe construction; walls are 38 inches thick. Local art collection. (Mon, Wed & Fri–Sun) Guided tours (inquire for schedule). Admission included in 2-day ticket.

   Pacific House (1847). Custom House Plaza. A museum of California history and Holman American Indian artifact collection. (Daily, inquire for hrs; closed major hols) **Free.**

4. **Colton Hall Museum** (1849) and **Old Monterey Jail** (1854). Pacific St, between Madison & Jefferson Sts, in Civic Center, 2nd fl. Built as a town hall and public school by the Reverend Walter Colton, alcalde (mayor or judge) of Monterey Dist during the American occupation of California, 1846–1848. Classic Revival design of stone and adobe mortar. The first constitution of California (in Spanish and English) was written here. Changing exhibits. The jail, a single story addition of granite, was added to the building in 1854 at which time Colton Hall served as the Monterey County Courthouse. (Daily; closed Jan 1, Thanksgiving, Dec 25) Phone 646-5640. **Free.**

5. **Presidio of Monterey.** Pacific St, N of Scott St. Home of Defense Language Institute. Developed in 1902 as cantonment for troops returning from the Philippine Insurrection. Monument to John Drake Sloat, commander of American troops that captured Monterey (1846); statue in honor of Fray Junipero Serra. There are twelve historic sites and monuments on Presidio Hill; brochure and map are available. The Presidio Museum has artifacts and dioramas depicting the history of Presidio Hill from the Ohlone Indian period through the Spanish, Mexican and American eras. Hrs vary, phone 647-5414 or the Presidio of Monterey Public Affairs Office at 647-5104. **Free.**

6. **Monterey Bay Aquarium.** 886 Cannery Row. One of the largest aquariums in the US; 100 exhibits of the sea life and habitats along the shores of California's Monterey Bay include sea otters, sharks and a 3-story-tall kelp forest. While construction continues on a new wing to house the Outer Bay exhibit, twice wkly live video broadcasts, "Live from Monterey Canyon," of work in progress are transmitted from waters up to 3,300 feet deep to a screen in the aquarium auditorium (Mon & Tues afternoons). (Daily; closed Dec 25) Phone 648-4888. ¢¢¢¢

7. **Monterey Peninsula Museum of Art.** 559 Pacific St. Displays early California and American art, folk, ethnic and tribal art, Asian art. Photography exhibits; changing exhibitions of major American artists. Docent-guided tour avail (Sun afternoon). (Daily exc Mon; closed Jan 1, Thanksgiving, Dec 25) Donation. Phone 372-7591.

8. **La Mirada.** 720 Via Mirada. Original residence of Jose Castro, prominent Californian during the Mexican period, and later Frank Work, who added a collection of art and antiques to the 2½-acre estate. Garden and house tours (Wed & Sat afternoons; 3 departures each day). ¢¢

9. **Maritime Museum of Monterey.** Located in the Stanton Center at #5 Custom House Plaza, adj to Fisherman's Wharf. Seven major theme areas provide exhibits on maritime and naval history of the area, including sailing ship era and whaling industry; ship models; maritime artifacts, interactive exhibits; paintings; research library;

model workshop for restoration and building replicas of historic vessels. The jewel of the museum collection is the 16-ft tall intricately crafted first order Fresnel Lens from the old lighthouse at Point Sur. Also here is a 100-seat theater featuring an orientation film and re-enactments. (Daily exc Mon, extended hrs in summer; closed Jan 1, Thanksgiving, Dec 25) Phone 373-AHOY (2469). ¢¢

10. Seventeen-Mile Drive. A famous scenic drive between Monterey and Carmel (see) along Pacific Coast past Seal Rock, Lone Cypress, Cypress Point and Spyglass Hill and Pebble Beach golf courses. This private community in Del Monte Forest is known around the world for its natural beauty. Road may be entered at several points; follow the red-and-yellow center lines and the 17-Mile Drive signs. Toll ¢¢¢

11. Fisherman's Wharf. On Monterey Harbor. Restaurants, shops, tour boat departure area.

12. Marina. Foot of Figueroa St. Berths for 420 vessels up to 50 feet long; two launching ramps. Municipally owned. (Office closed Jan 1, Thanksgiving, Dec 25) Phone 646-3950.

13. Sightseeing tours.

    Gray Line bus tours. Contact 350 8th St, San Francisco 94103; phone 415/558-9400 or 800/826-0202.

    CCInc Auto Tape Tours. These 90-minute cassettes offer mile-by-mile self-guided tours to Fresno (142 mi) with highlights of the Coastal Range, San Joaquin Valley, historic stagecoach route to San Luis Reservoir; to San Luis Obispo (138 mi) with scenic points of interest in Carmel, Point Lobos State Reserve, Big Sur, Hearst Castle at San Simeon; to San Francisco (139 mi) with historic account and scenic details of Santa Cruz Mountains, giant redwood forest; to Mariposa (151 mi) with description of the Salinas and San Joaquin valleys highlighting the trip to Mariposa, gateway to Yosemite National Park. Fourteen different tour tapes of California are available. Tapes may be purchased directly from CCInc, PO Box 227, 2 Elbrook Dr, Allendale, NJ 07401; 201/236-1666. ¢¢¢¢

(For further information contact the Monterey Peninsula Chamber of Commerce and Visitors & Convention Bureau, 380 Alvarado St, PO Box 1770, phone 649-1770; or the Visitors Center, Camino El Estero & Franklin Sts, phone 649-1770.)

Annual Events

AT&T–Pebble Beach National Pro-Amateur Golf Championship. Takes place on Pebble Beach, Cypress and Spyglass courses. Late Jan or early Feb.

Adobe Tour. Sponsored by the Monterey History & Art Assn. Self-guided walking tour visits approx 25 historic adobes and gardens. Contact 5 Custom House Plaza; 372-2608. Last Sat Apr.

Monterey County Fair. Fairgrounds & Exposition Park. 2004 Fairground Rd, corner of Fairground Rd & Garden Rd. Phone 372-1000. 6 days mid-Aug.

Monterey Jazz Festival. County Fairgrounds. Reserved seats only. Contact PO Box JAZZ; 373-3366. Mid-Sept.

Laguna Seca Raceway. 8 mi E on CA 68. International auto and motorcycle races. Includes ISMA races, historic races, and Indy cars. For specific dates and details phone 800/327-SECA.

(See Carmel, Pacific Grove, Pebble Beach, Salinas)

Motels

(Rates are often higher holidays, special events, some wkends)

★★**BAY PARK.** 1425 Munras Ave. 408/649-1020; FAX 408/373-4258. 80 rms, 3 story. No elvtr. Mid-June–Aug: S, D $79–$119; each addl $10; under 18 free; lower rates rest of yr. Crib free. TV. Heated pool; whirlpool. Restaurant 7 am–9 pm. Rm serv. Bar 11 am–10 pm; entertain-

ment, dancing Fri & Sat. Ck-out noon. Meeting rms. Sundries. Some refrigerators. Cr cds: A, C, D, DS, MC, V, JCB.

★★**BEST WESTERN STEINBECK LODGE.** 1300 Munras Ave. 408/373-3203. 32 rms, 2 story. No A/C. June–Oct: S, D $65–$79; each addl $10; lower rates rest of yr. TV; cable. Heated pool. Complimentary continental bkfst. Restaurant nearby. Ck-out 11 am. Cr cds: A, D, DS, MC, V.

★★**CANNERY ROW INN.** 200 Foam St. 408/649-8580; FAX 408/649-2566. 32 rms, 2 story. No A/C. Mar–Sept: S, D $65–$150; each addl $10; under 12 free; higher rates wknds; lower rates rest of yr. Pet accepted. TV; cable. Complimentary continental bkfst. Complimentary coffee in rms. Ck-out noon. Meeting rms. Covered parking. Whirlpool. Refrigerators, fireplaces. Balconies. Opp ocean. Cr cds: A, MC, V.

★★**CYPRESS GARDENS INN.** 1150 Munras Ave. 408/373-2761; res: 800/433-4732. 46 rms, 2 story. No A/C. Late June–Oct: S, D $84–$104; each addl $10; suite $175–$250; under 12 free; lower rates rest of yr. Crib free. TV; cable. Heated pool; whirlpool. Complimentary continental bkfst. Ck-out noon. Private patios, balconies. Cr cds: A, C, D, DS, ER, MC, V, JCB.

✔★★**CYPRESS TREE INN.** 2227 N Fremont St. 408/372-7586; FAX 408/372-2940. 55 rms, 2 story, 12 kits. No A/C. S, D, kits. $52–$78; each addl $6; suites $95–$185. Crib $6. Pet accepted, some restrictions. TV; cable. Complimentary coffee at bakery 6:30 am–noon. Ck-out 11 am. Coin lndry. Sundries. Whirlpool, hot tub. Refrigerators; hot tub in suites. Private patios, balconies. Picnic table, grill. Cr cds: MC, V.

★**EL ADOBE INN.** 936 Munras Ave. 408/372-5409; res: 800/433-4732. 26 rms, 2 story. No A/C. Late June–Oct: S, D $74–$95; each addl $10; under 12 free; lower rates rest of yr. Crib free. Pet accepted; $5. TV; cable. Complimentary continental bkfst. Ck-out noon. Whirlpool. Sun deck. Cr cds: A, C, D, DS, MC, V.

★★**HOLIDAY INN EXPRESS.** 443 Wave St. 408/372-1800. 43 rms, 3 story. No A/C. May–Oct: S, D $95–$165; each addl $10; under 19 free; higher rates Fri, Sat; lower rates rest of yr. Crib free. TV; cable. Complimentary continental bkfst. Complimentary coffee in rms. Ck-out noon. Meeting rm. Covered parking. Whirlpool. Refrigerators avail. Ocean 1 blk. Cr cds: A, C, D, DS, MC, V, JCB.

★★**MARIPOSA INN.** 1386 Munras Ave. 408/649-1414. 51 rms, 3 story. S, D $68–$98; each addl $8; suites $95–$170; under 18 free; golf plans. Crib $6. TV. Heated pool; whirlpool. Complimentary continental bkfst. Restaurant opp from 7 am. Ck-out noon. Covered parking. Some refrigerators. Balconies. Cr cds: A, C, D, DS, MC, V.

★★**MERRITT HOUSE.** 386 Pacific St. 408/646-9686. 25 rms, 2 story. S, D $120–$130; each addl $15; suites $175–$195; under 10 free. Crib $5. TV; cable. Continental bkfst. Ck-out noon. Some refrigerators. Patios, balconies. Fireplaces. Suites in adobe house (1830). Garden. Cr cds: A, C, D, MC, V.

★★**MONTEREY BAY INN.** 242 Cannery Row. 408/373-6242; res: 800/424-6242. 47 rms, 3 story. No A/C. June–Oct: S, D $129–$269; lower rates rest of yr. Crib free. TV. Complimentary continental bkfst in rms. Restaurant nearby. Ck-out noon. Meeting rms. Bellhops. Whirlpool. Minibars. Balconies. On ocean. Cr cds: A, C, D, DS, MC, V.

✔★**PADRE OAKS.** 1278 Munras Ave. 408/373-3741. 20 rms. No A/C. Mid-June–Aug: S $60–$80; D $65–$90; each addl $5; lower rates rest of yr. Crib $5. TV; cable. Heated pool. Complimentary continental bkfst. Restaurant nearby. Ck-out 11 am. Cr cds: A, DS, MC, V.

[icons]

★★**SAND DOLLAR INN.** *755 Abrego St. 408/372-7551; res: 800/982-1986.* 63 rms, 3 story. S, D $74–$114; each addl $10; suites $99–$124; under 12 free. Crib free. TV; cable. Heated pool; whirlpool. Complimentary continental bkfst. Restaurant open 24 hrs. Ck-out noon. Coin lndry. Some refrigerators, wet bars, fireplaces. Some private patios, balconies. Cr cds: A, C, D, MC, V.

[icons]

Motor Hotels

★★**BEST WESTERN MONTEREY BEACH.** *2600 Sand Dunes Dr, near Monterey Peninsula Airport. 408/394-3321; FAX 408/393-1912.* 196 rms, 4 story. June–Oct: S, D $90–$170; suites $280; under 18 free; lower rates rest of yr. Crib free. TV; cable. Pool; whirlpool. Restaurant 7 am–9:30 pm. Rm serv. Bar 11–1 am; entertainment. Ck-out noon. Meeting rms. Bellhops. Valet serv. Concierge. Valet parking. Free airport transportation. Tennis privileges. Golf privileges, greens fee $45. Some refrigerators. Ocean view; beach access. Cr cds: A, C, D, DS, MC, V, JCB.

[icons]

★★**BEST WESTERN VICTORIAN INN.** *487 Foam St. 408/373-8000; FAX 408/373-8000, ext 401.* 68 rms, 3 story. June–Oct: S, D $109–$229; each addl $10; under 12 free; lower rates rest of yr. TV; cable. Complimentary continental bkfst. Ck-out noon. Meeting rms. Whirlpool. Bathrm phones, refrigerators, fireplaces. Private patios, balconies. Victorian furnishings. 2 blks from bay. Cr cds: A, C, D, DS, MC, V, JCB.

[icons]

★★**CASA MUNRAS.** *(Box 1351) 700 Munras Ave. 408/375-2411; res: 800/222-2558 (exc CA), 800/222-2446 (CA); FAX 408/375-1365.* 151 rms, 2 story. No A/C. S, D $86–$135; each addl $15; suites $161–$350; under 12 free. Crib free. TV; cable. Heated pool. Restaurant 7 am–9 pm. Bar 4:30 pm–1 am; entertainment Thurs–Sun. Ck-out noon. Meeting rms. Bellhops. Barber, beauty shop. Many fireplaces. Former garden estate. Cr cds: A, C, D, MC, V.

[icons]

✔★**DAYS INN.** *(1400 Del Monte Blvd, Seaside 93955) NE off CA 1. 408/394-5335; FAX 408/394-7125.* 143 rms, 5 story. June–Sept: S $65–$87; D $76–$99; each addl $10; under 18 free; wkly rates; lower rates rest of yr. Crib free. TV; cable. Heated pool. Restaurant 6 am–10 pm. Wine, beer. Ck-out noon. Meeting rms. Valet serv. Sundries. Cr cds: A, D, DS, MC, V.

[icons]

★★★**HYATT REGENCY.** *1 Old Golf Course Rd. 408/372-1234; FAX 408/375-3960.* 575 rms, 1–4 story. No A/C. S $135–$175; D $160–$200; suites $225–$1,000. Crib free. TV; cable, in-rm movies avail. 2 heated pools; poolside serv. Supervised child's activities (summer & hols; rest of yr Fri, Sat evenings only). Restaurant 7 am–11 pm. Bar 11–1:30 am. Ck-out noon, ck-in 3 pm. Convention facilities. Bellhops. Valet serv. Concierge. Beauty salon. 6 tennis courts, pro. 18-hole golf, greens fee $37, putting green. Bicycles. Exercise equipt; weights, bicycles, whirlpool, sauna. Exercise course. Many refrigerators. Situated on 23 landscaped acres. *LUXURY LEVEL:* **REGENCY FLOOR.** 33 rms, 2 floors. S, D $175–$225; each addl $25. Private lounge. Library. Complimentary continental bkfst, refreshments.
Cr cds: A, C, D, DS, MC, V, JCB.

[icons]

Hotels

★★**DOUBLETREE AT FISHERMAN'S WHARF.** *2 Portola Plaza, at Fisherman's Wharf. 408/649-4511; FAX 408/372-0620.* 374 rms, 7 story. No A/C. S $125–$170; D $145–$190; each addl $15; suites $225–$650; Easter, Thanksgiving, Christmas packages; under 18 free. Crib free. TV; cable. Heated pool; whirlpool, poolside serv. Restaurants 6 am–10 pm; Fri & Sat to 11 pm. Bar 5:30 pm–2 am; entertainment, dancing. Ck-out noon. Convention facilities. Concierge. Shopping arcade. Valet or self-parking. Health club privileges. Minibars. Balconies. Near wharf. Cr cds: A, C, D, DS, ER, MC, V, JCB.

[icons]

★★★**MARRIOTT.** *350 Calle Principal. 408/649-4234; FAX 408/372-2968.* 341 rms, 10 story. S, D $130–$170; each addl $20; suites $195–$550; under 18 free; packages avail. Crib free. Valet parking $8. TV. Heated pool. Restaurant 6:30–1 am. Ck-out noon. Meeting rms. Concierge. Drugstore. Barber, beauty shops. Exercise equipt; weights, bicycles, whirlpool, sauna. Refrigerators; bathrm phone in suites. Cr cds: A, C, D, DS, ER, MC, V, JCB.

[icons]

★★**MONTEREY PLAZA.** *400 Cannery Row. 408/646-1700; res: 800/631-1339 (exc CA), 800/334-3999 (CA); FAX 408/646-0285.* 290 rms, 4 story. S, D $108–$270; each addl $20; suites $200–$300; under 12 free; package plans avail. Garage, valet parking $10. TV; cable, in-rm movies avail. Restaurant 6:30 am–10 pm. Bar 11:30 am–midnight. Ck-out 1 pm. Concierge. Exercise equipt; weight machine, bicycles. Minibars, bathrm phones. Private patios, balconies. On Monterey Bay; beach access. Located on oceanfront on historic Cannery Row. Cr cds: A, C, D, DS, MC, V, JCB.

[icons]

Inns

★★★**HOTEL PACIFIC.** *300 Pacific St. 408/373-5700; res: 800/554-5542.* 103 rms, 4 story. May–Oct: S, D $144–$214; each addl $20; under 10 free; lower rates rest of yr. TV; cable. Complimentary continental bkfst, refreshments. Dining rm 11 am–2:30 pm, 5–10 pm. Rm serv. Ck-out noon, ck-in 4 pm. Meeting rms. Bellhops. Valet serv. Concierge. Covered parking. Whirlpools. Refrigerators, fireplaces. Private patios, balconies. Original art, antiques, fireplace in lobby. 3 gardens; hand-carved fountains. Cr cds: A, C, D, DS, MC, V.

[icons]

★★★**JABBERWOCK.** *598 Laine St, at Hoffman St. 408/372-4777.* 7 rms, 4 share bath, 3 story. No A/C. No rm phones. S, D $100–$180. Complimentary full bkfst, refreshments. Ck-out noon, ck-in 3 pm. Library; antiques. ½-acre gardens; waterfalls. Former convent. Cr cds: MC, V.

[icons]

★★**MONTEREY HOTEL.** *406 Alvarado St. 408/375-3184; res: 800/727-0960; FAX 408/373-2899.* 45 rms, 4 story, 6 suites. No A/C. S, D $99–$109; each addl $10; suites $129–$149; under 12 free; special seasonal rates avail. Crib free. Garage $3.50. TV; cable. Complimentary continental bkfst, afternoon tea. Ck-out noon, ck-in 3 pm. Meeting rms. Valet serv. Some refrigerators, wet bars. Fireplace in some suites. Cr cds: A, C, D, DS, ER, MC, V, JCB.

[icons]

★★★★**OLD MONTEREY INN.** *500 Martin St. 408/375-8284; res: 800/350-2344.* 10 rms, 1 cottage. No A/C. No rm phones; cordless phone avail. S, D $160–$220; suite, cottage $220; 3rd person in suite $50 addl. Complimentary full bkfst, wine & afternoon tea. Ck-out noon, ck-in 2:30–8 pm. Fireplaces. English country house (1929) situated on oak-studded hillside near the bay; 1¼ acres of gardens. Individually decorated rms; antiques. Down comforters & pillows; some featherbeds. Totally nonsmoking. Cr cds: MC, V.

[icons]

SPINDRIFT. (New general manager, therefore not rated) *652 Cannery Row. 408/646-8900; res: 800/841-1879.* 41 rms, 4 story. No A/C. May–Oct: S, D $149–$319; under 10 free; lower rates rest of yr. TV. Complimentary continental bkfst, afternoon tea, wine. Dining rm 11:30 am–10 pm. Rm serv. Bar. Ck-out noon, ck-in 4 pm. Meeting rm. Bellhops. Concierge. Valet parking. Rolls Royce limo avail. Bathrm phones, refrigerators, honor bars, fireplaces. Some balconies. On private beach. Individually decorated rms, marble baths, Oriental rugs; elegant, traditional furnishings; antiques, artwork. Roof-top garden with sweeping views of Monterey Bay. Cr cds: A, C, D, DS, MC, V.

Restaurants

✔ ★ ★**ABALONETTI SEAFOOD TRATTORIA.** 57 Fisherman's Wharf. 408/373-1851. Hrs: 11 am–10 pm; wkends to 11 pm. Closed Dec 25. Res accepted. No A/C. French, Italian menu. Bar 10 am–11 pm. Semi-a la carte: lunch $6.95–$13.95, dinner $9.95–$15.95. Child's meals. Specializes in calamari, grilled fish, seafood pasta, pizza baked in wood-burning oven. Outdoor dining. Exhibition kitchen. Harbor view. Cr cds: A, C, D, DS, ER, MC, V, JCB.

✔ ★**AMARIN.** 807 Cannery Row, on 2nd floor. 408/373-8811. Hrs: 11 am–10 pm. Closed Jan 1, Thanksgiving, Dec 25. Res accepted. No A/C. Thai menu. Wine, beer. Semi-a la carte: lunch $5.50–$6.25, dinner $7.25–$10.95. Specialties: p'ad Thai, musaman, squid with cilantro root. Contemporary Thai decor. Totally nonsmoking. Cr cds: A, C, D, DS, MC, V, JCB.

★ ★**BINDEL'S.** 500 Hartnell St. 408/373-3737. Hrs: 5–10 pm; Sat to 10:30 pm; Sun brunch 10 am–3 pm. Res accepted. Bar. Complete meals: dinner $10.95–$18.95. Sun brunch $8.95–$10.95. Specializes in fresh fish, prime rib, lamb, regional dishes. Own pasta, sorbet. Parking. Renovated historic 1840s adobe house. Cr cds: A, C, D, DS, MC, V.

★ ★**CAFE FINA.** 47 Fisherman's Wharf. 408/372-5200. Hrs: 11:30 am–2:30 pm, 5–10 pm; Sat & Sun 11:30 am–3 pm, 5–10 pm. Closed Easter, Thanksgiving, Dec 25. Res accepted. No A/C. Italian menu. Bar. A la carte entrees: lunch $6–$15, dinner $10–$35. Child's meals. Specializes in fresh Monterey Bay seafood, pasta, meat dishes. Collection of family photos displayed. View of bay. Cr cds: A, C, D, DS, MC, V.

★ ★**CHART HOUSE.** 444 Cannery Row. 408/372-3362. Hrs: 5–10 pm; Fri to 11 pm; Sat 4–11 pm; Sun 4–10 pm. Res accepted. Bar. Semi-a la carte: dinner $12.95–$25.95. Specializes in fresh seafood, steak, prime rib. Salad bar. Parking. Ocean view. Cr cds: A, D, DS, MC, V.

★ ★**CIBO.** 301 Alvarado St. 408/649-8151. Hrs: 5–10 pm; Fri & Sat to 10:30 pm. Res accepted. No A/C. Italian menu. Bar to 1 am. Semi-a la carte: dinner $6.95–$18.95. Specializes in lasagne, seafood pasta, antipasto misto. Mediterranean decor. Cr cds: A, C, D, MC, V.

✔ ★**CLOCK GARDEN.** 565 Abrego. 408/375-6100. Hrs: 10 am–11 pm; early-bird dinner 4–6 pm; Sun brunch to 3 pm. Closed Jan 1, Thanksgiving, Dec 25. Res accepted. No A/C. Bar to 1 am. Semi-a la carte: lunch $4.75–$7.95, dinner $6.95–$17.95. Sun brunch $3.95–$9.95. Child's meals. Specializes in honey-glazed spareribs, prime rib, shrimp fettucine. Own soups. Parking. Outdoor dining. Gardens, fountains. Clock & bottle collection. Cr cds: A, D, MC, V.

★ ★**FISHERY.** 21 Soledad Dr. 408/373-6200. Hrs: 5–9 pm; early-bird dinner 5–6 pm. Closed Sun, Mon. Res accepted. Asian, Amer menu. Bar. Semi-a la carte: dinner $12.95–$17.95. Specializes in fresh fish, steak, Malaysian curried calamari, Thai fish. Own desserts. Oriental artifacts, prints. Cr cds: A, D, DS, MC, V.

★ ★**FRESH CREAM.** 100 F Heritage Harbor. 408/375-9798. Hrs: 6–10 pm; Fri also 11:30 am–2 pm. Closed Dec 25. Res accepted. French menu. Bar. Wine cellar. A la carte entrees: lunch $8.95–$12.95, dinner $25–$40. Specialties: carré d'agneau à la Dijonnaise, canard rôti au cassis. Own baking. Five dining rms, all with harbor view. Cr cds: C, MC, V.

★**KIEWEL'S CAFE.** 100A Heritage Harbor. 408/372-6950. Hrs: 11 am–9 pm; Sun from 3 pm; Sat & Sun brunch 9 am–3 pm. Res accepted. No A/C. Bar. A la carte entrees: lunch $4.50–$14.95, dinner $9.95–$21.95. Sun brunch $3.95–$9.95. Child's meals. Specializes in steak, seafood, pasta, baked desserts. Parking. Outdoor dining. Casual dining; harbor view. Cr cds: MC, V.

★**RAPPA'S.** Old Fisherman's Wharf, at end of wharf. 408/372-7562. Hrs: 11 am–9:30 pm; Fri & Sat to 10 pm. Closed Thanksgiving, Dec 25. Res accepted. Italian menu. Bar. A la carte entrees: lunch $5.50–$8.95, dinner $7.95–$15. Specialties: cioppino, bouillabaisse, seafood, pasta. Casual dining. Scenic view of bay. Family-owned. Cr cds: D, DS, MC, V.

★ ★**SARDINE FACTORY.** 701 Wave St. 408/373-3775. Hrs: 5–10:30 pm; Fri & Sat to 11 pm; Sun 2–10 pm. Closed wk of Dec 25. Res accepted. Bar. Wine cellar. A la carte entrees: dinner $15–$30. Specialties: fresh abalone, linguini & seafood, Monterey Bay prawns, steak. Parking. Three separate dining rms; two wine cellar rooms. Historic building was originally built as a canteen for sardine workers. Cr cds: A, C, D, MC, V, JCB.

 ★**SIAMESE BAY.** 131 Webster St. 408/373-1550. Hrs: 11 am–3 pm, 5–10 pm; Sat & Sun from 5 pm. Thai menu. Wine, beer. Semi-a la carte: lunch $4–$6, dinner $6–$9. Specializes in shrimp soup, curry, Thai vegetarian cuisine. Own ice cream. Ceiling fans; photographs of Thailand. Thai decor. Cr cds: A, MC, V.

★**SPADARO'S.** 650 Cannery Row. 408/372-8881. Hrs: 11:30 am–3:30 pm, 5–10 pm. Closed Dec 24 & 25. Res accepted. Italian menu. Bar. A la carte entrees: lunch $4.95–$12.95, dinner $9.95–$19.95. Specializes in fresh fish, pasta, chicken. Display of historic photos. On the beach overlooking Monterey Bay. Cr cds: A, MC, V.

★ ★**TARPY'S ROADHOUSE.** 2999 Monterey-Salinas Hwy (CA 68), at Canyon Del Rey, near Monterey Peninsula Airport. 408/647-1444. Hrs: 11:30 am–10 pm; Sun brunch 10 am–3 pm. Closed Thanksgiving, Dec 25. Res accepted. Bar. A la carte entrees: lunch $4.50–$11, dinner $6.50–$18. Sun brunch $6–$12. Specializes in rabbit, chicken, steak, fresh seafood. Parking. Outdoor dining. Located in historic country stone house; dining area is former wine tasting room. Fireplaces. Cr cds: A, DS, MC, V.

★ ★**TRIPLES.** 220 Olivier St. 408/372-4744. Hrs: 6–9:30 pm; Fri & Sat to 10 pm. Closed Thanksgiving, Dec 25. Res accepted. No A/C. California, French menu. Bar. A la carte entrees: dinner $12.95–$19.95. Specialties: crab cakes, rack of lamb, steak tartare, Grand Marnier soufflé. California decor. Jacket. Cr cds: A, MC, V.

★**WHARFSIDE.** 60 Old Fisherman's Wharf. 408/375-3956. Hrs: 11 am–10 pm. Closed Easter, Thanksgiving, Dec 25. Res accepted. Italian menu. Semi-a la carte: lunch $5.95–$8.95, dinner $8.75–$26. Specializes in fresh seafood, bouillabaisse, combination cioppino. Own ravioli. View of Monterey Bay, yacht harbor. Cr cds: A, D, MC, V.

Morro Bay (G-2)

Pop: 9,664 **Elev:** 200 ft **Area code:** 805 **Zip:** 93442

At the harbor entrance to this seaport town is Morro Rock, a 576-foot volcanic dome discovered by Juan Rodriguez Cabrillo in 1542. A large commercial fishing fleet sails from here and many boats dock along the Embarcadero.

What to See and Do

1. **Morro Bay State Park.** S of town. Approx 2,400 acres on Morro Bay. Fishing, boating. 18-hole golf course (fee). Picnicking, cafe. Hiking. Tent & trailer camping (showers, dump station; water & electric hookups). Standard fees. Phone 772-2560. On White Point is

Museum of Natural History. State Park Rd. Films, slide shows, displays; nature walks. (Daily; closed Jan 1, Thanksgiving, Dec 25) Phone 772-2694. ¢

Other natural features are Morro Bay Heron Rookery, Montana de Oro State Park, Morro Strand State Beach, Los Osos Oaks Reserve and Morro Rock.

2. **Morro Bay Aquarium.** 595 Embarcadero. Displays 300 live marine specimens. (Daily) Phone 772-7647. ¢

3. **Harbor cruises.** 1205 Embarcadero. One-hour narrated tours of bay on sternwheeler *Tiger's Folly II*, departing from Harbor Hut Dock. Phone 772-2257. ¢¢¢

4. **Central Coast Cruises.** 501 Embarcadero. Nature, sunset and whale-watching cruises. Sr citizen rate. Phone 541-1435 or 800/773-BOAT. ¢¢¢–¢¢¢¢¢

(For further information contact the Chamber of Commerce, 895 Napa, A-1, PO Box 876; 772-4467 or 800/231-0592.)

(See Atascadero, Paso Robles, Pismo Beach, San Luis Obispo)

Motels

★★**BAY VIEW LODGE.** *225 Harbor St, at Market St. 805/772-2771; res: 800/742-8439 (CA).* 22 rms, 2 story. No A/C. June–Sept & wkends: S $60–$74; D $68–$75; each addl $8; higher rates graduation wkend; lower rates wkdays rest of yr. Crib $4. TV; cable, in-rm movies. Coffee in rms. Restaurant nearby. Ck-out 11 am. Whirlpool. Refrigerators, fireplaces. Ocean view from some rms. Bay 1 blk. Cr cds: A, MC, V.

Ⓢ Ⓘ

★★★**BEST WESTERN EL RANCHO.** *2460 Main St. 805/772-2212.* 27 rms. Easter–Labor Day: S, D $54–$89; each addl $7; under 12 free; lower rates rest of yr. Crib $5. TV; cable. Heated pool. Restaurant 7 am–10 pm. Ck-out 11 am. Coin lndry. Refrigerators. Grill. Redwood lobby, etched glass door. Opp ocean. Cr cds: A, C, D, DS, MC, V.

⩙ Ⓢ Ⓘ SC

★★**BLUE SAIL INN.** *851 Market St. 805/772-2766; res: 800/336-0707 (CA).* 48 rms, 1–2 story. No A/C. S, D $60–$95; suites $95–$120; lower rates Jan–Mar. Crib $7. TV; cable. Complimentary coffee in rms. Restaurant adj 7 am–10 pm. Ck-out 11 am. Covered parking. Whirlpool. Refrigerators, wet bars; some fireplaces. Balconies. Picnic tables. Bay view. Cr cds: A, D, DS, MC, V.

D Ⓢ Ⓘ

★★**BREAKERS.** *(Box 1447) 780 Market St, at Morro Bay Blvd. 805/772-7317; res: 800/932-8899 (CA).* 25 rms, some A/C, 2–3 story. No elvtr. S, D $70–$96; each addl $10. Crib $4. TV; cable. Heated pool; whirlpool. Complimentary coffee in rms. Restaurant opp 7 am–10 pm. Ck-out noon. Refrigerators. Some fireplaces. Bay view from many rms. Ocean 1 blk. Cr cds: A, C, D, DS, MC, V.

D ⩙ Ⓢ Ⓘ

★★**HARBOR HOUSE INN.** *1095 Main St. 805/772-2711; res: 800/247-5076.* 46 rms, 2 story. No A/C. Memorial Day wkend–Sept: S $60–$70; D $60–$75; under 18 free; lower rates rest of yr. Crib $5. TV; cable, in-rm movies. Complimentary coffee in rms. Restaurant opp open 24 hrs. Ck-out 11 am. Whirlpool. Some refrigerators. Balconies. Bay 3 blks. Cr cds: A, D, DS, MC, V.

D Ⓢ Ⓘ

★★**LA SERENA INN.** *(PO Box 1711) 990 Morro Ave. 805/772-5665; res: 800/248-1511.* 37 rms, 3 story, 5 suites. May–mid-Oct: S, D $68.50–$88.50; each addl $5; suites $105–$150; lower rates rest of yr. Crib $5. TV; cable. Complimentary continental bkfst. Restaurant nearby. Ck-out 11 am. Meeting rm. Covered parking. Sauna. Many refrigerators. Balconies. Ocean view. Cr cds: A, MC, V.

D Ⓢ Ⓘ SC

✔★**SEA AIR INN.** *845 Morro Ave. 805/772-4437.* 25 rms, 2 story, 3 suites. No A/C. May–Sept: S $38–$60; D $40–$75; each addl $5; suites $75–$100; under 5 free; lower rates rest of yr. TV; cable. Compli-

mentary coffee in rms. Restaurant adj 7 am–10 pm. Ck-out 11 am. Beauty shop. Refrigerator in suites. Ocean 1 blk. Cr cds: A, DS, MC, V.

Ⓢ Ⓘ SC

★★**THE TWIN DOLPHIN.** *590 Morro Ave. 805/772-4483.* 31 rms, 3 story. May–Oct: S, D $55–$80; each addl $5; suites $80–$100; lower rates rest of yr. Crib $5. TV; cable. Complimentary continental bkfst. Restaurant nearby. Ck-out noon. Meeting rm. Covered parking. Whirlpool. Refrigerators avail. Balconies. Ocean 1 blk. Cr cds: DS, MC, V.

D Ⓢ Ⓘ

✔★**VILLAGER.** *1098 Main St, at Beach St. 805/772-1235; res: 800/444-0782.* 22 rms, 2 story. No A/C. S $35–$95; D $40–$95; each addl $6; higher rates: wkends, Poly graduation, mid-state fair. Crib $6. TV; cable. Complimentary coffee in rms. Restaurant opp open 24 hrs. Ck-out 11 am. Whirlpool. Some refrigerators. Ocean 3 blks. Cr cds: A, D, DS, MC, V.

Ⓢ Ⓘ SC

Hotel

★★★**INN AT MORRO BAY.** *State Park Rd, adj to Morro Bay Golf Course. 805/772-5651; res: 800/321-9566; FAX 805/772-4779.* 96 rms, 2 story. No A/C. S, D $85–$225. Crib free. TV; cable. Heated pool; poolside serv. Restaurant 7 am–2 pm, 5–9 pm; summer to 10 pm. Bar 11 am–midnight; entertainment, dancing. Ck-out noon. Meeting rms. Concierge. Golf privileges. Many refrigerators, fireplaces. Private patios, balconies. Picnic tables. On Morro Bay. Public 18-hole golf course adj. Cr cds: A, C, D, DS, MC, V, JCB.

⊷ 🚲 ⩙ Ⓢ Ⓘ SC

Restaurants

✔★★★**GALLEY.** *899 Embarcadero. 805/772-2806.* Hrs: 11 am–9 pm. Closed late Nov–Dec 25. Res accepted. Beer. Wine cellar. Semi-a la carte: lunch $3.95–$11. Complete meals: dinner from $12.75. Child's meals. Specializes in fresh fish, shellfish. Parking. Overlooks Morro Bay and Morro Rock. Family-owned since 1966. Cr cds: MC, V.

★★**ROSE'S LANDING.** *725 Embarcadero. 805/772-4441.* Hrs: 11:30 am–3 pm, 5–9 pm; Fri to 10 pm; Sat 4–10 pm; Sun 4–9 pm; early-bird dinner Mon–Fri 5–6:30 pm, Sat & Sun 4–6 pm. Res accepted. Bar noon–midnight. Semi-a la carte: lunch $5.95–$9.95, dinner $7.95–$38.95. Child's meals. Specializes in steak, seafood, pasta. Entertainment Wed–Sun in summer. Parking. View of bay. Cr cds: A, MC, V.

SC

Mother Lode Country (C-2,3 – D-2,3)

Three hundred eighteen miles long and only a few miles wide, this strip of land stretching through nine counties from the Sierra foothills was the scene of the gold rush of the mid-19th century. Discovery of gold at Coloma in 1848 touched off a wave of migration to the West that accelerated the development and population of all the western states by several decades. The enormous gold-bearing quartz vein was surface-mined until the end of the century; a few mines still exist, but it is now necessary to penetrate deep into the earth. In this narrow stretch of country have developed frontier and mining camp legends that are part of the warp and woof of the American West.

Today the scenic Mother Lode country is dotted with ghost towns, old mine shafts, rusting machinery and ancient buildings. Recreational gold panning is a favorite pastime. CA 49, a delightful but not high-speed highway, connects many of the towns where the 49ers panned for gold. Many picnic and camping areas can be found here. Map available from Chamber of Commerce offices throughout Mother Lode Country. For further information, contact the El Dorado County Chamber of Commerce, 542 Main St, Placerville, 95667 or phone 916/621-5885. (For Auto Tour of Mother Lode Country see SACRAMENTO.)

(For accommodations see Auburn, Grass Valley, Jackson, Nevada City, Placerville, Sonora, Truckee)

Mountain View (E-2)

Pop: 67,460 **Elev:** 97 ft **Area code:** 415

(See Palo Alto, Santa Clara)

Motels

★ ★ **BEST WESTERN MOUNTAIN VIEW INN.** *2300 El Camino Real W (94040).* 415/962-9912; FAX 415/962-9011. 72 units, 3 story, 10 suites. No elvtr. S $62–$72; D $65–$75; each addl $5; suites, kit. units $75–$150; under 12 free; wkly, special wkend rates. Crib free. TV; in-rm movies avail. Pool. Complimentary continental bkfst. Complimentary coffee in rms. Restaurant opp 6 am–midnight. Ck-out 11 am. Coin lndry. Meeting rms. Valet serv. Airport, RR station transportation. Exercise equipt; weight machine, bicycles, whirlpool, sauna. Refrigerators. Cr cds: A, C, D, DS, MC, V, JCB.

★ ★ **RESIDENCE INN BY MARRIOTT.** *1854 El Camino Real W (94040).* 415/940-1300; FAX 415/969-4997. 112 kit. suites, 2 story. S, D $139–$163; wkly, wkend, monthly rates. Pet accepted; $50 non-refundable and $6 per day. TV; cable. Heated pool; whirlpool. Complimentary continental bkfst. Restaurant nearby. Ck-out noon. Coin lndry. Meeting rm. Valet serv. Sundries. Lawn games. Health club privileges. Refrigerators. Private patios, balconies. Picnic tables, grills. Cr cds: A, C, D, DS, MC, V, JCB.

✔ ★ **RODEWAY INN.** *55 Fairchild Dr (94043).* 415/967-6856; FAX 415/964-4542. 50 rms, 2 story. S $55–$65; D $60–$70; each addl $5; under 18 free. Crib free. TV; cable, in-rm movies. Pool; whirlpool. Complimentary continental bkfst. Complimentary coffee in rms. Restaurant nearby. Ck-out 11 am. Coin lndry. Meeting rms. Valet serv. Refrigerators. Cr cds: A, C, D, DS, ER, MC, V, JCB.

Mt Diablo State Park (E-2)

(5 mi E of I-680, Danville, on Diablo Rd)

A spiraling road leads to the summit of Mt Diablo (3,849 ft), the highest peak in the San Francisco Bay region. From here, on a clear day one can see 200 miles in each direction. The mountain is dotted with rock formations containing fossilized shells. Hiking trails wind from ridge to ridge throughout the more than 19,000 acres of the park. Near the south entrance are unusual rock formations known as the Devil's Slide and the Wind Caves. There are more than 100 miles of unpaved roads and 68 miles of trails available to hikers and horseback riders. Also available are picnic and camping facilities. Standard fees. Phone 510/837-2525.

(For accommodations see Fremont, Pleasanton, Santa Clara, also see Livermore)

Mt Shasta (B-2)

Pop: 3,460 **Elev:** 3,554 ft **Area code:** 916 **Zip:** 96067

Set in Strawberry Valley, Mt Shasta offers a central location to fishing in nearby lakes and streams and to gem, mineral and fossil hunting in the surrounding area. City water from a nearby spring is so pure that, even untreated, it can be used as distilled water.

A Ranger District office of the Shasta-Trinity National Forests (see REDDING) is located in Mt Shasta.

What to See and Do

1. **Mt Shasta.** E of I-5, in Shasta-Trinity National Forests (see REDDING). Perpetually snow-covered double peak towering to 14,162 feet. Five glaciers persist on the slopes, feeding the McCloud and Sacramento rivers. A highway climbs the slope to 7,840 feet for a magnificent view. White bark pine, the famous Shasta lily and majestic stands of red fir are found at various heights.

2. **State Fish Hatchery.** 1 mi W off I-5, Central Mt Shasta exit. Raises trout; in continuous operation since 1888. (Daily) Phone 926-2215. **Free.** Also here is

   Sisson Museum. Features exhibits on area history, mountain climbing, fish hatchery. (Daily; closed Jan 1, Easter, Dec 25) Also annual quilt shows. Phone 926-5508. **Free.**

3. **Lake Siskiyou.** 2½ mi SW, off I-5. Box Canyon Dam impounds this lake of 430 acres. On W shore of lake is

   Lake Siskiyou Camp-Resort. Bordered by Box Canyon Recreation Area. Swimming beach; fishing; boating (rentals, ramp, marina). Hiking. Picnicking. Lodging. Snack bar; restaurant; store. Camping (tent & RV sites; hookups, rentals; dump station). Contact PO Box 276; phone 926-2618. Day use per person ¢; Camping ¢¢¢¢–¢¢¢¢¢

4. **Campgrounds.** The US Forest Service maintains the following

   Castle Lake. 12 mi SW, ¼ mi from Castle Lake. 6 units. Swimming; fishing. Picnicking. No trailers. **Sims Flat.** 7½ mi S of Castella, 1 mi E of I-5. 20 units. Fishing. **McBride Springs.** 5 mi E of Mt Shasta. 9 units. All open yr-round. Fee at Sims and McBride. For additional information on these and other campgrounds contact the Shasta-Trinity National Forests, 204 Alma St; phone 926-4511.

5. **Mt Shasta Ski Park.** 10 mi SE on CA 89. Two triple chairlifts, 1 surface lift; patrol, school, rentals; cafeteria, bar. 21 runs; longest run 1.2 mi; vertical drop 1,100 ft. (Thanksgiving–mid-Apr, daily) Night skiing (Wed–Sat), snowboarding. Phone 926-8610 or -8686 (snow conditions). ¢¢¢¢¢

(For further information contact the Chamber of Commerce/Convention & Visitors Bureau, 300 Pine St; 926-4865 or 800/926-4865.)

(See Dunsmuir, Redding, Yreka)

Motels

★ ★ ★ **BEST WESTERN TREE HOUSE.** *(Box 236) Lake St, just E of I-5 Central Mt Shasta exit.* 916/926-3101; FAX 916/926-3542. 95 rms, 2–3 story. S $56; D $76–$82; each addl $8; suites $80–$149. Crib free. TV; cable. Indoor pool. Restaurant 6:30 am–2 pm, 5–9:30 pm; Sun to 1:30 pm, 4–9 pm. Bar from 10 am. Ck-out noon. Meeting rms. Downhill/x-country ski 10 mi. View of Mt Shasta. Cr cds: A, C, D, DS, MC, V.

✔ ★ **FINLANDIA.** *1612 S Mt Shasta Blvd.* 916/926-5596. 9 air-cooled rms, 4 A/C, 1–2 story, 3 kits. S $28; D $30–$32; each addl $4; suites $40–$48; kit. units $4 addl. Crib $2. TV; cable. Complimentary morning coffee on request. Ck-out 11 am. Free bus depot transportation. Downhill ski 9 mi; x-country ski 8 mi. Picnic table, grill. Lake view from some rms. Cr cds: A, D, MC, V.

✔ ★SWISS HOLIDAY LODGE. *(Box 335) S Mt Shasta Blvd, 2 mi S at jct CA 89, I-5 McCloud exit. 916/926-3446.* 21 air-cooled rms, 2 story. May–Oct: S $36.95–$42.95; D $36.95–$56.95; each addl $4; suite $90; lower rates rest of yr. Crib $5. Pet accepted. TV; cable. Heated pool (seasonal); whirlpool. Complimentary coffee in rms. Ck-out 11 am. Downhill/x-country ski 10 mi. Refrigerators avail. Free community kitchen. Picnic tables, grills. View of Mt Shasta. Cr cds: A, D, DS, MC, V.

Restaurant

✔ ★ ★PIEMONT. *1200 S Mt Shasta Blvd. 916/926-2402.* Hrs: 5–9:30 pm; Fri, Sat to 10 pm in summer; Sun 1–9:30 pm; winter 5–9 pm. Closed Mon; Dec 24–25; also 4–6 wks Jan, Feb. Res accepted. Italian, Amer menu. Bar. Complete meals: dinner $8.25–$15.95. Child's meals. Specializes in ravioli, chicken, steak. Own pasta. Parking. Family-owned since 1940. Cr cds: MC, V.

Muir Woods National Monument (E-1)

(17 mi N of San Francisco, off CA 1)

This was the first area in the National Park system to preserve a virgin stand of redwoods *(Sequoia sempervirens)*, the tallest type of tree on earth. Every effort has been made to preserve this area as close as possible to what it was when the first white man saw it in 1850. The monument lies at the south foot of Mt Tamalpais. Two parcels of land, totaling more than 465 of the monument's 553 acres were donated to the United States by William and Elizabeth Thacher Kent and named in honor of John Muir, famous traveler and naturalist. The first parcel of land was donated in 1908.

Charred stumps and deep scars on living trees are proof that fires regularly occurred prior to white man's arrival, about 1850. During mid-December to mid-March, depending on winter rains, visitors can see mature salmon and steelhead trout fighting their way up the rapids of Redwood Creek to the spawning beds. There are 6 miles of trails; visitors must stay on trails. The following are not permitted: pets, picnicking, fishing, camping, hunting and possession of firearms. No fires may be built. There are 1½ miles of flat, asphalt trail to provide access for the disabled. The park is open every day, 8 am to sunset; there is no admission charge. Because the area is so popular, during the summer months it is best to drive there before 11 am or after 5 pm. Limited parking for oversize vehicles and large RVs. Contact the Site Manager, Muir Woods Natl Monument, Mill Valley 94941; 415/388-2595.

(For accommodations see Corte Madera, Mill Valley, San Francisco, Sausalito)

Napa (D-2)

Pop: 61,842 **Elev:** 17 ft **Area code:** 707

As gateway to the fertile Napa Valley, an area renowned for its fine wines, the town of Napa is a popular stopping-off point for tourists.

What to See and Do

1. **Napa Valley Wine Train.** Scenic trips aboard turn-of-the-century Pullman cars and 1950s diesel Steamliners. The 3-hour, 36-mile round-trip journey departs from Napa to St Helena and passes through Napa Valley vineyards. Lunch, brunch and dinner also served (fee). Reservations recommended one month in advance. Contact 1275 McKinstry St, 94559; phone 253-2111 or 800/522-4142. ¢¢¢¢¢

2. **Wineries.** For tour map showing area wineries contact the Convention & Visitors Bureau, 1310 Town Center Mall; phone 226-7459.

(For further information contact the Chamber of Commerce, 1556 First St, 94559, phone 226-7455 or the Convention & Visitors Bureau, 1310 Town Center Mall, 94559, phone 226-7459.)

(See Calistoga, St Helena, Sonoma, Yountville)

Motels

★ ★CHABLIS LODGE. *3360 Solano Ave (94558). 707/257-1944; res: 800/443-3490; FAX 707/226-6862.* 34 rms, 2 story, 7 kits. Apr–Oct: S, D $64–$89; kit. units $69–$79; each addl $5; under 16 free; higher rates Fri, Sat & hols; lower rates rest of yr. Crib $5. TV; cable. Heated pool; whirlpool. Complimentary continental bkfst. Complimentary coffee in rms. Restaurant nearby. Ck-out 11 am. Refrigerators. Picnic tables. Spacious rooms. Cr cds: A, D, DS, MC, V.

★STEELE PARK RESORT. *1605 Steele Canyon Rd, (94558), in Steele Park, 5 mi E of jct CA 121, 128. 707/966-2123; res: 800/522-2123; FAX 707/255-2727.* 24 rms, 4 with kit., 16 kit. cottages. S, D $75–$85; each addl $10; cottages $85–$125; under 18, $5; under 3 free; wkly rates. TV, some B/W. Pool. Playground. Restaurant 8 am–6 pm, Sat to 9 pm. Bar. Ck-out noon. Coin lndry. Sundries. Tennis. Private patios, balconies. Picnic tables. On lake. Marina. RV hookups. Cr cds: A, MC, V.

✔ ★TRAVELODGE NAPA VALLEY. *2nd & Coombs Sts (94559). 707/226-1871.* 44 rms, 2–3 story. May–Oct: S $60–$75; D $65–$95; each addl $10; under 17 free; higher rates Fri, Sat in season; lower rates rest of yr. TV. Pool. Complimentary morning coffee. Restaurant nearby. Ck-out noon. Cr cds: A, C, D, DS, MC, V.

Motor Hotels

★ ★BEST WESTERN INN. *100 Soscol Ave (94558). 707/257-1930; FAX 707/255-0709.* 68 rms, 3 story. Apr–Nov: S $65–$89; D $89–$109; each addl $5; suites $125–$150; lower rates rest of yr. Crib $5. Pet accepted. TV; cable. Heated pool; whirlpool. Coffee in rms. Restaurant open 24 hrs. Ck-out 11 am. Meeting rm. Private patios, balconies. Cr cds: A, C, D, DS, ER, MC, V, JCB.

★THE CHATEAU. *4195 Solano Ave (94558). 707/253-9300; res: 800/253-6272 (CA); FAX 707/253-0906.* 115 rms, 2 story. Apr–Oct: S $85; D $95; each addl $10; suites $140–$160; under 12 free; lower rates rest of yr. Crib free. TV; cable. Heated pool; whirlpool. Complimentary continental bkfst. Restaurant adj. Ck-out noon. Meeting rms. Some refrigerators. Hot-air balloon rides. Cr cds: A, C, D, DS, MC, V.

★ ★JOHN MUIR INN. *1998 Trower Ave (94558). 707/257-7220; res: 800/522-8999; FAX 707/258-0943.* 59 units, 3 story. S, D $75–$95; each addl $10; suites $100–$150; kits. $80–$120; under 14 free; mid-wk rates. Crib free. TV; cable, in-rm movies avail. Pool; whirlpool. Complimentary continental bkfst. Complimentary coffee in rms. Restaurant nearby. Meeting rms. Valet serv. Some refrigerators. Cr cds: A, C, D, DS, MC, V.

★ ★SHERATON INN NAPA VALLEY (formerly Clarion Inn). *3425 Solano Ave (94558). 707/253-7433; FAX 707/258-1320.* 191 rms, 2 story. Apr–mid-Nov: S, D $69–$149; each addl $10; suites $225–$450;

under 18 free; lower rates rest of yr. TV; cable, in-rm movies avail. Heated pool; whirlpool, poolside serv. Restaurant 7 am–11 pm. Rm serv. Bar; entertainment, dancing Thurs–Sat. Ck-out noon. Meeting rms. Bellhops. Valet serv. Sundries. Gift shop. Lighted tennis. Refrigerators avail. Some private patios, balconies. Cr cds: A, C, D, DS, ER, MC, V, JCB.

Hotel

★ ★ ★INN AT NAPA VALLEY (formerly Crown Sterling Suites). *1075 California Blvd (94559). 707/253-9540; FAX 707/253-9202.* 205 suites, 3 story. May–Oct: S, D $159–$179; each addl $15; under 12 free; higher rates some wkends; lower rates rest or yr. Crib free. TV; cable. 2 pools, 1 indoor; whirlpool, sauna, steam rm, poolside serv. Complimentary full bkfst. Complimentary coffee in rms. Restaurants 11 am–10 pm. Bar to 1 am; entertainment. Ck-out noon. Meeting rms. Concierge. Refrigerators, wet bars. Cr cds: A, C, D, DS, ER, MC, V, JCB.

Inns

★ ★ ★BEAZLEY HOUSE. *1910 First St (94559). 707/257-1649.* 11 rms, 2 story. S $97.50–$167.50; D $110–$190; each addl $25. Complimentary full bkfst, evening tea & sherry. Ck-out 11:30 am, ck-in 3:30-6:30 pm. Meeting rm. Whirlpool in 5 rms; fireplace in 6 rms. Built 1902; furnished with antiques; library. Totally nonsmoking. Cr cds: MC, V.

★ ★ ★COUNTRY GARDEN. *1815 Silverado Trail (94558). 707/255-1197; FAX 707/255-3112.* 8 rms, 2 story, 1 cottage. No rm phones. Apr–Nov, wkends: D $140–$190; each addl $25; lower rates rest of yr. Children over 16 yrs only. Champagne bkfst. Complimentary evening snacks, wine. Ck-out 11:30 am, ck-in 3 pm. Lawn games. Fireplaces; some in-rm whirlpools. Private patios, balconies. Picnic tables. View of river. Built 1855; antiques. On 1½ acres of woodland; rose garden; aviary. Totally nonsmoking. Cr cds: MC, V.

★ ★ ★LA RESIDENCE COUNTRY INN. *4066 St Helena Hwy N (CA 29) (94558). 707/253-0337; FAX 707/253-0382.* 20 rms, 18 baths, 2–3 story. Apr–Nov: S, D $90–$155; each addl $20; suites $190; lower rates rest of yr. TV avail. Heated pool; whirlpool. Complimentary full bkfst. Ck-out 11 am, ck-in 2 pm. Meeting rm. Balconies. Large rms, antiques, fireplaces. Gothic-revival architecture. Built 1870. Cr cds: D, MC, V.

★ ★OLD WORLD INN. *1301 Jefferson St (94559). 707/257-0112; res: 800/966-6624.* 8 rms, 2 story. Apr–Nov: S, D $110–$145; lower rates rest of yr. Complimentary full bkfst; tea, wine & refreshments in evening. Ck-out 11:30 am, ck-in 3-6 pm. Whirlpool. Built ca 1900; Scandinavian country decor; antiques. Garden. Totally nonsmoking. Cr cds: A, DS, MC, V.

Resort

★ ★ ★SILVERADO. *1600 Atlas Peak Rd (94558). 707/257-0200; res: 800/532-0500; FAX 707/257-5400.* 280 rms, 2 story. Mar–late Nov: S, D $130–$150; kit. suites $175–$600; each addl $15; hol, golf, tennis packages; lower rates rest of yr. Crib free. TV; cable, in-rm movies avail. 9 pools, some heated; whirlpool. Complimentary coffee, tea in suites. Restaurant 6:30 am–5 pm; dining rms 6–11 pm. Bar 11–1 am, Fri & Sat to 2 am; entertainment, dancing Wed–Sun. Ck-out noon, ck-in 5 pm. Coin lndry. Meeting rms. Concierge. Sundries. Golf, tennis

pro shops. Valet parking. Lighted tennis $14, pro. 36-hole golf, greens fee $95 (includes cart), pro, putting greens, driving range. Refrigerators, minibars, fireplaces. Private patios, balconies. Attractive grounds on 1,200 acres. Cr cds: A, C, D, DS, MC, V, JCB.

Restaurants

★CHANTERELLE. *804 First St. 707/253-7300.* Hrs: 11 am–4 pm, 5–9:30 pm; Sun to 9 pm; Sun brunch to 2:30 pm. Closed Jan 1, Dec 25. Res accepted. Continental menu. Bar. Semi-a la carte: lunch $5.50–$12.50, dinner $13.50–$19. Complete meals: lunch $15, dinner $27.50. Sun brunch $13.75. Parking. Cr cds: MC, V.

★ ★LA BOUCANE. *1778 Second St. 707/253-1177.* Hrs: 5:30–10:30 pm. Closed Sun; major hols; also Jan. Res accepted; required wkends. Bar. Semi-a la carte: dinner $15–$28. Specialties: salmon poached in cream & champagne, rack of lamb, roast duckling. Parking. House built 1885. Cr cds: MC, V.

★ ★ ★RUFFINO'S. *645 First St. 707/255-4455.* Hrs: 11:30 am–2 pm, 5–10 pm; Sat from 5 pm; Sun 4–9:30 pm. Closed Wed; Jan 1, Thanksgiving, Dec 24–26. Res accepted. Italian menu. Bar. Semi-a la carte: lunch $5–$8, dinner $8–$21.50. Child's meals. Specializes in steak, veal, pasta, fresh seafood. Family-owned. Cr cds: MC, V.

Needles (H-6)

Founded: 1882 **Pop:** 5,191 **Elev:** 488 ft **Area code:** 619 **Zip:** 92363

Founded as a way station for the Santa Fe Railroad, this town took its name from the needlelike peaks visible 15 miles away in Arizona. The town is shady with palms, cottonwoods, tamarisks and pepper trees. Nearby are many mines and ghost towns. With marinas on the Colorado River and recreational areas under development, the area is attracting anglers, boaters and campers.

What to See and Do

1. **Moabi Regional Park.** 11 mi SE via I-40, on the Colorado River. Swimming beach and lagoon, waterskiing; fishing; boating (boat rentals, launches, marina). Camping (fee; hookups, hot showers); laundry, general store. Peninsula, riverfront camping. Pets on leash only. Water, rest rms only. Fee per vehicle. Contact Park Moabi Rd; 326-3831.

2. **Providence Mountains State Recreation Area.** 40 mi W on I-40, then 17 mi NW on Essex Rd. Spectacular scenery including 300-square-mile area of desert. Two of the Mitchell Caverns are open to the public—El Pakiva and Tecopa; both contain fine examples of stalactites and stalagmites. El Pakiva has rare shields or palettes (round plate-like protrusions from the walls). Cavern tours (mid-Sept–mid-June, daily; fee). Visitors are advised to bring adequate clothing, food and water. There are trails to the surrounding area near the visitor center. Developed and RV camping (fee). Park open all yr. Contact the Ranger Office, Box 1, Essex 92332; 389-2303. Parking per vehicle ¢; Camping ¢¢¢¢; Cavern tours ¢¢

(For further information contact the Chamber of Commerce, Front & G Streets, PO Box 705; 326-2050.)

Annual Event

Rodeo. S to Lilly Hill Dr, Clary Dr exit at New Needles Rodeo Grounds. IRA sanctioned. Late Apr.

Restaurant

✔ ★**HUNGRY BEAR.** *1906 W Needles Hwy. 619/326-2988.* Hrs: 5 am–10:30 pm. Closed Dec 25. Bar 10–2 am. Semi-a la carte: bkfst $3–$7, lunch $3.95–$7, dinner $4.95–$14.95. Child's meals. Specializes in steak, seafood, homemade pastries. Salad bar. Parking. Route 66 motif in dining rm. Cr cds: A, C, D, DS, MC, V.

Nevada City (D-2)

Settled: 1849 **Pop:** 2,855 **Elev:** 2,525 ft **Area code:** 916 **Zip:** 95959

Two years after gold was discovered here, 10,000 miners were working every foot of ground within a radius of three miles. The gravel banks are said to have yielded $8 million in gold dust and nuggets in two years. Of the major gold rush towns, Nevada City remains one of the most picturesque, its residential areas dotted with multigabled frame houses. Principal occupations are lumbering, tourism, government, electronics and craft shops. The gold mines were closed in 1942.

A Ranger District office of the Tahoe National Forest is located here.

What to See and Do

1. **National Hotel.** 211 Broad St. Three stories, with balconies and balustrades reaching over the sidewalks. Victorian furnishings. Conducted a prosperous bar business during 1860s and 1870s. Still operates dining room (see RESTAURANT) and saloon. Phone 265-4551.

2. **Firehouse No. 1** (1861). 214 Main St. On display are Donner Party relics, Joss House altar, Maidu Indian artifacts and furniture, clothing and photos of early settlers. (Daily; closed Jan 1, Thanksgiving, Dec 25; also Wed in winter) Donation. Phone 265-5468 or -5179.

3. **Historic Miners Foundry** (1856). 325 Spring St. Group of stone, brick and frame buildings. The Pelton Wheel was originally tested and manufactured here (1878). Special events, theater and concerts are held here. Phone 265-5383 or 265-5040.

4. **Nevada Theatre** (1865). Broad St. The Foothill Theatre Company performs several productions in this historic theater. (Mar–Dec) For schedule, reservations contact PO Box 1812; phone 265-8587.

5. **Malakoff Diggins State Historic Park.** 15 mi NE off CA 49 at Tyler-Foote Crossing. Gold mining town on 3,000 acres. Museum with hydraulic mining exhibits (Apr–Oct). Swimming; fishing. Hiking, bridle trails. Picnicking. Camping, cabins. Standard fees. Phone 265-2740. Day use per vehicle ¢¢

6. **Walking tours.** Booklets describing historical buildings and sites may be obtained at the Chamber of Commerce.

(For further information contact the Chamber of Commerce, 132 Main St; 265-2692.)

Annual Events

International Teddybear Convention. Phone 265-5804. First wkend Apr.

Nevada City Classic Bicycle Tour. A 40-mile senior race and a 20-mile junior race through the city's hilly streets. Father's Day wkend.

Constitution Day Parade. Phone 265-2692. Sept 13.

Seasonal Events

Fall Color Spectacular. Colorful maples, aspens, fruit trees, poplars, firs, cedars and pines. Phone 265-2692. Mid-Oct–mid-Nov.

Victorian Christmas. Street fair with costumes, crafts, music, entertainment. For details phone 265-2692. 3 Wed nights & 1 Sun preceding Christmas.

(See Auburn, Grass Valley, Marysville, Oroville)

Motel

✔ ★★**NORTHERN QUEEN INN.** *400 Railroad Ave. 916/265-5824; FAX 916/265-3720.* 85 rms, 1–2 story, 8 kit. cottages, 8 kit. chalets. S, D $50–$55; each addl $3; kit. cottages $80–$90; kit. chalets $90–$105. TV; cable. Heated pool; whirlpool. Coffee, tea in rms. Restaurant 7 am–9 pm. Ck-out 11 am. Refrigerators. Picnic tables, grills. Vintage railroad cars and locomotives. On 16 wooded acres; stream. Cr cds: A, C, D, MC, V, JCB.

Inns

★★**FLUMES'S END.** *317 S Pine. 916/265-9665.* 6 rms, 3 story. S, D $80–$140. TV in lobby; cable. Complimentary full bkfst, coffee & afternoon refreshments. Restaurant nearby. Ck-in 2–6 pm. Whirlpool. Balconies. Picnic tables. Victorian inn built 1863. On stream; historic water flume on property. Gold rush ambience. Totally nonsmoking. Cr cds: A, MC, V.

★**RED CASTLE.** *109 Prospect St. 916/265-5135.* 7 rms, 4 story. No rm phones. Dec–Mar: S, D $90–$95; wkly rates; higher rates: wkends & hols (min stay required); lower rates rest of yr. Children over 12 yrs only. Complimentary full bkfst, coffee, tea. Restaurant nearby. Ck-out 11 am, ck-in 4 pm. Balconies. Built in 1860, historic inn is fine example of domestic Gothic; restored and furnished with antiques and period pieces. Terraced gardens; fountain pool. Totally nonsmoking. Cr cds: MC, V.

Restaurants

✔ ★★**CREEKSIDE CAFE.** *101 Broad St, at Sacramento St. 916/265-3445.* Hrs: 11:30 am–2 pm; Sat & Sun 9 am–3 pm. Closed Jan 1, Dec 25. Res accepted. Bar. Semi-a la carte: bkfst $3.95–$12, lunch $3.95–$10, dinner $11–$16. Child's meals (lunch). Specializes in fresh roasted turkey breast, fresh seafood. Own breads. Entertainment Thurs–Sun. Parking. Outdoor dining (lunch). Cr cds: MC, V.

★★**VICTORIAN DINING ROOM.** *211 Broad St. 916/265-4551.* Hrs: 7 am–2:30 pm, 5:30–9:30 pm (June–Sept to 10 pm); Sat to 3 pm; Sun brunch 7 am–3 pm. Res accepted. Continental menu. Bar 10–2 am. Semi-a la carte: bkfst, lunch $3.95–$6.95, dinner $10.95–$17.50. Sun brunch $6.25–$13.95. Child's meals. Specializes in prime rib. Own desserts. Entertainment Fri & Sat; pianist Sat & Sun in summer. Parking. Victorian decor. In historic hotel (1852). Totally nonsmoking. Cr cds: A, MC, V.

Newport Beach (J-4)

Pop: 66,643 **Elev:** 25 ft **Area code:** 714

This seaside community, sometimes referred to as the American Riviera, is famous for elegant waterfront villas, smart shops and restaurants, and beautiful Pacific Coast scenery. With a 6-mile-long beach and a fine harbor, it offers a variety of water activities. Vacation attractions are largely clustered around the Balboa peninsula, a 6-mile finger of land running east and west. Behind it is Newport Harbor, with 12 miles of waterways and eight islands.

What to See and Do

1. **Newport Harbor Art Museum.** 850 San Clemente Dr. Permanent and changing exhibits of modern and contemporary art, with an emphasis on California art since the second World War. Bookshop; Sculpture Garden Cafe (Mon–Fri). Museum (daily exc Mon; closed hols). Phone 759-1122. ¢¢

2. **Sherman Library & Gardens.** 5 mi S via Pacific Coast Hwy, Dahlia Ave exit to 2647 E Coast Hwy in Corona del Mar. Botanical gardens set amidst fountains and sculpture. Historical library has a research center for the study of Pacific Southwest. (Daily; closed Jan 1, Thanksgiving, Dec 25) Phone 673-2261. ¢

(For further information contact the Newport Harbor Area Chamber of Commerce, 1470 Jamboree Rd, 92660; 729-4400.)

Annual Events

Newport SeaFest. Mid-Sept.

Christmas Boat Parade. Newport Beach Harbor. Mid-Dec.

(See Huntington Beach, Irvine, Laguna Beach, Long Beach)

Motel

★★**BEST WESTERN BAY SHORES INN.** 1800 W Balboa Blvd (92663). 714/675-3463; FAX 714/675-4977. 21 rms. Mid-June–early Sept: S $99; D $104; each addl $7; suite $219; under 10 free; lower rates rest of yr. Crib free. TV; in-rm movies. Complimentary continental bkfst. Restaurant nearby. Ck-out noon. Sun deck. Some ocean, bay views. Beach ½ blk. Cr cds: A, C, D, DS, MC, V.

Hotels

★★★★**FOUR SEASONS.** 690 Newport Center Dr (92660). 714/759-0808; res: 800/332-3442, 800/268-6282 (CAN); FAX 714/759-0568. 285 rms, 20 story. S, D $155–$225; each addl $30; suites $300–$1,500; under 18 free; wkend rates; honeymoon, anniversary, golf packages. Valet parking $12.50. TV; cable. Pool; poolside serv. Restaurants 6:30 am–10 pm (also see PAVILION). Afternoon tea 3–5 pm. Rm serv 24 hrs. Bar 11–1 am; entertainment. Ck-out noon. Convention facilities. Concierge. Gift shop. John Wayne Airport transportation. Lighted tennis, pro. Golf privileges. Exercise rm; instructor, weights, bicycles, whirlpool, sauna. Massage. Bathrm phones, refrigerators. In-rm movies in suites. Balconies. Luxury hotel; view of ocean, harbor. Cr cds: A, C, D, ER, MC, V, JCB.

★★★**HOTEL MERIDIEN.** 4500 MacArthur Blvd (92660). 714/476-2001; FAX 714/476-0153. 435 rms, 10 story. S $135–$165; D $145–$175; each addl $15; suites $235–$800; under 16 free. TV; cable. Pool; poolside serv. Restaurant 11:30 am–10:30 pm. Rm serv 24 hrs. Bar 4 pm–2 am; entertainment. Ck-out noon. Meeting rms. Concierge. Gift shop. Free John Wayne Airport transportation. Lighted tennis, pro, pro shop. Golf privileges. Exercise equipt; weights, bicycles, whirlpool and sauna. Lawn games. Bathrm phones, minibars. Some balconies. Ziggurat-like building with sharp, angular design; distinctive European-style decor. *LUXURY LEVEL:* CLUB LEVEL. 44 rms. S $165; D $175. Concierge. Private lounge, honor bar. Complimentary continental bkfst, refreshments.
Cr cds: A, C, D, DS, ER, MC, V.

★★★**MARRIOTT HOTEL & TENNIS CLUB.** 900 Newport Center Dr (92660), at Fashion Island. 714/640-4000; FAX 714/640-5055. 574 rms, 16 story. S $139–$170; D $139–$175; each addl $15; 1–2-bedrm suites $250–$419; under 12 free; wkend, tennis package plans. Crib free. Pet accepted. TV; cable. 2 heated pools; poolside serv. Restaurant 6:30 am–11 pm. Bar 11–2 am. Ck-out noon. Convention

facilities. Coin lndry. Gift shop. Valet parking avail. Free John Wayne Airport transportation. 8 lighted tennis courts, pro, tennis club. Golf privileges. Exercise rm; instructor, weights, bicycles, whirlpool, sauna. Refrigerators avail. Private patios, balconies. Beautiful landscaping. Shopping center opp. *LUXURY LEVEL:* CONCIERGE LEVEL. 46 rms. S $149; D $169. Concierge. Private lounge. Bathrm phones. Complimentary continental bkfst, refreshments.
Cr cds: A, C, D, DS, MC, V, JCB.

★★★**MARRIOTT SUITES.** 500 Bayview Circle (92660), off Jamboree Rd. 714/854-4500; FAX 714/854-3937. 250 suites, 9 story. S, D $149–$169; each addl $10; under 18 free; wkend rates. Crib free; TV; cable. Indoor/outdoor pool; poolside serv. Restaurant 6:30 am–10:30 pm. Bar noon–midnight. Ck-out noon. Meeting rms. Free John Wayne Airport transportation. Exercise equipt; weight machines, bicycles, whirlpool, sauna. Refrigerators. Private patios, balconies. Cr cds: A, C, D, DS, ER, MC, V, JCB.

✔★★**SHERATON NEWPORT BEACH.** 4545 MacArthur Blvd (92660). 714/833-0570; FAX 714/833-3927. 338 rms, 7 & 10 story. S $79–$140; D $79–$150; each addl $15; suites $300–$350; under 18 free. Crib free. TV. Heated pool; whirlpool, poolside serv. Restaurant 6:30 am–10 pm; dining rm 11:30 am–2 pm, 6–10 pm. Rm serv to 1 am. Bar 11–2 am; entertainment Fri–Sat. Ck-out 1 pm. Convention facilities. Gift shop. Free John Wayne Airport transportation. 2 lighted tennis courts. Health club. Balconies. Cr cds: A, C, D, DS, MC, V.

Inns

★★★**DORYMAN'S.** 2102 W Ocean Front (92663), at foot of Newport Pier. 714/675-7300. 10 rms, 3 suites. S, D $135–$175; suites $185–$275. TV; cable. Complimentary continental bkfst. Complimentary coffee in rms. Dining rm 5:30–9:30 pm. Rm serv. Ck-out noon, ck-in 4 pm. Fireplaces. Opulently decorated with French and Amer antiques; sitting rm; sun deck. On ocean with pier opp. Cr cds: A, C, D, MC, V.

★★★**LITTLE INN ON THE BAY.** 617 Lido Park Dr (92663). 714/673-8800; FAX 714/673-1500. 30 rms, 2 story. S, D $98–$140; each addl $15; suites $150–$180. Crib free. TV. Pool. Complimentary bkfst, refreshments. Ck-out noon, ck-in 3 pm. Meeting rm. Refrigerator in suites. Patios, balconies. Complimentary bay cruise, bicycles. Country decor; view of bay. Cr cds: A, C, D, DS, MC, V.

★★★**PORTOFINO BEACH HOTEL.** 2306 W Ocean Front (92663), 2 blks N of Newport Pier. 714/673-7030; FAX 714/723-4370. 18 rms, 2 story, 8 suites. D $100–$150; suites $210–$235; under 16 free; package plans. TV. Complimentary continental bkfst. Dining rm 5:30–11 pm. Rm serv from 6 pm. Ck-out noon, ck-in 3 pm. Some fireplaces. Restored ocean-front hotel (1923); library/sitting rm; many antiques. Cr cds: A, C, D, MC, V.

Resort

★★★**HYATT NEWPORTER.** 1107 Jamboree Rd (92660). 714/729-1234; FAX 714/644-1552. 410 rms, 3 story, four 3-bedrm villas. S, D $119–$174; each addl $15; suites $300–$450; villas for 1–6 (with 3 baths, private pool, fireplace), $650; under 18 free. Crib free. TV; cable. 3 heated pools; poolside serv. Supervised child's activities (Fri & Sat evenings). Dining rm 6 am–10:30 pm. Rm serv to 12:30 am. Bar 11–2 am; entertainment Tues–Sat. Ck-out noon, ck-in 4 pm. Convention facilities. Concierge. Gift shop. Barber, beauty shop. Free John Wayne Airport transportation. Lighted tennis privileges, pro. 18-hole golf privileges, 9-hole golf. Exercise equipt; weights, bicycles, whirlpool. Bicycle rentals. Lawn games. Boating nearby. Wet bar in suites. Private patios, balconies. 26 acres, beautiful landscaping, lush gardens, overlooking bay and harbor. Ocean 1 mi. Cr cds: A, C, D, MC, V.

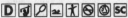

Restaurants

✔ ★★**AMELIA'S ON BALBOA ISLAND.** *(311 Marine Ave, Balboa Island)* Take Jamboree across bridge to island. *714/673-6580.* Hrs: 11:30 am–2:30 pm, 5–10 pm; Sun brunch 10:30 am–2:30 pm. Closed some major hols. Res accepted. Italian menu. Wine, beer. Semi-a la carte: lunch $5–$9, dinner $9–$18. Sun brunch $4–$9. Specialties: crab-stuffed abalone, baby calamari with fresh bay scallops. Strolling guitarist Fri & Sat. Wood-beamed ceilings; antique mirrors. One of the original restaurants on Balboa Island. Cr cds: A, C, D, DS, MC, V, JCB.

D

★★**THE CANNERY.** *3010 Lafayette. 714/675-5777.* Hrs: 11:30–2 am; Sun from 10 am; Sun brunch to 2:30 pm. Closed Thanksgiving, Dec 25. Res accepted. Bar to 2 am. Semi-a la carte: lunch $4.95–$12, dinner $16–$23. Sun brunch $8.95–$12.50. Child's meals. Specializes in steak, abalone, fresh fish of the day. Seafood bar. Entertainment. Valet parking. Outdoor dining. Converted cannery (1934). View of harbor, fishing boats. Brunch, dinner cruises avail. Cr cds: A, C, D, DS, MC, V, JCB.

D

✔ ★★**CANO'S.** *2241 Pacific Coast Hwy. 714/631-1381.* Hrs: 11:30 am–2:30 pm, 5–10 pm; Fri & Sat to 11 pm; Sun 5–10 pm; Sun brunch 10 am–3 pm. Res accepted. Semi-a la carte: lunch $4.95–$11.95, dinner $10.95–$19.95. Sunset dinners (Mon–Fri, 5–6 pm) $8.95. Sun brunch $11.95–$14.95. Specializes in fresh seafood. Entertainment. Valet parking. Overlooks Newport Harbor. Mediterranean decor with Mexican flair. Cr cds: A, C, D, MC, V.

★**CHARLEY BROWN'S.** *151 E Pacific Coast Hwy. 714/675-5790.* Hrs: 11:30 am–10 pm; Fri & Sat to 11 pm; Sun 5–10 pm; Sun brunch from 10 am. Res accepted. Bar to midnight. Semi-a la carte: lunch $5.99–$9.99, dinner $6.99–$26.99. Sun brunch $16.95. Specializes in steak, fresh seafood. Dining on board vintage 1890s riverboat in Newport Harbor. Cr cds: A, D, DS, MC, V, JCB.

★**MARRAKESH.** *1100 W Pacific Coast Hwy. 714/645-8384.* Hrs: 5–11 pm. Closed Dec 25. Res accepted. Moroccan menu. Bar. Complete meals: dinner $18–$22.50. Specializes in multi-course dinners, chicken, fish, rabbit. Belly dancing Thurs–Sun. Valet parking. Tent-like interior. Seating on low couches; Moroccan-style dining. Menu recited. Cr cds: A, C, D, DS, MC, V.

★★**PAVILION.** *(See Four Seasons Hotel) 714/759-0808.* Hrs: 6:30–10:30 am, 11:30 am–2 pm, 6–11 pm; Sun brunch 10 am–2 pm. Res accepted. California/Italian cuisine. Bar 11 am–midnight. A la carte entrees: bkfst $8.50–$15, lunch $9–$15, dinner $16–$25. Sun brunch $39. Specializes in fish, lamb, grilled veal chop. Own pastries. Valet parking. Outdoor dining. Veranda dining. Overlooks garden. Jacket. Cr cds: A, C, D, DS, ER, MC, V, JCB.

D

★★★**THE RITZ.** *880 Newport Center Dr, at Fashion Island. 714/720-1800.* Hrs: 11:30 am–3 pm, 6–10 pm; Fri to 11 pm; Sat 5:30–11 pm. Closed Sun. Res accepted. Continental menu. Bar. Wine cellar. A la carte entrees: lunch $6.95–$15, dinner $18–$33. Specialties: bouillabaisse, roast duck, rack of lamb. Own baking. Pianist. Valet parking. Turn-of-the-century decor. Cr cds: A, D, MC, V.

D

✔ ★★**ROYAL KHYBER.** *1000 Bristol St N. 714/752-5200.* Hrs: 11:30 am–2:30 pm, 5:30–10:30 pm; Sun brunch to 3 pm. Res accepted. Indian menu. Bar. Buffet: lunch $7.95. A la carte entrees: lunch $5.75–$8.75. Complete meals: dinner $17–$20. Sun brunch $12.95. Specialties: moghlai, tandoori. Parking. Exotic east Indian decor, fountains. Cr cds: A, D, MC, V.

★★**SAPORI.** *1080 Bayside Dr. 714/644-4220.* Hrs: 11:30 am–10 pm; Fri & Sat 5–11 pm. Closed Jan 1, Easter, Dec 25. Res accepted. Italian menu. Bar. A la carte entrees: lunch $4.50–$14.50, dinner $8.50–$20.50. Specializes in seafood, gourmet pizza, pasta. Parking. Outdoor dining. Cr cds: A, D, DS, MC, V.

D

★**TALE OF THE WHALE.** *400 Main St, at Balboa Peninsula. 714/673-4633.* Hrs: 7 am–11 pm; Sat & Sun brunch to 4 pm. Closed Dec 25. Bar 10–2 am. Semi-a la carte: bkfst, lunch $3.95–$8.95, dinner $10.95–$24.95. Sat & Sun brunch $3.95–$9.50. Specializes in seafood. Own muffins. Entertainment Thurs–Sat. In historic Balboa Pavilion (1905) overlooking bay. Cr cds: A, C, D, DS, MC, V.

★★**VILLA NOVA.** *3131 W Pacific Coast Hwy. 714/642-7880.* Hrs: 5 pm–2 am; Sun from 4 pm. Res accepted. Italian menu. Piano bar. A la carte entrees: dinner $9.50–$25. Child's meals. Specializes in pasta, veal, seafood, chicken. Valet parking. Hand-painted murals. Private boat dockage. Overlooks Newport Bay. Family-owned. Cr cds: A, C, D, DS, MC, V, JCB.

North Hollywood (L.A.) *

Elev: 385 ft **Area code:** 818
*11 mi NW of Downtown Los Angeles (H-4) on Hollywood Frwy (US 101, CA 170).

This community is a neighborhood of Los Angeles, but is regarded by many as a separate entity.

(For general information and attractions see Los Angeles and Hollywood.)

Motor Hotels

★★**BEST WESTERN MIKADO.** *12600 Riverside Dr (91607),* US 101 Laurel Canyon Blvd exit, N to Riverside Dr, then W. *818/763-9141; FAX 818/752-1045.* 58 rms, 2 story, 3 kits. S $70–$75; D $85–$90; each addl $10; suites, kit. units $100–$150; under 12 free. Crib $10. TV. Pool; whirlpool. Complimentary full bkfst. Restaurants 11:30 am–2:30 pm, 5:30–9:30 pm; Fri, Sat to 10 pm; Sun, Mon to 9 pm. Rm serv. Bar. Ck-out 1 pm. Bathrm phones. Cr cds: A, C, D, DS, ER, MC, V, JCB.

★★**BEVERLY GARLAND HOTEL.** *4222 Vineland Ave (91602),* US 101 Vineland Ave exit, ½ mi S. *818/980-8000; res: 800/238-3759; FAX 818/766-5230.* 258 rms, 6–7 story. S $79–$99; D $89–$109; each addl $10; suites $189–$350; under 18 free; wkend rates. Crib free. TV; cable. Heated pool; wading pool, poolside serv. Playground. Restaurant 6 am–midnight. Rm serv. Bar 11–1:30 am. Ck-out noon. Convention facilities. Bellhops. Valet serv. Gift shop. Free Burbank airport transportation. Lighted tennis. Private patios, balconies. Cr cds: A, C, D, DS, ER, MC, V, JCB.

Restaurant

★★**FUNG LUM.** *222 Universal Terrace Pkwy, opp Universal Studios. 818/763-7888.* Hrs: 11:30 am–2:30 pm, 5–10 pm; Fri, Sat to 11 pm; Sun 11 am–10 pm; Sun brunch to 3 pm. Res accepted. Chinese menu. Bar. Semi-a la carte: lunch $8–$15, dinner $10–$25. Sun brunch $11.95. Specialties: lemon chicken, minced squab. Valet parking. Chinese palace-style building. Cr cds: A, C, D, MC, V, JCB.

Oakdale (E-2)

Pop: 11,961 **Elev:** 155 ft **Area code:** 209 **Zip:** 95361

Oakdale's birth is linked to gold and the railroad. An important town along the freight lines to the Mother Lode towns, it was founded by the Stockton & Visalia Railroad Co in 1871. Beef and dairy cattle and a variety of produce support the area now.

What to See and Do

1. **Woodward Reservoir.** 5 mi N at 14528 26 Mile Rd. Swimming, waterskiing; fishing, duck hunting; boating (moorings, marina). Picnicking, concession (Apr–mid-Sept). Camping, showers. (Daily) Phone 847-3304. Per vehicle (day use) ¢¢; Camping ¢¢¢–¢¢¢¢

2. **Industrial tour. Hershey Chocolate USA.** 120 S Sierra Ave, SE corner of jct CA 108 & 120. Visitors' Reception Center and 30-minute factory tours. (Mon–Fri; closed major hols) No cameras. Phone 848-5100. **Free.**

(For further information contact the Chamber of Commerce, 590 N Yosemite Ave; 847-2244.)

Annual Events

PRCA Rodeo. Early Apr.

Chocolate Festival. Mid-May.

California Daily Team Roping Championships. Oakdale Saddle Club Rodeo grounds, CA 120. 3rd wkend Sept.

(See Modesto)

Motel

★★**RAMADA INN.** *825 East F St. 209/847-8181; FAX 209/847-9546.* 70 rms, 2 story. May–Sept: S $71–$91; D $77–$97; each addl $6; suites $126–$197; under 18 free; lower rates rest of yr. TV; cable. Heated pool; whirlpool. Complimentary coffee in rms. Restaurant 5:30 am–11 pm. Bar 11 am–midnight. Ck-out noon. Meeting rms. Cr cds: A, C, D, DS, MC, V, JCB.

Oakland (E-1)

Founded: 1850 **Pop:** 372,242 **Elev:** 42 ft **Area code:** 510

Oakland lies just across the bay from San Francisco. The port of Oakland has excellent facilities and caters to heavy Pacific trade. More than 1,500 factories help make Alameda County a leading manufacturing center. The Bay Area Rapid Transit system (BART) links suburban areas and Oakland with San Francisco. Once part of the Rancho San Antonio, 48,000-acre domain of former Spanish cavalry sergeant Luis Maria Peralta, it was acquired as a townsite by Horace W. Carpentier, who named it for the evergreen oaks that marked the landscape.

What to See and Do

1. **Lake Merritt.** In heart of downtown Oakland. Largest natural body of saltwater in the world completely within any city (155 acres), surrounded by drives and handsome buildings. Boat rentals, sightseeing launch (wkends, some hols). Sailing lessons, day camps. Special events include sailing regattas. Phone 444-3807. Per car (wkends) ¢ Adjoining lake is

Lakeside Park. Car entrance at Belleview & Grand Aves. Approx 120 acres. Picnic areas, free children's play area; lawn bowling, putting greens; trail and show gardens, duck-feeding area; bandstand concerts (summer, Sun & hols). Parking free (exc Feb–Oct, wkends & hols). Phone 273-3092. Also here are

Children's Fairyland. Belleview & Grand Aves. Everything child-size, with tiny buildings depicting fairyland tales. Many contain live animals and birds. Carousel, Ferris wheel, train and trolley rides, children's bumper boats and puppet theater (fee for some activities). (Summer, daily; spring & fall, Wed–Sun; winter, Sat & Sun only; closed Jan 1, Thanksgiving, Dec 25) Phone 452-2259. ¢¢

Trial and Show Gardens. 666 Bellevue Ave. Demonstration Gardens; includes cactus, fuchsia, dahlia, chrysanthemum, Polynesian, palm, herb and Japanese gardens. (Daily; closed Jan 1, Thanksgiving, Dec 25) Phone 273-3208. **Free.**

Rotary Nature Center. North America's oldest wildlife refuge (1870); nature and conservation exhibits; native birds; films, illustrated lectures or walks (wkends); animal feeding area. (Daily) **Free.**

2. **Oakland Museum.** 1000 Oak St, near Lake Merritt. Galleries, gardens cover four city blocks; exhibits on natural science, history and art interpret land and people of California. Great Hall exhibits (fee). (Wed–Sun; closed major hols) Phone 834-2413 (recording) or 238-3401. For tour information phone 238-3514. **Free.**

3. **The Oakland Museum Sculpture Court at City Center.** 1111 Broadway, at 12th St. One-person exhibitions by contemporary California sculptors are mounted quarterly. (Daily; closed hols) **Free.**

4. **Kaiser Center.** 300 Lakeside Dr. This complex was founded by industrialist Henry J. Kaiser and remains the home of Kaiser Aluminum & Chemical Corporation. The Kaiser Building is of aluminum and glass construction. Changing art exhibits on mezzanine; remarkable 3½-acre rooftop garden with trees, shrubs, flowers, pool and fountains. (Daily exc Sun; closed major hols) Cafeterias, restaurants. Phone 271-6146. **Free.**

5. **Camron-Stanford House** (1876). 1418 Lakeside Drive, on the shores of Lake Merritt. Once the home of the Camron family and later the Stanford family, this building served as the Oakland Public Museum from 1910 until 1967. Today the house operates as a resource center and museum with authentic period furnishings, sculpture and paintings. Slide program; library. Guided tours. (Wed & Sun) Free the 1st Sun of each month. Sr citizen rate. Phone 836-1976. ¢

6. **Jack London Square.** Formed by Clay, Franklin, Embarcadero and the Oakland Estuary. Colorful waterfront area where the author worked. **Heinold's First and Last Chance saloon,** 56 Jack London Square, at the foot of Webster St, is where London spent much of his time and wrote his most famous novels. Several restaurants and the reconstructed cabin in which the author weathered the Klondike winter of 1898 reflect characters and situations from his life and books. Adj is **Jack London Village,** foot of Alice St. Shops, restaurants, marina area. (Daily) Phone 272-1100.

7. **Paramount Theatre.** 2025 Broadway. Impressive, restored 1931 art deco movie palace, home of Oakland Ballet. Hosts organ pops series and a variety of musical performances. 90-minute tours start from Box Office (1st & 3rd Sat of each month; no tours hols). Phone 465-6400 (box office, event information, tours).

8. **Skyline Blvd.** On top of Berkeley-Oakland Hills; superb views of entire East Bay area.

9. **Joaquin Miller Park.** Joaquin Miller Rd. Site of the "Hights," former house of Joaquin Miller, "Poet of the Sierras." Four monuments erected by Miller to Moses, General Frémont, Robert & Elizabeth Browning and a funeral pyre for himself. Fountain and statuary from 1939 World's Fair. Park is also site of Woodminster Amphitheater, scene of Woodminster Summer Musicals (see SEASONAL EVENTS). Hiking and picnic areas. Phone 238-3187. (Daily) **Free.**

10. **Oakland Zoo in Knowland Park.** 98th Ave/Golf Links Rd exit off I-580. Situated on 525 acres, the zoo houses 330 native and exotic animals, a children's petting zoo and "Simba Pori," a 1½-acre habitat with a pride of 6 lions, and Siamang Island. Also here are

children's rides and picnic areas. Free parking 1st Mon of each month exc hols. Sr citizen rate. (Daily) Phone 632-9523. General admission ¢¢

11. Dunsmuir House and Gardens (1899). 2960 Peralta Oaks Ct. A 37-room Colonial-revival mansion; 40 acres of trees, lawns, shrubs and gardens; special events (Apr–Dec). Guided tours (Apr–Sept, Wed & Sun). Sr citizen rate. Phone 562-0328. ¢¢

12. Northern California Center for Afro-American History and Life. 5606 San Pablo Ave. Artifacts, photographs, exhibit and archive on black history in the US, with emphasis on California. (Tues–Fri; closed major hols) Phone 658-3158. **Free.**

13. East Bay Regional Park District. Headquarters at 2950 Peralta Oaks Court. Organization maintains more than 75,000 acres in 50 parks and recreation areas in Alameda and Contra Costa counties. Facilities include swimming, fishing, archery, boating, riding, picnic grounds, campgrounds and other pastimes. Most parks are open daily. Phone 526-PARK. The park system includes

Anthony Chabot Regional Park & Lake Chabot. Park: E & S via 35th Ave & Redwood Rd; Lake Chabot: S on I-580 to Fairmont Ave, then E to Lake Chabot Rd and left to parking area. Park offers 4,927 acres for hiking and riding, horse rentals; marksmanship range for rifle, pistol and trapshooting; 18-hole golf course. Camping: motor home and tent camping (fee); for reservations phone 652-CAMP. Park entrances along Skyline Blvd, between Redwood & Golf Links Rd and along Redwood Rd E of Skyline Blvd; stables and hiking along on Skyline Blvd. At Lake Chabot there are fishing and boating facilities (rentals); bicycle trails and picnic areas. Wheelchair accessible trail and pier. Per vehicle ¢¢ Adj is

Redwood Regional Park. E off Skyline Blvd on Redwood Rd. Redwood groves, evergreens, chaparral and grassland on 1,830 acres. Hiking; nature study. Picnicking, playfields, children's playground. Creek with native rainbow trout. Per vehicle ¢¢

Martin Luther King, Jr Regional Shoreline. S on I-880 to Hegenberger exit, then NW on Doolittle Dr. On 1,219 acres, near Oakland Intl Airport. Sunning beach; fishing; boating (two-lane launching ramp). Hiking trails, bird watching. Picnicking, children's playfields, beach cafe. Nature study. **Free.**

14. Gray Line bus tours. Contact 350 8th St, San Francisco 94103; 415/558-7373.

(For information on upcoming events phone the entertainment hotline, 835-ARTS. For further information contact the Convention and Visitors Bureau, 1000 Broadway, Suite 200, 94607, phone 839-9000 or 800/262-5526.)

Seasonal Events

Woodminster Summer Amphitheater. Joaquin Miller Park (see #9). For information phone 531-9597. June–Sept.

Professional sports. Athletics (baseball), Golden State Warriors (basketball), Oakland-Alameda County Coliseum Complex. Phone 639-7700.

(See Berkeley, Hayward, San Francisco, San Francisco Airport Area, San Mateo, Sausalito)

Motels

★★**BEST WESTERN THUNDERBIRD INN.** *233 Broadway (94607), at 3rd St.* 510/452-4565; FAX 510/452-4634. 103 rms, 2–3 story, no ground floor rms. S $70; D $80; each addl $10; under 12 free. Crib free. TV. Heated pool; saunas. Complimentary continental bkfst, coffee. Restaurant adj open 24 hrs. Ck-out noon. Meeting rm. Bellhops. Garage. Some balconies. Cr cds: A, C, D, DS, ER, MC, V, JCB.

☐ D ☐ ⊗ Ⓢ SC

✔ ★★**HAMPTON INN OAKLAND AIRPORT.** *8465 Enterprise Way (94621), near Intl Airport.* 510/632-8900; FAX 510/632-4713. 149 rms, 3 story. S $64–$73; D $69–$75; under 18 free. Crib free. Pet accepted, some restrictions. TV; cable. Heated pool; whirlpool. Complimentary continental bkfst, coffee. Restaurant nearby. Meeting rm. Valet serv. Sundries. Free airport, BART station transportation. Refrigerators avail. Cr cds: A, D, DS, MC, V.

☐ D ☐ ☐ ✕ ⊗ Ⓢ SC

★★**SAN LEANDRO MARINA INN.** *(68 San Leandro Marina, San Leandro 94577)* 1¼ mi SW of I-880 Marina exit. 510/895-1311; res: 800/786-7783; FAX 510/483-4078. 131 units, 3 story. S $82–$98; D $83–$99; suites $99–$102; under 18 free. TV; cable. Heated pool; whirlpool. Complimentary continental bkfst. Restaurant nearby. Ck-out noon. Meeting rms. Sundries. Free airport transportation. Some refrigerators, wet bars. Private patios, balconies. Cr cds: A, C, D, MC, V.

☐ D ☐ ⊗ Ⓢ SC

Motor Hotels

★★★**HILTON OAKLAND AIRPORT.** *1 Hegenberger Rd (94621), 5 mi SW, I-880 Hegenberger-Coliseum exit, at Intl Airport.* 510/635-5000; FAX 510/635-0244. 362 rms, 3 story. S $115–$135; D $135–$155; each addl $20; suites $275–$568; wknd rates. Crib free. TV; cable. Heated pool; poolside serv. Restaurants 6 am–10 pm. Rm serv. Bar 10:30–2 am; entertainment, dancing Fri, Sat. Ck-out noon. Meeting rms. Bellhops. Gift shop. Free airport transportation. Exercise equipt; weights, bicycles. Some bathrm phones. Refrigerators avail. Private patios. Cr cds: A, C, D, DS, ER, MC, V, JCB.

☐ D ☐ ☐ ✕ ⊗ Ⓢ SC

★★**HOLIDAY INN-OAKLAND AIRPORT.** *500 Hegenberger Rd (94621).* 510/562-5311; FAX 510/636-1539. 285 rms, 2–6 story. S $95; D $105; each addl $10; suites $159–$229; under 12 free. Crib free. Pet accepted. TV; cable. Pool. Restaurant 6 am–10 pm. Bar 2 pm–2 am. Ck-out noon. Coin lndry. Meeting rms. Bellhops. Sundries. Gift shop. Airport, Coliseum transportation. Exercise equipt; weight machine, bicycles. Cr cds: A, C, D, DS, MC, V, JCB.

☐ D ☐ ☐ ☐ ☐ ⊗ Ⓢ SC

Hotels

★★★**CLAREMONT RESORT & TENNIS CLUB.** *Domingo & Ashby Aves (94623).* 510/843-3000; res: 800/323-7500; FAX 510/843-6239. 239 rms, some rms with shower only, 6 story. S $155–$195; D $175–$215; suites $295–$720; under 14 free; wknd packages. Crib free. TV; cable. 2 heated pools; poolside cafe, lifeguard. Restaurants 7 am–10 pm; totally nonsmoking. Rm serv 6:30 am–midnight. Bar; combo, dancing Fri, Sat. Ck-out noon. Convention facilities. Gift shop. Beauty shop. Valet parking. Oakland airport transportation avail. Lighted tennis, pro. Golf privileges. Exercise rm; instructor, weight machine, bicycles, whirlpool, sauna, steam rm. Health spa facilities. Some refrigerators, wet bars. Extensive art collection. Scenic location; spacious grounds. Cr cds: A, C, D, DS, MC, V, JCB.

☐ D ☐ ☐ ☐ ☐ ☐ ☐ ⊗ Ⓢ SC

★★★**LAKE MERRITT.** *1800 Madison (94612), at Lakeside Dr.* 510/832-2300; res: 800/933-4683; FAX 510/832-7150. 50 units, 41 suites. S $89–$119; D $89–$159; each addl $10; suites, kit. suites $119–159; under 12 free; wknd rates. Valet parking $9. Pet accepted. TV; cable. Complimentary continental bkfst. Complimentary coffee in rms. Restaurant 7 am–9:30 pm. Bar. Ck-out 11 am. Meeting rms. Concierge. Health club privileges. Refrigerators, minibars. Restored Mediterranean/art deco landmark (1927) offers outstanding views of Lake Merritt. In quiet residential neighborhood, 3 blks from financial district. Cr cds: A, D, DS, MC, V.

☐ ☐ ⊗ Ⓢ SC

★★**PARC OAKLAND HOTEL.** *1001 Broadway (94607).* 510/451-4000; res: 800/338-1338; FAX 510/835-3466. 488 rms, 21 story. S $105–$130; D $125–$150; each addl $20; suites from $325; under 18 free; wknd plans. Crib free. Pet accepted, some restrictions; $25. TV; cable. Heated pool; whirlpool. Restaurants 6:30 am–10:30 pm. Bar 11–1 am; entertainment. Convention facilities. Concierge. Gift shop. Airport transportation. Refrigerators. Cr cds: A, C, D, DS, ER, MC, V, JCB.

✔ ★ ★ **WASHINGTON INN.** *495 10th St (94607), opp Oakland Convention Center.* 510/452-1776; res: 800/477-1775; 800/464-1776 (CA). 47 units, 5 story, 8 suites. S, D $89–$99; suites $129–$218. Covered parking $9.50. TV; cable. Complimentary full bkfst. Restaurant 7 am–2 pm. Bar 4:30–11 pm, closed Sat & Sun. Ck-out noon. Meeting rm. Refrigerator in suites. Wet bars. Renovated 1913 hotel with turn-of-the-century bar. Cr cds: A, D, MC, V.

★ ★ ★ **WATERFRONT PLAZA.** *10 Washington St (94607), at Jack London's Waterfront.* 510/836-3800; res: 800/729-3638; FAX 510/832-5695. 144 rms, 5 story, 27 suites. S $135–$160; D $150–$175; suites $200–$325; under 16 free; honeymoon packages. Crib free. Valet parking, in/out $8. TV; in-rm movies. Heated pool. Restaurant (see JACK'S). Rm serv to 10 pm. Bar 10–1 am. Ck-out noon. Meeting rms. Concierge. Exercise equipt; weights, bicycles, whirlpool, sauna. Bathrm phones, minibars. Some rms with fireplace. Balconies. Many rms with view of San Francisco skyline. 2 boat slips avail. Cr cds: A, C, D, DS, ER, MC, V, JCB.

Restaurants

★ ★ ★ **CHEF PAUL'S.** *4179 Piedmont Ave.* 510/547-2175. Hrs: 5 pm–midnight. Closed Mon. Res accepted. Eclectic French-Swiss menu. Extensive wine list. Semi-a la carte: dinner $29. Complete meal: dinner $35. Specializes in seafood, tasting menu. Outdoor dining. Elegant atmosphere. Chef-owned. Cr cds: A, MC, V.

✔ ★ **EL TORITO.** *67 Jack London Square.* 510/835-9260. Hrs: 11 am–10 pm; Fri & Sat to midnight; Sun 10 am–10 pm; Sun brunch to 2 pm. Closed Thanksgiving, Dec 25. Res accepted. Mexican menu. Bar 11–2 am, Sun 10 am–midnight. Semi-a la carte: lunch $5–$8, dinner $6–$12. Sun brunch $9.95. Child's meals. Specializes in tacos, fajitas, chimichangas. Outdoor dining. Spanish decor. Cr cds: A, C, D, DS, MC, V.

★ ★ **GULF COAST GRILL.** *736 Washington St.* 510/836-3663. Hrs: 11 am–2:30 pm, 5–9 pm; Fri to 11 pm; Sat 5–11 pm; Sun 11 am–9 pm. Closed Mon. Res accepted. Creole, Cajun menu. Bar. Semi-a la carte: lunch $7–$11, dinner $11–$18. Specialties: jambalaya, gumbo, smoked chicken & catfish. Historic building in Old Oakland. Totally nonsmoking. Cr cds: A, DS, MC, V.

★ ★ **JACK'S.** *(See Waterfront Plaza Hotel)* 510/444-7171. Hrs: 6:30 am–10 pm; early-bird dinner 5–6:30 pm. Res accepted. Continental menu. Bar 10–2 am. A la carte entrees: bkfst $4–$12, lunch $8–$16, dinner $15–$20. Specialties: scampi a la Jack, steak, pasta, seafood. Entertainment Wed & Fri–Sun. Valet parking. On the waterfront; 2 boat slips avail for temporary dockage. Cr cds: A, C, D, DS, ER, MC, V, JCB.

✔ ★ ★ **L.J. QUINN'S LIGHTHOUSE.** *51 Embarcadero Cove.* 510/536-2050. Hrs: 11:30 am–2:30 pm, 5:30–9 pm; Fri to 10 pm; Sat 5:30–10 pm; Sun 11:30 am–3 pm, 4:30–9 pm; early-bird dinner 5:30–7 pm. Closed Jan 1. Res accepted. No A/C. Bar. Semi-a la carte: lunch $5.95–$13.95, dinner $5.95–$16.50. Sun brunch $5.95–$11. Child's meals. Specializes in prawn dishes, pasta, steak. Parking. Outdoor dining. In historic Oakland Harbor Lighthouse (1890); nautical decor. Cr cds: D, DS, MC, V.

✔ ★ **ÓSUMO.** *532 Grand Ave.* 510/834-7866. Hrs: 11:30 am–2 pm, 5–9 pm; Fri, Sat 5–10 pm; Sun 5–9 pm; early-bird dinner Mon–Thurs 5–6 pm. Closed some major hols. Res accepted. No A/C. Japanese menu. Wine, beer. Semi-a la carte: lunch $5.25–$6.50, dinner $8.50–$13.95. Child's meals. Specialties: sashimi, tempura, honey lime chicken. Japanese decor. Totally nonsmoking. Cr cds: A, MC, V.

★ **OVERLAND HOUSE GRILL.** *101 Broadway, at Jack London Square.* 510/268-9222. Hrs: 11 am–10 pm; Fri, Sat to 11 pm; Sun brunch 10 am–3 pm. Closed some major hols. Res accepted. Bar to midnight. Semi-a la carte: lunch $6.95–$17.75, dinner $7.50–$17.75. Sun brunch $6.25–$15. Specializes in fresh pasta, seafood. Parking. Antiques. Family-owned. Cr cds: A, D, MC, V.

★ ★ **PESCATORE.** *57 Jack London Square.* 510/465-2188. Hrs: 11:30 am–10:30 pm; Sat, Sun from 11 am; Sun brunch to 3 pm. Closed Mon; Jan 1, Thanksgiving, Dec 25. Res accepted. Italian menu. Bar. Semi-a la carte: lunch $10.25–$14, dinner $10.25–$22. Sun brunch $9.50–$17. Specializes in pasta, seafood. Outdoor dining. Nautical decor. On waterfront. Cr cds: A, C, D, DS, MC, V.

★ ★ **SCOTT'S SEAFOOD GRILL & BAR.** *2 Broadway, at Jack London Square.* 510/444-3456. Hrs: 11 am–10 pm; Fri, Sat to 11 pm; Sun to 9 pm; Sun brunch to 3 pm. Closed Dec 25. Res accepted. Bar. Semi-a la carte: lunch $10.95–$22.50, dinner $12.50–$22.50. Sun brunch $10.95–$18.95. Specialties: grilled petrale sole, Norwegian salmon. Pianist. Jazz trio Sun brunch. Valet parking. Patio dining. On estuary; view of harbor, San Francisco. Cr cds: A, C, D, DS, MC, V.

★ **SILVER DRAGON.** *835 Webster St.* 510/893-3748. Hrs: 11:30 am–9 pm. Closed Thanksgiving, Dec 25. Cantonese menu. Bar. Semi-a la carte: lunch, dinner $10–$18. Specialties: Peking duck, stuffed crab claws, crispy-skin chicken. Cr cds: A, MC, V.

★ ★ ★ **TRADER VIC'S.** *(9 Anchor Dr, Emeryville) 3 mi NW, ½ mi W of I-80 Powell St, Emeryville exits.* 510/653-3400. Hrs: 11:30 am–2:30 pm, 5–9:30 pm; Fri to 11 pm; Sat 5–11 pm; Sun 4:30–9 pm. Closed some major hols. Res accepted. Polynesian menu. Bar. A la carte entrees: lunch $7–$13, dinner $14–$25. Specialties: peach blossom duck, Indonesian rack of lamb. Valet parking. Chinese barbecue oven. Polynesian decor. Bay view. Family-owned. Cr cds: A, C, D, MC, V.

Oceanside (J-4)

Pop: 128,398 **Elev:** 47 ft **Area code:** 619

Camp Pendleton, a US Marine base, borders this city on the north. I-5 goes through the camp property for about 18 miles.

What to See and Do

1. **Marina.** 1540 Harbor Dr N. Accommodates 915 pleasure boats; angler's weigh station; sportfishing boats operate daily; limited RV beach camping; cruises to Catalina; restaurants.

2. **Mission San Luis Rey de Francia** (1798). 4½ mi E on CA 76. Founded by Father Lasuén, it was named for Louis IX, crusader and ruler of France from 1226 to 1270. It was 18th of the chain. "King of Missions," largest of the 21 early California missions, it has a large collection of Spanish vestments, cloister gardens, Indian cemetery, first pepper tree (1830) and other historic artifacts. Picnicking. Self-guided tours. Museum (daily; closed Jan 1, Thanksgiving, Dec 25). Phone 757-3651. ¢¢

3. **Antique Gas & Steam Engine Museum.** 7 mi E via Oceanside Blvd, at 2040 N Santa Fe Ave in Vista. Agricultural museum on 40 acres of rolling farmland, featuring early farming equipment, steam and

gas engines. Special shows 3rd & 4th wkends in June & Oct (fee). (Daily; closed Dec 25) Phone 941-1791. **Free.**

(For further information contact the Chamber of Commerce, Tourism Promotion, 928 N Hill St, 92054; 721-1101.)

(See Carlsbad, Escondido, San Clemente)

Motels

★ ★ ★**BEST WESTERN OCEANSIDE INN.** *1680 Oceanside Blvd (92054). 619/722-1821; FAX 619/967-8969.* 80 rms, 2 story. S $59–$90; D $65–$85; each addl $6; suites $80–$110. Crib free. TV; cable. Heated pool; whirlpool, saunas. Complimentary continental bkfst. Ck-out noon. Meeting rms. Valet serv. Sundries. Some bathrm phones. Refrigerator in suites. Private patios, balconies. Cr cds: A, C, D, DS, ER, MC, V, JCB.

★ ★**EL CAMINO INN.** *3170 Vista Way (92056). 619/757-2200; res: 800/458-6064.* 43 rms, 2 story. No A/C. S, D $49.95–$55.95; each addl $5; wkly rates; golf package plans. Crib $5. TV; cable. Heated pool. Playground. Complimentary continental bkfst. Restaurant 7:30 am–3 pm, Fri & Sat 5:30–8:30 pm; closed Mon. Bar 10 am–6 pm; wkends to 10 pm. Ck-out noon. Tennis $3. 18-hole golf, greens fee $32–$37, pro. Exercise equipt; weights, bicycles, whirlpool. Private patios, balconies. Cr cds: A, C, D, MC, V.

✔ ★**SANDMAN.** *1501 Carmelo Dr (92054). 619/722-7661.* 82 rms, 2 story. June–Sept: S $39–$50; D $45–$55; each addl $4–$5; lower rates rest of yr. Crib free. Pet accepted, some restrictions. TV; cable. Heated pool. Complimentary coffee in rms. Restaurant opp open 24 hrs. Ck-out noon. Some rms overlook marina. Cr cds: A, C, D, MC, V, JCB.

Ojai (H-3)

Pop: 7,613 **Elev:** 746 ft **Area code:** 805 **Zip:** 93023

The Ojai Valley was first farmed by citrus and cattle ranchers after the Civil War. In the 1870s, publicity in Eastern newspapers initiated its popularity as a tourist haven and winter resort. Attracted by its quiet, rural beauty and proximity to urban centers, many artists, writers and other creative people make their home in the Ojai Valley.

A Ranger District office of the Los Padres National Forest (see KING CITY, SANTA BARBARA) is located here.

What to See and Do

1. **Ojai Valley Historical Society and Museum.** 109 South Montgomery St. Displays of animals, birds, local history, artifacts of the Chumash Indians; changing exhibits; research library. (Wed–Mon afternoons; closed Jan 1, July 4, Thanksgiving, Dec 25) Phone 646-2290. **Free.**

2. **Lake Casitas Recreation Area.** 5 mi W on CA 150. Fishing; boating (rentals, trailer rentals). Picnicking, concession. Camping (fee; for reservations phone 649-1122; hookups); trailer storage (fee). Pets on leash only (fee); no firearms. Nearby are beaches, golf courses and tennis courts. Contact 11311 Santa Ana Rd, Ventura 93001; 649-2233.

(For further information contact the Ojai Valley Chamber of Commerce, PO Box 1134, 93024; 646-8126.)

Annual Events

Tennis Tournament. Libbey Park. Oldest tennis tournament in the same location in the US (since 1899). Late Apr.

Ojai Festivals. Ojai Libbey Park Bowl. Outdoor concerts. Phone 646-2094. Wkend after Memorial Day.

Ojai Shakespeare Festival. Ojai Bowl in Libbey Park. Outdoor evening and matinee performances of two Shakespeare plays, with pre-show Elizabethan entertainment. Phone 646-9455. Aug.

Ojai Studio Artists Tour. Recognized artists open their studios to the public. Phone 646-8126. Oct.

(See Oxnard, Santa Barbara, Ventura)

Motel

★ ★**BEST WESTERN CASA OJAI.** *1302 E Ojai Ave. 805/646-8175; FAX 805/640-8247.* 45 rms, 2 story. Mid-May–mid-Sept: S $75–$115; D $80–$115; each addl $5; under 12 free; lower rates rest of yr. TV; cable. Heated pool; whirlpool. Complimentary continental bkfst. Coffee in rms. Restaurant nearby. Ck-out noon. Some refrigerators. Cr cds: A, D, DS, MC, V.

Resort

★ ★ ★**OJAI VALLEY INN & COUNTRY CLUB.** *Country Club Rd. 805/646-5511; res: 800/422-OJAI; FAX 805/646-7969.* 212 units, 3 story. EP: S, D $195–$260; each addl $25; suites, cottages $335–$850; family rates. Pet accepted; $25 per stay. TV; cable. 2 heated pools; poolside serv. Playground. Supervised child's activities (summer & hols). Coffee & tea in rms. Restaurant (public by res): 6:30–10:30 am, 11:30 am–2:30 pm, 6:30–10 pm. Box lunches, snack bar, picnics. Rm serv 24 hrs. Bar 11:30 am–midnight. Ck-out noon, ck-in 4 pm. Meeting rms. Concierge. Sports dir. Lighted tennis, pro. 18-hole golf, greens fee from $76, pro, putting green, driving range. Bicycles. Lawn games. Hiking, horseback riding, mountain biking; hay rides. Aviary. Children's petting zoo. Soc dir; entertainment, dancing wkends. Exercise rm; instructor, weights, stair machine, whirlpool, sauna, steam rm. Refrigerators, minibars; some fireplaces. Many private patios, balconies. On 200 acres. Mountain views. Cr cds: A, D, DS, MC, V.

Restaurants

★ ★ ★**L'AUBERGE.** *314 El Paseo St, at Rincon St. 805/646-2288.* Hrs: 5:30–9 pm; Sat & Sun brunch 11 am–2:30 pm. Closed Tues; Jan 1, Dec 25. Res accepted. Country French, Belgian menu. Beer. Wine list. Semi-a la carte: dinner $15.50–$19. Sat & Sun brunch $8.75. Child's meals. Specializes in frogs' legs, sweetbreads, fish. Own desserts, cheesecake. Parking. Outdoor dining. In old house; country French decor. Cr cds: A, MC, V.

★ ★ ★**RANCH HOUSE.** *102 Besant Rd. 805/646-2360.* Hrs: dinner sittings at 6 pm & 8:30 pm; Sun sittings at 1 pm, 3:30 pm, 6 pm & 7:30 pm; Apr–Sept: Wed–Sat 11:30 am–1:30 pm. Closed Mon & Tues; Jan 1, Dec 24. Res accepted. Continental menu. Beer. Wine cellar. A la carte entrees: lunch $5.75–$11.95, dinner $18.95–$23.95. Child's meals. Specialties: crab voisin, chicken champagne, beef Bali Hai. Own baking. Parking. Outdoor dining. Wine terrace. Bakery. Family-owned. Cr cds: A, DS, MC, V.

★ ★**ROGER KELLER'S.** *331 E Ojai Ave. 805/646-7266.* Hrs: 11:30 am–2 pm, 5–10 pm; Fri & Sat to 10:30 pm; Sun 11:30 am–3 pm, 5–10 pm. Closed Dec 25. Res accepted. Bar. Semi-a la carte: lunch $5.50–$9.95, dinner $5.50–$20. Child's meals. Specializes in fresh fish, pasta, vegetarian dishes. Own soups. Cr cds: A, D, MC, V.

Ontario (H-4)

Founded: 1882 **Pop:** 133,179 **Elev:** 988 ft **Area code:** 909

What to See and Do

1. **Museum of History and Art, Ontario.** 225 S Euclid Ave. Regional history and fine arts exhibits. (Wed–Sun afternoons; closed major hols) Phone 983-3198. **Free.**

2. **Planes of Fame Air Museum.** 5 mi S via Euclid Ave, 7000 Merrill Ave in Chino. Exotic collection of more than 60 operable historic military aircraft, including Japanese Zero, ME-109G, B-17. Aircraft rides. (Daily; closed Thanksgiving, Dec 25) Phone 597-3722. ¢¢¢

3. **Cucamonga-Guasti Regional Park.** 800 N Archibald Ave. Swimming (Memorial Day–Labor Day, fee; lifeguards in season); water slide (Memorial Day–Labor Day, fee); fishing (fee); paddleboat rentals; picnicking, playground. (Daily; closed Jan 1, Thanksgiving, Dec 25) Phone 945-4321. Parking ¢¢

4. **Prado Regional Park.** 8 mi S via Euclid Ave; 6 mi S of Pomona Frwy. Fishing; nonpower boat rentals. Horseback riding (rentals; fee); golf. Picnicking. Camping. (Daily; closed Dec 25) Phone 597-4260. Per car ¢¢; Per person ¢

5. **Industrial tour. Graber Olive House.** 315 E 4th St. Tour of sorting, canning, packaging areas. Mini-museum, gourmet food and gift shop. (Daily; closed major hols) Phone 983-1761. **Free.**

(For further information contact the Visitors and Convention Bureau, 421 N Euclid, 91762; 984-2450.)

(See Claremont, Pomona)

Motels

★★**COUNTRY SIDE SUITES.** 204 N Vineyard Ave (91764), I-10 exit Vineyard Ave S, near Intl Airport. 909/986-8550; res: 800/248-4661; FAX 909/986-4227. 107 kit. suites, 2 story. Suites $59–$92; under 13 free; wkend, wkly rates. Crib free. TV; cable. Heated pool; whirlpool. Complimentary full bkfst, coffee. Restaurant adj open 24 hrs. Ck-out noon. Coin lndry. Meeting rms. Valet serv. Free airport transportation. Health club privileges. Cr cds: A, C, D, DS, MC, V.

⊡ ⇌ ✕ ⊗ ⊚ SC

✔★**EXPRESS INN.** 1841 East G Street (91764), I-10 Vineyard Ave exit S, near Intl Airport. 909/988-0602; res: 800/382-8318. 67 units, 3 story, 16 suites. S, D $39–$45; suites $45–$50; under 18 free. Crib free. TV; cable. Pool; whirlpool. Complimentary continental bkfst, coffee. Restaurant adj 6 am–1 pm, 5–10:30 pm. Ck-out 11 am. Coin lndry. Meeting rms. Free airport transportation. Many refrigerators. Cr cds: A, C, D, DS, MC, V.

⊡ ⇌ ✕ ⊗ ⊚ SC

★★**RESIDENCE INN BY MARRIOTT.** 2025 East D St (91764), I-10 Vineyard Ave exit S, near Intl Airport. 909/983-6788; FAX 909/983-3843. 200 kit. units, 2 story. Kit. units $69–$129; under 16 free. Pet accepted; $35 and $6 per day. TV; cable. Heated pool; whirlpool. Complimentary continental bkfst, refreshments. Restaurant nearby. Ck-out noon. Coin lndry. Meeting rms. Valet serv. Free airport transportation. Paddle tennis. Refrigerators; some fireplaces. Balconies. Picnic tables, grills. Cr cds: A, C, D, DS, ER, MC, V.

⊡ ⛵ ⇌ ✕ ⊗ ⊚ SC

✔★**SUPER 8 LODGE.** 514 N Vineyard Ave (91761), I-10 Vineyard Ave exit S, near Intl Airport. 909/983-2886; FAX 909/988-2115. 135 rms, 3 story. S $43; D $43–$46; each addl $5; suites $56; under 12 free. Crib free. TV; cable. Pool; whirlpool. Complimentary coffee. Restaurant adj open 24 hrs. Ck-out 11 am. Free airport transportation. Cr cds: A, C, D, DS, MC, V.

⊡ ⇌ ✕ ⊗ ⊚ SC

Motor Hotels

★★**INNSUITES ONTARIO AIRPORT.** 3400 Shelby St (91764), I-10 Haven Ave exit N, near Intl Airport. 909/466-9600; res: 800/642-2617; FAX 909/941-1445. 150 kit. suites, 3 story. Suites $71–$87; 1-bedrm suites $92–$108; wkly rates. Crib free. Pet accepted, some restrictions. TV; cable, in-rm movies. Heated pool. Complimentary continental bkfst Mon–Fri, full bkfst Sat & Sun. Complimentary coffee in rms. Restaurant 6–10 pm. Rm serv. Bar 5–11 pm; Sat & Sun from 4 pm. Ck-out noon. Coin lndry. Meeting rms. Valet serv. Sundries. Gift shop. Free airport transportation. Exercise equipt; bicycles, rowers, whirlpool, sauna. Game rm. Some balconies. Picnic tables. Cr cds: A, C, D, DS, MC, V.

⊡ ⛵ ⇌ 🏃 ✕ ⊗ ⊚ SC

★★★**RED LION HOTEL.** 222 N Vineyard Ave (91764), I-10 Vineyard Ave exit S, near Intl Airport. 909/983-0909; FAX 909/983-8851. 340 rms, 3 story. S $109–$129; D $119–$149; each addl $15; suites $315–$500; under 18 free; wkend rates. Crib $10. Pet accepted, some restrictions. TV; cable, in-rm movies avail. Heated pool; poolside serv (May–Sept). Restaurant 6 am–11 pm; dining rm 11:30 am–2 pm, 5–10 pm; Sat 5–11 pm; Sun 9 am–2 pm, 5–10 pm. Rm serv. Bar 11–2 am; entertainment, dancing. Ck-out 1 pm. Meeting rms. Bellhops. Valet serv. Gift shop. Free airport transportation. Exercise equipt; weight machine, bicycles, whirlpool. Cr cds: A, C, D, DS, ER, MC, V.

⊡ ⛵ ⇌ 🏃 ✕ ⊗ ⊚ SC

Hotels

✔★★**DOUBLETREE CLUB HOTEL.** 429 N Vineyard Ave (91761), I-10 Vineyard Ave exit S, near Intl Airport. 909/391-6411; FAX 909/391-2369. 171 rms, 6 story. S, D $59–$94; each addl $10; suites $150; under 12 free. Crib free. TV; cable. Heated pool. Complimentary full bkfst. Restaurant 5–9 pm. Bar to 11 pm. Ck-out 1 pm. Meeting rms. Free airport transportation. Exercise equipt; weights, bicycles, whirlpool. Cr cds: A, C, D, DS, ER, MC, V, JCB.

⊡ ⇌ 🏃 ✕ ⊗ ⊚ SC

★★★**HILTON ONTARIO AIRPORT.** 700 N Haven Ave (91764), I-10 Haven Ave exit N, near Intl Airport. 909/980-0400; FAX 909/948-9309. 308 rms, 10 story. S $105; D $115; each addl $15; family rates. Crib free. TV; cable, in-rm movies. Heated pool; poolside serv. Restaurants 6 am–midnight. Bars 11:30–1 am; dancing. Ck-out noon. Convention facilities. Concierge. Gift shop. Free airport transportation. Exercise equipt; weights, bicycles whirlpool. **LUXURY LEVEL: CONCIERGE.** 46 units, 2 suites, 2 floors. S $125; D $135; suites $355–$460. Concierge. Privage lounge, honor bar. Whirlpool, wet bar in suites. Complimentary continental bkfst, refreshments.
Cr cds: A, C, D, DS, ER, MC, V.

⊡ ⇌ 🏃 ✕ ⊗ ⊚ SC

★★★**MARRIOTT.** 2200 E Holt Blvd (91761), I-10 Vineyard Ave exit, S to Holt then 2 blks E, near Intl Airport. 909/986-8811; FAX 909/391-6151. 300 rms, 3 story. S $69–$124; D $69–$134; each addl $10; suites $250–$475; wkend packages. Crib free. Pet accepted, some restrictions. TV; cable, in-rm movies. Heated pool; poolside serv. Restaurants open 24 hrs. Rm serv 6 am–11 pm. Bar 4 pm–2 am. Ck-out noon. Convention facilities. Concierge. Gift shop. Free airport transportation. Lighted tennis. Exercise rm; instructor, weights, bicycles, whirlpool, sauna, steam rm. Racquetball & basket ball courts. Cr cds: A, C, D, DS, MC, V.

⊡ ⛵ ⛳ ⇌ 🏃 ✕ ⊗ ⊚ SC

Restaurant

★★★**ROSA'S.** 425 N Vineyard Ave, I-10 Vineyard Ave exit S. 909/391-1971. Hrs: 11:30 am–10 pm; Sat from 5 pm; Sun 5–9 pm. Closed some major hols. Res accepted. Italian menu. Bar. Wine cellar. Semi-a la carte: lunch $6.95–$15.50, dinner $8.50–$27. Specializes in fresh fish, pasta. Pianist. Mediterranean villa atmosphere. Cr cds: A, C, D, MC, V.

Orange *

Founded: 1868 **Pop:** 110,658 **Elev:** 187 ft **Area code:** 714
Just N of Santa Ana (J-4) on CA 35 (Costa Mesa Frwy).

What to See and Do

Tucker Wildlife Sanctuary. 15 mi SE via Chapman Ave, Santiago Canyon Rd. 12-acre refuge for native plants and birds, including several species of hummingbirds (seasonal); observation porch, nature trails, museum displays. Picnic areas. (Daily exc Dec 25) Phone 649-2760. ¢

(See Anaheim, Santa Ana)

Motels

★★**RESIDENCE INN BY MARRIOTT.** *201 N State College Blvd (92668), off I-5 Chapman Ave exit. 714/978-7700; FAX 714/978-6257.* 104 kits., 2 story. S $89–$110; D $99–$125; family, wkly rates. Crib free. TV; cable. Heated pool; whirlpool. Complimentary continental bkfst. Complimentary coffee in rms. Restaurant nearby. Ck-out noon. Coin lndry. Meeting rms. Valet serv. Sundries. Airport, RR station, bus depot transportation. Some balconies. Picnic tables, grills. Anaheim Stadium ½ mi N. Cr cds: A, C, D, DS, ER, MC, V, JCB.

★★**WOODFIN SUITES.** *720 The City Dr S (92668), CA 22 The City Dr exit, 1 blk S. 714/740-2700; res: 800/237-8811; FAX 714/971-1692.* 124 suites, 3 story. Suites $79–$185; under 13 free; monthly rates. Crib free. TV; cable, in-rm movies. Heated pool; whirlpool. Complimentary full bkfst. Complimentary coffee in rms. Ck-out noon. Coin lndry. Meeting rms. Valet serv. Sundries. Gift shop. Free Disneyland transportation. Refrigerators, wet bars. Grills. Cr cds: A, C, D, DS, ER, MC, V, JCB.

Hotels

★★★**DOUBLETREE-ORANGE COUNTY.** *100 The City Dr (92668), CA 22 The City Dr exit, then ½ mi N. 714/634-4500; FAX 714/978-3839.* 454 units, 20 story. S $120–$140; D $140–$160; each addl $20; suites $250–$575; under 18 free. Crib free. Garage; self-park $4, valet park $6. TV; cable, in-rm movies. Heated pool; whirlpool, poolside serv. Restaurant 6 am–11 pm. Bar from 11 am. Ck-out noon. Convention facilities. Gift shop. Free airport, Disneyland transportation. Lighted tennis. Bathrm phone, refrigerator in suites. Cr cds: A, C, D, DS, ER, MC, V, JCB.

★★★**HILTON SUITES-ANAHEIM/ORANGE.** *400 N State College Blvd (92668), off I-5 Chapman Ave exit (N) or I-5 The City Dr or State College Blvd (S). 714/938-1111; FAX 714/938-0930.* 230 suites, 10 story. Suites $115–$175; family rates. Crib free. TV; cable, in-rm movies. Indoor pool. Complimentary full bkfst. Complimentary coffee in rms. Restaurant 11:30 am–1:30 pm, 5:30–10 pm; wknd hrs vary. Rm serv 5:30–10 pm. Bar 4 pm–midnight. Ck-out noon. Meeting rms. Gift shop. Free Disneyland transportation. Exercise equipt; weight machine, bicycles, whirlpool, sauna. Refrigerators. Some balconies. 10-story triangular atrium. Anaheim Stadium ½ mi N. Cr cds: A, C, D, DS, ER, MC, V, JCB.

Restaurant

✔★★**YEN CHING.** *574 S Glassell St, CA 22 Glassell St exit, 1 blk N. 714/997-3300.* Hrs: 11:30 am–2:30 pm, 4:30–9:30 pm; Fri to 10:30 pm; Sat noon–10:30 pm; Sun noon–9:30 pm. Res accepted. Chinese menu. Wine, beer. A la carte entrees: lunch $5.75–$7.50, dinner $8.90–$13.95. Specializes in mandarin dishes. Parking. Cr cds: A, MC, V.

Oroville (C-2)

Settled: 1850 **Pop:** 11,960 **Elev:** 174 ft **Area code:** 916 **Zip:** 95965

Water-oriented recreation, tourism and hunting predominate in Oroville—where the lure of gold once held sway and "too many gambling houses to count" catered to the wants of miners. Miners' Alley is a historic remnant of those days when Oroville was the second largest city in California.

Oroville, in addition to being the portal to the Sierra's great watershed, the Feather River, also has orange and olive groves, which thrive in the area's thermal belt. Fruit and olive processing, as well as lumber, contribute much to the community's economy.

A Ranger District office of the Plumas National Forest (see QUINCY) is located in Oroville.

What to See and Do

1. **Chinese Temple** (1863). 1500 Broderick St, at Elma. The "Temple Beside the River," largest of the authentic temples in California, has a tapestry hall and display room. It is all that remains of a Chinatown that was second in size only to San Francisco's. (Daily; closed Dec 15–Jan) Phone 538-2496. ¢

2. **Historic Judge C. F. Lott House** (1856). 1067 Montgomery St, in Lott-Sank Park. Authentically restored; period furnishings. Picnic area. (Sun–Tues & Fri, afternoons; closed Dec 15–Jan) Phone 538-2497. ¢

3. **Feather River Fish Hatchery.** 5 Table Mountain Blvd, on N bank of Feather River. Raises salmon and steelhead. Underwater viewing chamber (Sept–Jan); hatchery (daily). Phone 538-2222. **Free.**

4. **Oroville Dam & Reservoir.** 7 mi E on CA 162, then 3 mi N on Canyon Dr. This 770-foot-high earth-filled dam impounds Lake Oroville with a 167-mile shoreline. The dam is a vital part of the $3.2 billion California State Water Project. Phone 538-2200. For tours of Power Plant contact Dept of Water Resources, PO Box 939; 534-2436. **Free.**

   Visitor Center & Overlook. 9 mi E on CA 162, 2½ mi N on Kelly Ridge Rd. Exhibits, slide shows, films; observation tower. (Daily; closed Jan 1, Thanksgiving, Dec 25) Phone 538-2219. **Free.**

   Lake Oroville State Recreation Area. In several sections. **Forebay-South.** 3 mi W, CA 70 Grand Ave exit. Powerboats allowed (fee for boat launch); no camping. (Daily; fee) **Forebay-North.** 1 mi W, CA 70 Garden Dr exit. Swimming; bathhouse; no powerboats. (Daily; fees) **Loafer Creek Campground.** 9 mi E via CA 162. Swimming; camping (fee). (Daily, Apr–Oct) All three recreation areas have fishing; boat ramps; hiking trails; picnicking. Standard fees. Two marinas: **Lime Saddle** and **Bidwell Canyon.** Also camping facilities at Bidwell Canyon (campground all yr; full RV hookup; fees). **Spillway.** 7 mi E via CA 162, N via Canyon Dr, 3 mi W across dam. Wayside camping; launch ramp. (Daily; fees) Reservations for both campgrounds available through Mistix 800/444-7275. Contact park headquarters for swimming and launching status; phone 538-2200.

5. **Feather Falls.** 25 mi NE in Plumas National Forest (see QUINCY). Sixth highest in U.S. 3½-mi trail leads to a 640-ft drop of the Fall River into the canyon just above the Middle Fork of the Feather

River in Feather Falls Scenic Area. Allow 4–6 hrs for round trip and carry drinking water. Phone 675-2462.

(For further information contact the Chamber of Commerce, 1789 Montgomery St; 533-2542.)

Annual Events

Old Time Fiddlers' Contest. Northern California Regional Championship. Late Mar.

Fabulous Feather Fiesta Days. Parades. Early May.

Bidwell Bar Days. Gold panning, pioneer arts & crafts. May.

(See Chico, Marysville)

Motels

★★**BEST WESTERN GRAND MANOR INN.** *1470 Feather River Blvd.* 916/533-9673; FAX 916/533-5862. 54 rms, 3 story. S $58; D $64–$75; suites $97–$125; under 12 free. Crib $6. TV; cable. Pool. Complimentary continental bkfst, coffee. Restaurant nearby. Ck-out 11 am. Coin lndry. Meeting rms. Exercise equipt; weights, bicycles, whirlpool, sauna. Refrigerators. Many balconies. Cr cds: A, C, D, DS, MC, V.

✔★**VILLA.** *1527 Feather River Blvd.* 916/533-3930. 20 rms. S $48; D $50–$54; each addl $4. Crib free. TV; cable. Pool. Coffee in rms. Restaurant nearby. Ck-out 11 am. Cr cds: A, C, D, MC, V.

Restaurant

✔★★**DEPOT.** *2191 High St.* 916/534-9101. Hrs: 11 am–2:30 pm, 4–9:30 pm; Fri to 10 pm; Sat 10 am–2 pm, 4–10 pm; Sun 10 am–2 pm, 3:30–9:30 pm; early-bird dinner Mon–Sat 4–5:30 pm. Closed Dec 25. Bar 11–2 am. Semi-a la carte: bkfst $3.25–$8.50, lunch $3.95–$8.50, dinner from $4.95. Child's meals. Specialties: broiled halibut, chicken Cordon Bleu, prime rib. Salad bar. Entertainment Fri–Sat. Parking. Outdoor dining. In 1908 Western Pacific railroad depot. Cr cds: A, DS, MC, V.

Oxnard (H-3)

Pop: 142,216 **Elev:** 52 ft **Area code:** 805 **Zip:** 93030

What to See and Do

1. **Carnegie Art Museum.** 424 South C Street. Regional and international visual and fine arts. (Thurs–Sun) Phone 385-8157 (recording). ¢¢

2. **Channel Islands National Park** (see). HQ at 1901 Spinnaker Dr, Ventura 93001.

3. **CEC/Seabee Museum.** Naval Construction Battalion Center, Channel Islands Blvd & Ventura Rd, SW off US 101 in Port Hueneme. Enter on Ventura Rd at Sunkist St, S of Channel Islands Blvd. Memorabilia of the US Navy Seabees, who are the construction battalions of the Navy; uniforms, Antarctic display, South Pacific artifacts, underwater diving display, outrigger canoes, World War II dioramas, weapons, flags; southeast Asian musical instruments, cultural items, hunting and farming implements; officer's artifacts. (Mon–Sat, also Sun afternoons; closed hols) Phone 982-5163 or -5167. **Free.**

4. **Channel Islands Harbor.** End of Peninsula Rd off Channel Islands Blvd. Public recreation includes boating, fishing, swimming,

beaches; parks, barbecue & picnic facilities; playgrounds, tennis courts; charter boat and bicycle rentals. Also here is

Fisherman's Wharf. Channel Islands Blvd. A New England-style village with specialty shops, restaurants and transient docking for pleasure boaters.

(For further information contact the Visitors Center, 715 South A Street; 483-7960.)

Annual Events

Strawberry Festival. Channel Islands Harbor. Waiters' race, wine tasting, entertainment, crafts, strawberry foods, free ferry rides. 3rd wkend May.

Point Mugu Airshow. Pacific Coast Hwy (CA 1) or I-101 (Ventura Frwy) W to Las Posas exit. Military aircraft demonstration, parachutists & displays; civilian/foreign aerobatics. Special seating/accommodations for the physically disabled; interpreter for the hearing impaired. Phone (activated in Aug) 989-8786 or -8094 (all yr). Late Oct.

(See Ventura)

Motel

★★★**COUNTRY INN AT PORT HUENEME.** *(350 E Hueneme Rd, Port Hueneme 93041) CA 1 Hueneme Rd exit, E to Ventura Rd; or US 101 to Ventura Rd exit, then 6 mi S to Hueneme Rd.* 805/986-5353; res: 800/447-3529; FAX 805/986-4399. 135 kit. units, 3 story. S from $85; D from $95; each addl $8; suites $155; under 12 free. TV; cable, in-rm movies. Pool; whirlpool. Complimentary full bkfst. Ck-out noon. Coin lndry. Refrigerators. Near ocean. Nautical decor. Cr cds: A, C, D, DS, MC, V.

Motor Hotel

✔★★★**CASA SIRENA RESORT.** *3605 Peninsula Rd.* 805/985-6311; res: 800/228-6026 (CA); FAX 805/985-4329. 273 rms, 2–3 story. No A/C. S $79–$89; D $89–$99; each addl $10; suites $139–$275; kit. units $139; under 18 free; package plans. Crib free. TV. Heated pool; poolside serv. Playground. Complimentary morning coffee. Restaurant 6:30 am–10 pm. Rm serv to 9:30 pm. Bar 10–1:30 am; Sun to 11:30 pm. Ck-out noon. Convention facilities. Bellhops. Valet serv. Sundries. Barber, beauty shop. Free airport, RR station, bus depot transportation. Lighted tennis. Putting green. Exercise equipt; weights, bicycles, whirlpool, sauna. Game rm. Refrigerators. Private patios, balconies. Marina. View of harbor. Park adj. Cr cds: A, C, D, DS, ER, MC, V.

Hotels

★★★**HILTON INN.** *600 Esplanade Dr, adj to US 101 Vineyard exit.* 805/485-9666; FAX 805/485-2061. 160 rms, 6 story. S $70–$95; D $83–$110; each addl $10; suites $100–$175; family rates. Crib free. TV; in-rm movies. Pool; whirlpool, sauna, poolside serv. Restaurant 6:30 am–10 pm. Bar 11–2 am, Sun to midnight; entertainment, dancing. Ck-out noon. Meeting rms. Shopping arcade. Barber, beauty shop. Tennis. Health club privileges. Refrigerators. Balconies. Cr cds: A, C, D, DS, ER, MC, V, JCB.

★★★**MANDALAY BEACH RESORT.** *2101 Mandalay Beach Rd.* 805/984-2500; res: 800/433-4600; FAX 805/984-8339. 250 suites, 3 story. May–Aug: S $139–$229; D $154–$244; each addl $15; under 12 free; lower rates rest of yr. TV; cable. Pool; whirlpool, poolside serv. Supervised child's activities (summer Fri & Sat). Complimentary full bkfst. Coffee in rms. Restaurant 11 am–3 pm, 5–10 pm. Rm serv 6–1 am. Bar 11–2 am; pianist. Ck-out noon. Convention facilities. Concierge. Gift shop. Free local airport transportation. Lighted tennis. Bicycle rentals.

Refrigerators. Private patios, balconies. 7½ acres; on beach. Cr cds: A, C, D, DS, MC, V.

D 🛇 ⚓ ☂ 🛇 ⊘

★ ★ ★RADISSON SUITE. 2101 W Vineyard Ave. 805/988-0130; FAX 805/983-4470. 250 kit. suites, 1–2 story. S $85–$109; D $95–$119; under 17 free; golf, tennis packages. Crib free. TV; cable, in-rm movies. 2 heated pools; poolside serv. Complimentry coffee in rms. Restaurant 6:30 am–10 pm. Bar 11–1 am; entertainment. Ck-out noon. Coin lndry. Convention facilities. Concierge. Gift shop. Free airport, RR station, bus depot transportation. Lighted tennis, pro. 18-hole golf, pro, greens fee $20–$22, driving range. Exercise equipt; weight machine, bicycles, whirlpools. Some wood-burning fireplaces. Balconies. Picnic tables, grills. Located on 15 acres; gazebo. Summer home of the LA Raiders. Cr cds: A, C, D, DS, ER, MC, V.

D 🛇 🏊 ⚓ ☂ 🛇 ⊘ SC

Pacific Beach (San Diego) (K-4)

Area code: 619 Zip: 92109

This community is an integral part of San Diego, but is regarded by many as a separate entity.

(For general information and attractions see San Diego.)

Motor Hotel

★ ★ ★PACIFIC TERRACE INN. 610 Diamond St. 619/581-3500; res: 800/344-3370; FAX 619/274-3341. 73 rms, 3 story, 40 kits. Mid-June–Sept: S $150–$200; D $160–$210; each addl $10; suites $235–$425; studio rms $235–$285; kit. units $170–$425; lower rates rest of yr. Crib free. TV; cable. Heated pool; whirlpool. Complimentary continental bkfst; coffee in rms. Restaurant nearby. Ck-out 11 am. Meeting rm. Bellhops. Covered parking. Refrigerators, minibars. Bathrm phone in suites. Private patios, balconies. On beach. Cr cds: A, C, D, DS, MC, V, JCB.

D 🏊 🛇 ⊘ SC

Hotel

★ ★ ★CATAMARAN RESORT. 3999 Mission Blvd. 619/488-1081; res: 800/288-0770, 800/233-8172 (CAN). 312 rms, 2–12 story, 120 kits. S, D $120–$180; each addl $15; suites $175–$250. Crib free. TV; cable. Heated pool; poolside serv. Restaurant 6:30 am–10 pm, Fri & Sat to 11 pm. Bar 11–2 am; entertainment, dancing Wed–Sat. Ck-out noon. Meeting rms. Exercise equipt; weights, bicycles, whirlpool. Sailboats. Beach activities. Many refrigerators. Private patios, balconies. Opp ocean. Resort hotel on Mission Bay. Cr cds: A, C, D, DS, ER, MC, V.

D 🏊 ☂ 🛇 ⊘

Restaurants

✔ ★ ★McCORMICK'S. 4190 Mission Blvd. 619/581-3938. Hrs: 11:30 am–3 pm, 5–10 pm; Fri to 11 pm; Sat 10 am–3 pm, 5–11 pm; Sun brunch 9 am–3 pm. Closed Dec 25. Res accepted. Bar to 2 am. Semi-a la carte: lunch $3.95–$7.95, dinner $5.95–$16.95. Sun brunch $9.95. Child's meals. Specializes in seafood. Entertainment Mon–Fri 5:30–7:30 pm. Parking. Outdoor dining. View of Pacific Ocean from upper deck. Cr cds: A, C, D, DS, MC, V.

D

★ ★OLD OX. 4474 Mission Blvd. 619/275-3790. Hrs: 11 am–2:30 pm, 5–10 pm; Fri & Sat to 11 pm; Sat & Sun brunch 10 am–2:30 pm. Closed Dec 25. Res accepted. Bar to 1:30 am. Semi-a la carte: lunch

$5.95–$10.95, dinner $10.95–$16.95. Sat & Sun brunch $5–$9. Specializes in prime rib, steak, fresh fish. Parking. Outdoor dining. Cr cds: A, MC, V.

Pacific Grove (F-1)

Pop: 16,117 Elev: 0–300 ft Area code: 408 Zip: 93950

What to See and Do

1. **Pacific Grove Museum of Natural History.** 165 Forest Ave. Natural history of Monterey County, including birds, shells, mammals, Indian exhibits; native plants garden. (Daily exc Mon; closed most major hols) (See ANNUAL EVENTS) Phone 648-3116 or -3119 (recording). **Free.**

2. **Point Piños Light Station** (1855). Asilomar Ave at Lighthouse Ave. Oldest continuously operating lighthouse on Pacific Coast. (Jan 2–late Nov, Sat & Sun afternoons) Phone 648-3116 or -3119 (recording). **Free.**

3. **Ocean View Blvd.** Five-mile scenic road along rocky, flower-bordered shoreline.

4. **Asilomar State Beach and Conference Center.** 800 Asilomar Blvd. A 105-acre beach front conference center, historical landmark and park. Recreational facilities, meeting rooms, accommodations. Contact PO Box 537; phone 372-8016 for details on the conference center.

(For further information contact the Chamber of Commerce, Central & Forest Aves, PO Box 167M; 373-3304.)

Annual Events

Good Old Days. Parade, fair, entertainment, quilt show, contests. Late Apr.

Wildflower Show. Pacific Grove Museum of Natural History (see #1). 3rd wkend Apr.

Feast of Lanterns. Lantern-lit processions on land and sea, barbecue; pageant. Late July.

Butterfly Parade. Celebrates arrival of thousands of Monarch butterflies. Mid-Oct.

Marching Band Festival. Parade, field show; competition of statewide high school championship bands. Early Nov.

Christmas at the Inns. Tour of old Victorian inns decorated for the holidays. Usually 2nd Tues Dec.

(See Carmel, Carmel Valley, Monterey, Pebble Beach)

Motels

✔ ★ ★ASILOMAR CONFERENCE CENTER. (Box 537) 800 Asilomar Blvd, at Asilomar State Beach. 408/372-8016; FAX 408/372-7227. 313 rms, 1–2 story. No A/C. S $61–$65; D $71–$75; each addl $16; suites $116. Crib free. Heated pool. Restaurant 7:30–9 am, noon–1 pm, 6–7 pm. Ck-out noon. Convention facilities. Some free covered parking. Rec rm. Lawn games. Balconies. Wooded grounds; on beach. Designed 1913. No cr cds accepted.

D 🏊 ⊘

★QUALITY INN. 1111 Lighthouse Ave. 408/646-8885; FAX 408/646-5976. 49 units, 2 story, 5 suites. May–Oct: S $90–$145; D $100–$155; each addl $10; suites $170–$325; under 18 free; higher rates: hols, special events; lower rates rest of yr. Crib $10. TV; cable. Heated pool; whirlpool, sauna. Complimentary continental bkfst. Complimentary coffee in rms. Restaurant opp 7 am–10 pm. Ck-out noon.

Meeting rms. Refrigerator in suites. Beach 3 blks. Cr cds: A, C, D, DS, MC, V.

★**SUNSET.** *133 Asilomar Blvd. 408/375-3936.* 20 rms, 1–2 story, 12 kits. No A/C. Mid-May–mid-Oct: S, D & kit. units $65–$95; each addl $6; suites $75–$90; lower rates rest of yr. Crib $5. TV; cable. Complimentary continental bkfst. Complimentary coffee in rms. Restaurant nearby. Ck-out 11 am. Whirlpool. Fireplace in some rms. Cr cds: MC, V.

⊛

✔ ★**WILKIE'S.** *1038 Lighthouse Ave. 408/372-5960; res: 800/253-5707.* 24 rms, 2 story, 2 kits. No A/C. June–Oct: S, D $65–$85; each addl $5; kit. units addl $10; higher rates: hols, special events; lower rates rest of yr. TV; cable. Complimentary coffee in rms. Ck-out 11 am. Ocean view from some rms. Cr cds: A, DS, MC, V.

Inns

★★**CENTRELLA.** *612 Central Ave. 408/372-3372.* 20 rms, 2 share bath, 3 story, 5 suites in cottages. No A/C. S, D $125; each addl $15; suites $150; cottage suites $175–$185; under 12 free in cottages. Children over 12 yrs only in main house. Crib avail. TV in cottages, suites; cable. Complimentary continental bkfst, afternoon wine, sherry. Ck-out 11 am, ck-in 2 pm. Refrigerator in suites. Private patios. Built 1889; Victorian architecture, decor. Near ocean. Cr cds: D, MC, V.

⊡ ⊛

★★**GOSBY HOUSE.** *643 Lighthouse Ave. 408/375-1287.* 22 rms, 20 with bath, 2 kit. units. No A/C. S, D $85–$150; each addl $15. Complimentary buffet bkfst, evening refreshments. Picnic lunches. Ck-out noon, ck-in 2 pm. Meeting rm. Bellhops. Some fireplaces. 4 verandas. 2-story Queen Anne/Victorian mansion built in 1887 by cobbler from Nova Scotia. Wine cellar. Cr cds: A, MC, V.

⊛ ⊛

★★**GREEN GABLES.** *104 5th St. 408/375-2095.* 11 rms, 7 with bath, 2 story, 6 rms in main bldg, 5 rms in carriage house. No A/C. S, D $100–$160. Complimentary full bkfst, afternoon tea. Ck-out noon, ck-in 2 pm. Queen Anne-style mansion (1888); on Monterey Bay. Cr cds: A, MC, V.

⊛ ⊛

★★**MARTINE.** *255 Ocean View Blvd. 408/373-3388.* 20 rms, 3 story. S, D $125–$230; each addl $35. Complimentary full bkfst, refreshments. Ck-out 11 am, ck-in 2 pm. Meeting rms. Game rm. Refrigerators; some fireplaces. Victorian, Mediterranean-style home built 1899. Antiques. Opp ocean. Cr cds: MC, V.

⊡ ⊛ ⊛

★**OLD ST ANGELA.** *321 Central Ave. 408/372-3246.* 9 rms, 6 baths. No rm phones. D $90–$150; each addl $10; suites $105–$150. Complimentary full bkfst, wine, cheese. Ck-out 11:30 am, ck-in 3–6 pm. Cape Cod decor with country pine antiques; enclosed solarium. On Monterey Peninsula. Totally nonsmoking. Cr cds: MC, V.

⊛ ⊛

★★**PACIFIC GROVE.** *581 Pine Ave. 408/375-2825.* 16 rms, in 2 houses, 3 story. July–Oct: S, D $87.50–$147.50; lower rates rest of yr. TV. Complimentary continental bkfst. Ck-out noon, ck-in 2 pm. Some refrigerators. Restored Queen Anne-style house (1905). Totally nonsmoking. Cr cds: A, D, DS, MC, V.

⊡ ⊛ ⊛

★★★★**SEVEN GABLES.** *555 Ocean View Blvd. 408/372-4341.* 14 rms, 2–3 story. No rm phones. S, D $105–$205. Complimentary full bkfst, afternoon tea. Ck-out noon, ck-in 2:30–10 pm. Some refrigerators. Landmark Victorian mansion built 1886; elegantly furnished with

European antiques. Spectacular location on Monterey Bay. Ocean view from all rms. Totally nonsmoking. Cr cds: MC, V.

Restaurants

★★**CENTRAL 1-5-9 RESTAURANT & MARKET.** *15th St, between Lighthouse & Central Aves. 408/372-2235.* Hrs: 11 am–9 pm. Closed Sun; July 4, Thanksgiving, Dec 25. Res accepted; required wkends. Wine, beer. A la carte entrees: lunch $6.25–$10, dinner $12–$15. Specializes in grilled fish, duck, rabbit. Totally nonsmoking. Cr cds: A, D, MC, V.

✔ ★★**EL COCODRILO.** *701 Lighthouse Ave. 408/655-3311.* Hrs: 4–10 pm. Closed Tues; Thanksgiving, Dec 25. Res accepted. Central American, Caribbean menu. Bar. Semi-a la carte: dinner $8.50–$12.95. Specialties: prawns Diablo, snapper Mardi Gras, chicken fettucine. Tropical atmosphere. Cr cds: MC, V.

✔ ★★★**FANDANGO.** *223 17th St. 408/372-3456.* Hrs: 11 am–2:30 pm, 5:30–10 pm; Sun 10 am–2:30 pm, 5:30–10 pm. Res accepted. No A/C. Continental menu. Bar. A la carte entrees: lunch $5.25–$9, dinner $10.75–$14.75. Specializes in fresh seafood, paella, rack of lamb. Parking. Outdoor dining. Casual southern European decor; fireplaces. Cr cds: A, C, D, DS, MC, V.

★**FISHWIFE.** *1996½ Sunset Dr, at Asilomar State Beach. 408/375-7107.* Hrs: 11 am–10 pm; Sun from 10 am; Sun brunch to 4 pm. Closed Tues; Thanksgiving, Dec 25. Res accepted. Caribbean menu. Wine, beer. Semi-a la carte: lunch $4.95–$6.95, dinner $7.95–$11.95. Sun brunch $4.95–$6.95. Child's meals. Specialties: sea garden salad with Cajun spices, prawns Belize. Parking. Caribbean decor. Cr cds: MC, V.

★★**GERNOT'S VICTORIA HOUSE.** *649 Lighthouse Ave. 408/646-1477.* Hrs: 5:30–9:30 pm. Closed Mon; Dec 25. Res accepted. No A/C. Wine, beer. Semi-a la carte: dinner $16–$20. Specializes in veal, game, local seafood. Restored Queen Anne Victorian mansion (1896). Cr cds: A, MC, V.

★★★**MELAC'S.** *663 Lighthouse Ave. 408/375-1743.* Hrs: 11:30–2 pm, 5:30–9:30 pm; Sat from 5:30 pm. Closed Sun, Mon; Dec 25. Res accepted. French, California menu. Wine list. A la carte entrees: lunch $7.50–$15, dinner $18.95–$25. Specializes in lamb, veal, seafood. Own pastries. French country decor; fireplace. Totally nonsmoking. Cr cds: A, C, D, DS, MC, V.

★★★**OLD BATH HOUSE.** *620 Ocean View Blvd. 408/375-5195.* Hrs: 5–10:30 pm; Sat from 4 pm; Sun from 3 pm. Res accepted. No A/C. Continental menu. Bar 4 pm–midnight. Semi-a la carte: dinner $15.75–$29. Specialties: unique seafood, game & beef dishes, fresh Dungeness crab, lobster cakes, hot pecan ice cream fritters. Own pastries. Parking. In 1930s Victorian-style building overlooking Lover's Point. Cr cds: A, C, D, DS, MC, V.

✔ ★★**PEPPERS MEXICALI CAFE.** *170 Forest Ave. 408/373-6892.* Hrs: 11:30 am–10 pm; Fri & Sat to 11 pm. Closed Tues; some major hols. Res accepted. Mexican, Latin Amer menu. Bar. Semi-a la carte: lunch, dinner $5.50–$10.95. Specializes in fresh seafood, fajitas, tamales. Own tamales, chips, salsa. Southwestern decor; Latin Amer artifacts. Cr cds: A, C, D, DS, MC, V.

★**THE TINNERY.** *631 Ocean View Blvd. 408/646-1040.* Hrs: 8–1 am. Res accepted. No A/C. Bar. Semi-a la carte: bkfst $4.99–$8.50, lunch $4.99–$10.99, dinner $7.99–$16.99. Child's meals. Specializes in seafood, pizza, pasta. Parking. Outdoor dining. Entertainment. Ocean view. Cr cds: A, C, D, DS, MC, V.

✔ ★**VITO'S.** *1180 Forest Hill Shopping Center. 408/375-3070.* Hrs: 5–10 pm. Closed Thanksgiving, Dec 25. Res accepted. No A/C. Italian menu. Wine, beer. Semi-a la carte: dinner $9–$15. Specializes in pasta, veal, gnocchi. Cr cds: A, MC, V.

Palmdale (H-4)

Pop: 68,842 **Elev:** 2,659 ft **Area code:** 805 **Zip:** 93550

The Angeles National Forest is west and south of town (see PASADENA).

(See Lancaster)

Motor Hotel

★★**RAMADA.** *300 W Palmdale Blvd. 805/273-1200; FAX 805/947-9593.* 135 rms, 4 story. S $48; D $53; each addl $5; under 12 free. Crib free. TV; cable, in-rm movies avail. Pool; whirlpool. Restaurant 6 am–9 pm; wkends from 7 am. Rm serv. Bar 4–10 pm, Fri & Sat to 1:30 am; entertainment, dancing exc Sun. Ck-out noon. Coin lndry. Meeting rms. Valet serv. Refrigerators avail. Cr cds: A, D, DS, MC, V.

Palm Desert (J-5)

Pop: 23,252 **Elev:** 243 ft **Area code:** 619 **Zip:** 92260

What to See and Do

1. **Palms to Pines Highway.** Scenic CA 74 goes south and west toward Idyllwild and Hemet (see both).

2. **The Living Desert.** 47-900 S Portola Ave. This 1,200-acre wildlife and botanical park contains interpretive exhibits from the world's deserts. Animals include mountain lions, zebras, bighorn sheep, coyotes, reptiles and birds. Indian exhibits; picnic areas, nature trails; gift shop; nursery. Special programs on wkends. (Sept–mid-June) Sr citizen rate. Phone 346-5694. **¢¢¢**

(For further information contact the Chamber of Commerce, 72-990 CA 111; 346-6111.)

Annual Event

Bob Hope Chrysler Classic. Golf pros and celebrities play at four country clubs at Bermuda Dunes, La Quinta, Palm Desert and Indian Wells. Mid-Jan.

Motels

✔★**HOLIDAY INN EXPRESS.** *74675 CA 111. 619/340-4303; FAX 619/340-4303, ext 377.* 131 rms, 3 story. Jan–May: S, D $95–$189; suites $95–$340; under 18 free; lower rates rest of yr. Crib free. TV; cable. Heated pool; whirlpool. Complimentary continental bkfst. Restaurant adj. Ck-out noon. Valet serv. Tennis. Lawn games. Some refrigerators. Balconies. Picnic tables. Cr cds: A, C, D, DS, ER, MC, V, JCB.

★★**NEW INN.** *(42-325 Adams St, Bermuda Dunes 92201) W on CA 111, N on Washington St. 619/345-2577; res: 800/472-3715; FAX 619/360-1123.* 40 kit. villas, 26 suites. Nov–June: S, D $90–105; suites $125–$250; 2-night min wkends; lower rates rest of yr. Crib free. TV. Heated pool; whirlpool. Complimentary continental bkfst wkends. Complimentary coffee in rms. Restaurant nearby. Ck-out noon. Concierge. Free airport transportation. Tennis privileges. 18-hole golf privileges. Patios. Cr cds: A, DS, MC, V.

✔★★**TRAVELERS INN.** *72-322 CA 111. 619/341-9100; FAX 619/773-3515.* 115 rms, 3 story. Mid-Jan–May: S $70–$85; D $80–$95; each addl $7; suites $120–$135; under 13 free; lower rates rest of yr. Crib free. TV; cable. Heated pool; whirlpool. Complimentary continental bkfst. Restaurant nearby. Ck-out 11 am. Meeting rm. Valet serv. Free airport transportation. Putting green. Some refrigerators. Private patios, balconies. Cr cds: A, C, D, DS, ER, MC, V.

★★**VACATION INN.** *74-715 CA 111. 619/340-4441; res: 800/231-8675; FAX 619/773-9413.* 130 rms, 3 story. Jan–May: S, D $82–$108; each addl $10; under 12 free; lower rates rest of yr. Crib free. TV; in-rm movies avail. Heated pool; whirlpool. Continental bkfst. Complimentary coffee in rms. Restaurant nearby. Bar to 2 am; entertainment, dancing. Ck-out noon. Meeting rm. Tennis. Putting green. Refrigerators. Private patios, balconies. Cr cds: A, C, D, DS, ER, MC, V.

Motor Hotels

★★★**EMBASSY SUITES.** *74-700 CA 111. 619/340-6600; FAX 619/340-9519.* 196 suites, 3 story. Jan–May: S, D $154–$220; each addl $15; exec suites $229; under 12 free; lower rates rest of yr. Crib free. TV; cable. Heated pool; poolside serv. Complimentary full bkfst. Coffee in rms. Restaurant 11:30 am–2:30 pm, 5–10 pm. Rm serv 11 am–11 pm. Bar to 2 am; entertainment, dancing Wed–Sat. Ck-out noon. Meeting rms. Gift shop. Lighted tennis. Putting green. Exercise equipt; weights, bicycles, whirlpool. Refrigerators. Some balconies. Courtyard. Cr cds: A, C, D, DS, MC, V.

★★★**ERAWAN GARDEN RESORT.** *(76-477 CA 111, Indian Wells 92210) 3 mi E of CA 74. 619/346-8021; res: 800/237-2926; FAX 619/568-0541.* 218 rms, 2 story. Jan–May: S, D $90–$140; 1-bedrm suites $180–$220; 2-bedrm suites $250–$290; under 12 free; package plans; lower rates rest of yr. Crib free. TV; cable. 2 pools, heated; wading pool, whirlpools, sauna, poolside serv. Complimentary coffee. Restaurant 7 am–10 pm. Rm serv. Bar 10–2 am; entertainment, dancing Wed–Sun. Ck-out noon. Convention facilities. Bellhops. Valet serv. Concierge. Shopping arcade. Sundries. Barber, beauty shop. Tennis privileges. Golf privileges, putting green. Lawn games. Refrigerators; some wet bars. Oriental motif. Cr cds: A, C, D, DS, MC, V.

Hotel

★★★**INDIAN WELLS.** *(76-661 CA 111, Indian Wells 92210) 3 mi E of CA 74. 619/345-6466; res: 800/248-3220; FAX 619/772-5083.* 152 rms, 3 story. Jan–Apr: S, D $99–$189; suites $199–$289; lower rates rest of yr. TV; cable. Heated pool; whirlpool. Restaurant 6 am–10 pm. Bar 11–2 am; entertainment Wed–Sat. Ck-out noon. Meeting rms. Concierge. Free valet parking. Tennis privileges. 18-hole golf privileges, putting green, driving range. Lawn games. Health club privileges. Honor bars. Balconies. Cr cds: A, C, D, DS, MC, V, JCB.

Resorts

★★★★**HYATT GRAND CHAMPIONS.** *(44-600 Indian Wells Lane, Indian Wells 92210) SE, just off CA 111. 619/341-1000; FAX 619/568-2236.* 316 rms in main building, 5 story, 20 Italian-style garden villas, 1- & 2-bedrm. Mid-Dec–May: S, D $220–$300; each addl $25; villas $725–$925; under 18 free; golf, tennis plans; lower rates rest of yr. Crib free. Valet parking (fee). TV; cable. 4 heated pools; wading pool, poolside serv. Supervised child's activities. Dining rms 6:30 am–10 pm. Box lunches, snack bar, picnics. Rm serv 24 hrs. Bar 11–1 am. Ck-out noon (Sun 8 pm), ck-in 4 pm. Convention facilities. Beauty shop. Sports dir. 12 tennis courts including 2 clay, 2 grass & 8 hard surface, pro. 36-hole golf, greens fee $30–$100, pro, putting green, driving range. Bicycles. Lawn games. Entertainment, dancing. Exercise rm; instructor, weight machines, bicycles, whirlpool, sauna, steam rm. Aerobics. Massage. Full service health spa. Refrigerators, honor bars. Some fireplaces. Private patios, balconies. Butler serv in villas 6 am–11 pm. Situated on 35 acres, with elaborate landscaping; scenic view from all rms. Unique Moorish-style architecture. *LUXURY LEVELS:* REGENCY CLUB & PENTHOUSE. 24 suites. S, D $325–$375. Concierge. Private lounge. Wet bars. Complimentary continental bkfst, refreshments. Cr cds: A, C, D, DS, MC, V, JCB.

[D] [icons] SC

★ ★ ★ ★ MARRIOTT'S DESERT SPRINGS RESORT & SPA. *74855 Country Club Dr. 619/341-2211; res: 800/228-9290; FAX 619/341-1872.* 895 rms, 8 story. EP, late Dec–Memorial Day: S, D $250–$320; each addl $10; suites $600–$2,000; under 18 free; golf, tennis, spa package rates; lower rates rest of yr. Crib free. Garage: valet parking (fee); public parking free. TV; cable. 3 heated pools; poolside serv. Supervised child's activities. Dining rms 7 am–10 pm. Box lunches, snack bar, picnics. Bar 11–2 am. Ck-out noon, ck-in 4 pm. Convention facilities. Concierge. Shopping arcade. Barber, beauty shop. Sports dir. 20 hard tennis courts, 7 lighted, 3 clay, 2 grass. 36-hole golf, greens fee $100–$110, pro, championship putting course, putting green, driving range. Boats. Lawn games. Soc dir; entertainment, dancing. Exercise rm; instructor, weight machines, bicycles, whirlpool, sauna, steam rm. Massage. Full service European health spa. Minibars. Private patios, balconies. Situated on 420 acres, surrounded by 35 acres of waterways & lakes, including a 23,000-sq-ft sunning beach. Lush gardens & landscaping. Inside main lobby is 8-story atrium with waterfall. Man-made lake with boat dock; from here, guests may board boats for transportation to the resort's restaurants and bars. Cr cds: A, C, D, DS, ER, MC, V, JCB.

[D] [icons] SC

★ ★ ★ SHADOW MOUNTAIN RESORT & RACQUET CLUB. *45750 San Luis Rey. 619/346-6123; res: 800/472-3713; FAX 619/346-6518.* 125 units, 2 story. Mid-Feb–Apr: S, D $124–$160; each addl $15; condos $193–$415; under 18 free; lower rates rest of yr. Crib $15. TV; cable. 4 heated pools; poolside serv. Free supervised child's activities. Bar. Ck-out noon, ck-in 3 pm. Coin lndry. Meeting rms. Valet serv. Concierge. 16 tennis courts, 4 lighted, pro, pro shop. 18-hole golf privileges. Exercise equipt; weights, bicycles, whirlpools, sauna. Masseuse. Lawn games. Bicycle rentals. Private patios, balconies. Home of the Desert Tennis Academy. Cr cds: A, MC, V.

[D] [icons] SC

★ ★ ★ STOUFFER ESMERALDA. *(44-400 Indian Wells Lane, Indian Wells 92210) SE off CA 111. 619/773-4444; FAX 619/773-9250.* 560 units, 7 story, 44 suites. Late Dec–May: S, D $260–$380; each addl $25; suites $500–$2,500; under 18 free; tennis, golf plans; honeymoon package; lower rates rest of yr. Crib free. Pet accepted, some restrictions. TV; cable. 2 pools; wading pool, poolside serv. Supervised child's activities. Dining rms 6:30 am–11 pm (also see SIROCCO). Rm serv 24 hrs. Bar noon–2 am; entertainment, dancing. Ck-out noon, ck-in 3 pm. Coin lndry. Meeting rms. Bellhops. Valet serv. Concierge. Gift shops. Airport transportation. Sports dir. Lighted tennis, pro. 36-hole golf, greens fee $90–$100, pro, putting green, driving range. Tennis & golf clinics; equipt rentals. Private beach. Hiking. Bicycle rentals. Lawn games. Game rm. Fully equipped health/fitness center. Exercise rm; instructor, weight machine, bicycles, whirlpool, sauna, steam rm. Masseuse. Bathrm phones, minibars; some wet bars. Some suites with woodburning fireplace. Balconies. 350-acre golf resort nestled in the foothills of the Santa Rosa Mountains. Cr cds: A, C, D, DS, ER, MC, V, JCB.

[D] [icons] SC

Restaurants

★ ★ ★ A TOUCH OF MAMA'S. *74-063 CA 111. 619/568-1315.* Hrs: 6–10:30 pm. Closed Dec 24. Res accepted. Italian, continental menu. Bar. Semi-a la carte: dinner $11.95–$23.95. Specialties: osso buco, veal piccata, chicken basilica. Guitarist. Mural of Lago de Como. Cr cds: A, MC, V.

[D]

★ ★ CEDAR CREEK INN. *73-445 El Paseo. 619/340-1236.* Hrs: 11 am–9 pm. Closed Thanksgiving, Dec 24, 25. Bar. Semi-a la

carte: lunch $5.25–$11, dinner $12.95–$24.95. Specializes in fresh fish, prime rib, steak. Salad bar. Own soups. Outdoor dining. Extensive dessert menu. Cr cds: A, MC, V.

[D]

★ ★ CLUB 74. *73-061 El Paseo. 619/568-2782.* Hrs: 11:30 am–2:30 pm, 5:30–10 pm. Res accepted. French menu. Bar. A la carte entrees: lunch $6–$16, dinner $16–$28. Specialties: L.I. duckling, escargot, salade Niçoise. Pianist. On 2nd floor, overlooking El Paseo, with view of valley. Jacket. Cr cds: A, C, D, DS, MC, V.

[D]

★ ★ ★ DOMINICK MANCUSO'S TRATTORIA. *73-520 El Paseo. 619/346-0445.* Hrs: 6–10 pm. Closed Jan 1, Thanksgiving, Dec 25. Res required. Italian menu. Bar to 11 pm. Wine cellar. Semi-a la carte: dinner $13.95–$26.95. Child's meals. Specialties: osso buco, cioppino, stuffed veal chop. Pianist & vocalist. Valet parking. Outdoor dining in garden-like patio area. Two separate dining areas; original artwork. Cr cds: A, MC, V.

[D]

✔ ★ DON DIEGO'S. *(74-969 CA 111, Indian Wells) E on CA 111. 619/340-5588.* Hrs: 11 am–9 pm; Fri, Sat to 10 pm; early-bird dinner 4–6 pm; Sun brunch 10 am–2 pm. Closed Thanksgiving, Dec 25. Res accepted. Mexican menu. Bar. A la carte entrees: lunch $5.95–$12.95, dinner $8.95–$17.95. Sun brunch $10.95. Child's meals. Specializes in fajitas, carnitas. Parking. Outdoor dining. Casual dining. Mexican decor. Cr cds: A, D, DS, MC, V.

★ ★ LA QUINTA CLIFFHOUSE. *78-250 CA 111. 619/360-5991.* Hrs: 5–9:30 pm; Fri & Sat to 10 pm; Sun brunch (seasonal) 10 am–2 pm. Closed Dec 25. Res accepted. Bar. Semi-a la carte: dinner $8.95–$21.95. Child's meals. Specialties: citrus-glaze seafood, Szechwan fish, steak. Valet parking. Outdoor dining. Situated on a hillside. 3 separate dining ares, 2 with valley view. Southwestern decor, western artifacts & memorabilia. Cr cds: A, MC, V.

[D] SC

★ ★ ★ LE PAON. *45640 CA 74. 619/568-3651.* Hrs: 6–10 pm. Closed Thanksgiving. Res accepted. French, continental menu. Bar. Wine cellar. A la carte entrees: dinner $16–$28. Specializes in veal, steak Diane, venison. Pianist & vocalist. Valet parking. Outdoor dining. Formal, elegant dining; rose garden. Cr cds: A, C, D, MC, V.

[D]

★ ★ LG'S STEAKHOUSE. *74-225 CA 111. 619/779-9799.* Hrs: from 5 pm. Res accepted. Bar. A la carte entrees: dinner $12–$28. Child's meals. Specializes in 9 varieties of steak, fresh fish, broasted chicken. Valet parking. Pueblo-style structure with 4 separate dining areas; Southwestern decor, artifacts. Cr cds: A, DS, MC, V, JCB.

[D] SC

★ THE NEST. *(75-188 CA 111, Indian Wells) E of Cook St. 619/346-2314.* Hrs: 5–10:30 pm. Closed Easter, Thanksgiving, Dec 25; also July–Aug. Continental menu. Bar to 12:30 am. Semi-a la carte: dinner $8.50–$19.50. Specializes in fresh fish, pasta. Entertainment 7 pm–midnight. Parking. Newspaper menu. Bistro atmosphere, Parisian decor. Cr cds: A, C, D, DS, MC, V.

✔ ★ PASTA ITALIA. *44-491 Town Center Way. 619/341-1422.* Hrs: 11:30 am–2:30 pm, 5–10 pm; Fri, Sat to 10:30 pm; Sun 5–10 pm. Closed Thanksgiving, Dec 25. Res accepted. Italian menu. Bar. A la carte entrees: lunch $6.95–$12.95, dinner $6.95–$15.95. Specializes in pasta, non-cholesterol dishes, tiramisu. Guitarist wknds. Parking. Outdoor dining. Old World trattoria atmosphere. Family-owned. Cr cds: A, MC, V.

[D]

★ ★ RISTORANTE MAMMA GINA. *73-705 El Paseo. 619/568-9898.* Hrs: 11:30 am–2 pm, 5:15–10 pm; Fri, Sat to 10:30 pm; Sun from 5:15 pm. Closed Jan 1, Easter, Thanksgiving, Dec 25; also Aug. Res required. Italian menu. Bar. A la carte entrees: lunch $6.90–$13.90, dinner $12.40–$26.90. Specializes in pasta, veal. Pianist. Valet parking. Contemporary and Italian decor. Cr cds: A, C, D, MC, V.

★ ★ ★ROBERT CUNARD'S. *73-101 CA 111. 619/773-3337.* Hrs: 5:30–11 pm; summer 6–10 pm. Res accepted. Continental menu. Bar to 2 am. Wine cellar. Semi-a la carte: dinner $9.50–$26. Specializes in fresh seafood, veal, fresh pasta. Entertainment Thurs–Sat. Valet parking. Bi-level dining area. Cr cds: A, MC, V.

★ ★RUSTY PELICAN. *72-191 CA 111. 619/346-8065.* Hrs: 11 am–2:30 pm, 5–10 pm; early-bird dinner 5–6:30 pm; Sun brunch 10 am–2 pm. Bar 5 pm–midnight. Semi-a la carte: lunch $5.95–$12.95, dinner $10.50–$29.95. Specializes in fresh fish, beef, pasta. Seafood bar. Lagoon with waterfall. Cr cds: A, C, D, DS, MC, V.

★ ★SIROCCO. *(See Stouffer Esmeralda Resort) 619/773-4444.* Hrs: 6–10 pm. Res accepted. Mediterranean cuisine. Bar. Wine cellar. A la carte entrees: dinner $10.50–$24. Specialties: bouillabaisse, paella, fresh seafood. Own baking. Valet parking. Classical Mediterranean decor. Two display wine rooms at entry. Overlooks golf course. Cr cds: A, C, D, DS, ER, MC, V, JCB.

Palm Springs (J-5)

Founded: 1876 **Pop:** 40,181 **Elev:** 466 ft **Area code:** 619

Discovered in 1774 by a Spanish explorer, this site was dourly dubbed Agua Caliente (hot water). One hundred years later it was the location of a stagecoach stop and a drowsy, one-store railroad town. Today, after a second hundred years, Palm Springs is known as "America's foremost desert resort." Originally the domain of Cahuilla Indians, the city has been laid out in a checkerboard pattern, with nearly every other square mile still owned by the tribe.

What to See and Do

1. **Palm Canyon.** 6½ mi S on S Palm Canyon Dr. Approx 3,000 native palm trees line a stream bed. Magnificent views from the canyon floor or from points above the canyon. Picnic tables. (Early Sept–June, daily) Phone 325-5673. **¢¢**

2. **Palm Springs Aerial Tramway.** 2 mi N on CA 111, then 4 mi W on Tramway Rd. World's longest double-reversible, single-span aerial tramway. Two 80-passenger cars make 2½-mile trip ascending to 8,516-foot elevation on Mt San Jacinto. Picnicking, camping in summer; cafeteria at summit. (Daily; closed 2 wks beginning 1st Mon Aug) Phone 325-1391 (recording). **¢¢¢¢¢**

3. **Palm Springs Golf Course.** 1885 Golf Club Dr, 3 mi SE on CA 111. (Daily) Phone 328-1005 or -1956. There are 70 other courses within a 15-mile radius of the city, making this area the "Winter Golf Capital of the World." **¢¢¢¢¢**

4. **Palm Springs Desert Museum.** 101 Museum Dr. Natural science and art exhibits; performing arts; features art of the American West, contemporary art and Native American basketry, film retrospectives. (Mid-Sept–June, daily exc Mon; closed Jan 1, Thanksgiving, Dec 25) 1st Tues each month admission free. Phone 325-7186 or -0189. **¢¢**

5. **Village Green Heritage Center.** 221 S Palm Canyon Dr. Consists of two 19th-century houses exhibiting artifacts from early Palm Springs. **McCallum Adobe** (ca 1885) is the oldest building in city and houses extensive collection of photographs, paintings, clothes, tools, books and Indian ware. **Miss Cornelia's "Little House"** (ca 1890) was constructed of rail ties from the defunct Palmdale Railway and is furnished with authentic antiques. (Mid-

Oct–May, Wed–Sun; rest of yr, by appt; closed major hols) Phone 323-8297. Per house **¢**

6. **Moorten's Botanical Garden.** 1701 S Palm Canyon Dr. Approx 3,000 varieties of desert plants; nature trails. World's first "cactarium" contains several hundred species of cactus and desert plants from around the world. Guide maps to desert wildflowers. (Daily; closed some major hols) Phone 327-6555. **¢**

7. **Oasis Waterpark.** 5 mi S off I-10, at 1500 Gene Autry Trail. This 22-acre water park has 12 water slides, inner tube ride, wave pool and beach sand volleyball courts. (Mid-Mar–early Sept, daily; early Sept–late Oct, wkends) Sr citizen rate. Phone 325-7873 or 327-0499. **¢¢¢¢¢**

8. **Gray Line bus tours.** Contact 333 S Indian Canyon Rd, Ste C, 92262; 325-0974.

(For further information and bikeway maps, contact the Convention and Visitors Bureau, 69930 CA 111, Suite 201, Rancho Mirage, 92270; 770-9000.)

Motels

✔ ★ARROWHEAD ARMS. 715 San Lorenzo Rd (92264). 619/325-9723; FAX 619/325-4357. 15 rms, 9 kits. S, D $39–$89; each addl $20; suites $89; wkly, monthly rates. TV; in-rm movies avail. Heated pool; whirlpool. Complimentary coffee. Ck-out noon. Refrigerators. Some private patios. Cr cds: A, MC, V.

★ ★BEST WESTERN HOST. 1633 S Palm Canyon Dr (92264). 619/325-9177. 72 rms, 3 story. Late Dec–mid-June: S $78–$98; D $78–$98; each addl $6; under 12 free; higher rates: hols, wkends; lower rates rest of yr. Crib $5. TV; cable. Heated pool; whirlpool. Complimentary continental bkfst. Restaurant nearby. Ck-out noon. Refrigerators avail. Cr cds: A, C, D, DS, ER, MC, V, JCB.

★ ★ ★COURTYARD BY MARRIOTT. 1300 Tahquitz Canyon Way (92262), near Municipal Airport. 619/322-6100; FAX 619/322-6091. 149 rms, 3 story. Mid-Dec–May: S, D $114–$124; suites $134; under 12 free; lower rates rest of yr. Crib free. TV; cable. Heated pool. Complimentary coffee in rms. Restaurant 6:30–11:30 am. Bar noon–11 pm. Ck-out noon. Coin lndry. Meeting rms. Valet serv. Free airport transportation. Tennis & golf privileges. Exercise equipt; weight machine, bicycles. Refrigerator in suites. Balconies. Cr cds: A, C, D, DS, MC, V.

★ ★DAYS INN SUITES. (69-151 E Palm Canyon Dr, Cathedral City 92234) 1 blk E of Date Palm Dr on CA 111. 619/324-5939; FAX 619/324-3034. 97 kit. suites, 3 story. Jan–May: kit. suites $83–$157; under 16 free; higher rates wkends; lower rates rest of yr. Crib free. TV; cable. Heated pool; whirlpool. Complimentary continental bkfst. Restaurant opp open 24 hrs. Ck-out noon. Coin lndry. Meeting rms. Valet serv. Airport transportation. Tennis & golf privileges. Cr cds: A, C, D, MC, V.

★EL RANCHO LODGE. 1330 E Palm Canyon Dr (92264), near Municipal Airport. 619/327-1339. 19 rms, 5 kit. suites. Jan–May: S, D $61–$80; kit. suites $131; lower rates rest of yr. TV; cable. Heated pool; whirlpool. Complimentary continental bkfst. Restaurant opp open 24 hrs. Ck-out noon. Coin lndry. Refrigerators. Some private patios. Cr cds: A, DS, MC, V.

★ ★ ★FOUR SEASONS APARTMENT HOTEL. 290 San Jacinto Dr (92262). 619/325-6427. 11 rms, 9 suites. Feb–Mar: S, D $105; each addl $15; studio rms $115; suites $130–$170; monthly rates; lower rates rest of yr. TV. Heated pool; whirlpool. Restaurant nearby. Ck-out noon. Tennis privileges. Golf privileges. Refrigerators. All rms individually decorated. Cr cds: MC, V.

✔ ★**GOLDEN PALM VILLA.** *601 Grenfall Rd (92264), near Municipal Airport.* 619/327-1408; *res:* 800/833-5675; *FAX* 619/327-7273. 21 rms, 15 kits. Sept–June: S, D $60–$90; each addl $15; kit. units addl $6 (3-day min). Adults only. Closed June–Aug. TV. 2 heated pools; 2 whirlpools. Complimentary coffee in rms. Ck-out 11 am. Coin lndry. Free airport, bus depot transportation. Golf privileges. Lawn games. Refrigerators. Grills. Cr cds: A, DS, MC, V.

[icons]

✔ ★ ★**HAMPTON INN.** *2000 N Palm Canyon Dr (92262).* 619/320-0555; *FAX* 619/320-2261. 96 rms, 2 story. Jan–May: S $54–$74; D $69–$79; suites $89; under 18 free; higher rates: special events, hols, wkends; lower rates rest of yr. Crib free. TV; cable. Heated pool; whirlpool. Complimentary coffee. Restaurant nearby. Ck-out noon. Meeting rms. Valet serv. Tennis privileges. Golf privileges. Some refrigerators. Spanish-style architecture. Cr cds: A, C, D, DS, MC, V.

[icons]

★ ★ ★**LA SIESTA VILLAS.** *247 W Stevens Rd (92262).* 619/325-2269; *FAX* 619/778-6533. 16 villas (1–2-bedrm). Oct–May: villas $99–$165; wkly, monthly rates; lower rates rest of yr. Adults only. TV. Heated pool; whirlpool. Complimentary continental bkfst wkends. Restaurant nearby. Ck-out noon. Valet serv. Concierge. Covered parking. Tennis & golf privileges. Refrigerators, fireplaces. Private patios. Grills. Tropical setting. Cr cds: MC, V.

[icons]

✔ ★ ★**MIRA LOMA.** *1420 N Indian Canyon Dr (92262).* 619/320-1178; *res:* 800/722-3082; *FAX* 619/320-5308. 14 rms, 6 kits. Dec–Apr: S, D $50–$65; each addl $10; suites $110–$115; kit. units $65; monthly rates; lower rates rest of yr. Adults only. TV. Heated pool. Complimentary coffee in rms. Ck-out noon. Free airport transportation. Refrigerators. Cr cds: A, C, D, DS, MC, V, JCB.

[icons]

✔ ★**MOTEL 6.** *660 S Palm Canyon Dr (92262), near Municipal Airport.* 619/327-4200. 149 rms, with shower only, 3 story. Sept–mid-Apr: S $35.99; D $41.99; each addl $6; under 17 free; lower rates rest of yr. Crib free. TV; cable. Heated pool. Restaurant nearby. Ck-out noon. Cr cds: A, C, D, DS, MC, V.

[icons]

★ ★**PALM TEE.** *1590 E Palm Canyon Dr (92264), near Municipal Airport.* 619/327-1293. 15 rms, 1–2 story, 9 kits. Nov–May: S, D $56–$120; each addl $10; suites $77–$120; kit. units $65; higher rates hols (3-night min); lower rates rest of yr. Children over 16 yrs only (winter). TV. Heated pool; whirlpool. Complimentary continental bkfst. Coffee in rms. Restaurant nearby. Ck-out noon. Bellhops. Airport transportation. Refrigerators. Private patios, balconies. Cr cds: A, DS, MC, V.

[icons]

★ ★**QUALITY INN.** *1269 E Palm Canyon Dr (92264).* 619/323-2775; *FAX* 619/323-4234. 144 rms, 2 story, 8 suites. Late Dec–May: S, D $65–$105; suites $95–$155; under 18 free; lower rates rest of yr. Crib avail. TV; cable. Heated pool; wading pool, whirlpool. Complimentary coffee in rms. Restaurant adj open 24 hrs. Ck-out noon. Coin lndry. Meeting rm. Free airport transportation. Many refrigerators. Grill. Cr cds: A, C, D, DS, ER, MC, V, JCB.

[icons]

★ ★**SHILO INN.** *1875 N Palm Canyon Dr (92262).* 619/320-7676; *FAX* 619/320-9543. 124 rms, 2 story. Jan–May: S, D $90–$120; each addl $12; kit. units $140–$155; under 12 free; wkly, monthly rates; lower rates rest of yr. Crib free. TV; cable. 2 heated pools. Complimentary continental bkfst. Ck-out noon. Coin lndry. Meeting rm. Valet serv. Free local airport transportation. Exercise equipt; weights, bicycles, whirlpool, sauna, steam rm. Bathrm phones, refrigerators. Private patios, balconies. Cr cds: A, C, D, DS, ER, MC, V, JCB.

[icons]

★ ★ ★ ★**SUNDANCE VILLAS.** *303 W Cabrillo Rd (92262), 1 blk E of Palm Canyon Dr & 1 blk N of Racquet Club Rd.* 619/325-3888; *FAX* 619/323-3029. 19 kit. villas. Mid-Dec–May: villas $295–$450; wkly rates;

lower rates rest of yr. Crib $15. TV; cable, in-rm movies. Pool; whirlpool, sauna. Restaurant nearby. Ck-out 1 pm. Valet serv. Concierge. Free airport transportation. Lighted tennis. Golf privileges. Health club privileges. Wet bars. Fireplaces. Patios. Grills. Each private villa also has its own swimming pool, whirlpool, enclosed yard and 2-car garage. Cr cds: A, D, MC, V.

[icons]

✔ ★**SUPER 8.** *1900 N Palm Canyon Dr (92262).* 619/322-3757; *FAX* 619/323-5290. 63 rms, 2 story. Late Dec–Mar: S $55.88; D $65.88–$69.88; each addl $5; suites $89.88; under 12 free; lower rates rest of yr. Crib free. TV; cable. Heated pool; whirlpool. Complimentary continental bkfst, coffee. Restaurant nearby. Ck-out 11 am. Refrigerators. Cr cds: A, C, D, DS, MC, V.

[icons]

★**TRAVELODGE.** *333 E Palm Canyon Dr (92264).* 619/327-1211. 158 rms, 2 story. Jan–mid-June: S $55–$75; D $65–$85; each addl $10; higher rates: special events, hols, wkends; lower rates rest of yr. Crib free. TV; cable. 2 pools, heated; whirlpool. Complimentary coffee in rms. Restaurant adj open 24 hrs. Ck-out noon. Coin lndry. Lawn games. Private patios, balconies. Cr cds: A, C, D, DS, ER, MC, V, JCB.

[icons]

★**VAGABOND INN.** *1699 S Palm Canyon Dr (92264), jct E Palm Canyon Dr.* 619/325-7211; *FAX* 619/322-9269. 120 rms, 3 story. Jan–May: S, D $36–$76; higher rates: hols (2-night min), date festival, golf classics; lower rates rest of yr. Crib $3. TV. Heated pool; whirlpool, sauna, poolside serv. Complimentary coffee in rms. Restaurant nearby. Ck-out noon. Refrigerators avail. Cr cds: A, C, D, DS, ER, MC, V, JCB.

[icons]

✔ ★**WESTWARD HO.** *1701 E Palm Canyon Dr (92264), near Municipal Airport.* 619/320-2700; *res:* 800/854-4345; *FAX* 619/322-5354. 207 rms, 2 story. Mid-Dec–May: S $41.90; D $52.90; higher rates: Easter, Memorial Day, Labor Day; lower rates rest of yr. Crib $10. TV; cable. Heated pool; whirlpool. Restaurant open 24 hrs. Bar 10 am–midnight. Ck-out 11 am. Coin lndry. Cr cds: A, DS, MC, V.

[icons]

Motor Hotels

★ ★ ★**AUTRY RESORT HOTEL.** *4200 E Palm Canyon Dr (92264), near Municipal Airport.* 619/328-1171; *res:* 800/443-6328; *FAX* 619/324-7280. 173 rms, 2 story, 11 bungalows. Jan–Apr: S, D $135–$195; each addl $25; suites $195; bungalows $300; under 12 free; package plans; lower rates rest of yr. Crib free. TV; cable. 3 heated pools; 2 whirlpools, sauna, poolside serv. Restaurant 7 am–10:30 pm. Rm serv 24 hrs. Bar 10–2 am; entertainment, dancing. Ck-out noon. Meeting rms. Concierge. Sundries. Gift shop. Beauty, barber shop. Free airport transportation. Tennis, pro, school. Golf privileges. Masseur. Bathrm phones, refrigerators. Private patios, balconies. Cr cds: A, C, D, DS, ER, MC, V, JCB.

[icons]

★ ★**LAS BRISAS.** *222 S Indian Canyon Dr (92262).* 619/325-4372; *res:* 800/346-5714; *FAX* 619/320-1371. 90 rms, 3 story, 8 suites. Jan–Apr: S, D $85–$115; each addl $10; suites $99–$135; under 17 free; lower rates rest of yr. Crib free. TV; cable. Pool; whirlpool, poolside serv. Complimentary continental bkfst. Coffee in rms. Restaurant nearby. Bar 6–2 am. Ck-out noon. Coin lndry. Meeting rms. Refrigerators. Cr cds: A, C, D, DS, MC, V.

[icons]

★ ★ ★**RIVIERA RESORT AND RACQUET CLUB.** *1600 N Indian Canyon Dr (92262).* 619/327-8311; *res:* 800/444-8311; *FAX* 619/327-4323. 480 rms, 2–3 story. Mid-Jan–mid-Apr: S, D $135–$195; each addl $20; suites $195–$475; under 18 free; lower rates rest of yr. Crib free. Pet accepted, some restrictions. TV; cable. 2 heated pools; poolside serv. Restaurant 6:30 am–10 pm. Rm serv. Bar 11–2 am; entertainment Fri & Sat; dancing Thurs–Sun. Ck-out noon. Convention facilities. Bellhops. Valet serv. Concierge. Sundries. Gift shop. Beauty shop. Free valet parking. Free airport transportation. Lighted tennis. Golf privileges. Exercise equipt; weight machine, bicycles, whirlpools. Health club privileges. Bicycle rentals. Lawn games. Many minibars, bathrm phones; some refrigerators, wet bars. Balconies. Cr cds: A, C, D, DS, MC, V.

☐ ☐ ☐ ☐ ☐ ☐ ☐ ☐ ☐ SC

SPA HOTEL & MINERAL SPRINGS. (Remodeling incomplete when inspected, therefore not rated) *100 N Indian Canyon Dr (92263), near Municipal Airport.* 619/325-1461; res: 800/854-1279; FAX 619/325-3344. 230 rms, 5 story. Jan–May: S, D $155–$175; each addl $20; suites from $250; under 12 free; lower rates rest of yr. Crib $10. TV. 3 pools; 2 hot mineral pools; poolside serv. Restaurant 7 am–9:30 pm. Rm serv. Bar 10–2 am. Ck-out 1 pm. Meeting rms. Bellhops. Concierge. Sundries. Gift shop. Barber, beauty shop. Free valet parking. Free airport transportation. Lighted tennis, pro. 18-hole golf privileges. Exercise equipt; weights, bicycles, whirlpool, sauna, steam rm. Some bathrm phones, refrigerators. Private patios, balconies. Cr cds: A, C, D, DS, MC, V.

☐ ☐ ☐ ☐ ☐ ☐ ☐ ☐ ☐ SC

Hotels

★ ★ ★**HILTON.** *400 E Tahquitz Canyon Way (92262), near Municipal Airport.* 619/320-6868; FAX 619/320-2126. 260 rms, 3 story. Dec–May: S, D $205–$305; each addl $15; suites $265–$685; studio rms $155; kit. condos $235–$345; under 18 free; lower rates rest of yr. Crib free. TV; cable. Heated pool; 2 whirlpools, sauna, poolside serv. Supervised child's activities. Restaurant 6 am–10 pm. Bar 4 pm–2 am. Ck-out noon. Convention facilities. Concierge. Gift shop. Barber, beauty shop. Valet parking. Free airport transportation. 6 lighted tennis courts, pro, shop. Golf privileges. Refrigerators, minibars. Private patios, balconies. Cr cds: A, C, D, DS, ER, MC, V, JCB.

☐ ☐ ☐ ☐ ☐ ☐ ☐ SC

★ ★ ★**HYATT REGENCY SUITES PALM SPRINGS.** *285 N Palm Canyon Dr (92262), near Municipal Airport.* 619/322-9000; res: 800/233-1234; FAX 619/325-4027. 192 suites, 6 story. Jan–Apr: suites $199–$450; each addl $25; under 18 free; mid-wk rates; lower rates rest of yr. Crib free. Pet accepted, some restrictions; $50 refundable. TV; cable. Pool; poolside serv. Restaurants 7 am–11 pm. Bar 11–1 am; entertainment Wed–Sun. Ck-out noon. Meeting rms. Concierge. Valet parking. Free airport transportation. Tennis & golf privileges. Exercise equipt; weight machine, bicycles, whirlpool. Massage. Bathrm phones, refrigerators, wet bars. Private patios, balconies. Shopping plaza adj. Cr cds: A, C, D, DS, ER, MC, V, JCB.

☐ ☐ ☐ ☐ ☐ ☐ ☐ ☐ SC

★ ★ ★**MARQUIS.** *150 S Indian Canyon Dr (92262), near Municipal Airport.* 619/322-2121; res: 800/223-1050; FAX 619/322-4365. 166 rms, 101 kit. villas, 3 story. Jan–Apr: S, D $140–$205; villas $245–$675; wkly, monthly rates; golf, tennis packages; lower rates rest of yr. Underground parking; free valet parking; overnight parking $5. Crib free. TV; cable. 2 pools; poolside serv. Restaurants 6:30 am–11 pm. Rm serv 24 hrs. Bar 11–2 am; entertainment wkends. Ck-out noon. Convention facilities. Concierge. Gift shop. Free airport transportation. Lighted tennis, pro. Golf privileges. Exercise equipt; weight machine, bicycles, whirlpool. Masseuse. Bathrm phones. Private patios, balconies. View of San Jacinto Mountains. Eight-acre resort. Cr cds: A, C, D, DS, MC, V, JCB.

☐ ☐ ☐ ☐ ☐ ☐ ☐ ☐

★ ★**RAMADA HOTEL RESORT.** *1800 E Palm Canyon Dr (92264), at Sunrise Way.* 619/323-1711; res: 800/245-6907 (exc CA), 800/245-6904 (CA); FAX 619/322-1075. 255 rms, 3 story. Feb–May: S, D $79–$139; each addl $15; suites $125–$200; under 18 free; higher rates: wkends, hols; lower rates rest of yr. Crib free. TV. Heated pool; poolside serv. Restaurant 6:30 am–10 pm. Bar 11 am–midnight; entertainment wkends. Ck-out noon. Coin lndry. Meeting rms. Gift shop. Free airport transportation. Tennis & golf privileges. Exercise equipt; weights, bi-

cycles, whirlpools, sauna. Many refrigerators; wet bar in suites. Balconies. Cr cds: A, C, D, DS, ER, MC, V, JCB.

☐ ☐ ☐ ☐ ☐ ☐ ☐ ☐ SC

★ ★ ★**WYNDHAM.** *888 E Tahquitz Canyon Way (92262), near Municipal Airport.* 619/322-6000; FAX 619/322-5351. 410 units, 5 story, 158 suites. Jan–May: S, D $185–$245; each addl $25; suites $205–$230; under 17 free; golf plans; lower rates rest of yr. Crib $15. TV; cable. Pool; wading pool; poolside serv. Coffee in rms. Restaurant 6 am–11 pm. Bar 11–1:30 am; entertainment Thurs–Sat. Ck-out noon. Convention facilities. Concierge. Shopping arcade. Barber, beauty shop. Free valet parking. Free airport transportation. Tennis privileges. Golf privileges. Exercise equipt; weight machines, bicycles, whirlpool, sauna. Game rm. Private patios, balconies. Covered walkway to convention center. Cr cds: A, C, D, DS, ER, MC, V, JCB.

☐ ☐ ☐ ☐ ☐ ☐ ☐ ☐

Inns

★ ★**CASA CODY.** *175 S Cahuilla Rd (92262).* 619/320-9346. 17 rms, 15 kit. suites. Late Dec–late Apr: S, D $65–$190; each addl $10; monthly, wkly rates; lower rates rest of yr. Crib $10. TV; cable. 2 heated pools; whirlpool. Complimentary continental bkfst. Restaurant nearby. Ck-out 11 am, ck-in 2 pm. Refrigerators; many fireplaces. Many private patios. Cr cds: A, D, MC, V.

☐ ☐ ☐ SC

★ ★ ★**INGLESIDE.** *200 W Ramon Rd (92264).* 619/325-0046; res: 800/772-6655; FAX 619/325-0710. 29 rms. Oct–May: S, D $85–$275; suites $295–$550; villas $125–$375; penthouses $95–$125; lower rates rest of yr. Pet accepted, some restrictions. TV; cable. Heated pool; whirlpool, poolside serv. Complimentary continental bkfst. Restaurant (see MELVYN'S INGLESIDE). Rm serv. Bar; entertainment. Ck-out 1 pm, ck-in 2 pm. Valet serv. Concierge. Free airport transportation. Health club privileges. In-rm steam baths, whirlpools, refrigerators; some fireplaces. Some private patios. Hacienda atmosphere; courtyard, fountain. Rms individually decorated; many antiques. Cr cds: A, DS, MC, V.

☐ ☐ ☐ ☐ ☐

★ ★ ★**VILLA ROYALE.** *1620 Indian Trail (92264), near Municipal Airport.* 619/327-2314; res: 800/245-2314 (exc CA). 32 rms, 19 suites. Oct–early July: D $75–$300; each addl $25; suites $135–$300; lower rates rest of yr. Adults only. TV. Pools; whirlpool. Dining rm 11:30 am–2:30 pm, 5:30–11 pm. Rm serv. Bar 4:30–11 pm. Ck-out noon, ck-in 2 pm. Meeting rms. Airport transportation. Many refrigerators. Private patios. Some fireplaces. Located on 3½ acres with series of interior couryards. Rms decorated with objets d'art from Morocco, France, England, Holland, Spain and Greece. European atmosphere. Cr cds: A, MC, V.

☐ ☐ ☐

Resorts

★ ★ ★**DOUBLETREE.** (Box 1644, 92263) *Vista Chino at Landau Blvd.* 619/322-7000; FAX 619/322-6853. 289 rms, 4 story, 100 condos (1–3 bedrm). Jan–late Apr: S, D $200–$230; each addl $15; suites $300–$750; condos $225–$325; under 19 free; wkly, monthly rates in condos; golf, tennis plans; lower rates rest of yr. Crib free. TV; cable. Heated pool; wading pool, poolside serv. Dining rm 6:30 am–11 pm. Rm serv. Bar 10–2 am; entertainment, dancing Fri–Sun. Ck-out noon, ck-in 3 pm. Grocery, package store 3 mi. Convention facilities. Concierge. Gift shop. Barber, beauty shop. Free airport, bus depot transportation. Lighted tennis, pro. 27-hole golf, greens fee $65–$85, pro, putting greens, driving range. Lawn games. Exercise equipt; weight machines, bicycles, whirlpool, sauna. Masseuse. Refrigerators. Private patios, balconies. On 347 acres; panoramic mountain view. Cr cds: A, C, D, DS, ER, MC, V, JCB.

☐ ☐ ☐ ☐ ☐ ☐ ☐ ☐ SC

★ ★ ★LA MANCHA PRIVATE VILLAS AND COURT CLUB. *(Box 340, 92263) 444 Avenida Caballeros, near Municipal Airport.* 619/323-1773; res: 800/255-1773; FAX 619/323-5928. 54 kit. villas, 1–2 story, 11 minisuites. Dec–Apr: minisuites $145–$185; villas $195–$950; extended stay rates; golf, tennis, honeymoon packages; lower rates rest of yr. Crib $25. TV; cable, in-rm movies avail. Pool; poolside serv. Dining rm 7 am–2 pm, 5:30–10 pm. Box lunches, picnics. Rm serv. Bar 8 am–11 pm. Ck-out 11 am, ck-in 2 pm. Grocery, coin lndry, package store 1 mi. Meeting rms. Concierge. Gift shop. Free airport transportation. Sports dir. Lighted tennis, pro. Golf privileges, putting green. Bicycles. Lawn games. Exercise equipt; weights, bicycles, whirlpool, sauna, steam rm. Some fireplaces. Private patios, balconies. Grills. Most villas with private pool, whirlpools and/or spa; some villas with private tennis court. Extensive grounds. Cr cds: A, C, D, DS, MC, V.

★ ★LAWRENCE WELK'S DESERT OASIS. *34567 Cathedral Canyon Dr (92234).* 619/321-9000; res: 800/824-8224 (CA); FAX 619/321-6200. 162 villas, 2 story. Mid-Dec–May: suites $219–$269; each addl $20; under 18 free; golf, tennis plans; lower rates rest of yr. Crib free. TV; cable. Heated pool; poolside serv. Coffee in rms. Dining rm 7 am–10 pm. Bar 10:30 am–midnight; entertainment, dancing. Ck-out 11 am, ck-in 4 pm. 10 tennis courts, 7 lighted, pro. 27-hole golf, pro, greens fee $80, putting green, driving range. Pro shop. Exercise equipt; weights, bicycles, whirlpool. Refrigerators. Private patios, balconies. Cr cds: A, DS, MC, V.

★ ★ ★MARRIOTT'S RANCHO LAS PALMAS. *(41000 Bob Hope Dr, Rancho Mirage 92270) SE on CA 111.* 619/568-2727; res: 800/458-8786; FAX 619/568-5845. 450 rms, 2 story. Jan–Apr: S, D $210–$240; each addl $10; suites $330–$1,000; under 18 free; AP, MAP avail; golf package plan; varied lower rates rest of yr. Pet accepted, some restrictions. TV; cable. 3 pools, heated; wading pool, poolside serv, lifeguard. Playground. Supervised child's activities. Dining rm 6 am–10 pm (also see CABRILLO). Rm serv 24 hrs; limited serv midnight–6 am. Box lunches, snack bar. Bar 11–2 am. Ck-out noon, ck-in 4 pm. Convention facilities. Concierge. Gift shop. Barber, beauty shop. Lighted tennis, pro. Tennis school. 27-hole golf, greens fee $85, pro, putting green, driving range (free balls). Bicycle rentals. Soc dir; entertainment, dancing. Exercise equipt; weights, bicycles, whirlpool. Massage. Some refrigerators, minibars. Private patios, balconies. Large, luxurious rms, spacious grounds, garden. Horseback riding nearby. Cr cds: A, C, D, DS, ER, MC, V, JCB.

★ ★RACQUET CLUB. *2743 N Indian Canyon Dr (92263).* 619/325-1281; res: 800/367-0947 (exc CA), 800/423-6588 (CA); FAX 619/325-3249. 150 units. Jan–May: S, D $129–$169; each addl $25; suites $195–$595; villas $129–$179; cottages $119–$169; monthly rates; lower rates rest of yr. Crib $15. Pet accepted, some restrictions. TV; cable. 4 pools; poolside serv. Dining rm 7:30 am–10 pm. Rm serv. Bar 11–2 am. Ck-out noon, ck-in 3 pm. Boutique. Free airport transportation. 12 lighted tennis courts, pro. Golf privileges. Lawn games. Entertainment, dancing Fri & Sat. Exercise equipt; weights, bicycles, whirlpool, sauna, steam rm. Many refrigerators; some fireplaces, private pools. Private patios, balconies. Cr cds: A, MC, V.

★ ★ ★THE RITZ-CARLTON, RANCHO MIRAGE. *(68-900 Frank Sinatra Dr, Rancho Mirage 92270) 11 mi SE via CA 111.* 619/321-8282; FAX 619/321-6928. 240 rms, 3 story. Mid-Dec–early June: S, D $275–$395; each addl $25; suites $650–$1,700. Crib free. TV; cable. Heated pool; poolside serv. Supervised child's activities. Dining rm 7 am–11 pm (also see THE CLUB GRILL). Box lunches, snack bar, picnics. Afternoon tea 2:30–5 pm. Rm serv 24 hrs. Bar 10:30–1 am. Ck-out noon, ck-in 3 pm. Grocery, coin lndry, package store 2 mi. Convention facilities. Gift shop. Underground valet parking. Airport transportation. Free transportation to golf facilities. Lighted tennis, pro, pro shop. 18-hole golf privileges, greens fee $60–$170. Lawn games. Exercise rm; instructor; weight machines, bicycles, whirlpool, sauna, steam rm. Massage. Bathrm phones, refrigerators, honor bars. Private patios, balconies. Located on a secluded plateau in the foothills of the Santa Rosa

Mountains; lush gardens; gazebo; panoramic view of desert. *LUXURY LEVEL:* RITZ-CARLTON CLUB. 33 rms. S, D $395; suites $750. Concierge. Private lounge. Minibars; wet bar in suites. Complimentary continental bkfst, refreshments.
Cr cds: A, C, D, DS, ER, MC, V, JCB.

★ ★ ★THE WESTIN MISSION HILLS. *(Dinah Shore Dr, Rancho Mirage 92270) At Bob Hope Dr.* 619/328-5955; res: 800/544-0287; FAX 619/321-2955. 512 units in 16 buildings, 2 story, 40 suites. Late Dec–May: S, D $189–$305; each addl $25; suites $329–$1,000; under 18 free; golf & tennis plans; lower rates rest of yr. Crib free. TV; cable. 3 heated pools; poolside serv, lifeguard (main pool); 60-ft water slide. Playground. Supervised child's activities (ages 4–12 yrs). Dining rms 6 am–11 pm. Box lunches. Snack bar. Deli. Rm serv 24 hrs. Bars 8–2 am; entertainment. Ck-out noon, ck-in 4 pm. Convention facilities. Bellhops. Valet serv. Concierge. Gift shop. Clothing shops (women's & children's). Tennis & golf shops. Airport transportation. Sports dir. 7 tennis courts, lighted, pro. Pete Dye & Gary Player championship 18-hole golf courses, pro, 6 putting greens, 2 double-sided practice ranges. Bicycles (rentals). Lawn games include croquet, shuffleboard, volleyball. Soc dir. Game rm. Exercise equipt; weight machines, treadmill, whirlpool, steam rm. Health and fitness center; massage, herbal wraps, skin care, beauty salon; aerobics and weight training. Fully stocked minibars. Set on 360 acres, with lagoons, waterways and lush landscaping; the resort's architecture is classic Moroccan in design. Most rms offer panoramic views of golf course fairways, surrounding mountains and water features. *LUXURY LEVEL:* ROYAL OASIS CLUB. 32 rms, 2 floors. S, D $385; 2-bedrm suite $1,050. Concierge. Private lounge. Bathrm phones. Complimentary continental bkfst, refreshments.
Cr cds: A, C, D, DS, ER, MC, V, JCB.

Restaurants

★ ★ ★CABRILLO. *(See Marriott's Rancho Las Palmas Resort)* 619/568-2727. Hrs: 6–10 pm. Res accepted. International flavors menu. Bar. Wine list. A la carte entrees: dinner $13.95–$19.95. Child's meals. Specialties: wood-smoked barbecued shrimp, seared salmon saffron, seared medallions of pork, creme brulée. Own baking. Valet parking. Old Spanish mission decor. Some tableside cooking. Cr cds: A, C, D, DS, ER, MC, V, JCB.

✔ ★CACTUS CORRAL. *(67-501 E Palm Canyon Dr, Cathedral City) E on CA 111.* 619/321-8558. Hrs: 6 pm–2 am. Closed Dec 24, 25. Bar. Semi-a la carte: dinner $6.95–$14.95. Specializes in barbecue, steak. Country & Western entertainment. Southwestern decor. Cr cds: A, C, D, DS, MC, V.

★ ★CAFE ST. JAMES. *254 N Palm Canyon Dr.* 619/320-8041. Hrs: 5:30–11 pm. Closed Mon; Jan 1, Thanksgiving, Dec 25; also Aug–mid-Sept. Continental menu. Bar. A la carte entrees: dinner $14–$24. Specializes in seafood, pasta. Veranda dining. Rotating menu. Cr cds: A, DS, MC, V.

★ ★CEDAR CREEK INN. *1555 S Palm Canyon Dr.* 619/325-7300. Hrs: 11 am–9 pm. Closed some major hols. Res accepted. Bar to 11 pm. Semi-a la carte: lunch $5.95–$10.95, dinner $5.95–$23. Specialties: chicken papaya salad, rack of lamb, homemade desserts. Entertainment Fri & Sat. Parking. Outdoor dining. Old World country garden atmosphere. Cr cds: A, MC, V.

★ ★ ★THE CLUB GRILL. *(See The Ritz-Carlton, Rancho Mirage Resort)* 619/321-8282. Hrs: 6–11 pm. Closed Sun & Mon. Res accepted. Continental menu. Bar. A la carte entrees: dinner $18–$28. Specializes in seafood, sautéed veal chop, rack of lamb, grilled steak. Own baking. Entertainment. Valet parking. Braille menu. European decor. Jacket. Cr cds: A, C, D, DS, ER, MC, V, JCB.

★ ★ ★DAR MAGHREB. *(42300 Bob Hope Dr, Rancho Mirage) Approx 10 mi S on CA 111. 619/568-9486.* Hrs: 6–11 pm; July–Aug wkends only. Res accepted. Moroccan menu. Bar 6 pm–midnight. Semi-a la carte: dinner $12.50–$29.50. Child's meals. Specialties: b'stila, lemon chicken, lamb brochettes. Own baking. Parking. Servers in traditional Moroccan costume; belly dancer. Moroccan draperies, artwork. Cr cds: C, D, MC, V.

D

★ ★DOMINICK'S. *(70-030 CA 111, Rancho Mirage) 619/324-1711.* Hrs: 5–11 pm. Closed Dec 25; also Aug. Res accepted. Italian, continental menu. Bar to 2 am. Semi-a la carte: dinner $9.95–$23. Specializes in steak, chops, seafood. Piano bar. Valet parking. South seas motif. Cr cds: A, C, D, MC, V.

D

★ ★ ★EVELEEN'S. *664 N Palm Canyon Dr. 619/325-4766.* Hrs: 5:30–10 pm. Closed Sun; Jan 1, Thanksgiving, Dec 25; also July. Res accepted; required Sat. French menu. Bar. Wine cellar. A la carte entrees: lunch $8–$16, dinner $12.50–$28. Specialties: fois de canard a l'aille, steak tartare, steak Eveleen. Salad bar. Parking. Outdoor dining. Tableside food preparation. Intimate dining. Cr cds: A, C, D, DS, ER, MC, V, JCB.

D

★ ★FLOWER DRUM. *424 S Indian Canyon Dr. 619/323-3020.* Hrs: 11:30 am–3 pm, 4–10:30 pm; Fri, Sat to 11 pm; early-bird dinner 4–6 pm. Res accepted. Chinese menu. Bar to 11 pm. A la carte entrees: lunch $4.95–$12.95, dinner $8.95–$28. Specializes in chicken, duck, seafood. Chinese costumed dancing Wed–Sat. Hosts Chinese New Year's Celebration (Jan & Feb). Goldfish stream. Rock gardens. Cr cds: A, MC, V.

★ ★GREAT WALL. *362 S Palm Canyon Dr. 619/322-2209.* Hrs: 11:30 am–3 pm, 4:30–10 pm; wkends to 10:30 pm. Res accepted. Chinese menu. Bar. A la carte entrees: lunch $4.95–$6.95, dinner $6.25–$28. Specialties: Chinese chicken salad, house pan-fried noodle, triple delight, general's chicken. Outdoor dining (in season). Oriental decor; authentic Chinese watercolors; large tapestry of the Great Wall. Cr cds: A, C, D, DS, MC, V.

D

★ ★KOBE JAPANESE STEAK HOUSE. *(69-838 CA 111, Rancho Mirage) On CA 111. 619/324-1717.* Hrs: 5 pm–midnight; early-bird dinner 5–6 pm. Closed Thanksgiving. Res accepted. Teppan cooking. Bar. Complete meals: dinner $12.95–$25.95. Child's meals. Specializes in steak, seafood, chicken. Sushi bar. Entertainment Thurs–Sat (seasonal). Valet parking. Tableside preparation. Japanese farmhouse decor. Cr cds: A, C, D, MC, V, JCB.

D

★LAM'S GARDEN. *622 N Palm Canyon Dr 619/325-8860.* Hrs: noon–10 pm. Closed Mon. Res accepted. Chinese menu. A la carte entrees: lunch $3.95–$4.75, dinner $6.25–$13.75. Specializes in Cantonese and Szechwan dishes. Chinese decor. Cr cds: A, MC, V.

★ ★LAS CASUELAS NUEVAS. *(70-050 CA 111, Rancho Mirage) On CA 111. 619/328-8844.* Hrs: 11 am–10 pm; Fri, Sat to 11 pm. Sun brunch 10 am–2 pm. Closed Thanksgiving, Dec 25. Res accepted. Mexican menu. Bar. Semi-a la carte: lunch $6.15–$11.25, dinner $9.50–$22.95. Sun brunch $14.95. Specialties: crab enchiladas, lobster Ensenada, chicken fajitas. Salad bar (lunch). Entertainment Tues–Sun. Valet parking. Patio dining. Cr cds: A, C, D, DS, MC, V.

D

✔ ★ ★LAS CASUELAS TERRAZA. *222 S Palm Canyon Dr. 619/325-2794.* Hrs: 11 am–closing; Sun from 10 am. Closed Thanksgiving, Dec 25. Res accepted. Mexican menu. Bar. Semi-a la carte: lunch $5.75–$8.95, dinner $6.15–$12.95. Child's meals. Specialties: relleno vaquero, shrimp enchiladas, fajitas. Guitarist, vocalist. Parking. Outdoor dining. Antique bar. Cr cds: A, DS, MC, V.

D

★ ★ ★LE VALLAURIS. *385 W Tahquitz Canyon Way. 619/325-5059.* Hrs: 11:30 am–3 pm, 6–11 pm. Res accepted. French menu. Bar to 2 am. Wine cellar. A la carte entrees: lunch $10–$18.50, dinner $22–$28. Specializes in veal, lamb, pastries. Own baking. Pianist. Valet parking. Menu changes daily. Outdoor dining. Scenic view. French tapestries. Cr cds: A, C, D, DS, MC, V.

★ ★LORD FLETCHER INN. *(70-385 CA 111, Rancho Mirage) 10 mi E on CA 111. 619/328-1161.* Hrs: 5–10:30 pm. Closed Sun; also July–Aug. Res accepted. Continental menu. Bar. Complete meals: dinner $16.50–$19.50. Specializes in short ribs, prime rib with Yorkshire pudding, chicken dumplings, seafood. Valet parking. In authentic English inn. Family-owned. Cr cds: MC, V.

✔ ★LOUISE'S PANTRY. *124 S Palm Canyon Dr. 619/325-5124.* Hrs: 7 am–9 pm. Closed July–Aug. Semi-a la carte: bkfst $3–$4.25, lunch $3.65–$5.95, dinner $7.95–$8.95. Specializes in lamb shank, chicken & dumplings, meat loaf. Own desserts. Cr cds: C, MC, V.

★ ★LYONS ENGLISH GRILLE. *233 E Palm Canyon Dr. 619/327-1551.* Hrs: 4–11 pm; early-bird dinner 4:30–6 pm. Res accepted. English menu. Bar. Semi-a la carte: dinner $9.95–$19.95. Specializes in steak, prime rib, fresh seafood. Own desserts. Pianist. Valet parking. Old English decor; stained glass. Family-owned. Cr cds: A, C, D, MC, V.

★ ★ ★MELVYN'S INGLESIDE. *(See Ingleside Inn) 619/325-2323.* Hrs: noon–3 pm, 6–11 pm; Sat & Sun champagne brunch 9 am–3 pm. Res accepted. Continental menu. Bar 10–2 am. Wine cellar. Semi-a la carte: lunch $8.95–$13.95, dinner $16.95–$22.95. Champagne brunch $13.95–$16.95. Specialties: veal Ingleside, chicken Charlene, steak Diane; mixed seafood grill. Pianist, vocalist. Valet parking. Historic building; 2 main dining areas. Luncheon casual; evenings semi-formal. Cr cds: MC, V.

★ ★PERRINA'S. *340 N Palm Canyon Dr. 619/325-6544.* Hrs: 5–11 pm. Closed Mon; Thanksgiving, Dec 25. Res accepted. Italian, continental menu. Bar to 1 am. Semi-a la carte: dinner $8.95–$23.95. Specialties: milk-fed veal, baked mostaccioli, scampi. Pianist. Photos of sports celebrities. Family-owned. Cr cds: A, C, DS, MC, V.

★ ★SCOMA'S. *(69-620 CA 111, Rancho Mirage) E on CA 111. 619/328-9000.* Hrs: 5–11 pm. Closed Thanksgiving; also July & Aug. Res accepted. Italian menu. Bar. A la carte entrees: dinner $12–$24. Specializes in seafood, pasta. Pianist exc Mon. Valet parking. Bi-level dining; contemporary decor, art. Cr cds: A, C, D, DS, MC, V, JCB.

D

✔ ★SIAMESE GOURMET. *4711 E Palm Canyon Dr. 619/328-0057.* Hrs: 11:30 am–2:30 pm, 5 pm–closing; Sun from 5 pm; Sun brunch (Jan–May) 11 am–2:30 pm. Res accepted. Thai menu. Wine, beer. A la carte entrees: lunch $4.95–$9.95, dinner $7.95–$15.95. Specializes in curries, seafood. Parking. Cr cds: A, C, D, MC, V.

D

★ ★SORRENTINO'S. *1032 N Palm Canyon Dr. 619/325-2944.* Hrs: 5–11 pm; off-season 5:30–10 pm. Closed Thanksgiving. Res accepted. Italian menu. Bar. Complete meals: dinner $10.95–$30. Specializes in seafood, veal, steak. Pianist. Valet parking. Outdoor dining. Family-owned since 1944. Cr cds: A, C, D, MC, V.

★ ★ ★WALLY'S DESERT TURTLE. *(71-775 CA 111, Rancho Mirage) W on CA 111. 619/568-9321.* Hrs: 6–10 pm; Fri 11:30 am–2 pm, 6–10 pm. Closed mid-June–Sept. Res accepted. Continental menu. Bar. Wine cellar. A la carte entrees: lunch $12–$20, dinner $17–$30. Specializes in Dover sole, rack of lamb, duck. Pianist. Valet parking. Two-level dining with elevated terrace. Jacket. Cr cds: A, DS, MC, V.

D

★ ★ ★WILDE GOOSE. *(67-938 E Palm Canyon Dr, Cathedral City) 2 mi E on CA 111. 619/328-5775.* Hrs: 5:30 pm–closing. Res accepted. Continental menu. Bar. Semi-a la carte: dinner $9.95–$28.95. Specializes in prime beef, duck, seafood. Pianist, vocalist Thurs–Sun in season. Valet parking. European country inn decor. Cr cds: A, C, D, DS, MC, V.

★ ★ZORBA'S. *(42434 Bob Hope Dr, Rancho Mirage) E on CA 111, in shopping center. 619/340-3066.* Hrs: 11 am–2:30 pm, 5–10 pm;

Sun from 5 pm. Closed July–Aug. Res accepted. Greek menu. Bar. Semi-a la carte: lunch $4.95–$8.95, dinner $9.95–$29.95. Specialties: rack of lamb, moussaka, shrimp a la Mykonos. Belly dancer. Outdoor dining. Greek decor. Cr cds: A, C, D, DS, MC, V.

Palm Springs Area (J-5)

Area code: 619

What was once one of the country's favorite vacation towns has become one of America's most popular resort regions. Tourism experienced a remarkable boom in the years since the first Hollywood celebrities built their winter houses here. The beautiful scenery and ideal weather that attracted those first vacationers are still present, but as the area's popularity has increased they have been accompanied by an ever growing number of hotels, inns, resorts, shopping malls, golf courses, recreation sites and performing arts facilities. No longer is the area solely a retreat for the famous and wealthy. Although there are more luxurious restaurants, resorts and stores than ever before, it is now also quite easy to take full advantage of the area's attractions while on a restricted budget. The more than two million people who visit each year come mostly to relax, soak up the sun and enjoy the climate. It is also possible to enjoy everything from cross-country skiing atop Mt San Jacinto to camping among the tall cactus at Joshua Tree National Monument (see). The following towns, all within a short distance of the city of Palm Springs, provide this great variety of recreation: Desert Hot Springs, Idyllwild, Palm Desert and Palm Springs (see all).

Palo Alto (E-1)

Founded: 1889 **Pop:** 55,900 **Elev:** 23 ft **Area code:** 415

A tall and ancient redwood tree stands at the northwest entrance to the city. Nearly two centuries ago, Spanish explorers used it as a landmark, calling it Palo Alto ("tall tree"). Stanford University is a major economic factor. The city is also one of the nation's most important electronics development and research centers.

What to See and Do

1. **Stanford University** (1891). (13,549 students) Near El Camino Real (CA 82). Founded by Senator and Mrs. Leland Stanford in memory of their only son, it has become one of the great universities of the world. Phone 723-2300. Features of the campus include

   Hoover Tower. Library houses collection begun by President Herbert Hoover during the First World War. At 250 feet high, the carillon platform on 14th floor offers panoramic view of campus and peninsula (daily; closed hols, school breaks). Information desk (daily; closed hols, school breaks) Phone 723-2053 or -2560. Observation platform ¢

   Stanford Medical Center. A $21 million cluster of buildings on a 56-acre site, designed by internationally famous architect Edward Durell Stone. Tours (Thurs, by appt). Phone 723-7167.

   Thomas Welton Stanford Art Gallery. Changing exhibits. (Daily exc Mon; closed major hols) Phone 723-2842. **Free.**

   Stanford Stadium. Home of Stanford Cardinals football. Site of 1994 World Cup Soccer matches (see SAN FRANCISCO).

   Stanford Guide Service. Information booth at main entrance to Quadrangle (daily; closed hols, school breaks) and in Hoover Tower. Free one-hour campus tours leave information booth (twice daily; closed hols, school breaks). Maps and brochures are at both locations. Phone 723-2560 or -2053 during office hours.

2. **Trees** for which Palo Alto is famous. **El Palo Alto.** Palo Alto Ave near Alma St. "The Tall Tree" that gives city its name. Also, 60 varieties along Hamilton Ave, blocks between 100 & 1500.

3. **Palo Alto Junior Museum.** 1451 Middlefield Rd. Displays expose children to art, science, history and anthropology through a variety of media; hands-on exhibits and workshops. Zoo on grounds. (Daily exc Mon; closed some hols) Phone 329-2111. **Free.**

   Lucy Evans Baylands Nature Interpretive Center. 2775 Embarcadero Rd, E of US 101. Nature preserve at edge of salt marsh. Naturalist-guided walking tours; slide shows; bicycling; birdwatching. (Tues–Sun; closed Thanksgiving, Dec 25) Phone 329-2506. **Free.**

4. **Winter Lodge.** 3009 Middlefield Rd. Only outdoor ice rink in the US west of the Sierra Nevada Mountains. Skate rentals. (Sept–Apr; closed Easter, Thanksgiving, Dec 25) Phone 493-4566. ¢¢

(For further information contact the Chamber of Commerce, 325 Forest Ave, 94301; 324-3121.)

(See Fremont, Redwood City, Santa Clara, Saratoga)

Motels

★**COUNTRY INN.** 4345 El Camino Real (94306). 415/948-9154; FAX 415/949-4190. 27 rms, 12 A/C, 1–2 story, 13 kits. S, D $38–$55; each addl $6; kit. units $5–$10 addl. Crib $5. TV; cable. Heated pool. Complimentary continental bkfst. Restaurant adj open 24 hrs. Ck-out 11 am. Cr cds: A, C, D, DS, MC, V, JCB.

★★**STANFORD TERRACE INN.** 531 Stanford Ave (94306). 415/857-0333; res: 800/729-0332; FAX 415/857-0343. 79 units, 2–3 story, 14 kits. S $98; D $103; each addl $10; kit. suites $115–$180; under 12 free. TV; cable. Pool. Complimentary continental bkfst. Coffee in rms. Restaurant nearby. Ck-out noon. Coin lndry. Meeting rms. Free garage. Stanford Univ opp. Cr cds: A, C, D, MC, V.

✔★**TOWN HOUSE.** 4164 El Camino Real (94306). 415/493-4492; res: 800/458-8696; FAX 415/493-3418. 23 rms. S $39–$42; D $42–$47; each addl $4. Crib avail. TV; cable. Complimentary continental bkfst. Complimentary coffee in rms. Restaurant nearby. Ck-out 11 am. Refrigerators. Cr cds: A, C, D, MC, V.

Motor Hotels

★★**BEST WESTERN CREEKSIDE INN.** 3400 El Camino Real (94306). 415/493-2411; FAX 415/493-6787. 136 rms, 1–4 story, 8 kits. S $69–$79; D $71–$81; each addl $3; kit. units $84. Crib avail. TV; cable. 2 pools, 1 heated. Coffee in rms. Continental bkfst. Restaurant 6:30 am–11 pm; Sat, Sun from 7 am. Bar from 11 am. Ck-out noon. Meeting rms. Valet serv. Airport transportation. Many refrigerators. Many private patios, balconies. Cr cds: A, C, D, DS, ER, MC, V, JCB.

★★★**DINAH'S GARDEN HOTEL.** 4261 El Camino Real (94306). 415/493-2844; res: 800/227-8220; FAX 415/856-4713. 107 rms, 1–3 story, 20 suites. S $72; D $72–$92; suites $100–$160. Crib free. TV; cable. 2 pools, heated; poolside serv. Restaurant 6:30 am–11 pm. Rm serv. Ck-out noon. Coin lndry. Valet serv. Sundries. Exercise equipt; bicycle, stair machine, sauna. Refrigerators. Many private patios, terraces. On 5 acres; lagoons. Cr cds: A, C, D, DS, MC, V.

★★**HOLIDAY INN.** 625 El Camino Real (94301), at University Ave, opp Stanford Univ. 415/328-2800; FAX 415/327-7362. 343 units, 4 story, 6 kits. S $109–$129; D $119–$139; each addl $10; suites $210–$400; kit. units $122–$144; under 18 free; wkend rates. Crib free. TV; cable. Pool. Restaurant 6:30 am–10 pm. Rm serv. Bar 11 am–midnight. Ck-out noon. Meeting rms. Bellhops. Exercise equipt;

bicycles, stair machine. Some bathrm phones, in-rm whirlpools; refrigerators avail. Some private patios, balconies. Cr cds: A, C, D, DS, MC, V.

Hotels

★ ★ ★ GARDEN COURT. *520 Cowper St (94301), downtown. 415/322-9000; res: 800/824-9028; FAX 415/324-3609.* 61 rms, 4 story, 13 suites. S, D $185–$400; each addl $15; suites $200–$400. Crib free. Covered parking $8. TV; cable. Continental bkfst. Restaurant 7 am–11 pm. Bar 11:30 am–midnight. Ck-out noon. Meeting rms. Concierge. Bicycles, tennis racquets, exercise equipt avail. Fireplace, whirlpool, wet bar in some rms. Private patios, balconies. Luxury hotel, elegant furnishings; open-air, flower-laden courtyard reminiscent of a European village square. Cr cds: A, D, MC, V, JCB.

★ ★ ★ HYATT RICKEYS. *4219 El Camino Real (94306). 415/493-8000; FAX 415/424-0836.* 14 rms, 12 with bath, in 2 houses, 6 story. S $115–$155; D $140–$180; suites $185–$380; under 18 free; wknd rates. Crib free. Pet accepted, some restrictions; $100 and $25 per day. TV; cable. Pool; poolside serv. Restaurant 6:30 am–10 pm. Bar 11–1:30 am; dancing. Ck-out noon. Convention facilities. Airport transportation. Health club privileges. Lawn games. Putting green. Fireplace in many suites. Refrigerators avail. Some balconies. On 22 acres with gardens, pond, lagoon. Cr cds: A, C, D, DS, MC, V, JCB.

Inn

✔ ★ COWPER INN. *705 Cowper St (94301), at Forest St. 415/327-4475; FAX 415/329-1703.* 14 rms, 12 with bath, in 2 houses, 2 story. No A/C. S, D $55–$105; each addl $10. Crib free. TV; cable. Complimentary continental bkfst, coffee. Restaurant nearby. Ck-out 11 am, ck-in 1 pm. Restored shingle craftsman-style houses near downtown. Totally nonsmoking. Cr cds: A, MC, V.

Restaurant

★ ★ SCOTT'S SEAFOOD GRILL & BAR. *2300 E Bayshore Rd, US 101 exit Embarcadero E to Bayshore Rd. 415/856-1046.* Hrs: 11:30 am–9:30 pm; Mon to 9 pm; Sat from 5 pm; early-bird dinner Mon–Fri 4–6 pm, Sat 5–6 pm. Closed Sun; some major hols. Res accepted. Bar. A la carte entrees: lunch, dinner $10.95–$23.95. Specializes in seafood. Parking. Cape Cod decor. Family-owned. Cr cds: A, C, D, DS, MC, V.

Pasadena (H-4)

Founded: 1874 **Pop:** 131,591 **Elev:** 865 ft **Area code:** 818

Home of the world-famous Tournament of Roses, Pasadena was first chosen as a health refuge for weary Midwesterners and later as a winter retreat for Eastern millionaires. Today it is a cultural center and scientific and industrial frontier because of its many research, development and engineering industries, including NASA's Jet Propulsion Laboratory. The name "Pasadena" comes from the Chippewa dialect; it means "Crown of the Valley."

What to See and Do

1. **Norton Simon Museum of Art.** 411 W Colorado Blvd. Paintings, tapestries and sculpture from Renaissance to mid-20th century; sculptures of Southeast Asia and India. (Thurs–Sun, mid-afternoon–early evening) Sr citizen rate. Phone 449-6840. ¢¢

2. **Pasadena Historical Society.** 470 W Walnut St. Housed in 18-room Fenyes Estate (1905); contains original furnishings, antiques, paintings and accessories. The mansion gives a glimpse of the elegant lifestyle that existed on Orange Grove Boulevard at the turn of the century. Mansion, Finnish Folk Art Museum and library archives have extensive photo and San Gabriel Valley historic collections. Tours (Thurs–Sun afternoons; closed Aug & major hols) Phone 577-1660. ¢¢

3. **Rose Bowl.** Rose Bowl Dr off Arroyo Blvd between I-210 and CA 134. One of the country's most famous football stadiums, seats 104,000. Home of UCLA Bruins football team; scene of annual Rose Bowl game and other events throughout the year. Phone 577-3106.

4. **Pacific Asia Museum.** 46 N Los Robles Ave. Changing exhibits of traditional and contemporary Asian and Pacific Basin art; Chinese Imperial Palace-style building and Chinese courtyard garden; research library; bookstore. Docent tours (Sun afternoon). (Wed–Sun afternoons) Phone 449-2742. ¢¢

5. **The Gamble House** (1908). 4 Westmoreland Pl. Exemplary of the mature California bungalow designs of American architects Greene & Greene; interiors of teakwood, mahogany, maple and cedar; gardens. Guided tour (Thurs–Sun, afternoons; closed major hols) Sr citizen rate. Phone 793-3334 or 213/681-6427. ¢¢

6. **Angeles National Forest.** N, E & S via US 210, CA 2, 118, 39, I-5. Approx 700,000 acres, including San Gabriel and Sheep Mountain wildernesses. More than 100 camp and picnic grounds; many streams and lakes for fishing; hiking, winter sports. Contact Office of Information, 701 N Santa Anita Ave, Arcadia 91006; 574-5200. Recreation use fee is charged for some activities, also some campsites. **Free.** Also here is

Crystal Lake Recreation Area. Fishing. Nature, hiking trails. Picnicking, store. Tent & trailer camping (fee). Amphitheater programs (summer). Visitors Center has maps and interpretive materials (Sat, Sun). Long trailers (over 22 ft) and recreational vehicles not recommended (steep roads). Phone 910-1149.

(For further information contact the Convention & Visitors Bureau, 171 S Los Robles, 91101; 795-9311.)

Annual Event

Tournament of Roses. Spectacular floral parade on Colorado Blvd attracts more than a million people. Afternoon capped at the Rose Bowl. Special tournament events during preceding wk. Phone 449-ROSE. Jan 1.

Special Event

World Cup 94. Rose Bowl. (Also see LOS ANGELES). Mid-June–mid-July.

(See Claremont, Glendale, Los Angeles Area, Pomona, San Marino)

Motels

(Rates are usually higher late Dec–early Jan, Rose Parade and Festival)

✔ ★ BEST WESTERN COLORADO INN. *2156 E Colorado Blvd (91107). 818/793-9339; FAX 818/568-2731.* 77 rms, 3 story. S $47–$54; D $50–$66; each addl $5; under 12 free. Crib free. TV; cable. Heated pool; whirlpool. Complimentary continental bkfst, coffee. Restaurant nearby. Ck-out noon. Coin lndry. Valet serv. Refrigerators. Some balconies. Cr cds: A, C, D, DS, MC, V.

★ COMFORT INN. *2462 E Colorado Blvd (91107). 818/405-0811; FAX 818/796-0966.* 50 rms, 3 story. S $50–$57; D $55–$58; each addl $5; under 18 free; Rose Parade 3-night min. Crib free. TV; cable, in-rm movies. Heated pool. Complimentary continental bkfst. Ck-out noon.

Coin lndry. Meeting rm. Exercise equipt; bicycles, rowing machine, whirlpool, sauna. Refrigerators. Cr cds: A, C, D, DS, ER, MC, V, JCB.

[D] [≈] [🏃] [⊘] [◎] [SC]

★SAGA. *1633 E Colorado Blvd (91106).* 818/795-0431. 69 rms, 3 story. S $49; D $54–$56; each addl $5; suites $68–$73; under 12 free; Rose Parade 3-day min. Crib free. TV. Heated pool. Complimentary continental bkfst. Ck-out noon. Valet serv. Cr cds: A, D, MC, V.

[≈] [◎] [SC]

Motor Hotel

★★HOLIDAY INN. *303 E Cordova St (91101).* 818/449-4000; FAX 818/584-1390. 320 rms, 5 story. S $89–$108; D $101–$120; each addl $12; suites $225–$275; under 19 free; Rose Parade (4-day min); wkend rates. Pet accepted. TV; cable. Heated pool; poolside serv. Restaurant 6 am–10 pm. Rm serv. Bar 5 pm–2 am. Ck-out noon. Bellhops. Gift shop. Garage. Los Angeles Intl, Hollywood-Burbank airport transportation. Lighted tennis. Some patios, balconies. Cr cds: A, C, D, DS, MC, V, JCB.

[D] [🏊] [⊘] [≈] [⊘] [◎] [SC]

Hotels

★★★DOUBLETREE AT PLAZA LAS FUENTES. *191 N Los Robles Ave (91101).* 818/792-2727; FAX 818/795-7669. 350 rms, 12 story. S $89–$300; D $89–$325; each addl $10; suites $250–$750; under 16 free; wkend rates. Crib free. Garage parking $4; valet $8. TV; cable. Heated pool; poolside serv. Restaurant 6:30 am–11 pm. Rm serv 24 hrs. 2 bars 11–1 am; entertainment. Ck-out noon. Convention facilities. Concierge. Gift shop. Airport transportation. Exercise rm; instructor, weight machine, bicycles, whirlpool, sauna, steam rm. Some balconies. City hall adj. *LUXURY LEVEL.* 25 rms. S $119–$310; D $134–$325; suites $550–$750. Private lounge, honor bar. Complimentary continental bkfst, refreshments, newspaper. Cr cds: A, C, D, DS, ER, MC, V, JCB.

[D] [≈] [🏃] [⊘] [◎] [SC]

★★★HILTON. *150 S Los Robles Ave (91101).* 818/577-1000; FAX 818/584-3148. 291 rms, 13 story. S $110–$160; D $130–$190; each addl $15; suites $175–$450; family, wkend rates; Rose Parade (4-day min). Crib free. Pet accepted, some restrictions; $25. Garage $5/day. TV; cable. Heated pool. Restaurant 6:30 am–11 pm. Bar 11–2 am; entertainment. Ck-out 1 pm. Meeting rms. Concierge. Gift shop. Barber, beauty shop. Garage parking. Exercise equipt; weight machine, stair machine. Minibars; some bathrm phones. Cr cds: A, C, D, DS, ER, MC, V, JCB.

[D] [🏊] [≈] [🏃] [⊘] [◎]

THE RITZ-CARLTON HUNTINGTON, PASADENA. (4-Star 1993; New owners, therefore not rated) *1401 S Oak Knoll Ave (91106), I-210 Lake Ave exit, 2 mi S to Oak Knoll Ave.* 818/568-3900; FAX 818/568-3159. 383 rms, 2–8 story, 26 suites, 6 cottages. S, D $145–$240; suites, cottages $350–$800; under 18 free; special package plans. Crib free. Valet parking $12. TV; cable, in-rm movies. Heated pool; poolside serv. Supervised child's activities (June–Aug). Restaurants 6:30 am–2:30 pm, 5–10 pm. Rm serv 24 hrs. Bar; entertainment. Ck-out noon. Convention facilities. Concierge. Gift shop. Beauty shop. Limo transportation arranged. Lighted tennis, pro. Golf privileges. Exercise rm; instructor, weight machines, bicycles, whirlpool, sauna. Massage. Health club privileges. Lawn games. Bathrm phones, minibars; many balconies. Built in 1907 as a fashionable resort and restored to its turn-of-the-century elegance; contains an abundance of fine art and antiques. Located on 23 acres in the foothills of the spectacular San Gabriel Mountains. Elaborately landscaped grounds include the celebrated Picture Bridge and the Japanese and Horseshoe Gardens, recreated in their original splendor. *LUXURY LEVEL: RITZ-CARLTON CLUB.* 37 units, 7 suites, 2 floors. S $240; suites $500–$2,500. Concierge.

Private lounge, honor bar. Complimentary continental bkfst, refreshments, food presentations 5 times daily. Cr cds: A, C, D, DS, ER, MC, V, JCB.

[D] [🍴] [🏊] [≈] [🏃] [⊘] [◎]

Restaurants

★★BECKHAM PLACE. *77 W Walnut St.* 818/796-3399. Hrs: 11:30 am–2:30 pm, 5:30–9:30 pm; Fri, Sat 5:30–10 pm; Sun 5–9:30 pm. Closed Memorial Day, July 4, Labor Day, Dec 25. Res accepted. Bar 11 am–11:30 pm; Fri & Sat 5 pm–midnight. Semi-a la carte: lunch $6.75–$11.75, dinner $12.75–$18.95. Child's meals. Specializes in prime rib, fresh seafood. Own English trifle. Valet parking. English inn decor; antiques. Cr cds: A, MC, V.

[D]

★★BISTRO 45. *45 S Mentor Ave.* 818/795-2478. Hrs: 11:30 am–2 pm, 6–10 pm; Fri to 11 pm; Sat 5:30–midnight; Sun 5–9 pm. Closed Mon; Jan 1, Thanksgiving, Dec 25. Res accepted. French menu. Bar. A la carte entrees: lunch $5.50–$13, dinner $15–$21. Own pastries. Valet parking. Seasonal menu. Art deco atmosphere. Cr cds: A, C, D, MC, V.

[D]

★★CHRONICLE. *897 Granite Dr.* 818/792-1179. Hrs: 11:30 am–2:30 pm; 5–10 pm; Fri, Sat to 11 pm; early-bird dinner 5–6:30 pm. Closed some major hols. Res accepted. Continental menu. Bar. Wine cellar. Complete meals: lunch $8.50–$13, dinner $13–$24. Specializes in seafood, saddle of lamb, grilled steak. Valet parking. Early San Francisco decor; antiques. Cr cds: A, C, D, DS, MC, V.

[D]

✔★CROCODILE CAFE. *140 S Lake Ave, I-210 Lake Ave S exit.* 818/449-9900. Hrs: 11 am–11 pm; Fri, Sat to midnight; Sun, Mon to 10 pm. Closed Thanksgiving, Dec 25. A la carte entrees: lunch, dinner $2.95–$8.95. Specializes in pizza, oak-grilled hamburgers. Patio dining. Contemporary room open to kitchen. Cr cds: A, C, D, MC, V.

[D]

✔★GRANDVIEW PALACE. *590 S Fair Oaks Ave, at jct California Blvd.* 818/578-9385. Hrs: 11 am–10 pm. Res accepted. Chinese menu. Wine, beer. Semi-a la carte: lunch $4.75–$5.25, dinner $6.25–$12. Specializes in Hunan beef & spicy chicken, Imperial shrimp. Valet parking (wkends). Aquarium with tropical fish. Cr cds: MC, V.

[D]

★★MALDONADO'S. *1202 E Green St.* 818/796-1126. Hrs: 11:30 am–2:30 pm, dinner sittings 6 pm & 9 pm; Sun 5–8 pm. Closed Mon; major hols. Res accepted. French, continental menu. Bar. Wine cellar. Complete meals: lunch $9.50–$15. Semi-a la carte: dinner $21–$28. Specializes in lamb, fresh fish. Own baking. After-dinner entertainment featuring professional singers, musicians from Broadway productions or opera houses; $10 per person. Valet parking. Jacket (dinner). Cr cds: A, MC, V.

[D]

★MI PIACE. *25 E Colorado Blvd.* 818/795-3131. Hrs: 11 am–11 pm; Fri, Sat to 1 am. Closed Thanksgiving, Dec 25. Res accepted. Italian menu. Bar. A la carte entrees: lunch $9–$12, dinner $17–$19. Specializes in traditional Southern Italian dishes. Valet parking. Outdoor dining. Casual trattoria atmosphere. Cr cds: A, MC, V.

[D]

★★MIYAKO. *139 S Los Robles Ave, lower level of Livingstone Hotel.* 818/795-7005 or 213/681-3086. Hrs: 11:30 am–2 pm, 5:30–9:30 pm; Fri, Sat 5:30–10 pm; Sun 4–9 pm. Closed July 4, Thanksgiving, Dec 25. Res accepted. Japanese menu. Bar. Semi-a la carte: lunch $5.95–$11.95, dinner $8.95–$21.95. Child's meals. Specializes in shrimp tempura, beef sukiyaki, teriyaki dishes. Parking. Japanese & Western seating. Boat dinners. Family-owned. Cr cds: A, MC, V.

✔ ★THE PEPPERMILL. *795 E Walnut St.* 818/449-1214. Hrs: 11:30 am–10 pm; Mon to 9:30 pm; Fri, Sat to 10:30 pm; Sun 10:30 am–9:30 pm; early-bird dinner 4–6 pm; Sun brunch 10:30 am–3 pm. Closed Thanksgiving, Dec 25. Res accepted. Continental menu. Bar. Semi-a la carte: lunch $4.95–$11.95, dinner $6.25–$16.95. Sun brunch $7.95–$9.95. Child's meals. Specializes in prime rib, steak, seafood. Salad bar. Parking. Cr cds: A, DS, MC, V.

★ ★★THE RAYMOND. *1250 S Fair Oaks Ave.* 818/441-3136. Hrs: 11:30 am–2:30 pm, 6–9:30 pm; Fri to 10 pm; Sat 5:45–10 pm; Sun 4:30–8 pm; Sat brunch 11 am–2:30 pm; Sun brunch 10 am–2:30 pm. Closed Mon; Jan 1, July 4, Thanksgiving, Dec 25. Res accepted. Bar. Wine cellar. A la carte entrees: lunch $9–$13, dinner $20–$27. Specialties: Long Island roast duckling, grilled king salmon. Classical musician (dinner & Sun brunch). Patio dining. Turn-of-the-century caretaker's cottage; wood floors, lace curtains, fireplace. Totally nonsmoking. Cr cds: A, C, D, MC, V.

D

Paso Robles (G-2)

Pop: 18,600 (est) **Elev:** 721 ft **Area code:** 805 **Zip:** 93446

Franciscan Fathers named this city for the great oak trees in the area, at the southern end of the fertile Salinas River Valley. Lying between mountains on the west and barley and grape fields on the east, Paso Robles is also noted for its almond tree orchards.

What to See and Do

1. **Lake Nacimiento Resort.** 17 mi NW on Lake Nacimiento Dr (G14), off US 101. Swimming, waterskiing; fishing; boating (dock, landing, dry storage, rentals), marina (all yr, daily). Picnicking, lodge, cafe, general store (closed same days as marina). Camping (fee). Park (daily). Phone 238-3256 or 800/323-3839 (CA).

2. **Lake San Antonio Recreation Area.** 28 mi NW off US 101, between Nacimiento & Lockwood on Interlake Rd. Swimming, waterskiing; fishing; boating (marina, launching, rentals). Picnicking, snack bar, grocery; laundromat. Camping; trailer facilities (off-season rates mid-Sept–mid-May). Pets on leash only; fee. Fee for activities. Phone 472-2311. Per vehicle (up to eight persons) ¢¢

3. **Mission San Miguel Arcángel** (1797). 7 mi N via US 101, Mission St in San Miguel. Sixteenth in chain of the 21 Franciscan missions; interior is in excellent condition; frescoes by Esteban Munras and his Native American helpers (1821); museum. Picnic facilities. (Daily; closed Jan 1, Easter, Thanksgiving, Dec 25). (See ANNUAL EVENTS) Donation for self-guided tour. Phone 467-3256.

4. **Wineries.** For a brochure describing many of the wineries in the Paso Robles appellation, tours and tasting rooms, contact the Chamber of Commerce.

(For further information contact the Chamber of Commerce, 1225 Park St; 238-0506.)

Annual Events

Wine Festival. Wine tasting, food, entertainment. 3rd Sat May.

California Mid-State Fair. Rodeo, horse show, amusements, entertainment. Aug.

Mission San Miguel Arcángel Fiesta (see #3). Barbecue. 3rd Sun Sept.

(See Atascadero)

Motels

★ ★★ADELAIDE MOTOR INN. *1215 Ysabel Ave, at 24th St.* 805/238-2770; res: 800/549-7276; FAX 805/238-3497. 67 rms, 1–2 story. May–mid-Oct: S, D $39–$50; each addl $5; lower rates rest of yr. Crib $3. TV; cable. Heated pool. Restaurant adj 7 am–10:30 pm. Bar. Ck-out noon. Coin lndry. Meeting rm. Valet serv. Sundries. Free airport, bus depot transportation. Refrigerators. Picnic tables, grills. Cr cds: A, C, D, DS, MC, V.

★ ★★BEST WESTERN BLACK OAK. *1135 24th St.* 805/238-4740; FAX 805/238-0726. 110 units, 2 story. Mid-May–mid-Oct: S, D $51–$68; each addl $6; suites $96–$107; lower rates rest of yr. Crib $3. TV; cable. Pool; whirlpool, sauna. Playground. Complimentary coffee in rms. Restaurant 6 am–8:30 pm; dining rm 5–10:30 pm. Bar 11 am–midnight. Ck-out noon. Coin lndry. Free local airport transportation 8 am–8 pm. Refrigerators. Picnic table, grills. Cr cds: A, C, D, DS, MC, V.

✔ ★MELODY RANCH. *939 Spring St.* 805/238-3911. 19 rms. S $32–$40; D $38–$44; each addl $2. Crib $2. TV; cable. Heated pool. Complimentary coffee in rms. Restaurant adj 7 am–10 pm. Ck-out noon. Picnic table. Cr cds: A, C, D, MC, V.

Restaurant

★ ★JOSHUA'S. *512 13th St, at Vine.* 805/238-7515. Hrs: 11 am–2:30 pm, 5–9 pm; Fri & Sat to 10 pm; Sun 10 am–2 pm, 5–9 pm; early-bird dinner 3–6 pm; Sun brunch 10 am–2 pm. Res accepted. Bar 11:30 am–11 pm. Semi-a la carte: lunch $4.25–$8.95, dinner $7.95–$21.95. Sun brunch $13.95. Child's meals. Specializes in rack of lamb, fresh seafood, oak-grilled steak. Own dressings. Parking. Patio dining. Local wines. Converted church. Cr cds: MC, V.

D

Pebble Beach (F-1)

Pop: 5,000 (est) **Elev:** 0–37 ft **Area code:** 408 **Zip:** 93953

Pebble Beach is noted for its scenic beauty, the palatial houses of its residents and the Pebble Beach golf courses, where the annual National Pro-Amateur Golf Championship is held (see MONTEREY).

(See Carmel, Monterey, Pacific Grove)

Resorts

★ ★ ★ ★INN & LINKS AT SPANISH BAY. *(Box 1418) 2700 Seventeen Mile Dr.* 408/647-7500; res: 800/654-9300; FAX 408/647-7443. 270 units, 4 story. S, D $245–$350; suites $550–$1,650; children free; golf, tennis plans. Service charge $17 per day per rm. Crib free. TV; cable. Heated pool; whirlpool, sauna, poolside serv. Dining rm 6:30 am–10 pm (also see BAY CLUB). Box lunches. Picnics. Rm serv 24 hrs. Bar 10–1 am. Ck-out noon, ck-in 4 pm. Landry facility. Package store. Convention facilities. Concierge. Shops, specialty stores. Free valet parking. Free airport transportation. Lighted tennis. 72-hole golf, greens fee $135–$225 (incl cart), pro, putting green, driving range. Private beach. Bicycle rentals. Equestrian center. Hiking trails. Health club privileges. Minibars. Fireplaces. Private patios, balconies. Picnic tables, grills. Located on 236 acres, surrounded by golf; guests enjoy preferred tee times at Pebble Beach's prestigious golf courses. Complimentary shuttle service to the lodge. Cr cds: A, C, D, MC, V.

★ ★ ★THE LODGE AT PEBBLE BEACH. *3 mi N of Carmel on Seventeen Mile Dr.* 408/624-3811; FAX 408/624-6357. 161 rms, 1–3 story. S, D $295–$450; suites $875–$1,800; under 18 free. Service charge $15 per day per rm. Crib free. TV; cable. Heated pool; wading pool, poolside serv, lifeguard in summer. Supervised child's activities (June–Aug). Afternoon tea. Restaurant (see CLUB XIX). Box lunches, snacks. Rm serv 24 hrs. Bar 11–1 am. Ck-out noon, ck-in 4 pm. Convention facilities. Valet serv. Concierge. Shopping arcade; bank, post office. Barber, beauty shop. Valet parking. Free airport transportation. Tennis. 3 golf courses, par-3 golf, greens fee $125–$225, putting green, 2 driving ranges. Private beach. Exercise equipt; weights, bicycles, whirlpool, sauna, steam rm. Massage. Refrigerators, honor bars, fireplaces; some wet bars. Private patios, balconies. Rms overlook beach, golf course. Equestrian center with 34 mi of trails. Lavish resort on Carmel Bay. Extensive grounds; shuttle service throughout resort and to Spanish Bay. Cr cds: A, C, D, MC, V.

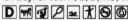

Restaurants

★ ★ ★ **BAY CLUB.** *(See Inn & Links at Spanish Bay Resort)* 408/647-7500. Hrs: 6–10 pm. Res accepted. Northern Italian menu. Bar 2 pm–1 am. Wine cellar. A la carte entrees: dinner $18–$40. *Prix fixe:* 4-course dinner $40; with wine $60. Specializes in fresh seafood, pasta. Own baking, pasta. Entertainment. Valet parking. Ocean view. Cr cds: A, C, D, MC, V.

★ ★ **CLUB XIX.** *(See The Lodge at Pebble Beach Resort)* 408/624-3811. Hrs: 11:30 am–3:30 pm, 6:30–10:30 pm. Res accepted. French country menu. Bar. Wine cellar. A la carte entrees: lunch $12–$25, dinner $22–$35. Specializes in terrine of seared duck foie gras, petite abalone, saffron pasta, rack of lamb. Own baking. Parking. Outdoor dining. English country decor. Overlooks ocean, golf course. Jacket (dinner). Cr cds: A, C, D, MC, V.

Petaluma (D-1)

Pop: 43,184 **Elev:** 12 ft **Area code:** 707 **Zip:** 94952

What to See and Do

1. **Petaluma Adobe State Historic Park.** 3325 Adobe Rd, 3 mi E of US 101 on CA 116. Restored adobe ranch house, built 1834-45 for General M. G. Vallejo, combines Monterey Colonial style with the traditional Spanish-Mexican plan. (Daily; closed Jan 1, Thanksgiving, Dec 25) ¢

2. **Petaluma Historical Library & Museum.** 20 Fourth St. Built with a grant from Andrew Carnegie in 1906, the museum contains one of California's only free standing glass domes. Permanent and changing exhibits of Petaluma history. (Thurs–Mon; closed major hols) Phone 778-4398. **Free.**

3. **The Great Petaluma Mill.** 6 Petaluma Blvd N. Refurbished historic grain mill housing 30 shops and two restaurants intermingled with remnants of the riverboat era of the building. (Daily; closed Dec 25) Phone 762-1149.

4. **Sightseeing Cruise.** 255 Weller St. 300-passenger paddlewheeler *Petaluma Queen* offers several types of cruises, including brunch, dinner/dance, sunset. (Wed–Sun) Phone 762-2100. ¢¢¢¢–¢¢¢¢¢

5. **Industrial tours.**

   California Cooperative Creamery and Store. 711 Western Ave, at Baker St. Cheese factory; tours every hour (late morning–early afternoon). Video. (Daily exc Sun; closed Jan 1, Thanksgiving, Dec 25) Phone 778-1234. **Free.**

Marin French Cheese Company. 7500 Red Hill Rd, ¼ mi S of jct Novato Blvd & Petaluma-Point Reyes Rd. Manufacturer of soft ripening cheeses, including Camembert, Brie, Breakfast and Schloss. Guided tours (daily; closed Jan 1, Thanksgiving, Dec 25). Phone 762-6001. **Free.**

(For further information contact the Chamber of Commerce, 215 Howard St; 762-2785.)

Annual Events

Sonoma-Marin Fair. Agricultural fair, carnival, rodeo, entertainment. 5 days late June.

World Wrist Wrestling Championships. Veteran's Memorial Bldg, 1094 Petaluma Blvd S. 2nd Sat Oct.

(See Guerneville, Napa, Santa Rosa, Sonoma)

Motel

★ ★ **QUALITY INN.** 5100 Montero Way, US 101 Penngrove exit. 707/664-1155; FAX 707/664-8566. 110 rms, 2 story, 4 suites. S $59–$89; D $59–$119; each addl $5; suites $99–$140; under 18 free. Crib $5. TV; cable, in-rm movies avail. Heated pool; whirlpool, sauna. Complimentary continental bkfst. Restaurant adj 5:30 am–midnight. Ck-out noon. Coin lndry. Valet serv. Refrigerators. Cr cds: A, C, D, DS, ER, MC, V, JCB.

Restaurants

★ **DE SCHMIRE.** 304 Bodega Ave. 707/762-1901. Hrs: 5:30–10 pm; Sun to 9 pm. Closed most major hols. Res accepted. No A/C. Continental menu. Wine, beer. Complete meals: dinner $16–$19. Child's meals. Specialties: ahi baked in nut crust, chicken Zanzibar, chicken Dijonaise. Parking. European bistro atmosphere; open kitchen. Eclectic mix of European, California, Asian cuisine. No cr cds accepted.

✔ ★ **STEAMER GOLD LANDING.** 1 Water St. 707/763-6876. Hrs: 11:30 am–9 pm; Fri & Sat to 10:30 pm; Sun 5–9 pm; Sun brunch 10:30 am–5 pm. Closed Thanksgiving, Dec 25. Res accepted. Semi-a la carte: lunch $6.75–$10.95, dinner $8.95–$16. Sun champagne brunch $7.95–$11.50. Specializes in seafood, corned beef, prime rib. Entertainment. Parking. Outdoor dining. Located in historic Great Petaluma Mill on the Petaluma River. Cr cds: A, MC, V.

Pine Valley (K-5)

Settled: 1869 **Pop:** 1,297 **Elev:** 3,736 ft **Area code:** 619 **Zip:** 92062

What to See and Do

Cleveland National Forest. Surrounds town. Nearly 420,000 acres; dense chaparral environment with conifers at higher levels, tree-like manzanitas, Palomar Observatory (see ESCONDIDO). Fishing. Hiking, riding, nature trails, guided walks. Picnicking. Camping. Includes Laguna Mountain Recreation Area, 10 mi NE of I-8 on County S1. Use fees are charged at developed recreation sites. Contact Forest Supervisor, 10845 Rancho Bernardo Rd, San Diego, 92127-2107; 673-6180.

(For accommodations see El Cajon, San Diego)

Pinnacles National Monument (F-2)

(35 mi S of Hollister, off CA 25 or 35 mi NE of King City, off US 101; also 11 mi E of Soledad, off US 101)

Geologic activity formed a large volcano 23 million years ago—Pinnacles is the eroded remnant. The volcano formed where two plates of the earth's crust grind together along the San Andreas fault; one portion has remained near the point of origin, while the other has shifted 195 miles northward. The former section now lies between Gorman and Lancaster; the latter section, traveling at a rate of two centimeters a year, is the Pinnacles—an area of three square miles eroded by wind, rain, heat, frost and chemical action. Also here are the canyons of Bear Gulch and Chalone Creek, containing talus caves or "covered canyons," formed by large blocks of rock that have slipped from the steep walls. In all, the monument covers 25 square miles, is four miles wide and seven miles long. It has a variety of bird life, including the prairie falcon, turkey vulture and golden eagle.

Hiking is the main activity, with well-defined trails (some strenuous). High Peaks Trail follows the spectacular cliffs and pinnacles; the North Chalone Peak Trail reaches 3,305 feet, the highest point in the monument. Trails in the caves area are shorter but equally interesting.

There are picnic areas with barbecue grills on both the east and west sides. Visitors must bring their own fuel. No wood fires permitted during high fire season (usually June–Oct). Pets on leash only; not permitted on trails. There is limited camping on west side (June–January only) and there is a private campground outside east entrance (phone 408/389-4462). A service station and camper store are also available there. Interpretive programs on east side (mid-Feb–Memorial Day, wkends). There is no through road; access to the east entrance is via Hollister, off CA 25 or via King City, off US 101. The west entrance is reached via Soledad, off US 101. Visitor center on east side. For campground and visitor information phone 408/389-4485. Golden Eagle Passport (see INTRODUCTION). Per vehicle ¢¢

(For accommodations see King City, Salinas)

Pismo Beach (G-2)

Pop: 7,669 **Elev:** 33 ft **Area code:** 805 **Zip:** 93449

This town is famous for its 23 miles of scenic beach. Ocean fishing, dunes, swimming, surfing, diving, golf, horseback riding and camping make the area popular with vacationers. Pismo Beach is also in a growing wine region. It is the last Pacific oceanfront community where autos can still be driven on the beach (access ramps are at two locations along the beach). A more dramatic and rugged coastline is found at Shell Beach, to the north, which has been incorporated into Pismo Beach.

What to See and Do

1. **Monarch Butterfly Grove.** Pismo State Beach, 1 mi S via CA 1, North Beach Campground exit. The state's largest winter site for Monarch butterflies; they can be seen in the grove located at the North Beach Campground (Nov–March, daily; dependent on butterfly migration). Phone 489-1869. Campground parking per vehicle ¢¢¢

2. **Pismo Dunes State Vehicular Recreation Area.** 2 mi S via CA 1, Pier Ave exit. Operated by the state park system to provide location for off-highway vehicle use (vehicle access to the beach is not common in California). (Daily) Sr citizen rate. Phone 473-7220. Per car ¢¢

3. **Lopez Recreational Area.** 12 mi SE via US 101, Grand Ave exit. On lake created by Lopez Dam. Swimming, waterskiing, water slide,

windsurfing; fishing; boating. Hiking trail. Picnicking. Primitive camping, tent & trailer sites (hookups, dump station; fee). Summer campfire programs, boat tours. Phone 489-2095. Day use, per vehicle ¢¢

4. **Wineries of the Edna Valley & Arroyo Grande Valley.** Several wineries, many with public tasting rms and offering tours, may be found along the county roads of Edna Valley and Arroyo Grande Valley; approx 5–8 mi NE and SE via CA 227 off US 101. Many are free; fee at some. Contact the Chamber of Commerce for winery maps; phone 541-5868.

(For further information contact the Convention & Visitors Bureau, 581 Dolliver St; 773-4382 or 800/443-7778 within CA.)

(See San Luis Obispo, Santa Maria)

Motels

★★★**SEA CREST.** *2241 Price St. 805/773-4608; res: 800/782-8400 (CA).* 160 rms, 4 story. Memorial Day–Labor Day: S, D $75–$95; each addl $5; suites $105–$135; lower rates rest of yr. Crib $5. TV; cable. Heated pool; whirlpools. Coffee in rms. Restaurant 8 am–10 pm. Ck-out noon. Coin lndry. Meeting rms. Lawn games. Refrigerators. Private patios, balconies. Picnic tables, grills. On beach; ocean view from some rms, walkway to the beach. Sun deck. Cr cds: A, C, D, DS, MC, V, JCB.

✔★★**SEA GYPSY.** *1020 Cypress, at Wadsworth St. 805/773-1801; res: 800/592-5923; FAX 805/773-9286.* 77 units, 3 story. S $35–$99; D $40–$99; each addl $10; suites $70–$176; lower rates winter. Crib free. TV; cable. Heated pool; whirlpool. Complimentary morning coffee in lobby. Ck-out noon. Coin lndry. Refrigerators. Private patios, balconies. On ocean, sand beach. Cr cds: A, DS, MC, V.

Motor Hotels

★★**BEST WESTERN SHORE CLIFF LODGE.** *2555 Price St. 805/773-4671; FAX 805/773-2341.* 99 units, 2–3 story, 9 kits. May–Sept: S, D $95–$105; each addl $10; suites $210; kit. units $105; under 18 free; lower rates rest of yr. Crib free. TV; cable. Heated pool; whirlpool; sauna. Coffee in rms. Restaurant 7 am–9 pm; wknds to 10 pm. Rm serv. Bar 11–2 am; entertainment, dancing Thurs–Sun. Ck-out 11 am. Meeting rms. Lighted tennis. Private patios, balconies with ocean view. Spiral staircase to beach. Cr cds: A, C, D, DS, ER, MC, V, JCB.

✔★★★**KON TIKI INN.** *1621 Price St. 805/773-4833; FAX 805/773-6541.* 86 rms, 3–4 story. Late Mar–late Sept: S, D $74–$88; each addl $14; lower rates rest of yr. Crib $7. TV; cable. Heated pool. Restaurant 7 am–9 pm. Bar 10–midnight; entertainment, dancing. Ck-out noon. Coin lndry. Meeting rm. Lighted tennis. Exercise equipt; weights, stair machine, whirlpools, sauna. Refrigerators; some fireplaces. Private patios, balconies. On ocean; stairway to beach. Cr cds: A, MC, V.

★★★**QUALITY SUITES.** *651 Five Cities Dr. 805/773-3773; FAX 805/773-5177.* 133 suites, 2 story. Apr–mid-Sept: S, D $89–$118; each addl $9; under 18 free; lower rates rest of yr. Crib free. TV; cable, in-rm movies. Heated pool; wading pool, whirlpool. Complimentary full bkfst. Ck-out noon. Coin lndry. Meeting rms. Sundries. Gift shop. Putting green. Refrigerators. Cr cds: A, C, D, DS, ER, MC, V, JCB.

★★**SANDCASTLE INN.** *100 Stimson Ave, at beach. 805/773-2422; res: 800/822-6606; FAX 805/773-0771.* 59 rms, 3 story. Memorial Day–Sept: S, D $100–$155; suites $175–$250; under 12 free; lower rates rest of yr. Crib free. TV; cable, in-rm movies. Complimentary continental bkfst, coffee. Ck-out noon. Whirlpool. Refrigerators; some fireplaces. Patios, balconies. On beach. Cr cds: A, C, D, DS, MC, V, JCB.

★ ★ ★**SEA VENTURE.** *100 Ocean View Ave. 805/773-4994; res: 800/237-7804 (exc CA), 800/662-5545 (CA); FAX 805/773-4693.* 52 rms, 3 story. S, D $89–$178; up to 2 addl free. Crib $15. TV; cable. Coffee in rms. Complimentary continental bkfst. Restaurant 4–10 pm. Rm serv. Bar. Ck-out noon. Bathrm phones, refrigerators, wet bars. Some private balconies with whirlpools. On ocean; panoramic view. Cr cds: A, C, D, DS, MC, V.

★ ★ ★**SPYGLASS INN.** *2705 Spyglass Dr. 805/773-4855; res: 800/824-2612 (CA); FAX 805/773-5298.* 82 rms, 1–2 story. S, D $70–$125; each addl $10; suites, kit. units $120–$150; under 12 free; higher rates wkends. TV; cable, in-rm movies. Pool; whirlpool. Coffee in rms. Restaurant 7 am–2 pm, 4–9:30 pm. Bar 10–2 am; entertainment, dancing Thurs–Sat. Ck-out noon. Meeting rm. Miniature golf. Many private patios, balconies with ocean view. Cr cds: A, C, D, DS, ER, MC, V, JCB.

Hotel

★ ★ ★**THE CLIFFS AT SHELL BEACH.** *2757 Shell Beach Rd. 805/773-5000; res: 800/826-5838 (exc CA), 800/826-7827 (CA); FAX 805/773-0764.* 166 rms, 5 story, 27 suites. S, D $115–$185; suites $170–$310; under 13 free; wkend packages; golf plans. Crib free. TV; cable, in-rm movies. Heated pool; poolside serv. Coffee in rms. Restaurant 7 am–10 pm. Bar 10–2 am; entertainment, dancing. Ck-out noon. Coin lndry. Meeting rms. Gift shop. Valet parking. Free airport, RR station, bus depot transportation. Exercise rm; instructor, weight machine, bicycles, whirlpool, sauna. Lawn games. Bathrm phones; some refrigerators. Whirlpool in suites. Private patios, balconies. On cliff overlooking beach. Cr cds: A, C, D, DS, MC, V, JCB.

Restaurants

★ ★**F. McLINTOCKS.** *750 Mattie Rd. 805/773-1892.* Hrs: 11:30 am–10 pm; Sun 9 am–9:30 pm; early-bird dinner Mon–Fri 3–6 pm, Sat & Sun 2–4 pm; Sun brunch 9 am–1:30 pm. Closed Jan 1, Thanksgiving, Dec 24, 25. Res accepted Sun–Thurs. Bar. Semi-a la carte: lunch $4.35–$11.25. Complete meals: dinner $7.95–$28.50. Sun brunch $9.95–$14.10. Child's meals. Specializes in steak, seafood, oak pit barbecue. Guitarist (seasonal). Parking. Unique ranch-era decor includes 1921 Ford Model T truck, 6-foot-high stuffed buffalo, old farm implements, blacksmith & branding iron gear. Cr cds: DS, MC, V.

D

✔ ★ ★**ROSA'S.** *491 Price St. 805/773-0551.* Hrs: 11:30 am–2 pm, 4–10 pm; Fri to 10:30 pm; Sat 4–10:30 pm; Sun 4–10 pm. Closed Thanksgiving, Dec 25. Res accepted. Italian menu. Wine, beer. Semi-a la carte: lunch $2.95–$6.95, dinner $6.25–$12.95. Child's meals. Specializes in pasta, seafood, chicken, veal. Parking. Extensive floral display. Cr cds: A, DS, MC, V.

D

Placerville (D-2)

Founded: 1848 **Pop:** 8,355 **Elev:** 1,866 ft **Area code:** 916 **Zip:** 95667

This one-time rough-and-tough gold town was first known as Dry Diggin's (because the gravel had to be carried to water to be washed for gold) and later as Hangtown (because of the number of hangings necessary to keep law and order). At one time the town rivaled San Francisco and nurtured three notables: Mark Hopkins, railroad magnate; Philip D. Armour, meat-packing magnate; and John Studebaker,

automobile magnate. A few mines still function, but lumbering, agriculture and recreation are the main industries.

What to See and Do

1. **Gold Bug Mine.** In Hangtown's Gold Bug Park. Municipally owned double-shaft gold mine with exposed vein; restored gold stampmill. Picnic area. Guided tours avail (res required). (May–mid-Sept, daily; mid-Mar–Apr & mid-Sept–Nov, wkends) Phone 642-5232. ¢

2. **El Dorado County Historical Museum.** 100 Placerville Dr. Displays and exhibits of early Gold Rush days, when Miwok, Maidu and Washoe Indians inhabited the area. (Wed–Sat; closed hols) Phone 621-5865. **Free.**

3. **Marshall Gold Discovery State Historic Park.** 8 mi NW on CA 49 in Coloma. Marks place where James Marshall found flecks of gold in tailrace of Sutter's Mill in January of 1848. By the next year more than $10 million in gold had been taken from the American River's South Fork. Park includes Gold Discovery Museum (daily; closed Jan 1, Thanksgiving, Dec 25), Marshall's cabin and monument where he is buried, Thomas House Museum, operating replica of Sutter's mill, blacksmith shop and several other buildings. Fishing. Nature and hiking trails. Picnicking, concession. Park (daily). Sr citizen rate. Phone 622-3470. Per vehicle ¢¢

4. **Eldorado National Forest.** 25 mi E via US 50. Approx 786,000 acres. Includes the 105,364-acre Mokelumne Wilderness, located between CA 4 and CA 88, and the popular 63,475-acre Desolation Wilderness, located immediately west of Lake Tahoe. Campgrounds have varying fees and facilities; all are closed in winter. Contact the Information Center, 3070 Camino Heights Dr, Camino 95709; 644-6048.

(For further information contact the El Dorado County Chamber of Commerce, 542 Main St; 621-5885.)

Annual Events

Wagon Train Week. Celebrations each night along wagon train trek (US 50) from Nevada to Placerville. Sat celebrations at fairgrounds; parade on Sun. Mid-June.

El Dorado County Fair. Fairgrounds, SW on US 50. 1st wkend Aug.

(See Auburn, Sacramento)

Motel

★ ★**BEST WESTERN PLACERVILLE INN.** *6850 Greenleaf Dr, S of US 50 at Missouri Flat Rd. 916/622-9100; FAX 916/622-9376.* 105 rms, 3 story. No elvtr. S $59–$69; D $71–$81; each addl $6; suites $130; under 12 free. Crib free. Pet accepted; $10. TV; cable. Heated pool; whirlpool. Coffee in rms; complimentary coffee in lobby. Restaurant adj open 24 hrs. Ck-out 11 am. Meeting rms. Some patios, balconies. Cr cds: A, C, D, DS, MC, V.

Restaurant

✔ ★**LILLIAN RUSSELL ROOM.** *In Sam's Town, 3333 Coach Lane, W on US 50 to Cameron Park exit. 916/677-2273 or 933-1671.* Hrs: 7 am–10 pm; Fri & Sat to 11 pm. Closed Dec 25. Res accepted. Bar 8 am–midnight, Fri, Sat to 2 am. Semi-a la carte: bkfst $3.25–$6.95, lunch $3.25–$7.25, dinner $7.25–$14.95. Child's meals. Specializes in prime rib, châteaubriand. Parking. Gay 90s decor, paintings, antiques. Old-fashioned general store, 19th-century museum & Sam's Town-Honky Tonk Room cafeteria in building; entertainment Fri–Sun. Family-owned. Cr cds: A, MC, V.

Pleasanton *

Settled: 1851 **Pop:** 50,553 **Elev:** 352 ft **Area code:** 510 **Zip:** 94566
4 mi W of Livermore (E-2) on I-580.

Named for the friend of an early settler, Pleasanton was once called "the most desperate town in the West," for its many bandits and desperados. Phoebe Apperson Hearst founded the PTA in Pleasanton.

What to See and Do

1. **Eugene O'Neill National Historic Site.** 7 mi W of I-680, near Danville. Winner of the Nobel Prize and four Pulitzer Prizes, O'Neill wrote some of his finest works at Tao House, including the autobiographical *Long Day's Journey Into Night* and *A Moon For the Misbegotten*. A blend of Chinese philosophy and Spanish-style architecture, Tao House was to be O'Neill's "final home and harbor." The house commands a spectacular view of the hills and orchards of the San Ramon Valley and Mt Diablo. Tours (Wed–Sun, morning and afternoon; by res only). Shuttle service provided from Danville. Contact Superintendent, PO Box 280, Danville 94526; 838-0249.   **Free.**

2. **Alameda County Fairgrounds.** 4501 Pleasanton Ave, I-680 at Bernal Ave. Exhibit area; 9-hole golf course. Events and activities. Oldest racetrack west of the Mississippi River. Thoroughbred racing during county fair (see ANNUAL EVENT); satellite-broadcast races year-round. Phone 426-7600.

3. **Behring Auto Museum.** 7 mi N on I-680 to Crow Canyon Rd in San Ramon, then 4 mi E to Camino Tassajara, then 1 blk E, turn left on Blackhawk Plaza Dr. Display of 110 classic and rare automobiles, many custom-built. Modern sculpture building; library. (Daily exc Mon) Sr citizen rate. Phone 736-2277.   ¢¢;   Adj is

   Berkeley Museum of Art, Science and Culture. Houses university collections of anthropology, paleontology and changing art exhibits. (Daily exc Mon) Combination ticket with Auto Museum avail   ¢¢¢

(For further information contact the Convention & Visitors Bureau, 450 Main St; 846-8910.)

Annual Event

Alameda County Fair. Fairgrounds, jct I-680 & I-580, Bernal Ave exit. Horse racing, exhibitions, carnival, theatrical shows. Phone 426-7600. Late June–mid-July.

(See Fremont, Hayward, Livermore, Oakland)

Motel

★ ★ ★**COURTYARD BY MARRIOTT.** 5059 Hopyard Rd. 510/463-1414; FAX 510/463-0113. 145 rms, 3 story, 14 suites. S $86; D $96; each addl (after 4th person) $10; suites $101–$111; under 18 free; wkly, wkend rates. Crib free. TV; cable. Heated pool. Complimentary coffee in rms. Restaurant 7:30 am–1 pm; wkends 6:30–10 am. Bar 5–11 pm. Ck-out 1 pm. Coin lndry. Meeting rms. Valet serv. Sundries. Exercise equipt; weight machine, bicycles, whirlpool. Refrigerator in suites. Balconies. Cr cds: A, C, D, DS, MC, V.

⬛ ⬛ ⬛ ⬛ ⬛ ⬛ SC

Hotels

★ ★**DOUBLETREE CLUB.** 5990 Stoneridge Mall Rd, just S of I-580, Foothill Rd exit. 510/463-3330; FAX 510/463-3330, ext 644. 171 rms, 6 story. S $87–$115; D $97–$125; each addl $10; suites $135–$170; under 12 free; wkend, hol rates. Pet accepted, some restrictions; $15 non-refundable. TV; cable. Heated pool (summer). Complimentary full bkfst, evening refreshments. Bar. Ck-out 1 pm. Meeting

rms. Exercise equipt; weights, bicycles, sauna. Refrigerator in suites. Cr cds: A, C, D, DS, ER, MC, V, JCB.

⬛ ⬛ ⬛ ⬛ ⬛ ⬛ ⬛ SC

★ ★ ★**HILTON AT THE CLUB.** 7050 Johnson Dr, at jct I-580, I-680, Hopyard exit off I-580. 510/463-8000; FAX 510/463-3801. 300 rms, 5 story. S, D $69–$119; each addl $10; suites $200–$300; family, wkend rates. Crib free. Pet accepted, some restrictions; $15. TV; cable. Heated pool; poolside serv. Supervised child's activities. Restaurant 6 am–11 pm. Bar 11–1:30 am. Ck-out noon. Meeting rms. Gift shop. Barber, beauty shop. Valet parking. Indoor tennis, pro. Exercise rm; instructor, weights, bicycles, sauna. Bathrm phones. *LUXURY LEVEL:* **EXECUTIVE LEVEL.** 30 rms, 1 suite. S, D $125; suite $400. Private lounge. Complimentary newspaper.
Cr cds: A, C, D, DS, ER, MC, V, JCB.

⬛ ⬛ ⬛ ⬛ ⬛ ⬛ ⬛ ⬛ SC

✔ ★ ★ ★**HOLIDAY INN.** 11950 Dublin Canyon Rd, just W of jct I-580, I-680, Foothill Rd exit. 510/847-6000; FAX 510/463-2585. 244 rms, 6 story. S $76–$95; D $86–$105; each addl $10; suites $200–$300; under 18 free; wkend rates. Crib free. Pet accepted, some restrictions. TV; cable, in-rm movies avail. Heated pool. Restaurant 6 am–10 pm. Bar noon–midnight. Ck-out noon. Coin lndry. Convention facilities. Gift shop. Exercise equipt; weight machine, bicycle, whirlpool. Refrigerators avail. Cr cds: A, C, D, DS, MC, V, JCB.

⬛ ⬛ ⬛ ⬛ ⬛ ⬛ SC

★ ★ ★**SHERATON INN.** 5115 Hopyard Rd. 510/460-8800; FAX 510/847-9455. 214 units, 2 story. S $85–$115; D $95–$125; each addl $10; suites $125–$225; under 17 free. Crib free. TV; cable. Pool; whirlpool, poolside serv. Restaurant 6:30 am–10 pm. Bar 11–1 am; dancing Tues–Sat. Ck-out 1 pm. Meeting rms. Some refrigerators. Private patios, balconies. Atrium lobby; stained glass. Garden setting; lagoon. Cr cds: A, C, D, DS, MC, V.

⬛ ⬛ ⬛ ⬛ SC

Restaurant

★**PLEASANTON HOTEL.** 855 Main St. 510/846-8106. Hrs: 11:30 am–2 pm, 5–9 pm; Fri, Sat to 10 pm; Sun brunch to 2 pm. Closed Memorial Day, Labor Day & Dec 25. Res accepted. Bar. A la carte entrees: lunch $4.95–$10.95, dinner $8.95–$16.95. Sun brunch $15.95. Specializes in fresh fish, pasta, veal. Band Wed–Sun; big band Sun. Parking. Patio dining. Victorian dining room in 1851 hotel that was once a stagecoach stop and gambling house. Cr cds: A, D, DS, MC, V.

⬛

Pomona (H-4)

Pop: 131,723 **Elev:** 850 ft **Area code:** 909

What to See and Do

1. **California State Polytechnic University, Pomona** (1938). (19,000 students) 3801 W Temple Ave. Kellogg West Continuing Education Center has conference facilities with observation deck (daily). Phone 869-7659. On campus is the renowned

   Kellogg Arabian Horse Center. Also houses Equine Research Center. One-hour performances (Oct–June, 1st Sun each month; no shows Easter). Stable (daily; free). Phone 869-2224. Shows   ¢

2. **Adobe de Palomares** (1850–54). 491 E Arrow Hwy, 1 mi N on Garey Ave off San Bernardino Frwy. Grounds, furnished 13-room adobe house illustrate romantic "Days of the Dons." Indian artifacts, baskets. (Sun or by appt; closed major hols) Phone 623-2198. **Free.**

(For further information contact the Chamber of Commerce, 363 S Park Ave, Suite 104, 91766; 622-1256.)

Annual Event

Los Angeles County Fair. Fairplex, 1101 W McKinley Ave. Thoroughbred racing, carnival, exhibits, free stage shows, food booths, monorail. Contact PO Box 2250, 91769; 623-3111. Mid-Sept–early Oct.

(See Claremont, Ontario, Pasadena)

Motor Hotel

★ ★ ★**SHILO INN HILLTOP SUITES.** *3101 Temple Ave (91768). 909/598-7666; FAX 909/598-5654.* 130 suites, 3 story. Suites $99–$119; each addl $10; under 12 free. Crib $5. TV; cable, in-rm movies. Heated pool; poolside serv. Complimentary continental bkfst. Restaurant 6 am–11 pm. Rm serv. Bar 11–2 am; entertainment Fri & Sat. Ck-out noon. Coin lndry. Meeting rms. Bellhops. Valet serv. Sundries. Airport transportation. Exercise equipt; weight machine, bicycle, whirlpool, sauna, steam rm. Bathrm phones, refrigerators, wet bars. Cr cds: A, C, D, DS, ER, MC, V, JCB.

Hotel

★**RADISSON INN DIAMOND BAR** (formerly Days Hotel). *(21725 E Gateway Dr, Diamond Bar 91765) CA 57 Grand Ave exit to Golden Springs Dr, then SW to E Gateway Dr. 909/860-5440; FAX 909/860-8224.* 175 rms, 6 story. S $89–$99; D $99–$109; each addl $10; suites $110–$120; under 12 free. TV; cable. Heated pool; whirlpool, poolside serv. Restaurant 6 am–noon, 5–10 pm. Bar. Ck-out noon. Meeting rms. Airport transportation. Some balconies. Cr cds: A, C, D, DS, ER, MC, V.

Restaurant

★ ★**D'ANTONIO'S.** *(808 N Diamond Bar Blvd, Diamond Bar) CA 57 exit Temple Ave E, then S on Diamond Bar Blvd. 909/860-3663.* Hrs: 11 am–10 pm; Fri to 11 pm; Sat noon–11 pm; Sun noon–10 pm. Closed some major hols. Res accepted. Italian menu. Wine, beer. Semi-a la carte: lunch $5.65–$15.95, dinner $6.35–$22.95. Child's meals. Specializes in fresh pasta, homemade pizza, veal. Parking. Cr cds: A, C, D, MC, V.

Porterville (G-3)

Pop: 29,563 **Elev:** 459 ft **Area code:** 209 **Zip:** 93257

What to See and Do

Sequoia National Forest. 20 mi E via CA 190. Precipitous canyons, spectacular views of the Sierra Nevada and more than 30 groves of giant sequoias on 1,123,685 acres. Largest tree of any National Forest is here; the Boole Tree stands 269 feet and is 90 feet in circumference. (The General Sherman Tree in Sequoia National Park is a few feet taller). The forest contains the 306,000-acre Golden Trout, 94,695-acre Dome Land, 10,500-acre Jennie Lake, 63,000-acre South Sierra and the 45,000-acre Monarch wilderness areas. Activities include swimming; lake and stream fishing for trout, hunting; whitewater rafting in the Kern and Kings rivers. Hiking, riding and backpacking trails in wilderness areas (permit required). Cross-country skiing, snowshoeing and snowmobiling in winter. Picnicking. Camping (no reservations) at 45 areas; 14-day/month limit; no electric hookups or other utility connections; campgrounds (fees vary). Contact Forest Supervisor, 900 W Grand Ave; 784-1500.

Quincy (C-3)

Pop: 4,271 **Elev:** 3,432 ft **Area code:** 916 **Zip:** 95971

What to See and Do

1. **Plumas National Forest.** Beautiful 1½ million-acre forest in Feather River Country. Feather Falls (640-ft drop), sixth highest waterfall in US, accessible by 3.5-mile trail (see OROVILLE). CA 70, which runs approximately 150 miles through the forest, is a designated National Scenic Byway. Groomed cross-country skiing, snowmobile trails. Interpretive trails; hiking, backpacking. Fishing, boating; hunting (deer, bear, game birds). Picnicking. Camping (May–Oct, fee); reservations for some campsites can be made by phoning 800/283-CAMP. Contact the Forest Supervisor, 159 Lawrence St, PO Box 11500; 283-2050.

2. **Plumas County Museum.** 500 Jackson St. Period rooms, changing historical displays, artifacts and photographs featured in main gallery; permanent exhibit of baskets woven by area's native Maidu Indians. Mezzanine gallery features contemporary cultural displays by county artisans, historical exhibits and Western Pacific and local RR colletions. Archival collection of Plumas County documents. (May–Sept, daily; rest of yr, Mon–Fri) Phone 283-6320. **Free.**

(For further information contact the Plumas County Chamber of Commerce, PO Box 11018; 283-6345.)

Annual Event

Plumas County Fair. Plumas County Fairgrounds. Held annually since 1859. Horse shows, stock car races, Pacific Coast Loggers Championship Show, country/western entertainment; parade, pageant; 4-H livestock auction. Phone 283-6272. 2nd wk Aug.

(See Chester)

Motels

★**LARIAT LODGE.** *2370 E Main St. 916/283-1000; res: 800/999-7199.* 20 rms. 6 A/C. S $35–$50; D $44–$57; each addl $7; family units $70–$78. Crib $5. TV; cable. Heated pool. Complimentary coffee in rms. Restaurant nearby. Ck-out 11 am. X-country ski 17 mi. Cr cds: A, C, D, DS, MC, V.

✔ ★ ★**RANCHITO.** *2020 E Main St. 916/283-2265.* 30 rms, 4 kits. No A/C. S $38.50–$41.50; D $45–$49.50; each addl $9; kit. units for 2–4, $56–$72.50. Crib $6. TV; cable. Complimentary coffee in rms. Restaurant nearby. Ck-out 11 am. X-country ski 17 mi. Private patios. Picnic tables. Some adobe buildings; Spanish decor. Shaded gardens, brook, 2 wooded acres. Cr cds: A, C, D, DS, MC, V.

Restaurants

✔ ★ ★**MOON'S.** *497 Lawrence. 916/283-0765.* Hrs: 4–10 pm. Closed Mon; most major hols. Res accepted. Italian, Amer menu. Wine, beer. Semi-a la carte: dinner $5.25–$15.50. Specialties: chicken cacciatore, mushrooms St Thomas, pizza, Angus beef. Own desserts. Parking. Patio dining. Restored early 1900s building. Totally nonsmoking. Cr cds: MC, V.

★ ★ ★**OLSEN'S CABIN.** *(Graeagle 96103)* ¼ mi W of Graeagle on County A14. *916/836-2801.* Hrs: 8 am–2:30 pm; Fri & Sat also 6–9:30 pm (Jan–Mar). Closed Sun & Mon; also Nov & Dec. Res accepted. Bar. Complete meals: bkfst from $6.50, lunch, dinner $7.50–$25. Child's meals. Specialties: waffles, French toast, home-roasted meats. Salad bar. Own baking. Parking. In historic log cabin. Gift shop. Totally non-smoking. Cr cds: MC, V.

Rancho Bernardo

(see San Diego)

Rancho Cordova *

Pop: 48,731 **Elev:** 126 ft **Area code:** 916
5 mi E of Sacramento off US 50.

(For information about this area contact the Chamber of Commerce, 11070 White Rock Rd, Suite 170, 95670; 638-8700.)

(See Sacramento)

Motels

★★**BEST WESTERN HERITAGE INN.** *11269 Point East Dr (95742), SE of jct US 50 & Sunrise Blvd.* 916/635-4040; FAX 916/635-7198. 124 rms, 3 story. S $55–$70; D $60–$75; each addl $5; under 12 free. TV; cable. Pool; sauna. Complimentary full bkfst Mon–Sat. Restaurant 6–9 am, 5–10 pm; Sun 10 am–2 pm. Rm serv. Bar 4 pm–midnight. Ck-out 11 am. Meeting rms. Valet serv. Free airport, RR station, bus depot transportation. Some refrigerators, in-rm whirlpools. Cr cds: A, C, D, DS, ER, MC, V, JCB.

★**COMFORT INN.** *3240 Mather Field Rd (95670), S of jct US 50 & Mather Field Rd.* 916/363-3344; FAX 916/362-0903. 112 rms, 4 story. S $54; D $59; suites $65–$75; under 14 free. Pet accepted; $100. TV; cable. Pool; whirlpool. Coffee in rms. Restaurant adj 7 am–9 pm. Ck-out noon. Coin lndry. Meeting rms. Airport transportation. Health club privileges. Some refrigerators. Mather AFB ½ mi. Cr cds: A, C, D, DS, ER, MC, V, JCB.

★★★**COURTYARD BY MARRIOTT.** *10683 White Rock Rd (95670), SW of jct US 50 & Zinfandel Dr.* 916/638-3800; FAX 916/638-6776. 144 rms, 3 story. S, D $78–$88; suites $90–$102; under 18 free; wkend rates. TV; cable. Heated pool (seasonal). Restaurant 6:30 am–2 pm, 5–10 pm. Rm serv from 5 pm. Bar 4–11 pm. Ck-out 1 pm. Coin lndry. Meeting rms. Valet serv. Sundries. Exercise equipt; weights, bicycles, whirlpool. Some refrigerators. Private patios, balconies. Cr cds: A, C, D, DS, MC, V.

✔★**ECONOMY INNS OF AMERICA.** *12249 Folsom Blvd (95670), SW of jct US 50 & Hazel Ave.* 916/351-1213; FAX 916/351-1817. 124 rms, 2 story. S $34.90; D $42.90–$49.90; each addl (up to 4) $7. Pet accepted. TV; cable. Pool. Complimentary continental bkfst, coffee. Restaurant adj open 24 hrs. Ck-out 11 am. Some balconies. Cr cds: A, MC, V.

✔★**INNCAL.** *10800 Olson Dr (95670), NE of jct US 50 & Zinfandel Dr.* 916/638-2500. 148 rms, 3 story, 42 suites. No elvtr. S $30–$40; D $36–$46; each addl $6; suites $46; under 12 free. TV; cable. Heated pool (seasonal). Complimentary coffee in lobby. Restaurant adj. Ck-out 11 am. Meeting rm. Cr cds: A, C, D, MC, V, JCB.

Motor Hotel

★★**QUALITY SUITES.** *11260 Point East Dr (95742), SE of jct US 50 & Sunrise Blvd.* 916/638-4141; FAX 916/638-4287. 127 suites, 3 story. S $80–$90; D $95–$110; each addl $7; under 16 free; wkend rates. Crib free. TV; cable. Heated pool. Complimentary full bkfst. Restaurant nearby. Rm serv (lunch, dinner). Bar 5–11 pm. Ck-out noon. Coin lndry. Meeting rms. Valet serv. Gift shop. Exercise equipt; bicycles, treadmill, whirlpool. Bathrm phones, minibars; some refrigerators. Some private patios. Cr cds: A, C, D, DS, ER, MC, V, JCB.

Hotel

★★★**SHERATON SUNRISE.** *11211 Point East Dr (95742), S of jct US 50 & Sunrise Blvd.* 916/638-1100; FAX 916/638-5803. 265 rms, 11 story. S $79–$110; D $89–$120; each addl $10; suites $250–$300; under 17 free. TV. Heated pool. Restaurant 6 am–10:30 pm. Bar 11–2 am, Sun to 11 pm; dancing. Ck-out noon. Convention facilities. Concierge. Gift shop. Free airport, RR station, bus depot transportation. Exercise equipt; weights, bicycles, whirlpool. *LUXURY LEVEL:* **TOWER CLUB.** 25 rms. S $110; D $120; suites $300. Private lounge.
Cr cds: A, C, D, DS, MC, V, JCB.

Restaurants

✔★**BROOKFIELD'S.** *11135 Folsom Blvd, SW of jct US 50 & Sunrise Blvd.* 916/638-2046. Hrs: 6:30 am–11 pm; Fri, Sat to midnight. Closed July 4, Thanksgiving, Dec 25. Mexican, Amer menu. Wine, beer. Semi-a la carte: bkfst, lunch $3–$7, dinner $5–$10. Child's meals. Specializes in own pastries, breads. Parking. Coffee shop atmosphere. Cr cds: A, DS, MC, V.

★★★**SLOCUM HOUSE.** *(7992 California Ave, Fair Oaks) 3 mi N on Sunrise Blvd, opp Community Center.* 916/961-7211. Hrs: 11:30 am–2 pm, 5:30–10 pm; Sun brunch 10:30 am–2 pm. Closed Mon; Jan 1. Res accepted. Continental menu. Bar. Wine list. A la carte entrees: lunch $8–$10.50. Semi-a la carte: dinner $18–$22.50. Sun brunch $8–$10.50. Specializes in seafood, wild game. Jazz quartet Fri & Sat in summer. Parking. Outdoor dining. Historic 1920s luxury house; art deco decor; original marble/oak fireplace. Hillside setting, among trees and flowers. Cr cds: A, C, D, DS, MC, V.

Rancho Cucamonga (H-4)

Pop: 101,409 **Elev:** 1,110 ft **Area code:** 909 **Zip:** 91730

The original residents, the Serrano Indians, called this area Cucamonga or "sandy place." Later, it was part of the vast Rancho de Cucamonga. Violent deaths and long legal battles caused the eventual sale of the land to several wine and citrus industries in 1871.

What to See and Do

Casa de Rancho Cucamonga (Rains House). Corner of Hemlock and Vineyard. Oldest burned-brick house in San Bernardino County (ca 1860); was home to wealthy and socially prominent John and Merced Rains. (Wed–Sun) Phone 989-4970. **Free.**

(For further information contact the Chamber of Commerce, 8280 Utica Ave, Suite 160; 987-1012.)

Annual Event

Grape Harvest Festival. Wine tasting, grape stomping contest, carnival, displays, entertainment. Early Oct.

(For accommodations see Claremont, Ontario, Pomona)

Restaurants

★★**MAGIC LAMP INN.** *8189 E Foothill Blvd. 909/981-8659.* Hrs: 11:30 am–2:30 pm, 5–10:30 pm; Sat from 5 pm; Sun 5–9:30 pm. Closed Dec 25 & 26. Res accepted. Continental menu. Bar 11:30–2 am. Wine list. Semi-a la carte: lunch $4.50–$12.95, dinner $7.95–$29.95. Child's meals. Specializes in prime rib, seafood. Entertainment Wed–Sat. Parking. Cr cds: A, C, D, MC, V.

★★**SYCAMORE INN.** *8318 Foothill Blvd. 909/982-1104.* Hrs: 11:30 am–2:30 pm, 5–10 pm; Fri to 11 pm; Sat 5–11 pm; Sun 11 am–10 pm. Closed Dec 25. Res accepted. Continental menu. Bar 11:30 am–11 pm. Semi-a la carte: lunch $5.95–$12.95, dinner $10.95–$41.95. Child's meals. Specializes in prime rib, certified black Angus steak. Pianist wkends. Parking. Historic stagecoach inn/stop (1848), surrounded by sycamore trees. Cr cds: A, C, D, DS, MC, V.

Rancho Santa Fe (J-4)

Pop: 5,000 (est) **Elev:** 245 ft **Area code:** 619 **Zip:** 92067

(See Del Mar)

Resorts

★★★**THE INN AT RANCHO SANTA FE.** *(Box 869) 5951 Linea del Cielo, 4 mi E of I-5 Lomas Santa Fe Dr, Solana Beach. 619/756-1131; res: 800/654-2928; FAX 619/759-1604.* 89 units in lodge, cottages. S, D $80–$185; each addl $20; suites $250–$470. Crib $20. Pet accepted. TV. Heated pool; poolside serv. Restaurant 7:30–10:30 am, noon–2:30 pm, 6:30–9:30 pm. Rm serv. Box lunches. Bar 11 am–11 pm. Ck-out noon, ck-in 3 pm. Grocery 2 blks. Meeting rms. Bellhops. Tennis. 18-hole golf privileges. Exercise equipt; weights, stair machine. Lawn games. Some refrigerators, fireplaces, wet bars. Many private patios. On 20 acres of landscaped grounds. Beach house in Del Mar avail for day use. Cr cds: A, C, D, MC, V.

★★★★**RANCHO VALENCIA.** *(Box 9126) 5921 Valencia Circle. 619/756-1123; res: 800/548-3664; FAX 619/756-0165.* 43 suites. S $280–$320; D $295–$600; 3-bedrm hacienda from $2,000; tennis clinic plans, golf plans. Crib free. TV; cable. Heated pool; poolside serv. Complimentary coffee in rms. Restaurant 6:30 am–10 pm. Box lunches. Picnics. Bar from 10 am. Ck-out noon, ck-in 4 pm. Guest lndry. Meeting rms. Bellhops. Valet serv. Gift shop. Free airport transportation; RR station transportation. 18 tennis courts, pro. 18-hole golf privileges adj. Exercise equipt; weights, treadmill. Bicycle rentals. Lawn games; professional croquet lawn. Soc dir. Bathrm phones, refrigerators, minibars, wet bars, fireplaces. Secluded accommodations reminiscent of early California haciendas; Spanish architecture, private terraces and spacious interiors. Cr cds: A, C, D, MC, V, JCB.

Restaurants

★★★**DELICIAS.** *6106 Paseo Delicias. 619/756-8000.* Hrs: 11 am–2:30 pm, 6–9 pm; Mon from 6 pm; wkends 6–10 pm. Closed Jan 1, July 4, Dec 25. Res accepted. Bar to 11 pm. Wine list. A la carte entrees: lunch $8–$14, dinner $18–$26. Specialties: smoked salmon pizza, Chinese duck. Outdoor dining. French country-style decor. Outdoor fireplace. Cr cds: A, D, DS, MC, V.

★★★**MILLE FLEURS.** *Country Square Courtyard. 619/756-3085.* Hrs: 11:30 am–2:30 pm, 6–10 pm. Closed Dec 25. Res required Fri & Sat. Nouvelle cuisine. Bar. Wine list. Semi-a la carte: lunch $14–$20, dinner $25–$34. Own pastries. Pianist Wed–Sat. Outdoor dining (lunch). Portuguese decor. Menu changes daily. Cr cds: A, D, MC, V.

Red Bluff (C-2)

Pop: 12,363 **Elev:** 340 ft **Area code:** 916 **Zip:** 96080

A marketing center for the products of the upper Sacramento Valley, the town is named for the reddish sand and gravel cliffs in the vicinity. The first settlers came for gold, but found wealth in wheat fields and orchards instead. As river steamers discharged passengers and freight, the city also became a transportation center for the mines around it. Now lumbering, agriculture and wood products are important industries. One notable pioneer of Red Bluff, William Ide (see #1), led the Bear Flag Revolt against Mexico.

What to See and Do

1. **William B. Ide Adobe State Historic Park.** 2 mi NE off I-5 Wilcox Rd exit. Restored version of adobe house of William B. Ide, only president of the California Republic. Collection of household artifacts. Picnicking. Demonstrations on process of adobe brickmaking, pioneer crafts in summer. (Daily; closed Jan 1, Thanksgiving, Dec 25) Phone 527-5927. ¢¢

2. **Kelly-Griggs House Museum** (1880s). 311 Washington St, at Ash St. Renovated Victorian house with period furnishings; Pendleton Gallery of Art; Chinese and Indian artifacts; historical exhibits. Map of auto tours of Victorian Red Bluff avail (fee). (Thurs–Sun, afternoons; closed major hols) Phone 527-1129.   **Free.**

3. **Fishing.** In Sacramento River. Steelhead, salmon, trout. Sam Ayer Park and Dog Island Fishing Access, 1 mi N on Sacramento River. Footbridge to 11-acre island; nature trails, picnicking. Phone 527-6220.   **Free.**

4. **Lassen Volcanic National Park** (see). 45 mi E on CA 36.

5. **City River Park.** On the Sacramento River, between Reeds Creek Bridge & Sycamore St. Swimming pool (June-Aug, daily exc Sun; fee); boat ramp. Picnic areas, playgrounds. Band concerts (summer, Mon). Phone 527-6220.   **Free.**

(For further information contact the Red Bluff-Tehama County Chamber of Commerce, 100 Main St, PO Box 850; 527-6220 or 800/655-6225.)

Annual Events

Red Bluff Roundup. RCA approved. One of the biggest two-day rodeos in the West. 3rd wkend Apr.

Tehama County Fair. 4 days late July.

(See Redding)

Motels

✔ ★ ★**LAMPLIGHTER LODGE.** *210 S Main St. 916/527-1150.* 51 rms, 1–2 story, 5 family units. S $34–$38; D $44–$48; each addl $4; family units, studio rms $56. Crib $4. TV; cable. Heated pool. Complimentary continental bkfst. Restaurant 6:30 am–9 pm. Ck-out 11:30 am. Cr cds: A, C, D, DS, MC, V.

★**VALUE LODGE.** *30 Gilmore Rd. 916/529-2028; res: 800/ 341-8000; FAX 916/527-1702.* 60 rms, 2 story. Apr–Sept: S $40–$46; D $44–$50; each addl $4; under 12 free; lower rates rest of yr. Crib free. Pet accepted. TV; cable. Pool. Complimentary coffee in rms. Restaurant opp open 24 hrs. Ck-out 11 am. Coin lndry. Health club privileges. Some refrigerators. Cr cds: A, C, D, DS, MC, V.

Redding (B-2)

Founded: 1872 **Pop:** 66,462 **Elev:** 557 ft **Area code:** 916

The hub city of Northern California's vast scenic Shasta-Cascade Region is located at the top of the Sacramento Valley, in the shadow of Mount Shasta—with the rugged Coast Range on the west, the Cascades on the north and the Sierra Nevada on the east. The city was founded when the California and Oregon Railroad chose the site as its northern terminus; it became the county seat in 1884. Lumber and tourism are its principal industries. The Sacramento River flows directly through the city, providing popular pastimes such as fishing, rafting and canoeing.

What to See and Do

1. **Lake Redding-Caldwell Park.** Rio Dr, N on Market St, on N shore of Sacramento River. An 85-acre park; boat ramp, swimming pool. Picnic facilities. Falls of the lake are lighted in summer. Phone 225-4095. (See ANNUAL EVENTS) **Free.** In Caldwell Park is the

   Redding Museum of Art & History. 56 Quartz Hill Rd. Rotating fine arts and regional history exhibits. (Daily exc Mon; closed major hols) Phone 225-4155. **Free.**

2. **Lake Shasta Caverns.** 16 mi N on I-5, then 1½ mi E on Shasta Cavern Rd. Stalactites, stalagmites, flowstone deposits; 58°F. Guided tour includes boat ride across McCloud Arm of Lake Shasta and bus ride up mountain to cavern entrance. (Daily; closed Thanksgiving, Dec 25). Phone 238-2341 or 800/795-CAVE. ¢¢¢¢

3. **Shasta State Historic Park.** 6 mi W on CA 299. Remains of gold rush town with several well-preserved original buildings; historical museum; art gallery. Picnicking. (Thurs–Mon; closed Jan 1, Thanksgiving, Dec 25) Phone 243-8194. ¢

4. **Coleman National Fish Hatchery.** S on I-5 to Cottonwood, 5 mi E on Balls Ferry Rd to Ash Creek Rd, 1 mi to Gover Rd, 2½ mi to Coleman Fish Hatchery Rd. Chinook (king) salmon and steelhead trout are raised here to help mitigate the loss of spawning area due to construction of Shasta Dam. (Daily) Phone 365-8622. **Free.**

5. **Shasta-Trinity National Forests.** N, E & W via CA 299, I-5. More than 2 million acres contain portions of the Trinity Alps Wilderness, Mt Shasta Wilderness, Castle Crags Wilderness, Chanchelulla Wilderness and the Yolla Bolly-Middle Eel Wilderness. Picnicking; camping (fee). For a recording of recreation information phone 246-5338. For further information contact the Forest Supervisor, 2400 Washington Ave, 96001; 246-5313.

6. **Whiskeytown-Shasta-Trinity National Recreation Area, Whiskeytown Unit.** 8 mi W via CA 299. Water sports; fishing; boating (marinas). Picnicking, snack bars. Camping (fee), campfire programs. Phone 241-6584. **Free.** Contains areas surrounding

   Clair A. Hill Whiskeytown Dam and Whiskeytown Lake. Part of the Central Valley Project; forms lake with a 36-mile shoreline.

Camping (mid-May–mid-Sept, 14-day limit; rest of yr, 30 days; fee). Information center NE of dam at jct CA 299 & Kennedy Memorial Dr; 246-1225. Contact Box 188, Whiskeytown 96095; 241-6584.

   Shasta Dam and Power Plant. 5 mi W of I-5. Three times as high as Niagara Falls: 602 feet high, 3,460 feet long. Roadway and sidewalks along the crest; view of Mt Shasta. Visitor center. Waters of three rivers back up to form Shasta Lake, 35 miles long with a 365-mile shoreline. (Memorial Day–Labor Day, daily; rest of yr, Mon–Fri) Schedule may vary; phone 275-4463.

   Trinity Dam and Clair Engle Lake. 22 mi NW via CA 299 W. Large earthfill dam (465 ft high) creates lake, known locally as Trinity Lake, 20 miles long with 145-mile shoreline.

   (For information on Shasta and Trinity areas, contact US Forest Service, 2400 Washington Ave, 96001; phone 246-5313.)

   Lewiston Dam and Lake. 17 mi NW on CA 299, then 6 mi N on unnumbered roads. Regulator and diversion point for water to Whiskeytown Dam near Shasta.

7. **Waterworks Park.** Jct I-5 & CA 299E. Water theme park with 3 giant serpentine slides, Raging River inner tube ride, activity pool, kiddie water playground. (Memorial Day–Labor Day, daily) Phone 246-9550. ¢¢¢¢

8. **Lassen Volcanic National Park (see).** 44 mi E on CA 44.

   (For further information contact the Convention and Visitors Bureau, 777 Auditorium Dr, 96001; 225-4100 or 800/874-7562.)

Annual Events

Shasta Dixieland Jazz Festival. 1st wkend Apr.

Children's Lawn Festival. Caldwell Park (see #1). Children and adults participate in various activities including weaving, bread baking, cow milking and acorn grinding; also Native American games. Late Apr or early May.

Exchange Club Air Show. Late May.

Rodeo Weekend. 3rd wkend May.

Shasta District Fair. 11 mi S on US 99, I-5 in Anderson. 3rd wkend June.

(See Burney, Mt Shasta, Red Bluff, Weaverville)

Motels

★ ★ ★**BEST WESTERN HILLTOP INN.** *2300 Hilltop Dr (96002). 916/221-6100; FAX 916/221-2867.* 115 rms, 2 story. S $69–$79; D $79–$89; each addl $10; suites $95–$115; under 12 free. Crib free. TV; cable, in-rm movies avail. Heated pool; wading pool; whirlpool. Complimentary buffet bkfst. Restaurant 11 am–11 pm; dining rm 5:30–10 pm. Bar 11 am–midnight. Ck-out noon. Coin lndry. Meeting rms. Bellhops in summer. Valet serv. Health club privileges. Cr cds: A, C, D, DS, MC, V.

✔ ★**BEST WESTERN HOSPITALITY HOUSE.** *532 N Market St (96003). 916/241-6464.* 62 rms, 2 story. Mid-May–mid-Oct: S $42–$52; D $46–$56; each addl $6; lower rates rest of yr. TV; cable. Pool. Complimentary coffee in rms. Restaurant 6 am–10 pm; winter to 8 pm. Ck-out 11 am. Cr cds: A, C, D, DS, MC, V.

★ ★**BRIDGE BAY RESORT.** *10300 Bridge Bay Rd (96003), 12 mi N. 916/275-3021; res: 800/752-9669; FAX 916/275-8365.* 40 rms, 2 story, 5 kits. May–Sept: S, D $69–$89; each addl $8; kits. $110; kit. suites $140–$150; under 5 free; lower rates rest of yr. Crib $6. TV; cable. Heated pool. Restaurant 7 am–2 pm, 5–10 pm. Bar (in season) 11–2 am. Ck-out 11 am. Gift shop. Some refrigerators. Some grills. On Lake Shasta; boats, houseboats, moorage. Cr cds: MC, V.

✔ ★ ★**RIVER INN.** *1835 Park Marina Dr (96001). 916/241-9500; res: 800/995-4341; FAX 916/241-5345.* 79 rms, 2–3 story. No elvtr. S from $42; D from $48; each addl $5; under 12 free. Crib $5. Pet accepted. TV; cable, in-rm movies avail. Pool; whirlpool, sauna. Coffee in rms. Restaurant 6 am–9 pm. Bar 11–2 am. Ck-out 11 am. Refrigerators; some wet bars. Private patios, balconies. Picnic tables. Cr cds: A, C, D, DS, MC, V.

★★VAGABOND INN. *536 E Cypress Ave (96002).* 916/223-1600; FAX 916/221-4247. 71 rms, 2 story. Mid-Mar–mid-Oct: S $55; D $60–$65; each addl $5; under 19 free; lower rates rest of yr. Crib free. TV; cable. Pool. Complimentary continental bkfst, coffee. Restaurant open 24 hrs. Ck-out noon. Valet serv. Some refrigerators. Cr cds: A, C, D, DS, ER, MC, V, JCB.

Motor Hotels

★★DAYS HOTEL. *2180 Hilltop Dr (96002).* 916/221-8200; FAX 916/223-4727. 139 rms, 3 story. S $49–$79; D $59–$89; each addl $10; suites $125–$150; under 18 free. Crib free. TV; cable. Pool; whirlpool. Restaurant 6 am–2 pm, 5–10 pm. Rm serv. Bar from 4:30 pm; entertainment, dancing Fri, Sat. Ck-out noon. Meeting rms. Valet serv. Beauty shop. Free airport, RR station, bus depot transportation. Private patios, balconies. Cr cds: A, C, D, DS, ER, MC, V.

★★PARK TERRACE INN (formerly Holiday Inn). *1900 Hilltop Dr (96002).* 916/221-7500; FAX 916/222-3008. 165 rms, 2 story. S $64; D $71; each addl $7; suites $125; under 19 free. Crib free. TV; cable. Indoor pool; wading pool. Restaurant 6 am–10 pm. Rm serv. Bar 2 pm–1:30 am; entertainment, dancing. Ck-out noon. Coin lndry. Meeting rms. Bellhops. Valet serv. Sundries. Free airport, RR station, bus depot transportation. Exercise equipt; bicycles, treadmill, whirlpool, sauna. Holidome. Game rm. Some refrigerators. Cr cds: A, C, D, DS, MC, V, JCB.

★★★RED LION HOTEL. *1830 Hilltop Dr (96002).* 916/221-8700; FAX 916/221-0324. 194 rms, 2 story. May–Sept: S $85–$125; D $100–$140; each addl $15; suites $250; under 18 free; package plans; lower rates rest of yr. Crib free. Pet accepted. TV; cable, in-rm movies avail. Heated pool; wading pool; whirlpool, poolside serv. Restaurant 6 am–11 pm; dining rm 11:30 am–2 pm, 5–10 pm; Fri, Sat to 11 pm. Rm serv. Bar 11–2 am; entertainment, dancing Thurs–Sat. Ck-out 1 pm. Meeting rms. Bellhops. Sundries. Free airport, RR station, bus depot transportation. Putting green. Health club privileges. Private patios, balconies. Cr cds: A, C, D, DS, ER, MC, V, JCB.

Unrated Dining Spot

JJ NORTH'S GRAND BUFFET. *2244 Hilltop Dr.* 916/221-6200. Hrs: 11 am–9 pm; Sun from 8 am. Closed Dec 25. Complete meals: bkfst, lunch $5.29, dinner $6.99–$7.50. Specializes in fried chicken, baked ham, roast beef. Salad bar. Beverage & dessert bar. Parking. Contemporary Western decor. Cr cds: MC, V.

Redlands (H-4)

Founded: 1888 **Pop:** 60,394 **Elev:** 1,302 ft **Area code:** 909

Named for the color of the earth in the area and known for many years as the Navel Orange Center, Redlands still handles a large volume of citrus fruits, but has diversified its industry in recent years to achieve greater economic prosperity and stability.

What to See and Do

1. **Prosellis Bowl.** Eureka & Vine Sts. Also known as the Redlands Bowl; the free concerts held here every Tues and Fri in summer have earned it the name Little Hollywood Bowl.

2. **Asistencia Mission de San Gabriel** (1830). 26930 Barton Rd, 2 mi W. Restored adobe with Indian and early pioneer exhibits, historic scenes of the valley; cactus garden; wishing well, bell tower, wedding chapel and reception room. (Wed–Sat, also Tues & Sun afternoons; closed Jan 1, Thanksgiving, Dec 25) Phone 793-5402 or 798-8570. **Free.**

3. **Lincoln Memorial Shrine.** 125 W Vine St, in Smiley Park. George Grey Barnard's Carrara marble bust of Lincoln; murals by Dean Cornwell; painting by Norman Rockwell; manuscripts, books, artifacts relating to Lincoln and the Civil War. (Tues–Sat, afternoons; closed most hols) Phone 798-7632. **Free.**

4. **San Bernardino County Museum.** 2024 Orange Tree Ln. Mounted collection of birds & bird eggs of Southern California; reptiles, mammals. Pioneer and Indian artifacts; rocks & minerals; paleontology. Changing art exhibits. On grounds are steam locomotive, garden of cacti and succulents. (Daily exc Mon; closed Jan 1, Thanksgiving, Dec 25) Phone 798-8570.

5. **Kimberly Crest House and Gardens** (1897). 1325 Prospect Drive. French chateau-style house and accompanying carriage house on 6.5 acres. Former house of John Kimberly, forefounder of the Kimberly-Clark Corporation. Structure is representative of the "Mansion Era" of Southern California; 1930s furnishings. Italian gardens and citrus grove on grounds. Guided tours. (Thurs–Sun; closed Easter, Dec 25; also Aug) Phone 792-2111. ¢¢

(For further information contact the Chamber of Commerce, One E Redlands Blvd, 92373; 793-2546.)

(See Big Bear Lake, Lake Arrowhead, Ontario, Riverside, San Bernardino)

Motel

✔★★★BEST WESTERN SANDMAN. *1120 W Colton Ave (92374),* I-10 Tennessee St exit, 1 blk S. 909/793-2001; FAX 909/792-7612. 66 rms, 2 story, 7 kits. S $38–$55; D $46–$60; each addl $4; kit. units $5 addl. TV; cable. Heated pool; whirlpool. Complimentary continental bkfst. Restaurant adj 6 am–midnight. Ck-out 11 am. Cr cds: A, C, D, DS, MC, V.

Restaurant

★★JOE GREENSLEEVES. *222 N Orange St.* 909/792-6969. Hrs: 5–9:30 pm; Fri also 11 am–1:30 pm; Sun 4:30–8:30 pm. Closed Mon; major hols. Res accepted. Wine, beer. A la carte entrees: lunch (Fri only) $5.50–$10, dinner $14–$22. Specialties: fresh rabbit, wild game. Parking. Nautical atmosphere; large, cedar-carved replica of sloop on display. Totally nonsmoking. Cr cds: A, MC, V.

Redondo Beach (J-3)

Pop: 60,167 **Elev:** 59 ft **Area code:** 310

This is a recreation and vacation center featuring a 2½-mile beach and the popular King Harbor, which houses 1,700 craft.

What to See and Do

Redondo Pier. Western end of Torrance Blvd. Sailing, scuba diving and windsurfing, also rentals and lessons, off beach at south of pier or at the marina north of pier. Adj is

International Boardwalk. Collection of shops and restaurants featuring goods and food from all over the world.

(For further information contact the Chamber of Commerce, 1215 N Catalina Ave, 90277; 376-6911.)

Annual Event

International Surf Festival. At Redondo, Hermosa, Manhattan & Torrance beaches. Events include lifeguard skills, "flying disc" and sand-castle competitions; outrigger canoe race; rough-water swim and beach run. Early Aug.

(For other general information and attractions see Los Angeles.)

Motels

★★**BEST WESTERN SUNRISE AT REDONDO BEACH MARINA.** 400 N Harbor Dr (90277). 310/376-0746. 111 rms, 3 story. S, D $75–$95; each addl $10; suites $125–$145; under 16 free; wkend rates. Crib free. TV; cable. Heated pool; whirlpool. Complimentary coffee in rms. Restaurant 6 am–10 pm. Ck-out noon. Meeting rms. Valet serv. Refrigerators. Opp ocean. Cr cds: A, C, D, DS, MC, V.

D ⊠ ⊗ ⊚ SC

★★**HOTEL HERMOSA.** (2515 Pacific Coast Hwy, Hermosa Beach 90254) N on Pacific Coast Hwy, at corner of Artesia Blvd. 310/318-6000; res: 800/331-9979; FAX 310/318-6936. 81 units, 3 story, 8 suites. S $59–$125; D $69–$125; each addl $10; suites $99–$109; under 12 free. Crib free. TV; cable. Heated pool. Complimentary continental bkfst. Complimentary coffee in rms. Restaurant nearby. Ck-out 11 am. Coin lndry. Meeting rms. Exercise equipt; weight machine, stair machine. Bathrm phones, refrigerators; some wet bars. Attractive landscaping; Japanese garden. Beach 5 blks. Cr cds: A, D, DS, MC, V.

D ⊠ ⊁ ⊗ ⊚ SC

✔★**TRAVELODGE.** 206 S Pacific Coast Hwy (90277). 310/318-1811; FAX 310/379-0190. 37 rms, 3 story, 2 suites. S $54–$60; D $60–$68; each addl $6; suites $85–$95; under 17 free. Crib free. TV. Heated pool; whirlpool. Complimentary continental bkfst, coffee. Restaurant nearby. Ck-out 11 am. Refrigerators. Beach 2 blks. Cr cds: A, C, D, DS, ER, MC, V, JCB.

D ⊠ ⊗ ⊚ SC

Motor Hotels

★**PALOS VERDES INN.** 1700 S Pacific Coast Hwy (90277). 310/316-4211; res: 800/421-9241 (exc CA); FAX 310/316-4863. 110 rms, 4 story. May–Sept: S, D $90–$120; each addl $10; suites $175–$210; under 18 free; lower rates rest of yr. Crib free. TV. Heated pool; whirlpool. Restaurants 7 am–midnight. Rm serv. Bar 10–2 am; entertainment, dancing. Ck-out noon. Meeting rm. Bellhops. Valet serv. Refrigerator in suites. Many balconies. Most rms with ocean view. Cr cds: A, C, D, MC, V, JCB.

⊠ ⊗ ⊚ SC

★★**PORTOFINO HOTEL & YACHT CLUB.** 260 Portofino Way (90277). 310/379-8481; res: 800/468-4292; FAX 310/372-7329. 192 rms, 3 story, 23 suites, 20 kits. S, D $140–$200; each addl $10; suites $245–$275; kits. $2,200–$3,000/month; under 12 free; wkend, fishing plans. Crib free. TV; cable. Heated pool; poolside serv. Restaurant 6 am–3 pm, 4–10 pm. Rm serv. Bar 11–1 am; entertainment Thurs–Sun. Ck-out noon. Meeting rms. Bellhops. Valet serv. Gift shop. Free airport transportation. Lighted tennis privileges, pro. Exercise equipt; weights,

bicycles, whirlpool. Refrigerators, minibars. On ocean. Cr cds: A, C, D, MC, V, JCB.

D ⊷ ⊘ ⊠ ⊁ ⊗ ⊚ SC

Hotel

★★★**HOLIDAY INN CROWNE PLAZA.** 300 N Harbor Dr (90277). 310/318-8888; FAX 310/376-1930. 340 rms, 5 story. S, D $130–$150; each addl $20; suites $275–$625; under 19 free. Crib $10. Covered parking $6. TV; cable. Pool; poolside serv. Restaurant 6–11:30 am, 5–10:30 pm. Rm serv 24 hrs. Bar 11 am–midnight, Fri & Sat to 2 am; dancing Fri & Sat. Ck-out noon. Convention facilities. Concierge. Gift shop. Lighted tennis. Exercise equipt; weight machine, bicycles, sauna. Health club privileges. Game rm. Refrigerators, minibars. Private patios, balconies. Opp ocean. Large deck overlooks harbor. **LUXURY LEVEL: CONCIERGE LEVEL.** 36 rms, 3 suites. S, D $150. Concierge. Private lounge, honor bar. Complimentary continental bkfst, refreshments, newspaper.
Cr cds: A, C, D, DS, MC, V, JCB.

D ⊷ ⊘ ⊠ ⊁ ⊗ ⊚ SC

Restaurants

✔★**AJETIS.** (425 Pier Ave, Hermosa Beach) N on Pacific Coast Hwy, W on Pier Ave. 310/379-9012. Hrs: 5–10 pm; Sun to 9 pm. Closed Mon; Jan 1, July 4, Dec 25. Res accepted. No A/C. Balkan menu. Wine, beer. Complete meals: dinner $8.95–$17.95. Child's meals. Specialties: roast leg of lamb, spicy lamb stew, chicken & dumplings. Acoustical guitarist Tues, Thurs & Fri. European atmosphere, fireplace. Cr cds: MC, V.

★★★**CHEZ MELANGE.** 1716 S Pacific Coast Hwy. 310/540-1222. Hrs: 7 am–3 pm, 5–11 pm; Sun 5–10 pm; Sun brunch 8 am–2:30 pm. Res required. Bar from 11 am. Wine cellar. Semi-a la carte: bkfst $3.50–$8, lunch $6.95–$10.95, dinner $7.95–$22.95. Sun brunch $6.95–$12.95. Champagne & oyster bar. Specializes in California eclectic cuisine. Own baking, pasta, sausages. Parking. Cr cds: A, MC, V.

★★**LE BEAUJOLAIS.** 522 Pacific Coast Hwy. 310/543-5100. Hrs: 11:30 am–3 pm, 5:30–10 pm. Sat & Sun brunch 10 am–3 pm. Res accepted. French menu. Serv bar. A la carte entrees: lunch $5.95–$15.95, dinner $15.95–$26.95. Sat, Sun brunch $3.95–$10.95. Specializes in rack of lamb, duck, fresh fish. Intimate dining. Elegant decor. Cr cds: A, C, D, DS, MC, V.

D

Redwood City (E-1)

Settled: 1854 **Pop:** 66,072 **Elev:** 15 ft **Area code:** 415

In the center of the booming commercial and industrial peninsula area, Redwood City has the only deepwater bay port south of San Francisco on the peninsula. Once a Spanish ranch, it was settled by S.M. Mezes, who called it Mezesville; lumbermen who cut the nearby virgin redwoods renamed it Redwood City. It was incorporated in 1867 and is the seat of San Mateo County.

What to See and Do

1. **Methuselah Redwood.** Junipero Serra Frwy via Woodside Rd exit, W on CA 84 to Skyline Blvd, 4 mi N. Tree more than 1,500 years old, measures 55 feet in circumference. Trunk has been blackened by repeated fires.

2. **Marinas. Port of Redwood City Yacht Harbor,** 451 Seaport Blvd, phone 306-4150. **Docktown Marina,** foot of Maple St, phone 365-3258. **Pete's Harbor,** Uccelli Blvd, at foot of Whipple Ave, phone 366-0922.

3. Lathrop House. 627 Hamilton St. Victorian house and furnishings. (Tues–Thurs; open some Sun for special activities; closed hols, Aug, late Dec) Phone 365-5564. **Free.**

(For further information contact the Chamber of Commerce, 1675 Broadway, 94063, 364-1722; or the San Mateo County Convention and Visitors Bureau, 111 Anza Blvd, Suite 410, Burlingame 94010, 348-7600.)

Annual Event

San Mateo County Fair & Floral Fiesta. Aug.

(See Belmont, Palo Alto, San Francisco Airport Area, San Mateo)

Motels

★★**BEST WESTERN EXECUTIVE SUITES.** *25 5th Ave (94063). 415/366-5794; FAX 415/365-1429.* 28 rms, 2 story, 5 suites. S $75–$85; D $85–$95; each addl $8; suites $125–$150. Crib $5. TV; cable. Complimentary continental bkfst. Complimentary coffee in rms. Restaurant nearby. Ck-out noon. Coin lndry. Bathrm phones, refrigerators; some minibars. Cr cds: A, C, D, DS, MC, V.

★**COMFORT INN.** *1818 El Camino Real (94063). 415/599-9636; FAX 415/369-6481.* 52 rms, 2 story, 11 suites, 9 kit. units. May–Oct: S $55–$65; D $70–$85; each addl $5; suites $85–$90; kit. units $90; lower rates rest of yr. TV; cable, in-rm movies. Pool; whirlpool, sauna. Complimentary continental bkfst, coffee. Restaurant nearby. Ck-out 11 am. Meeting rms. Cr cds: A, C, D, DS, ER, MC, V, JCB.

✔★**CONTINENTAL GARDEN.** *2650 El Camino Real (94061). 415/369-0321; res: 800/556-1177 (exc CA), 800/453-7070 (CA).* 70 rms, 2 story, 19 kits. S $42–$48; D, kit. units $56–$68; each addl $6. Crib $6. TV; cable. Heated pool; whirlpool. Complimentary continental bkfst. Restaurant nearby. Ck-out 11 am. Coin lndry. Refrigerators. Some private patios, balconies. Picnic tables. Gazebo. Cr cds: A, C, D, MC, V.

★**HOWARD JOHNSON.** *485 Veterans Blvd (94063), at US 101 Whipple Ave exit. 415/365-5500; FAX 415/365-1119.* 126 rms, 2 story. S, D $59–$89; each addl $5; under 18 free; wkend rates. Crib free. Pet accepted, some restrictions. TV; cable. Heated pool; wading pool. Restaurant 6 am–noon. Rm serv. Ck-out noon. Meeting rms. Bellhops. Free airport, hospital transportation. Balconies. Cr cds: A, C, D, DS, ER, MC, V, JCB.

Hotel

★★★**SOFITEL.** *223 Twin Dolphin Dr (94065). 415/598-9000; res: 800/SOFITEL; FAX 415/598-0459.* 319 units, 9 story. S $135; D $150; each addl $20; suites $250; under 18 free. Crib free. TV; cable. Pool. Restaurant 6 am–11 pm. Rm serv 5:30–2 am. Bar 10–2 am; entertainment exc Sun. Ck-out noon. Convention facilities. Concierge. Gift shop. Free airport transportation. Exercise rm; instructor, weights, bicycles, whirlpool, sauna, steam rm. Minibars. Elegant atmosphere; Baccarat chandeliers. Cr cds: A, C, D, DS, MC, V, JCB.

Redwood Highway (A-1 – C-1)

US 101 runs for 387 miles through scenic countryside where 97 percent of the world's sequoias grow. The bulk of the giant redwood trees, *Sequoia sempervirens,* are from Leggett north to the Oregon state line. The Humboldt Redwoods State Park (see) runs on both sides of the highway; many of the major groves are here, including the spectacular Avenue of the Giants north of Phillipsville, south of Pepperwood. Other concentrations of redwoods are at **Grizzly Creek Redwoods State Park,** 18 miles E of US 101 on CA 36, camping (standard fees), picnicking, swimming, fishing; and at Redwood National Park (see CRESCENT CITY), which takes in Prairie Creek Redwoods State Park, 6 miles north of Orick on US 101, Del Norte Coast Redwoods State Park, 7 miles south of Crescent City, and Jedediah Smith Redwoods State Park, 9 miles northeast of Crescent City.

The Redwood Highway, a major thoroughfare, has four lanes at many points. Since summer traffic is heavy, it may be difficult to get overnight lodging along the way—plan ahead.

(For further information contact the Redwood Empire Assn, 785 Market St, 15th Floor, San Francisco 94103; 415/543-8334; to receive a 56-page Visitors Guide, enclose $3 for postage and handling.)

(For accommodations see Crescent City, Eureka)

Richardson Grove State Park (C-1)

(8 mi S of Garberville on US 101)

One of California's beautiful redwood parks, Richardson Grove covers a 1,000-acre tract along the south fork of the Eel River. Swimming; fishing (Oct–Jan). Hiking trails. Picnicking, store (summer). Camping. Visitor center (summer); nature programs offered daily in summer. Standard fees. Phone 707/247-3318.

(For accommodations see Garberville)

Riverside (J-4)

Founded: 1870 **Pop:** 226,505 **Elev:** 858 ft **Area code:** 909

In 1873 a resident of the new town of Riverside obtained from the US Department of Agriculture two cuttings of a new type of orange, a mutation which had suddenly developed in Brazil. These cuttings were the origin of the vast navel orange groves that make this the center of the "Orange Empire."

What to See and Do

1. **Riverside Municipal Museum.** 3720 Orange St. Area history, anthropology and natural history displays; changing exhibits. (Daily exc Mon; closed major hols) Phone 782-5273. **Free.**

2. **Riverside Art Museum.** 3425 7th St. Changing exhibits of historical and contemporary sculpture, painting and graphics; lectures, demonstrations, juried shows, sales gallery. Housed in 1929 Mediterranean-style YWCA building designed by Julia Morgan. (Daily exc Sun; closed major hols) Phone 684-7111. ¢

3. **Chinese Memorial Pavilion.** 3581 7th St, on Riverside Public Library grounds. Dedicated to Chinese pioneers of the West and those who contributed to the growth of Riverside.

4. **Heritage House** (1891). 8193 Magnolia Ave. Restored Victorian mansion. (Tues, Thurs & Sun; closed July, Aug) Phone 689-1333. **Free.**

5. **Parent Washington Navel Orange Tree.** Magnolia & Arlington Aves. Propagated from one of the original trees from Bahia, Brazil, planted in 1873.

6. **Castle Amusement Park.** 3500 Polk St, CA 91 between Tyler and La Sierra exits. Features 80-year-old Dentzel carousel with hand-carved animals; antique cars. Ride Park with 30 rides & attractions (Fri, early–late evening; Sat, noon–late evening; Sun, noon–early evening). Four 18-hole miniature golf courses and video arcade (daily). Fee for activities. Phone 785-4140 (recording).

7. **Mount Rubidoux Memorial Park.** W end of 9th St, ½ mi W. According to legend, the mountain was once the altar of Cahuilla and Serrano sun worship. A cross rises on the peak in memory of Fray Junipero Serra, founder of the California missions. The World Peace Tower stands on the side of the mountain. Hiking. (Daily, weather permitting: vehicular traffic allowed Sun–Wed; closed to vehicles Thurs–Sat) Phone 782-5301. (See ANNUAL EVENTS)

8. **University of California at Riverside** (1954). (8,800 students) 900 University Ave. Centers around 161-foot Carillon Tower; Botanic Garden featuring flora from all parts of the world. For tours of campus phone 787-4531, for other inquiries phone 787-5185. The university also maintains the University Art Gallery, 3701 Canyon Crest Dr, and the

9. **California Museum of Photography.** 3824 Main St. Large collection of photographic equipment, prints, stereographs, memorabilia. Interactive gallery, walk-in camera; library. (Wed–Sat, also Sun afternoons; closed Jan 1, Dec 25) Free admission Wed. Phone 787-4787. ¢

10. **Orange Empire Railway Museum.** 2201 South A Street, 14 mi S via I-215 in Perris. More than 150 rail vehicles and pieces of off-rail equipment; railroad and trolley memorabilia; picnicking. Trolley rides (Sat, Sun & major hols; fee). Grounds (daily; closed Thanksgiving, Dec 25). Phone 657-2605. ¢¢

(For further information contact the Visitors and Convention Bureau, 3443 Orange St, 92501; 787-7950.)

Annual Events

Easter Sunrise Pilgrimage. Mt Rubidoux Memorial Park (see #7). First nonsectarian sunrise service in US; continuous since 1909. Easter Sun.

Cinco de Mayo Week. Citywide celebration. Parades, cultural events, barbecue, sports events. Phone 787-7950. May.

(See San Bernardino)

Motels

✔ ★**DYNASTY SUITES.** 3735 Iowa Ave (92507) 909/369-8200; FAX 909/369-2807. 33 rms, 2 story, 29 suites. S, D $39.95–$44.95; each addl $5; suites $39.95–$79.95; family rates. Crib free. TV; cable. Heated pool. Complimentary continental bkfst, coffee. Restaurant opp 11 am–10 pm. Ck-out noon. Refrigerators. Cr cds: A, C, D, DS, MC, V.

★≝⊘◎SC

✔ ★**ECONO LODGE.** 1971 University Ave (92507). 909/684-6363; FAX 909/684-9228. 45 rms, 2–3 story, 6 kits. No elvtr. S $32–$49; D $35–$52; kit. units $3 addl. Crib $5. Pet accepted. TV; cable, in-rm movies avail. Pool. Complimentary coffee. Restaurant adj 8 am–10:30 pm. Ck-out 11 am. Sun deck. Cr cds: A, C, D, DS, MC, V, JCB.

🅿≝⊘◎SC

★ ★**HAMPTON INN.** 1590 University Ave (92507). 909/683-6000; FAX 909/782-8052. 115 rms, 2 story. S $52–$59; D $57–$64; under 18 free. Crib free. TV. Heated pool. Complimentary continental bkfst, coffee. Restaurant nearby. Ck-out noon. Meeting rms. Valet serv. Refrigerators avail. Cr cds: A, C, D, DS, MC, V.

D≝⊘◎SC

Hotels

★**DAYS INN.** 1510 University Ave (92507). 909/788-8989; FAX 909/787-6783. 163 rms, 6 story. S $49–$69; D $59–$79; each addl $10; under 18 free; wkly, monthly rates. Crib free. TV; cable. Heated pool; whirlpool. Restaurant 6 am–1:30 pm, 5–10 pm. Bar 5 pm–midnight. Ck-out noon. Meeting rms. Some balconies. Cr cds: A, C, D, DS, ER, MC, V.

D≝⊘◎SC

★ ★ ★**MISSION INN.** 3649 Seventh St (92501), CA 91 University Ave exit. 909/784-0300; res: 800/843-7755; FAX 909/683-1342. 243 rms, 15 with shower only, 5 story, 35 suites. S $80–$130; D $95–$145; each addl $15; suites $175–$425; under 15 free; special package plans. TV; cable. Heated pool. Restaurant 7 am–10 pm. Bar; entertainment Fri & Sat. Meeting rms. Gift shop. Free airport transportation. Exercise equipt; weight machine; some balconies. Historic building was originally a 2-story, 12-rm boarding house (1876); expanded over the years. Renovated, unique Spanish-style architecture; courtyard fountains, gardens; stained-glass windows; many antiques. 2 wedding chapels, mission bells. Cr cds: A, C, D, DS, MC, V, JCB.

D≝🕴⊘◎SC

★ ★**SHERATON.** 3400 Market St (92501). 909/784-8000; FAX 909/369-7127. 285 rms, 12 story. S $84–$94; D $94–$104; each addl $10; suites $135–$275; under 18 free. Crib free. TV; cable. Heated pool. Restaurant 6:30 am–3 pm, 5–10 pm. Bar 11–2 am; entertainment, dancing (Sat evening). Ck-out noon. Convention facilities. Gift shop. Free airport transportation. Exercise equipt; weight machine, bicycle, whirlpool. Some wet bars; refrigerators avail. Some balconies. Cr cds: A, C, D, DS, MC, V, JCB.

D≝🕴⊘◎SC

Restaurants

★ ★**GÉRARD'S.** 9814 Magnolia Ave, CA 91 Tyler St exit N, 4 blks E on Magnolia. 714/687-4882. Hrs: 5–9:30 pm. Closed Mon; most major hols. Res accepted. French menu. Wine, beer. Semi-a la carte: dinner $11.50–$18.50. Specialties: pepper-steak/filet mignon flambé, bouillabaise/shellfish stew au safran. Parking. Country French decor; intimate dining area. Some antiques. Family-owned since 1969. Totally nonsmoking. Cr cds: A, MC, V.

★ ★**MARIO'S PLACE.** 1725 Spruce St. 909/684-7755. Hrs: 11:30–2 am; Sat 5:30 pm–2:30 am; Sun from 5 pm. Res accepted. Northern Italian, Southern French menu. Bar. Semi-a la carte: lunch $6–$14, dinner $14–$24. Menu changes frequently; seasonal offerings. Entertainment. Parking. Fireplaces; many intimate dining areas. Cr cds: A, C, D, MC, V.

D

★**REUBEN'S.** 3640 Central Ave, CA 91 Central Ave exit N. 909/683-3842. Hrs: 11:30 am–9:30 pm; Fri from 10 pm; Sat 4–10 pm; Sun 4:30–9 pm; early-bird dinner Mon–Sat 5–7 pm; Sun brunch 9:30 am–2 pm. Res accepted. Bar. Semi-a la carte: lunch $4.99–$9.99, dinner $10.99–$18.99. Sun champagne brunch $6.95–$10.95. Child's meals. Specializes in seafood, plank steak for two. Parking. Cr cds: A, C, D, DS, MC, V.

SC

Roseville (D-2)

Pop: 44,685 **Elev:** 160 ft **Area code:** 916 **Zip:** 95678

(See Rancho Cordova, Sacramento)

Motel

✔ ★ ★**HERITAGE INN.** 204 Harding Blvd. 916/782-4466; FAX 916/782-4461. 101 rms, 2 story. S $51–$61; D $54–$65; each addl $4; under 12 free; wkly rates. Crib $4. TV; cable. Pool; whirlpool. Complimentary coffee in rms. Restaurant adj 6 am–10 pm. Ck-out 11 am.

Meeting rms. Valet serv. Many bathrm phones, refrigerators. Cr cds: A, C, D, DS, MC, V.

Motor Hotel

★★FIRST CHOICE INNS. *(4420 Rocklin Rd, Rocklin 95677) W on I-80 exit Rocklin Rd N. 916/624-4500; res: 800/462-2400; FAX 916/624-5982.* 90 rms, 3 story. May–Sept: S, D $60–$95; each addl $5; suites, kit. units $85–$125; under 12 free; lower rates rest of yr. Crib free. Pet accepted; $12 per day. TV; cable. Pool; whirlpool. Complimentary full bkfst wkdays. Complimentary coffee in rms. Restaurant adj open 24 hrs. Ck-out noon. Coin lndry. Meeting rms. Valet serv. Refrigerators; minibar in suites. Cr cds: A, C, D, DS, MC, V.

Sacramento (D-2)

Settled: 1839 **Pop:** 369,365 **Elev:** 25 ft **Area code:** 916

Capital of the state since 1854, Sacramento is known to flowers lovers as the "Camellia Capital of the World." It is the marketing center for 11 counties in the Sacramento Valley, producing a cash farm income approaching 11 percent of the state's income.

Modern Sacramento started when Captain John A. Sutter established New Helvetia, a colony for his Swiss compatriots. Sutter built a fort here and immigrants came. He prospered in wheat raising, flour milling, distilling and in a passenger and freight boat service to San Francisco. The discovery of gold at Coloma in 1848 (see PLACERVILLE), brought ruin to Sutter. Workers deserted to hunt gold, and he soon lost possession of the fort. The next year his son, who had been deeded family property near the boat line terminus, laid out a town there, naming it Sacramento City. At the entrance to the gold rush country, its population rocketed to 10,000 within seven months. Chosen as California's capital in 1854, the new capitol building was constructed at a cost of more than $2.6 million over a 20-year period.

Transportation facilities were important in the city's growth. In 1860, the Pony Express made Sacramento its western terminus. Later, Sacramento's "Big Four"—Mark Hopkins, Charles Crocker, Collis P. Huntington and Leland Stanford—financed the building of the Central Pacific Railroad over the Sierras. Deepwater ships reach the city via a 43-mile-long channel from Suisun Bay. Sacramento's new port facilities handle an average of 20 ships a month carrying import and export cargo from major ports around the world.

What to See and Do

1. **State Capitol.** 10th & L Streets. The Capitol provides a unique combination of past and present under one roof. It has been the home of California's lawmaking branch of government since the Capitol opened in 1869. The main building has been restored to recreate its turn-of-the-century ambience and to ensure its safety. The Legislature still meets in the restored Senate and Assembly chambers. Nine historic offices include exhibits from the State Library and State Archives. The more modern east annnex contains the offices of the legislators and the governor. The building is surrounded by a 40-acre park with hundreds of varieties of trees, shrubs and flowers. Free guided tours of building (daily, on the hour). Park tours (June–Sept, daily). Capitol (daily; closed Jan 1, Thanksgiving, Dec 25). **Free.**

2. **Governor's Mansion.** 16th & H Streets. Once owned by Joseph Steffens, father of Lincoln Steffens, a turn-of-the-century journalist. Every governor from 1903 through 1967 lived here. Guided tours (daily; closed Jan 1, Thanksgiving, Dec 25) Phone 323-3047. ¢

3. **Sutter's Fort State Historic Park.** 2701 L Street. Restored in the late 1800s. Exhibits depict Sutter's life; kitchen. Special craft and living history demonstration days. (Daily; closed Jan 1, Thanksgiving, Dec 25) Admission includes self-guided audio tour. Phone 445-4422. ¢   Also here is the

   State Indian Museum. 2618 K Street. Displays include dugout canoes, weapons, pottery, basketry; changing exhibits. (Hrs same as park) Films (Sat & Sun). Phone 324-0971. ¢

4. **Old Sacramento Historic District** (ca 1850–70). Adj central business district between I-5 & I St bridge. This 28-acre area of historic buildings along the banks of the Sacramento River has been restored to its 1850–70 period of the pony express, the arrival of the Central Pacific Railroad and the gold rush. Special events held throughout the year. The area also has shops and restaurants. Most buildings closed Jan 1, Thanksgiving, Dec 25. For recorded information, including the Governor's Mansion and Sutter's Fort State Historic Park, phone 324-0539. **Free.**   Includes

   Hastings Building. 2nd & J Streets. Western terminus of the Pony Express and original home of the California Supreme Court.

   Old Eagle Theatre. Front & J Streets. Guided tours (by appt). Period plays (Fri & Sat; fee). Phone 446-6761.

   California State Railroad Museum. 125 I Street. The largest part of this complex is the **Museum of Railroad History**, which houses 21 pieces of rolling stock and a total of 40 exhibits covering all aspects of railroading. (Daily; closed Jan 1, Thanksgiving, Dec 25) Phone 448-4466. ¢¢   Also part of the State Railroad Museum, and included in museum admission fee, is the

   Central Pacific Passenger Depot. 930 Front St. (Same days as railroad museum)

5. **Sacramento History Museum.** 101 I Street, in Old Sacramento. Regional history exhibits, including gold ore specimens and restored artifacts; hands-on exhibits; video computers. (Wed–Sun; closed some major hols) Phone 264-7057. ¢¢

6. **Towe Ford Museum.** 2200 Front St. Collection of 180 antique Ford automobiles from 1903 to 1953, including a rare 1904 Model B touring car. (Daily; closed Jan 1, Thanksgiving, Dec 25) Sr citizen rate. Phone 442-6802. ¢¢¢

7. **Crocker Art Museum.** 216 O Street. Original restored Victorian Gallery (1872), reconstructed Mansion Wing and Herold Wing housing E.B. Crocker collection; European and American paintings; master drawings; Asian art; decorative arts; changing exhibits. (Wed–Sun; closed Jan 1, July 4, Thanksgiving, Dec 25) Museum bookstore/gift shop. Phone 264-5423. ¢¢

8. **Sacramento Science Center.** 3615 Auburn Blvd. Hands-on science exhibitions; planetarium (fee); Discovery Trail featuring California plant species. Planetarium shows & special events (wkends). (Wed–Sun; closed some hols) Phone 277-6180 (recording). ¢¢

9. **William Land Park.** Freeport Blvd between 13th Ave & Sutterville Rd. Wading pool (summer, daily); fishing (children under 16 only). Nine-hole golf course. Picnic facilities, supervised playground, ballfields. Amusement area near zoo has pony, amusement rides (summer, daily). **Sacramento Zoo,** in the park at Land Park Dr & Sutterville Rd, has more than 340 specimens representing more than 150 species of exotic animals displayed in a 15-acre botanical garden setting (daily, mid-morning–mid-afternoon; closed Dec 25). Fairytale Town children's theme park (daily). Fee for activities. Phone 264-5200 or -5885 (zoo recording). Zoo ¢¢; Fairytale Town ¢¢

10. **California State University, Sacramento** (1947). (25,000 students) 6000 J Street, on the banks of the American River. A replica of the Golden Gate bridge serves as a footbridge across the river. Phone 278-6156.

11. **CCInc Auto Tape Tours.** These 90-minute cassettes offer mile-by-mile self-guided tours to Mariposa (188 mi) with landmarks of early West and gold rush country; to Reno (132 mi) through Mother Lode country, then over the Sierras via Donner Pass; to South Lake Tahoe (217 mi) with stories of the 49ers and pioneers, colorful history of the boomtown days of Carson City and Virginia City; to San Francisco (166 mi) through the Napa Valley and "wine country," Sonoma, Sausalito, across the Golden Gate Bridge. Fourteen different tour tapes of California are available. Tapes may be

purchased directly from CCInc, PO Box 227, 2 Elbrook Dr, Allendale, NJ 07401; 201/236-1666. **¢¢¢¢**

12. Industrial tour. Blue Diamond Growers Visitors Center. 17th & C Streets. 25-minute video (daily exc Sun). Phone 446-8439. **Free.**

13. Cal Expo. 5 mi NE at 1600 Exposition Blvd, borders Business Loop I-80. Multipurpose facility for variety of activities including various consumer shows, auto racing and concerts. (See ANNUAL EVENTS) Phone 263-3000 (recording).

(For details on recreation and further information contact the Convention & Visitors Bureau, 1421 K Street, 95814; 264-7777.)

Annual Events

Camellia Festival. 10 days early Mar.

Sacramento Jazz Festival. Venues throughout city. Cabaret, concert and jam sessions. Phone 372-5277. Memorial Day wkend.

California State Fair. California Exposition grounds (see #13). Includes traditional state fair activities; exhibits, livestock, carnival food, entertainment on 10 stages, Thouroughbred racing and 1-mile monorail. Phone 263-3000 (recording). Late Aug–early Sept.

Seasonal Event

Music Circus. Tent at 14th & H Streets. Summer professional musical theater. (Daily) Phone 557-1999. July–Sept.

(See Davis, Rancho Cordova)

Motels

(All rates are generally higher during conventions, state fair and other special events)

★★**BEST WESTERN HARBOR INN.** *(1250 Halyard Dr, West Sacramento 95691) S off I-80 Business, Harbor Blvd exit. 916/371-2100; FAX 916/373-1507.* 138 rms, 2–4 story, 19 suites. S $55–$65; D $62–$72; each addl $5; suites $67–$79; under 12 free. Crib free. TV; cable. Heated pool; 2 whirlpools. Complimentary coffee in rms. Restaurant adj 7 am–11 pm. Ck-out noon. Meeting rms. Valet serv. Free airport, RR station, bus depot transportation. Some refrigerators, in-rm whirlpools. Private patios, balconies. Cr cds: A, D, DS, MC, V.

✔★**DAYS INN.** *200 Jibboom St (95814). 916/448-8100; FAX 916/447-3621.* 173 rms, 3 story. S $52–$58; D $56–$70; each addl $10; under 18 free; wkly rates. Pet accepted, some restrictions; $25. TV; cable. Pool; poolside serv (seasonal). Restaurant 5 am–11 pm. Wine, beer. Ck-out noon. Meeting rms. Free airport, RR station, bus depot transportation. On Sacramento River. Cr cds: A, C, D, DS, MC, V.

★★**DISCOVERY MOTOR INN.** *350 Bercut Dr (95814). 916/442-6971; res: 800/952-5516 (CA); FAX 916/444-2809.* 100 rms, 2 story. S $62–$81; D $47–$135; each addl $5; suites $100–$135; under 12 free. Crib free. TV; cable. Pool; whirlpool. Complimentary continental bkfst. Coffee in rms. Restaurant adj open 24 hrs. Ck-out 11 am. Meeting rms. Valet serv. Free airport transportation. Some refrigerators, minibars. Private patios, balconies. Cr cds: A, C, D, DS, ER, MC, V.

✔★**ECONO LODGE.** *1319 30th St (95816), at N Street. 916/454-4400; FAX 916/736-2812.* 83 rms, 3 story. S $44; D $44–$50; each addl $5; under 16 free. Crib free. TV. Pool. Coffee in lobby. Restaurant adj open 24 hrs. Ck-out noon. Cr cds: A, C, D, DS, MC, V.

✔★★**LA QUINTA.** *4604 Madison Ave (95841). 916/348-0900; FAX 916/331-7160.* 129 rms, 3 story. S $54–$61; D $62–$67; each addl $5; suites $85; under 18 free. Crib free. Pet accepted, some restrictions. TV; cable. Pool. Continental bkfst in lobby 6–10 am. Restaurant adj open

24 hrs. Ck-out noon. Meeting rms. Fireplace in lobby. Cr cds: A, C, D, DS, MC, V.

★★**RESIDENCE INN BY MARRIOTT.** *1530 Howe Ave (95825). 916/920-9111; FAX 916/921-5664.* 176 kit. units, 2 story. Kit. units $98–$118; each addl $10; under 12 free; wkly rates. Crib free. TV. Pool; whirlpools. Complimentary continental bkfst. Ck-out noon. Coin lndry. Meeting rms. Sundries. Free airport, RR station, bus depot transportation. Balconies. Cr cds: A, C, D, DS, MC, V, JCB.

★**VAGABOND INN.** *909 3rd St (95814). 916/446-1481; FAX 916/448-0364.* 107 rms, 3 story. S $63–$67; D $70; each addl $5; under 17 free. Crib free. Pet accepted; $5 per day. TV; cable. Pool. Complimentary continental bkfst, coffee. Restaurant adj open 24 hrs. Ck-out noon. Meeting rm. Valet serv. Free airport, RR station, bus depot transportation. Cr cds: A, C, D, DS, ER, MC, V, JCB.

Motor Hotels

★★**BEVERLY GARLAND HOTEL.** *1780 Tribute Rd (95815). 916/929-7900; res: 800/972-3976; FAX 916/921-9147.* 205 rms, 3 story. S $70–$85; D $80–$95; each addl $10; 2-story suites $115–$200; under 18 free; lower rates July–Aug. Crib free. TV; cable. Heated pool; whirlpool, poolside serv (seasonal). Restaurant 6 am–10 pm; Sun to 9 pm. Rm serv. Bar 11:30–2 am. Ck-out noon. Coin lndry. Meeting rms. Bellhops. Free airport, RR station, bus depot transportation. Private patios, balconies. Cr cds: A, C, D, DS, MC, V.

★★**CLARION.** *700 16th St (95814). 916/444-8000; FAX 916/442-8129.* 239 rms, 2–4 story. S $89–$99; D $99–$109; each addl $15; suites $135–$265; under 18 free; wknd rates. Crib free. TV; cable, in-rm movies. Pool; poolside serv. Restaurant 6:30 am–2 pm, 5–10 pm. Rm serv to midnight. Bar 11–1 am. Ck-out noon. Meeting rms. Bellhops. Valet serv. Sundries. Free airport, RR station, bus depot transportation. Health club privileges. Some refrigerators. Some private patios, balconies. Cr cds: A, C, D, DS, ER, MC, V, JCB.

★★★**FOUNTAIN SUITES.** *321 Bercut Dr (95814), E off I-5 Richards Blvd exit. 916/441-1444; res: 800/767-1777 (CA); FAX 916/441-6530.* 300 suites, 3 story. S $84–$104; D $94–$119; deluxe suites $300; under 12 free. Crib free. TV; cable. Heated pool; whirlpool. Complimentary continental bkfst, coffee. Restaurant adj open 24 hrs. Rm serv. Bar 4 pm–1 am. Ck-out noon. Coin lndry. Convention facilities. Bellhops. Valet serv. Sundries. Free airport, RR station, bus depot transportation. Health club privileges. Some refrigerators. Cr cds: A, C, D, DS, MC, V.

★★★**RADISSON.** *500 Leisure Lane (95815), off CA 160 Canterbury Rd exit. 916/922-2020; FAX 916/649-9463.* 309 rms, 2 story. S, D $94–$104; each addl $10; suites $184–$335; under 18 free; wknd rates. Crib avail. Pet accepted; $100. TV; cable. Pool; poolside serv. Restaurant 6 am–11 pm. Rm serv 24 hrs. Bar 10–2 am; entertainment, dancing Tues–Sat. Ck-out noon. Convention facilities. Bellhops. Valet serv. Concierge. Sundries. Gift shop. Free valet parking. Free airport, RR station, bus depot transportation. Exercise equipt; weight machine, stair machine, whirlpool. Some refrigerators. Balconies. On small, private lake. Cr cds: A, C, D, DS, ER, MC, V, JCB.

★★★**RED LION HOTEL.** *2001 Point West Way (95815). 916/929-8855; FAX 916/924-4913.* 448 rms, 4 story. S $94–$104; D $109–$119; each addl $15; suites $160–$450; under 18 free. Crib free. Pet accepted, some restrictions. TV. Heated pool; poolside serv. Restaurant 6 am–midnight. Rm serv. Bars 11–2 am; entertainment, dancing. Ck-out 1 pm. Meeting rms. Bellhops. Valet serv. Gift shop. Free airport, RR station, bus depot transportation. Game rm. Exercise equipt; weight machine, stair machine. Bathrm phone, refrigerator, minibar, whirlpool in suites. Balconies. Cr cds: A, C, D, DS, ER, MC, V, JCB.

★ ★ **RED LION SACRAMENTO INN.** *1401 Arden Way (95815). 916/922-8041; FAX 916/922-0386.* 376 rms, 2–3 story. S $99–$109; D $114–$124; each addl $15; suites $150–$445; under 18 free. Crib free. TV; cable. 3 pools; wading pool, poolside serv. Restaurant 6 am–10 pm. Rm serv. Bar 11–2 am; entertainment, dancing Tues–Sat. Ck-out 1 pm. Meeting rms. Bellhops. Sundries. Gift shop. Free airport, RR station, bus depot transportation. Putting green. Exercise equipt; weights, bicycles. Some bathrm phones, in-rm whirlpools, refrigerators. Private patios, balconies. Cr cds: A, C, D, DS, MC, V, JCB.

Hotels

★ ★ ★ **HILTON INN-SACRAMENTO.** *2200 Harvard St (95815). 916/922-4700; FAX 916/922-8418.* 325 rms, 12 story. S $72–$112; D $82–$129; each addl $10; suites $250–$485; wkend rates. Crib free. Pet accepted, some restrictions; $25. TV; cable. Heated pool; poolside serv. Restaurant 6 am–11 pm. Bar 11:30–2 am; dancing. Ck-out 1 pm. Convention facilities. Gift shop. Free airport, RR station, bus depot transportation. Exercise equipt; weights, bicycles, whirlpool, sauna. Refrigerator in suites. Some minibars. Some balconies. Cr cds: A, C, D, DS, ER, MC, V, JCB.

✔ ★ ★ ★ **HOLIDAY INN-CAPITOL PLAZA.** *300 J Street (95814). 916/446-0100; FAX 916/446-0100, ext 2133.* 368 rms, 15 story. Jan–June & Sept–Nov: S $82–$94; D $84–$96; each addl $8; suites $175–$550; under 12 free; lower rates rest of yr. Crib free. Pet accepted. TV; cable, in-rm movies. Pool; sauna. Restaurant 6 am–2 pm; dining rm 5:30–11 pm. Bar 11–2 am; entertainment Tues–Sat. Ck-out noon. Meeting rms. Concierge. Gift shop. Health club privileges. Some bathrm phones, refrigerators. Cr cds: A, C, D, DS, MC, V, JCB.

★ ★ ★ **HYATT REGENCY.** *1209 L Street (95814), opp State Capitol. 916/443-1234; FAX 916/321-6699.* 500 rms, 15 story. S $140–$180; D $165–$205; each addl $20; suites $195–$550; under 18 free; wkly, wkend rates. Crib free. Valet parking $10/day, garage $6/day. TV; cable. Heated pool; wading pool, poolside serv. Supervised child's activities (Fri & Sat evenings). Restaurant 6 am–midnight. Bar 11–2 am; entertainment, dancing Tues–Sat. Ck-out noon. Convention facilities. Concierge. Shopping arcade. Airport, RR station, bus depot transportation. Exercise equipt; weight machine, bicycles, whirlpool. Minibars. Balconies. **LUXURY LEVEL: REGENCY CLUB.** 63 rms. S $185; D $205; suites $250–$850. Private lounge, honor bar. Complimentary continental bkfst.
Cr cds: A, C, D, DS, MC, V, JCB.

Inns

★ ★ ★ **AMBER HOUSE.** *1315 22nd St (95816). 916/444-8085; res: 800/755-6526.* 9 rms in two houses, 2 story. S, D $85–$195. TV; cable. Complimentary full bkfst 7–10:30 am. Rm serv. Ck-out noon, ck-in 4 pm. Free airport, RR station, bus depot transportation. Whirlpool in some rms. Houses built 1905 and 1913; rms individually decorated; antiques; library. Totally nonsmoking. Cr cds: A, C, D, DS, MC, V.

★ ★ ★ ★ **STERLING HOTEL.** *1300 H Street (95814), 2 blks N of Sacramento Convention Center, downtown. 916/448-1300; res: 800/365-7660; FAX 916/448-8066.* 12 rms, 3 story. S, D $95–$175; each addl $15; higher rates wkends. Crib free. TV; cable. Complimentary coffee in sitting rm. Dining rm (see CHANTERELLE). Rm serv. Serv bar. Ck-out 11 am, ck-in 3 pm. Meeting rms. Bellhops. Valet serv. Complimentary covered parking. Health club privileges. In-rm whirlpools. Some refrigerators. Some balconies. Individually decorated rms. On the grounds is

a unique glass structure imported from England, used for meetings & social gatherings. Totally nonsmoking. Cr cds: A, D, MC, V.

★ ★ ★ **VIZCAYA.** *2019 21st St (95818). 916/455-5243; res: 800/445-6102.* 9 rms, 3 story. S, D $79–$225. TV; cable. Complimentary full bkfst. Rm serv. Ck-out 11 am, ck-in 3 pm. Street parking. Some in-rm whirlpools, fireplaces. Picnic tables. Landscaped gardens, Victorian gazebo. Built 1899; Italian marble in bathrms. Sitting rm; antiques. Brick patio. Totally nonsmoking. Cr cds: A, C, MC, V.

Restaurants

★ ★ ★ **ALDO'S.** *2914 Pasatiempo Lane. 916/483-5031.* Hrs: 11:30 am–2:30 pm, 6–10:30 pm; Sun to 2:30 pm. Res accepted. French, Italian menu. Bar 11–1 am. Semi-a la carte: lunch $6.50–$15, dinner $13.75–$26.40. Specialties: chicken Jerusalem, flaming steak, tournedos Rossini. Pianist 6:30 pm–1 am. Lavish decor; art display. Family-owned. Cr cds: A, C, D, MC, V.

★ ★ ★ **CHANTERELLE.** *(See Sterling Hotel Inn) 916/442-0451.* Hrs: 7–9 am, 11:30 am–2 pm, 5:30–8:30 pm; Sun 8:30 am–2 pm, 5:30–8:30 pm. Closed some major hols. Res accepted. California, French menu. Setups. Wine list. Semi-a la carte: bkfst $6.50–$8.50, lunch $7.50–$10.50, dinner $12.50–$18. Sun brunch $12.50. Specialty: veal with chanterelle mushrooms. Own baking. Totally nonsmoking. Cr cds: A, MC, V.

★ ★ **CHINOIS EAST/WEST.** *2232 Fair Oaks Blvd. 916/648-1961.* Hrs: 11:30 am–10 pm; Fri & Sat to 11 pm; Sun 4:30–10 pm; Sat brunch 11:30 am–2 pm. Closed Thanksgiving, Dec 25. Chinese, European menu. Bar. A la carte entrees: lunch, dinner $8.95–$20.95. Specialties: whole prawn potstickers, laughing buns with grilled beef. Own desserts. Parking. Outdoor dining. Family-owned. Cr cds: A, C, DS, MC, V, JCB.

★ ★ **CHRISTOPHE'S FRENCH RESTAURANT.** *(6608 Folsom-Auburn Rd, Folsom) 18 mi NE on US 50, at Greenback, in shopping mall. 916/988-2208.* Hrs: 5–10 pm. Closed Mon; some major hols. Res accepted. French menu. Bar. Semi-a la carte: dinner $16.50–$23.50. Specializes in rack of lamb, filet mignon. Outdoor dining (seasonal). Intimate dining area; view of woods. Totally nonsmoking. Cr cds: MC, V.

★ ★ ★ **FIREHOUSE.** *1112 2nd St. 916/442-4772.* Hrs: 11:30 am–2:15 pm, 5:30–10 pm; Sat from 5:30 pm. Closed Sun; major hols. Res accepted. Continental menu. Bar 11:30 am–midnight. A la carte entrees: lunch $10–$15, dinner $35–$40. Specializes in rack of lamb with eggplant, lobster with morels, artichokes and asparagus. Courtyard dining (lunch). Antiques, crystal. In Old Sacramento; restored landmark firehouse (1853). Family-owned. Cr cds: A, MC, V.

✔ ★ **JOSE'S.** *(5451 Fair Oaks Blvd, Carmichael) 10 mi NE, midway between Arden & Camino, at Garfield. 916/485-7800.* Hrs: 10–2 am; Sun brunch to 2 pm. Closed Thanksgiving, Dec 25. Res accepted. Mexican menu. Serv bar. Semi-a la carte: lunch $3.95–$8.95, dinner $4.95–$12.95. Sun brunch $6.95. Specialties: steak Chicano, huevos rancheros, vegetarian dishes. Entertainment Thurs–Sat. Parking. Outdoor dining. Mexican cantina atmosphere. Cr cds: A, C, D, MC, V.

✔ ★ **LEMON GRASS.** *601 Monroe St. 916/486-4891.* Hrs: 11:30 am–2 pm, 5:30–9:30 pm; Fri, Sat 5–10 pm; Sun 5–9 pm. Closed some major hols. Vietnamese, Thai menu. Bar. Semi-a la carte: lunch $5–$12, dinner $9–$15. Child's meals. Specializes in grilled seafood. Parking. Outdoor dining. Original art. Cr cds: A, D, MC, V.

✔ ★ ★ **MARRAKECH.** *1833 Fulton Ave. 916/486-1944.* Hrs: 5:30–10 pm. Closed Mon; Thanksgiving, Dec 25. Res accepted. Moroccan menu. Wine, beer. Complete meals: dinner $18.50. Specialties:

harira-lentil soup, pastilla, lamb dishes. Belly dancer Fri, Sat. Parking. Costumed waiters in desert atmosphere. Totally nonsmoking. Cr cds: A, MC, V.

★ ★ ★ MITCHELL'S TERRACE. *544 Pavilions Lane, 3 mi E on Fair Oaks Blvd, 2 blks E of Howe Ave. 916/920-3800.* Hrs: 11:30 am–2:30 pm, 6–10 pm; Sat from 6 pm. Closed Sun; Jan 1, Dec 25. Res accepted. French, Amer menu. Bar. Extensive wine list. A la carte entrees: lunch $9.50–$14.50, dinner $16–$25. Specializes in wild game, exotic seafood. Menu changes monthly. Jazz guitarist (dinner). Outdoor dining. On 2nd floor of shop; courtyard view. Totally nonsmoking. Cr cds: A, MC, V.

★ ★ PILOTHOUSE. *1000 Front St, aboard historic* Delta King *paddlewheeler. 916/441-4440.* Hrs: 11:30 am–2 pm, 5–10 pm; Sun brunch 10 am–2 pm. Res accepted. Bar. A la carte entrees: lunch $5.95–$11.95, dinner $11.95–$20.95. Sun brunch $16.95. Child's meals. Specializes in fresh fish, steak, pasta. Valet parking. Outdoor dining. Victorian decor. Totally nonsmoking. Cr cds: A, C, D, DS, MC, V.

✔ ★ RISTORANTE PIATTI. *571 Pavilions Lane, 2 blks E of Howe Ave. 916/649-8885.* Hrs: 11 am–10 pm; Fri & Sat to 11 pm. Closed Thanksgiving, Dec 25. Res accepted. Italian menu. Bar. A la carte entrees: lunch, dinner $8–$12. Child's meals. Specializes in roasted chicken, wood-fired pizza, fresh pasta. Valet parking. Outdoor dining. Mediterranean decor. Totally nonsmoking. Cr cds: A, MC, V.

★ RUSTY DUCK. *500 Bercut Dr, I-5 & Richards Blvd. 916/441-1191.* Hrs: 11:30 am–2:30 pm, 5–10 pm; Fri, Sat to 11 pm; Sun 10 am–3 pm, 4:30–10 pm; early-bird dinner Mon–Sat 5–6:30 pm. Res accepted. Bar; Fri, Sat to 1:30 am. Semi-a la carte: lunch $3.95–$10.95, dinner $9.95–$19.95. Child's meals. Specializes in fresh fish, prime rib. Oyster bar. Own pies, cheesecake. Soft rock band Fri, Sat. Parking. Rustic hunting lodge decor; fireplace. Cr cds: A, C, D, DS, MC, V.

★ ★ SILVA'S SHELDON INN. *(9000 Grant Line Rd, Elk Grove) 3 mi S on CA 99, left on Elk Grove Blvd to Grant Line Rd, NE 1 mi. 916/686-8330.* Hrs: 5–9:30 pm; Fri & Sat to 10:30 pm; Sun 4–8:30 pm. Closed Mon; some major hols; also wk of Jan 1 & wk of July 4. Bar from 4 pm. Complete meals: dinner $9–$17. Child's meals. Specializes in fresh fish, steak, Portuguese bean soup. Parking. In turn-of-the-century building. Totally nonsmoking. Cr cds: MC, V.

Unrated Dining Spot

RICK'S DESSERT DINER. *2322 K St. 916/444-0969.* Hrs: 10 am–11 pm; Fri, Sat to midnight. Closed Sun; Jan 1, Easter, Thanksgiving, Dec 24–26. A la carte: 75¢–$10. Specializes in desserts. Specialties: Chocolate OD, white chocolate almond torte. Outdoor dining. 1950s decor. Totally nonsmoking. No cr cds accepted.

St Helena (D-1)

Founded: 1853 **Pop:** 4,990 **Elev:** 257 ft **Area code:** 707 **Zip:** 94574

What to See and Do

1. **Silverado Museum.** 1490 Library Ln. Approx 8,500 items of Robert Louis Stevenson memorabilia; first and variant editions of author's works, original letters and manuscripts; paintings, sculptures, photographs. Special exhibits. (Daily exc Mon, afternoons; closed major hols) Phone 963-3757.   **Free.**
2. **Lake Berryessa.** 4 mi S on CA 29 to Rutherford, then E on CA 128. Man-made lake formed by Monticello Dam; 165 miles of shoreline.

Swimming, waterskiing; fishing. Picnicking, concession areas. Camping. Oak Shores has car top boat launch (fee). Contact Lake Berryessa Recreation Office, Bureau of Reclamation, PO Box 9332, Spanish Flat Station, Napa 94558; 966-2111.

3. **Wineries.**

Beaulieu Vineyard. 4 mi S on CA 29, at 1960 S St Helena Hwy, in Rutherford. Winery founded at the turn of the century. Tours and tastings (daily; closed major hols). Phone 963-2411.   **Free.**

Beringer Vineyards. 2000 Main St, N on CA 29. Established 1876. Underground cellars; Rhine House (1883). Tours with wine tasting (daily; closed major hols). Phone 963-4812 or -7115.   **Free.**

Inglenook-Napa Valley. 4 mi S on CA 29, in Rutherford. Founded in 1877–1879; neo-Gothic winery (1887) has vaulted cellars with wines dating to the 1880s. Museum and wine library; gift shop. Guided tours (daily; closed major hols). Phone 967-3359 or -3300. **Free.**

Franciscan Vineyards. 15 mi N via CA 29 in Rutherford, at 1178 Galleron Rd. Wine tasting and sales. (Daily; closed some hols) Phone 963-7111. Tastings (wkends)   ¢

Charles Krug Winery. 2800 Main St. Established 1861. Tours and wine tasting. Select tasting room (fee). (Thurs–Tues; closed major hols) Phone for schedule, 963-5057.   ¢¢

Louis M. Martini Winery. 254 S St Helena Hwy. Guided tours. Wine tasting. (Daily; closed major hols) Phone 963-2736 or 800/321-9463.   **Free.**

Merryvale Vineyards. 1000 Main St. Tasting room within restored 1930s building; 2,000- and 3,000-gallon oak casks on display. Merryvale produces distinct Chardonnays as well as Bordeaux-style red wine. Tours (daily, by appt; closed some major hols). Phone 963-7777 or -2225.   ¢¢

(For further information about the many wineries in the area contact the Chamber of Commerce, 1080 Main St, PO Box 124; 800/767-8528.)

(See Calistoga, Napa, Santa Rosa, Yountville)

Motel

✔ ★ ★ EL BONITA. *195 Main St. 707/963-3216; res: 800/541-3284 (CA); FAX 707/963-8838.* 42 rms, 6 kits. May–Oct: S $65–$110; D $73–$110; suites $105–$160; lower rates wkdays. Crib $5. Pet accepted, some restrictions; $8. TV; cable. Pool; whirlpool, sauna. Complimentary coffee in rms. Restaurant adj 6 am–3 pm. Ck-out 11:30 am. Refrigerators; some in-rm whirlpools. Cr cds: A, C, D, DS, MC, V.

Inns

★ ★ ★ AUBERGE DU SOLEIL. *(180 Rutherford Hill Rd, Rutherford 94573) N via CA 29 to Rutherford, E on CA 128 to Silverado Trail, then N to Rutherford Hill Rd. 707/963-1211; res: 800/348-5406; FAX 707/963-8764.* 48 rms, 2 story. Mid-Mar–mid-Dec: S, D $315–$900; each addl $40; lower rates rest of yr. TV; cable, in-rm movies. Pool; poolside serv. Dining rm (see AUBERGE DU SOLEIL). Rm serv 24 hrs. Bar 11–2 am. Ck-out noon, ck-in 3 pm. Meeting rm. Bellhops. Valet serv. Beauty shop. Tennis, pro avail. Bicycles avail. Exercise equipt; weights, treadmill, sauna, steam rm. Masseuse. Refrigerators. Fireplaces. Private patios, balconies. Nestled in a 33-acre hillside olive grove overlooking the Napa Valley; designed in the informal but elegant tradition of the finest European country inns. Cr cds: A, DS, MC, V.

★ CHESTELSON HOUSE. *1417 Kearney St. 707/963-2238.* 4 rms, 2 story, 1 suite. May–mid-Nov: S $80–$145; D $90–$145; each addl $25; 2-wk rates; lower rates rest of yr. TV $5. Complimentary full bkfst, afternoon & evening refreshments. Restaurant nearby. Ck-out 11 am, ck-in 3 pm. Street parking. Victorian house (1904) with wrap-around porch; library/sitting rm furnished with antiques. Totally nonsmoking. Cr cds: MC, V.

★ ★ ★**HARVEST.** *1 Main St. 707/963-9463; res: 800/950-8466; FAX 707/963-4402.* 54 rms, 2 story. Apr–Nov: S, D $100–$325; each addl $20; lower rates rest of yr. Crib $10. Pet accepted, some restrictions; $10. TV; cable. 2 heated pools; whirlpools. Complimentary continental bkfst, snacks. Ck-out 11 am, ck-in after 4 pm. Meeting rms. Bicycle rentals. Bathrm phones; many refrigerators, fireplaces, wet bars. Some private patios, balconies. Overlooks vineyards. Award-winning landscaping. Cr cds: A, DS, MC, V.

★ ★**HOTEL ST HELENA.** *1309 Main St. 707/963-4388; FAX 707/963-5402.* 18 units, 13 with bath, 2 story (no ground floor units). S, D $110–$200; each addl $10; mid-wk rates. TV in some rms, sitting rm. Complimentary continental bkfst. Restaurant adj 8:30 am–10 pm. Wine, beer. Ck-out noon, ck-in 4 pm. Gift shop. Victorian structure (1881). Cr cds: A, D, MC, V.

★**OLIVER HOUSE.** *2970 Silverado Trail N. 707/963-4089; res: 800/682-7888.* 4 suites, 2 story. Rm phones avail. Aug–Nov: suites $105–$210; each addl $15; 2-day min wkends; lower rates rest of yr. Complimentary continental bkfst. Ck-out 11 am, ck-in 3:30–6 pm. Lawn games. Balconies. Country-Swiss house with antique furnishings; fireplaces. Totally nonsmoking. Cr cds: A, MC, V.

★ ★ ★**RANCHO CAYMUS INN.** *(PO Box 78, Rutherford 94573, 1140 Rutherford Rd) Jct CA 29 & 128. 707/963-1777; res: 800/845-1777; FAX 707/963-5387.* 26 suites, 2 story, 5 kits. Apr–Nov (2-night min wkends): suites $115–$295; kit. units $225–$295; lower rates rest of yr. TV. Complimentary continental bkfst. Dining rm 8 am–3 pm. Ck-out noon, ck-in 3 pm. Meeting rms. Refrigerators. Some in-rm whirlpools, fireplaces. Private patios, balconies. Spanish-style architecture. Cr cds: A, MC, V.

★ ★**VILLA ST HELENA.** *2727 Sulphur Springs Ave. 707/963-2514.* 3 rms, 1 A/C, 3 story. S, D $145–$245. Adults only. Complimentary continental bkfst. Ck-out 11 am, ck-in 3 pm. In the foothill of Mayacamas Mts, with panoramic views of Napa Valley. Eclectic period furnishings; Mexican tile floors; paneled library; fireplaces. Cr cds: MC, V.

✔ ★**WHITE SULPHUR SPRINGS.** *3100 White Sulphur Springs Rd. 707/963-8588.* 28 rms in 2 bldgs, 14 share bath, 14 half-baths, 9 cottages, 4 with kit. No A/C. No rm phones. S, D $65; each addl $15; cottages $100; kit. cottages $125. Crib free. Complimentary continental bkfst, coffee. Ck-out noon, ck-in 3 pm. Meeting rms. Hiking. Bicycles (rentals). Lawn games. Picnic tables, grills. Rustic inn in secluded canyon surrounded by forests; a hot sulphur spring (87°F) flows out of the mountains into a rock-lined outdoor soaking pool. Totally nonsmoking. Cr cds: DS, MC, V.

★ ★ ★**WINE COUNTRY.** *1152 Lodi Lane. 707/963-7077; res: 800/473-3463; FAX 707/963-9018.* 24 units, 2–3 story. Mid-Apr–mid-Oct: S $77–$156; D $97–$176; each addl $20; suites $166–$211; lower rates rest of yr. Closed Dec 25. Pool; whirlpool. Complimentary continental bkfst. Ck-out noon, ck-in 2 pm. Gift shop. Many fireplaces; some refrigerators. Private patios, balconies. Handmade quilts in many rms; antiques. View of vineyards. Cr cds: A, MC, V.

Resort

★ ★ ★ ★**MEADOWOOD.** *900 Meadowood Lane, off Silverado Trail at Howell Mt Rd, Napa Valley area. 707/963-3646; res: 800/458-8080; FAX 707/963-3532.* 99 units, 51 suites. S, D $245–$385; each addl $25; suites $350–$1,500; under 12 free. Crib free. TV; cable. 2 pools; poolside serv. Coffee in rms. Dining rm 7:30 am–9:30 pm (also see THE RESTAURANT AT MEADOWOOD). Rm serv. 3 bars 10:30 am–midnight. Ck-out noon, ck-in 4 pm. Meeting rms. Pro shops. 7 tennis courts, pro. 9-hole golf, pro, putting green. World-class croquet facilities, pro. Exercise rm; instructor, weight machine, bicycles, whirlpool, sauna, steam rm. Masseuse. Spa & fitness center. Refrigerators, honor bar, fresh fruit; many fireplaces. Private patios, balconies. On 256 wooded acres of private reserve; hiking trail with par course; bicycle rentals. Cr cds: A, C, D, DS, MC, V.

Restaurants

★ ★ ★**AUBERGE DU SOLEIL.** *(See Auberge du Soleil Inn) 707/963-1211.* Hrs: 7–11 am, 11:30 am–2:30 pm, 6–9:30 pm. Res accepted. Bar 10–2 am. Wine country cuisine. A la carte entrees: bkfst $8.50–$20, lunch $10–$20, dinner $16–$30. Own baking. Valet parking. Outdoor dining. Country atmosphere. View of valley, vineyards. Cr cds: A, DS, MC, V.

★ ★ ★**THE RESTAURANT AT MEADOWOOD.** *(See Meadowood Resort) 707/963-3646.* Hrs: 11:30 am–2:30 pm, 5:30–10 pm; Sat also 7–11:30 am; Sun 7–11:30 am, 5:30–10 pm; Sun brunch 10:30 am–2:30 pm. Res accepted. French, California menu. Bar to midnight. Wine cellar. A la carte entrees: bkfst $8–$12, lunch $11.50–$15.50, dinner $17.50–$25. Sun brunch $14–$22.50. Specialties: crab cakes, foie gras, paella. Own baking. Parking. Outdoor dining. Jacket. Cr cds: A, C, D, DS, MC, V.

★ ★**SHOWLEY'S AT MIRAMONTE.** *1327 Railroad Ave, 1 blk E of Main St. 707/963-1200.* Hrs: 11 am–3 pm, 6–9:30 pm. Closed Mon; Thanksgiving, Dec 25. Res accepted; required wkends. Bar. Eclectic cuisine. A la carte entrees: lunch $6–$11, dinner $12–$19. Child's meals. Specialties: grilled duck breast, sweetbreads. Outdoor dining. Natural stone building (1858). Cr cds: A, DS, MC, V.

★ ★ ★**TERRA.** *1345 Railroad Ave. 707/963-8931.* Hrs: 6–9:30 pm; Fri & Sat to 10 pm. Closed Tues; some major hols. Res accepted. Southern French, northern Italian menu. Wine, beer. A la carte entrees: dinner $14.50–$19.50. Child's meals. Specialties: grilled filet of salmon with Thai red curry sauce & rice, grilled rare tuna with tomato eggplant compote & tahini sauce. Own pastries. Wine racks along walls. Cr cds: MC, V.

✔ ★ ★**TRA VIGNE.** *1050 Charter Oak Ave. 707/963-4444.* Hrs: noon–9:30 pm; Fri & Sat to 10:30 pm. Closed Thanksgiving, Dec 25. Res accepted. Northern Italian menu. Bar. A la carte entrees: lunch, dinner $4.95–$16.50. Specializes in fresh pasta, grilled dishes. Own desserts. Parking. Outdoor dining. Patio. Cr cds: DS, MC, V, JCB.

★ ★**TRILOGY.** *1234 Main St. 707/963-5507.* Hrs: noon–2 pm, 6–9 pm; Sat & Sun from 6 pm. Closed Mon; Thanksgiving, Dec 25. Res accepted. French, California menu. Wine, beer. A la carte entrees: lunch $3–$12, dinner $13–$19. Complete meals: dinner $32. Child's meals. Specializes in beef, seafood, lamb. Outdoor dining. Cr cds: MC, V.

Salinas (F-2)

Pop: 108,777 **Elev:** 53 ft **Area code:** 408

Birthplace of novelist John Steinbeck, many of whose works, including *East of Eden* (1952), *Tortilla Flat* (1935) and *Of Mice and Men* (1937), are set in the Salinas Valley area.

What to See and Do

1. *Hat in Three Stages of Landing.* Community Center, 940 N Main St. Sculpture by Claes Oldenburg. Concept of a straw hat tossed out of the rodeo grounds (adjacent) in three stages of landing on the field.
2. **Pinnacles National Monument** (see). Approx 25 mi S via US 101, then 11 mi E via CA 146.

(For further information contact the Chamber of Commerce, 119 E Alisal St, PO Box 1170, 93902; 424-7611.)

Annual Events

California Rodeo. Rodeo Grounds, 1034 N Main St, ¼ mi N off US 101. Parades, square dancing, entertainment, barbecue. Ramps to grandstand. Phone 757-2951. 3rd wkend July.

Steinbeck Festival. Sponsored by Steinbeck Center Foundation. Bus and walking tours of Steinbeck country; films, plays, readings and lectures about the author. Phone 753-6411. Aug.

International Airshow. 4 mi SE via US 101, at airport. Aerobatic displays, formation parachute jumping, precision close-formation flying by top US and international performers, including the US Navy's Blue Angels. Late fall, usually Oct.

(See Big Sur, Carmel, Monterey, Pacific Grove)

Motels

(Rates may be higher, no single rms avail during rodeo, special events)

★**COMFORT INN.** *144 Kern St (93905). 408/758-8850; FAX 408/758-3611.* 32 rms, 2 story. S $49–$98; D $54–$110; each addl $8; under 16 free; higher rates some wkends. Crib $8. TV; cable. Complimentary continental bkfst. Complimentary coffee in rms. Restaurant nearby. Ck-out 11 am. Bathrm phones. Cr cds: A, C, D, DS, ER, MC, V, JCB.

★★**LAUREL INN.** *801 W Laurel Dr (93906). 408/449-2474; res: 800/354-9831; FAX 408/449-2476.* 145 rms, 2 story. S $44–$80; D $52–$90. Crib $4. TV; cable, in-rm movies avail. Heated pool; whirlpool, sauna. Coffee in lobby. Restaurant adj open 24 hrs. Bar 11–2 am. Ck-out noon. Meeting rms. Valet serv. Some refrigerators, fireplaces. Cr cds: A, C, D, DS, MC, V.

✔★**VAGABOND INN.** *131 Kern St (93905). 408/758-4693; FAX 408/758-9835.* 70 rms, 2 story. S $48–$59; D $51–$59; each addl $5; under 18 free. Crib free. Pet accepted, some restrictions; $3. TV; cable. Heated pool. Complimentary continental bkfst, coffee. Restaurant adj open 24 hrs. Ck-out noon. Cr cds: A, C, D, DS, ER, MC, V.

Restaurant

★**PUB'S PRIME RIB.** *227 Monterey St. 408/424-2261.* Hrs: 11 am–10 pm; Sun 3–9 pm. Closed major hols. Res accepted. No A/C. Bar. Complete meals: lunch $5–$10, dinner $9–$17. Child's meals. Specializes in prime rib, skirt steak, sweetbreads. Own desserts. Parking. Cr cds: A, C, D, DS, MC, V.

Salton Sea State Recreation Area (J-5)

(N shore of Salton Sea, CA 111 at State Park Rd)

The Salton Sea, located in the Colorado Desert, is a popular inland boating and fishing area. In 1905, the Colorado River flooded through a broken canal gate into the Salton Basin, creating a vast new lake. Fishermen catch corvina, croakers, sargo and tilapia year round. A launch ramp is available and can accommodate any trailer boat. The recreation area covers 17,913 acres and has areas for swimming and waterskiing. There are nature trails for birdwatching, interpretive programs (Nov–May), picnic grounds and 148 developed campsites (dump station, hookups), plus two miles of primitive camping at Corvina Beach, Salt Creek and Bombay Beach campgrounds. Standard fees. Phone 619/393-3052 or -3059.

(For accommodations see Indio)

San Bernardino (H-4)

Founded: 1810 **Pop:** 164,164 **Elev:** 1,049 ft **Area code:** 909

Set amid mountains, valleys and deserts, San Bernardino is a mixture of Spanish and Mormon cultures. The city takes its name from the valley and mountains discovered by a group of missionaries in 1810 on the feast of San Bernardino of Siena. In 1851, a group of Mormons bought the Rancho San Bernardino and laid out the city, modeled after Salt Lake City. The group was recalled by Brigham Young six years later but the city continued to thrive. The area has a vast citrus industry. In April the fragrance and beauty of orange blossoms fill the nearby groves.

What to See and Do

1. **Rim of the World Highway** (CA 18). Scenic 45-mile mountain road leading to Big Bear Lake, Snow Summit, Running Springs, Lake Arrowhead, Blue Jay and Skyforest. Beaches on the lakes, fishing, hiking and riding trails, picnic grounds.
2. **Glen Helen Regional Park.** 2555 Devore Rd, 10 mi N, 1 mi W of I-215. Approx 500 acres. Swimming (fee), 2 flume water slides (fee); fishing (fee). Nature trail. Picnicking, playground. Group camping (fee). (Daily; closed Jan 1, Dec 25) Phone 880-2522. Per vehicle ¢¢
3. **San Bernardino National Forest.** 10 mi N via I-215, CA 18, 30, 38, 330. One of the most heavily used national forests in the country; stretches east from San Bernardino to Palm Springs. Includes the popular San Gorgonio Wilderness at the forest's east edge by Redlands, the small Cucamonga Wilderness in the west end of the San Bernardino Mountains and the San Jacinto Wilderness in the San Jacinto Mountains (permits required for wildernesses). Fishing, hunting; boating. Hiking. Skiing. Off-road vehicle trails. Picnicking. Camping (fees charged; reservations for camping accepted, as well as first come, first served basis). Contact Forest Supervisor, 1824 S Commercenter Circle, 92408; 383-5588. Campground reservations 800/283-CAMP. Camping ¢¢¢–¢¢¢¢¢
4. **Mountain High Ski Area.** 20 mi N on I-215 (US 395), then 9 mi NW on CA 138, then 8 mi SW, off CA 2 in Wrightwood. Two quad, 3 triple, 6 double chairlifts; patrol; school; rentals; snowmaking; concession areas, cafeterias. Longest run 1½ mi; vertical drop 1,600 ft. (Mid-Nov–mid-Apr, daily) Night skiing. Shuttle bus operates between east and west areas (free). Phone 619/249-5477. ¢¢¢¢¢

(For further information contact the San Bernardino Area Chamber of Commerce, 546 W 6th St, PO Box 658, 92402; 885-7515.)

Annual Event

National Orange Show. Fairgrounds, Mill & E Sts. Marks completion of winter citrus crop harvest. Held annually since 1915. Exhibits, sports events, entertainment. Contact Natl Orange Show Fairground; 888-6788. Apr or May.

Seasonal Event

Renaissance Faire. Glen Helen Regional Park, 10 mi N on I-215, exit Devore Rd. Re-creates an Elizabethan experience with costumed performers, booths, food and games. Phone 800/52-FAIRE. Late Apr-mid-June, wkends.

(See Anaheim, Lake Arrowhead, Redlands, Riverside)

Motels

★ ★**LA QUINTA.** *205 E Hospitality Lane (92408), I-10 exit Waterman Ave N.* 909/888-7571; FAX 909/884-3864. 153 rms, 3 story. S $52–$59; D $60–$67; each addl $8; under 18 free. Pet accepted, some restrictions. TV; cable, in-rm movies avail. Heated pool. Complimentary continental bkfst 6–10 am, Sat & Sun 6:30–10:30 am. Restaurant adj open 24 hrs. Ck-out noon. Meeting rms. Valet serv. Sundries. Health club privileges. Cr cds: A, C, D, DS, ER, MC, V, JCB.

✔ ★**SUPER 8-OAK CREEK INN.** *777 W 6th St (92410), 1 blk E of I-215.* 909/889-3561; FAX 909/884-7127. 57 rms, 2 story. S $38; D $40–$41; each addl $3; suites $45–$48. Crib $4. TV; cable. Heated pool; whirlpool, sauna. Complimentary continental bkfst. Restaurant opp 6 am–10 pm. Ck-out 11 am. Refrigerators. Cr cds: A, C, D, DS, MC, V, JCB.

Hotels

★ ★**HILTON.** *285 E Hospitality Lane (92408), I-10 exit Waterman Ave N.* 909/889-0133; FAX 909/381-4299. 247 rms, 7 story. S $85; D $95; each addl $10; suites $125–$300; family rates. Crib free. TV; cable, in-rm movies avail. Heated pool; whirlpool, poolside serv. Restaurant 6:30 am–10 pm; Sun 7 am–9 pm. Bar 11:30–1 am. Ck-out noon. Convention facilities. Gift shop. Free Ontario Intl Airport transportation. Health club privileges. Bathrm phones, refrigerators. Cr cds: A, C, D, DS, MC, V.

★ ★**RADISSON.** *295 North E St (92401).* 909/381-6181; FAX 909/381-5288. 231 rms, 12 story. S $65–$80; D $75–$90; each addl $10; suites $85–$245; under 12 free; ski plans. Crib free. TV; cable, in-rm movies. Coffee in rms. Restaurant 6:30 am–11 pm. Bar 11–1:30 am; entertainment Wed–Sat, dancing. Ck-out noon. Meeting rms. Gift shop. Free Ontario Intl Airport, RR station, bus depot transportation. Exercise equipt; weight machine, bicycles, whirlpool. Some refrigerators. Convention center adj. Cr cds: A, C, D, DS, MC, V, JCB.

Restaurants

✔ ★ ★**LOTUS GARDEN.** *111 E Hospitality Lane, I-10 exit Waterman Ave N.* 909/381-6171. Hrs: 11:30 am–9:30 pm; Fri, Sat to 10:30 pm. Closed Thanksgiving. Res accepted. Chinese menu. Bar. A la carte entrees: lunch, dinner $5.25–$14.50. Complete meals: dinner $8.95–$13.95. Lunch buffet $5.25. Child's meals. Specializes in mandarin dishes. Parking. Chinese decor; exterior resembles a Chinese temple. Cr cds: A, C, D, DS, MC, V.

★**YAMAZATO OF JAPAN.** *289 E Hospitality Lane, I-10 exit Waterman Ave N.* 909/888-3103. Hrs: 11:30 am–2 pm, 5–9:30 pm; Sat & Sun from 5 pm. Closed Thanksgiving, Dec 25. Res accepted. Japanese menu. Bar. Semi-a la carte: lunch $5.95–$12.95, dinner $10.95–$28.95. Child's meals. Specializes in teppanyaki, tempura. Sushi bar. Karaoke singing Sat & Sun. Parking. Authentic Japanese decor. Cr cds: A, MC, V.

San Clemente (J-4)

Pop: 41,100 **Elev:** 200 ft **Area code:** 714 **Zip:** 92672

What to See and Do

1. **San Clemente State Beach.** Califia Ave, off I-5. Swimming, lifeguard; fishing; hiking trail, picnicking; trailer hookups, camping. Camping reservations necessary. Phone 492-3156. Day use per vehicle ¢¢¢; Camping ¢¢¢¢¢

2. **Swimming. Municipal Pier & Beach.** ½ mi W of I-5. Swimming, surfing; picnicking, playground; fishing, bait and tackle shop at end of pier. (Daily; lifeguards) For information contact Division of Marine Safety, 100 Avenida Presidio; phone 361-8219. **Free.**

(For further information contact the Chamber of Commerce, 1100 N El Camino Real; 492-1131.)

Annual Event

San Clemente Summer Fiesta. Street party, ocean festival. July or Aug.

(See Anaheim, Laguna Beach, San Juan Capistrano)

Motels

★ ★ ★**RAMADA INN.** *35 Calle de Industrias, off I-5 Pico Ave exit, 1 blk W.* 714/498-8800; FAX 714/498-8800, ext 207. 110 rms, 3 story. S $73–$79; D $83–$89; each addl $10; suites $150; wkly rates. Crib $10. TV; cable. Heated pool. Complimentary bkfst buffet. Restaurant 6 am–2 pm, 5–10 pm. Ck-out noon. Meeting rms. Some refrigerators; wet bar in suites. Balconies. Cr cds: A, C, D, DS, ER, MC, V, JCB.

✔ ★ ★**TRAVELODGE SAN CLEMENTE BEACH.** *2441 S El Camino Real.* 714/498-5954; FAX 714/498-5954, ext 114. 19 rms, 3 suites. June–mid-Sept: S $55–$69; D $65–$85; each addl $4; suites $105–$135; lower rates rest of yr. Crib $4. TV; cable, in-rm movies avail. Complimentary continental bkfst, coffee. Restaurant nearby. Ck-out 11 am. Free covered parking. Refrigerators. Many private patios, balconies. Cr cds: A, C, D, DS, MC, V.

Motor Hotel

★ ★ ★**HOLIDAY INN.** *111 S Ave de Estrella.* 909/361-3000; FAX 909/361-2472. 72 rms, 3 story, 19 suites. S, D $65–$85; suites $125–$135; under 12 free; wkly, monthly rates. Crib free. Pet accepted; $10. TV; cable. Heated pool. Restaurant 7 am–2 pm, 5–10 pm. Rm serv. Bar. Ck-out noon. Meeting rms. Bellhops. Free garage parking. Exercise equipt; bicycles, rowers, whirlpool. Refrigerators; some wet bars. Balconies. Cr cds: A, C, D, DS, MC, V, JCB.

Hotel

★★QUALITY SUITES. *2481 S El Camino Real. 714/366-1000; FAX 714/366-1030.* 66 suites, 4 story. Mid-May–mid-Sept: S $89–$99; D $99–$109; each addl $10; under 18 free; lower rates rest of yr. Crib free. TV; cable, in-rm movies. Heated pool; whirlpool. Complimentary full bkfst, coffee. Restaurant nearby. No rm serv. Ck-out noon. Gift shop. Refrigerators. Wet bars. Some balconies. Cr cds: A, C, D, DS, ER, MC, V, JCB.

San Diego (K-4)

Founded: 1769 **Pop:** 1,110,549 **Elev:** 42 ft **Area code:** 619

The southernmost city in California gains a Mexican flavor from its proximity to Mexico's border town of Tijuana (see; for Border Crossing Regulations see INTRODUCTION). Like many California cities, San Diego stretches from the Pacific Ocean eastward over lovely rolling hills of 1,591 feet. It is a warm city where the sun nearly always shines; this balmy year-round climate encourages outdoor living. Within San Diego County are mountains as high as 6,500 feet, 70 miles of beaches, a desert area, resorts, flowers, palm trees and a lively cultural program. Several universities are located here.

For many years San Diego has been an important Navy center. Many Navy personnel, as well as others, retire here. It is a growing oceanography center and is also noted for avocado producing, electronics, ship, aircraft and missile building, manufacturing, education, health and biomedical research and tourism.

San Diego was "the place where California began" when the Portuguese conquistador Juan Rodriguez Cabrillo landed here in 1542. Since the first mission in California was built in San Diego in 1769, the city has grown steadily under the Spanish, Mexicans and North Americans.

Transportation

Car Rental Agencies: See toll-free numbers under Introduction.

Public Transportation: Buses, trolleys downtown, to East County and to Tijuana (San Diego Transit), phone 233-3004.

Rail Passenger Service: Amtrak 800/872-7245.

Airport Information

San Diego Intl Airport/Lindbergh Field: Information 231-2100; lost and found 231-5260; weather 289-1212; cash machines, East Terminal.

Terminals: West Terminal: American, Aero California, Delta, Midwest Express, Northwest, Reno Air, Sky West; East Terminal: Aero Mexico, Air West, Alaska, America West, Continental, Southwest, TWA, United, United Express, USAir, USAir Express

(Airlines and their terminal locations may change. Before leaving for the airport, you should phone the airline to confirm terminal location for your flight.)

What to See and Do

1. **Cabrillo National Monument.** 10 mi W of I-8 on Catalina Blvd (CA 209), at tip of Point Loma. Commemorates discovery of what is now the west coast of the US by explorer-navigator Juan Rodriguez Cabrillo. From the most southwesterly point in the continental US, the view stretches north to La Jolla, west to the Pacific, south to Mexico, east into San Diego County. The old lighthouse (1855) is a feature of the monument and vantage point for observing annual migration of gray whales (Dec–mid-Mar). Visitor center and museum; slide and film programs. (Daily) For information contact Superintendent, PO Box 6670, 92166; 557-5450. (See ANNUAL EVENTS) Per vehicle ¢¢

2. **Old Town.** Around the plaza at Mason St & San Diego Ave. Historic section of city with many restored or reconstructed buildings; old adobe structures, restaurants, shops. Guided walking tours (daily). Old Town includes Old Town San Diego State Historic Park (see #3) and

 Presidio Park. Presidio Dr off Taylor St. Site of the first mission in California. Mounds mark the original Presidio and fort. Inside is

 Junipero Serra Museum. In Presidio Park. Landmark of San Diego; the museum stands on top of the hill recognized as the site where California's first mission and presidio were established in 1769. The museum interprets the Spanish and Mexican periods of San Diego's history. (Daily exc Mon; closed major hols) Phone 297-3258. ¢¢

 Whaley House (1856). 2482 San Diego Ave, at Harney St. Once housed "The Tanner Troupe" theater company, and later served as the San Diego County Courthouse until the records were transferred to "New Town" on March 31, 1871. Restored and refurnished; on grounds are replica of Old Town drugstore; herb and rose gardens. (Daily; closed major hols) Sr citizen rate. Phone 298-2482. ¢¢

3. **Old Town San Diego State Historic Park.** This is an area within Old Town that is bounded by Congress, Wallace, Twigg and Juan Sts. Visitor center, 4002 Wallace St (daily; closed Jan 1, Thanksgiving, Dec 25). Phone 237-6770. ¢ Includes

 Seeley Stable. Calhoun St. Restoration of stables built in 1869 to serve US mail stage line; display of horse-drawn vehicles, historic Western artifacts. (Daily; closed Jan 1, Thanksgiving, Dec 25) ¢ Also nearby, and included in admission, is

 Casa de Estudillo (1820–29). 40001 Mason St. Restored example of one-story adobe town house; period furnishings. (Daily; closed Jan 1, Thanksgiving, Dec 25) Included in admission for Seeley Stable (see).

 San Diego *Union* **Historical Restoration.** 2626 San Diego Ave. Restored birthplace of the San Diego newspaper that first came off the press in 1868. (Daily exc Mon; closed Jan 1, Thanksgiving, Dec 25) Free.

4. **Mission Basilica San Diego de Alcala** (1769). 10818 San Diego Mission Rd. First California mission. Restored, still used for services. Museum has relics of early days of mission; tape tours include mission and grounds. (Daily; closed Thanksgiving, Dec 25) Sr citizen rate. Phone 281-8449. Museum ¢

5. **Gaslamp Quarter.** Downtown. A 16½-block national historic district bordered by Broadway on the north, 6th Ave on the east, K Street on the south and 4th Ave on the west. This area formed the city's business center at the turn of the century. Many Victorian buildings under restoration. Walking tours (Sat). Phone 233-5227. Walking tours ¢¢

6. **Balboa Park.** Center of city on 1,200 acres. Art galleries, museums, theaters, restaurants, recreational facilities and miles of garden walks, lawns, flowers, subtropical plants and ponds. Off Park Blvd are

 San Diego Zoo. More than 3,200 rare and exotic animals representing 800 species, many of which are displayed in new natural habitats such as Tiger River, Sun Bear Forest and Gorilla Tropics. **Children's Zoo** features petting paddock, animal nursery, animal exhibits at children's eye level. Walk-through aviaries. Animal shows daily; 40-min guided tour aboard double-deck bus; Skyfari aerial tramway. (Daily) Sr citizen rate. Phone 234-3153. ¢¢¢¢

 Starlight Bowl. Setting for musical, dance and theater events.

 House of Pacific Relations. Thirty-one nations offer cultural and art exhibits in 15 California/Spanish-style cottages. (Sun; also 1st Tues of month) Phone 234-0739. Free.

 Spreckels Outdoor Organ Pavilion. One of the largest in the world; 4,400 pipes. (Concerts: Sun, hols; also Tues–Thurs in July–Aug) (See ANNUAL EVENTS) Free.

 On Laurel St (El Prado) are

SAN DIEGO
AND VICINITY

MILES
0 1 2 3 4
0 2 3 6.4
KILOMETERS

© H.M. GOUSHA

M-4-UH-1132-S

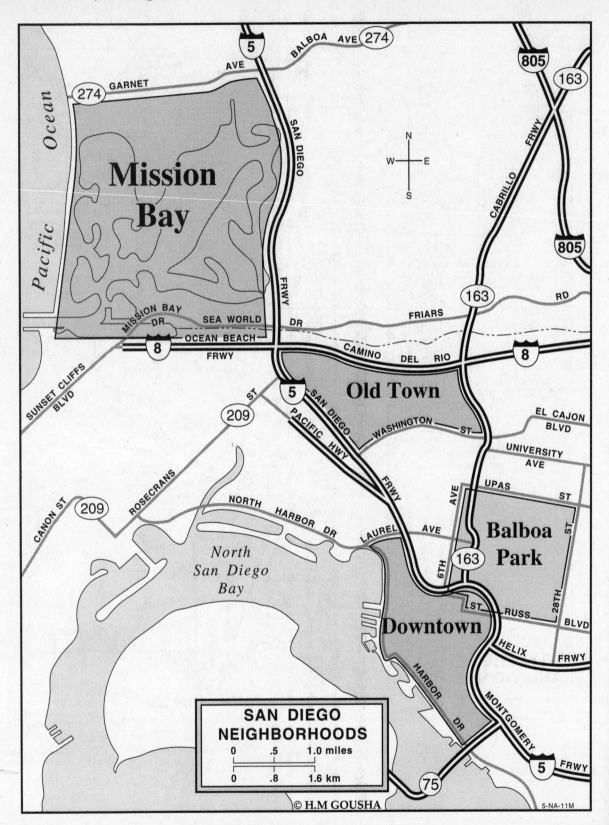

San Diego/California 236
Mission Bay
Pacific Ocean
274 GARNET AVE
5
BALBOA AVE 274
SAN DIEGO FRWY
805
163
CABRILLO FRWY
805
163
FRIARS RD
163
8
SEA WORLD DR
OCEAN BEACH FRWY
8
CAMINO DEL RIO
MISSION BAY DR
8
SUNSET CLIFFS BLVD
5
Old Town
SAN DIEGO FRWY
PACIFIC HWY
WASHINGTON ST
EL CAJON BLVD
209 ST
UNIVERSITY AVE
UPAS ST
209
CANON ST
ROSECRANS
NORTH HARBOR DR
LAUREL AVE
6TH AVE
163
Balboa Park
28TH ST
North San Diego Bay
RUSS BLVD
ST
Downtown
HELIX FRWY
HARBOR DR
MONTGOMERY
SAN DIEGO NEIGHBORHOODS
0   .5   1.0 miles
0   .8   1.6 km
75
5 FRWY
© H.M GOUSHA
5-NA-11M

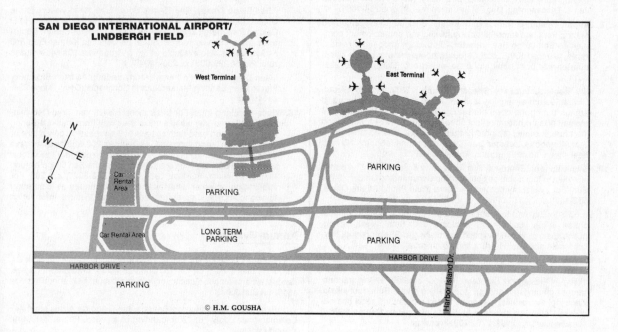

SAN DIEGO INTERNATIONAL AIRPORT/ LINDBERGH FIELD

West Terminal

East Terminal

N
W   E
S

Car Rental Area

PARKING

Car Rental Area

PARKING

PARKING

LONG TERM PARKING

PARKING

HARBOR DRIVE

HARBOR DRIVE

Harbor Island Dr.

PARKING

© H.M. GOUSHA

Natural History Museum. Exhibits of flora and fauna and minerology of southwestern US and Baja California; seismograph, Foucault pendulum; traveling exhibits; classes, nature outings. (Daily; closed Jan 1, Thanksgiving, Dec 25) Phone 232-3821. ¢¢–¢¢¢

Reuben H. Fleet Space Theater and Science Center. 1875 El Prado. Space Theater features Omnimax theater with large-format, educational science films and multimedia shows. Science Center is a museum of natural phenomena; more than 50 permanent exhibits engage the visitor in active exploration. Admission includes participatory exhibits in Science Center. (Daily) Sr citizen rate. Phone 238-1233 for information. ¢¢¢

San Diego Aerospace Museum. Aerospace Historical Center. Full-scale original and reproduction aircraft; moon rock exhibit. (Daily; closed Jan 1, Thanksgiving, Dec 25) Phone 234-8291. ¢¢ Admission includes

International Aerospace Hall of Fame. Portraits, memorabilia and special exhibits honoring the men and women around the world who have made significant contributions to aerospace progress. (Daily; closed Jan 1, Thanksgiving, Dec 25) Phone 232-8322.

San Diego Museum of Art. European and American paintings and decorative arts; Japanese, Chinese and other Oriental art, contemporary sculpture. (Daily exc Mon; closed Jan 1, Thanksgiving, Dec 25) Sr citizen rate. Free admission 3rd Tues of month. Phone 232-7931. ¢¢

Timken Museum of Art. Collection of European Old Masters, 18th- and 19th-century American paintings and Russian icons. Docent tours (Tues–Thurs or by appt). (Tues–Sat, also Sun afternoons; closed major hols, also Sept). Phone 239-5548. **Free.**

Museum of Photographic Arts. 1649 El Prado, Casa de Balboa. Changing exhibitions featuring 19th century, early–mid-20th century and contemporary works by world-renowned photographers.

(Daily; closed Jan 1, Martin Luther King Day, Labor Day, Thanksgiving, Dec 25; also Mon & Tues between each exhibition) Free guided tours (wkends). Phone 239-5262. ¢¢   In same building is

San Diego Hall of Champions Sports Museum. Exhibits on more than 40 sports in the area; theater; gift shop; Breitbard Hall of Fame and San Diego sports archives. (Daily; closed Jan 1, Thanksgiving, Dec 25) Phone 234-2544. ¢¢

Museum of Man. Exhibits on California and Hopi Indians, ancient Egypt, Maya culture, early man, mummies; human reproduction; changing exhibits. (Daily; closed Jan 1, Thanksgiving, Dec 25) Phone 239-2001. ¢¢

Old Globe Theatre. One of three uniquely different theaters of the Simon Edison Centre for the Performing Arts; productions staged include classical and contemporary comedy and drama of diverse styles in the 581-seat Old Globe Theatre, the 225-seat Cassius Carter Centre Stage and the 612-seat outdoor Lowell Davies Festival Theater. Performances (nightly exc Mon, also Sat & Sun matinees). For information on schedules and ticket prices contact Old Globe Theatre, PO Box 2171, 92112; 239-2255. ¢¢¢¢¢

N off Laurel St (El Prado), on Village Place is

Spanish Village Arts and Crafts Center. Artists and craftspeople work here with amateur critics observing. Studios surrounding patios (daily; closed Jan 1, Thanksgiving, Dec 25). Phone 233-9050. **Free.**

Recreational facilities in the park include

Golf. Municipal courses. Near 26th & A Sts. 18- & 9-hole courses; pro shop, restaurant, driving range, 3 putting greens; rental carts. (Daily) Phone 232-2470.

7. **Museum of Contemporary Art.** 1001 Kettner Blvd. Permanent and changing exhibits of contemporary painting, sculpture, design, photography and architecture. Bookstore. (Daily exc Mon; closed Jan 1, Thanksgiving, Dec 25) Sr Citizen rate. Phone 234-1001. ¢

8. **Seaport Village.** W Harbor Dr at Kettner Blvd, adj to Embarcadero Marina Park. A 14-acre shopping, dining and entertainment complex on San Diego Bay. Includes 75 specialty shops and restaurants; restored 1890 Looff Carousel; horse-drawn carriage rides; quarter-mile boardwalk along the waterfront. (Daily) Phone 235-4014.

9. **Villa Montezuma/Jesse Shepard House** (1887). 1925 K Street. Lavish Victorian mansion built for Jesse Shepard, musician and author, during the city's "Great Boom" (1886–88). More than 20 stained glass windows reflect Shepard's interest in art, music and literature; includes restored kitchen, antiques. Guided tours (Fri & Sun afternoons, last tour leaves at 4 pm; phone for appt). No high heel shoes; no photographs. Phone 239-2211. ¢¢

10. **Naval ship tour.** Broadway Pier, Broadway & Harbor Dr. The public is invited to tour a ship as guests of the Commanding Officer. (Sat & Sun) For availability contact the Naval Base Public Affairs Office, 532-1430 or -1431. **Free.**

11. **San Diego Bay and the Embarcadero.** Port for active Navy ships, cruise ships, commercial shipping and tuna fleet. Sailing, powerboating, waterskiing and sportfishing at Shelter Island, Harbor Island, the Yacht Harbor and Commercial Basin.

12. **Mission Bay Park.** N of San Diego River, reached via I-5. Aquatic park on 4,600 acres. Swimming, lifeguards (summer, daily), waterskiing in Fiesta and Sail bays; fishing; boating, sailing (rentals, ramps, landings, marinas); sportfishing fleet. Golf. Picnicking. Camping. For details, reservations and regulations send self-addressed, stamped envelope to Visitor Information Center, 2688 E Mission Bay Dr, 92109; 276-8200. In park is

   Sea World. Sea World Dr, exit W off I-5. This 150-acre marine park on Mission Bay features several shows and more than 20 exhibits and attractions. Baby Shamu in special Shamu show. Also new Dolphin Bay/Otter Outlook exhibit at Rocky Point Preserve. (Daily) Phone 226-3901 or 800/325-3150 (CA), 800/SEA-WRLD (exc CA). ¢¢¢¢¢

13. **Maritime Museum Association.** 1306 N Harbor Dr, on Embarcadero. Restored bark *Star of India* (1863) built at Ramsey on the Isle of Man and launched as the *Euterpe;* sailed under the British, Hawaiian (before it was part of the US) and United States flags. It sailed for the first time in fifty years on July 4, 1976. Also here are the steam ferry *Berkeley* (1898), with nautical exhibits and the luxury steam yacht *Medea* (1904). (Daily) Sr citizen rate. Phone 234-9153. ¢¢

14. **San Diego Wild Animal Park.** 30 mi NE via I-15 to Via Rancho Pkwy exit, follow signs. Operated by the Zoological Society of San Diego as a preservation area for endangered species. More than 2,400 African & Asian animals roam freely on the 2,100-acre preserve; five-mile guided Wgasa Bush Line monorail tour; Africa-inspired Nairobi Village featuring animal shows, hiking trail, animal and botanical exhibits. (Daily) Sr citizen rate. Phone 234-6541. ¢¢¢¢

15. **Sightseeing.**

    Gray Line bus tours. Contact 3855 Rosecrans St, 92110; 491-0011 or 800/331-5077 (exc CA).

    Southwest Coaches. Contact 1601 Newton Ave, 92113; 232-7579.

    San Diego Harbor Excursion. 1050 N Harbor Dr. One-hour (12-mi) narrated tour highlights Harbor Island, Coronado and the Navy Terminals at North Island and 32nd St. Two-hour (25-mi) narrated tour includes the above plus Shelter Island, Ballast Point (where Cabrillo is believed to have first landed in 1542), the harbor entrance, the ship yards and the Navy's submarine base. (Daily) Sr citizen rate. Phone 234-4111. One-hour tour ¢¢¢; Two-hour tour ¢¢¢¢

    Scenic drive. Many of the attractions noted above may be seen on a 59-mile loop marked by blue and yellow seagull signs. The drive takes two-and-one-half to three hours, includes waterfront,

Shelter Island, Cabrillo National Monument, Point Loma, Old Town, and the top of Mt Soledad, which has a magnificent view of entire area.

   San Diego Trolley. The 15-mile South Line takes visitors to the United States/Mexico border; 17-mile East Line takes visitors to El Cajon. Lines merge at the Imperial & 12th Transfer Center. Departures every 15 minutes from Santa Fe Depot at Kettner Blvd & C Street; tickets also available at 5th & Broadway. (Daily) Sr citizen rate. Phone 239-6051 or 233-3004. ¢

   San Diego-Coronado Ferry. Hourly departures from Broadway Pier to Ferry Landing Marketplace in Coronado. (Daily) Phone 234-4111. ¢¢

16. **Whale-watching trips.** For three months each year (mid-Dec–mid-Feb), California gray whales make their way from Alaska's Bering Sea to the warm bays and lagoons of Baja, passing only a mile or so off the San Diego shoreline. As many as 200 whales a day have been counted during the peak of the migration period. Trips to local waters and Baja lagoons are scheduled by the San Diego Natural History Museum, PO Box 1390, 92112; 232-3821, ext 203. For information on other whale-watching trips inquire at local sport fishing companies or at the International Visitors Information Center; 236-1212. ¢¢¢¢¢

Annual Events

Corpus Christi Fiesta. Mission San Antonio de Pala. 41 mi N via CA 163, I-15, then 7 mi E on CA 76. Open-air mass, procession; games, dances, entertainment; Spanish-style pit barbecue; held annually since 1816. 1st Sun June.

Festival of Bells. Mission Basilica San Diego de Alcala (see #4). Commemorates July 16, 1769 founding of mission. Phone 281-8449. Wkend mid-July.

Admission Day. Commemoration of California's entry into United States. Mariachi bands, singers, dancers, food. Phone 297-1183. Early Sept.

Cabrillo Festival. Cabrillo National Monument (see #1). Celebration of discovery of the west coast. Phone 557-5450. Last wkend Sept–early Oct.

Christmas on the Prado. Spreckels Outdoor Organ Pavilion and throughout Balboa Park (see #6). Fifty-foot-tall lighted tree, Nativity scenes; special programs. First wkend in Dec.

Christmas-Light Boat Parade. San Diego Harbor, Shelter Island Yacht Basin. Phone 222-4081. Late Dec.

Seasonal Events

Professional sports. Padres (baseball), Chargers (football), Jack Murphy Stadium, CA 163 to Friars Rd exit. Sockers (indoor soccer), Gulls (hockey), Sports Arena, 3500 Sports Arena Blvd.

Additional Visitor Information

The San Diego Convention & Visitors Bureau, International Visitor Information Center, 11 Horton Plaza, 1st & F Streets, 92101, phone 236-1212, offers general information brochures in English, French, German, Japanese, Portuguese and Spanish. *San Diego Magazine* may be obtained at newsstands and has up-to-date information on cultural events and articles of interest to visitors.

Note: For towns in the San Diego area see map. These towns and their accommodations are listed alphabetically.

San Diego Area Suburbs

The following San Diego area towns and suburbs are included in the *Mobil Travel Guide.* For information on any one of them, see the individual alphabetical listing. Carlsbad, Chula Vista, Coronado, Del Mar, El Cajon, Escondido, Oceanside, Rancho Sante Fe, San Ysidro.

City Neighborhoods

Many of the restaurants, unrated dining establishments and some lodgings listed under San Diego include neighborhoods as well as exact street addresses. A map showing these neighborhoods can be found immediately following the city map. Geographic descriptions of these areas are given, followed by a table of restaurants arranged by neighborhood.

Balboa Park: Northeast of downtown; south of Upas St, west of 28th St, north of St Russ Blvd and east of 6th Ave.

Downtown: South and west of I-5 and north and east of the San Diego Bay. **North of Downtown:** North of US 5.

Mission Bay: South of Garnet Ave, west of I-5, north of I-8 and Mission Bay Channel and east of the Pacific Ocean.

Old Town: South of I-8, west of CA 163, north of I-5 and Washington St and east of I-5.

Point Loma: Peninsula west of San Diego Bay and east of the Pacific Ocean.

SAN DIEGO RESTAURANTS BY NEIGHBORHOOD AREAS

(For full description, see alphabetical listings under Restaurants)

BALBOA PARK
Hob Nob Hill. 2271 1st Ave

DOWNTOWN
Anthony's Star of the Sea Room. 1360 Harbor Dr
Athens Market Taverna. 109 W F St
Bice Ristorante. 777 Front St
Corvette Diner Bar & Grill. 3946 5th Ave
Dobson's. 956 Broadway Circle
Fio's. 801 5th Ave
515 Fifth. 515 Fifth Ave
Harbor House. 831 W Harbor Dr
Karl Strauss' Old Columbia Brewery & Grill. 1157 Columbia St
Le Fontainebleau (The Westgate Hotel). 1055 Second Ave
Luigi Al Mare. 861 W Harbor Dr
Pacifica Grill & Rotisserie. 1202 Kettner Blvd
Panda Inn. 506 Horton Plaza
Rainwater's. 1202 Kettner Blvd
San Diego Pier Cafe. 885 W Harbor Dr
Särö. 926 Broadway Circle
Top of the Market. 750 N Harbor Dr

NORTH OF DOWNTOWN
À Dông. 3874 Fairmount Ave
Afghanistan Khyber Pass. 4647 Convoy St
Anthony's Fish Grotto. 11666 Avena Place
Benihana of Tokyo. 477 Camino del Rio South
Busalacchi's. 3683 5th Ave

California Cuisine. 1027 University Ave
Calliope's Greek Cafe. 3958 5th Ave
Celadon. 3628 5th Ave
City Delicatessen. 535 University Ave
D.Z. Akin's. 6930 Alvarado Rd
El Bizcocho (Rancho Bernardo Inn Resort). 17550 Bernardo Oaks Dr
El Indio Shop. 3695 India St
El Tecolote. 6110 Friars Rd
French Side of the West. 2202 Fourth Ave
Greek Corner. 5841 El Cajon Blvd
Imperial House. 505 Kalmia St
Kelly's. 500 Hotel Circle N
Michelangelo. 1878 Rosecrans St
Mister A's. 2550 5th Ave
Nati's. 1852 Bacon St
Saffron. 3731-B India St
Thee Bungalow. 4996 W Point Loma Blvd
Tom Ham's Lighthouse. 2150 Harbor Island Dr
Winesellar & Brasserie. 9550 Waples St, Suite 115

MISSION BAY
Baci Ristorante. 1955 W Morena Blvd
Belgian Lion. 2265 Bacon St

OLD TOWN
Cafe Coyote. 2461 San Diego Ave
Cafe Pacifica. 2414 San Diego Ave
Casa de Bandini. 2754 Calhoun St
Lino's. 2754 Calhoun St
Old Town Mexican Cafe & Cantina. 2489 San Diego Ave

POINT LOMA
Fairouz. 3166 Midway Dr

Note: When a listing is located in a town that does not have its own city heading, it will appear under the city nearest to its location. In these cases, the address and town appear in parenthesis immediately following the name of the establishment.

Motels

★★**BALBOA PARK INN.** *3402 Park Blvd (92103), in Balboa Park.* 619/298-0823; FAX 619/294-8070. 25 rms, 2 story, 17 kit. suites. S, D $75–$80; kit. suites $85–$175; under 12 free. Crib $5. TV; cable. Complimentary continental bkfst. Complimentary coffee in rms. Ck-out noon. Free lndry facilities. Refrigerators; some in-rm whirlpools. Many patios, balconies. Sun deck. Each rm is a ''theme'' rm, with individual decor. Cr cds: A, C, D, DS, MC, V.

✔★★**BEST WESTERN SEVEN SEAS.** *411 Hotel Circle S (92108), in Old Town.* 619/291-1300; FAX 619/291-6933. 309 rms, 2 story, 9 kit. units. S, D $49–$89; kit. units $59–$99; under 12 free. Crib free. Pet accepted, some restrictions; $10. TV; cable. Heated pool; whirlpool, poolside serv. Playground. Complimentary coffee in rms. Restaurant 6 am–midnight. Rm serv. Bar 10–2 am; entertainment, dancing Tues–Sat. Ck-out noon. Coin lndry. Meeting rms. Bellhops. Valet serv. Sundries. Gift shop. Free airport, RR station, bus depot transportation. Lawn games. Game rm. Some balconies. Cr cds: A, C, D, DS, ER, MC, V, JCB.

D ⊛ ≋ ⊗ ⊙ **SC**

✔ ★★**COMFORT SUITES-MISSION VALLEY.** 631 Camino del Rio S (92108), north of downtown. 619/294-3444; FAX 619/260-0746. 122 suites, 3 story. Suites $60–$80; under 17 free. Crib free. TV; cable. Heated pool. Complimentary continental bkfst, coffee. Restaurant adj 10 am–10 pm. Ck-out 11 am. Meeting rms. Coin lndry. Free airport transportation. Exercise equipt; weight machine, bicycles, whirlpool. Refrigerators. Cr cds: A, C, D, DS, ER, MC, V, JCB.

D ≋ ⊼ ⊗ ⊙ **SC**

★**DANA INN & MARINA.** 1710 W Mission Bay Dr (92109), in Mission Bay. 619/222-6440; res: 800/345-9995; FAX 619/222-5916. 196 rms, 2 story. Late May–mid-Sept: S $69–$119; D $79–$129; each addl $10; under 18 free; lower rates rest of yr. Crib free. TV; cable. Heated pool; whirlpool, poolside serv. Coffee in rms. Restaurant 7 am–10 pm. Rm serv. Bar. Ck-out noon. Coin lndry. Bellhops. Valet serv. Free airport, RR station, bus depot transportation. Tennis. Marina. Boat launch adj. Cr cds: A, C, D, DS, MC, V.

◪ ≋ ⊗ ⊙ **SC**

✔ ★**DAYS INN-HOTEL CIRCLE.** 543 Hotel Circle S (92108), in Old Town. 619/297-8800; FAX 619/298-6029. 280 rms, 3 story, 49 kit. units. S $49–$62; D $55–$73; each addl $10; kit. units $57–$79; under 18 free; wkly rates (kit. units); higher rates special events. Crib free. TV; cable. Heated pool; whirlpool. Restaurant 6:30 am–9 pm. Ck-out noon. Coin lndry. Bellhops. Valet serv. Sundries. Barber, beauty shop. Free airport, RR station, bus depot transportation. Refrigerators. Cr cds: A, C, D, DS, MC, V.

D ≋ ⊗ ⊙ **SC**

★★**FABULOUS INN.** 2485 Hotel Circle Place (92108), north of downtown. 619/291-7700; res: 800/824-0950 (exc CA), 800/647-1903 (CA); FAX 619/297-6179. 175 rms, 4 story. Mid-June–early Sept: S $56–$70; D $65–$75; suites $110–$140; under 18 free; lower rates rest of yr. Crib $10. TV; cable. Heated pool; whirlpool. Complimentary continental bkfst. Restaurant nearby. Ck-out noon. Coin lndry. Meeting rms. Free covered parking. Free airport, RR station transportation. Some refrigerators, in-rm whirlpools. Many balconies. Cr cds: A, C, D, DS, ER, MC, V.

D ≋ ⊗ ⊙ **SC**

★★**GROSVENOR INN.** 3145 Sports Arena Blvd (92110), near Lindbergh Field Intl Airport, in Point Loma. 619/225-9999; res: 800/232-1212 (exc CA), 800/222-2929 (CA); FAX 619/225-0958. 206 rms, 2 story. S $64–$74; D $66–$74; suites $165–$250. Crib $6. TV; cable. Heated pool; whirlpool. Coffee in rms. Restaurant 11 am–11 pm. Ck-out noon. Coin lndry. Meeting rms. Bellhops. Valet serv. Sundries. Free airport, RR station, bus depot transportation. Refrigerators. Shopping arcade adj. Cr cds: A, C, D, DS, MC, V.

D ≋ ⊠ ⊗ ⊙ **SC**

★★**HAMPTON INN.** 5434 Kearny Mesa Rd (92111), north of downtown. 619/292-1482; FAX 619/292-4410. 150 rms, 5 story. June–Aug: S, D $72–$83; under 18 free; lower rates rest of yr. Crib free. TV; cable, in-rm movies avail. Heated pool. Complimentary continental bkfst, coffee. Restaurant adj 7 am–11 pm. Ck-out 11 am. Coin lndry. Meeting rms. Valet serv. Some refrigerators. Cr cds: A, C, D, DS, MC, V.

D ≋ ⊗ ⊙ **SC**

✔ ★**HOWARD JOHNSON.** 4545 Waring Rd (92120), north of downtown. 619/286-7000; FAX 619/286-7000, ext 135. 96 rms, 2 story. June–Aug: S, D $50–$85; each addl $10; under 18 free; lower rates rest of yr. Crib free. Pet accepted. TV; cable. Heated pool. Restaurant 8 am–10 pm. Ck-out noon. Coin lndry. Meeting rm. Valet serv. Refrigerators avail. Private patios, balconies. Cr cds: A, C, D, DS, MC, V.

D ⊛ ≋ ⊗ ⊙ **SC**

★★**HUMPHREY'S HALF MOON INN.** 2303 Shelter Island Dr (92106), in Point Loma. 619/224-3411; res: 800/542-7400; FAX 619/224-3478. 182 rms, 2 story, 30 kit. units. Late May–early Sept: S $79–$139; D

$89–$149; each addl $10; kit. suites $119–$225; under 18 free; lower rates rest of yr. Crib free. TV; cable. Heated pool; whirlpool, poolside serv. Complimentary coffee in rms. Restaurant 6:30 am–10 pm. Rm serv. Bar 11–2 am; entertainment. Ck-out noon. Coin lndry. Meeting rms. Bellhops. Sundries. Free airport, RR station transportation. Bicycles. Lawn games. Refrigerators. Many private patios, balconies. South Sea island decor. Gardens. On marina; 3 slips. Cr cds: A, C, D, DS, MC, V.

D ≋ ⊗ ⊙ **SC**

✔ ★**LA QUINTA.** 10185 Paseo Montril (92129), north of downtown. 619/484-8800; FAX 619/538-0479. 120 rms, 3 story. S $53–$66; D $59–$75; each addl $5; suites $85; under 18 free. Crib free. Pet accepted. TV; cable. Heated pool. Complimentary continental bkfst in lobby. Restaurant adj open 24 hrs. Ck-out noon. Meeting rms. Cr cds: A, C, DS, ER, MC, V.

D ⊛ ≋ ⊗ ⊙ **SC**

★★**TRAVELODGE SPORTS ARENA.** 3737 Sports Arena Blvd (92110), opp Sports Arena, in Point Loma. 619/226-3711; FAX 619/224-9248. 307 rms, 3 story. May–Sept: S, D $52–$70; suites $75–$150; under 17 free; lower rates rest of yr. TV. Heated pool; whirlpool. Complimentary continental bkfst. Restaurant adj 6 am–11 pm. Rm serv. Ck-out noon. Coin lndry. Meeting rms. Bellhops. Some covered parking. Free airport transportation. Health club privileges adj. Some refrigerators. Cr cds: A, C, D, DS, ER, MC, V, JCB.

≋ ⊗ ⊙ **SC**

★★**VACATION INN.** 3900 Old Town Ave (92110), in Old Town. 619/299-7400; res: 800/451-9846; FAX 619/299-1619. 125 rms, 3 story. Mid-May–mid-Sept: S $85–$119; D $95–$119; each addl $10; suites $105–$160; under 17 free; lower rates rest of yr. Crib free. TV; cable. Heated pool; whirlpool. Complimentary continental bkfst. Complimentary coffee in rms. Restaurant opp 10 am–10 pm. Ck-out noon. Coin lndry. Meeting rms. Covered parking. Free airport, RR station transportation. Refrigerators; some wet bars. Some balconies. Cr cds: A, C, D, DS, ER, MC, V.

D ≋ ⊗ ⊙ **SC**

★**VAGABOND INN.** 625 Hotel Circle S (92108), north of downtown. 619/297-1691; FAX 619/692-9009. 87 rms, 2 story. Mid-May–mid-Sept: S $60–$72; D $65–$77; each addl $5; under 18 free; lower rates rest of yr. Crib free. Pet accepted; $5. TV; cable. 2 heated pools; whirlpool. Complimentary continental bkfst, coffee. Restaurant adj open 24 hrs. Ck-out noon. Cr cds: A, C, D, DS, ER, MC, V.

⊛ ≋ ⊗ ⊙ **SC**

Motor Hotels

★★★**BAY CLUB HOTEL & MARINA.** 2131 Shelter Island Dr (92106), in Point Loma. 619/224-8888; res: 800/833-6565 (CA), 800/672-0800 (exc CA); FAX 619/225-1604. 105 rms, 2 story. S $115–$175; D $130–$200; each addl $10; suites $210–$295; under 12 free; honeymoon, island getaway packages. Crib $10. TV; cable. Heated pool; poolside serv. Complimentary bkfst. Restaurant 6:30 am–11 pm. Rm serv. Bar 10 am–midnight. Ck-out noon. Meeting rms. Bellhops. Valet serv. Concierge. Sundries. Covered parking. Free airport, RR station, bus depot transportation. Exercise equipt; weight machine, bicycles, whirlpool. Refrigerators. Private patios, balconies. On bay; marina. Fishing from nearby pier. Cr cds: A, C, D, DS, ER, MC, V.

D ≋ ⊼ ⊗ ⊙ **SC**

★★★**BEST WESTERN HACIENDA HOTEL.** 4041 Harney St (92110), in Old Town. 619/298-4707; FAX 619/298-4707, ext 2460. 149 suites, 2–3 story. June–Aug: S $109–$119; D $119–$129; each addl $10; under 16 free; lower rates rest of yr. Crib free. TV; cable, in-rm movies. Heated pool; poolside serv. Complimentary coffee in rms. Restaurants 6 am–10 pm. Rm serv. Bar 11–1:30 am. Ck-out noon. Meeting rms. Bellhops. Valet serv. Concierge. Covered parking. Free airport, RR station, bus depot transportation. Exercise equipt; weights, bicycles, whirlpool. Refrigerators. Some private patios, balconies. Grills. Spanish architecture. Cr cds: A, C, D, DS, ER, MC, V.

D 🏊 🕴 ⊘ 🌐 SC

★★**BEST WESTERN SAN DIEGO CENTRAL.** 3805 Murphy Canyon Rd (92123), north of downtown. 619/277-1199; FAX 619/277-3442. 176 rms, 4 story, 19 suites. S $65-$85; D $75-$95; each addl $6; suites $93-$113; under 12 free; higher rates: Memorial Day, July 4, Labor Day. Crib free. TV; cable. Pool. Complimentary continental bkfst. Restaurant 6:30 am-9:30 pm. Rm serv. Bar 11-2 am. Ck-out noon. Coin lndry. Meeting rms. Free garage parking. Exercise equipt; weight machine, bicycles, whirlpool. Refrigerators. Wet bar in suites. Most suites with balcony. Cr cds: A, C, D, DS, ER, MC, V, JCB.

D 🏊 🕴 ⊘ 🌐 SC

★★DOUBLETREE-RANCHO BERNARDO. 11611 Bernardo Plaza Court (921), north of downtown. 619/485-9250; FAX 619/451-7948. 209 rms, 4 story. S $109; D $119; each addl $10; suites $150; under 10 free; wkend rates. Crib free. TV; cable. Heated pool. Restaurant 6-9 am, 5-10 pm; Sat & Sun from 7 am. Bar from 5 pm. Ck-out 1 pm. Meeting rms. Exercise equipt; weight machine, bicycles, whirlpool. Cr cds: A, C, D, DS, ER, MC, V, JCB.

D 🏊 🕴 ⊘ 🌐 SC

★★★**HANDLERY HOTEL & COUNTRY CLUB.** 950 Hotel Circle N (92108), I-8 Hotel Circle exit, north of downtown. 619/298-0511; res: 800/676-6567; FAX 619/298-9793. 217 rms, 2 story. S $75; D $85; each addl $10; suites $150-$190; under 12 free; golf packages. Crib free. TV; cable. 2 pools (1 lap pool); poolside serv. Coffee in rms. Restaurant open 24 hrs. Rm serv 7 am-10 pm. Bars 11-1 am; entertainment Fri & Sat. Ck-out noon. Lndry facilities. Meeting rms. Bellhops. Valet serv. Sundries. Gift shop. Barber, beauty shop. Tennis. 27-hole golf, greens fee $45 (incl cart), pro, putting green, driving range. Exercise equipt; weight machines, treadmill. Some balconies. Cr cds: A, C, D, DS, ER, MC, V, JCB.

🏌 ⛳ 🏊 🕴 ⊘ 🌐 SC

✔ ★★★**HOLIDAY INN RANCHO BERNARDO.** 17065 W Bernardo Dr (92127), north of downtown. 619/485-6530; FAX 619/485-6530, ext 324. 178 rms, 2-3 story, 13 kits. S, D $58-$76; each addl $10; suites $76-$125; kit. units $5 addl; under 18 free. Crib free. Pet accepted, some restrictions; $10. TV; cable. Heated pool. Complimentary bkfst. Coffee in rms. Restaurant opp 11 am-10 pm. Ck-out noon. Coin lndry. Meeting rms. Valet serv. Sundries. Some covered parking. Exercise equipt; weights, bicycles, whirlpool, sauna. Some refrigerators, in-rm whirlpools. Many private patios, balconies. Cr cds: A, C, D, DS, MC, V, JCB.

D 🐾 🏊 🕴 ⊘ 🌐 SC

✔ ★★**HOWARD JOHNSON.** 1430 7th Ave (92101), near Lindbergh Field Intl Airport, north of downtown. 619/696-0911; FAX 619/234-9416. 136 rms, 3 story. June-Sept: S $55-$70; D $65-$90; each addl $5; suites $90-$150; under 12 free; wkly rates; lower rates rest of yr. Crib free. Covered parking $3. TV; cable. Heated pool. Complimentary continental bkfst. Coffee in rms. Restaurant adj 6 am-10 pm. Ck-out noon. Free airport, RR station, bus depot transportation. Exercise equipt; weight machine, bicycles. Some balconies. Many balconies. Cr cds: A, C, D, DS, ER, MC, V.

🏊 🕴 ✕ ⊘ 🌐 SC

★★**QUALITY SUITES.** 9880 Mira Mesa Blvd (92131), at jct I-15, north of downtown. 619/530-2000; FAX 619/530-2000, ext 145. 130 suites, 4 story. Early July-Labor Day: suites $89-$159; each addl $10; under 18 free; lower rates rest of yr. Crib free. TV; cable, in-rm movies. Heated pool. Complimentary continental bkfst. Ck-out noon. Meeting rms. Gift shop. Exercise equipt; weights, bicycles, whirlpool. Refrigerators. Cr cds: A, C, D, DS, ER, MC, V, JCB.

D 🏊 🕴 ⊘ 🌐 SC

✔ ★★**RAMADA INN-HOTEL CIRCLE.** 2151 Hotel Circle S (92108), north of downtown. 619/291-6500; FAX 619/294-7531. 183 rms, 4 story. S $52-$99; D $59-$119; each addl $10; under 18 free. Crib free. TV; cable. Heated pool; whirlpool. Complimentary coffee in rms.

Restaurant 6:30-11 am, 5-10 pm. Rm serv. Bar 4:30-11 pm; Fri & Sat to midnight. Ck-out noon. Meeting rms. Bellhops. Valet serv. Some covered parking. Free airport, RR station, bus depot transportation. Refrigerators avail. Cr cds: A, C, D, DS, MC, V, JCB.

D 🏊 ⊘ 🌐 SC

★**RODEWAY INN.** 833 Ash St (92101), downtown. 619/239-2285; FAX 619/235-6951. 45 rms, 4 story. July-Aug: S $59-$69; D $64-$74; each addl $5; studio rms $50-$70; under 18 free; lower rates rest of yr. Crib free. TV; cable. Complimentary continental bkfst. Restaurant opp open 24 hrs. Ck-out noon. Meeting rm. Valet serv. Whirlpool, saunas. Some refrigerators. Some balconies. Cr cds: A, C, D, DS, ER, MC, V, JCB.

⊘ 🌐 SC

★★**SEAPOINT.** 4875 N Harbor Dr (92106), near Lindbergh Field Intl Airport, north of downtown. 619/224-3621; res: 800/345-9995; FAX 619/224-3629. 237 rms, 2-5 story. July-mid-Sept: S $59.50-$109.50; D $69.50-$119.50; each addl $10; suites $125-$145; under 18 free; lower rates rest of yr. Crib free. TV; cable. Heated pool. Complimentary coffee in rms. Restaurant adj 6 am-11 pm. Ck-out noon. Coin lndry. Meeting rms. Bellhops. Valet serv. Sundries. Free airport, RR station, bus depot transportation. Exercise equipt; weights, bicycles. Lawn games. Some refrigerators. Some private patios, balconies. Opp marina. Cr cds: A, C, D, DS, MC, V.

D 🏊 🕴 ✕ ⊘ 🌐 SC

★★**TOWN & COUNTRY.** 500 Hotel Circle N (92108), north of downtown. 619/291-7131; res: 800/854-2608; FAX 619/291-3584. 952 rms, 1-10 story. S $80-$120; D $90-$130; each addl $10; suites $250-$450; under 18 free. Crib free. TV; cable. 4 pools, 1 heated; whirlpool, poolside serv. Restaurant 6:30 am-9:30 pm. Rm serv. Bar 11-2 am; entertainment, dancing. Ck-out noon. Convention facilities. Bellhops. Valet serv. Barber. Lighted tennis privileges, pro. Golf privileges; driving range adj. Health club privileges. Some refrigerators. Some private patios, balconies. On 32 acres. Cr cds: A, C, D, DS, MC, V.

D 🏌 ⛳ 🏊 ⊘ 🌐 SC

Hotels

★★★**DOUBLETREE-HORTON PLAZA.** 910 Broadway Circle (92101), downtown. 619/239-2200; FAX 619/239-0509. 450 rms, 16 story. S $160-$185; D $175-$205; each addl $10; suites $300-$1,050; under 17 free; wkend & wkday packages. Crib free. Covered parking $8; valet $10. TV; cable. Heated pool; poolside serv. Restaurant 6:30 am-10 pm. Rm serv 24 hrs. Bar to 2 am; entertainment. Ck-out noon. Convention facilities. Concierge. Lighted tennis. Exercise rm; instructor, weight machines, bicycles, whirlpool, sauna. Bathrm phones, refrigerators, minibars. Some balconies. Connected to Horton Plaza. **LUXURY LEVEL: CONCIERGE LEVEL.** 55 units, 8 suites. Private lounge. Some wet bars. Complimentary continental bkfst, evening refreshments. Cr cds: A, C, D, DS, ER, MC, V, JCB.

D 🖋 🏊 🕴 ⊘ 🌐 SC

★★★**EMBASSY SUITES.** 601 Pacific Hwy (92101), near Seaport Village, west of downtown. 619/239-2400; FAX 619/239-1520. 337 suites, 12 story. Mid-June-mid-Sept: suites $129-$179; under 12 free; lower rates rest of yr. Crib free. Covered parking $7. TV; cable. Indoor pool. Complimentary full bkfst. Complimentary coffee in rms. Restaurant 11 am-10 pm. Bar to midnight. Ck-out noon. Coin lndry. Meeting rms. Gift shop. Barber, beauty shop. Free airport, RR station transportation. Exercise equipt; weight machine, bicycles, whirlpool, sauna. Refrigerators, minibars. Some balconies. San Diego Bay 1 blk. Cr cds: A, C, D, DS, MC, V, JCB.

D 🏊 🕴 ⊘ 🌐

★★★**HILTON BEACH AND TENNIS RESORT.** 1775 E Mission Bay Dr (92109), in Mission Bay. 619/276-4010; FAX 619/275-7991. 354 rms, 8 story. S $125-$205; D $145-$225; each addl $20; suites $325-$575; family, wkend rates. Crib free. Pet accepted. Heated pool; wading pool, poolside serv. Playground. Restaurant 6:30 am-11 pm. Bars 10:30 am-midnight & 5 pm-1:30 am; entertainment, dancing Tues–Sat. Ck-out noon. Coin lndry. Convention facilities. Gift shop. Beauty shop. Free airport transportation. Lighted tennis, pro. Putting greens. Exercise equipt; weights, bicycles, whirlpool, sauna. Rec rm. Lawn games. Some bathrm phones, refrigerators, minibars. Private patios, balconies. Dock; boats. On beach. Cr cds: A, C, D, DS, ER, MC, V, JCB.

[D] [symbols] SC

★★★HILTON-MISSION VALLEY. 901 Camino del Rio S (92108), off I-8 Mission Center Rd exit, north of downtown. 619/543-9000; FAX 619/543-9358. 350 rms, 14 story. S $99–$149; D $109–$159; each addl $10; suites $200–$400; under 18 free. Crib free. Pet accepted, some restrictions. TV; cable. Heated pool; poolside serv. Coffee in rms. Restaurant 6:30 am–10:30 pm. Bar 11–2 am. Ck-out noon. Convention facilities. Some covered parking. Free Mission Valley shopping transportation. Exercise equipt; weights, bicycles, whirlpool, sauna. Refrigerators. Large entrance foyer. Cr cds: A, C, D, DS, ER, MC, V, JCB.

[D] [symbols] SC

★★HOLIDAY INN-HARBOR VIEW. 1617 1st Ave (92101), downtown. 619/239-6171; FAX 619/233-6228. 203 rms, 16 story. S $88–$118; D $98–$128; each addl $10; under 19 free. Crib free. TV; cable. Heated pool. Coffee in rms. Restaurant 6 am–10 pm. Bar 11 am–midnight. Ck-out noon. Coin lndry. Meeting rms. Gift shop. Free airport, RR station transportation. Circular building. Cr cds: A, C, D, DS, ER, MC, V, JCB.

[D] [symbols] SC

★★HOLIDAY INN ON THE BAY. 1355 N Harbor Dr (92101), downtown. 619/232-3861; FAX 619/232-4924. 600 rms, 14 story. July–Aug: S $95–$135; D $105–$145; each addl $10; suites $250–$800; under 19 free; lower rates rest of yr. Crib free. Pet accepted, some restrictions. Parking $8/day. TV; cable. Heated pool. Restaurant 6 am–10 pm. Bar 11–1 am; entertainment Tues–Sat. Ck-out noon. Convention facilities. Shopping arcade. Airport, RR station transportation. Some bathrm phones, refrigerators. Balconies. Sun deck. Many bay view rms. Outside glass-enclosed elvtr. Cruise ship terminal opp. Cr cds: A, C, D, DS, MC, V, JCB.

[D] [symbols] SC

★★★THE HORTON GRAND. 311 Island Ave (92101), downtown. 619/544-1886; res: 800/542-1886; FAX 619/239-3823. 132 rms, 4 story. S $99–$109; D $119–$129; each addl $20; suites $159–$189; under 12 free. Crib free. Some covered parking, valet $7. TV; cable. Restaurant 7 am–10 pm. Tea 2:30–5:30 pm. Bar noon–11:30 pm; entertainment. Ck-out noon. Meeting rms. Concierge. Fireplaces; refrigerator in suites. Some balconies. Victorian building; built 1886. Antiques, oak staircase. Chinese Museum & Tea Room. Skylight in lobby; bird cages. Oldest building in San Diego. Cr cds: A, C, D, DS, MC, V.

[D] [symbols] SC

★HOTEL SAN DIEGO. 339 W Broadway (92101), downtown. 619/234-0221; res: 800/621-5380; FAX 619/232-1305. 220 rms, 6 story. S, D $59–$79; suites $99–$109; under 18 free; wkly rates. TV; cable. Restaurant adj 7 am–9 pm. No rm serv. Ck-out noon. Coin lndry. Meeting rms. Gift shop. Free airport, RR station, local transportation. Some refrigerators. Cr cds: A, C, D, DS, ER, MC, V, JCB.

[symbols] SC

★★HOTEL ST JAMES. 830 6th Ave (92101), in Gaslamp Quarter, downtown. 619/234-0155; res: 800/338-1616; FAX 619/235-9410. 99 air-cooled rms, 10 story, 12 suites, 7 kit. units. Mid-June–mid-Sept: S $75; D $85; suites, kit. units $99–$450; under 18 free; wkly rates; lower rates rest of yr. Crib free. Valet parking $7.50. Restaurant adj 6 am–midnight. Ck-out noon. Meeting rms. Concierge. Health club privileges. Built in 1913; handcrafted furnishings in a Southwestern motif. Cr cds: A, C, D, DS, MC, V.

[symbols] SC

★★HYATT ISLANDIA. 1441 Quivira Rd (92109), in Mission Bay. 619/224-1234; FAX 619/224-0348. 423 rms, 17 story. S, D $109–$170; suites $159–$2,000; under 18 free. Crib free. TV; cable.

Heated pool; whirlpool, poolside serv. Supervised child's activities (June–Sept). Restaurant 6 am–11 pm. Bar 11:30–2 am; entertainment Thurs–Sat. Ck-out noon. Convention facilities. Concierge. Airport transportation avail. Some refrigerators. Many private patios, balconies. Most rms with view of ocean or bay. Bicycle rentals. Marina; sport fishing; sailboat charters. Whale watching (Dec–Mar). Cr cds: A, C, D, DS, ER, MC, V, JCB.

[D] [symbols] SC

★★★HYATT REGENCY. One Market Place (92101), adj to Convention Center and Seaport Village, downtown. 619/232-1234; FAX 619/233-6464. 875 units, 40 story, 55 suites. S, D $139–$220; under 18 free. Crib free. Garage parking $8–$11. TV. Pool; poolside serv. Restaurant 6 am–midnight. Rm serv 24 hrs. Bar noon–1:30 am. Ck-out noon. Convention facilities. Concierge. Shopping arcade. Airport transportation. 4 tennis courts. Exercise rm; instructor, weight machine, bicycles, whirlpool, sauna, steam rm. Some refrigerators, minibars. Located on San Diego Bay; panoramic view of harbor and marina. LUXURY LEVEL: REGENCY CLUB. 53 rms, 10 suites, 7 floors. S $220; D $245. Concierge. Private lounge, honor bar. Complimentary continental bkfst, refreshments.
Cr cds: A, C, D, DS, ER, MC, V, JCB.

[D] [symbols] SC

★★★MARRIOTT HOTEL & MARINA. 333 W Harbor Dr (92101), adj to Seaport Village & Convention Center, downtown. 619/234-1500; FAX 619/234-8678. 1,355 rms, 26 story. S, D $159–$195; each addl $20; suites over $310; under 18 free; wkend rates. Crib free. Pet accepted. TV; cable. Pool; poolside serv. Restaurant 6:30 am–11 pm. Rm serv 24 hrs. Bar 11–2 am; entertainment. Ck-out noon. Coin lndry. Meeting rms. Concierge. Shopping arcade. Barber, beauty shops. 6 lighted tennis courts, pro. Exercise equipt; weight machines, treadmill, whirlpool, sauna. Game rm. Bathrm phones, minibars; some refrigerators. Some balconies. Luxurious; marble tile, large chandeliers in lobby. Bayside; marina. LUXURY LEVEL. 62 rms, 4 suites, 2 floors. S, D $179–$199; suites $310–$2,800. Private lounge. In-rm steam bath in some suites. Deluxe toiletry amenities. Complimentary continental bkfst, refreshments, newspaper.
Cr cds: A, C, D, DS, ER, MC, V, JCB.

[D] [symbols] SC

★★★MARRIOTT SUITES-DOWNTOWN. 701 A Street (92101), downtown. 619/696-9800; FAX 619/696-1555. 264 suites, 15 story. S, D $99–$174; under 18 free. Crib free. Pet accepted, some restrictions; $50. Garage $12, valet parking $10. TV; cable. Indoor pool. Complimentary coffee in rms. Restaurant 6:30 am–10 pm. Bar 10 am–midnight. Ck-out noon. Meeting rms. Gift shop. Free airport, RR station, bus depot transportation. Exercise equipt; weight machine, bicycles, whirlpool, sauna. Health club privileges. Refrigerators, minibars. Cr cds: A, C, D, DS, ER, MC, V, JCB.

[D] [symbols] SC

★★★PAN PACIFIC. 400 W Broadway (92101), near Lindbergh Field Intl Airport, downtown. 619/239-4500; res: 800/327-8585; FAX 619/239-3274. 436 rms, 25 story. S, D $140–$180; each addl $15; suites $260–$2,000; under 16 free. Crib free. Garage $8. TV; cable. Heated pool; poolside serv. Restaurant 6 am–10 pm. Bar 11–1 am; entertainment. Ck-out noon. Convention facilities. Concierge. Shopping arcade. Free airport, convention center transportation. Exercise rm; instructor, weight machine, bicycle, whirlpool, steam rm. Bathrm phones, minibars. Cr cds: A, C, D, DS, ER, MC, V, JCB.

[D] [symbols]

★★★RADISSON. 1433 Camino del Rio S (92108), north of downtown. 619/260-0111; FAX 619/260-0853. 260 rms, 13 story. S $85; D $95; each addl $10; under 17 free; wkend packages. Crib free. Pet accepted, some restrictions. TV; cable. Heated pool. Restaurant 6:30 am–10 pm. Bar 2 pm–1:30 am; entertainment. Ck-out noon. Convention facilities. Free airport transportation. Exercise equipt; weight machine, bicycles, whirlpool. Some balconies. LUXURY LEVEL: PLAZA CLUB. 24 rms, 11 suites, 2 floors. S, D $105–$115; suites $155–$300. Concierge.

Private lounge. Full wet bar in some suites. Complimentary continental bkfst, refreshments.
Cr cds: A, C, D, DS, ER, MC, V, JCB.

[D] [🍴] [≈] [🏃] [🚭] [⊘] [SC]

★ ★ ★RADISSON SUITE. *11520 W Bernardo Court (92127), north of downtown.* 619/451-6600; FAX 619/592-0253. 177 suites, 3 story. S, D $75–$130; each addl $10; under 12 free; golf plans. Crib $10. Pet accepted, some restrictions. TV; cable, in-rm movies. Heated pool. Complimentary full bkfst. Complimentary coffee in rms. Restaurant 6–9:30 am, 5–10 pm. Bar 5–10 pm. Ck-out noon. Coin lndry. Meeting rms. Tennis, golf privileges. Exercise equipt; weight machine, bicycles, whirlpool. Refrigerators, minibars. Cr cds: A, C, D, DS, ER, MC, V, JCB.

[D] [🍴] [⊘] [🛳] [🏊] [≈] [🏃] [🚭] [⊘] [SC]

★ ★RAMADA BAYVIEW. *660 K Street (92101), downtown.* 619/696-0234; FAX 619/231-8199. 312 rms, 21 story, 48 suites. Late May–early Sept: S $75–$130; D $85–$140; each addl $10; suites $140–$165; under 18 free; lower rates rest of yr. Crib free. Covered parking $6/night. TV; cable. Coffee in rms. Restaurant 6:30 am–10 pm. Bar 11–2 am; entertainment Fri, Sat. Ck-out noon. Coin lndry. Meeting rms. Gift shop. Free airport, RR station, bus depot transportation. Exercise equipt; weight machine, bicycles, whirlpool, sauna. Some bathrm phones. Balconies. View of San Diego Bay. Cr cds: A, C, D, DS, MC, V, JCB.

[D] [🏃] [🚭] [⊘] [SC]

★ ★ ★RED LION. *7450 Hazard Center Dr (92108), north of downtown.* 619/297-5466; FAX 619/297-5499. 300 rms, 11 story. S, D $130–$165; each addl $15; under 18 free. Crib free. Pet accepted. TV; cable. 2 pools, 1 indoor; poolside serv. Restaurant 6 am–11 pm. Bar 5 pm–2 am; entertainment, dancing Tues–Sat. Ck-out noon. Convention facilities. Gift shop. Garage parking; valet. Free airport, RR station, bus depot transportation. Lighted tennis, pro. Exercise equipt; weight machine, stair machine, whirlpool, sauna. Minibars. Some bathrm phone, wet bar in suites. Some balconies. *LUXURY LEVEL:* **EXECUTIVE LEVEL.** 21 rms, 4 suites. S, D $145–$180; suites $395–$495. Private lounge, honor bar. Complimentary continental bkfst, refreshments, newspaper.
Cr cds: A, C, D, DS, ER, MC, V, JCB.

[D] [🍴] [⊘] [🏊] [≈] [🏃] [🚭] [⊘] [SC]

★ ★ ★SHERATON HARBOR ISLAND. *1380 Harbor Island Dr (92101), near Lindbergh Field Intl Airport, north of downtown.* 619/291-2900; FAX 619/296-5297. 1,048 rms, 12 story. S, D $150–$170; each addl $20; suites $375–$1,100; under 18 free. Crib free. TV; cable. 3 pools, heated; 2 wading pools, poolside serv in summer. Playground. Complimentary coffee in rms. Restaurant 6 am–11 pm. Rm serv 24 hrs. Bar 11–1 am. Ck-out noon. Coin lndry. Convention facilities. Concierge. Shopping arcade. Free airport transportation. Lighted tennis, pro. Exercise rm; instructor, weights, bicycles, whirlpool, sauna. Bicycle rentals. Minibars. Bathrm phone in some suites. Balconies. All rms with view of marina, city or bay. Elaborate landscaping. Boat dock, beach; bicycles. Cr cds: A, C, D, DS, ER, MC, V, JCB.

[D] [↔] [⊘] [🏊] [≈] [🏃] [🏃] [🛳] [⊘] [SC]

✔ ★ ★TRAVELODGE HOTEL-HARBOR ISLAND. *1960 Harbor Island Dr (92101), near Lindbergh Field Intl Airport, north of downtown.* 619/291-6700; FAX 619/293-0694. 208 rms, 9 story. S, D $69–$139; each addl $10; suites $175–$350; under 17 free. Crib free. TV. Heated pool. Complimentary coffee in rms. Restaurant 6:30 am–2 pm, 5:30–10 pm. Bar 11–1 am. Ck-out noon. Meeting rms. Gift shop. Free airport transportation. Exercise equipt; weights, bicycles, whirlpool, sauna. Some refrigerators. Balconies. Cr cds: A, C, D, DS, ER, MC, V, JCB.

[D] [🏊] [🏃] [🏃] [🛳] [⊘] [⊘] [SC]

★ ★ ★U. S. GRANT. *326 Broadway (92101), downtown.* 619/232-3121; res: 800/237-5029 (exc CA), 800/334-6957 (CA); FAX 619/232-3626. 280 rms, 11 story, 60 suites. S $140–$160; D $160–$180; each addl $20; suites $245–$1,000. Crib $15. Valet parking $10. TV; cable. Cafe 6:30–10:30 am, 11:30 am–2:30 pm, 5:30–11 pm. Rm serv 24 hrs. Bar 11–2 am; entertainment Thurs–Sat. Ck-out noon. Concierge. Gift shop. Exercise equipt; weights, bicycles. Masseuse. Bathrm

phones, minibars. Antiques, artwork, period chandeliers and fixtures. 1910 landmark has been restored to its original elegance. Cr cds: A, C, D, DS, ER, MC, V, JCB.

[D] [🏃] [🚭] [⊘] [SC]

★ ★ ★ ★THE WESTGATE HOTEL. *1055 Second Ave (92101), downtown.* 619/238-1818; res: 800/221-3802; FAX 619/232-4526. 223 units, 19 story, some kits. S from $144; D from $154; each addl $20; suites from $300; under 12 free; wknd rates. Valet parking $8.50/day. Crib free. TV; cable. Complimentary coffee 6–10 am. Restaurant 6 am–11 pm (also see LE FONTAINEBLEAU). Afternoon tea. Rm serv 24 hrs. Bar 11–2 am; entertainment. Ck-out noon. Meeting rms. Concierge. Shopping arcade. Free airport, RR station, bus depot transportation; downtown transportation on request. Exercise equipt; weight machine, bicycles. Health club privileges. Bathrm phones, minibars. Cr cds: A, C, D, DS, ER, MC, V.

[🏃] [🚭] [⊘]

✔ ★WILLIAM PENN SUITE HOTEL. *511 F Street (92101), downtown.* 619/531-0833. 37 air-cooled rms, 14 with shower only, 4 story, 21 suites, 30 kit. units. June–Sept: S, D $79; suites $150; kit. units $79–$150; children free; wkly, monthly rates; lower rates rest of yr. Crib free. Valet parking $7.50. TV; cable. Complimentary continental bkfst. Restaurant opp 7 am–2 pm. No rm serv. Ck-out noon. No bellhops. Cr cds: A, C, D, DS, MC, V.

[🚭] [⊘] [SC]

Resorts

★ ★ ★DOUBLETREE CARMEL HIGHLAND GOLF & TENNIS RESORT. *14455 Penasquitos Dr (92129), north of downtown.* 619/672-9100; FAX 619/672-9166. 172 rms, 3 story, 14 suites. S, D $109–$169; each addl $10; suites $129–$179; under 12 free; golf, tennis, fitness plans. Crib $10. Pet accepted, some restrictions; $150. TV; cable. 2 pools; poolside serv, lifeguard (summer). Supervised child's activities (June–early Sept). Dining rms 6:30 am–10:30 pm. Rm serv. Bar 11–2 am; entertainment Thurs–Sat, dancing. Ck-out noon, ck-in 3 pm. Convention facilities. Bellhops. Concierge. Gift shop. Airport transportation. 6 lighted tennis courts, pro. 18-hole golf, greens fee $44–$54, pro, putting green. Exercise rm; instructor, weights, bicycles, whirlpool, 2 saunas, steam rm. Private patios, balconies. On 130 acres. Cr cds: A, C, D, DS, ER, MC, V, JCB.

[D] [🍴] [⊘] [🛳] [🏊] [≈] [🏃] [🚭] [⊘] [SC]

★ ★ ★ ★RANCHO BERNARDO INN. *17550 Bernardo Oaks Dr (92128), north of downtown.* 619/487-1611; res: 800/542-6096; FAX 619/673-0311. 287 rms, 3 story. Jan–June: S, D $185–$220; suites $275–$620; under 12 free; golf, tennis plans; lower rates rest of yr. TV; cable. 2 pools, heated; poolside serv. Free supervised child's activities (Aug; also Easter, Memorial Day wkend, July 4 wkend, Labor Day wkend, Thanksgiving hols & Christmas hols). Dining rm 6:30 am–10 pm (also see EL BIZCOCHO). Snack bar. Rm serv 6:30 am–midnight. Bars 11–1 am; entertainment, dancing Tues–Sat. Ck-out 1 pm. Convention facilities. Concierge. Gift shop. Drugstore. Airport transportation. Complimentary shuttle service to shopping mall. Lighted tennis, pro. Three 18-hole and one 27-hole golf courses, pro, putting green, driving range. Volleyball. Bicycles. Exercise rm; instructor, weight machine, bicycles, 7 whirlpools, sauna, steam rm. Masseuse. Many honor bars; some bathrm phones. Private patios, balconies. Beautifully appointed rms in mission-style building. Extensive grounds. Noted tennis and golf colleges. Complimentary tea, sherry, finger sandwiches 4–5 pm. Cr cds: A, C, D, DS, ER, MC, V, JCB.

[D] [🍴] [⊘] [🏊] [≈] [🏃] [🏃] [🛳] [⊘]

★ ★SAN DIEGO PRINCESS. *1404 W Vacation Rd (92109), in Mission Bay.* 619/274-4630; res: 800/542-6275; FAX 619/581-5929. 462 cottage rms, 153 kits. May–Aug: S, D $130–$150; each addl $15; suites $225–$345; kit. units $170–$180; lower rates rest of yr. Crib free. TV; cable. 5 pools, 2 heated; wading pool, poolside serv. Complimentary coffee in rms. Dining rms 7 am–10 pm. Rm serv. Bars 11–2 am; entertainment, dancing Tues–Sat. Ck-out noon, ck-in 4 pm. Coin lndry. Convention facilities. Valet serv. Concierge. Gift shop. Lighted tennis, pro. Putting green. Exercise rm; instructor, weights, stair machine, whirlpool, sauna, steam rm. Bicycles. Game rm. Lawn games. Boats; windsurfing. Some bathrm phones, refrigerators, minibars. Private patios. On beach. Botanical walk. Cr cds: A, DS, ER, MC, V.

Restaurants

✔ ★Á DÔNG. *3874 Fairmount Ave, north of downtown. 619/298-4420.* Hrs: 10 am–10 pm. Vietnamese & Chinese menu. Wine, beer. Semi-a la carte: lunch $3.75–$7.99, dinner $3–$14. Specialties: beef marinated with lemon grass, fried rice in earthen pot. Parking. Casual dining. Cr cds: A, C, MC, V.

✔ ★★AFGHANISTAN KHYBER PASS. *4647 Convoy St, north of downtown. 619/571-3749.* Hrs: 11 am–2:30 pm, 5–10 pm; Sun from 5 pm. Res accepted. Afghan menu. Wine, beer. Semi-a la carte: lunch $5.25–$8.25, dinner $10.95–$14.95. Buffet lunch (Mon–Fri): $6.95. Specializes in shish kebab, curries. Parking. Interior designed as an Afghan cave. Cr cds: A, DS, MC, V.

SC

★★ANTHONY'S FISH GROTTO. *11666 Avena Place, off Bernardo Center Dr in Rancho Bernardo, north of downtown. 619/451-2070.* Hrs: 11:30 am–8:30 pm. Closed major hols. Bar. Semi-a la carte: lunch $4–$13, dinner $6.90–$26. Child's meals. Specializes in fresh seafood. Parking. Overlooks Webb Lake Park. Family-owned. Cr cds: A, C, D, DS, MC, V.

D

★★★ANTHONY'S STAR OF THE SEA ROOM. *1360 Harbor Dr, downtown. 619/232-7408.* Hrs: 5:30–10:30 pm. Closed major hols. A la carte entrees: dinner $25–$44. Specialties: planked fish, stuffed fish, loin of swordfish. Valet parking. Harbor view. Family-owned. Jacket. Cr cds: A, C, D, DS, MC, V.

D

★★ATHENS MARKET TAVERNA. *109 W F Street, downtown. 619/234-1955.* Hrs: 11:30 am–11 pm; Fri & Sat to midnight. Closed Jan 1, Thanksgiving, Dec 25. Res accepted. Greek menu. Bar to 2 am. Semi-a la carte: lunch $4.75–$12.50, dinner $9.95–$19.95. Specializes in lamb, fish. Belly dancers Fri, Sat evenings. Cr cds: A, C, D, DS, MC, V.

★★★BACI RISTORANTE. *1955 W Morena Blvd, Mission Bay. 619/275-2094.* Hrs: 11:30 am–2:30 pm, 5:30–10 pm; Sat from 5:30 pm. Closed Sun; major hols. Res required Fri, Sat. Northern Italian menu. Bar. Wine list. A la carte entrees: lunch $6.95–$11.95, dinner $10.95–$17.95. Specializes in seafood, veal, pasta. Own baking, pasta. Parking. Intimate atmosphere; many art pieces, prints. Cr cds: A, C, D, DS, MC, V.

D

★★★BELGIAN LION. *2265 Bacon St, Mission Bay. 619/223-2700.* Hrs: 5:30–10 pm; Fri & Sat from 6 pm. Closed Sun, Mon; major hols. Res accepted. French, Belgian menu. Beer. Wine list. A la carte entrees: dinner $15–$18.50. Specialties: fresh fish, classic duck confit. Own pastries. Parking. Outdoor dining. Country Belgian decor. Cr cds: A, D, DS, MC, V.

★★BENIHANA OF TOKYO. *477 Camino del Rio South, north of downtown. 619/298-4666.* Hrs: 11:30 am–2 pm, 5–10 pm; Fri to 11 pm; Sat 5–11 pm; Sun 5–10 pm. Res accepted. Japanese menu. Bar. Semi-a la carte: lunch $6.95–$12.95, dinner $12.95–$24.75. Child's meals. Specializes in Japanese steak & seafood. Sushi bar. Valet parking. Japanese village settings. Cr cds: A, C, D, DS, MC, V, JCB.

D

★★★BICE RISTORANTE. *777 Front St, on top floor of Palladium, downtown. 619/239-2423.* Hrs: 11:30 am–2:30 pm, 6–11 pm; Fri to midnight; Sat noon–3 pm, 6 pm–midnight; Sun 5–10 pm. Res accepted. Milanese-style Italian menu. Bar. Wine list. A la carte entrees: lunch

$9–$15, dinner $9–$20. Specializes in homemade pasta. Valet parking. Cr cds: A, C, D, MC, V.

D

★★★BUSALACCHI'S. *3683 5th Ave, north of downtown. 619/298-0119.* Hrs: 11:30 am–2:15 pm, 5–10 pm; Fri & Sat to 11 pm. Closed Jan 1, Memorial Day, Dec 25. Res accepted. Italian menu. Wine, beer. A la carte entrees: lunch $7.75–$15, dinner $7.95–$21.95. Specializes in Sicilian dishes. Valet parking. Outdoor dining. Victorian-style house. Cr cds: A, C, D, DS, ER, MC, V.

✔ ★CAFE COYOTE. *2461 San Diego Ave, in Old Town Esplanade, in Old Town. 619/291-4695.* Hrs: 7:30 am–10 pm; Fri & Sat to 11 pm; Sun to 9 pm. Closed Dec 25. Res accepted. Mexican, Amer menu. Bar. Semi-a la carte: bkfst $2.95–$5.95, lunch $3.95–$8.95, dinner $4.95–$9.95. Child's meals. Specialties: blue corn pancakes, carnitas, carne asada. Own tortillas. Entertainment Fri–Sun on patio. Parking. Outdoor dining. Pictures, statues of Southwestern wildlife. Cr cds: A, D, DS, MC, V.

D

★★★CAFE PACIFICA. *2414 San Diego Ave, in Old Town. 619/291-6666.* Hrs: 11:30 am–2 pm, 5:30–10 pm; Sat & Sun from 5:30 pm; early-bird dinner 5:30–6:45 pm. Closed Thanksgiving, Dec 25. Res accepted. Bar. Semi-a la carte: lunch $6–$11, dinner $12–$18. Specializes in seafood. Valet parking. Near Old Spanish Cemetery. Cr cds: A, C, D, DS, MC, V.

D

★★CALIFORNIA CUISINE. *1027 University Ave, north of downtown. 619/543-0790.* Hrs: 11 am–10 pm; Sat & Sun from 5 pm. Closed Mon; Jan 1, Thanksgiving, Dec 25. Res accepted. French, California menu. Wine, beer. Semi-a la carte: lunch $5.50–$12, dinner $7–$18. Specializes in fresh seafood, game, salad. Outdoor dining. Menu changes daily. Original paintings change monthly. Cr cds: A, C, D, DS, MC, V.

✔ ★★CALLIOPE'S GREEK CAFE. *3958 5th Ave, north of downtown. 619/291-5588.* Hrs: 11:30 am–2:30 pm, 5–10 pm; Mon to 9 pm; Fri & Sat to 11 pm. Closed some hols. Res accepted. Greek menu. Wine, beer. Semi-a la carte: lunch $5.95–$9.95, dinner $10.95–$16.95. Specializes in fresh seafood, vegetarian dishes, traditional Greek dishes. Valet parking. Totally nonsmoking. Cr cds: A, C, D, DS, MC, V.

D

★★CASA DE BANDINI. *2754 Calhoun St, in Old Town. 619/297-8211.* Hrs: 11 am–10 pm; Sun from 10 am; winter to 9 pm. Closed Thanksgiving, Dec 25. Mexican menu. Bar. Semi-a la carte: lunch, dinner $5.50–$15.50. Child's meals. Specializes in seafood. Mariachi band. Parking. Outdoor dining. Early California atmosphere, garden patio with fountain. Adobe bldg (1827) once served as headquarters for Commodore Stockton. Cr cds: A, C, D, DS, MC, V.

★★CELADON. *3628 5th Ave, north of downtown. 619/295-8800.* Hrs: 11:30 am–2 pm, 5–10 pm. Closed Sun; Jan 1, Thanksgiving, Dec 25. Res accepted. Thai menu. Wine, beer. A la carte entrees: lunch $6.25–$12, dinner $8.25–$17. Specializes in shrimp, chicken, beef. Cr cds: A, MC, V.

★★DOBSON'S. *956 Broadway Circle, downtown. 619/231-6771.* Hrs: 11:30 am–3 pm, 5:30–10 pm; Thur–Sat to 11 pm. Closed major hols. Res accepted. Continental menu. Bar to 1:30 am. Semi-a la carte: lunch $5.50–$14, dinner $10–$27. Specializes in fresh seafood, veal. Own sourdough bread. Covered parking. Cr cds: A, MC, V.

★★★EL BIZCOCHO. *(See Rancho Bernardo Inn Resort) 619/487-1611.* Hrs: 6–10 pm; Fri & Sat to 10:30 pm; Sun brunch 10 am–2 pm. Res accepted. French menu. Bar. Extensive wine list. A la carte entrees: dinner $19–$28. Sun brunch $21. Specializes in roast duckling, rack of lamb, fresh salmon. Pianist. Valet parking. View of grounds with waterfall. Jacket (exc brunch). Cr cds: A, C, D, DS, MC, V.

✔ ★EL TECOLOTE. *6110 Friars Rd, north of downtown. 619/295-2087.* Hrs: 11 am–10 pm; Sun 4–9 pm. Closed Jan 1, Thanksgiving, Dec 25. Mexican menu. Serv bar. Semi-a la carte: lunch $2.25–$6.95, dinner $4.95–$10.95. Child's meals. Specialties: cheese-filled zucchinis, beef tongue Veracruz, mole poblano. Parking. Outdoor dining. Mexican artifacts, photographs, original art. Totally nonsmoking. Cr cds: DS, MC, V.

D

✔ ★**FAIROUZ.** *3166 Midway Dr, in Point Loma.* 619/225-0308. Hrs 11 am–10 pm. Closed Jan 1. Res required Fri & Sat. Greek, Lebanese menu. Bar. Semi-a la carte: lunch $3.95–$12.95, dinner $5–$13.95. Buffet: lunch $5.25, dinner $10.95. Specialties: hommos taboleh, kabobs. Parking. Paintings, prints available for purchase. Cr cds: A, D, DS, MC, V.

D

★ ★ ★**FIO'S.** *801 5th Ave, downtown.* 619/234-3467. Hrs: 11:30 am–3 pm, 5–11 pm; Fri & Sat to midnight. Closed Dec 25. Res accepted. Italian menu. Bar. Wine cellar. A la carte entrees: lunch, dinner $3.75–$17.95. Specializes in pasta, wood-fired pizza. European decor; original artwork depicting Palio of Siena. Cr cds: A, C, D, DS, MC, V.

D

★ ★**515 FIFTH.** *515 Fifth Ave, downtown.* 619/232-3352. Hrs: 5:15–10 pm; Fri & Sat to 11 pm; Sun to 9 pm. Closed most major hols. Res accepted. No A/C. Bar. A la carte entrees: dinner $7–$16. Specialties: char-broiled duck with roasted shallots & caramel-balsamic vinegar glaze; peanut-crusted pork tenderloin with ginger, garlic, lemon & dijon; linguine with salmon. Outdoor dining. Menu changes daily. Art deco decor. Cr cds: A, C, D, DS, MC, V.

D

★ ★**FRENCH SIDE OF THE WEST.** *2202 Fourth Ave, north of downtown.* 619/234-5540. Hrs: 11:30 am–2 pm, 5:30–9:30 pm; Fri & Sat 5:30–10:30 pm. Closed Dec 25. Res accepted; required Fri & Sat. Country French menu. Wine, beer. Complete meals: lunch $4–$7.50 or 3-course $12.50, dinner (5-course) $17.50, $19.50 or $23.50. Specializes in traditional French country cuisine. Parking. Outdoor dining. Rustic French country house decor. Cr cds: A, C, D, DS, MC, V.

D

★ ★**HARBOR HOUSE.** *831 W Harbor Dr, in Seaport Village, downtown.* 619/232-1141. Hrs: 11:30 am–10 pm; Fri & Sat to 11 pm; Sun brunch 10:30 am–2:30 pm. Res accepted. Bar from 11 am. A la carte entrees: lunch $6.95–$9.95, dinner $11.95–$18.95. Sun brunch $7.95–$11.95. Child's meals. Specializes in fresh seafood broiled over mesquite. Parking. View of harbor, boat docks, Coronado Bay Bridge. Cr cds: A, DS, MC, V.

D

★ ★**HOB NOB HILL.** *2271 1st Ave, in Balboa Park.* 619/239-8176. Hrs: 7 am–8 pm. Closed Sat; major hols. Res accepted. Wine, beer. A la carte entrees: bkfst $1.10–$9.95. Complete meals: lunch $5.45–$9.95, dinner $5.45–$11.95. Child's meals. Specializes in prime rib, corned beef, roast turkey. Family-owned. Cr cds: A, DS, MC, V.

★ ★**IMPERIAL HOUSE.** *505 Kalmia St, north of downtown.* 619/234-3525. Hrs: 11 am–4 pm, 5–10 pm; Mon to 2 pm; Fri & Sat to 11 pm; early-bird dinner Mon–Fri 5–6:30 pm. Closed Sun; most major hols. Res accepted. Continental menu. Bar to 11 pm; Fri & Sat to 12:30 am. A la carte entrees: lunch $6–$11, dinner $12–$20. Specializes in rack of lamb, pepper steak, seafood. Pianist Wed–Sat. Valet parking. Old world decor. Family-owned. Cr cds: A, C, D, DS, MC, V.

✔ ★**KARL STRAUSS' OLD COLUMBIA BREWERY & GRILL.** *1157 Columbia St, downtown.* 619/234-2739. Hrs: 11:30 am–10 pm; Thurs, Fri & Sat to midnight. Closed most major hols. Res accepted. Bar. Semi-a la carte: lunch $8–$10, dinner $8–$12. Specialties: hamburgers, mixed grill, German-style sausage. Brew own beer; some seasonal varieties. View of microbrewery from restaurant. Cr cds: MC, V.

D

★ ★**KELLY'S.** *500 Hotel Circle N, north of downtown.* 619/291-7131 ext 3806. Hrs: 11 am–11 pm; Sat, Sun & hols from 4 pm; early-bird dinner 4–6:30 pm. Closed Easter, Thanksgiving, Dec 25. Bar to 2 am; Sat & Sun from 4 pm. Semi-a la carte: lunch $3.50–$7.50, dinner

$5.75–$23.95. Specialties: châteaubriand, steak. Entertainment. Parking. Waterfalls. Cr cds: A, C, D, DS, MC, V, JCB.

★ ★ ★**LE FONTAINEBLEAU.** *(See The Westgate Hotel)* 619/238-1818. Hrs: 11:45 am–2 pm, 6–10 pm; Sun brunch 10 am–2 pm. Res accepted. Continental menu. Bar. Wine cellar. Semi-a la carte: lunch $7.95–$16.75, dinner $19.50–$30. Complete meals: dinner $24.95. Sun brunch $24.95. Child's meals. Specializes in seafood, veal. Pianist, harpist. Valet parking. Lavish French period setting. Original 17th-century oils; antiques. Cr cds: A, C, D, DS, ER, MC, V.

D

✔ ★ ★**LINO'S.** *2754 Calhoun St, in Old Town.* 619/299-7124. Hrs: 11 am–10 pm; winter to 9 pm. Closed Thanksgiving, Dec 25. Res accepted. Italian menu. Bar. Semi-a la carte: lunch $5.25–$8.25, dinner $5.75–$14.95. Child's meals. Specializes in veal, chicken, shrimp. Own pasta. Parking. Outdoor dining. Cr cds: A, C, D, DS, ER, MC, V, JCB.

★ ★**LUIGI AL MARE.** *861 W Harbor Dr, in Seaport Village, downtown.* 619/232-7581. Hrs: 11 am–10 pm. Res accepted. Italian menu. Bar. A la carte entrees: lunch $6.95–$12.95, dinner $10.95–$19.95. Child's meals. Specializes in seafood, fresh pasta. Outdoor dining. View of San Diego Harbor. Cr cds: A, DS, MC, V.

D

★**MICHELANGELO.** *1878 Rosecrans St, north of downtown.* 619/224-9478. Hrs: 11 am–10 pm; Fri & Sat to 10:30 pm; Sun 4–10 pm; early-bird dinner 4–5:30 pm. Closed most major hols. Res accepted. Northern Italian menu. Wine, beer. Semi-a la carte: lunch $4–$13, dinner $7–$17. Specializes in veal, homemade pasta. Parking. Italian-style decor. Cr cds: A, DS, MC, V.

★ ★ ★**MISTER A'S.** *2550 5th Ave, on 12th floor of Financial Center, north of downtown.* 619/239-1377. Hrs: 11 am–2:30 pm, 6–10:30 pm. Closed some major hols. Res accepted. Continental menu. Bar 11–2 am; Sat, Sun from 5 pm. Wine list. Semi-a la carte: lunch $6–$13.50, dinner $16.95–$28.95. Specialties: beef Wellington, rack of lamb, fresh fish. Entertainment Wed–Sat. Valet parking. Rococo decor; oil paintings. Rooftop dining; panoramic view. Family-owned. Jacket (dinner). Cr cds: A, C, D, DS, MC, V.

✔ ★**NATI'S.** *1852 Bacon St, north of downtown.* 619/224-3369. Hrs: 11 am–9 pm; Sat & Sun from 9 am; winter to 8 pm, Fri to 9 pm, Sat 9 am–9 pm, Sun 9 am–8 pm. Closed some major hols. Mexican menu. Bar. Semi-a la carte: bkfst $3–$6.50, lunch, dinner $4.35–$8.50. Specializes in chiles rellenos, sour cream tostadas, carne asada. Parking. Outdoor dining. Cr cds: MC, V.

★**OLD TOWN MEXICAN CAFE & CANTINA.** *2489 San Diego Ave, in Old Town.* 619/297-4330. Hrs: 7 am–11 pm. Closed Thanksgiving, Dec 25. Mexican menu. Bar to 1 am. A la carte entrees: bkfst $2.95–$5.95, lunch, dinner $2.25–$11. Specialties: carnitas, Old Town pollo, Mexican-style ribs, homemade tortillas. Child's meals. Parking. Patio dining. Cr cds: A, D, DS, MC, V.

D

★ ★**PACIFICA GRILL & ROTISSERIE.** *1202 Kettner Blvd, near train depot, downtown.* 619/696-9226. Hrs: 11:30 am–2:30 pm, 5–10 pm; Fri to 10:30 pm; Sat 5–10:30 pm; Sun 5–9:30 pm. Closed some major hols. Res accepted. Bar. Wine list. Semi-a la carte: lunch $5–$9, dinner $10–$19. Specializes in seafood, pasta, steak, rotisserie chicken. Own desserts. Valet parking. Cr cds: A, C, D, DS, MC, V.

✔ ★ ★**PANDA INN.** *506 Horton Plaza, on top floor, downtown.* 619/233-7800. Hrs: 11 am–10 pm; Fri & Sat to 11 pm. Closed Thanksgiving. Res accepted. Mandarin menu. Bar. Semi-a la carte: lunch $5–$9, dinner $6–$14. Specialties: sweet & pungent shrimp, orange-flavored beef. Parking. Outdoor dining. Several dining areas, all with Chinese art pieces, 1 with entire ceiling skylight; pandas depicted in stained-glass windows. Cr cds: A, D, MC, V.

D

★ ★ ★**RAINWATER'S.** *1202 Kettner Blvd, near train depot, downtown.* 619/233-5757. Hrs: 11:30 am–midnight; Sat 5 pm–midnight;

Sun 5–11 pm. Closed Thanksgiving, Dec 24, 25. Res accepted. Bar. Wine list. Semi-a la carte: lunch $8–$15, dinner $15–$40. Specializes in fresh seafood, prime steaks. Own pastries. Valet parking. Outdoor dining. Cr cds: A, C, D, MC, V.

✔ ★ ★ SAN DIEGO PIER CAFE. *885 W Harbor Dr, in Seaport Village, downtown.* 619/239-3968. Hrs: 7 am–9 pm; Fri & Sat to 10 pm. Wine, beer. Semi-a la carte: bkfst $4–$7.95, lunch $6.95–$13.95, dinner $7.95–$16.95. Child's meals. Specializes in fresh fish broiled over mesquite fire. Outdoor dining. On harbor pier. Cr cds: A, DS, MC, V.

★ ★ SÄRÖ. *926 Broadway Circle, downtown.* 619/232-7173. Hrs: 11 am–10 pm; Sat & Sun 5–10:30 pm; early-bird dinner Mon–Fri 3–6 pm. Closed some major hols. Res accepted Sat & Sun. Swedish, International menu. Bar. Semi-a la carte: lunch $6–$15, dinner $7–$20. Outdoor dining. 2-story dining rm; main floor & balcony dining areas. Cr cds: A, D, MC, V.

★ ★ THEE BUNGALOW. *4996 W Point Loma Blvd, north of downtown.* 619/224-2884. Hrs: 5:30–9:30 pm; wkends to 10 pm. Closed Mon; Jan 1, July 4, Dec 24. Res accepted. Extensive wine list. Continental menu. Semi-a la carte: dinner $9–$19.95. *Prix fixe* (Wed–Thurs & Sun): dinner $9.95. Specializes in roast duck, rack of lamb, fresh seafood. Parking. In converted house. Many special wine dinners planned throughout the year. Totally nonsmoking. Cr cds: A, DS, MC, V.

★ ★ TOM HAM'S LIGHTHOUSE. *2150 Harbor Island Dr, north of downtown.* 619/291-9110. Hrs: 11:15 am–3:30 pm, 5–10:30 pm; Sat 5–11 pm; Sun 4–10 pm; early-bird dinner Mon–Fri 5–6:30 pm, Sat 5–6 pm, Sun 4–6 pm; Sun brunch 10 am–2 pm. Closed Dec 25. Res accepted. Bar 11–2 am. Semi-a la carte: lunch $3.95–$13.95, dinner $9.95–$30. Sun brunch $9.95. Child's meals. Specializes in steak, seafood. Salad bar (lunch). Entertainment Wed–Sat. Parking. Early California, Spanish decor. View of bay, San Diego skyline. Official Coast Guard No. 9 beacon. Family-owned. Cr cds: A, C, D, DS, MC, V.

[SC]

★ ★ TOP OF THE MARKET. *750 N Harbor Dr, downtown.* 619/234-4867. Hrs: 11 am–10 pm; Fri & Sat to 10:30 pm; Sun brunch 10 am–3 pm. Closed Thanksgiving, Dec 25. Res accepted. Bar to 11 pm. Semi-a la carte: lunch $5.75–$23, dinner $10.25–$31. Sun brunch $12–$15. Child's meals. Specializes in seafood. Oyster, sushi bar. Parking. Outdoor dining. Pictures of turn-of-the-century fishing scenes. Retail fish market lower floor. Cr cds: A, D, DS, MC, V.

★ ★ ★ WINESELLAR & BRASSERIE. *9550 Waples St, Suite 115, 2nd fl, north of downtown.* 619/450-9576. Hrs: 11:30 am–2 pm, 6–10 pm; Sun 5–9 pm. Closed Mon; Jan 1, Easter, Thanksgiving, Dec 25. Res accepted; required Fri–Sun. Contemporary French menu. Bar. Extensive wine list. A la carte entrees: lunch $5–$14, dinner $8–$19. Complete meals (Tues–Thurs): 3-course dinner with 3 glasses of specially selected wine $29. *Prix fixe:* dinner (Sun only) $17.95. Menu changes daily. Parking. Intimate, formal dining. Cr cds: A, DS, MC, V.

Unrated Dining Spots

AESOP'S TABLES. *8650 Genesee Ave, in Costa Verde Center.* 619/455-1535. Hrs: 11 am–10 pm; Sun from 4 pm. Closed major hols. Greek, Middle Eastern menu. Bar. Semi-a la carte: lunch $4–$9.95, dinner $5–$12.95. Patio dining. Cr cds: A, C, D, DS, MC, V.

CITY DELICATESSEN. *535 University Ave, north of downtown.* 619/295-2747. Hrs: 7 am–midnight; Fri, Sat to 2 am. Closed Dec 25; Yom Kippur. Jewish-style delicatessen. Wine, beer. A la carte entrees: bkfst, lunch $4.50–$8.50, dinner $4.50–$9.95. Child's meals. Own baking. Delicatessen and bakery. Photos and portraits of entertainers. Cr cds: MC, V.

CORVETTE DINER BAR & GRILL. *3946 5th Ave, downtown.* 619/542-1001. Hrs: 7 am–midnight. Closed Jan 1, Easter, Dec 24 eve, 25. Bar. Semi-a la carte: bkfst $1.95–$3.95, lunch $4.85–$7.95, dinner $5.50–$9.95. Specializes in hamburgers, chicken-fried steak. DJ. 1950s-style diner with soda fountains. Corvette in center of room. Cr cds: A, DS, MC, V, JCB.

D.Z. AKIN'S. *6930 Alvarado Rd, north of downtown.* 619/265-0218. Hrs: 7 am–9 pm; Fri, Sat to 11 pm. Closed July 4, Thanksgiving, Dec 25; some Jewish hols. Semi-a la carte: bkfst $3.50–$6, lunch $6–$8, dinner $8–$12. Specializes in delicatessen items. Own pastries. Parking. Cr cds: MC, V.

EL INDIO SHOP. *3695 India St, north of downtown.* 619/299-0333. Hrs: 8 am–9 pm. Mexican menu. Semi-a la carte: bkfst $3–$4, lunch, dinner $5–$7. Outdoor dining. Cafeteria-style. Tortilla factory in kitchen. Family-owned. Cr cds: DS, MC, V.

GREEK CORNER. *5841 El Cajon Blvd, north of downtown.* 619/287-3303. Hrs: 11 am–10 pm. Greek, Middle Eastern menu. Wine, beer. Semi-a la carte: lunch, dinner $6–$10. Specializes in Greek dishes, Middle Eastern vegetarian dishes. Parking. Outdoor dining. Greek cafe-style dining. Cr cds: MC, V.

SAFFRON. *3731-B India St, north of downtown.* 619/574-0177. Hrs: 11 am–9 pm. Closed Sun; Jan 1, Thanksgiving, Dec 25. Thai menu. A la carte entrees: lunch, dinner $3.75–$12. Specializes in Thai grilled chicken. Take-out with outdoor dining. Picnic baskets avail. Cr cds: MC, V.

San Fernando Valley Area (H-3)

North and west of Los Angeles (see) and bounded by the Santa Monica, Santa Susana and San Gabriel mountains is the area known as the San Fernando Valley. The Los Angeles River, which flows through the valley, has its source in the mountains. Once primarily an agricultural area, the San Fernando Valley has diversified into a haven for light industry and commuters to Los Angeles.

The valley was explored by the Spanish in 1769; they found "a very pleasant and spacious valley". . . "with many live oaks and walnuts." The arrival of the Southern Pacific railroad in 1876, linking Los Angeles to San Francisco, temporarily boosted agricultural production. However, production decreased following the Second World War, when the land was divided into housing tracts. At one time, the valley gained 15,000–20,000 new residents per year, rivaling the spectacular growth of Los Angeles.

The following towns and Los Angeles neighborhoods in the San Fernando Valley area are included in the *Mobil Travel Guide.* For additional information on any of them, see the individual alphabetical listing: North Hollywood, San Fernando, Studio City, Van Nuys, Woodland Hills.

San Fernando (H-3)

Pop: 22,580 **Elev:** 1,061 ft **Area code:** 818

A Ranger District office of the Angeles National Forest (see PASADENA) is located here.

What to See and Do

1. **Mission San Fernando Rey de España** (1797). 15151 San Fernando Mission Blvd. Restored 17th mission of chain; collections of Indian artifacts, furniture, woodcarvings, gold-leaf altars. A 35-bell carillon rings with an ancient melody sung by Native Americans in

mission days. Guided tours (Sat). (Daily; closed Thanksgiving, Dec 25) Phone 361-0186.   ¢¢   Also here, and included in the general admission, is the

Archival Center. Located in the west garden of the mission, the center houses ecclesiastical and historical documents; medals and mitres; relics of early California missionaries; changing exhibits. (Mon, Thurs & Fri, early afternoon)

2. **Lopez Adobe** (1882). 1100 Pico St. Two-story home of Geronimo and Catalina Lopez, early residents of San Fernando. Spanish shawls, bags, dolls; Victorian furnishings. Guided tours. (Wed, Sat & Sun; closed hols & last wk Dec) Phone 361-5050 or 365-9990. **Free.**

(For further information contact the Chamber of Commerce, 519 S Brand Blvd, 91340; 361-1184.)

San Francisco (E-1)

Founded: 1776 **Pop:** 723,959 **Elev:** 63 ft **Area code:** 415

Nearly everyone who comes to San Francisco falls in love with it. A city of sea, hills and parks, cable cars, a bustling waterfront, bridges that span mighty spaces—all freshened by clean Pacific breezes and warmed by a cooperative sun and a romantic fog—San Francisco is alive and lovely. Heart of a great Pacific empire, it is the true capital of the West.

This city of precipitous hills stretches seven miles across in each direction, rimmed on three sides by water. Its awe-inspiring bay, 500 square miles, equal in beauty to the Bay of Naples, constitutes one of the most nearly perfect natural harbors on earth. Rome has its 7 hills; San Francisco was built on 43 hills. The city encompasses a total of 129.4 square miles, of which only 46.6 square miles are land. Within its boundaries are islands—Yerba Buena, Treasure and Alcatraz—plus the Farallon group 32 miles west, part of the city since 1872.

San Francisco is one of nature's few "air-conditioned cities"—relatively warm in winter and cool in summer. Weather Bureau statistics show sunshine in 66 out of every 100 possible hours. The average mean temperatures for San Francisco are 50°F in winter; 55°F in spring; 62°F in summer; and 60°F in fall.

Gateway to the Orient, San Francisco is a melting pot of Occidental and Oriental cultures. Its population is descended from peoples of almost every nation of the world and every state of the Union. Leading national groups are Italian, German, Irish, Chinese, English, Russian, Latin American, Japanese, Korean and Filipino. More than 500 churches, temples and meetinghouses conduct services in 23 different tongues. Fifty periodicals are published in 13 languages.

San Francisco is an important financial center and headquarters of one of the largest banks in the world (Bank of America). Although no longer considered the air hub of the West (Los Angeles now holds that title), the city still plays a major role in the nation's air travel; San Francisco International Airport, a $250 million air gateway to the world, is located 14½ miles south off Bayshore Freeway and US 101. The San Francisco Bay Area ranks second on the West Coast in waterborne commerce. The Port of San Francisco is a $100 million public utility with a 7½-mile stretch of ship-berthing space, 229 acres of covered and open wharf area and a total of 43 piers. More than 1,500 San Francisco firms engage in international trade.

Hellenic in setting and climate, European in its intellectual and cultural scope, American in its vigor and informality and Oriental in its tranquility, San Francisco is indeed an exciting "Baghdad by the Bay." Author and raconteur Gene Fowler said, "Every man should be allowed to love two cities—his own and San Francisco."

San Francisco's lusty history began with early Portuguese, English and Spanish explorers penetrating the Bay. In 1775 the Spanish ship *San Carlos* sailed through the Golden Gate to drop the first anchor off San Francisco. On March 28, 1776, a mission site was selected and dedicated to St Francis of Assisi. The little village of Yerba Buena developed near the mission, but slumbered until 1836, when the port grew into an important trading post.

In 1846, the USS *Portsmouth* dropped anchor in the cove; Captain John B. Montgomery and 70 men came ashore and hoisted the Stars and Stripes, marking the end of Mexican rule. The next year the village changed its name to San Francisco, taking its cue from the mission.

A year later, gold was discovered in Sutter's millrace on the American River at Coloma. This had tremendous impact on San Francisco; few of the inhabitants remained, and, as the news spread around the world, a torrent of people and ships descended on the city. A year later, 6,000 miners were digging and San Francisco was a wild tent city of 20,000 rough, tough transients. An average of 50 sailing ships a month anchored in San Francisco Bay; many were deserted by crews eager for gold.

A few farsighted men realized that fortunes could be made in San Francisco as well as in the gold camps. Their foresight is reflected today in many of the city's distinguished stores.

Meanwhile, thirsty for gold, the East was migrating to California. With the aid of imported Chinese labor, 2,000 miles of railroad track crossed the nation's two greatest mountain ranges to join East and West. Shipping to the Orient flourished and small industries prospered.

Young and raw, San Francisco spent the last half of the 19th century as an exciting mix of growing metropolis, frontier and boom town. Then, on April 18, 1906, came the great earthquake (8.6 on the Richter scale) and fire. Raging unchecked for three days, the fire wiped out the entire business area and burned out 497 blocks of buildings in the heart of the city. Losses amounted to some 2,500 lives and nearly $350 million. With the ashes still warm, the city started rebuilding; it was largely completed by 1915, when the city celebrated the opening of the Panama Canal with the Panama Pacific International Exposition.

The opening of the San Francisco-Oakland Bay Bridge in 1936, followed by the Golden Gate Bridge in 1937 and the completion of the Bay Area Rapid Transit System (BART) have tied the cities of the Bay Area together.

A significant historical event took place April 25–June 26, 1945, when delegates from the nations of the world assembled here to found the United Nations. San Francisco became the birthplace of the UN—another facet of its cosmopolitan personality.

In sightseeing, dining, nightlife, shopping and all other tourist adventures, San Francisco is rivaled—and perhaps not exceeded—only by New York City.

From the Twin Peaks area, the center of the city, Market Street bisects the eastern segment of San Francisco, ending at the Ferry Building and the Embarcadero. The business section, "the Wall Street of the West," is a cluster of skyscrapers extending from Kearny Street to the waterfront and south of Market Street from New Montgomery Street north to Jackson Street. Chinatown, Nob Hill, Telegraph Hill and Fisherman's Wharf fan out north of Market Street. Russian Hill gives a panoramic view of San Francisco Bay. Here is Lombard Street, known as "the crookedest street in the world"—lined by hydrangea gardens and handsome residences, it makes nine hairpin turns in a single block. The Presidio, several museums and Golden Gate Bridge are on the northwest side of the peninsula.

One formula for a systematic exploration is to start with a guided three-and-a-half-hour "around San Francisco" sightseeing bus tour. (These tours can be booked through your hotel.) Note the places you want to visit at greater length, then explore in detail. Use your own car or rent one to reach outlying areas and to explore across the bridges. The San Francisco hills are not for fainthearted drivers, but they're not as bad as they look. Be sure to turn your wheels in toward the curb and set your brake when parking.

San Francisco also has its scenic "49-Mile Drive," marked with blue and white seagull signs. This begins at City Hall in the Civic Center (Van Ness Ave & McAllister St), then twists around the entire city and leads to most of the spectacular sights. You can pick this up and follow its signs at any point or obtain a map of the drive from the San Francisco

SAN FRANCISCO
BAY AREA

© H.M. GOUSHA

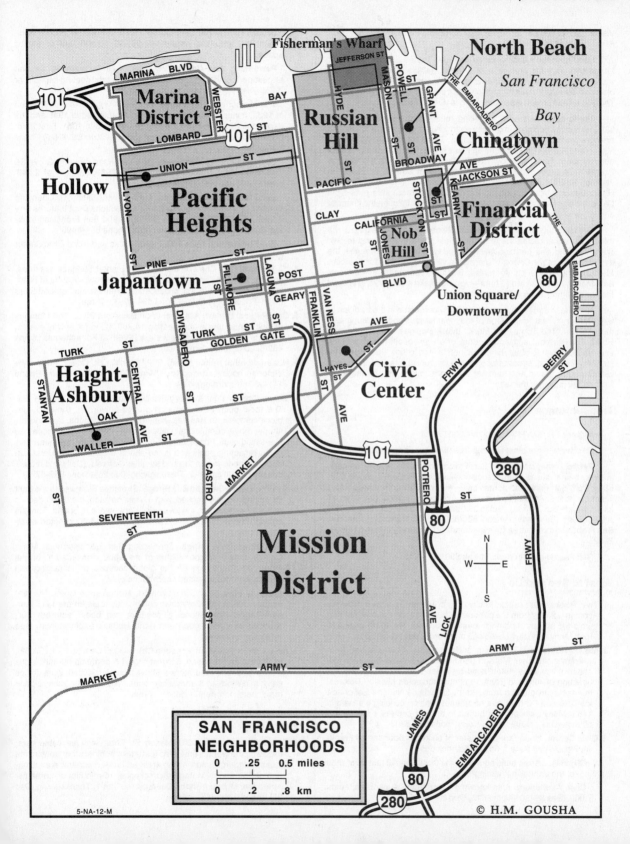

Fisherman's Wharf

North Beach

San Francisco

Bay

MARINA BLVD

Marina District

WEBSTER ST

LOMBARD ST

101

BAY ST

JEFFERSON ST

Russian Hill

POWELL ST

MASON ST

HYDE ST

GRANT AVE

Chinatown

Cow Hollow

UNION ST

LYON ST

Pacific Heights

PACIFIC

BROADWAY

AVE

JACKSON ST

KEARNY ST

Financial District

CLAY

CALIFORNIA ST

STOCKTON ST

PINE ST

Japantown

FILLMORE ST

LAGUNA ST

POST

JONES ST

Nob Hill

Union Square/
Downtown

DIVISADERO ST

TURK ST

GOLDEN GATE

STANYAN ST

TURK ST

CENTRAL AVE

Haight-Ashbury

OAK ST

WALLER

GEARY

FRANKLIN ST

VAN NESS AVE

ST

BLVD

AVE

HAYES ST

Civic Center

POTRERO

FRWY

80

EMBARCADERO

BERRY ST

101

280

CASTRO ST

MARKET

SEVENTEENTH ST

ST

Mission District

80

JAMES LICK FRWY

N
W   E
S

ARMY ST

ARMY ST

MARKET

SAN FRANCISCO NEIGHBORHOODS

0   .25   0.5 miles

0   .2   .8 km

EMBARCADERO

280

5-NA-12-M

© H.M. GOUSHA

Visitor Information Center, lower level of Hallidie Plaza, Powell & Market Sts.

San Francisco's famous cable cars (designated a National Historic Landmark) were the brainchild of Andrew Hallidie. The inaugural run was made down Clay from Jones Street on August 2, 1873. The century-old cable car system was temporarily shut down in 1982 for renovations. The $60 million project was completed in June, 1984.

These cable cars offer a thrilling roller-coaster experience (fare $2). The natives hop on and off with abandon, but visitors are advised to be more cautious. Also, avoid rush hours. There are three lines: Powell-Mason and Market Streets goes up Powell, over Nob Hill, along Columbus Avenue to Taylor and down to Bay Street at Fisherman's Wharf; the Powell-Hyde cable runs from Powell and Market Streets, up Powell to Jackson Street, west on Jackson to Hyde, north on Hyde over Russian Hill to Beach Street at Aquatic Park; the California cable runs from California and Market Streets to Van Ness Avenue, through the financial district, past Chinatown and over Nob Hill.

The city's diverse restaurants number nearly 3,300. The gold of the mining camps attracted some of the finest chefs in the world to San Francisco and this heritage persists today. Chinatown features the exotic cuisine of the Orient; Fisherman's Wharf is famous for seafood. Mexican, Italian, French, Armenian, Russian, Japanese, Vietnamese, East Indian, American are all here—you can make a culinary trip around the world without leaving San Francisco.

Nightlife in San Francisco is only partly carried on in the tradition of the "Barbary Coast" days. One of the most famous cocktail lounges in the world is "The Top of the Mark" (Mark Hopkins Inter-Continental Hotel). The Fairmont, across the street, offers an equally fine view of the city, as do several other high-rise hotels and office buildings. The theaters have long, successful seasons. In sports, the San Francisco Giants play in spring and summer and both college and professional football are played in the fall.

Transportation

Airport: See SAN FRANCISCO AIRPORT AREA.

Car Rental Agencies: See toll-free numbers under Introduction.

Public Transportation: In San Francisco—cable cars, streetcars, subway trains, buses (San Francisco Municipal Railway), phone 673-6864; from San Francisco across bay—subway trains (Bay Area Rapid Transit), phone 788-2278; from San Francisco across bay—ferries (Golden Gate Bus Transit), phone 332-6600; from San Francisco to Palo Alto—buses (Samtrans), phone 800/660-4-BUS; transportation from San Francisco to bay-area towns—buses (AC Transit), phone 510/839-2882.

Rail Passenger Service: Amtrak 800/872-7245.

What to See and Do

1. **Twin Peaks.** Near center of city. The breathtaking view it provides comes not only from the panorama, but also from the breezes that whip the hilltops. The north peak is 903 feet, the south peak 910 feet. Many apartment buildings and homes dot the hillsides.

2. **Mission Dolores** (1776). 16th & Dolores Sts. Fountainhead from which the city grew. Mission San Francisco de Asis was sixth in a chain of missions established by Franciscan fathers under the direction of Junipero Serra. (It is now known as Mission Dolores, the name being taken from nearby Laguna de Nuestra Señora de los Dolores.) Cornerstone of present mission building was laid in 1782. Many pioneers are buried in ancient cemetery beside the church. (Daily; closed major hols) Phone 621-8203. ¢

3. **Civic Center.** 11-square-blk cluster of buildings bounded by Franklin, 7th, Golden Gate & Hayes Sts. Includes

   City Hall. Classic building with dome more than 13 feet taller than that of the Capitol in Washington, DC.

   Civic Auditorium. Also known as Exposition Auditorium; seats 7,000. (See SEASONAL EVENTS) Opp is

Brooks Hall. Under Civic Center Plaza; connected to Civic Auditorium by ramp and escalators; 90,000 square feet of exhibit space.

Performing Arts Center. Van Ness Ave & Grove St. Second largest performing arts center in US, with a total seating capacity of 7,233. Also here is

War Memorial/Opera House. Van Ness Ave & Grove St. Opened in 1932, it was here that the UN was established in 1945 and the Japanese Peace Treaty Conference was held in 1951. First civic-owned opera house in the country. (See SEASONAL EVENTS) Phone 864-3330. Adj is

Louise M. Davies Symphony Hall. Van Ness Ave and Grove St. This $30 million concert hall opened in 1980; capacity of 2,743. (See SEASONAL EVENTS) Phone 431-5400.

San Francisco Public Library. Larkin & McAllister Sts. Changing exhibits on 2nd & 3rd floors. Special Collections Dept features rare books and many volumes on California and San Francisco (daily exc Sun). (Daily exc Sun; closed hols) Phone 557-4400.

The Federal and State Buildings are also part of the Civic Center group.

4. **"A World of Oil."** Chevron USA Inc, 555 Market St. Plaza has trees, shrubs, fountains and flowers. Petroleum exhibit in lobby of building tells how oil is found, produced and refined. Self-guided tours (Mon–Fri; no tours hols). Phone 894-4086. **Free.**

5. **Cow Palace.** Geneva Ave, 1 mi W off Bayshore Blvd. World famous exhibit center and arena, seating 14,700. Used for sports events, exhibits and concerts. (See ANNUAL EVENTS) For schedule phone 469-6000 or -6065 (box office).

6. **Haas-Lilienthal House** (1886). 2007 Franklin St. Queen Anne-style Victorian house. Guided tour (Wed, Sun). Sr citizen rate. Phone 441-3004 (recording). ¢¢

7. **Japan Center.** Post & Geary Sts, between Fillmore & Laguna Sts. The focal point of an expanding Japantown, this three-square-block complex houses Japanese restaurants, baths, bookstores, shops; movie complex, art galleries and hotel. Peace Pagoda has five-tiered roof. Peace Plaza, paved in slate, has Japanese gardens, reflecting pools and is the site of traditional Japanese entertainment during spring and summer festivals. (Daily; most businesses closed Jan 1–3, Thanksgiving, Dec 25) Phone 922-6776.

8. **San Francisco-Oakland Bay Bridge.** Stretches 8½ miles to the East Bay cities. Double-decked, with 5 lanes on each; the upper deck is one-way westbound, the lower deck one-way eastbound. Tunnels through Yerba Buena Island in midbay. Auto toll collected westbound only.

9. **The Golden Gate Bridge.** Connecting San Francisco with Marin County. One of famous sights of the world, conceded to be the most beautiful bridge on the globe because of its setting and design. Auto toll collected southbound only.

10. **Palace of Fine Arts.** 3601 Lyon St. Monumental Greco-Romanesque rotunda with Corinthian colonnades; built for the 1915 Panama-Pacific International Exposition; has been restored. Surrounded by duck lagoon and park. Houses Exploratorium (see #19). Grounds **free.**

11. **Acres of Orchids (Rod McLellan Co).** 1450 El Camino Real (CA 82), in South San Francisco. Largest orchid & gardenia nursery in the world; scientific laboratories show cloning. Guided tours (twice daily: mid-morning & early afternoon). Visitor center (daily; closed major hols). Phone 871-5655. **Free.**

MUSEUMS

12. **Cable Car Museum.** 1201 Mason St. Three antique cable cars, including the world's first. Also features machinery that powers the cables. Underground viewing area, artifacts, mechanical explanation of operations, vintage photographs, 16-min film on cable car operation. Museum shop. (Daily; closed Jan 1, Thanksgiving, Dec 25) Phone 474-1887. **Free.**

13. San Francisco Museum of Modern Art. 401 Van Ness Ave, at McAllister St, 3rd & 4th floors of Veterans Building, in Civic Center area (see #3). 20th-century art on permanent exhibit, also traveling exhibitions; concerts, lectures, special events. (Daily exc Mon; closed major hols) Free admission 1st Tues of month. Sr citizen rate. Phone 252-4000. ¢¢

14. Wells Fargo Bank History Museum. 420 Montgomery St. Artifacts and displays dating from the Gold Rush to the 1906 earthquake to present-day banking; Concord Stagecoach. (Mon–Fri; closed hols) Phone 396-2619. **Free.**

15. Treasure Island Museum. 2 mi E via Oakland Bay Bridge, Treasure Island exit, at Bldg #1. Exhibits on history of the Navy, Marines and Coast Guard in the Pacific from 1813. Also exhibits on 1939–40 Golden Gate International Exposition, for which island was built, and *China Clipper* flying boats of 1935–1946. (Daily; closed Jan 1, Easter, Thanksgiving, Dec 25) Phone 395-5067. **Free.**

16. Ferry Building. Embarcadero at the foot of Market St. Ferries to Sausalito and Larkspur leave from Ferry Plaza end of building (Pier ½); ferries to Oakland, Alameda, Vallejo and Tiburon leave from terminal at north. Also here is a waterfront promenade. Ferries ¢¢

17. Randall Museum. 199 Museum Way. Includes live animal room (Tues–Sat, limited hrs; phone for schedule); seismograph; San Francisco natural history exhibits; model railroad. Nature walks (Sat afternoons) on 16-acre hill. (Tues–Sat, mid-morning–late afternoon; closed hols) Phone 554-9600. **Free.**

18. National Maritime Museum (see #27).

19. Exploratorium. 3601 Lyon St, housed in the Palace of Fine Arts (see #10). Hands-on museum dedicated to providing insights into scientific and natural phenomena. More than 700 participatory exhibits on science, art and human perception. Changing exhibits. (Daily exc Mon; closed Thanksgiving, Dec 25) Sr citizen rate. 1st Wed of month free. Phone 561-0360. ¢¢¢

20. M.H. deYoung Memorial Museum. Golden Gate Park (see #25). Features 17th- to 20th-century American art. Paintings from collection of John D. Rockefeller III; British art; tribal rugs from Central Asia; African, Oceanic and ancient art. Cafe. (Wed–Sun) Sr citizen rate. 1st Wed of month free. Phone 863-3330. ¢¢   In the west wing is the

  Asian Art Museum. The Avery Brundage Collection; art from China, India, Japan, Korea and southeast, central and western Asia; traveling exhibitions; displays rotate often. (Wed–Sun) Sr citizen rate. Free admission 1st Sat morning & 1st Wed of month. Phone 668-8921. ¢¢

21. California Academy of Sciences, Natural History Museum & Aquarium. Golden Gate Park (see #25). Includes Morrison Planetarium (shows daily; fee; no shows Thanksgiving, Dec 24, 25); Steinhart Aquarium and the Fish Roundabout; African Safari Hall, Cowell Hall (main entrance), Wild California, Earth & Space Hall, Hall of Human Cultures, Gem & Mineral Hall and "Life through Time," a hall devoted to the evidence for evolution. Also Far Side of Science Gallery, featuring more than 160 cartoons by Gary Larson. Cafeteria. (Daily) Sr citizen rate. Admission free 1st Wed of month. Phone 750-7145 (recording). ¢¢¢

22. Ripley's Believe It or Not Museum. 175 Jefferson St, at Fisherman's Wharf. Oddities collected from US and abroad; video displays; walk-through kaleidoscope. (Daily) Phone 771-6188. ¢¢¢

23. The Mexican Museum. Fort Mason Center, Bldg D, Laguna & Marina Blvds. Pre-Hispanic, Colonial, Folk, contemporary Mexican and Mexican-American art. Permanent and changing exhibits. Gift shop. (Wed–Sun, afternoons; closed some hols & late Dec) Sr citizen rate. Admission free 1st Wed of month. Phone 441-0404 or -0445. ¢¢

24. Old Mint. 5th & Mission Sts. Outstanding example of Federal Classic-revival architecture; period rooms, authentic 1869 coin press. Pyramid of gold bars, monetary treasures and Old West artifacts. (Mon–Fri; closed hols) Phone 744-6830. **Free.**

RECREATIONAL AREAS

25. Golden Gate Park. Bounded by Lincoln Way, Stanyan & Fulton Sts & Great Hwy. Once a 1,017-acre sand waste, from 1887 the area was developed by John McLaren, master botanist and landscaper, into one of the most beautiful parks in the world. Park contains more than 10,000 trees and shrubs, a restored Dutch windmill, statues and monuments, 11 gardens, 2 waterfalls, 11 lakes and 40 picnic areas. Also, McLaren Rhododendron Dell (free), a conservatory on Kennedy Dr near Arguello Blvd (daily; fee), a Music Concourse near Fulton St & 8th Ave entrance (band concerts: Sun, hols, weather permitting), the Strybing Arboretum and Botanical Garden, King Dr & 9th Ave (daily, free). Fee for some activities. Phone 666-7200. Other park attractions include

  Prayerbook Cross (1894). Kennedy Dr. Commemorates first prayer service in English language held on Pacific Coast, conducted by Sir Francis Drake's chaplain.

  Spreckels Lake. Kennedy Dr & 36th Ave. Used primarily for sailing model boats.

  Stow Lake. Stow Lake Dr off Kennedy Dr, near 16th Ave. Surrounds Strawberry Hill. View of park and city. One-hour boat rentals (fee): electric motorboat, rowboat, pedal boat.

  Mary Connolly Children's Playground. Near King Dr & 3rd Ave. Innovative play equipment, Herschel Spillman Carrousel (1912-14) (fee); picnic area.

  Buffalo paddock. A 10-acre enclosure with bison.

  Sports. 9-hole golf course (fee), 47th Ave off Fulton St, phone 751-8987; 3 lawn bowling greens, 21 tennis courts (fee), 3 fly and plug casting pools; 2 indoor and 2 outdoor handball courts; archery field; horseshoe courts; trotting track, bicycle track, running trails, baseball diamonds (fee).

  Japanese Tea Garden. Oriental landscaping; includes a teahouse, gift shop, pagoda, Buddha, several ponds, streams, footbridges. In spring, cherry blossoms, azaleas and flowering shrubs are in bloom. (Daily). ¢

26. Golden Gate National Recreation Area. Within the 74,000 acres of the recreation area are most of the shoreline of San Francisco, the countryside extending 20 miles north in Marin County and a 1,047-acre parcel in San Mateo County to the south. The Golden Gate Bridge connects the two segments of the park. The most popular visitor areas are the former penitentiary on Alcatraz Island, the historic Cliff House, Fort Point National Historic Site, Muir Woods National Monument (see) and the cultural-entertainment center, Fort Mason Center. The area has 28 miles of shoreline with many beaches, lagoons, rugged headlands, meadows, fortifications, valleys, hillsides, picnic facilities and 100 miles of trails are within the area Congress designated in 1972 as one of the first urban national parks. (Hrs vary, but most areas are always open during the day.) For general recreation area information, phone 556-0560 or write Golden Gate National Recreation Area, Fort Mason, Building 201, San Francisco 94123. Some of the park areas include

  Ocean Beach. 3½ mi of beach on San Francisco's Pacific shore. **Free.**

  Seal Rocks & Cliff House. Restaurants at the Cliff House (1909) overlook the ocean, the Marin Coast to the north and the Seal Rocks habitat of sea lions. Visitor information center (limited hrs). **Free.**

  China Beach. Wind-protected cove with swimming beach. **Free.**

  Baker Beach. Sandy beach on the western shore of the Presidio. **Free.**

  Fort Point National Historic Site. Long Ave & Marine Dr, under southern end of Golden Gate Bridge in the Presidio. This restored Civil War-era fort houses an exhibit explaining story of the fort; also a museum with military artifacts. Guided tours. (Wed–Sun; closed Jan 1, Thanksgiving, Dec 25) For information contact District Ranger, PO Box 29333, Presidio of San Francisco 94129; 556-1693. **Free.**

Golden Gate Promenade. Bay shoreline between Fort Point and Fort Mason provides an area to walk, run and observe; also off-leash dog walking permitted.

Fort Mason Center. Two piers and other buildings of the former Army port of embarkation are a cultural and entertainment center with restaurants (phone 441-5706). Building E houses the J. Porter Shaw Library of the National Maritime Museum (Tues evenings & Wed–Fri afternoons, also Sun mid-morning–early evening; phone 556-9870). The last surviving intact Liberty ship, the SS *Jeremiah O'Brien*, is moored at Pier 3; phone 441-3101.

Fort Mason. Old Army Post, once the Army's western headquarters, is now headquarters for the Golden Gate National Recreation Area. Jogging, bicycling and exercise courses.

Muir Beach. Protected cove in the ocean coastline, picnicking. (Daily) Phone 868-0942.

Tennessee Valley and Beach. Secluded, protected beach on ocean. Approx 1½-mile walk from parking. (Daily) Phone 331-1540.

Mt Tamalpais State Park. 13 mi N via CA 1, then 6 mi W on Panoramic Hwy. (See MILL VALLEY)

Muir Woods National Monument (see). Adj to Mt Tamalpais State Park, at the base of the mountain.

Stinson Beach. North to Bolinas. (Daily)

Alcatraz Island. In San Francisco Bay, 1¼ mi from shore. Once a famous maximum security Federal penitentiary, closed in 1963. Former inmates include Al Capone, "Machine Gun" Kelly, public enemy #1 Al Karpis and Robert Stroud, the "Birdman of Alcatraz." Boats leave Pier 41 near Fisherman's Wharf every half-hour (all-yr). Tours include long uphill walk. Self-guided tour; slide show; taped audio tour (fee). For reservations contact Ticketron; or phone the Red & White Fleet, 546-2805. Ferry ¢¢¢

27. **San Francisco Maritime National Historical Park.** Adj to Fort Mason. Includes

Aquatic Park. Cove contains a swimming beach and municipal pier for fishing. Here are most of the historic ships and the

National Maritime Museum. Foot of Polk St. Collection of ship models, relics & gear; figureheads, scrimshaw, photographs of historic Pacific Coast vessels and early San Francisco. (Daily; closed federal hols) Phone 556-3002. **Free.** Included as part of the museum are

Hyde Street Pier Historic Ships. Foot of Hyde St. Collection of five historic merchant ships, including SV *Balclutha*, a sailing ship built in 1886 and restored as a Cape Horn trader. (Daily; closed federal hols) Sr citizens free. Phone 556-3002. ¢¢

USS *Pampanito*. Pier 45, Fisherman's Wharf. Restored World War II fleet submarine. (Daily) Sr citizen rate. For information phone 929-0202. ¢¢

28. **San Francisco Zoo.** Sloat Blvd at 45th Ave. Zoo with over 1,000 animals, including unique Primate Discovery Center with 14 species of rare and exotic monkeys. Also here, Prince Charles, a rare white tiger, African wild dogs; Koala Crossing, Gorilla World, African Scene and Insect Zoo. Children's Zoo with barnyard and nursery; 25-min train tour on the Zebra Zephyr; carousel. Nature trail in summer. Zoo (daily). Fee for activities. Sr citizen rate. Phone 753-7083 (recording) or -7080. ¢¢¢

29. **Sigmund Stern Memorial Grove.** Sloat Blvd & 19th Ave. Natural amphitheater enclosed by eucalyptus trees. Free outdoor concerts in summer (see SEASONAL EVENTS). Picnic tables and barbecue pits nearby.

SPECIAL AREAS

30. **Market St.** Runs from Ferry Building to base of Twin Peaks. San Francisco's best-known street, lined with business establishments and center for municipal transportation.

31. **Montgomery St.** Called the "Wall Street of the West," it's the West's financial hub. Tall buildings form a canyon beginning at Market St and extending to within a block of the Embarcadero.

32. **Jackson Square.** Washington, Jackson & Pacific Sts from Montgomery to Battery St. Historic District; many buildings date back to the mid-1800s. Includes 1 Jackson Pl (formerly a paper warehouse)—a compound of shops, showrooms, and gaslit courtyards.

33. **Union Square.** Bounded by Geary, Powell, Post & Stockton Sts. Public park above four-story subsurface parking garage, first of its kind in the nation. Square is in midst of city's fashionable downtown shopping center. Stores (daily).

34. **Nob Hill.** A 376-ft crest at Sacramento & Jones Sts.

35. **The Embarcadero.** Wide thoroughfare paralleling waterfront behind the docks from China Basin to Fisherman's Wharf, about 3½ miles. Between Montgomery St and the Ferry Building is the new Embarcadero Center. On the Embarcadero at the foot of Market St is the Ferry Building (see #16).

36. **Chinatown.** A "little Cathay" with more than 80,000 people. Largest community of its kind outside Asia. Grant Ave, its main thoroughfare, has been called the "Street of 25,000 Lanterns." Points of interest include

St Mary's Square. Bufano's stainless steel statue of Sun Yat-sen, founder of Republic of China. Nearby is Old St Mary's Church (1853).

Chinese Culture Center. 750 Kearny St, 3rd floor. Art exhibitions, Chinese cultural performances, gift shop; docent-guided walks through the Chinese community. Gallery (Tues–Sat; closed hols). Chinese Heritage Walk (Sat; fee). Also Culinary/Luncheon Walk (Wed; fee). Phone 986-1822. **Free.**

37. **Telegraph Hill** (284 ft). Lombard above Kearny St. Topped by 210-foot Coit Memorial Tower, monument to Volunteer Firemen of 1850s and 1860s. Murals decorating 1st and 2nd floors can also be seen from the outside. Elevator to top. (Daily; closed Thanksgiving, Dec 25) The hill itself is occupied by artists' studios and expensive homes.

38. **Ghirardelli Square.** North Point, Beach & Larkin Sts, W of Fisherman's Wharf. Charming shopping-restaurant complex with live theater on site of Ghirardelli Chocolate factory. Informal entertainment; arts and crafts, women's and children's fashions, sports clothes, ski equipment and many other interesting stores and buildings.

39. **Fisherman's Wharf.** Foot of Taylor St. Center of multimillion-dollar commercial fishing industry and location of many seafood restaurants.

40. **The Cannery.** 2801 Leavenworth St, at Beach St. Complex of shops, restaurants and markets housed in old fruit-processing factory; informal entertainment on the mall.

41. **Alcatraz Island** (see #26).

42. **Cow Hollow.** Union St between Van Ness Ave & Lyon St. Originally the location of a milk-producing area populated mostly by cows, this has been developed into an area of specialty shops, art galleries and bookshops. Many shops are in restored Victorian houses. Numerous restaurants in area.

43. **The Presidio.** Richardson Ave & Lombard St, NW corner of city. Wooded tract of 1,450 acres, fortified since 1776 and now US Army Installation. The present Officer's Club contains sections of the first building to be erected in San Francisco. Markers indicate points of historical interest; hiking. Museum (daily exc Mon); Lincoln Blvd. Phone 561-3660 or -3843. **Free.**

44. **Pier 39.** Two blocks E of Fisherman's Wharf. Approx 100 specialty shops, 12 restaurants, bay cruises, motorized cable car, city tours, free entertainment, waterfront park, 350-berth marina. Re-creates early San Francisco Barbary Coast. Shops (daily); restaurants (daily). Phone 981-7437.

SIGHTSEEING TOURS

45. **CCInc Auto Tape Tours.** These 90-minute cassettes offer mile-by-mile self-guided tours to Monterey (139 mi) along Skyline Blvd, atop Santa Cruz Mountains, to Henry Cowell Redwoods, Monte-

rey's Fisherman's Wharf and Cannery; to Sacramento (166 mi) with a visit to Sausalito, Muir Woods, wineries in the Napa Valley, the historic state capital; to the Wine Country (160 mi) through Sausalito, Muir Woods, a winery tour, dramatic re-creation of the great San Francisco earthquake. Fourteen different tour tapes of California are available. Tapes may also be purchased directly from CCInc, PO Box 227, 2 Elbrook Dr, Allendale, NJ 07401; 201/236-1666. ¢¢¢¢

46. Near Escapes. Auto audio tape tour of San Francisco; also walking audio tape tour of Chinatown. Package includes route map. Tapes may be purchased directly from Near Escape Tapes, PO Box 193005-G, 94119; 386-8687. ¢¢¢¢

47. San Francisco Bay cruises.

Red & White Fleet. Fisherman's Wharf, at Pier 43½ . Bay Cruises. (Daily) Sr citizen rate. Phone 546-2896. ¢¢¢

Blue & Gold Fleet. Adj to Fisherman's Wharf, Pier 39. Offers 1¼-hr cruise. (Daily) Sr citizen rate. Phone 705-5444. ¢¢¢¢

Hornblower Dining Yachts. Pier 33, along the Embarcadero. Luxury dining yachts cruise San Francisco Bay. Flagship is the *California Hornblower,* a 183-foot, 1,000-passenger vessel with 3 decks. Luncheon, dinner/dance, wkend champagne brunch and special event cruises avail. Reservations required. Phone 394-8900, ext 7 or 788-8866, ext 7. ¢¢¢¢¢

48. Gray Line bus tours. Contact 350 8th St, 94103; 585-7373 or 800/826-0202.

Annual Events

Chinese New Year. Chinatown (see #36). Largest and most colorful celebration of this occasion held in US. Week-long activities include Golden Dragon Parade, lion dancing, carnival, cultural exhibits. For more information, contact Chinese Chamber of Commerce, 730 Sacramento St, 94108; 982-3000. Late Jan–late Feb.

Cherry Blossom Festival. Japan Center (see #7). Japanese music, dancing, flower arranging, doll & sword exhibits, bonsai show, martial arts, calligraphy, origami, Akita dog exhibit, tea ceremony, children's village, arts & crafts, films, food bazaar, parade. Phone 563-2313. 2 wkends Apr.

Carnaval. Mission District. Phone 826-1401 or 861-3101. May.

Grand National Rodeo, Horse & Stock Show. Cow Palace (see #5). Late Oct–early Nov.

Seasonal Events

San Francisco Ballet. War Memorial/Opera House (see #3). For information phone 703-9400. Repertory season early Feb–early May; *Nutcracker,* Dec.

Midsummer Music Festival. Sigmund Stern Memorial Grove (see #29), 19th Ave & Sloat Blvd. Sun afternoons. Phone 252-6252. Mid-June–mid-Aug.

Pop concerts. Civic Auditorium (see #3). Check newspapers for schedule. July.

San Francisco Opera. War Memorial/Opera House (see #3). Contact Box Office, Opera House, 94102; 864-3330. Some summer presentations and 14 wks beginning early Sept.

San Francisco Symphony Orchestra. Louise M. Davies Symphony Hall (see #3). Obtain tickets in lobby and at major ticket agencies. Phone 431-5400 (box office). Also special events. Sept–July.

Professional sports. Giants (baseball), 49ers (football), Candlestick Park, Gilman Ave, E of Bayshore Frwy. Stadium has seating capacity of 60,000.

Special Event

World Cup 94. San Francisco will be one of nine US cities to host games of the XV World Cup soccer tournament. This will be the first time the event is held in North America. Stanford Stadium in Palo Alto (see) will be the site of six matches. Tickets avail through Ticketmaster. For further information phone World Cup Public Information, 310/277-9494. Mid-June–mid-July.

Additional Visitor Information

The San Francisco Convention & Visitors Bureau, PO Box 429097, 94102-9097, phone 391-2000, handles written inquiries. Tourist guides may be obtained by mail (postage & handling fee) or at the San Francisco Visitor Information Center, Hallidie Plaza, Powell & Market Sts on lower plaza level. Phone 391-2001 for a daily recording of events.

San Francisco Magazine, available at newsstands, has up-do-date information on cultural events and articles of interest to visitors.

San Francisco Area Suburbs

The following cities, towns and suburbs in the San Francisco area are included in the *Mobil Travel Guide.* For information on any one of them, see the individual alphabetical listing. Berkeley, Corte Madera, Fremont, Hayward, Los Gatos, Martinez, Menlo Park, Mill Valley, Mountain View, Oakland, Palo Alto, Redwood City, San Jose, San Mateo, San Rafael, Santa Clara, Saratoga, Sausalito, Sunnyvale, Tiburon.

San Francisco Airport Area

For additional accommodations, see SAN FRANCISCO AIRPORT AREA, which follows SAN FRANCISCO.

City Neighborhoods

Many of the restaurants, unrated dining establishments and some lodgings listed under San Francisco include neighborhoods as well as exact street addresses. A map showing these neighborhoods can be found following the city map. Geographic descriptions of these areas are given, followed by a table of restaurants arranged by neighborhood.

Chinatown: South of Broadway, west of Kearny St, north of California St and east of Stockton St; along Grant Ave.

Civic Center: South of Golden Gate Ave, west of 7th St, north of Hayes St and east of Franklin St.

Cow Hollow: Area along Union St between Van Ness Ave on the east and Lyon St on the west.

Financial District: South of Jackson St, west of San Francisco Bay, north of Market St and east of Chinatown (Kearny St).

Fisherman's Wharf: On San Francisco Bay, west of Powell St, north of Bay St and east of Hyde St; at foot of Taylor St.

Haight-Ashbury: Between University of San Francisco and University of California San Francisco; South of Oak St (Panhandle of Golden Gate Park), west of Buena Vista Park, north of Waller St and east of Golden Gate Park.

Japantown: South of Pine St, west of Laguna St, north of Geary Blvd and east of Fillmore St.

Marina District: South of Marina Blvd, west of Webster St, north of Lombard St and east of the Palace of Fine Arts and Lyon St.

Mission District: Area around Mission Dolores; south of Market St and I-101, west of Potrero Ave, north of Army St and east of Castro St.

Nob Hill: On and around crest at Sacramento and Jones Sts.

North Beach: South of Fisherman's Wharf, west of Telegraph Hill, north of Chinatown and east of Russian Hill.

Pacific Heights: South of Lombard St, west of Lyon St, north of Pine St and east of Van Ness Ave.

Richmond District: South of the Presidio, west of Arguello Blvd, north of Golden Gate Park and east of the Pacific Ocean.

Russian Hill: South of Jefferson St, west of Mason St, north of Pacific Ave and east of Van Ness Ave.

Union Square: South of Post St, west of Stockton St, north of Geary St and east of Powell St. **North of Union Square:** North of Post St. **South of Union Square:** South of Geary St. **West of Union Square:** West of Powell St.

SAN FRANCISCO RESTAURANTS
BY NEIGHBORHOOD AREAS

(For full description, see alphabetical listings under Restaurants)

CHINATOWN

Empress of China. 838 Grant Ave

Kan's. 708 Grant Ave

The Pot Sticker. 150 Waverly Place

Yamato. 717 California St

CIVIC CENTER

Hayes Street Grill. 320 Hayes St

Stars. 150 Redwood Alley

Undici. 374 11th St

Zuni Cafe. 1658 Market St

COW HOLLOW

Bontá. 2223 Union St

Prego. 2000 Union St

Yoshida-Ya. 2909 Webster St

FINANCIAL DISTRICT

Agua. 252 California St

Bix. 56 Gold St

Blue Fox. 659 Merchant St

Carnelian Room. 555 California St

Ciao. 230 Jackson St

Circolo. 161 Sutter St

Cypress Club. 500 Jackson St

Ernie's. 847 Montgomery St

Fog City Diner. 1300 Battery St

Harbor Village. 4 Embarcadero Center

Hunan. 924 Sansome St

Just Desserts. 3 Embarcadero Center

Mac Arthur Park. 607 Front St

Palio d'Asti. 640 Sacramento St

Park Grill (Park Hyatt Hotel). 333 Battery St

Schroeder's. 240 Front St

Silks (Mandarin Oriental Hotel). 222 Sansome St

Splendido. Embarcadero Center Four

Tadich Grill. 240 California St

Tommy Toy's. 655 Montgomery St

Waterfront. Pier 7

Yank Sing. 427 Battery St

FISHERMAN'S WHARF

A. Sabella's. 2766 Taylor St

Bobby Rubino's. 245 Jefferson St

Chic's Place. Pier 39

Franciscan. Pier 43½

Gaylord India. 900 North Point St

Ghirardelli Chocolate Manufactory. 900 North Point St

Lolli's Castagnola. 286 Jefferson St

Mandarin. 900 North Point St

Scoma's. Pier 47

Swiss Louis. Pier 39

JAPANTOWN

Elka (Miyako Hotel). 1625 Post St

Isobune. 1737 Post St

Mifune. 1737 Post St

MARINA DISTRICT

Angkor Palace. 1769 Lombard St

Balboa Cafe. 3199 Fillmore St

Greens. Building A, Fort Mason

La Pergola. 2060 Chestnut St

North India. 3131 Webster St

Scott's Seafood Grill and Bar. 2400 Lombard St

MISSION DISTRICT

Ramis Cafe. 1361 Church St

NOB HILL

The Big 4 (Huntington Hotel). 1075 California St

The Dining Room (The Ritz-Carlton, San Francisco Hotel). 600 Stockton St

Fournou's Ovens (Stouffer Stanford Court Hotel). Nob Hill

Le Club. 1250 Jones St

Nob Hill (Mark Hopkins Inter-Continental Hotel). 1 Nob Hill

Rue Lepic. 900 Pine St

Vanessi's. 1177 California St

NORTH BEACH

Amelio's. 1630 Powell St

Basta Pasta. 1268 Grant St

Caffe Roma. 414 Columbus Ave

Enrico's Sidewalk Cafe. 504 Broadway

Fior d'Italia. 601 Union St

Julius Castle. 1541 Montgomery St

Moose's. 1652 Stockton St

North Beach. 1512 Stockton St

The Shadows. 1349 Montgomery St

PACIFIC HEIGHTS

Harris'. 2100 Van Ness Ave

Le Castel. 3235 Sacramento St

Pacific Heights Bar & Grill. 2001 Fillmore St

Trio Cafe. 1870 Fillmore St

RICHMOND DISTRICT

Alejandro's. 1840 Clement

Dynasty Fantasy. 6139 Geary Blvd

Flower Lounge. 5322 Geary Blvd

Khan Toke Thai House. 5937 Geary Blvd

RUSSIAN HILL

Acquerello. 1722 Sacramento St

Frascati. 1901 Hyde St

Golden Turtle. 2211 Van Ness Ave

House of Prime Rib. 1906 Van Ness Ave

I Fratelli. 1896 Hyde St

UNION SQUARE

Campton Place (Campton Place Kempinski Hotel). 340 Stockton

NORTH OF UNION SQUARE

Café Latté. 100 Bush St

Fleur de Lys. 777 Sutter St

Geordy's. 1 Tillman Place

Janot's. 44 Campton Place

Lascaux. 248 Sutter St

SOUTH OF UNION SQUARE

The Acorn. 1256 Folsom St

Donatello (The Donatello Hotel). 501 Post St

Etrusca. 121 Spear St

Fino. 1 Cosmo Place

Fringale. 570 Fourth St

Kuleto's. 221 Powell St

Marrakech Moroccan. 419 O'Farrell St

Wu Kong. 101 Spear St

WEST OF UNION SQUARE

China Moon Cafe. 639 Post St

David's. 474 Geary St

Dottie's True Blue Cafe. 522 Jones St

French Room (Four Seasons Clift Hotel). 495 Geary St

New Joe's. 347 Geary St

Pacific Grill (Pan Pacific Hotel). 500 Post St

Postrio (The Prescott Hotel Inn). 545 Post St

Salmagundi. 442 Geary St

Note: When a listing is located in a town that does not have its own city heading, it will appear under the city nearest to its location. In these cases, the address and town appear in parenthesis immediately following the name of the establishment.

Motels

✔ ★ ★**BEST WESTERN CIVIC CENTER.** *364 Ninth St (94103), in Civic Center area.* 415/621-2826; FAX 415/621-0833. 57 rms, 2 story. No A/C. May–Oct: S $68–$85; D $75–$95; each addl $7; under 13 free; lower rates rest of yr. Crib free. TV; cable. Heated pool. Complimentary coffee in rms. Restaurant 7 am–2 pm. Ck-out noon. Coin lndry. Airport transportation. Refrigerators. Cr cds: A, C, D, DS, ER, MC, V, JCB.

★ ★**BUENA VISTA MOTOR INN.** *1599 Lombard St (94123), at Gough, in Cow Hollow.* 415/923-9600; res: 800/835-4980; FAX 415/441-4775. 49 rms, 3 story. Mid-May–mid-Oct: S $80; D $85; under 12 free; lower rates rest of yr. Crib free. TV. Complimentary coffee in rms. Restaurant adj 6 am–10 pm. Ck-out noon. Airport transportation. Cr cds: A, C, D, DS, MC, V.

✔ ★**CAPRI.** *2015 Greenwich St (94123), at Buchanan, in Marina District.* 415/346-4667; FAX 415/346-3256. 46 units, 3 story. No A/C. S, D $54–$72; each addl $8; suites, kit. units $78–$146. Crib $4. TV. Restaurant nearby. Ck-out noon. Some covered parking. Cr cds: A, C, D, DS, MC, V.

★ ★**CHELSEA MOTOR INN.** *2095 Lombard St (94123), at Fillmore St, north of Union Square.* 415/563-5600; FAX 415/567-6475. 60 rms, 3 story, no ground floor rms. S $73; D $78–$86; each addl $7; under 5 free. Crib free. TV; cable. Complimentary coffee in rms. Restaurant nearby. Ck-out noon. Free covered parking. Airport transportation. Cr cds: A, C, D, MC, V.

★ ★**COLUMBUS MOTOR INN.** *1075 Columbus Ave (94133), in North Beach.* 415/885-1492; FAX 415/928-2174. 45 rms, 5 story. S, D $92–$110; each addl $7–$10. Crib free. TV; cable. Complimentary coffee in rms. Restaurant nearby. Ck-out noon. Free covered parking. Fisherman's Wharf 4 blks. Cr cds: A, C, D, MC, V.

★**COVENTRY MOTOR INN.** *1901 Lombard St (94123), in Marina District.* 415/567-1200; FAX 415/921-8745. 69 rms, 3 story. S $73–$86; D $76–$86; each addl $7; under 6 free. Crib free. TV; cable. Complimentary coffee in rms. Restaurant nearby. Ck-out noon. Free covered parking. Cr cds: A, C, D, MC, V.

✔ ★ ★ ★**COW HOLLOW MOTOR INN.** *2190 Lombard St (94123), in Marina District.* 415/921-5800; FAX 415/922-8515. 117 rms, 2–4 story, 12 suites. S $73; D $78; each addl $7; suites $175–$245; under 5 free. Crib free. TV; cable. Restaurant adj 7 am–2:30 pm. Ck-out noon. Free covered parking. Health club privileges. Cr cds: A, C, D, MC, V.

★ ★**DAYS INN.** *2600 Sloat Blvd (94116), south of Union Square.* 415/665-9000; FAX 415/665-5440. 33 rms, 2 story. July–mid-Sept: S $80–$100; D $85–$105.50; suites $130; under 12 free; lower rates rest of yr. Crib free. TV; cable. Complimentary continental bkfst, coffee. Restaurant nearby. Ck-out 11 am. Refrigerators. Cr cds: A, C, D, DS, MC, V.

✔ ★**DAYS INN-DOWNTOWN.** *895 Geary St (94109), at Larkin, west of Union Square.* 415/441-8220; FAX 415/771-5667. 73 rms, 4 story. S, D $60–$100; each addl $10; under 12 free. Crib free. TV; in-rm movies. Complimentary continental bkfst. Complimentary coffee in rms. Ck-out noon. Free garage parking. Airport transportation. Cr cds: A, C, D, DS, MC, V.

Ⓢ Ⓘ SC

★★**HOWARD JOHNSON.** *580 Beach St (94133), at Fisherman's Wharf.* 415/775-3800; FAX 415/441-7307. 128 rms, 4 story. S $89–$129; D $99–$139; suites $130–$160; under 17 free. Crib free. Covered parking (fee). TV; cable, in-rm movies. Restaurant 7–11 am. Ck-out noon. Coin lndry. Bellhops. Valet serv. Minibars. Cr cds: A, C, D, DS, ER, MC, V, JCB.

Ⓓ Ⓢ Ⓘ SC

★★**LOMBARD MOTOR INN.** *1475 Lombard St (94123), in Cow Hollow.* 415/441-6000; res: 800/835-3639; FAX 415/441-4291. 48 rms, 3 story. May–Sept: S $65–$95; D $78–$97; each addl $6; under 11 free; lower rates rest of yr. Crib free. TV. Complimentary coffee in rms. Restaurant opp open 24 hrs. Ck-out noon. Airport transportation. Cr cds: A, C, D, DS, MC, V.

Ⓢ Ⓘ SC

✔ ★★**PACIFIC HEIGHTS INN.** *1555 Union St (94123), in Cow Hollow.* 415/776-3310; res: 800/523-1801; FAX 415/776-8176. 40 rms, 2 story, 17 kits. No A/C. S, D $59–$85; suites $75–$95; family rates. Crib free. TV; cable. Complimentary continental bkfst. Complimentary coffee in rms. Restaurant opp open 24 hrs. Ck-out noon. Bellhops. Refrigerators, in-rm steam and whirlpool baths. Cr cds: A, C, D, DS, MC, V.

Ⓢ Ⓘ SC

★★**PHOENIX.** *601 Eddy St (94109), at Larkin St, in Civic Center area.* 415/776-1380; res: 800/248-9466; FAX 415/885-3109. 44 rms, 2 story. No A/C. S, D $89; suites $129–$139; under 12 free. Crib free. TV; cable. Heated pool; poolside serv. Complimentary continental bkfst. Restaurant 7:30 am–2:30 pm, 6–10 pm; wknds to 11 pm; closed Mon. Rm serv. Bar from 5 pm. Ck-out noon. Meeting rms. Concierge. Sundries. Health club privileges. Some refrigerators. Private patios, balconies. Cr cds: A, C, D, DS, MC, V.

☀ Ⓘ SC

✔ ★★**ROYAL PACIFIC.** *661 Broadway (94133), in Chinatown.* 415/781-6661; res: 800/545-5574; FAX 415/781-6688. 74 rms, 12 A/C, 5 story. Apr–Nov: S, D $72–$76; each addl $5; suites $89–$99; lower rates rest of yr. Crib $5. TV. Complimentary coffee in rms. Restaurant nearby. Ck-out noon. Coin lndry. Sauna. Refrigerators avail. Some balconies. Cr cds: A, C, D, MC, V.

Ⓢ Ⓘ

★★**SEAL ROCK INN.** *545 Point Lobos Ave (94121), at 48th Ave, west of Union Square.* 415/752-8000. 27 rms, 4 story, 11 kit. units. Mid-May–mid-Sept: S $75–$100; D $80–$105; deposit required; each addl $8; kit. units $5 addl; under 16, $4; lower rates rest of yr. Crib $2. TV; cable. Pool. Complimentary coffee in rms. Restaurant 6:30 am–4 pm; Sat & Sun to 6 pm. Ck-out 11 am. Sundries. Covered parking. Lawn games. Refrigerators; some fireplaces. Ocean view. Near Golden Gate Park. Cr cds: A, C, D, MC, V.

☀ Ⓘ

★★**VAGABOND INN-MIDTOWN.** *2550 Van Ness Ave (94109), in Russian Hill.* 415/776-7500; FAX 415/776-5689. 132 rms, 5 story. No A/C. S $75–$120; D $85–$150; each addl $5; suites, kit. units $150–$200; under 19 free; higher rates special events. Crib free. TV; cable. Heated pool. Complimentary continental bkfst. Restaurant open 24 hrs. Bar 5 pm–midnight. Ck-out noon. Meeting rm. Valet serv. Free covered parking. Airport transportation. Some refrigerators. Some balconies. Cr cds: A, C, D, DS, ER, MC, V.

Ⓓ ☀ Ⓢ Ⓘ SC

★★**WHARF.** *2601 Mason St (94133), at Fisherman's Wharf.* 415/673-7411; res: 800/548-9918; FAX 415/776-2181. 51 rms, 3–4 story. No A/C. May–Oct: S, D $88–$130; kit. suite $225–$275; lower rates rest of yr. Crib free. TV; cable. Complimentary coffee in lobby. Restaurant nearby. Ck-out 11 am. Concierge. Airport transportation. Some balconies. Cr cds: A, C, D, DS, MC, V.

Ⓢ Ⓘ SC

Motor Hotels

★★**BEST WESTERN AMERICANIA.** *121 Seventh St (94103), in Civic Center area.* 415/626-0200; FAX 415/626-3974. 143 rms, 4 story, 24 suites. No A/C. June–Sept: S $87–$99; D $99–$115; each addl $10; suites $110–$175; under 12 free; lower rates rest of yr. Crib free. TV; cable. Heated pool. Coffee in rms. Restaurant 6:30 am–10 pm. Rm serv. Bar 11 am–midnight. Ck-out noon. Coin lndry. Meeting rms. Valet serv. Exercise equipt; weight machine, stair machine, sauna. Some refrigerators. Cr cds: A, C, D, DS, ER, MC, V, JCB.

☀ ⚆ Ⓢ Ⓘ SC

★★**BEST WESTERN CANTERBURY HOTEL & WHITEHALL INN.** *750 Sutter St (94109), near Taylor St, on Nob Hill.* 415/474-6464; FAX 415/474-5856. 250 rms in 2 bldgs, 4 & 10 story, 14 suites. S $85–$190; D $95–$119; each addl $10; suites $125–$175; under 18 free; wkend, honeymoon plans. Garage parking $11.50 in/out. TV; cable. Pool privileges. Complimentary coffee in rms. Restaurant 6:30 am–10:30 pm. Rm serv. Bar; entertainment. Ck-out noon. Meeting rms. Gift shop. Airport transportation. Exercise equipt; weight machine, bicycles. Minibars; many refrigerators. Cr cds: A, C, D, DS, MC, V, JCB.

Ⓓ ⚆ Ⓢ Ⓘ SC

★★**BEST WESTERN MIYAKO INN.** *1800 Sutter St (94115), in Japantown.* 415/921-4000; FAX 415/923-1064. 125 rms, 8 story. S $85–$93; D $95–$103; each addl $10; suites $150–$250; under 18 free. Crib free. TV. Restaurant 7 am–10 pm. Ck-out noon. Bellhops. Valet serv. Airport transportation. In-rm steam baths. Balconies. Cr cds: A, C, D, DS, MC, V, JCB.

Ⓢ Ⓘ SC

★★**HOLIDAY INN-FISHERMAN'S WHARF.** *1300 Columbus Ave (94133), at Fisherman's Wharf.* 415/771-9000; FAX 415/771-7006. 580 rms, 5 story. June–Nov: S $135–$185; D $140–$190; each addl $5; suites $300–$400; under 19 free; lower rates rest of yr. Crib free. Pet accepted. TV; cable. Heated pool; poolside serv. Restaurant 6:30 am–10 pm. Rm serv. Ck-out noon. Coin lndry. Meeting rms. Bellhops. Valet serv. Sundries. Some refrigerators. Cr cds: A, C, D, DS, MC, V, JCB.

Ⓓ 🐾 ☀ Ⓢ Ⓘ SC

★★★**HYDE PARK SUITES.** *2655 Hyde St (94109), at Fisherman's Wharf.* 415/771-0200; res: 800/227-3608; FAX 415/346-8058. 24 kit. suites, 3 story. No A/C. S, D $165–$220; each addl $10; under 12 free. Garage in/out $12. TV; cable. Complimentary continental bkfst. Ck-out noon. Coin lndry. Concierge. Airport transportation. Refrigerators, honor bars. Private patios; some balconies. Ghirardelli Square 1 blk. Cr cds: A, C, D, DS, MC, V, JCB.

Ⓘ SC

★★**RAMADA HOTEL AT FISHERMAN'S WHARF.** *590 Bay St (94133), at Fisherman's Wharf.* 415/885-4700; FAX 415/771-8945. 232 rms, 4 story. May–Oct: S $135–$170; D $150–$185; each addl $15; suites $240–$255; under 19 free; lower rates rest of yr. Crib free. Garage in/out $7. TV; cable. Restaurant 6:30 am–10 pm. Rm serv. Bar 4 pm–midnight. Ck-out noon. Meeting rms. Valet serv. Sundries. Gift shop. Refrigerator in suites. Cr cds: A, C, D, DS, ER, MC, V, JCB.

Ⓓ ⚆ Ⓢ Ⓘ SC

★★★**SHERATON AT FISHERMAN'S WHARF.** *2500 Mason St (94133), at Fisherman's Wharf.* 415/362-5500; FAX 415/956-5275. 525 rms, 4 story. S, D $155–$230; each addl $20; suites from $425; under 17 free; package plans. Crib free. Pet accepted, some restrictions. Garage $12. TV; cable, in-rm movies. Heated pool. Restaurant 6:30 am–10 pm; Fri, Sat to 11 pm. Rm serv 24 hrs. Bar; entertainment Fri, Sat. Ck-out noon. Convention facilities. Valet serv. Concierge. Gift shop. Barber, beauty shop. Health club privileges. Cr cds: A, C, D, DS, MC, V, JCB.

🐾 ☀ Ⓢ Ⓘ SC

★★**TRAVELODGE HOTEL.** *250 Beach St (94133), at Fisherman's Wharf.* 415/392-6700. 250 rms, most rms with shower only, 4 story, 4 suites. Some A/C. S, D $95–$155; each addl $10; suites $150–$350; under 17 free. Crib free. TV; cable. Heated pool; poolside serv. Complimentary coffee in rms. Restaurant 6:30–2 am. Ck-out noon. Meeting rm. Gift shop. Airport transportation. Refrigerators avail. Balconies. Opp bay. Cr cds: A, C, D, DS, MC, V.

D ⊛ ⊗ ⊚ SC

Hotels

✔ ★ALEXANDER INN. 415 O'Farrell St (94102), at Taylor St, west of Union Square. 415/928-6800; res: 800/843-8709. 48 rms, 3 story. No A/C. S, D $48–$72; under 12 free. TV. Complimentary continental bkfst. Coffee in rms. Ck-out 11 am. Coin lndry. Airport transportation. Cable car turntable 2 blks. Cr cds: A, D, DS, MC, V, JCB.

⊗ ⊚ SC

★ ★ ★ANA. 50 Third St (94103), south of Union Square. 415/974-6400; res: 800/ANA-HOTELS; FAX 415/543-8268. 667 rms, 36 story. S $170–$235; D $195–$260; each addl $25; suites $300–$1,500; under 12 free; wkend rates. Crib free. Valet, garage parking $21. TV. Restaurant 6:30 am–11:30 pm. Bar 11–1:30 am; entertainment. Ck-out noon. Convention facilities. Concierge. Gift shop. Tennis privileges. Exercise equipt; weight machine, bicycles, sauna, steam rm. Bathrm phones, minibars. Cr cds: A, C, D, DS, ER, MC, V, JCB.

D ⊠ ⊘ T ⊗ ⊚ SC

★ATHERTON. 685 Ellis St (94109), at Larkin St, west of Union Square. 415/474-5720; res: 800/227-3608; FAX 415/474-8256. 74 rms, 6 story. No A/C. S, D $61–$81; each addl $10; under 12 free. Crib free. TV. Restaurant 7 am–2:30 pm; Sun 8 am–1 pm. Bar 4 pm–2 am. Ck-out noon. Meeting rm. Airport, RR station, bus depot transportation. Cr cds: A, C, D, DS, ER, MC, V, JCB.

⊚

★ ★BEDFORD. 761 Post St (94109), west of Union Square. 415/673-6040; res: 800/227-5642; FAX 415/563-6739. 144 rms, 17 story. No A/C. S, D $109; each addl $10; 2-bedrm family unit $155; under 12 free. Crib free. Valet parking $15. TV; cable, in-rm movies. Coffee in rms. Restaurant 7–10 am, 6–9 pm. Bar 5 pm–midnight. Ck-out 1 pm. Meeting rms. Refrigerators, honor bars. Cr cds: A, C, D, DS, ER, MC, V, JCB.

⊗ ⊚ SC

★ ★BERESFORD. 635 Sutter St (94102), north of Union Square. 415/673-9900; res: 800/533-6533; FAX 415/474-0449. 114 rms, 7 story. No A/C. S $79; D $89; each addl $5; family units $94–$104; under 12 free. Crib free. Pet accepted, some restrictions. Garage parking $15 in/out; valet parking $15. TV; cable. Complimentary bkfst. Restaurant 7 am–2 pm, 5:30–10:30 pm; Sun & Mon to 2 pm. No rm serv. Bar 7–1 am, Sun to 2 pm. Ck-out noon. Airport transportation. Health club privileges. Refrigerators, honor bars. Cr cds: A, C, D, DS, MC, V, JCB.

🐾 ⊗ ⊚ SC

★BERESFORD ARMS. 701 Post St (94109), west of Union Square. 415/673-2600; res: 800/533-6533; FAX 415/474-0449. 90 rms, 8 story, 40 kit. units. No A/C. S $79; D $89; each addl $10; suites $105–$130. Crib free. Valet parking $15 in/out. TV. Complimentary continental bkfst in lobby, also tea & refreshments 4:30–5:30 pm. Ck-out noon. No rm serv. Airport transportation. Some bathrm phones, in-rm whirlpools, honor bars. Cr cds: A, C, D, DS, MC, V, JCB.

D ⊗ ⊚ SC

✔ ★ ★BRITTON. 112 7th St (94103), near Civic Center area. 415/621-7001; res: 800/444-5819; FAX 415/626-3974. 79 rms, 5 story. June–Sept: S $59–$69; D $61–$80; each addl $7; suites $78–$83; lower rates rest of yr. Crib free. TV. Restaurant 6 am–10 pm. Ck-out noon. Coin lndry. Barber. Convention Center 3 blks. Cr cds: A, C, D, DS, ER, MC, V, JCB.

D ⊗ ⊚ SC

★CALIFORNIAN. 405 Taylor St (94102), at O'Farrell St, west of Union Square. 415/885-2500; res: 800/227-3346; FAX 415/673-5784. 245 rms, 17 story. No A/C. S $84; D $94; each addl $10; suites

$95–$165; under 12 free. Crib free. TV; cable. Complimentary coffee in rms. Restaurant 7 am–3 pm; dining rm 6:30 am–11 pm. Bar 11 am–midnight. Ck-out noon. Meeting rms. Barber. Cr cds: A, C, D, ER, MC, V, JCB.

⊗ ⊚ SC

★ ★ ★CAMPTON PLACE KEMPINSKI. 340 Stockton St (94108), on Union Square. 415/781-5555; res: 800/426-3135; FAX 415/955-5536. 120 rms, 7–17 story, 10 suites. S, D $200–$350; suites $450–$850; under 18 free. Crib free. Valet parking $19/24 hrs. Pet accepted; $25. TV; cable, in-rm movies avail. Restaurant (see CAMPTON PLACE). Rm serv 24 hrs. Bar 10 am–11 pm; Fri, Sat to midnight. Ck-out 2 pm. Meeting rms. Concierge 24 hrs. Butler services. Airport transportation; complimentary morning limo service downtown. Racquetball, health club nearby, by arrangement. Bathrm phones; refrigerators avail. Rooftop garden. Lavish decor; antiques, artwork. A small luxury hotel in the European tradition. Cr cds: A, C, D, MC, V, JCB.

D ⊘ 🐾 ⊗ ⊚

★ ★CARLTON. 1075 Sutter St (94109), north of Union Square. 415/673-0242; res: 800/227-4496; FAX 415/673-4904. 165 rms, 9 story. No A/C. S, D $94; 3rd person in rm $12 addl; under 12 free. Crib free. Parking opp in/out $8. TV; in-rm movies. Coffee in rms. Complimentary afternoon tea, evening wine. Restaurant 7–11 am, 5–9 pm. Ck-out 1 pm. Meeting rm. Airport, RR station, bus depot transportation; free Financial District and civic center transportation. Honor bars. Cr cds: A, C, D, DS, MC, V, JCB.

⊗ ⊚ SC

★ ★CARTWRIGHT. 524 Sutter St (94102), at Powell St, north of Union Square. 415/421-2865; res: 800/227-3844; FAX 415/421-2865. 114 rms, 34 A/C, 8 story. S $99–$109; D $109–$119; suites $150–$160; under 3 free. Crib free. Parking in/out $12. TV; cable. Complimentary afternoon tea, cakes. Restaurant 7–11 am. Ck-out 1 pm. Meeting rm. Airport transportation. Game rm/library. Many refrigerators. Antiques. Cr cds: A, C, D, DS, ER, MC, V, JCB.

⊗ ⊚

★ ★CHANCELLOR. 433 Powell St (94102), south of Union Square. 415/362-2004; res: 800/428-4748; FAX 415/362-1403. 140 rms, 16 story. No A/C. S $97; D $114; each addl $20; suites $165. Crib free. Garage ½ blk $16. TV; cable. Restaurant 7 am–3 pm, 5–9:30 pm. Bar 11–1 am. Ck-out noon. Meeting rm. Gift shop. Airport transportation. Tallest building in the city when constructed (1914) after the San Francisco earthquake in 1906. Cr cds: A, C, D, DS, ER, MC, V, JCB.

⊗ ⊚ SC

★COMFORT INN-BY THE BAY. 2775 Van Ness Ave (94109), north of Union Square. 415/928-5000; FAX 415/441-3990. 134 rms, 11 story. July–early Sept: S $83–$128; D $95–$140; each addl $12; under 18 free; lower rates rest of yr. Crib free. Garage parking in/out $5. TV; in-rm movies avail. Complimentary continental bkfst. Ck-out noon. Meeting rm. Airport transportation. Exercise equipt; bicycle, rower. Cr cds: A, C, D, DS, ER, MC, V, JCB.

D T ⊗ ⊚ SC

★ ★DIVA. 440 Geary St (94102), west of Union Square. 415/885-0200; res: 800/553-1900; FAX 415/346-6613. 108 rms, 7 story. S, D $119; each addl $10; suites $299–$300; under 12 free. Crib free. Valet parking, in/out $16. TV; in-rm movies. Complimentary California continental bkfst. Restaurant 11:30 am–10 pm; Fri, Sat to 11 pm; Sun 1–9 pm. Rm serv 7 am–11 pm. Ck-out noon. Meeting rms. Concierge. Exercise equipt; weight machines, bicycles. Bathrm phones, refrigerators, honor bars. Cr cds: A, C, D, DS, ER, MC, V, JCB.

D T ⊗ ⊚ SC

★ ★ ★THE DONATELLO. 501 Post St (94102), south of Union Square. 415/441-7100; res: 800/227-3184; FAX 415/885-8842. 95 rms, 14 story. S, D $155–$175; each addl $25; suites $325–$525; under 11 free; wkend rates. Crib free. Garage, in/out $16. TV; in-rm movies. Restaurant (see DONATELLO). Bar 5 pm–1 am. Ck-out noon. Meeting rms. Concierge. Exercise equipt; weights, bicycles, whirlpool, sauna, steam rm. Bathrm phones; some refrigerators, minibars. Some balconies. Spacious rms with plants. Complimentary newspaper, shoeshine. Italian Renaissance decor; antiques; classic elegance. Grand piano in lobby; pianist. Cr cds: A, C, D, DS, MC, V, JCB.

D 🔒 ✦ ⊘ ⊛

✔ ★★**ESSEX.** *684 Ellis St (94109), at Larkin St, west of Union Square.* 415/474-4664; res: 800/453-7739 (exc CA), 800/443-7739 (CA); FAX 415/441-1800. 96 rms, 7 story. No A/C. S $49; D $59; each addl $10; suites $80; under 12 free. TV. Complimentary coffee in lobby. Ck-out noon. Airport transportation. Some balconies. Civic Center 3 blks. Cr cds: A, MC, V.

⊛ **SC**

★★★**FAIRMONT HOTEL & TOWER.** *California & Mason Sts (94106), on Nob Hill.* 415/772-5000; FAX 415/781-3929. 600 rms, 8 & 24 story. S, D $150–$295; each addl $30; suites $475–$6,000; under 13 free; wkend rates. Crib free. Garage, in/out $23/day, valet. TV; cable. Restaurant 6 am–11 pm. Rm serv 24 hrs. Bars; entertainment, dancing. Ck-out 1 pm. Convention facilities. Concierge. Shopping arcade. Barber, beauty shop. Airport, free financial district transportation. Exercise rm; instructor, weight machine, weights, sauna. Bathrm phones, minibars, whirlpools. Some suites with private patio. Spacious lobby. Outside glass-enclosed elvtr to Fairmont Crown Room. Panoramic view of city; rooftop garden. Cr cds: A, C, D, DS, MC, V, JCB.

D 🔒 ✦ ⊘ ⊛

★★★★**FOUR SEASONS CLIFT.** *495 Geary St (94102), at Taylor St, west of Union Square.* 415/775-4700; FAX 415/441-4621. 329 rms, 17 story. S $205–$320; D $205–$350; each addl $30; suites $365–$690; under 18 free; wkend rates. Crib free. Pet accepted. Valet parking $22. TV; cable, in-rm movies avail. Restaurant (see FRENCH ROOM); lobby tea service Mon–Sat 3–5 pm. Rm serv 24 hrs. Bar 11–2 am; pianist 5:30 pm–1:30 am, Sun to 10 pm; also lobby lounge Mon–Fri 3–10 pm. Ck-out 1 pm. Valet serv 24 hrs. Concierge. Free limo to financial district. Exercise equipt; bicycles, treadmill. Bathrm phones, refrigerators, minibars. Tastefully furnished rms; lovely large suites. Electric blankets on request; specialized child's amenity package. In-rm FAX avail. Hotel with Old World charm; personalized service. Cr cds: A, C, D, ER, MC, V, JCB.

D 🔒 🐾 ✦ ⊘ ⊛

★★**GALLERIA PARK.** *191 Sutter St (94104), in Financial District.* 415/781-3060; res: 800/792-9639; FAX 415/433-4409. 177 rms, 8 story. S, D $105–$150; suites $155–$375; family, wkend rates. Garage in/out $15. TV; cable, in-rm movies avail. Restaurant 7 am–11 pm. Bar. Ck-out noon. Meeting rms. Concierge. Shopping arcade. Airport transportation. Refrigerators, honor bars. Atrium lobby with unique sculptured fireplace. Cr cds: A, C, D, DS, ER, MC, V, JCB.

D 🎿 ⊘ ⊛ **SC**

★★★★**GRAND HYATT SAN FRANCISCO.** *345 Stockton St (94108), on Union Square.* 415/398-1234 res: 800/233-1234; FAX 415/392-2536. 693 rms, 36 story, 33 suites. S, D $195–$240; each addl $25; suites $350–$1,550; under 19 free; honeymoon, hol and other package plans. Crib free. Valet parking, garage in/out $23. TV; cable, in-rm movies avail. Restaurant 6:30 am–11 pm. Rm serv 24 hrs. Bar 11–2 am; entertainment. Ck-out 3 pm. Convention facilities. Concierge. Shopping arcade. Barber, beauty shop. Airport, RR station, bus depot transportation. Complimentary limo serv. Tennis privileges. Exercise equipt; weight machine, bicycles. Masseuse. Refrigerators, minibars; many bathrm phones; some wet bars. *LUXURY LEVEL:* REGENCY CLUB. 85 rms, 7 suites, 4 floors. S, D $219–$270; suites $350–$950; wkend plans. Concierge. Private lounge, honor bar. In-rm movies, wet bar in suites. Complimentary continental bkfst, refreshments. Cr cds: A, C, D, DS, ER, MC, V, JCB.

D 🔏 ✦ ⊘ ⊛ **SC**

✔ ★**GRANT PLAZA.** *465 Grant St (94108), in Chinatown.* 415/434-3883; res: 800/472-6899; FAX 415/434-3886. 72 rms, 6 story. S $37–$45; D $42–$65; each addl $7; under 10 free. Crib $7. Garage (fee). TV. Restaurant adj open 24 hrs. No rm serv. Ck-out noon. Cr cds: A, C, D, ER, MC, V, JCB.

⊛

★★★**HANDLERY UNION SQUARE.** *351 Geary St (94102), west of Union Square.* 415/781-7800; res: 800/843-4343; FAX 415/781-0269. 376 rms, 8 story. Some A/C. S, D $125–$135; each addl $10; suites $155–$320; under 15 free. Crib free. Garage in/out $13.50. TV; cable, in-rm movies avail. Heated pool; sauna, poolside serv. Complimentary morning coffee & tea. Restaurant 7 am–11 pm. Rm serv 7–10:30 am, 5–10 pm. Bar 10 am–11:30 pm. Ck-out noon. Meeting rms. Concierge. Gift shop. Barber, beauty shop. Airport transportation. *LUXURY LEVEL:* HANDLERY CLUB. 93 rms, 8 floors. S $150; D $160; each addl $10; suites $300–$480. Private lounge. Minibars. Complimentary coffee & tea. Cr cds: A, C, D, DS, ER, MC, V, JCB.

D ≈ ⊘ ⊛ **SC**

★★**HARBOR COURT.** *165 Steuart St (94105), east of Union Square.* 415/882-1300; res: 800/346-0555; FAX 415/882-1313. 131 rms, 5 story. Apr–mid-Nov: S, D $120–$160; wkend rates; lower rates rest of yr. Crib free. Parking in/out $15. TV; cable. Indoor pool; lifeguard. Restaurant 7 am–11 pm. Rm serv 5–9 pm. Bar to 2 am; entertainment exc Sun. Ck-out noon. Concierge. Free transportation to Financial District. Exercise rm; instructor, weights, bicycles, whirlpool, sauna. Refrigerators, minibars. Victorian decor. On waterfront. Cr cds: A, C, D, DS, ER, MC, V, JCB.

D ≈ ✦ ⊘ ⊛ **SC**

★★★**HILTON & TOWERS.** *333 O'Farrell St, south of Union Square.* 415/771-1400; FAX 415/771-6807. 1,910 rms, 19, 23 & 46 story. S $170–$210; D $195–$235; each addl $25; suites from $350; wkend packages. Garage, in/out $20; valet $30. TV; cable. Pool on 16th floor in garden court. Restaurants 6 am–midnight. Bars 10:30–1:30 am; dancing. Ck-out noon. Convention facilities. Shopping arcade. Barber, beauty shop. Exercise equipt; weights, bicycles, sauna. Masseuse. Balconies. Some penthouse suites with solarium. 16th floor lanai rms; some rms on floors 17–19 overlook pool area. 46-story tower with distinctive rms. *LUXURY LEVEL:* TOWER. 130 units, 4 suites, 2 floors. S $250; D $275. Concierge. Private lounge. Minibars. Complimentary continental bkfst, refreshments. Cr cds: A, C, D, DS, MC, V, JCB.

D ≈ ✦ ⊘ ⊛

★★**HOLIDAY INN-CIVIC CENTER.** *50 8th St (94103), at Market St, in Civic Center area.* 415/626-6103; FAX 415/552-0184. 389 rms, 14 story. S $94–$134; D $104–$144; each addl $15; suites $200–$350; under 19 free; wkend rates. Crib free. TV; cable. Heated pool. Restaurant 6 am–10 pm. Bar. Ck-out noon. Coin lndry. Meeting rms. Gift shop. Free garage parking. Airport transportation. Health club privileges. Balconies. Cr cds: A, C, D, DS, MC, V, JCB.

D ≈ ⊘ ⊛ **SC**

★★**HOLIDAY INN-GOLDEN GATEWAY.** *1500 Van Ness Ave (94109), at California St, in Russian Hill.* 415/441-4000; FAX 415/776-7155. 499 rms, 26 story. June–Oct: S, D $105–$148; each addl $15; suites $185–$460; under 19 free; lower rates rest of yr. Crib free. Parking in/out $10. TV; cable, in-rm movies avail. Heated pool. Restaurant 6:30 am–10:30 pm. Bar; entertainment, dancing. Ck-out noon. Convention facilities. Gift shop. Airport transportation. Some refrigerators. On cable car line. Cr cds: A, C, D, DS, MC, V, JCB.

≈ ⊘ ⊛ **SC**

★★**HOLIDAY INN-UNION SQUARE.** *480 Sutter St (94108), north of Union Square.* 415/398-8900; FAX 415/989-8823. 401 rms, 30 story. S $135–$175; D $160–$195; each addl $25; suites $165–$700; under 19 free; wkend rates. Crib free. Parking in/out $14. TV; in-rm movies avail. Restaurant 6:30 am–10:30 pm. Bar; pianist Tues–Sat. Rm serv. Ck-out noon. Convention facilities. Bellhops. Valet serv. Gift shop. Refrigerator in suites. Cr cds: A, C, D, DS, MC, V, JCB.

D ⊘ ⊛ **SC**

★★★**HOTEL NIKKO.** *222 Mason St (94102), west of Union Square.* 415/394-1111; FAX 415/421-0455. 522 rms, 25 story, 33 suites. S $205–$265; D $225–$285; each addl $25; suites $375–$1,300; under 18 free; wkend rates. Crib free. Covered parking, in/out $22; valet. TV; cable. Indoor pool; poolside serv. Restaurant 6:30 am–10 pm. Rm serv

24 hrs. Bar 11–2 am; entertainment Tues–Sat. Ck-out noon. Convention facilities. Concierge. Drugstore. Barber, beauty shop. Free transportation to financial district. Exercise rm; instructor, weight machines, bicycles, whirlpool, steam rm, sauna. Full-service fitness center. In-rm steam baths, minibars. 2-story marble staircase in lobby frames cascading waterfall. *LUXURY LEVEL:* NIKKO FLOORS. 68 rms, 14 suites, 3 floors. S $265; D $285; suites from $475. Private lounge. Wet bars. Complimentary bkfst, refreshments.
Cr cds: A, C, D, ER, MC, V, JCB.

★ ★ ★HOTEL TRITON. *342 Grant Ave (94108), east of Union Square.* 415/394-0500; res: 800/433-6611; FAX 415/394-0555. 140 rms, 7 story. S, D $119–$159 each addl $10; suites $169–$209; under 16 free; wkly rates. Crib free. Valet, in/out parking $16. TV; cable, in-rm movies avail. Complimentary morning coffee & tea, evening wine. Restaurants 6:30 am–midnight. Rm serv 24 hrs. Bar from 11 am. Ck-out noon. Meeting rms. Airport transportation. Health club privileges. Minibars. Whimsical sophisticated design; showcase for local artists. Cr cds: A, C, D, DS, ER, MC, V, JCB.

★ ★HOTEL UNION SQUARE. *114 Powell St (94102), west of Union Square.* 415/397-3000; res: 800/553-1900; FAX 415/399-1874. 131 rms, 6 story. S, D $99–$109; each addl $10; suites $129–$280; under 12 free. Garage in/out $16. TV; cable, in-rm movies. Complimentary continental bkfst. Restaurant adj 11 am–11 pm. Bar noon–2 am. Ck-out noon. Airport, Financial District transportation. Honor bars; some wet bars. Penthouse suites with refrigerator, deck. Cr cds: A, C, D, DS, ER, MC, V, JCB.

★ ★ ★HUNTINGTON. *1075 California St (94108), top of Nob Hill.* 415/474-5400; res: 800/227-4683 (exc CA), 800/652-1539 (CA); FAX 415/474-6227. 100 rms, 12 story, 40 suites. No A/C. S $165–$215; D $185–$235; suites $250–$650; under 6 free. Crib free. Garage, in/out $16.50. TV; cable. Restaurant (see THE BIG 4). Rm serv 6 am–midnight. Bar 11:30–12:30 am; pianist. Ck-out noon. Meeting rms. Concierge. Free downtown, financial district & Fisherman's Wharf transportation. Health club privileges. Minibars. Wet bar in most rms; some kits. Complimentary tea or sherry upon arrival. Exquisite rms, individually decorated; many rms with view of city, bay. Built 1924; site of the Tobin house. Cr cds: A, C, D, DS, MC, V.

★ ★HYATT AT FISHERMAN'S WHARF. *555 North Point St (94133), at Fisherman's Wharf.* 415/563-1234; FAX 415/749-6122. 313 rms, 5 story. Apr–Oct: S $155–$175; D $180–$200; suites $275–$525; under 19 free; wkend rates; lower rates rest of yr. Crib free. Garage $13 in/out. TV; cable, in-rm movies. Heated pool. Restaurant 6–11 am, 5–10 pm; Fri & Sat to 11 pm. Bar 4 pm–midnight, Fri & Sat noon–2 am. Ck-out noon. Coin lndry. Meeting rms. Concierge. Gift shop. Airport transportation. Exercise equipt; weights, bicycles, whirlpool, sauna. Some bathrm phones. Cable car line opp. Cr cds: A, C, D, DS, ER, MC, V, JCB.

★ ★ ★HYATT REGENCY. *5 Embarcadero Center (94111), Market & Drumm Sts, in Financial District.* 415/788-1234; FAX 415/398-2567. 803 rms, 15 story. S $149–$245; D $215–$245; each addl $30; suites $350–$995; under 18 free; package plans. Crib free. Covered parking, valet $20. TV; cable, in-rm movies avail. Coffee in rms. Restaurant 6–1:30 am. Rm serv 24 hrs. Bars; entertainment; revolving rooftop restaurant/bar. Ck-out noon. Convention facilities. Concierge. Shopping arcade. Airport, RR station, bus depot transportation. Exercise equipt; bicycles, stair machine. Health club privileges. Refrigerators. Balconies. Spacious 15-story atrium in lobby. *LUXURY LEVEL:* REGENCY CLUB. 54 rms. S $215–$295; D $245–$295. Private lounge, honor bar. Complimentary continental bkfst, refreshments.
Cr cds: A, C, D, DS, MC, V.

★ ★ ★INN AT THE OPERA. *333 Fulton St (94102), in Civic Center area.* 415/863-8400; res: 800/325-2708 (exc CA), 800/423-9610

(CA); FAX 415/861-0821. 30 rms, 7 story, 18 suites. No A/C. S $110–$160; D $120–$170; suites $165–$210. Crib free. Parking $18. TV; cable. Complimentary bkfst. Restaurant 7–10 am, 11:30 am–2 pm, 5:30–10:30 pm. Rm serv 24 hrs. Bar to 10 pm, Fri & Sat to 1 am; entertainment Tues–Sat. Ck-out noon. Concierge. Refrigerators, minibars. Elegant European decor. In Performing Arts Center. Cr cds: A, MC, V.

★ ★JULIANA. *590 Bush St (94108), north of Union Square.* 415/392-2540; res: 800/328-3880; FAX 415/391-8447. 106 rms, 9 story. S, D $119–$160; suites $140–$160; monthly rates. Crib free. TV; cable. Restaurant 7–10:30 am, 5:30–11 pm. Bar. Ck-out noon. Free Financial District transportation. Refrigerators, honor bars. Cr cds: A, C, D, DS, ER, MC, V, JCB.

✔ ★ ★ ★KENSINGTON PARK. *450 Post St (94102), south of Union Square.* 415/788-6400; res: 800/553-1900; FAX 415/399-9484. 86 rms, 12 story. S, D $89–$115; each addl $10; suites $160–$350; under 13 free; theater packages. Crib free. Pet accepted, some restrictions; $200. Valet parking $16. TV. Complimentary continental bkfst, also tea/sherry in afternoon. Ck-out noon. Meeting rms. Free downtown transportation. Bathrm phones; some refrigerators. Renovated 1924 hotel. Grand piano in lobby. Traditional English decor. Cr cds: A, D, DS, ER, MC, V, JCB.

★ ★KING GEORGE. *334 Mason St (94102), west of Union Square.* 415/781-5050; res: 800/288-6005; FAX 415/391-6976. 143 rms, 9 story. No A/C. S $97; D $107; each addl $10; suites $185; under 12 free; 2-night packages. Crib free. Garage, in/out $15.50. TV; in-rm movies avail. Continental bkfst, afternoon tea. Restaurant 7–10 am, 3–6:30 pm. Rm serv 24 hrs. Bar; entertainment. Ck-out noon. Meeting rms. Concierge. Airport, RR station, bus depot transportation. Health club privileges. Union Square 1 blk. Cr cds: A, C, D, DS, ER, MC, V, JCB.

✔ ★ ★LOMBARD. *1015 Geary St (94109), at Polk St, west of Union Square.* 415/673-5232; res: 800/227-3608; FAX 415/885-2802. 101 rms, 6 story. No A/C. S, D $85–$91; each addl $10; under 12 free. Crib free. Valet parking in/out $10/day. TV. Complimentary coffee, tea, sherry. Restaurant 7–11 am, 5:30–9 pm. Ck-out noon. Meeting rm. Airport, bus depot transportation. Free downtown transportation. Game rm. Refrigerators. Sun deck. Cr cds: A, C, D, DS, ER, MC, V, JCB.

★ ★MAJESTIC. *1500 Sutter St (94109), at Gough St, in Pacific Heights.* 415/441-1100; res: 800/869-8966; FAX 415/673-7331. 58 rms, 5 story. S, D $115–$150; each addl $15; suites $205. Covered parking $12. TV. Restaurant 7 am–2 pm, 5:45–10 pm; closed Mon lunch. Bar 11 am–midnight; pianist. Ck-out noon. Meeting rms. Concierge. Free downtown transportation. Many fireplaces; some refrigerators. Each rm individually decorated with antiques, custom furnishings. Restored Edwardian hotel (1902); antique tapestries. Cr cds: A, D, MC, V.

★ ★ ★MANDARIN ORIENTAL. *222 Sansome (94104), between Pine & California Sts, in Financial District.* 415/885-0999; res: 800/622-0404; FAX 415/433-0289. 160 rms, 11 story; on floors 38–48 of the twin towers in the First Interstate Center. S, D $255–$390; suites $540–$1,200; under 12 free; wkend rates. Crib free. Covered parking $19.50. TV; cable, in-rm movies avail. Restaurant (see SILKS). Rm serv 24 hrs. Bar 11 am–11 pm; entertainment from 3 pm exc Sun. Ck-out noon. Meeting rms. Concierge. Health club privileges. Bathrm phones, refrigerators, minibars. Unique location; all guest rms occupy twin towers of Center and are linked on each floor by a spectacular sky bridge; panoramic view of bay and skyline. Lobby level business center. Cr cds: A, C, D, DS, MC, V, JCB.

★ ★ ★MARK HOPKINS INTER-CONTINENTAL. *1 Nob Hill (94108), on Nob Hill.* 415/392-3434; res: 800/327-0200; FAX 415/421-

3302. 391 rms, 19 story. S $180–$250; D $200–$280; each addl $30; suites $410–$2,000; under 14 free; wknd rates. Crib free. Garage, in/out $20/day. TV; cable, in-rm movies. Restaurant 6:30 am–3 pm, 6–10:30 pm (also see NOB HILL). Rm serv 24 hrs. Bars noon–2 am. Ck-out 1 pm. Convention facilities. Concierge. Airport transportation. Complimentary limo service 7:30 am–noon. Exercise equipt; bicycles, treadmill. Minibars. Some balconies. Complimentary newspaper, shoeshine. California landmark; on site of the Mark Hopkins mansion. Panoramic view from glass-walled Top of the Mark. *LUXURY LEVEL:* **CLUB INTER-CONTINENTAL.** 19 rms, 3 suites. S $275; D $305; suites $375–$1,000. Concierge. Private lounge, honor bar. Wet bar, in-rm movies in suites. Complimentary continental bkfst, refreshments. Cr cds: A, C, D, ER, MC, V, JCB.

★ ★ ★ **MARRIOTT.** 55 4th St (94103), opp Moscone Convention Center, south of Union Square. 415/896-1600; FAX 415/777-2799. 1,500 rms, 39 story, 133 suites. S, D $129–$235; each addl $30; suites $300–$2,000; under 18 free. Crib free. Garage $24, in/out 24 hrs. TV; cable, in-rm movies. Indoor pool; poolside serv. Restaurant 6:30 am–11 pm; Fri, Sat to midnight. Bar 10:30–2 am. Ck-out noon. Convention facilities. Concierge. Gift shop. Airport, RR station, bus depot transportation. Exercise equipt; weight machine, bicycles, whirlpool, sauna, steam rm. Minibars; some bathrm phones. Refrigerator, wet bar in suites. Some balconies. Six-story atrium lobby. *LUXURY LEVEL:* **CONCIERGE LEVEL.** 99 rms, 6 suites, 2 floors. S $225; D $240; suites $350–$650. Private lounge, honor bar. Wet bar. Bathrm phones. Complimentary continental bkfst, refreshments. Cr cds: A, C, D, DS, ER, MC, V, JCB.

★ ★ ★ **MARRIOTT FISHERMAN'S WHARF.** 1250 Columbus Ave (94133), at Fisherman's Wharf. 415/775-7555; FAX 415/474-2099. 255 rms, 5 story. S, D $164; each addl $20; suites $235–$495; under 18 free; wknd rates. Crib free. Valet parking in/out $18. TV; cable. Restaurant 6:30 am–10 pm. Bar 2 pm–midnight. Ck-out noon. Meeting rms. Gift shop. Free morning downtown transportation (Mon–Fri). Airport transportation. Exercise equipt; weight machine, bicycles, sauna. Honor bars; some bathrm phones. Marble floor in lobby. Cr cds: A, C, D, DS, ER, MC, V, JCB.

★ ★ ★ **MIYAKO.** 1625 Post St (94115), in Japantown. 415/922-3200; res: 800/533-4567; FAX 415/921-0417. 218 rms, 5 & 16 story. S $99–$129; D $129–$159; each addl $20; suites $189–$279; under 18 free. Crib free. Garage in/out $8. TV; cable, in-rm movies. Restaurant (see ELKA). Bar 10–1 am. Ck-out 1 pm. Meeting rms. Concierge. Shopping arcade. Airport transportation. Health club privileges. Minibars. Refrigerator in suites; sauna in suites. Balconies. Shiatsu massage avail. Japanese decor; authentic Japanese furnishings in some rms. Cr cds: A, C, D, DS, ER, MC, V, JCB.

★ ★ **MONTICELLO INN.** 127 Ellis St (94102), south of Union Square. 415/392-8800; res: 800/669-7777; FAX 415/398-2650. 91 rms, 5 story, 36 suites. S, D $120–$135; suites $145–$280. Crib free. Valet parking $15. TV; cable. Complimentary continental bkfst. Restaurant 11 am–midnight. Ck-out noon. Concierge. Airport, RR station, bus depot, downtown transportation. Refrigerators. 18th-century decor. Renovated hotel built 1906. Cr cds: A, C, D, DS, ER, MC, V, JCB.

✔ ★ **MOSSER VICTORIAN.** 54 Fourth St (94103), south of Union Square. 415/986-4400; res: 800/227-3804; FAX 415/495-7653. 165 rms, 80 with bath, 8 story. No A/C. S $39–$79; D $49–$89; each addl $10; suites $99–$129; under 12 free; wkly rates. Crib free. TV; cable. Complimentary continental bkfst. Restaurant 10–1 am. No rm serv. Bar to 2 am. Ck-out 11 am. Coin lndry. Airport transportation. Health club privileges. Cr cds: A, MC, V.

★ ★ **NOB HILL LAMBOURNE.** 725 Pine St (94108), on Nob Hill. 415/433-2287; res: 800/274-8466; FAX 415/433-0975. 20 kit. units,

3 story, 6 suites. No A/C. S, D $175; suites $250; family, monthly rates. Crib avail. Garage; valet, in/out $18. TV; cable, in-rm movies. Complimentary continental bkfst. Complimentary coffee in rms. Restaurant opp 6:30 am–11 pm. No rm serv. Ck-out noon. Concierge. Airport, RR station, bus depot transportation. Health club privileges. Wet bars. Balconies. Cr cds: A, C, D, DS, MC, V.

★ ★ ★ **ORCHARD.** 562 Sutter St (94102), north of Union Square. 415/433-4434; res: 800/433-4434; FAX 415/433-3695. 94 rms, some A/C, 7 story. S, D $110–$130; each addl $10; suites $195–$225. Crib free. Garage $15 in/out. TV; cable. Restaurant 7 am–2 pm; Sat & Sun to noon. Bar 4:30–10 pm, closed Sun & Mon. Ck-out noon. Concierge. Airport transportation. Health club privileges. Minibars. Renovated hotel; many furnishings imported from Europe. Cr cds: A, C, D, DS, MC, V, JCB.

✔ ★ **PACIFIC BAY INN.** 520 Jones St (94102), between O'Farrell St and Geary Blvd, west of Union Square. 415/673-0234; res: 800/445-2631; FAX 415/673-4781. 84 rms, 7 story. No A/C. S $55; D $65–$75; wkly rates. Covered parking, in/out $12. TV. Restaurant 7 am–2 pm; closed Wed. No rm serv. Ck-out 11 am. Airport, RR station, bus depot transportation. Some refrigerators. Cr cds: A, D, DS, MC, V.

★ ★ ★ ★ **PAN PACIFIC.** 500 Post St (94102), west of Union Square. 415/771-8600; res: 800/533-6465 (CA); FAX 415/398-0267. 330 units, 21 story, 19 suites, 2 with kit. S, D $185–$325; suites $550–$1,500; under 18 free; special wkend rates. Crib free. Garage, in/out $20; valet parking. Pet accepted. TV; cable, in-rm movies. Supervised child's activities. Restaurant 6:30 am–10 pm (also see PACIFIC GRILL). Rm serv 24 hrs. Bar 11–2 am; entertainment 5–10 pm. Ck-out 4 pm. Meeting rms. Personal valet serv. Concierge. Gift shop. Airport transportation; limo serv avail. Exercise equipt; weights, bicycles. Health club privileges. Bathrm phones. Complimentary newspaper. Third-floor atrium lobby highlighted by spectacular 17-story skylight; extensive use of marble; 3 fireplaces; fountain; commissioned sculptures. Cr cds: A, C, D, DS, ER, MC, V, JCB.

★ ★ ★ **PARC FIFTY-FIVE.** 55 Cyril Magnin St (94102), Market at 5th St, south of Union Square. 415/392-8000; FAX 415/296-9764. 1,006 rms, 32 story. S $155–$175; D $170–$190; each addl $15; suites $340–$1,200; under 19 free; wkend rates. Crib free. Garage, in/out $21. TV; cable. Restaurants 6:30 am–11 pm. Bar 11–1 am; pianist. Ck-out noon. Convention facilities. Concierge. Drugstore. Barber, beauty shops. Exercise equipt; weights, bicycles, sauna, steam rm. Bathrm phones. Marble floor, Oriental carpets in lobby. *LUXURY LEVEL:* **CONCIERGE CLUB.** 68 rms, 15 suites. S $195; D $210; suites $450–$1,200. Private lounge, honor bar. Some in-rm whirlpools. Complimentary continental bkfst, refreshments. Cr cds: A, C, D, DS, ER, MC, V, JCB.

★ ★ ★ **PARK HYATT.** 333 Battery St (94111), at Clay St, in Financial District. 415/392-1234; FAX 415/421-2433. 360 rms, 24 story, 37 suites. S, D $240–$290; each addl $25; suites $295–$2,000; under 18 free; wkend rates. Crib free. Pet accepted, some restrictions. Covered valet parking, in/out $19. TV; cable. Restaurant (see PARK GRILL); afternoon tea and evening caviar service. Rm serv 24 hrs. Bar 11–1 am; entertainment. Ck-out noon. Meeting rms. Concierge. Airport transportation. Exercise equipt available for in-rm use. Health club privileges. Bathrm phones, minibars. Some balconies. Reference library with national and international publications. Complimentary newspaper, shoeshine. Located in Embarcadero Center. Offers neoclassical formality. Cr cds: A, C, D, DS, ER, MC, V, JCB.

★ ★ **QUALITY HOTEL & CONFERENCE CENTER** (formerly Cathedral Hill). 1101 Van Ness Ave (94109), at Geary Blvd, west of Union Square. 415/776-8200; res: 800/227-4730 (exc CA), 800/622-0855 (CA); FAX 415/441-2841. 400 rms, 8 story. S $105–$240; D $125–$240; each addl $20; suites $400–$600; under 18 free; wkend package. Crib free. Garage parking $10 in/out. TV; cable. Heated pool. Restaurant 6:30 am–10:30 pm. Bar 11–1 am. Ck-out noon. Convention facilities. Concierge. Shopping arcade. Barber, beauty shop. Airport transportation. Many bathrm phones; some refrigerators. Balconies; some private patios. Art gallery. Cr cds: A, C, D, DS, MC, V, JCB.

D ⚏ 🚭 Ⓢ SC

★ ★ **RAPHAEL.** *386 Geary St (94102), west of Union Square.* 415/986-2000; res: 800/821-5343; FAX 415/397-2447. 152 rms, 12 story. S $92–$112; D $102–$122; each addl $10; suites $135–$195; under 18 free. Crib free. Parking in/out $14.75. TV; cable, in-rm movies avail. Complimentary morning coffee. Restaurant 7 am–midnight. Bar 11 am–midnight. Ck-out 1 pm. Airport transportation. Health club privileges. Bathrm phones. Cr cds: A, C, D, DS, MC, V.

🚭 Ⓢ

★ ★ ★ ★ ★ **THE RITZ-CARLTON, SAN FRANCISCO.** *600 Stockton St (94108), at California St, on Nob Hill.* 415/296-7465; FAX 415/296-8559. 336 rms, 9 story, 44 suites. S, D $205–$335; suites $450–$3,000; under 18 free; wkend packages. Crib avail. Garage; valet $23, in/out $20. TV; in-rm movies. Indoor pool; whirlpool, sauna. Supervised child's activities. Restaurant 6:30 am–11 pm. Rm serv 24 hrs. Bar 10:30–2 am; entertainment. Ck-out noon. Convention facilities. Concierge. Gift shop. Complimentary limo service within city. European spa service. Bathrm phones, minibars; some wet bars. Elegant furnishings. Rooms surround outdoor inner courtyard. Public areas decorated with fine art and antiques. Located at a cable car stop on the eastern slope of Nob Hill, this neoclassical building achieved San Francisco city landmark status in 1984 and is included on the list of Architecturally Significant Structures. *LUXURY LEVEL:* **RITZ-CARLTON CLUB.** 67 rms, 15 suites, 2 floors. S, D $335–$500. Concierge. Private lounge, honor bar. Complimentary continental bkfst, refreshments.
Cr cds: A, C, D, DS, ER, MC, V, JCB.

D ⚏ 🚭 Ⓢ SC

★ ★ **SAVOY.** *580 Geary St (94102), west of Union Square.* 415/441-2700; res: 800/227-4223; FAX 415/441-2700, ext 297. 83 rms, 7 story. No A/C. S $99–$109; D $109–$129; each addl $10; suites $149–$189; under 14 free. Crib free. Valet parking in/out $16. TV. Complimentary continental bkfst. Afternoon tea, cookies, sherry. Restaurant 6:30–9:30 am, 5:30–10:30 pm. Bar. Ck-out noon. Meeting rm. Concierge. Cr cds: A, C, D, DS, ER, MC, V, JCB.

🚭 Ⓢ SC

✔ ★ **SHEEHAN.** *620 Sutter St (94102), west of Union Square.* 415/775-6500; res: 800/848-1529; FAX 415/775-3271. 68 rms, 58 with bath, 6 story. No A/C. S $40–$80; D $55–$95; each addl $10; under 12 free. Crib free. Garage $12. TV; cable. Indoor pool; lifeguard. Complimentary continental bkfst. Tea rm 7 am–9 pm. No rm serv. Ck-out 11 am. Meeting rms. Beauty shop. Airport transportation. Exercise equipt; weight machines, rowers. Cr cds: A, C, D, MC, V, JCB.

D ⚏ 🏃 🚭 Ⓢ SC ✔

★ ★ **SHERATON PALACE.** *2 New Montgomery St (94105), at Market St, east of Union Square.* 415/392-8600; FAX 415/543-0671. 550 rms, 8 floors. S $195–$295; D $215–$315; each addl $20; suites $400–$2,000; family, wkend rates. Crib free. Valet parking, in/out $20. TV; cable, in-rm movies. Indoor pool; poolside serv. Restaurant 6:30–1 am. Rm serv 24 hrs. Bar from 11 am; entertainment. Ck-out noon. Convention facilities. Concierge. Shopping arcade. Airport transportation. Exercise rm; instructor, weights, treadmill, whirlpool, sauna. Health spa. Bathrm phones, refrigerators. Cr cds: A, C, D, DS, ER, MC, V, JCB.

D ⚏ 🏃 🚭 Ⓢ SC

★ ★ **SIR FRANCIS DRAKE.** *450 Powell St (94102), north of Union Square.* 415/392-7755; res: 800/227-5480; FAX 415/391-8719. 417 rms, 21 story. S $85–$125; D $95–$135; each addl $10; suites $265–$500; under 18 free; wkend rates; package plans. Crib free. Pet accepted. Valet parking in/out $20. TV; cable, in-rm movies avail. Restaurant 6:30 am–10 pm. Bar 11:30–1 am, Sun to 10 pm; dancing. Ck-out noon. Meeting rms. Concierge. Shopping arcade. Airport, bus depot

transportation. Exercise equipt; weights, bicycles. Some honor bars. Cr cds: A, C, D, DS, MC, V, JCB.

D 🅿 🏃 🚭 Ⓢ SC

★ ★ ★ ★ **STOUFFER STANFORD COURT.** *Nob Hill (94108).* 415/989-3500; res: 800/227-4736 (exc CA), 800/622-0957 (CA); FAX 415/986-8195. 402 rms, 8 story. S $195–$295; D $225–$325; each addl $30; 1-bedrm suites $315–$735; 2-bedrm suites $475–$1,750; under 18 free. Crib free. Pet accepted. Valet parking, in/out $22/day. TV; cable, in-rm movies. Restaurant 6:30 am–2:30 pm (also see FOURNOU'S OVENS). Afternoon tea in lobby. Rm serv 24 hrs. Bars 11–1 am. Ck-out noon. Meeting rms. Concierge. Shopping arcade. Free limo service. Health club privileges. Marble bathrms with phone, TV & special amenities. Antiques. Lavish hotel with glass-domed courtyard carriage entry. Antiques & artwork in lobby. Cr cds: A, C, D, DS, MC, V, JCB.

🅿 🚭 Ⓢ

★ ★ **TUSCAN INN AT FISHERMAN'S WHARF.** *425 North Point St (94133), at Fisherman's Wharf.* 415/561-1100; res: 800/648-4626; FAX 415/561-1199. 220 rms, 4 story, 12 suites. S, D $158–$178; each addl $20; suites $198; under 19 free; package plans avail. Crib free. Pet accepted, some restrictions; $100. Garage in/out $13/day. TV; cable, in-rm movies. Complimentary continental bkfst. Restaurant 7 am–10 pm. Bar. Ck-out noon. Meeting rms. Concierge. Airport transportation. Free Financial District transportation Mon–Fri. Health club privileges. Minibars. European-style "boutique hotel" following the tradition of a classic inn. 3 blks from San Francisco Bay. Cr cds: A, C, D, DS, MC, V, JCB.

D 🅿 🚭 Ⓢ SC

★ ★ **VILLA FLORENCE.** *225 Powell St (94102), south of Union Square.* 415/397-7700; res: 800/553-4411; FAX 415/397-1006. 183 rms, 7 story, 36 suites. S, D $134; suites $149–$154; under 16 free; Christmas, honeymoon package plans. Crib free. Garage parking in/out $16. TV; cable. Coffee in rms. Restaurant 7 am–midnight. Bar. Ck-out noon. Meeting rms. Concierge. Free Financial District transportation. Airport transportation. Refrigerators. Cr cds: A, C, D, DS, ER, MC, V, JCB.

🚭 Ⓢ SC

★ ★ **VINTAGE COURT.** *650 Bush St (94108), north of Union Square.* 415/392-4666; res: 800/654-1100; FAX 415/433-4065. 106 rms, 65 A/C, 8 story. S, D $125; each addl $10; under 12 free. Crib free. Garage in/out $15. TV; cable, in-rm movies avail. Complimentary continental bkfst 7–10 am. Complimentary coffee, wine. Restaurant 6–9:30 pm. Bar 6–10 pm. Ck-out noon. Meeting rm. Airport transportation. Health club privileges. Refrigerators. Sitting area each floor. Built 1912. Cr cds: A, C, D, DS, ER, MC, V, JCB.

D 🚭 Ⓢ SC

★ ★ ★ **WARWICK REGIS.** *490 Geary St (94102), west of Union Square.* 415/928-7900; res: 800/827-3447; FAX 415/441-8788. 80 rms, 8 story. S, D $99–$225; each addl $10; suites $150–$225; under 16 free. Crib free. Valet parking in/out $17. TV; in-rm movies avail. Complimentary continental bkfst. Restaurants 7–10 am, 6–10 pm. Bar 11–2 am. Ck-out 1 pm. Meeting rms. Refrigerators; some fireplaces. Balconies. Louis XVI decor. Built 1911. Cr cds: A, C, D, DS, ER, MC, V, JCB.

D 🚭 Ⓢ SC

★ ★ ★ **THE WESTIN ST FRANCIS.** *335 Powell St (94102), on Union Square.* 415/397-7000; FAX 415/774-0124. 1,200 rms in hotel & tower, 12 & 32 story. S $150–$230; D $180–$260; each addl $30; suites $300–$1,500; under 18 free. Crib free. Pet accepted, some restrictions. Garage in/out, valet parking $21. TV. Restaurants 6 am–midnight. Rm serv 24 hrs. Bars 11–2 am; entertainment, dancing. Ck-out 1 pm. Convention facilities. Concierge. Barber, beauty shop. Shopping arcade. Airport transportation; limo to Financial District. Refrigerators, minibars; bathrm phone in suites. Attractively furnished rms. Landmark hotel built 1904, on Union Square. 32-story tower with outside glass-enclosed elvtrs. Cable car stop. Cr cds: A, C, D, DS, MC, V, JCB.

D 🅿 🚭 Ⓢ SC

★ ★ **YORK.** *940 Sutter St (94109), lower Nob Hill.* 415/885-6800; res: 800/227-3608; FAX 415/885-2115. 96 rms, 7 story. S, D

$95–$110; each addl $10; suites $175; under 12 free. Valet parking $12. TV; cable. Complimentary continental bkfst. Complimentary coffee in rms, afternoon refreshments. Bar 5 pm–midnight, closed Sun, Mon; entertainment. Ck-out noon. Meeting rm. Airport, RR station transportation. Free wkday morning downtown transportation. Exercise equipt; weights, bicycles. Honor bars; some refrigerators. Renovated 1922 hotel; marble floors, ceiling fans. Hitchcock's *Vertigo* filmed here. Cr cds: A, C, D, DS, ER, MC, V, JCB.

🧍 💲 🅰 SC

Inns

★★ALAMO SQUARE. 719 Scott St (94117), west of Union Square. 415/922-2055; res: 800/345-9888; FAX 415/931-1304. 15 rms in 2 bldgs, 10 with shower only, 3 story. No A/C. S, D $85–$135; each addl $25; suites $150–$250; wkly rates; higher rates wkends (2-night min). Crib free. TV in some rms; cable. Complimentary full bkfst, coffee, tea, wine. Restaurant nearby. Ck-out noon, ck-in 2–6 pm. Concierge. Bellhop. Airport transportation. Health club privileges. Balconies. Picnic tables. Inn complex includes two restored Victorian mansions, 1895 Queen Anne and 1896 Tudor Revival, located in historic district. Antique furnishings, some wood-burning fireplaces; stained-glass skylight. Garden. Overlooks hilltop park; panoramic view of city skyline. Totally nonsmoking. Cr cds: A, D, MC, V, JCB.

💲 🅰

★ALBION HOUSE. 135 Gough St (94102), south of Union Square. 415/621-0896; FAX 415/621-0154. 8 rms, 2 story. S, D $75–$135; suite $145. TV. Complimentary full bkfst 8:30–10:30 am, afternoon tea. Restaurant nearby. Ck-out noon, ck-in 2 pm. Built 1906; individually decorated rms, antiques; piano in parlor. Cr cds: A, DS, MC, V.

🅰 SC

✔ ★AMSTERDAM. 749 Taylor St (94108), west of Union Square. 415/673-3277; res: 800/637-3444; FAX 415/673-0453. 31 rms, some share bath, 3 story. No elvtr. S $45–$69; D $50–$75; each addl $5; under 11 free. Crib free. Garage $13 in/out. TV; cable. Complimentary continental bkfst. Restaurant opp 6 am–11 pm. Ck-out 11 am, ck-in noon. Cr cds: A, MC, V.

💲 🅰

★★ANDREWS HOTEL. 624 Post St (94109), west of Union Square. 415/563-6877; res: 800/926-3739; FAX 415/928-6919. 48 rms, 7 story. No A/C. S, D $82–$106; each addl $10; suites $119. Parking adj, $13 in/out. TV. Complimentary continental bkfst on each floor, wine. Dining rm 5:30–10 pm. Ck-out noon, ck-in 3 pm. European decor; impressionist prints. Built 1905. Cr cds: A, MC, V.

💲 🅰

★★ARCHBISHOPS MANSION. 1000 Fulton St (94117), at Steiner St, south of Union Square. 415/563-7872; res: 800/543-5820; FAX 415/885-3193. 15 rms, 3 story. S, D $115–$185; each addl $20; suites $195–$285. TV; cable. Complimentary continental bkfst, coffee, tea, wine. Restaurant nearby. Ck-out 11:30 am, ck-in 3 pm. Bellhops. Concierge. Stained-glass skylight over stairwell. Built 1904; antiques. Individually decorated rms. Cr cds: A, MC, V.

🅰

★★INN AT UNION SQUARE. 440 Post St (94102), west of Union Square. 415/397-3510; res: 800/288-4346; FAX 415/989-0529. 30 rms, 6 story. No A/C. S $110–$160; D $120–$180; each addl $15; suites $170–$400. Crib free. Valet parking in/out $18. TV; cable. Complimentary continental bkfst, refreshments. Afternoon tea. Rm serv 5–9:30 pm. Ck-out noon, ck-in 2 pm. Bellhops. Concierge. Sitting area, fireplace most floors; antiques. Robes in all rms. Penthouse suite with fireplace, bar, whirlpool, sauna. Totally nonsmoking. Cr cds: A, D, MC, V, JCB.

🅳 💲 🅰 SC

★★THE INN SAN FRANCISCO. 943 S Van Ness Ave (94110), in Mission District. 415/641-0188; res: 800/359-0913; FAX 415/641-1701. 22 rms, 17 baths, 3 story. No A/C. S, D $75–$175; each addl $20;

suites $155–$175. Limited parking avail; $10. TV. Complimentary continental bkfst, coffee, tea, sherry. Restaurant nearby. Ck-out noon, ck-in 2 pm. Airport transportation. Whirlpool. Refrigerators. Balconies. Library. Italianate mansion (1872) near Mission Dolores; ornate woodwork, fireplaces; antique furnishings; garden with redwood hot tub, gazebo; view of city, bay from rooftop sun deck. Cr cds: A, C, D, DS, MC, V.

🅰

★★MANSIONS HOTEL. 2220 Sacramento St (94115), in Pacific Heights. 415/929-9444; res: 800/826-9398; FAX 415/567-9391. 21 rms, 3 story. No A/C. S $74–$225; D $89–$350. Pet accepted. Complimentary full bkfst, wine/sherry. Dining rm (res required) 6–9 pm; closed Mon. Rm serv 7:30 am–midnight. Ck-out noon, ck-in 2 pm. Bellhops. Airport transportation. Game rm. Music rm. Evening magic concerts. Some balconies. Old mansion (1887); Victorian memorabilia, antiques. Garden; fresh flowers in rms. Large collection of Buffano sculptures. Cr cds: A, D, DS, MC, V.

🐾 🅰

✔ ★★MARINA INN. 3110 Octavia St (94123), at Lombard St, north of Union Square. 415/928-1000; res: 800/274-1420; FAX 415/928-5909. 40 rms, 4 story. S, D $65–$85; each addl $10. TV; cable. Complimentary continental bkfst, afternoon sherry. Ck-out noon, ck-in 2 pm. Bellhops. Barber, beauty shop. Restored 1928 bldg; English country ambiance. Cr cds: A, MC, V.

🅳 🅰

★MILLEFIORI. 444 Columbus Ave (94133), in North Beach. 415/433-9111; FAX 415/362-6292. 15 rms, 2–3 story. S $65–$75; D $85–$110; each addl $10; under 5 free. TV. Complimentary continental bkfst. Restaurant adj 7–1 am. Ck-out noon, ck-in from 7:30 am. Individually decorated rms. Cr cds: A, C, D, MC, V.

💲 🅰

★★★PETITE AUBERGE. 863 Bush St (94108), north of Union Square. 415/928-6000; FAX 415/775-5717. 26 rms, 5 story. No A/C. S, D $110–$160; each addl $15; suite $220. Crib free. Valet parking in/out $17. TV; cable. Complimentary full bkfst, coffee, tea refreshments. Ck-out noon, ck-in 2 pm. Bellhops. Airport transportation. Some fireplaces. French country inn ambiance. Cr cds: A, C, D, MC, V.

🅰

★★★★THE PRESCOTT HOTEL. 545 Post St (94102), west of Union Square. 415/563-0303; res: 800/283-7322; FAX 415/563-6831. 166 rms, 7 story, 16 suites. S, D $160; each addl $10; suites $210–$600; hol rates. Crib free. Covered valet parking, in/out $15. TV; cable, in-rm movies avail. Pool privileges. Dining rm (see POSTRIO). Complimentary morning coffee and tea, evening wine and hors d'oeuvres. Rm serv 6 am–midnight. Bar 11–2 am. Ck-out noon, ck-in 3 pm. Concierge. Airport transportation. Free morning Financial District transportation. Health club privileges. Minibars; some wet bars. Lobby has hearth-style fireplace, red fir wainscoting and alabaster chandeliers. Union Square shopping 1 blk. *LUXURY LEVEL:* CLUB LEVEL. 44 rms, 21 suites, 4 floors. S, D $180; suites $230. Concierge. Private lounge, honor bar. Complimentary use of exercise equipt (stationary bike or rower) for in-rm use. Complimentary continental bkfst, refreshments, shoeshine. Cr cds: A, C, D, DS, ER, MC, V, JCB.

🅳 💲 🅰 SC

★★★QUEEN ANNE. 1590 Sutter St (94109), west of Union Square. 415/441-2828; res: 800/227-3970; FAX 415/775-5212. 49 rms, 4 story. No A/C. S, D $99–$150; each addl $10; suites $175–$275; under 12 free; wkly rates. Parking in/out $12. TV. Crib $5. Complimentary continental bkfst, afternoon tea & sherry. Ck-out noon, ck-in 3 pm. Meeting rm. Bellhops. Bathrm phones; some wet bars, fireplaces. Restored boarding school for young girls (1890); palms, stained glass, many antiques, carved staircase. Cr cds: A, C, D, MC, V.

💲 🅰

✔ ★SAN REMO. 2237 Mason St (94133), in North Beach. 415/776-8688; res: 800/352-7366; FAX 415/776-2811. 62 rms, shared baths, 2 story. No rm phones. S $35–$45; D $55–$85; each addl $10;

wkly rates. Parking $8. Dining rm 8–10 am, 5–10 pm; closed Mon. Bar 4 pm–midnight. Ck-out 11 am, ck-in 2 pm. Lndry facilities. Italianate Victorian bldg; antiques, art. Cr cds: A, C, D, MC, V, JCB.

★ ★ ★ ★ SHERMAN HOUSE. 2160 Green St (94123), Pacific Heights, north of Union Square. 415/563-3600; res: 800/424-5777; FAX 415/563-1882. 14 rms, 4 story. No elvtr. S, D $235–$375; suites $550–$750; under 18 free. Garage $16. TV; cable. Dining rm 7 am–10 pm. Rm serv 24 hrs. Ck-out noon, ck-in 2 pm. Concierge. Butler service. Bathrm phones; many wet bars. Roman tub, whirlpool in some rms. Private patios, balconies. Built 1876. Each rm individually designed, furnished in French Second Empire, Biedermeier or English Jacobean motifs & antiques. Marble, wood-burning fireplaces; canopy beds; private garden. Cr cds: A, D, MC, V.

★ ★ ★ STANYAN PARK. 750 Stanyan St (94117), in Haight-Ashbury. 415/751-1000; FAX 415/668-5454. 36 rms, 3 story, 6 kits. No A/C. S, D $82–$102; suites $120–$180. Municipal parking lot $5. TV. Complimentary continental bkfst, afternoon coffee, tea & cookies. Ck-out noon. Bellhops. Refrigerator in suites. Restored Victorian hotel. Cr cds: A, C, D, DS, MC, V.

★ ★ VICTORIAN INN ON THE PARK. 301 Lyon St (94117), in Haight-Ashbury. 415/931-1830; res: 800/435-1967; FAX 415/931-1830. 12 rms, 4 story. No A/C. No elvtr. S, D $94–$154; each addl $20; suites $154–$300. Parking $9. TV in lounge, rm TV avail. Complimentary continental bkfst, coffee, sherry & refreshments. Ck-out noon, ck-in 2 pm. Some fireplaces. Historic building (1897); Victorian decor throughout. Cr cds: A, D, DS, MC, V.

★ ★ WASHINGTON SQUARE. 1660 Stockton St (94133), in North Beach. 415/981-4220; res: 800/388-0220; FAX 415/397-7242. 15 rms, 11 with bath, 2 story. No A/C. S, D $85–$180; each addl $10. Valet parking $17. TV avail. Complimentary continental bkfst, afternoon tea, wine. Bkfst rm serv on request. Ck-out noon, ck-in 2 pm. Bellhops. Concierge. Individually decorated rms with English & French country antiques. Opp historic Washington Square. Totally nonsmoking. Cr cds: A, D, MC, V, JCB.

★ ★ WHITE SWAN. 845 Bush St (94108), north of Union Square. 415/775-1755; FAX 415/775-5717. 26 rms, 5 story. S, D $145–$160; each addl $15; suite $250. Crib free. Valet parking in/out $17. TV; cable. Complimentary full bkfst, wine/sherry. Restaurant nearby. Ck-out noon, ck-in 2 pm. Airport transportation. Refrigerators. Country English theme; antiques, fireplaces. Each rm individually decorated. Garden. Cr cds: A, MC, V.

Restaurants

★ ★ A. SABELLA'S. 2766 Taylor St, at Fisherman's Wharf. 415/771-6775. Hrs: 11 am–11 pm. Closed Dec 25. Res accepted. Italian, Amer menu. Bar. A la carte entrees: lunch $7.25–$13.75, dinner $11.50–$37. Child's meals. Specialties: filet de sole Grenoblois, halibut Luciano, fettucine Angelina. Own cakes, cheesecake. Pianist evenings. Dinner theater Fri & Sat (7:30 pm). Overlooks wharf. Family-owned. Cr cds: A, D, MC, V, JCB.

★ ★ THE ACORN. 1256 Folsom St, south of Union Square. 415/863-2469. Hrs: 11:30 am–2:30 pm, 6–10 pm; Sat from 6 pm; Sat brunch & Sun 10:30 am–3 pm. Closed Mon; Jan 1, Dec 25. Res accepted. No A/C. Bar. A la carte entrees: lunch $6.50–$13, dinner $13–$20. Sat & Sun brunch $6–$14. Specializes in fresh organic produce, seafood, pastas. Patio dining. Two dining rms, art deco. Totally nonsmoking. Cr cds: A, DS, MC, V.

★ ★ ★ ACQUERELLO. 1722 Sacramento St, in Russian Hill. 415/567-5432. Hrs: 6–10:30 pm. Closed Sun, Mon; most major hols. Res accepted. Regional Italian menu. Wine, beer. A la carte entrees: dinner $7–$30. Specializes in pasta, seafood. Menu changes every 6 wks. Intimate dining in restored chapel (ca 1930); high-beamed ceiling decorated with gold foil. Local artwork on display. Totally nonsmoking. Cr cds: C, D, DS, MC, V.

D

★ ★ ★ AGUA. 252 California St, in Financial District. 415/956-9662. Hrs: 11:30 am–2:30 pm, 5:30–10:30 pm; Fri to 11 pm; Sat 5:30–11 pm. Closed Sun; most major hols. Res accepted. Bar. A la carte entrees: $12–$15, dinner $19–$31. Complete meals: dinner $55. Specialties: medallions of ahi tuna (rare) with foie gras in wine sauce, Dungeness crab cakes. Valet parking (dinner). Cr cds: A, D, MC, V.

D

★ ★ ALEJANDRO'S. 1840 Clement, in Richmond District. 415/668-1184. Hrs: 5–11 pm; Fri & Sat to midnight; Sun 4–11 pm. Closed Jan 1–2, Thanksgiving, Dec 25–26. Res accepted. Mexican, Spanish, Peruvian menu. Bar. A la carte entrees: dinner $9–$18. Specialties: paella marinera, paella Valenciana, tapas. Flamenco guitarist/vocalist exc Sun. Spanish decor; pottery display. Cr cds: A, C, D, DS, MC, V.

★ ★ ★ AMELIO'S. 1630 Powell St, in North Beach. 415/397-4339. Hrs: 5:30–10:30 pm. Closed Dec 25; also 1st 2 wks Jan. Res accepted. No A/C. French menu. Bar. Wine cellar. A la carte entrees: dinner $20–$28. Prix fixe: dinner $70. Specialties: woven pasta with shellfish, Maine lobster, Grand Marnier soufflé in orange shell. Own baking. Valet parking. Traditional San Francisco dining. Intimate, distinctive. Jacket. Cr cds: A, C, D, DS, MC, V.

★ ANGKOR PALACE. 1769 Lombard St, in Marina District. 415/931-2830. Hrs: 5–10:30 pm. Closed Jan 1, Dec 25. Res accepted wkends. Cambodian menu. Wine, beer. A la carte entrees: dinner $6–$40. Complete meals: dinner $20. Specialties: stuffed chicken legs, barbecued jumbo river prawns, mixed seafood curry platter, royal fire pot of beef, squid, prawns, clams, octopus, fish slices and vegetables. Cambodian decor; gold canopy throne, highly polished wood, antiques. Cr cds: A, MC, V.

D

✔ ★ BALBOA CAFE. 3199 Fillmore St, in Marina District. 415/921-3944. Hrs: 11 am–11 pm; Sat & Sun brunch 10:30 am–3 pm. Bar to 2 am. A la carte entrees: lunch, dinner $7.95–$14.95. Sat, Sun brunch $7–$14.95. Built 1897. Cr cds: A, C, D, DS, MC, V.

✔ ★ BALISTRERI'S. (1922 Palmetto Ave, Pacifica) 8 mi SW on I-280 to CA 1, then 4 mi S to Palmetto Ave. 415/738-0113. Hrs: 5:30–10 pm. Closed Mon; Jan 1, July 4, Thanksgiving, Dec 24–25. Res accepted wkends. No A/C. Italian menu. Wine, beer. Semi-a la carte: dinner $9.25–$16.95. Child's meals. Specializes in veal, pasta, seafood. Cr cds: MC, V.

✔ ★ ★ BASTA PASTA. 1268 Grant St, in North Beach. 415/434-2248. Hrs: 11:30–1:45 am. Closed some major hols. Res accepted. Italian menu. Bar. Semi-a la carte: lunch $6.95–$14.25. A la carte entrees: dinner $7.95–$15.25. Specializes in pizza baked in wood-burning oven, pasta, veal, chicken. Valet parking. Outdoor (rooftop) dining. Main dining rm on 2nd floor. Cr cds: A, C, D, DS, MC, V, JCB.

D

★ ★ ★ THE BIG 4. (See Huntington Hotel) 415/771-1140. Hrs: 7–10 am, 11:30 am–3 pm, 5:30–10:30 pm; Sat & Sun 7–11 am, 5:30–10:30 pm. Res accepted. Bar 11:30–12:30 am. Wine cellar. Contemporary continental cuisine. A la carte entrees: bkfst $4–$13.50, lunch $7.50–$14.50, dinner $8.50–$22.50. Complete meal: bkfst $15. Specialties: seasonal wild game dishes, lamb sausage with black pepper papardelle noodles, petrale sole with sweet corn and sun-dried tomatoes. Pianist evenings. Valet parking. Turn-of-the-century atmosphere. Cr cds: A, C, D, DS, MC, V.

★ ★ BIX. 56 Gold St, in Financial District. 415/433-6300. Hrs: 11:30 am–11 pm; Fri to midnight; Sat 5:30–midnight; Sun 6–10 pm. Closed major hols. Res accepted. Bar to 1 am. A la carte entrees: lunch

$8–$20, dinner $14–$24. Specializes in classic American dishes, seafood. Jazz nightly. Valet parking (dinner). Art deco decor with grand piano; some seating on balcony. Cr cds: A, D, DS, MC, V, JCB.

D

★ ★ ★ **BLUE FOX.** *659 Merchant St, in Financial District. 415/981-1177.* Hrs: 6–10 pm. Closed Sun; major hols; also Dec 25–Jan 1. Res accepted. Italian menu. Bar. Wine cellar. A la carte entrees: dinner $21–$28. *Prix fixe:* dinner $39.50 & $55. Specializes in classic Italian cuisine. Pianist some wkends. Valet parking. Jacket. Cr cds: A, C, D, DS, MC, V.

✔ ★ **BOBBY RUBINO'S.** *245 Jefferson St, at Fisherman's Wharf. 415/673-2266.* Hrs: 11 am–11 pm; Sat to midnight. Res accepted. No A/C. Bar. Semi-a la carte: lunch $3.95–$15.95, dinner $5.95–$16.95. Child's meals. Specializes in barbecued dishes, fresh fish. Casual dining, on two levels. View of fishing fleet. Cr cds: A, D, DS, MC, V, JCB.

SC

★ ★ **BONTÀ.** *2223 Union St, in Cow Hollow. 415/929-0407.* Hrs: 5:30–10:30 pm; Sun 5–10 pm. Closed Mon; some major hols. Res accepted. No A/C. Italian menu. Wine, beer. A la carte entrees: dinner $9.50–$15.75. Child's meals. Storefront dining rm. Totally nonsmoking. Cr cds: MC, V.

✔ ★ **CAFFE ROMA.** *414 Columbus Ave, in North Beach. 415/391-8584.* Hrs: 7 am–11:15 pm; Fri & Sat to 1:15 am; Fri, Sat & Sun brunch to 2 pm. Closed Dec 25. Res accepted. Italian menu. Bar. A la carte entrees: bkfst $3.80–$8, lunch, dinner $5.25–$10. Brunch $3.25–$8.50. Specializes in pizza, pasta dishes, oversize salads. Outdoor dining. Murals on ceiling & walls. Cr cds: MC, V.

D

★ ★ **CAMPTON PLACE.** *(See Campton Place Kempinski Hotel) 415/955-5555.* Hrs: 7 am–2:30 pm, 5:30–10 pm; Fri to 10:30 pm; Sat 8 am–2:30 pm, 5:30–10:30 pm; Sun 8 am–2:30 pm, 4:30–10 pm. Res accepted. Contemporary American cuisine with regional emphasis. Bar 10 am–11 pm; Fri, Sat to midnight. Extensive wine list. A la carte entrees: bkfst $9–$15, lunch $13–$18, dinner $18–$28. *Prix fixe:* Sun dinner $29. Sun brunch $9–$16.50. Child's meals. Own baking. Menu changes frequently to reflect fresh seasonal ingredients. Valet parking. Brass wall sconces; Oriental antiques. Jacket (dinner). Cr cds: A, C, D, DS, MC, V, JCB.

D

★ ★ **CARNELIAN ROOM.** *52nd floor of Bank of America Center, 555 California St, in Financial District. 415/433-7500.* Hrs: 6–10 pm; Sun brunch 10 am–2:30 pm. Closed Jan 1, Thanksgiving, Dec 25. Res accepted. Bar from 3 pm; Sun from 10 am. Wine cellar. A la carte entrees: dinner $19–$36. *Prix fixe:* dinner $32. Sun brunch $22.50. Vintage 18th-century decor; antiques. Panoramic view of city. Jacket. Cr cds: A, C, D, DS, MC, V, JCB.

D

✔ ★ **CHIC'S PLACE.** *Pier 39, at Fisherman's Wharf. 415/421-2442.* Hrs: 9 am–11 pm. Res accepted. No A/C. Bar. Semi-a la carte: bkfst $4.50–$6.95, lunch $6.95–$10.95, dinner $8.95–$17.95. Specializes in seafood. Own desserts. Parking (Pier 39 garage). View of bay, Alcatraz, Golden Gate Bridge. Cr cds: A, C, D, DS, MC, V.

★ **CHINA MOON CAFE.** *639 Post St, west of Union Square. 415/775-4789.* Hrs: 11:30 am–2:15 pm, 5:30–10 pm; Sun from 5:30 pm. Closed major hols. Res accepted; required before theater. Chinese menu. Wine. A la carte entrees: lunch $12–$15, dinner $25–$30. Specialties: pot-browned noodle pillow, spring rolls. Art deco cafe. Cr cds: MC, V.

★ ★ **CIAO.** *230 Jackson St, at Front St, in Financial District. 415/982-9500.* Hrs: 11:30 am–11 pm; Fri & Sat to midnight; Sun 4–10:30 pm. Closed Thanksgiving, Dec 25. Res accepted. No A/C. Italian menu. Serv bar. A la carte entrees: lunch, dinner $9–$16. Specializes in mesquite-grilled fresh fish and meats, homemade pasta. Cr cds: A, D, MC, V.

D

★ ★ **CIRCOLO.** *161 Sutter St, in Financial District. 415/362-0404.* Hrs: 11:30 am–3 pm, 5–11 pm; Sat from 5 pm. Closed Sun; most major hols. Res accepted. Mediterranean menu. Bar. A la carte entrees: lunch, dinner $8–$16. Specializes in fresh pasta. Jazz Mon–Fri 5–9 pm. Outdoor dining. Elegant fine dining. Cr cds: A, C, D, MC, V.

D

★ ★ **CYPRESS CLUB.** *500 Jackson St, in Financial District. 415/296-8555.* Hrs: 11:30 am–2:30 pm, 5:30–10 pm; Fri & Sat to 11 pm. Closed Jan 1, July 4, Dec 25. Res accepted. Contemporary Amer menu. Bar 11–2 am. Wine list. A la carte entrees: lunch $5–$15, dinner $20–$25. Menu changes daily. Whimsical, 1940s-style design. Cr cds: A, D, DS, MC, V, JCB.

D

★ ★ ★ **THE DINING ROOM.** *(See The Ritz-Carlton, San Francisco Hotel) 415/296-7465.* Hrs: 6:30 am–11 pm; Sun brunch 10:30 am–3 pm. Res accepted. Mediterranean menu. Bar. Wine cellar. Semi-a la carte: bkfst $2.50–$14.50, lunch $4.50–$16, dinner $4.50–$19. Sun brunch $38. Child's meals. Specializes in regional Northern California/Mediterranean cuisine. Entertainment. Valet parking. Outdoor dining. Cr cds: A, C, D, DS, ER, MC, V, JCB.

D

★ ★ ★ **DONATELLO.** *(See The Donatello Hotel) 415/441-7182.* Hrs: 7–10:30 am, 5:30–10:30 pm. Res required Fri & Sat. Northern Italian menu. Bar. Wine list. A la carte entrees: bkfst $6.50–$15, dinner $18–$25. *Prix fixe:* dinner $50–$65. Specialties: roasted saddle of rabbit, homemade stuffed pasta with spinach, ricotta & amaretti, veal carpaccio with black truffels vinaigrette, creative Italian dishes. Own baking, pasta, sauces. Valet parking. Marble and mirrored dining rms, artwork. Classic regional Italian cuisine. Private entrance to dining room from hotel. Jacket. Cr cds: A, C, D, MC, V, JCB.

D

★ ★ **DYNASTY FANTASY.** *6139 Geary Blvd, at 25th Ave, in Richmond District. 415/386-3311.* Hrs: 11:30 am–10 pm. Closed Mon; Thanksgiving, Dec 25. Res accepted; required hols. Chinese menu. Wine, beer. A la carte entrees: lunch, dinner $6.50–$20. Specialties: apple chicken, trout in ginger & scallion sauce, Grand Marnier prawns. 3 floors. Cr cds: A, DS, MC, V, JCB.

D

★ ★ ★ **ELKA.** *(See Miyako Hotel) 415/922-7788.* Hrs: 6:30 am–10 pm; Sat & Sun brunch 11 am–2:30 pm. Res accepted; required Thurs–Sat (dinner). Franco-Japanese menu. Bar. Wine cellar. A la carte entrees: bkfst $6.50–$9.50, lunch $7–$10, dinner $14–$24. Sat & Sun brunch $6.50–$9.50. Specialties: coriander-encrusted ahi tuna, Japanese bento boxes. Parking. Mix of modern American and Oriental decor. Cr cds: A, D, MC, V.

D

★ ★ **EMPRESS OF CHINA.** *Top floor of China Trade Center Bldg, 838 Grant Ave, in Chinatown. 415/434-1345.* Hrs: 11:30 am–3 pm, 5–11 pm. Chinese menu. Res accepted. Bar. A la carte entrees: lunch $7.50–$10.50, dinner $12.50–$29. Complete meals (for 2 or more persons): lunch $8.50–$13.50, dinner $16.95–$33.95. Specialties: regional delicacies of China. Oriental decor; ancient art objects. View of city, Telegraph Hill. Jacket (dinner). Cr cds: A, D, MC, V.

★ **ENRICO'S SIDEWALK CAFE.** *504 Broadway, in North Beach. 415/982-6223.* Hrs: 11:30–2 am; Sun brunch to 3 pm. Closed Jan 1, Dec 25. Res accepted. No A/C. Mediterranean menu. Bar. A la carte entrees: lunch $7.25–$15, dinner $8–$17. Entertainment. Outdoor dining. Bistro with glass wall, large terrace. Cr cds: A, MC, V.

D

★ ★ ★ **ERNIE'S.** *847 Montgomery St, in Financial District. 415/397-5969.* Hrs: 11:30 am–2:30 pm, 6–10:30 pm; Memorial Day–Labor Day from 6 pm. Closed major hols; also 1st 2 wks Jan. Res accepted. Contemporary French cuisine. Bar from 5:30 pm. Wine cellar. A la carte entrees: lunch $13.50–$17.50, dinner $24–$30. *Prix fixe:* dinner $38–$68. Specialties: dungeness crab & asparagus cake with tomato gelee, roast rack of lamb with spring vegetables, fricassee of Maine lobster with ginger and sauternes, grilled salmon with sweet mustard. Own baking. Validated parking (lunch); valet parking (dinner). Parisian decor. Popular with celebrities. Jacket. Cr cds: A, C, D, MC, V, JCB.

★★ETRUSCA. *121 Spear St, near Ferry Building, south of Union Square.* 415/777-0330. Hrs: 11:30 am–3 pm, 5:30–10 pm; Fri & Sat to 11 pm. Closed Thanksgiving, Dec 25. Res accepted. Northern Italian menu. Bar. A la carte entrees: lunch $4.50–$17.50, dinner $4.50–$19.50. Specialties: umbrichelle all'Etrusca, pesce Etrusca, coniglio con funghi. Valet parking. Ceiling panels depict ancient Etrusca. Cr cds: A, DS, MC, V.

D

✔★★FINO. *1 Cosmo Place, south of Union Square.* 415/928-2080. Hrs: 5:30–10 pm. Closed major hols. Res accepted. Southern Italian menu. Bar. Semi-a la carte: dinner $8.50–$16.95. Specializes in fresh seafood, fresh pasta. Valet parking. Descending staircase leads to dining area; marble fireplace. Cr cds: A, MC, V.

★★FIOR D'ITALIA. *601 Union St, in North Beach.* 415/986-1886. Hrs: 11:30 am–10:30 pm. Closed Thanksgiving. Res accepted. No A/C. Northern Italian menu. Bar. A la carte entrees: lunch $7–$16.50, dinner $9–$18. Specializes in veal, risotto, homemade pasta. Valet parking. On Washington Square Park. Family-owned. Cr cds: A, C, D, DS, MC, V, JCB.

D

★★★FLEUR DE LYS. *777 Sutter St, north of Union Square.* 415/673-7779. Hrs: 6–10 pm. Closed Sun; Jan 1, July 4, Thanksgiving, Dec 25. Res required. French menu. Bar. Wine list. A la carte entrees: dinner $26–$32. *Prix fixe:* dinner $62.50. Specialties: salmon baked in tender corn pancake topped with caviar, Maine lobster & macaroni au gratin, oven-roasted lamb loin, chocolate creme brulee. Valet parking. French provincial decor; unusual tapestry ceiling. Jacket. Cr cds: A, C, D, MC, V.

D

★★FLOWER LOUNGE. *5322 Geary Blvd, at 17th Ave, in Richmond District.* 415/668-8998. Hrs: 11 am–2:30 pm, 5–9:30 pm; Sat & Sun from 10 am. Res accepted. Chinese menu. Bar. A la carte entrees: lunch $1.80–$12.95, dinner $4–$30. Complete meals: dinner (for 4) $78. Oriental decor. Cr cds: A, D, MC, V.

D

★★FOG CITY DINER. *1300 Battery St, in Financial District.* 415/982-2000. Hrs: 11:30 am–11 pm; Fri & Sat to midnight. Closed July 4, Thanksgiving, Dec 25. Res accepted. No A/C. Bar. A la carte entrees: lunch, dinner $9–$20. Specializes in seafood. Outdoor dining. Railroad dining car atmosphere. Cr cds: D, DS, MC, V, JCB.

D

★★★★FOURNOU'S OVENS. *(See Stouffer Stanford Court Hotel)* 415/989-1910. Hrs: 6:30 am–2:30 pm, 5:30–10 pm; Fri & Sat to 10:30 pm; Sun brunch 10 am–2:30 pm. Res accepted; required hols. New American cuisine. Bar from 5 pm. Extensive wine cellar. A la carte entrees: bkfst $7.50–$13.50, dinner $9–$28. Table d'hôte: dinner $25–$45. Sun brunch $12–$16. Child's meals. Specializes in rack of lamb, farm-raised meats, nightly poultry & fish selections. Own breads, pasta. Valet parking. Several dining areas. On Nob Hill; view of cable cars from dining room. Cr cds: A, C, D, DS, MC, V, JCB.

D

★★FRANCISCAN. *Pier 43½ , at Fisherman's Wharf.* 415/362-7733. Hrs: 11 am–10:30 pm; Fri & Sat to 11 pm. Closed Thanksgiving, Dec 25. Res accepted. Bar. A la carte entrees: lunch, dinner $8.50–$30. Child's meals. Specialties: bouillabaisse, halibut à la Florentine, prawns Marsala. Own cheesecake. Announcement of passing ships. View of bay, city. Cr cds: A, MC, V.

D

★FRASCATI. *1901 Hyde St, in Russian Hill.* 415/928-1406. Hrs: 5–10:30 pm. Closed Dec 25. Res accepted. No A/C. Roman, Northern Italian menu. Wine list. A la carte entrees: dinner $7.50–$17.95. Specialties: stuzzicarello della casa (appetizer plate),

petti di pollo al funghi de bosco, fresh pastas, risotto. Valet parking. Outdoor dining. Storefront location; bistro atmosphere. Cr cds: A, DS, MC, V.

★★★FRENCH ROOM. *(See Four Seasons Clift Hotel)* 415/775-4700. Hrs: 6:30 am–11 pm; Sun 11 am–2 pm. Res accepted; required Sun & hols. California continental menu. Bar. Award-winning wine list. A la carte entrees: bkfst $8–$12, lunch $10–$20, dinner $22–$32. *Prix fixe:* 4-course dinner $29.50. Sun brunch $32.50. Child's meals. Specializes in beef, veal, lamb, fresh seafood specials. Pianist. Valet parking. Classic decor. Jacket. Cr cds: A, C, D, ER, MC, V, JCB.

D

✔★★FRINGALE. *570 Fourth St, south of Union Square.* 415/543-0573. Hrs: 11:30 am–3 pm, 5:30–10:30 pm; Sat from 5:30 pm. Closed Sun; some major hols. Res accepted. No A/C. French menu. Bar. A la carte entrees: lunch $3–$11.75, dinner $3–$14.75. Upscale bistro fare. Atmosphere of European country cafe. Cr cds: A, MC, V.

D

★★GAYLORD INDIA. *900 North Point St, in Ghirardelli Square, at Fisherman's Wharf.* 415/771-8822. Hrs: 11:45 am–1:45 pm, 5–10:45 pm; early-bird dinner Mon–Thurs 5–6:30 pm; Sun brunch noon–2:45 pm. Closed Thanksgiving, Dec 25. Res accepted. Indian menu. Bar. Semi-a la carte: lunch $9.25–$13.25, dinner $9.95–$21. Complete meals: dinner $22–$28.75. Specializes in tandoori dishes, Indian desserts. Parking. Spectacular view of bay. Cr cds: A, C, D, DS, MC, V, JCB.

★★★GEORDY'S. *1 Tillman Place, north of Union Square.* 415/362-3175. Hrs: 11:30 am–2:30 pm, 5:30–10:30 pm. Closed Sun; major hols. Res accepted. Serv bar. Wine list. Semi-a la carte: lunch $5.50–$16, dinner $5.50–$19.50. Specializes in American cuisine with French and Mediterranian influences. Valet parking. Dining rms on two levels, connected by short flight of stairs; upper level has banquettes, mirrored walls. Restaurant's main entrance is set back off the west side of Grant Ave, between Sutter and Post Sts. Cr cds: A, C, D, DS, MC, V.

D

★★GOLDEN TURTLE. *2211 Van Ness Ave, at Broadway, in Russian Hill.* 415/441-4419. Hrs: 11:30 am–3 pm, 5–11 pm. Closed Mon. Res accepted. Vietnamese menu. Wine, beer. A la carte entrees: lunch $7.50–$17.95, dinner $8.50–$18.95. Specialties: imperial beef, spicy calamari sauté, chili chicken, lemon-grass beef & pork, pan-fried Dungeness crab. Carved wooden panels depict scenes of Vietnamese culture. Cr cds: A, DS, MC, V.

D

✔★★GREENS. *Building A at Fort Mason, in Marina District.* 415/771-6222. Hrs: 11:30 am–2 pm, 5:30–9:30 pm; Fri & Sat 11:30 am–2:15 pm, 6–9:30 pm; Sun brunch 10 am–2 pm. Closed Mon; Jan 1, July 4, Thanksgiving, Dec 25. Res accepted. Vegetarian menu. Bar. A la carte entrees: lunch $7–$12, dinner $9–$12.50. *Prix fixe:* dinner (Fri & Sat) $36. Sun brunch $7–$11. Occasional entertainment. Parking. View of bay. Totally nonsmoking. Cr cds: DS, MC, V.

D

★★★HARBOR VILLAGE. *4 Embarcadero Center, in Financial District.* 415/781-8833. Hrs: 11 am–2:30 pm, 5:30–9:30 pm; Sat from 10:30 am; Sun & hols from 10 am. Res accepted. Chinese menu. Bar. Wine list. A la carte entrees: lunch $2.40–$26, dinner $8–$26. Specializes in Hong Kong-style seafood. Parking. Formal Chinese decor. Cr cds: A, C, D, MC, V, JCB.

D

★★HARRIS'. *2100 Van Ness Ave, in Pacific Heights.* 415/673-1888. Hrs: 6–10 pm; Sat & Sun from 5 pm. Closed Jan 1, Dec 25. Res accepted. A la carte entrees: dinner $16.95–$23.50. Specializes in beef, fresh seafood, Maine lobster. Jazz Fri & Sat. Valet parking. Cr cds: A, D, DS, MC, V, JCB.

D

★★HAYES STREET GRILL. *320 Hayes St, in Civic Center area.* 415/863-5545. Hrs: 11:30 am–2 pm, 5–10 pm; Fri to 11 pm; Sat

6–11 pm. Closed Sun; major hols. Res accepted. Bar. A la carte entrees: lunch $12–$18, dinner $13–$25. Specializes in fresh seafood, salads, charcoal-grilled fish. Cr cds: A, D, DS, MC, V.

★ ★ ★ **HOUSE OF PRIME RIB.** *1906 Van Ness Ave, at Washington St, in Russian Hill.* 415/885-4605. Hrs: 5:30–10 pm; Fri & Sat from 5 pm; Sun from 4 pm; hols from 3 pm. Res accepted. Bar. Wine list. A la carte entrees: dinner $17.95. Semi-a la carte: dinner $18.75–$22.25. Child's meals. Specializes in corn-fed, 21-day aged prime rib of beef, seafood. Prime rib carved at table. Valet parking. Early American decor. Cr cds: A, MC, V.

★ **HUNAN.** *924 Sansome St, in Financial District.* 415/956-7727. Hrs: 11:30 am–9:30 pm. Closed Jan 1, July 4, Thanksgiving, Dec 25. Res accepted. No A/C. Hunan menu. Bar. A la carte entrees: lunch, dinner $5–$9.50. Specializes in smoked Hunan dishes. Chinese decor. Cr cds: A, C, D, DS, MC, V.

✔ ★ **I FRATELLI.** *1896 Hyde St at Green, in Russian Hill.* 415/474-8603. Hrs: 5–10 pm. Closed major hols, Dec 31. Italian menu. Bar. A la carte entrees: dinner $8–$15. Child's meals. Specializes in homemade pasta. Cafe atmosphere; photos of Italian street scenes. Cr cds: MC, V.

★ ★ **JANOT'S.** *44 Compton Pl, off Stockton St, north of Union Square.* 415/392-5373. Hrs: 11:30 am–2:30 pm, 6–10 pm. Closed Sun. Res accepted. French menu. Bar. A la carte entrees: lunch $8–$17, dinner $13–$20. Specialties: grilled quail & spinach salad, confit of duck leg & watercress salad, grilled chicken breast, grilled lamb chops with flageolets. Bi-level dining area, high ceilings, modern decor. Cr cds: A, MC, V.

★ ★ ★ **JULIUS CASTLE.** *1541 Montgomery St, on Telegraph Hill, in North Beach.* 415/362-3042. Hrs: 5–10 pm. Res accepted. No A/C. Contemporary French menu. Bar. A la carte entrees: dinner $19–$26. Specializes in veal, rack of lamb, seafood. Own pastries, pasta, ice cream. Valet parking. Turreted castle overlooking San Francisco Bay. Cr cds: A, C, D, DS, MC, V.

★ ★ **KAN'S.** *708 Grant Ave (upstairs), in Chinatown.* 415/982-2388. Hrs: 11:30 am–10 pm; Sun from 3 pm. Closed Thanksgiving, Dec 25. Res accepted. Cantonese menu. Bar. Complete meals (2 or more): lunch $6.50–$11, dinner $14–$21. A la carte entrees: lunch from $5.50, dinner from $7.50. 9-course Peking duck dinner for 8, $26/person (24-hr notice). Specialties (24-hr notice): melon cup soup, rock cod à la Kan. Famous Chinese restaurant; popular with celebrities. Cr cds: A, C, D, DS, MC, V, JCB.

★ ★ **KHAN TOKE THAI HOUSE.** *5937 Geary Blvd, in Richmond District.* 415/668-6654. Hrs: 5–11 pm. Closed Labor Day, Thanksgiving, Dec 25. Res accepted. Thai menu. Wine, beer. A la carte entrees: dinner $4.95–$12.50. Complete meal: dinner $14.95. Specialties: pong pang (seafood), haa sa hai (chicken and beef). Thai classical dancing performance Sun (8 pm). Thai decor and furnishings. Totally nonsmoking. Cr cds: A, MC, V.

★ ★ **KULETO'S.** *221 Powell St, south of Union Square.* 415/397-7720. Hrs: 7–10:30 am, 11:30 am–11 pm; Sat & Sun from 8 am. Closed Labor Day, Thanksgiving, Dec 25. Res accepted. Northern Italian menu. Bar 10 am–midnight. Complete meals: bkfst $4.50–$8.95. A la carte entrees: lunch, dinner $7.50–$16.95. Specializes in grilled fish, chicken, pasta. Italian decor. Cr cds: A, C, D, DS, ER, MC, V, JCB.

✔ ★ ★ **LA PERGOLA.** *2060 Chestnut St, in Marina District.* 415/563-4500. Hrs: 5:30–10:30 pm; Fri & Sat to 11 pm. Closed most major hols. Res accepted. No A/C. Northern Italian menu. Wine, beer. A la carte entrees: dinner $12–$15. Cr cds: A, D, MC, V, JCB.

★ ★ ★ **LASCAUX.** *248 Sutter St, north of Union Square.* 415/391-1555. Hrs: 11:30 am–3 pm, 5–10 pm; Sat from 5 pm; Sun 4:30–9 pm. Closed major hols. Res accepted. Mediterranean menu. Bar. Wine cellar. A la carte entrees: lunch $8–$17, dinner $12–$24. Specializes in grilled fish, spit-roasted lamb, pork, venison. Own pastries, pasta. Jazz. Fireplace, candlelight, flowers in romantic grotto-like setting of stone and stucco; kitchen rotisserie on view from dining rm. Cr cds: A, D, MC, V.

★ ★ ★ **LE CASTEL.** *3235 Sacramento St, in Pacific Heights.* 415/921-7115. Hrs: 5:30–10 pm. Closed Mon; major hols. Res accepted. No A/C. French menu. Wine cellar. A la carte entrees: dinner $16–$19. *Prix fixe:* 4-course dinner $27.50. Specialties: homard frais aux pâstes et la sauce nantua, confit de canard Alsacien, roast squab, fresh fish of the day. Own baking. Valet parking. Jacket. Cr cds: A, C, D, MC, V.

★ ★ ★ ★ **LE CLUB.** *(Clay Jones Apt) 1250 Jones St, on Nob Hill.* 415/771-5400. Hrs: 5:30–11 pm. Closed Sun, Mon; major hols. Res accepted. French menu. Bar. Wine list. A la carte entrees: dinner $18–$25. Child's meals. Specialties: northern California cuisine with a Mediterranean influence. Own baking. Valet parking. Florentine mirrors, wood paneling. Jacket. Cr cds: A, C, MC, V.

★ ★ **LOLLI'S CASTAGNOLA.** *286 Jefferson St, at Fisherman's Wharf.* 415/776-5015. Hrs: 9 am–11 pm. Closed Dec 25. Bar. Semi-a la carte: bkfst $3.95–$9.95, lunch, dinner $5.95–$26.45. Child's meals. Specializes in seafood. Valet parking lunch. Outdoor dining. View of fishing fleet. Cr cds: A, C, D, DS, MC, V, JCB.

★ ★ **MAC ARTHUR PARK.** *607 Front St, in Financial District.* 415/398-5700. Hrs: 11:30 am–3:30 pm, 5–10:30 pm; Fri to 11 pm; Sat from 5 pm; Sun 4:30–10 pm. Closed Thanksgiving, Dec 25. Res accepted. No A/C. Bar. A la carte entrees: lunch, dinner $7.95–$18.95. Specializes in barbecued ribs, mesquite-grilled fish. Valet parking. Outdoor dining. Cr cds: A, C, D, MC, V.

★ ★ **MANDARIN.** *900 North Point St, in Ghirardelli Square, at Fisherman's Wharf.* 415/673-8812. Hrs: 11:30 am–11 pm. Closed Thanksgiving, Dec 25. Res accepted. Northern Chinese, mandarin menu. Bar. Semi-a la carte: lunch $8.95–$13, dinner $13–$35. Complete meals: dinner $16–$38. Mandarin banquet for 8 or more, $25–$38 each. Specialties: minced squab, beggar's chicken (1-day notice), Peking duck (1-day notice). Valet parking. Chinese decor; beautifully tiled floor, artifacts. 19th-century structure. View of bay. Cr cds: A, C, D, MC, V, JCB.

★ ★ **MARRAKECH MOROCCAN.** *419 O'Farrell St, south of Union Square.* 415/776-6717. Hrs: 6–10 pm. Res accepted. Moroccan menu. Bar. *Prix fixe:* dinner $19.95–$23.95. Specialties: chicken with lemon, lamb with honey, couscous fassi, b'stila, Le Diner Menara. Belly dancing. Valet parking. Seating on floor pillows or low couches. Moroccan decor. Unusual dining experience. Cr cds: A, DS, MC, V.

★ ★ **MOOSE'S.** *1652 Stockton St, between Union & Filbert Sts, in North Beach.* 415/989-7800. Hrs: 11:30 am–2:30 pm, 5:30–10 pm; Fri & Sat to 11 pm; Sun brunch 10:30 am–3 pm. Closed some major hols. Res accepted. Bar. Wine cellar. A la carte entrees: lunch $4.25–$12.95, dinner $4.25–$16.95. Sun brunch $2.95–$12.95. Child's meals. Specializes in Mediterranean, Italian cuisine with California elements. Jazz pianist evenings. Valet parking. Exhibition kitchen. Dining rm accented with terrazzo tile and ceramics; expansive views of Washington Square Park. Large bronze "moose" near entry. Cr cds: A, MC, V.

★ ★ **NEW JOE'S.** *347 Geary St, west of Union Square.* 415/989-6733. Hrs: 7 am–11 pm. Closed Dec 25. Res accepted. Contemporary Italian menu. Bar. A la carte entrees: bkfst $5–$8, lunch $6–$14, dinner $10–$19. Child's meals. Specialties: risotto del marinaio, pizza Danesa with ricotta cheese, dill, smoked salmon and caviar, fresh seafood. Mahogany paneling and moldings. Mural of city. Cr cds: A, C, D, DS, MC, V, JCB.

★ ★ ★NOB HILL. *(See Mark Hopkins Inter-Continental Hotel)* *415/616-6944.* Hrs: 6:30 am–3 pm, 6–10:30 pm; early-bird dinner 6–7 pm; Sun brunch noon–2 pm. Res accepted. Bar. Wine list from 36 states. A la carte entrees: bkfst $5–$15, lunch $7.50–$19, dinner $18–$26.50. *Prix fixe:* lunch $17.50, dinner $25. Sun brunch $28. Child's meals. Specialties: steamed or grilled salmon, sautéed duck foie gras, grilled lamb. Valet parking. 19th-century club atmosphere; oak-paneled walls. Cr cds: A, C, D, ER, MC, V, JCB.

D

★ ★ ★NORTH BEACH. *1512 Stockton St, at Columbus, in North Beach. 415/392-1700.* Hrs: 11:30 am–11:45 pm. Closed some major hols. Res accepted. Italian menu. Wine cellar. A la carte entrees: lunch $8.50–$24, dinner $10.75–$29. Complete meals: lunch, dinner from $22.95. Specializes in fresh fish, veal, pasta. Valet parking. Cr cds: A, C, D, DS, MC, V, JCB.

★ ★NORTH INDIA. *3131 Webster St, at Lombard St, in Marina District. 415/931-1556.* Hrs: 11:30 am–2:30 pm, 5–11 pm; Sat from 5 pm; Sun 5–10 pm. Res accepted. Northern Indian menu. Bar. Semi-a la carte: lunch $6.95–$9.95, dinner $9.95–$22.50. Child's meals. Specializes in tandoori seafood, lamb & poultry, fresh vegetables. Own desserts. Paintings of Moghul and Bengal lancers. Kitchen tours. Cr cds: A, C, D, MC, V.

D

★ ★ ★PACIFIC GRILL. *(See Pan Pacific Hotel) 415/771-8600.* Hrs: 7 am–10 pm; Sun brunch 10 am–2 pm. Res accepted. California comfort menu. Bar 11:30–2 am. Wine list. A la carte entrees: bkfst $5–$10, lunch $7.50–$14, dinner $15–$20. Sun brunch $10–$15. Child's meals. Specializes in crab cakes, Caesar salad, lamb shank. Pianist. Valet parking. Modern decor; atrium setting in lobby of hotel. Cr cds: A, C, D, DS, ER, MC, V, JCB.

D

★ ★PACIFIC HEIGHTS BAR & GRILL. *2001 Fillmore St, in Pacific Heights. 415/567-3337.* Hrs: 11:30 am–9:30 pm; Fri & Sat to 10:30 pm; Mon & Tues 5:30–9:30 pm. Closed Dec 24 & 25. Res accepted. Bar 11:30 am–midnight; Fri & Sat to 1 am. A la carte entrees: dinner $9.95–$15.95. Specialties: bistro-style food, oysters. Own pastries. Cr cds: A, C, D, MC, V.

★ ★PALIO D'ASTI. *640 Sacramento St, at Montgomery St, in Financial District. 415/395-9800.* Hrs: 11:30 am–9:30 pm; Thurs & Fri to 10 pm; Sat 5–10 pm. Closed Sun; major hols. Res accepted. Italian menu. Bar. A la carte entrees: lunch $9–$18, dinner $9–$20. Child's meals. Specialties: mezzelune alla monferrina, crespelle di pollo alla Piemontese. Valet parking. Exhibition pasta-making and pizza-making kitchens; wood-burning ovens. Cr cds: A, D, DS, MC, V.

D

★ ★ ★PARK GRILL. *(See Park Hyatt Hotel) 415/296-2933.* Hrs: 6:30 am–11 pm; Sun brunch 10 am–2 pm. Res accepted. Bar 11–1 am. Wine list. A la carte entrees: bkfst $7–$12, lunch $8–$16, dinner $15–$26. Sun brunch $23. Child's meals. Specializes in mixed grills. Own baking. Pianist. Valet parking. Outdoor dining. Club rm atmosphere; original art. Cr cds: A, C, D, DS, ER, MC, V, JCB.

D

★ ★ ★POSTRIO. *(See The Prescott Hotel Inn) 415/776-7825.* Hrs: 7–10 am, 11:30 am–2 pm, 5:30–10 pm; Sat & Sun from 5:30 pm; Sat & Sun brunch 9 am–2 pm. Closed July 4, Thanksgiving, Dec 25. Res required. California, Oriental menu. Bar 11:30–2 am. Wine list. A la carte entrees: bkfst $5–$15, lunch $10–$18, dinner $18–$30. Specialties: Chinese duck, roasted salmon. Own baking. Valet parking. Bi-level seating under skylight; custom Oriental light fixtures. Cr cds: A, C, D, MC, V.

D

✔ ★THE POT STICKER. *150 Waverly Place, in Chinatown. 415/397-9985.* Hrs: 11:30 am–9:45 pm. Closed Thanksgiving; also Dec 20–25. Res accepted. No A/C. Hunan/Mandarin menu. A la carte entrees: lunch, dinner $5.25–$18. Complete meals: lunch $3.50–$4.95,

dinner $7.95–$9.95. Specialties: pot stickers, Szechwan crispy fish, orange spareribs. Cr cds: A, MC, V.

★ ★PREGO. *2000 Union St, in Cow Hollow. 415/563-3305.* Hrs: 11:30 am–midnight. Closed Thanksgiving, Dec 25. Res accepted. Northern Italian menu. Bar to 1 am. A la carte entrees: lunch, dinner $8.79–$18.95. Specialties: carpaccio, agnolotti d'aragosta, pizza baked in wood-burning oven, meats & fowl cooked on a rotisserie. Cr cds: A, C, D, MC, V.

✔ ★RAMIS CAFE. *1361 Church St, in Mission District. 415/641-0678.* Hrs: 11:30 am–3 pm, 4–10 pm; Sat & Sun from 4 pm; Sat & Sun brunch 8 am–4 pm. Closed Thanksgiving, Dec 25. Res accepted. Middle Eastern, California menu. Wine, beer. A la carte entrees: lunch $1–$10.95, dinner $9.95–$14.95. Sat & Sun brunch $4.50–$8.95. Specialties: sesame chicken pasta, cheese blintzes. Patio dining. Built 1903; changing art display monthly. Totally nonsmoking. Cr cds: DS, MC, V.

★ ★RUE LEPIC. *900 Pine St, at Mason St, on Nob Hill. 415/474-6070.* Hrs: 11:30 am–2:30 pm, 5:30–10 pm; Fri to 11 pm; Sat 5:30–11 pm; Sun 5:30–10 pm. Closed most major hols. Res accepted; required wkends. French menu. A la carte entrees: lunch $6–$13, dinner $17–$21. Complete meals: dinner $31–$35. Specialties: roast medallion of veal with mushroom sauce, Maine lobster, roasted rack of lamb with garlic. Totally nonsmoking. Cr cds: A, MC, V.

★SCHROEDER'S. *240 Front St, in Financial District. 415/421-4778.* Hrs: 11 am–9 pm; Sat from 4:30 pm. Closed Sun; major hols. Res accepted. Bavarian, Amer menu. Bar. Semi-a la carte: lunch $7–$16, dinner $8.50–$18.50. Child's meals. Specializes in baked chicken & noodles, sauerbraten, Wienerschnitzel. Menu changes daily. German decor, murals. Established 1893. Family-owned. Cr cds: A, D, DS, MC, V.

SC

★SCOMA'S. *Pier 47, at Fisherman's Wharf. 415/771-4383.* Hrs: 11:30 am–11 pm. Closed Thanksgiving, Dec 24, 25. Italian, continental menu. Bars. A la carte entrees: lunch, dinner $11–$25. Child's meals. Specialties: calamari, cioppino, scampi. Valet parking. View of fishing fleet. Originally fisherman's shack. Family-owned. Cr cds: A, C, D, DS, MC, V, JCB.

D

★ ★SCOTT'S SEAFOOD GRILL AND BAR. *2400 Lombard St, in Marina District. 415/563-8988.* Hrs: 11:30 am–10:30 pm; Fri & Sat to 11 pm; Sun brunch 9:30 am–3 pm. Closed Thanksgiving, Dec 25. Res accepted. Bar. A la carte entrees: lunch $7.50–$16.50, dinner $8.50–$18.50. Sun brunch $6.50–$16.50. Specialties: petrale sole, fried calamari, seafood sauté. Cr cds: A, DS, MC, V.

D

★ ★ ★THE SHADOWS. *1349 Montgomery St, on Telegraph Hill, in North Beach. 415/982-5536.* Hrs: 5–10 pm. Closed Thanksgiving, Dec 25. Res required. No A/C. Country French menu. Bar. A la carte entrees: dinner $18–$24. Specializes in duck, lamb, fresh seafood. Own pastries, pasta, ice cream. Valet parking. Chalet overlooking San Francisco Bay. Cr cds: A, C, D, DS, MC, V.

★ ★ ★SILKS. *(See Mandarin Oriental Hotel) 415/986-2020.* Hrs: 7–10:30 am, 11:30 am–2 pm, 6–10 pm. Res accepted. Bar 11 am–11 pm. Wine list. A la carte entrees: bkfst $5.75–$18, lunch $15–$25, dinner $25–$40. *Prix fixe:* dinner $70. Specializes in California cuisine with Asian accents. Own pastries. Valet parking. Silk paintings. Cr cds: A, C, D, DS, MC, V, JCB.

D

★ ★SPLENDIDO. *Embarcadero Center Four, promenade level, in Financial District. 415/986-3222.* Hrs: 11:30 am–2:30 pm, 5:30–10 pm; Thurs & Fri to 10:30 pm; Sat 5:30–10:30 pm; Sun 5:30–10 pm. Closed major hols. Res accepted. Mediterranean menu. Bar. A la carte entrees: lunch $11.50–$15.75, dinner $13–$17.95. Specializes in seared pepper tuna, baked goods. Own pasta, sausages, ice cream. Outdoor dining. Cr cds: A, C, D, DS, MC, V.

D

★ ★ ★STARS. 150 Redwood Alley, between Golden Gate Ave and McAllister St, in Civic Center area. 415/861-7827. Hrs: 11:30 am–2:30 pm, 5:30–11:30 pm; Sun brunch 11 am–2:30 pm. Closed Thanksgiving, Dec 25. Res accepted. Bar from 11 am; wkends from 4 pm. A la carte entrees: lunch $8–$18, dinner $19.50–$28. Sun brunch $4–$14.50 Pianist. Daily changing menu. Oyster bar. Bistro decor. Cr cds: A, D, MC, V.

D

★ ★SWISS LOUIS. Pier 39, at Fisherman's Wharf. 415/421-2913. Hrs 11:30 am–10 pm; Sat & Sun brunch 10:30 am–3:30 pm. Closed Dec 25. Res accepted. No A/C. Italian menu. Bar. Semi-a la carte: lunch $9.50–$15, dinner $11.50–$25. Sat & Sun brunch $10.50. Child's meals. Specializes in veal dishes, seafood. Own desserts. View of bay, Golden Gate Bridge. Cr cds: A, C, D, DS, MC, V, JCB.

D

★TADICH GRILL. 240 California St, in Financial District. 415/391-1849. Hrs: 11 am–9 pm; Sat from 11:30 am. Closed Sun; major hols. Bar. A la carte entrees: lunch, dinner $12–$25. Child's meals. Specializes in fresh seafood. Also counter serv. Turn-of-the-century decor. Established in 1849; family-owned since 1928. Cr cds: MC, V.

★ ★ ★TOMMY TOY'S. 655 Montgomery St, in Financial District. 415/397-4888. Hrs: 11:30 am–3 pm, 6–9:30 pm; Sat & Sun from 6 pm. Closed Jan 1, Dec 25. Res accepted; required wkends. Chinese menu. Bar. A la carte entrees: lunch $11.95–$14.95, dinner $12.95–$16.95. Table d'hôte: lunch $11.95. Prix fixe: dinner $38–$48. Specializes in seafood, breast of duckling. Valet parking (dinner). 19th-century Chinese decor. Antiques. Jacket. Cr cds: A, C, D, DS, MC, V.

D

✔ ★ ★UNDICI. 374 11th St, at Harrison St, in Civic Center area. 415/431-3337. Hrs: 6–10 pm; Fri & Sat to 11 pm. Closed Sun; major hols. Res accepted. Southern Italian, Sicilian menu. Bar from 5:30 pm. A la carte entrees: dinner $9–$16. Specializes in pasta, pizza, fresh seafood. Rustic Italian courtyard atmosphere; faux stone walls, trompe l'oeil grapevines, antique wrought-iron gates. Cr cds: A, D, MC, V.

D

★ ★VANESSI'S. 1177 California St, on Nob Hill. 415/771-2422. Hrs: 11:30 am–10 pm; Fri to 11 pm; Sat 4:30–11 pm; Sun 4:30–10 pm; early-bird dinner 4:30–6:30 pm. Closed major hols. Res accepted. Italian, Amer menu. Bar. A la carte entrees: lunch $7–$14, dinner $8–$19. Specializes in homemade pasta, fresh fish, veal dishes. Valet parking. Open kitchen; exhibition cooking. Cr cds: A, D, MC, V.

D

★ ★WATERFRONT. Pier 7, the Embarcadero at Broadway, in Financial District. 415/391-2696. Hrs: 11:30 am–10:30 pm; Sun brunch 10 am–3 pm. Closed July 4, Dec 25. Res accepted. No A/C. Bar 11 am–10:30 pm. A la carte entrees: lunch $8–$21, dinner $11–$38. Sun brunch $6.95–$12. Specializes in seafood from around the world, including fresh abalone. Valet parking. Outdoor dining. View of harbor. Cr cds: A, C, D, DS, MC, V.

★ ★WU KONG. 101 Spear St, in Rincon Center, south of Union Square. 415/957-9300. Hrs: 11 am–2:30 pm, 5:30–10 pm. Res accepted. Chinese menu. Bar. A la carte entrees: lunch $5.95–$15.95, dinner $7.95–$20. Complete meals: lunch $8–$12, dinner $15–$30. Specializes in dim sum. Valet parking. Outdoor dining. Oriental decor. Atrium with fountain. Cr cds: A, D, MC, V, JCB.

D

★ ★YAMATO. 717 California St, in Chinatown. 415/397-3456. Hrs: 11:45 am–2 pm, 5–10 pm; Sat & Sun from 5 pm. Closed Mon; Jan 1, Thanksgiving, Dec 25. Res accepted. Japanese menu. Bar. A la carte entrees: lunch, dinner $7.75–$23. Complete meals: lunch $7.75–$11.75, dinner $10.50–$23. Specializes in sukiyaki, tempura, chicken or steak teriyaki. Sushi bar. Traditional Japanese decor. Indoor gardens. Some rms with floor & well seating. Family-owned. Cr cds: A, C, D, MC, V, JCB.

✔ ★ ★YANK SING. 427 Battery St, in Financial District. 415/781-1111. Hrs: 11 am–3 pm; Sat & Sun 10 am–4 pm. Res accepted.

Chinese menu. Bar. A la carte entrees: lunch $12–$15. Specialties: dim sum cuisine. Tableside carts in addition to menu. Cr cds: A, D, MC, V.

★YOSHIDA-YA. 2909 Webster St, in Cow Hollow. 415/346-3431; or -3432. Hrs: 5–10:30 pm; Fri, Sat to 11 pm. Closed Jan 15, July 4, Thanksgiving eve & Thanksgiving Day, Dec 25. Japanese menu. Bar. Complete meals: dinner $15–$25. Specialties: sushi, yakitori. Oriental decor; traditional dining upstairs, Japanese style downstairs. Cr cds: A, C, D, DS, MC, V, JCB.

D

★ ★ZUNI CAFE. 1658 Market St, in Civic Center area. 415/552-2522. Hrs: 7:30 am–midnight; Sun to 11 pm; Sun brunch 11 am–3 pm. Closed Mon; some hols. Res accepted. Bar. A la carte entrees: bkfst $3–$5, lunch $7.50–$15, dinner $20–$35. Sun brunch $7.50–$15. Own desserts. Pianist Fri & Sat. Outdoor dining. Changing art displays. Cr cds: A, MC, V.

D

Unrated Dining Spots

CAFÉ LATTÉ. 100 Bush St, 2nd fl, north of Union Square. 415/989-2233. Hrs: 7–9:30 am, 11:30 am–3 pm. Closed Sat, Sun; major hols. No A/C. Nouvelle California/northern Italian menu. Wine, beer. Avg ck: bkfst $3.50, lunch $7. Specializes in fresh fish, fresh pasta, salads. Stylish cafeteria in landmark art deco skyscraper; mirrored deco interior with marble counters, tray ledges, floors. Cr cds: A, C, D, MC, V.

DAVID'S. 474 Geary St, west of Union Square. 415/771-1600. Hrs: 7–1 am; Sat, Sun from 8 am. Closed Jewish high hols. Jewish deli menu. Beer, wine. Semi-a la carte: bkfst $3.35–$9.75, lunch $4.95–$9.95, dinner from $6.95. Complete meal: dinner $16.95. Specializes in chopped chicken liver, stuffed cabbage, cheese blintzes. Cr cds: A, C, D, MC, V, JCB.

DOTTIE'S TRUE BLUE CAFE. 522 Jones St, west of Union Square. 415/885-2767. Hrs: 8 am–2 pm. Closed Wed. No A/C. Wine, beer. Semi-a la carte: bkfst $3–$7.50, lunch $3.50–$7.50. Specializes in all-American bkfst. Traditional coffee shop. No cr cds accepted.

GHIRARDELLI CHOCOLATE MANUFACTORY. 900 North Point St, on grounds of Ghirardelli Square, at Fisherman's Wharf. 415/771-4903. Hrs: 10 am–midnight; winter to 11 pm; Fri, Sat to midnight. Closed Thanksgiving, Dec 25. Soda fountain & candy shop. Specializes in Emperor Norton ice cream, earthquake sundae, premium chocolates. Own candy making, ice cream toppings. Parking. Located in former chocolate factory; built in late 1890s. Totally nonsmoking. Cr cds: MC, V.

ISOBUNE. 1737 Post St, in Japantown. 415/563-1030. Hrs: 11:30 am–10 pm. Closed Jan 1–3, Dec 25. Japanese sushi menu. Wine, beer. A la carte entrees: lunch $5–$8, dinner $10–$12. Specializes in sashimi. Dining at counter; selections pass in front of diners on small boats. Cr cds: MC, V.

JUST DESSERTS. 3 Embarcadero Center, in lobby, in Financial District. 415/421-1609. Hrs: 7 am–6 pm; Sat 9 am–5 pm. Closed Sun; most major hols. A la carte entrees: pastries, cakes, muffins $2.50–$4. Specializes in cheesecake. Own baking. Outdoor dining. Modern cafe atmosphere. Cr cds: MC, V.

D SC

MIFUNE. 1737 Post St, in Japantown. 415/922-0337. Hrs: 11 am–9:30 pm. Closed Jan 1–3, Thanksgiving, Dec 25. Japanese menu. A la carte entrees: lunch, dinner $3.50–$13. Specializes in noodle dishes. Own noodles. Validated parking. Cr cds: A, C, D, DS, MC, V.

SALMAGUNDI. 442 Geary St, west of Union Square. 415/441-0894. Hrs: 8 am–11:30 pm; Sun 11 am–9 pm. Closed Thanksgiving, Dec 25. Wine, beer. Soup, salad, roll $3–$7; dessert extra; pasta torte. Specialty: oven-baked onion soup. Own soups. Cr cds: A, MC, V.

D SC

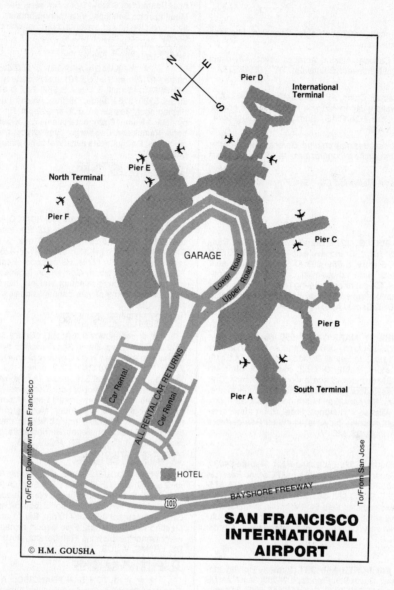

North Terminal

Pier F

Pier E

Pier D

International Terminal

GARAGE

Lower Road

Upper Road

Pier C

Pier B

South Terminal

Pier A

To/From Downtown San Francisco

Car Rental

ALL RENTAL CAR RETURNS

Car Rental

HOTEL

To/From San Jose

101

BAYSHORE FREEWAY

SAN FRANCISCO INTERNATIONAL AIRPORT

© H.M. GOUSHA

TRIO CAFE. *1870 Fillmore St, in Pacific Heights.* 415/ 563-2248. Hrs: 8 am–6 pm; Sun 10 am–4 pm. Closed Mon; Easter, Thanksgiving; also Dec 24–Jan 2. Eclectic menu. Bar. A la carte entrees: bkfst, lunch $4–$6. Outdoor dining in cafe setting. Store front entrance. Totally nonsmoking. No cr cds accepted.

San Francisco Airport Area *

17 mi S of San Francisco (E-1) via US 101.

Services and Information

Information: 415/761-0800.

Lost and Found: 415/876-2261.

Weather: 415/936-1212.

Cash Machines: South Terminal, business center.

Club Lounges: Admirals Club (American), North Terminal; Crown Room (Delta), South Terminal; Presidents Club (Continental), South Terminal; Red Carpet Club (United), North Terminal; WorldClub (Northwest), South Terminal.

Terminals

North Terminal: American, American Eagle, Canadian, Midwest Express, United, United Express

South Terminal: Air Canada, Alaska, America West, American Trans Air, Continental, Delta, Northwest, Southwest, TWA, USAir, USAir Express

International Terminal: Air China, Air France, Alaska, British Airways, China Airlines, Hawaiian, Japan Airlines, Lufthansa, Mexicana, Northwest, Philippine Airlines, QANTAS, Russian Intl, Singapore, TACA, United, UTA, Varig, VASP

(Airlines and their terminal locations may change. Before leaving for the airport, you should phone the airline to confirm terminal location for your flight.)

(See Hayward, Oakland, Redwood City, San Francisco, San Mateo)

Motels

★★**COMFORT SUITES.** *(121 E Grand Ave, South San Francisco 94080) 3 mi N on US 101, E Grand Ave exit.* 415/589-7766; FAX 415/588-2231. 165 suites, 3 story. S $59–$69; D $69–$89; each addl $10; under 18 free. TV; cable, in-rm movies avail. Complimentary continental bkfst. Coffee in rms. Ck-out noon. Meeting rms. Bellhops. Valet serv. Free airport, RR station transportation. Whirlpool. Health club privileges. Refrigerators. Grill. Cr cds: A, C, D, DS, ER, MC, V.

[D] [X] [⊘] [◎] [SC]

★★**COURTYARD BY MARRIOTT.** *(1050 Bayhill Dr, San Bruno 94066) 1½ mi N on US 101 to jct I-380 W, then 1 mi W to El Camino Real South (CA 82), then 1 blk S to Bayhill Dr.* 415/952-3333; FAX 415/952-4707. 147 rms, 2–3 story. S $92; D $102; each addl (after 4th person) $10; suites $105–$115; under 13 free; lower rates wkends. Crib free. TV; cable, in-rm movies. Indoor pool. Complimentary coffee in rms. Restaurant 6:30 am–10 pm. Rm serv. Bar 11 am–11 pm. Ck-out 1 pm. Coin lndry. Meeting rms. Valet serv. Sundries. Free airport transportation. Exercise equipt; weight machine, bicycles, whirlpool. Refrigerators avail. Balconies. Cr cds: A, C, D, DS, MC, V.

[D] [≈] [🏃] [X] [⊘] [◎]

✔★★**MILLWOOD INN.** *(1375 El Camino Real, Millbrae 94030) 1 mi SE on US 101, then ½ mi W on Millbrae Ave to El Camino Real (CA 82), then 1 mi NW.* 415/583-3935; res: 800/345-1375; FAX 415/875-4354. 34 rms, 2 story. S $52–$62; D $58–$68; suites $66–$82; kit. units $54/wk addl; wkly rates exc summer. Crib $4. TV; cable, in-rm movies. Complimentary continental bkfst. Coffee in rms. Restaurant nearby. Ck-out 11 am. Coin lndry. Valet serv. Bathrm phones, refrigerators. Cr cds: A, C, D, DS, ER, MC, V, JCB.

[X] [◎]

★★**RAMADA INN NORTH-AIRPORT** (formerly Holiday Inn-Airport). *(245 S Airport Blvd, South San Francisco 94080) 2 mi N on US 101, off S Airport Blvd exit.* 415/589-7200; FAX 415/588-5007. 319 rms, 2 story. S $70–$100; D $73–$110; each addl $10; under 18 free; wkend rates. Crib free. Pet accepted, some restrictions. TV; cable, in-rm movies. Pool. Restaurant 5:30 am–10:30 pm. Rm serv. Bar; entertainment, dancing Tues–Sat. Ck-out 2 pm. Coin lndry. Meeting rms. Bellhops. Sundries. Barber shop. Free airport transportation. Cr cds: A, C, D, DS, ER, MC, V, JCB.

[D] [🐾] [≈] [X] [⊘] [◎] [SC]

Motor Hotels

★★**BEST WESTERN EL RANCHO INN.** *(1100 El Camino Real, Millbrae 94030) 1 mi SE on US 101, then ½ mi W on Millbrae Ave to El Camino Real (CA 82), then 1 mi NW.* 415/588-8500; FAX 415/871-7150. 300 rms, most A/C, 1–3 story. S $74–$84; D $84–$94; each addl $5; kit. units, suites $110–$150; under 18 free. Crib free. Pet accepted, some restrictions; $6. TV; cable, in-rm movies. Heated pool. Coffee in

rms. Restaurant 6 am–11 pm. Rm serv. Bar. Ck-out 1 pm. Coin lndry. Meeting rms. Bellhops. Valet serv. Sundries. Free airport transportation. Exercise equipt; weights, bicycles, whirlpool. Some refrigerators. Cr cds: A, C, D, DS, ER, MC, V, JCB.

[D] [🐾] [≈] [🏃] [X] [⊘] [◎] [SC]

★★**RAMADA-AIRPORT.** *(1250 Old Bayshore Hwy, Burlingame 94010) 1 mi S on US 101, exit Broadway.* 415/347-2381; FAX 415/348-8838. 145 rms, 3 story. S $82–$96; D $88–$102; each addl $10; suites $120–$160; under 18 free; wkend rates. Crib free. TV; cable. Heated pool. Restaurant 6:30 am–10 pm. Rm serv 6:30–9:30 am, 6–10 pm. Bar 11 am–10 pm; entertainment. Ck-out noon. Meeting rm. Bellhops. Valet serv. Concierge. Free airport transportation. Health club privileges. Refrigerators avail. Wet bar in suites. Cr cds: A, C, D, DS, ER, MC, V, JCB.

[D] [≈] [🏃] [X] [⊘] [◎] [SC]

Hotels

★★★**CLARION-SAN FRANCISCO AIRPORT.** *(401 E Millbrae Ave, Millbrae 94030) 1 mi SE on US 101, then E on Millbrae Ave.* 415/692-6363; FAX 415/697-8735. 440 rms, 2–6 story. S $90–$125; D $110–$135; each addl $10; suites $175–$250; under 16 free; wkend rates. Crib free. TV; cable. Heated pool. Restaurant 6 am–11 pm. Bar 10–2 am. Ck-out noon. Convention facilities. Gift shop. Free airport transportation. Exercise equipt; weights, bicycles, whirlpool. Refrigerator in suites. Some private patios, balconies. Cr cds: A, C, D, DS, ER, MC, V, JCB.

[D] [≈] [🏃] [X] [⊘] [◎] [SC]

★★★**CROWN STERLING SUITES-SOUTH SAN FRANCISCO.** *(250 Gateway Blvd, South San Francisco 94080) 3 mi N on US 101, E Grand Ave exit, then N on Gateway Blvd.* 415/589-3400; res: 800/676-7602; FAX 415/876-0305. 312 suites, 10 story. S $119–$129; D $129–$139; each addl $10; under 13 free; wkend rates. Crib free. TV; cable, in-rm movies. Indoor pool. Complimentary full bkfst. Complimentary coffee in rms. Restaurant 11 am–11 pm. Bar 10–1 am; entertainment. Ck-out 1 pm. Coin lndry. Meeting rms. Gift shop. Free airport transportation. Exercise equipt; weight machine, bicycle, whirlpool, sauna. Health club privileges. Refrigerators, minibars. Balconies. Bay 4 blks. Cr cds: A, C, D, DS, ER, MC, V, JCB.

[D] [≈] [🏃] [X] [⊘] [◎] [SC]

✔★★**DOUBLETREE.** *(835 Airport Blvd, Burlingame 94010) 2 mi S on US 101.* 415/344-5500; FAX 415/340-8851. 291 rms, 8 story. S $99–$129; D $109–$139; each addl $10; suites $150–$300; under 17 free. Crib free. Pet accepted, some restrictions; $20 non-refundable. TV; cable. Restaurant 6:30 am–10 pm. Bar 11 am–11:30 pm. Ck-out noon. Meeting rms. Gift shop. Free airport transportation. Exercise equipt; weight machine, bicycles. Refrigerator, wet bar in suites. Cr cds: A, C, D, DS, ER, MC, V, JCB.

[D] [🐾] [🏃] [X] [⊘] [◎] [SC]

★★★**HILTON SAN FRANCISCO AIRPORT.** *(Box 8355, San Francisco 94128) At San Francisco Intl Airport.* 415/589-0770; FAX 415/589-4696. 527 rms, 3 story. S $139–$169; D $155–$185; each addl $16; suites $275–$500; family, wkend rates. Crib free. TV; cable. Heated pool; poolside serv. Restaurant 6 am–11 pm. Bar; entertainment. Ck-out noon. Convention facilities. Concierge. Free airport transportation. Exercise equipt; weights, bicycles, whirlpool. Minibars; bathrm phone in suites. Balconies. Cr cds: A, C, D, DS, ER, MC, V, JCB.

[D] [≈] [🏃] [X] [⊘] [◎] [SC]

★★★**HOLIDAY INN-CROWNE PLAZA.** *(600 Airport Blvd, Burlingame 94010) 1½ mi S on US 101 to Broadway exit, then E to Airport Blvd, then 1 mi along bay.* 415/340-8500; FAX 415/343-1546. 405 rms, 15 story. S $114–$124; D $124–$134; each addl $10; suites $250–$300; under 18 free; wkend rates. Crib free. TV; cable, in-rm movies. Indoor pool. Restaurant 6 am–midnight. Bar 11–1:30 am; entertainment. Ck-out noon. Coin lndry. Meeting rms. Gift shop. Free covered parking. Free airport transportation. Exercise equipt; weights, bicycles, whirlpool, sauna. Refrigerators avail. *LUXURY LEVEL:* CROWNE LEVEL. 30

rms, 2 suites. S $119; D $129; suites $300. Wet bar. Complimentary continental bkfst, refreshments, newspaper. Cr cds: A, C, D, DS, MC, V, JCB.

★ ★ ★HYATT REGENCY-SAN FRANCISCO AIRPORT. *(1333 Bayshore Hwy, Burlingame 94010) Off US 101 Broadway exit.* 415/347-1234; FAX 415/696-2669. 793 rms, 9 story. S $129–$205; D $154–$230; each addl $25; suites $200–$720; under 18 free; wkend rates. Crib free. Valet parking $9. TV; cable. Heated pool. Supervised child's activities (Fri, Sat evenings). Restaurant 6:30 am–11 pm. Rm serv 24 hrs. Deli open 24 hrs. Bar 11–1 am. Ck-out noon. Convention facilities. Concierge. Gift shop. Free airport transportation. Exercise equipt; weight machine, bicycles, whirlpool, sauna. Some bathrm phones, wet bars. Refrigerators avail. Atrium. *LUXURY LEVEL:* REGENCY CLUB. 72 rms, 4 suites. S $180; D $180–$205; suites $600–$720. Private lounge, honor bar. Bathrm phones. Complimentary continental bkfst, evening refreshments. Cr cds: A, C, D, DS, ER, MC, V, JCB.

★ ★ ★MARRIOTT AIRPORT. *(1800 Old Bayshore Hwy, Burlingame 94010) 1 mi SE on US 101, then E on Millbrae Ave to Old Bayshore Hwy, then SE, on San Francisco Bay.* 415/692-9100; FAX 415/692-8016. 683 rms, 11 story. S $159; D $179; suites $450–$600; under 18 free; wkend, wkly rates. Crib free. Pet accepted, some restrictions. Valet parking $10. TV; cable, in-rm movies. Indoor pool; poolside serv. Restautant 6 am–11 pm. Rm serv 24 hrs. Bar; entertainment, dancing. Ck-out noon. Coin lndry. Convention facilities. Concierge. Gift shop. Free airport transportation. Exercise equipt; weights, bicycles, whirlpool, sauna. Some bathrm phones, refrigerators. *LUXURY LEVEL:* CONCIERGE LEVEL. 55 rms. S, D $179. Private lounge. Wet bar. Bathrm phones. Free bkfst, refreshments. Cr cds: A, C, D, DS, ER, MC, V, JCB.

★ ★SHERATON. *(1177 Airport Blvd, Burlingame 94010) 1½ mi S on US 101 to Broadway exit, then E to Airport Blvd.* 415/342-9200; FAX 415/342-1655. 301 rms, 10 story. S $99–$119; D $114–$129; each addl $15; suites $175–$250; under 18 free; wkend rates. Crib free. Pet accepted, some restrictions. TV; cable, in-rm movies. Indoor/outdoor pool. Restaurant 6 am–11 pm. Bar; entertainment, dancing. Ck-out 1 pm. Coin lndry. Convention facilities. Concierge. Gift shop. Barber, beauty shop. Free airport transportation. Free covered parking. Exercise equipt; weights, bicycles, whirlpool. Cr cds: A, C, D, DS, ER, MC, V.

★ ★ ★THE WESTIN-SAN FRANCISCO AIRPORT. *(One Old Bayshore Hwy, Millbrae 94030) 1 mi SE on US 101, then E on Millbrae Ave to Old Bayshore Hwy.* 415/692-3500; FAX 415/872-8111. 392 rms, 7 story. S, D $119–$179; each addl $20; suites $350–$500; under 18 free; wkend rates. Crib free. Pet accepted, some restrictions. Valet parking $7. TV; cable. Indoor pool; poolside serv. Restaurant 6 am–10 pm. Rm serv 24 hrs. Bar 11 am–midnight; entertainment. Ck-out 1 pm. Convention facilities. Concierge. Gift shop. Free airport transportation. Exercise equipt; weight machine, bicycles, whirlpool, sauna. Refrigerators, minibars. *LUXURY LEVEL:* EXECUTIVE CLUB. 75 rms. S, D $149–$189; each addl $20. Private lounge. Complimentary continental bkfst, refreshments, newspaper. Cr cds: A, C, D, DS, ER, MC, V, JCB.

Restaurants

★ ★ ★EMPRESS COURT. *(433 Airport Blvd, Burlingame) 1½ mi SE on US 101 to Broadway exit, then NE to Airport Blvd, then 1 mi E along bay.* 415/348-1122. Hrs: 11:30 am–2 pm, 5–10 pm; Fri & Sat to 10:30 pm. Res accepted. Chinese menu. Bar. Complete meals (4 or more): lunch from $5.95, dinner $16.95–$35. A la carte entrees: dinner from $9.95. Peking banquet for 4, $27.95 each. Specialties: barbecued baby quail and minced squab, Szechwan spice beef, lemon chicken.

Parking. Lavish Sung dynasty decor; aviary, pond. On 5th floor; view of bay. Cr cds: A, D, DS, MC, V.

★ ★VANESSI'S. *(1095 Rollins Rd, Burlingame) S via US 101, Broadway exit.* 415/342-4922. Hrs: 11:30 am–10 pm; Sat & Sun from 4 pm. Closed Memorial Day, July 4, Thanksgiving, Dec 25. Res accepted. Northern Italian menu. Bar. Semi-a la carte: lunch $6–$12, dinner $10–$25. Specializes in fresh seafood, pasta. Pianist Fri & Sat. Valet parking. Totally nonsmoking. Cr cds: A, D, MC, V.

San Gabriel *

Pop: 37,120 **Elev:** 430 ft **Area code:** 818
Just N of I-10, 11 mi E of Downtown Los Angeles (H-4).

(For accommodations see Arcadia, Pasadena)

Restaurant

★ ★CLEARMAN'S STEAK 'N STEIN INN. *7269 N Rosemead Blvd, at Huntington Dr.* 818/287-1424. Hrs: 5–10 pm; Sun 3–9 pm. Closed Mon & Tues; July 4, Thanksgiving, Dec 25. Res accepted. Bar. Semi-a la carte: dinner $11.95–$26.95. Specializes in prime rib, seafood, chicken. Parking. Fireplace in lounge; stained-glass windows; art display. Family-owned. Cr cds: A, DS, MC, V.

San Jose (E-2)

Founded: 1777 **Pop:** 782,248 **Elev:** 87 ft **Area code:** 408

At the south end of San Francisco Bay, 50 miles from San Francisco, San Jose is known as the "Capital of Silicon Valley." San Jose was founded as "Pueblo de San Jose de Guadalupe" in the name of Charles III of Spain; the first American flag was raised above the town hall in 1846. The city was one of the first to be incorporated in California. Before California was even a state, San Jose became the first state capital; the first state legislature assembled here on December 15, 1849. In recent years it has become an important electronic and aerospace center. It is also the home of San Jose State University.

What to See and Do

1. **Winchester Mystery House.** 525 S Winchester Blvd, at I-280 & CA 17. Started in 1884 by widow of the firearms manufacturer. Told by a medium that she would never die as long as she kept building, Sarah Winchester kept a crew of carpenters busy 24 hours a day until her death in 1922, 38 years later. The expenditures cost more than $5 million. The mansion includes 160 rooms, thousands of doors and windows, 40 stairways (most with 13 steps, many that go nowhere), blank walls, blind chimneys, trapdoors and secret passageways. Sixty-five-minute guided mansion tour; self-guided gardens and outlying buildings tour. Guided tours (daily; closed Dec 25); admission to Historic Museum of Winchester Rifles included in tour. Sr citizen rate. Phone 247-2101 (24-hr info). ¢¢¢¢¢

2. **Rosicrucian Park.** Park & Naglee Aves. Headquarters of the English Grand Lodge of the Rosicrucian Order, AMORC; worldwide philosophical fraternity. Phone 947-3600. **Free.** On grounds are

   Rosicrucian Planetarium & Science Center. The feature exhibit "Geological Gems" looks at mineral properties, crystals, quartz, gemstones and rock types. (Hrs vary, phone for schedule; children under age 5 are not admitted to planetarium shows) Phone 947-3634. **Free.** Planetarium shows ¢¢

Egyptian Museum. One of largest collections of Egyptian antiquities west of the Mississippi; mummy collection includes those of children, adults and animals; replica of a nobleman's tomb. Also art gallery with contemporary works on display. (Daily; closed Jan 1, Thanksgiving, Dec 25) Phone 947-3636   ¢¢¢

3. The Tech Museum of Innovation. 145 W San Carlos St. Offers visitors a fascinating interactive experience in new technologies. See how a microchip works and watch a giant chip process your command; experience a space flight over Mars; learn about robotics and how machines behave like people. (Tues–Sun; closed Jan 1, Thanksgiving, Dec 25) Sr citizen rate. Phone 279-7150.   ¢¢¢

4. The Children's Discovery Museum. 180 Woz Way, in Guadalupe River Park. Provides children and their families with "hands-on" exhibits that explore the relationships between the natural and created worlds, and among people of different cultures and times. Exhibits include the Streets, a ⅝ scale replica of an actual city, with street lights, parking meters, fire hydrants; Waterworks allows operation of pumps and valves to move water through a reservoir system. (Tues–Sat, also Sun afternoon) Sr citizen rate. Phone 298-5495.   ¢¢¢

5. American Museum of Quilts & Textiles. 766 S 2nd St. Regularly changing exhibits feature quilts and other textiles from around the world. Museum's collection includes quilts and coverlets from the 19th century. Explores the role of quilts in cultural traditions, the lives of their makers, and their significance as historical documents. (Tues–Sat; closed Jan 1, July 4, Thanksgiving, Dec 25) Phone 971-0323.

6. San Jose Museum of Art. 110 S Market St. International exhibits featuring contemporary art; docent tours; historic building. (Wed–Sun; closed most hols) Phone 294-2787.   ¢

7. Peralta Adobe and Fallon House. 175-186 W St John St. Built in 1797, the Peralta adobe is the last remaining home of the first pueblo (city) in California. The Fallon house is a Victorian home built for a wealthy resident. Both homes are furnished in the period. (Daily) Phone 287-2290.   ¢

8. Kelley Park. Keyes St at Senter Rd. Phone 277-4661. Includes

Happy Hollow Park and Zoo. 1300 Senter Rd. On 12 acres. Themed children's rides; creative play areas; zoo and contact area; special events. (Daily; no admittance during last hr open; closed Dec 25) Sr citizen rate. Phone 292-8188. General admission   ¢¢

San Jose Historical Museum. At South Kelley Park, 1600 Senter Rd. Original and replica structures have been placed on the grounds to re-create most elements of early San Jose. Outdoor exhibits include original pioneer houses, doctor's office, print shop, fruit barn, 1927 gas station; replicas of early landmarks, including hotel, stables, trolley barn, firehouse, bank, 117-foot electric light tower, operating ice cream store and 1880 Chinese Temple with original altar. Indoor hotel exhibits trace history of area's Indian, Spanish, Mexican and Chinese background. Museum (daily; closed Jan 1, Thanksgiving, Dec 25). Sr citizen rate. Phone 287-2290.   ¢

Japanese Friendship Garden. 1500 Senter Rd. A 6½-acre Japanese Stroll Garden patterned after Korakuen Park in Okayama, Japan; on two levels with a waterfall dropping from lake on upper level into one of two lakes on lower level; 22 symbolic features include bridges and lanterns; teahouse; three-quarter-mile paved walkway trail. (Daily) Phone 295-8383.   **Free.**

9. Alum Rock Park. 16240 Alum Rock Ave, 6 mi E. These 720 acres are known as "Little Yosemite" because of the natural formations. Hiking, bicycle and bridle trails. Picnic grounds, playground. (Daily) Phone 259-5477. Parking fee per vehicle (wkends and hols)   ¢¢ Also in park is

Youth Science Institute. 16260 Alum Rock Ave. Natural science classes, exhibits and nature trips. (Tues–Sat) Phone 258-4322.   ¢

10. Municipal Rose Garden. Naglee & Dana Aves. Approximately 5,000 rose plants on 6 acres, peak blooming in late Apr–May. Picnicking. (Daily) Phone 277-4661.   **Free.**

11. Overfelt Gardens. McKee Rd, W of Jackson Ave, via US 101 and I-680. This 33-acre botanical preserve includes extensive natural areas, a formal botanic garden and a wildlife sanctuary. Migratory waterfowl and other wildlife inhabit three lakes; wooded areas with wild flowers; Chinese Cultural Garden has a bronze and marble statue of Confucius overlooking a reflecting pond, an ornate Chinese gate and three Chinese pavilions—all a gift from the Chinese community. (Daily) No pets or bicycles. Phone 926-5555 or 251-3323.   **Free.**

12. Lick Observatory. 25 mi SE on CA 130 at Mt Hamilton. Main building has astronomical exhibits, guide lectures and 36-inch refracting telescope. At a 120-inch reflecting telescope there is a Visitors Gallery with a self-guided tour. Maintained by the Univ of California at Santa Cruz. (Daily; closed Thanksgiving & day after, Dec 24–25) Phone 274-5061.   **Free.**

13. Raging Waters. 2333 S White Road, in Lake Cunningham Regional Park. Water theme amusement park with more than 35 water park attractions, including the Shark, a double tube ride; river rides; Wacky Water Works, a children's activity area; water slides; lagoon and a beach. (Mid-June–Labor Day, daily; mid-May–mid-June & after Labor Day–Sept, Sat & Sun) Sr citizen rate. Phone 270-8000.   ¢¢¢¢

14. Mirassou Winery. 3000 Aborn Rd. Produces vintage wines and champagnes. Wine tasting and tours. (Mon–Sat, also Sun afternoons; closed some hols) Phone 274-4000.   **Free.**

15. J. Lohr Winery. 1000 Lenzen Ave. Producer of J. Lohr varietal wines. Tasting room (daily, mid-morning–mid-afternoon; closed hols). Tours (wkends, 2 departures: late morning & early afternoon). Phone 288-5057.   **Free.**

(For further information contact the Convention & Visitors Bureau, 333 W San Carlos St, Suite 1000, 95110, phone 295-9600 or 295-2265 for 24-hr recording; or phone the Visitor Information Center, 283-8833.)

Annual Events

San Jose America Festival. Food booths, arts & crafts; rides and games, entertainment. Phone 279-1775. Early July.

Obon Festival. Japanese-American outdoor celebration with hundreds of costumed dancers and Taiko drummers; games, food, crafts. Phone 293-9292. Early or mid-July.

Santa Clara County Fair. Exposition Center, 344 Tully Rd, 3 mi S off US 101. Phone 295-3050. Late July–mid-Aug.

Tapestry in Talent's Festival of the Arts. Downtown. Multi-cultural arts festival celebrates the arts and ethnic diversity of Santa Clara County. Phone 293-9727. Early Sept.

Firefighters Rodeo. Santa Clara County Fairgrounds, via US 101. PRCA cowboys from US, Canada and Australia compete for prize money in six events. Phone 395-3612. 4th wkend Sept.

(See Fremont, Livermore, Santa Clara, Santa Cruz, Saratoga)

Motels

✔ ★ ★ **BEST WESTERN GATEWAY INN.** *2585 Seaboard Ave (95131), near Intl Airport.* 408/435-8800; FAX 408/435-8879. 146 rms, 2 story. S $59–$84; D $64–$89; each addl $5; under 12 free; wkly rates. Crib free. Pet accepted, some restrictions; $10 non-refundable. TV; cable. Pool; whirlpool. Complimentary continental bkfst. Ck-out noon. Meeting rms. Valet serv. Sundries. Free airport transportation. Refrigerators. Cr cds: A, C, D, DS, MC, V, JCB.

★ ★ **COMFORT INN SAN JOSE.** *2118 The Alameda (95126).* 408/243-2400; FAX 408/243-5478. 40 minisuites, 2 story. S $57–$60; D $70; suites $65–$120; under 10 free. Crib avail. TV; cable, in-rm movies. Heated pool; whirlpool. Complimentary continental bkfst, coffee. Coffee in rms. Restaurant nearby. Ck-out 11 am. Valet serv. Refrigerators, minibars; some bathrm phones, in-rm whirlpools. Cr cds: A, C, D, MC, V.

★ ★ ★ **COURTYARD BY MARRIOTT.** (10605 N Wolfe Rd, Cupertino 95014) 5 mi N on I-280 exit Wolfe Rd, 1 blk N. 408/252-9100; FAX 408/252-0632. 149 rms, 3 story, 12 suites. S $68–$93; D $66–$103; suites $80–$115; under 18 free. Crib free. TV; cable. Heated pool. Complimentary coffee in rms. Restaurant 6:30–11 am. Ck-out 1 pm. Coin lndry. Meeting rms. Exercise equipt; weight machine, bicycle, whirlpool. Some refrigerators. Balconies. Cr cds: A, C, D, DS, MC, V.

[D] [symbols] SC

★ ★ **EXECUTIVE INN SUITES.** (1300 Camden Ave, Campbell 95008) S on I-880 Camden Ave exit. 408/559-3600; res: 800/888-3611; FAX 408/371-5721. 38 units, 35 suites, 2 story. S $68–$72; D $75–$85; each addl $7; under 18 free. Crib free. Pet accepted, some restrictions. TV; cable, in-rm movies. Complimentary continental bkfst, coffee. Restaurant nearby. Ck-out noon. Free lndry facilities. Exercise equipt; bicycle, rowing machine. Refrigerators; many bathrm phones, minibars. Balconies. Cr cds: A, C, D, DS, MC, V.

[D] [symbols] SC

★ ★ **RESIDENCE INN BY MARRIOTT.** (2761 S Bascom Ave, Campbell 95008) Off I-880 exit Camden Ave at Curtner Ave. 408/559-1551; FAX 408/371-9808. 80 kit. suites, 2 story. Kit. suites $129–$154. Crib free. Pet accepted, some restrictions. $50 and $6 per pet. TV; cable. Heated pool; whirlpool. Complimentary continental bkfst. Ck-out noon. Coin lndry. Meeting rm. Valet serv. Free airport transportation. Health club privileges. Bicycles. Refrigerators, fireplaces. Balconies. Grills. Cr cds: A, C, D, DS, MC, V, JCB.

[D] [symbols] SC

✔ ★ **RODEWAY INN.** 2112 Monterey Hwy (95112). 408/294-1480; FAX 408/947-0343. 95 rms, 2–3 story, 13 kits. S $45–$70; D $50–$78; each addl $5; kit. units $50–$85. Crib free. TV; cable. Pool. Coffee in rms. Restaurant open 24 hrs. Ck-out 11 am. Coin lndry. Valet serv. Refrigerators. On 3 tree-shaded acres. Cr cds: A, C, D, DS, MC, V, JCB.

[symbols] SC

★ ★ **SUMMERFIELD SUITES.** 1602 Crane Ct (95122), off US 101, 1st St exit, then right on Brokaw Rd, ¼ mi NE to Bering Dr, then S to Crane Ct, near Intl Airport. 408/436-1600; res: 800/833-4353; FAX 408/436-1075. 98 kit. units, 2–3 story. S, D $119–$149. Pet accepted, some restrictions; $50 non-refundable and $5–$10 per day. Complimentary continental bkfst. Complimentary coffee in rms. Restaurant nearby. Ck-out noon. Coin lndry. Meeting rms. Valet serv. Free airport transportation. Exercise equipt; weight machine, bicycles, whirlpool. Lawn games. Some fireplaces. Picnic tables, grills. Cr cds: A, C, D, DS, MC, V, JCB.

[D] [symbols]

Motor Hotels

★ ★ ★ **CAMPBELL INN.** (675 E Campbell Ave, Campbell 95008) W off I-880, CA 17 at Campbell Ave. 408/374-4300; res: 800/582-4300; FAX 408/379-0695. 74 rms, 2 story, 25 suites. S $109–$119; D $119; suites $140–$275; under 12 free; lower rates wkends, hols. Pet accepted, some restrictions; $10 per night. TV; cable, in-rm movies. Heated pool; whirlpool. Complimentary full buffet bkfst. Ck-out noon. Bellhops. Valet serv. Concierge. Free airport, RR station, bus depot transportation. Lighted tennis. Touring bicycles. Game rm. Bathrm phones, refrigerators. Steam bath, fireplace in suites. Private patios, balconies. Picnic tables. Cr cds: A, C, D, MC, V.

[symbols] SC

★ ★ ★ **HOLIDAY INN.** 399 Silicon Valley Blvd (95138). 408/972-7800; FAX 408/972-0157. 150 rms, 3 story, 24 suites. S, D $89–$134; each addl $10; suites $95–$150; under 17 free. Crib free. TV; cable, in-rm movies. Pool. Complimentary coffee in lobby. Restaurant adj 6 am–10 pm. Rm serv. Bar; entertainment. Ck-out noon. Meeting rms. Valet serv. Free airport, RR station, bus depot transportation. Exercise

equipt; weight machine, stair machine. Health club privileges. Refrigerators avail. Cr cds: A, C, D, DS, MC, V.

[D] [symbols] SC

★ ★ **HOLIDAY INN PARK CENTER PLAZA.** 282 Almaden Blvd (95113), at San Carlos St. 408/998-0400; FAX 408/289-9081. 231 rms, 9 story. S $90–$100; D $100–$110; each addl $10; suites $190–$285; under 18 free. Crib free. Pet accepted. TV; cable. Pool. Restaurant 6 am–10 pm. Rm serv 7 am–2 pm, 5–10 pm. Bar 11:30–1:30 am; entertainment Tues–Sat. Ck-out noon. Meeting rms. Valet serv. Gift shop. Free airport, RR station, bus depot transportation. Exercise equipt; weight machine, treadmill. Cr cds: A, C, D, DS, MC, V, JCB.

[D] [symbols] SC

★ ★ ★ **PRUNEYARD INN.** (Box 925, 1995 S Bascom Ave, Campbell 95009) Off I-880 (CA 17) Hamilton Ave exit, in Pruneyard Shopping Center. 408/559-4300; res: 800/582-4300; FAX 408/559-9919. 116 rms, 3 story, 11 kits. S $109–$175; D $119–$185; each addl $12; suites $245; kits. $120–$132; under 12 free; wkend rates. Crib free. TV; cable, in-rm movies. Heated pool; whirlpool, sauna. Complimentary continental bkfst. Ck-out noon; wkends 11 am. Meeting rms. Bellhops. Valet serv. Concierge. Free airport, RR station, bus depot transportation. Lighted tennis. Bathrm phones, refrigerators, minibars; some fireplaces. Cr cds: A, C, D, MC, V.

[D] [symbols] SC

Hotels

★ ★ ★ **BEVERLY HERITAGE.** (1820 Barber Lane, Milpitas 95035) Just off I-880, on Montague Expy in Oak Creek Business Pk. 408/943-9080; res: 800/443-4455; FAX 408/432-8617. 196 rms, 3 story. S $97–$140; D $107–$150; each addl $10; suites $117–$300; under 18 free; wkend package plans. Crib free. TV; cable, in-rm movies. Heated pool; wading pool, poolside serv. Complimentary continental bkfst. Restaurant 6:30 am–11 pm. Bar from 11 am. Ck-out noon. Meeting rms. Free airport transportation. Exercise equipt; weights, stair machine, whirlpool. Health club privileges. Bathrm phones; some refrigerators. Mountain bikes avail. Cr cds: A, C, D, DS, ER, MC, V, JCB.

[D] [symbols] SC

✔ ★ ★ **CROWN STERLING SUITES.** (901 E Calaveras Blvd, Milpitas 95035) 10 mi N on I-880. 408/942-0400; res: 800/433-4600; FAX 408/262-8604. 267 suites, 9 story. S $89–$137; D $89–$151; each addl $15; under 12 free; wkend rates. TV; cable. Indoor pool; whirlpool, sauna, poolside serv. Complimentary full bkfst. Restaurant 11 am–10 pm. Bar. Ck-out 1 pm. Convention facilities. Shopping arcade. Free airport transportation. Health club privileges. Private patios, balconies. Atrium. Cr cds: A, C, D, DS, MC, V.

[D] [symbols] SC

★ ★ ★ ★ **THE FAIRMONT AT FAIRMONT PLAZA.** 170 S Market St (95113), downtown. 408/998-1900; res: 800/527-4727; FAX 408/287-1648. 544 rms, 20 story, 41 suites. S, D $135–$195; each addl $25; suites $400–$1,500; anniversary, hol packages. Covered parking $8/day. TV; cable. Heated pool; poolside serv. Restaurant 6 am–midnight; Sat & Sun to 1 am (also see LES SAISONS AT FAIRMONT PLAZA). Rm serv 24 hrs. Bar 11–1:30 am; entertainment, dancing. Ck-out 1 pm. Convention facilities. Concierge. Shopping arcade. Courtesy airport transportation. Exercise rm; instructor, weight machines, bicycles, sauna, steam rm. Massage. Bathrm phones, minibars. Private patios. Landmark hotel; adj to Plaza Park. Cr cds: A, C, D, DS, MC, V, JCB.

[D] [symbols]

★ ★ ★ **HOTEL DE ANZA.** 233 W Santa Clara St (95113), at Almaden Blvd. 408/286-1000; res: 800/843-3700; FAX 408/286-0500. 101 units, 10 story, 6 suites. S $130–$155; D $135–$155; each addl $15; suites $250–$750; under 18 free; wkend rates. Valet parking $3–$5. TV; cable, in-rm movies. Complimentary coffee in rms. Restaurant 7 am–11 pm. Rm serv 24 hrs. Bar 10:30–2 am; entertainment, dancing Tues–Sat. Ck-out noon. Meeting rms. Gift shop. Free airport, RR station, bus depot transportation. Exercise equipt; weight machine, bicycles. Health club privileges. Bathrm phones, refrigerators, minibars; some wet bars. Balconies. Historic landmark building (ca 1930); restored art deco exterior. Cr cds: A, C, D, MC, V, JCB.

★★**HOTEL SAINTE CLAIRE.** *302 S Market St (95113).* 408/295-2000; res: 800/824-6835; FAX 408/279-5803. 170 rms, 6 story, 18 suites. Feb-Oct: S $104–$140; D $104–$165; each addl $15; suites $150–$795; under 12 free; wkly rates; lower rates rest of yr. Crib free. Valet, garage parking $6. TV; cable. Restaurants 7 am–10 pm. Rm serv 24 hrs. Bar 11:30 am–11 pm; entertainment Fri, Sat, Sun, dancing. Ck-out noon. Meeting rms. Concierge. Gift shop. Free airport, RR station, bus depot transportation. Exercise rm; instructor, weights, bicycles. Bathrm phones, refrigerators, minibars. Renovation of 1926 hotel. Cr cds: A, C, D, DS, ER, MC, V, JCB.

★★★**HYATT.** *1740 N 1st St (95112), near Intl Airport.* 408/993-1234; FAX 408/453-0259. 470 rms, 2–3 story. S $129; D $154; each addl $25; suites $199–$599; under 18 free; wkend rates. Pet accepted, some restrictions; $100 refundable. TV; cable. Heated pool; poolside serv. Restaurant 5:30 am–midnight. Bar 11–2 am; entertainment. Ck-out noon. Meeting rms. Concierge. Gift shop. Barber, beauty shop. Free airport transportation. Exercise equipt; weight machine, bicycle, whirlpool. Some refrigerators; wet bar in suites. Many private patios, balconies. *LUXURY LEVEL:* **REGENCY FLOORS.** 53 rms, 3 floors. S, D $154–$179. Private lounge, honor bar. Bathrm phones. Complimentary full bkfst, refreshments.
Cr cds: A, C, D, DS, MC, V, JCB.

✓★★★**LE BARON.** *1350 N 1st St (95112), near Intl Airport.* 408/453-6200; res: 800/538-6818 (exc CA), 800/662-9896 (CA); FAX 408/437-9693. 327 rms, 9 story. S, D $71–$135; each addl $10; suites $135–$700; under 12 free; wkend rates. Pet accepted, some restrictions. TV; cable. Heated pool; poolside serv. Coffee in rms. Restaurant 6 am–11 pm. Rm serv 24 hrs. Bar. Ck-out noon. Convention facilities. Gift shop. Barber, beauty shop. Free airport transportation. Exercise equipt; weights, bicycles. Refrigerator avail. Some bathrm phones. Cr cds: A, C, D, DS, ER, MC, V, JCB.

★★★**RADISSON PLAZA.** *1471 N 4th St (95112), near Intl Airport.* 408/452-0200; FAX 408/437-8819. 186 rms, 5 story. S $110–$118; D $133; each addl $10; suites $275–$375; under 12 free. Crib free. TV; cable. Heated pool; poolside serv. Complimentary coffee in rms. Restaurant 6:30 am–11 pm. Bar 10:30–1 am. Ck-out noon. Meeting rms. Gift shop. Covered parking. Free airport, RR station, bus depot transportation. Exercise equipt; bicycles, rowing machine, whirlpool. Some bathrm phones, refrigerators, minibars, in-rm whirlpools. Many private patios, balconies. *LUXURY LEVEL:* **PLAZA CLUB.** Ext 4045. 40 rms. S $135; D $145; suites $225–$375. Concierge. Private lounge. Complimentary continental bkfst, refreshments.
Cr cds: A, C, D, DS, ER, MC, V, JCB.

★★★**RED LION HOTEL.** *2050 Gateway Pl (95110), off US 101, 1st St exit/Brokaw Rd, near Intl Airport.* 408/453-4000; FAX 408/437-2899. 505 rms, 10 story. S $79–$147; D $79–$167; each addl $15; suites $450–$600; under 18 free; wkly rates. Pet accepted, some restrictions; $15 refundable. TV; cable. Heated pool; poolside serv. Restaurants 6 am–midnight. Rm serv. Bar to 1:30 am; entertainment, dancing. Ck-out 1 pm. Convention facilities. Bellhops. Valet serv. Concierge. Gift shop. Barber, beauty shop. Free airport, RR station transportation. Exercise equipt; weights, stair machines, sauna. Refrigerator in suites. Balconies. Cr cds: A, C, D, DS, ER, MC, V.

✓★★★**SHERATON.** *(1801 Barber Lane, Milpitas 95035) N on I-880, exit Montague Expy, W on Montague, N on McCarthy, E on Barber Lane.* 408/943-0600; FAX 408/943-0484. 229 rms, 9 story, 60 suites. S $85–$130; D $85–$140; each addl $10; suites $145–$250; under 18 free; wkend packages. Crib free. Heated pool; poolside serv.

Complimentary coffee in rms. Restaurant 6 am–10 pm. Bar 11–2 am; entertainment, dancing exc Sun. Ck-out 1 pm. Meeting rms. Concierge. Gift shop. Free airport transportation. Exercise equipt; weight machine, bicycles, whirlpool. Health club privileges. Bathrm phones. Refrigerator, wet bar in suites. Balconies. *LUXURY LEVEL:* **CONCIERGE FLOOR.** 25 rms, 3 suites. S $140–$150; D $150–$160; suites $155–$250. Private lounge. Wet bars. Bathrm phones. Complimentary continental bkfst, refreshments.
Cr cds: A, C, D, DS, MC, V.

Inn

★★**BRIAR ROSE.** *897 E Jackson St (95112).* 408/279-5999. 6 rms, 4 baths, 2 story. No A/C. S, D $65–$125; each addl $10; under 5 free. TV avail. Complimentary full bkfst, tea. Restaurant nearby. Ck-out 11 am, ck-in 3–8 pm. Street parking. Restored Victorian farm house (1875); antique furnishings; garden with pond, fountain. Cr cds: A, MC, V.

Restaurants

★**BO TOWN.** *409 S 2nd St.* 408/295-2125. Hrs: 11 am–10 pm. Closed Chinese New Year. Res accepted. Chinese, Vietnamese menu. Wine, beer. A la carte entrees: lunch, dinner $4.25–$20. Specializes in seafood. Parking. Cr cds: MC, V.

★★**EMILE'S.** *545 S 2nd St.* 408/289-1960. Hrs: 11:30 am–2 pm, 6–10 pm. Closed Sun, Mon; most major hols. Res accepted. Contemporary French menu. Bar. A la carte entrees: lunch $7.50–$15, dinner $12–$25. Specializes in fish. French country decor. Cr cds: A, C, D, DS, MC, V.

★★**EULIPIA.** *374 S 1st St.* 408/280-6161. Hrs: 11:30 am–1:30 pm, 5:30–9 pm; Fri & Sat 5:30–10 pm; Sun 4:30–9 pm. Closed major hols. Res accepted. A la carte entrees: lunch $7.95–$13.50, dinner $8.50–$16.50. Specialty: chicken breast with brie. Totally non-smoking. Cr cds: A, C, D, DS, MC, V.

★★**FUNG LUM.** *(1815 S Bascom Ave, Campbell) 2 mi S on US 280, Bascom Ave exit.* 408/377-6955. Hrs: 11:30 am–2 pm, 5–10 pm; Fri to 10:30 pm; Sat 11:30 am–2:30 pm, 5–10:30 pm; Sun 11 am–9 pm; Sat & Sun brunch to 3 pm. Chinese menu. A la carte entrees: lunch $5–$12, dinner $10–$20. Buffet: lunch (Sun) $10.95. Sat & Sun brunch $10.95. Specializes in lemon chicken, spareribs. Parking. Formal Chinese decor. Family-owned. Cr cds: A, C, D, MC, V.

✓★**HOCHBURG VON GERMANIA.** *261 N 2nd St.* 408/295-4484. Hrs: 11:30 am–2 pm, 5–9:30 pm; Sat 5–10 pm; Sun 5–9:30 pm. Closed major hols. Res accepted. No A/C. German menu. Bar. Semi-a la carte: lunch $6–$10, dinner $11–$19. Specializes in veal, pork, steak. Parking. Outdoor dining. German decor; medieval setting. Cr cds: A, DS, MC, V.

★★★**LES SAISONS AT FAIRMONT PLAZA.** *(See The Fairmont at Fairmont Plaza Hotel)* 408/998-1900. Hrs: 6–10:30 pm; early-bird dinner 5:30–7 pm. Res accepted. Bar. Wine list. Semi-a la carte: dinner $26–$48. Specializes in California cuisine. Seasonal menu. Own baking. Harpist. Valet parking. Elegant room. Award-winning wine selection. Jacket. Cr cds: A, C, D, DS, MC, V, JCB.

★★**LOU'S VILLAGE.** *1465 W San Carlos St.* 408/293-4570. Hrs: 11:30 am–10 pm; Sat 4:30–11 pm. Closed Sun & Mon; Jan 1, Dec 25. Res accepted. Bar. Semi-a la carte: lunch $7.95–$17, dinner

$10.95–$24.95. Child's meals. Specializes in seafood, veal, pasta. Own desserts. Parking. Nautical decor. Family-owned. Cr cds: A, DS, MC, V.

★★ORIGINAL JOE'S. 301 S 1st St. 408/292-7030. Hrs: 11–1:30 am. Closed some major hols. Italian, Amer menu. Bar. A la carte entrees: bkfst $5.50–$8.95, lunch $4.50–$12.95. Semi-a la carte: dinner $6.95–$21.95. Child's meals. Family-owned. Cr cds: DS, MC, V.

✔ ★TACOS AL PASTOR. 400 S Bascom Ave. 408/275-1619. Hrs: 10 am–9 pm; wkends from 8:30 am. Closed Mon. No A/C. Wine, beer. Semi-a la carte: bkfst $5.05–$5.79, lunch, dinner $5.49–$8.59. Specialties: plato al Pastor, carne en su Jugo. Parking. Mexican taqueria; murals on walls. No cr cds accepted.

San Juan Bautista (F-2)

Pop: 1,570 **Elev:** 150 ft **Area code:** 408 **Zip:** 95045

The San Andreas Fault intersects this little town, providing residents with a few minor tremors and a topic of speculation, but little worry; most of the buildings have been standing more than 150 years. San Juan Bautista began in 1797 with the Spanish mission (see #1). The town that spread around the mission prospered as a center of cattle ranching and commerce from a nearby lode of quicksilver. However, in 1870 the Southern Pacific Railroad ran the region's first tracks through a nearby town and San Juan Bautista began to decline. Today, tourists and artists contribute to the economy of the town.

What to See and Do

1. **San Juan Bautista State Historic Park.** 2nd St, 3 mi E of US 101. Phone 623-4881. Here are

   Plaza Stable (1861) houses collection of restored horse-drawn carriages, blacksmith and wagonwright equipment and tools; **Castro-Breen House** (1841) (self-guided tours); **Plaza Hall** (1868) used as a residence, assembly place and dance hall; **Plaza Hotel**, restored. Picnicking. (Daily; closed Jan 1, Thanksgiving, Dec 25) All buildings ¢

   Mission San Juan Bautista (1797). 2nd & Mariposa Sts. Fifteenth and largest mission church built by the Franciscans. Church, finished in 1812 and still in use, contains many original items. The museum has old vestments, music books, barrel organ, relics and original kitchen and dining room. Cemetery has graves of 4,300 Indians. (Daily; closed most major hols) Donation. Phone 623-4528.

2. **Pinnacles National Monument** (see). 8 mi E on CA 156, then 35 mi S on CA 25.

   (For further information contact the Chamber of Commerce, PO Box 1037; 623-2454.)

Annual Events

Early Days Celebration. Commemorates founding of Mission; food, entertainment, history demonstrations. Mid-June.

San Benito County Saddle Horse Show, Parade & Rodeo. 8 mi W on CA 156 to Hollister, then 8 mi S on CA 25. Phone 628-3421. Late June.

(See Gilroy, Salinas)

Motel

★SAN JUAN INN. 410 Alameda St, jct CA 156. 408/623-4380. 42 rms, 2 story. S $45; D $55–$60; each addl $6. Crib free. TV;

cable. Heated pool; whirlpool. Restaurant opp 7 am–10 pm. Ck-out noon. Cr cds: A, D, MC, V.

Restaurants

★CADEMARTORI'S. 600 1st St, 4 blks N of CA 156. 408/623-4511. Hrs: 11:30 am–2 pm, 5–9 pm; Fri & Sat to 10 pm; Sun 1–9 pm. Closed Mon; Dec 24, 25. Res accepted. No A/C. Italian, Amer menu. Bar. Semi-a la carte: lunch $5.75–$13.95, dinner $11.95–$19.95. Child's meals. Specialties: saltimbocca, cannelloni. Own pasta. Parking. Patio dining. In old parish hall of Mission San Juan Bautista; view of San Juan Valley. Family-owned. Cr cds: A, D, MC, V.

✔ ★DOÑA ESTHER. 25 Franklin St. 408/623-2518. Hrs: 11 am–10 pm; Sat & Sun from 9 am. Closed Easter, Thanksgiving, Dec 25. Res accepted. No A/C. Mexican menu. Bar. Semi-a la carte: bkfst $4–$6.25, lunch $3.50–$8.75, dinner $3.50–$9.75. Buffet: lunch $5.95. Specializes in fish, authentic Mexican dishes. Guitarist & vocalist Fri-Sun. Outdoor dining. Cr cds: A, DS, MC, V.

San Juan Capistrano (J-4)

Founded: 1776 **Pop:** 26,183 **Elev:** 104 ft **Area code:** 714 **Zip:** 92675

Because of its colorful mission and its euphonious name, this town has been romanticized in song, legend, short stories and movies. Perched between mountains and ocean, San Juan Capistrano developed around the mission and today is occupied, in part, by descendants of early Mexican settlers. At one time the village declared war on Mexico.

What to See and Do

1. **Mission San Juan Capistrano.** 2 blks W of I-5, Ortega Hwy exit. Famous for its swallows, which depart each year on St John's Day, October 23, and return on St Joseph's Day, March 19. Founded by Fray Junipero Serra in 1776 and named for St John of Capistrano, the Crusader, the church was built in the form of a cross and was one of the most beautiful of all California missions. The arched roof, five domes, nave, cloister and belfry collapsed during the 1812 earthquake. Pillars, arches, the garden and quadrangle remain. Self-guided tour includes the Serra Chapel (still in use), oldest building in California, ruin of the Great Stone Church, padres' living quarters, soldiers' barracks and three museum rooms exhibiting artifacts from Native American and early Spanish culture. Also the site of a major North American archaeological dig. (Daily; closed Easter, Thanksgiving, Dec 25) Phone 248-2048. ¢¢

2. **O'Neil Museum.** 31831 Los Rios St. Housed in a restored Victorian house, museum features collections of historical photographs, rare books, period furniture and clothing, Indian artifacts; also genealogical information. (Tues–Fri & Sun; closed major hols) Phone 493-8444. ¢

3. **Ronald W. Caspers Wilderness Park.** 33401 Ortega Hwy, I-5 Ortega exit, approx 8 mi E on Ortega Hwy. Wilderness on 8,060 acres. Riding and hiking trails, nature center. Camping (fee). Inquire in advance for camping and trail use information and restrictions. (Daily) No pets. No one under age of 18 yrs allowed in park. Phone 728-0235 or 831-2174. Day use per vehicle ¢

4. **Regional Library and Cultural Center.** 31495 El Camino Real. Architecturally noteworthy post-modern building, designed by Michael Graves, combines Spanish, Egyptian, Greek and pre-Columbian American influences in its design. (Daily exc Sun; tours by appt) Phone 493-1752. **Free.**

5. Tour of old adobes. Sponsored by the San Juan Capistrano Historical Society. Contact the Historical Society, 31831 Los Rios St; 493-8444. ¢

(For further information contact the Chamber of Commerce, 31682 El Camino Real; 493-4700.)

Annual Events

Festival of Whales. Dana Point Harbor, in Dana Point. Educational and entertainment events saluting visit of California gray whales. Phone 496-1555. Late Feb–mid-Mar, wkends.

Fiesta de las Golondrinas. Celebrates the return of the swallows to the mission (see #1); dance pageant, art exhibits. St Joseph's Day, Mar.

(See Anaheim, Laguna Beach, San Clemente)

Motels

 ★ ★**BEST WESTERN CAPISTRANO INN.** *27174 Ortega Hwy.* *714/493-5661; FAX 714/661-8293.* 108 rms, 2 story. Mar–Sept: S, D $69–$75; each addl $6; kit. units $70–$75; under 13 free; lower rates rest of yr. Crib $5. Pet accepted, some restrictions. TV; cable. Heated pool; whirlpool. Complimentary full bkfst (Mon–Fri). Complimentary coffee in rms. Restaurant adj open 24 hrs. Bar 11–2 am. Ck-out noon. Meeting rm. Some balconies. Cr cds: A, C, D, DS, ER, MC, V, JCB.

D ⊁ ⊠ ⊘ ⊚ SC

★ ★**HOLIDAY INN EXPRESS-CANA POINT EDGEWATER.** *(34744 Coast Hwy, Capistrano Beach 92624)* S on I-5 exit Camino Los Ramblas, left on Doheny Park Rd to Coast Hwy, ½ mi S on left. *714/240-0150; FAX 714/240-4862.* 30 rms, 3 story, 5 suites. June–Sept: S $85–$120; each addl $10; suites $120–$135; under 19 free; wkly rates; lower rates rest of yr. Crib free. TV; cable. Complimentary continental bkfst, coffee. Restaurant adj noon–10 pm. Ck-out 11:30 am. Free covered parking. Whirlpool, sauna. Refrigerators, wet bars. Some balconies. Many rms with ocean view. Cr cds: A, C, D, DS, MC, V, JCB.

D ⊘ ⊚ SC

Restaurants

★ ★**EL ADOBE DE CAPISTRANO.** *31891 Camino Capistrano. 714/493-1163.* Hrs: 11:30 am–10 pm; Fri & Sat to 11 pm; Sun 10:30 am–10 pm; early-bird dinner Mon–Fri 4–6 pm. Res accepted. Mexican, Amer menu. Bar. Semi-a la carte: lunch $4.50–$10.50, dinner $5.25–$16.95. Sun brunch $5.25–$10.75. Child's meals. Specialty: President's choice. Entertainment Fri–Sun. Parking. Spanish adobe courthouse (1776). Cr cds: A, DS, MC, V.

★ ★ ★**L'HIRONDELLE.** *31631 Camino Capistrano, opp Old Mission. 714/661-0425.* Hrs: 5–9 pm; Fri, Sat to 10 pm; early-bird dinner Tues–Thurs & Sun 5–6:30 pm; Sun brunch 11 am–2 pm. Closed Mon; Dec 25. Res accepted. French, Belgian menu. Wine, beer. Semi-a la carte: dinner $12.50–$16.95. Sun brunch $10.95. Specializes in braised duckling, rabbit, sweetbreads. Own baking. Parking. Accordionist at brunch. Many antiques. Cr cds: A, C, D, MC, V.

★**SARDUCCI'S CAFE & GRILL.** *31751 Camino Capistrano. 714/493-9593.* Hrs: 8 am–10 pm; Fri & Sat to 11 pm; early-bird dinner Mon–Fri 4–7 pm; Sun brunch 8 am–4 pm. Closed Jan 1, Thanksgiving, Dec 25. Res accepted. Wine, beer. Semi-a la carte: bkfst $2.50–$6.95, lunch $3.95–$6.95, dinner $8.95–$16.95. Sun brunch $7.95. Child's meals. Specializes in pasta, seafood. Outdoor dining on large patio. Cr cds: A, DS, MC, V.

D

 ★**WALNUT GROVE.** *26871 Ortega Hwy, adj to Mission. 714/493-1661.* Hrs: 6 am–9:45 pm. Closed Dec 25. Wine, beer. Semi-a la carte: bkfst $2.25–$9.95, lunch $3.50–$7.95, dinner $6.95–$14.95.

Child's meals. Specializes in home-style cooking. Parking. Family-owned. Cr cds: A, C, D, MC, V.

SC

San Luis Obispo (G-2)

Founded: 1772 **Pop:** 41,958 **Elev:** 234 ft **Area code:** 805

Father Junípero Serra, who established the mission in 1772, saw a resemblance to a bishop's mitre in two nearby volcanic peaks and named the mission San Luis Obispo de Tolosa (St Louis, Bishop of Toulouse). After the thatched mission roofs burned several times, a tilemaking technique was developed that soon set the style for all California missions. Located in a bowl-shaped valley, the town depends on government employment, tourism, agriculture, retail trade and its university population.

What to See and Do

1. Mission San Luis Obispo de Tolosa. 782 Monterey St, between Chorro & Broad Sts. Fifth of the California missions, founded in 1772, still serves as the parish church. 8-room museum contains extensive Chumash Indian collection and artifacts from early settlers. First olive orchard in California planted here; two original trees still stand. (Daily; closed Jan 1, Easter, Thanksgiving, Dec 25) Donation. Phone 543-6850.

2. San Luis Obispo County Historical Museum (1905). 696 Monterey St, near mission. Local history exhibits; decorative arts; turn-of-the-century parlor re-creation. (Wed–Sun; closed major hols) Phone 543-0638. **Free.**

3. Ah Louis Store (1874). 800 Palm St. Leader of the Chinese community, Ah Louis was an extraordinary man who achieved prominence at a time when Orientals were given few opportunities. The two-story building, which served as the Chinese bank, post office and general merchandise store, was the cornerstone of the Chinese community. (Mon–Sat, afternoons; closed hols) Phone 543-4332.

4. Children's Museum. 1010 Nipomo St, jct Monterey St. A "hands-on" museum for children pre-school through elementary school (must be accompanied by an adult); houses many interactive exhibits; themes change monthly. (Mid-June–Aug, Fri–Sun, also Tues from mid-morning–mid-afternoon and Thurs from early afternoon–early evening; rest of yr, Thurs–Sun, hrs vary; closed most major hols) Phone 544-KIDS. ¢

5. California Polytechnic State University (1901). (17,000 students) N edge of town. On campus are three art galleries, working livestock and farm units, horticultural, architectural and experimental displays. Campus tours (Mon, Wed & Fri; res required). Phone 756-2792. **Free.** Also here is

Shakespeare Press Printing Museum. Graphic Arts Bldg. Collection of 19th-century printing presses, type and related equipment; demonstrations for prearranged tours. (Mon–Fri, by appt; closed hols) Phone 756-1108. **Free.**

(For further information contact the Chamber of Commerce, 1039 Chorro St, 94301-3278; 781-2777.)

Annual Events

La Fiesta de San Luis Obispo. Parade, barbecues, Spanish Market Place, entertainment. Mid-May.

Renaissance Faire. Celebration of the Renaissance; period costumes, food booths, entertainment, arts & crafts. July.

Mozart Festival. Recitals, chamber music, orchestra concerts & choral music. Held at various locations throughout the county, including

Mission San Luis Obispo de Tolosa and Cal Poly State University campus. Contact PO Box 311; 781-3008. Late July–early Aug.

(See Morro Bay, Pismo Beach)

Motels

✔ ★★BEST WESTERN OLIVE TREE INN. *1000 Olive St (93405).* 805/544-2800. 38 rms, 2 story, 6 kits. No A/C. S $43–$53; D $49–$65; each addl $4–$6; suites $68–$92; kits. $74–$98. Crib $6. TV; cable. Heated pool; sauna. Restaurant 6:30 am–2 pm. Ck-out 11 am. Coin lndry. Sundries. Balconies. Cr cds: A, C, D, DS, MC, V.

★★CAMPUS. *404 Santa Rosa St (93405).* 805/544-0881; res: 800/447-8080 (CA). 35 rms, some A/C, 2 story. Mid-May–Sept: S, D $49–$89; each addl $5; higher rates: hols & special events; lower rates rest of yr. Crib $5. Pet accepted, some restrictions; $5 per day. TV; cable. Heated pool. Complimentary coffee in rms. Restaurant nearby. Ck-out 11 am. Coin lndry. Meeting rm. Refrigerators; some in-rm whirlpools. Cr cds: A, C, D, DS, MC, V.

★HOWARD JOHNSON. *1585 Calle Joaquin (93405).* 805/544-5300; FAX 805/541-2823. 64 rms, 2 story. June–Sept: S, D $49–$99; under 18 free; lower rates rest of yr. Crib free. Pet accepted, some restrictions; $10. TV; cable, in-rm movies. Heated pool; wading pool. Complimentary coffee. Restaurant 6:30 am–10 pm. Bar. Ck-out noon. Coin lndry. Many refrigerators. Private patios, balconies. Cr cds: A, C, D, DS, ER, MC, V, JCB.

✔ ★LAMP LIGHTER INN. *1604 Monterey St (93401).* 805/547-7777; res: 800/547-7787; FAX 805/547-7787. 40 rms, 2–3 story, 3 cottages. No elvtr. Early June–Labor Day: S, D $49–$64; each addl $6; suites, cottages $64–$69; higher rates special events; lower rates rest of yr. TV; cable, in-rm movies avail. Heated pool; whirlpool. Complimentary bkfst. Complimentary coffee in rms. Restaurant nearby. Ck-out noon. Coin lndry. Refrigerators. Cr cds: A, DS, MC, V.

★★SANDS. *1930 Monterey St (93405).* 805/544-0500; res: 800/441-4657; FAX 805/544-3529. 56 rms, 1–2 story, 14 suites. May–Sept: S, D $59–$89; each addl $5; suites $69–$99; under 12 free; higher rates: special events & hols; lower rates rest of yr. Crib $5. Pet accepted, some restrictions; $5 per day. TV; cable, many in-rm movies. Heated pool. Complimentary continental bkfst. Restaurant adj 6 am–10 pm. Ck-out 11 am. Coin lndry. Meeting rms. Sundries. Some covered parking. Free airport, RR station, bus depot transportation. Refrigerators. Private patios, balconies. Picnic tables, grill. Delicatessen. Cr cds: A, C, D, DS, MC, V.

✔ ★★VILLA SAN LUIS. *1670 Monterey St (93401).* 805/543-8071. 14 rms, 1–2 story. June–Oct: S, D $43–$58; each addl $3; higher rates: university events, major hols; lower rates rest of yr. Crib free. TV; cable, in-rm movies. Heated pool in season. Complimentary coffee in rms. Restaurant nearby. Ck-out 11 am. Cr cds: C, DS, MC, V, JCB.

Motor Hotels

★★MADONNA INN. *100 Madonna Rd (93405).* 805/543-3000; res: 800/543-9666; FAX 805/543-1800. 109 rms, 1–4 story. Some A/C. No elvtr. S $72; D $82–$130; suites $110–$170. Crib free. TV; cable. Restaurant 7 am–10 pm, dining rm from 5:30 pm. Bar noon–midnight; entertainment, dancing Tues–Sat. Ck-out noon. Meeting rm. Sundries. Gift shops. Fireplace in suites. Some balconies. Individually decorated rms, each in motif of different nation or period. On hill with mountain view. No cr cds accepted.

★★★QUALITY SUITES. *1631 Monterey St (93401).* 805/541-5001; FAX 805/546-9475. 138 suites, 3 story. May–Labor Day: S $109–$119; D $119–$129; each addl $10; under 18 free; higher rates special events; lower rates rest of yr. Crib free. TV; cable, in-rm movies. Heated pool; wading pool, whirlpool. Complimentary full bkfst. Restaurant 6:30–9:30 am, 6–8 pm; wkends 7–10 am. Ck-out noon. Coin lndry. Meeting rm. Valet serv. Sundries. Gift shop. Airport, RR station, bus depot transportation. Refrigerators. Private patios, balconies. Grills. Cr cds: A, C, D, DS, ER, MC, V, JCB.

Hotel

★★★EMBASSY SUITES. *333 Madonna Rd (93405).* 805/549-0800; FAX 805/543-5273. 195 suites, 4 story. S, D $109–$250; each addl $10; under 12 free. Crib free. TV; cable, in-rm movies. Indoor pool. Complimentary full bkfst. Coffee in rms. Restaurant 6:30 am–10 pm. Bar 11 am–11 pm. Ck-out noon. Coin lndry. Meeting rms. Shopping arcade. Free airport, RR station, bus depot transportation. Exercise equipt; weights, bicycles, whirlpool. Minibars; some bathrm phones. Balconies. Atrium lobby; glass elevators. Cr cds: A, C, D, DS, MC, V.

Inns

✔ ★ADOBE. *1473 Monterey St (93401).* 805/549-0321; res: 800/676-1588. 15 rms, 2 story, 7 kit. units. No A/C. May–Sept: S $45–$79; D $55–$89; each addl $6; under 5 free; lower rates rest of yr. TV; cable. Complimentary full bkfst 8:30–10 am. Restaurant nearby. Ck-out 11 am, ck-in 2 pm. Meeting rm. Southwestern-style bed & breakfast inn. Cr cds: A, DS, MC, V.

★★★APPLE FARM. *2015 Monterey St.* 805/544-2040; res: 800/374-3705; FAX 805/541-5497. 67 rms, 3 story. July–mid-Sept, wkends, hols: S, D $140–$200; each addl $15; under 18 free; honeymoon packages; lower rates rest of yr. Crib free. TV; cable. Pool; whirlpool. Bkfst in rms. Restaurant (see APPLE FARM). Ck-out noon, ck-in 4 pm. Valet serv. Gift shop. Free airport, RR station, bus depot transportation. Fireplaces. Some balconies. Sitting rm. Antiques. Bakery, millhouse. Cr cds: A, DS, MC, V.

Restaurants

✔ ★★APPLE FARM. *(See Apple Farm Inn)* 805/544-6100. Hrs: 7 am–9:30 pm. Wine, beer. Semi-a la carte: bkfst $3.25–$5.95, lunch $3.95–$6.95, dinner $3.95–$14.95. Specializes in fish, soups, apple dumplings. Salad bar. Patio dining. Gift shop, bakery; water-powered grist mill. Totally nonsmoking. Cr cds: A, DS, MC, V.

★IZZY ORTEGA'S. *1850 Monterey St, near the university.* 805/543-3333. Hrs: 11:30 am–9 pm; Fri to 9:30 pm; Sat 11 am–9:30 pm; Sun 11 am–9 pm; Sun brunch 11:30 am–3 pm. Closed Jan 1, Thanksgiving, Dec 24 & 25. Res accepted. Mexican menu. Bar. Semi-a la carte: lunch $3.75–$9.95, dinner $5.95–$9.95. Child's meals. Specialties: fajitas, chili relleños, nachos. Parking. Outdoor dining. Authentic Mexican decor; cantina atmosphere. Totally nonsmoking. Cr cds: DS, MC, V.

San Marino *

Pop: 12,959 **Elev:** 566 ft **Area code:** 818 **Zip:** 91108
3 mi W of Arcadia (H-4) on Huntington Dr.

What to See and Do

1. **Huntington Library, Art Collections and Botanical Gardens.** 1151 Oxford Rd. Comprehensive collection of British and French 18th- and 19th-century art and American art. Home of Gainsborough's *Blue Boy*, a Shakespeare First Folio, Ellesmere manuscript of Chaucer's *Canterbury Tales* and manuscript of Franklin's autobiography; 150-acre botanical gardens. (Daily exc Mon; closed hols) Phone 405-2141 (recording) or -2100. ¢¢

2. **El Molino Viejo** (ca 1816). 1120 Old Mill Rd. First gristmill to be operated by water in southern California. Changing exhibits of paintings and prints of California and the West. Southern California headquarters of California Historical Society. (Daily exc Mon; closed hols) Phone 449-5450. **Free.**

(For further information contact the Chamber of Commerce, 2304 Huntington Dr; 286-1022.)

(For accommodations see Arcadia, Los Angeles)

Restaurant

✔ ★**COLONIAL KITCHEN.** 1110 Huntington Dr. 818/289-2449. Hrs: 7 am–9 pm. Semi-a la carte: bkfst $2.95–$6.55, lunch $3.95–$6.35, dinner $6.95–$12.95. Child's meals. Parking. Colonial decor. Cr cds: MC, V.

San Mateo (E-1)

Settled: 1851 **Pop:** 85,486 **Elev:** 28 ft **Area code:** 415

Once a stop between the chain of missions established by Fray Junipero Serra, San Mateo is now a busy suburban area within easy access to both the coast and the bay.

What to See and Do

1. **Japanese Garden.** In Central Park, 5th & Laurel Aves. Collection of *koi* (carp), bonsai specimens; pagoda from Toyonaka, Japan; teahouse. (Daily; closed Dec 25) Phone 377-4640. **Free.**

2. **Coyote Point Museum.** 1651 Coyote Point Dr, 1 mi E via US 101; northbound exit Dore Ave; southbound exit Poplar Ave. Museum features four-level exhibition including ecological concepts, dioramas, computer games, live insect colonies, aquarium displays. Two-acre Wildlife Center features native bay area animals, walk-through aviaries and native plants. (Daily exc Mon; closed Jan 1, Thanksgiving, Dec 24 & 25) Free admission 1st Wed of month. Sr citizen rate. Phone 342-7755. ¢¢

3. **Horse racing.** Bay Meadows Racecourse, Bayshore Frwy (US 101), CA 92 & Hillsdale Blvd. Turf club, clubhouse, grandstand and infield park. Thoroughbred racing (late Aug–late Jan, Wed–Sun). Parking fee. Phone 574-7223 for admission prices and schedule.

4. **Woodside Store** (1854). 10 mi SW via I-280 then E on CA 84 (Woodside Rd) to Kings Mt & Tripp Rds in Woodside. First store between San Jose and San Francisco. The building, once used as a post office and general store, still contains original equipment and furnishings. (Tues, Thurs, Sat & Sun afternoons) Tours by appt. Phone 851-7615. **Free.** Also in Woodside is

   Fioli Gardens. Cañada Rd. This was a filming location for *Dynasty* TV program. Georgian-style mansion and 16 acres of gardens. Guided tours of mansion (Feb–Nov, Tues–Sat; reservation required; no children under 12 yrs). Sr citizen rate. Phone 364-2880. ¢¢¢¢

(For further information contact the San Mateo County Convention & Visitors Bureau, 111 Anza Blvd, Suite 410, Burlingame 94010; 348-7600 or 800/288-4748.)

Annual Event

San Mateo County Fair & Floral Fiesta. Expo Center. Phone 574-FAIR. Aug.

(See Redwood City, San Francisco Airport Area)

Motor Hotels

✔ ★**DUNFEY.** 1770 S Amphlett Blvd (94402), at jct US 101, CA 92W. 415/573-7661; res: 800/843-6664 (exc CA), 800/238-6339 (CA); FAX 415/573-0533. 270 rms, 3 story. S $59–$110; D $59–$120; each addl $10; suites $155–$275; under 17 free; wknd rates. Crib free. Pet accepted; $75 refundable. TV; in-rm movies avail. Heated pool. Restaurant 6:30 am–10 pm; Fri & Sat to 10:30 pm. Rm serv. Bar 4 pm–midnight. Ck-out 1 pm. Meeting rms. Gift shop. Free airport transportation. Some refrigerators; wet bar in suites. Cr cds: A, C, D, DS, MC, V.

D P ≈ ⊗ ⊛ SC

★**QUALITY HOTEL-AIRPORT SOUTH.** 4000 S El Camino Real (94403). 415/341-0966; FAX 415/573-0164. 300 rms, 2–5 story. S $69–$89; D $72–$97; each addl $8; suites $115–$225; under 18 free. Crib free. TV; cable. Pool; poolside serv. Complimentary coffee in rms. Restaurant open 24 hrs. Rm serv. Bar 10–2 am; pianist, dancing Thurs–Sat. Ck-out 1 pm. Convention facilities. Bellhops. Gift shop. Barber, beauty shop. Free airport transportation. Exercise equipt; weight machine, stair machine. Some refrigerators. Some balconies. Cr cds: A, C, D, DS, ER, MC, V, JCB.

D ≈ ✳ ⊗ ⊛ SC

San Pedro (L.A.) (J-3)

Elev: 20 ft **Area code:** 310

Nestled in the Palos Verdes hills, this community is a neighborhood of Los Angeles, but is regarded by many as a separate entity.

What to See and Do

1. **Cabrillo Marine Museum.** 3720 Stephen White Dr. Extensive marine life displayed in 34 seawater aquaria; interpretive displays, environmental conservation, multimedia shows, "Touch Tank." (Daily exc Mon; closed Thanksgiving, Dec 25) Seasonal grunion programs, whale-watching, tidepool tours. Access to beaches, picnic areas, fishing pier, launching ramp (beach parking fee). Phone 548-7562. **Free.**

2. **Ports o' Call Village.** E at Berth 77. Area with many specialty shops and a number of restaurants, all with waterfront dining.

3. **Los Angeles Maritime Museum.** Berth 84, foot of 6th St at Los Angeles Harbor. Features scale models of ships, numerous displays and artifacts from sailing vessels of all types. Models include the *Titanic* and movie studio models from the films *The Poseidon Adventure* and *Mutiny on the Bounty*. (Daily exc Mon; closed hols) Donation. Phone 548-7618.

(For further information contact the Chamber of Commerce, 390 W 7th St, 90731; 832-7272.)

(See Los Angeles)

Motel

✔ ★ ★**BEST WESTERN SUNRISE.** 525 S Harbor Blvd (90731). 310/548-1080; FAX 310/519-0380. 112 rms, 3 story. S, D $58–$72; each addl $8; suites $99; under 12 free. Crib free. TV; cable. Heated pool; whirlpool. Complimentary continental bkfst. Ck-out noon. Meeting rms.

Bellhops. Valet serv. Some bathrm phones, refrigerators, wet bars. Near cruise terminal; harbor view. Cr cds: A, C, D, DS, MC, V, JCB.

Hotels

★★**DOUBLETREE.** *2800 Via Cabrillo Marina (90731).* 310/514-3344; FAX 310/514-8945. 226 rms, 3 story. S $79–$109; D $89–$119; each addl $10; suites $195–$325; under 16 free; wkend rates. Crib free. TV; cable. Heated pool. Complimentary continental bkfst. Restaurant 6 am–11 pm. Bar 4 pm–1 am; entertainment Fri, Sat. Ck-out 1 pm. Meeting rms. Concierge. Gift shop. Barber, beauty shop. Lighted tennis. Exercise equipt; weight machine, bicycles, whirlpool, sauna. Refrigerators avail. On marina. Cr cds: A, C, D, DS, ER, MC, V, JCB.

★★★**SHERATON LOS ANGELES HARBOR.** *601 S Palos Verdes St (90731).* 310/519-8200; FAX 310/519-8421. 244 rms, 10 story, 54 suites. S, D $95–$119; each addl $10; suites $135–$695; under 14 free. Crib free. Pet accepted, some restrictions. TV. Heated pool. Restaurant 6 am–10:30 pm. Rm serv 24 hrs. Bar; entertainment. Ck-out noon. Meeting rms. Gift shop. Airport transporation. Exercise equipt; weights, bicycles, whirlpool, sauna. Minibars. *LUXURY LEVEL.* 28 rms, 2 suites. S, D $119; suites $135–$695; Concierge. Private lounge, honor bar. TV; cable, in-rm movies. Complimentary continental bkfst, refreshments.
Cr cds: A, C, D, DS, MC, V, JCB.

Inn

★★**GRAND COTTAGES.** *815-829 S Grand Ave (90731).* 310/548-1240. 4 cottages. S $75; D $90; up to 3 persons, $105. TV; cable, in-rm movies. Complimentary continental bkfst, tea/champagne, refreshments. Complimentary coffee in rms. Ck-out noon, ck-in 4 pm. Meeting rms. Many fireplaces. Antiques. Totally nonsmoking. Cr cds: A, D, MC, V.

Restaurant

★★**NIZETICH'S.** *1050 Nagoya Way, Berth 80.* 310/514-3878. Hrs: 11:30 am–2:30 pm, 5:30–10 pm; Fri & Sat 5:30–11 pm; Sun 5–10 pm. Closed Dec 25. Res accepted. Bar. Semi-a la carte: lunch $4.75–$13.95, dinner $13.95–$22.50. Chef specials daily. Parking. Outdoor dining. Elegant dining with view of harbor. Jacket. Cr cds: A, MC, V.

D

Unrated Dining Spot

BABOUCH. *810 S Gaffey.* 310/831-0246. Hrs: 5–10 pm. Closed Mon; July 4, Thanksgiving, Dec 25. Res accepted. Moroccan menu. Complete meals: dinner $20 (includes show). Child's meals. Specialties: bastilla, lamb with honey and roasted almonds, cous-cous, chicken with lemon. Moroccan-style dining with no silverware in exotic, tent-like atmosphere; velvet couches, low brass tables, tapestries. Cr cds: A, MC, V.

San Rafael (E-1)

Founded: 1817 **Pop:** 48,404 **Elev:** 34 ft **Area code:** 415

Built around an early Spanish mission, San Rafael is one of several residential communities across the Golden Gate Bridge, north of San Francisco. It is the commercial, cultural and governmental hub of scenic Marin County.

What to See and Do

1. **Mission San Rafael Arcángel.** 1104 5th Ave at A St, 3 blks W of US 101. The 20th in a chain of California missions; built in 1817 and rebuilt in 1949. Chapel (daily). Gift shop. Phone 456-3016. **Free.**

2. **Marin County Civic Center.** 2 mi N on N San Pedro Rd off US 101. Complex designed by Frank Lloyd Wright; one of his last major projects. (Mon–Fri; closed hols) Tours (res required). Phone 499-6104. **Free.**

(For further information contact the Chamber of Commerce, 817 Mission Ave, 94901; 454-4163.)

(See San Francisco)

Motel

✔★★**FRIENDSHIP INN VILLA INN.** *1600 Lincoln Ave (94901).* 415/456-4975; res: 800/424-4777. 60 rms, 2 story, 9 kits. S $62.50–$65.50; D $67.50–$74.50; kit. units $5 addl (3-day min); suite $112; under 12 free. Crib free. TV; cable. Indoor pool; whirlpool. Restaurant 7 am–2 pm, 5–10 pm; Sun to 2 pm. Rm serv. Bar 11 am–11 pm. Ck-out noon. Coin lndry. Valet serv. Refrigerators. Cr cds: A, C, D, DS, MC, V.

Motor Hotels

★★★**HOLIDAY INN MARIN.** *1010 Northgate Dr (94903),* off US 101 at Freitas Pkwy exit. 415/479-8800; FAX 415/479-8800, ext 528. 204 rms, 4 story. S $79–$97; D $89–$97; each addl $10; suites $200–$300; under 16 free; wkend rates. Crib free. Pet accepted, some restrictions. TV; cable, in-rm movies avail. Heated pool; poolside serv. Restaurant 6:30 am–2:30 pm, 5:30–10 pm. Rm serv. Bar 4:30 pm–2 am; entertainment, dancing Tues–Sat. Ck-out noon. Meeting rms. Bellhops. Valet serv. Concierge. Gift shop. Barber, beauty shop. Airport transportation. Exercise equipt; weights, bicycles, whirlpool. Some refrigerators. *LUXURY LEVEL:* **EXECUTIVE REGISTRY.** 29 rms. S $110; D $122. Private lounge. Wet bar. Complimentary continental bkfst, refreshments. Cr cds: A, C, D, DS, MC, V, JCB.

✔★**QUALITY INN-MARIN.** *(215 Alameda del Prado, Novato 94949)* 2 mi N on US 101. 415/883-4400. 104 rms, 3 story. S $64–$129; D $68–$129; each addl $5; under 16 free. Crib free. TV; cable, in-rm movies avail. Pool; hot tub. Complimentary continental bkfst. Restaurant nearby. Ck-out noon. Meeting rms. Valet serv. Barber, beauty shop. Airport transportation. Some refrigerators. Balconies. Cr cds: A, C, D, DS, ER, MC, V, JCB.

Restaurants

✔★★**ADRIANA'S.** *999 Andersen Dr, off US 101, Francisco Blvd exit.* 415/454-8000. Hrs: 11:30 am–2:30 pm, 5–9:30 pm; early-bird dinner 5–6 pm. Closed major hols. Res accepted. Italian menu. Wine, beer. Semi-a la carte: lunch $9–$13, dinner $9.50–$13.95. Child's meals. Specialties: linguine tutto mare, caciucco (bouillabaise), grilled seafood. Own pasta. Parking. Outdoor dining. Totally nonsmoking. Cr cds: A, D, MC, V, JCB.

D

★★**LA PETITE AUBERGE.** *704 4th St.* 415/456-5808. Hrs: 5–10 pm; Fri-Sun 11 am–2 pm, 5–10 pm; early-bird dinner 5–6 pm. Closed Mon; Dec 25. French, continental menu. Bar. Semi-a la carte: lunch $8–$12.50. A la carte entrees: dinner $11.95–$20. Specialties:

frogs' legs, beef Wellington, rack of lamb, souflé Grand Marnier. Outdoor dining. Cr cds: A, C, D, MC, V.

San Simeon (G-2)

Pop: 250 (est) **Elev:** 20 ft **Area code:** 805 **Zip:** 93452

San Simeon is a historical old whaling village. About 100 years ago, death-defying forays took place off these rocky shores when whales were spotted. Sea lion, sea otter and whale-watching is popular during northward migration in March, April and May; and also during December and January, when southward migration occurs. Deep-sea fishing is especially popular all year.

What to See and Do

Hearst-San Simeon State Historical Monument (see).

(For further information contact the Chamber of Commerce, PO Box 1; 927-3500.)

(See Cambria, Morro Bay, Paso Robles)

Motels

★ ★ ★**BEST WESTERN CAVALIER INN.** *9415 Hearst Dr.* 805/927-4688; FAX 805/927-0497. 90 rms, 2 story. No A/C. S, D $69–$121; each addl $6. Crib free. TV; cable, in-rm movies. 2 heated pools. Restaurant 7 am–10 pm; summer to 11 pm. Rm serv. Serv bar. Ck-out noon. Coin Indry. Meeting rms. Shopping arcade. Exercise equipt; bicycles, rowing machine, whirlpool. Refrigerators, minibars; many wet bars, fireplaces. Many private patios, balconies. On ocean. Cr cds: A, C, D, DS, ER, MC, V, JCB.

★ ★**BEST WESTERN GREEN TREE INN.** *9450 Castillo Dr.* 805/927-4691; FAX 805/927-1473. 117 rms, 2 story. Mid-June–Sept: S, D $80–$110; each addl $10; family units $90–$110; suites $175–$210; lower rates rest of yr. Crib free. TV; cable. Indoor pool; whirlpool. Continental bkfst 7–10 am. Restaurant adj 7 am–9 pm. Ck-out noon. Coin Indry. Meeting rm. Lighted tennis. Game rm. Rec rm. Cr cds: A, C, D, DS, ER, MC, V, JCB.

D ⊘ ≈ ⊗ ⊙ **SC**

★ ★**SAN SIMEON PINES RESORT.** *(Box 117) 7200 Moonstone Beach Dr.* 805/927-4648. 60 rms, 1–2 story. No A/C. S, D $68–$94. TV; cable. Pool. Complimentary coffee. Restaurant nearby. Ck-out 11 am. Meeting rm. 9-hole par 3 golf course. Hiking. Lawn games. Many fireplaces. Some patios. 8 wooded acres on ocean. Cr cds: A, MC, V.

D ⊸ ⊸ ⚲ ≈ ⚘ ⊗ ⊙

Santa Ana (J-4)

Pop: 293,742 **Elev:** 110 ft **Area code:** 714

What to See and Do

1. **The Bowers Museum of Cultural Art.** 2002 N Main St. Over 80,000 objects in its collection, which focuses on the artworks of pre-Columbian, Oceanic, Native American, African and Pacific Rim cultures. (Daily exc Mon; closed Jan 1, Thanksgiving, Dec 25) Phone 567-3600. ¢¢

2. **Santa Ana Zoo at Prentice Park.** 1801 E Chestnut, I-5 to 1st St exit. Playgrounds, picnic area; zoo. (Daily; closed Jan 1, Dec 25) Phone 836-4000. ¢

(For further information contact the Chamber of Commerce, PO Box 205, 92702; 541-5353.)

(See Anaheim, Irvine, Long Beach, Newport Beach, Orange)

Motor Hotels

✔ ★ ★**COMFORT SUITES.** *2620 Hotel Terrace Dr (92705).* 714/966-5200; FAX 714/979-9650. 130 suites, 3 story. S $59; D $69; each addl $10; under 18 free; wkly rates. Crib free. TV; cable. Heated pool; whirlpool. Continental bkfst. Ck-out noon. Coin Indry. Meeting rms. Bellhops. Valet serv. Free airport transportation. Health club privileges. Refrigerators, minibars. Cr cds: A, C, D, DS, MC, V, JCB.

D ≈ ⊗ ⊙ **SC**

★ ★**QUALITY SUITES.** *2701 Hotel Terrace Dr (92705).* 714/957-9200; FAX 714/641-8963. 177 suites, 3 story. S $85; D $95; each addl $10; under 18 free; wkend rates. Crib free. TV; cable, in-rm movies. Heated pool; whirlpool. Complimentary full bkfst. Ck-out noon. Bellhops. Valet serv. Gift shop. Free airport, RR station, bus depot transportation. Health club privileges. Minibars. Private patios, balconies. Cr cds: A, C, D, DS, ER, MC, V, JCB.

D ≈ ⊗ ⊙ **SC**

★ ★ ★**RAMADA GRAND.** *2726 S Grand Ave (92705).* 714/966-1955; FAX 714/966-1889. 183 rms, 3 story. S $69–$89; D $79–$99; each addl $6; under 18 free. Crib free. TV; cable. Heated pool; poolside serv. Complimentary full bkfst. Restaurant 6:30 am–11 pm; wkends 7:30 am–10 pm. Rm serv. Bar 5–10:30 pm. Ck-out noon. Coin Indry. Meeting rms. Valet serv. Free local airport transportation. Exercise equipt; weights, bicycles, whirlpool. Many refrigerators. Some private patios. Cr cds: A, C, D, DS, ER, MC, V, JCB.

D ≈ ⚲ ⊗ ⊙ **SC**

Hotels

★ ★ ★**CROWN STERLING SUITES.** *1325 E Dyer Rd (92705).* 714/241-3800. 308 suites, 10 story. S, D $129; each addl $10; under 13 free; wkend rates. Crib free. TV; cable. Pool; whirlpool, sauna. Complimentary full bkfst. Restaurant 11 am–11 pm. Bar to 1 am; entertainment. Ck-out 1 pm. Meeting rms. Gift shop. Free local airport transportation. Refrigerators. Balconies. Cr cds: A, C, D, DS, MC, V.

D ≈ ⊗ ⊙ **SC**

★ ★**DOUBLETREE CLUB.** *7 Hutton Centre Dr (92707), near John Wayne Airport.* 714/751-2400; FAX 714/662-7935. 170 rms, 6 story. S $79–$109; D $89–$119; each addl $10; suites $150–$200; under 12 free; wkend rates. Crib free. TV; cable. Heated pool. Complimentary continental bkfst. Restaurant 6–9 am, 5–10 pm; Sat & Sun 7–10 am, 5–10 pm. Bar 5 pm–midnight. Ck-out 1 pm. Meeting rms. Free airport transportation. Exercise equipt; weights, bicycles, whirlpool. Refrigerators. Cr cds: A, C, D, DS, ER, MC, V, JCB.

D ≈ ⚲ ✕ ⊗ ⊙ **SC**

Restaurants

★ ★ ★**ANTONELLO.** *3800 S Plaza Dr, in South Coast Plaza Village.* 714/751-7153. Hrs: 11:30 am–2 pm, 5:45–10 pm; Fri to 11 pm; Sat 5:45–11 pm. Closed Sun; major hols. Res accepted. Northern Italian menu. Bar. Wine list. A la carte entrees: lunch $6.75–$13.50, dinner $15.25–$35. Specializes in seafood, veal, pasta. Own baking, pasta. Valet parking. Jacket. Cr cds: A, D, MC, V.

★ ★ ★**GUSTAF ANDERS.** *In South Coast Plaza Village, opp South Coast Plaza on the Bear St side.* 714/668-1737. Hrs: 11:30 am–2 pm, 5:30–10 pm; Fri & Sat to midnight; Sun 5:30–10 pm. Closed Memorial Day, July 4, Labor Day. Res accepted. Swedish, continental menu.

Bar. Wine list. A la carte entrees: lunch $10–$20, dinner $20–$40. Child's meals. Specialties: gravad lax, parsley salad with sun-dried tomatoes, filet of beef with Stilton/red wine sauce. Understated elegance. Outdoor dining. Totally nonsmoking. Cr cds: A, C, D, MC, V.

Santa Barbara (H-3)

Founded: 1769 **Pop:** 85,571 **Elev:** 37–850 ft **Area code:** 805

Spanish charm hangs over this city, with its colorful street names, Spanish and Moorish-style architecture, adobe buildings and beautiful houses and gardens on the slopes of the Santa Ynez Mountains. It faces east and west on the Pacific Ocean along the calmest stretch of the California coast. Although the Spanish explorer Vizcaino entered the channel on Saint Barbara's Day, December 4, 1602, and named the region after the saint, a Portuguese navigator, Juan Rodriguez Cabrillo is credited with the discovery of the channel in 1542. Its large harbor and breakwater can accommodate many boats and offers boat rentals and excursions. A Ranger District office of the Los Padres National Forest (see #12) is located in Santa Barbara.

What to See and Do

1. **Mission Santa Barbara.** E Los Olivos & Upper Laguna Sts, 2 mi N. Founded in 1786, the present church was completed in 1820. Known as "Queen of the Missions" because of its architectural beauty, the 10th California mission stands on a slight elevation and at one time served as a beacon for sailing ships. Its twin-towered church and monastery represent the earliest phase of Spanish Renaissance architecture. Self-guided tours. Display rooms exhibit mission building arts, mission crafts and examples of Indian and Mexican art. (Daily; closed some hols) Phone 682-4713. ¢

2. **Santa Barbara County Courthouse.** 1100 Anacapa St. Resembles a Spanish-Moorish palace. Considered one of the most beautiful buildings in the West. (Daily; closed Dec 25) Guided tours (Mon–Sat, afternoon; Wed & Fri, also mid-morning). Phone 962-6464. **Free.**

3. **Santa Barbara Museum of Natural History.** 2559 Puesta del Sol Rd, beyond mission. Exhibits of fauna, flora, geology and prehistoric life of the Pacific coast; lectures, shows, planetarium. (Daily; closed Jan 1, Thanksgiving, Dec 25) Sr citizen rate. Phone 682-4711. ¢¢

4. **Santa Barbara Historical Museum.** 136 E de la Guerra St. Documents, paintings, costumes and artifacts from three cultures: Spanish, Mexican and American. Large, gilded Chinese *Tong* shrine. Library. (Daily exc Mon; closed some hols) Phone 966-1601. **Free.**

5. **Santa Barbara Museum of Art.** 1130 State St. Collections of ancient and Asian art; 19th-century French art; American and European paintings and sculpture; 20th-century art; photography collection; changing exhibits; lectures; guided tours. (Daily exc Mon; closed most hols) Phone 963-4364. ¢¢

6. **El Paseo.** Opp City Hall, De la Guerra St between State & Anacapa Sts. Courtyards and passageways similiar to old Spain. Shops, art galleries, restaurants.

7. **El Presidio de Santa Barbara State Historic Park.** 123-129 E Cañon Perdido. Original and reconstructed buildings of the last presidio (military & government outpost) built by Spain in the New World. Museum displays, slide show. (Daily; closed some hols) Phone 965-0093. **Free.**

8. **Santa Barbara Botanic Garden.** 1212 Mission Canyon Rd, 1¼ mi N of mission. Native trees, shrubs and wild flowers of California on 65 acres; Old Mission Dam (1806). Guided tours. (Daily) Phone 682-4726. ¢¢

9. **Moreton Bay fig tree.** Chapala & Montecito Sts. Believed to be largest of its kind in the US. Planted in 1877, it is considered possible for the tree to attain a branch spread of 160 feet. A Santa Barbara city engineer estimated that 10,450 persons could stand in its shade at noon.

10. **Santa Barbara Zoo.** 500 Niños Dr, just off US 101. Zoo with walk-through aviary, monkeys, big cats, elephants and other exhibits; miniature railroad (fee); snack bar; picnic, barbecue sites. (Daily; closed Thanksgiving, Dec 25) Sr citizen rate. Phone 962-6310 or -5339. ¢¢

11. **University of California, Santa Barbara** (1944). (18,500 students) Approx 10 mi N on US 101, in Goleta. An 815-acre seaside campus. For tours phone 893-2485. For current performing arts activities on campus phone 893-3535. On campus is

    Art Museum. Arts Building. Sedgwick collection of Old Master and Baroque period paintings, Morgenroth collection of Renaissance medals and plaques; Dreyfus collection of Mid-Eastern and pre-Columbian artifacts; changing exhibits. (Daily exc Mon) **Free.**

12. **Los Padres National Forest.** N of town. Forest of 1,724,000 acres encompassing the La Panza, Santa Ynez, San Rafael, Santa Lucia and Sierra Madre Mountains. The vegetation ranges from chaparral to oak woodlands to coniferous forests, which include the Santa Lucia fir, the rarest and one of the most unusual firs in North America. Also contains the mountainous 149,000-acre San Rafael Wilderness, the 64,700-acre Dick Smith Wilderness and the 21,250-acre Santa Lucia Wilderness. (Legislation signed in 1992 added 400,000 acres of the forest to the wilderness acreage.) There is also the Sespe Condor Refuge. Fishing for trout in 485 miles of streams; hunting. Hiking and riding on 1,750 miles of trails. Camping. Contact the District Ranger Office, Star Route, Los Prietos 93105, phone 967-3481; or the Forest Supervisor 6144 Calle Real, Goleta 93117, phone 683-6711. (See KING CITY)

13. **Stearn's Wharf.** 3 block extension of State St. Oldest operating wharf on the West Coast. Restaurants, shops, sport fishing pier, beautiful view of harbor and city. Wharf open 24 hours.

14. **Island & Coastal Fishing Trips.** Scuba diving trips; whale-watching in season. For further information phone 963-3564. ¢¢¢¢–¢¢¢¢¢

15. **Carpinteria State Beach.** 12 mi SE on US 101. Swimming, lifeguard (summer), fishing. Picnicking. Camping (some hookups, dump station). Standard fees. Phone 684-2811.

(For further information contact the Conference & Visitors Bureau, 510-A State St, 93101; 966-9222 or 800/927-4688.)

Annual Events

Santa Barbara International Orchid Show. Earl Warren Showgrounds, US 101 & Las Positas Rd. Late Mar.

Summer Sports Festival (Semana Nautica). More than 50 land and water sports. Late June–early July.

Santa Barbara National Horse Show. Earl Warren Showgrounds. Mid-July.

Old Spanish Days Fiesta. City-wide. Recreates city's history from Indian days to arrival of American troops. 5 days early Aug.

(See Ojai, Solvang, Ventura)

Motels

★**AMBASSADOR BY THE SEA.** *202 W Cabrillo Blvd (93101).* 805/965-4577; FAX 805/965-9937. 32 rms, 2 story, 2 kits. No A/C. May–Sept: S, D $88–$168; each addl $10; kit. units $20 addl; lower rates rest of yr. TV. Heated pool. Complimentary continental bkfst. Restaurant nearby. Ck-out noon. Sun decks. Large fountain patio. Beach opp. Cr cds: A, C, D, DS, ER, MC, V.

★★**BEST WESTERN PEPPER TREE INN.** *3850 State St (93105).* 805/687-5511; FAX 805/682-2410. 150 rms, 1–2 story. S $90–$110; D $96–$116; suites $116–$126; each addl $6. Crib free. TV; cable, in-rm movies. 2 heated pools. Complimentary coffee in rms.

Restaurant 6 am–11 pm. Rm serv. Bar 10–2 am. Ck-out noon. Coin Indry. Meeting rms. Concierge. Sundries. Gift shop. Barber, beauty shop. Free airport transportation. Exercise equipt; weight machines, bicycles, whirlpools, sauna, steam rm. Refrigerators. Private patios, balconies. Cr cds: A, C, D, DS, ER, MC, V, JCB.

★ ★CASA DEL MAR. *18 Bath St (93101). 805/963-4418; res: 800/433-3097; FAX 805/966-4240.* 20 rms, 2 story, some kits. June–Sept: S, D $65–$115; each addl $10; suites $105–$155; under 13 free; wkly, monthly off-season rates; lower rates rest of yr. Pet accepted, some restrictions; $10 per day. TV; cable. Complimentary continental bkfst, coffee. Ck-out noon. Whirlpool. Many fireplaces. Near ocean. Cr cds: A, D, MC, V.

★ ★CATHEDRAL OAKS LODGE. *4770 Calle Real (93110), at US 101 exit Turnpike Rd. 805/964-3511; res: 800/654-1965; FAX 805/964-0075.* 126 rms, 2 story. S $74–$98; D $84–$98; each addl $10; suites $110–$150; under 12 free. Crib free. TV; cable, in-rm movies. Heated pool; whirlpool. Complimentary continental bkfst. Coffee in rms. Restaurant 6 am–10 pm. Ck-out noon. Coin Indry. Meeting rms. Valet serv. Airport transportation. Refrigerators avail. Private patios, balconies. Cr cds: A, C, D, MC, V.

★ ★COAST VILLAGE INN. *1188 Coast Village Rd (93108). 805/969-3266; res: 800/257-5131.* 25 rms, 1–2 story, 2 kits. No A/C. Mid-May–mid-Sept: S, D $70–$85; each addl $5; suites, kit. units $75–$95; higher rates hols, wkends; lower rates rest of yr. TV; cable. Heated pool. Complimentary continental bkfst. Ck-out 11 am. Totally nonsmoking. Cr cds: A, MC, V.

★ ★FRANCISCAN INN. *109 Bath St (93101). 805/963-8845; FAX 805/564-3295.* 53 rms, 2 story, 25 kit. suites. Mid-May–mid-Sept: S, D $65–$155; each addl $8; kit. suites $85–$155; monthly, wkly rates; lower rates rest of yr. Crib free. TV; cable, in-rm movies avail. Heated pool; whirlpool. Complimentary continental bkfst. Restaurant nearby. Ck-out noon. Coin Indry. Valet serv. Many refrigerators. Balconies. Beach, marina 1 blk. Cr cds: A, D, ER, MC, V.

★ ★MARINA BEACH. *21 Bath St (93101). 805/963-9311.* 31 rms, 18 kits. No A/C. Mid-May–mid-Sept: S $45–$120; D $55–$140; each addl $5; suites $65–$200; lower rates rest of yr. Crib $5. TV; cable. Complimentary continental bkfst. Complimentary coffee in rms. Restaurant nearby. Ck-out noon. Beach ½ blk. Cr cds: A, C, D, DS, MC, V.

★ ★QUALITY SUITES. *5490 Hollister Ave (93111), near Municipal Airport. 805/683-6722; FAX 805/683-4121.* 75 rms, 2 story. July–Sept: S, D $120–$180; each addl $10; under 18 free; lower rates rest of yr. Crib free. Pet accepted, some restrictions; $10. TV; cable, in-rm movies. Heated pool; whirlpool. Complimentary full bkfst. Complimentary coffee in rms. Ck-out noon. Meeting rms. Bellhops. Valet serv. Sundries. Gift shop. Free airport transportation. Tennis privileges. 18-hole golf privileges. Health club privileges. Bicycles (rentals). Refrigerators, wet bars. Balconies. Cr cds: A, C, D, DS, ER, MC, V, JCB.

★ ★TRAVELODGE SANTA BARBARA BEACH. *22 Castillo St (93101). 805/965-8527; FAX 805/965-6125.* 19 rms, 1–2 story. May–mid-Sept: S $70–$120; D $80–$120; each addl $10; under 17 free; higher rates: special events, wkends; lower rates rest of yr. Crib free. TV; cable. Complimentary coffee in rms. Restaurant nearby. Ck-out 11 am. Some private patios. Park opp; beach ½ blk. Cr cds: A, C, D, DS, ER, MC, V.

Lodge

★ ★ ★EL ENCANTO HOTEL & GARDEN VILLAS. *1900 Lasuen Rd (93103). 805/687-5000; res: 800/346-7039 (CA); FAX 805/687-3903.* 84 cottages. Some A/C. S, D $120–$280; cottage suites $180–$380. Crib free. TV; cable. Heated pool. Coffee in rms. Restaurant 7 am–9:30 pm. Rm serv 7 am–9 pm. Bar 11 am–midnight; entertainment. Ck-out noon. Meeting rm. Bellhops. Concierge. Free valet parking. Free airport, RR station transportation. Tennis, pro. Golf privileges. Minibars. Some fireplaces. Private patios, balconies. Formal gardens. Ocean view. Cr cds: A, D, MC, V.

Motor Hotels

★ ★ ★RADISSON HOTEL SANTA BARBARA (formerly Sheraton). *1111 E Cabrillo Blvd (93103). 805/963-0744; FAX 805/962-0985.* 174 rms, 3 story. July–early Oct: S, D $139–$210; each addl $15; suites $250–$610; under 17 free; higher rates hols; lower rates rest of yr. Crib free. TV; cable. Heated pool; poolside serv. Restaurants 6:30 am–10:30 pm. Bar 11–1 am; entertainment Fri & Sat. Ck-out noon. Meeting rms. Bellhops. Valet serv. Concierge. Gift shop. Free covered parking. Golf privileges. Exercise equipt; weight machines, bicycles, whirlpool. Minibars; some refrigerators. Balconies. Ocean opp. Cr cds: A, C, D, DS, MC, V, JCB.

★ ★ ★SANTA BARBARA INN. *901 E Cabrillo Blvd (93103). 805/966-2285; res 800/231-0431; FAX 805/966-6584.* 71 rms, 4 story. No A/C. Apr–Oct: S, D $99–$189; each addl $15; kit. units $10 addl; suites $200–$395; lower rates rest of yr. Crib free. TV; cable. Heated pool; whirlpool, poolside serv. Coffee in rms. Restaurant 7 am–10 pm. Rm serv. Bar 11 am–11 pm. Ck-out noon. Meeting rms. Bellhops. Valet serv. Free valet parking. Tennis privileges. Golf privileges. Health club privileges. Bathrm phones, refrigerators; many wet bars. Balconies. Adj to beach, ocean. Cr cds: A, C, D, DS, MC, V.

Hotels

★ ★ ★FESS PARKER'S RED LION RESORT. *633 E Cabrillo Blvd (93103). 805/564-4333; FAX 805/962-8198.* 360 rms, 3 story. S, D $185–$285; each addl $15; suites $345–$680; under 18 free; package plans. Pet accepted, some restrictions. TV; cable. Heated pool; poolside serv. Restaurants 6:30 am–11 pm. Bar 5 pm–1 am; entertainment, dancing. Ck-out noon. Coin Indry. Convention facilities. Valet serv. Concierge. Barber, beauty shop. Valet parking. Free airport transportation. Lighted tennis, pro. Golf privileges, greens fee $30–$60, pro, putting green. Exercise equipt; weight machines, stair machine, sauna. Game rm. Lawn games. Minibars. Private patios, balconies. Atrium lobby. On 24 acres; ocean opp. Cr cds: A, C, D, DS, MC, V.

★ ★ ★ ★FOUR SEASONS BILTMORE. *1260 Channel Dr (93108). 805/969-2261; FAX 805/969-4212.* 234 rms, 2 story, 18 suites. No A/C. S, D $190–$395; suites from $450; under 18 free. Crib free. Pet accepted. Valet parking (fee). TV; cable, in-rm movies. 2 pools, heated; poolside serv. Restaurant 6:30 am–11 pm (also see LA MARINA). Rm serv 24 hrs. Bar 11:30–1 am; entertainment, dancing. Ck-out noon. Meeting rms. Concierge. Gift shop. Drugstore. Beauty shop. Lighted tennis, pro. Golf privileges, putting green. Exercise rm; instructor, bicycles, treadmill, whirlpool, steam rm. Masseuse. Complete health club. Opp beach; cabanas. Bicycles. Lawn games. Bathrm phones, minibars; many fireplaces. Many private patios, balconies. On 21 acres. View of ocean, mountains, gardens. Cr cds: A, C, D, DS, ER, MC, V, JCB.

★ ★ ★MONTECITO INN. *1295 Coast Village Rd (93108). 805/969-7854; res: 800/843-2017; FAX 805/969-0623.* 52 rms. No A/C. S, D $130–$175; suites $185–$245; 2-night min wkends, hols. Crib $10. TV;

cable, in-rm movies. Heated pool. Complimentary continental bkfst 7–10 am. Restaurant 11:30 am–2:30 pm, 5:30–10 pm. Ck-out noon. Meeting rm. Free valet parking. Exercise equipt; weights, treadmill, sauna. Bicycles. Refrigerators avail. Established in 1928 by Charlie Chaplin & Fatty Arbuckle; inspiration for Richard Rodgers' "There's a Small Hotel." Beach 3 blks. Free sightseeing trolley passes. Cr cds: A, C, D, DS, ER, MC, V.

Inns

★ ★ ★ **CHESHIRE CAT.** *36 W Valerio (93101), off US 101 Mission exit. 805/569-1610; FAX 805/682-1876.* 14 rms, 2 story, 5 suites. S, D $119–$139; suites $169–$249; higher rates: wkends, hols. TV & in-rm movies in 2 rms. Complimentary full bkfst, tea, cognac. Restaurant nearby. Ck-out noon, ck-in 3–6 pm. Concierge. Whirlpool in gazebo. Some in-rm whirlpools. Lawn games. Bicycles. Picnic tables. Sitting rm; antiques. Built 1880s. *Alice in Wonderland* theme. Totally nonsmoking. Cr cds: MC, V.

★ ★ **GLENBOROUGH INN & COTTAGE.** *1327 Bath St (93101). 805/966-0589.* 11 rms in 3 houses, 5 with bath, 2 story. No A/C. Mid-May–mid-Sept: S, D $80–$110; each addl $25; suites $145–$170; lower mid-wk rates rest of yr. Children over 12 yrs only. Complimentary full bkfst in rms, coffee, refreshments. Ck-out 11 am, ck-in 3–6 pm. Hot tub. Some fireplaces. Turn-of-the-century home furnished with antiques; garden. Totally nonsmoking. Cr cds: A, C, D, DS, MC, V.

★ ★ ★ **INN ON SUMMER HILL.** *(PO Box 376, 93067; 2520 Lillie Ave, Summerland) S on US 101, left on Evans, right on Lillie Ave. 805/969-9998; res: 800/845-5566.* 16 rms, 2 story, 1 suite. S, D $160–$195; each addl $20; suite $225–$275. TV; cable, in-rm movies. Complimentary full bkfst. Complimentary coffee in rms. Restaurant nearby. Ck-out 11 am, ck-in 3 pm. Whirlpool. Bathrm phones, refrigerators, fireplaces, canopy beds. Balconies. New England-style inn with ocean view. Totally nonsmoking. Cr cds: A, MC, V.

★ ★ **THE OLD YACHT CLUB.** *431 Corona del Mar Dr (93103). 805/962-1277; res: 800/676-1676 (exc CA), 800/549-1676 (CA); FAX 805/962-3989.* 9 rms, 2 story. No A/C. D $85–$150; mid-wk rates in winter. Complimentary full bkfst, evening refreshments. Ck-out 11 am, ck-in 2 pm. Bicycles. Former headquarters of Santa Barbara Yacht Club (1912); antiques, Oriental rugs. Totally nonsmoking. Cr cds: A, D, DS, MC, V.

★ ★ ★ **SIMPSON HOUSE.** *121 E Arrellaga St (93101). 805/963-7067; res: 800/676-1280; FAX 805/564-4811.* 14 rms, 8 A/C, 1–2 story. May–mid-Oct: D $105–$160; each addl $25; suites $195–$205; cottages $200/$250; wkly rates; lower rates rest of yr. TV in some rms. Complimentary full bkfst, tea & wine. Ck-out 11 am, ck-in 3 pm. Lawn games. Sitting rm with fireplace. Balconies. Picnic tables. Historic landmark, built 1874; Eastlake-style Victorian house, original barn converted to guest rms. Gardens. Totally nonsmoking. Cr cds: A, DS, MC, V.

★ ★ **TIFFANY.** *1323 De la Vina St (93101). 805/963-2283.* 7 rms, 5 with bath, 3 story, 2 suites. No rm phones. S, D $105–$195; suite $195; mid-wk rates off-season. Complimentary full bkfst, refreshments. Ck-out 11 am, ck-in 3–7 pm. Whirlpool in suites. Restored Victorian house (1898); antique furnishings; many fireplaces; garden. Totally nonsmoking. Cr cds: A, MC, V.

★ ★ **UPHAM.** *1404 De la Vina St (93101). 805/962-0058; res: 800/727-0876; FAX 805/963-2825.* 49 rms, 2 story. No A/C. S, D $100–$170; each addl $10; suites $155–$325; under 12 free. Crib $10. TV; cable. Complimentary continental bkfst, wine. Dining rm 11:30 am–2 pm. Ck-out noon, ck-in 3 pm. Meeting rms. Valet serv. Whirl-

pool in master suite. Fireplace in cottages. Some private patios. Historic Victorian hotel established 1871. Period furnishings include antique armoires, beds. One-acre garden with roses, camellias. Cr cds: A, C, D, DS, MC, V.

★ ★ ★ **VILLA ROSA.** *15 Chapala St (93101). 805/966-0851; FAX 805/962-7159.* 18 rms, 2 story, 3 kits. July–Sept, wkends: S, D $90–$190; suite, kit. units $160–$190; mid-wk, winter rates; lower rates rest of yr. Children over 14 yrs only. TV avail; cable. Heated pool; whirlpool. Complimentary continental bkfst, refreshments. Ck-out noon, ck-in 3 pm. Some refrigerators, fireplaces. Balconies. Spanish architecture; southwestern decor. Near beach. Cr cds: A, MC, V.

Guest Ranch

★ ★ ★ **SAN YSIDRO RANCH.** *900 San Ysidro Lane (93108). 805/969-5046; res: 800/368-6788; FAX 805/565-1995.* 44 cottages units, 1 kit. 12 A/C. S, D $195–$350; suites $425–$695. Crib free. Pet accepted; $45 per stay. TV; cable, in-rm movies. Heated pool; wading pool, poolside serv. Playground. Coffee in rms. Dining rm 7 am–9:30 pm. Rm serv 24 hrs. Box lunches. Bar 5 pm–midnight, wkends from 1 pm; entertainment. Ck-out noon, ck-in 3 pm. Grocery 1 mi. Meeting rms. Bellhop. Gift shop. Tennis. Golf privileges. Driving range. Summer activities. Horses (fee), riding trails. Exercise rm; instructor (wkends), bicycles, stair machine. Lawn games. Refrigerators, fireplaces; some in-rm whirlpools. Some screened porches. 550 acres in mountains. Cr cds: A, MC, V.

Restaurants

★ ★ **ANDRIA'S HARBORSIDE.** *336 W Cabrillo Blvd. 805/966-3000.* Hrs: 6 am–midnight; wkends to 1 am. Res accepted. Continental menu. Bar. Wine list. Semi-a la carte: bkfst $3.95–$5.95, lunch $3.95–$8.95, dinner $7.95–$18.95. Specializes in mesquite charbroiled fresh seafood, steak, chicken, pasta. Own desserts. Entertainment. Parking. Oyster bar. Cr cds: A, DS, MC, V.

★ ★ **BRIGITTE'S.** *1325 State St. 805/966-9676.* Hrs: 11:30 am–2:30 pm, 5–10 pm; Fri & Sat to 11 pm; Sun 5–10 pm. Closed some major hols. Bar. A la carte entrees: lunch, dinner $5.50–$11.50. Specialties: angel hair with bay scallops and goat cheese-walnut pesto, gourmet pizza, fresh fish. California-style bistro; bakery/deli. Cr cds: MC, V.

★ ★ ★ **DOWNEY'S.** *1305 State St. 805/966-5006.* Hrs: 11:30 am–1:45 pm, 5:30–9 pm; Fri & Sat to 9:30 pm; Sun 5:30–9 pm. Closed Mon; some major hols. Res accepted. Wine. A la carte entrees: lunch $8.75–$10.50, dinner $17.95–$22.95. Specialties: grilled lamb loin, abalone with citrus sauce, local swordfish with fresh papaya vinaigrette. Jazz Fri evenings. Contemporary decor. Cr cds: A, MC, V.

★ ★ ★ **LA MARINA.** *(See Four Seasons Biltmore Hotel) 805/969-2261.* Hrs: 6–10 pm; Sun brunch 10 am–2 pm. Res accepted. No A/C. Bar 11:30–1 am. Wine cellar. A la carte entrees: dinner $14–$30. *Prix fixe:* dinner $37.50. Sun brunch $35. Specialties: roast Maine lobster, Santa Barbara bouillabaisse, rack of meadow lamb. Menu changes wkly. Own baking. Valet parking. Vaulted wood-beam ceilings. Ocean view. Braille menu. Cr cds: A, C, D, DS, ER, MC, V, JCB.

★ ★ ★ **MICHAEL'S WATERSIDE.** *50 Los Patos Way. 805/969-0307.* Hrs: 6–9 pm; Fri & Sat to 9:30 pm. Closed Sun; also 1 wk Jan. Res accepted. California, French menu. Bar. Wine cellar. Semi-a la carte: dinner $17.50–$28. Specialties: Gruyere cheese souffle, Channel Island abalone, carmelized apple tart. Own baking. Parking. Victorian cottage

(1872); country French decor. Overlooks bird refuge. Cr cds: A, C, D, MC, V.

D

★★**PALACE CAFE.** *8 E Cota St. 805/966-3133.* Hrs: 5:30–11 pm; Fri & Sat to midnight. Res accepted. Cajun, Caribbean menu. Serv bar. Semi-a la carte: dinner $11.75–$24. Child's meals. Specialties: crawfish etouffée, blackened redfish, Louisiana bread pudding soufflé. New Orleans Mardi Gras atmosphere with Carribbean flavor. Cr cds: A, MC, V.

D

✔★**PALAZZIO.** *1151 Coast Village Rd. 805/969-8565.* Hrs: 11:30 am–2 pm, 5:30–11 pm; Fri & Sat to midnight; Sun 11 am–5:30 pm. Closed Thanksgiving, Dec 25. Res accepted. Italian menu. Wine, beer. A la carte entrees: lunch, dinner $5.95–$10.95. Specialties: capellini shrimp, classic tiramisu, fusilli roasted eggplant. Parking. Outdoor dining. Totally nonsmoking. Cr cds: MC, V.

D

✔★**STATE A.** *1201 State St. 805/966-1010.* Hrs: 10 am–midnight. No A/C. Continental menu. Bar. Semi-a la carte: lunch $3.95–$6.45, dinner $5.45–$8.45. Specializes in hamburgers, international salads. Salad bar. Entertainment Wed–Sat. Outdoor dining. Cr cds: A, MC, V.

D

★★**STEAMERS.** *214 State St. 805/966-0260.* Hrs: 11:30 am–3 pm, 5–10 pm; Fri & Sat to 11 pm. Res accepted. Wine, beer. Semi-a la carte: lunch $4.95–$8.95, dinner $9.95–$19.95. Child's meals. Specializes in fresh fish, pasta, steak. Parking. Outdoor dining. Former fish processing plant. Cr cds: A, MC, V.

D

★★★**WINE CASK.** *813 Anacapa St. 805/966-9463.* Hrs: 11:30 am–2:30 pm, 5–10 pm; Sat & Sun from 5 pm. Closed some major hols. Res accepted. Beer. Wine cellar. A la carte entrees: lunch $4–$10.50, dinner $10.50–$18. Child's meals. Specializes in seafood, chicken, pasta, grilled meat. Seasonal menu. Extensive wine selection. Valet parking. Patio dining. Bistro atmosphere. Totally nonsmoking. Cr cds: A, MC, V.

Santa Clara (E-2)

Founded: 1777 **Pop:** 93,613 **Elev:** 88 ft **Area code:** 408

Santa Clara, the "Mission City," is in the heart of Silicon Valley, just 50 minutes south of San Francisco.

What to See and Do

1. **Triton Museum of Art.** 1505 Warburton Ave, opp Civic Center. Permanent and changing exhibits of 19th- and 20th-century American and contemporary works; sculpture garden; landscaped grounds on seven acres. (Daily; closed some hols) Phone 247-3754.   **Free.**

2. **Santa Clara University** (1851). (7,900 students) On both sides of The Alameda between Bellomy & Franklin Sts. Oldest institution of higher learning in California, founded in 1851. Self-guided tour of the Mission Gardens, which includes the Adobe Lodge and Wall (restored) from the 1822–25 mission. Olive trees and grinding stones in the gardens also date to the early mission period. Phone 554-4764. On campus are

   Mission Santa Clara de Asís (1777). The modern mission, dedicated in 1928, is an enlarged and adapted replica of the original mission. The present roof contains 12,000 cover tiles salvaged from earlier missions. Of the four mission bells in the tower, one was a gift from Carlos IV of Spain in 1798, and survived the 1926 fire; another was a gift from Alfonso XIII of Spain in 1929. Sur-

rounded by beautiful gardens and restored Adobe Lodge and Wall; part of the 1822 mission quadrangle. (Mon–Fri) Phone 554-4023.   **Free.**

   De Saisset Museum. Rotating exhibits (all-yr); California Historical Collection focuses on pre-contact Indian period, Mission period, and early years of the university. (Daily exc Mon) Phone 554-4528.   **Free.**

3. **Paramount's Great America.** Great America Pkwy, off I-101. On this 100-acre park is a blend of movie magic with theme park thrills. Features an array of thrilling rides, live stage shows and entertainment; Paramount's Great America's premier movie themed attraction, "Top Gun," is a mind boggling inverted roller coaster. Also featured are Star Trek, Addams Family and Conehead characters as well as Yogi Bear, Fred Flintstone, Scooby Doo, and others. Among a number of shows is "Paramount on Ice," highlighting the many movie and television productions of Paramount. Also spectacular is the IMAX theater, and the world's tallest double decker-carousel, Carousel Columbia, which is near the park's entrance. There is also Smurf Woods, just for small children. (Mid-Mar–Oct; inquire for schedule) Admission includes all rides and attractions. Phone 988-1800 (recording) or -1776.   ¢¢¢¢¢

(For further information contact the Convention & Visitors Bureau, 2200 Laurelwood Rd, 2nd fl, PO Box 387, 95052; 296-7111.)

Annual Event

Parade of Champions. 1st Sun Oct.

(See Fremont, Livermore, San Jose, Saratoga)

Motels

✔★★**BEST WESTERN INN SANTA CLARA.** *4341 El Camino Real (95051).* 408/244-3366. 52 rms, 1–2 story. S $49–$56; D $59–$65; each addl $4. Crib free. TV; cable, in-rm movies avail. Pool. Continental bkfst 7–10 am. Coffee in rms. Restaurant nearby. Ck-out noon. Refrigerators. Cr cds: A, C, D, DS, MC, V.

D ⚓ 🚫 ⏰ **SC**

★**ECONO LODGE SILICON VALLEY.** *2930 El Camino Real (95051).* 408/241-3010; FAX 408/247-0623. 70 units, 2 story, 17 kits. S $50–$80; D $53–$90; each addl $5; suites $70–$95; kit. units $70–$95; under 18 free. Crib $5. Pet accepted; $5. TV; cable, in-rm movies. Heated pool. Complimentary continental bkfst. Complimentary coffee in rms. Restaurant adj. Ck-out 11:30 am. Valet serv. Refrigerators. Some balconies. Cr cds: A, C, D, DS, MC, V, JCB.

🐾 ⚓ 🚫 ⏰ **SC**

★**HOWARD JOHNSON.** *5405 Stevens Creek Blvd (95051), at jct I-280 Lawrence Expy exit.* 408/257-8600; FAX 408/446-2936. 95 rms, 2 story. S $72–$90; D $78–$96; under 18 free. Crib free. Pet accepted, some restrictions. TV; cable. Heated pool; wading pool. Restaurant adj 6 am–10 pm. Ck-out noon. Coin lndry. Meeting rm. Valet serv. Balconies. Cr cds: A, C, D, DS, ER, MC, V, JCB.

D 🐾 ⚓ 🚫 ⏰ **SC**

★★**MARIANI'S INN.** *2500 El Camino Real (95051).* 408/243-1431; res: 800/553-8666; FAX 408/243-5745. 121 units, 1–2 story, 53 kits. S $60–$68; D $67–$75; each addl $8; kit. suites $71–$79; under 12 free. Crib free. TV; cable. Heated pool; sauna. Complimentary continental bkfst. Restaurant 6:30 am–11 pm. Rm serv. Bar from 11 am; entertainment, dancing Tues–Sat. Ck-out 11 am. Meeting rms. Valet serv. Sheltered barbecue area. Cr cds: A, C, D, DS, MC, V.

D ⚓ 🚫 ⏰ **SC**

✔★**VAGABOND INN.** *3580 El Camino Real (95051), at jct CA 82, Lawrence Expy.* 408/241-0771; FAX 408/247-3386. 70 rms, 2 story. S $45; D $55; each addl $5; under 19 free. Crib free. Pet accepted; $5. TV; cable. Heated pool. Complimentary continental bkfst, coffee, tea.

Restaurant nearby. Ck-out noon. Coin lndry. Meeting rm. Valet serv. Cr cds: A, C, D, DS, ER, MC, V.

Motor Hotel

★ ★ ★ **QUALITY SUITES.** *3100 Lakeside Dr (95054).* 408/748-9800; FAX 408/748-1476. 220 suites, 7 story. S, D $109–$149; each addl $10; under 16 free; wkly rates; lower rates wkends. Crib free. TV; cable, in-rm movies. Heated pool. Complimentary full bkfst. Complimentary coffee in rms. Restaurant nearby. Ck-out noon. Coin lndry. Meeting rms. Bellhops. Sundries. Gift shop. Free garage parking. Free airport, RR station, bus depot transportation. Minibars. Cr cds: A, D, DS, MC, V, JCB.

Hotels

★ ★ ★ **EMBASSY SUITES.** *2885 Lakeside Dr (95054), just off US 101, exit Bowers Ave/Great America.* 408/496-6400; FAX 408/988-7529. 257 suites, 10 story. S $159; D $175; each addl $15; under 12 free; wkend rates. Crib free. TV; cable. Indoor pool. Complimentary full bkfst. Restaurant 11 am–10 pm. Bar to 1:30 am. Ck-out 1 pm. Meeting rms. Gift shop. Exercise equipt; weights, bicycles, whirlpool, sauna. Free airport, RR station, Great America transportation. Refrigerators. Cr cds: A, C, D, DS, MC, V, JCB.

★ ★ **MARRIOTT.** *2700 Mission College Blvd (95054), 5 mi N, ½ mi E of US 101 at Great America Pkway exit.* 408/988-1500; FAX 408/727-4353. 754 rms, 14 story. S $69–$155; D $69–$165; suites $400; studio rms $145; under 18 free; wkend plans. Crib free. Pet accepted. TV; cable. Indoor/outdoor pool; poolside serv. Restaurants 6 am–11 pm. Rm serv to 1:30 am. Bar 11:30–2 am. Ck-out 11 am. Convention facilities. Gift shop. Free San Jose airport transportation. Lighted tennis. Exercise equipt; weight machines, bicycles, whirlpool. Game rm. Rec rm. Some refrigerators; bathrm phone in suites. Some private patios, balconies. *LUXURY LEVEL:* CONCIERGE LEVEL. 66 rms, 4 floors. S $165; D $180. Private lounge, honor bar. Complimentary continental bkfst, refreshments.
Cr cds: A, C, D, DS, ER, MC, V, JCB.

★ ★ ★ **WOODCREST.** *5415 Stevens Creek Blvd (95051), at I-280.* 408/446-9636; res: 800/862-8282; FAX 408/446-9739. 60 rms, 4 story. MAP: S $114; D $129; each addl $15; suites $124–$225; under 12 free; wkend rates. Crib free. TV; cable, in-rm movies. Complimentary bkfst buffet 6:30–10 am. Bar 5:30–10:30 pm. Ck-out noon. Meeting rms. Covered parking. Health club privileges. Bathrm phones; some fireplaces; refrigerator, wet bar in suites. Resembles French country estate with courtyard. Cr cds: A, C, D, MC, V.

Inn

★ ★ **MADISON STREET.** *1390 Madison St (95050).* 408/249-5541. 6 rms, 4 baths. S, D $60–$85; MAP avail. TV avail. Pool; whirlpool. Complimentary full bkfst. Ck-out noon, ck-in 4 pm. Airport, RR station, bus depot transportation. Picnic tables, grills. Victorian furnishings (1895); library, antiques, bearclaw tubs. Garden. Totally nonsmoking. Cr cds: A, D, DS, MC, V.

Restaurants

★ **FISH MARKET.** *3775 El Camino Real.* 408/246-3474. Hrs: 11 am–9:30 pm; Fri & Sat to 10 pm; Sun noon–9:30 pm. Closed Easter, Thanksgiving, Dec 25. Bar. Semi-a la carte: lunch $4.95–$25.95, dinner

$6.25–$26.95. Specializes in fresh mesquite-broiled seafood, desserts. Oyster bar. Parking. Nautical decor. Cr cds: A, C, D, DS, MC, V.

✔ ★ ★ **LA GALLERIA.** *2798 El Camino Real.* 408/296-6800. Hrs: 11:30 am–9 pm; Fri to 9:30 pm; Sat 5–9:30 pm. Closed Sun; Thanksgiving, Dec 25. Res accepted. Northern Italian menu. Wine, beer. Semi-a la carte: lunch $5–$13.95, dinner $6–$14.95. Specialties: osso buco Milanese, fettucine alla Galleria. Parking. Cr cds: A, C, D, DS, ER, MC, V, JCB.

★ **LA PALOMA.** *2280 El Camino Real.* 408/247-0990 or -0991. Hrs: 11 am–10 pm; Sun 4–9 pm. Closed July 4, Thanksgiving, Dec 25. Res accepted. Mexican menu. Bar. Semi-a la carte: lunch, dinner $11.95–$16.95. Child's meals. Specialties: pollo al cilantro, burrito ranchero. 1-hr dinner show Fri–Sun; res required. Parking. Mexican village decor. Cr cds: A, C, D, DS, MC, V.

Santa Cruz (E-1)

Founded: 1840 **Pop:** 49,040 **Elev:** 20 ft **Area code:** 408

Santa Cruz is a bustling seaside resort and arts and crafts center with 29 miles of public beaches. Large brussel sprout, strawberry, artichoke and begonia crops and apple harvests in the nearby Pajaro Valley make agriculture a major industry in the area. The present town is predated by the village of Branciforte, which it has now assimilated. Branciforte was founded in 1797 as a colonial venture of the Spanish government. Lacking financial support, the village failed to develop, and its shiftless colonists made much trouble for the nearby mission. The Santa Cruz Valley was given its name, Holy Cross, by Don Gaspar de Portola and Father Crespi, who discovered it in 1769.

What to See and Do

1. **Municipal Wharf.** Extends ½ mi into Monterey Bay. One of few piers of this type to permit auto traffic. Restaurants, gift shops, fish markets, charter boats; free fishing area.

2. **Santa Cruz Beach Boardwalk.** Half-mile long. Only remaining beachside amusement park on the West Coast. Includes famous Cocoanut Grove ballroom, Neptune's Kingdom with entertainment and attractions, restaurants, shops, outdoor shows at beach bandstand, miniature golf, arcades, games & rides and the Giant Dipper roller coaster and 1911 Looff carousel. Boardwalk (Memorial Day–Labor Day, daily; rest of yr, wkends & hols; closed Dec 25, 26). Neptune's Kingdome (daily; closed Dec 24 & 25). For hrs phone 423-5590. All-day unlimited ride pass ¢¢¢¢¢

3. **Santa Cruz City Museum of Natural History.** 1305 E Cliff Dr. Natural and cultural history of the northern Monterey Bay region. California Indian exhibits; tidepool aquarium. (Daily exc Mon; closed major hols) Phone 429-3773. ¢

4. **Santa Cruz Mission State Historical Park.** 130 School St. Casa Adobe (Neary-Rodriguez Adobe) is the only remaining building of the old Santa Cruz Mission; the date of construction is between 1822 and 1824; displays. (By appt) Phone 425-5849. ¢

5. **West Cliff Drive.** On N shoreline of Santa Cruz Beach. One of the most renowned ocean drives in the state.

6. **Felton covered bridge.** Built in 1892; spans San Lorenzo River 80 ft above the water.

7. **University of California, Santa Cruz** (1965). (10,000 students) NW section of town. Made up of 8 colleges on a 2,000-acre campus overlooking Monterey Bay. The Institute of Marine Sciences offers guided tours of the Long Marine Laboratory. Art galleries, astronomical exhibits, agroecology farm. Phone 459-2495.

8. **The Mystery Spot.** 1953 Branciforte Dr, 2½ mi N. Area 150 feet in diameter that "defies" conventional laws of gravity, perspective; balls roll uphill, trees grow sideways. Discovered in 1939. Guided tours. (Daily) Phone 423-8897. ¢¢

9. **Roaring Camp & Big Trees Narrow-Gauge Railroad.** 6 mi N on Graham Hill Rd in Felton. Authentic 19th-century narrow-gauge steam locomotives carry passengers up North America's steepest railroad grades through groves of giant redwoods. Stopover at Bear Mt for picnicking, hiking; round trip 6 mi, 1¼ hrs. Historic townsite with 1880s depot, old-time general store, covered bridge. Trains leave Roaring Camp depot, ½ mi SE of Felton at jct Graham Hill & Roaring Camp Rds. (Schedule varies; additional trains wkends, hols and in summer) Chuckwagon barbecue (May–Oct, wkends). (See ANNUAL EVENTS) For additional information and schedule phone 335-4400. ¢¢¢¢ Also here is

Santa Cruz, Big Trees & Pacific Railway. 1920s-era railroad operating vintage passenger coaches over spectacular rail route between redwoods at Roaring Camp and beach and boardwalk at Santa Cruz. A 2½-hr round trip excursion through tunnel, over trestles and along rugged San Lorenzo River Canyon on its way to the beach at Santa Cruz. Historic railroad dates back to 1875. (June–Sept, daily; May & Oct, wkends & hols) For information and schedule phone 335-4400. ¢¢¢¢

10. **State parks.**

Natural Bridges Beach. W of city limits on W Cliff Dr. Ocean-formed sandstone arch; winter site for monarch butterflies. Fishing. Nature trail. Picnicking. Displays of local tidepool life. Day use only. Standard fees. Phone 423-4609.

Wilder Ranch. 3 mi NW on CA 1. Coastal terraces, pocket beaches and historic farm on 3,000 acres. Nature, hiking, biking, bridle trails. Interpretive displays. Farm and blacksmith demonstrations. Day use only. Standard fees. Phone 688-3241 or 426-0505.

Seacliff Beach. 5 mi S on CA 1. Fishing pier leads to "The Cement Ship," sunk here in 1929 to serve as an amusement center. Swimming beach, seasonal lifeguards; fishing. Picnicking. Campsites (full hookups); no tents. Standard fees. Phone 688-3241 or -3222; for reservations phone Mistix, 800/444-7275.

Forest of Nisene Marks. 6 mi SE on CA 1 to Aptos, then N on Aptos Creek Rd. Seismologists identified the epicenter of the October, 1989 earthquake (7.1 magnitude) in this 10,000-acre state park. Diagonal fault ridges are evident although the earthquake epicenter can barely be distinguished. Hiking, bicycling. Picnicking. Primitive camping (6-mi hike to campsite). Phone 335-4598.

Big Basin Redwoods (see). 23 mi N via CA 9, 236.

Henry Cowell Redwoods. 5 mi N on CA 9. These 1,737 acres contain some of the finest specimens of coast redwood in the world, including one tree that has a base large enough to shelter several people. Self-guided nature trail, hiking, bridle trails. Picnicking. Camping. Some campfire programs and guided walks conducted by rangers. Standard fees. Phone 335-4598.

11. **Bargetto Winery.** 3535 N Main St, E on CA 1, exit Capitola/Soquel exit, right on Main St in Soquel. Family winery with tours and tasting (daily; closed Jan 1, Easter, Thanksgiving, Dec 25). Tasting room, 700 Cannery Row, Suite L, Monterey 93940; phone 373-4053. Phone 475-2258. **Free.**

(For further information contact the Santa Cruz County Conference and Visitors Council, 701 Front St, 95060; 425-1234.)

Annual Events

Cabrillo Music Festival. Santa Cruz Civic Auditorium. Considered one of the best small music festivals in the country. Presents a variety of classical and contemporary works performed by artists from the international concert stage. Phone 662-2701. Late July–early Aug.

National Begonia Festival. 5 mi E, in Capitola. Height of blooming season. Fishing derbies, parade. Late Aug–early Sept.

Santa Cruz County Fair. Santa Cruz Fairgrounds. Phone 688-3384. Early–mid-Sept.

Mountain Man Rendezvous. Re-enactment of an early day rendezvous with participants authentically costumed as trappers and traders as they gather to exchange products, swap tales and engage in old-time games. Thanksgiving wkend.

Seasonal Event

Shakespeare/Santa Cruz Festival. UCSC Campus (see #7). Presentation of Shakespearean and contemporary plays by professional actors; indoor and outdoor performances. Thurs–Sun, late July–late Aug.

(See Los Gatos, Santa Clara)

Motels

★ ★**BEST WESTERN SEACLIFF INN.** *(7500 Old Dominion Ct, Aptos 95003) 5 mi S on CA 1, exit Seacliff Beach, 1 blk E then left. 408/688-7300; FAX 408/685-3603.* 140 rms, 2 story. Mid-Mar–mid-Oct: S $79–$99; D $89–$109; each addl $10; suites $135–$180; under 12 free; higher rates: hols, Watsonville Fly-in, Begonia Festival; lower rates rest of yr. Crib free. TV; cable, in-rm movies. Heated pool; whirlpool, poolside serv. Complimentary coffee in rms. Restaurant 7 am–2 pm, 5–10 pm. Rm serv. Bar 11–2 am; entertainment, dancing Fri, Sat. Ck-out noon. Meeting rms. Bellhops. Refrigerator, minibar in suites. Balconies. Picnic tables. Beach ½ mi. Cr cds: A, C, D, DS, ER, MC, V.

D ⊠ ⊘ ⊚ SC

✔ ★**CAROUSEL.** *110 Riverside Ave (95060). 408/425-7090; FAX 408/427-3400.* 34 rms, 3 story. No A/C. Late Mar–early Sept: S, D $56–$95; vacation packages; higher rates: spring break, Easter, some hols; lower rates rest of yr. Crib $5. TV; cable. Complimentary continental bkfst, coffee. Restaurant nearby. Ck-out 11 am. Balconies. Ocean nearby; swimming beach. Cr cds: A, C, D, DS, MC, V.

D ⊠ ⊘ ⊚

✔ ★**INNCAL.** *320 Ocean St (95060), at Broadway Ave. 408/458-9220; res: 800/446-6225.* 62 rms, 3 story, 6 suites. June–Sept: S $43–$55; D $49–$60; suites $65; under 12 free; lower rates rest of yr. Crib $5. TV. Complimentary coffee in lobby. Restaurant nearby. Ck-out 11 am. Coin lndry. Meeting rms. Near ocean, beach, boardwalk. Cr cds: A, C, D, DS, MC, V.

D ⊘ ⊚ SC

★ ★**RIVERSIDE GARDEN INN.** *600 Riverside Ave (95060). 408/458-9660; FAX 408/426-8775.* 79 rms, 3 story, 9 suites. Mid-June–Sept: S, D $58–$98; each addl $10; suites $127–$175; under 12 free; higher rates wkends; lower rates rest of yr. Crib free. TV; cable. Pool; whirlpool. Complimentary continental bkfst. Ck-out 11 am. Meeting rm. Private patios, balconies. Beach 4 blks. Cr cds: A, C, D, DS, MC, V.

D ⊠ ⊘ ⊚

★ ★**SEA & SAND INN.** *201 West Cliff Dr (95060). 408/427-3400.* 20 air-cooled rms, 2 story, 2 kit. suites. June–Aug: S, D $105–$175; each addl $10; kit. suites $175–$190; under 12 free; wkly rates; Oct–Mar (2-night min Sat); lower rates rest of yr. Crib $10. TV; cable, in-rm movies. Complimentary continental bkfst, coffee. Restaurant adj 7 am–10 pm. Ck-out 11 am. Some in-rm whirlpools. Balconies. Grills. On cliffs overlooking Monterey Bay. Ocean swimming, beach. Cr cds: A, D, ER, MC, V.

➡ ⊠ ⊘ ⊚

Motor Hotels

★ ★ ★**CHAMINADE.** *(PO Box 2788, 95063-2788) One Chaminade Lane, CA 1 Soquel Dr exit, N on Paul Sweet Rd to Chaminade Lane. 408/475-5600; res: 800/283-6569; FAX 408/476-4942.* 152 rms, 2 story. S $125–$135; D $125–$145; each addl $25; under 14 free; some special rates Nov–Mar. TV; cable. Heated pool; poolside serv. Restaurant 7 am–9:30 pm. Bar 11–1:30 am; entertainment Fri, Sat. Ck-out noon. Meeting rms. Concierge. Gift shop. Free valet parking. Lighted tennis. Golf privileges 5 mi, pro. Exercise rm; instructor, weights, bicycles, whirlpool, steam rm, sauna. Game rm. Lawn games. Private patios, balconies. Picturesque setting in Santa Cruz Mts. Cr cds: A, C, D, DS, ER, MC, V.

★**DREAM INN.** *175 West Cliff Dr (95060), adj to boardwalk amusement park.* 408/426-4330; res: 800/662-3838 (CA); FAX 408/427-2025. 164 rms, 1–10 story. Mid-May–mid-Sept: S, D $110–$205; suites $225–$265; under 12 free; lower rates rest of yr. Crib free. TV; in-rm movies. Heated pool; whirlpool, sauna, poolside serv. Coffee in rms. Restaurant 6:30 am–5 pm. Rm serv. Bar 11–2 am. Ck-out noon. Meeting rms. Bellhops. Valet serv. Game rm. Minibars. Private balconies. Overlooks beach. Cr cds: A, C, D, DS, ER, MC, V.

★★**HOLIDAY INN.** *611 Ocean St (95060), at Dakota Ave, adj to boardwalk amusement park.* 408/426-7100; FAX 408/429-1044. 167 rms, 5 story. July–Sept: S, D $99–$125; each addl $10; under 18 free; lower rates rest of yr. Crib free. TV; cable. Heated pool. Restaurant 6:30 am–10 pm. Rm serv. Bar from 11 am; entertainment, dancing Fri, Sat. Ck-out noon. Meeting rms. Bellhops. Exercise equipt; weight machine, bicycle, whirlpool. Cr cds: A, C, D, DS, MC, V.

Inns

★★★**BABBLING BROOK.** *1025 Laurel St (95060).* 408/427-2437; res: 800/866-1131; FAX 408/427-2457. 12 rms. S, D $85–$150; each addl $15. Children over 12 yrs only. TV; cable. Complimentary full bkfst buffet, wine & cheese, tea & cookies. Ck-out noon, ck-in 3 pm. Some wood-burning stoves. Some balconies. Former gristmill & tannery. Country French decor. Garden walkways, waterfalls. Boardwalk 7 blks. Cr cds: A, C, D, DS, MC, V.

★**CHATEAU VICTORIAN.** *118 First St (95060).* 408/458-9458. 7 rms, 2 story. No A/C. No rm phones. D $105–$135. Continental bkfst, coffee. Restaurant nearby. Ck-out noon, ck-in 3:30–6:30 pm. Picnic tables. Victorian house; fireplaces. 1 blk to beach. Totally nonsmoking. Cr cds: A, MC, V.

★★★★**INN AT DEPOT HILL.** *(250 Monterey Ave, Capitola-By-The-Sea 95010) S via CA 1, Capitola-Soquel exit to Bay Ave or Park Ave exit to Monterey Ave.* 408/462-3376; FAX 408/462-2697. 8 rms, 2 story, 4 suites. No A/C. S, D $155–$195; each addl $25; suites $195–$250; under 3 free; 2-night min Sat. TV; cable, in-rm movies. Complimentary full bkfst, wine & hors d'oeuvres. Complimentary coffee in rms. Restaurant nearby. Rm serv. Ck-out 11:30 am, ck-in 3 pm. Balconies. Elegant furnishings; each rm with distinctive decor, wood-burning fireplace. 5 rms have hot tub on private patio. Former turn-of-the-century railroad depot (1901) transformed into a sophisticated seaside inn. Unique trompe l'oeil in dining rm creates the illusion of the dining car of a train. Patio with reflecting pond is surrounded by flowers, ferns and vines. Ocean 2 blks; swimming beach. Totally nonsmoking. Cr cds: A, MC, V.

Restaurants

★★★**CHEZ RENÉE.** *(9051 Soquel Dr, Aptos) 8 mi E on CA 1 to Rio del Mar exit, then ¼ mi W on Soquel Dr.* 408/688-5566. Hrs: 11:30 am–2 pm, 5:30–10 pm. Closed Sun, Mon; Jan 1, Thanksgiving, Dec 25; also 1st wk Jan & last wk Oct. Res required. California French menu. Bar. Wine cellar. Semi-a la carte: lunch $5.95–$8.95, dinner

$13.95–$22.95. Specializes in duck, lamb, fresh fish, pasta. Own pastries. Parking. Outdoor dining. French country atmosphere; antiques, Steuben glass. Cr cds: MC, V.

★★**CROW'S NEST.** *2218 E Cliff Dr.* 408/476-4560. Hrs: 11:30 am–2:30 pm, 5:30–9:30 pm; Sat 11:30 am–3 pm, 5–10 pm; Sun 11 am–3 pm, 5–9 pm. Closed Dec 25. Res accepted. Bar. A la carte entrees: lunch $5.95–$12.50, dinner $6.95–$24.95. Child's meals. Specializes in fresh seafood, steak. Salad bar. Oyster bar upper level. Entertainment. Parking. Outdoor dining. On beach, at yacht harbor; view of bay. Cr cds: A, C, D, DS, MC, V.

★**GILBERTS SEAFOOD GRILL.** *Municipal Wharf #25.* 408/423-5200. Hrs: 11:30 am–10 pm; Fri & Sat to 11 pm. Res accepted. Bar. Semi-a la carte: lunch $5.95–$14.95, dinner $7.95–$28.95. Child's meals. Specializes in seafood, pasta. Parking. View of Monterey Bay and beach from wharf. Cr cds: A, C, D, MC, V.

✔ ★**IDEAL FISH.** *106 Beach St.* 408/423-5271. Hrs: 4:30–10 pm; Fri & Sat to 11 pm; early-bird dinner 4:30–6:30 pm. Closed Jan 1, Thanksgiving, Dec 24, 25. Res accepted. Bar. Semi-a la carte: dinner $6.95–$17.95. Specializes in seafood, pasta. On beach; nautical decor. Gift shop. Cr cds: A, C, D, MC, V.

★★★**SHADOWBROOK.** *(1750 Wharf Rd, Capitola) 4 mi S on CA 1, ½ mi S on 41st Ave, ½ mi E on Capitola Rd.* 408/475-1511. Hrs: 5–10 pm; Sat 4–11 pm; Sun 10 am–2:30 pm, 4–9 pm. Res accepted. Bar from 4 pm; wkends from 10 am. Complete meals: dinner $12.95–$23.95. Sun brunch $7.95–$12.50 Child's meals. Specializes in seafood, prime rib. Own baking. Parking. Garden stairway to restaurant; garden decor. Overlooks river. "Cable car" from parking lot to restaurant. Cr cds: A, C, D, DS, MC, V.

★★★**THEO'S.** *(3101 N Main St, Soquel) W on CA 1 Soquel/Capitola exit.* 408/462-3657. Hrs: 6–9:30 pm. Res accepted. French menu. Wine cellar. A la carte entrees: dinner $8.95–$18.95. Specializes in duck, lamb, fresh seafood. Own pastries. Parking. Outdoor dining. French country decor. Organic garden. Uses locally grown produce. Cr cds: DS, MC, V.

Santa Maria (G-2)

Pop: 61,284 **Elev:** 216 ft **Area code:** 805

A Ranger District office of the Los Padres National Forest (see KING CITY, SANTA BARBARA) is located in Santa Maria.

What to See and Do

Santa Maria Historical Museum. 616 S Broadway. Early settler and Chumash Indian artifacts. (Tues–Sat; closed major hols) Phone 922-3130. **Free.**

(For further information contact the Chamber of Commerce, 614 S Broadway, 93454; 925-2403.)

Annual Events

Elks Rodeo & Parade. Fairgrounds. 1st wkend June.

Santa Barbara County Fair. Santa Maria Fairgrounds. 9 days late June–early July.

(See Lompoc, San Luis Obispo, Solvang)

Motels

★ ★ ★**BEST WESTERN BIG AMERICA.** *1725 N Broadway (93454).* 805/922-5200; FAX 805/922-9865. 106 units, 2 story, 16 suites. May–Sept: S $50–$70; D $60–$75; suites $70–$90; under 18 free; wkly rates; lower rates rest of yr. Crib free. TV; cable, in-rm movies. Heated pool; whirlpool. Complimentary continental bkfst. Restaurant 6 am–9 pm. Rm serv. Bar. Ck-out noon. Meeting rms. Valet serv. Free airport, bus depot transportation. Refrigerators, wet bars. Cr cds: A, C, D, DS, MC, V.

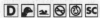

✔ ★ ★**HOWARD JOHNSON.** *210 S Nicholson Ave (93454), at Main St.* 805/922-5891; FAX 805/928-9222. 62 rms, 2 story. S, D $49–$69; under 18 free. Crib free. Pet accepted. TV; cable. Heated pool; wading pool, whirlpool. Restaurant 6 am–10 pm. Ck-out noon. Coin lndry. Meeting rms. Private patios, balconies. Grill. Cr cds: A, C, D, DS, ER, MC, V, JCB.

★ ★**RAMADA SUITES.** *2050 N Preisker Lane (93454), CA 101 Broadway exit.* 805/928-6000; FAX 805/928-0356. 210 kit. suites, 4 story. S, D $49–$150; each addl $10; under 18 free. Crib free. Pet accepted, some restrictions; $15. Heated pool; whirlpool. Supervised child's activities (seasonal). Complimentary coffee in rms. Restaurant 6 am–10 pm. Bar 11 am–midnight. Ck-out noon. Coin lndry. Meeting rms. Valet serv. Sundries. Health club privileges. Balconies. Cr cds: A, C, D, DS, MC, V, JCB.

Motor Hotel

★ ★ ★**SANTA MARIA INN.** *801 S Broadway (93454).* 805/928-7777; res: 800/462-4276; FAX 805/928-5690. 166 rms, 2–6 story. S $70–$130; D $80–$140; each addl $8; suites $150–$340; under 12 free; wine tour packages. Crib free. TV; cable, in-rm movies. Heated pool; whirlpool, sauna, poolside serv in season. Restaurant (see SANTA MARIA INN). Rm serv. Bar 10:30–2 am; entertainment. Ck-out noon. Bellhops. Valet serv. Shopping arcade. Barber, beauty shop. Airport transportation. Pitch and putt course. Refrigerators; some bathrm phones, fireplaces. Private patios, balconies. 1917 inn preserves bygone era; antique fountain, English antiques, stained glass. Cr cds: A, C, D, DS, MC, V, JCB.

Restaurant

★ ★ ★**SANTA MARIA INN.** *(See Santa Maria Inn Motor Hotel)* 805/928-7777. Hrs: 6:30 am–10 pm; early-bird dinner 5–6:30 pm; Sun brunch 10 am–2 pm. Res accepted. Bar. Wine cellar. Semi-a la carte: bkfst $3.95–$9.25, lunch $4.95–$8.25, dinner $10.95–$20.95. Sun brunch $11.95. Child's meals. Specializes in prime rib, fresh seafood, Santa Maria barbecue. Parking. Outdoor dining. Cr cds: A, C, D, DS, MC, V, JCB.

Santa Monica (H-3)

Founded: 1875 **Pop:** 86,905 **Elev:** 101 ft **Area code:** 310

With its wide, white beaches, continual sunshine and casual ambiance, Santa Monica is one of southern California's undiscovered beachside resorts. Located at the end of famed Wilshire Boulevard, Santa Monica is perhaps best known for its popular bay. Here the scenery of palm trees, beach and mountains has been popular for years in snapshots, movies and postcards.

What to See and Do

1. **Palisades Park.** Ocean Ave from Colorado Ave to Adelaide Dr. Parks, paths and gardens on 26 acres overlooking the ocean. Senior recreation center (all yr). Phone 458-8310.

2. **Santa Monica State Beach.** Considered one of the best in Los Angeles area; 3.3 miles long; lifeguards, surfing, volleyball, bike path, play equipment, snack bars. Phone 458-8310. Parking ¢¢¢

3. **Santa Monica Pier.** On Ocean Ave at the foot of Colorado Ave. Restaurants, shops; also antique carousel with 46 hand-carved horses housed in restored building (1916). Phone 458-8900.

4. **Santa Monica Heritage Museum.** 2612 Main St. Built along palisades in 1894. Moved to present site and restored. Houses changing history exhibits; contemporary art and photo gallery. (Wed–Sun; closed hols) Phone 392-8537. ¢

5. **Museum of Flying.** At Santa Monica Airport. Historical and current aviation exhibits, models and memorabilia; Donald Douglas Library and Archives. Most aircraft on display are in fully operational condition. Special events, exhibitions. (Wed–Sun; closed hols) Phone 392-8822. ¢¢

(For further information contact the Convention and Visitors Bureau, 1400 Ocean Ave, 90401; 393-7593.)

(See Beverly Hills, Buena Park, Fullerton, Los Angeles, Malibu, Marina Del Rey)

Motel

✔ ★**COMFORT INN.** *2815 Santa Monica Blvd (90404).* 310/828-5517. 101 rms, 3 story. June–Sept: S $65–$75; D $75–$85; each addl $10; under 18 free; lower rates rest of yr. Crib $10. TV; cable. Heated pool. Complimentary coffee. Ck-out noon. Cr cds: A, C, D, DS, MC, V.

Hotels

★ ★ ★**GUEST QUARTERS.** *1707 4th St (90401).* 310/395-3332; FAX 310/452-7399. 253 suites, 8 story. May–Sept: S $145–$165; D $165–$185; each addl $20; under 18 free; wkly rates; package plans; lower rates rest of yr. Crib free. Garage parking $10, valet $12. TV; cable. Heated pool; poolside serv. Complimentary coffee in rms. Restaurant 6:30 am–10 pm. Bar 5 pm–12:30 am; entertainment. Ck-out noon. Coin lndry. Convention facilities. Gift shop. Airport transportation. Exercise equipt; weight machine, bicycles, whirlpool, sauna. Game rm. Refrigerators, minibars. Beach 4 blks. Some rms with ocean view. Cr cds: A, C, D, DS, MC, V, JCB.

★ ★ ★ ★**LOEWS SANTA MONICA BEACH.** *1700 Ocean Ave (90401), west of downtown.* 310/458-6700; FAX 310/458-6761. 352 rms, 8 story, 35 suites. S, D $195–$400; each addl $20; suites $350–$2,500; under 17 free; package plans. Valet parking $14; self-park $12. TV; cable. Indoor/outdoor pool; poolside serv. Supervised child's activities. Restaurants 6 am–11 pm. Rm serv 24 hrs. Bar 10–1 am; entertainment. Ck-out noon. Convention facilities. Concierge. Shopping arcade. Barber, beauty shop. Tennis privileges. Golf privileges. Exercise rm; instructor, weights, bicycles, whirlpool, sauna, steam rm. Masseuse. Bicycle and roller skate rentals. Bathrm phones, minibars; some wet bars. Balconies. Atrium. Beach approx 50 yds. Cr cds: A, C, D, MC, V, JCB.

★ ★**SHANGRI-LA.** *1301 Ocean Ave (90401).* 310/394-2791; FAX 310/451-3351. 55 units, 7 story, 47 kits. No A/C. S, D $110–$205; each addl $15; suites $140–$450. Crib $15. TV. Complimentary continental bkfst, afternoon tea. Ck-out noon. Balconies. Large terrace. Beach opp. Cr cds: A, C, D, DS, MC, V, JCB.

★★★**SHERATON MIRAMAR.** *101 Wilshire Blvd (90401). 310/ 576-7777; FAX 310/458-7912.* 303 rms, 1–10 story. S, D $195–$300; each addl $20; suites $225–$900; under 17 free; wkend rates. Crib free. TV; cable, in-rm movies avail. Heated pool; poolside serv. Coffee in rms. Restaurant 6:30 am–midnight. Rm serv 24 hrs. Bar; pianist. Ck-out noon. Meeting rms. Concierge. Shopping arcade. Airport transportation. Bathrm phones, minibars. Beach opp. Cr cds: A, C, D, DS, ER, MC, V, JCB.

SHUTTERS ON THE BEACH. (Too new to be rated) *1 Pico Blvd (90405). 310/458-0330; res: 800/334-9000; FAX 310/458-4589.* 198 rms in 3 bldgs, 7 story, 12 suites. S $250–$350; D $275–$375; each addl $25; suites $650–$2,000; under 12 free; wkend plans. Crib free. Pet accepted, some restrictions; $50. Valet parking $15. TV. Heated pool; poolside serv. Restaurant 6:30 am–11 pm. Rm serv 24 hrs. Bar. Ck-out noon. Meeting rms. Concierge. Gift shop. Exercise equipt; weight machine, bicycles, whirlpool, steam rm. Full health facilities. Minibars. Balconies. Named for the distinctive sliding shutter doors in all guest rms. Located on the ocean; beachfront boardwalk. Cr cds: A, C, D, DS, MC, V.

Inn

✔★★★**CHANNEL ROAD.** *219 W Channel Rd (90402). 310/459-1920.* 14 rms, 3 story, 2 suites. No A/C. S, D $85–$180; suites $165–$200; family, wkly rates. Crib free. TV; cable. Complimentary full bkfst, coffee. Restaurant opp 7 am–11 pm. Rm serv. Ck-out noon, ck-in 3 pm. Whirlpool. Bicycles. Colonial-revival house built in 1910; library, fireplaces, antiques. Cr cds: A, MC, V.

Restaurants

★**BOB BURNS.** *202 Wilshire Blvd. 310/393-6777.* Hrs: 11:30 am–11 pm; Fri & Sat to midnight; Sun brunch to 3 pm. Closed Dec 25. Res accepted. Continental menu. Bar to midnight, Fri & Sat to 2 am. Semi-a la carte: lunch $8–$16, dinner $13–$26. Sun brunch $9.50–$15.95. Child's meals. Specializes in fresh fish, lamb chops, roast duckling, beef. Pianist. Valet parking. Fireplace. Cr cds: A, C, D, DS, MC, V.

★★**BORDER GRILL.** *1445 4th St. 310/451-1655.* Hrs: 5:30–10:30 pm; Fri & Sat to midnight. Closed Jan 1, Easter, Thanksgiving, Dec 25. Res accepted. Mexican menu. Bar. A la carte entrees: dinner $10–$22. Specializes in seafood and shellfish. 2-story murals. Cr cds: A, MC, V.

★**BROADWAY BAR & GRILL.** *1460 3rd St Promenade. 310/393-4211.* Hrs: 11:30 am–11 pm; wkends to midnight; Sun brunch 11:30 am–3 pm. Closed Dec 25. Res accepted. Bar to 2 am Fri, Sat. A la carte entrees: lunch $7.95–$13.95, dinner $8.95–$22. Sun brunch $7.95–$13.95. Specializes in pork chops, steak, fresh fish. Outdoor dining. Antique oak bar. Cr cds: A, MC, V.

✔★**BROADWAY DELI.** *1457 3rd St Promenade. 310/451-0616.* Hrs: 7 am–midnight; Fri & Sat to 1 am. Closed Dec 25. International menu. Bar. A la carte entrees: bkfst $5–$8, lunch $6–$12, dinner $12–$16. Specializes in: rotisserie-cooked herb chicken, honey roast pork, crème brulée, fruit cobbler. Valet parking. Contemporary decor. Gourmet market on premises. Cr cds: A, MC, V.

★★**CAFE ATHENS.** *1000 Wilshire Blvd. 310/395-1000.* Hrs: 11:30 am–midnight; Sat 4 pm–12:30 am; Sun 4–11 pm. Closed Mon. Res accepted. Greek, Amer menu. Bar; Fri, Sat to 2 am. A la carte entrees: lunch $6.95–$14, dinner $11.95–$18.75. Specialties: stuffed grape leaves, baby lamb, moussaka. Greek music; singing & dancing. Cr cds: A, C, D, MC, V.

★★**CHARTREUSE.** *1909 Wilshire Blvd. 310/453-3333.* Hrs: 11:30 am–2 pm, 6–9:30 pm. Closed Sun; major hols. Res accepted.

French menu. Bar. A la carte entrees: lunch $8.50–$18. Semi-a la carte: dinner $12–$20. Specialties: roast duck, grilled whitefish. Parking. Cr cds: A, MC, V.

★★**CHINOIS ON MAIN.** *2709 Main St. 310/392-9025.* Hrs: 6–10:30 pm; Wed–Fri also 11:30 am–2 pm; Sun 5:30–10 pm. Closed some major hols. Res required. Chinese, French menu. Bar. A la carte entrees: lunch $9.50–$18.50, dinner $19.50–$29.50. Specialties: sizzling catfish, curried oysters. Valet parking. Unique ultramodern decor. Cr cds: A, D, MC, V.

✔★**FISH COMPANY.** *174 Kinney St. 310/392-8366.* Hrs: 11:30 am–10 pm; Fri & Sat to 11 pm. Closed Thanksgiving, Dec 25. Res accepted. California menu. Bar. Semi-a la carte: lunch $7–$10, dinner $10–$17. Child's meals. Specializes in fresh fish, Alaskan king crab legs, filet mignon. In restored railroad station (ca 1920). Nautical decor; copper wall resembling side of ship, large salt water aquarium. Cr cds: A, MC, V.

✔★★**JOE'S.** *(1023 Abbot Kinney Blvd, Venice) S on Main St. 310/399-5811.* Hrs: 11 am–3 pm, 6–11 pm. Closed Mon; Jan 1, Thanksgiving, Dec 25. Res accepted. Wine, beer. A la carte entrees: lunch $7–$10, dinner $13–$16. Specialties: shiitake mushrooms with mozzarella cheese and roasted red peppers, salmon sauteed with wild rice and red wine sauce. Contemporary art work. Cr cds: MC, V.

★★**LE PETIT MOULIN.** *714 Montana Ave. 310/395-6619.* Hrs: 11:30 am–2:30 pm, 5:30–10 pm. Closed Jan 1. Res required. French menu. Wine. Semi-a la carte: lunch $4.95–$9.95, dinner $9.95–$20.95. Wine-maker dinners $35–$40. Specializes in veal, fresh seafood, lamb. Own desserts. Parking. French provincial decor. Family-owned. Cr cds: A, MC, V.

★★**MADAME WU'S GARDEN.** *2201 Wilshire Blvd. 310/828-5656.* Hrs: 11:30 am–10 pm; Fri to 11 pm; Sat 5–11 pm; Sun 3–10 pm. Closed Thanksgiving, Dec 25. Res accepted. Chinese menu. Bar. A la carte entrees: lunch $7.25–$8.95, dinner $9.50–$30. Complete meals: dinner $17–$31. Specialties: Peking duck, mandarin dishes. Valet parking. Family-owned. Cr cds: A, C, D, MC, V.

★★★**MICHAEL'S.** *1147 3rd St. 310/451-0843.* Hrs: noon–2 pm, 6:30–10 pm. Closed Sun & Mon; most major hols. Res accepted. French, Amer menu. Bar. Wine cellar. A la carte entrees: lunch $12.50–$22.50, dinner $18–$26.50. Serv charge 15%. Specialties: spaghettini with lobster, grilled California quail with Maui onions, chocolate/caramel torte. Own pastries. Valet parking. Outdoor dining. Contemporary decor; modern art collection. Garden. Cr cds: A, D, DS, MC, V, JCB.

★★★**OPUS.** *2425 W Olympic Blvd. 310/829-2112.* Hrs: 11:45 am–2:30 pm, 6–10 pm; Fri & Sat to 10:30 pm; Sun 5–9 pm. Closed Jan 1, Dec 25. Res required. Modern French menu. Bar. Wine list. A la carte entrees: lunch $8–$13, dinner $20–$25. Specialties: crisped red snapper with roasted garlic, carpaccio of tuna with mushrooms, crisped loin of lamb with porcini mushrooms. Parking. Outdoor dining. Contemporary decor. Overlooks fountain and lake. Cr cds: A, MC, V.

★★★**72 MARKET ST.** *(72 Market St, Venice) S on Main St to Market. 310/392-8720.* Hrs: 11:30 am–2:30 pm, 6–10 pm; Fri to 11 pm; Sat 6–11 pm; Sun brunch 11 am–2:30 pm. Closed Jan 1, July 4, Thanksgiving, Dec 25. Res accepted. Bar. A la carte entrees: lunch $7–$12, dinner $12–$25. Sun brunch $6–$12. Specialties: steak tartare of filet mignon, meat loaf, chili. Oyster bar. Own baking. Pianist. Valet parking. Two dining rms: high-tech, industrial; chic supper club. Celebrity haunt. Cr cds: A, MC, V.

★★★**VALENTINO.** *3115 Pico Blvd. 310/829-4313.* Hrs: 5:30–10:30 pm; Fri also noon–3 pm; Fri, Sat to 11:30 pm. Closed Sun; most major hols. Res accepted. Italian menu. Bar. A la carte entrees:

dinner $20–$29.50. Specialties: nodino di vitello, fresh seafood. Own baking, pasta. Valet parking. Cr cds: A, C, D, MC, V.

Santa Nella *

Pop: summer (est) 500 **Area code:** 209 **Zip:** 95322
11 mi NW of Los Banos (F-2) at jct I-5, CA 33 and 75 mi S of Stockton (E-2) on I-5.

Motels

★★**BEST WESTERN ANDERSEN'S INN.** *12367 S CA 33, at jct I-5, CA 33. 209/826-5534.* 94 rms, 2 story. S $56–$64; D $62–$68; each addl $7; under 12 free. Crib free. TV; cable. Heated pool. Complimentary continental bkfst, coffee. Restaurant adj 7 am–10 pm. Ck-out noon. Private patios, balconies. Cr cds: A, C, D, DS, MC, V.

✓★★**HOLIDAY INN MISSION DE ORO.** *13070 S CA 33 (95322), jct I-5 & CA 33. 209/826-4444; FAX 209/826-8071.* 159 rms, 2 story. S $39.95–$59.95; D $49.95–$64.95; each addl $10; under 13 free. TV; cable. Heated pool; whirlpool. Playground. Restaurant 6:30 am–10 pm. Rm serv. Bar 2 pm–2 am; dancing Fri, Sat. Ck-out noon. Coin lndry. Meeting rms. Sundries. Some private patios, balconies. Cr cds: A, C, D, DS, MC, V, JCB.

Restaurant

★★**PEA SOUP ANDERSEN'S.** *12411 S CA 33, off jct I-5 & CA 33. 209/826-1685.* Hrs: 7 am–10 pm; Fri–Sun to 11 pm; Sun brunch 10 am–2 pm. Res accepted. Bar; Fri, Sat to midnight. Semi-a la carte: bkfst $2–$6.30, lunch, dinner $3.75–$20. Sun brunch $7.95. Child's meals. Specializes in pea soup, deep-dish apple pie. Parking. Gift and wine shop. Danish decor, windmill, heraldic flags. Cr cds: A, C, D, DS, ER, MC, V, JCB.

Santa Rosa (D-1)

Settled: 1829 **Pop:** 113,313 **Elev:** 167 ft **Area code:** 707

Surrounded by vineyards and mountains, the county seat of Sonoma County is within minutes of more than 100 wineries. The rich soil and even climate of the Sonoma Valley lured famed horticulturist Luther Burbank here to develop innumerable new and better plants. Many farm and ranch products originate from the area today.

What to See and Do

1. **Sonoma County Museum.** 425 7th St. Regional history and art museum of Sonoma County and northern California. Changing exhibits. Guided tours (by appt). Special events throughout year. (Wed–Sun; closed hols) Sr citizen rate. Phone 579-1500. ¢

2. **Luther Burbank Home & Gardens.** Santa Rosa & Sonoma Aves. Features work of the famous horticulturist who lived and worked in Santa Rosa. Site includes greenhouse, gardens, carriage house exhibits. Gift shop. Home tours (Apr–Oct, Wed–Sun). Gardens (daily; free). Phone 524-5445. Home tours ¢

3. **Snoopy's Gallery.** 1665 W Steele Ln. Houses a museum of Charles Schulz's original drawings of the *Peanuts* characters; awards and

trophies. Gift shop. (Daily; closed some hols) Phone 546-3385. **Free.**

(For further information contact the Sonoma County Convention and Visitors Bureau, 10 4th St, 95401; 575-1191 or 800/326-7666.)

Annual Events

Luther Burbank Rose Festival. 3 days of art and flower shows, parade. Mid-May.

Sonoma County Fair. Horse racing daily exc Sun, exhibits, stock shows, rodeos, entertainment. Phone 545-4200. Late July–early Aug.

Scottish Gathering and Games. Bagpipe bands & competition; Western US Highland Dance championships; US Invitational Heavy Event & Caber Toss. Fri–Sun, Labor Day wkend.

(See Calistoga, Healdsburg, Petaluma, Sonoma)

Motels

✓★★**BEST WESTERN GARDEN INN.** *1500 Santa Rosa Ave (95404), off US 101. 707/546-4031.* 78 rms. May–Oct: S, D $59–$77; each addl $6; under 12 free; lower rates rest of yr. Crib free. Pet accepted, some restrictions; $10. TV; cable. 2 pools, 1 heated. Coffee in rms. Restaurant 6:30–11 am. Coin lndry. Refrigerators. Private patios. Cr cds: A, C, D, DS, MC, V.

★★★**FOUNTAINGROVE INN.** *101 Fountaingrove Pkwy (95403), exit US 101 at Mendocino Ave. 707/578-6101; res: 800/222-6101 (CA); FAX 707/544-3126.* 85 units, 2 story. S $75; D $85; each addl $10; suites $125–$175; under 13 free. Crib free. TV; cable, in-rm movies avail. Heated pool; whirlpool, poolside serv. Complimentary bkfst buffet. Restaurant 11:30 am–2:30 pm, 5–9:30 pm. Rm serv from 7 am. Entertainment. Ck-out noon. Meeting rms. Bellhops. Valet serv. Sundries. Local airport, bus depot transportation. Tennis privileges. 18-hole golf privileges, greens fee $35–$60. Refrigerators. Redwood sculpture, waterfall in lobby. Equestrian theme. Cr cds: A, C, D, DS, MC, V.

★★★**LOS ROBLES LODGE.** *925 Edwards Ave (95401). 707/545-6330; res: 800/255-6330; FAX 707/575-5826.* 105 units, 2 story. May–Oct: S $75–$90; D $85–$100; each addl $5; under 12 free; lower rates rest of yr. Crib free. Pet accepted, some restrictions. TV; cable, in-rm movies avail. Heated pool; whirlpool, wading pool, poolside serv. Complimentary coffee in rms. Restaurant 6 am–10 pm. Rm serv. Bar 11–1 am; entertainment, dancing. Ck-out noon. Coin lndry. Meeting rms. Valet serv. Free local airport transportation. Refrigerators. Private patios, balconies; many overlook pool. Cr cds: A, C, D, DS, MC, V.

✓★**SUPER 8.** *2632 Cleveland Ave (95403). 707/542-5544; FAX 707/542-9738.* 100 rms, 3 story. Apr–Oct: S $43–$45; D $47–$52; each addl $3; suites $55–$75; under 12 free; lower rates rest of yr. Crib free. TV; cable. Pool. Complimentary continental bkfst 7–10 am. Restaurant 6 am–10 pm. Ck-out 11 am. Cr cds: A, C, D, DS, MC, V.

★★★**VINTNERS INN.** *4350 Barnes Rd (95403). 707/575-7350; res: 800/421-2584; FAX 707/575-1426.* 44 rms, 2 story. S, D $108–$195; each addl $10; under 6 free. Crib $6. TV; in-rm movies avail. Complimentary continental bkfst. Restaurant 11:30 am–2 pm, 5:30–9:30 pm; Sat & Sun from 5:30 pm; Sun brunch 10:30 am–2 pm. Rm serv. Bar. Ck-out noon. Meeting rms. Bellhops. Concierge. Tennis privileges. Golf privileges, greens fee $32–$55 (incl cart), pro. Whirlpool. Health club privileges. Refrigerators; many fireplaces. Private patios, balconies. Views of vineyards, courtyard. Cr cds: A, C, D, MC, V.

Motor Hotels

★★★DOUBLETREE. *3555 Round Barn Blvd (95403), US 101 exit at Mendocino Ave.* 707/523-7555; FAX 707/545-2807. 247 rms, 3 story. S, D $79–$129; each addl $10; suites $150–$195; under 18 free; golf plans. Crib free. TV; cable, in-rm movies avail. Pool; whirlpool, poolside serv in summer. Restaurant 6:30 am–10 pm. Rm serv. Bar 2:30 pm–1:30 am. Ck-out noon. Valet serv. Local airport transportation. Tennis privileges. 18-hole golf privileges, pro, greens fee $45–$70. Bathrm phones; some refrigerators. Some private patios. Outstanding views. Cr cds: A, C, D, DS, ER, MC, V, JCB.

★★★FLAMINGO. *2777 4th St (95405).* 707/545-8530; res: 800/848-8300; FAX 707/528-1404. 136 rms, 2 story. Apr–Oct: S, D $66–$94; each addl $11; suites $106–$186; under 12 free (up to 2); monthly rates; lower rates rest of yr. Crib free. TV; cable, in-rm movies. Pool; wading pool, whirlpool, poolside serv. Restaurant 7 am–10 pm. Rm serv. Bar; pianist, dancing. Ck-out 11 am. Meeting rms. Shopping arcade. Beauty shop. 5 tennis courts. Golf privileges. Exercise rm; instructor, weight machines, bicycles, whirlpool, steam rm, sauna. Lawn games. Some refrigerators. Balconies. Gardens. Cr cds: A, D, MC, V, JCB.

Hotel

★★HOTEL LA ROSE. *308 Wilson St (95401).* 707/579-3200; res: 800/LA ROSE8; FAX 707/579-3247. 49 rms, 4 story, 8 suites. S $60–$85; D $70–$95; each addl $10; suites $85–$95; under 12 free. Crib free. TV; cable. Restaurant 11:30 am–2 pm, 5:30–9 pm; Sat from 5:30 pm; closed Sun, Mon. Bar 5–11 pm, closed Sun, Mon. Ck-out noon. Meeting rms. On Railroad Square. Cr cds: A, MC, V.

Inns

★★GABLES. *4257 Petaluma Hill Rd (95404).* 707/585-7777. 3 rms, 3 suites, 1 cottage. No A/C. No rm phones. S, D $95; each addl $25; suites $115–$175. Complimentary full bkfst, coffee. Ck-out 11 am, ck-in 3:30–6 pm. Picnic tables. House of 15 gables in Gothic-revival style (1877) with unusual keyhole window in each gable. Interior boasts 12-ft ceilings, Italian marble fireplaces and spectacular mahogany spiral staircase. Antique furnishings & fixtures. Whirlpool in cottage. Totally nonsmoking. Cr cds: A, DS, MC, V.

★★PYGMALION HOUSE. *331 Orange St (95401).* 707/526-3407. 5 rms, 2 story. No rm phones. S $50–$75; D $55–$75; each addl $15; TV in sitting rm; cable. Complimentary full bkfst, coffee, tea & refreshments. Restaurant nearby. Ck-out 11 am, ck-in after 3 pm. Antiques. Library. Victorian house built 1886. Totally nonsmoking. Cr cds: A, MC, V.

Restaurants

★★CRICKLEWOOD. *4618 Old Redwood Hwy.* 707/527-7768. Hrs: 11:30 am–2:30 pm, 5–9:30 pm; Fri to 10 pm; Sat & Sun 5–10 pm. Closed Easter, Thanksgiving, Dec 25. Bar to 10 pm. Semi-a la carte: lunch $4.95–$6.95, dinner $8.95–$20. Specializes in prime rib, steak, seafood. Salad bar. Parking. Outdoor dining. Cr cds: A, MC, V.

✔★★THE GOOD EARTH. *610 3rd St.* 707/523-3060. Hrs: 8 am–9:30 pm; Fri & Sat to 10:30 pm; Sun brunch to 2 pm. Closed Dec 25. Continental menu. Wine, beer. Semi-a la carte: bkfst $2.55–$5.95, lunch $4.15–$9.25, dinner $7.95–$9.95. Sun brunch $8.25. Child's meals.

Specializes in soups, pasta, seafood, chicken. Classical guitarist. Braille menu. Totally nonsmoking. Cr cds: D, MC, V.

✔★★LA GARE. *208 Wilson St, at Railroad Square.* 707/528-4355. Hrs: 5:30–10 pm; Fri & Sat from 5 pm; Sun 5–9 pm. Closed Mon; Jan 1, Thanksgiving, Dec 25. Res accepted. French, Swiss menu. Semi-a la carte: dinner $7.95–$14.95. Child's meals. Specializes in baked salmon, pepper steak. Totally nonsmoking. Cr cds: A, C, D, MC, V.

★★LISA HEMENWAY'S. *714 Village Court Mall, in Montgomery Village.* 707/526-5111. Hrs: 11:30 am–2:30 pm, 5:30–9:30 pm; Sun brunch 10 am–2 pm. Closed Jan 1, Thanksgiving, Dec 25. Res accepted. Semi-a la carte: lunch $7.95–$13.95, dinner $15.95–$22. Sun brunch $2.95–$14.95. Specializes in seafood, pasta, salads, Sonoma County dishes. Outdoor dining. Cr cds: D, DS, MC, V.

★★MARSHALL HOUSE. *835 Second St.* 707/542-5305. Hrs: 11:30 am–2:30 pm, 5–9 pm; Fri & Sat to 10:30 pm. Closed Mon. German menu. Wine, beer. A la carte entrees: lunch $7–$12, dinner $11–$17. Specialties: sauerbraten, Wienerschnitzel, potato pancakes, apple strudel. Outdoor dining. Home cooking. In Victorian house; English flower garden. Cr cds: MC, V.

★★MIXX. *135 Fourth St.* 707/573-1344. Hrs: 11:30 am–2 pm, 5:30–10 pm; Fri to 10:30 pm; Sat 5:30–10:30; Sun 5:30–9:30 pm. Closed Dec 25. Res accepted. Bar from 5 pm. Semi-a la carte: lunch $3.50–$10, dinner $3.95–$18.95. Child's meals. Specializes in fresh fish, local lamb, pasta. Own desserts. Art deco decor. Totally nonsmoking. Cr cds: A, D, MC, V.

✔★OLD MEXICO EAST. *4501 Montgomery Dr.* 707/539-2599. Hrs: 11 am–10 pm; Fri & Sat to 11 pm; Sun to 9 pm. Res accepted. Mexican, Amer menu. Bar to midnight. Semi-a la carte: lunch $5, dinner $6.50–$14. Child's meals. Specialties: prawns rancheros, chimichangas, quesadillas. Parking. Outdoor dining. Family-owned. Cr cds: A, MC, V.

★PROSPECT PARK. *515 Fourth St.* 707/526-2662. Hrs: 5–10 pm; Fri & Sat to 11 pm. Closed Jan 1, Labor Day, Thanksgiving, Dec 25. Res accepted. Bar to 2 am. Complete meals: dinner $12.95–$17.95. Child's meals. Specializes in roast duckling, pasta, seafood. Parking. Cr cds: A, D, MC, V.

★RUSSIAN RIVER VINEYARDS. *(5700 Gravenstein Hwy, Forestville)* 8 mi W on Guerneville Rd, 1 mi N on CA 116. 707/887-1562. Hrs: 11:30 am–2:30 pm; 5:30–9:30 pm; Sun brunch 10:30 am–2:30 pm; off-season days vary. Res accepted. No A/C. California, Greek menu. Complete meals: lunch $7–$8.50, dinner $12–$20. Sun brunch $8–$10.50. Child's meals. Specializes in Greek dishes. Entertainment. Parking. Outdoor dining. Own herb garden. Garden area with many native plants. Family-operated winery and restaurant. Cr cds: A, D, DS, MC, V.

San Ysidro (San Diego) (K-4)

Area code: 619 **Zip:** 92073

Just across the border from Tijuana, San Ysidro reflects the combined influences of the United States and Mexico. (For Border Crossing Regulations see INTRODUCTION.)

This community is an integral part of San Diego, but is regarded by many as a separate entity.

(For general information and attractions see San Diego.)

Motels

★**AMERICANA INN & SUITES.** *815 W San Ysidro Blvd, just off I-5, 2 mi N of border.* 619/428-5521; FAX 619/428-0693. 125 units, 2 story, 12 suites. July–Sept: S $38–$40; D $45–$50; each addl $5; suites $59–$89; under 16 free; lower rates rest of yr. Crib free. TV; cable. Heated pool; whirlpool. Complimentary continental bkfst. Restaurant adj open 24 hrs. Ck-out noon. Coin lndry. Refrigerators, wet bars. Cr cds: A, C, D, DS, MC, V.

✔★**ECONOMY INNS OF AMERICA.** *230 Via de San Ysidro.* 619/428-6191. 122 rms, 2 story. S $25–$30; D $35–$40. Pet accepted. TV; cable. Heated pool. Restaurant adj open 24 hrs. Ck-out 11 am. Cr cds: A, MC, V.

Saratoga (E-1)

Pop: 28,061 Elev: 455 ft Area code: 408 Zip: 95070

Originally called McCartysville, in honor of the man who built a toll road for the lumber wagons here and established the town, the name changed to Bank Mills when a gristmill was opened here. Finally, when mineral springs were found nearby, the local citizenry took matters in their own hands and voted for the name of Saratoga, after the springs at Saratoga, New York.

What to See and Do

1. **Villa Montalvo** (1912). 15400 Montalvo Rd, ½ mi S, just off CA 9. Mediterranean-style summer house of Senator James D. Phelan. Now a cultural center with art galleries, concerts, plays, lectures, poetry readings, artists in residence. Formal gardens with hiking trails, arboretum, outdoor amphitheater and Carriage House Theatre. Tours (Apr–Sept, Thurs & Sat). Grounds (daily; free). Galleries (Thurs & Fri, afternoons; Sat & Sun, late morning–mid-afternoon; closed Jan 1, Thanksgiving, Dec 25). Sr citizen rate. Phone 741-3421. Tours ¢¢

2. **Historical Museum.** 20450 Saratoga-Los Gatos Rd. Exhibits housed in a turn-of-the-century store depict local history dating from 1850. (Wed–Sun afternoons; closed hols) Phone 867-4311. **Free.**

3. **Hakone Gardens.** 21000 Big Basin Way. Japanese gardens, pond, bridge, Japanese-style houses, waterfall, picnic area. (Daily; closed legal hols) Phone 741-4994. Mar–Oct: Gardens **free;** Wkend parking ¢¢; Rest of yr: Parking **free;** Gardens ¢

4. **Big Basin Redwoods State Park** (see). 18 mi W on CA 9.

(For further information contact the Chamber of Commerce, 20460 Saratoga-Los Gatos Rd; 867-0753.)

Seasonal Events

Villa Montalvo Performing Arts Season (see #1). Phone 741-3428. Apr–Sept.

"Music at the Vineyards." Classical concerts performed on stage built in front of the old Paul Masson Mountain Winery. Also "Vintage Sounds" jazz series. June–Sept.

(See Palo Alto, Redwood City, San Jose, Santa Clara, Sunnyvale)

Inn

★★★**THE INN AT SARATOGA.** *20645 4th St, downtown.* 408/867-5020; res: 800/338-5020; FAX 408/741-0981. 46 rms, 5 story, 4 suites. S, D $145–$440; suites $295–$495; under 18 free. Crib free. TV; cable. Complimentary continental bkfst, coffee, tea & wine. Restaurant adj 7 am–10 pm. Ck-out noon, ck-in 3 pm. Bellhops. Valet serv. Concierge. Health club privileges. Bathrm phones. Balconies. Patio. All rms are oversized, each overlooking Saratoga Creek and a wooded park. Cr cds: A, D, MC, V.

Restaurants

★★★**LA MÈRE MICHELLE.** *14467 Big Basin Way.* 408/867-5272; or -2011. Hrs: 11:30 am–2 pm, 6–9:30 pm; Fri & Sat 6–10 pm; Sun 5:30–9 pm. Closed Mon; major hols. Res accepted; required wkends. French menu. Bar. Wine list. A la carte entrees: lunch $7.50–$13.50, dinner $16.50–$23.50. Specializes in veal, quail. Own pastries. Parking. Guitarist Fri & Sat. Elegant French decor. Family-owned. Cr cds: A, C, D, DS, ER, MC, V, JCB.

★★★**PLUMED HORSE.** *14555 Big Basin Way.* 408/867-4711. Hrs: 6–10 pm. Closed Sun; hols. Res accepted. Continental menu. Bar 4 pm–2 am. Wine cellar. A la carte entrees: dinner $14–$45. Complete meals: dinner $25–$58. *Prix fixe:* dinner $40. Specializes in fresh game birds, venison, rack of lamb. Own pastries. Jazz trio. Parking. Elegant country decor; originally a stable (1883). Totally nonsmoking. Cr cds: A, C, D, MC, V.

Sausalito (E-1)

Settled: 1800 Pop: 7,152 Elev: 14 ft Area code: 415 Zip: 94965

Sausalito, a picturesque town above San Francisco Bay, is an art colony and residential suburb in the shadow of the Golden Gate Bridge. Whalers first used the cove here. The town's name is a corruption of the Spanish for willows, which flourished here at one time. Sausalito's springs were San Francisco's major source of water for many years.

What to See and Do

1. **Village Fair.** 777 Bridgeway, opp Yacht Harbor. Fascinating and colorful 3-story complex of specialty shops selling unusual crafts, artifacts & imports. The building was once a Chinese gambling hall, opium den and a distillery for bootleg whiskey. Cafeteria. (Daily; closed Thanksgiving, Dec 25) Phone 332-1902.

2. **San Francisco Bay & Delta Hydraulic Model.** 2100 Bridgeway. Hydraulic model reproduces tidal action, currents and mixing of salt and fresh water and indicates trends in sediment deposition; the 850-square-mile bay-delta area is duplicated in a 3-acre building. Interactive exhibits, 9-min orientation video and 45-min general information audio tour. Self-guided tour; audio tours avail in 6 languages: English, French, German, Japanese, Spanish and Russian. (Memorial Day–Labor Day, daily exc Mon; rest of yr, Tues–Sat) Model in operation only during testing; for schedule phone 332-3870 (recording). **Free.**

(For further information contact the Chamber of Commerce, PO Box 566; 332-0505.)

Annual Event

Sausalito Art Festival. Labor Day wkend.

(See San Francisco, Tiburon)

Motel

★ ★ **ALTA MIRA.** *(Box 706) 125 Bulkley Ave. 415/332-1350; FAX 415/331-3862.* 35 rms, 2 story, 14 cottages. No A/C. S, D, cottages $75–$175; each addl $10. Restaurant 7 am–11 pm. Rm serv. Bar. Ck-out noon. Bellhops. Valet parking. Fireplace in cottages. Some balconies. On hillside above city; view of bay from many rms. Cr cds: A, C, D, MC, V, JCB.

Inns

★ ★ ★ **CASA MADRONA.** *801 Bridgeway. 415/332-0502; res: 800/288-0502; FAX 415/332-2537.* 30 rms, 5 cottages, 2 with kit. S, D $105–$225; each addl $10; cottages $145–$165. Parking $5. Complimentary continental bkfst, wine & cheese. Restaurant (see CASA MADRONA). Rm serv. Ck-out noon, ck-in 3 pm. Meeting rm. Bellhops. Valet serv. Concierge. Airport transportation avail. Whirlpool. Refrigerators, fireplaces. Many balconies, decks. Victorian house (1885); antiques. Cr cds: A, D, DS, MC, V.

★ ★ **SAUSALITO HOTEL.** *16 El Portal. 415/332-4155; FAX 415/332-3542.* 15 rms, 10 with bath, on 2nd story. No A/C. S, D $75–$175; suites $180–$210. TV. Complimentary continental bkfst. Ck-out noon, ck-in 2 pm. Built 1915. Victorian decor; antiques. Bay or park view from most rms. Cr cds: A, C, D, MC, V, JCB.

Restaurants

★ ★ **ANGELINO.** *621 Bridgeway. 415/331-5225.* Hrs: 11:30 am–10 pm; Fri–Sun to 11 pm. Closed Thanksgiving, Dec 25. Res accepted; required wkends. Italian menu. Bar. A la carte entrees: lunch $14–$25, dinner $18–$28. Specializes in seafood, pasta dishes. Cr cds: A, MC, V.

★ ★ ★ **CASA MADRONA.** *(See Casa Madrona Inn) 415/331-5888.* Hrs: 11:30 am–2:30 pm, 6–10 pm; Sat & Sun from 6 pm; Sun brunch 10:30 am–3 pm. Res accepted. Wine list. A la carte entrees: lunch $8–$15, dinner $13–$20. Sun brunch $19.50. Specializes in California regional cuisine. Own baking, desserts. Pianist. Valet parking. Outdoor dining. French country decor. View of bay. Cr cds: A, D, DS, MC, V.

★ **FLYNN'S LANDING.** *303 Johnson St. 415/332-0131.* Hrs: 11:30 am–10 pm. Closed Thanksgiving, Dec 25. Res accepted. No A/C. Bar. A la carte entrees: lunch $7.95–$12.95, dinner $12.95–$16.95. Specializes in seafood, pasta. Nautical decor. On waterfront. Cr cds: A, MC, V.

★ ★ **HORIZONS.** *558 Bridgeway. 415/331-3232.* Hrs: 11 am–11 pm; Sat & Sun from 10 am. Closed Thanksgiving, Dec 25. Res accepted. No A/C. Bar. Semi-a la carte: lunch, dinner $6.50–$25. Daily brunch $7.25–$14. Specializes in fresh seafood. Entertainment Tues & Wed evenings. Valet parking. Outdoor dining. View of San Francisco & East Bay. Family-owned. Cr cds: A, MC, V.

★ ★ **SCOMA'S.** *588 Bridgeway. 415/332-9551.* Hrs: 11:30 am–9:30 pm; Tues & Wed from 5:30 pm. Closed Jan 1, Thanksgiving, Dec 24 & 25. Italian menu. Bar. Semi-a la carte: lunch $7–$13.50, dinner $12.50–$19. Child's meals. Specializes in seafood, pasta. Landmark Victorian building at end of wharf; view of bay. Family-owned. Cr cds: A, C, D, MC, V.

★ **SEVEN SEAS.** *682 Bridgeway. 415/332-1304.* Hrs: 8 am–11 pm; Sat & Sun brunch noon–3 pm. Res accepted. No A/C. Bar. Semi-a la carte: bkfst $1.50–$9.25, lunch & dinner $5.95–$22.95. Sun brunch $7.50–$10.75. Specializes in pizza, seafood, steak. Outdoor dining. Coffee bar, ice cream, pastry at entrance; "greenhouse" dining area has movable roof to open or close as weather permits. Family-owned. Cr cds: A, D, MC, V.

✔ ★ ★ **SPINNAKER.** *100 Spinnaker Dr, at end of Anchor St. 415/332-1500.* Hrs: 11 am–11 pm; Sun brunch to 3 pm. Closed Thanksgiving, Dec 24–25; also 2nd wk Jan. Res accepted. Bar. A la carte entrees: lunch $7.95–$15.95, dinner $8.95–$18. Sat & Sun brunch $6.75–$12. Child's meals. Specialties: bouillabaise, fresh seafood, fresh pasta. Valet parking. View of bridges and bay. Family-owned. Cr cds: A, C, D, MC, V.

✔ ★ ★ **WINSHIPS.** *670 Bridgeway. 415/332-1454.* Hrs: 8 am–9:30 pm; Mon & Tues to 4 pm; early-bird dinner Wed–Sun 5–7:30 pm; Sun brunch 8 am–1 pm. Closed Thanksgiving, Dec 25. Res accepted. Bar. Semi-a la carte: bkfst $5.95–$11.95, lunch $5.75–$14.45, dinner $7.95–$15.45. Sun brunch $3.50–$9.45. Child's meals. Specializes in fresh seafood, pasta. Nautical decor; ship models, marine artifacts. Family-owned. Totally nonsmoking. Cr cds: A, C, D, DS, MC, V.

Sequoia & Kings Canyon National Parks (F-4)

(55 mi E of Fresno on CA 180; 35 mi E of Visalia on CA 198)

Although independently established, Sequoia and Kings Canyon National Parks are geographically and administratively one. Lying across the heart of the Sierra Nevada in eastern central California, they comprise more than 1,300 square miles and include some 75 isolated groves of spectacular giant sequoias, towering granite peaks, deep canyons and hundreds of alpine lakes. Giant sequoias reach their greatest size and are found in the largest numbers here. Mount Whitney, 14,495 feet, is the highest point in the lower 48 states. Some rocks of the foothill and summit area indicate that this whole region once lay under the ocean.

Allow plenty of driving time due to the gradient into and out of the mountains. Gasoline is available all year in both parks, as are limited groceries. Camping (no trailer hookups) is restricted to designated areas. Many of the campgrounds are closed by snow, October–late May. Routes to Sequoia and Kings Canyon National Parks involve some travel over steep grades, which may extend driving times. Winter visitors should carry tire chains. Entry fee valid for 7 days. For information contact Sequoia and Kings Canyon National Parks, Three Rivers 93271; 209/565-3134 or -3341.

What to See and Do

1. **Foothills, Lodgepole and Grant Grove Visitor Centers.** Exhibits, photos, data about the parks; expert advice on how to organize sightseeing. Schedules of campfire talks and guided trips are posted here. (Daily) Phone: Foothills 209/565-3134; Lodgepole 209/565-3782; Grant Grove 209/335-2856.

2. **Giant Forest.** One of the finest groves of giant sequoias. The General Sherman Tree is the largest living thing on earth. At 275 feet high and 103 feet in circumference, it is estimated to be 2,300–2,700 years old. Moro Rock, Crescent Meadow, Crystal Cave and Tokopah Valley are in this section of the park. Horses, pack animals available at Wolverton Pack Station.

3. **General Grant Grove.** Includes the General Grant Tree, 267 feet tall with a circumference of 108 feet. Saddle rides.

4. **Redwood Mountain Grove.** Includes the Hart Tree, a large sequoia; accessible by trail.

5. **Cedar Grove.** In canyon of S Fork of Kings River. Towering peaks rise a mile high above the stream. Horses, pack animals. Road closed Nov–Apr.

6. **The high country.** Vast region of wilderness, mountains, canyons, rivers, lakes and meadows, accessible by trail. The Sierra Crest forms the eastern boundary.

7. **Boyden Cavern.** Located in King's River Canyon, between Grant Grove and Cedar Grove. A 45-minute tour on lighted, handrail-equipped trail through ornate chambers with massive stalagmites, stalactites and columns. (May–Oct; daily) Sr citizen rate. For further information contact PO Box 78, Vallecito 95251; 209/736-2708. ¢¢¢

8. **Fishing** for trout is excellent in a few lakes and streams; the most popular spots are along Kings River and the forks of the Kaweah River. Some stores in the park sell state fishing licenses.

(See Porterville, Three Rivers)

Motels

(Note: All accommodations within Sequoia and Kings Canyon National Parks are operated by Guest Services, Inc under concession from the Dept of the Interior and are listed for those wishing to stay in the park proper. Reservations are advised and should be made through the central office, phone 209/561-3314 or write to Sequoia Guest Services, Reservations Manager, PO Box 789, Three Rivers 93271.)

★**CEDAR GROVE LODGE.** *(Box 789, Three Rivers 93271) At end of CA 180, 30 mi E of General Grant Grove.* 209/561-3314. 18 rms, 2 story. No rm phones. May–Sept: S, D $77.50; each addl $6; under 12 free. Closed rest of yr. Crib $7.50. Restaurant 7 am–9 pm. Ck-out 11 am. Coin lndry. Gift shop. Picnic tables, grills. Cr cds: MC, V.

★**GIANT FOREST LODGE.** *(Box 789, Three Rivers 93271) 17¼ mi N of park entrance on CA 198.* 209/561-3314; FAX 209/565-3249. 244 rms in motel, cottages, rustic cabins, 101 with bath. No A/C. No rm phones. Rustic cabins (closed in winter): semi-housekeeping (no equipt; patio with woodburning stove); some without electricity; no bath. Late May–Oct: S, D $35–$111; each addl $6; lower rates rest of yr. Crib $7.50. Restaurant 7 am–9 pm; dining rm (May–Oct) 7–11 am, 4:30–9 pm. Bar 5–11 pm. Ck-out 11 am. Sundries. Gift shop. X-country ski on site. Sledding, tobogganing. Some balconies. In Sequoia Natl Park. Cr cds: MC, V.

★**STONY CREEK LODGE.** *(Box 789, Three Rivers 93271) Generals Hwy, Sequoia & Kings Canyon Natl Parks.* 209/561-3314; FAX 209/565-3249. 11 rms, 2 story. No A/C. No rm phones. Late May–mid-Sept: S, D $77.50; each addl $6; under 12 free. Closed rest of yr. Restaurant 7 am–9 pm. Ck-out 11 am. Coin lndry. Gift shop. Cr cds: MC, V.

Solvang (H-2)

Founded: 1911 **Pop:** 4,741 **Elev:** 495 ft **Area code:** 805 **Zip:** 93463

Founded by Danes from the Midwest in 1911, a corner of Denmark has been re-created here. Solvang is a community of picturesque Danish-style buildings, which include four windmills. Rich Danish pastries and Danish imports are featured in its shops.

What to See and Do

1. **Old Mission Santa Inés** (1804). 1760 Mission Dr. Established by Fray Estevan Tapis as the 19th mission. A gold adobe building with red-tiled roof, garden and arched colonnade in front. Used as a

church; many artifacts, manuscripts and vestments on exhibit; recorded tour. (Daily; closed hols) Phone 688-4815. ¢

2. **Lake Cachuma Recreation Area.** 6 mi E on CA 246, then 6 mi S on CA 154. Swimming pool (summer); fishing; boating (rentals). General store. Camping (hookups). Fees for some activities. (Daily) Phone 688-8780 (recording). Per vehicle day-use ¢¢

(For further information contact the Conference & Visitors Bureau, 1511-A Mission Dr, PO Box 70; 800/468-6765.)

Annual Event

Danish Days Festival. Danish folk dancing, singing, band concerts; parade on Sat. 3rd wkend Sept.

Seasonal Event

Solvang Theaterfest. 420 Second St. The Pacific Conservatory of the Performing Arts (PCPA) presents musicals, dramas, new works and classics in an outdoor theater. Contact PCPA Theaterfest, PO Box 1700, Santa Maria 93456; 922-8313. Early June–early Sept.

(See Lompoc, Santa Barbara)

Motels

(Rates are generally higher during special celebrations)

✔ ★ ★ ★**BEST WESTERN ANDERSEN'S INN.** *(Box 197, Buellton 93427) On CA 246, just W of US 101.* 805/688-3216; FAX 805/688-9767. 97 rms, 2 story. May–Sept: S $47–$57; D $58–$62; each addl $6; lower rates rest of yr. Crib $3. TV; cable. Heated pool; whirlpool. Complimentary continental bkfst, coffee. Restaurant 5 am–10 pm. Bar from 11 am. Ck-out noon. Sundries. Putting green. Some refrigerators. Private patios. Gazebo. Cr cds: A, C, D, DS, ER, MC, V.

★ ★**BEST WESTERN KRONBORG INN.** *1440 Mission Dr.* 805/688-2383. 39 rms, 2 story. June–Sept: S, D $65–$85; each addl $5; under 12 free; higher rates special hols (2-night min); lower rates rest of yr. Crib free. Pet accepted, some restrictions. TV; cable. Pool; whirlpool. Complimentary continental bkfst. Complimentary coffee in rms. Restaurant nearby. Ck-out 11 am. Refrigerators. Balconies. Cr cds: A, C, D, DS, MC, V.

★ ★**CHIMNEY SWEEP INN.** *1554 Copenhagen Dr.* 805/688-2111; res: 800/824-6444; FAX 805/688-8824. 28 units, 1–2 story, 6 kit. cottages. S, D $65–$90; each addl $10; suites $100–$125; kit. cottages $135–$215. Crib $5. TV; cable. Complimentary continental bkfst. Coffee in rms. Ck-out 11 am. Whirlpool. Whirlpool with kit. cottages. Cr cds: A, DS, MC, V.

★ ★ ★**DANISH COUNTRY INN.** *1455 Mission Dr.* 805/688-2018; res: 800/44-RELAX; FAX 805/688-1156. 82 rms, 3 story, 9 suites. S $105–$115; D $115–$125; each addl $10; suites $150; under 12 free. Crib free. TV; cable, in-rm movies. Heated pool; whirlpool. Complimentary full bkfst. Restaurant 6–9:30 am; Sat & Sun from 7 am. Ck-out noon. Meeting rms. Refrigerators. Balconies. Country inn elegance. Sitting rm. Antiques. Cr cds: A, C, D, DS, MC, V, JCB.

✔ ★ ★**RAMADA INN AT THE WINDMILL.** *(114 E CA 246, Buellton 93427) 3 mi W, at jct US 101 & CA 246.* 805/688-8448; FAX 805/686-1338. 108 rms, 2 story. Mar–Aug: S $42–$74; D $48–$82; suites $104; under 18 free; lower rates rest of yr. Crib free. TV; cable, in-rm movies. Heated pool; whirlpool. Complimentary continental bkfst wkends, coffee. Bar 4 pm–midnight. Ck-out noon. Coin lndry. Meeting rms. Sundries. Patios, balconies. Danish-style architecture. Cr cds: A, C, D, DS, MC, V, JCB.

★ ★**ROYAL COPENHAGEN.** *1579 Mission Dr. 805/688-5561; res: 800/624-6604 (CA).* 48 units, 1–2 story. S, D $60–$80; each addl $6; suites $95. Crib $6. TV; cable. Heated pool. Complimentary continental bkfst. Restaurant nearby. Ck-out 11 am. Danish motif. Cr cds: A, MC, V.

★ ★**SVENDSGAARD'S DANISH LODGE.** *1711 Mission Dr. 805/688-3277; res: 800/341-8000; 800/733-8757 (CA).* 48 rms, 3 story, 4 kits. S, D $55–$100; each addl $6; suites, kit. units $63–$104. Crib free. TV; cable. Heated pool; whirlpool. Complimentary continental bkfst. Restaurant nearby. Ck-out 11 am. Refrigerators; some gas or electric fireplaces. Private balconies. Sun deck. Mission opp. Cr cds: A, C, D, DS, MC, V, JCB.

Hotels

★ ★ ★**HOLIDAY INN.** *(555 McMurray Rd, Buellton 93427) At jct US 101 & CA 246. 805/688-1000; FAX 805/688-0380.* 149 units, 4 story. S $89; D $95; each addl $10; suites $155–$250; family rates. Crib free. TV; cable. Heated pool; poolside serv in summer. Coffee in rms. Restaurants 7 am–10 pm. Bar. Ck-out noon. Coin lndry. Meeting rms. Airport, bus depot transportation. Tennis. Exercise rm; instructor, weights, bicycles, whirlpool. Game rm. Rec rm. Minibars. Balconies. Picnic tables. Elaborate landscaping; fountains. 3 movie theaters. Cr cds: A, C, D, DS, MC, V, JCB.

★ ★ ★**SOLVANG ROYAL SCANDINAVIAN INN.** *(Box 30) 400 Alisal Rd. 805/688-8000; res: 800/624-5572; FAX 805/688-0761.* 133 rms, 3 story. June–Sept: S, D $95–$135; each addl $10; suites $135–$245; under 18 free; lower rates rest of yr. Crib free. TV; cable. Heated pool; whirlpool. Restaurant 7 am–10 pm. Bar 11–2 am; entertainment, dancing. Ck-out 11 am. Meeting rms. Refrigerator, wet bar in suites. Many patios, balconies. Custom-made Danish furniture. Cr cds: A, C, D, DS, ER, MC, V, JCB.

Inns

★ ★ ★ ★**LOS OLIVOS GRAND HOTEL.** *(PO Box 526, 2860 Grand Ave, Los Olivos 93441) 2 mi E of US 101 on CA 154. 805/688-7788; res: 800/446-2455; FAX 805/688-1942.* 21 rms, 2 story. Wkends: S, D $210–$255; suite $325; lower rates mid-wk. Crib free. TV; cable. Heated pool; whirlpool, poolside serv. Coffee in rms. Complimentary continental bkfst. Dining rm 11:30 am–2:30 pm, 5–9 pm; Sat & Sun 8 am–3 pm, 5–9 pm. Rm serv. Ck-out noon, ck-in 3 pm. Meeting rms. Bellhops. Valet serv. Fireplaces. Library. Elegant furnishings; many antiques. Bicycles avail. Elaborate landscaping; arbor, gazebo. Luxury hideaway located in the Santa Ynez Valley. Cr cds: A, DS, MC, V.

★ ★ ★**PETERSEN VILLAGE INN.** *1576 Mission Dr. 805/688-3121; res: 800/321-8985 (CA); FAX 805/688-5732.* 42 rms, 3 story. S, D $95–$165; suites $145–$220. Children over 7 yrs only. TV; cable. Complimentary European buffet bkfst 7:30–11:30 am. Complimentary coffee, tea in rms. Dining rm 8 am–9 pm. Pianist; complimentary wine. Ck-out 1 pm, ck-in 3 pm. Bellhops. Whirlpool, fireplace in suites. Some private patios, balconies. Replica of old Danish village; 28 shops on premises; garden area. Cr cds: A, MC, V.

Guest Ranch

★ ★ ★**ALISAL.** *1054 Alisal Rd, 2½ mi S. 805/688-6411; FAX 805/688-2510.* 73 units. No A/C. No rm phones. MAP (2-day min): S $230–$350; D $270–$350; each addl $65; package plans. Crib $30. TV in lounge; cable. Heated pool; whirlpool, poolside serv in season, lifeguard in summer. Supervised child's activities (June–mid-Sept & hols). Coffee in rms. Dining rm 8–9:45 am, 6:30–8:30 pm (jacket dinner); closed to public. Cookouts in season, picnic lunches, bkfst rides. Snack bar at golf course. Bars 11 am–midnight. Ck-out 1 pm, ck-in 4 pm. Coin lndry. Bellhops. Tennis, pro. 18-hole golf, greens fee $45, cart $22, pro, putting green. Sailboats, rowboats, windsurfing. Indoor, outdoor games. Hayrides. Horseback riding. Trail rides. Adult, child rec rms. Dancing, entertainment nightly. Winery tours. Fireplaces, refrigerators. Library. 10,000-acre working ranch, up to 2,000 head of cattle. Large private lake. Cr cds: A, MC, V.

Restaurants

★ ★★**MASSIMI RISTORANTE.** *1588 Mission Dr. 805/688-0027.* Hrs: 5:30–9:30 pm. Closed Mon; Jan 1, Dec 25. Res accepted. Italian menu. Wine, beer. Semi-a la carte: dinner $11–$20. Specialties: osso buco, veal chop Florentine, quail with polenta & mushrooms. Outdoor dining. Italian country decor. Totally nonsmoking. Cr cds: MC, V.

✔ ★**MUSTARD SEED.** *1655 Mission Dr. 805/688-1318.* Hrs: 8 am–2:30 pm, 4:30–9 pm; Sat-Mon from 4:30 pm. Closed Jan 1, Dec 25. Res accepted. Wine, beer. Semi-a la carte: bkfst $3.25–$6.25, lunch $3.95–$6.25, dinner $6.95–$10.95. Child's meals. Specializes in omelets, soup, salad. Parking. Outdoor dining. Casual dining. Cr cds: MC, V.

Sonoma (D-1)

Founded: 1823 **Pop:** 8,121 **Elev:** 84 ft **Area code:** 707 **Zip:** 95476

Mission San Francisco Solano (1823) was secularized under Mariano Guadalupe Vallejo in 1834. Vallejo had been sent by Governor Figueroa to investigate Russian activities at Fort Ross (see FORT ROSS STATE HISTORIC PARK). This mission was the last and most northerly of the 21 Franciscan missions in California and the only one established under Mexican rule.

On June 14, 1846, Sonoma was the scene of the Bear Flag Revolt—establishing the California Republic, which lasted until July 9.

What to See and Do

1. **Sonoma State Historic Park.** General Vallejo's house (1851-80), W Spain St & 3rd St W; Mission San Francisco Solano (1823-46), barracks (1840-46), E Spain St & 1st St E; other buildings on and near Sonoma Plaza. Picnicking. (Daily; closed Jan 1, Thanksgiving, Dec 25) Phone 938-1519. ¢

2. **Jack London State Historic Park.** 8½ mi W on CA 12, then 1½ mi W of Glen Ellen on London Ranch Rd. Memorial, "House of Happy Walls," and grave of author. Wolf House ruins, Jack London cottage; farm building; winery structure ruins located in beautiful Valley of the Moon. Hiking trails. Park (daily). Museum (daily; closed Jan 1, Thanksgiving, Dec 25). Sr citizen rate. Phone 938-5216. Per vehicle ¢¢

3. **Sonoma Depot Museum.** 270 1st St W. Rebuilt train depot (1880) houses historical artifacts; display scenes depicting Sonoma heritage, including "Manifest Destiny 1846," focusing on Bear Flag Revolt; also Rand Room, featuring railroad items; changing exhibits. (Wed–Sun afternoons; closed Jan 1, Thanksgiving, Dec 25) Phone 938-9765. ¢

4. **Train Town.** 20264 Broadway. Steam-powered miniature railroad makes 20-min run through landscaped park with animals, waterfalls and historic replica structures. (June–Sept, daily; rest of yr, Fri–Sun) Sr citizen rate. Phone 938-3912. ¢¢

5. **Haraszthy Villa.** E via Napa St, then N on Old Winery Rd, in Bartholomew Memorial Park. Villa built in 1861 by Count Agoston Haraszthy has been re-created; also vineyard and gazebo. Picnicking.

(Wed, Sat & Sun; mid-morning–mid-afternoon) Phone 938-2244. **Free.**

6. Wineries.

Sebastiani Vineyards & Winery. 389 4th St E. Large collection of carved casks. Guided tours; tasting room and aging cellars may be visited. (Daily; closed major hols) Phone 938-5532 or 800/888-5532. **Free.**

Buena Vista Winery. 18000 Old Winery Rd, 1½ mi E. Cellars built in 1857. Historical panels; tasting room; art gallery; picnic area. Concerts in summer; special events. Tours (daily; closed Jan 1, Thanksgiving, Dec 25). Phone 938-1266 or 800/926-1266. **Free.**

Gloria Ferrer Champagne Caves. 23555 CA 121, 6 mi S. Guided tours through "champagne caves" (inquire for schedule); wine tasting. (Daily; closed Thanksgiving, Dec 25; also early Jan) Phone 996-7256. **¢¢**

Chateau St Jean. 10 mi N, at 8555 Sonoma Hwy (CA 12), in Kenwood. Self-guided tours, tasting. Picnic area. (Daily; closed major hols) Phone 833-4134. **Free.**

7. Sears Point Raceway. CA 37 & CA 121. Motor sports entertainment, including NASCAR Cup, NHRA drag racing, SCCA pro and amateur road races, AMA and AFM motorcycle events, vintage car races, amateur drag racing, car clubs. Under 12 yrs with adult only. (Daily; closed Dec 25) Phone 938-8448. **¢¢¢¢–¢¢¢¢¢**

(For further information contact the Sonoma Valley Visitors Bureau, 453 1st St E; 996-1090.)

Annual Event

Valley of the Moon Vintage Festival. California's oldest wine festival. Parades, wine tasting, folk dancing. Usually last full wkend Sept.

(See Calistoga, Napa, Petaluma, St Helena, Santa Rosa)

Motels

★ ★**BEST WESTERN SONOMA VALLEY INN.** *550 2nd St W. 707/938-9200; FAX 707/938-0935.* 72 rms, 2 story. S, D $79–$145; each addl $10; under 12 free; golf plans. Crib free. TV; cable. Pool; whirlpool. Complimentary continental bkfst. Ck-out noon. Lndry facilities. Valet serv. Refrigerators; many fireplaces; some in-rm whirlpools. Private patios, balconies. Cr cds: A, C, D, DS, ER, MC, V, JCB.

✔ ★**EL PUEBLO.** *896 W Napa St. 707/996-3651.* 38 units, 2 story. Apr–Oct: S, D from $57; lower rates rest of yr. Crib $5. TV. Heated pool. Complimentary coffee in rms. Restaurant opp. Ck-out noon. Cr cds: A, MC, V.

Hotel

★ ★ ★**SONOMA MISSION INN & SPA.** *(PO Box 1447) 18140 Sonoma Hwy, Valley of the Moon area. 707/938-9000; res: 800/358-9022 (exc CA), 800/862-4945 (CA); FAX 707/938-4250.* 170 rms, 2–3 story. Apr–late Oct: S, D $170–$350; each addl $30; suites $475–$650; lower rates rest of yr. Crib free. TV; cable, in-rm movies. 2 heated pools. Restaurant 7 am–10 pm (also see THE GRILLE). Bar 11–1 am; entertainment. Ck-out noon. Meeting rms. Concierge. Beauty shop. Airport transportation to San Francisco avail. Lighted tennis, pro. 18-hole golf privileges. Exercise rm; instructor, weights, bicycles, whirlpool, sauna, steam rm. Natural hot artesian mineral water in both pools and whirlpool. Full European-style spa. Refrigerators, honor bars. Some private patios, balconies. Early morning guided country hikes. Country inn built 1927; restored. Spanish mission-style architecture. Cr cds: A, C, D, MC, V.

Inns

✔ ★**MAGLIULO'S.** *691 Broadway. 707/996-1031.* 5 rms, 2 with bath, 1 A/C. No rm phones. S, D $75–$85. Continental bkfst 8–10 am. Restaurant (see MAGLIULO'S). Bar to 11 pm. Ck-out noon, ck-in 3 pm. Century-old Victorian home; some antiques. Totally nonsmoking. Cr cds: DS, MC, V.

★ ★ ★**TROJAN HORSE.** *19455 Sonoma Hwy (CA 12). 707/996-2430; res: 800/899-1925.* 6 rms. No rm phones. May–Oct: S, D $110–$130; each addl $20; mid-wk rates; lower rates rest of yr. Crib $10. Complimentary full bkfst, evening refreshments. Restaurant nearby. Rm serv. Ck-out 11:30 am, ck-in 3 pm. Whirlpool. Picnic tables. Restored pioneer family home (1887); period antiques. Totally nonsmoking. Cr cds: A, MC, V.

★ ★**VICTORIAN GARDEN.** *316 E Napa St. 707/996-5339; res: 800/543-5339.* 4 rms, 2 story. No rm phones. D $79–$139. Complimentary California bkfst. Ck-out noon, ck-in 2–5 pm. Pool. Private patios. Picnic tables. Former farmhouse (1870); gardens. Cr cds: A, D, ER, MC, V.

Restaurants

★ ★**DEPOT 1870.** *241 1st St W. 707/938-2980.* Hrs: 11:30 am–2 pm, 5–9 pm; Sat & Sun from 5 pm. Closed Mon & Tues; Jan 1, Dec 25. Res accepted. Northern Italian menu. Beer, wine. Semi-a la carte: lunch $6.75–$13.50, dinner $7.75–$17.50. Child's meals. Parking. Outdoor dining around pool. Historic stone building (1870); originally a hotel, later a saloon and private residence. Restored in 1962. Herb garden. Cr cds: A, D, DS, MC, V.

★ ★ ★**THE GRILLE.** *(See Sonoma Mission Inn & Spa Hotel) 707/938-9000.* Hrs: 11:30 am–2:30 pm, 6–10 pm; Sun brunch 9 am–2 pm. Res accepted. Bar 11–1 am. Extensive wine cellar. A la carte entrees: lunch $10–$19, dinner $15–$29. Sun brunch $12–$22. Complete meals: dinner $35. Specializes in wine country cuisine featuring local seafood, game, produce. Own baking. Pianist. Valet parking. Outdoor poolside dining. Totally nonsmoking. Cr cds: A, C, D, MC, V.

✔ ★**LA CASA.** *121 E Spain St. 707/996-3406.* Hrs: 11:30 am–9 pm; Fri &, Sat to 10 pm. Closed Easter, Thanksgiving, Dec 25. Res accepted. Mexican menu. Bar. Semi-a la carte: lunch, dinner $4–$11. Specializes in fresh snapper Veracruz, tamales, chimichangas. Mexican decor. Outdoor dining. Cr cds: A, C, D, MC, V.

★ ★**MAGLIULO'S.** *(See Magliulo's Inn) 707/996-1031.* Hrs: 11 am–9 pm; Sun brunch to 2:30 pm. Closed Dec 25. Res accepted; required Sat. Italian, Amer menu. Bar. A la carte entrees: lunch, dinner $3.95–$16.95. Sun brunch $5.95–$12.95. Child's meals. Specialties: chicken Marsala, veal scaloppini. Parking. Outdoor dining. Provincial decor. Cr cds: DS, MC, V.

★ ★**PIATTI.** *405 First St W. 707/996-2351.* Hrs: 11:30 am–2:30 pm, 5–10 pm; Sat & Sun 11 am–10 pm. Res accepted. Italian menu. Bar. A la carte entrees: lunch $7.50–$11.95, dinner $8.95–$15.95. Child's meals. Specialties: ravioli with lemon cream, lasagne al pesto. Outdoor dining. Italian country atmosphere. Cr cds: A, MC, V.

✔ ★**SONOMA GROVE.** *19315 Sonoma Hwy (CA 12). 707/996-5777.* Hrs: 11:30 am–10 pm. Closed Thanksgiving, Dec 24 & 25. Bar to midnight. Semi-a la carte: lunch $4.50–$9.50, dinner $7.50–$16. Child's meals. Specializes in prime rib, lamb, veal, seafood. Own baklava. Parking. Cr cds: A, MC, V.

Sonora (E-3)

Settled: 1848 **Pop:** 4,153 **Elev:** 1,825 ft **Area code:** 209 **Zip:** 95370

Mexican miners named this the Sonoran Camp for their home state. Mexicans, Chileans and Americans did not mix well and the camp became peaceful only after the Latins fled the wild Yankees. At the Big Bonanza, richest pocket mine in the Mother Lode, $160,000 in nearly pure gold was harvested in a single day. Stretching across seven hills, this colorful town, the seat of Tuolumne County, was the setting for several tales by Mark Twain and Bret Harte.

What to See and Do

1. **Columbia State Historic Park.** 4 mi N via CA 49 & Parrotts Ferry Rd. The 1850 gold town of Columbia is being restored to its early glory. The gold boom brought stages, freight wagons, brick stores, all the facilities of civilization and thousands of gold-hungry miners. Operating gold mine tour; gold panning; stagecoach ride; concessions (fees). Free slide show in museum. Guided tours (summer, wknds). While still in the process of restoration, most of the buildings are open (daily; closed Thanksgiving, Dec 25; some shops closed wkdays in winter). Phone 532-4301. Among the 40 buildings on the self-guided tour are

    Firehouse. Tuolumne Engine Co #1 and pumper "Papeete." **Free.**

    Schoolhouse (1860). One of the oldest of its kind in the state; in use until 1937; authentically refurnished. **Free.**

    Eagle Cotage *(sic)*. Reconstructed boardinghouse. Outside viewing only.

    City Hotel. Refitted as period restaurant and hotel.

2. **Railtown 1897 State Historic Park.** 3 mi S in Jamestown. Steam passenger train rides (daytime, 1 hr; evening, 2 hrs) over the Sierra foothills. Roundhouse tour. Park (daily). Rides (Mar–Nov, Sat, Sun & hols). Reservations are necessary. Combination tickets are avail. For information contact Railtown, PO Box 1250, Jamestown 95327; 984-3953. Tours ¢¢ Rides ¢¢¢

3. **Moaning Cavern.** 5350 Moaning Cave Rd, 12 mi N near Vallecito. Discovered in 1849. View formations from 100-foot spiral staircase. Walking tour (45 min). Vistors may also descend into the cavern via 180-foot rope rappel; or take a 3-hr tour into the undeveloped cavern depths (by appt). Display of Native American and mining artifacts. (Daily) Phone 736-2708. ¢¢

4. **Mercer Caverns.** 10 mi N on CA 49, then 5 mi NE on CA 4. Stalagmites, stalactites, aragonite, other formations in caves discovered in 1885. Ten rooms; lighted walkways; 55°F; 45-min guided tours. (June–Sept, daily; rest of yr, wkends & school hols; closed Thanksgiving, Dec 25) Picnic area. Phone 728-2101. ¢¢

5. **Stanislaus National Forest.** NE & SE of town. More than 890,000 acres; contains Emigrant Wilderness, Carson-Iceberg Wilderness and a portion (22,917 acres) of the Mokelumne Wilderness. The forest has many developed recreation sites with swimming; fishing; boating, rafting. Hiking, bridle trails. Winter sports. Picnicking. More than 40 developed campgrounds (fee). For further information contact the Forest Supervisor's Office, 19777 Greenley Rd; 532-3671 or the Summit Ranger District Office at 965-3434.

6. **Skiing.**

    Bear Valley. 17 mi NW on CA 49, then 50 mi E on CA 4. Two triple, 7 double chairlifts, 2 surface lifts; patrol, school, rentals; restaurant, cafeteria, concession area, bar; lodging. Longest run 3 mi; vertical drop 1,900 ft. (Nov–Apr, daily) Cross-country skiing also available in area (phone 753-2834). Half-day rates. Phone 753-2301, -2308 (snow phone). ¢¢¢¢¢

    Dodge Ridge. 30 mi E on CA 108. Two triple, 5 double chairlifts, 4 rope tows; patrol, school, rentals; cafeteria, bar; day-lodge, nursery. 28 runs; longest run 2¼ mi; vertical drop 1,600 ft. Snowboard-

ing. (Mid-Nov–mid-Apr, daily) Phone 965-3474 or -4444 (snow conditions, 24 hrs). ¢¢¢¢¢

7. **Don Pedro Lake Recreation Area.** 13 mi S off CA 120. A 26-mile-long lake impounded by 580-ft dam. Swimming (fee); fishing; boat launching (marinas). Picnicking. Camping (fee; hookups). No pets. (Daily) Fee for activities. Phone 852-2396. Per vehicle ¢¢

8. **New Melones Lake Recreation Area.** 10 N via CA 49, situated between Angels Camp, Sonora and Columbia. When full, the lake offers more than 100 mi of shoreline for water and fishing sports, as well as 7-lane launch ramps, fish cleaning facilities and a marina. During low lake levels, river rafting is popular on the Stanislaus River. Improved camping & day use facilities avail in the Glory Hole and Tuttletown recreation areas. (All yr, daily; some sections of day use areas & campgrounds may be closed during winter) Standard fees. Phone 536-9094 or 800/446-1333.

(For further information contact the Tuolumne County Visitors Bureau, PO Box 4020; 800/446-1333.)

Annual Events

Fireman's Muster. Columbia State Historic Park (see #1). Antique fire engines, pumping contests. Early May.

Mother Lode Roundup Parade and Rodeo. Mother Lode Fairgrounds on CA 108. Mother's Day wkend.

Mother Lode Fair. Fairgrounds. 4 days mid-July.

Wild West Film Fest & Rodeo. Fairgrounds. Last wkend Sept.

(See Modesto, Oakdale)

Motel

✔ ★★**GUNN HOUSE.** 286 S Washington St. 209/532-3421. 24 rms, 23 A/C, 2–3 story. No rm phones. No elvtr. S $45; D $55–$75. TV. Heated pool. Continental bkfst in lounge. Restaurant opp 6–10 pm. Bar 4 pm–midnight, closed Sun. Ck-out noon. Refrigerators. Built 1850; restored in authentic Victorian decor; antiques. Cr cds: A, DS, MC, V.

Motor Hotel

★**SONORA INN.** 160 S Washington St. 209/532-2400; res: 800/321-5261; FAX 209/532-4542. 64 rms, 3 story. S, D $40–$70; each addl $5; suites $109–$185; under 10 free; ski plans. Crib $5. TV; cable. Pool. Restaurant open 24 hrs. Ck-out 11 am. Meeting rms. Sundries. Some refrigerators. Cr cds: A, C, D, DS, MC, V.

Inns

★★**BARRETTA GARDENS.** 700 S Barretta St. 209/532-6039. 5 rms, 2 story. S, D $80–$95. TV in parlor. Complimentary full bkfst, refreshments. Ck-out 11 am, ck-in 3–5 pm. Whirlpool. Antiques. 3 parlors, one with fireplace. Victorian house (1903). Cr cds: A, MC, V.

★★**CITY HOTEL.** (Box 1870, Columbia 95310) N on CA 49, on Main St. 209/532-1479. 10 rms, 2 story. No rm phones. S $65–$90; D $70–$95; each addl $10; theater packages avail. Crib free. Complimentary continental bkfst, sherry. Restaurant (see CITY HOTEL). Bar. Ck-out noon, ck-in 2 pm. Concierge. Balconies. Restored Gold Rush-era hotel (1856). Many antiques. Cr cds: A, MC, V.

★★**FALLON.** (Box 1870, Columbia 95310) 3 mi N on CA 49. 209/532-1470. 14 rms, 2 story. No rm phones. S, D $45–$90; suite $130; theater packages. Crib free. Continental bkfst. Ck-out noon, ck-in 2 pm.

Meeting rms. Concierge. Balconies. Established 1857; in Columbia State Historic Park. Cr cds: A, MC, V.

★★**JAMESTOWN HOTEL.** *(Box 539, Jamestown 95327) On Main St, 3 mi W on CA 108. 209/984-3902.* 8 air-cooled rms, 2 story. No rm phones. S, D $55–$85; lower rates Oct–April (Sun–Thurs). Complimentary continental bkfst. Restaurant (see JAMESTOWN HOTEL). Bar 11 am–10:30 pm. Ck-out noon, ck-in 2 pm. Balconies. Restored gold rush era-style hotel (1859). Antique furnishings, lace curtains. Cr cds: A, DS, MC, V.

★**NATIONAL HOTEL.** *(PO Box 502, Jamestown 95327) On Main St, 3 mi W on CA 108. 209/984-3446.* 11 rms, 5 with bath, 2 story. No rm phones. S, D $65–$80; each addl $8; higher rates Fri, Sat. Children over 10 yrs only. TV avail. Complimentary continental bkfst. Dining rm 10 am–10 pm; Sun 11 am–9 pm. Rm serv. Ck-out noon, ck-in 2 pm. Free local airport transportation. Balconies. Continuously operated since 1859. Cr cds: MC, V.

Restaurants

★★★**CITY HOTEL.** *(See City Hotel Inn) 209/532-1479.* Hrs: 5–9 pm; Sun brunch 11 am–2 pm. Closed Mon; Dec 25. Res accepted. Contemporary French menu. Bar to 11 pm. A la carte entrees: dinner $13–$19. Complete meals: dinner $28.50. Sun brunch $11–$14. Specializes in California French cuisine, Caesar salad. Own baking, desserts. Parking. Restored Gold Rush-era hotel (1856). Cr cds: A, MC, V.

★★★**HEMINGWAY'S.** *362 S Stewart St. 209/532-4900.* Hrs: 11:30 am–2:30 pm, 5 pm–closing. Closed Mon; Jan 1, Thanksgiving, Dec 24, 25. Res accepted. Continental menu. Beer. Wine list. Semi-a la carte: lunch $6–$15, dinner $20–$35. Complete meals: dinner $35. Specialties: Mahagony duckling, tournedos of veal. Own desserts. Dinner theater Fri, Sat. Outdoor dining. Rotating menu. Country European cafe. Ernest Hemingway theme. Cr cds: A, MC, V.

✔★★★**JAMESTOWN HOTEL.** *(See Jamestown Hotel Inn) 209/984-3902.* Hrs: 11:30 am–2:30 pm, 5–9 pm; Fri, Sat to 10 pm; Sun 4–9 pm; Sun brunch 10 am–2:30 pm. Res accepted. Bar 11 am–midnight. Wine list. Semi-a la carte: lunch $4.95–$9.95, dinner $7.95–$17.95. Sun brunch $6.25–$10.95. Specializes in prime rib, fresh seafood, pasta. Seasonal entertainment on patio. Outdoor dining. Historic building (1859); 19th-century bar. Victorian decor; antiques. Cr cds: A, DS, MC, V.

South Lake Tahoe (Lake Tahoe Area) (D-3)

Pop: 21,586 **Elev:** 6,260 ft **Area code:** 916

(For general information, map and attractions see Lake Tahoe Area; also see Stateline, NV.)

Motels

(For casinos and casino restaurants see Stateline, NV)

★★★**BEST WESTERN STATION HOUSE INN.** *901 Park Ave (96150). 916/542-1101; FAX 916/542-1714.* 102 rms, 2 story. June–Oct, hols: S, D $88–$98; each addl $10; suites $125–$200; under 6 free; ski plan; lower rates rest of yr. Crib $5. TV; cable. Heated pool; whirlpool, poolside serv. Complimentary full bkfst Oct–May. Restaurant 7:30–10:30 am, 5:30–10 pm; closed Wed. Bar from 4:30. Ck-out noon.

Meeting rms. Valet serv. Downhill ski 1 mi; x-country ski 14 mi. Private beach 2½ blks. Cr cds: A, C, D, DS, MC, V.

✔★**CEDAR LODGE.** *(Box 4547, 96157) 4069 Cedar Ave. 916/544-6453; res: 800/222-1177 (CA).* 35 rms, 2 story. Mid-June–mid-Sept, wknds, hols: S, D $42–$88; each addl $10; ski & golf plans; lower rates rest of yr. TV; cable. Heated pool; whirlpool (winter). Complimentary coffee in lobby. Restaurant nearby. Ck-out noon. Downhill ski 1 mi; x-country ski 15 mi. Some fireplaces. Beach privileges 4 blks. Cr cds: MC, V.

★★**FLAMINGO LODGE.** *3961 Lake Tahoe Blvd (96150). 916/544-5288; res: 800/544-5288.* 90 rms, 2 story. Mid-June–mid-Sept: S $69–$89; D $74–$89; each addl $10; kit. suites $104–$159; under 18 free; ski plan; higher rates: wknds, hols; lower rates rest of yr. Crib $10. TV; cable. Heated pool in season; whirlpools, sauna. Coffee in rms. Restaurant adj 6:30 am–midnight; summer & hols 7 am–9 pm. Ck-out noon. Coin lndry. Downhill ski 1 mi; x-country ski 5 mi. Refrigerators; some wet bars. Cr cds: A, C, D, DS, MC, V.

★★★**INN BY THE LAKE.** *3300 Lake Tahoe Blvd (96150). 916/542-0330; res: 800/877-1466; FAX 916/541-6596.* 99 rms, 3 story. June–Sept: S, D $98–$148; suites $175–$330; ski & golf plans; lower rates rest of yr. Crib $8. TV; cable, in-rm movies avail. Heated pool; whirlpool, sauna. Complimentary continental bkfst. Coffee in rms. Restaurant adj open 24 hrs. Ck-out noon. Coin lndry. Meeting rm. Valet serv. Sundries. Downhill ski 1½ mi; x-country ski 10 mi. Some refrigerators, wet bars, bathrm phones. Balconies. Lake opp. Cr cds: A, C, D, DS, MC, V.

✔★**MATTERHORN.** *(PO Box 7277, 96158) 2187 Lake Tahoe Blvd. 916/541-0367.* 18 rms, 2 story. No A/C. Mid-June–mid-Sept, wknds, hols: S, D $38–$58; kit. units $10 addl; lower rates rest of yr. Pet accepted; $20 and $5 per day. TV; cable. Heated pool. Complimentary coffee in lobby. Ck-out noon. Free airport transportation. Downhill ski 3 mi; x-country ski 10 mi. Hot tub. Near marina. Cr cds: A, DS, MC, V.

★**PACIFICA LODGE.** *(Box 4298, 96157) 931 Park Ave. 916/544-4131.* 67 rms, 2 story. June–Sept: S, D $65–$80; each addl $6; suites $90–$150; kits. $150; under 12 free; higher rates major hols; lower rates rest of yr. Crib $5. TV; cable. Heated pool; whirlpool. Complimentary continental bkfst. Restaurant nearby. Ck-out 11 am. Downhill ski 1 mi; x-country ski 14 mi. Some refrigerators, fireplaces, in-rm whirlpools. Some balconies. Private beach access. Cr cds: A, C, D, DS, MC, V, JCB.

★★**ROYAL VALHALLA.** *(Drawer GG, 96157) 4104 Lakeshore Blvd. 916/544-2233; res: 800/999-4104; FAX 916/544-1436.* 80 rms, 3 story, 30 kits. (some equipt). No A/C. June–Sept: S, D $76–$96; each addl $5; suites $76–$198; kit. units $5 addl; under 12 free; higher rates some hols; lower rates rest of yr. TV; cable. Heated pool. Complimentary continental bkfst. Complimentary coffee in rms. Restaurant nearby. Ck-out 11 am. Coin lndry. Sundries. Downhill ski 1½ mi; x-country ski 14 mi. Rec rm. Many private patios, balconies. Private beach. Cr cds: A, C, D, MC, V.

★**SOUTH SHORE INN.** *(Box 6470, 96157) 3900 Pioneer Trail. 916/544-1000.* 22 units, 2 story. No A/C. Mid-June–Sept, wknds, hols: S, D $48–$82; each addl $8; lower rates rest of yr. TV; cable. Complimentary coffee in lobby. Restaurant nearby. Ck-out 11 am. Some covered parking. Downhill ski 1 mi; x-country ski 14 mi. Sun deck. Cr cds: MC, V.

★★**TAHOE CHALET INN.** *3860 Lake Tahoe Blvd (96150). 916/544-3311; res: 800/821-2656; FAX 916/544-4069.* 66 units, 2 story,

14 suites, 6 kits. Some A/C. Mid-June–Sept & mid-Dec–Mar: S $58–$82; D $82–$88; suites $118–$220; kit. units addl $12; fishing, ski, golf plans; higher rates some hols; lower rates rest of yr. TV; cable. Pool. Complimentary continental bkfst, coffee. Restaurant nearby. Ck-out 11 am. Coin lndry. Meeting rms. Downhill ski 2½ mi. Exercise equipt; bicycle, rowing machine, whirlpool, sauna. Game rm. Many refrigerators. Some bathrm phones, wet bars. Some rms with in-rm whirlpool, fireplace. ¼ mi to lake. Cr cds: A, C, D, DS, MC, V.

✦ ★TAHOE SANDS INN. *(Box 18692, 96151) 3600 US 50, at Ski Run Blvd.* 916/544-3476; res: 800/237-8882; FAX 916/542-4011. 110 rms, 2 story. No A/C. Mid-May–mid-Sept, mid-Dec–Mar: S, D $58–$78; each addl $6; suites $85–$190; under 12 free; higher rates hols; lower rates rest of yr. Pet accepted; $6. TV; cable, in-rm movies avail. Pool (seasonal). Playground. Restaurant 6:30 am–2 pm. Bar 4 pm–2 am. Ck-out noon. Meeting rms. Casino, ski area transportation. Downhill ski 1 mi; x-country ski 14 mi. Hot tub. Lawn games. Some fireplaces. Some balconies. Cr cds: A, C, D, DS, MC, V, JCB.

✦ ★TRAVELODGE SOUTH TAHOE. *(Box 70512, 96156) 3489 Lake Tahoe Blvd.* 916/544-5266; FAX 916/544-6985. 59 rms, 2 story. S, D $49–$83; each addl $5; under 18 free; higher rates: wkends, hols. TV; cable. Heated pool. Complimentary coffee in rms. Restaurant adj 7 am–11 pm. Ck-out noon. Downhill ski 2 mi; x-country ski 11 mi. Cr cds: A, C, D, DS, ER, MC, V, JCB.

Motor Hotel

★★LAKELAND VILLAGE. *(Box 1356, 96156) 3535 Lake Tahoe Blvd, 1 mi SW of CA-NV state line on US 50.* 916/541-7711; res: 800/822-5969; FAX 916/541-6278. 212 kit. units, 2–3 story. July–Aug, mid-Dec–Mar, hols (2-day min): S, D $85–$145; town houses $165–$280; ski, summer plans; lower rates rest of yr. Crib free. TV; cable. 2 pools, heated; wading pool, 2 whirlpools, sauna. Playground. Coffee in rms. Restaurant adj 7 am–10 pm. Ck-out 11 am. Coin lndry. Meeting rms. Some garage parking. Casino transportation. Tennis, pro. Downhill ski 1½ mi; x-country ski 14 mi. 1½–2 baths in most units. Refrigerators, fireplaces. Private patios, balconies. Pier; dock. Private sand beach. Spacious grounds, 19 acres. Cr cds: A, MC, V.

Hotel

★★★EMBASSY SUITES. *4130 Lake Tahoe Blvd (96150).* 916/544-5400; FAX 916/544-4900. 400 suites, 9 story. Jan–Mar & July–Aug: S, D $139–$179; under 12 free; ski, golf plans; higher rates hols; lower rates rest of yr. Crib free. TV; cable, in-rm movies. Indoor pool; poolside serv. Complimentary full bkfst. Complimentary coffee in rms. Restaurant 11 am–11 pm. Bar 11–2 am; entertainment, dancing. Ck-out noon. Coin lndry. Convention facilities. Concierge. Gift shop. Free garage parking. Free airport transportation. 18-hole golf privileges, greens fee $40. Downhill ski 1 mi; x-country ski 5 mi. Exercise equipt; bicycles, treadmill, whirlpool, sauna. Refrigerators, minibars, wet bars; some bathrm phones. Some balconies. Cr cds: A, C, D, DS, ER, MC, V, JCB.

Restaurants

★CAFE FIORE. *1169 Ski Run Blvd, #5.* 916/541-2908. Hrs: 5:30–10 pm; June–Sept also 11 am–2 pm. Closed some major hols. Res accepted. Italian menu. Wine, beer. Semi-a la carte: lunch $5–$12, dinner $11.50–$20. Child's meals. Specializes in scampi, pasta. Parking. Outdoor dining. Totally nonsmoking. Cr cds: A, MC, V.

★★DORY'S OAR. *1041 Fremont Ave.* 916/541-6603. Hrs: 5–10 pm. Closed Thanksgiving, Dec 25. Res accepted. Bar 4:30–11 pm.

Semi-a la carte: dinner $11.25–$33.95. Specializes in fresh lobster & salmon. Cr cds: A, C, D, DS, MC, V.

★★★EVANS AMERICAN GOURMET. *536 Emerald Bay Rd.* 916/542-1990. Hrs: 6–10 pm. Closed Sun; Thanksgiving, Dec 25. Res accepted. Beer. Wine list. Semi-a la carte: dinner $14.95–$21.95. Specializes in fresh seafood, creative cuisine. Parking. Small house converted into restaurant. Totally nonsmoking. Cr cds: MC, V.

✦ ★PETRELLO'S. *900 Emerald Bay Rd.* 916/541-7868. Hrs: 6–10 pm; winter from 5 pm. Closed Jan 1, Easter, Thanksgiving, Dec 25. Res accepted. Italian menu. Bar. Semi-a la carte: dinner $8.50–$14.50. Child's meals. Specializes in chicken, seafood. Mix of California ranch and French designs. Parking. Totally nonsmoking. Cr cds: MC, V.

★★★SWISS CHALET. *2540 Lake Tahoe Blvd, 4 mi W of CA-NV state line on US 50.* 916/544-3304. Hrs: 5–10 pm. Closed Mon; Easter, Thanksgiving, Dec 25. Res accepted. Continental menu. Bar from 4 pm. Semi-a la carte: dinner $13.95–$24.95. Child's meals. Specializes in veal dishes, steak, fresh seafood. Own baking. Parking. Swiss decor. Family-owned. Cr cds: A, MC, V.

South San Francisco

(see San Francisco Airport Area)

Squaw Valley

(see Lake Tahoe Area)

Stockton (E-2)

Founded: 1849 **Pop:** 210,943 **Elev:** 13 ft **Area code:** 209

Connected to San Francisco Bay by a 78-mile deepwater channel, Stockton is an important inland port with giant ore-loading facilities and grain terminals accessible to large ships. In its early days as the gateway to the Mother Lode country, it became a "city of a thousand tents." Many of the 49ers settled here and became rich when irrigation systems turned the surrounding countryside into fertile grain fields.

What to See and Do

1. **Haggin Museum.** 1201 N Pershing Ave, at Rose St in Victory Park. State and local historical exhibits; 19th-century European and American paintings and decorative arts; Native American arts. Guided tours (Sat or by appt); changing exhibits. (Daily exc Mon, afternoons; closed Jan 1, Thanksgiving, Dec 25) Donation. Phone 462-4116 or -1566.

2. **Municipal recreation facilities.** The city maintains 50 parks, tennis courts, playgrounds, swimming pools, picnic areas; 2 golf courses; boat launching facilities and berths; ice arena; community and sr citizen centers. Fee for activities. Phone 944-8206.

   Pixie Woods. In Louis Park, W end of Monte Diablo Blvd. Mother Goose and Fairyland characters; puppet shows in Toadstool Theatre; train, boat and merry-go-round rides. (June–Labor Day, Wed–Sun; late Feb–May & after Labor Day–late Oct, Sat, Sun & hols, including Easter wk) Phone 944-8206. ¢

(For further information contact the Convention and Visitors Bureau, 46 W Fremont St, 95202; 943-1987 or 800/350-1987.)

Annual Events

Stockton Asparagus Festival. Musical entertainment, asparagus food dishes, car show, wagon rides. Phone 943-1987. Late Apr.

San Joaquin County Fair. Horse racing, agricultural and livestock displays, entertainment. Phone 466-5041. June.

Obon Festival and Bazaar. Street dance, food, exhibits, authentic Japanese costumes, colorful decorations at the Buddhist Temple. Phone 466-6701. Late July.

Greek Festival. Food, music, dancing. Phone 478-7564. Sept.

(See Lodi, Modesto)

Motels

★★**BEST WESTERN CHARTER WAY INN.** *550 W Charter Way (95206), at jct CA 4, I-5.* 209/948-0321. 80 rms, 2 story. S $45–$55; D $50–$60; each addl $5; under 12 free. Crib $4. TV; cable. Pool. Complimentary coffee in rms. Restaurant adj open 24 hrs. Ck-out noon. Some refrigerators. Cr cds: A, C, D, DS, ER, MC, V.

✔★**INNCAL.** *3473 Hammer Lane (95209).* 209/473-2000. 122 rms, 3 story, 10 suites (no equipt). No elvtr. S $29.95–$39.95; D $34.95–$41.95; each addl $5; suites, kit. units $39.95–$44.95. TV; cable. Pool. Complimentary coffee in lobby. Restaurant adj open 24 hrs. Ck-out 11 am. Coin lndry. Meeting rms. Cr cds: A, C, MC, V, JCB.

★**TRAVELERS INN.** *2654 W March Lane (95207).* 209/478-4300; res: 800/633-8300; FAX 209/478-1872. 124 rms, 3 story. S $44; D $50; each addl $4; suites $75; under 11 free. Crib free. TV; cable. Pool; whirlpool. Complimentary coffee in lobby. Restaurant open 24 hrs. Ck-out 11 am. Meeting rms. Valet serv. Refrigerator, wet bar in suites. Cr cds: A, C, D, MC, V.

✔★**VAGABOND INN.** *33 N Center St (95202).* 209/948-6151; FAX 209/948-1220. 99 rms, 3 story. S $35–$40; D $40–$45; each addl $5; under 19 free. Crib $3. Pet accepted. TV. Pool. Coffee in rooms. Restaurant adj. Ck-out noon. Meeting rm. Refrigerators avail. Near marina. Cr cds: A, C, D, DS, ER, MC, V, JCB.

Hotel

★★★**HILTON STOCKTON.** *2323 Grand Canal Blvd (95207).* 209/957-9090; FAX 209/473-8908. 198 rms, 5 story. S $78–$102; D $90–$114; each addl $12; suites $250–$275; under 18 free; wkly, wkend rates. Crib free. TV. Pool. Restaurant 6:30 am–11 pm. Bar 11–2 am; entertainment, dancing Tues–Sat. Ck-out 1 pm. Meeting rms. Shopping arcade. Health club privileges. Some balconies. Cr cds: A, C, D, MC, V.

Restaurant

★★**JOE & RICK'S LE BISTRO.** *3121 W Benjamin Holt Dr, in Marina Shopping Ctr.* 209/951-0885. Hrs: 11:30 am–3 pm, 5:30–10 pm; Sat from 5:30 pm; Sun 5–9 pm. Closed some major hols. Res accepted. French, Amer menu. Bar. Semi-a la carte: lunch $9.95–$13.50, dinner $15.95–$37. Specializes in fresh fish, soufflés, European-style cuisine. Own desserts. Parking. Cr cds: A, C, D, DS, MC, V.

Studio City (L.A.) (H-3)

Area code: 818 **Zip:** 91604

This community, located in the San Fernando Valley, is a neighborhood of Los Angeles, but is regarded by many as a separate entity.

(For general information and attractions see Los Angeles.)

Motor Hotel

★★★**SPORTSMEN'S LODGE HOTEL.** *12825 Ventura Blvd, at Coldwater Canyon Rd.* 818/769-4700; res: 800/821-1625 (CA), 800/821-8511 (exc CA), 800/341-6363 (CAN); FAX 213/877-3898. 200 rms, 2–5 story. S $100–$110; D $110–$120; each addl $10; suites $165–$290; under 18 free. Crib free. TV; cable. Heated pool; poolside serv. Restaurant 6:30 am–10 pm. Rm serv. Bars 11–1 am. Ck-out noon. Meeting rms. Bellhops. Valet serv. Gift shop. Barber, beauty shop. Free Burbank airport transportation. Exercise equipt; weight machine, bicycles, whirlpool. Private patios, balconies. Gardens; ponds. Cr cds: A, C, D, DS, ER, MC, V.

Restaurants

★★**LA LOGGIA.** *11814 Ventura Blvd, vicinity of Laurel Canyon Blvd.* 818/985-9222. Hrs: 11:30 am–2:30 pm, 5:30–11 pm. Sat from 5:30 pm; Sun 5–10 pm. Closed most major hols. Res accepted. Italian menu. Bar. A la carte entrees: lunch, dinner $7.95–$15.95. Specializes in fresh pasta, Northern Italian dishes. Own pasta. Valet parking. Menu changes monthly. Trattoria setting. Cr cds: A, C, D, MC, V.

★★**ST. MORITZ.** *11720 Ventura Blvd, vicinity Laurel Canyon Blvd.* 818/980-1122. Hrs: 11:30 am–2:30 pm, 5–10 pm; wkends from 5 pm. Closed Jan 1, July 4, Dec 25. Res accepted. Continental menu. Bar. Complete meals: lunch $7.50–$15, dinner $14.50–$23.50. Specializes in Wienerschnitzel, roast rack of lamb, fresh seafood. Valet parking. Outdoor dining. Semi-formal dining; European decor. Cr cds: A, C, D, DS, MC, V.

★★**WINE BISTRO.** *11915 Ventura Blvd, vicinity Laurel Canyon Blvd.* 818/766-6233. Hrs: 11:30 am–10:30 pm; Sat from 5:30 pm. Closed Sun; major hols. Res accepted. French, continental menu. Bar. Semi-a la carte: lunch $9.50–$12.50, dinner $14.95–$21.95. Specializes in fresh fish, duck. Valet parking. Cr cds: A, C, D, DS, MC, V.

Sunnyvale (E-2)

Pop: 117,229 **Elev:** 130 ft **Area code:** 408

What to See and Do

Sunnyvale Historical Museum. 235 E California Ave, in Martin Murphy Jr Park. Houses historical artifacts and pictures of area as well as information on pioneering families. (Tues, Thurs & Sun; closed major hols) Phone 749-0220. **Free.**

(See Santa Clara)

Motels

★★**AMBASSADOR BUSINESS INN.** *910 E Fremont Ave (94087), at Wolfe Rd.* 408/738-0500; res: 800/538-1600; FAX 408/245-4167. 204 kit. units, 2 story. S $72; D $78–$86; suites $105–$125; under 12 free; wkly rates. Crib free. TV; cable, in-rm movies. Heated pool;

whirlpool. Complimentary continental bkfst. Coffee in rms. Restaurant nearby. Ck-out noon. Coin lndry. Meeting rm. Valet serv. In-rm whirlpool in suites. Grills. Cr cds: A, C, D, MC, V.

⊠ ⊘ ⊚ SC

✔ ★★COMFORT INN. *595 N Mathilda Ave (94086), S off US 101.* 408/749-8000; FAX 408/749-0367. 52 rms, 2 story. S $67–$85; D $67–$87; each addl $5; under 16 free; wkend rates. Crib free. TV; cable, in-rm movies. Complimentary continental bkfst. Complimentary coffee in rms. Restaurant nearby. Ck-out noon. Free lndry facilities. Whirlpool, sauna. Refrigerators; some in-rm whirlpools. Cr cds: A, C, D, DS, ER, MC, V, JCB.

D ⊚ SC

★★HOLIDAY INN. *1217 Wildwood Ave (94089).* 408/245-5330; FAX 408/732-2628. 176 rms, 2 story. S $94–$114; D $104–$124; under 19 free; wkend rates. Crib free. TV; cable. Heated pool; poolside serv. Coffee in rms. Restaurants 6 am–10 pm; Sat & Sun from 7 am. Rm serv. Bars; entertainment Mon–Fri. Ck-out noon. Coin lndry. Meeting rms. Bellhops. Valet serv. Concierge. Free airport transportation. Health club privileges. Cr cds: A, C, D, DS, MC, V, JCB.

D ⊠ ⊘ ⊚ SC

★★RESIDENCE INN BY MARRIOTT-SILICON VALLEY I. *750 Lakeway (94086).* 408/720-1000; FAX 408/737-9722. 231 kit. units, 2 story. S $124–$132; D $139–$149. Pet accepted; $100 non-refundable and $6 per day. TV; cable. Heated pool; whirlpools. Complimentary continental bkfst; Thurs barbecue. Restaurant nearby. Ck-out noon. Coin lndry. Meeting rm. Valet serv. Free local airport transportation. Health club privileges. Lawn games. Picnic tables, grills. Cr cds: A, C, D, DS, MC, V, JCB.

D ☞ ⊠ ⊘ ⊚ SC

★★SHERATON SUNNYVALE INN. *1100 N Mathilda Ave (94089).* 408/745-6000; FAX 408/734-8276. 174 units, 2 story. S $95–$120; D $105–$130; each addl $10; under 18 free; wkend rates. Crib free. TV; cable. Heated pool; poolside serv. Complimentary coffee in rms. Restaurant 6:30 am–10 pm; Sat from 5 pm, Sun 7:30 am–2 pm. Rm serv. Bar noon–2 am; entertainment, dancing. Ck-out 1 pm. Meeting rms. Bellhops. Valet serv. Airport transportation. Exercise equipt; weights, bicycles, whirlpool. Bathrm phones. Refrigerators avail. Cr cds: A, C, D, DS, MC, V, JCB.

D ⊠ ☨ ⊘ ⊚ SC

★★SUMMERFIELD SUITES. *900 Hamlin Ct (94089), just E of US 101 Mathilda Ave (N) exit.* 408/745-1515; res: 800/833-4353; FAX 408/745-0540. 138 kit. suites, 2–3 story. S $79–$129; D $99–$159; family rates. Crib free. Pet accepted, some restrictions; $10. TV; cable, in-rm movies. Pool. Complimentary continental bkfst. Complimentary coffee in rms. Restaurant nearby. Ck-out noon. Coin lndry. Meeting rms. Valet serv. Sundries. Free airport transportation. Exercise equipt; weight machine, bicycle, whirlpool. Health club privileges. Many fireplaces. Grills. Cr cds: A, C, D, DS, MC, V, JCB.

D ☞ ⊠ ☨ ⊘ ⊚ SC

★★SUNDOWNER INN. *504 Ross Dr (94089).* 408/734-9900; res: 800/223-9901; FAX 408/747-0580. 105 units, 2 story. S, D $92–$102; each addl $10; suites $98–$104; wkend rates. Crib free. TV; in-rm movies. Heated pool. Complimentary continental bkfst. Restaurant 6–2 am; Sat, Sun from 9 am. Bar; entertainment Tues–Sat. Ck-out noon. Meeting rms. Valet serv. Exercise equipt; weights, bicycles, sauna. Library. Refrigerators. Cr cds: A, C, D, DS, MC, V, JCB.

D ⊠ ☨ ⊘ ⊚ SC

✔ ★VALU INN. *852 W El Camino Real (94087), at Hollenbeck Rd.* 408/773-1234; res: 800/527-2810; FAX 408/773-0420. 59 rms, 3 story. S $54–$61; D $56–$66; each addl $5; under 10 free; wkly rates. Crib free. TV; cable. Complimentary continental bkfst, coffee. Restaurant adj 9 am–9 pm. Ck-out 11 am. Some in-rm whirlpools, refrigerators. Some balconies. Cr cds: A, D, DS, MC, V.

D ⊘ SC

Motor Hotels

★★★HILTON SUNNYVALE. *1250 Lakeside Dr (94086).* 408/738-4888; FAX 408/737-7147. 374 rms, 2–3 story. S $110–$155; D $125–$170; each addl $15; suites $250; family, wkend rates. Crib free. TV. Heated pool; poolside serv. Restaurants 6 am–10 pm. Rm serv. Bars 10–2 am. Ck-out noon. Bellhops. Valet serv. Convention facilities. Gift shop. Free airport transportation. Exercise equipt; weights, bicycles, whirlpool, sauna. Bathrm phones. Park, duck pond. Cr cds: A, C, D, DS, ER, MC, V, JCB.

D ⊠ ☨ ☨ ⊘ ⊚ SC

★★★RADISSON HAUS INN. *1085 E El Camino Real (94087).* 408/247-0800; FAX 408/984-7120. 136 rms, 3 story. S $105–$135; D $115–$145; each addl $10; suites $135–$145; under 16 free; wkend rates. Crib free. TV; cable. Heated pool. Restaurant 6 am–2 pm, 5:30–10 pm. Rm serv. Bar from 5 pm. Ck-out noon. Meeting rms. Bellhops. Valet serv. Free garage parking. Free airport, RR station, bus depot transportation. Health club privileges. Exercise equipt; weight machine, bicycles, whirlpool. Minibars. Atrium. Cr cds: A, C, D, DS, ER, MC, V, JCB.

D ⊠ ☨ ⊘ ⊚ SC

★★WOODFIN SUITES. *635 E El Camino Real (94087).* 408/738-1700; res: 800/237-8811; FAX 408/738-0840. 88 kit. suites, 2 story. Kit. suites $109–$145; monthly rates. Crib free. Pet accepted, some restrictions; $400 deposit. TV; in-rm movies. Heated pool; whirlpool. Complimentary full bkfst. Restaurant adj 6:30 am–10:30 pm. Ck-out noon. Coin lndry. Valet serv. Free airport transportation. Cr cds: A, C, D, DS, ER, MC, V.

D ☞ ⊠ ⊚ SC

Restaurant

★★MICHAELS. *830 E El Camino Real.* 408/245-2925. Hrs: 11 am–3 pm, 5:30–10 pm; Fri & Sat 5–10:30 pm; Sun 5–9 pm. Closed Jan 1, July 4, Dec 25. Res accepted. Bar; piano bar 7:30–11:30 pm. Semi-a la carte: lunch $6–$15, dinner $12–$32. Child's meals. Specializes in New England & Pacific seafood. Valet parking. Traditional European decor. Family-owned. Cr cds: A, D, MC, V.

D

Susanville (C-3)

Settled: 1853 **Pop:** 7,279 **Elev:** 4,258 ft **Area code:** 916 **Zip:** 96130

Susanville is currently a trading center for an area producing livestock, lumber, alfalfa, garlic and strawberries. There is fine hunting for deer, bear, antelope, pheasant, grouse, quail, ducks and geese, and fishing in many lakes and rivers in the surrounding hills and mountains. Lassen National Forest (see #1) headquarters and a Ranger District office are located here. In 1856, Susanville was the capital of the Republic of Nataqua, an area of 50,000 square miles. Isaac Roop, the town's first settler, helped establish the republic, which later joined the Nevada Territory. Roop was first Provisional Governor of Nevada and later senator. California surveys showed the area was part of Plumas County. The locals refused to join and holed up in Roop's house in 1864. After a day of gunfighting, California won back what is now Lassen County. Susanville was named by Roop in honor of his only daughter.

What to See and Do

1. **Lassen National Forest.** 7 mi W on CA 36. More than 1 million acres. Swimming; excellent trout fishing in lakes and streams, hunting. Cross-country and downhill skiing, snowmobiling. The Thousand Lakes, Caribou and Ishi wildernesses offer backpacking and primitive camping. For further information contact the Forest Supervisor, 55 S Sacramento St; phone 257-2151. In the forest area is

2. Eagle Lake. 2 mi W on CA 36, then 15 mi N on County A1, in Lassen National Forest. Called by scientists "the lake that time forgot," this 26,000-acre lake was formed by the receding waters of a primeval lake larger than Lake Erie. It is the second largest natural lake in California and home to Eagle Lake trout, a species averaging 3–5 lbs that has adapted to living in the lake's alkaline water. Gallatin Beach, at south end of lake, provides swimming, waterskiing, Five campgrounds are available (fee). Marina has boat rentals. For additional information contact Supervisor, Lassen National Forest, 55 S Sacramento St; 257-2151.

    Gallatin Marina, adj to Lassen National Forest Campgrounds. Fishing, boating (ramps, rentals); groceries. (Late May–mid-Oct) Phone 257-2151.

3. Bizz Johnson Trail. Begins ½ mi S via S Weatherlow St, left on Richmond Rd to Susanville Depot Trailhead; parking avail. Multi-purpose trail winding 24.5 mi from Susanville to Mason Station, 4 mi N of Westwood. Transverses rugged Susan River Canyon on former railroad route. Fishing on river. Hiking, bicycling, horseback riding. Cross-country skiing. Camping. Phone 257-0456.   **Free.**

4. Roop's Fort & Lassen Historical Museum. N Weatherlow St. Fort (1854), built by Isaac Roop, was the state capitol of the Nataqua Republic. (May–Oct, Mon–Fri) Phone 257-3292.   **Free.**

5. Wilderness Areas. Caribou Peak. 35 mi W via CA 36 and County A21. Gentle rolling forested terrain with many small crystal lakes. Many small cinder cones. **Thousand Lakes.** 25 mi E & S of Burney via CA 299, 89, Forest Road 26. Contrasting topography; hiking trails. **Ishi Wilderness.** Ishi. 35 mi W & S of Chester via CA 36, 32. Dotted with rocl)utcroppings and bizarre pillar lava formations. Camping in all areas. For information contact Lassen National Forest, 55 S Sacramento; 257-2151.

    (For further information contact the Chamber of Commerce, 84 N Lassen St, PO Box 338; 257-4323.)

Annual Event

    Lassen County Fair. Fairgrounds, off Russell Ave & Main St. Livestock and horse shows; rodeos; parade, livestock auction; entertainment. Phone 257-4104. Late Aug.

Motel

    ★★**BEST WESTERN TRAILSIDE INN.** *(PO Box 759) 2785 Main St. 916/257-4123; FAX 916/257-2665.* 90 rms, 2 story. Apr–Oct: S, D $44–$84; each addl $5; lower rates rest of yr. TV; cable. Heated pool. Restaurant open 24 hrs. Rm serv 24 hrs. Ck-out 11 am. Meeting rm. X-country skiing 2 mi. Cr cds: A, C, D, DS, MC, V.

    🚹 🏊 🚭 🅿 **SC**

Tahoe City (Lake Tahoe Area) (D-3)

Pop: 2,500 (est) **Elev:** 6,240 ft **Area code:** 916 **Zip:** 95730

At north end of Lake Tahoe.

    (For general information, map and attractions see Lake Tahoe Area.)

Motel

    ✔★★**TRAVELODGE TAHOE CITY.** *(Box 84) 455 N Lake Blvd. 916/583-3766; FAX 916/583-8045.* 47 rms, 2 story. No A/C. July–Labor Day: S $70; D $81–$91; each addl $5; under 17 free; higher rates:

wkends, hols; lower rates rest of yr. Crib free. TV; cable. Pool; whirlpool, sauna. Complimentary coffee, tea in rms. Restaurant adj 6 am–10 pm. Ck-out 11 am. Downhill ski 5 mi; x-country ski 2 mi. Sun deck. Some balconies. Lake opp. Golf adj. Cr cds: A, C, D, DS, ER, MC, V, JCB.

    🚹 🏊 🚭 🅿 **SC**

Inn

    ★**THE COTTAGE.** *(Box 66) 1690 W Lake Blvd, 2 mi S of CA 89. 916/581-4073.* 17 units. No A/C. No rm phones. Mid-June–mid-Sept: S, D $100–$150; wkly; ski rates; higher rates hols; lower rates rest of yr. Children over 12 yrs only. Complimentary full bkfst; afternoon coffee, tea/wine. Restaurant nearby. Ck-out 11 am, ck-in 3 pm. Downhill/x-country ski 3 mi. Sauna. Lawn games. Picnic tables, grills. On lake, beach. Library. Fireplaces. Rustic cabins in the woods. Totally nonsmoking. Cr cds: C, D, MC, V.

    🚹 🚶 🚭 🅿 **SC**

Resorts

    ★**GRANLIBAKKEN.** *(Box 6329) 1 mi W, at end of Granlibakken Rd. 916/583-4242; res: 800/543-3221 (CA); FAX 916/583-7641.* 53 kit. units, 3 story. No elvtr. S, D $80–$115; each addl $20; 2-bedrm, 3-bedrm units $195–$250. Crib $5. TV. Heated pool (seasonal); wading pool, whirlpool, sauna. Complimentary full bkfst. Snack bar (winter). Ck-out 11 am, ck-in 4 pm. Grocery, package store 1 mi. Coin lndry. Convention facilities. Airport, RR station, bus depot transportation. Tennis. Downhill/x-country ski on site. Rental equipt. Sledding. Hiking. Many fireplaces. Many balconies. Cr cds: A, D, MC, V.

    🚹 🎾 🏊 🚭 🅿

    ★★**RESORT AT SQUAW CREEK.** *(PO Box 3333, 400 Squaw Creek Rd, Olympic Valley 96146) 6 mi N on CA 89, Squaw Valley exit. 916/583-6300; res: 800/327-3353; FAX 916/581-6632.* 405 units, 9 story, 205 suites, 18 kits. Mid-Dec–mid-Apr: S, D $250–$275; suites $350–$855; under 13 free; lower rates rest of yr. Crib free. TV. 3 heated pools; wading pool, poolside serv, lifeguard. Supervised child's activities. Coffee in rms. Dining rms 6:30 am–11 pm. Rm serv. Bar 11–1 am. Ck-out 11 am, ck-in 3 pm. Package store. Grocery 2 mi. Coin lndry 6 mi. Convention facilities. Bellhops. Valet serv. Concierge. Gift shop. Beauty shop. Airport transportation. Sports dir. Lighted tennis, pro. Golf, greens fee $100, pro. Aquatic center features 250-ft waterfall, waterslide and stream. Downhill/x-country ski on site. Rental equipt. Ice skating. 7 mi of landscaped hiking and bicycle paths; bicycle rentals avail. Exercise rm; instructor, bicycles, weight machine, whirlpools, saunas. Health & fitness center. Situated among the trees on the side of Papoose Peak, this 620-acre resort offers year-round recreational activities. Cr cds: A, C, D, DS, MC, V.

    D 🐴 🚹 🚣 🎾 🏊 🚶 🚭 🅿 **SC**

Restaurants

    ★★★**SWISS LAKEWOOD.** *(5055 W Lake Blvd, Homewood) 6 mi S on CA 89. 916/525-5211.* Hrs: 5:30–10:30 pm; summer also 11:30 am–3:30 pm. Closed Mon exc hols. Res required. French, continental menu. Bar. Semi-a la carte: lunch $5.95–$11.50, dinner $16.50–$24. Parking. Outdoor dining. Swiss, European decor; many antiques; wagon wheel chandeliers. Totally nonsmoking. Cr cds: A, MC, V.

    ★★**WOLFDALE'S CUISINE UNIQUE.** *640 N Lake Blvd. 916/583-5700.* Hrs: 6–10 pm. Closed Tues Sept–June. Res accepted. California Japanese menu. Bar from 5:30 pm. A la carte entrees: dinner $12–$19. Child's meals. Specializes in seafood. Parking. Outdoor dining. Built 1889 on south shore, moved to north shore in 1901. Garden. Totally nonsmoking. Cr cds: MC, V.

    D

Tahoe Vista (Lake Tahoe Area) (D-3)

Pop: 1,144 **Elev:** 6,232 ft **Area code:** 916 **Zip:** 95732

At north end of Lake Tahoe.

(For general information, map and attractions see Lake Tahoe Area.)

Motels

✔ ★**CEDAR GLEN LODGE.** *(Box 188) 6589 Northlake Blvd, 1½ mi W of CA 267 on CA 28.* 916/546-4281; res: 800/341-8000. 31 rms in 2-story motel, cottages, 14 kits. No A/C. Mid-June–mid-Sept, Dec–Apr: S, D $45–$60; each addl $5; kit. units, cottages $70–$105; wkly rates; lower rates rest of yr. Crib free. TV; cable. Heated pool; whirlpools, sauna. Playground. Complimentary continental bkfst. Complimentary coffee in rms. Restaurant nearby. Ck-out 11 am. Downhill ski 8 mi; x-country ski 4 mi. Some refrigerators. Private patios. Picnic tables, grills. Beach opp. Cr cds: A, DS, MC, V.

★**COTTONWOOD LODGE.** *(Box 86) 6542 N Lake Blvd.* 916/546-2220. 17 rms in cabins, 13 kits. (many ovens). No A/C. June–mid-Sept, wkends, hols, Christmas wk: S, D $74–$94; each addl $5; kit. units $10 addl (3-day min); kit. cottages for 2–5, $110 (3-day min); lower rates rest of yr. Crib $5. TV; cable. Pool; whirlpool, sauna. Complimentary coffee in rms. Ck-out 11 am. Downhill ski 15 mi; x-country ski 10 mi. Picnic tables, grill. On 2 acres; pond. Private beach, pier. Cr cds: A, C, D, DS, MC, V.

★**FRANCISCAN LAKESIDE LODGE.** *6944 N Lake Blvd.* 916/546-7234; res: 800/564-6754 (CA). 58 kit. units, 10 cabins. No A/C. Mid-May–mid-Oct: S, D $50–$160; lower rates rest of yr. Crib $5. TV; cable. Heated pool (seasonal). Playground. Restaurant nearby. Ck-out 11 am. Downhill/x-country ski 15 mi. Free boat buoys. Some fireplaces. Picnic tables, grills. On lake. Cr cds: A, MC, V.

★**HOLIDAY HOUSE.** *(Box 229) 7276 N Lake Blvd.* 916/546-2369. 7 kit. apts, 2 story. No A/C. Late June–Labor Day & hols: S, D $110; each addl $10; wkly rates; ski plans; lower rates rest of yr. TV; cable. Coin lndry. Downhill ski 15 mi; x-country ski 10 mi. Whirlpool. Refrigerators. Balconies. Picnic tables, grills. Panoramic view of lake and mountains. On lake. Marina adj. Cr cds: A, C, D, MC, V, JCB.

✔ ★**VILLA VISTA.** *(Box 47) 6750 N Lake Blvd.* 916/546-1550; FAX 916/546-4100. 13 rms, 10 kits. No A/C. S, D $65; each addl $10; studio rms $75–$85; kit. units for 1–4, $75–$130; wkly rates in summer. Crib free. TV; cable. Heated pool. Coffee in rms. Ck-out 11 am. Coin lndry. Downhill ski 15 mi; x-country ski 10 mi. Health club privileges. Refrigerators. Private patios. Picnic tables, grill. Sun deck. On private sand beach; moorage. Cr cds: A, MC, V.

Inn

★★★**TAHOE VISTA INN & MARINA.** *(Box 157) 7252 N Lake Blvd, ¾ mi W of jct CA 267 & CA 28.* 916/546-7662; res: 800/662-3433; FAX 916/546-7963. 7 kit. suites, 3 A/C. Jan–Mar & mid-June–Sept: S, D $152–$240; lower rates rest of yr. TV; cable. Complimentary coffee in rms. Restaurant (see CAPTAIN JON'S). Ck-out noon, ck-in 3 pm. Downhill/

x-country ski 15 mi. Some in-rm whirlpools, fireplaces. Balconies. On Lake Tahoe. Cr cds: MC, V.

Restaurants

★★**CAPTAIN JON'S.** *(See Tahoe Vista Inn & Marina)* 916/546-4819. Hrs: 11 am–9 pm (summer), dinner sittings: 6 & 9 pm. Closed Mon; also Nov until Thanksgiving. Res accepted. Country French menu. Bar 3 pm–2 am, summer from 11 am. Semi-a la carte: lunch $7–$12, dinner $12–$29. Specializes in seafood. Valet parking. Nautical decor. Outdoor dining. On lakefront. Cr cds: A, C, D, MC, V.

★**COL. CLAIR'S.** *6873 N Lake Blvd.* 916/546-7358. Hrs: 5–10 pm. Res accepted. Bar to midnight. A la carte entrees: dinner $9.95–$19.95. Specialties: cajun dishes, blackened prime rib, barbecued beer shrimp, fresh fish, jambalaya. Parking. Outdoor dining. In restored house; hanging antique lamps, leaded glass. Cr cds: A, MC, V.

★★**LA PLAYA.** *7046 N Lake Blvd.* 916/546-5903. Hrs: 11 am–3 pm (June–Oct), 5:30–10 pm; Sun brunch 10 am–3 pm. Res accepted. No A/C. Bar. Semi-a la carte: lunch $5.95–$12.95, dinner $13.50–$25. Sun brunch $5.95–$14.50. Specializes in seafood, rack of lamb, steak. Patio dining. French country atmosphere. View of lake, mountains. On lakefront. Cr cds: A, C, D, MC, V, JCB.

★★★**LE PETIT PIER.** *7250 N Lake Blvd.* 916/546-2508 or -4464. Hrs: 6–10:30 pm. Res accepted. French, Amer menu. Bar. Wine list. A la carte entrees: dinner $17.50–$25. *Prix fixe:* dinner $42.50. Specialties: pheasant à la Souvaroff for two, beef Wellington. Own pastries. Entertainment Fri–Sun. Valet parking. Outdoor balcony dining. Formal French atmosphere. View of mountains, Lake Tahoe. Totally nonsmoking. Cr cds: A, D, MC, V, JCB.

Tehachapi (G-3)

Pop: 5,791 **Elev:** 3,973 ft **Area code:** 805 **Zip:** 93581

Tehachapi was founded when the railroad made its way through the pass between the San Joaquin Valley and the desert to the east. The Tehachapi Pass, east of town, is one of the windiest areas in the world; of the approximately 15,000 wind turbines located in the state, 5,000 are located here. The best time to see the turbines spinning is late afternoon, when heating on the nearby Mojave Desert is greatest. Historians believe the name Tehachapi is derived from a Native American word meaning "sweet water and many acorns," but others believe it means "windy place." Both are true of the area.

What to See and Do

Tehachapi Loop. NW of town. Visitors as well as railroad buffs enjoy watching trains (with 85 or more boxcars) pass over themselves when rounding the "Tehachapi Loop." Built in 1875–1876, the loop makes it possible for trains to gain the needed elevation in a short distance. It can be seen by taking Woodford-Tehachapi Rd to a viewpoint just above the loop.

(For information about this area, contact the Greater Tehachapi Chamber of Commerce, PO Box 401; 822-4180.)

Annual Events

Indian Pow Wow. Indian cultural and religious gathering of various tribes. Open to public viewing: Indian dance competition, arts & crafts, museum display of artifacts. Usually last wkend June.

Mountain Festival and PRCA Rodeo. Includes arts & crafts, food booths, parade, events. Usually 3rd wkend Aug.

(See Bakersfield)

Motels

✔ ★**BEST WESTERN MOUNTAIN INN.** *416 W Tehachapi Blvd.* 805/822-5591; FAX 805/822-6197. 75 rms, 2 story. S $45–$55; D $49–$59; each addl $3; under 18 free. Crib free. TV; cable. Pool. Restaurant open 24 hrs. Ck-out noon. Coin lndry. Meeting rm. Some refrigerators. Model trains in restaurant. Cr cds: A, C, D, DS, MC, V.

[D] [symbols]

★ ★**TEHACHAPI-SUMMIT.** *(PO Box 140) 500 Steuber Rd.* 805/823-8000; FAX 805/823-8006. 81 units, 2 story, 7 suites. S $49–$52; D $56–$59; each addl $7; suites $61–$64; kit. unit $89–$99; under 18 free. Crib $5. TV; cable. Heated pool; whirlpool. Complimentary coffee in rms. Restaurant 5:30 am–9:30 pm. Bar 3–11 pm; Fri, Sat to 2 am; entertainment, dancing Fri & Sat. Ck-out 11 am. Meeting rms. Gift shop. Balconies. Cr cds: A, D, MC, V.

[D] [symbols] [SC]

Lodge

★ ★**SKY MOUNTAIN RESORT.** *18100 Lucaya, 15 mi W on CA 202 to Cummings Valley, then follow signs to Stallion Springs.* 805/822-5581; res: 800/244-0864; FAX 805/822-4055. 63 rms in main bldg, 2 story, 21 kit. cottages (1–2 bedrms). S, D, suites $70–$185; each addl $10; kit. cottages $155–$185; under 12 free; golf plans. Crib $10. Pet accepted. TV; cable. Heated pool. Playground. Supervised children's activities (seasonal). Dining rm 7:30 am–1:30 pm, 6–8:30 pm. Bar 4–10 pm, wkend hrs vary; entertainment, dancing. Ck-out noon, ck-in 3 pm. Meeting rms. Free shuttle transportation avail. Sports dir. Lighted tennis, pro. 18-hole golf, greens fee $20–$30, pro, putting green, driving range. Hiking. Bicycles (rentals). Lawn games. Exercise equipt; bicycles, weight machine, whirlpool, sauna. Balconies. Situated atop hill; overlooks golf course, lakes, forests. Cr cds: A, DS, MC, V.

[D] [symbols] [SC]

Temecula *

Pop: 27,099 **Elev:** 1,006 ft **Area code:** 909
Approx 15 mi NE of Fallbrook (J-4) on I-15

The Temecula Valley, bordered on the west by Camp Pendleton Marine Corps Base and the Cleveland National Forest, is approximately midway between Los Angeles and San Diego. This area is the "Napa Valley" of southern California; many fine wineries are located here.

(For information about this area, contact the Temecula Valley Chamber of Commerce, 27450 Ynez Rd, #104, 92591; 676-5090.)

Annual Event

Balloon and Wine Festival. Wine tasting, hot air balloon race, musical entertainment, children's activities. Phone 676-4713 or -6713. Early May.

(See Fallbrook)

Motel

✔ ★**RAMADA INN.** *28980 Front St (92592).* 909/676-8770; FAX 909/699-3400. 70 rms, 2 story. S $44–$59; D $49–$64; each addl $5; under 17 free; wkly rates. Crib free. Pet accepted, some restrictions. TV; cable, in-rm movies avail. Heated pool; whirlpool. Complimentary continental bkfst, coffee, tea fruit in lobby. Restaurant adj 6 am–10 pm.

Ck-out noon. Meeting rm. Refrigerators, wet bars; some bathrm phones. Cr cds: A, C, D, DS, ER, MC, V, JCB.

[D] [symbols] [SC]

Lodge

★ ★ ★**TEMECULA CREEK INN.** *44501 Rainbow Canyon Rd (92592).* 909/694-1000; res: 800/962-7335; FAX 909/676-3422. 80 rms in 5 bldgs, 2 story. S, D $115–$125; each addl $30; suites $135–$150; under 12 free. Crib free. TV; cable. Heated pool; whirlpool; poolside serv. Complimentary coffee in rms. Dining rm 6:30 am–10 pm. Bar 9:30 am–11 pm. Ck-out noon, ck-in 3 pm. Meeting rms. Bellhops. Tennis. 27-hole golf; greens fee $35–$50, pro, putting green, driving range. Lawn games. Refrigerators, minibars. Balconies. Cr cds: A, C, D, DS, MC, V.

[symbols]

Hotel

★ ★**EMBASSY SUITES** (formerly Doubletree Suites). *29345 Rancho California Rd (92591), adj I-15.* 909/676-5656; FAX 909/699-3928. 136 suites, 4 story. S $79–$129; D $89–$139; each addl $10; under 18 free. Crib free. TV; cable, in-rm movies. Heated pool; poolside serv. Restaurant 6:30 am–9:30 pm. Bar noon–midnight; entertainment Fri & Sat. No rm serv. Ck-out noon. Meeting rms. Gift shop. Exercise equipt; weight machine, stair machine, whirlpool. Refrigerators, wet bars. Many balconies. Cr cds: A, C, D, DS, ER, MC, V, JCB.

[D] [symbols] [SC]

Inn

★ ★**LOMA VISTA.** *33350 La Serena Way (92591), 4½ mi E of I-15, off Rancho California Rd.* 909/676-7047. 6 rms, 2 story. No rm phones. S, D $95–$125; each addl $25; family rates. TV in sitting rm. Complimentary full bkfst, coffee, tea/sherry. Restaurant opp 11 am–9 pm. Ck-out 11 am, ck-in 3 pm. Some balconies. Totally nonsmoking. Mission-style house surrounded by citrus groves and vineyards. Cr cds: DS, MC, V.

[symbols]

Restaurants

✔ ★**BANK OF MEXICAN FOOD.** *28645 Front St, at Main.* 909/676-6160. Hrs: 11 am–9 pm. Closed Easter, Thanksgiving, Dec 25. Res accepted. Mexican menu. Wine, beer. Complete meals: lunch $3.95–$8.95, dinner $5.95–$8.95. Child's meals. In refurbished bank building (1913). Cr cds: MC, V.

[D]

★ ★**CAFE CHAMPAGNE.** *32575 Rancho California Rd, at Culbertson Winery, 4 mi E of I-15.* 909/699-0088. Hrs: 11 am–9 pm. Closed Jan 1, Thanksgiving, Dec 24, 25. California eclectic menu. Bar. A la carte entrees: lunch $7.95–$17.95, dinner $14.95–$22.95. Specialties: mesquite-grilled foods, award-winning sparkling wines. Parking. Outdoor dining. View of vineyard. Herb garden. Cr cds: MC, V.

[D]

Thousand Oaks (H-3)

Pop: 104,352 **Elev:** 800 ft **Area code:** 805

What to See and Do

Stagecoach Inn Museum Complex. 51 S Ventu Park Rd, ½ mi S of US 101 in Newbury Park. Reproduction of 1876 building with Victorian furnishings; contains Chumash Indian display; pioneer artifacts;

changing exhibits; carriage house with antique vehicles; gift shop. Tri-Village consists of Chumash hut, Spanish adobe and pioneer house representing three early cultures in Conejo Valley. One-room schoolhouse. Nature trail. (Wed–Fri & Sun afternoons; closed Easter, Thanksgiving, Dec 25) Phone 498-9441. ¢

(For further information contact the Conejo Valley Chamber of Commerce, 625 W Hillcrest Dr, 91360; 499-1993.)

(See Los Angeles)

Motels

✔ ★BEST WESTERN OAKS LODGE. *12 Conejo Blvd (91360). 805/495-7011; FAX 805/495-0647.* 76 rms, 2 story, some kits. S $47–$57; D $52–$62; each addl $5; kit. units $5 addl (7-night min); under 12 free. Crib $3. TV; cable. Heated pool; whirlpool. Complimentary continental bkfst. Restaurant adj 11–2 am. Ck-out noon. Airport transportation avail. Some refrigerators, wet bars. Private patios. Cr cds: A, C, D, DS, ER, MC, V, JCB.

★★CLARION-SIMI VALLEY. *(1775 Madera Rd, Simi Valley 93065) N on CA 23, E on Olsen to Madera Rd. 805/584-6300; FAX 805/527-9969.* 120 rms, 2 story. S $70–$90; D $80–$100; each addl $10; suites $130–$300; under 17 free; monthly rates. TV; cable. Heated pool; whirlpool. Complimentary full bkfst. Complimentary coffee in rms. Restaurant 6:30–9:30 am. Rm serv. Bar 5–10 pm. Ck-out noon. Coin lndry. Meeting rms. Bellhops. Valet serv. Airport transportation avail. Health club privileges. Some refrigerators. Private patios, balconies. Garden courtyard with waterfall. Cr cds: A, C, D, DS, ER, MC, V, JCB.

Motor Hotel

★★★WESTLAKE INN HOTEL. *(31943 Agoura Rd, Westlake Village 91361) ¼ mi S of Ventura Frwy (US 101), Westlake Blvd (E), Lindero Cyn Rd (W) exit. 818/889-0230 or 805/496-1667; res: 800/535-9978 (CA); FAX 818/879-0812.* 75 units, 2 story. S $79–$89; D $89–$99; each addl $10; suites $120–$225; under 12 free. Crib free. TV; cable. Heated pool. Complimentary continental bkfst. Coffee in rms. Restaurant 6:30 am–9 pm; dining rm 11:30 am–2:30 pm, 5–10 pm; Sun 10 am–2:30 pm, 5–9 pm. Bar 11:30–2 am; entertainment. Ck-out noon. Meeting rms. Valet serv. Lighted tennis. 18-hole golf, greens fee $14–$22, carts $16. Fireplace in suites. Private patios, courtyards. Balconies overlook lake. Spacious grounds. Cr cds: A, C, D, DS, MC, V.

Hotel

★★★HYATT WESTLAKE PLAZA. *(880 S Westlake Blvd, Westlake Village 91361) Off Ventura Frwy (US 101), Westlake Blvd exit. 805/497-9991; FAX 805/379-9392.* 256 rms, 5 story. S $118–$140; D $133–$165; each addl $25; suites $140–$350; under 18 free; wkend rates; package plans. Crib free. TV; cable. Heated pool; poolside serv. Restaurant 6:30 am–10:30 pm. Rm serv 24 hrs. Bar 11–1 am; entertainment, dancing. Ck-out 1 pm. Meeting rms. Concierge. Gift shop. Free valet parking. Tennis, golf privileges. Exercise equipt; weights, bicycles, whirlpools. Bicycle rentals. Refrigerators avail (fee). Private patios, balconies. Garden atrium. Spanish mission-style architecture. Cr cds: A, C, D, DS, ER, MC, V, JCB.

Restaurant

★CORRIGAN'S STEAK HOUSE. *556 E Thousand Oaks Blvd. 805/495-5234.* Hrs: 11 am–10:30 pm; Sat & Sun from 9 am. Closed Thanksgiving, Dec 25. Res accepted. Bar to midnight. Semi-a la carte: bkfst $3.75–$10.50, lunch $5.75–$10.95, dinner $8.95–$20.95. Specializes in steak, seafood, chili. Steaks by the ounce. Old time Western decor; Western movies memorabilia. Cr cds: MC, V.

Three Rivers (F-3)

Pop: 2,000 (est) **Elev:** 1,200 ft **Area code:** 209 **Zip:** 93271

(See Sequoia & Kings Canyon National Parks)

Motels

★★BEST WESTERN HOLIDAY LODGE. *(Box 129) 40105 Sierra Dr, 8 mi W of Sequoia & Kings Canyon National parks' entrance, on CA 198. 209/561-4119; FAX 209/561-3427.* 44 rms, 1–2 story. S $48–$74; D $50–$74; each addl $4; suites $72–$84. Crib $4. Pet accepted. TV; cable. Pool; whirlpool. Playground. Continental bkfst 7–10 am. Complimentary coffee in rms. Ck-out 11 am. Sundries. Refrigerators; some fireplaces. Balconies. Grills. Cr cds: A, C, D, DS, MC, V, JCB.

✔ ★SIERRA LODGE. *43175 Sierra Dr. 209/561-3681; res: 800/367-8879; FAX 209/561-3264.* 22 units, 3 story, 5 kit. suites. No elvtr. May–Sept: S, D $48–$60; each addl $3; suites $75–$145; lower rates rest of yr. Pet accepted. TV. Pool. Complimentary continental bkfst. Complimentary coffee in rms. Restaurant nearby. Ck-out 11 am. Meeting rms. Refrigerators; some fireplaces. Balconies. Cr cds: A, C, D, MC, V, JCB.

Tiburon *

Pop: 7,532 **Elev:** 90 ft **Area code:** 415 **Zip:** 94920
*3 mi E of US 101 on CA 131, 7 mi S of San Rafael (E-1).

What to See and Do

China Cabin. Beach Rd, Belvedere Cove, near jct Tiburon Blvd. Elegant social saloon of the 19th-century transpacific steamship SS *China*. The 20-by-40-foot cabin was removed in 1886 and used as a waterfront cottage until 1978. Completely restored; intricate woodwork, gold leaf, cut glass windows brass & crystal chandeliers; period furnishings. Tours (Apr–Oct, Wed & Sun afternoons or by appt) Phone 435-1853. **Free.**

(See Mill Valley, San Francisco, San Rafael, Sausalito)

Motel

★★TIBURON LODGE. *1651 Tiburon Blvd, on CA 131. 415/435-3133; res: 800/762-7770 (exc CA), 800/842-8766 (CA); FAX 415/435-2451.* 101 rms, 3 story, 4 kit. suites. May–Sept: S $95–$180; D $110–$250; each addl $15; kit. suites $125–$175; under 12 free; lower rates rest of yr. Crib free. Pet accepted, some restrictions; $15. TV; cable. Heated pool. Restaurant 7–11 am; Sat, Sun 7 am–1 pm. Rm serv. Ck-out noon. Meeting rms. Bellhops. Valet serv. Refrigerators. Some in-rm whirlpools. Some private patios, balconies. San Francisco ferry 1 blk. Cr cds: A, C, D, DS, MC, V.

Tijuana, Baja California, Mexico *

Pop: 600,000 (est) **Elev:** 15 ft
Just S of U.S.–Mexico Border on I-5, 6 mi S of Chula Vista (K-4).

Tijuana has all the characteristics of the Mexican border town: recreation that is Latin in flavor, yet tailored to North American desires; a mixture of two cultures resulting in a spirited vitality. A great deal of enjoyment can be found here, as is indicated by the host of people who cross the border from Los Angeles and San Diego daily. Trolley and tour bus transportation to the border is available from San Diego (see). (For Border Crossing Regulations see INTRODUCTION.)

What to See and Do

1. **Mexitlan.** Ocampo & 2nd Ave, downtown. Mexico's miniature museum, with over 150 scale models of Mexican cathedrals, pyramids, monuments, buildings and colonial towns. Entertainment stage features Mexican musicians and dancers. Also shopping and dining avail. (Wed–Sun) Phone 011-52-66/38-41-01 or 619/531-1112. ¢¢

2. **Bullfights.** Plaza Monumental, Calle Segunda, W side of town in Playas de Tijuana section. El Toreo de Tijuana, Agua Caliente Blvd, S side of town. (Approx May–Sept, Sun) Admission charged.

3. **Horse & greyhound racing.** Hipodromo de Agua Caliente. Agua Caliente Blvd. Thoroughbred racing (Sat & Sun). Admission charged. Greyhound racing (nightly exc Tues). **Free.**

4. **Jai Alai.** Downtown at Fronton Palacio, Revolucion Ave & 7th St. Ancient Basque game with parimutuel betting; restaurant. (Games: nightly exc Wed) Admission charged.

5. **Tijuana Cultural Center.** Paseo de los Héroes. Complex housing Omnitheater (fee) with film presentations on Mexico, museum, concert hall, open-air shows with mariachis, regional dancers, Papantla Fliers. Gift shop. (Daily) Tours ¢¢

(For further information contact the Tijuana & Baja Tourism and Convention Bureau, 7860 Mission Center Court, Suite 202, San Diego 92108; 619/298-4105 or 800/225-2786.)

Motor Hotels

✔ ★ ★**BEST WESTERN HOTEL COUNTRY CLUB.** *Blvd Agua Caliente & Tapachula, adj to Caliente Race Track.* 011-52-66/81-77-33; FAX 011-52-66/81-76-92. 135 rms, 3 story, 31 suites. S, D $49–$60; each addl $5; suites $60–$82; under 12 free. TV; cable. Heated pool; whirlpool, sauna, poolside serv. Restaurant 7:30 am–10:30 pm. Rm serv. Bar; entertainment Fri–Sun. Ck-out 1 pm. Meeting rms. Bellhops. Valet serv. Sundries. Some refrigerators. Some balconies. Cr cds: A, MC, V.

★ ★**BEST WESTERN HOTEL HACIENDA DEL RIO.** *(Mailing address: PO Box 5356, Chula Vista 91912) Blvd Sanchez Taboada #10606.* 011-52-66/84-86-44; FAX 011-52-66/84-86-20. 131 rms, 3 story. S, D $75–$81; each addl $5; suites $85–$90; wkly rates. TV; cable. Pool. Restaurant open 24 hrs. Rm serv 7 am–10 pm. Ck-out 1 pm. Meeting rms. Valet serv. Sundries. Exercise equipt; weight machine, bicycles. Cr cds: A, MC, V.

Hotels

★ ★**GRAND HOTEL TIJUANA** (formerly Fiesta Americana Tijuana). *(PO Box BC, Chula Vista 91912) 4500 Blvd Agua Caliente.* 011-52-66/81-70-00; res: 800/GRAND-TJ; FAX 011-52-66/81-70-16. 422 rms, 22 story. S, D $95; each addl $15; under 12 free. Crib free. TV; cable. Pool; whirlpool. Restaurant open 24 hrs. Bar noon–2 am; entertainment, dancing. Ck-out 1 pm. Convention facilities. Concierge. Shopping arcade. Barber, beauty shop. Free covered parking. 2 tennis courts. Golf privileges, greens fee $25–$40, pro. Health club privileges. Some refrigerators. *LUXURY LEVEL:* **GRAND CLUB.** 40 rms, 5 suites, 3 floors. S, D $125; suites $240–$695. Private lounge. Minibars. Complimentary continental bkfst, refreshments. Cr cds: A, D, MC, V.

★ ★**RADISSON PARAÍSO.** *(Mailing address: PO Box 43-1588, San Ysidro 92143) Blvd Agua Caliente #1.* 011-52-66/81-72-00; res: 800/333-3333; FAX 011-52-66/86-36-39. 192 rms, 10 story. S $75; D $85; each addl $10; suites $160–$500; under 12 free; wkly rates. Crib free. TV; cable. Heated pool; whirlpool. Complimentary continental bkfst. Restaurant 7 am–11 pm. Bar; entertainment Tues–Sat. Ck-out 1 pm. Barber, beauty shop. Golf privileges. Some refrigerators. Balconies. Cr cds: A, D, MC, V.

Restaurants

★**LA COSTA.** *150 7th St (Galeana).* 011-52-66/85-84-94. Hrs: 10 am–midnight. Bar. Seafood only. Semi-a la carte: lunch, dinner $9.50–$27. Parking. Nautical decor. Cr cds: MC, V.

★ ★**LA ESPADAÑA.** *10813 Blvd Sánchez Taboada.* 011-52-66/34-14-88/89. Hrs: 7:30 am–11 pm; Sun to 10 pm. Closed Jan 1, May 1, Dec 25; also Thurs & Fri before Easter. Mexican menu. Bar. Semi-a la carte: bkfst $4–$7, lunch, dinner $10–$18. Specializes in steak, shrimp, spare ribs. Parking. Old hacienda atmosphere; wooden beam ceilings, adobe walls. Antiques. Cr cds: MC, V.

★ ★**PEDRIN'S.** *1115 Avenida Revolucion.* 011-52-66/85-40-62/52. Hrs: 10 am–midnight. Mexican menu. Bar. Complete meals: lunch, dinner $8.50–$26. Specializes in Mexican seafood. Parking. 2-level dining area; contemporary decor; skylight. Cr cds: MC, V.

✔ ★ ★**VICTOR'S.** *Blvd Sanchez Tabardo & Joaquin Coausel.* 011-52-66/34-33-09. Hrs: 7–1 am; Sun brunch 9 am–4 pm. Res accepted. Mexican, Amer menu. Bar. Semi-a la carte: bkfst $2.50–$11, lunch, dinner $3.50–$16. Sun brunch $7. Specializes in carne asada, enchiladas. Parking. Formal and casual dining areas. Family-owned. Cr cds: MC, V.

Torrance *

Pop: 133,107 **Elev:** 84 ft **Area code:** 310
8 mi W of Long Beach (J-4) on I-405 (San Diego Frwy).

(For general information and attractions see Los Angeles.)

Motels

★ ★ ★**COURTYARD BY MARRIOTT.** *2633 Sepulveda Blvd (90505), at Crenshaw Blvd.* 310/533-8000. 149 rms, 3 story. S, D $59–$69; suites $79–$89; under 18 free; wkend rates. Crib free. TV; cable. Heated pool. Complimentary coffee in rms. Restaurant 6:30 am–10 pm. Bar 11 am–11 pm. Ck-out 1 pm. Coin lndry. Meeting rms. Valet serv. Exercise equipt; weight machine, bicycles, whirlpool. Balconies. Cr cds: A, C, D, MC, V.

✔ ★**RAMADA INN.** *(850 E Dominguez, Carson 90746) 1 blk off San Diego Frwy (I-405), Avalon Blvd exit.* 310/538-5500; FAX 310/715-2957. 167 rms, 2 story. S $55–$65; D $65–$75; each addl $10; suites $85–$185; under 18 free. Crib $10. TV; cable. Pool. Restaurant 7 am–9:30 pm. Rm serv. Bar 11–2 am. Ck-out 1 pm. Meeting rms. Valet serv. Sundries. Cr cds: A, C, D, DS, MC, V.

★★**SUMMERFIELD SUITES.** *19901 Prairie Ave (90503). 310/371-8525; res: 800/833-4353; FAX 310/542-9628.* 144 kit. suites, 3 story. Kit. suites $129–$159; under 12 free. Crib avail. Pet accepted. TV; cable, in-rm movies. Heated pool. Complimentary continental bkfst. Complimentary coffee in rms. Restaurant nearby. Ck-out noon. Coin lndry. Meeting rm. Sundries. Airport transportation. Exercise equipt; weight machine, bicycles, whirlpool. Picnic tables, grills. Cr cds: A, C, D, DS, MC, V, JCB.

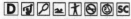

Hotel

★★★**MARRIOTT.** *3635 Fashion Way (90503). 310/316-3636; FAX 310/543-6076.* 487 rms, 17 story. S $125–$149; D $145–$169; suites from $275; under 18 free; wkend rates. Crib free. Valet parking $7/day; self-park free. TV; cable. Indoor/outdoor pool; poolside serv. Restaurant 6:30 am–10 pm; Fri & Sat to 11 pm. Bars 11–2 am; entertainment, dancing. Ck-out 1 pm. Meeting rms. Concierge. Gift shop. Barber, beauty shop. Tennis & golf privileges. Exercise equipt; weight machines, bicycles, whirlpool, sauna. Some bathrm phones. Balconies. Opp shopping center. *LUXURY LEVEL:* **CONCIERGE LEVEL.** 69 rms, 2 floors. S $149; D $169. Private lounge, honor bar. Complimentary continental bkfst, refreshments. Cr cds: A, C, D, DS, ER, MC, V.

Restaurants

★★**FINO.** *24530 Hawthorne Blvd. 310/373-1952.* Hrs: 5–10 pm; Fri & Sat to 10:30 pm. Closed July 4, Thanksgiving, Dec 25. Res accepted. Bar. A la carte entrees: dinner $8–$19.95. Specialties: tapas, polenta, bruschetta, homemade tortellini. Parking. Outdoor dining. Mediterranean decor. Cr cds: A, MC, V.

★★**VELVET TURTLE.** *3210 W Sepulveda Blvd. 310/534-1701.* Hrs: 11:30 am–10 pm; Fri to 10:30 pm; Sat 5–10:30 pm; Sun 10 am–9:30 pm; Sun brunch to 3 pm. Continental menu. Bar. A la carte entrees: lunch $7.25–$12.95. Complete meals: dinner $13.95–$20.95. Sun brunch $12.95. Specialties: beef Wellington, prime rib, rack of lamb. Cr cds: A, C, D, DS, MC, V.

Trinidad (B-1)

Pop: 362 **Elev:** 40 ft **Area code:** 707 **Zip:** 95570

When leaders of a Spanish expedition landed here on June 18, 1775, it was Trinity Sunday, so the leaders named the area Trinidad. The city was founded in 1850 and was a port of entry for supplies packed into the upriver gold country. Offshore is Prisoner Rock; in the old days, constables took drunks here and gave them two options: swim the sobering length ashore or dry up here.

What to See and Do

1. **Telonicher Marine Laboratory.** 570 Ewing St, at Edwards St. Marine teaching and research facility of Humboldt State University. Touch-tank with local tidepool marine life; display aquariums. Self-guided tours of hallway exhibits. (Sept–May, daily; rest of yr, Mon–Fri; schedule may vary; closed academic hols) Phone 677-3671. **Free.**

2. **Patrick's Point State Park.** 5 mi N on US 101. On 650 acres. Ocean fishing, beachcombing, tidepooling. Hiking trails. Picnicking. Camping facilities in unusual rain-forest type of growth; reserva-

tions through Mistix suggested. Museum exhibits, naturalist programs, Yorok Indian Village. Standard fees. Phone 677-3570.

(See Eureka)

Motel

★★**BISHOP PINE LODGE.** *1481 Patrick's Point Dr. 707/677-3314.* 13 cottage units (1–2-rm), 10 kits. No A/C. Apr–mid-Oct, hols: S, D $60–$100; each addl $5; kit. units $5 addl; wkly rates mid-Oct–Mar; lower rates rest of yr. Crib $5. TV; cable. Playground. Complimentary coffee. Ck-out 11 am. Free airport transportation. Exercise equipt; bicycle, treadmill. Picnic tables, grills, outside fireplace. Fish storage. Gazebo. Rustic cottages surrounded by wild azaleas, wooded grounds; forest trails & ocean. Cr cds: A, DS, MC, V.

Inn

★★**LOST WHALE.** *3452 Patrick's Point Dr. 707/677-3425.* 6 rms, private bath. No A/C. No rm phones. May–Oct & major hols: S $80–$120; D $90–$130; each addl $10–$15; wedding packages; lower rates rest of yr. Crib free. Complimentary full bkfst, coffee, tea/sherry. Ck-out 11 am, ck-in 3–6 pm. Whirlpool. Balconies. Ocean view. Private beach. On four acres; farm animals. Totally nonsmoking. Cr cds: MC, V.

Restaurant

★★**MERRYMAN'S.** *100 Moonstone Beach Rd, 3 mi S, US 101 Westhaven (N), 6th Ave (S) exits. 707/677-3111.* Hrs: 5–9:30 pm; Sun from 4 pm. Closed major hols; also wkdays Oct–Mar. No A/C. Bar. Complete meals: dinner $9.95–$19.75. Child's meals. Specializes in seafood, beef. Parking. At outlet of Little River; ocean view. Totally nonsmoking. No cr cds accepted.

Truckee (D-3)

Pop: 3,484 **Elev:** 5,820 ft **Area code:** 916 **Zip:** 96161

Once a lumbering camp, now a railroad and recreation center, Truckee becomes important in winter as the gateway to one of California's best winter sports areas. In 1913 the first California ski club was organized; today more than 20 ski clubs make their headquarters here. Truckee is surrounded by Tahoe National Forest; a Ranger District office of the forest is located here.

What to See and Do

1. **Donner Memorial State Park.** 2 mi W on Old US 40. A 353-acre area that serves as monument to Donner Party, stranded here in October, 1846 by early blizzards. Of a party of 81 who pitched camp, only 48 survived. Emigrant Trail Museum has exhibits on Donner Party, construction of first transcontinental railroad, geology of the Sierra Nevada, wildlife and Indians (daily; closed Jan 1, Thanksgiving, Dec 25; fee). Swimming, fishing. Nature trail. Cross-country ski trail. Picnicking. Camping (Memorial Day–Labor Day). Ranger, naturalist programs (seasonal). Park (daily). Standard fees. Phone 582-7892.

2. **Donner Lake.** 3 mi W on US 40. Sparkling blue lake surrounded by mountain slopes of Sierras. Nearby is Donner Pass, main route into California for more than a century.

3. **Skiing.**

    Boreal. 10 mi W on I-80, Castle Peak exit. 2 quad, 2 triple, 6 double chairlifts; patrol, school, rentals; snowmaking; cafeteria, bar; lodge. 41 runs; longest run 1 mi; vertical drop 600 ft. (Nov–May, daily) Night skiing. Phone 426-3666 for snow conditions. ¢¢¢¢¢

Donner Ski Ranch. 10 mi W, 3½ mi off I-80 at Soda Springs exit. Triple, 3 double chairlifts; patrol, school, rentals; bar, restaurant, cafeteria. Longest run 1 mi; vertical drop 720 ft. (Nov–May, daily) Phone 426-3635. ¢¢¢¢–¢¢¢¢¢

Northstar. 6 mi S on CA 267 via I-80. Two quad, 3 triple, 3 double chairlifts, gondola; patrol, school, rentals; snowmaking; cafeteria, restaurants, bars; lodging. Longest run 3 mi; vertical drop 2,200 ft. Cross-country skiing; rentals. (Nov–Apr, daily) Half-day rates. Summer activities include tennis, 18-hole golf, mountain biking, horseback riding and swimming. Phone 562-1010 or 800/533-6787. ¢¢¢¢¢

Royal Gorge Cross Country Ski Resort. 12 mi W on I-80. Approx 80 cross-country trails over 200 miles of rolling terrain. Patrol, school, rentals; restaurants; 2 lodges. Longest trail 14 mi. (Mid-Nov–mid-May) Phone 426-3871. ¢¢¢¢¢

Soda Springs. 1 mi off I-80, Norden exit. Double, triple chairlifts; patrol, school, rentals. Longest run 1 mi; vertical drop 650 ft. (Nov–Apr, Sat, Sun & hols) Phone 426-3666. ¢¢¢¢¢

Sugar Bowl. 11 mi W on I-80. Quad, 6 double chairlifts, gondola; patrol, school, rentals; restaurant, cafeterias, bar; nursery, lodging. 47 runs; longest run 1.5 mi; vertical drop 1,500 ft. (Nov–Apr, daily) Phone 426-3651 or -3847 (snow conditions). ¢¢¢¢¢

Tahoe Donner. 6 mi NW off I-80. Two double chairlifts, rope tow; patrol, school, rentals; cafeteria, restaurant, bar. (Dec–Apr, daily; closed Easter) Cross-country trails (fee). Phone 587-9444 or -9494 (snow conditions). ¢¢¢¢¢

(For further information contact the Truckee-Donner Chamber of Commerce, 10065 Donner Pass Rd, PO Box 2757; 587-2757.)

Annual Events

(Some events may be postponed and rescheduled due to weather conditions.)

Cross-country skiing marathon. Citizens presidential cup race. Mid-Feb.

Truckee-Tahoe Airshow. Late June.

Fourth of July Community Celebration. Parade, fireworks. July 4.

Truckee Rodeo. 2nd wkend Aug.

(See Tahoe City, Tahoe Vista)

Motels

✔ ★★**BEST WESTERN TRUCKEE-TAHOE.** *11331 CA 267. 916/587-4525; FAX 916/587-8173.* 100 rms, 2 story. S $58; D $65; each addl $7; under 12 free; golf, fishing, ski packages; higher rates hol wkends. Crib free. TV; cable. Heated pool. Complimentary continental bkfst. Restaurant nearby. Ck-out 11 am. Meeting rms. Downhill ski 5 mi. Exercise equipt; weight machine, bicycles, whirlpool, sauna. Cr cds: A, C, D, DS, ER, MC, V.

★★**DONNER LAKE VILLAGE RESORT.** *15695 Donner Pass Rd. 916/587-6081; res: 800/621-6664; FAX 916/587-8782.* 66 rms, 2 story. No A/C. July–Sept, mid-Dec–Apr: S, D $90–$125; each addl $5; suites $125–$205; under 12 free; higher rates hols; lower rates rest of yr. Crib free. TV; cable. Complimentary coffee in rms. Ck-out 11 am. Meeting rms. Downhill ski 4 mi; x-country ski 7 mi. Sauna. Balconies, grills. On lake; marina. Cr cds: A, C, D, DS, MC, V.

Resort

★★**NORTHSTAR-AT-TAHOE.** *(Box 2499) 6 mi S on CA 267. 916/562-1113; res: 800/533-6787; FAX 916/587-0215.* 31 rms in 3-story lodge, 183 kit. town houses, 16 houses (3–5-bedrm). No A/C. Mid-Nov–mid-Apr: S, D $125–$200; town houses $165–$350; houses $300–$450; ski, golf plans; higher rates: Dec 25, special events; lower rates rest of yr. Crib $5. TV; cable. Heated pool (seasonal). Supervised child's activities (July–Labor day, mid-Nov–Mar). Coffee in rms. Bar. Ck-out 11 am, ck-in 5 pm. Grocery, delicatessen. Coin lndry. Meeting rms. Free RR station, bus depot transportation exc hols. Sports dir. Tennis, pro. 18-hole golf, pro, greens fee $60 (incl cart); putting green, driving range. Downhill/x-country ski on site. Soc dir (summer). Game rm. Exercise equipt; weights, bicycles, whirlpool, sauna. Many fireplaces. Private decks, balconies. Picnic tables. Cr cds: A, DS, MC, V.

Restaurants

★★**THE LEFT BANK.** *10098 Donner Pass Rd. 916/587-4694.* Hrs: 11:30 am–10 pm; Sun brunch from 10 am. Closed Tues. Res accepted. French menu. Bar. Semi-a la carte: lunch $6–$13, dinner $14–$20. Sun brunch $7–$14. Specializes in seafood, French country dishes. Art, antiques. Cr cds: A, MC, V.

★**O'B'S PUB.** *10050 Donner Pass Rd. 916/587-4164.* Hrs: 11:30 am–10:30 pm; Sat & Sun brunch 10 am–2 pm. Bar. Semi-a la carte: lunch $5–$8. A la carte entrees: dinner $8–$14. Specializes in seafood, prime rib. Built in early 1900s; many antiques, wood-burning stove. Totally nonsmoking. Cr cds: D, MC, V.

Ukiah (C-1)

Settled: 1855 **Pop:** 14,599 **Elev:** 639 ft **Area code:** 707 **Zip:** 95482

In the center of a valley that the Indians called Ukiah, or Deep Valley, this is the seat of Mendocino County. It is the trading place of an agricultural area that produces a $75 million annual crop of pears, grapes and other products. Recreational activities include golf, tennis and fishing.

What to See and Do

1. **Lake Mendocino.** 3 mi NE, off US 101. Artificial lake produced by Coyote Dam, which controls Russian River. Dedicated in 1959, the lake provides swimming, waterskiing; fishing; boating (ramps, docks). Hiking. Picnicking. Camping (fee). Interpretive programs. (Apr–Sept, daily; closed rest of yr exc some campgrounds) Pets on leash only. No camping reservations accepted. Phone 462-7581 or -7582.

2. **Cow Mountain Recreation Area.** SE of Lake Mendocino. This 50,000-acre recreation area is highlighted by a 3,200-foot mountain. Deer hunting. Hiking, equestrian and off-road vehicle trails. Picnicking. Camping. Trailers & large recreational vehicles not recommended for use in area due to primitive roads. Temporary wet-weather road closures Oct–May. (Daily) Phone 462-3873. **Free.**

3. **Grace Hudson Museum.** 431 S Main St. Permanent exhibits on Pomo Indians; regional artists and photographers; early 20th-century paintings by Mendocino County artist Grace Hudson. Changing exhibits. **The Sun House** (1911) is the six-room craftsman house of Grace and John Hudson. Tours. (July 4–Labor Day, daily exc Mon; rest of yr, Wed–Sun) Phone 462-3370. **Free.**

4. **Wineries.**

   Dunnewood Vineyards. 2399 N State St. Winery tours (by appt). Tasting Room (daily; closed hols). Picnic area. Phone 462-2987. **Free.**

Parducci Wine Cellars. 501 Parducci Rd. Guided tours; wine tasting (daily; closed hols). Phone 462-3828. **Free.**

(For further information contact the Greater Ukiah Chamber of Commerce, 495-E E Perkins St; 462-4705.)

Annual Event

Mendocino County Fair & Apple Show. Boonville. 3 days mid- or late Sept.

(See Clear Lake Area)

Motels

★ ★ **BEST WESTERN INN.** *601 Talmage Rd E. 707/462-8868; FAX 707/468-9043.* 40 rms, 2 story. May–Sept: S, D $48–$65; each addl $5; lower rates rest of yr. Crib $5. TV; cable. Pool. Complimentary continental bkfst. Complimentary coffee in rms. Restaurant nearby. Ck-out noon. Meeting rm. Many refrigerators. Cr cds: A, C, D, DS, MC, V, JCB.

✔ ★ ★ **DISCOVERY INN.** *1340 N State St. 707/462-8873; FAX 707/462-1249.* 154 rms, 2 story. S $40–$55; D $47–$60; each addl $5; suites $65–$75; kit. units $60–$85. Crib free. TV; cable. Heated pool; whirlpool, sauna. Restaurant 6 am–11 pm. Ck-out noon. Meeting rms. Tennis. Lawn games. Refrigerators. Cr cds: A, C, D, DS, MC, V.

★ **TRAVELODGE.** *406 S State St. 707/462-8611.* 40 rms, 2 story. May–Sept: S, D $42–$56; each addl $5; higher rates: hols, special events; lower rates rest of yr. TV; cable. Pool. Complimentary continental bkfst. Complimentary coffee in rms. Restaurant opp 9 am–10 pm. Ck-out 11 am. Some refrigerators. Cr cds: A, C, D, DS, MC, V.

Vacaville (D-2)

Pop: 71,479 **Elev:** 179 ft **Area code:** 707 **Zip:** 95688

(See Fairfield)

Motels

✔ ★ **BEST WESTERN HERITAGE INN.** *1420 E Monte Vista Ave. 707/448-8453.* 41 rms, 2 story. S $42; D $46; each addl $7; under 12 free. Crib $4. TV; cable. Pool. Complimentary continental bkfst, coffee. Restaurant adj open 24 hrs. Ck-out 11 am. Refrigerators avail. Cr cds: A, C, D, DS, MC, V.

★ **DAYS INN.** *1571 E Monte Vista Ave. 707/448-6482; FAX 707/452-8857.* 87 rms, 1–2 story. Mid-June–mid-Sept: S $39.95–$48.95; D $55–$65; each addl $5; kit. units $65; under 12 free; wkly rates; lower rates rest of yr. Pet accepted, some restrictions; $5. TV; cable. Pool; whirlpool. Complimentary continental bkfst, coffee. Restaurant adj open 24 hrs. Ck-out 11 am. Coin lndry. Meeting rms. Some refrigerators. Cr cds: A, C, D, DS, MC, V.

★ ★ **QUALITY INN.** *950 Leisure Town Rd Overpass, just off I-80. 707/446-8888; FAX 707/449-0109.* 120 rms, 2 story. S, D $49–$56; each addl $5; under 18 free. Crib free. TV; cable. Pool. Complimentary continental bkfst. Restaurant opp 6 am–11 pm. Ck-out 11 am. Cr cds: A, C, D, DS, ER, MC, V, JCB.

Restaurants

★ **BLACK OAK.** *320 Orange Dr. 707/448-1311.* Hrs: 6 am–11 pm. Res accepted; required major hols. Continental menu. Wine, beer. Semi-a la carte: bkfst $2.75–$8.75, lunch $5.65–$8.25, dinner $5.45–$11.45. Child's meals. Specializes in American, Mexican, Italian and Chinese dishes. Parking. Totally nonsmoking. Cr cds: A, DS, MC, V.

✔ ★ ★ **COFFEE TREE.** *100 Nut Tree Pkwy, just N off I-80. 707/448-8435.* Hrs: 6 am–11 pm; Fri & Sat to midnight. Closed Dec 25. Wine, beer. Semi-a la carte: bkfst $3.95–$8.55, lunch, dinner $3.95–$14.95. Child's meals. Specializes in omelettes, salads, strawberry shortcake. Own desserts, breads. Parking. Colorful decor; art display. Family-owned. Cr cds: A, D, MC, V.

★ ★ **NUT TREE.** *I-80, Monte Vista exit. 707/448-6411.* Hrs: 7 am–9 pm. Closed Dec 25. Res accepted. Bar. Semi-a la carte: bkfst $3.25–$7.95, lunch $6.95–$12.95, dinner $8.95–$15.95. Child's meals. Specializes in seafood, pasta, exotic fruits. Pianist. Parking. Outdoor dining. Built on the site of a fruit ranch, the restaurant is now part of a complex consisting of a private airport, park, bakery, produce store, coffee shop and retail store. Named in honor of a tree planted a century ago, in 1962 the area was officially designated by the US Postal Service as Nut Tree, California. Totally nonsmoking. Cr cds: A, C, D, DS, MC, V.

Valencia (H-3)

Pop: 30,000 (est) **Area code:** 805 **Zip:** 91355

What to See and Do

1. **Six Flags Magic Mountain.** 26101 Magic Mt Pkwy, off I-5, Magic Mt Pkwy exit. Family theme park on 260 acres featuring more than 100 rides, shows and attractions. Eight major rollercoasters, including Psyclone, Flashback and Viper; water rides; animal and musical shows; shops, concessions. A 6½-acre area for children features 13 scaled-down rides, animal farm and petting zoo. (Memorial Day–Labor Day, daily; rest of yr, wkends and school hols) Sr citizen rate. Phone 255-4100 or 818/367-5965 (L.A.). ¢¢¢¢¢

2. **Pyramid Lake Recreation Area.** 20 mi N on I-5. Lake with swimming, waterskiing, windsurfing; fishing; boating (rentals, ramp). Picnicking, concession. Camping. (Daily; closed major hols) Phone 257-2790 (24-hr recording). Per vehicle ¢¢–¢¢¢

(See Los Angeles)

Motels

★ ★ **BEST WESTERN RANCH HOUSE INN.** *27413 N Tourney Rd, opp Six Flags Magic Mountain. 805/255-0555; FAX 805/255-2216.* 184 rms in 4 buildings, 2 story. Jan–Aug: S, D $69–$99; each addl $10; under 18 free; lower rates rest of yr. Crib free. Pet accepted. TV; cable. 2 pools, 1 heated; wading pool. Restaurant 6 am–10 pm. Rm serv. Bar 4 pm–2 am; entertainment. Ck-out noon. Coin lndry. Meeting rms. Free transportation to Six Flags Magic Mountain. Refrigerators avail. Cr cds: A, C, D, DS, MC, V.

★ ★ **HAMPTON INN.** *(25259 The Old Road, Santa Clarita 91381) I-5 exit Lyons Ave W to Chiquella Lane, then S. 805/253-2400; FAX 805/253-1683.* 130 rms, 4 story. May–Sept: S $69–$79; D $79–$89; lower rates rest of yr. Crib free. Pet accepted, some restrictions; $8 per day. TV; cable. Heated pool; whirlpool. Complimentary coffee in lobby. Restaurant adj open 24 hrs. Ck-out noon. Coin lndry. Meeting rm. Valet serv. Sundries. Health club privileges. Some refrigerators. Some balconies. Cr cds: A, C, D, DS, MC, V.

★HILTON GARDEN INN. 27710 The Old Road, opp Six Flags Magic Mountain. 805/254-8800; FAX 805/254-9399. 152 rms, 2 story. May–Sept: S $89–$109; D $99–$119; each addl $10; suites $198; lower rates rest of yr. Crib free. Pet accepted, some restrictions. TV; cable. Heated pool; poolside serv. Complimentary coffee in rms. Restaurant 6:30 am–10 pm. Rm serv. Bar. Ck-out noon. Coin lndry. Meeting rms. Exercise equipt; weights, bicycles, whirlpool. Some bathrm phones; refrigerators avail. Balconies. Picnic tables, grills. Cr cds: A, C, D, DS, MC, V, JCB.

Vallejo (D-1)

Founded: 1851 Pop: 109,199 Elev: 50 ft Area code: 707

This was California's capital in 1852 for about a week; and again, a year later, for just over one month. Despite the departure of the legislature in 1853 for Benicia, the town prospered because the United States purchased Mare Island for a Navy yard in 1854. The Mare Island Naval Shipyard is a 2,300-acre spread of land between the Mare Island Strait and San Pablo Bay.

What to See and Do

1. **Vallejo Naval and Historical Museum.** 734 Marin St, located in the old City Hall building. Two galleries house changing exhibits on local history. Two additional galleries house permanent exgibits on Navy and Mare Island Naval Shipyard history. Naval exhibits include models, murals and a functioning submarine periscope. Also here is a local history research library (by appt) and a book/gift shop. (Tues–Sat; closed some major hols) Sr citizen rate. Phone 643-0077. ¢

2. **Marine World Africa USA.** Jct I-80 & CA 37, Marine World Pkwy. Wildlife theme park. Major shows featuring killer whales, dolphins, sea lions, tigers, exotic and predatory birds and waterski/boat show. Participatory exhibits include Elephant Encounter, Butterfly World, giraffe feedings and lorikeet feedings. (Memorial Day–Labor Day, daily; rest of yr, Wed–Sun) Sr citizen rate. Phone 643-ORCA (recording). ¢¢¢¢

3. **Benicia Capitol State Historic Park.** 1st & G Sts, 6 mi SE, in Benicia. Building has been restored and furnished in style of 1853–54, when it served as state capitol. (Daily; closed Jan 1, Thanksgiving, Dec 25) Phone 745-3385. ¢

(For further information contact the Convention & Visitors Bureau, Suite 270, Georgia St Plaza, 301 Georgia St, 94590; 642-3653.)

Annual Events

Solano County Fair. Fairgrounds, Fairgrounds Dr, N off I-80. Phone 648-3247. July.

Whaleboat Regatta. Marina Vista Park. Phone 644-5551. Early Oct.

(See Berkeley, Fairfield, Martinez, Oakland)

Motels

★★BEST WESTERN HERITAGE INN. (1955 E 2nd St, Benicia 94510) 6 mi E off I-780 2nd St exit. 707/746-0401; FAX 707/745-0842. 100 rms, 3 story. S, D $60–$95; each addl $5; suites $85–$95; kit. units $60–$70; under 12 free; wkly, monthy rates. Crib free. Pet accepted, some restrictions; $50 refundable. TV; cable. Pool; whirlpool. Complimentary continental bkfst. Coffee in rms. Restaurant nearby. Ck-

out 11 am. Meeting rms. Valet serv. In-rm whirlpools; some refrigerators, wet bars. Balconies. Cr cds: A, C, D, DS, MC, V.

✔ ★★COMFORT INN. 1185 Admiral Callaghan Lane (94591), I-80 Columbus Pkwy exit. 707/648-1400; FAX 707/552-8623. 80 units, 2 story, 10 suites. June–Sept: S $54–$65; D $59–$69; each addl $7; suites $75–$150; under 18 free; lower rates rest of yr. Crib free. TV. Heated pool. Complimentary continental bkfst, coffee. Restaurant nearby. Ck-out 11 am. Coin lndry. Meeting rm. Sundries. Exercise equipt; weights, bicycles, sauna. Some refrigerators. Cr cds: A, C, D, DS, ER, MC, V.

★★RAMADA INN. 1000 Admiral Callaghan Lane (94591), I-80 at Columbus Pkwy exit. 707/643-2700; FAX 707/642-1148. 131 rms, 3 story, 36 suites. May–Sept: S $63–$79; D $68–$86; each addl $7; suites $87–$120; under 18 free. Crib free. Pet accepted; $20. TV; cable. Pool; whirlpool. Complimentary continental bkfst. Complimentary coffee in rms. Restaurant nearby. Ck-out noon. Coin lndry. Meeting rms. Valet serv. Free Marine World transportation. Health club privileges. Refrigerators. Picnic tables, grill. Cr cds: A, C, D, DS, ER, MC, V, JCB.

Inns

★★CAPTAIN DILLINGHAM'S. (145 East D St, Benicia 94510) 4 mi SE via I-780, exit 2nd St. 707/746-7164; res: 800/544-2278 (CA). 9 rms, 2 story, 1 suite. S, D $70–$125; suite $160–$170; under 5 free. Pet accepted. TV. Complimentary full bkfst, refreshments. Ck-out noon, wkends 1 pm, ck-in 3 pm. Antiques. Library. Refrigerators, in-rm whirlpools. Private patios, balconies. Picnic tables, grills. Cape Cod decor. English country garden. Former residence of a New England sea captain. Cr cds: A, C, D, MC, V.

★ ★UNION HOTEL. (401 First St, Benicia 94510) 4 mi SE via I-780, exit 2nd St. 707/746-0100; FAX 707/746-6458. 12 rms, 3 story. S, D $70–$120; hol, wkend rates. TV. Complimentary continental bkfst. Dining rm 11:30 am–2:30 pm, 6–9:30 pm; Sun brunch 9:30 am–2:30 pm. Bar 10–2 am; entertainment Wed–Sun. Ck-out noon, ck-in 3 pm. Concierge. In-rm whirlpools. Victorian architecture (1882), period furnishings. Cr cds: A, C, D, DS, MC, V.

Restaurant

✔ ★THE WHARF. 295 Mare Island Way, Georgia St Wharf. 707/648-1966. Hrs: 11:30 am–9 pm; Fri & Sat to 10 pm; Sun 4–9 pm. Closed Mon; some major hols. Res accepted. Bar to 1 am. Semi-a la carte: lunch $3.95–$11.95, dinner $8.50–$14.95. Child's meals. Specializes in fresh seafood. Own desserts. Entertainment Tues–Sat. Parking. Nautical decor; view of estuary, shipyards. Family-owned. Cr cds: C, D, MC, V.

Van Nuys (L.A.) *

Area code: 818
*Just N of US 101, 14 mi NW of Downtown Los Angeles (H-4).

This community in the San Fernando Valley is an integral part of Los Angeles, but is regarded by many as a separate entity.

(For general information and attractions see Los Angeles.)

Motel

✔ ★TRAVELODGE. 6909 Sepulveda Blvd (91405). 818/787-5400; FAX 818/782-0239. 74 rms, 3 story. S, D $49–$79; each addl $6;

under 12 free. TV. Pool. Complimentary continental bkfst. Restaurant nearby. Ck-out noon. Refrigerators. Cr cds: A, C, D, DS, ER, MC, V, JCB.

Motor Hotels

★ ★ ★ **BEST WESTERN AIRTEL PLAZA.** *7277 Valjean Ave (91406), I-405 Sherman Way W exit. 818/997-7676; FAX 818/785-8864.* 268 rms, 3–5 story. S $109–$119; D $119–$129; each addl $10; suites $150–$600; under 18 free. Crib free. TV; cable, in-rm movies. Heated pool; poolside serv. Restaurant 6 am–10 pm. Rm serv. Bar 10–2 am; entertainment, dancing. Ck-out noon. Convention facilities. Bellhops. Exercise equipt; weight machine, bicycles, whirlpool. Some refrigerators. Some private patios, balconies. Cr cds: A, C, D, DS, ER, MC, V, JCB.

★ ★ **HOLIDAY INN.** *8244 Orion St (91406), I-405 at Roscoe Blvd. 818/989-5010; FAX 818/781-6453.* 130 rms, 7 story. S $75–$110; D $87–$122; each addl $12; under 18 free. Crib free. TV; cable. Heated pool; poolside serv. Restaurant 6 am–2 pm, 5:30–10 pm. Rm serv. Bar 4 pm–midnight. Ck-out noon. Coin lndry. Meeting rms. Bellhops. Valet serv. Airport transportation. Exercise equipt; bicycle, stair machine. Cr cds: A, C, D, DS, MC, V, JCB.

Hotel

★ **RADISSON VALLEY CENTER.** *(15433 Ventura Blvd, Sherman Oaks 91403) Jct US 101 & I-405, adj to Galleria Mall. 818/981-5400; FAX 818/981-3175.* 215 units, 14 story, 5 suites. S, D $79–$140; each addl $10; suites $225–$395; under 18 free. Crib free. Garage $5. TV; cable. Heated pool; poolside serv. Complimentary continental bkfst 5:30–6:30 am. Restaurant 6:30 am–10 pm. Bar 11–2 am; entertainment Fri & Sat. Ck-out noon. Convention facilities. Concierge. Gift shop. Barber. Airport transportation. Exercise equipt; bicycles, weight machine, whirlpool. Bathrm phones. Balconies. Picnic tables. Cr cds: A, C, D, DS, ER, MC, V, JCB.

Ventura *(H-3)*

Founded: 1782 **Pop:** 93,483 **Elev:** 50 ft **Area code:** 805

What was once a little mission surrounded by huge stretches of sagebrush and mustard plants is now the busy city of Ventura. The sagebrush and mustard have been replaced by citrus, avocado and other agriculture, but the mission still stands. With the Pacific shore at its feet and rolling foothills at its back, Ventura attracts a steady stream of vacationers. It is in the center of the largest lemon-producing county in the US.

What to See and Do

1. **San Buenaventura State Beach.** Approx 115 acres on a sheltered sweep of coast. Offers swimming, lifeguard (summer); surf fishing. Coastal bicycle trail access point. Picnicking, concession. Standard fees. Phone 654-4610.
2. **San Buenaventura Mission** (1782). 211 E Main St, off US 101. Ninth California mission and the last founded by Fray Junipero Serra. Massive, with a striped rib dome on the bell tower; restored. Garden with fountain. Museum (enter through gift shop at 225 E Main St) features original wooden bell. Museum (daily; closed major hols). Church and gardens (daily). Phone 643-4318 or 648-4496. ¢

3. **Ventura County Museum of History and Art.** 100 E Main St. Collection of Native American, Spanish and pioneer artifacts; George Stuart Collection of Historical Figures; changing exhibits of local history and art; outdoor areas depicting the county's agricultural history; educational programs, research library; gift shop. (Daily exc Mon; closed Jan 1, Thanksgiving, Dec 25) Phone 653-0323 or -5469. ¢
4. **Albinger Archaeological Museum.** 113 E Main St. Preserved archaeological exploration site and visitor center in downtown area. Evidence of Indian culture 3,500 years old; Chumash Indian village site, settled approx A.D. 1500; foundation of original mission; Chinese and Mexican artifacts; audiovisual programs. (Wed–Sun; closed some hols) Phone 648-5823. **Free.**
5. **Camping. Emma Wood State Beach**, North Beach. Access from W Pacific Coast Hwy, state beaches exit northbound US 101. Swimming, surfing; fishing. 2 RV group camping sites, 61 primitive camp sites. Standard fees. Phone 654-4610. **McGrath State Beach.** 3 mi S off Harbor Blvd. Swimming; fishing. Nature trail. 170 developed campsites. Standard fees. Phone 654-4744. For local camping information, phone 654-4610.
6. **Olivas Adobe** (1847). 4200 Olivas Park Dr, off US 101 Victoria Ave exit. Restored with authentic furnishings; displays; gardens; visitor center, video. Tours (by appt). House open for viewing (Sat, Sun). Grounds (daily; closed some hols). Special programs monthly. Phone 644-4346. **Free.**
7. **Ortega Adobe** (1857). 215 W Main St. Restored and furnished adobe built on the Camino Real. Furnished with rustic handmade furniture from the 1850s. Tours (by appt). Grounds (daily). Phone 648-5823. **Free.**
8. **Ventura Harbor.** 1603 Anchors Way Dr. Accommodates more than 1,500 boats; 3 marinas, launch ramp, mast up dry storage boat yard, drydock and repair facilities, fuel docks, guest slips. Sportfishing and island boats; sailboat rentals; cruises (see #11). Swimming, fishing; hotel, shops, restaurants; Channel Islands National Park headquarters. Phone 642-8538.
9. **Channel Islands National Park** (see).
10. **Channel Islands National Park Visitor's Center.** 1901 Spinnaker Dr. Displays, exhibits and scale models of the five islands; marine life exhibit; observation tower; film of the islands (25 min). (Daily; closed Thanksgiving, Dec 25) Phone 658-5730. **Free.**
11. **Island Packer Cruises.** Boat leaves Ventura Harbor (see #8) for picnic, sightseeing and recreational trips to Channel Islands National Park. Reservations required. (Memorial Day–Sept, 5 islands; rest of yr, 2 islands) For details contact 1867 Spinnaker Dr, 93001; 642-7688 (recording) or -1393 (reservations). ¢¢¢¢¢

(For further information contact the Visitor & Convention Bureau Information Center, 89-C S California St, 93001; 648-2075.)

Annual Event

Ventura County Fair. Ventura Fairgrounds. Parade, rodeo, carnival, entertainment, livestock auction. Aug.

Seasonal Event

Whale watching. Dec–Mar.

(See Ojai, Oxnard, Santa Barbara, Thousand Oaks)

Motels

★ ★ ★ **CLARION CORRIA CLOCKTOWER INN.** *181 E Santa Clara St (93001). 805/652-0141; FAX 805/643-1432.* 49 rms, 2 story. S, D $70–$100; each addl $10; under 12 free. TV. Complimentary continental bkfst. Restaurant 11 am–2:30 pm, 5–9:30 pm; wkend hrs vary; closed Sun. Rm serv. Ck-out noon. Meeting rms. Some fireplaces. Private patios, balconies. Near beach. Southwestern decor. Renovated firehouse in park setting; atrium, walkways. Cr cds: A, C, D, DS, ER, MC, V, JCB.

★ ★ ★ **COUNTRY INN.** *298 S Chestnut St (93001). 805/653-1434; res: 800/44-RELAX; FAX 805/648-7126.* 120 kit. units, 3 story. S $79–$89; D $89–$99; each addl $10; suites $110–$159; under 12 free. TV; cable, in-rm movies. Heated pool; whirlpool. Complimentary full bkfst 7–9:30 am. Ck-out noon. Coin lndry. Meeting rm. Valet serv. Bathrm phones; some fireplaces. Private patios, balconies. Country decor. Opp ocean. Cr cds: A, C, D, DS, MC, V, JCB.

★ ★ ★ **PIERPONT INN.** *550 San Jon Rd (93001). 805/643-6144; res: 800/285-4667; FAX 805/641-1501.* 72 rms, 2–3 story. No A/C. No elvtr. S, D $69–$79; each addl $10; cottages $125–$175; under 12 free. Crib free. TV; cable, in-rm movies. Heated pool. Complimentary continental bkfst. Restaurant 6:30 am–2 pm, 4:30–10 pm. Rm serv. Bar 10–2 am. Ck-out noon. Meeting rms. Tennis privileges. Health club privileges. Some fireplaces. Many private verandas, balconies. Established in 1908. Overlooks Pierpont Bay. Cr cds: A, C, D, DS, ER, MC, V.

✔ ★ **VAGABOND INN.** *756 E Thompson Blvd (93001). 805/648-5371.* 82 rms, 2 story. S $46–$52; D $50–$75; each addl $5; higher rates special events. Crib free. TV; cable, in-rm movies. Heated pool; whirlpool. Playground. Complimentary continental bkfst. Restaurant open 24 hrs. Ck-out noon. Meeting rm. Cr cds: A, C, D, DS, MC, V.

Motor Hotel

★ ★ **HOLIDAY INN.** *450 E Harbor Blvd (93001). 805/648-7731; FAX 805/653-6202.* 260 rms, 12 story. S $80–$90; D $90–$100; each addl $10; suites $105–$200; under 19 free. TV; cable, in-rm movies. Heated pool; wading pool, poolside serv in summer. Restaurant 6 am–11 pm; wkends from 6:30 am; revolving rooftop dining rm Fri & Sat 5–11 pm. Rm serv. Bar noon–2 am; entertainment, dancing exc Sun. Ck-out noon. Coin lndry. Meeting rms. Bellhops. Valet serv Mon–Fri. Gift shop. Exercise equipt; weight machine, rowing machine. Game rm. Balconies with coastline view. On beach. Cr cds: A, C, D, DS, MC, V, JCB.

Hotel

★ ★ **DOUBLETREE.** *2055 Harbor Blvd (93001). 805/643-6000; FAX 805/643-7137.* 285 rms, 4 story. S $89–$119; D $99–$129; each addl $10; suites $175–$350; under 18 free; package plans. Pet accepted, some restrictions; $50. TV; cable. Heated pool; whirlpool. Restaurant 6:30 am–10:30 pm, Sat & Sun from 7 am. Bar 2–11 pm. Ck-out noon. Convention facilities. Gift shop. Exercise equipt; weights, bicycles, whirlpool, sauna. Balconies. Beach 1 blk. Cr cds: A, C, D, DS, ER, MC, V, JCB.

Inn

★ ★ **LA MER.** *411 Poli St (93001). 805/643-3600.* 4 rms, 2½ story, 1 suite. No A/C. No rm phones. S $80–$150; D $85–$155; suite $150–$155; mid-wk rates. Children over 13 yrs only. Complimentary Bavarian buffet bkfst, wine & champagne. Ck-out noon, ck-in 4 pm. Antique horse-drawn carriage rides. Library. Antiques. Each rm individually decorated to represent a European country. Private patios. Overlooks ocean. Totally nonsmoking. Cr cds: MC, V.

Restaurants

✔ ★ ★ **BJ'S.** *545 E Thompson Blvd. 805/643-1232.* Hrs: 11:30 am–10 pm; Fri to 10:30 pm; Sat 4:30–10:30 pm; Sun 4–9:30 pm. Closed Memorial Day, Labor Day. Res accepted. Bar. Semi-a la carte: lunch from $4.95, dinner from $10.95. Child's meals. Specializes in steak, seafood, pasta. Pianist in bar Thurs–Sat. Parking. Contemporary decor. Cr cds: A, D, DS, MC, V.

★ **SPORTSMAN.** *53 S California St. 805/643-2851.* Hrs: 11 am–10 pm; Sat from 9 am; Sun 9 am–9 pm. Closed major hols. Res accepted. Bar. Semi-a la carte: bkfst $3.45–$8.95, lunch $3.95–$7.95, dinner $7.95–$26.95. Specializes in charcoal-broiled steak, seafood, prime rib. Open kitchen. Cr cds: A, MC, V.

Victorville (H-4)

Founded: 1878 **Pop:** 40,674 **Elev:** 2,715 ft **Area code:** 619

You may never have been in Victorville, but you've probably seen the town before—it has been the setting for hundreds of cowboy movies. This aspect of the town's economy has waned, replaced by light industry. On the edge of the Mojave Desert, the town serves as a base for desert exploration. The presence of lime has attracted four major cement plants to the vicinity.

What to See and Do

1. **Mojave Narrows Regional Park.** 2 mi S on I-15, then 4 mi E on Bear Valley Cutoff, 3 mi N on Ridgecrest. Fishing, boating. Hiking and bridle trails. Picnicking, snack bar. Camping (fee). Park (daily; closed Dec 25). Contact PO Box 361, 92392; 245-2226. Per vehicle ¢¢
2. **Roy Rogers-Dale Evans Museum.** 15650 Seneca Rd. Western-style fort depicting the personal and professional lives of the Rogers. (Daily; closed Thanksgiving, Dec 25) Sr citizen rate. Phone 243-4547 or -4548. ¢¢

(For further information contact the Chamber of Commerce, 14174 Green Tree Blvd, 92393; 245-6506.)

Annual Events

Huck Finn Jubilee. At Mojave Narrows Regional Park (see #1). River-raft building, fence painting, bluegrass and clogging activities; food. Father's Day wkend.

San Bernardino County Fair. 14800 7th St. Rodeo, livestock and agricultural exhibits, carnival. Phone 951-2200. Late July–early Aug.

(See Barstow, Big Bear Lake, Lake Arrowhead)

Motels

★ ★ **BEST WESTERN GREEN TREE INN.** *14173 Green Tree Blvd (92392). 619/245-3461; FAX 619/245-7745.* 168 rms, 2–3 story. S $52–$56; D $52–$60; each addl $6; suites $62–$78; kit. units, studio rms $48–$58; under 12 free. Crib free. TV; cable. Heated pool; wading pool, whirlpool, poolside serv. Complimentary coffee in rms. Restaurant open 24 hrs; dining rm 5–10 pm; Fri, Sat to 11 pm. Rm serv. Bar 11–2 am; entertainment, dancing. Ck-out 1 pm. Meeting rms. Shopping arcade. Refrigerators. 18-hole golf adj. View of desert, mountains. Cr cds: A, C, D, DS, ER, MC, V, JCB.

✔ ★ **TRAVELODGE NORTH.** *16868 Stoddard Wells Rd (92392). 619/243-7700; FAX 619/243-4432.* 96 rms, 2 story. S $27; D $36–$42; suites $81; each addl $5; under 17 free; wkly rates. Crib free.

TV; cable. Heated pool. Complimentary coffee in lobby. Restaurant opp open 24 hrs. Ck-out noon. Coin Indry. Cr cds: A, C, D, DS, MC, V.

Restaurant

★★CHATEAU CHANG. *15425 Anacapa Rd. 619/241-3040.* Hrs: 11:30 am–2:30 pm, 5:30–9:30 pm; Sat 5:30–10:30 pm. Closed Sun; some major hols. Res accepted. French, continental menu. Bar. Semi-a la carte: lunch $5.50–$6.50, dinner $8.75–$24.95. Specialties: flaming filet mignon, roast duck with orange sauce, whole lobster Thermidor. Parking. Contemporary decor; gray marble floors; saltwater aquarium. Cr cds: A, MC, V.

Visalia (F-3)

Pop: 75,636 **Elev:** 331 ft **Area code:** 209

What to See and Do

1. **Sequoia and Kings Canyon National Parks** (see). Approx 50 mi E on CA 198. Due to gradient into and from the mountains, allow minimum of 1–5 hours driving time to the visitors center.fro

2. **Tulare County Museum.** Mooney Grove, 27000 Mooney Blvd. Ten buildings set in a 140-acre park house historical exhibits. Park features *End of the Trail* statue by James Earl Fraser. Museum has Indian artifacts, early farm equipment, antique guns, clocks, dolls; log cabin. (Thurs–Mon; closed some hols) Phone 733-6616. Park entry (per car) ¢;   Museum ¢

3. **Agricultural tours.** Tulare County is one of the largest agricultural areas in the nation. Contact Convention and Visitors Bureau for tour details.

(For further information contact the Convention & Visitors Bureau, 720 W Mineral King Ave, 93291; 734-5876.)

(See Hanford, Porterville, Three Rivers)

Motel

✔★ECONO LODGE. *1400 S Mooney Blvd (93277).* 209/732-6641; FAX 209/739-7520. 49 rms, 2 story. S $40–$45; D $45–$50; each addl $5. Crib $4. TV; cable. Pool. Coffee in rms. Restaurant 5:30 am–2 pm. Ck-out 11 am. Some refrigerators. Cr cds: A, C, D, DS, ER, MC, V, JCB.

Hotel

★★★RADISSON. *300 S Court St (93291).* 209/636-1111; FAX 209/636-8224. 200 rms, 8 story. S, D $85–$110; each addl $6; suites $200–$400. Crib free. TV; cable. Pool; poolside serv. Restaurant 6 am–2:30 pm, 5–10 pm. Rm serv 6–2 am. Bar 11–2 am; entertainment Fri, Sat. Ck-out noon. Meeting rms. Concierge. Gift shop. Free airport, RR station transportation. Exercise equipt; weights, bicycles, whirlpool. Game rm. Refrigerators, minibars. Wet bar in suites. Some balconies. Cr cds: A, C, D, DS, ER, MC, V, JCB.

Inn

★★SPALDING HOUSE. *631 N Encina (93291).* 209/739-7877. 3 suites, 2 story. No rm phones. S $75; D $85. Crib free. TV in living rm. Complimentary full bkfst. Restaurant nearby. Ck-out noon, ck-in 3

pm. Historic Colonial-revival house built 1901; fully restored. Elegant furnishings; some fireplaces, antiques. LIbrary; piano in music rm; sitting rm. Totally nonsmoking. Cr cds: MC, V.

Restaurants

★★BULLENE'S. *208 W Main St.* 209/739-8136. Hrs: 11 am–3 pm, 5:30–10 pm. Closed Sun; major hols. Res accepted; required wkends. Bar to midnight. Semi-a la carte: lunch $6–$10, dinner $10.95–$20.95. Child's meals. Specializes in seafood, pasta. Own desserts. Jazz, classical flamenco guitarist Thurs–Sat. Parking. Cr cds: A, MC, V.

★★★THE VINTAGE PRESS. *216 N Willis.* 209/733-3033. Hrs: 11:30 am–2 pm, 6–10:30 pm; Fri, Sat to 11 pm. Closed Sun; Dec 25. Res accepted. California menu. Bar 11–2 am. Semi-a la carte: lunch $6.95–$14.95, dinner $16.95–$34.50. Child's meals. Specializes in fresh seafood. Parking. Outdoor dining. Antiques. Family-owned. Cr cds: A, C, D, MC, V.

Walnut Creek (E-2)

Pop: 60,569 **Elev:** 135 ft **Area code:** 510

(See Berkeley, Concord, Oakland)

Motel

★★WALNUT CREEK MOTOR LODGE. *1960 N Main St (94596).* 510/932-2811; res: 800/824-0334 (CA). 71 rms, 2 story, 8 kits. S $65–$80; D $75–$90; each addl $10; suites $80–$90; kit. units $75–$85; family rates. Crib $10. Pet accepted, some restrictions. TV; cable, in-rm movies avail. Pool; whirlpool. Coffee in rms. Restaurant adj 11 am–10 pm. Ck-out 11 am. Valet serv. Cr cds: A, C, D, MC, V.

Motor Hotel

★★★★BEST WESTERN LAFAYETTE PARK. *(3287 Mt Diablo Blvd, Lafayette 94549)* 2 mi W on CA 24 to Pleasant Hill Rd S exit, then 1 blk to Mt Diablo Blvd. 510/283-3700; FAX 510/284-1621. 139 rms, 4 story. S, D $135–$175; suites $225–$300. TV; cable. Heated pool; poolside serv. Restaurant 6:30 am–10 pm. Evening refreshments. Rm serv 24 hrs. Bar 11 am–midnight. Ck-out noon. Meeting rms. Concierge. Valet serv avail. Free covered parking. Exercise equipt; weight machines, stair machine, whirlpool, sauna. Bathrm phones, refrigerators, minibars. Some private patios. Cr cds: A, C, D, DS, MC, V.

Hotels

★★DOUBLETREE. *2355 N Main St (94596).* 510/934-2000; FAX 510/934-6374. 337 rms, 6 story. S $104–$135; D $115–$140; suites $150–$500; under 18 free; wkend rates. Crib free. TV; cable. Pool; whirlpool. Restaurant 6 am–11 pm. Bar 2 pm–1 am; jazz trio Tues–Sat. Ck-out noon. Meeting rms. Concierge. Airport transportation. Bathrm phones; some refrigerators. Balconies. Cr cds: A, C, D, DS, ER, MC, V, JCB.

★★MARRIOTT-SAN RAMON. *(2600 Bishop Dr, San Ramon 94583)* Off I-680, 5 mi N of I-580 interchange at Bishop Ranch. 510/867-9200; FAX 510/830-9326. 368 rms, 6 story. S, D $125–$135; suites

$300–$600; under 18 free; wkend rates; honeymoon packages. Crib free. Pet accepted. TV; cable. Pool. Restaurant 6 am–10 pm. Bar 11:30–2 am; entertainment. Ck-out noon. Coin lndry. Convention facilities. Concierge. Sundries. Airport transportation avail. Exercise equipt; weights, bicycles, whirlpool, sauna. Wet bar in suites. View of Mt Diablo. Cr cds: A, C, D, DS, ER, MC, V, JCB.

Restaurants

★★MUDD'S. (10 Boardwalk, San Ramon) I-680 exit Crow Canyon Rd W to Park Place. 510/837-9387. Hrs: 11:30 am–2:30 pm, 5:30–9 pm; Sat 5–10 pm; Sun 5–9 pm; Sun brunch 10 am–2 pm. Closed Jan 1, Memorial Day, Dec 25. Res accepted; required wkends, hols. Bar 11:30 am–10:30 pm. Semi-a la carte: lunch $6–$12, dinner $12–$20. Sun brunch $6–$10. Specializes in fresh seafood, homemade pasta. Parking. Outdoor dining. Cedarwood ceilings. 2-acre garden. Cr cds: A, D, MC, V.

★★★TOURELLE CAFE. (3565 Mt Diablo Blvd, Lafayette) 3 mi W via CA 24. 510/284-3565. Hrs: 11:30 am–11 pm; Sun brunch 10 am–2:30 pm. Closed some major hols. Res accepted. Country European menu. Bar. A la carte entrees: lunch, dinner $7–$20. Sun brunch $7–$15. Child's meals. Specializes in veal, steak, seafood, pizza. Jazz Fri, Sat. Valet parking. Outdoor dining. Country French decor. Cr cds: A, C, D, MC, V.

Weaverville (B-1)

Founded: 1849 Pop: 3,370 Elev: 2,011 ft Area code: 916 Zip: 96093

Weaverville's birth was linked with the discovery of gold. Within a few years the town's population had jumped to 3,000—half of it composed of Chinese miners. A Ranger District office of the Shasta-Trinity National Forests (see REDDING) is located here.

What to See and Do

1. **Weaverville Joss House State Historic Park.** Main & Oregon Sts, on CA 299. Temple, built in 1874 by Chinese during gold rush, contains priceless tapestries and gilded wooden scrollwork. Hourly guided tours (Thurs–Mon; closed Jan 1, Thanksgiving, Dec 25). Phone 623-5284. ¢

2. **J.J. Jackson Memorial Museum.** 508 Main St, on CA 299. Local historical exhibits. (Apr–Nov, daily; rest of yr, Tues) Phone 623-5211. **Free.**

3. **Highland Art Center.** 503 Main St. Exhibits by local and other artists include paintings, photography, sculpture, textiles and pottery. (Tues–Sat) Phone 623-5111. **Free.**

4. **Scott Museum of Trinity Center.** 30 mi NE via CA 3, in town of Trinity Center. Artifacts and exhibits depicting pioneer life include early transportation display, barbed wire collection, farming tools, household items, Indian artifacts and baskets. (Mid-May–mid-Sept, Tues–Sat; closed some hols). Phone 266-3378. **Free.**

5. **Trinity Alps Wilderness Area.** 15 mi N in Shasta-Trinity National Forests (see REDDING). Reached from Canyon Creek, Stuart Fork, Swift Creek, North Fork, New River or Coffee Creek. Unsurpassed alpine scenery, called US counterpart of Swiss Alps. Backpacking, fishing, pack trips. Resort areas on fringes. Wilderness permit necessary (free); obtain at Ranger District Office, PO Box 1190; phone 623-2121. **Free.**

(For further information contact the Chamber of Commerce, 317 Main St, PO Box 517; 623-6101 or 800/623-3753.)

(For accommodations see Redding)

West Covina *

Pop: 96,086 Elev: 381 ft Area code: 818
On I-10, 9 mi W of Pomona (H-4).

(See Pomona)

Motels

★COMFORT INN. 2804 E Garvey Ave S (91791). 818/915-6077; FAX 818/339-4587. 58 rms, 3 story. S $44–$74; D $49–$79; each addl $5; under 18 free. Crib $5. Pet accepted, some restrictions. TV; cable. Heated pool; whirlpool. Complimentary continental bkfst. Restaurant nearby. Ck-out 11 am. Meeting rms. Valet serv. Refrigerators; some in-rm whirlpools. Cr cds: A, C, D, DS, ER, MC, V, JCB.

✓★EL DORADO MOTOR INN. 140 N Azusa Ave (91791). 818/331-6371; FAX 818/858-9345. 82 rms, 2 story. S, D $34–$42; each addl $10; suites $60–$90; under 12 free. Crib free. TV; cable. Heated pool; wading pool. Complimentary coffee in lobby. Restaurant nearby. Bar 10–2 am; dancing. Ck-out noon. Private patios, balconies. Cr cds: A, C, D, DS, MC, V.

★★HAMPTON INN. 3145 East Garvey Ave N (91791). 818/967-5800; FAX 818/331-8819. 127 rms, 5 story. S $50–$60; D $55–$65; under 18 free. Crib free. Pet accepted. TV; cable. Heated pool. Complimentary continental bkfst, coffee. Restaurant adj 11 am–11 pm. Ck-out noon. Meeting rms. Health club privileges. Cr cds: A, C, D, DS, MC, V.

Motor Hotels

★★★EMBASSY SUITES. 1211 E Garvey St (91724). 818/915-3441; FAX 818/331-0773. 264 kit. suites, 3 story. S, D $109–$220; each addl $10; under 12 free; wkend rates. Crib free. TV; cable. 2 pools, 1 heated. Complimentary full bkfst 6–9:30 am; wkends 7–10:30 am. Bar 11–1:30 am; entertainment, dancing. Ck-out 1 pm. Coin lndry. Bellhops. Valet serv. Gift shop. Lighted tennis. Exercise equipt; weight machine, bicycles. Some in-rm steam baths. Balconies. Grills. Mexican tile floor, murals in lobby. Cr cds: A, C, D, DS, MC, V, JCB.

✓★★HOLIDAY INN. 3223 E Garvey Ave N (91791), at San Bernardino Frwy (I-10) Barranca or Grand Ave exit. 818/966-8311; FAX 818/339-2850. 134 rms, 5 story. S $49–$83; D $49–$87; each addl $10; under 19 free. Crib free. TV; cable. Heated pool. Restaurant 6 am–2 pm, 5–10 pm. Rm serv. Bar 4:30–10 pm. Ck-out noon. Coin lndry. Meeting rms. Health club privileges. Refrigerators. Cr cds: A, C, D, DS, ER, MC, V, JCB.

Hotel

★★★SHERATON INDUSTRY HILLS RESORT. (1 Industry Hills Pkwy, City of Industry 91744) CA 60, exit Azusa Ave, then 1½ mi N to Industry Hills Pkwy. 818/965-0861; FAX 818/964-9535. 294 rms, 11 story. S $95–$145; D $110–$160; each addl $15; suites $250–$450; studio rms $150; under 17 free; wkend rates; golf, package plans. Crib free. TV; cable. 2 pools, heated; whirlpool, sauna, steam rm. Restaurant 6 am–11 pm; dining rm 11 am–10 pm; Sat from 5 pm. Bar 11–2 am; entertainment, dancing. Ck-out noon. Convention facilities. Concierge. Lighted tennis, 17 courts, pro. Two 18-hole golf courses, pro, driving

range. Some refrigerators. *LUXURY LEVEL.* 41 rms, 8 suites. S, D $125–$145. Wet bars.
Cr cds: A, C, D, DS, ER, MC, V, JCB.

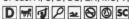

Restaurant

★**REUBEN'S.** *2200 E Garvey Ave, S of I-10 Azusa Ave or Citrus Ave exit. 818/332-6247.* Hrs: 11:30 am–9 pm; Fri to 10 pm; Sat 5–10 pm; Sun 4–9 pm; early-bird dinner 5–7 pm. Closed Dec 25. Res accepted. Bar. Semi-a la carte: lunch $4.95–$9.95, dinner $9.95–$19.95. Complete meals: dinner $10.95–$15.95. Child's meals. Specializes in prime rib, seafood, chicken, pasta. Entertainment Sun 5–9 pm. Parking. Cr cds: A, C, D, DS, MC, V, JCB.

Unrated Dining Spot

CLIFTON'S CAFETERIA. *1200 W Covina Pkwy, in West Covina Fashion Plaza. 818/960-4741.* Hrs: 11 am–8 pm; Sun to 7:30 pm. Closed July 4. Avg ck: lunch, dinner $5.25. Specializes in top round of beef, turkey, ham. Antiques. Family-owned. Cr cds: MC, V.

Westwood Village (L.A.) *

Area code: 310
Just N of CA 2 (Santa Monica Blvd), 4 mi NE of Santa Monica (H-3).

This community is an integral part of Los Angeles, but is regarded by many as a separate entity.

What to See and Do

Westwood Memorial Cemetery. Glendon Ave, 1 blk E of Westwood Blvd. Graves of movie stars Marilyn Monroe, Peter Lorre and Natalie Wood. (Daily)

(For general information and attractions see Los Angeles.)

Motel

★★**HOTEL DEL CAPRI.** *10587 Wilshire Blvd (90024). 310/474-3511; res: 800/44-HOTEL; FAX 310/470-9999.* 80 units, 2–4 story, 46 kit. suites. S $85; D $95–$105; each addl $10; kit. suites $110–$140. Crib $10. TV; cable. Heated pool. Complimentary continental bkfst. Restaurant nearby. Ck-out noon. Guest lndry. Bellhops. Valet serv. Bathrm phones, refrigerators; some in-rm whirlpools. Cr cds: A, C, D, MC, V.

Hotels

★★**HILGARD HOUSE, A CLARION CARRIAGE INN.** *927 Hilgard Ave (90024). 310/208-3945.* 47 rms, 4 story. S $99–$109; D $109–$119; each addl $10; under 6 free. Crib free. TV. Complimentary continental bkfst. Ck-out noon. Free covered parking. Refrigerators. Cr cds: A, C, D, MC, V.

★★**HOLIDAY INN-WESTWOOD PLAZA.** *10740 Wilshire Blvd (90024). 310/475-8711.* 294 rms, 19 story. S $120–$140; D $130–$145; each addl $10; suites $200–$250; under 18 free. Crib free. Pet accepted.

TV; cable. Heated pool; poolside serv. Restaurant 6:30 am–10 pm. Bar 4 pm–midnight. Ck-out noon. Meeting rms. Concierge. Gift shop. Valet parking. Free UCLA transportation. Exercise equipt; weights, bicycles, whirlpool, sauna. Game rm. Refrigerators. Cr cds: A, C, D, DS, MC, V, JCB.

★★★★**WESTWOOD MARQUIS HOTEL & GARDEN.** (4-Star 1993; New general manager, therefore not rated) *930 Hilgard Ave (90024), west of downtown L.A. 310/208-8765; res: 800/421-2317; FAX 310/824-0355.* 258 suites (1–3 bedrm), 16 story. S, D $220–$650; wkend rates. Crib free. TV; cable, in-rm movies. 2 heated pools. 4 restaurants; dining rm 6:30 am–11 pm (also see DYNASTY ROOM). Afternoon tea. Rm serv 24 hrs. Bar 10–2 am; pianist, harpist. Ck-out noon. Meeting rms. Concierge. Maid serv 24 hrs. Barber, beauty shop. Gift shop. Garage; valet parking. Complimentary limo to Beverly Hills. Exercise rm; instructor, weights, bicycles, sauna, steam rm. Massage. Complete spa facilities. Refrigerators, minibars. Butler service in penthouse suites. Individually decorated suites. European elegance. Cr cds: A, C, D, MC, V, JCB.

Restaurants

★★★**DYNASTY ROOM.** *(See Westwood Marquis Hotel) 310/208-8765.* Hrs: 6–10:30 pm. Res accepted. Continental menu. Bar 10–1:30 am. A la carte entrees: dinner $17.50–$25. Specialties: potato pancake with smoked salmon and cavier, Peking-style roast duck, seafood mixed grill. Harpist. Valet parking. Elegant dining; collection of Ming dynasty ceramics. Cr cds: A, C, D, MC, V, JCB.

★**MONTY'S.** *1100 Glendon Ave. 310/208-8787.* Hrs: 11 am–3 pm, 5 pm–1 am; Sat & Sun 5 pm–midnight. Closed Thanksgiving, Dec 25. Res accepted. Bar to 2 am, Sat & Sun from 5 pm. Semi-a la carte: lunch $6–$16, dinner $13–$50. Specializes in prime rib, steak, seafood. Entertainment. Valet parking. Located on top floor of building; panoramic view. Cr cds: A, C, D, MC, V.

Whittier (J-4)

Founded: 1887 **Pop:** 77,671 **Elev:** 365 ft **Area code:** 310

This Quaker-founded community was named for John Greenleaf Whittier, the Quaker poet. At the foot of the rolling Puente Hills, this residential city was once a citrus empire. It is the home of Whittier College.

What to See and Do

1. **Richard Nixon Library & Birthplace.** 18001 Yorba Linda Blvd, in Yorba Linda. Archives and original home of the 37th president of the United States. Nine-acre grounds include the library's main hall with display of gifts from world leaders, life-size statues; video forum allows guests to ask questions via "touchscreen"; 75-seat amphitheater; reflecting pool; First Lady's garden. Only privately-funded presidential library in the country. Nixon grew up in Yorba Linda before moving to Whittier and graduating from Whittier College. (Daily; closed Jan 1, Thanksgiving, Dec 25) Sr citizen rate. Phone 714/993-3393. ¢¢

2. **Rose Hills Memorial Park.** 3900 S Workman Mill Rd. Gardens and cemetary covering 2,500 acres. Pageant of Roses Garden has more than 7,000 rose bushes of more than 600 varieties in bloom most of the year; Japanese gardens with a lake, arched bridge and meditation house. (Daily) Phone 692-1212 or 699-0921. **Free.**

(For further information contact the Chamber of Commerce, PO Box 4188, 90602; 698-9554.)

(See Anaheim, Buena Park, West Covina)

Hotel

★ ★ ★ **HILTON.** *7320 Greenleaf Ave (90602). 310/945-8511; FAX 310/945-6018.* 202 units, 8 story. S $95–$125; D $110–$140; each addl $10; suites $125–$475; family, wkly, wkend rates. Crib free. TV; cable. Heated pool; poolside serv. Coffee in rms. Restaurant 5:30 am–10:30 pm. Bar 11–2 am; entertainment, dancing Tues–Sat. Ck-out noon. Meeting rms. Gift shop. Free Disneyland, Knotts Berry Farm transportation. Exercise equipt; weight machine, bicycle, whirlpool. Some refrigerators. Some private patios. Courtyard. Cr cds: A, C, D, DS, ER, MC, V.

D 🏊 🏃 🚭 🌐 SC

Restaurant

★ **SEAFARE INN.** *16363 E Whittier Blvd. 310/947-6645.* Hrs: 11:30 am–9 pm; Fri 11 am–10 pm. Closed Mon; major hols. Wine, beer. Semi-a la carte: lunch $2.95–$5.95, dinner $5.25–$24. Child's meals. Seafood dishes only. Parking. Nautical decor. Family-owned. Totally nonsmoking. No cr cds accepted.

Willits (C-1)

Pop: 5,027 **Elev:** 1,364 ft **Area code:** 707 **Zip:** 95490

Nestled in the Little Lake Valley, Willits is the hub of three railroads: the California Western "Skunk Train" (see FORT BRAGG), the North Coast Railroad and the Northwestern Pacific.

What to See and Do

Mendocino County Museum. 400 E Commercial St. History of area depicted by artifacts, including unique collection of Pomo baskets; stagecoaches, redwood logging tools; contemporary art shows. Special programs. (Wed–Sat; closed major hols exc July 4) Phone 459-2736. **Free.**

(For further information contact the Chamber of Commerce, 239 S Main St; 459-7910.)

(See Fort Bragg, Mendocino, Ukiah)

Motels

★ **HOLIDAY LODGE.** *1540 S Main St. 707/459-5361; res: 800/835-3972.* 16 rms. Mid-May–Sept: S $43; D $48–$57; each addl $5; lower rates rest of yr. Crib free. TV; cable. Pool. Complimentary coffee in rms. Restaurant opp 8 am–11 pm. Ck-out 11 am. Cr cds: A, D, MC, V.

🏊 🚭 🌐 SC

✔ ★ **LARK.** *1411 S Main St. 707/459-2421.* 22 rms. May–Oct: S $36–$38; D $38–$42; each addl $4–$6; suites $46–$52; holiday plans; lower rates rest of yr. Crib free. TV; cable. Heated pool. Coffee in rms. Restaurant adj 6:30 am–9:30 pm. Ck-out 11 am. Free RR station, bus depot transportation. Near Skunk Train. Cr cds: A, C, D, DS, MC, V, JCB.

🏊 🚭 SC

Willows (C-2)

Pop: 5,988 **Elev:** 135 ft **Area code:** 916 **Zip:** 95988

What to See and Do

Mendocino National Forest. Approx 25 mi W via CA 162. More than 1 million acres. Swimming; fishing for steelhead and trout; boating at 2,000-acre Pillsbury Lake. Hiking, bridle and off-road vehicle trails. Camping (fee at more developed sites; some water; high elevation sites closed in winter). Hang gliding. Contact the Forest Supervisor, 420 E Laurel St; phone 934-3316. For recorded information on road conditions and recreation phone 934-2350.

Motels

★ ★ ★ **BEST WESTERN GOLDEN PHEASANT INN.** *249 N Humboldt Ave. 916/934-4603; FAX 916/934-7542.* 104 rms. S $45–$55; D $51–$61; each addl $5; suites $78. Crib $4. TV; cable. 2 heated pools; sauna. Complimentary continental bkfst. Restaurant 6 am–11 pm. Rm serv. Bar from 10 am. Ck-out noon. Coin lndry. Meeting rms. Gift shop. Free local airport, bus depot transportation. Spacious lawn; waterfall. Cr cds: A, C, D, DS, ER, MC, V, JCB.

D 🏊 🚭 🌐 SC

★ **COMFORT INN.** *(PO Box 729, 400 C St, Williams 95987) Approx 30 mi S on I-5. 916/473-2381; FAX 916/473-2418.* 61 rms, 2 story, 9 suites. S $43; D $48; each addl $5; suites $43–$58; under 18 free. Crib $5. TV; cable. Pool; whirlpool. Complimentary continental bkfst, coffee. Restaurant nearby. Ck-out noon. Cr cds: A, C, D, DS, ER, MC, V.

D 🏊 🚭 🌐 SC

✔ ★ **CROSS ROADS WEST.** *452 N Humboldt Ave. 916/934-7026.* 41 rms, 2 story. Many rm phones. S $26; D $33–$36; each addl $6; under 5 free. Pet accepted. TV; cable. Pool. Complimentary morning coffee. Restaurant adj 11 am–9 pm. Ck-out 11 am. Cr cds: A, DS, MC, V.

🐾 🏊 🚭 🌐 SC

Woodland Hills (L.A.) (H-3)

Elev: 460 ft **Area code:** 818

This community, located in the San Fernando Valley, is a neighborhood of Los Angeles, but is regarded by many as a separate entity.

(For general information and attractions see Los Angeles.)

Motels

★ ★ **CLARION SUITES-WARNER PALMS.** *(20200 Sherman Way, Canoga Park 91306) 2 mi N of US 101, off Winnetka Ave. 818/883-8250; FAX 818/883-8268.* 100 rms, 3 story, 88 kit. suites. S, D $59; each addl $10; kit. suites $79–$99; under 18 free; wkly, monthly rates. Crib free. TV; cable. Pool. Complimentary full bkfst. Complimentary coffee in rms. Restaurant nearby. Ck-out noon. Coin lndry. Meeting rms. Valet serv. Deli. Airport transportation. Lighted tennis. Health club privileges. Refrigerators. Courtyard. Cr cds: A, C, D, DS, ER, MC, V, JCB.

🔑 🏊 🚭 🌐 SC

★ ★ ★ **COUNTRY INN AT CALABASAS.** *(23627 Calabasas Rd, Calabasas 91302) 2 mi W on US 101 Pkwy Calabasas exit. 818/222-5300; res: 800/447-3529; FAX 818/591-0870.* 122 rms, 3 story. S $95–$105; D $105–$110; each addl $10; kit. suites $200–$220; under 12 free. Crib free. TV; in-rm movies. Heated pool; whirlpool. Complimentary full bkfst, coffee. Restaurant nearby. Ck-out noon. Coin lndry. Meeting rms. Valet serv. Refrigerators, wet bars. Cr cds: A, C, D, DS, MC, V, JCB.

D 🏊 🚭 🌐 SC

✔ ★ **VAGABOND INN.** *20157 Ventura Blvd (91364), US 101 Winnetka Ave exit, S to Ventura Blvd. 818/347-8080; FAX 818/716-5333.* 95 rms, 3 story. Mid-May–mid-Sept: S $54–$59; D $59–$64; each addl $5; under 19 free; lower rates rest of yr. Crib free. Pet accepted, some restrictions; $5. TV; cable. Heated pool; whirlpool. Complimentary continental bkfst. Restaurant adj open 24 hrs. Ck-out noon. Meeting rm. Valet serv. Cr cds: A, C, D, DS, ER, MC, V.

✔ ★WARNER GARDENS. 21706 Ventura Blvd (91364), US 101 Canoga Ave exit, S to Ventura Blvd. 818/992-4426; res: 800/824-9292; FAX 818/704-1062. 40 rms, 2 story. S $46; D $49-$54; suites $54-$60; under 14 free; wkly, monthly rates. Crib free. TV; cable. Heated pool; whirlpool. Complimentary continental bkfst, coffee. Restaurant adj 8 am-8 pm. Ck-out 11 am. Valet serv. Cr cds: A, C, D, MC, V.

Hotels

★★★HILTON & TOWERS-WARNER CENTER. 6360 Canoga Ave (91367), US 101 Canoga Ave exit, N 1 mi. 818/595-1000; FAX 818/595-1090. 318 rms, 14 story. S $119-$129; D $129-$139; each addl $10; suites $300-$800; family rates. Crib free. Valet parking $7. TV; cable. Heated pool. Restaurant 6 am-11 pm. Bar 11-1 am; entertainment exc Sun. Ck-out noon. Convention facilities. Concierge. Airport transportation. Lighted tennis. Exercise rm; instructor, weights, bicycles, sauna, steam rm. Minibars. Some balconies. *LUXURY LEVEL:* **TOWERS.** 44 rms, 6 suites, 2 floors. S $139-$149; D $149-$159. Private lounge, honor bar. Whirlpool in suites. Complimentary continental bkfst, refreshments, newspaper. Cr cds: A, C, D, DS, ER, MC, V, JCB.

★★MARRIOTT-WARNER CENTER. 21850 Oxnard St (91367), US 101 Topanga Canyon Blvd exit N to Oxnard. 818/887-4800; FAX 818/340-5893. 461 rms, 17 story. S, D $129; suites $150-$1,500; under 18 free; wkend rates. Crib free. Pet accepted. Garage; valet parking $7. TV; cable. Indoor/outdoor pool; poolside serv. Restaurant 6:30 am-11 pm. Bar; pianist, dancing. Ck-out noon. Convention facilities. Gift shop. Airport transportation. Tennis privileges. Exercise equipt; weights, bicycles, whirlpool, sauna. Balconies. *LUXURY LEVEL:* **CONCIERGE LEVEL.** 82 rms, 3 floors. S, D $139. Private lounge. In-rm movies avail. Complimentary continental bkfst, refreshments, newspaper. Cr cds: A, C, D, DS, MC, V, JCB.

Restaurants

✔ ★CAPRI. 21926 Ventura Blvd, US 101 Topanga Canyon Blvd exit S to Ventura Blvd. 818/883-3401. Hrs: 11 am-10 pm; Sat, Sun 5:30-10:30 pm. Closed Thanksgiving, Dec 25. Res accepted. Italian menu. A la carte entrees: lunch $5.95-$11.50. Semi-a la carte: dinner $8.95-$18. Parking. Cr cds: A, DS, MC, V.

★★LE SANGLIER. (5522 Crebs Ave, Tarzana) US 101, Reseda exit then 4 blks W on Ventura Blvd. 818/345-0470. Hrs: 5:30-10:30 pm; Sun to 10 pm. Closed Mon; major hols. Res accepted. French menu. Bar. Semi-a la carte: dinner $17-$27. Specializes in French country cuisine. Parking. French hunting lodge interior. Cr cds: A, C, D, MC, V.

Yosemite National Park (E-3)

(67 mi NE of Merced on CA 140; 62 mi N of Fresno on CA 41; 13 mi SW of Lee Vining on CA 120) **Area code:** 209 **Zip:** 95389

John Muir, the naturalist instrumental in the founding of this national park, wrote that here are "the most songful streams in the world. . . the noblest forests, the loftiest granite domes, the deepest ice sculptured canyons." Nearly 4 million people visit Yosemite year round, and most

agree with Muir. An area of 1,170 square miles, it is a park of lofty waterfalls, sheer cliffs, high wilderness country, alpine meadows, lakes, snowfields, trails, streams and river beaches. There is a variety of magnificent waterfalls during spring and early summer. Yosemite's granite domes are unsurpassed in number and diversity. Entrance fee is $5/car, $3/person. Phone 372-0200 for information on weather, camping and road conditions. Routes to Yosemite National Park involve some travel over steep grades, which may extend driving times.

For general park information contact PO Box 577, Yosemite National Park; 372-0200 or 372-0265. For lodging information contact Yosemite Park and Curry Co, Yosemite National Park; 252-4848. For recorded camping information phone 372-0200. Camping reservations taken by Mistix for Yosemite Valley (800/365-CAMP) and other campgrounds (see #13).

What to See and Do

1. **Yosemite Valley.** Surrounded by sheer walls, waterfalls, towering domes and peaks. One of the most spectacular views is from Tunnel View, looking up the Valley to Clouds Rest. El Capitan (7,569 ft) on the left, Bridalveil Falls on the right. The east end of the Valley, beyond Camp Curry and the stables, is closed to automobiles, but is accessible by foot, bicycle and, in summer, shuttle bus (free); special placards permit the disabled to drive in restricted area when the route is drivable. The placards are available at visitor centers and entrance stations.

2. **Waterfalls.** Reaching their greatest proportions in mid-May, they may, in dry years, dwindle to trickles or disappear completely by late summer. The Upper Yosemite Falls drop 1,430 feet; the lower falls drop 320 feet. With the middle Cascades they have a combined height of 2,425 feet and are the fifth highest waterfalls in the world. Others are Ribbon Falls, 1,612 feet; Vernal Falls, 317 feet; Bridalveil Falls, 620 feet; Nevada Falls, 594 feet; and Illilouette Falls, 370 feet.

3. **The Giant Sequoias.** Located principally in three groves. Mariposa Grove is near the south entrance to the park; toured on foot or by 50-passenger trams (May-early Oct; fee). Merced and Tuolumne groves are near Crane Flat, northwest of Yosemite Valley. The Grizzly Giant in Mariposa Grove is estimated to be 2,700 years old and is 209 feet high and 34.7 feet in diameter at its base.

4. **Pioneer Yosemite History Center.** A few miles from Mariposa Grove in Wawona. Has a covered bridge, historic buildings, wagons and other exhibits. Living history program in summer; guided tours in spring and fall.

5. **Glacier Point.** Offers one of the best panoramic views in Yosemite. From here the crest of the Sierra Nevada can be viewed, as well as Yosemite Valley 3,214 feet below. Across the valley are Yosemite Falls, Royal Arches, North Dome, Basket Dome, Mt Watkins and Washington Column; up the Merced Canyon are Vernal and Nevada Falls; Half Dome, Grizzly Peak, Liberty Cap and the towering peaks along the Sierran crest and the Clark Range mark the skyline. (Road closed in winter)

6. **The High Country.** The Tioga Rd (closed in winter, approx mid-Nov-Memorial Day) crosses the park and provides the threshold to a vast wilderness accessible via horseback, or on foot to mountain peaks, passes and lakes. Tuolumne Meadows is the major trailhead for this activity; one of the most beautiful and largest of the subalpine meadows in the High Sierra, 55 miles from Yosemite Valley by way of Big Oak Flat and Tioga Rds. Group horse and hiking trips start from Tuolumne Meadows (exc winter), follow the High Sierra Loop, and fan out to mountain lakes and peaks. Each night's stop is at a High Sierra Camp; the pace allows plenty of time to explore at each camp.

7. **Visitor Center.** At Park Headquarters in Yosemite Valley. Orientation slide program on Yosemite (daily). Exhibits on geology and ecology; naturalist-conducted walks and evening programs offered throughout the year on varying seasonal schedules. Indian cultural demonstrators (summer, daily). Phone 372-0299.

The Indian Cultural Museum, located in the building west of the Valley visitor center, portrays the cultural history of the Yosemite Indians. Consult *Yosemite Guide* for hours. Adj is

Yosemite Fine Arts Museum. Gallery featuring contemporary art exhibits and the Yosemite Centennial. Consult *Yosemite Guide* for hours.

8. **Happy Isles Nature Center.** E end of Yosemite Valley. Exhibits on ecology and natural history. (Summer, daily)

9. **Walks and hikes.** Conducted all yr in the Valley and Mariposa Grove (weather conditions permitting) and, during summer, at Glacier Point, Tuolumne Meadows, Wawona, White Wolf and Crane Flat. All-day guided hikes leave several times per week from Tuolumne Meadows.

10. **Campfire programs.** At several campgrounds; in summer, naturalists present nightly programs on park-related topics and provide tips on how to enjoy the park. Evening programs all year in the Valley only.

11. **Yosemite Mountain-Sugar Pine Railroad.** 4 mi S of S park entrance on CA 41. Four-mile historic narrow-gauge steam train excursion through scenic Sierra National Forest. Picnic area. Museum; gift shops. Logger steam train (mid-May–Sept, daily; early May & Oct, wkends). Jenny Railcars (Apr–Oct, daily). Evening steam train, outdoor barbecue, live entertainment (June–Sept, Sat evenings; reservations advised). For reservations and information phone 683-7273. ¢¢¢–¢¢¢¢¢

12. **Winter sports** are centered around the Badger Pass Ski Area, 23 mi from Yosemite Valley on Glacier Point Rd. Four chairlifts, rope tow; patrol, rentals; snack stand; sun deck; nursery (min age 3 yrs); instruction (over 4 yrs). (Thanksgiving–mid-Apr, daily, weather permitting) Cross-country skiing. Ice-skating (fee) in Yosemite Valley; snowcat tours; scheduled competitions. Naturalists conduct snowshoe and ski tours (fee) in the Badger Pass area. Phone 372-1330 or -1000 for snow conditions. Lift ticket ¢¢¢¢¢

13. **Camping.** Limited to 30 days in a calendar year; June–Sept 15, camping in Yosemite Valley is limited to seven days, in the rest of the park to 14 days. Campsites in five valley campgrounds, Hodgdon Meadow, Crane Flat and half of Tuolumne Meadows campgrounds may be reserved through Mistix. Other park campgrounds are on a first-come, first-served basis, as are all campgrounds in Oct–Apr. Winter camping only in the valley and Wawona.

14. **Hiking and backpacking** on 773 miles of maintained trails. Wilderness permits are required for all overnight backcountry trips.

15. **Boating.** No motors permitted.

16. **Swimming.** Prohibited at Hetch Hetchy Reservoir and in some areas of the Tuolumne River watershed. Swimming pools are maintained at Camp Curry, Yosemite Lodge and Wawona.

17. **Fishing.** California fishing regulations pertain to all waters. State license, inland waters stamp and trout stamp are required.

(See Lee Vining)

Motels

(**Note:** All accommodations *within* Yosemite National Park are operated by the Yosemite Park & Curry Co, under supervision of the National Park Service. Reservations are advised and should be made through the central reservations office, 209/252-4848. The company maintains a wide variety of accommodations here. Riding horses, pack trips. Grocery, drugstore, barber, coin lndry, other facilities are at a central area in Yosemite Valley. Accommodations outside the park are privately operated.)

★ ★**BEST WESTERN YOSEMITE GATEWAY INN.** *(40530 CA 41, Oakhurst 93644) 1 mi N of jct CA 49, CA 41. 209/683-2378; FAX 209/683-3813.* 118 rms, 2 story, 16 suites, 11 kits. Early May–late Sept: S, D $72–$84; each addl $6; suites $110; kit. units $5–$10 addl; wkly rates off-season; higher rates late Dec; lower rates rest of yr. Crib $2. TV; cable. Indoor pool; whirlpool, sauna. Restaurant adj 7 am–9:30 pm. Bar.

Ck-out 11 am. Coin lndry. Meeting rm. Some refrigerators. Balconies. Picnic table, grill. Cr cds: A, C, D, DS, ER, MC, V, JCB.

◻ 🅳 ⌇ 🛇 ⊘

✔ ★**MARIPOSA LODGE.** *(Box 733, 5052 CA 140, Mariposa 95338) At jct CA 140, CA 49. 209/966-3607; res: 800/341-8000; FAX 209/742-7038.* 44 rms, 31 rms with shower only. Apr–Oct: S $50–$55; D $65–$70; each addl $6; lower rates rest of yr. Crib $6. Pet accepted, some restrictions; $6. TV; cable. Heated pool; whirlpool. Complimentary coffee. Restaurant adj 7 am–9 pm. Ck-out 11 am. Free local airport transportation. Gazebo. Cr cds: A, C, D, DS, MC, V.

🅳 🐾 ⌇ ⊘

✔ ★ ★**MINERS INN RESORT.** *(Box 246, Mariposa 95338) At jct CA 49, 140. 209/742-7777; res: 800/237-7277 (CA); FAX 209/966-2343.* 64 rms, 2 story. Apr–Sept: S $50–$55; D $65–$70; each addl $6; lower rates rest of yr. Crib free. TV; cable. Pool. Complimentary coffee in rms. Restaurant adj 6:30 am–10 pm. Ck-out 11 am. Cr cds: A, C, D, DS, MC, V.

🅳 ⌇ 🛇 ⊘ SC

★ ★**NARROW GAUGE INN.** *(CA 41, Fish Camp 93623) 2 mi S of Fish Camp on CA 41, outside park; 4 mi from S entrance. 209/683-7720.* 26 rms, 3 story. No A/C. No rm phones. Apr–Oct: S, D $85–$120; each addl $5. Closed rest of yr. Crib $6. TV. Heated pool. Restaurant 7:30 am–9 pm. Bar from 5:30 pm. Ck-out 11 am. Sundries. Gift shop. Hot tub. Balconies. Narrow-gauge steam railroad rides. View of mountains. Cr cds: A, C, D, MC, V.

⌇ ⊘

★ ★**SHILO INN.** *(40644 CA 41, Oakhurst 93644) 15 mi S on CA 41. 209/683-3555; FAX 209/683-3386.* 80 rms, 4 story. Apr–Sept: S, D $85–$115; each addl $10; under 12 free; lower rates rest of yr. Crib free. TV; cable, in-rm movies avail. Heated pool. Complimentary continental bkfst. Restaurant adj 7 am–9 pm. Ck-out noon. Coin lndry. Exercise equipt; weights, bicycles, sauna, steam rm. Bathrm phones, refrigerators. Some patios, balconies. Cr cds: A, C, D, DS, ER, MC, V, JCB.

🅳 ⌇ 🏃 🛇 ⊘ SC

★**YOSEMITE GOLD RUSH INN.** *(4994 Bullion St, Mariposa 95338) 1 blk S of jct CA 49, 140. 209/966-4344; res: 800/321-5261; FAX 209/966-4655.* 61 rms, 3 story. No elvtr. Mar–Oct: S, D $60–$72; each addl $6; suites $175–$350; under 6 free; lower rates rest of yr. Crib free. TV; cable. Heated pool; whirlpool. Complimentary continental bkfst, coffee. Restaurant opp 11 am–9 pm. Ck-out 11 am. Meeting rm. Some refrigerators. Cr cds: A, MC, V.

⌇ 🛇 ⊘ SC

Lodges

★ ★ ★**MARRIOTT'S TENAYA LODGE AT YOSEMITE.** *(Box 159, Fish Camp 93623; 1122 CA 41) 2 mi S of Yosemite Natl Park south gate on CA 41, near Fish Camp. 209/683-6555; res: 800/635-5807; FAX 209/683-8684.* 242 rms, 3 story, 20 suites. Mid-May–mid-Sept: S, D $184–$210; suites $250–$350; under 18 free; lower rates rest of yr. Crib free. TV; cable. 2 pools, 1 indoor. Supervised child's activities (Memorial Day–Labor Day). Complimentary bkfst. Dining rm 7–11 am, 6–10 pm; Mon–Wed from 6 pm. Deli 7 am–11 pm. Rm serv. Ck-out noon, ck-in 3 pm. Coin lndry. Convention facilities. Bellhops. Valet serv. Concierge. Sundries. Gift shops. X-country ski on site. Exercise equipt; bicycles, treadmill, whirlpool, saunas, steam rm, massage. Game rm. Guided hikes and mountain tours. Bicycle rentals. Bathrm phones. Wet bar in suites. On river; water sports. Southwest, Indian decor; rustic with an elegant touch. Cr cds: A, D, DS, MC, V, JCB.

🅳 🏊 ⌇ 🏃 🏃 🛇 ⊘ SC

✔ ★ ★**WAWONA.** *(Box 2005) 5 mi NE of S entrance on CA 41, 27 mi from Park HQ. 209/252-4848.* 104 rms, 50 with bath, 2 story. No A/C. No rm phones. Mid-Apr–late Dec: S, D $59.75–$79.75; each addl $10; schedule varies rest of yr. Crib avail. TV in lounge. Heated pool. Dining rm 7:30–10 am, noon–1:30 pm, 6–8:30 pm (res required dinner).

No rm serv. Bar 5:30–11 pm. Ck-out 11 am. Meeting rm. Tennis. 9–18-hole golf, greens fee $12–$17.50, putting green. Saddle trips, stage-coach rides. Historic summer hotel. Totally nonsmoking. Cr cds: C, D, DS, MC, V, JCB.

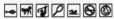

Hotels

★ ★ ★**AHWAHNEE.** *14 mi E of entrance on CA 140, 1 mi E of Yosemite Village.* 209/252-4848. 99 rms, 6 story, 24 cottages. S, parlor $196.50; D $201.50; each addl $20; 3–12 yrs free. TV. Heated pool. Afternoon tea 5–5:30 pm. Dining rm (res required for dinner; jacket). Rm serv 7 am–10 pm. Bar noon–11:30 pm; entertainment. Ck-out noon. Meeting rms. Concierge. Gift shops. Free valet parking. Tennis. Some balconies, fireplaces. Stone building with natural wood interior, Native American decor. Tire chains may be required by Park Service Nov–Mar to reach lodge. Cr cds: C, D, DS, MC, V, JCB.

★ ★**YOSEMITE LODGE.** *On CA 41/140, 1 mi W of Park HQ.* 209/252-4848. 290 hotel rms, most with bath, 2 story; 189 cabins, 100 with bath. No A/C. Apr–Oct, hotel: S, D $76–$90 (with bath), $54 (no bath); cabins: S, D $67 (with bath); $47 (no bath); each addl $6–$12; lower rates rest of yr. Crib $5. Pool; lifeguard. Restaurant 6:30 am–8 pm; dining rm 7–11 am, 5–9 pm. Bar noon–11:30 pm. Ck-out 11 am. Meeting rms. Sundries. Gift shop. Valley tours. Cr cds: C, D, MC, V, JCB.

Inn

★ ★ ★ ★**CHÂTEAU DU SUREAU.** *(PO Box 577, 48688 Victoria Lane, Oakhurst 93644)* ¼ mi S of jct CA 49 & 41. 209/683-6860; FAX 209/683-0800. 9 rms, 2 story. EP: D $250–$350 and 10% service charge. No TV. Pool. Complimentary coffee in rms and in library. Complimentary full bkfst. Restaurant adj 11:30 am–1 pm, 5:30–8:30 pm. Ck-out noon, ck-in 2 pm. Concierge. Bellman. Lawn games. Balconies. Picnic tables. Luxurious hillside estate situated on 7 acres; landscaped grounds with several fountains, walking paths. French chateau-style house has a stone turret; antique French furnishings, many canopied beds; spiral staircase of limestone; fireplaces. Circular music tower has French grand piano and soaring ceiling with a trompe l'oeil fresco. Totally nonsmoking. Cr cds: DS, MC, V.

Cottage Colonies

★**CURRY VILLAGE.** *On CA 41/140, 1 mi E of Park HQ in Yosemite Valley.* 209/252-4848 res: 209/372-1233; FAX 209/372-4816. 18 motel rms, 182 cabins, 102 with bath, 427 tents. No A/C. No rm phones. Motel: S, D $76; cabins: $48 (no bath); $63 (with bath); tents: S, D $33; each addl $4–$7.50. Crib $5. Heated pool; lifeguard. Dining rm 7–10 am, 5:30–8 pm; snack bar. Bar noon–9 pm in summer. Ck-out 11 am, ck-in after 5 pm. Meeting rms. Bellhops. Ice skating. Bicycle rentals. Cr cds: C, D, DS, MC, V, JCB.

★ ★**PINES RESORTS.** *(Box 329, Bass Lake 93604)* 14 mi S of entrance, approx 5 mi off CA 41 on North Shore Rd, next to post office. 209/642-3121; res: 800/350-7463; FAX 209/642-3902. 84 kit. units, 2 story. No A/C. Apr–Oct: S, D $125–$165; each addl $10; under 16 free; lower rates rest of yr. TV; cable, in-rm movies avail. Pool. Restaurant nearby. Bar 11–2 am; entertainment, dancing Fri–Sat. Ck-out noon, ck-in 3 pm. Grocery 1 blk. Meeting rms. Tennis. Exercise equipt; weights, bicycle, whirlpool, sauna. Boating. All-wood chalets, most with fireplaces. Private patios. Picnic tables, grills. ½ blk to lake. Cr cds: C, D, DS, MC, V.

Restaurants

★ ★**CHARLES STREET DINNER HOUSE.** *(Box 1211, Mariposa 95338)* On CA 140 at 7th St. 209/966-2366. Hrs: 5–9 pm. Closed Mon & Tues; Thanksgiving, Dec 24 & 25; also Jan. Res accepted. Beer. Wine cellar. Semi-a la carte: dinner $11.50–$29.50. Specializes in steak, fresh seafood. Own desserts. 19th-century house. Cr cds: A, C, DS, MC, V.

SC

★ ★ ★**ERNA'S ELDERBERRY HOUSE.** *(Box 2413, Oakhurst 93644)* Victoria Lane & CA 41. 209/683-6800. Hrs: 11:30 am–1 pm, 5:30–8:30 pm; Sat & Sun from 5:30 pm; Sun brunch 11 am–1 pm. Closed Tues; also Mon in summer. Res accepted. Continental menu. Bar. Wine cellar. Complete meals: lunch $14, dinner $45 and $53. Sun brunch $24. Menu changes daily. Menu recited. Own baking. Classical harpist special hols. Parking. Terrace dining. Elegant dining in European country estate atmosphere; each dining area individually decorated; many oil paintings; tapestry, furnishings imported from France. Cr cds: MC, V.

Yountville (D-1)

Settled: 1831 **Pop:** 3,259 **Elev:** 97 ft **Area code:** 707 **Zip:** 94599

In the heart of the Napa Valley, Yountville has retained the turn-of-the-century charm of a quiet farming community. The town dates from 1831 with the settlement of George Yount, a North Carolina trapper. Although now a major tourist destination, surrounded by world-famous wineries, the town has successfully protected its rural atmosphere and historic character, reflected in its quaint hotels, restaurants and shops.

What to See and Do

1. **Vintage 1870.** 6525 Washington St. Restored brick winery complex houses 5 restaurants, a bakery and more than 40 specialty shops. Wine tasting cellar. Entertainment and holiday demonstrations in Dec. Picnic areas. (Daily; closed Jan 1, Easter, Thanksgiving, Dec 25) Phone 944-2451. **Free.**

2. **Wineries.**

   Domaine Chandon. W of CA 29, California Dr. Subsidiary of French producers of champagne and cognac. Visitors observe all phases of the *méthode champenoise*, the classic French method of producing champagnes. Guided tours, salon, retail sales, restaurant. Tasting (fee). (May–Oct, daily; rest of yr, Wed–Sun) Phone 944-2280 (tour) or -2892 (restaurant). **Free.**

   Robert Mondavi. 7801 St Helena Hwy, N in Oakville. Graceful, mission-style building. Guided tours, wine tasting. Reservations recommended. (Daily; closed some hols) Phone 963-9611. **Free.**

(For further information contact the Chamber of Commerce, PO Box 2064; 944-0904.)

(See Napa, St Helena)

Motor Hotels

★ ★ ★**BEST WESTERN NAPA VALLEY LODGE.** *(Box L)* ½ blk E of CA 29 Madison exit. 707/944-2468; FAX 707/944-9362. 55 rms, 2 story. S $115–$155; D $125–$165; each addl $10; suites $130–$195. Crib free. TV; cable. Heated pool. Complimentary continental bkfst. Complimentary coffee in rms. Restaurant nearby. Ck-out noon. Meeting rms. Bellhops. Valet serv. Exercise equipt; weights, bicycles, whirlpool, sauna. Refrigerators, minibars, fireplaces. Private patios, balconies. Park opp. Cr cds: A, C, D, DS, MC, V.

★★★**VINTAGE INN.** *(Box 2536) 6541 Washington St. 707/944-1112; res: 800/351-1133; FAX 707/944-1617.* 80 rms in 9 buildings, 1–2 story. S $129–$169; D $139–$179; each addl $25; suites $179–$199; cottages $169–$189. Crib avail. Pet accepted; $25. TV; cable. Heated pool; whirlpool. Complimentary continental bkfst with champagne. Afternoon tea 3–5 pm. Coffee in rms. Restaurant adj 11:30 am–10 pm. Bar 10 am–10 pm. Ck-out noon. Meeting rms. Concierge. Bellhops. Valet serv exc Sun. Napa airport transportation. Tennis. Refrigerators. In-rm whirlpools, fireplaces. Verandas. Vineyard, mountain views. Stream on property. Cr cds: A, C, D, MC, V.

Inns

★**NAPA VALLEY RAILWAY INN.** *6503 Washington St. 707/944-2000.* 9 rms. Apr-Oct: S, D $95–$105; each addl $15; under 5 free; lower rates rest of yr. Complimentary coffee, tea. Restaurant opp. Ck-out 11 am, ck-in 3 pm. Unique lodging in elegantly restored turn-of-the-century railroad cars; bay windows, skylights; private entrance. Vineyards nearby. Cr cds: MC, V.

★ ★**OLEANDER HOUSE.** *(PO Box 2937) 7433 St Helena Hwy (CA 29), 3 mi N of town on the W side of the street. 707/944-8315; res: 800/788-3057.* 4 rms, 2 story. No rm phones. S, D $115–$160; each addl $25; higher rates wkends & hols (2-night min). TV in sitting rm. Complimentary full bkfst, coffee. Restaurant adj 11 am–10 pm. Ck-out 11 am, ck-in 1 pm. Whirlpool. Balconies. Individually decorated rms; woodburning fireplaces. Rose garden. Totally nonsmoking. Cr cds: MC, V.

Restaurants

★**CAFE KINYONI.** *6525 Washington St, in Vintage 1870 shopping complex. 707/944-2788.* Hrs: 11:30 am–3 pm; Sun brunch 9:30 am–3 pm. Closed Jan 1, Dec 25. Res accepted. Bar. Semi-a la carte: lunch $2–$7.95. Sun brunch $6.95–$11.95. Specialties: peanut chicken salad, grilled chicken with mango chutney and jack cheese in french roll. Outdoor dining. Original art. Totally nonsmoking. Cr cds: A, MC, V.

★ ★**COMPADRES MEXICAN BAR & GRILL.** *6539 Washington St. 707/944-2406.* Hrs: 11 am–10 pm; Fri 10 am–11 pm; Sat 9 am–11 pm; Sun 9 am–10 pm. Closed Thanksgiving, Dec 25. Res accepted. Mexican menu. Bar. Semi-a la carte: lunch, dinner $5.95–$18.95. Specializes in carnitas, grilled meat & seafood. Parking. Outdoor dining. Atrium; fireplace. Cr cds: A, MC, V.

✔ ★**DINER.** *6476 Washington St. 707/944-2626.* Hrs: 8 am–3 pm, 5:30–9 pm. Closed Mon; July 4, Thanksgiving, Dec 25. No A/C. Mexican, Amer menu. Wine, beer. Complete meals: bkfst, lunch $4–$9.50, dinner $6–$15. Child's meals. Specialties: German potato pancakes, huevos jalisco, chicken & cream enchiladas, Mexican shellfish soup. Parking. Organic bakery on premises. No cr cds accepted.

★ ★ ★**DOMAINE CHANDON.** *1 California Dr, just W of CA 29 Yountville, Veteran's Home exit. 707/944-2892.* Hrs: 11:30 am–2:30 pm, 6–9 pm. Closed Mon & Tues (exc May–Oct open for lunch); Dec 24, 25; also month of Jan. Res accepted. French, California menu. Wine list. A la carte entrees: lunch $12–$16, dinner $21–$28. Specialties: smoked red trout fillet, tuna pepper steak, Monterey Bay sardines on basil potatoes. Menu changes daily. Own desserts. Outdoor dining at lunch (May–Nov). Rural setting at winery. Totally nonsmoking. Cr cds: A, C, D, DS, MC, V.

★ ★**MUSTARD'S GRILL.** *7399 St Helena Hwy. 707/944-2424.* Hrs: 11:30 am–10 pm; Nov-Apr to 9 pm. Closed Thanksgiving, Dec 25. Res accepted; required Sat, Sun. Bar. A la carte entrees: lunch, dinner $7.95–$17.95. Specializes in smoked and grilled fish, fowl, beef. Parking. Totally nonsmoking. Cr cds: C, D, DS, MC, V, JCB.

Yreka (A-2)

Founded: 1851 **Pop:** 6,948 **Elev:** 2,625 ft **Area code:** 916 **Zip:** 96097

Yreka (Why-RE-ka) was known in gold rush days as Thompson's Dry Diggings, later as Shasta Butte City, and finally, since 1852, as Yreka. Yreka today is the seat of Siskiyou County and a trade center for ranchers, lumbermen and miners. Many historic buildings may be seen in the Historic Preservation District, in the vicinity of Miner and Third Streets. Hunting and fishing are popular in the area.

What to See and Do

1. **Siskiyou County Museum.** 910 S Main St. Exhibits of Siskiyou County from prehistoric era, Indians, trappers, gold rush, transportation, logging, agriculture. First and second floors include period rooms and environments. Research library on premises. (Summer, daily exc Sun; rest of yr, Tues–Sat) Phone 842-3836. ¢ Also on grounds is

   Outdoor Museum. On 2½ acres with pioneer cabin, school house, blacksmith shop, logging skid shack, miner's cabin, church, operating general store. (Summer, daily exc Sun) **Free.**

2. **County Gold Exhibit.** County Courthouse, 311 4th St. Extensive display of gold nuggets taken from mines in Siskiyou County. (Memorial Day wkend–Labor Day, daily exc Sun; rest of yr, Mon–Fri; closed hols) Phone 842-8340. **Free.**

3. **Yreka Western Railroad.** 300 E Miner St. Steam engine-powered 1915 historic train takes visitors on a 3-hr tour of the Shasta Valley. (Memorial Day–Labor Day, Wed–Sun; 1 departure mid-morning) Phone 842-4146. ¢¢¢

4. **Iron Gate Dam and Lake.** 13 mi NE on I-5, then 6 mi E on Klamath River Road. Water sports, fishing, boating (ramps, launching facilities). Picnicking. Camping.

5. **Klamath National Forest.** E & W of town via CA 263, turn left onto CA 96. Approx 1.72 million acres, of which 1.69 million acres are in California and the remainder in Oregon. Within the forest are the Klamath, Scott, Salmon, Siskiyou and Marble mountain ranges and the Klamath, Scott and Salmon rivers. Camping; hunting, hiking; fishing, white water boating on the three rivers; cross-country skiing. The western section of the forest also includes the

   Marble Mountain Wilderness. Access off CA 96. 241,000 acres. Once part of the flat bottom of a shallow ocean, volcanic upheaval and the erosive action of rivers and glaciers have since combined to form what is now one of the most attractive wilderness areas in California. Marble Mountain itself is composed primarily of prehistoric marine invertebrate fossils. Camping, hiking; fishing in many streams and 79 trout-stocked lakes. Fire permit for this wilderness area is required and may be obtained at the Supervisor's office or any Ranger District Office. Contact the Forest Supervisor, 1312 Fairlane Rd; 842-6131. Also at the Supervisor's office is the

   Klamath National Forest Interpretive Museum. Lookout Model; displays of wildlife, mining, timber production, fire management. (Mon–Fri; closed hols) **Free.**

(For further information contact the Chamber of Commerce, 117 Miner St; 842-1649 or 800/ON-YREKA for recording.)

(See Mt Shasta)

Motels

★ ★**BEST WESTERN MINER'S INN.** *122 E Miner St. 916/842-4355; FAX 916/842-4480.* 135 rms, 2 story, 15 kit. suites. S $44; D $49–$55; each addl $5; kit. suites $85–$95. Crib $3. Pet accepted. TV; cable. 2 heated pools. Complimentary coffee in rms. Restaurant adj open 24 hrs. Ck-out noon. Meeting rms. Balconies; some patios. Cr cds: A, C, D, DS, MC, V.

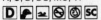 ★ ★ **KLAMATH MOTOR LODGE.** *1111 S Main St. 916/842-2751.* 28 rms, 1–2 story. S $36; D $40–$42; each addl $3; suites $60. Crib $3. TV; cable, in-rm movies avail. Heated pool. Coffee in rms. Restaurant nearby. Ck-out 11 am. Refrigerators. Picnic table. Gardens. Cr cds: A, C, D, MC, V.

Restaurant

★ ★ **MING'S.** *210 W Miner St. 916/842-3888.* Hrs: 11:30 am–11 pm; Sat, Sun from noon. Closed Thanksgiving, Dec 25; also Sun in winter. Res accepted. Chinese, Amer menu. Bar. Semi-a la carte: lunch $3.95–$5.95, dinner $5.95–$24.95. Lunch buffet (Mon–Fri) $4.95. Child's meals. Specialties: teriyaki steak, barbecued spareribs. Parking. In historic district. Oriental decor. Family-owned. Cr cds: A, D, DS, MC, V.

D

Nevada

Population: 1,201,833
Land area: 109,895 square miles
Elevation: 470–13,143 feet
Highest point: Boundary Peak (Esmeralda County)
Entered Union: October 31, 1864 (36th state)
Capital: Carson City
Motto: All for our country
Nickname: Silver State
State flower: Sagebrush
State bird: Mountain bluebird
State tree: Single-leaf piñon and bristlecone pine
State fair: Mid-August, 1994, in Reno
Time zone: Pacific

Famous for gambling and glamorous nightlife, Nevada also has a rich history and tradition, magnificent scenery and some of the wildest desert country on the continent.

Tourism is still the lifeblood of Nevada, with some 30 million visitors a year coming for a vacation or convention. Because of its central location and lack of inventory tax on goods bound out of state, Nevada is becoming increasingly important as a warehousing center for the western states.

Gambling (Nevadans call it "gaming") was first legalized in the Depression year of 1931, the same year residency requirements for obtaining a divorce were relaxed. Gaming is strictly controlled and regulated in Nevada, and casinos offer each bettor a fair chance to win. Taxes derived from the casinos account for nearly half of the state's revenue.

Most Nevadans feel it is preferable to license, tax and regulate gambling strictly than to tolerate the evils of bribery and corruption that inevitably accompany illegal gambling activities. While the state enforces numerous regulations, such as those barring criminals and prohibiting cheating, it *does not* control odds on the various games.

Although Nevada has little rainfall and few rivers, water sports are popular on a few large lakes, both natural and man-made. These include Lakes Tahoe, Mead, Lahontan, Pyramid Lake and Walker Lake.

Mining and ranching have always been important facets of Nevada's economy. Sheep raising became important when millions of sheep were needed to feed the hungry miners working Nevada's Comstock Lode and California's Mother Lode. Most of these sheepherders were Basque. Although today's sheepherder is more likely Peruvian or Mexican, the Basques are still an important influence in the state.

Because of Nevada's arid land, cattle have to roam over a wide area; therefore, ranches average more than 2,000 acres in size. Most

Nevada beef cattle are shipped to California or the Midwest for fattening prior to marketing.

Known for its precious metals, Nevada produces more than $2.2 billion worth of gold and silver a year. Eerie ghost towns still hint at the romantic early days of fabulous gold and silver strikes that made millionaires overnight and generated some of the wildest history in the world. In the southern part of the state, the deserted mining camps of Rhyolite, Johnnie, Goodsprings and Searchlight, to name a few, still delight explorers and rockhounds.

The fur traders of the 1820s and 1830s, Jedediah Smith, Peter Ogden and Joseph Walker and the Frémont expeditions, guided by Kit Carson in 1843 and 1845, were the first to report on the area that is now Nevada.

The Mormons established a trading post in 1851. Now called Genoa, this was Nevada's first non-Indian settlement. Gold was found along the Carson River in Dayton Valley in May of 1850. A decade later the fabulous Comstock Lode (silver and gold ore) was discovered. The gold rush was on and Virginia City mushroomed into a town of 20,000. Formerly a part of Utah and New Mexico Territory, ceded by Mexico in 1848, Nevada became a territory in 1861, a state in 1864. Before Europeans arrived, Nevada was the home of the Paiute, the Shoshone and the Washoe, and even earlier, the Basketmakers.

Note: It is illegal to pick many types of wildflowers in Nevada. It is also illegal in this dry land to toss away lighted cigarette butts.

National Park Service Areas

Nevada has Lake Mead National Recreation Area (see), and part of Death Valley National Monument (see under California). Great Basin National Park (see) was established late in 1986 and includes Lehman Caves, a portion of Humboldt National Forest and a large stand of rare bristlecone pines.

National Forests

The following is an alphabetical listing of National Forests and towns they are listed under.

Humboldt National Forest (see ELKO): Forest Supervisor in Elko; Ranger offices in Buhl, ID, Ely, Mountain City*, Wells*, Winnemucca.

Toiyabe National Forest (see RENO): Forest Supervisor in Sparks; Ranger offices in Austin, Bridgeport, CA, Carson City, Las Vegas, Tonopah.
*Not described in text

State Recreation Areas

The following towns list state recreation areas in their vicinity under What to See and Do; refer to the individual town for directions and park information.

Listed under **Austin:** see Berlin-Ichthyosaur State Park.

Listed under **Caliente:** see Beaver Dam, Cathedral Gorge, Echo Canyon and Spring Valley state parks.

Listed under **Ely:** see Cave Lake State Recreation Area and Ward Charcoal Ovens Historic State Momument.

Listed under **Fallon:** see Lahontan State Recreation Area.

Listed under **Hawthorne:** see Walker Lake State Recreation Area.

Listed under **Incline Village:** see Lake Tahoe Nevada State Park.

Listed under **Las Vegas:** see Floyd Lamb and Spring Mountain Ranch state parks.

Listed under **Lovelock:** see Rye Patch State Recreation Area.

Listed under **Valley of Fire State Park:** see Valley of Fire State Park.

Listed under **Yerington:** see Fort Churchill State Historic Park.

Water-related activities, hiking, riding, various other sports, picnicking and visitor centers, as well as camping, are available in many of these areas. "Roughing" it may be necessary in remote areas. Camping on a first-come, first-served basis; $4–$5/night (Apr–Oct), $3–$5/night (Nov–Mar). Boat launching $2–$5; annual permit $50 (covers all fees, including boat launching). Inquire locally about road conditions for areas off paved highways. Carry drinking water in remote areas. Pets on leash only. For detailed information contact Nevada Division of State Parks, Capitol Complex, Carson City 89710; 702/687-4370 or -4384.

Fishing & Hunting

Nevada's streams and lakes abound with trout, bass, mountain whitefish and catfish. Most fishing areas are open year-round. There are some exceptions; inquire locally. Nonresident license: $45.50 for 1 year or $17.50 for a 3-day and $30.50 for a special 10-day visitors' permit. Special use stamp ($3) for Lake Mead, Lake Mohave and the Colorado River; $5 trout stamp required to take or possess trout.

There is an abundance of wildlife—mule deer, quail, ducks, geese and partridges. Deer hunting season lasts 4 to 5 weeks from the first 2 weekends in October; season varies in some counties. Nonresident hunting license: $100.50 plus $155 for deer tag and processing. Deer hunting with bow and arrow: nonresidents $100.50 for license and $155 for tag and processing. Hunts usually held August 8 through September 4, prior to rifle season.

For digest of fishing and hunting regulations write to the Nevada Department of Wildlife, PO Box 10678, Reno 89520.

Skiing

Listed under **Incline Village:** see Diamond Peak Ski Resort and Mt Rose Ski Area.

Safety Belt Information

Safety belts are mandatory for all persons anywhere in vehicle. Children under 5 years and under 40 pounds in weight must be in an approved safety seat anywhere in vehicle. For further information phone 702/687-5300.

Interstate Highway System

The following alphabetical listing of Nevada towns in *Mobil Travel Guide* shows that these cities are within 10 miles of the indicated Interstate highways. A highway map, however, should be checked for the nearest exit.

INTERSTATE 15: Las Vegas, Overton.

INTERSTATE 80: Battle Mountain, Elko, Lovelock, Reno, Winnemucca.

Additional Visitor Information

The Complete Nevada Traveler: A Guide to the State (Gold Hill Publishing), a reprint of the American Guide Series publication, is a helpful reference for those planning to visit Nevada. *Nevada Magazine,* an illustrated bimonthly magazine, and the *Nevada's Events Guide* (free), may be obtained by contacting the Nevada Commission on Tourism, Capitol Complex, Carson City 89710; 800/NEVADA-8.

For information about the Lake Mead area write the Public Affairs Officer, Lake Mead National Recreation Area, Boulder City 89005.

Information on rock hunting, camping, fishing and hunting, water sports, gambling, ghost towns, mining, agriculture, the state capitol and museum may also be obtained from the Commission on Tourism (see above).

Gambling

Gambling is limited to those 21 or over. Children are welcome in restaurants, and many casinos have child-care facilities.

Austin (C-3)

Settled: 1862 **Pop:** 350 (est) **Elev:** 6,525 ft **Area code:** 702 **Zip:** 89310

Austin was the mother town of central and eastern Nevada mining. For a time its strike did not attract hordes because of the phenomenal character of the Comstock Lode in booming Virginia City. By 1867, however, the number of ore-reduction mills had increased to 11, and 6,000 claims had been filed.

Many of its old buildings have deteriorated and fallen down, but Austin firmly denies that it is a ghost town. Rather, it is a relic of Nevada's greatest days of fame and glory looking toward a future of renewed mining activity made possible through improved methods for using low-grade ore.

A Ranger District office of the Toiyabe National Forest (see RENO) is located here.

What to See and Do

1. **The Lander County Courthouse.** Oldest country courthouse in the state and one of the plainest. Its sturdy construction, without frills, suited the early residents.
2. **Other old buildings.** Stores, churches, hotel and saloons. Stokes Castle is a century-old, three-story stone building that can be seen for miles.

3. **The Reese River** *Reveille.* Published continuously since May 16, 1863; complete files are preserved.

4. **Berlin-Ichthyosaur State Park.** 50 mi SW via US 50, then 30 mi S on NV 361 to Gabbs, then 22 mi E on NV 844, in Toiyabe National Forest. Approx 1,070 acres. Fossilized remains of marine reptiles, some up to 50 feet long, with fish-shaped bodies and long narrow snouts. The ghost town of Berlin is also here. Picnicking. Camping facilities (dump station). Open year-round. Standard fees. Phone 964-2440.

5. **Hickison Petroglyph Recreation Site.** 24 mi E on US 50. Native American drawings carved in stone (ca 1000 B.C.–A.D. 1500); near former pony express trail. Picnicking. Camping; no drinking water available. (Daily) Phone 635-4000. **Free.**

(For further information write the Chamber of Commerce, PO Box 212; 964-2200)

(For accommodations see Battle Mountain)

Battle Mountain (B-3)

Settled: 1868 **Pop:** 3,542 **Elev:** 4,512 ft **Area code:** 702 **Zip:** 89820

Motels

✔ ★**COLT SERVICE CENTER.** *650 W Front St, on I-80 Business. 702/635-5424; res: 800/343-0085; FAX 702/635-0085.* 72 rms, 2 story. May–Sept: S $38–$50; D $45–$50; each addl $5; under 12 free; lower rates rest of yr. TV; cable. Coffee in lobby. Restaurant adj open 24 hrs. Ck-out 11 am. Picnic table, grill. Western theme. Cr cds: A, C, D, DS, MC, V.

D Ⓢ Ⓞ SC

★ ★**HOLIDAY INN EXPRESS.** *521 E Front St, on I-80 Business. 702/635-5880; FAX 702/635-5788.* 72 rms, 2 story. June–Aug: S $48–$53; D $53–$58; each addl $5; under 19 free; lower rates rest of yr. Crib free. Pet accepted. TV; cable. Heated pool; whirlpool. Complimentary continental bkfst. Complimentary coffee in lobby. Restaurant adj 11 am–9 pm. Ck-out noon. Coin lndry. Meeting rms. Refrigerators. Cr cds: A, C, D, DS, MC, V, JCB.

 🅟 ⓜ Ⓢ Ⓞ SC

★**OWL CLUB.** *(PO Box 179) 155 S Reese St. 702/635-5155.* 18 rms, 2 story. S $34; D $38–$40; each addl $5. TV; cable. Restaurant adj open 24 hrs. Ck-out 11 am. Cr cds: A, DS, MC, V.

Ⓞ

Boulder City (F-5)

Founded: 1931 **Pop:** 12,567 **Elev:** 2,500 ft **Area code:** 702 **Zip:** 89005

Boulder City owes its birth to the construction of the mighty Hoover Dam, which spans the Colorado River. A free movie on the project is shown daily, at 45-minute intervals, at the Hoover Dam Museum; for information phone 294-1988.

This is a well-planned model city built by the federal government to house personnel and serve as headquarters for Reclamation, Park Service and Bureau of Mines forces operating in the area.

(For further information contact the Chamber of Commerce, 1497 Nevada Hwy; 293-2034.)

Annual Events

Boulder Damboree. Central Park. July 4.

Art in the Park. Wilbur Sq, Bicentennial & Escalante Parks. 1st full wkend Oct.

(See Henderson, Lake Mead National Recreation Area, Las Vegas)

Motels

★**EL RANCHO.** *725 Nevada Hwy. 702/293-1085; FAX 702/293-6685.* 39 rms. S, D $60–$80; family, wlky rates. Pool. Complimentary coffee in lobby. Restaurant adj 6 am–midnight. Ck-out 11 am. Meeting rms. Refrigerators. Cr cds: A, C, D, DS, ER, MC, V.

D ⓜ Ⓞ

✔ ★**GOLD STRIKE INN & CASINO.** *E on US 93, 3 mi W of Hoover Dam. 702/293-5000; res: 800/245-6380.* 155 rms, 3 story. S, D $29; each addl $3.24; under 12 free. Crib $3. TV. Restaurant open 24 hrs. Bar; entertainment Thurs–Sun. Ck-out 11 am. Gift shop. Casino. Some private patios, balconies. Outstanding view of Lake Mead. Cr cds: A, C, D, DS, MC, V.

D 🅟 Ⓢ Ⓞ SC

★**SUPER 8.** *704 Nevada Hwy. 702/294-8888.* 114 kit. units, 3 story. S $39.88–$79.88; suites $69.88–$200.88; wkly, monthly rates. Crib $5. TV; cable. Indoor pool; whirlpool. Restaurant 6 am–11 pm. Rm serv. Bar. Ck-out noon. Meeting rms. Game rm. Picnic tables. Cr cds: A, C, D, DS, MC, V.

D ⓜ Ⓢ Ⓞ SC

Caliente (D-5)

Pop: 1,111 **Elev:** 4,395 ft **Area code:** 702 **Zip:** 89008

This is a ranch and recreation center situated in a fertile valley.

What to See and Do

State parks and recreation areas.

Beaver Dam. 6 mi N on US 93, then 28 mi E on improved gravel road. (Check conditions locally; trailers over 24 ft not recommended.) More than 2,200 acres set amid pine forests and lofty cliffs. Fishing. Hiking. Picnicking. Camping. Standard fees. (Apr–Oct) Phone 728-4467.

Cathedral Gorge. 14 mi N on US 93. This 1,633-acre park is a long, narrow valley cut into tan bentonite clay formations. Peculiar erosion has created unique patterns, fluting the gorge walls and forming isolated towers that resemble cathedral spires. Hiking. Picnicking. Camping facilities. Standard fees.

Echo Canyon. 25 mi N on US 93, then 4 mi E on NV 322, then 10 mi SE on NV 323. A 920-acre park. Swimming; fishing on 65-acre reservoir (daily); boat launching. Picnicking. Camping (dump station). Standard fees. Phone 962-5103.

Spring Valley. 26 mi N on US 93 to Pioche, then 18 mi E on NV 322. A 1,630-acre park. Boating and fishing on Eagle Valley Reservoir. Picnicking. Camping (dump station). Standard fees. (Daily) Phone 962-5102 or 728-4467.

(For further information contact the Chamber of Commerce, PO Box 533; 726-3129.)

Annual Events

Lincoln County Homecoming. Barbecue, celebrity auction, art show. Memorial Day wkend.

Lincoln County Fair and Rodeo. 2nd wkend Aug.

Meadow Valley Western Days. Hayrides, rodeo, talent show. 3rd wkend Sept.

(For accommodations see Las Vegas, Overton)

Carson City (C-1)

Founded: 1858 **Pop:** 40,443 **Elev:** 4,687 ft **Area code:** 702 **Zip:** 89701

State capital and a county itself, Carson City is situated near the edge of the forested eastern slope of the Sierra Nevada in Eagle Valley. It was first called Eagle Ranch and later renamed for Kit Carson. It became the social center for nearby settlements and shared Wild West notoriety in the silver stampede days of the last century. Fitzsimmons knocked out Corbett here in 1897. Movies of the event (first of their kind) grossed $1 million.

A Ranger District office of the Toiyabe National Forest (see RENO) is located here.

What to See and Do

1. **State Capitol** (1871). N Carson St. Large stone structure with Doric columns and a silver dome. Houses portraits of past Nevada governors. (Mon–Fri) Near the capitol are

   State Library Building. 401 N Carson St. Files of Nevada newspapers and books about the state. (Mon–Fri; closed hols) **Free.**

   Nevada State Museum. N Carson and Robinson Sts. Former US Mint. Exhibits of coins, guns, minerals, pioneer memorabilia, mining operations; life-size displays of Nevada ghost town, Native American camp with artifacts and walk-through "Devonian sea." A 300-foot mine tunnel with displays runs beneath the building. (Daily; closed Jan 1, Thanksgiving, Dec 25) Phone 687-4810. ¢

   Warren Engine Company No. 1 Fire Museum. 111 N Curry St. Currier and Ives series "The Life of a Fireman," old photographs, antique fire-fighting equipment, state's first fire truck (restored), 1863 Hunneman handpumper, 1847 4-wheel cart. (Mon–Fri, afternoons; closed hols) Children under 18 must be accompanied by adult. Phone 887-2210. **Free.**

   Nevada State Railroad Museum. S Carson at Fairview Dr. Exhibits 22 freight and passenger cars, as well as 3 steam locomotives that once belonged to the Virginia and Truckee Railroad. Houses pictorial history gallery and artifacts of the famed Bonanza Road. Motor-rail car rides (summer wkends; fee) and steam-engine rides (summer hols & some wkends; fee). Museum (Wed–Sun). Phone 687-6953. Museum ¢

2. **Bowers Mansion** (1864). 10 mi N in Washoe Valley. The Bowers built this $200,000 granite house with the profits from a gold and silver mine. Their resources were soon depleted, leaving them penniless and forcing Mrs. Bower to become the "Washoe seeress," telling fortunes for a living. Half-hour guided tours of 16 rooms with many original furnishings. (Memorial Day–Labor Day, daily; May, Sept & Oct, wkends) Swimming pool (Memorial Day–Labor Day; fee) and picnicking in adj park. Phone 849-0201. Tours ¢¢

3. **Skiing.** (See LAKE TAHOE AREA, CA)

   (For information on guided walking tours and other attractions contact the Carson City Convention & Visitors Bureau, 1900 S Carson St, Suite 200; 687-7410 or 800/638-2321.)

Annual Event

Nevada Day Celebration. Commemorates admission to the Union. Grand Ball, parades, exhibits. 4 days late Oct.

(See Incline Village, Reno, Stateline, Virginia City; also see Lake Tahoe Area, CA)

Motels

★**HARDMAN HOUSE MOTOR INN.** 917 N Carson St. 702/882-7744; res: 800/626-0793; FAX 702/887-0321. 62 rms, 3 story. May–Oct: S $40–$60; D $45–$65; each addl $6; suites $80–$100; higher rates: wkends, hols, air races; lower rates rest of yr. Crib free. TV; cable. Complimentary coffee in lobby. Restaurant nearby. Ck-out noon. Garage parking. Some refrigerators; some wet bars. Cr cds: A, D, DS, MC, V.

★**MILL HOUSE INN.** 3251 S Carson St. 702/882-2715. 24 rms. May–Oct: S $40–$50; D $45–$55; each addl $5; under 12 free; higher rates: wkends, hols; lower rates rest of yr. Crib $5. TV; cable. Heated pool (seasonal). Complimentary coffee in lobby. Restaurant nearby. Ck-out 11 am. Picnic tables. Cr cds: A, DS, MC, V.

✔ ★**NUGGET.** 651 N Stewart St. 702/882-7711. 60 rms, 2 story. S $35–$45; D $40–$55; each addl $5; under 6 free. TV; cable. Complimentary coffee in lobby. Restaurant nearby. Ck-out noon. Cr cds: A, DS, MC, V.

Restaurants

★ ★**ADELE'S.** 1112 N Carson St. 702/882-3353. Hrs: 11 am–midnight. Closed Sun; also wk of Dec 25–mid-Jan. Res accepted. A la carte entrees: lunch $6.95–$15.95, dinner $17.95–$30. Specializes in seafood, roast duck. Entertainment Thurs & Fri. Parking. Extensive wine selection. Barbary Coast decor in Second Empire house. Cr cds: A, MC, V.

D

✔ ★ ★**CARSON NUGGET STEAK HOUSE.** In Carson Nugget Casino, 507 N Carson St. 702/882-1626. Hrs: 5–10 pm. Res accepted. Bar open 24 hrs. Semi-a la carte: dinner $8–$15. Child's meals. Specializes in seafood, prime rib, steak. Parking. Western decor. Also on premises are buffet dining rm & coffee shop open 24 hrs. Cr cds: A, C, D, DS, MC, V.

D SC

★**SILVANA'S.** 1301 N Carson St. 702/883-5100. Hrs: 5–10 pm. Closed Sun & Mon; Dec 25; also Feb. Res accepted. Italian menu. Bar. Semi-a la carte: dinner $10.95–$19.95. Specializes in pasta, seafood, steak. Parking. Contemporary decor. Cr cds: A, C, D, MC, V.

D

Crystal Bay

(see Incline Village)

Elko (B-4)

Settled: ca 1870 **Pop:** 14,736 **Elev:** 5,067 ft **Area code:** 702 **Zip:** 89801

On the Humboldt River, Elko is the center of a large ranching area. Originally a stopping point for wagon trains headed for the West Coast, its main sources of revenue today are tourism, ranching, mining and railroads.

What to See and Do

1. **Northeastern Nevada Museum.** 1515 Idaho St. Three galleries feature art, historical, Native American and nature exhibits of area. Pioneer vehicles and original 1860 pony express cabin on grounds. (Daily; closed Jan 1, Thanksgiving, Dec 25) Phone 738-3418. **Free.**

2. **Licensed casinos, nightclubs.** Particularly along Idaho Street.

3. **Humboldt National Forest.** 20 mi SE on NV 228 (Ruby Mountain District), or 70 mi N on NV 225 (Mountain City & Jarbridge Districts). Some of the features of this more than 2 million-acre forest are its

eight wilderness areas, spectacular canyons, streams and old mining camps. Fishing; hunting. Picnicking. Camping (May–Oct; fee). For further information contact Supervisor, 976 Mountain City Hwy; 738-5171. ¢¢

(For further information regarding fishing, hunting and ghost towns contact the Chamber of Commerce, 1601 Idaho St; 738-7135.)

Annual Events

Cowboy Poetry Gathering. Last full wkend Jan.

National Basque Festival. Contests in weightlifting, sheephooking, other skills of mountaineers; dancing, feast. Wkend early July.

County Fair and Livestock Show. Horse racing. 4 days Labor Day wkend.

Motels

✔ ★ **BEST WESTERN AMERITEL EXPRESS.** *837 E Idaho St. 702/738-7261; FAX 702/738-0118.* 49 rms, 2 story. Mid-May–Sept: S $44–$54; D $54–$64; each addl $5; suites $79; higher rates special events; varied lower rates rest of yr. Crib $4. TV; cable. Heated pool. Complimentary continental bkfst. Ck-out 11 am. Cr cds: A, D, DS, MC, V.

⊠ ◎ ⊚ SC

★ **HOLIDAY INN.** *3015 E Idaho St. 702/738-8425.* 170 rms, 4 story. Apr–Oct: S $61–$70, D $69–$87; each addl $8; higher rates: Cowboy Poetry Gathering, Mining Exposition; lower rates rest of yr. Crib free. Pet accepted. TV; cable. Indoor pool. Coffee in rms. Restaurant 6 am–10 pm. Rm serv. Bar 4 pm–midnight. Ck-out noon. Coin lndry. Meeting rms. Valet serv. Free airport, RR station, bus depot transportation. Exercise equipt; weight machine, bicycles, whirlpool. Cr cds: A, C, D, DS, MC, V, JCB.

D ⊠ ⊠ 🏃 ◎ ⊚ SC

★ ★ **RED LION INN & CASINO.** *2065 E Idaho St. 702/738-2111; FAX 702/753-9859.* 223 rms, 3 story. S $64; D $74; each addl $10; suites $255; under 16 free. Crib free. Pet accepted. TV; cable. Heated pool. Coffee in rms. Restaurant open 24 hrs. Bar; entertainment, dancing. Ck-out noon. Gift shop. Barber, beauty shop. Free airport transportation. Game rm. Casino. Cr cds: A, C, D, DS, ER, MC, V.

D ⊠ ⚬ ◎ ⊚ SC

★ ★ **SHILO INN.** *2401 Mountain City Hwy, near JC Harris Airport. 702/738-5522; FAX 702/738-6247.* 70 rms, 2 story, 16 kit. units. Apr–Oct: S, D $70; kit. units $90; under 12 free; wkly rates; higher rates special events; lower rates rest of yr. Crib free. Pet accepted; $6. TV; cable. Indoor pool. Complimentary continental bkfst. Restaurant nearby. Ck-out noon. Coin lndry. Meeting rm. Sundries. Free airport, RR station, bus depot transportation. Exercise equipt; weight machine, bicycles, whirlpool, sauna. Bathrm phones, refrigerators, wet bars. Cr cds: A, C, D, DS, ER, MC, V.

D ⊠ ⚬ 🏃 ✕ ◎ ⊚ SC

✔ ★ **SUPER 8.** *1755 E Idaho St. 702/738-8488.* 75 rms, 2 story. Late May–Sept: S $37.88–$41.88; D $46.88; each addl $3; under 12 free; higher rates special events; lower rates rest of yr. Crib free. TV; cable. Complimentary coffee in lobby. Restaurant opp. Ck-out 11 am. Cr cds: A, C, D, DS, MC, V.

D ◎ ⊚ SC

Ely (C-4)

Settled: 1868 **Pop:** 4,756 **Elev:** 6,427 ft **Area code:** 702 **Zip:** 89301

Although founded in 1868 as a silver mining camp, Ely's growth began in 1906 with the arrival of the Nevada Northern Railroad, which facilitated the development, in 1907, of large-scale copper mining. Gold and silver

are still mined in Ely. The seat of White Pine County, it is the shopping and recreational center of a vast ranching and mining area. The city is surrounded by mountains that offer deer hunting, trout fishing and winter skiing. High elevation provides a cool, sunny climate.

A Ranger District office of the Humboldt National Forest (see ELKO) is located here.

What to See and Do

1. **Nevada Northern Railway Museum.** 11th St E & Avenue A. Located in the historic Nevada Northern Railway Depot (1906). Original oak furniture, filing cabinets and telephones. The railroad, which operated until 1983, never replaced anything, which makes the Nevada Northern one of the best preserved shortline railroads in the US. Guided walking tour avail (45 min). Rides on original steam passenger train with turn-of-the-century wooden coaches to old mining and smelting towns (call for dates; fee). Museum (Memorial Day wkend–Labor Day, Wed–Sun). Phone 289-2085. Museum ¢¢; Train excursions ¢¢¢¢

2. **White Pine Public Museum.** 2000 Aultman St. 1905 coach and 1909, 1917 steam locomotives, early-day relics and mementos, mineral display. (Daily) Phone 289-4710. **Free.**

3. **Ward Charcoal Ovens Historic State Monument.** 5 mi SE on US 6, 50, 93, then 11 mi W on unnumbered gravel road. Six stone beehive charcoal ovens used during the 1870 mining boom. Hunting in season. Picnicking.

4. **Cave Lake State Recreation Area.** 8 mi S on US 93, then 7 mi E on Success Summit Rd, NV 486. A 1,240-acre area; 32-acre reservoir provides swimming; fishing (trout); boating. Picnicking. Camping (dump station). (Daily; access may be restricted in winter) Standard fees. Phone 728-4467.

5. **Humboldt National Forest** (see ELKO).

(For further information contact the White Pine Chamber of Commerce, Professional Building, 636 Aultman St; 289-8877.)

Annual Events

Auto races. Open road auto races. 3rd wkend May & Sept.

Pony Express Days. Horse racing, parimutuel betting. Last 2 wkends Aug.

White Pine County Fair. Last wkend Aug.

Motels

✔ ★ ★ **COPPER QUEEN.** *701 Avenue I, at jct Us 50, US 93 & US 6. 702/289-4884.* 63 rms, 2 story. S $43–$50; D $48–$57; each addl $5. Crib free. Indoor pool; whirlpool. TV; cable. Restaurant 6 am–10 pm. Bar. Ck-out noon. Free shuttle to airport. Casino. Cr cds: A, C, D, MC, V.

⚬ ◎ ⊚ SC

✔ ★ **JAILHOUSE MOTEL & CASINO.** *5th & High Sts. 702/289-3033; res: 800/841-5430.* 47 rms, 2 story. S $40; D $42–$51; each addl $5. Crib free. TV; cable. Restaurant 5 am–9 pm. Ck-out 11 am. Casino. Cr cds: A, C, D, DS, MC, V.

D ◎ SC

Fallon (C-2)

Pop: 6,438 **Elev:** 3,963 ft **Area code:** 702 **Zip:** 89406

What to See and Do

Lahontan State Recreation Area. 18 mi W on US 50. Approx 30,000 acres with a 16-mile-long reservoir. Water sports; fishing; boating (launching, ramps). Picnicking. Camping (dump station). Standard fees. Phone 867-3500.

(For further information contact the Chamber of Commerce, 100 Campus Way; 423-2544.)

Annual Event

All Indian Rodeo. Rodeo events, parade, powwow, Native American dances, arts, games. Phone 423-2544. 3rd wk July.

Motels

★★**BEST WESTERN BONANZA INN.** *855 W Williams Ave.* *702/423-6031.* 75 rms, 2 story. S $40; D $50; each addl $5; suite $59–$76; under 12 free. Crib $5. Pet accepted; $20. TV; cable. Pool. Restaurant 5 am–10 pm. Bar open 24 hrs. Ck-out noon. Coin lndry. Casino. Cr cds: A, C, D, DS, MC, V.

🐾 ⛱ 🈂 🎴 SC

★**COMFORT INN.** *1830 W Williams Ave. 702/423-5554;* *FAX 702/423-0663.* 49 rms, 2 story. Apr–Oct: S, D $45–$60; suites $60–$100; under 18 free; lower rates rest of yr. Crib free. TV; cable. Pool. Complimentary continental bkfst. Restaurant opp open 24 hrs. Ck-out noon. Sundries. Refrigerators avail. Cr cds: A, C, D, DS, ER, MC, V, JCB.

D ⛱ 🈂 🎴 SC

✔★**WESTERN.** *125 S Carson St. 702/423-5118.* 22 rms, 2 story. S $32; D $38; each addl $5. Crib $4. Pet accepted, some restrictions. TV. Heated pool. Complimentary coffee in lobby. Restaurant nearby. Ck-out 11 am. Some refrigerators. Cr cds: A, C, D, MC, V.

🐾 ⛱ 🈂 🎴 SC

Gardnerville (C-1)

Pop: 2,177 **Elev:** 4,746 ft **Area code:** 702 **Zip:** 89410

Gardnerville lies just east of Minden, seat of Douglas County. The two are considered contiguous towns.

What to See and Do

Mormon Station State Historic Park. 4 mi N via US 395, then 4 mi W on NV 57 in Genoa. Fort/stockade. Museum exhibits relics of the early pioneer days and the first white settlement in state. Also picnicking, tables, stoves. (Mid-May–mid-Oct, daily) Phone 782-2590.

(For further information contact the Carson Valley Chamber of Commerce, 1524 US 395 N, Suite 1; 782-8144 or 800/727-7677.)

Annual Event

Carson Valley Days. 2nd wkend June.

(See Carson City, Stateline; also see Lake Tahoe Area, CA)

Motor Hotel

✔★★★**CARSON VALLEY INN.** *(1627 US 395, Minden 89423) N* *on US 395. 702/782-9711; res: 800/321-6983; FAX 702/782-7472.* 154 rms, 2 bldgs, 4 story. Registration in rear bldg. June–Oct: S, D $49–$69; each addl $6; suites $139–$149; under 12 free; ski, golf packages; higher rates: wknds, hols; lower rates rest of yr. Crib free. TV. Supervised child's activities. Restaurant open 24 hrs. Rm serv 6 am–10 pm. Bar open 24 hrs; entertainment, dancing. Ck-out noon. Meeting rms. Bellhops. Downhill ski 15 mi; x-country ski 18 mi. Whirlpool. Game rm.

Some bathrm phones, refrigerators. Casino. Stained-glass chapel. Cr cds: A, C, D, DS, MC, V.

D ⛱ 🈂 🎴 SC

Inn

★★**THE NENZEL MANSION.** *1431 Ezell St. 702/782-7644.* 4 air-cooled rms, 2 share bath, 3 story. No rm phones. S, D $80–$95; each addl $10; family & wkly rates. Crib free. TV in sitting rm; cable. Complimentary full bkfst. Restaurant nearby. Ck-out 11 am, ck-in 3 pm. Downhill ski 18 mi; x-country ski 20 mi. Picnic tables, grills. Built 1910; period furnishings. No cr cds accepted.

🐾 🈂 🎴

Great Basin National Park (C-5)

(5 mi W of Baker on NV 488)

Established as a national park in 1986, Great Basin includes Lehman Caves (formerly Lehman Caves National Monument), Wheeler Peak (elev 13,063 ft), the park's only glacier, and Lexington arch, a natural limestone arch more than six stories tall. The park consists of 77,092 acres of diverse scenic, ecologic and geologic attractions.

Of particular interest in the park is Lehman Caves, a large limestone solution cavern. The cave contains numerous limestone formations, including shields and helectites. Temperature in the cave is 50°F; jackets are recommended. Guided tours of the caves (daily; closed Jan 1, Thanksgiving, Dec 25)

The 12-mile Wheeler Peak Scenic Drive reaches to the 10,000-foot elevation on Wheeler Peak. From there, hiking is possible to the summit of the peak at 13,063 feet. Backcountry hiking and camping are permitted. The Lexington Arch is located at the south end of the park.

Camping is allowed at three campgrounds located along the Wheeler Peak Scenic Drive: the Wheeler Peak Campground, the Upper Lehman Creek Campground and the Lower Lehman Campground. Baker Creek Campground is located approximately 5 miles from park headquarters. Picnic facilities are available near park headquarters.

Park headquarters and the Visitor Center are located at Lehman Caves (daily exc Jan 1, Thanksgiving, Dec 25; extended hrs in summer). Also here is a souvenir and snack shop (Easter–mid-Oct; daily). For further information contact the Superintendent, Great Basin National Park, Baker 89311; 702/234-7331.

Hawthorne (C-2)

Pop: 4,162 **Elev:** 4,320 ft **Area code:** 702 **Zip:** 89415

Hawthorne, seat of Mineral County, is a truly Western desert town on a broad plain rimmed by beautiful mountains where gold has been mined. The area is inviting to people who like to explore the ''old'' Nevada.

What to See and Do

Walker Lake. 12 mi N on US 95. Named for the trapper and scout Joseph Walker, this is a remnant of ancient Lake Lahontan. It is 15 miles long and 5 miles wide. Swimming, water skiing. Fishing is good for cutthroat trout in these alkaline and saline waters. Boating (landing). Camping sites. The US Bureau of Land Management maintains one recreational area: Sportsman's Beach (boat launching, camping; free). Phone 885-6000. Also here is

Walker Lake State Recreation Area. Approx 280 acres. Swimming; fishing; boating (launching ramp). Picnicking, shade structures.

(For further information contact the Chamber of Commerce, 5th & F Street, PO Box 1635; 945-5896.)

Motels

✔ ★**EL CAPITAN LODGE & CASINO.** *(Box 1000) 1 blk E of US 95.* 702/945-3321; FAX 702/324-6229. 103 rms, 1–2 story. S $28–$40; D $34–$44; each addl $5; under 12 free. Crib free. TV. Heated pool. Restaurant open 24 hrs. Bar open 24 hrs. Ck-out 1 pm. Meeting rms. Sundries. Game rm. Refrigerators. Casino. Cr cds: A, C, D, DS, MC, V.

★**SAND N SAGE.** *(PO Box 2325) 1301 E 5th St, 1 blk NE of US 95.* 702/945-3352. 37 rms, 2 story. S $28–$33; D $37–$40; each addl $4; kit. units $6 addl. TV; cable. Pool. Complimentary coffee in lobby. Restaurant nearby. Ck-out 11 am. Some refrigerators. Balconies. Cr cds: A, DS, MC, V.

Henderson (E-5)

Settled: 1942 **Pop:** 64,942 **Elev:** 1,960 ft **Area code:** 702 **Zip:** 89015

The industrial center of Nevada, Henderson is on level desert terrain, midway between Boulder City (see) and Las Vegas (see). It was originally created to provide housing for the employees of a wartime magnesium plant. The fastest growing city in Nevada, it has become the third largest city in the state.

What to See and Do

Clark County Heritage Museum. 1830 S Boulder Hwy. Exhibit Center with county ''time line.'' Railroad, early residence exhibits; commercial print shop, outdoor mining, farming display; gift shop. (Daily) Phone 455-7955. ¢

(For further information contact the Chamber of Commerce, 100 E Lake Mead Dr; 565-8951.)

Annual Event

Industrial Days. 5 days Apr.

(See Boulder City, Lake Mead National Recreation Area, Las Vegas)

Motel

✔ ★**BEST WESTERN LAKE MEAD.** *85 W Lake Mead Dr.* 702/564-1712; FAX 702/564-7642. 58 rms, 2 story. S $41–$51; D $46–$56; each addl $5; wkly rates; higher rates hols. Crib free. TV; cable. Heated pool. Restaurant nearby. Ck-out 11 am. Coin lndry. Some refrigerators. Cr cds: A, C, D, DS, MC, V.

Restaurant

✔ ★**RAINBOW CLUB.** *122 Water St.* 702/565-9777. Open 24 hrs. Bar. Semi-a la carte: bkfst 99¢–$3.75, lunch $2.50–$3.75, dinner $3.95–$8.75. Specializes in steak, chicken, seafood. In casino. No cr cds accepted.

Incline Village *

* 2 mi E of Crystal Bay (C-1) on NV 28. **Pop:** 7,1119 **Elev:** 6,360 ft **Area code:** 702 **Zip:** 89451

What to See and Do

1. **Lake Tahoe Nevada State Park.** On NV 28. Approx 14,200 acres on the eastern shore of beautiful Lake Tahoe consisting of five management areas. Gently sloping sandy beach, swimming; fishing; boating (ramp). Hiking. Mountain biking. X-country skiing. Picnic tables, stoves. No camping. Standard fees. (Daily) Phone 831-0494.

2. **Ponderosa Ranch and Western Theme Park.** On Tahoe Blvd (NV 28). Cartwright House seen in the *Bonanza* television series. Frontier town; vintage autos; breakfast hayrides (fee); amusements May–Oct. Convention facilities. (Daily) Phone 831-0691. ¢¢¢

3. **Skiing.**

Diamond Peak Ski Resort. Jct NV 28, Country Club Dr. Quad, 6 double chairlifts; patrol, school, rentals, snowmaking; cafeteria, bar; lodge. 35 runs; longest run approx 2.5 miles; vertical drop 1,840 feet. (Mid-Nov–mid-Apr, daily) Phone 832-1177 for fees, 831-3211 for snow conditions. ¢¢¢¢¢

Mount Rose Ski Area. 12 mi NE on NV 431. Quad, 3 triple, 1 double chairlift; patrol, rentals, school; bar, cafeteria and deli; sport shop. Longest run 2½ miles; vertical drop 1,440 feet. (Mid-Nov–mid-Apr, daily) Phone 849-0704 or 800/SKI-ROSE (exc NV). ¢¢¢¢¢

(For further information contact the Visitor & Convention Bureau, 969 Tahoe Blvd; 832-1606 or 800/GO-TAHOE.)

(See Stateline; also see Lake Tahoe Area, CA)

Motel

✔ ★**INN AT INCLINE.** *(PO Box 4545) 1003 Tahoe Blvd (NV 28).* 702/831-1052; res: 800/824-6391. 38 rms, 2 story. No A/C. Mid-Jan–mid-Mar, mid-June–Sept: S, D $79–$99; each addl $10; under 13 free; lower rates rest of yr. Crib free. TV; cable. Indoor pool. Complimentary continental bkfst. Restaurant nearby. Ck-out 11 am. Downhill ski 1 mi; x-country ski 6 mi. Exercise equipt; weights, bicycles, whirlpool, sauna. Game rm. Some balconies. Private beach. Cr cds: A, DS, MC, V, JCB.

Hotel

★★★★**HYATT REGENCY LAKE TAHOE.** *(Box 3239, 89450) Lakeshore Blvd and Country Club Dr.* 702/832-1234; FAX 702/831-7508. 458 rms, 12 story. Feb–Mar, May–Oct, wkends, hols: S, D $239; each addl $10; suites $495–$895; under 18 free; ski, tennis packages; lower rates rest of yr. Crib free. TV; cable, in-rm movies. Heated pool; poolside serv. Supervised child's activities (daily in season; Fri, Sat evenings off-season). Coffee in rms. Restaurant open 24 hrs (also see HUGO'S ROTISSERIE). Rm serv 24 hrs. Bar. Ck-out 11 am. Convention facilities. Concierge. Shopping arcade. Free valet parking. Tennis. Downhill ski 1½ mi; x-country ski 6 mi. Exercise rm; instructor, weights, bicycles, whirlpool, sauna, steam rm. Massage. Private beach. Game rm. Rec rm. Lawn games. Bicycles avail. Minibars; some refrigerators, fireplaces. Some balconies. Wet bar in suites. Casino. *LUXURY LEVEL: REGENCY CLUB.* 56 rms, 2 story. S, D $279. Private lounge. Complimentary continental bkfst, refreshments.
Cr cds: A, C, D, DS, ER, MC, V, JCB.

Inn

★★**HAUS BAVARIA.** *(PO Box 3308) 593 N Dyer Circle. 702/ 831-6122; res: 800/GO-TAHOE.* 5 rms, 2 story. No A/C. No rm phones. July–mid-Sept: S $80; D $90; wkly rates, ski plan; lower rates rest of yr. Children over 12 yrs only. TV in sitting rm; cable. Complimentary full bkfst, tea, sherry. Ck-out 11 am, ck-in 2 pm. Downhill ski 1½ mi; x-country ski 5 mi. Library. Balconies. Alpine-style building. View of Sierra Nevadas. Totally nonsmoking. Cr cds: A, DS, MC, V.

⓱ Ⓢ Ⓢ **SC**

Restaurants

★★★**HUGO'S ROTISSERIE.** *(See Hyatt Regency Lake Tahoe Hotel) 702/831-1111.* Hrs: 5:45–10 pm; Fri & Sat to 11 pm; Sun brunch 10 am–3 pm. Res accepted. Bar 4 pm–midnight. A la carte entrees: dinner $19.50–$31. Sun brunch $12.95. Specializes in spit-roasted duckling, fresh seafood. Salad bar. Own baking. Make your own soft ice cream sundaes. Pianist Thurs–Sun. Parking. Cr cds: A, C, D, DS, ER, MC, V, JCB.

D

✔★**LAS PANCHITAS.** *930 Tahoe Blvd (NV 28), in Raley's Shopping Center. 702/831-4048.* Hrs: 11 am–10 pm; Sat & Sun from noon. Closed Thanksgiving, Dec 25. Mexican menu. Serv bar. Semi-a la carte: lunch $3.95–$10.95, dinner $4.95–$16.50. Specialties: fajitas, chile rellenos. Outdoor dining. Rustic Mexican decor. Cr cds: A, DS, MC, V.

D

★★**SPATZ.** *341 Ski Way. 702/831-8999.* Hrs: 11:30 am–2 pm, 6–10 pm; Sun from 6 pm. Closed late Oct–mid-Nov. Res accepted. California continental menu. Bar. Semi-a la carte: lunch $6–$10.50, dinner $14–$19.50. Specializes in seafood. Own soups. Pianist Fri–Sun. Parking. Views of lake, mountains. Cr cds: DS, MC, V.

D

Lake Mead National Recreation Area (E-5 – F-5)

(4 mi E of Boulder City on US 93, 466)

This 2,337-square-mile tract extends along the Colorado River from Grand Canyon National Park to a point below Davis Dam. It is a land of colorful deserts, high plateaus, narrow canyons and two magnificent lakes. Lake Mead, impounded by Hoover Dam (726 feet high), is by volume one of the largest man-made reservoirs; 110 miles long, with a shoreline of 550 miles when full, with a maximum depth of 500 feet. Lake Mohave, formed behind Davis Dam, is 67 miles long with a shoreline of 150 miles.

The dams are part of an irrigation, reclamation and power project of the federal government. More than nine million people use the recreational facilities yearly. The Alan Bible Visitor Center on US 93 is open daily except Jan 1, Thanksgiving and Dec 25.

What to See and Do

1. **Hoover Dam.** About 8 mi E of Boulder City on US 93. Tour of dam and powerhouse (daily; closed Dec 25). Exhibit building houses model of a generating unit and topographical model of Colorado River Basin. Phone 293-8367. Tour **¢**

2. **Davis Dam.** (See BULLHEAD CITY, AZ).

3. **Lake Mead Cruises.** Lake Mead Marina. 7 mi E of Boulder City on Lakeshore Dr, at Lake Mead Resort Area. One-and-one-half-hour sightseeing cruise to Hoover Dam on paddlewheeler *Desert Prin-*

cess. Breakfast and dinner cruises available. (Daily exc Dec 25) Concessioner of National Park Service. For details phone 293-6180. **¢¢¢¢**

4. **Swimming, fishing, boating, camping, hiking.** Developed areas in Arizona: Willow Beach on Lake Mohave, 18 mi S of Hoover Dam (no camping); Temple Bar on Lake Mead, 50 mi E of Hoover Dam; Katherine on Lake Mohave, 3 mi N of Davis Dam (campgrounds, stores, restaurants, motels, marinas, boat ramps in these areas). Developed areas in Nevada: Boulder Beach on Lake Mead, 6 mi NE of Boulder City; Las Vegas Bay, 10 mi NE of Henderson; Callville Bay, 24 mi NE of Henderson; Overton Beach, 9 mi S of Overton; Echo Bay, 23 mi S of Overton; Cottonwood Cove, 14 mi E of Searchlight. (All these sites, except Willow Beach and Overton Beach, have campgrounds, $6/site/night; stores, restaurants, marinas and boat ramps at most.) For information contact Superintendent, Lake Mead National Recreation Area, 601 Nevada Hwy, Boulder City 89005-2426; 702/293-8906.

(For accommodations see Boulder City, Overton)

Lake Tahoe

(see Lake Tahoe Area, CA)

Las Vegas (E-4)

Settled: 1905 **Pop:** 258,295 **Elev:** 2,020 ft **Area code:** 702

Las Vegas, Nevada's largest city, became a major entertainment center after World War II. Near Hoover Dam and Lake Mead National Recreation Area (see), the city has public buildings and entertainment facilities designed to attract vacationers. Famous for glittering nightclubs, bars, gambling casinos and plush hotels, Las Vegas also offers tennis, racquetball, bowling, water sports, snow skiing, golf, fishing and hunting, hiking and riding trails and tours to nearby points of interest. The townsite covers 53 square miles on a plain encircled by distant mountains. Beyond its suburban fringe lies the desert.

Two natural springs and green meadows made the Las Vegas valley a favorite camping place in the 1840s for caravans following the Old Spanish Trail from Santa Fe to California. It was first settled by the Spanish in 1829. American settlement began in 1855, when Brigham Young sent 30 settlers to build a fort and stockade here. The Mormons tried mining in the area but found that the ore was hard to smelt and the metal made poor bullets. Later this "lead" was discovered to be a galena ore carrying silver.

The Mormons abandoned the settlement in 1857; from 1862 to 1899 it was operated as a ranch. Las Vegas was really born in 1905, with the advent of the railroad. A tent town sprang up; streets were laid out, and permanent buildings followed. In 1911 the city of Las Vegas was created by an act of the legislature.

A Ranger District office of the Toiyabe National Forest (see RENO) is located here.

Transportation

Las Vegas McCarran Intl Airport: Information 261-5733; weather 734-2010.

Car Rental Agencies: See toll-free numbers under Introduction.

Public Transportation: Las Vegas Transit, 384-3540.

Rail Passenger Service: Amtrak 800/872-7245.

What to See and Do

1. **The Strip.** Las Vegas Blvd, S of town. Las Vegas' biggest attraction, with dazzling casinos, roulette wheels, luxurious hotels, glamor-

LAS VEGAS AND VICINITY

© H.M. GOUSHA

M-B-UH-1057-S

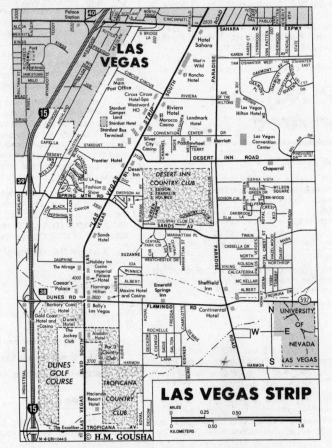

LAS VEGAS STRIP

© H.M. GOUSHA

M-4-UH-1044-S

ous chorus lines and top entertainers. Some shows are free; some require buying food or drink. Make reservations.

2. **Convention Center.** Paradise Rd, S of town. The largest single-level convention center in the country; 1.3 million square feet of exhibit and meeting space.

3. **Liberace Museum.** 1775 E Tropicana Ave, 2½ mi E of Strip. Displays memorabilia of Liberace's career, including antique and custom cars, miniature and full-size pianos, the world's largest rhinestone and a portion of his million-dollar wardrobe. Showcases contain awards, gifts from fans and dignitaries and personal items. (Daily; closed Jan 1, Thanksgiving, Dec 25) Sr citizen rate. Phone 798-5595. ¢¢

4. **Las Vegas Art Museum.** 3333 W Washington Ave. The main gallery features local, national and international artists. Changing monthly exhibits. (Daily exc Mon; closed hols) Phone 647-4300. **Free.**

5. **Las Vegas Natural History Museum.** 900 Las Vegas Blvd N. Wildlife collection featuring animated dinosaurs and shark exhibits. (Daily; closed Dec 25) Sr citizen rate. Phone 384-3466. ¢¢

6. **Nevada State Museum and Historical Society.** 700 Twin Lakes, in Lorenzi Park. Exhibits explore the growth of southern Nevada from Spanish explorers to present. The natural history of the area is presented in the Hall of Biological Science. Changing exhibits on art, history of the region. (Daily; closed Jan 1, Thanksgiving, Dec 25) Phone 486-5205. ¢

7. **University of Nevada, Las Vegas** (1957). (19,500 students) 4505 Maryland Pkwy, 1½ mi E of Strip. Campus tours arranged in advance by calling 895-3443. For university activities open to the public, phone 739-3131. On campus are

   Marjorie Barrick Museum of Natural History. Exhibits of the biology, geology and archaeology of the Las Vegas area, including live desert animals. (Daily exc Sun; closed major hols) Phone 895-3381. **Free.**

   The Flashlight. A 38-foot-tall steel sculpture by Claes Oldenburg and Coosje von Bruggen.

   Artemus W. Ham Concert Hall. A 1,900-seat theater featuring yearly Charles Vanda Master Series of symphony, opera and ballet. Jazz and popular music concerts also performed here. Box office phone 895-3801.

   Donna Beam Fine Art Gallery. Exhibits by professional artists, faculty, students; emphasis on contemporary art. (Mon–Fri; closed major hols) Phone 895-3893. **Free.**

   Judy Bayley Theatre. Varied theatrical performances all yr. Sr citizen rate. Box office 895-3801.

   Thomas and Mack Center. 18,500-seat events center features concerts, ice shows, rodeos, sporting events. Phone 895-3900.

8. **Guinness World of Records Museum.** 2780 Las Vegas Blvd S. Interactive computers bring the famous Guinness book to life. Displays; rare videos; special exhibit on Las Vegas. Gift shop. (Daily) Phone 792-0640. ¢¢

9. **Imperial Palace Auto Collection.** 3535 Las Vegas Blvd, on 5th-floor parking area of hotel. More than 200 antique and classic cars on display. Large collection of Duesenbergs. Also cars belonging to Adolf Hitler, the King of Siam, Eleanor Roosevelt, Howard Hughes, Al Capone. (Daily) Sr citizen rate. Phone 731-3311 or 794-3174. ¢¢¢

10. **Wet 'n Wild.** 2601 Las Vegas Blvd S. Aquatic amusement park featuring 75-foot water slide; rafting (rentals), flumes, water cannons, whirlpools, whitewater rapids, waterfalls, pools, lagoon, 4-foot waves and children's activities. Picnicking; snack bars. (Apr–Sept, daily) Phone 737-3819. ¢¢¢¢¢

11. **Red Rock Canyon National Conservation Area.** 18 mi W on W Charleston Blvd. Spectacular view of the area's steep canyons and red and white hues of the Aztec sandstone formation. Picnicking, hiking trails, rock climbing; 13-mile scenic drive (daylight hrs only); limited primitive camping. Visitor center; nature walks led by Bureau of Land Management ranger-naturalists. Phone 363-1921. **Free.** Nearby is

Spring Mountain Ranch State Park. Approx 18 mi W on W Charleston Blvd. Visitor center at main ranch house (Fri–Mon; closed Jan 1, Dec 25) has brochures with self-guided tours of park and interpretive trails. Picnicking. (Daily) Phone 875-4141. Per vehicle ¢¢¢

12. **Mt Charleston Recreation Area.** 15 mi NW on US 95, then 21 mi W on NV 157, which leads to Toiyabe National Forest (see RENO). Picnicking. Camping. (Winter) Phone for conditions, 331-6444.

13. **Floyd Lamb State Park.** 10 mi N via US 95. Approx 2,000 acres. Small lakes; fishing. Picnicking. No overnight camping. Phone 486-5413. Per vehicle ¢¢

14. **Valley of Fire State Park** (see).

15. **Southern Nevada Zoological Park.** 1775 N Rancho Dr. Apes, monkeys, leopard, tiger; exotic bird collection, Southwestern desert animals and a petting zoo. Also here is an endangered species breeding program. (Daily; closed Jan 1, Thanksgiving, Dec 25) Phone 647-4685. ¢¢–¢¢¢

16. **Bonnie Springs Old Nevada.** 20 mi W via W Charleston Blvd. Historic Western mining town features narrow-gauge railroad, museums, shops, entertainment; 1890 melodramas. Also restaurants, motel; riding stables and a petting zoo. (Daily) Sr citizen rate. Phone 875-4191. ¢¢¢

17. **Scenic Airlines.** Sightseeing flights through Grand Canyon in 19-seat aircraft; panoramic, nontinted windows for undistorted color photography. Service from Las Vegas (daily). Contact 241 E Reno Ave, 89119; 739-1900.

18. **Gray Line bus tours.** Tours of southern Nevada and Utah and northern Arizona. For information contact 1550 S Industrial Rd, 89102; 384-1234.

Annual Events

Helldorado Festival. Rodeos, parades, beauty contest. Don western garb. Mid–late May.

Las Vegas Invitational. PGA tournament with more than $1 million in prize money. Oct.

National Finals Rodeo. Thomas and Mack Center. Nation's richest professional rodeo, featuring 15 finalists in 7 rodeo disciplines. Dec.

Additional Visitor Information

Information may be obtained from the Las Vegas Convention/Visitors Authority, located at the Convention Center, 3150 Paradise Rd, 89109, phone 892-0711

(See Boulder City, Henderson)

Motels

(Note on accommodations: Rates are likely to vary upward in Las Vegas at peak occupancy and sometimes a minimum of three days occupancy is required. In addition, minimum rates quoted are generally available only from Sun through Tues, sometimes on Wed, rarely on holidays. This is *not* true of all accommodations but is true of many. We urge you to check the rate on any room you occupy and to make certain no other special conditions apply. Show reservations are available at most accommodations.)

✔ ★**ARIZONA CHARLIE'S.** *740 S Decatur Ave (89107), west of the Strip. 702/258-5200; res: 800/342-2695.* 100 rms, 3 story. S, D $28–$45; higher rates conventions. Crib free. TV. Pool; poolside serv, lifeguard. Restaurant open 24 hrs. Bar. Ck-out noon. Bellhops. Valet serv. Gift shop. Casino. Cr cds: A, C, D, DS, MC, V.

D ⓐ ⊠ ⊗ ⓞ

★★**BEST WESTERN McCARRAN INN.** *4970 Paradise Rd (89119), near McCarran Intl Airport, east of the Strip. 702/798-5530; FAX 702/798-7627.* 97 rms, 3 story. S, D $40–$57; each addl $7; suites

$65–$75; under 12 free; higher rates: national hols, major events. Crib $8. TV. Pool. Complimentary bkfst. Restaurant nearby. Coin lndry. Ck-out noon. Meeting rms. Free daytime airport transportation. Cr cds: A, C, D, DS, ER, MC, V, JCB.

[D] [≈] [✕] [⊘] [◎] [SC]

✔ ★CENTER STRIP INN. *3688 Las Vegas Blvd S (89109), on the Strip.* 702/739-6066; *res:* 800/777-7737; *FAX* 702/736-2521. 92 rms, 2 story, 46 suites. S, D $29.95–$89.95; each addl $6; suites $59–$125; under 16 free. Crib free. TV; in-rm movies. Pool. Complimentary continental bkfst. Restaurant adj open 24 hrs. Ck-out noon. Refrigerators. Cr cds: A, C, D, DS, ER, MC, V, JCB.

[≈] [⊘] [◎] [SC]

★COMFORT INN. *211 E Flamingo Rd (89109), east of the Strip.* 702/733-7800; *FAX* 702/733-7353. 120 rms, 2 story. S, D $45–$85; under 17 free. TV; cable. Pool. Complimentary continental bkfst. Restaurant adj open 24 hrs. Ck-out 11 am. Cr cds: A, C, D, DS, MC, V.

[≈] [⊘] [◎] [SC]

★COMFORT INN-AIRPORT. *5075 Koval Lane (89119), near McCarran Intl Airport, east of the Strip.* 702/736-3600. 106 rms, 2 story. S, D $38–$90; under 18 free. Crib free. TV; cable. Pool. Complimentary continental bkfst, coffee. Restaurant adj open 24 hrs. Ck-out 11 am. Cr cds: A, C, D, DS, ER, MC, V, JCB.

[D] [≈] [✕] [⊘] [◎] [SC]

✔ ★DAYS INN. *707 E Fremont (89101).* 702/388-1400; *FAX* 702/388-9622. 146 units, 3 story, 7 suites. Feb–Nov: S $28–$100; D $32–$100; each addl $10; suites $60–$150; under 18 free; lower rates rest of yr. Crib free. TV. Pool. Restaurant open 24 hrs. Ck-out noon. Cr cds: A, C, D, DS, MC, V, JCB.

[≈] [⊘] [◎] [SC]

★★FAIRFIELD INN BY MARRIOTT. *3850 Paradise Rd (89109), near McCarran Intl Airport, east of the Strip.* 702/791-0899. 129 rms, 4 story. S $43.95–$49.95; D $50.95–$56.95; each addl $9; under 18 free. Crib free. TV; cable. Heated pool; whirlpool. Complimentary continental bkfst, coffee in lobby. Restaurant adj 7 am–10 pm. Ck-out noon. Meeting rms. Free airport transportation. Cr cds: A, C, D, DS, MC, V.

[D] [≈] [✕] [⊘] [◎] [SC]

★LA QUINTA MOTOR INN. *3782 Las Vegas Blvd S (89109), on the Strip.* 702/739-7457. 114 rms, 3 story. S $45–$62; D $53–$70; each addl $8; under 18 free. Crib free. TV; cable. Heated pool. Restaurant nearby. Ck-out noon. Free airport transportation. Cr cds: A, C, D, DS, MC, V.

[D] [≈] [⊘] [◎] [SC]

★★RESIDENCE INN BY MARRIOTT. *3225 Paradise Rd (89109), near McCarran Intl Airport, east of the Strip.* 702/796-9300. 192 kit. suites, 1–2 story. S $90–$119; D $120–$165; family rates. Crib free. Pet accepted, some restrictions; $40–$60 deposit and $7 per day. TV. Heated pool; whirlpool. Complimentary continental bkfst. Complimentary coffee in rms. Restaurant adj 6:30 am–9 pm. Ck-out noon. Coin lndry. Meeting rms. Free airport transportation. Lighted tennis. Balconies. Picnic tables, grills. Cr cds: A, C, D, DS, MC, V, JCB.

[D] [🐾] [✐] [≈] [✗] [✕] [⊘] [◎] [SC]

★★RODEWAY INN. *3786 Las Vegas Blvd S (89109), on the Strip.* 702/736-1434; *FAX* 702/736-6058. 97 rms, 2 story. S, D $46–$95; under 17 free; suites $75–$150. Crib free. Pet accepted, some restrictions; $10. TV. Heated pool. Coffee in rms. Restaurant adj open 24 hrs. Ck-out noon. Valet serv. Cr cds: A, C, D, DS, ER, MC, V, JCB.

[🐾] [≈] [⊘] [◎] [SC]

✔ ★TRAVELODGE-LAS VEGAS DOWNTOWN. *2028 E Fremont St (89101).* 702/384-7540; *FAX* 702/384-0408. 58 rms, 2 story. S $30–$50; D $30–$55; each addl $5; family rates. Crib free. TV; cable. Heated pool. Complimentary coffee in rms. Restaurant nearby. Ck-out noon. Cr cds: A, C, D, DS, ER, MC, V, JCB.

[≈] [⊘] [◎] [SC]

Motor Hotels

★★COURTYARD BY MARRIOTT. *3275 Paradise Rd (89109), near McCarran Intl Airport, east of the Strip.* 702/791-3600; *FAX* 702/796-7981. 149 rms, 3 story, 12 suites. Sept–mid-Dec: S $82–$110; D $92–$120; each addl $10; under 16 free; higher rates: conventions, hol wkends; lower rates rest of yr. Crib free. TV; cable. Heated pool. Complimentary coffee in rms. Restaurant 6:30 am–2 pm, 5–10 pm. Bar 4–11 pm. Ck-out 1 pm. Coin lndry. Meeting rms. Valet serv. Free airport transportation. Exercise equipt; weights, bicycles, whirlpool. Some refrigerators. Balconies. Cr cds: A, C, D, DS, MC, V.

[D] [≈] [✗] [✕] [⊘] [◎] [SC]

★★HOLIDAY INN (formerly Emerald Springs Inn). *325 E Flamingo Rd (89109), near McCarran Intl Airport, east of the Strip.* 702/732-9100; *FAX* 702/731-9784. 150 units, 3 story, 117 suites. Mid-Sept–May: S, D $69–$175; each addl $15; suites $95–$165; under 19 free; higher rates: hols, major conventions; lower rates rest of yr. Crib free. TV; cable. Heated pool; whirlpool, poolside serv. Complimentary full bkfst. Complimentary coffee in rms. Restaurant 6:30 am–10 pm. Bar 4 pm–2 am. Ck-out noon. Meeting rms. Concierge. Free airport, casino transportation. Health club privileges. Refrigerators. Wet bars. Cr cds: A, C, D, DS, MC, V, JCB.

[D] [≈] [✕] [⊘] [◎] [SC]

★★SHEFFIELD INN. *3970 Paradise Rd (89109), near McCarran Intl Airport, east of the Strip.* 702/796-9000. 228 units, 3 story, 171 kits. S, D $98; kits. $98–$200; under 18 free. Crib free. TV; cable, in-rm movies. Pool. Complimentary continental bkfst. Ck-out noon. Coin lndry. Meeting rms. Bellhops. Valet serv. Free airport transportation. In-rm whirlpools. Refrigerators. Private patios, balconies. Cr cds: A, C, D, DS, ER, MC, V.

[D] [≈] [✕] [⊘] [◎] [SC]

✔ ★WESTWARD HO HOTEL & CASINO. *2900 Las Vegas Blvd S (89109), on the Strip.* 702/731-2900; *res:* 800/634-6803 (exc NV). 777 rms, 2–4 story. S, D $37–$67; each addl $15; 2-bedrm apt $81–$111; package plan. Crib $15. TV. 4 pools, 1 heated; whirlpools. Restaurant open 24 hrs. Rm serv. Bars open 24 hrs; entertainment. Ck-out 11 am. Free airport transportation. Some refrigerators. Casino. Cr cds: MC, V.

[D] [≈] [◎]

Hotels

★★★ALEXIS PARK RESORT. *(Box 95698, 89109) 375 E Harmon Ave, near McCarran Intl Airport, 1 mi E of the Strip.* 702/796-3300; *res:* 800/582-2228 (exc NV); *FAX* 702/796-4334. 500 suites, 2 story. 1-bedrm $85–$500; 2-bedrm $475–$1,150; each addl $15; under 18 free. Crib free. Pet accepted, some restrictions; $15. TV; cable. 3 heated pools; poolside serv. Restaurant 6–11 pm (also see PEGASUS). Bar 10–1 am; entertainment. Ck-out noon. Convention facilities. Concierge. Gift shop. Barber, beauty shop. Lighted tennis, pro. Golf privileges nearby. Putting green. Exercise equipt; weights, bicycles, whirlpool, sauna, steam rm. Refrigerators, minibars; some bathrm phones, in-rm whirlpools. Cr cds: A, C, D, DS, MC, V, JCB.

[D] [🐾] [🏌] [✐] [≈] [✗] [✕] [⊘] [◎]

★★BALLY'S. *3645 Las Vegas Blvd S (89109), on the Strip.* 702/739-4111; *res:* 800/634-3434; *FAX* 702/794-2413. 2,813 rms, 26 story. S, D $86–$180; each addl $15; suites $180–$1,500; under 18 free; package plans. Crib free. TV. Heated pool; whirlpool, sauna, poolside serv. Restaurant, bar open 24 hrs; entertainment. Ck-out 11 am. Convention facilities. Shopping arcade. Barber, beauty shop. Lighted tennis, pro. Game rm. Some bathrm phones, refrigerators. Casino, wedding chapel. Cr cds: A, C, D, DS, MC, V, JCB.

[D] [✐] [≈] [⊘] [◎]

★★BARBARY COAST. *3595 Las Vegas Blvd S (89109), on the Strip.* 702/737-7111; *res:* 800/634-6755 (exc NV); *FAX* 702/737-6304. 200 rms, 8 story. S, D $50–$75; each addl $5; suites $200–$300;

under 12 free. TV; cable. Restaurant, bar open 24 hrs. Ck-out noon. Gift shop. Free valet, covered parking. Casino. Cr cds: A, C, D, DS, MC, V, JCB.

D 🚭 ⌚

★ ★ ★ ★ **CAESARS PALACE.** *3570 Las Vegas Blvd S (89109), 1 blk E of I-15 Dunes/Flamingo exit, on the Strip. 702/731-7110; res: 800/634-6001 (exc NV); FAX 702/731-6636.* 1,518 rms, 14–22 story. S $95–$160; D $110–$175; each addl $15; suites $170–$875; under 13 free. TV; cable. 2 heated pools; lifeguard. Restaurant, bars open 24 hrs (also see PALACE COURT and SPAGO). Circus Maximus, star entertainment; dancing. Ck-out noon. Convention facilities. Concierge. Shopping arcade. Barber, beauty shop. Parking free. Tennis, pro. Exercise rm; instructor, weight machines, bicycles, whirlpool, sauna, steam rm. Massage. Solarium. Racquetball. Handball, squash courts. Game rm. Casino. Omnimax Theater: movies. Bathrm phones; many whirlpools; some refrigerators. Many bi-level suites with wet bar. Cr cds: A, C, D, DS, MC, V, JCB.

D 🏌 🏊 🏃 🍷 🚭 ⌚

✔ ★ ★ **CALIFORNIA HOTEL & CASINO.** *(PO Box 630, 89125) 1st & Ogden Aves, I-95 Casino Center exit. 702/385-1222; res: 800/634-6255.* 635 rms, 9–11 story. S, D $40–$60; each addl $5; under 12 free; package plans. Crib free. TV. Pool. Restaurant, bar open 24 hrs; dining rms 5:30–11 pm. Ck-out noon. Gift shop. Refrigerators; some wet bars. Casino. Cr cds: A, D, DS, MC, V.

D 🏊 ⌚

★ ★ **CARRIAGE HOUSE.** *105 E Harmon Ave (89109), east of the Strip. 702/798-1020; FAX 702/798-1020, ext 112.* 150 kit. suites, 9 story. S, D $85–$190; children free; wkly rates; higher rates: special events, hols. Crib free. TV; cable. Heated pool; whirlpool. Complimentary coffee in rms. Restaurant 7–10 am, 5–11 pm. Bar 5–11 pm; entertainment. Ck-out 11 am. Coin lndry. Free airport, casino transportation. Tennis. Cr cds: A, D, DS, ER, MC, V.

🏌 🏊 🚭 ⌚ SC

✔ ★ ★ **CIRCUS-CIRCUS HOTEL & CASINO.** *(Box 14967, 89114) 2880 Las Vegas Blvd S, on the Strip. 702/734-0410; res: 800/634-3450; FAX 702/734-5897.* 2,800 rms, 3–29 story. S, D $19–$49; each addl $6; suites $45–$100; under 12 free. Crib $6. TV. 2 heated pools; poolside serv, lifeguard. Restaurants, bars open 24 hrs; entertainment. Ck-out 11 am. Shopping arcade. Barber, beauty shop. Casino, performing circus and midway housed together in tent-like structure. Cr cds: A, C, D, DS, MC, V.

D 🏊 🚭 ⌚

★ ★ **DESERT INN.** *(Box 14577, 89109) 3145 Las Vegas Blvd S, on the Strip. 702/733-4444; res: 800/634-6906 (exc NV); FAX 702/733-4774.* 821 rms, 2–14 story. S, D $90–$175; each addl $15; suites $250–$1,500. Crib free. TV; cable. Heated pool; poolside serv, lifeguard. Restaurant (see MONTE CARLO). Rm serv 24 hrs. Bars open 24 hrs; Crystal Room, theater, star entertainment. Ck-out noon. Convention facilities. Concierge. Shopping arcade. Barber, beauty shop. Free valet parking. Lighted tennis, pro. 18-hole golf, greens fee, putting green, driving range. Exercise rm; instructor, weights, bicycles, whirlpool, sauna, steam rm. Wet bar in suites; bathrm phones, refrigerators. Private patios, balconies, 10 whirlpools. Casino. Resort hotel on 160 acres. Cr cds: A, C, D, DS, MC, V, JCB.

D 🏌 🏌 🏊 🏃 🏃 🍷 🚭 ⌚

✔ ★ **EL CORTEZ.** *(Box 680, 89125) 600 E Fremont St. 702/385-5200; res: 800/634-6703.* 308 rms, 15 story. S, D $23–$40; each addl $3. Crib free. TV. Restaurant 4:30–11 pm. Rm serv 7 am–7 pm. Bar open 24 hrs. Ck-out noon. Meeting rms. Shopping arcade. Barber, beauty shop. Free valet parking. Casino. Cr cds: A, C, D, DS, MC, V, JCB.

D 🚭 ⌚

★ ★ **EXCALIBUR.** *3850 Las Vegas Blvd S (89119), on the Strip. 702/597-7777; res: 800/937-7777.* 4,032 rms, 28 story. S, D $39–$85; each addl $7; suites $110; higher rates: wkends, hols. Crib $7.

TV. 2 heated pools; poolside serv, lifeguard. Restaurants open 24 hrs. Dinner theater. Limited rm serv. Bar open 24 hrs; entertainment. Ck-out 11 am. Shopping arcade. Barber, beauty shop. Whirlpool in suites. Casino. Castle-like structure with medieval/old English interiors based upon legend of King Arthur and Round Table. Cr cds: A, C, D, DS, MC, V.

D 🏊 🚭 ⌚

★ ★ **FOUR QUEENS.** *(Box 370, 89125) 202 E Fremont, at Casino Center Blvd. 702/385-4011; res: 800/634-6045; FAX 702/383-0631.* 700 rms, 19 story. S, D $47–$59; each addl $8; suites $85–$95; under 12 free. TV. Restaurant open 24 hrs; dining rm 6 pm–midnight. Bar; entertainment, jazz Mon evenings. Ck-out noon. Meeting rms. Garage parking. Wet bar in suites. Casino. Cr cds: A, C, D, DS, MC, V.

D 🚭 ⌚ SC

★ **FREMONT.** *200 E Fremont St (89125). 702/385-3232; res: 800/634-6182.* 452 rms, 14 story. S, D $36–$60; package plan. TV. Restaurant, bars open 24 hrs. Ck-out noon. Gift shop. Casino. Cr cds: A, C, D, DS, MC, V, JCB.

🚭 ⌚

✔ ★ ★ **GOLD COAST.** *4000 W Flamingo Rd (89103), at Valley View Blvd, west of the Strip. 702/367-7111; res: 800/331-5334; FAX 702/367-8575.* 722 rms, 10 story. S, D $35–$50; suites $100–$400; family rates; package plan. TV. Pool. Supervised child's activities. Restaurant, bar open 24 hrs; entertainment, dancing. Ck-out noon. Convention facilities. Barber, beauty shop. Free valet parking. Game rm. Bowling. Some bathrm phones. Casino. Movie theaters. Cr cds: A, C, D, DS, ER, MC, V, JCB.

D 🚭 ⌚

★ ★ ★ ★ **GOLDEN NUGGET.** *(Box 610, 89125) 129 E Fremont St, at Casino Center. 702/385-7111; res: 800/634-3454 (exc NV); FAX 702/386-8362.* 1,907 rms, 18–22 story. S, D $58–$150; each addl $12; under 12 free; suites, minisuites $210–$750. Crib free. TV; cable. Heated pool; poolside serv, lifeguard. Restaurant open 24 hrs (also see LILY LANGTRY'S). Bar; entertainment. Ck-out noon. Meeting rms. Gift shop. Barber, beauty shop. Exercise rm; instructor, weight machines, bicycles, whirlpool, sauna, steam rm. Massage. Casino. Some bathrm phones. Cr cds: A, C, D, DS, MC, V.

D 🏊 🏃 🚭 ⌚

✔ ★ **HACIENDA RESORT.** *(Box 98506, 89114) 3950 Las Vegas Blvd S, on the Strip. 702/739-8911; res: 800/634-6713 (exc NV); FAX 702/798-8289.* 1,140 rms, 2–11 story. S, D $28–$78; each addl $10; suites $125–$350; lower rates June–Aug, Dec. Crib free. TV. Pool; poolside serv, lifeguard. Restaurants, bar open 24 hrs; entertainment. Ck-out 11 am. Convention center. Shopping arcade. Barber, beauty shop. Free valet parking. Lighted tennis, pro. Game rm. Some refrigerators. Casino. Full-serv RV park. Cr cds: A, C, D, DS, MC, V.

D 🏌 🏊 🚭 ⌚

★ ★ ★ **HARRAH'S.** *3475 Las Vegas Blvd S (89109), on the Strip. 702/369-5000; FAX 702/369-6014.* 1,725 rms, 35 story. Feb–May, Sept–Nov, last wk Dec: S, D $69–$89; each addl $10; suites $190–$355; under 12 free; higher rates special events; lower rates rest of yr. Crib free. TV; cable. Pool; poolside serv, lifeguard. Restaurant, bar open 24 hrs; entertainment exc Sun. Ck-out noon. Coin lndry. Convention facilities. Shopping arcade. Barber, beauty shop. Valet parking; covered parking free. Exercise equipt; weights, bicycles, whirlpool, sauna. Game rm. Balconies. Casino. Cr cds: A, C, D, DS, MC, V, JCB.

D 🏊 🏃 🚭 ⌚

★ ★ **HILTON.** *(Box 15087, 89114) 3000 Paradise Rd, east of the Strip. 702/732-5111; FAX 702/794-3611.* 3,174 rms, 30 story. S, D $85–$205; each addl $20; 1–2 bedrm suites from $295; lanai suites $275–$295. Crib free. TV. Rooftop heated pool; poolside serv, lifeguard. Restaurant, bars open 24 hrs; 13 dining rms; dancing; star entertainment. Ck-out noon. Convention facilities. Shopping arcade. Barber, beauty shop. Free valet parking. 8½-acre recreation deck includes lighted tennis, pro. Golf privileges, greens fee $80, putting green. Exercise equipt; weights, bicycles, whirlpool, sauna. Game rm. Some bathrm phones, refrigerators. Private patios, balconies. Casino. Cr cds: A, C, D, DS, MC, V, JCB.

[D] [icons]

★ ★ ★HILTON FLAMINGO. *3555 Las Vegas Blvd S (89109), on the Strip. 702/733-3111; res: 800/732-2111 (exc NV); FAX 702/733-3528.* 3,527 rms, 28 story. S, D $63–$133; each addl $16; suites $200–$440; family rates; package plan; lower rates Dec–Jan. Crib free. TV; cable. 2 pools; poolside serv, lifeguard. Restaurant, bar open 24 hrs; stage show, dancing. Ck-out noon. Convention center. Concierge. Shopping arcade. Barber, beauty shop. Free valet parking. Tennis privileges. Exercise equipt; weight machines, bicycles, whirlpools, sauna, steam rm. Some bathrm phones. Refrigerators avail. Casino. Cr cds: A, C, D, DS, ER, MC, V, JCB.

[D] [icons]

★ ★HOWARD JOHNSON PLAZA SUITES. *4255 Paradise Rd (89109), near McCarran Intl Airport, east of the Strip. 702/369-2400; FAX 702/369-3770.* 202 suites, 6 story. S, D $95–$250; each addl $15; under 18 free. Crib free. TV; cable. Heated pool; poolside serv. Complimentary coffee in rms. Restaurant 6 am–2 pm, 5–10 pm. Bar 11 am–midnight. Ck-out noon. Meeting rms. Concierge. Gift shop. Free airport transportation. Exercise equipt; weights, bicycles, whirlpool, sauna. Minibars. Cr cds: A, C, D, DS, ER, MC, V, JCB.

[D] [icons]

★IMPERIAL PALACE. *3535 Las Vegas Blvd S (89109), on the Strip. 702/731-3311; res: 800/634-6441 (exc NV), 800/351-7400 (NV); FAX 702/735-8528.* 2,700 rms, 19 story. S, D $45–$125; each addl $12; suites $105–$325; package plan; higher rates hols. Crib $12. TV. Heated pool; whirlpool, poolside serv, lifeguard. Restaurant, bar open 24 hrs; entertainment. Ck-out noon. Convention facilities. Shopping arcade. Barber, beauty shop. Free valet, covered parking. Some bathrm phones, refrigerators. Private balconies. Casino. Antique auto exhibit. Cr cds: A, C, D, DS, MC, V.

[D] [icons]

★ ★LADY LUCK CASINO. *206 N 3rd St (89101). 702/477-3000; res: 800/523-9582; FAX 702/477-3002.* 791 rms, 17 & 25 story. Feb–Mar & Sept–Oct: S, D $45–$150; suites $60–$200; package plans; lower rates rest of yr. TV; cable. Pool. Restaurant, bar open 24 hrs. Ck-out noon. Free garage parking. Refrigerators. Casino. Cr cds: A, C, D, DS, MC, V, JCB.

[D] [icons]

★ ★ ★MIRAGE. *3400 Las Vegas Blvd S (89109), on the Strip. 702/791-7111; res 800/627-6667; FAX 702/791-7446.* 3,049 rms, 30 story. S, D $79–$259; each addl $15; suites $300–$3,000; under 12 free. Crib free. TV; cable. 2 heated pools. Restaurant open 24 hrs. Bar; entertainment, dancing. Ck-out noon. Convention facilities. Concierge. Shopping arcade. Barber, beauty shop. Valet parking. 18-hole golf, driving range. Exercise rm; instructor, weights, bicycles. Bathrm phone, refrigerator, wet bar in suites. Casino. Atrium features tropical rain forest; behind front desk is 20,000-gallon aquarium with sharks and tropical fish. On 100 acres with dolphin and white tiger habitats. Cr cds: A, C, D, DS, ER, MC, V.

[D] [icons]

✔ ★ ★ ★PALACE STATION HOTEL & CASINO. *2411 W Sahara (89102), at I-15, west of the Strip. 702/367-2411; res: 800/634-3101 (exc NV).* 1,028 rms, 21 story. S, D $39–$99; each addl $10; suites $150–$750; under 12 free. Crib free. TV; cable. 2 heated pools; whirlpools. Restaurants, bars open 24 hrs; entertainment. Ck-out noon. Gift shop. Garage parking. Game rm. Casino, bingo. Cr cds: A, C, D, DS, ER, MC, V.

[D] [icons] SC

★ ★RAMADA-SAN REMO. *115 E Tropicana Ave (89109), near McCarran Intl Airport, east of the Strip. 702/739-9000; FAX 702/736-1120.* 711 rms, 18 story, 45 suites. S, D $55–$125; each addl $10; suites $75–$350; under 18 free; higher rates: hols, conventions. Crib $10. TV. Heated pool; poolside serv. Restaurant open 24 hrs, dining rm

5–11 pm. Bar; entertainment. Ck-out noon. Meeting rms. Gift shop. Free garage parking. Balconies. Casino. Cr cds: A, C, D, DS, ER, MC, V, JCB.

[D] [icons] SC

★ ★ ★RIO SUITE HOTEL & CASINO. *(Box 14160, 89114) I-15 at Flamingo Rd, west of the Strip. 702/252-7777; res: 800/PLAY-RIO; FAX 702/252-7670.* 424 suites, 20 story. Suites $85–$101; under 12 free; mid-wk rates. Crib free. TV; cable. Heated pool. Complimentary coffee in rms. Restaurant open 24 hrs, dining rm 5–11 pm. Bar; entertainment. Ck-out noon. Convention facilities. Concierge. Shopping arcade. Barber, beauty shop. Exercise equipt; weights, bicycles. Refrigerators. Building facade of red and blue glass trimmed in neon. Casino. Cr cds: A, C, D, MC, V.

[D] [icons] SC

★ ★RIVIERA. *(Box 14528, 89109) 2901 Las Vegas Blvd S, on the Strip. 702/734-5110; res: 800/634-6753 (exc NV); FAX 702/794-9663.* 2,100 rms, 2–24 story. S, D $59–$95; each addl $12; suites $125–$500; under 12 free; package plan. Crib free. TV; cable. Heated pool; poolside serv, lifeguard. Restaurant, bar open 24 hrs; Versailles Room, name entertainment. Ck-out noon. Convention facilities. Shopping arcade. Barber, beauty shop. Lighted tennis. Exercise equipt; weights, bicycles, whirlpool, sauna, steam rm. Some refrigerators. Bathrm phone in some suites. Some balconies. Casino. Cr cds: A, C, D, MC, V, JCB.

[D] [icons]

★ ★SAHARA. *2535 Las Vegas Blvd S (89109), on the Strip. 702/737-2111; res: 800/634-6666; FAX 702/791-2027.* 2,035 rms, 2–27 story. S, D $55–$95; each addl $10; suites $200–$300; under 12 free; package plans. Crib $10. TV. 2 pools, heated; poolside serv, lifeguard. Restaurant, bar open 24 hrs. Congo Theatre, star entertainment & revue, dancing. Ck-out noon. Convention facilities. Shopping arcade. Barber, beauty shop. Free covered parking. Many bathrm phones. Private patios, balconies. Casino. Cr cds: A, C, D, DS, MC, V.

[D] [icons] SC

✔ ★ ★SAM'S TOWN. *(Box 12001, 89122) 5111 Boulder Hwy, at E Flamingo Rd & Nellis Blvd, east of the Strip. 702/456-7777; res: 800/634-6371.* 197 rms, 3 story. S, D $28–$40; each addl $5; suites $90–$100; under 12 free; higher rates wkends; package plan. Crib free. TV. Heated pool. Restaurant, bar open 24 hrs; entertainment, dancing. Ck-out noon. Shopping arcade. Casino. Cr cds: A, C, D, DS, MC, V.

[D] [icons]

★ ★SANDS. *3355 Las Vegas Blvd (89109). 800/634-6901; FAX 702/733-5620.* 715 rms, 18 story. S $29–$109; D $59–$109; suites $150–$1,500; under 12 free. Heated pool; poolside serv, lifeguard. Restaurant 10–1 am. Rm serv 24 hrs. Ck-out noon. Coin lndry. Convention facilities. Concierge. Shopping arcade. Barber, beauty shop. Airport, RR station transportation. Exercise rm; instructor, weights, bicycles, whirlpool. Health club privileges. Lawn games. Many refrigerators. Balconies. Cr cds: A, C, D, DS, ER, MC, V.

[D] [icons]

✔ ★ ★SANTA FE HOTEL & CASINO. *4949 N Rancho Dr (89130). 702/658-4900; res: 800/872-6823; FAX 702/658-4919.* 200 rms, 4 story. S, D $36–$50; each addl $5; under 13 free; higher rates some hols. TV; cable. Free supervised child's activities. Restaurant open 24 hrs. Bar; entertainment. Ck-out noon. Meeting rm. Gift shop. Downhill/x-country ski 20 mi. Game rm. Bowling lanes. Ice rink. Cr cds: A, C, D, DS, MC, V.

[D] [icons]

✔ ★ ★SHOWBOAT. *2800 E Fremont St (89104). 702/385-9123; res: 800/826-2800 (exc NV); FAX 702/383-9238.* 484 rms, 19 story. S, D $26–$85; each addl $5; suites $85–$255; under 12 free. Crib $5. TV. Heated pool; lifeguard. Restaurants, bar open 24 hrs. Ck-out noon. Meeting rms. Gift shop. Barber, beauty shop. Free airport, RR station, bus depot transportation. Game rm. Casino; bingo parlor. 106-lane bowling. Cr cds: A, C, D, MC, V.

[D] [icons]

★★STARDUST RESORT & CASINO. 3000 Las Vegas Blvd S (89109), on the Strip. 702/732-6111; res: 800/634-6757; FAX 702/732-6296. 2,341 rms, 2-32 story. Jan-May, Oct-Nov: S, D $24-$100; suites $150-$225. Crib free. TV. 2 pools; lifeguard, poolside serv. Restaurants, bar open 24 hrs; entertainment. Ck-out noon. Convention facilities. Shopping arcade. Barber, beauty shop. Game rm. Some bathrm phones, refrigerators. Some private patios, balconies. Casino. Cr cds: A, C, D, DS, ER, MC, V, JCB.

D 🖾 🛇 ⊘

★★TROPICANA. 3801 Las Vegas Blvd S (89109), near McCarran Intl Airport, on the Strip. 702/739-2222; res: 800/634-4000 (exc NV); FAX 702/739-2469. 1,900 rms, 22 story. S, D $55-$129; each addl $10. TV. Pool; poolside serv, lifeguard. Restaurant, bar open 24 hrs; Tiffany Theatre, entertainment. Ck-out noon. Convention facilities. Concierge. Shopping arcade. Barber, beauty shop. Exercise equipt; weights, bicycles, whirlpool, sauna. Some bathrm phones, refrigerators. Private patios, balconies. Casino. Cr cds: A, C, D, DS, MC, V, JCB.

D 🖾 🛉 ✈ 🛇 ⊘ SC

Restaurants

✔★★ALPINE VILLAGE INN/RATHSKELLER. 3003 Paradise Rd, 1 blk east of the Strip. 702/734-6888. Hrs: 5-11 pm. Res accepted. German, Swiss menu. Bar. Semi-a la carte: dinner $3.75-$15.50. Complete meals: dinner $9.50-$18.50. Child's meals. Specialties: Bavarian chicken supreme soup, sauerbraten, Wienerschnitzel, fondue Bourguignonne. Valet parking. Alpine chalet decor. Family-owned. Cr cds: A, C, D, DS, MC, V.

D

★★★ANDRE'S. 401 S 6th St. 702/385-5016. Hrs: 6-11 pm. Closed major hols; also 3-4 wks July. Res accepted. French menu. Bar. Wine cellar. A la carte entrees: dinner $19-$32. Specializes in fresh fish, duck, pastries. Own baking. Valet parking. Outdoor dining. Country French decor. No jeans. Cr cds: A, C, D, MC, V.

D

★BATTISTA'S HOLE IN THE WALL. 4041 Audrie St, east of the Strip. 702/732-1424. Hrs: 4:30-11 pm. Closed Thanksgiving; also 15 days mid-Dec. Res accepted. Italian menu. Bar. Complete meals: dinner $12.95-$26.95. Specializes in fresh pasta, Battista-style cioppino. Parking. Warm, casual atmosphere. Family-owned. Cr cds: A, C, D, DS, MC, V.

D

✔★CAFE MILANO. 3900 Paradise Rd. 702/732-2777. Hrs: 11 am-3 pm, 5-10 pm. Closed Sun. Res accepted. Italian menu. Wine. Semi-a la carte: lunch $4.95-$12.50, dinner $9.50-$19.95. Parking. Outdoor dining. Cr cds: C, D, DS, ER, MC, V.

D

✔★CHAPALA. 2101 S Decatur Blvd, in shopping center. 702/871-7805. Hrs: 11 am-11 pm; Fri, Sat to midnight. Closed Jan 1, Thanksgiving, Dec 25. Res accepted. Mexican menu. Bar. Semi-a la carte: lunch, dinner $3.25-$10. Specialties: fajitas, enchilada ranchero. Cr cds: MC, V.

D

★★★CHIN'S. 3200 Las Vegas Blvd S, on the Strip. 702/733-8899. Hrs: 11 am-10 pm; Sun from noon. Closed Thanksgiving, Dec 24 & 25. Res accepted. Cantonese menu. Bar. Wine cellar. A la carte entrees: lunch $7.95-$10.95, dinner $12-$28. Complete meals: lunch $12-$15, dinner $27.50-$50. Specialties: Chin's beef, strawberry chicken, shrimp puffs, crispy pudding. Valet parking. Cr cds: A, MC, V.

D

★★★CIPRIANI. 2790 E Flamingo Rd. 702/369-6711. Hrs: 11:30 am-2 pm, 6-10:30 pm; Sat from 6 pm. Closed Thanksgiving, Dec 25. Res accepted. Italian menu. Serv bar. Semi-a la carte: lunch $5.90-$12, dinner $10.95-$34. Complete meals: dinner $49.95. Specialties: scaloppina Monte Bianco, medallion of beef Piemontese, grilled

seafood. Harpist Fri, Sat. Parking. Florentine atmosphere. Cr cds: A, C, D, DS, MC, V.

D

✔★COUNTRY INN. 1401 Rainbow Blvd. 702/254-0520. Hrs: 7 am-10 pm; wkends to 11 pm. Closed Dec 25. Wine, beer. Semi-a la carte: bkfst $2.25-$6.95, lunch, dinner $3.25-$13.95. Specializes in turkey, fish, steak. Parking. Cr cds: A, C, D, DS, MC, V.

D

★DI MARTINO'S. 2797 S Maryland Pkwy. 702/732-1817. Hrs: 4:30-10 pm. Closed some major hols. Res accepted. Italian menu. Bar. Complete meals: dinner $7.95-$18.95. Child's meals. Specializes in ravioli, cavatelli, Italian cheesecake. Stained-glass windows, Tiffany-style lamps. Cr cds: A, MC, V.

★★GOLDEN STEER STEAK HOUSE. 308 W Sahara Ave, west of the Strip. 702/384-4470. Hrs: 5 pm-midnight. Closed Thanksgiving, Dec 25. Res accepted. Bar. Semi-a la carte: dinner $20-$34. Specializes in steak, seafood, Italian specialties. Valet parking. 1890s Western decor. Family-owned. Cr cds: A, C, D, DS, MC, V.

D

★★★LILY LANGTRY'S. (See Golden Nugget Hotel) 702/385-7111. Hrs: 6-11 pm. Res accepted. Cantonese menu. Bar. Wine cellar. A la carte entrees: dinner $10-$26. Specialties: lobster Cantonese, Chinese pepper steak, Szechwan shrimp, moo goo gai pan. Own baking. Valet parking. Oriental decor. Cr cds: A, C, D, DS, MC, V, JCB.

D

★★MARRAKECH. 3900 Paradise Rd. 702/737-5611. Hrs: 5:30-11 pm. Closed Dec 25. Res accepted. Moroccan menu. Bar. Complete meal: dinner $23.95. Child's meals. Specialty: shrimp scampi. Belly dancers. Valet parking. Colorful French Moroccan decor. Cr cds: A, MC, V.

D

★★★MONTE CARLO. (See Desert Inn Hotel) 702/733-4524 or 733-4525. Hrs: 6-11 pm. Closed Tues, Wed. Res required. French menu. Serv bar. Wine cellar. Semi-a la carte: dinner $25-$35. Specializes in boneless roast duckling, stuffed veal chop, quail, sea bass Kiev. Own baking. Valet parking. Elegant decor reminiscent of 18th-century France, Palace of Versailles; murals by Evans & Brown. Jacket. Cr cds: A, C, D, DS, MC, V, JCB.

D

★★★PALACE COURT. (See Caesars Palace Hotel) 702/731-7110. Hrs: 6-11 pm. Res required. French, continental menu. Extensive wine list. A la carte entrees: dinner $28-$55. Specializes in French gourmet dishes, lobster, veal. Own baking; own smoked salmon. Valet parking. Stained-glass dome ceiling. Jacket. Cr cds: A, C, D, MC, V.

D

★★★PEGASUS. (See Alexis Park Resort Hotel) 702/796-3300. Hrs: 6-11 pm. Res accepted. French, continental menu. Bar. Wine list. A la carte entrees: dinner $13.50-$75. Specialties: lobster Princess, médaillons de veau. Classical guitarist. Valet parking. Italian crystal chandelier; arched windows overlooking waterfall and garden. Jacket. Cr cds: A, C, D, DS, MC, V.

D

★★PHILIPS SUPPER HOUSE. 4545 W Sahara. 702/873-5222. Hrs: 5-11 pm; early-bird dinner 4:30-6:30 pm. Res accepted. Continental menu. Bar. Complete meals: dinner $14.95-$36.95. Specializes in Black Angus beef. Parking. Victorian decor. Cr cds: A, C, D, DS, MC, V.

D

★★PIERO'S. 355 Convention Center Dr, east of the Strip. 702/369-2305. Hrs: 5:30-11 pm. Closed Thanksgiving, Dec 24, 25. Res accepted. Northern Italian menu. Bar. Semi-a la carte: dinner $17-$55. Specializes in veal, fettucine, linguine, fresh fish. Valet parking. Cr cds: A, C, D, MC, V.

★★PORT TACK. *3190 W Sahara, 1¼ mi west of the Strip.* 702/873-3345. Hrs: 11–5 am; early-bird dinner 4–6:30 pm. Closed major hols. Bar. Semi-a la carte: lunch $5.95–$9, dinner $10.95–$32.95. Child's meals. Specializes in steak, fresh fish. Salad bar. Valet parking. Nautical/Spanish decor. Cr cds: A, C, D, DS, MC, V.

D

✔★SHALIMAR. *3900 Paradise Rd, in shopping mall, east of the Strip.* 702/796-0302. Hrs: 11:30 am–2 pm, 5:30–10 pm; Sat, Sun from 5:30 pm. Res accepted. Northern Indian menu. Serv bar. Buffet: lunch $5.95. A la carte entrees: dinner $7.95–$13.95. Specialties: chicken tandoori, lamb Shalimar, lamb & seafood curries. Contemporary decor. Cr cds: A, C, D, MC, V.

D

★★★SPAGO. *3500 Las Vegas Blvd S, in Caesars Palace Hotel.* 702/369-0360. Hrs: 11:30–12:30 am. Closed July 4, Dec 25. Res accepted. Varied menu. Bar. Wine cellar. A la carte entrees: lunch $6.50–$12.50. Complete meals: dinner $30–$50. Specialties: pizza, chicken salad. Jazz pianist. Parking. Modern artwork. Art deco, wrought iron design. Counterpart of famous restaurant in West Hollywood. Cr cds: A, C, D, DS, ER, MC, V.

D

★★★TILLERMAN. *2245 E Flamingo, east of the Strip.* 702/731-4036. Hrs: 5–11 pm. Closed major hols. Wine list. Semi-a la carte: dinner $13.95–$32.95. Specializes in fresh fish, steak, pasta. Parking. Atrium, garden, loft dining areas. Cr cds: A, C, D, DS, MC, V.

D

★TONY'S GRECO-ROMAN. *220 W Sahara Ave, west of the Strip.* 702/384-5171. Hrs: 11 am–11 pm. Closed Thanksgiving. Res accepted. Greek, Italian menu. Wine, beer. Semi-a la carte: lunch $3.75–$7.95, dinner $7.50–$18.95. Parking. Cr cds: A, D, DS, MC, V.

✔★VINEYARD. *3630 Maryland Pkwy, 1 mi east of the Strip.* 702/731-1606. Hrs: 11 am–10 pm; Fri, Sat to 11 pm. Closed major hols. Italian, Amer menu. Serv bar. Semi-a la carte: lunch $5.95–$11.50, dinner $6.95–$14.95. Complete meals: dinner for two, $25. Child's meals. Specializes in veal parmigiana, breast of chicken. Salad bar. Parking. Italian marketplace decor. Cr cds: A, D, MC, V.

SC

★YOLIE'S CHURRASCARIA. *3900 Paradise Road, east of the Strip.* 702/794-0700. Hrs: 11:30 am–3 pm, 5:30–11 pm. Res required. Brazilian menu. Bar. Semi-a la carte: lunch $3.95–$11.95, dinner $12.95–$20.95. Child's meals. Specializes in steak, skewered lamb. Parking. Outdoor dining. Cr cds: A, C, D, DS, MC, V.

D

Laughlin (F-5)

Pop: 4,791 **Elev:** 520 ft **Area code:** 702 **Zip:** 89029

This resort community offers a pleasant change of pace from the dazzle of Las Vegas. In many ways, it resembles Las Vegas in its earlier days. Many hotels and casinos line the Colorado River; most provide ferry service to and from parking facilities on the Arizona side. But Laughlin offers other diversions as well; water sports such as fishing, waterskiing and swimming in nearby Lake Mojave are popular.

(For information about this area contact the Chamber of Commerce, PO Box 2280; 800/227-5245.)

Annual Event

Laughlin Riverdays. Miss Laughlin Beauty Pageant, carnival, golf tournament. Mid-May.

(See Bullhead City, AZ, Kingman, AZ; also see Needles, CA)

Motor Hotel

✔★★PIONEER HOTEL & CASINO. *(Box 29664) On Casino Dr, 3 mi S of Davis Dam.* 702/298-2442; res: 800/634-3469. 415 rms, 3 story. S, D $28–$45. Crib free. TV. Pool. 2 restaurants open 24 hrs. Bar. Ck-out noon. Gift shop. Free airport transportation. Lighted tennis. Game rm. Some refrigerators. On river; some riverfront rms. Cr cds: MC, V.

D ⚓ ≈ 🚭 ⊘

Hotels

★★BEST WESTERN RIVERSIDE RESORT. *(PO Box 500) 1650 Casino Way, 2 mi NW on AZ 68, 2 mi S of Davis Dam.* 702/298-2535; FAX 702/298-2614. 660 rms, 14 story. S, D $34–$64; each addl $8; suites $75–$300. Crib $10. TV; cable, in-rm movies avail. 2 pools. Restaurant open 24 hrs. Rm serv 24 hrs. Bars; entertainment, dancing exc Mon. Ck-out 11 am. Convention facilities. Free local airport transportation. Bathrm phones. Balconies. Movie theaters. Casino. Bus depot on premises. Boat dockage on Colorado River; RV spaces. Cr cds: A, C, D, DS, MC, V.

D ≈ 🚭 ⊘ ⊛

✔★★COLORADO BELLE. *(Box 2304) 2100 Casino Dr.* 702/298-4000; res: 800/458-9500. 1,232 rms, 6 story. S, D $25–$69. Crib $7. TV. Heated pool; whirlpool. Restaurant open 24 hrs. Limited rm serv. Bar; entertainment. Ck-out 11 am. Shopping arcade. Free airport transportation. Casino. Adj to replica of three-deck Mississippi paddlewheeler. Cr cds: A, C, D, DS, MC, V.

D ≈ 🚭 ⊘ ⊛

✔★EDGEWATER HOTEL/CASINO. *(Box 30707) 2020 Casino Dr.* 702/298-2453; res: 800/677-4837. 1,450 rms, 6–26 story. S, D $23–$54; each addl (after 4th person) $7; suites $75–$125; under 12 free. Crib $7. TV. Pool; whirlpool. Restaurant open 24 hrs. Bar; entertainment. Ck-out 11 am. Gift shop. Covered parking. Free airport transportation. Some balconies. On river. Cr cds: A, C, D, DS, MC, V.

D ≈ 🚭 ⊘ ⊛

✔★GOLD RIVER GAMBLING HALL & RESORT. *(Box 77700) 2700 S Casino Dr.* 702/298-2242; res: 800/835-7903. 1,003 rms, 3–25 story. S, D $25–$55; suites $85–$300. Crib free. TV. Heated pool; whirlpool. Restaurant open 24 hrs. Bar; entertainment, dancing. Ck-out 11 am. Convention facilities. Shopping arcade. Free valet parking. Free airport transportation. Game rm. Cr cds: A, C, D, DS, ER, MC, V, JCB.

D ≈ 🚭 ⊘ ⊛

GOLDEN NUGGET. *(Too new to be rated) 2300 Casino Dr.* 702/298-7111; res: 800/950-7700; FAX 702/298-7122. 300 rooms, 4 story. May–Sept: S, D $21–$49; suites $150; under 12 free; higher rates hols. Crib free. TV; cable. Pool; whirlpool, sauna, poolside serv. Restaurants 9 am–7 pm. Bar. Ck-out noon. Concierge. Shopping arcade. Free airport transportation. On Colorado River. Cr cds: A, C, D, DS, MC, V.

D ≈ 🚭 ⊘ SC

★★HILTON FLAMINGO-LAUGHLIN. *1900 S Casino Dr.* 702/298-5111; FAX 702/298-5129. 2,000 rms, 18 story. Mar–Oct: S, D $29–$95; each addl $7; suites $200–$275; family rates; higher rates: wkends, hols; lower rates rest of yr. Crib $7. TV; cable. Heated pool. Restaurant open 24 hrs. Rm serv 6 am–11 pm. Bar; entertainment. Ck-out 11 am. Meeting rms. Shopping arcade. Beauty shop. Free garage parking. Free airport transportation. Lighted tennis. Game rm. Wet bar in suites. Casino. On 18-acre site along Colorado River. Cr cds: A, C, D, DS, ER, MC, V, JCB.

D ⚓ ≈ 🚭 ⊘

★★RAMADA EXPRESS. *(Box 77771) 2121 Casino Dr.* 702/298-4200. 406 rms, 12 story. S, D $25–$59; suites $150–$200; under 18 free; higher rates: hols, gaming tournaments. Crib $7. TV; cable. Heated pool; poolside serv. Restaurant open 24 hrs. No rm serv. Bar; entertainment, dancing. Ck-out 11 am. Gift shop. Valet parking. Free airport transportation. Game rm. Refrigerator, wet bar in suites. Opp river.

Railroad station theme; full-size train runs around hotel. Cr cds: A, C, D, DS, MC, V.

Lovelock (B-2)

Settled: early 1840s **Pop:** 2,069 **Elev:** 3,977 ft **Area code:** 702 **Zip:** 89419

The 49ers stopped in Lovelock Valley on their way west. There was plenty of feed for weary oxen and horses because beavers had dammed the Humboldt River, thus providing a steady water supply. The travelers mended their wagons and made other preparations for the 36-hour dash across the dreaded 40-mile desert to Hot Springs.

A deep layer of rich, black loam, left in the Lovelock Valley as the waters of an ancient lake receded, spreads over more than 40,000 acres. This soil, irrigated from the Rye Patch Reservoir, supports rich farms and productive ranches. Lovelock, the seat of Pershing County, was named for an early settler, George Lovelock, across whose ranch the original Central Pacific Railroad was built. Ore mines, mineral deposits and a seed-processing plant in the area contribute to the growth of modern Lovelock.

What to See and Do

1. **Courthouse Park.** The only round courthouse still in use. Shaded picnic grounds; swimming pool. (May–Aug, daily; closed Sept–Apr) Phone 273-7874. ¢
2. **Rye Patch State Recreation Area.** 23 mi N on I-80. Approx 27,500 acres on 200,000-acre reservoir; swimming, waterskiing; fishing; boating (launching ramps). Picnicking. Camping (dump station). Standard fees. Phone 538-7321.

(For further information contact the Pershing County Chamber of Commerce, NV 40W/Marzen Lane, PO Box 821; 273-7213.)

Annual Event

Frontier Days. Parade, races, rodeo. 1st wkend Aug.

Lunar Crater (D-4)

(Near US 6 between Tonopah and Ely)

This is a vast field of cinder cones and frozen lava. The crater is a steep-walled pit, 400 feet deep and three-quarters of a mile in diameter, created by volcanic action about 1,000 years ago. The earth exploded violently, heaving cinders, lava and rocks the size of city blocks high into the air. Awed by the remains, pioneers named the pit Lunar Crater.

Overton (E-5)

Pop: 3,000 (est) **Elev:** 1,270 ft **Area code:** 702 **Zip:** 89040

An old Mormon settlement, Overton is located at the site of an ancient civilization that, 1,200 years ago, extended for 30 miles along the Muddy River. Some of this area is now covered by Lake Mead.

What to See and Do

1. **Lost City Museum of Archaeology.** 1 mi S on NV 169. An agency of the Nevada State Museum, it is located on a restored portion of Pueblo Grande de Nevada. The museum has an extensive collection of ancient Native American artifacts, fossils and semiprecious gems. There is also a picnic area. The curator and staff have travel tips and information on the area; gift shop. (Daily; closed Jan 1, Thanksgiving, Dec 25) Phone 397-2193. ¢
2. **Lake Mead National Recreation Area** (see). SE via NV 169.
3. **Valley of Fire State Park** (see). Approx 15 mi SW via NV 169.

(See Las Vegas)

Motel

★**ECHO BAY RESORT.** *North Shore Rd. 702/394-4000; res: 800/752-9669 (exc NV).* 52 rms, 2 story. S, D $69–$84; each addl $6; under 5 free. Crib free. TV. Restaurant 7 am–10 pm. Bar noon–11 pm. Ck-out 11 am. Coin lndry. Sundries. Boat rentals; fishing supplies. Private patios, balconies. On lake. Cr cds: MC, V.

Pyramid Lake (B-1)

(36 mi N of Reno on NV 33)

Surrounded by rainbow-tinted, eroded hills, this is a remnant of prehistoric Lake Lahontan, which once covered 8,400 square miles in western Nevada and northeastern California. The largest natural lake in the state, Pyramid is about 30 miles long and from 7 to 9 miles wide, with deep-blue sparkling waters. It is fed by scant water from the diverted Truckee River and by brief floods in other streams. Since the Newlands Irrigation Project deprives it of water, its level is receding.

General John C. Frémont gave the lake its name when he visited the area in 1844, apparently taking it from the tufa (porous rock) islands that jut up from the water. One, 475 feet high, is said by Native Americans to be a basket inverted over an erring woman. Though turned to stone, her "breath" (wisps of steam from a hot spring) can still be seen. Another is called Stone Mother and Basket. At the north end there is a cluster of sharp spires known as the Needles. Anahoe Island, in the lake, is a sanctuary and breeding ground for more than 10,000 huge white pelicans.

An air of mystery surrounds the area, bred by the murmuring waves, the spires and domes with their wisps of steam, and the ever-changing tints of the folded, eroded hills. At nearby Astor Pass, railroad excavations uncovered a horse skull, fragmentary remains of an elephant, bison and camel, all believed to have lived on the lakeshore in prehistoric times.

Pyramid Lake abounds with Lahonton cutthroat trout; it is one of the top trophy trout lakes in the United States. All rights belong to the Native Americans. For information about roads, fishing and boat permits, contact the Sutcliffe Ranger Station or Pyramid Lake Fisheries, Star Rte, Sutcliffe 89510; phone 702/476-0500. Camping, boating and fishing at Pyramid Lake is considered by many to be the best in the state.

Visitor centers, located in the hatcheries at Sutcliffe and between Nixon and Wadsworth, describe the land, lake and people through photographs and displays (daily).

(For accommodations see Reno)

Reno (C-1)

Founded: 1868 **Pop:** 133,850 **Elev:** 4,498 ft **Area code:** 702

Reno, "the biggest little city in the world," renowned as a gambling and vacation center, is an important distribution and merchandising area, the home of the University of Nevada–Reno and a residential city. Between the steep slopes of the Sierra and the low eastern hills, Reno spills across the Truckee Meadows. The neon lights of the nightclubs, gambling casinos and bars give it a glitter that belies its quiet acres of fine houses, churches and schools. The surrounding area is popular for sailing, boating, horseback riding and deer and duck hunting.

Reno was known as Lake's Crossing and was an overland travelers' camping place even before the gold rush. It grew with the exploitation of the Comstock Lode and became a city in May, 1868, with a public auction of real estate by a railway agent. Within a month there were 100 houses. A railroad official named the town in honor of a Union officer of the Civil War, General Jesse Lee Reno. In 1871 it became the seat of Washoe County.

Many Nevadans resent Reno's reputation as a divorce capital. They point out that many more couples are married than divorced at the Washoe Courthouse. A six-month divorce law had been on the books since 1861, before Nevada became a state. The six-week law became effective in the 1930s.

What to See and Do

1. **University of Nevada-Reno** (1874). (12,000 students) 9th and N Virginia Sts. The campus covers 200 acres on a plateau overlooking the Truckee Meadows, in the shadow of the Sierra Nevada Mountains. Opened in Elko, it was moved to Reno and reopened in 1885. Tours of campus. Phone 784-4941. On campus are

   Fleischmann Planetarium. Northern Nevada's only planetarium, this facility features star shows, movies, astronomy museum, telescope viewing (Fri evenings) and more. (Daily; closed Jan 1, Thanksgiving, Dec 25) Phone 784-4811. ¢¢¢

   Nevada Historical Society Museum. 1650 N Virginia St. Prehistoric and modern Native American artifacts; ranching, mining and gambling artifacts. Carson City Mint materials; audiovisual programs; museum tours; research and genealogy library (Tues–Sat). Museum (daily exc Sun; closed hols, Oct 31). Donation. Phone 688-1190.

   Mackay School of Mines Museum. Minerals, rocks, fossils and mining memorabilia. (Mon–Fri; closed hols)   **Free.**

2. **William F. Harrah Foundation National Automobile Museum.** 10 S Lake St. More than 200 vehicles on display. Theater presentation; period street scenes. (Daily; closed Thanksgiving, Dec 25) Sr citizen rate. Phone 333-9300. ¢¢¢

3. **Nevada Museum of Art.** 160 W Liberty St. Changing art exhibits by international, national, regional and local artists. (Daily exc Mon; closed hols) Phone 329-3333. ¢¢

4. **Pyramid Lake** (see). 36 mi N on NV 33.

5. **Toiyabe National Forest.** 10 mi W on I-80, then W on NV 27. Approx 3 million acres, partly in California. Big-game hunting, saddle and pack trips, trout fishing, campsites (fees vary), picnicking, winter sports. Berlin-Ichthyosaur State Park (see AUSTIN), Lake Tahoe (see CALIFORNIA) and Mt Charleston Recreation Area (see LAS VEGAS) are in the forest. For further information contact Public Affairs Officer, 1200 Franklin Way, Sparks 89431; 331-6444.

6. **Sightseeing tours.**

   CCInc Auto Tape Tours. These 90-minute cassettes offer mile-by-mile self-guided tours to South Lake Tahoe (61 mi) with stories of the Comstock Lode, ghost towns, colorful history of boomtown days of Virginia City and Carson City (smallest state capital); and to Sacramento (132 mi) over the Sierras via Donner Pass, then through the Mother Lode Country. Tapes may be purchased directly from CCInc, 2 Elbrook Dr, PO Box 227, Allendale, NJ 07401; 201/236-1666. ¢¢¢¢

   Gray Line bus tours. To Virginia City, Ponderosa Ranch, Lake Tahoe and other nearby points. For information contact 2570 Tacchino St, 89512; 329-1147.

   Reno-Tahoe Tours. Historic tours to Virginia City and Lake Tahoe from Reno hotels. For information contact 1325 Airmotive Way, PO Box 20985, 89515; 322-9044. ¢¢¢¢¢

(For further information contact Chamber of Commerce Hospitality Center or the Reno-Tahoe Visitors Center, 275 N Virginia St. Travelers may also contact the Chamber of Commerce at PO Box 3499, 89505;

329-3558. For information on cultural events contact the Sierra Arts Foundation, 200 Flint St, PO Box 2814, 89501; 329-1324.)

Annual Events

Winter Carnival. University of Nevada hosts 12 top collegiate ski teams. Phone 784-6589. Feb.

Rodeo. Downtown contests and celebrations on closed streets. Phone 329-3877. 5 days mid-June.

Nevada State Fair. Fairgrounds, Wells St. Phone 322-4424. Mid-Aug.

National Championship Air Races. Stead Air Field. Phone 328-6570. 4 days mid-Sept.

(See Carson City, Incline Village, Virginia City)

Motels

(Note on accommodations: Rates are likely to vary upward in Reno at peak occupancy and sometimes a minimum of three days occupancy is required. In addition, minimum rates quoted are generally available only from Mon through Thurs. We urge you to check the rate on any room you occupy and to make certain no other special conditions apply.)

★**COLONIAL MOTOR INN.** *232 West St (89501). 702/786-5038; res: 800/255-7366 (western states); FAX 702/323-4588.* 100 rms, 5 story. Mar–Nov: S, D $48–$52; each addl $10; lower rates rest of yr. Crib free. TV. Heated pool; sauna. Complimentary coffee in rms. Restaurant nearby. Ck-out noon. Sundries. Some covered parking. Sun deck. Cr cds: A, C, D, MC, V.

⊠ Ⓞ SC

✔ ★**DAYS INN.** *701 E 7th St (89512). 702/786-4070; FAX 702/329-4338.* 137 rms, 4 story. S $30–$50; D $45–$65; each addl $10; under 12 free; wkly rates. Crib free. Pet accepted; $6 per night. TV. Heated pool (seasonal). Restaurant 6 am–10 pm. Ck-out noon. Sundries. Some refrigerators. Cr cds: A, C, D, DS, MC, V.

D ⊠ ⊿ Ⓞ Ⓞ SC

★★**LA QUINTA INN-AIRPORT.** *4001 Market St (89502), off US 395 between Villanova & Vassar Sts, near Reno Cannon Intl Airport. 702/348-6100; FAX 702/348-5794.* 130 rms, 2 story. May–Oct: S $48–$58; D $53–$63; each addl $8; under 18 free; lower rates rest of yr. Crib free. Pet accepted. TV; cable. Heated pool. Complimentary continental bkfst, coffee in lobby. Restaurant adj open 24 hrs. Ck-out noon. Meeting rms. Valet serv. Free airport transportation. Cr cds: A, C, D, DS, MC, V.

D ⊿ ⊠ ✕ Ⓞ Ⓞ SC

✔ ★**NEVADA INN.** *330 E 2nd (89501). 702/323-1005; res: 800/999-9686.* 43 rms, 2 story. May–Oct: S, D $30–$35; each addl $5; wkly rates off season; higher rates: hols, special events; lower rates rest of yr. TV. Heated pool. Coffee in lobby. Restaurant nearby. Ck-out 11 am. Covered parking. Cr cds: A, DS, MC, V.

⊠ Ⓞ SC

★★**RODEWAY INN.** *2050 Market St (89502), US 395S exit Mill St W, near Reno Cannon Intl Airport. 702/786-2500; FAX 702/786-3884.* 210 units, 4 story, 70 kits. Late May–Oct: S $57, D $67; each addl $9; kit. suites $77–$89; under 18 free; wkly rates; higher rates hols & special events; lower rates rest of yr. Crib free. Pet accepted; $5 per day. TV; cable. Heated pool; whirlpool, sauna. Complimentary continental bkfst. Restaurant nearby. Ck-out noon. Coin lndry. Meeting rm. Valet serv. Airport transportation. Cr cds: A, C, D, DS, ER, MC, V, JCB.

D ⊿ ⊠ ✕ Ⓞ Ⓞ SC

✔ ★**VAGABOND INN.** *3131 S Virginia St (89502). 702/825-7134; FAX 702/825-3096.* 130 rms, 2 story. May–Oct: S $39–$59; D $49–$69; each addl $5; under 18 free; higher rates: air races, horse shows, hols; lower rates rest of yr. Crib free. Pet accepted, some restrictions; $5 per day. TV; cable. Heated pool. Complimentary continental bkfst. Restaurant adj 11 am–10 pm. Ck-out noon. Meeting rm. Airport, RR station, bus depot transportation. Some private patios, balconies. Cr cds: A, C, D, DS, MC, V.

[icons]

Motor Hotels

★ ★ **BEST WESTERN AIRPORT PLAZA.** *1981 Terminal Way (89502), at Reno Cannon Intl Airport.* 702/348-6370; FAX 702/348-9722. 270 rms, 3 story. S $62–$96; D $72–$105; each addl $10; suites $102–$230; kit. units $275; under 12 free; higher rates: hols, special events. Crib free. TV. Heated pool. Restaurant 5:30 am–11 pm. Rm serv. Bar 11–2 am. Ck-out noon. Meeting rms. Bellhops. Valet serv. Free airport transportation. Exercise equipt; weights, bicycles, whirlpool, sauna. Game rm. Some fireplaces. Minicasino. Cr cds: A, C, D, DS, MC, V.

[icons]

✔ ★ **COLONIAL HOTEL INN & CASINO.** *250 N Arlington (89501).* 702/322-3838; res: 800/336-7366 (western states); FAX 702/323-4588. 168 rms, 9 story. Mar–Nov: S, D $48–$55; each addl $10; lower rates rest of yr. Crib free. TV. Heated pool; sauna. Restaurant 6 am–midnight. Bar 7:30–1:30 am. Ck-out noon. Meeting rms. Sundries. Some covered parking. Sun deck. Casino. Cr cds: A, C, D, MC, V.

[icons]

★ ★ **HOLIDAY INN-CONVENTION CENTER.** *5851 S Virginia St (89502).* 702/825-2940; FAX 702/826-3835. 150 rms, 2 story. Apr–Oct: S, D $45–$55; each addl $5; under 18 free; higher rates: wkends, hols; lower rates rest of yr. Pet accepted. TV; cable. Heated pool; whirlpool. Coffee in rms. Restaurant 6:30 am–10 pm. Rm serv. Bar from 11 am. Ck-out noon. Coin lndry. Meeting rms. Bellhops. Airport transportation. Cr cds: A, C, D, DS, MC, V, JCB.

[icons]

★ ★ **JOHN ASCUAGA'S NUGGET COURTYARD.** *(1225 B Street, Sparks 89431) Adj to John Ascuaga's Nugget Hotel, 3 mi E off I-80, exit 17NE.* 702/356-3300; res: 800/648-1177; FAX 702/356-4198. 157 rms, 5 story. S, D $65–$69; under 10 free. Crib free. TV. Heated pool; poolside serv. Complimentary coffee in lobby. Restaurant adj open 24 hrs. Ck-out 11 am. Meeting rms. Bellhops. Valet serv. Sundries. Free airport transportation. Health club privileges. Some balconies. Wedding chapel. Casino in adj hotel. Cr cds: A, C, D, DS, MC, V.

[icons]

✔ ★ ★ **TRUCKEE RIVER LODGE.** *501 W 1st St (89503).* 702/786-8888; res: 800/635-8950; FAX 702/348-4769. 214 rms, 6 story. May–Oct: S $31; D $36–$53; wkly rates; higher rates hols; lower rates rest of yr. Pet accepted; $10 per day. TV; cable. Complimentary coffee in rms. Restaurant 7:30 am–midnight; Thur–Sat to 2 am. Ck-out noon. Coin lndry. Valet serv. Free garage parking. Airport transportation. Exercise equipt; weights, bicycles. Refrigerators. Near river. Totally nonsmoking. Cr cds: A, C, D, DS, MC, V.

[icons]

Hotels

★ ★ **CIRCUS-CIRCUS.** *(PO Box 5880, 89513) 500 N Sierra St.* 702/329-0711; res: 800/648-5010; FAX 702/329-0599. 1,624 rms, 22 & 27 story. Apr–Oct: S, D $37; each addl $6; minisuites $52; under 12 free; ski plans; higher rates: wkends, hols; lower rates rest of yr. Crib $6. TV; cable. Restaurant open 24 hrs. Bar; entertainment. Ck-out noon. Gift shop. Free covered valet parking. Rec rm. Casino. Midway, arcade games. Free circus acts. Cr cds: A, C, D, DS, MC, V.

[icons]

★ ★ ★ **CLARION.** *3800 S Virginia St (89502).* 702/825-4700; FAX 702/826-7860. 303 rms, 12 story. May–Oct: S, D $49–$125; each addl $6; suites $75–$250; under 18 free; ski, golf rates; some wkend rates; higher rates: hols, special events; lower rates rest of yr. Crib free.

TV; cable. Heated pool. Restaurant open 24 hrs. Bar; entertainment. Ck-out 11 am. Meeting rms. Free valet parking. Free airport transportation. Exercise equipt; weights, bicycles, whirlpool, sauna. Casino. Cr cds: A, C, D, DS, ER, MC, V, JCB.

[icons]

★ ★ **COMSTOCK.** *200 W 2nd St (89501), downtown.* 702/329-1880; res: 800/468-4866. 310 rms, 16 story. July–Nov: S, D $48–$64; each addl $5; suites $90–$300; under 12 free; higher rates: wkends, special events; lower rates rest of yr. Crib free. TV; cable. Heated pool. Restaurant open 24 hrs. Rm serv 6–11 am. Bar open 24 hrs. Ck-out 11 am. Meeting rms. Free valet parking. Airport transportation. Exercise equipt; bicycles, stair machine, whirlpool, sauna. Whirlpool in some suites. Casino. Cr cds: A, C, D, DS, ER, MC, V.

[icons]

★ ★ **ELDORADO HOTEL/CASINO.** *345 N Virginia St (89501), at 4th St.* 702/786-5700; res: 800/648-5966 (exc NV); FAX 702/348-7513. 783 rms, 25 story. July–Oct: S, D $69–$89; each addl $10; suites $110–$150; under 14 free; higher rates: wkends, hols; lower rates rest of yr. Crib free. TV; cable. Heated pool; whirlpool, poolside beverage serv. Restaurant open 24 hrs. Rm serv 24 hrs. Bar; entertainment (show lounge). Ck-out noon. Convention facilities. Concierge. Gift shop. Garage; free valet parking. Wet bar in some suites; some bathrm phones, refrigerators. Casino. Cr cds: A, C, D, DS, MC, V.

[icons]

★ ★ **FITZGERALD'S.** *255 N Virginia St (89501).* 702/786-3663; res: 800/648-5022 (exc NV); FAX 702/786-7180. 351 rms, 16 story. May–Oct: S, D $36–$88; each addl $8; suites $90–$120; under 13 free; higher rates: wkends, hols; lower rates rest of yr. TV; cable. Restaurants open 24 hrs. Rm serv 7 am–8 pm. Bars open 24 hrs; entertainment. Ck-out noon. Free valet parking. X-country ski 18 mi. Casino. Cr cds: A, C, D, DS, MC, V.

[icons]

★ ★ ★ **HARRAH'S.** *(Box 10, 89520) 210 N Center St, at 2nd St, downtown.* 702/786-3232; res: 800/648-3773 (exc NV), 800/329-4422 (NV); FAX 702/329-4455. 565 rms, 24 story, no rms on 1st 5 floors. May–Oct: S, D $85–$130; each addl $10; suites $210–$375; under 15 free; higher rates wkends; lower rates rest of yr. Crib free. Pet accepted, some restrictions. TV; cable. Heated pool (seasonal); lifeguard in season. Restaurant open 24 hrs. Bars; name entertainment. Ck-out noon. Convention facilities. Shopping arcade. Barber, beauty shop. Covered parking; valet. Free airport, bus depot transportation. Exercise rm; instructor, weight machines, bicycles, whirlpool, sauna, steam rm. Massage. Game rm. Rec rm. Casino. Some bathrm phones. Some private patios. Cr cds: A, C, D, DS, MC, V, JCB.

[icons]

★ ★ **HILTON FLAMINGO.** *(Box 1291, 89504) 255 N Sierra St, downtown.* 702/322-1111; FAX 702/785-7086. 604 rms, 20 story. May–Sept: S, D $59–$99; each addl $15; suites $145–$395; under 19 free; higher rates hols; lower rates rest of yr. Crib free. TV; cable. Restaurant open 24 hrs. Bars; entertainment. Ck-out 11 am. Convention facilities. Gift shop. Barber, beauty shop. Free valet parking. Exercise equipt; weights, bicycles. Casino. Arcade games. Cr cds: A, C, D, DS, ER, MC, V, JCB.

[icons]

HILTON RENO (formerly Bally's). (New general manager, therefore not rated) *2500 E 2nd St (89595), near Reno Cannon Intl Airport.* 702/789-2000; FAX 702/789-2418. 2,001 rms, 27 story. S, D $69–$119; each addl $10; suites $130–$544; package plan. Crib free. TV. Heated pool (seasonal); poolside serv, lifeguard. Restaurants open 24 hrs. Bars; entertainment. Ck-out noon. Convention facilities. Meeting rms. Shopping arcade. Barber, beauty shop. Free valet parking. Free airport transportation. Lighted indoor & outdoor tennis, pro. Exercise rm; instructor, weights, bicycles, whirlpool, steam rm, sauna. Rec rm. Bowling. Indoor golf simulator. Some bathrm phones, refrigerators; wet bars. Movie theaters. Casino. Cr cds: A, C, D, DS, ER, MC, V, JCB.

[icons]

★ ★ ★ **JOHN ASCUAGA'S NUGGET.** *(1100 Nugget Ave, Sparks 89431) 3 mi E off I-80, exit 17 NE. 702/356-3300; res: 800/648-1177 (exc NV); FAX 702/356-4198.* 610 rms, 28 story. S, D $89–$115; each addl $10; suites $135–$450; under 12 free. Crib free. TV. Indoor/outdoor pool. Restaurants, bars open 24 hrs; entertainment; dancing. Ck-out 11 am. Convention facilities. Concierge. Gift shop. Free valet parking. Exercise equipt; weights, bicycles, whirlpool. Casino. *LUXURY LEVEL:* **EXECUTIVE LEVEL.** 60 rms, 10 suites. S, D $100–$115; suites $265–$550. Bathrm phones. Cr cds: A, C, D, DS, MC, V.

D ⊛ ⚊ ⚐ ⊘ ⊚ SC

★ ★ ★ **PEPPERMILL HOTEL CASINO.** *2707 S Virginia St (89502), 3 mi S on US 395, near Reno Cannon Intl Airport. 702/826-2121; res: 800/648-6992; FAX 702/825-5737.* 632 rms, 15 story. S, D $49–$94; each addl $10; suites $79–$450; under 15 free. Crib free. TV. Heated pool. Restaurant open 24 hrs. Bars open 24 hrs; entertainment. Ck-out noon. Meeting rms. Gift shop. Barber, beauty shop. Some covered parking. Free airport transportation. Exercise equipt; weights, bicycles, whirlpool, sauna. Minibars. Casino. Cr cds: A, C, D, DS, MC, V, JCB.

D ⚊ ⚐ ⚔ ⊘ ⊚

★ **RAMADA INN.** *6th & Lake Sts (89501). 702/788-2000; FAX 702/348-1860.* 232 rms, 11 story. June–Oct: S, D $45–$85; each addl $8; suites $80–$160; under 12 free; lower rates rest of yr. TV; cable. Restaurant 6 am–10 pm. Bar open 24 hrs; entertainment Tues–Sat. Ck-out noon. Free airport, RR station, bus depot & casino transportation. Game rm. Bathrm phone, wet bar in suites. Cr cds: A, C, D, DS, MC, V.

D ⊘ ⊚ SC

Restaurants

★ ★ ★ **CASANOVA'S.** *1695 S Virginia St. 702/786-6633.* Hrs: 11:30 am–2:30 pm, 5–10 pm; Fri to 11 pm; Sat, Sun 5:30–11 pm. Closed July 4, Dec 25. Res accepted. Northern Italian menu. Bar to 3 am; entertainment Fri, Sat. A la carte entrees: lunch $3.95–$9.95. Semi-a la carte: dinner $11–$20. Child's meals. Specializes in pasta, seafood, wild game. English Victorian decor; antique fixtures, leaded & stained glass. Cr cds: A, D, MC, V.

D

✔ ★ ★ **FAMOUS MURPHYS.** *3127 S Virginia St. 702/827-4111.* Hrs: 11 am–2 pm, 5–10 pm; Sat & Sun from 5 pm; early-bird dinner 5–6:30 pm; Sun brunch 10 am–2 pm. Res accepted. Bar to 4 am. Semi-a la carte: lunch $4.95–$12.95, dinner $9.95–$17.95. Sun brunch $6.25–$12.95. Child's meals. Specializes in steak, seafood, pasta. Salad bar. Oyster, seafood bar. Parking. Pub atmosphere. Cr cds: A, D, DS, MC, V.

★ ★ **GLORY HOLE.** *4201 W 4th St. 702/786-1323.* Hrs: 5–11 pm. Closed Thanksgiving. Bar. Semi-a la carte: dinner $9–$29.95. Specializes in steak, fresh seafood, chicken. Salad bar. Parking. Old West saloon, mining camp decor. Cr cds: A, MC, V.

★ ★ **ICHIBAN.** *635 N Sierra, downtown. 702/323-5550.* Hrs: 11 am–2:30 pm, 5–10 pm; Fri to 11 pm; Sat 5–11 pm; Sun 5–10 pm. Closed Easter Sun, July 4, Dec 25. Res accepted. Japanese menu. Bar. A la carte entrees: lunch $3.95–$7.95, dinner $6.50–$20, teppanyaki dinners $10.50–$23. Child's meals. Specializes in steak, shrimp, teriyaki chicken. Sushi bar. Cr cds: A, C, D, DS, MC, V.

D SC

★ ★ ★ ★ **PIMPAREL'S LA TABLE FRANÇAISE.** *3065 W 4th St, 2 mi west of downtown. 702/323-3200.* Hrs: 6–10 pm. Closed Sun, Mon; Jan 1, Thanksgiving, Dec 25. Res accepted. French menu. Bar. Wine list. A la carte entrees: dinner $18.50–$30. Menu changes wkly; based on fresh, seasonal ingredients. Own baking. Parking. Country French inn atmosphere. Beamed ceiling, stone & beam fireplace; antiques, artwork. Cr cds: A, MC, V.

D

✔ ★ ★ **RAPSCALLION.** *1555 S Wells Ave. 702/323-1211.* Hrs: 11:30 am–10 pm; Fri & Sat 5–10:30 pm; Sun brunch 10 am–2 pm. Closed Thanksgiving, Dec 25. Res accepted. Bar 11–1 am; Sat to 2 am; Sun from 10 am. A la carte entrees: lunch, dinner $5.95–$14.95. Sun brunch $4.95–$7.95. Child's meals. Specializes in seafood. Parking. Outdoor dining. 1890s San Francisco decor. Cr cds: A, MC, V.

South Lake Tahoe

(see South Lake Tahoe, CA)

Sparks

(see Reno)

Stateline (C-1)

Pop: 1,379 **Elev:** 6,360 ft **Area code:** 702 **Zip:** 89449

This area is best known for its famous high-rise casino/hotels, cabarets and fine dining, but as an integral part of Tahoe's "south shore" it is also appreciated for its spectacular natural beauty. Alpine beaches and Sierra forests afford visitors an endless variety of year-round recreation. There are several excellent public golf courses in the area.

(For general information, map and attractions see Lake Tahoe Area, CA; also see Incline Village, NV)

Motel

(All distances and directions are given from the CA-NV state line)

✔ ★ **LAKESIDE INN & CASINO.** *(Box 5640) ½ mi NE on US 50, at Kingsbury Grade. 702/588-7777; res: 800/624-7980; FAX 702/588-4092.* 123 rms, 2 story. June–Sept: S, D $69–$89; each addl $10; suites $120–$235; package rates in winter; under 16 free; lower rates rest of yr. Crib free. TV; cable. Heated pool (seasonal). Complimentary coffee in rms. Restaurant open 24 hrs. Bar; entertainment. Ck-out noon. Meeting rms. Valet serv. Sundries. Downhill ski 2 mi; x-country ski 16 mi. Game rm. Wet bar in suites. Casino. Cr cds: A, D, DS, MC, V.

⛷ ⚊ ⊘ ⊚ SC

Hotels

★ ★ ★ **CAESAR'S TAHOE.** *(Box 5800) 1 blk N on US 50. 702/588-3515; res: 800/648-3353; FAX 702/586-2068.* 440 rms, 15 story. Mid-June–Sept: S, D $115–$200; each addl $10; suites $650–$970; executive suites $300; under 12 free; ski package; lower rates rest of yr. Crib free. TV; cable. Indoor pool; poolside serv. Restaurants open 24 hrs. Bar; entertainment, dancing. Ck-out noon. Convention facilities. Concierge. Shopping arcade. Barber, beauty shop. Free valet parking. Lighted tennis, pro. Downhill ski 1 mi; x-country ski 15 mi. Exercise rm; instructor, weights, bicycles, whirlpool, steam rm, sauna. Racquetball. Game rm. Bathrm phones; some refrigerators. Casino. Cr cds: A, C, D, MC, V, JCB.

D ⚽ ⊘ ⚊ ⚐ ⊘ ⊚ SC

★ ★ ★ ★ **HARRAH'S HOTEL CASINO.** *(Box 8) On US 50, downtown. 702/588-6611; res: 800/648-3773; FAX 702/586-6607.* 534 rms, 18 story. Mid-June–mid-Sept: S, D $139–$175; each addl $20; suites $179–$850; under 15 free; ski, summer package plans; higher rates wkends & hols; lower rates rest of yr. Crib free. Pet accepted. TV; cable. Indoor pool; poolside serv. 7 restaurants; bars open 24 hrs; theater-restaurant; entertainment, dancing. Ck-out noon. Convention facilities. Concierge. Shopping arcade. Barber, beauty shop. Free covered valet parking. Downhill ski 1 mi; x-country ski 15 mi. Exercise rm; instructor, weights, bicycles, whirlpool, sauna, steam rm. Game rm. Casino. Youth center. Each rm has 2 bathrms with phone & TV. Beverage & snack dispenser in rms; snacks, liquor, etc. Butler serv in suites. Cr cds: A, C, D, DS, ER, MC, V, JCB.

⬜🐕♿🏊🍴🏃🚭🕐

★ ★ ★ **HARVEY'S RESORT.** *(Box 128) On US 50, downtown. 702/588-2411; res: 800/648-3361; FAX 702/588-6643.* 740 rms, 19 story. July–Aug: S, D $99–$195; each addl $20; suites $179–$525; package plans; higher rates wkends & hols; lower rates rest of yr. Crib free. TV; cable. Pool. 8 restaurants (also see SAGE ROOM). Rm serv 24 hrs. 6 bars open 24 hrs; entertainment; dancing. Ck-out noon. Convention facilities. Concierge. Shopping arcade. Barber, beauty shop. Covered parking; free valet and self-park. Airport, recreation area transportation. Tennis. Downhill ski 3 mi; x-country ski 14 mi. Exercise equipt; weights, bicycles, whirlpool, sauna. Massage. Game rm. Rec rm. Casino. Bathrm phones; many minibars; wet bar in suites. Cr cds: A, C, D, DS, MC, V.

⬜🐕♿🏊🍴🏃🚭🕐 SC

★ ★ **LAKE TAHOE HORIZON.** *(Box C) 1 blk NE on US 50. 702/588-6211; res: 800/648-3322; FAX 702/588-3110.* 539 rms, 15 story. Mid-June–mid-Sept, hols: S, D $90–$125; each addl $10; suites $300–$400; lower rates rest of yr. Crib free. TV; cable, in-rm movies. Heated pool (seasonal); wading pool, whirlpool, poolside serv, lifeguard. Restaurants, bars open 24 hrs; buffet; entertainment. Ck-out noon. Convention facilities. Concierge. Shopping arcade. Barber, beauty shop. Free garage parking. Downhill ski 1 mi; x-country ski 15 mi. Game rm. Wet bar in suites; steam bath in some rms. Some balconies. Casino. Cr cds: A, C, D, DS, MC, V.

⬜🐕♿🏊🚭🕐 SC

Resort

★ ★ ★ **RIDGE TAHOE.** *(Box 5790) 400 Ridge Club Dr. 702/588-3553 or -3131; FAX 702/588-7099.* 443 condo units, 11 story, 249 kit. suites. Dec–mid-Apr: S, D $155; kit. suites $225; kit. cottages (2-bedrm) $330; wkly rates, ski plans; lower rates rest of yr. Crib free. TV; cable. Indoor/outdoor pool. Playground. Supervised child's activities (June–Aug). Dining rm 6–10 pm. Bar 4–10 pm. Ck-out 10 am, ck-in 4 pm. Grocery. Package store. Meeting rms. Concierge. Gift shop. Covered parking. Sports dir. Indoor tennis; pro. Putting green. Downhill/x-country ski ¼ mi; equipt rental. Hiking. Soc dir. Rec rm. Game rm. Exercise rm; instructor, weights, bicycles, whirlpool, sauna. Some balconies. Some picnic tables, grills. Cr cds: A, D, DS, MC, V.

⬜🐕♿🏊🍴🏃🚭🕐

Restaurants

★ ★ **CHART HOUSE.** *392 Kingsbury Grade, 2 mi E on US 50. 702/588-6276.* Hrs: 5:30–10 pm; Sat 5–10:30 pm. Res accepted. Bar from 5 pm; Sat from 4:30 pm. Semi-a la carte: dinner $14.95–$35.95. Child's meals. Specializes in teriyaki sirloin, prime rib, seafood. Salad bar. Parking. View of lake. Cr cds: A, C, D, DS, MC, V.

⬜

★ ★ ★ **SAGE ROOM.** *(See Harvey's Resort Hotel) 702/588-2411.* Hrs: 6–10 pm; Fri & Sat to 11 pm. Res accepted. Continental, Amer menu. Bar. Wine cellar. Semi-a la carte: dinner $19–$35. Specializes in steak, seafood, game (in season). Own baking. Valet parking. Dining rm interior is part of original Wagon Wheel Saloon & Gambling Hall; handhewn beams, redwood ceilings, Remington bronzes, Western decor. Family-owned. Cr cds: A, C, D, DS, MC, V.

⬜

Tonopah (D-3)

Settled: 1900 **Pop:** 3,616 **Elev:** 6,030 ft **Area code:** 702 **Zip:** 89049

Founded by prospector Jim Butler in 1900 and named by his wife, Tonopah was a high-spirited but unusually orderly camp in its early days. "Tono" is a shrub of the greasewood family, the roots of which can be eaten; "pah" means water in the Shoshone language. There are a couple of gold mines and a silver mine in the vicinity. The Tonopah Test Range is approximately 35 miles east. A Ranger District office of the Toiyabe National Forest (see RENO) is located here, as well as a detached area office of the Bureau of Land Management.

What to See and Do

1. **Mizpah Hotel** (1907). 100 Main St. Old mining hotel completely restored to its original Victorian style. Phone 482-6202.

2. **Central Nevada Museum.** Logan Field Rd. Historical, mining and gem displays. (Daily, afternoons; closed Dec 25) Donation. Phone 482-9676.

3. **Rock collecting.** Rich variety of minerals.

(For further information contact the Chamber of Commerce, 301 Brougher St, PO Box 869; 482-3859.)

Motels

★ ★ **BEST WESTERN HI DESERT INN.** *(PO Box 351) 320 S Main St (US 95). 702/482-3511.* 62 rms, 2 story. S $40; D $46–$52; each addl $6. Crib $8. TV; cable. Pool; whirlpool. Complimentary continental bkfst, coffee. Restaurant nearby. Ck-out 11 am. Cr cds: A, C, D, DS, MC, V.

 🚭🕐 SC

✔ ★ **SILVER QUEEN.** *(PO Box 311) 255 S Main (US 95). 702/482-6291.* 85 rms, 1–2 story. No elvtr. S, D $28–$35; each addl $4; kit. units $38. Crib $4. Pet accepted. TV; cable. Pool. Restaurant adj 6 am–10 pm. Bar 11 am–midnight. Ck-out 11 am. Cr cds: A, C, D, DS, MC, V.

🐕🚭🕐

Motor Hotel

✔ ★ **STATION HOUSE HOTEL & CASINO.** *(PO Box 1351) 1100 Erie Main St. 702/482-9777; FAX 702/482-8762.* 75 rms, 2 story. S $33; D $35; each addl $2; suites $60–$80; under 4 free. Crib free. TV; cable. Complimentary coffee in rms. Restaurant open 24 hrs. Bar; entertainment, dancing exc Mon. Ck-out 11 am. Meeting rms. Bellhops. Shopping arcade. Barber, beauty shop. Free bus depot transportation. Cr cds: A, C, D, DS, MC, V.

 SC

Valley of Fire State Park (E-5)

(37 mi NE of Las Vegas on I-15, then 18 mi SE on NV 169)

This park offers a geologically incredible 38,480-acre area, which gains its name from the red, Jurassic-period sandstone formed 150 million years ago. Fine examples of Native American petroglyphs can be seen throughout the park. Picnicking. Camping (dump station). Group use areas, visitor center. Standard fees. Phone 702/397-2088.

(For accommodations see Las Vegas, Overton)

Virginia City (C-1)

Settled: 1859 **Pop:** 750 **Elev:** 6,220 ft **Area code:** 702 **Zip:** 89440

Nevada's most famous mining town, Virginia City once had a population of about 25,000 people and was one of the richest cities in North America. Its dazzling career coincided with the life of the Comstock Lode, which yielded more than $1 billion worth of silver and gold. In the 1870s Virginia City had 4 banks, 6 churches, 110 saloons, an opera house, numerous theaters and the only elevator between Chicago and San Francisco. Great fortunes, including those of Hearst and Mackay, were founded here.

Virginia City is perched on the side of Mt Davidson, where a diagonal slit marks the Comstock Lode. The site is beautiful, and the air is so clear that the blue and purple masses of the Stillwater Range can be seen 120 miles away. Nearer are the green fields and cottonwoods along the Carson River and the white sands of Forty Mile Desert. Gold was found in this area in 1848, but the big silver strike was made in 1859.

Visitors can tour mines and old mansions, some of which have been restored (Easter week, Memorial Day–Oct, daily); visit several museums and saloons (daily); stroll through the local shops and ride on the steam-powered V&T Railroad (May–Sept).

What to See and Do

The Castle (1868). 70 South B Street. Built by Robert N. Graves, a mine superintendent of the Empire Mine, this Victorian mansion was once referred to as the "house of silver door knobs." Filled with international riches; original furnishings. (Memorial Day wkend–Oct; daily) Phone 847-0275. ¢¢

(The Visitors' Bureau on C Street shows an 18-minute film, *Story of Virginia City,* and has information on tours to mines and other points of interest; phone 847-0177. The Chamber of Commerce, located on South C Street, PO Box 464, provides information maps & brochures; phone 847-0311.)

Annual Event

Camel Races. Mid-Sept.

(For accommodations see Carson City, Reno)

Wendover

(see Wendover, UT)

Winnemucca (A-2)

Settled: ca 1850 **Pop:** 6,134 **Elev:** 4,299 ft **Area code:** 702 **Zip:** 89445

Originally called French Ford, the town was renamed for the last great chief of the Paiutes, who ruled the area. Winnemucca was first settled by a Frenchman who set up a trading post. Many Basques live here. A Ranger District office of the Humboldt National Forest (see ELKO) is located here.

What to See and Do

Humboldt Museum. Jungo Rd and Maple Ave. Historical museum features Native American artifacts; bottles; pioneers' home items, tools, utensils; local history; antique auto display; old country store. (Mon–Fri & Sat afternoons; closed major hols) Donation. Phone 623-2912.

(For further information contact the Humboldt County Chamber of Commerce, 30 W Winnemucca; 623-2225.)

Motels

★★**BEST WESTERN GOLD COUNTRY INN.** 921 W Winnemucca Blvd. 702/623-6999; res: 800/436-5306; FAX 702/623-9190.

71 rms, 2 story. June–Labor Day: S, D $65–$75; each addl $10; under 12 free; lower rates rest of yr. Crib $5. Pet accepted, some restrictions. TV; cable. Heated pool. Complimentary coffee in lobby. Restaurant adj open 24 hrs. Ck-out noon. Cr cds: A, C, D, DS, ER, MC, V.

✔ ★**LA VILLA.** 390 Lay St. 702/623-2334; FAX 702/623-0158. 37 rms, 2 story. May–Labor Day: S $38; D $48–$55; each addl $3; suites $65; lower rates rest of yr. Pet accepted. TV; cable. Continental bkfst in lobby. Restaurant nearby. Ck-out 11 am. Coin lndry. Cr cds: A, DS, MC, V.

★★**RED LION INN & CASINO.** 741 W Winnemucca Blvd. 702/623-2565; FAX 702/623-5702. 107 units, 2 story. June–Oct: S, D $68–$78; each addl $10; suites $95–$150; under 13 free; lower rates rest of yr. Crib $5. Pet accepted, some restrictions. TV. Heated pool. Restaurant open 24 hrs. Bar. Ck-out noon. Game rm. Some balconies. Casino. Cr cds: A, C, D, DS, ER, MC, V.

★★**THUNDERBIRD.** 511 W Winnemucca Blvd, at Garrison St. 702/623-3661; FAX 702/623-4234. 50 rms, 2 story. June–Labor Day: S $50; D $55; each addl $5; lower rates rest of yr. Crib $5. Pet accepted. TV; cable. Heated pool. Coffee in lobby. Restaurant nearby. Ck-out noon. Cr cds: A, C, D, DS, MC, V.

✔ ★**VAL-U INN.** 125 E Winnemucca Blvd. 702/623-5248; res: 800/443-7777; FAX 702/623-4722. 80 rms, 3 story. No elvtr. Mid-May–Sept: S $42–$45; D $48–$53; each addl $4; lower rates rest of yr. Crib $4. Pet accepted; $5. TV; cable. Heated pool; sauna, steam rm. Continental bkfst in lobby. Restaurant nearby. Ck-out noon. Cr cds: A, C, D, DS, MC, V.

Restaurants

✔ ★**BIDART'S RISTORANTE & CANTINA.** 47 E Winnemucca Blvd. 702/623-3021. Hrs: 10 am–10 pm; Sat from 7 am. Closed Sun; major hols. Mexican, Italian menu. Bar. Semi-a la carte: bkfst $3–$6, lunch $3.95–$7.75, dinner $8.50–$12.95. Specializes in ravioli, chimichangas, deep-fried ice cream. Cantina atmosphere. Cr cds: A, DS, MC, V.

★**ORMACHEA'S.** 180 Melarky St. 702/623-3455. Hrs: 6–9:30 pm. Closed Sun & Mon; some major hols. Basque, Amer menu. Bar. Complete meals: dinner $10.25–$17. Specializes in Basque dishes. Parking. Paintings, watercolors, prints of local scenery. Cr cds: MC, V.

Yerington (C-1)

Pop: 2,367 **Elev:** 4,384 ft **Area code:** 702 **Zip:** 89447

The town was first named Pizen Switch, presumably because of the bad whiskey being sold. Wovoka, the Paiute messiah, grew up in this area. In 1889 Wovoka claimed to have had a vision in which he was instructed to teach a new dance that would oust the white intruders and restore to the Native Americans their lands and old way of life. Spread of the Ghost Dance cult sparked rumors of an uprising. Trouble with the Sioux in 1890 resulted in the arrrival of federal troops. When the "ghost shirts" failed to protect their wearers during the massacre at Wounded Knee, the Ghost Dance cult died out.

What to See and Do

1. Fort Churchill State Historic Park. 25 mi N on US 95A, then 1 mi W on Old Fort Churchill Rd. This post was established when the rush to the Comstock began, as protection against the Paiutes. It was garrisoned from 1860 to 1869. Adobe walls of the old buildings exist in a state of arrested decay. The visitor center has displays. Camping facilities on 1,232 acres. Standard fees. Phone 577-2345.

2. **Lyon County Museum.** 215 S Main. Complex includes a general store, natural history building, blacksmith shop, schoolhouse. (Sat, Sun; closed Thanksgiving, Dec 25) For wkday tours phone 463-3341, ext 255. **Free.**

(For further information contact the Mason Valley Chamber of Commerce, 227 S Main St; 463-3721.)

Utah

Population: 1,722,850	
Land area: 84,990 square miles	
Elevation: 2,200–13,528 feet	
Highest point: Kings Peak (Duchesne County)	
Entered Union: January 4, 1896 (45th state)	
Capital: Salt Lake City	
Motto: Industry	
Nickname: Beehive State	
State flower: Sego lily	
State bird: California gull	
State tree: Blue spruce	
State fair: September 8–18, 1994, in Salt Lake City	
Time zone: Mountain	

Utah is named for the Ute people, a nomadic Shoshonean tribe that populated these regions before the days of westward expansion. The state presents many natural faces, with arid desert dominating the west and south, high, rugged mountains in the east and north and the deep, jagged canyons of the Colorado and Green rivers. Utah contains examples of almost all water and land forms, many unique to the state. This natural diversity, although stimulating to the artistic eye, created an environment inhospitable to early settlers. Tribes of Ute, Piute and Shoshone were the only people living in the region when the first white men, two Franciscan priests, passed through the area in 1776 en route to California from New Mexico. In 1819, British fur trappers began voyaging into northern Utah; by 1824 rugged mountain men—people like Canadians Étienne Provost and Peter Skene Ogden, for whom some of Utah's towns and rivers are named—were venturing into Utah's wilds. Although these men traversed and explored much of the state, it took the determination and perseverance of a band of religious fugitives, members of the Church of Jesus Christ of Latter-Day Saints, to conquer the wilderness that was Utah and permanently settle the land.

Brigham Young, leader of the Mormon followers, once remarked "If there is a place on this earth that nobody else wants, that's the place I am hunting for." On July 24, 1847, upon entering the forbidding land surrounding the Great Salt Lake, Young exclaimed "This is the place!" Immediately the determined settlers began to plow the unfriendly soil and build dams for irrigation. Hard work and tenacity were put to the test as the Mormons struggled to convert the Utah wilderness into productive land. With little to work with—what the settlers did not have, they did without—the Mormons gradually triumphed over the land, creating the safe haven they were searching for.

The Mormon church was founded by Joseph Smith on April 6, 1830, in New York State. The religion, based on writings inscribed on golden plates said to have been delivered to Smith by an angel and translated by him into *The Book of Mormon*, drew a large following.

Moving from New York to Ohio and Missouri, and then driven from Missouri and later Illinois, the church grew despite persecution and torture. When Smith was killed in Illinois, Young took over. With a zealot's determination, he headed farther west in search of a place of refuge. He found it in the Salt Lake area of Utah. Growing outward from their original settlement, Mormon pioneers and missionaries established colonies that were to become many of Utah's modern-day cities. During 1847, as many as 1,637 Mormons came to Utah, and by the time the railroad penetrated the region, more than 6,000 had settled in the state. Before his death in 1877, 30 years after entering the Salt Lake Valley, Brigham Young had directed the founding of more than 350 communities.

While the Mormon church undoubtedly had the greatest influence on the state—developing towns in an orderly fashion with wide streets, planting straight rows of poplar trees to provide wind breaks and introducing irrigation throughout the desert regions—the church members were not the only settlers. In the latter part of the 19th century, the West's fabled pioneer era erupted. The gold rush of 1849–50 sent gold seekers pouring through Utah on their way to California. The arrival of the Pony Express in Salt Lake City in 1860 brought more immigrants, and when the mining boom hit the state in the 1870s and 1880s, Utah's mining towns appeared almost overnight. In 1900 there were 277,000 Utahns; now the population stands at more than 1,700,000, with more than 75 percent living within 50 miles of Salt Lake City. The Mormon Church continues to play an important role, with close to 60 percent of the state's people belonging to the Church.

Utah's natural diversity has made it a state of magnificent beauty, with more than 3,000 lakes, miles of mountains, acres upon acres of forests and large expanses of deserts. Its main heights, 13,000 feet or more, are reached by plateaus and mountains lifted during the Cascade disturbance of the Cenozoic period. In northern Utah, the grandeur of the Wasatch Range, one of the most rugged mountain ranges in the United States, cuts across the state north to south; the Uinta Range, capped by the white peaks of ancient glaciers, is the only major North American range that runs east to west. In the western third of the state lies the Great Basin, a land-locked drainage area that, at one time, was half covered by a large, ancient sea. At its peak, Lake Bonneville was 1,050 feet deep, 145 miles wide and 346 miles long. The Great Salt Lake and Sevier Lake are saltwater remnants of Bonneville, and Utah Lake is a freshwater remnant. To the east, the Bonneville Salt Flats lie where the ancient lake had retreated. To the east and west extends the Colorado River Plateau, or Red Plateau. This red rock country, renowned for its brilliant coloring and fantastic rock formations, is also home to one of the largest concentrations of national parks and monuments. With its many aspects, Utah is a land designed for the traveler who loves the Western outdoors and can appreciate the awesome accomplishments of the pioneers who developed it.

National Park Service Areas

Five national parks—Arches, Bryce Canyon, Canyonlands, Capitol Reef, and Zion (see all)—and six national monuments—Cedar Breaks, Dinosaur, Natural Bridges, Rainbow Bridge, Timpanogos Cave (see all) and Hovenweep (see BLANDING)—preserve a number of Utah's geologically and archaeologically fascinating areas. Golden Spike National Historic Site (see BRIGHAM CITY) marks the spot where the first transcontinental railroad was completed in 1869. In addition, most of Glen Canyon National Recreation Area (see LAKE POWELL) is in Utah.

National Forests

The following is an alphabetical listing of National Forests and towns they are listed under.

Ashley National Forest (see VERNAL): Forest Supervisor in Vernal; Ranger offices in Duchesne*, Dutch John*, Manila*, Roosevelt, Vernal.

Dixie National Forest (see CEDAR CITY): Forest Supervisor in Cedar City; Ranger offices in Cedar City, Escalante*, Panguitch, St George, Teasdale*.

Fishlake National Forest (see RICHFIELD): Forest Supervisor in Richfield; Ranger offices in Beaver, Fillmore, Loa, Richfield.

Manti-LaSal National Forest (see MOAB, MONTICELLO and PRICE): Forest Supervisor in Price; Ranger offices in Ephraim*, Ferron*, Moab, Monticello, Price.

Uinta National Forest (see PROVO): Forest Supervisor in Provo; Ranger offices in Heber City, Pleasant Grove*, Spanish Fork*.

Wasatch-Cache National Forest (see LOGAN and SALT LAKE CITY): Forest Supervisor in Salt Lake City; Ranger offices in Kamas*, Logan, Mountain View, WY*, Ogden, Salt Lake City.
*Not described in text

State Recreation Areas

The following towns list state recreation areas in their vicinity under What to See and Do; refer to the individual town for directions and park information.

Listed under **Garden City:** see Bear Lake State Park.

Listed under **Green River:** see Goblin Valley State Park.

Listed under **Heber City:** see Deer Creek and Wasatch Mountain state parks.

Listed under **Kanab:** see Coral Pink Sand Dunes State Park.

Listed under **Loa:** see Escalante State Park.

Listed under **Logan:** see Hyrum Lake State Park.

Listed under **Moab:** see Dead Horse Point State Park.

Listed under **Nephi:** see Yuba State Park.

Listed under **Ogden:** see Willard Bay State Park.

Listed under **Park City:** see Rockport State Park.

Listed under **Price:** see Scofield State Park.

Listed under **Provo:** see Utah Lake State Park.

Listed under **St George:** see Gunlock and Snow Canyon state parks.

Listed under **Salina:** see Palisade State Park.

Listed under **Vernal:** see Steinaker State Park.

Water-related activities, hiking, riding, various other sports, picnicking and visitor centers, as well as camping, are available in many of these areas. Day-use fee, including picnicking, boat launching and museums: $1 (walk-ins); $3/carload. Camping (mid-Apr–Oct; some primitive sites available rest of yr), $5–$13/site/night; most sites 14-day max. Advance reservations may be obtained at all developed state parks; phone 801/322-3770 (Salt Lake City) or 800/322-3770. Pets on leash only. Sr citizen and disabled permit (free; UT residents only). For information on park facilities and permits, contact the Division of Parks & Recreation, 1636 W North Temple, Salt Lake City 84116; 801/538-7222.

Fishing & Hunting

Hunting license $5; nonresident big game hunting license $195 (includes tag for one buck deer); additional permit for bull elk $300; once-in-a-lifetime permit for moose, buffalo, desert bighorn sheep, $1,000; upland game mandatory habitat stamp (over 16 yrs) $5. For special permits write for information and apply from early–late May. Small game permits $40. Deer, elk, ducks, geese, pheasants, mourning doves and grouse are favorite quarry.

More than 3,000 lakes and hundreds of miles of mountain streams are filled with rainbow, German brown, cutthroat, Mackinaw and brook trout; there are also catfish, walleyed pike, bass, crappie and bluegill. Nonresident fishing license season permit (12 years and over) $40; 5-day permit $15; 1-day permit $5.

Further information may be obtained from the Division of Wildlife Resources, 1596 W North Temple, Salt Lake City 84116; 801/538-4700.

Skiing

The following towns list ski areas in their vicinity under What to See and Do; refer to the individual town for directions and information.

Listed under **Alta:** see Alta Ski Area.

Listed under **Beaver:** see Elk Meadows on Mt Holly Ski Area.

Listed under **Cedar City:** see Brian Head Ski Resort ‡.

Listed under **Garden City:** see Beaver Mountain Ski Area.

Listed under **Ogden:** see Nordic Valley Ski Resort, Powder Mountain Ski Resort, Snowbasin Ski Area.

Listed under **Park City:** see Deer Valley Resort, Park City Ski Area, ParkWest Resort, White Pine Touring Center‡‡.

Listed under **Provo:** see Sundance Ski Area ‡.

Listed under **Salt Lake City:** see Brighton Resort ‡, Solitude Resort ‡.

Listed under **Snowbird:** see Snowbird Ski and Summer Resort.
‡ Also cross-country trails
‡‡ Only cross-country trails

A booklet and further information may be obtained from Utah Travel Council, Council Hall, Capitol Hill, 300 N State St, Salt Lake City 84114; 801/538-1030.

River Expeditions

See Bluff, Green River, Moab, Salt Lake City, Vernal. For a directory of professional outfitters and river runners write Utah Travel Council,

Council Hall, Capitol Hill, 300 N State St, Salt Lake City 84114; 801/538-1030.

Safety Belt Information

Safety belts are mandatory for all persons in front seat of vehicle. Children under age 8 must be in an approved passenger restraint anywhere in the vehicle: ages 2–7 may use a regulation safety belt; under age 2 must use an approved safety seat. For further information phone 801/538-6120.

Interstate Highway System

The following alphabetical listing of Utah towns in *Mobil Travel Guide* shows that these cities are within 10 miles of the indicated interstate highways. A highway map, however, should be checked for the nearest exit.

> **INTERSTATE 15:** Beaver, Brigham City, Cedar City, Fillmore, Nephi, Ogden, Payson, Provo, St George, Salt Lake City.

> **INTERSTATE 70:** Green River, Salina.

> **INTERSTATE 80:** Salt Lake City, Wendover.

Additional Visitor Information

Utah Travel Council, Council Hall, Capitol Hill, 300 N State St, Salt Lake City 84114, will furnish excellent, extensive information on every section of the state and on special and annual events; phone 801/538-1030.

There are several visitor centers in Utah, with information and brochures about points of interest. Major centers may be found at the following locations: Utah Field House of Natural History, 235 E Main St, Vernal; St George Information Center, Dixie Center; Echo Information Center, 2 mi E of jct I-80E, I-80N; Thompson Information Center, on I-70, 45 mi west of Utah-Colorado border; Brigham City Information Center, I-15, 5 mi N.

The Utah Division of Fine Arts, E South Temple, Salt Lake City 84102, phone 801/533-5895, provides information on local and state-wide artists, museums, galleries and exhibits.

Alta (B-3)

Pop: 397 **Elev:** 8,600 ft **Area code:** 801 **Zip:** 84092

Founded around silver mines in the 1870s, Alta was notorious for constant shoot-outs in its 26 saloons. The town became the center of a noted ski area in 1937, with the opening of Utah's first ski resort. Historic markers identify the original townsite, and unusual wildflowers are found in Albion Basin.

What to See and Do

Alta Ski Area. On UT 210 in Little Cottonwood Canyon. Two triple, 6 double chairlifts, 4 rope tows; patrol, school, rentals; lodges, restaurant, cafeteria. Longest run 3½ mi, vertical drop 2,000 ft. (Mid-Nov–Apr, daily) Half-day rates. Phone 742-3333 or 572-3939 (snow conditions). ¢¢¢¢¢

(See Heber City, Park City, Salt Lake City)

Motels

★**ALTA LODGE.** On UT 210, in Little Cottonwood Canyon. 801/742-3500 or 322-4631 (Salt Lake City area); res: 800/748-5025; FAX 801/742-3500, ext 301. 57 rms, 50 with bath, 3 story. No A/C. No elvtr.

MAP, Nov–Apr: S $136–$225; D $98.50–$143.50/person; each addl $75; men's, women's dorms $86; under 12, $50; under 6, $24; under 5 free; EP avail in summer; lower rates June–mid-Oct; special rates Apr. Closed rest of yr. TV in lobby; cable. Restaurant 6:30–9 pm. Bar (winter). Ck-out 11 am. Meeting rms. Coin lndry. Downhill/x-country ski on site. Rec rm. Whirlpool, sauna. Fireplaces. Balconies. Sun deck. Accept cr cds (summer).

★★**RUSTLER LODGE.** On UT 210, in Little Cottonwood Canyon. 801/742-2200 or 532-2020 (Salt Lake City area); res: 800/451-5223; FAX 801/742-3832. 57 rms, 3 story. No A/C. No elvtr. MAP: S $99–$279; D $69–$159/person; each addl $65; suites $139–$209/person; under 12 special rates; higher rates Christmas & mid-Mar. Closed May–Oct. Crib avail. TV in rec rm; cable. Heated pool; whirlpool, saunas. Restaurant 7:30–9:15 am, 12:30–1:30 pm, 6:30–8:30 pm. Private club 4–11 pm. Ck-out noon. Coin lndry. Meeting rms. Bellhops. Downhill/x-country ski on site. Rec rm. Wet bars. No cr cds accepted.

Arches National Park (D-4)

(5 mi NW of Moab on US 191 to paved entrance road)

This timeless, natural landscape of giant stone arches, pinnacles, spires, fins and windows was once the bed of an ancient sea. Over time, erosion laid bare the skeletal structure of the earth, making this 114-square-mile area a spectacular outdoor museum. This wilderness, which contains the greatest density of natural arches in the world, was named a national monument in 1929 and a national park in 1971. More than 200 arches have been cataloged, ranging in size from three feet wide to the 105-foot-high, 291-foot-wide Landscape Arch.

The arches, other rock formations and views of the Colorado River with the peaks of the LaSal Mountains in the distance, can be reached by car, but hiking is suggested as the best way to explore. Petroglyphs from the primitive peoples that roamed this section of Utah from A.D. 700–1200 can be seen at the Delicate Arch trailhead. This is a wildlife sanctuary; no hunting is permitted. Hiking, rock climbing or camping in isolated sections should not be undertaken unless first reported to a park ranger at the visitor center (check locally for hours). Twenty-one miles of paved roads are open year round. Graded and dirt roads should not be attempted in wet weather. Devil's Garden Campground, 18 mi north of the visitor center off US 191, provides 52 individual and 2 group camp sites (March–mid-October, fee; rest of year, free; water available only March–mid-October). There is an entrance fee of $4/car; Golden Eagle, Golden Age and Golden Access passports accepted (see INTRODUCTION). For further information contact the Superintendent, PO Box 907, Moab 84532; 801/259-8161.

(For accommodations see Moab)

Beaver (D-2)

Settled: 1856 **Pop:** 1,998 **Elev:** 5,898 ft **Area code:** 801 **Zip:** 84713

Seat of Beaver County, this town is a national historic district with more than 200 houses of varied architectural styles and periods. It is also the birthplace of Butch Cassidy (1866).

Problems arose in Beaver's early days when tough gentile prospectors (in Utah, anyone not a Mormon was called a "gentile"), who came with a mining boom, derided the Mormons, who owned woolen mills. There was little harmony until the boom was over, but millions in gold, silver, lead, copper, tungsten, zinc, bismuth and sulphur had been mined by then. Now, irrigation has brought farming to Beaver. Dairying and stock-raising, as well as recreation, hunting and fishing, are important to the economy.

What to See and Do

1. **Fishlake National Forest.** (See RICHFIELD) E on UT 153. A Ranger District office of the forest is located in Beaver.
2. **Elk Meadows on Mt Holly Ski Area.** 18 mi E on UT 153. Triple, double chairlifts. School; rentals; shops, cafe, lodging. Longest run 2 mi; vertical drop 1,200 ft. (Mid-Nov–Mar, daily) Phone 438-5433. ¢¢¢¢¢

(For further information contact the Beaver County Travel Council, PO Box 372; 438-2975.)

Annual Event

Pioneer Days. Features parade, entertainment, horse racing; other events. Late July.

(See Cedar City, Richfield)

Motels

★★**BEST WESTERN PAICE INN.** (PO Box 897) 161 S Main St. 801/438-2438. 24 rms, 2 story. Mid-May–Sept: S $38–$44; D $40–$48; each addl $2; varied lower rates rest of yr. Crib $2. Pet accepted. TV; cable, in-rm movies. Heated pool; whirlpool, sauna. Restaurant 7 am–10 pm. Ck-out 11 am. Downhill ski 18 mi. Cr cds: A, C, D, DS, MC, V.

✔★**DE LANO.** (PO Box 1088) 480 N Main St. 801/438-2418. 10 rms. May–Oct: S $28–$32; D $32–$51; each addl $3; varied lower rates rest of yr. Crib $2. Pet accepted. TV; cable. Restaurant nearby. Ck-out 11 am. Coin lndry. Meeting rm. Covered parking. Downhill ski 18 mi. Cr cds: A, DS, MC, V.

★★**QUALITY INN.** (PO Box 1461) 1540 S 450 West. 801/438-5426. 52 rms, 2 story. June–Oct: S $36–$45; D $40–$50; each addl $4; suites $50–$55; under 18 free; ski plans; lower rates rest of yr. Crib $4. TV; cable. Indoor pool. Restaurant adj 6 am–10 pm. Ck-out 11 am. Downhill/x-country ski 18 mi. Cr cds: A, C, D, DS, MC, V.

★**SLEEPY LAGOON.** (Box 636) ½ mi N of I-15, South Beaver exit. 801/438-5681. 21 rms, 12 A/C, 9 air-cooled. May–Sept: S, D $38–$48; each addl $4; varied lower rates rest of yr. Crib free. TV. Heated pool. Coffee in rms. Restaurant nearby. Ck-out 11 am. Small pond. Downhill ski 18 mi. Cr cds: A, MC, V.

Restaurants

✔★**ARSHEL'S.** 711 N Main St. 801/438-2977. Hrs: 6 am–9:45 pm; Nov–Mar to 9 pm. Closed Thanksgiving, Dec 25. Res accepted. Semi-a la carte: bkfst $1.30–$4.95, lunch, dinner $2.65–$10. Specialties: chicken-fried steak, honey pecan chicken & shrimp. Parking. Cr cds: MC, V.

★★**COTTAGE INN.** 171 S Main St. 801/438-5855. Hrs: 7 am–10 pm. Closed Dec 25. Res accepted. Semi-a la carte: bkfst $2.50–$6.95, lunch $3.95–$8.95, dinner $3.95–$11.95. Child's meals. Specializes in prime rib (Fri, Sat), chicken-fried steak. Parking. Victorian-style interior with handcrafted doll case, antiques, carvings. Cr cds: MC, V.

Blanding (E-4)

Settled: 1905 **Pop:** 3,162 **Elev:** 6,105 ft **Area code:** 801 **Zip:** 84511

In 1940, with a population of 600, Blanding was the largest town in a county the size of Connecticut, Rhode Island and Delaware combined. Although surrounded by ranches and grazing areas, the city is a gateway to hunting and fishing grounds and national monuments. The sites can be explored by jeep or horseback along the many trails, or by boat through the waters of Glen Canyon National Recreation Area. A pueblo ruin, inhabited between A.D.800–1200, is now a state park within the city limits (see #1).

What to See and Do

1. **Edge of the Cedars State Park.** 1 mi NW off US 191. Excavated remnants of ancient dwellings and ceremonial chambers fashioned by the Anasazi. Artifacts and pictographs; museum of Native American history and culture. Visitor center. (Daily) Phone 678-2238. ¢
2. **Natural Bridges National Monument** (see). 4 mi S on US 191, then 40 mi W on UT 95.
3. **Glen Canyon National Recreation Area/Lake Powell.** 4 mi S on US 191, then 85 mi W on UT 95 & UT 276. (See LAKE POWELL)
4. **Hovenweep National Monument.** Approx 13 mi S on US 191, then 9 mi E on UT 262 and 6 mi E on county roads to Hatch Trading Post, follow signs 16 mi to Square Tower. Monument consists of six units of prehistoric ruins; the best preserved are the remains of pueblos (small cliff dwellings) and towers at Square Tower. Self-guided trail; park ranger on duty; visitor area (daily); camping (all-yr; limited facilities in winter). Camping ¢¢¢

(For brochures and maps of historic sites in the area contact the San Juan County Travel Council, 117 S Main St, Box 490, Monticello 84535; 587-3235 or 800/574-4FUN.)

(For accommodations see Bluff, Monticello)

Bluff (E-4)

Founded: 1880 **Pop:** 360 (est) **Elev:** 4,320 ft **Area code:** 801 **Zip:** 84512

Bluff's dramatic location between the sandstone cliffs along the San Juan River, its Anasazi ruins among the canyon walls and its Mormon pioneer past all combine to make it an interesting stop along scenic US 163 between the Grand Canyon and Mesa Verde national parks.

What to See and Do

1. **Tours of the Big Country.** Trips to Monument Valley, the Navajo Reservation and into canyons of southeastern Utah explore desert plant and wildlife, history, geology and Anasazi archaeology of this area. Naturalist-guided walking or four-wheel-drive tours. Half-day, full-day or overnight trips. (Apr–Oct) Contact Recapture Lodge, 672-2281. ¢¢¢¢
2. **Wild Rivers Expeditions.** Fun and educational trips on the archaeologically rich San Juan River through Glen Canyon National Recreation Area (see LAKE POWELL) and Cataract Canyon of the Colorado River. Geological formations, fossil beds and sites of 12,000-year-old early Paleo-Indians, through Anasazi to modern Navajo villages. (Apr–Oct) Phone 672-2244 or 800/422-7654 (exc UT). ¢¢¢¢

(For brochures and maps of historical sites in the area contact the San Juan County Travel Council, 117 S Main St, Box 490, Monticello 84535; 587-3235 or 800/574-4-FUN.)

Annual Event

Bluff Indian Day. Indian games, arts & crafts, competitive dancing, contests, horse races. 3rd wkend Apr.

(See Blanding)

Motel

✔ ★ ★ **RECAPTURE LODGE AND PIONEER HOUSE.** *(Box 309)* On US 191. 801/672-2281. 28 air-cooled rms, 1–2 story, 4 kits. (equipt avail). S $26–$36; D $28–$42; each addl $3–$6; kit. units $2–$5 addl. Crib free. TV. Heated pool; whirlpool. Playground. Continental bkfst in lobby. Restaurant opp 7 am–9 pm. Ck-out 11 am. Coin lndry. Lawn games. Bicycle rentals. Some refrigerators. Balconies. Picnic tables, grills. Sun decks. Also units for groups, families at Pioneer House (historic building). Geologist-guided tours; slide shows. ½ mi to San Juan River. Cr cds: A, DS, MC, V.

Brigham City (A-3)

Settled: 1851 **Pop:** 15,644 **Elev:** 4,439 ft **Area code:** 801 **Zip:** 84302

Renamed for Brigham Young in 1877, when he made his last public address here, this community was first known as Box Elder because of the many trees of that type that grew in the area. The city is situated at the base of the towering Wasatch Mountains.

What to See and Do

1. **Brigham City Mormon Tabernacle** (1881). 251 S Main St. The tabernacle, one of the most architecturally interesting buildings in Utah, has been in continuous use since 1881. Guided tours (May–Oct, Mon–Fri). Phone 723-5376.   **Free.**
2. **Brigham City Museum-Gallery.** 24 N 3rd W. Permanent history exhibits, rotating art exhibits; displays include furniture, clothing, books, photographs and documents reflecting the history of the Brigham City area since 1851. (Tues–Fri, also Sat afternoons) Phone 723-6769.   **Free.**
3. **Golden Spike National Historic Site.** 30 mi W via UT 83 & county road. Site where America's first transcontinental railroad was completed on May 10, 1869. Visitor center, movies, exhibits (daily; closed Jan 1, Thanksgiving, Dec 25). Self-guided auto tour along old railroad bed. Summer interpretive program includes presentations and operating replicas of steam locomotives "Jupiter" and "119" (May–early Oct, daily). (See ANNUAL EVENTS) Golden Eagle, Golden Age, Golden Access passports accepted (see INTRODUCTION). Contact Chief Ranger, PO Box 897; 471-2209. May–early Oct: per person ¢;   per car ¢¢

(For further information contact the Chamber of Commerce, 6 N Main St, PO Box 458; 723-3931.)

Annual Events

Driving of Golden Spike. Re-enactment of driving of golden spike in 1869 (see #3). At Promontory, site where the Central Pacific and Union Pacific met. Locomotive replicas used. May 10.

Railroaders Festival. Golden Spike National Historic Site (see #3). Relive the rush to complete transcontinental railroad. Professional railroaders pursue world record in spike driving. 2nd Sat Aug.

Peach Days Celebration. Parade; arts & crafts; carnival; car show; entertainment. 1st wkend after Labor Day.

(See Logan, Ogden)

Motel

✔ ★ **HoJo INN.** 1167 S Main St. 801/723-8511. 44 rms, 2 story. S $40–$43; D $49; each addl $4; under 18 free. Crib free. Pet accepted, some restrictions. TV; cable. Indoor pool; whirlpool. Complimentary continental bkfst. Restaurant adj 7 am–10 pm; closed Tues. Ck-out noon. Cr cds: A, C, D, DS, ER, MC, V, JCB.

Restaurants

✔ ★ **IDLE ISLE.** 24 S Main. 801/734-9062. Hrs: 7 am–8 pm. Closed Jan 1, Dec 25. Res accepted. Semi-a la carte: bkfst $2.25–$4.50, lunch, dinner $3–$9. Child's meals. Specializes in homemade custard, pies, baked chicken. Parking. Features soda fountain, homemade candy. Family-owned. Cr cds: MC, V.

★ ★ **MADDOX RANCH HOUSE.** *(1900 S US 89, Perry)* 2 mi S on US 89/91. 801/723-8545. Hrs: 11 am–9:30 pm. Closed Sun, Mon; Thanksgiving, Dec 25. Res accepted. Semi-a la carte: lunch, dinner $6.95–$21.95. Child's meals. Specializes in chicken, beef, seafood. Pianist Fri, Sat evenings. Parking. Western decor. Family-owned. Cr cds: DS, MC, V.

Bryce Canyon National Park (E-3)

(7 mi S of Panguitch on US 89, then 19 mi SE on UT 12)

Bryce Canyon is a 56-square-mile area of colorful, fantastic cliffs created by millions of years of erosion. Towering rocks worn to odd, sculptured shapes stand grouped in striking sequences. The Paiute, who once lived nearby, called this "the place where red rocks stand like men in a bowl-shaped canyon." Although termed a canyon, Bryce is actually a series of "breaks" in 12 large amphitheaters—some plunging as deep as 1,000 feet into the multicolored limestone. The formations appear to change color as the sunlight strikes from different angles and seem incandescent in the late afternoon. The famous Pink Cliffs were carved from the Claron Formation; shades of red, orange, white, gray, purple, brown and soft yellow appear in the strata. Rim Drive follows 17 miles along the eastern edge of the Paunsaugunt Plateau, where the natural amphitheaters are spread out below; plateaus covered with evergreens and valleys filled with sagebrush stretch away into the distance.

The visitor center at the entrance station has complete information on the park, including orientation shows, geologic displays and detailed maps (daily; closed Jan 1, Thanksgiving, Dec 25). Park is open year round; in winter, park road is open to most viewpoints. There is an entrance fee of $5/car; Golden Eagle, Golden Age and Golden Access Passports are accepted (see INTRODUCTION). For further information contact the Superintendent, Bryce Canyon 84717; 801/834-5322.

What to See and Do

1. **Talks** by rangers about history, geology, fauna, flora at campgrounds in the evening. (May–Sept)
2. **Hikes** with ranger naturalists into canyon. (May–Sept)
3. **Riding.** Horses available, escorted trips early morning, afternoon (spring, summer & fall). Fee.
4. **Van tour of three major viewpoints.** (May–Oct) Inquire at lodge for fees and schedule.
5. **Camping.** North Campground, E of park headquarters; Sunset Campground, 2 mi S of park headquarters. 14-day limit at both

sites; fireplaces, picnic tables, rest rms, water available. (Apr–Thanksgiving wkend) ¢¢¢

Motels

(Air conditioning is rarely necessary at this elevation)

★★★**BEST WESTERN RUBY'S INN.** *(Box 1, Bryce 84764) ½ mi N of park entrance on UT 63. 801/834-5341.* 316 rms, 1–2 story. June–Sept: S, D $70; each addl $5; suites, kit. units $105; varied lower rates rest of yr. Crib free. Pet accepted. TV; cable. Indoor pool. Restaurant 6:30 am–10 pm; winter hrs vary. Private club, setups. Ck-out 11 am. Coin lndry. Shopping arcade. Game rm. X-country ski opp. Picnic tables. Rodeo in summer; general store. Lake on property. Trailer park. Cr cds: A, C, D, DS, MC, V.

★★**BRYCE CANYON LODGE.** *(Box 400, Cedar City 84720) On UT 63, 3 mi S of UT 12. 801/834-5361; res: 801/586-7686.* 114 units in cabins, motel. May–mid-Oct: motel units $65; cabin units $75; each addl $5; suites $99. Closed rest of yr. Crib $5. Restaurant 6:30–10 am, 11:30 am–2:30 pm, 5:30–9:30 pm. Ck-out 11 am. Coin lndry. Bellhops. Sundries. Gift shop. Trail rides on mules, horses avail. Private patios. Emergency medical facility. Post office in lobby. Original 1923 building. Cr cds: A, C, D, DS, MC, V.

✔★★**BRYCE CANYON PINES.** *(Box 43, Bryce 84764) 6 mi NW of park entrance on UT 12. 801/834-5441; FAX 801/834-5330.* 50 rms, most A/C, 1–2 story. May–Oct: S, D $50–$70; each addl $5; suites $85–$110; kit. cottage $85; varied lower rates rest of yr. Crib $5. TV; cable. Heated pool. Restaurant 6:30 am–9:30 pm. Ck-out 11 am. Some fireplaces. Early Amer decor. Cr cds: D, DS, MC, V.

Restaurant

★**FOSTER'S.** *(Box 21) 3 mi NW of park entrance on UT 12. 801/834-5227.* Hrs: 7 am–10 pm; Dec–Mar from 2 pm. Beer. Semi-a la carte: bkfst 99¢–$4.25, lunch $1.25–$6.75, dinner $7.99–$22.50. Child's meals. Specializes in seafood, prime rib. Salad bar. Parking. Bakery adj. Cr cds: A, DS, MC, V.

Canyonlands National Park (D-4)

(N district: 9 mi N of Moab on US 191, then 21 mi SW on UT 313; S district: 12 mi N of Monticello on US 191, then 38 mi W on UT 211.)

Spectacular rock formations, canyons, arches, spires, pictograph panels, Native American ruins and desert flora are the main features of this 337,570-acre area. Set aside by Congress in 1964 as a national park, the area is largely undeveloped. Road conditions vary; primary access roads are paved and maintained, others are safe only for four-wheel-drive vehicles. For backcountry road conditions and information phone 259-7164. Three districts are open to the public:

Island in the Sky, North District, south of Dead Horse Point State Park (see MOAB) has Grand View Point, Upheaval Dome and White Rim Trail Road. This section is accessible by passenger car via UT 313, by four-wheel drive vehicle on dirt roads and by mountain bike.

Needles, South District, has hiking trails and four-wheel-drive roads to Angel Arch, the Needles, Chesler Park and the confluence of the Green and Colorado rivers. Also here are prehistoric ruins and rock art. This section is accessible by passenger car via UT 211, by four-wheel drive vehicle on dirt roads and by mountain bike.

Maze, West District, is accessible by hiking or by four-wheel drive vehicles using unimproved roads. The most remote and least visited section of the park, this area received its name from the many maze-like canyons. Horseshoe Canyon, a separate unit of the park nearby, is accessible via UT 24 and 30 miles of two-wheel drive dirt road. Roads usually passable only mid-March through mid-November.

Canyonlands is excellent for whitewater trips down the Green and Colorado rivers. Permits are required for private trips (fee; contact Chief Ranger's office); commercial trips (see MOAB). Campgrounds, with tent sites only, are located at Island in the Sky (free) and Needles (fee); water is available only at Needles. Visitor Contact Stations are in each district (daily). There is an entrance fee of $4/car. Golden Eagle, Golden Age, Golden Access passports accepted (see INTRODUCTION). For further information contact Superintendent, 125 W 200 South, Moab 84532; 801/259-7164.

(For accommodations see Moab, Monticello)

Capitol Reef National Park (D-3)

(10 mi E of Richfield on UT 119, then 76 mi SE on UT 24)

Capitol Reef, at an elevation ranging from 3,900–8,800 feet, is composed of red sandstone cliffs capped with domes of gray-white sandstone. Located in the heart of Utah's slickrock country, the park is actually a 75-mile section of the Waterpocket Fold, a 100-mile-long upthrust of sedimentary rock created during the formation of the Rocky Mountains. Pockets in the rocks collect thousands of gallons of water each time it rains. Capitol Reef was so named because the rocks formed a natural barrier to pioneer travel and the gray-white sandstone domes resemble the dome of the US Capitol.

Part of a nearly 242,000-square-mile area, this park was the home from A.D. 700–1250 of an ancient people who grew corn along the Fremont River. Petroglyphs can be seen on some of the sandstone walls.

The park can be approached from either east or west via UT 24, a paved road. There is a visitor center on this road about seven miles from the west boundary and eight miles from the east (daily; closed some major hols). A 25-mile scenic drive starts from this point (some parts unpaved). There are evening programs and guided walks (Memorial Day–Labor Day; free). Three campgrounds are available: Fruita, approximately 1½ mi S off UT 24, provides 70 tent and trailer sites year round (fee); Cedar Mesa, 23 mi S off UT 24, and Cathedral, 28 mi N off UT 24, offer a minimum of primitive tent sites with access depending on weather (free; no facilities). There is an entrance fee of $4/car. Golden Eagle, Golden Age, Golden Access passports accepted (see INTRODUCTION). For further information contact the Superintendent, Torrey 84775; 801/425-3791.

(See Loa)

Motels

★**CAPITOL REEF INN.** *(Box 100, 360 W Main St, Torrey 84775) 10 mi W of park on UT 24, ½ mi W of Torrey. 801/425-3271.* 10 rms. Apr–Oct: S, D $34–$38; each addl $4. Closed rest of yr. Pet accepted. TV. Playground. Restaurant 7–11 am, 5–9 pm. Ck-out 11 am. Gift shop. Cr cds: DS, MC, V.

✔★**SUNGLOW.** *(63 E Main St, Bicknell 84715) W of park on UT 24. 801/425-3821.* 18 rms, 10 A/C. Mar–mid-Nov: S $25–$28; D $34; each addl $2–$4. Closed rest of yr. Crib free. TV; cable. Restaurant 6:30 am–10 pm. Ck-out 11 am. Cr cds: A, DS, MC, V.

Cedar Breaks National Monument (E-2)

(23 mi E of Cedar City via UT 14)

Cedar Breaks National Monument's major formation is a spectacular, multicolored, natural amphitheater created by the same forces that sculpted Utah's other rock formations. The amphitheater, shaped like an enormous coliseum, is 2,000 feet deep and more than 3 miles in diameter. It is carved out of the Markagunt Plateau and is surrounded by Dixie National Forest (see CEDAR CITY). Cedar Breaks, at an elevation of more than 10,000 feet, was established as a national monument in 1933. It derives its name from the surrounding cedar trees and the word "breaks," which means "badlands." Although similar to Bryce Canyon National Park, Cedar Breaks' formations are fewer but more vivid and varied in color. Young lava beds, resulting from small volcanic eruptions and cracks in the earth's surface, surround the Breaks area; the heavy forests include bristlecone pines, one of the oldest trees on the earth. Here, as soon as the snow melts, wildflowers bloom profusely and continue to bloom throughout the summer.

Rim Drive, a five-mile scenic road through the Cedar Breaks' High Country, provides views of the monument's formations from four different overlooks. The area is open mid-May–mid-Oct, weather permitting. Point Supreme Campground, 2 miles north of south entrance, provides 30 tent and trailer sites (mid-June–mid-Sept, fee; water, rest rms). The visitor center offers geological, historical and environmental exhibits (Memorial Day–mid-Oct, daily); interpretive activities (mid-June–Labor Day). There is an entrance fee of $4/car. Golden Eagle, Golden Age, Golden Access passports accepted (see INTRODUCTION). For further information contact the Superintendent, PO Box 749, Cedar City 84720; 801/586-9451.

(For accommodations see Cedar City)

Cedar City (E-2)

Settled: 1851 **Pop:** 13,443 **Elev:** 5,834 ft **Area code:** 801 **Zip:** 84720

In 1852, Cedar City produced the first iron made west of the Mississippi. The blast furnace operation was not successful, however, and stock-raising soon overshadowed it, although iron is still mined west of the city on a limited basis. A branch line of the Union Pacific entered the region in 1923 and helped to develop the area. Now a tourist center because of its proximity to Bryce Canyon and Zion national parks (see both), Cedar City takes pride in its abundant natural wonders; streams and lakes have rainbow trout and the Markagunt Plateau provides deer and mountain lion hunting. Headquarters and a Ranger District office of the Dixie National Forest (see #4) are located here.

What to See and Do

1. **Kolob Canyons Visitor Center.** 17 mi S on I-15. This section of Zion National Park (see) provides a 7-mile hike to the Kolob Arch, world's largest, with a span of 310 feet. A five-mile scenic drive offers spectacular views of rugged peaks and sheer canyon walls 1,500 feet high. (Daily; closed Jan 1, Dec 25) Phone 586-9548. **Free.**

2. **Cedar Breaks National Monument** (see). 23 mi E via UT 14.

3. **Zion National Park** (see). 60 mi SE via I-15 & UT 9.

4. **Dixie National Forest.** 12 mi E on UT 14 to forest boundary or 17 mi SW on I-15, then W. Table Cliff Point offers a view of four states—Colorado, Arizona, Nevada and Utah. Camping, picnicking, winter sports (see #5), lake and stream fishing, boating, hunting for deer, elk and cougar on 1.9 acres. For information contact the Supervisor, PO Box 627, 84721; 865-3200.

5. **Brian Head Ski Resort.** 19 mi NE on I-15 to Parowan, then 11 mi SE on UT 143, in Dixie National Forest. Five triple, 2 double chairlifts; patrol; school, lessons, rentals; restaurants, cafeterias, bars; nursery; ski shops, grocery, gift shops; lodging. Longest run ½ mi, vertical drop 1,400 ft. (Mid-Nov–late Apr, daily) Cross-country trails, rentals. Snowmobiling. Phone 677-2035. ¢¢¢¢¢

6. **Iron Mission State Park.** N via I-15, at city limits. Site of the first pioneer iron foundry west of the Mississippi; extensive collection of horse-drawn vehicles and wagons from Utah pioneer days, Native American artifacts. (Daily; closed Jan 1, Thanksgiving, Dec 25) Phone 586-9290. ¢

7. **Southern Utah University** (1897). (4,500 students) 351 W Center. Braithwaite Fine Arts Gallery (daily exc Sun; free). (See ANNUAL and SEASONAL EVENTS) Phone 586-7700.

8. **Sightseeing trips. Cedar City Air Service.** Trips include Cedar Breaks National Monument and Grand Canyon, Zion and Bryce Canyon national parks (see all); other trips avail. (Daily) Phone 586-3881. ¢¢¢¢¢

(For further information contact the Chamber of Commerce, 286 N Main St, PO Box 220; 586-4484.)

Annual Events

Utah Summer Games. Olympic-style athletic events for amateur athletes. Phone 586-7228. June.

Renaissance Fair. Main St City Park. Entertainment, food and games, all in the style of the Renaissance. Held in conjunction with opening of Utah Shakespearean Festival (see SEASONAL EVENTS). Early July.

Seasonal Events

Utah Shakespearean Festival. Southern Utah University campus (see #7). Shakespeare presented on outdoor stage that is replica of 16th-century Tiring House and 750-seat indoor facility. Nightly exc Sun; preplay activities. Children over 5 yrs only; babysitting at festival grounds. Phone 586-7878 (box office). Late June–early Sept.

American Folk Ballet Summer Festival. Southern Utah University Centrum (see #7). Matinee and nightly performances. Phone 586-7872 (box office). Mid-July.

Motels

✔ ★ ★ **BEST WESTERN TOWN & COUNTRY INN.** *189 N Main St, near Municipal Airport.* 801/586-9900; FAX 801/586-1664. 157 rms, 2 story. S $46–$65; D $48–$70; each addl $4; suites $75–$140. Crib free. TV. 2 pools; 1 indoor; whirlpool. Restaurant 7 am–10 pm. Ck-out 11 am. Coin lndry. Meeting rm. Free airport transportation. Game rm. Cr cds: A, C, D, DS, MC, V.

🏊 ✕ 🚫 Ⓖ SC

★ ★ **COMFORT INN.** *250 N 1100 West.* 801/586-2082; FAX 801/586-3193. 94 rms, 2 story. June–Sept: S $55; D $64; each addl $5; under 12 free; lower rates rest of yr. Crib free. TV; cable. Heated pool. Complimentary continental bkfst. Restaurant adj 6 am–11 pm. Ck-out 11 am. Meeting rms. Free airport transportation (by appt). Cr cds: A, C, D, DS, ER, MC, V.

🅿 🏊 🚫 Ⓖ SC

★ ★ ★ **HOLIDAY INN.** *1575 W 200 North, near Municipal Airport.* 801/586-8888; FAX 801/586-1010. 100 rms, 2 story. June–Sept: S $73; D $77–$87; each addl $10; suites $95–$150; under 19 free; ski rates; lower rates rest of yr. Crib free. TV; cable. Heated pool. Restaurant 6 am–11 pm. Rm serv. Ck-out noon. Coin lndry. Meeting rms. Free airport, bus depot transportation. Exercise equipt; weights, rowing machine, whirlpool, sauna, steam rm. Cr cds: A, C, D, DS, MC, V.

★QUALITY INN. *18 S Main St. 801/586-2433.* 50 rms, 3 story. No elvtr. June–Sept: S, D $58–$72; each addl $4; under 17 free; lower rates rest of yr. Crib $4. TV; cable. Pool. Complimentary continental bkfst (winter). Restaurant adj 6 am–11 pm. Ck-out 11 am. Cr cds: A, C, D, DS, ER, MC, V, JCB.

✔ ★RODEWAY INN. *281 S Main St. 801/586-9916.* 48 rms, 2 story. June–Sept: S $53; D $56–$70; each addl $4; suites $66–$74; under 18 free; lower rates rest of yr. Crib free. Pet accepted. TV; cable. Heated pool; sauna. Restaurant adj 6 am–10 pm; winter to 9:30 pm. Ck-out noon. Meeting rm. Free airport transportation. Game rm. Cr cds: A, C, D, DS, ER, MC, V, JCB.

Restaurant

★MILT'S STAGE STOP. *(Box 1684) 5 mi E on UT 14 in Cedar Canyon. 801/586-9344.* Hrs: 5–10 pm; winter from 6 pm. Closed Thanksgiving, Dec 25. Res accepted. Bar. Semi-a la carte: dinner $10.75–$27. Child's meals. Specializes in steak, seafood. Salad bar. Parking. Rustic decor. Cr cds: A, C, D, DS, MC, V.

Dinosaur National Monument (B-4)

(7 mi N of Jensen on UT 149)

On August 17, 1909, paleontologist Earl Douglass discovered thousands of dinosaur bones in this area, several of them nearly complete skeletons. Since then, this location has provided more skeletons, skulls and bones of Jurassic-period dinosaurs than any other dig in the world. The dinosaur site comprises only 80 acres of this 325-square-mile area, which lies at the border of Utah and Colorado. The back country section, most of which is in Colorado, is a land of fantastic and deeply eroded canyons of the Green and Yampa rivers. The entire area was named a national monument in 1915.

Utah's Dinosaur Quarry section can be entered from the junction of US 40 and UT 149, north of Jensen, 13 miles east of Vernal; approximately 7 miles north on UT 149 is the fossil exhibit. Another 4 miles north is Split Mountain Campground, with 35 tent & trailer sites available, and 1 mile farther is Green River Campground, with 90 tent & trailer sites available mid-May–mid-September. A smaller campground, Rainbow Park, provides a small number of tent sites from May–November. Lodore, Deerlodge and Echo Park campgrounds are available in Colorado. A fee is charged at Split Mountain and Green River (water and rest rooms available). Access to the Colorado back country section is via Harpers Corner Road, starting at monument headquarters on US 40, 2 miles east of Dinosaur, Colorado. This 32-mile surfaced road ends at Harpers Corner. From there a 1-mile foot trail leads to a promontory overlooking the Green and Yampa rivers, more than 2,500 feet below.

Because of snow, some areas of the monument are closed approximately mid-November–mid-April. There is an entrance fee of $5/car. Golden Eagle, Golden Age, Golden Access passports accepted (see INTRODUCTION). For further information contact the Superintendent, PO Box 210, Dinosaur, CO 81610; 303/374-2216 (headquarters).

What to See and Do

1. **Dinosaur Quarry Information Center.** Remarkable fossil deposit exhibit of 150-million-year-old dinosaur remains; preparation laboratory on display. (Daily; closed Jan 1, Thanksgiving, Dec 25)

2. **Picnicking, hiking, fishing.** Harpers Corner area has picnic facilities, also picnicking at campgrounds. Self-guided nature trails (all-yr), guided nature walks. State fishing license required; boating permit required (obtainable only by advance lottery at the Headquarters Boating Office).

3. **River rafting.** On Green and Yampa rivers, by advance permit from National Park Service or with concession-operated guided float trips. Information at Superintendent's office.

4. **Backpacking.** By permit obtainable at visitor centers; few marked trails.

(For accommodations see Vernal)

Fillmore (C-2)

Settled: 1856 **Pop:** 1,956 **Elev:** 5,135 ft **Area code:** 801 **Zip:** 84631

Fillmore, the seat of Millard County and Utah's territorial capital until 1856, is today a trading center for the surrounding farm and livestock region. It is a popular hunting and fishing area. A Ranger District office of the Fishlake National Forest is located here.

What to See and Do

1. **Territorial Statehouse State Park.** 50 W Capitol Ave. Utah's first territorial capitol, built in the 1850s of red sandstone, is now a museum with extensive collection of pioneer furnishings, pictures, Native American artifacts and early documents; also rose garden. (Daily; closed Jan 1, Thanksgiving, Dec 25) Phone 743-5316. ¢

2. **Fishlake National Forest.** E on improved gravel road (see RICHFIELD).

(For further information contact the Chamber of Commerce, PO Box 1214; or the City of Fillmore, 75 W Center, PO Box 687; 743-5233.)

(See Nephi, Richfield)

Motel

✔ ★ ★ BEST WESTERN PARADISE INN. *(Box 368) 1025 N Main St. 801/743-6895.* 80 rms, 2 story. Mid-May–Oct: S $40; D $44; each addl $2; varied lower rates rest of yr. Crib $4. Pet accepted. TV. Heated pool; whirlpool. Restaurant 6 am–10 pm; summer to 11 pm. Ck-out 11 am. Cr cds: A, C, D, DS, MC, V, JCB.

Garden City (A-3)

Settled: 1875 **Pop:** 193 **Elev:** 5,960 ft **Area code:** 801 **Zip:** 84028

As was the case with many of Utah's towns, Garden City was settled by Mormon pioneers sent here from Salt Lake City. Today, it is a small resort town on the western shore of Bear Lake (see #1).

What to See and Do

1. **Bear Lake.** E of city. Covering 71,000 acres on the border of Utah and Idaho, this body of water is the state's second largest freshwater lake. Approx 20 miles long and 200 feet deep, it offers good fishing for mackinaw, rainbow trout and the rare Bonneville Cisco. Boat rentals at several resorts; sailboat regattas in the summer. On the west shore is

Bear Lake State Park. 2 mi N on US 89. Three park areas include state marina on west shore of lake, Rendezvous Beach on south shore and Eastside area on east shore. Swimming, beach, waterskiing; fishing, ice fishing; boating (ramp, dock), sailing. Hiking, mountain biking. Cross-country skiing, snowmobiling. Picnicking. Tent & trailer sites (rest rms, showers, hookups, dump station; fee). Visitor center. (Daily) Phone 946-3343. Per vehicle ¢¢

2. **Beaver Mt Ski Area.** 15 mi W via US 89. Three double chairlifts; patrol, school, rentals; day lodge, cafeteria. 16 runs; vertical drop 1,600 ft. (Dec–early Apr, daily) Phone 753-0921 or -4822 (snow conditions). Sr citizen & half-day rates avail. ¢¢¢¢¢

(For further information contact the Bear Lake Convention & Visitors Bureau, PO Box 26, Fish Haven, ID 83287; 208/945-2333 or 800/448-2327.)

(For accommodations see Logan)

Green River (C-4)

Settled: 1878 **Pop:** 866 **Elev:** 4,079 ft **Area code:** 801 **Zip:** 84525

Originally a mail relay station between Ouray, Colorado, and Salina, Utah, Green River now produces premium watermelons and cantaloupes on land irrigated by the Green River, one of Utah's largest rivers.

What to See and Do

1. **Goblin Valley State Park.** 12 mi W on I-70 (US 50), then 30 mi S on UT 24. Mile-wide basin filled with intricately eroded sandstone formations resembling gnomes, mushrooms or anything else a fertile imagination can dream up. Hiking, camping (rest rms, showers, dump station). (Daily) Phone 564-3633. ¢¢

2. **Arches National Park** (see). 23 mi E on I-70 (US 50), then 54 mi S on US 191.

3. **River trips.** On the Colorado, Green, San Juan and Dolores rivers.

   Adventure River Expeditions. PO Box 2133, Salt Lake City 84110; 943-0320 or 800/331-3324. ¢¢¢¢¢

   Colorado River & Trail Expeditions, Inc. PO Box 57575, Salt Lake City 84157-0575; 261-1789 or 800/253-7328. ¢¢¢¢¢

   Holiday River and Bike Expeditions. 544 E 3900 South, Salt Lake City 84107; 266-2087 or 800/624-6323 (exc UT). ¢¢¢¢¢

   Moki Mac River Expeditions. PO Box 21242, Salt Lake City 84121; 268-6667 or 800/284-7280. ¢¢¢¢¢

   Western River Expeditions. 7258 Racquet Club Dr, Salt Lake City 84121; 942-6669 or 800/453-7450. ¢¢¢¢¢

(For further information contact the Green River Travel Council, 885 E Main St; 564-3526.)

Annual Event

Melon Days. 3rd wkend Sept.

Motels

★ ★**BEST WESTERN RIVER TERRACE.** *(Box 420) 880 E Main St. 801/564-3401.* 51 rms, 2–3 story. No elvtr. Mid-May–Oct: S $51–$70; D $62–$100; each addl $2; family rates; varied lower rates rest of yr. TV; cable. Heated pool. Restaurant adj 6 am–10 pm. Ck-out 11 am. Bus depot transportation. Exercise equipt; stair machine, treadmill. Private patios, balconies. On river. Cr cds: A, C, D, DS, MC, V.

🏧 🏖 🏃 🚳 🌀

★**RODEWAY INN WESTWINDS.** *(PO Box 304) 525 E I-70 Business Loop. 801/564-3421.* 42 rms, 2 story. May–Oct: S, D $55–$60; each addl $5; suites $55–$60; under 18 free; lower rates rest of yr. Crib free. TV; cable. Restaurant adj open 24 hrs. Ck-out 11 am. Coin lndry. Meeting rms. Game rm. Some in-rm whirlpools. Cr cds: A, C, D, DS, ER, MC, V, JCB.

D 🚳 🌀 SC

Restaurant

✔ ★**TAMARISK.** *870 E Main St. 801/564-8109.* Hrs: 6 am–10 pm. Closed Thanksgiving, Dec 25. Semi-a la carte: bkfst $2.20–$6.95, lunch, dinner $3.75–$13.95. Buffet: bkfst $4.95, dinner $6.95. Child's meals. Specializes in chicken, steak, fish. Salad bar. Parking. Country-style cafe; view of Green River. Cr cds: A, C, D, DS, MC, V.

D SC

Heber City (B-3)

Settled: 1859 **Pop:** 4,782 **Elev:** 5,595 ft **Area code:** 801 **Zip:** 84032

In a fertile mountain-ringed valley, Heber City was once a commercial and livestock shipping center. Unusual crater mineral springs, called hot pots, are located four miles west near Midway. Mt Timpanogos, one of the most impressive mountains in the state, is to the southwest in the Wasatch Range. Good picnicking, fishing and hunting areas abound. A Ranger District office of the Uinta National Forest (see PROVO) is located here.

What to See and Do

1. **State Fish Hatchery.** 4 mi W on UT 113, then S, near Midway. (Daily) Children with adult only. Phone 654-0282. **Free.**

2. **Timpanogos Cave National Monument** (see). 16 mi SW on US 189, then 12 mi NW on UT 92.

3. **Wasatch Mountain State Park.** 2 mi NW off UT 220 or 224. Located in Heber Valley. Approx 25,000 acres. Fishing; boating. Hiking; 27-hole golf. Snowmobiling, cross-country skiing. Picnicking, restaurant. Camping (fee; hookups, dump station). Visitor center. (Daily) Standard fees. Phone 654-0532.

4. **Deer Creek State Park.** 8 mi SW on US 189. Swimming; fishing; boating (ramp). Camping (rest rms, showers; dump and fish cleaning stations). (Daily) Phone 654-0171. Day-use per vehicle ¢¢

5. **Piute Creek Outfitters.** 12 mi NE via US 189, in Kamas. Guided horse pack trips of 4–10 days into the High Uinta Mountains. Fishing and hunting. (July–Oct) Phone 783-4317 or 800/225-0218. ¢¢¢¢¢

(For further information contact Heber Valley Chamber of Commerce, PO Box 427; 654-3666.)

Annual Events

Cutter, snowmobile and dog sled races. 1st wkend Feb.

Wasatch County Fair. Parades, exhibits, livestock shows, rodeos, dancing. 2nd wkend Aug.

Swiss Days. 4 mi W in Midway. "Old country" games, activities, costumes. Fri & Sat before Labor Day.

(See Alta, Park City, Provo, Salt Lake City)

Motels

★**DANISH VIKING LODGE.** *989 S Main St. 801/654-2202; res: 800/544-4066 (exc UT).* 34 rms, 1-2 story, 3 kits. Mid-May–mid-Sept & Christmas season: S $32–$66; D $36–$74; each addl $4; kit. units $45–$74; ski, honeymoon packages; lower rates rest of yr. Crib $3. TV; cable. Outdoor pool; whirlpool, sauna. Playground. Complimentary coffee in lobby. Restaurant nearby. Ck-out 11 am. Coin lndry. Downhill ski 12 mi; x-country ski 7 mi. Refrigerators. Picnic tables, grills. Cr cds: A, C, D, DS, MC, V.

♿ 🏖 🚳 🌀 SC

✔ ★**NATIONAL 9 HIGH COUNTRY INN.** *1000 S Main St. 801/654-0201; res: 800/345-9198 (exc UT).* 38 rms. May–Sept: S $38; D

$40–$48; each addl $2; lower rates rest of yr. Crib $3. TV; cable. Heated pool; whirlpool. Playground. Complimentary continental bkfst. Restaurant 6 am–10 pm. Ck-out 11 am. Coin lndry. Downhill ski 20 mi; x-country ski 5 mi. Refrigerators. Picnic table. View of mountains. Cr cds: A, C, D, DS, MC, V.

Resort

★ ★ ★**HOMESTEAD.** (700 N Homestead Dr, Midway 84049) 5 mi W of US 40. 801/654-1102; res: 800/327-7220; FAX 801/654-5087. 117 rms, 1–2 story, 9 suites. S, D $75–$129; each addl $10; suites $145–$220; ski, golf packages. TV; cable, in-rm movies. 2 pools, 1 indoor; whirlpool, sauna. Restaurant (see SIMON'S FINE DINING). Bar. Ck-out 11 am, ck-in 3 pm. Meeting rms. Gift shop. Lighted tennis. 18-hole golf. X-country ski 10 mi. Horse stables. Wagon & buggy rides. Lawn games. Historic country inn (1886); spacious grounds, duck ponds. Cr cds: A, C, D, DS, MC, V.

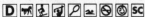

Restaurant

★ ★ ★**SIMON'S FINE DINING.** (See Homestead Resort) 801/654-1102. Hrs: 5:30–10 pm; Sun brunch 10:30 am–3 pm. Res accepted. Wine list. Complete meals: dinner $12.95–$26.95. Sun brunch $13.95. Child's meals. Daily specials. Pianist. Parking. Outdoor dining. Fireplaces. View of valley. Cr cds: A, C, D, DS, MC, V.

Kanab (E-2)

Founded: 1870 **Pop:** 3,289 **Elev:** 4,909 ft **Area code:** 801 **Zip:** 84741

Located at the base of the Vermillion Cliffs, this city began around Fort Kanab, built in 1864. Indians, however, forced the abandonment of the fort. Later, Mormon missionaries made Kanab a permanent settlement. Although the city's regular economy revolves around lumber, cattle, sheep and farm produce, since 1922 more than 100 Hollywood productions have used the sand dunes, canyons and lakes surrounding Kanab as their settings. Some movie-set towns can still be seen. Kanab is within a 1½-hour drive from the north rim of the Grand Canyon, Zion and Bryce Canyon national parks, Cedar Breaks and Pipe Spring national monuments and Glen Canyon National Recreation Area.

What to See and Do

1. **Pipe Spring National Monument** (see in ARIZONA). 7 mi S on US 89, then 14 mi W on AZ 389, in Arizona.
2. **Zion National Park** (see). 17 mi NW on US 89, then 25 mi W on UT 9.
3. **Glen Canyon National Recreation Area/Lake Powell.** 68 mi E via US 89, at Wahweap Basin Marina (see PAGE, AZ); access in Utah at Bullfrog Marina (see LAKE POWELL).
4. **Coral Pink Sand Dunes State Park.** 14 mi NW on US 89, then 12 mi S on county road. Six square miles of very colorful, windswept sandhills. Hiking. Picnicking. Tent & trailer sites (fee; showers, dump station). Off-hwy vehicles allowed; exploring, photography. (Daily) Phone 874-2408. Day-use per vehicle ¢¢
5. **Grand Canyon Scenic Flights.** 2½ mi S on US 89-A. Flights to Grand Canyon during daylight hrs; flight covering Bryce Canyon, and Zion National Parks, Lake Powell and Coral Pink Sand Dunes. (All-yr, by reservation) Phone 644-2904. ¢¢¢¢¢

(For further information contact Kane County Travel Council, 41 S 100 East; 644-5033.)

Seasonal Event

Melodrama. Old Barn Theater. Phone 644-2601. Late May–late Sept.

Motels

★ ★**BEST WESTERN RED HILLS.** 125 W Center St. 801/644-2675. 72 rms, 2 story. May–Oct: S $65; D $70; each addl $5; lower rates rest of yr. Crib $5. TV; cable. Heated pool; whirlpool. Restaurant opp 6 am–10 pm. Ck-out 11 am. Meeting rm. Refrigerators. Some balconies. Cr cds: A, C, D, DS, MC, V.

★ ★**FOUR SEASONS MOTOR INN.** (Box 308) 22 N 300 West. 801/644-2635. 41 rms, 2 story. Apr–Oct: S $56; D $63; each addl $6; lower rates rest of yr. Crib free. TV; cable. Pool; wading pool. Restaurant 6:30 am–10:30 pm. Ck-out 11 am. Sundries. Gift shop. Cr cds: A, C, DS, MC, V.

✔ ★ ★**PARRY LODGE.** 89 E Center St. 801/644-2601; res: 800/748-4104. 89 rms, 1–2 story. May–Oct: S $54.50; D $63; each addl $6; family rates; varied lower rates rest of yr. Pet accepted. TV; cable. Heated pool. Restaurant 7 am–noon, 5–10 pm. Ck-out 11 am. Coin lndry. Autographed pictures of movie stars displayed in lobby. Cr cds: A, DS, MC, V.

★ ★**SHILO INN.** 296 W 100 North. 801/644-2562; FAX 801/644-5333. 119 rms, 2–3 story. Mid-Apr–Sept: S, D $68–$78; each addl $5; lower rates rest of yr. Crib $10. TV; cable. Heated pool; whirlpool. Complimentary continental bkfst, coffee. Restaurant opp 7 am–10:30 pm. Ck-out noon. Coin lndry. Meeting rms. Sundries. Gift shop. Free airport transportation. Many refrigerators. Cr cds: A, C, D, DS, MC, V.

Restaurants

★**CHEF'S PALACE.** 153 W Center St. 801/644-5052. Hrs: 6 am–11 pm; winter to 9 pm. Closed Dec. Res accepted. Semi-a la carte: bkfst $2.90–$7.85, lunch $2.90–$5.75, dinner $5–$38. Child's meals. Specializes in prime rib, charcoal-broiled steak. Salad bar. Parking. Cr cds: A, C, D, DS, MC, V.

✔ ★**HOUSTON'S TRAIL'S END.** 32 E Center St. 801/644-2488. Hrs: 6 am–10 pm. Closed Thanksgiving, Dec 25; also Jan & Feb. Semi-a la carte: bkfst $2.65–$5.75, lunch $4.50–$6.75, dinner $5–$13.50. Child's meals. Specializes in chicken-fried steak, shrimp. Salad bar. Rustic, Western decor; "burned-wood" walls, wagon wheel lamps. Cr cds: A, DS, MC, V.

Lake Powell (D3 – E3)

(Approximately 90 mi SW of Blanding)

Lake Powell, formed by the Glen Canyon Dam on the Colorado River, is located in Glen Canyon National Recreation Area. It stretches 186 miles, has more than 1,900 miles of shoreline, is the second-largest man-made lake in the US and is located in the second-largest canyon in the US. The lake is named for John Wesley Powell, the one-armed explorer who, in 1869, successfully navigated the Colorado River through Glen Canyon and the Grand Canyon and later became director of the US Geological Survey.

What to See and Do

1. **Glen Canyon National Recreation Area (Bullfrog Marina).** Access from the north via UT 95 to UT 276. This 1.2 million-acre, year-round recreation area offers swimming; fishing; boating, boat tours & trips, boat rentals & repairs; picnicking; camping, tent & trailer sites (full hookups; fee); lodgings. A ranger station and visitors center offering summer campfire programs is located in Bullfrog on UT 276 (Apr–Oct, daily); phone 801/684-2243. Additional access and recreational activities are available at Hite Marina, north end of lake, just off UT 95; Halls Crossing Marina, across the lake from Bullfrog on UT 276, accessible by ferry; Dangling Rope Marina, 50 miles downlake (south) from Bullfrog, accessible only by boat; and Wahweap Lodge and Marina, at far south end of lake near Page, AZ (see). A visitors center and headquarters for the recreation area are located in in Page, AZ. Phone 602/645-2511.

2. **Lake Powell Ferry.** Approx 3-mile trip between Bullfrog and Hall's Crossing saves 130 miles driving around lake. (Daily; reduced hrs in winter) Contact Utah Travel Council, Council Hall/Capitol Hill, Salt Lake City 84114; 801/538-1030 or 684-2261 (Lake Powell). Passenger vehicles ¢¢¢–¢¢¢¢¢; Passengers on foot ¢

3. **Boat trips on Lake Powell.** From Bullfrog or Halls Crossing marinas, both on UT 276. Trips include Canyon Explorer tour (2.5 hrs) and all-day Rainbow Bridge National Monument tour; also houseboat and powerboat rentals. Advance reservations advised. (Daily) Phone Lake Powell Resorts & Marinas, 602/278-8888.

4. **Rainbow Bridge National Monument** (see). On east shore of Lake Powell, 50 miles by boat from Bullfrog Marina, Halls Crossing Marina and Wahweap Lodge and Marina.

(For further information contact Lake Powell Resorts & Marinas/ARA Leisure Services, 2916 N 35th Ave, Suite 8, Phoenix, AZ 85017, phone 602/278-8888; or the Page/Lake Powell Chamber of Commerce, PO Box 727, Page, AZ 86040, phone 602/645-2741.)

(See Page, AZ)

Lodge

★★**DEFIANCE HOUSE.** *(Box 4055, Bullfrog 84533)* ¼ mi *from Bullfrog Marina, at top of hill. 801/684-2233; res: 800/528-6154; FAX 801/684-2312.* 56 units, 2 story, 8 cottages. Many rm phones. Mid-May–Sept: S $72–$80; D $80.50–$90; each addl $8.50; suites $95–$105; cottages $90–$130; under 12 free; boating tour plans; lower rates rest of yr. Crib $6. TV; cable. Playground. Dining rm 7 am–8 pm; summer to 10:30 pm. Bar 5–9 pm; summer to 10:30 pm. Ck-out 11 am. Coin lndry. Sundries. Gift shop. Balconies. Anasazi Indian motif; decor, artifacts. On lake; swimming. Cr cds: A, C, D, DS, MC, V.

Loa (D-3)

Pop: 444 Elev: 7,060 ft Area code: 801 Zip: 84747

This town was named Loa because of the volcano-like appearance of a nearby mountain. A Ranger District office of the Fishlake National Forest (see RICHFIELD) is located here.

What to See and Do

1. **Capitol Reef National Park** (see). Approx 23 mi E via UT 24.

2. **Escalante State Park.** 65 mi S via UT 12, then 1 mi W, near Escalante. Petrified forest; mineralized wood and dinosaur bones. Swimming; fishing; boating (ramps) at reservoir. Hiking; brid watching. Picnicking. Camping (rest rms, showers, dump station). (Daily) Standard fees. Phone 826-4466.

Lodge

★★★**ROAD CREEK INN.** *90 S Main St. 801/836-2485; res: 800/388-7688; FAX 801/836-2489.* 12 rms, 3 story, 2 suites. May–Oct: S, D $56–$59; each addl $6; suites $77; under 12 free; lower rates rest of yr. Crib free. TV; cable. Complimentary full bkfst. Restaurant 11:30 am–10 pm. Rm serv. Ck-out 11 am. Meeting rm. Whirlpool, sauna. Rec rm. Fish/hunt guides. Restored 1912 general store building; inn-like amenities. Totally nonsmoking. Cr cds: A, MC, V.

Logan (A-3)

Founded: 1855 Pop: 32,762 Elev: 4,535 ft Area code: 801 Zip: 84321

Logan, situated in the center of beautiful Cache Valley, is surrounded by snowcapped mountains. The city received its name from an early trapper, Ephraim Logan. Begun by Mormons who were dedicated to living from fruits of the soil, little else was sold in Logan's early days except timber and farm produce. The change to a more industrialized economic base came about slowly. Now the city of Logan is the location of four cheese factories, five electronics plants, book printing, plastics, baking and meat packing plants, as well as specialized woodworking and women's clothing manufacturers.

What to See and Do

1. **Mormon Tabernacle** (1873). Main & Center Sts. Gray limestone example of early Mormon building; seats 2,000. (Mon–Fri)

2. **Mormon Temple** (1884). 175 N 300 East. The site for this massive, castellated limestone structure was chosen by Brigham Young, who also broke ground for it in 1877. Grounds are open year round, but the temple is closed to the general public.

3. **Utah State University** (1888). (15,000 students) 5th North & 7th East Sts. On campus is the Nora Eccles Harrison Museum of Art (Mon–Fri; closed hols, also Thanksgiving wkend, Dec 22–Jan 2; free). (See ANNUAL EVENTS) For tours of campus phone 750-1129 or -1623.

4. **Daughters of the Utah Pioneers Museum.** 160 N Main, in Chamber of Commerce Bldg. Exhibits depict Utah's past. (Hrs vary, phone ahead) Phone 752-2161. **Free.**

5. **Ronald V. Jensen Living Historical Farm.** 5 mi S on US 89/91, in Wellsville. Agricultural museum with typical Mormon family farm of World War I era; 120 acres of fields, meadows, orchards and gardens; artifacts and machinery; costumed interpreters. (June–Aug, Tues–Sat) Sr citizen rate. (See ANNUAL EVENTS) Phone 245-4064. ¢

6. **Wasatch-Cache National Forest, Logan Canyon.** E on US 89 Natl Forest (scenic byway). Fishing. Back country trails, hunting. Winter sports. Picnicking. Camping. Fees are charged at most recreation sites. A Ranger District office is located in Logan at 860 N 1200 East; 753-2772.

7. **Hyrum State Park.** 12 mi S, off US 89/90. A 450-acre reservoir with beach swimming, waterskiing; fishing; boating (ramp, dock), sailing. Picnicking. Camping (trailer parking). (Apr–Oct) Standard fees. Phone 245-6866. Day-use per vehicle ¢¢

8. **Hardware Ranch.** 8 mi S via UT 165 to Hyrum/Blacksmith Fork Canyon, then 17 mi E via UT 101. In the winter, up to 800 wild elk congregate here for their annual winter "hand-out." Stored hay is carried onto the grounds by horse-drawn sled; several hours each day are required for dispersal. Feeding elk may be observed from the visitor center area, or, when snow is adequate, sleigh rides into the midst of the herds are available. Sleigh rides (Jan–Feb, wkends); wagon rides (mid-Dec–mid-Mar). Visitor center

(Dec–early Mar, daily). Phone 245-3131 (recording) or -5896. Rides ¢¢

(For further information contact the Cache Chamber of Commerce/ Bridgerland Travel Region, 160 N Main; 752-2161 or 800/882-4433.)

Annual Events

Festival of the American West. Utah State University campus (see #3). Historical pageant; pioneer and Indian crafts fair, art exhibition, antique quilt show; frontier town; medicine man show; log construction; Dutch-oven cook-off. Phone 750-1738. Late July–early Aug.

Steam Threshing Bee. Ronald V. Jensen Living Historical Farm (see #5). Late July–early Aug.

Cache County Fair. Rodeo, horse races, exhibits. Early Aug.

(See Brigham City, Garden City)

Motels

★★**BEST WESTERN BAUGH.** *153 S Main St. 801/752-5220; FAX 800/462-4154.* 77 rms, 1–2 story. S $36–$56; D $40–$60; each addl $4. Crib $4. TV; cable. Heated pool. Restaurant 6 am–10 pm; Sun 8 am–2 pm. Ck-out noon. Meeting rm. Picnic tables. Fireplaces. Sun deck. Cr cds: A, C, D, DS, MC, V.

≈ Ⓢ ⊘ SC

★★**COMFORT INN.** *447 N Main St. 801/752-9141.* 83 rms, 2 story. S $38–$42; D $42–$48; each addl $4; suites $55; under 12 free. Crib $5. TV; cable. Indoor pool; whirlpool. Restaurant adj 6–1 am. Ck-out noon. Coin lndry. Meeting rms. Valet serv. X-country ski 20 mi. Refrigerator in suites. Cr cds: A, C, D, DS, ER, MC, V, JCB.

D ⇙ ≈ Ⓢ ⊘ SC

✔ ★**DAYS INN.** *364 S Main St. 801/753-5623.* 48 rms, 2 story, 21 kit. units. S $32–$34; D $38–$42; each addl $4; suites $45–$55; kit. units $41; under 12 free; wkly rates avail. Crib free. TV; cable, in-rm movies. Complimentary continental bkfst. Restaurant nearby. Ck-out 11 am. Coin lndry. X-country ski 20 mi. Many refrigerators; some in-rm whirlpools. Cr cds: A, D, DS, MC, V.

⇙ ≈ Ⓢ ⊘ SC

Inn

★★**CENTER STREET BED & BREAKFAST.** *169 E Center St. 801/752-3443.* 12 rms in 3 buildings, 7 A/C, 4 air-cooled, 3 story, 10 suites. No rm phones. S, D $43–$48; suites $64–$146. Adults only. TV; cable, in-rm movies. Complimentary full bkfst. Restaurant nearby. Ck-out noon, ck-in 3 pm. X-country ski 20 mi. Lobby in historic mansion (1879); Oriental rugs, period furniture. Special theme suites, such as penthouse suite and space odyssey, are uniquely decorated. Totally nonsmoking. Cr cds: A, MC, V.

D ⇙ ⊘ Ⓢ

Unrated Dining Spot

BLUEBIRD. *19 N Main St. 801/752-3155.* Hrs: 8 am–8 pm; Fri & Sat to 10 pm. Closed Sun; Jan 1, July 4, Thanksgiving, Dec 24, 25. Res accepted. Semi-a la carte: bkfst $2–$6.50, lunch $3–$10.45, dinner $7.50–$11. Child's meals. Limited menu. Parking. 1920s decor; ice cream, candy factory. Cr cds: A, DS, MC, V.

Moab *(D-4)*

Founded: 1879 **Pop:** 3,971 **Elev:** 4,025 ft **Area code:** 801 **Zip:** 84532

The first attempt to settle this valley was made in 1855, but Moab, named after an isolated area in the Bible, was not permanently settled until 1880. Situated on the Colorado River at the foot of the LaSal Mountains, Moab was a sleepy agricultural town until after World War II, when uranium exploration and production and oil and potash development made it boom. Today, tourism and moviemaking help make it a thriving community. A Ranger District office of the Manti-LaSal National Forest (see #7) is located here, as are headquarters for Canyonlands and Arches national parks.

What to See and Do

1. **Dan O'Laurie Museum.** 118 E Center St. Exhibits on local history, archaeology, geology, uranium, minerals of the area. Walking tour information. (Daily exc Sun; closed Jan 1, July 4, Thanksgiving, Dec 25) Donation. Phone 259-7985.

2. **Hollywood Stuntmen's Hall of Fame.** 111 E 100 North. Museum preserves history of the stunt profession. Stunt-related memorabilia includes costumes, weapons and footprints of more than 300 stunt people and stars; action photographs, films and videos. (Daily; closed some major hols) Sr citizen rate. ¢–¢¢

3. **Arches National Park** (see). 5 mi NW on US 191.

4. **Canyonlands National Park** (see). N district: 9 mi N on US 191, then 21 mi SW on UT 313.

5. **Dead Horse Point State Park.** 9 mi NW on US 191, then 22 mi SW on UT 313. Named for promontory rising 2,000 feet above the Colorado River, which makes a huge bend here. Approx 5,200 acres in region of gorges, cliffs, buttes and mesas. Visitor center, museum. Picnicking; limited drinking water. Camping (electricity, dump station). Trailer parking. (Daily) Standard fees. Phone 259-2614.

6. **Hole 'n the Rock.** 15 mi S via US 191. A 5,000-square-foot dwelling carved into huge sandstone rock. Picnic area with stone tables and benches. (Daily; closed Jan 1, Thanksgiving, Dec 25) Phone 686-2250. Tours. ¢¢

7. **Manti-LaSal National Forest, LaSal Division.** 8 mi S on US 191, then 5 mi E. The land of the forest's LaSal Division is similar in color and beauty to some parts of the Grand Canyon, but also includes high mountains nearing 13,000 feet and pine and spruce forests. Swimming; fishing. Hiking, hunting. (See MONTICELLO, PRICE) For information contact the Ranger District office, 125 W 200 South, phone 259-7155; or the Forest Supervisor, 599 W Price River Dr, Price 84501, phone 637-2817. **Free.**

8. **Sightseeing tours.**

Scenic Air Tours. 18 mi N on US 191, at Canyonlands Field. Flights over Canyonlands National Park and various other tours. (All-yr; closed Jan 1, Thanksgiving, Dec 25) Contact Redtail Aviation, 259-7421 or 564-3412. ¢¢¢¢¢

Tag-A-Long Expeditions. 452 N Main St. One- to seven-day whitewater rafting trips on the Green and Colorado rivers; jetboat trips on the Colorado River; jetboat trips and four-wheel drive tours into Canyonlands National Park; winter four-wheel drive tours (Nov–Feb). Also Canyon Classics, one-day jetboat trips with cultural performing arts programs. Most trips (Apr–mid-Oct). Phone 259-8946 or 800/453-3292. ¢¢¢¢¢

Lin Ottinger's Scenic Tours. Moab Rock Shop, 600 N Main St. Full- and half-day tours of Canyonlands and Arches national parks, Dead Horse Point State Park and other areas; rockhounding and geology offered. Tours may involve some hiking (sturdy shoes recommended), minimum fare required. Free evening slide show at tour headquarters. (Mid-Apr–Oct, daily) Res suggested. Phone 259-7312. ¢¢¢¢¢

Canyonlands By Night. Leaves dock at bridge, 2 mi N on US 191. Two-hour boat trip with sound-and-light presentation highlights history of area. (May–mid-Oct, daily, leaves at sundown, weather permitting) Reservations required; tickets must be purchased at office, 1861 N US 191. Phone 259-5261. ¢¢¢¢¢

Trail rides. Pack Creek Ranch. Horseback rides, ranging from one to six hours, in red rock canyons including Arches and Canyonlands national parks. Guided tours for small groups; also overnight trips. (Mar–Oct; upon availability) Phone 259-5505. Per hour ¢¢¢¢¢

Rim Tours. Guided mountain bike tours in canyon country and the Colorado Rockies. Vehicle support for camping tours. Daily and overnight trips; combination bicycle/river trips available. Phone 259-5223 or 800/626-7335. ¢¢¢¢¢

9. **River trips.** On the Green and Colorado rivers, including Canyonlands National Park, Lake Powell (see both) and Cataract Canyon.

Adrift Adventures of Canyonlands. Oar, paddle and motorized trips available; 1–7-days. (Early Apr–late Oct) Phone 259-8594 or 800/874-4483. ¢¢¢¢¢

Colorado River & Trail Expeditions, Inc. Phone 261-1789 or 800/253-7328. ¢¢¢¢¢

Sheri Griffith River Expeditions. Choice of rafts: oarboats, motorized rafts, paddleboats, inflatable kayaks or whitewater canoes; 1–6-day trips; instruction available. (May–Sept) Sr citizen rate. Phone 259-8229 or 800/332-2439. ¢¢¢¢¢

North American River Expeditions–Canyonland Tours, Inc. Rafting, jetboat and jeep trips (Mar–Nov). Phone 259-5865 or 800/342-5938. ¢¢¢¢¢

Tex's Riverways. Flatwater canoe trips, 4–10 days. Confluence pick-ups available, jet boat cruises, all river services. (Mar–Oct) Phone 259-5101. ¢¢¢¢¢

10. **Canyonlands Field Institute.** Educational seminars/trips featuring geology, natural and cultural history, endangered species, Southwestern literature and landscape photography. Many programs use Canyonlands and Arches national parks as outdoor classrooms. For information contact PO Box 68, 84532; 259-7750. ¢¢¢¢–¢¢¢¢¢

(For further information contact the Grand County Travel Council, 805 N Main St, PO Box 550; 259-8825 or 800/635-6622.)

Annual Events

Jeep Safari. Easter wkend.

Butch Cassidy Days PRCA Rodeo. Mid-June.

Motels

✔ ★**BEST WESTERN GREEN WELL.** *105 S Main St. 801/259-6151.* 72 rms, 1–2 story. Mar–Oct: S, D $41–$89; each addl $5; varied lower rates rest of yr. Crib $4. TV; cable. Heated pool. Restaurant 7 am–2 pm. Ck-out 11 am. Cr cds: A, C, D, DS, MC, V.

★**BOWEN.** *169 N Main St. 801/259-7132; res: 800/874-5439.* 40 rms, 2 story. Apr–Oct: S $52; D $59; each addl $4; under 12 free; higher rates: Easter, hol wkends, July 4; lower rates rest of yr. Crib $3. TV; cable. Heated pool. Complimentary coffee in lobby. Ck-out 11 am. Cr cds: A, C, D, DS, MC, V.

★**LANDMARK.** *168 N Main St. 801/259-6147; res: 800/441-6147; FAX 801/259-5556.* 35 rms, 2 story, 3 suites. Mid-Mar–Oct: S $64; D $76; each addl $4; suites $86; family rates; lower rates rest of yr. Crib free. TV; cable. Heated pool; wading pool, whirlpool. Complimentary coffee in lobby. Restaurant adj 8 am–midnight. Ck-out 11 am. Coin lndry. Meeting rms. Cr cds: A, C, D, DS, MC, V.

Guest Ranch

★ ★**PACK CREEK RANCH.** *(PO Box 1270) 8 mi S on US 191 to La Sal Mt Loop Rd, head E to "T" intersection, then right 6 mi to Pack Creek turnoff. 801/259-5505; FAX 801/259-8879.* 9 kit. cottages (1, 2 & 3 bedrm). No A/C. No rm phones. Apr–Oct, AP: S, D $100–$125; lower rates rest of yr. Crib $10 (one-time fee). Pet accepted. Heated pool; wading pool, whirlpool, sauna. Dining rm 7–10 am, 6:30–8 pm. Picnics. Ck-out 11 am, ck-in 3 pm. Grocery, coin lndry, package store 16 mi. Meeting rms. X-country ski on site. Hiking. Picnic tables. A 300-acre ranch at foot of La Sal Mts. Features trail rides, pack trips, river excursions. Cr cds: A, DS, MC, V.

Restaurants

★ ★**GRAND OLD RANCH HOUSE.** *1266 N US 191. 801/259-5753.* Hrs: 5–10:30 pm. Closed Dec 25. Res accepted. German, Amer menu. Serv bar. Semi-a la carte: dinner $6.95–$28.95. Specialties: jägerschnitzel, prime rib. Salad cart. Historic building (1896). Antiques, old photos. Cr cds: A, C, D, MC, V.

★**MI VIDA.** *900 N US 191. 801/259-7146.* Hrs: 11 am–10:30 pm. Closed Dec 25. Serv bar. Semi-a la carte: lunch $3.29–$6.95, dinner $5.95–$32.95. Specializes in prime rib, mesquite-broiled steak, seafood. Salad bar. Outdoor dining. In house of prospector Charlie Steen, whose strike started the uranium boom of the 1950s. View of Colorado River; historic items from the boom days. Cr cds: A, C, D, MC, V.

Monticello (D-5)

Founded: 1887 **Pop:** 1,806 **Elev:** 7,066 ft **Area code:** 801 **Zip:** 84535

Highest county seat in Utah (San Juan County), Monticello was named for Thomas Jefferson's Virginia home. On the east slope of the Abajo Mountains, the elevation makes the weather delightful but the growing season short. Livestock raising, dry farming, uranium mining and oil and gas drilling are the chief industries. A Ranger District office of the Manti-LaSal National Forest (see #1) is located here.

What to See and Do

1. **Manti-LaSal National Forest, LaSal Division.** 2½ mi W. The forest land of this division ranges from red rock canyons to high alpine terrain. Ancient ruins and rock art contrast with pine and spruce forests and aspen-dotted meadows. Fishing, hiking, snowmobiling, cross-country skiing, hunting, camping. For further information contact the Ranger District Office, 496 E Central, phone 587-2041; or the Forest Supervisor, 599 W Price River Dr, Price 84501, phone 637-2817. (See MOAB, PRICE)

2. **Canyonlands National Park (see).** S district: 14 mi N on US 191, then 35 mi W on UT 211 to Squaw Flats Campground Area. Beyond this point are primarily foot trails and four-wheel drive areas.

3. **Canyon Rims Recreation Area.** 20 mi N on US 191. Anticline and Needles overlooks into Canyonlands National Park are located here, as are Wind Whistle & Hatch campgrounds.

(For further information contact the San Juan County Travel Council, 117 S Main St, PO Box 490; 587-3235 or 800/574-4FUN.)

Annual Events

Monticello Pioneer Days. Parade, booths, food, games, sports. Wkend nearest July 24.

San Juan County 4-H Fair. 2nd wkend Aug.

(See Blanding)

Motels

✔ ★**BEST WESTERN WAYSIDE INN.** *(Box 669) 195 E Central (US 666), 2 blks E of US 191. 801/587-2261.* 35 rms. May–late Oct: S $35–$53; D $40–$59; each addl $4; suites $78; under 12 free; lower rates rest of yr. Crib $2. TV; cable. Pool. Restaurant opp 6 am–10 pm.

Ck-out 11 am. Downhill/x-country ski 6 mi. Picnic tables. Cr cds: A, C, D, DS, MC, V.

🎿 ⛵ 🚫 🎦 SC

★ TRIANGLE H. *(Box 876) On US 666E, 2 blks E of US 191.* *801/587-2274.* 26 rms, 6 suites. S $22–$32; D $24–$44; each addl $3; suites $46–$58. Crib $3. TV; cable. Restaurant nearby. Ck-out 11 am. X-country ski 3 mi. Refrigerators avail. Cr cds: A, C, D, DS, MC, V.

🎿 🚫 🎦 SC

Monument Valley

(see Kayenta, AZ)

Natural Bridges National Monument (E-4)

(4 mi S of Blanding on US 191, then 40 mi W on UT 95)

This 7,439-acre area of fantastically eroded and colorful terrain, made a national monument in 1908, features three natural bridges, all with Hopi Indian names: Sipapu, a 268-foot span, and Kachina, a 204-foot span, are in White Canyon, a major tributary gorge of the Colorado River; Owachomo, a 180-foot span, is near Armstrong Canyon, which joins White Canyon. Sipapu is the second largest natural bridge in the world. From 650 to 2,000 years ago, the Anasazi people lived in this area, leaving behind cliff dwelling ruins and pictographs, which can be viewed today. The entire area is a wildlife sanctuary. Bridge View Drive, a nine-mile loop road, provides views of the three bridges from rim overlooks. There are hiking trails to each bridge and two within the canyon. In the park is a visitor center (daily; closed hols in winter) and a primitive campground with 13 tent sites (all-yr, free). Car and passenger ferry service across Lake Powell is available (see LAKE POWELL). There is a $4/car entrance fee; Golden Eagle, Golden Age, Golden Access passports accepted (see INTRODUCTION). For further information contact the Superintendent, PO Box 1, Lake Powell 84533; 801/259-5174.

Nephi (C-3)

Settled: 1851 **Pop:** 3,515 **Elev:** 5,133 ft **Area code:** 801 **Zip:** 84648

What to See and Do

Yuba State Park. 30 mi S via I-15, near Scipio. Waterskiing and walleyed pike fishing are the big attractions of this lake, as well as sandy beaches. Swimming, waterskiing; fishing, boating (ramps). Picnicking. Camping (rest rms, showers, dump station). (Daily) Phone 758-2611. Day-use per vehicle ¢¢

Annual Event

Ute Stampede. Three-day festival featuring horse and mammoth parades, carnival, rodeo, contests, arts & crafts, concessions. Phone 623-0822. 2nd wkend July.

(See Fillmore, Payson)

Motels

★ ★ BEST WESTERN PARADISE INN. *1025 S Main St. 801/* *623-0624.* 40 rms, 2 story. Mid-May–Oct: S $40; D $42; each addl $2;

lower rates rest of yr. Crib $4. TV; cable. Heated pool. Restaurant nearby. Ck-out 11 am. Cr cds: A, C, D, DS, ER, MC, V.

⛵ 🚫 🎦 SC

✔ ★ BUDGET HOST-ROBERTA'S COVE. *(Box 268) 2250 S* *Main St. 801/623-2629.* 43 air-cooled rms, 2 story. S $26–$40; D $32–$50.95; each addl $5; higher rates Ute Stampede (2d wkend July). Crib $3. TV; cable. Coffee in rms. Restaurant opp 6 am–midnight. Ck-out 11 am. Coin lndry. Free bus depot transportation. Cr cds: A, C, D, DS, MC, V.

D 🚫 🎦

Inn

★ ★ WHITMORE MANSION. *(PO Box 73) 110 S Main St. 801/* *623-2047.* 6 rms, 3 story, 2 suites. No A/C. No rm phones. S, D $45–$70; each addl $10. TV in sitting rm. Complimentary full bkfst, refreshments. Ck-out 11 am, ck-in 4 pm. Restored Queen Anne/Victorian-style mansion (1898); original leaded-glass windows; antique furnishings. Totally nonsmoking. Cr cds: MC, V.

🚫 🎦

Restaurant

✔ ★ CEDAR HOLLOW. *2087 S Main St. 801/623-2633.* Hrs: 6 am–10 pm. Closed Dec 25. Semi-a la carte: bkfst, lunch $3.50–$5.50, dinner $6.95–$12. Buffet: dinner (Fri-Sun) $7.95. Child's meals. Specializes in halibut, steak. Salad bar. Parking. Cr cds: A, C, D, DS, MC, V.

D

Ogden (B-3)

Settled: 1844 **Pop:** 63,909 **Elev:** 4,300 ft **Area code:** 801

The streets of Ogden, fourth largest city in Utah, were laid out by Brigham Young in traditional Mormon geometrical style: broad, straight and bordered by poplar, box elder, elm and cottonwood trees. In the 1820s and 1830s, Ogden was a rendezvous and wintering place for trappers, who wandered as far afield as California and Oregon. In 1846, Miles Goodyear, the first white settler, built a cabin and trading post, Fort Buenaventura, here. The next year he sold out to the Mormons. During the last 30 years of the 19th century, Ogden was an outfitting center for trappers and hunters heading north. Its saloons and gambling halls were typical of a frontier town, and there was considerable friction between the Mormons and the "gentiles." With the coming of the railroad, however, Ogden became one of the few cities in Utah whose inhabitants were not primarily Mormons.

Today, Ogden is a commercial and industrial center. Hill Air Force Base is nearby. Bernard DeVoto—American novelist, journalist, historian and critic, best known for his history of the western frontier—was born in Ogden, as was John M. Browning, inventor of the automatic rifle. Mt Ben Lomond, north of the city in the Wasatch Range, was the inspiration for the logo of Paramount Pictures. A Ranger District office of the Wasatch-Cache National Forest (see SALT LAKE CITY) is located in Ogden.

What to See and Do

1. **Daughters of Utah Pioneers Visitor Center & Relic Hall.** 2148 Grant Ave, in Tabernacle Square. Old handicrafts, household items, pioneer clothing and furniture and portraits of those who came to Utah prior to the railroad of 1869. Also Miles Goodyear's cabin, the first permanent house built in Utah. (Mid-May–mid-Sept, daily exc Sun) Phone 393-4460 or 621-5224.   **Free.**

2. **Weber State University** (1889). (15,000 students) Harrison Blvd, off US 89. On campus are Layton P. Ott Planetarium, with natural science museum and Foucault pendulum, shows (Wed; no shows

Aug; fee); and Stewart Bell Tower, with 183-bell electronic carillon, performances (daily; free). Campus tours. Phone 626-6000.

3. **Union Station–the Utah State Railroad Museum.** 2501 Wall Ave, center of Ogden. **Spencer S. Eccles Railroad Center** features some of the world's largest locomotives, model railroad, films, gem and mineral displays, guided tours by "conductors." **Browning-Kimball Car Museum** has classic American cars. **Browning Firearms Museum** contains the reconstructed original Browning gun shop and inventor's models. Also here is 500-seat theater for musical and dramatic productions and an art gallery; restaurant. Visitors Bureau for northern Utah located here. (June–Sept, daily; rest of the yr, daily exc Sun; closed Jan 1, Thanksgiving, Dec 25) Sr citizen rate. Phone 629-8444. ¢

4. **Hill Air Force Base Museum.** 4 mi S on I-15 exit 341, in Roy. More than 40 aircraft on display, some indoors and suspended from ceiling. Planes include B-29 Superfortress, SR-71 "Blackbird" reconnaissance plane, B-52 bomber, PT-71 Stearman; helicopters, jet engines, missiles; uniforms and other memorabilia. (Daily exc Mon, limited hrs Tues–Fri; closed Jan 1, Thanksgiving, Dec 25) Phone 777-6868. **Free.**

5. **Pine View Reservoir.** 9 mi E on UT 39 in Ogden Canyon in Wasatch-Cache National Forest (see SALT LAKE CITY). Boating, fishing, waterskiing. Camping, picnicking. Fees for activities.

6. **Skiing.**

Snowbasin. 10 mi E on UT 39, then S on UT 226 in Wasatch-Cache National Forest (see SALT LAKE CITY). 6,400–8,800 ft. Double, 4 triple chairlifts; patrol, school, rentals; food service. Longest run 3 mi, vertical drop 2,400 ft. (Late Nov–mid-Apr, daily) Phone 399-1135 or -0198 (snow conditions). ¢¢¢¢¢

Powder Mountain. 7 mi E on UT 39, then 4½ mi N on UT 158, in Eden. Three chairlifts, 3 surface tows; patrol, school, rentals; food service, lodging. (Mid-Nov–Apr, daily) Night skiing. Phone 745-3772. ¢¢¢¢¢

Nordic Valley. 7 mi E on UT 39, then N on UT 162. Two chairlifts; patrol, school, rentals; snack bar. Longest run 1½ mi, vertical drop 1,000 ft. (Dec–Apr, daily) Family night rates. Phone 745-3511. ¢¢¢¢¢

7. **Fort Buenaventura State Park.** 2450 A Ave. The exciting era of mountain men is brought to life on this 32-acre site, where the actual fort, Ogden's first settlement, was built in 1846 by Miles Goodyear. The fort has been reconstructed according to archaeological and historical research: no nails have been used in building the stockade; wooden pegs and mortise and tenon joints hold the structure together. (Apr–Nov) Phone 621-4808. Per vehicle ¢¢

8. **Willard Bay State Park.** 15 mi N via I-15, exit 360, near Willard. This park features a 9,900-acre lake. Swimming; fishing; boating (ramps), sailing. Picnicking. Tent & trailer sites (fee; showers, dump station). (Daily) Phone 734-9494. Day-use per vehicle ¢¢

(For further information contact the Convention & Visitors Bureau, 2501 Wall Ave, 84401; 627-8288 or 800/ALL-UTAH.)

Annual Events

Pioneer Days. Ogden Pioneer Stadium. Rodeo; concerts; vintage car shows; fireworks; chili cookoff. Nightly exc Sun. Mid–late July.

Utah Symphony Pops Concert. Lindquist Fountain/Plaza. Music enhanced by fireworks display. Late July.

(See Brigham City, Salt Lake City)

Motel

✔ ★ **MOTEL 6.** *1500 W Riverdale Rd (84405). 801/627-2880.* 110 rms, 2 story. June–Aug: S, D $33.99; each addl $6; suites $47.99; under 18 free; lower rates rest of yr. Crib free. TV; cable. Heated pool. Restaurant 6:30 am–2 pm, 5:30–10 pm. Bar 5:30 pm–1 am; entertain-

ment, dancing Wed–Sat. Ck-out noon. Coin lndry. Tennis. Some in-rm whirlpools. Cr cds: A, C, D, DS, MC, V.

Motor Hotel

★ ★ **HOLIDAY INN.** *3306 Washington Blvd (84401). 801/399-5671; FAX 801/621-0321.* 109 rms, 2 story. S $58; D $66; each addl $8; under 18 free. Crib free. TV. Indoor pool; whirlpool. Restaurant 6 am–2 pm, 5–10 pm. Rm serv. Bar 5 pm–midnight. Ck-out noon. Coin lndry. Meeting rm. Valet serv. Downhill/x-country ski 15 mi. Cr cds: A, C, D, DS, MC, V, JCB.

Hotels

★ ★ ★ **BEST WESTERN OGDEN PARK.** *247 24th St (84401). 801/627-1190; FAX 801/394-6312.* 290 rms, 8 story, 17 suites. S $65–$85; D $77–$97; suites $75–$125; wkend rates; ski plans. Crib free. TV; cable. Indoor pool. Complimentary full bkfst. Restaurant 6 am–10 pm. Rm serv 24 hrs. Private club noon–2 am; entertainment, dancing. Ck-out noon. Convention facilities. Concierge. Gift shop. Beauty shop. Free parking. Bus depot transportation. Exercise equipt; weight machine, bicycles, whirlpool. Game rm. Refrigerator in suites. Balconies. Cr cds: A, C, D, DS, MC, V.

★ ★ ★ **RADISSON SUITE.** *2510 Washington Blvd (84401). 801/627-1900; FAX 801/394-5342.* 144 rms, 11 story, 122 suites. S $55; D $65; each addl $10; suites $89–$195; under 16 free; ski packages. Crib free. TV; cable. Complimentary full bkfst. Complimentary coffee in rms. Restaurant 6 am–10 pm. Bar 11:30–1 am; entertainment. Ck-out noon. Coin lndry. Meeting rms. Gift shop. Barber. Free covered parking. Downhill/x-country ski 16 mi. Exercise equipt; weight machine, bicycles. Refrigerator, wet bar in suites. Cr cds: A, C, D, DS, MC, V.

Restaurant

★ ★ **YE LION'S DEN.** *3607 Washington Blvd. 801/399-5804.* Hrs: 11:30 am–2 pm, 5–9:30 pm; Fri to 10:30 pm; Sat 5–10:30 pm; Sun noon–7 pm. Closed Jan 1, Dec 25. Res accepted. Serv bar. Complete meals: lunch $4–$6.95, dinner $7.75–$30.95. Specializes in prime rib, steak, seafood. Parking. Open-hearth grill. Cr cds: A, MC, V.

Panguitch (D-2)

Settled: 1864 **Pop:** 1,444 **Elev:** 6,624 ft **Area code:** 801 **Zip:** 84759

A livestock, lumbering and farm town, Panguitch is also a center for summer tourists who come to see nearby Bryce Canyon National Park and Cedar Breaks National Monument. The Paiutes named the city, which means "big fish," because of the large fish they caught in nearby Panguitch Lake. A Ranger District office of the Dixie National Forest (see CEDAR CITY) is located here.

What to See and Do

1. **Panguitch Lake.** 17 mi SW on paved road in Dixie National Forest (see CEDAR CITY). This 8,000-foot-high lake, which fills a large volcanic basin, has fishing, resorts, public campgrounds (developed sites, fee); ice fishing, snowmobiling, cross-country skiing.

2. **Bryce Canyon National Park** (see). 7 mi S on US 89, then 19 mi SE on UT 12.

3. **Cedar Breaks National Monument** (see). 35 mi SW on UT 143 through Dixie National Forest (see CEDAR CITY).

4. **Anasazi Indian Village State Park.** 98 mi E on UT 12, near Boulder. Partially excavated village, believed to have been occupied from A.D. 1050–1200, is one of the largest ancient communities west of the Colorado River. Picnicking. Visitor center & museum (daily; closed Jan 1, Thanksgiving, Dec 25). (Daily) Phone 335-7308. ¢

(For further information contact the City of Panguitch, 55 S Main St, PO Box 77; 676-2311.)

Annual Event

Horse racing. Thoroughbred & quarterhorse races. Last wkend June.

Seasonal Event

Bryce Canyon Country Rodeo. Approx 17 mi SE via UT 12, on UT 63, in Rubys Inn. Phone 834-5337. Daily exc Sun, Memorial Day–Labor Day.

(See Cedar City)

Motel

★ ★ **BEST WESTERN NEW WESTERN.** *(PO Box 3) 2 E Center St. 801/676-8876.* 55 rms. Apr–Oct: S $40–$50; D $50–$60; each addl $5; suites $70–$100; lower rates rest of yr. Crib free. TV; cable. Heated pool. Restaurant nearby. Ck-out 11 am. Coin lndry. Some refrigerators. Some rms across street. Cr cds: A, C, D, DS, MC, V, JCB.

Restaurant

✔ ★ **FOY'S COUNTRY CORNER.** *100 N Main St. 801/676-8851.* Hrs: 6 am–9:30 pm. Closed Dec 25. Semi-a la carte: bkfst $2.25–$5, lunch $4–$7, dinner $6–$13. Specializes in steak, trout, chicken. Parking. Cr cds: A, MC, V.

Park City (B-3)

Founded: 1868 **Pop:** 4,468 **Elev:** 7,080 ft **Area code:** 801 **Zip:** 84060

Two soldiers struck silver here in 1868, starting one of the nation's largest silver mining camps, which reached a population of 10,000 before declining to a near ghost town when the silver market collapsed. Since then, however, Park City has been revived as a four-season resort area with skiing, golf, tennis, water sports and mountain biking.

What to See and Do

1. **Kimball Art Center.** Park and Heber Aves. Exhibits in various media by local and regional artists. (Daily) Phone 649-8882. **Free.**
2. **Egyptian Theatre** (1926). 328 Main St. Originally built as a silent movie and vaudeville house, now a year-round performing arts center with a full semi-professional theater season. (Wed–Sat; some performances other days) Phone 649-9371.
3. **Skiing.**
   Park City. Approx 2,200 acres; 83 novice, intermediate, expert slopes and trails; 650 acres of open-bowl skiing. Two quad, 5 double, 5 triple chairlifts, 4-passenger gondola; patrol, school, rentals; snowmaking; restaurants, cafeteria, bar; nursery. (Mid-Nov–mid-Apr, daily) Alpine slide, children's park, miniature golf in summer (fees). Phone 649-8111 or -9571 (snow report). Summer ¢¢; Winter ¢¢¢¢¢

Deer Valley Resort. 1 mi SE on Deer Valley Dr. Approx 1,000 skiable acres. Double, high-speed quad, 9 triple chairlifts; rental, patrol, school; restaurants, lounge; lodge, nursery. (Dec–Easter, daily) Phone 649-1000. ¢¢¢¢¢

ParkWest Resort. 3 mi NW on ParkWest Dr. 50 trails. 7 double chairlifts; patrol, school, rentals; snowmaking; restaurant, cafeteria, bar. (Dec–Apr, daily) Phone 649-5400. ¢¢¢¢¢

Brighton Resort. Approx 10 mi SW via UT 190 in Big Cottonwood Canyon (see SALT LAKE CITY).

Solitude Resort. Approx 12 mi SW via UT 190 in Big Cottonwood Canyon (see SALT LAKE CITY).

White Pine Touring Center. Approx 2 mi N via UT 224 to Park City Golf Course. Groomed cross-country trails (18 km) school, rentals; guided tours. (Nov–Apr, daily) Summer mountain biking; rentals. Phone 649-8710 or -8701 (winter). Winter ¢¢¢; Summer ¢¢¢¢¢

4. **Rockport State Park.** N on UT 248 & US 40, then 8 mi NE on I-80, Wanship exit. Approximately 1,000-acre park along east side of Rockport Lake. Opportunity for viewing wildlife, including bald eagles (winter) and golden eagles. Swimming, waterskiing, sailboarding; fishing; boating (rentals, launch). Picnicking; restaurant, concession. Cross-country ski trail (6 mi). Camping, tent and trailer sites. (Daily) Standard fees. Phone 336-2241.

(For further information contact the Chamber of Commerce/Convention and Visitors Bureau, 1910 Prospector Ave, Suite 103 or the Visitor Information Center, 528 Main St, PO Box 1630; 649-6100, -6104 or 800/453-1360.)

Annual Events

Sundance Film Festival. Week-long festival for independent film makers. Workshops, screenings and special events. Mid-Jan.

Snow Sculpture Contest. Off UT 248. During Park City Winterfest. Early Mar.

Art Festival. Main St. Open-air market featuring work of more than 200 visual artists. Also street entertainment. 1st wkend Aug.

Franklin Showdown Classic Golf Tournament. 8 mi N on UT 224, then W on I-80, at Park Meadows. PGA Invitational Golf tournament. 2nd wkend Aug.

Autumn Aloft Hot-Air Balloon Festival. Park Meadows Golf Course. 2nd wkend Sept.

(See Alta, Heber City, Salt Lake City)

Motel

✔ ★ **EDELWEISS HAUS.** *(Box 495) 1482 Empire Ave. 801/649-9342; res: 800/438-3855.* 45 kit. units, 4 story. Nov–Mar: S, D $55–$125; each addl $10; suites, kit. units $95–$300; higher rates Christmas wk; lower rates rest of yr. Crib free. TV; cable, in-rm movies avail. Heated pool; whirlpool, sauna. Restaurant nearby. Ck-out 10 am. Coin lndry. Downhill/x-country ski opp. Balconies, patios. Cr cds: A, MC, V.

Lodge

★ ★ **RESORT CENTER LODGE & INN.** *(PO Box 3449) 1415 Lowell Dr. 801/649-0800; res: 800/824-5331; FAX 801/649-1464.* 123 rms, 3 story. 98 suites. No A/C. Mid-Jan–Mar: S $125; D $165–$190; suites $175–$825; higher rates: Christmas, Presidents' Week; lower rates rest of yr. Crib free. TV; cable. Indoor/outdoor pool; whirlpool, sauna. Restaurant 4 pm–midnight. Bar. Ck-out 10 am. Meeting rms. Free valet parking. Tennis privileges. Downhill ski on site; x-country ski 1 mi. Refrigerators. Balconies. Cr cds: A, C, D, DS, MC, V.

Motor Hotels

✔ ★★OLYMPIA PARK HOTEL. *(Box 4439) 1895 Sidewinder Dr. 801/649-2900; res: 800/234-9003; FAX 801/649-4852.* 206 rms, 1–4 story. S $59–$129; D $69–$159; each addl $15; suites $90–$250; under 12 free; ski, golf, wkend plans. Crib free. TV; cable. Indoor pool; whirlpool, sauna. Restaurant 6:30 am–10 pm; summer hrs vary. Rm serv. Bar from 4 pm. Ck-out noon. Meeting rms. Bellhops. Valet serv. Concierge. Gift shop. Garage parking. Downhill/x-country ski ½ mi. Game rm. Balconies. Cr cds: A, D, DS, MC, V.

🄳 ♿ 🛥 🚭 ⏱ SC

★★★SHADOW RIDGE RESORT HOTEL. *(Box 1820) 50 Shadow Ridge Dr. 801/649-4300; res: 800/451-3031; FAX 801/649-5951.* 150 rms, 4 story, 50 suites. Nov–Apr: S, D $130–$520; family rates; ski, golf plans; higher rates mid-Dec–early Jan & mid-Feb; lower rates rest of yr. Crib free. TV; cable, in-rm movies avail. Heated pool; whirlpool, sauna. Ck-out 10 am. Lndry facilities. Meeting rms. Bellhops in season. Valet serv. Downhill ski opp; x-country ski ½ mi. Some refrigerators, fireplaces. Balconies. Golf course adj. Cr cds: A, C, D, DS, MC, V, JCB.

♿ 🛥 ⏱

★★★YARROW RESORT HOTEL & CONFERENCE CENTER. *(PO Box 1840) 1800 Park Ave. 801/649-7000; res: 800/327-2332; FAX 801/645-7007.* 181 rms, 2 story. S, D $89–$179; each addl $10; suites $199–$299; studio rms $99–$189; under 13 free; ski package plan; higher rates Dec 25–Jan 1. Crib free. TV; cable, in-rm movies. Heated pool; whirlpools, sauna. Restaurant 6:30 am–10:30 pm. Rm serv. Bar. Ck-out 11 am. Coin lndry. Meeting rms. Bellhops. Valet serv. Concierge. Free transportation to ski area. Downhill ski ¼ mi; x-country ski ½ mi. Balconies. Golf course opp. Cr cds: A, C, D, MC, V.

♿ 🛥 ⏱ SC

Inns

★★IMPERIAL HOTEL. *(PO Box 4106) 221 Main St. 801/649-1904; res: 800/669-UTAH; FAX 801/645-7421.* 11 rms, 3 story, 2 suites. No A/C. Mid-Nov–mid-Mar: S $85–$130; D $100–$145; each addl $15; suite $140; under 12 free; higher rates Christmas; lower rates June–mid-Nov. Closed rest of yr. TV; cable. Complimentary continental bkfst, coffee. Restaurant opp 11 am–11 pm. Ck-out 10:30 am, ck-in 3 pm. Downhill ski ½ mi; x-country ski 2 mi. Whirlpool. Restored boarding house (1904) in historic area. Cr cds: A, MC, V.

♿ 🚭 ⏱

★★OLD MINERS' LODGE. *(Box 2639) 615 Woodside Ave. 801/645-8068; res: 800/648-8068.* 10 rms, 2 story, 3 suites. No A/C. Some rm phones. Mid-Nov–mid-Apr: S, D $85–$120; each addl $15; suites $135–$155; higher rates mid-Dec–early Jan; lower rates rest of yr. Crib $5. Complimentary full bkfst, coffee, tea. Restaurant nearby. Ck-out noon, ck-in 2 pm. Concierge. Street parking. Downhill ski 1½ blks; x-country ski 1½ mi. Whirlpool. Lawn games. Picnic tables, grills. Renovated lodging house used by miners (1893); early Western decor, fireplace, antiques. Totally nonsmoking. Cr cds: A, DS, MC, V.

♿ 🚭 ⏱

★★★WASHINGTON SCHOOL. *(Box 536) 543 Park Ave. 801/649-3800; res: 800/824-1672; FAX 801/649-3802.* 15 rms, 3 story, 3 suites. No A/C. Mid-Dec–mid-Mar: S, D $200–$225; suites $250–$275; lower rates rest of yr. Children over 12 yrs only. TV in some rms; cable. Complimentary full bkfst. Restaurant nearby. Ck-out 10 am, ck-in 3 pm. Meeting rms. Street parking. Downhill ski 1½ blks; x-country ski 1½ mi. Whirlpool, sauna. Game rm. Historic, stone schoolhouse (1889); antiques, sitting rm with stone and carved wood fireplace, library, bell tower, turn-of-the-century country decor. Cr cds: A, DS, ER, MC, V.

♿ 🚭 ⏱ SC

Resorts

★★★DEER VALLEY LODGING. *(Box 3000) 1375 Deer Valley Dr. 801/649-4040; res: 800/453-3833; FAX 801/645-8419.* 275 condo units (1–6 bedrm), 1–5 story. Mid-Jan–Mar: condo units $250–$1,600; wkly, monthly rates (summer only); ski package plans; higher rates late Dec; lower rates rest of yr. Crib $10. TV; cable. Heated pool for some units. Ck-out 10 am, ck-in 4 pm. Grocery. Meeting rms. Valet serv. Free daily maid serv incl linens (winter). Concierge. Garages, underground parking. Free ski area transportation. Tennis privileges (summer). Downhill ski on site; x-country ski 1 mi. Soc dir. Refrigerators, fireplaces, washers & dryers; many in-rm whirlpools. Many private patios, balconies. Cr cds: A, MC, V.

🛬 ♿ ⌖ 🛥 🎿 🚭 ⏱ SC

★★PROSPECTOR SQUARE HOTEL. *(PO Box 1698) 2200 Sidewinder Dr. 801/649-7100; res: 800/453-3812 (exc UT); FAX 801/649-8377.* 230 units, 2–3 story, 150 kits. Late Nov–mid-Apr: S, D $99–$129; each addl $10; kit. studio rms $129–$159; 1–2-bedrm condos $175–$200; under 12 free; ski plan; lower rates rest of yr. Pool privileges. Restaurant 11:30 am–10 pm. Bar from 5:30 pm. Ck-out 11 am, ck-in 4 pm. Coin lndry 4 blks. Convention facilities. Valet serv. Sports dir. Ski area transportation. Tennis. Golf privileges. Downhill ski ½ mi; x-country ski ¼ mi. Racquetball courts. Health club privileges. Refrigerators. Some balconies. Picnic tables, grills. Cr cds: A, C, D, DS, MC, V.

♿ 🍴 ⌖ 🚭 ⏱ SC

STEIN ERIKSEN LODGE. *(4-Star 1993; New general manager, therefore not rated) (Box 3177) 7700 Stein Way, 4 mi SW on UT 224 to Park Ave, then Deer Valley Dr to Royal St. 801/649-3700; res: 800/453-1302; FAX 801/649-5825.* 120 rms, 12 rms in main lodge, 2 story, 40 kit. suites. Early Dec–early Apr: S, D $265–$500; each addl $30; kit. suites $540–$840; under 12 free; summer rates; ski rates; higher rates hol season; lower rates rest of yr. Crib free. TV; cable, in-rm movies avail. Heated pool; poolside serv. 2 dining rms (see GLITRETIND). 2nd dining rm open winter only (wild game menu). Rm serv 24 hrs. Box lunches. Bar; pianist in winter. Ck-out 11 am, ck-in 4 pm. Grocery 4 mi. Meeting rms. Concierge. Sundries. Boutique. Underground parking. Complimentary transportation to Park City. Tennis. Downhill ski on site; x-country ski 3 mi. Sleighing. Snowmobiles. Hot air balloons; mountain bikes avail. Lawn games. Exercise equipt; weight machines, bicycle, whirlpool, sauna. Masseuse. Bathrm phone, whirlpool, washer, dryer in most rms. Some refrigerators, fireplaces. Many balconies. Dramatic 5-story stone fireplace in lobby. Spectacular high mountain setting. Extensive grounds. Cr cds: A, D, MC, V.

🄳 ♿ ⌖ 🛥 🎿 🚭 ⏱ SC

Restaurants

★★★GLITRETIND. *(See Stein Eriksen Lodge Resort) 801/645-6484.* Hrs: 7 am–10 pm; Sun brunch (Apr–Dec) 11 am–2:30 pm. Res accepted. Bar 1–10 pm. Wine cellar. Semi-a la carte: bkfst $5–$15, lunch $6–$15, dinner $19–$45. Sun brunch $15.95. Child's meals. Specializes in fresh seafood. Own baking. Valet parking. Outdoor dining. European-style decor; oak-framed walls, exposed beams, three stone fireplaces. View of mountainsides. Cr cds: A, D, MC, V.

🄳

✔ ★TEXAS RED'S PIT BARBECUE AND CHILI PARLOR. *440 Main St. 801/649-7337.* Hrs: 11:30 am–10 pm. Bar. Semi-a la carte: lunch $3.95–$5.95, dinner $6.95–$14.95. Child's meals. Specializes in pit-barbecued ribs. Parking. Restored storefront (1910); Western decor. Cr cds: A, MC, V.

Payson (C-3)

Settled: 1850 **Pop:** 9,510 **Elev:** 4,648 ft **Area code:** 801 **Zip:** 84651

Payson sits at the foot of the Wasatch Mountains, near Utah Lake. Mormons first settled the area after spending a night on the banks of Peteneet Creek. The surrounding farmlands produce fruit, milk, grain and row crops; livestock is raised. Limestone and dolomite are dug in the vicinity for use in smelting iron.

What to See and Do

1. **Mt Nebo Scenic Loop Drive.** This 45-mile drive around the eastern shoulder of towering Mt Nebo (elevation 11,877 ft) is one of the most thrilling in Utah; Mt Nebo's three peaks are the highest in the Wasatch range. The road travels south through Payson and Santaquin canyons and then climbs 9,000 feet up Mt Nebo, offering a view of Devil's Kitchen, a brilliantly colored canyon. (This section of the drive not recommended for those who dislike heights.) The forest road continues south to UT 132; take UT 132 east to Nephi and then drive north on I-15 back to Payson.

2. **Payson Lake Recreation Area.** 12 mi SE on unnumbered road in Uinta National Forest (see PROVO). Fishing, camping, swimming, hiking, backpacking.

(For further information contact Chamber of Commerce, 439 West Utah Ave; 465-5200.)

Annual Events

Mt Nebo Clogging Competition. City Park, Main St. Nearly 800 persons compete in various events; exhibits. 1st wkend June.

Golden Onion Days. Includes community theater presentations, marathon, horse races, parade, fireworks and picnic. Labor Day wkend.

(See Nephi, Provo)

Motel

✔ ★ ★ **COMFORT INN.** 830 N Main St. 801/465-4861. 62 rms, 2 story, 6 kits. (no equipt). S $46-$52; D $52-$63; each addl $6; suites $99; under 18 free. Crib free. Pet accepted; $10. TV; cable. Indoor pool. Complimentary continental bkfst, coffee. Restaurant adj open 24 hrs. Ck-out 11 am. Coin lndry. Meeting rms. Exercise equipt; weight machine, bicycles, whirlpool, sauna. Cr cds: A, C, D, DS, ER, MC, V, JCB.

Price (C-4)

Settled: 1879 **Pop:** 8,712 **Elev:** 5,567 ft **Area code:** 801 **Zip:** 84501

Price, the seat of Carbon County, bases its prosperity on coal; more than 30 mine properties, as well as oil and natural gas fields, are within 30 miles. Farming and livestock are also important. Price was one of the stopping places for the Robbers Roost gang in the 1930s. Headquarters and a Ranger District office of the Manti-LaSal National Forest (see #3) are located here.

What to See and Do

1. **College of Eastern Utah Prehistoric Museum.** 155 E Main St. Dinosaur displays, archaeology exhibits; geological specimens. (Memorial Day-Labor Day, daily; April-late May, daily exc Sun; rest of yr, Tues-Sat; closed major hols) Donation. Phone 637-5060.

2. **Geology tours.** Self-guided tours of wilderness area, Nine Mile Canyon, Indian dwellings, paintings, San Rafael Desert, Dinosaur Pit, Little Grand Canyon. Maps avail at Chamber of Commerce office or the Carbon County Travel Council, located at CEU Prehistoric Museum (see #1), phone 637-3009. **Free.**

3. **Manti-LaSal National Forest, Manti Division.** 21 mi SW on UT 10, then NW on UT 31. Originally two forests—the Manti in central

Utah and the LaSal section in southeastern Utah—now under single supervision. A 1,327,631-acre area partially in Colorado, this forest has among its attractions high mountain scenic drives, deep canyons, riding trails, campsites, winter sports, fishing, and deer and elk hunting. Joe's Valley Reservoir on UT 29 and Electric Lake on UT 31 have fishing and boating. Areas of geologic interest, developed as a result of massive landslides, are near Ephraim. Some fees in developed areas. For further information contact the Ranger District office or the Forest Supervisor at 599 W Price River Dr, 637-2817. (See MOAB, MONTICELLO) **Free.**

4. **Price Canyon Recreation Area.** 15 mi N on US 6, then 3 mi W on unnumbered road. Overlooks; hiking; picnicking; camping (fee). Roads have steep grades. (May-mid-Oct, daily) Phone 637-4584. **Free.**

5. **Scofield State Park.** 24 mi N on US 6, then 10 mi W & S on UT 96. Utah's highest state park has a 2,800-acre lake that lies at an altitude of 7,616 feet. Fishing; boating (docks, ramps); camping (rest rms, showers). Snowmobiling, ice fishing, cross-country skiing in winter. (May-Oct) Standard fees. Phone 448-9449. Camping ¢¢¢

6. **Cleveland-Lloyd Dinosaur Quarry.** 22 mi S on UT 10, then approx 15 mi E on unnumbered road. Since 1928, more than 12,000 dinosaur bones, representing at least 70 different animals, have been excavated on this site. Visitor center, nature trail, picnic area. (Memorial Day-Labor Day, daily; Easter-Memorial Day, wkends only) Phone 637-4584. **Free.**

(For further information contact Carbon County Chamber of Commerce, 31 N 200 East, PO Box 764; 637-2788 or -8182.)

Motels

★ **CARRIAGE HOUSE INN.** 590 E Main St. 801/637-5660; res: 800/228-5732 (UT). 41 rms, 2 story. S $29.95; D $36; each addl $6. Crib free. TV; cable. Indoor pool; whirlpool. Restaurant nearby. Ck-out noon. Airport transportation. Cr cds: A, C, D, DS, MC, V.

✔ ★ **CREST.** 625 E Main St. 801/637-1532. 84 rms, 1-2 story. June-Sept: S $23.98-$27.50; D $28.95-$33.95; each addl $3; suites $37.50-$53; under 6 free; lower rates rest of yr. Crib free. TV; cable. Restaurant 6 am-3 pm. Ck-out 11 am. Cr cds: A, C, D, DS, MC, V.

★ ★ **DAYS INN.** 838 Westwood Blvd. 801/637-8880; FAX 801/637-7707. 148 rms, 2 story. S $49-$55; D $51-$56; each addl $6; suites $53-$98; under 17 free. Crib $5. TV. Indoor pool; whirlpool, sauna. Restaurant 6 am-10 pm. Rm serv. Bar. Ck-out noon. Meeting rms. Refrigerators avail. Cr cds: A, C, D, DS, MC, V.

✔ ★ **GREENWELL INN.** 655 E Main St. 801/637-3520; res: 800/666-3520; FAX 801/637-4858. 97 rms, 1-2 story. May-Sept: S $21.99-$38; D $32-$48; each addl $5; lower rates rest of yr. Crib $5. TV; cable. Complimentary continental bkfst. Restaurant adj 6 am-10 pm. Ck-out noon. Lndry facilities. Gift shop. Cr cds: A, C, D, DS, ER, MC, V.

Provo (B-3)

Settled: 1849 **Pop:** 86,835 **Elev:** 4,549 ft **Area code:** 801

Provo received its name from French-Canadian trapper Etienne Provost, who arrived in the area in 1825. Provost and his party of mountain men set up camp near the mouth of the Provo River, but skirmishes with Indians forced them to escape to the mountains. It wasn't until 1849 that the first permanent settlement, begun by a party of Mormons, was established. The Mormon settlers erected Fort Utah as their first building, and despite famine, drought, hard winters and the constant danger of Indian attack, they persisted and the settlement grew. Today, Provo is the seat of Utah County and the state's third largest city.

An important educational and commercial center, Provo's largest employer is Brigham Young University. Beyond that, the city boasts major steel and electronic component manufacturers, health care and municipal employers and other educational facilities. Provo lies in the middle of a lush, green valley: to the north stands 12,008-foot Mount Timpanogos; to the south is the perpendicular face of the Wasatch Range; to the east Provo Peak rises 11,054 feet; and to the west lies Utah Lake, backed by more mountains. Provo is the headquarters of the Uinta National Forest (see #9), and many good fishing, boating, camping and hiking spots are nearby.

What to See and Do

1. **Brigham Young University** (1875). (27,000 students) Founded by Brigham Young and operated by the Church of Jesus Christ of Latter-day Saints. This is one of the world's largest church-related institutions of higher learning, with students from every state and more than 90 foreign countries. One-hour, free guided tours arranged at Hosting Center (Mon–Fri; also by appt, phone 378-4678). Phone 378-1211. Buildings on campus (Mon–Fri; closed hols) include

   Harris Fine Arts Center. Houses B.F. Larsen Gallery and Gallery 303; periodic displays of rare instruments and music collection. Concert, theater performances. Phone 378-HFAC.   **Free.**   Adj is

   Museum of Art. Exhibits from the BYU Permanent Collection; traveling exhibits (some fees). Phone 378-2819.   **Free.**

   Eyring Science Center. Houses Summerhays Planetarium, 4th floor (fee); geological collection, extensive series of minerals and fossils. Phone 378-5396 or -4361 (planetarium).   **Free.**

   Monte L. Bean Life Science Museum. Exhibits and collections of insects, fish, amphibians, reptiles, birds, animals and plants. For tours phone 378-5051.   **Free.**

   Museum of Peoples and Cultures. Allen Hall, 710 N 100 East. Material from South America, the Near East and the southwestern US. Phone 378-6112.   **Free.**

2. **McCurdy Historical Doll Museum.** 246 N 100 East. More than 3,000 dolls of many varieties on exhibit; antique toys, miniatures and doll shop. Documentary film. Doll hospital. Tours. (Tues–Sat afternoons) Phone 377-9935.   ¢

3. **Pioneer Museum.** 500 W 600 North, on US 89. Outstanding collection of Utah pioneer relics and Western art. Pioneer Village. (June–early Sept, Mon–Fri afternoons; rest of yr, by appt) Phone 379-6609 or 377-7078.   **Free.**

4. **Springville Museum of Art.** 7 mi SE via I-15 exit 263, at 126 E 400 South, in Springville. Utah art history from 1852 to present, including paintings, drawings, sculpture. State competition in Apr, quilt show in June. Guided tours. (Tues–Sat, also Sun afternoons; closed Jan 1, Easter, Dec 25) Phone 489-2727.   **Free.**

5. **John Hutchings Museum.** 17 mi NW via I-15 or UT 89/91, at 685 N Center St, in Lehi. Six main collections include archaeology, ornithology and oology, paleontology, mineralogy and pioneer artifacts. Most of the items are from the Great Basin area. Rare sea shells, fossils, Native American artifacts. (Daily exc Sun; closed most hols) Sr citizen rate. Phone 768-7180.   ¢

6. **Utah Lake State Park.** 2 mi W on Center St, off I-15. Park situated on the eastern shore of Utah Lake, a 150-square-mile, freshwater remnant of ancient Lake Bonneville, which created the Great Salt Lake. Fishing, fish cleaning station; boating (ramp, dock). Ice skating (winter), roller skating (summer). Picnicking, play area. Camping (dump station). Visitor center. (Daily) Standard fees. Phone 375-0733.

7. **Camp Floyd and Stagecoach Inn State Parks.** 13 mi N on I-15 to Lehi, then 21 mi W on UT 73, in Cedar Valley. Only the cemetery remains as evidence of the pre-Civil War post that quartered the largest troop concentration in the US here between 1858–61.

Approx 400 buildings were constructed for troops deployed to the west in expectation of a Mormon rebellion. The nearby Stagecoach Inn has been restored with original period furnishings. Visitor center. (Easter wkend–mid-Oct; daily) Standard fees. Phone 768-8932.

8. **Sundance Ski Area.** 15 mi NE on US 189, North Fork Provo Canyon. 4 chairlifts; patrol, school, rentals; warming hut, 4 restaurants. Longest run 2 mi, vertical drop 2,150 ft. (Dec–Apr, daily) Cross-country trails. Phone 225-4107 or 800/892-1600 (exc UT).   ¢¢¢¢

9. **Uinta National Forest.** S and E of town. Scenic drives through the 950,000-acre forest; areas include Provo Canyon, Bridal Veil Falls, Deer Creek Dam and Reservoir, Diamond Fork Canyon, Hobble Creek Canyon, Strawberry Reservoir and the Alpine and Mt Nebo Scenic Loop (see PAYSON); roads give an unsurpassed view of colorful landscapes, canyons, waterfalls. Stream and lake fishing, hunting for deer and elk, camping and picnicking. Reservations are advised. For further information contact the Supervisor, 88 W 100 North, PO Box 1428, 84601; 377-5780.

10. **Bridal Veil Falls Sleytram.** 5 mi NE on US 189. Ride on 45° tramway rising 1,228 feet over 2 picturesque waterfalls. (Mid-May–mid-Oct, daily) Phone 373-5355.   ¢¢

11. **Timpanogos Cave National Monument** (see). 15 mi NE on UT 146 (State St), then 2 mi E on UT 29.

(For further information contact the Utah County Travel Council, 51 S University Ave, PO Box 912, 84603; 370-8390 or -8393.)

Annual Event

Freedom Festival. Bazaar, carnival, parades. Late June–early July.

(See Heber City, Payson, Salt Lake City)

Motels

★ ★**BEST WESTERN COTTONTREE INN.** *2230 North University Pkwy (84604).* 801/373-7044; FAX 801/375-5240. 80 rms, 2 story. S $60–$71; D $65–$76; each addl $5; suites $150; under 18 free. Crib free. TV; in-rm movies. Heated pool; whirlpool. Restaurant 11 am–10 pm. Ck-out noon. Meeting rms. Valet serv. Beauty shop. Downhill ski 15 mi. Balconies. View of river. Cr cds: A, C, D, DS, ER, MC, V.

★ ★**COMFORT INN UNIVERSITY.** *1555 N Canyon Rd (84604).* 801/374-6020; FAX 801/374-0015. 101 rms, 2 story, 6 suites. S $52–$64; D $59–$69; each addl $6; suites $95–$145; kit. unit $98; under 18 free; higher rates BYU special events. Crib free. Pet accepted, some restrictions. TV; cable. Indoor pool; whirlpool. Complimentary continental bkfst. Restaurant nearby. Ck-out 11 am. Coin lndry. Meeting rms. Sundries. Downhill/x-country ski 15 mi. Some refrigerators. Cr cds: A, C, D, DS, ER, MC, V.

★**DAYS INN.** *1675 N 200 West (84604).* 801/375-8600; FAX 801/374-6654. 49 rms, 2 story. S $48; D $53; each addl $5; kit. unit $50–$60; under 18 free. Crib free. Pet accepted. TV; cable. Heated pool. Complimentary continental bkfst in lobby. Restaurant adj 6 am–10 pm. Ck-out noon. Downhill/x-country ski 15 mi. Cr cds: A, D, DS, MC, V.

★ ★**HOLIDAY INN.** *1460 S University Ave (84601).* 801/374-9750; FAX 801/377-1615. 54 rms, 2 story. S, D $49–$55; under 18 free. Crib free. TV; cable. Pool; wading pool. Restaurant 6:30 am–10 pm. Rm serv. Ck-out noon. Meeting rms. Downhill ski 20 mi. Cr cds: A, C, D, DS, MC, V, JCB.

✔ ★ ★**HORNES' EAST BAY INN.** *1292 S University Ave (84601).* 801/374-2500; res: 800/326-0025. 116 rms, 2 story. S $30.95–$35.95; D $38.95–$49.95; each addl $6; suites $55–$65; cabin suite $125; family rates. Crib free. Pet accepted; $6 per day. TV. Heated pool. Ck-out noon. Coin lndry. Meeting rms. Downhill ski 20 mi. Exercise equipt; weight machine, bicycles. Game rm. Some in-rm whirlpools. Cr cds: A, C, D, DS, MC, V.

✔ ★NATIONAL 9 COLONY INN SUITES. *1380 S University Ave (84601).* 801/374-6800; res: 800/524-9999. 80 kit. suites, 2 story. May–Oct: S $30–$46; D $36–$56; each addl $4; wkly, monthly rates; lower rates rest of yr. Crib $4. Pet accepted, some restrictions; $15 refundable and $3 per day. TV; cable. Heated pool; sauna. Restaurant adj. Ck-out noon. Coin lndry. Downhill ski 20 mi. Cr cds: A, C, D, DS, MC, V.

Hotel

★ ★ ★SEVEN PEAKS RESORT. *101 W 100 North (84601).* 801/377-4700; res: 800/777-7144; FAX 801/377-4708. 232 rms, 9 story. S $70–$80; D $85–$95; each addl $8; suites $125–$300; under 18 free; ski, honeymoon packages; higher rates BYU special events. Crib free. TV; cable. Heated pool. Restaurant 6:30 am–10 pm. Private club 5 pm–midnight. Ck-out noon. Meeting rms. Gift shop. Free covered parking. Free RR station, bus depot transportation. Downhill ski 14 mi. Exercise equipt; weights, bicycles, whirlpool, sauna. Some refrigerators, wet bars. Cr cds: A, C, D, DS, MC, V.

Resort

★ ★SUNDANCE. *(RR 3, Box A-1, Sundance 84604)* 14 mi NE on US 189, NW on UT 92, in North Fork Provo Canyon. 801/225-4107; FAX 801/226-1937. 80 kit. units. Mid-Dec–Mar: S, D $90–$425; suites $175–$425; 2–3 bedrm cottages $325–$475; ski plans; lower rates rest of yr. TV. Dining rms 7:30 am–10 pm. Ck-out 11 am, ck-in 3 pm. Package store. Meeting rms. Downhill ski on site. Some fireplaces. Private patios. Handmade wooden furniture; Indian art. Rustic retreat surrounded by pristine wilderness. Cr cds: A, C, D, MC, V.

Restaurants

★BOMBAY HOUSE. *463 N University Ave.* 801/373-6677. Hrs: 11:30 am–2:30 pm, 5–10 pm; Fri to 10:30 pm; Sat noon–10:30 pm. Closed Sun; Dec 25. Res accepted. Indian menu. Buffet: lunch $5.95. A la carte entrees: dinner $8–$13. Child's meals. Specializes in barbecue, tandoori, curry. Parking. Indian atmosphere. Cr cds: A, C, D, DS, MC, V.

✔ ★LA DOLCE VITA. *61 N 100 East.* 801/373-8482. Hrs: 10:30 am–10 pm; Fri, Sat 11 am–10:30 pm. Closed Sun; most major hols. Italian menu. Semi-a la carte: lunch $1.99–$10, dinner $6–$10. Child's meals. Specialties: cotoletta alla Bolognese, tortellini alla panna, pasta. Parking. Italian murals on walls. Cr cds: A, DS, MC, V.

Ⓓ

Rainbow Bridge National Monument (E-3)

(NW of Navajo Mountain, approachable from Arizona)

Rising from the eastern shore of Lake Powell, Rainbow Bridge, the largest natural rock bridge in the world, was named a national monument in 1910, one year after its sighting was documented. Carved by a meander of Bridge Creek, this natural bridge stands 290 feet tall, spans 275 feet and stretches 33 feet at the top. One of the seven natural wonders of the world, Rainbow Bridge is higher than the nation's capitol and nearly as long as a football field. The monument is predominantly salmon pink in color, modified by streaks of black iron oxide. In the light of the late afternoon sun, the bridge becomes brilliant to see. Native Americans consider the area a sacred place; legend holds that the bridge is a rainbow turned to stone.

The easiest way to reach Rainbow Bridge is a half-day round-trip boat ride across Lake Powell from Page, AZ (see) or a full-day round-trip boat ride from Bullfrog and Halls Crossing marinas (see LAKE POWELL). The bridge also can be reached on foot or horseback via the Rainbow Trail through the Navajo Indian Reservation (see under ARIZONA; permit required). Fuel and camp supplies are available at Dangling Rope Marina, accessible by boat only, 10 miles downlake (south). For further information contact the Superintendent, Glen Canyon National Recreation Area, PO Box 1507, Page, AZ 86040; 602/645-2511.

Richfield (D-3)

Settled: 1863 Pop: 5,593 Elev: 5,330 ft Area code: 801 Zip: 84701

Brigham Young sent members of his church here to settle the area, but problems with Indians forced abandonment of the fledgling town for almost a year before the pioneers were able to regain their settlement. Located in the center of Sevier Valley, Richfield has become the commercial hub of the region. Today, some of the world's best beef is raised in and shipped from this area. Headquarters and a Ranger District Office of the Fishlake National Forest (see #1) are located here.

What to See and Do

1. **Fishlake National Forest.** This 1,424,000-acre forest offers fishing, hunting, hiking, picnicking and camping (fee). Fish Lake, 33 mi SE via UT 119 & UT 24, then 7 mi NE on UT 25, offers high-altitude angling on 6-mile-long, mile-wide lake covering 2,600 acres. Also campgrounds (mid-May–late Oct) and resorts (yr-round). Contact the Supervisor's Office, 115 East 900 North; 896-9233.

2. **Big Rock Candy Mountain.** 25 mi S on US 89, in Marysvale Canyon. Multicolored mountain that Burl Ives popularized in song.

3. **Capitol Reef National Park** (see). 10 mi E on UT 119, then 76 mi SE on UT 24.

4. **Fremont Indian State Park.** 20 mi SW via I-70, at 11550 W Clear Creek Canyon Rd, in Sevier. Museum and trails feature the Fremont Indians, who lived in the area from A.D. 300–1300 and then vanished. There is no explanation, only speculation, for their disappearance. Interpretive center highlights evolution of their culture; artifacts from nearby Five Fingers Hill; nature trails lead to panels of rock art and a reconstructed pit house dwelling and granary. Fishing. Camping. Picnicking. (Daily; closed Jan 1, Thanksgiving, Dec 25) Standard fees. Paved trails for the disabled. Phone 527-4631.

(For further information contact Chamber of Commerce, PO Box 327; 896-4241.)

(See Beaver, Fillmore, Salina)

Motels

✔ ★BEST WESTERN APPLE TREE INN. *145 S Main St.* 801/896-5481. 62 rms, 1–2 story. May–Oct: S $38–$48; D $45–$55; each addl $4; suites $50–$95; varied lower rates rest of yr. Crib $5. Pet accepted. TV; cable. Heated pool. Complimentary continental bkfst. Restaurant nearby. Ck-out noon. Meeting rm. Cr cds: A, C, D, DS, ER, MC, V.

★★**DAYS INN.** *333 N Main St. 801/896-6476.* 51 rms, 3 story. No elvtr. May–Oct: S $41–$58; D $58–$65; each addl $5; suites $50–$79; under 12 free; lower rates rest of yr. Crib $8. TV; cable. Heated pool. Restaurant 6 am–10 pm. Ck-out 11 am. Meeting rms. Sundries. Refrigerators. Cr cds: A, C, D, DS, MC, V.

[symbols]

★★**QUALITY INN.** *540 S Main St. 801/896-5465.* 57 rms, 2 story. Mid-June–Oct: S $36; D $58; each addl $6; suites $62–$80; kit. units $48–$66; under 17 free; lower rates rest of yr. Crib free. TV; cable. Heated pool. Restaurant adj 6–1 am. Ck-out noon. Meeting rms. Exercise equipt; weights, bicycle. Whirlpool in suites. Cr cds: A, C, D, DS, ER, MC, V, JCB.

[symbols]

✔★**ROMANICO INN.** *1170 S Main St. 801/896-8471.* 29 rms, 2 story. Mid-May–Sept: S $26–$32; D $32–$42; each addl $4; kit. cottages $3 addl; under 12 free; lower rates rest of yr. Crib $2. Pet accepted. TV; cable. Restaurant adj 5:30–10 pm. Ck-out noon. Coin lndry. Whirlpool. Some refrigerators. Cr cds: A, C, D, DS, ER, MC, V.

[symbols]

★★**WESTON INN.** *647 S Main St. 801/896-9271.* 40 rms, 2 story. June–Sept: S, D $38–$48; each addl $4; under 12 free; lower rates rest of yr. Crib free. TV; cable. Indoor pool; whirlpool. Restaurant 6 am–9 pm. Rm serv. Ck-out noon. Meeting rms. Sundries. Free bus depot transportation. Cr cds: A, C, D, DS, MC, V.

[symbols]

Restaurant

✔★**TOPSFIELD LODGE STEAKHOUSE.** *1200 S Main St, behind Richfield Plaza shopping center. 801/896-5437.* Hrs: 5:30–10 pm. Closed Sun; Thanksgiving, Dec 25. Serv bar. Semi-a la carte: dinner $5.95–$15.95. Child's meals. Specializes in steak, shrimp & filet. Salad bar. Own spicecake. Country decor; fireplace, tole-painted wall hangings. Parking. Cr cds: A, MC, V.

[symbols]

Roosevelt (B-4)

Settled: 1905 **Pop:** 3,915 **Elev:** 5,182 ft **Area code:** 801 **Zip:** 84066

Roosevelt, in the geographical center of Utah's "dinosaur land," was settled when the opening of Indian reservation lands prompted a flood of homesteaders to stake claims in the area. The town was named after Theodore Roosevelt, who had once camped on the banks of a nearby river. Nine Mile Canyon, with its Indian petroglyphs, can be reached from here. A Ranger District office of the Ashley National Forest (see VERNAL) is located in the town.

(For further information about this area contact the Chamber of Commerce, 48 S 200 East St, PO Box 1417; 722-4598.)

(See Vernal)

Motel

✔★**FRONTIER.** *75 S 200 East St. 801/722-2201; FAX 801/722-3640.* 54 units, 2 kits. S $28–$36; D $31–$36; each addl $3; kit. units $34–$42. Crib $2.50. Pet accepted. TV; cable. Restaurant 6 am–9:30 pm; Sun to 9 pm. Ck-out 11 am. Cr cds: A, D, DS, MC, V.

[symbols]

St George (E-2)

Founded: 1861 **Pop:** 28,502 **Elev:** 2,761 ft **Area code:** 801 **Zip:** 84770

Extending themselves to this hot, arid corner of southwest Utah, members of the Mormon Church built their first temple here and struggled to survive by growing cotton—hence the nickname "Dixie." With determination and persistence, members of the Church struggled against odds to construct the temple. The site, chosen by Brigham Young, turned out to be a bog, but another site was not selected. Instead, hundreds of tons of rocks were pounded into the mud until a stable foundation could be laid. Mormons from the north worked 40-day missions, and southern church members gave 1 day's labor in 10 until the temple was complete. The workers quarried 17,000 tons of rock by hand. A team of oxen hauled the stones to the construction site, and for 7 straight days, timber was hauled more than 80 miles from Mount Trumbull to construct the structure. Made of red sandstone plastered to a gleaming white, the Mormon temple is not only the town's landmark, but also a beacon for passing aircraft.

In St George, warm summers are balanced by mild winters and a long growing season. Tourists and sportsmen bring in important business. The seat of Washington County, St George is the closest town of its size to Zion National Park (see). A Ranger District office of the Dixie National Forest (see CEDAR CITY) is located here.

What to See and Do

1. **Temple Visitor Center.** 440 S 300 East. On grounds of temple; guided tour of center explains local history and beliefs of the Latter-day Saints; audiovisual program. (Daily; closed Dec 25) Phone 673-5181. **Free.**

2. **Tabernacle.** Main & Tabernacle Sts. Red sandstone structure built 1863–1876 with local materials; resembles colonial New England church. (Daily; closed Dec 25) Phone 673-5181. **Free.**

3. **Brigham Young Winter Home** (1873). 200 North & 100 West Sts. Two-story adobe house where the Mormon leader spent the last four winters of his life; period furnishings, garden. (Daily; closed Dec 25) Phone 673-2517 or -5181. **Free.**

4. **Daughters of Utah Pioneers Collection.** Memorial Bldg, 143 N 100 East. Regional memorabilia. (Daily exc Sun; closed hols) Donation. Phone 628-7274.

5. **Jacob Hamblin Home** (1863). 5 mi W off I-15, in Santa Clara. Native sandstone house of Hamblin, Mormon missionary to Native Americans for 32 years; pioneer furnishings. (Daily; closed Dec 25) Phone 673-2161 or -5181. **Free.**

6. **State parks.**

   Snow Canyon. 10 mi N on UT 18. Flat-bottomed gorge cut into multicolored Navajo sandstone; massive erosional forms, sand dunes, Native American petroglyphs. Hiking. Picnicking. Improved camping areas (some hookups, dump station), trailer parking. (Daily) Standard fees. Phone 628-2255 or 800/322-3770 (reservations).

   Gunlock. 16 mi NW on Old Hwy 91. Approx 450 undeveloped acres in scenic red rock country. A dam across the Santa Clara River has created a 240-acre lake, which offers swimming, waterskiing; fishing; boating (ramp). Picnicking. Primitive camping; no drinking water. (Daily) Phone 628-2255. **Free.**

7. **Pine Valley Chapel.** 30 mi N via UT 18, Central exit, in Dixie National Forest. White frame meeting house built in 1868 as an upside-down ship by Ebenezer Bryce, a shipbuilder by trade. The walls were completed on the ground, then raised and joined with wooden pegs and rawhide. Still in use, the chapel served as both church and schoolhouse until 1919. (Memorial Day–Labor Day, daily) **Free.**

8. Zion National Park (see). 42 mi NE on UT 9.

(For further information contact the Washington County Travel & Convention Bureau, 425 S 700 East, Dixie Center; 634-5747 or 800/869-6635.)

Annual Events

Washington County Fair. Aug.

Dixie Roundup. 3 days mid-Sept.

Motels

★★**BEST WESTERN CORAL HILLS.** *125 E St George Blvd.* 801/673-4844. 98 rms, 2 story. Feb–Oct: S $39–$49; D $44–$56; each addl $3; suites $65–$95; under 12 free; lower rates rest of yr. Crib $3. TV; cable. 2 pools, 1 indoor; wading pool. Restaurant opp 6 am–9:30 pm. Ck-out 11 am. Meeting rms. Exercise equipt; weight machine, bicycles, whirlpool. Rec rm. Balconies. Cr cds: A, C, D, DS, ER, MC, V.

[D] [≈] [🏃] [⊗] [◎] [SC]

✓★**CLARIDGE INN.** *1187 S Bluff St.* 801/673-7222. 50 rms, 2 story. S, D $33–$50; wkend rates. Crib $3. TV; cable. Heated pool; whirlpool. Complimentary continental bkfst. Restaurant opp open 24 hrs. Ck-out 11 am. Totally nonsmoking. Cr cds: A, DS, MC, V.

[D] [≈] [⊗] [◎]

★★**COMFORT SUITES.** *1239 S Main St.* 801/673-7000; FAX 801/628-4340. 123 suites, 2 story. Feb–Aug: S, D $49–$89; under 16 free; golf plans; higher rates: Easter, early Oct; lower rates rest of yr. Crib $5. TV; cable. Heated pool; whirlpool. Complimentary continental bkfst. Restaurant opp open 24 hrs. Ck-out 11 am. Meeting rms. Bathrm phones, refrigerators. Cr cds: A, C, D, DS, ER, MC, V, JCB.

[D] [≈] [⊗] [◎] [SC]

★★**DAYS INN FOUR SEASONS.** *747 E St George Blvd.* 801/673-6111. 96 rms, 2 story. S, D $45–$55; each addl $5; suites $80–$130; under 12 free. Crib free. TV; cable, in-rm movies. Indoor/outdoor pool; whirlpool. Restaurant 5–10 pm. Ck-out 11 am. Meeting rms. Lighted tennis. Sun deck. Cr cds: A, C, D, DS, MC, V.

[P] [≈] [◎] [SC]

★★★**HOLIDAY INN.** *850 S Bluff St, near Municipal Airport.* 801/628-4235; FAX 801/628-8157. 164 rms, 2 story. S $61–$120; D $69–$120; each addl $8; suites $100–$120; under 19 free. Crib free. TV; cable. Indoor/outdoor pool. Restaurant 6 am–10 pm. Rm serv. Wine, liquor. Ck-out 11 am. Coin lndry. Meeting rms. Bellhops. Valet serv. Shopping arcade. Airport transportation. Lighted tennis. Putting green. Exercise equipt; weight machines, bicycles, whirlpool, sauna. Game rm. Some refrigerators. Balconies. Cr cds: A, C, D, DS, MC, V, JCB.

[D] [P] [≈] [🏃] [✗] [⊗] [◎] [SC]

★**SINGLETREE INN.** *260 E St George Blvd.* 801/673-6161; res: 800/528-8890; FAX 801/673-7453. 49 rms, 2 story. S, D $44–$54. Crib free. TV; cable. Heated pool; whirlpool. Continental bkfst in lobby. Restaurant adj 11:30 am–10 pm. Ck-out 11 am. Cr cds: A, C, D, DS, MC, V.

[D] [≈] [⊗] [◎] [SC]

✓★**SLEEP INN.** *1481 S Sunland Dr, near Municipal Airport.* 801/673-7900; res: 800/627-5337. 68 rms, shower only, 2 story. Apr–Nov: S, D $30–$40; under 12 free; higher rates Easter; lower rates rest of yr. Crib free. TV; cable, in-rm movies. Heated pool; whirlpool. Restaurant nearby. Ck-out noon. Cr cds: A, C, D, DS, MC, V, JCB.

[D] [≈] [✗] [⊗] [◎] [SC]

✓★**SUN TIME INN.** *420 E St George Blvd.* 801/673-6181; res: 800/237-6253. 46 rms, 2 story. S $28–$36; D $39–$45; each addl $4; suites $50–$60; under 16 free; wkly rates. Crib free. TV; cable.

Heated pool. Restaurant adj 10 am–9:30 pm. Ck-out noon. Some refrigerators. Cr cds: A, DS, MC, V.

[D] [≈] [⊗] [◎] [SC]

✓★**TRAVELODGE EAST.** *175 N 1000 East St.* 801/673-4621. 40 rms, 2 story. S $35–$40; D $39–$44; each addl $4; suites $69–$76; under 18 free. Crib free. Pet accepted. TV; cable. Heated pool. Coffee in rms. Restaurant adj open 24 hrs. Ck-out noon. Some refrigerators. Cr cds: A, C, D, DS, ER, MC, V, JCB.

[🐾] [≈] [⊗] [◎] [SC]

Inn

★★★**GREENE GATE VILLAGE.** *76 W Tabernacle St.* 801/628-6999; res: 800/350-6999. 18 rms, 1–2 story, 7 suites, 3 kit. units. S, D, suites $45–$110; each addl $10–$15; kit. units $55–$85; wkly, monthly rates. Crib free. TV; cable. Pool; whirlpool. Complimentary full bkfst. Dining rm Thurs–Sat 6–8 pm. Ck-out 11 am, ck-in 3 pm. Free airport, bus depot transportation. Balconies; some fireplaces. Picnic tables, grills. Consists of 8 Victorian and pioneer houses from late 1800s; library, sitting rm, antiques, tole-painted furnishings. Totally nonsmoking. Cr cds: A, MC, V.

[D] [≈] [⊗] [◎]

Restaurants

★★★**ANDELIN'S GABLE HOUSE.** *290 E St George Blvd.* 801/673-6796. Hrs: 11:30 am–10 pm. Closed Sun; Jan 1, Thanksgiving, Dec 24 eve, Dec 25. Res accepted. Semi-a la carte: lunch $2.95–$8.95. Complete meals: dinner $4.95–$24.95. Child's meals. Specializes in prime rib, rack of pork, fresh fish. Own baking. Parking. Old English decor, antiques. Old family recipes. Totally nonsmoking. Cr cds: A, DS, MC, V.

✓★**DICK'S CAFE.** *114 E St George Blvd.* 801/673-3841. Hrs: 6 am–9:30 pm. Closed Dec 25. Semi-a la carte: bkfst $2.70–$8; lunch $3.45–$4.85, dinner $7.50–$14.95. Child's meals. Specializes in steak, chicken, seafood. Parking. Western decor. Since 1935. Cr cds: A, DS, MC, V.

★★**SULLIVAN'S ROCOCO STEAKHOUSE.** *511 S Airport Rd, opp airport.* 801/673-3305. Hrs: 5:30–10 pm. Closed Thanksgiving, Dec 24, 25. Serv bar. Semi-a la carte: dinner $5.95–$29.95. Specializes in steak, prime rib, seafood. Parking. Victorian decor; chandeliers. View of city and surrounding mountains. Cr cds: A, D, DS, MC, V.

[D]

Salina (C-3)

Settled: 1863 **Pop:** 1,943 **Elev:** 5,150 ft **Area code:** 801 **Zip:** 84654

What to See and Do

Palisade State Park. 20 mi N via US 89, then 2 mi E, near Sterling. Approx 200 acres. Swimming beaches, showers; fishing; nonmotorized boating, canoe rentals. Nature trail, hiking. 9-hole golf. Picnicking. Camping (dump station). Six Mile Canyon adj. Standard fees. Phone 835-7275.

Annual Event

Mormon Miracle Pageant. 30 mi N via US 89 in Manti, on Temple grounds. Portrays historical events of the Americas; cast of 600. Phone 835-3000. Early-mid-July.

(See Richfield)

Motels

★ ★ **BEST WESTERN SHAHEEN'S.** *1225 S State St. 801/529-7455.* 40 rms, 2 story. May–Nov: S $46; D $54; each addl $6; lower rates rest of yr. Crib $4. TV; cable. Heated pool. Restaurant 5:30 am–10 pm. Ck-out 11 am. Meeting rm. Sundries. Cr cds: A, C, D, DS, MC, V.

✔ ★ **SAFARI.** *1425 S State St. 801/529-7447.* 28 rms, 2 story. June–mid-Oct: S $37–$44; D $48–$52; each addl $6; under 12 free; lower rates rest of yr. Crib $4. TV; cable. Heated pool. Restaurant 6 am–midnight. Ck-out 11 am. Cr cds: A, C, D, DS, MC, V.

Restaurant

✔ ★ **MOM'S CAFE.** *10 E Main St. 801/529-3921.* Hrs: 7 am–10 pm. Closed Thanksgiving, Dec 25. Semi-a la carte: bkfst $1.75–$7.60, lunch $3.20–$8.25, dinner $6.25–¢12. Child's meals. Specialties: fish & chips, liver & onions, shrimp. Salad bar. Own pies. Parking. Homey atmosphere. Family-owned. Cr cds: MC, V.

Salt Lake City (B-3)

Founded: 1847 **Pop:** 159,936 **Elev:** 4,330 ft **Area code:** 801

On a hill at the north end of State Street stands Utah's classic capitol building. Three blocks south is Temple Square, with the famed Mormon Temple and Tabernacle. The adjacent block houses the headquarters of the Church of Jesus Christ of Latter-day Saints, whose members are often called Mormons. Salt Lake City, with its 10-acre blocks, 132-foot-wide, tree-lined streets and mountains rising to the east and west, is one of the most beautifully planned cities in the country.

Once a desert wilderness, Salt Lake City was built by Mormon settlers who sought refuge from religious persecution. Neither the barrenness of the land, drought nor a plague of crickets swerved these people from their purpose. Followers of Brigham Young arrived and named their new territory "Deseret." In these early days the Mormons began a variety of experiments in farming, industry and society, many of which were highly successful. Today, Salt Lake City is an industrious, businesslike city, a center for electronics, steel, missiles and a hundred other enterprises.

West of the city is the enormous Great Salt Lake, stretching 48 miles one way and 90 miles the other. It is less than 35 feet deep and between 15 and 20 percent salt—almost twice as salty as the ocean—humans bob like a cork and cannot sink in the water. The lake is what remains of ancient Lake Bonneville, once 145 miles wide, 350 miles long and 1,000 feet deep. As Lake Bonneville water evaporated over thousands of years, a large expanse of perfectly flat, solid salt was left. Today the Bonneville Salt Flats stretch west almost to Nevada.

Headquarters and a Ranger District office of the Wasatch–Cache National Forest (see #25) are located in Salt Lake City.

Salt Lake City was laid out in grid fashion, with Temple Square at the center. Most street names are coordinates on this grid: 4th South St is four blocks south of Temple Square, 7th East is seven blocks east. These are written as 400 South and 700 East.

Transportation

Car Rental Agencies: See toll-free numbers under Introduction.

Public Transportation: Buses (Utah Transit Authority), phone 287-4636.

Rail Passenger Service: Amtrak 800/872-7245.

Airport Information

Salt Lake City Intl Airport: Information 575-2460; lost and found 575-2427; weather 524-5133; cash machines, Terminal Unit 2, near gift shop opposite entrance to Concourse C; Crown Room (Delta), in connector between Concourse C and Concourse D.

Terminals: Concourse A: America West, American, Continental, Northwest; Concourse B: Delta, Sky West, TWA, United; Concourse C: Delta; Concourse D: Delta; Concourse S: Alaska Air, Alpine Air, Horizon.

(Airlines and their terminal locations may change. Before leaving for the airport, you should phone the airline to confirm terminal location for your flight.)

What to See and Do

1. **Temple Square.** North, South and West Temple Sts & Main St. (Daily) Visitor centers provide information, exhibits and guided tours (½- to 1-hr; daily; every 15 min). Phone 240-2534. **Free.** Tour includes

   Tabernacle (1867). The self-supporting roof, an elongated dome, is 250 feet long and 150 feet wide. The tabernacle organ has 11,623 pipes, ranging from ⅝ inch to 32 feet in length. The world-famous Tabernacle Choir may be heard at rehearsal (Thurs evening) or at broadcast time (Sun morning). Organ recitals (Mon–Sat, noon or Sun, afternoon). **Free.**

   Temple (1893). Used for sacred ordinances, such as baptisms and marriages. Closed to non-Mormons.

   Assembly Hall (1880). Tours (daily), concerts (Fri, Sat evenings).

   Seagull Monument (1913). Commemorates saving of the crops from crickets in 1848.

   Museum of Church History and Art. 45 N West Temple St. Exhibits of Latter-day Saints church history from 1820 to present. (Daily; closed Jan 1, Easter, Thanksgiving, Dec 25) Phone 240-3310. **Free.**

   Family History Library. 35 N West Temple. Largest genealogy library in the world aids in compilation of family histories. (Daily exc Sun) Phone 240-2331. **Free.**

2. **Brigham Young Monument** (1897). Intersection of Main & South Temple Sts.

3. **Lion House** (1856) and **Beehive House** (1854). 63 & 67 E South Temple. Family residences, offices and social centers for Brigham Young and his wives and children. Guided tours of Beehive House. (Daily; closed Jan 1, Thanksgiving, Dec 25) Phone 240-2977 (Lion House) or -2672 (Beehive House). **Free.**

4. **State Capitol** (1914). Head of State St. Constructed of Utah granite and Georgia marble, with a modern annex, capitol has a commanding view of the valley and Wasatch Mountains. Gold Room is decorated with bird's-eye marble and gold from Utah mines; ground floor has exhibits. Guided tours every 30 min (Tues–Thurs; hrs vary). Phone 538-3000. **Free.**

5. **Council Hall** (1864–66). Capitol Hill. Meeting place of territorial legislature and city hall for 30 years was dismantled and then reconstructed in 1963 at present location; Federal/Greek-revival style architecture. Visitor information center and office; memorabilia. (Daily; closed Jan 1, Thanksgiving, Dec 25) Phone 538-1030. **Free.**

6. **Governor's Mansion** (1902). 603 E South Temple St. Restored mansion of Thomas Kearns, wealthy Utah senator of early 1900s; decorated with Russian mahogany, Italian marble. Tours. (Early May–Nov, Tues afternoons; closed hols) Phone 538-1005. **Free.**

7. **Pioneer Memorial Museum.** 300 N Main St, W side of capitol grounds. Manuscripts, pioneer relics. Also here is **Carriage House,** with exhibits relating to transportation, including Brigham Young's wagon, mule-drawn vehicles, pony express items. One-hour guided tours. (June–Aug, daily; rest of yr, daily exc Sun; closed hols) Phone 538-1050. **Free.**

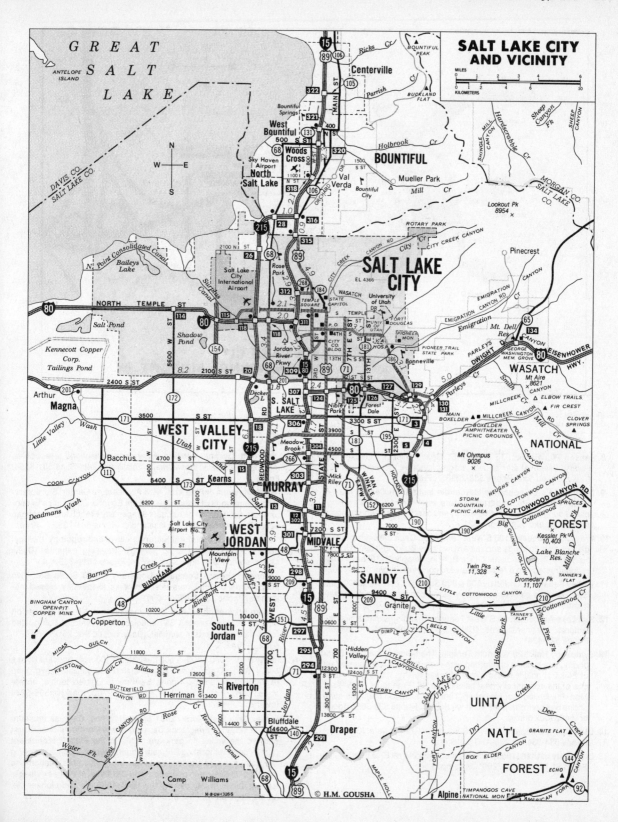

SALT LAKE CITY
AND VICINITY

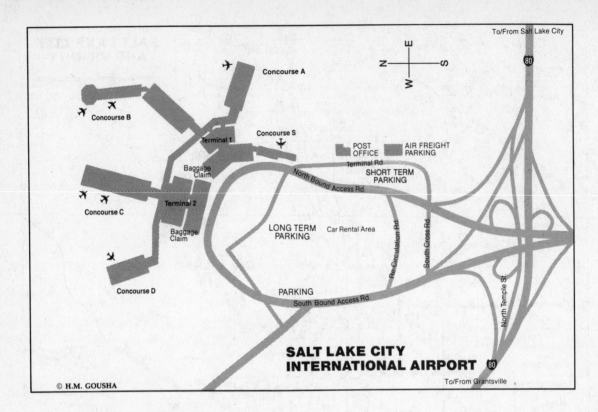

To/From Salt Lake City

Concourse A

N
E
S
W

Concourse B

Terminal 1

Concourse S

POST OFFICE   AIR FREIGHT PARKING

Terminal Rd.

Baggage Claim

North Bound Access Rd.

SHORT TERM PARKING

Concourse C

Terminal 2

LONG TERM PARKING   Car Rental Area

Re-Circulation Rd.

South Cross Rd.

North Temple St.

Baggage Claim

Concourse D

PARKING

South Bound Access Rd.

SALT LAKE CITY INTERNATIONAL AIRPORT 80

To/From Grantsville

© H.M. GOUSHA

8. **Hansen Planetarium.** 15 S State St. Space science museum and library. Seasonal star shows, stage plays (fee; schedule varies). (Daily; closed hols) Phone 538-2098.   **Free.**

9. **ZCMI (Zion's Co-operative Mercantile Institution) Center.** Main & South Temple Sts. Department store established in 1868 by Brigham Young anchors this 85-store, enclosed, downtown shopping mall. (Daily exc Sun) Phone 321-8743.

10. **Arrow Press Square.** 165 S West Temple St. Once the city's printing district, now buildings such as Arrow Press Building (1890), Upland Hotel (1910) and Midwest Office Building Supply (1910) have been reconstructed into a retail/restaurant complex. Phone 531-9700.

11. **Trolley Square.** Bounded by 500 & 600 South Sts and 600 & 700 East Sts. Ten-acre complex of trolley barns converted into entertainment/shopping/dining center. (Daily) Phone 521-9877.

12. **Salt Lake Art Center.** 20 S West Temple. Changing exhibits; school; lectures, seminars, films. (Daily; closed major hols) Donation. Phone 328-4201.

13. **Symphony Hall.** 123 W South Temple. The home of the Utah Symphony, this building is adorned with more than 12,000 square feet of 24-karat gold leaf and a mile of brass railing. It has been rated one of the acoustically best halls in the US. Free tours (May–Aug, Mon–Fri, limited hrs; rest of yr, Tues & Fri, limited hrs). The symphony has performances most weekends. Phone 533-5626 (tours) or -6408 (box office).

14. **Utah Opera Company.** 50 W 200 South St. Grand opera. (Oct–May) Phone 534-0842 or 355-ARTS (tickets).

15. **University of Utah** (1850). (25,900 students) 2½ mi E, at head of 200 South St. Phone 581-7200. On campus are

Marriott Library. Western Americana collection, rare books, manuscripts. (Daily; closed major hols & July 24) Phone 581-8558. **Free.**

Utah Museum of Fine Arts. Art & Architecture Center, S of library. Representations of artistic styles from Egyptian antiquities to contemporary American paintings; 19th-century French and American paintings, furniture. (Daily; closed hols) Phone 581-7332.   **Free.**

Utah Museum of Natural History. Halls of anthropology, biology, mineralogy, paleontology, geology; traveling exhibits. (Daily; closed some major hols; also July 24) Phone 581-4303.   ¢

Pioneer Theatre Company. University & 300 South Sts. Two auditoriums; dramas, musicals, comedies. (Sept–May; closed major hols) Phone 581-6270 or -6961.

State Arboretum of Utah. On campus. More than 9,000 trees on 150 acres, representing 350 species; conservatory. Self-guided tours. Special events in summer. (Daily; closed Dec 25) Phone 581-5322.   **Free.**

16. **Liberty Park.** 1300 South & 600 East Sts. In 100-acre park are Chase Mill (1852), Tracy Aviary (fee), children's garden playground (Apr–Sept), amusement park. Swimming. Lighted tennis, horseshoe courts. Picnicking. (Daily) Phone 972-7800 (park) or 596-5034 (aviary).   **Free.**

17. **Pioneer Trail State Park.** 2601 Sunnyside Ave. Day-use museum park at mouth of Emigration Canyon, where Mormon pioneers first entered the valley. In park are **"This Is the Place" Monument** (1947), commemorating Brigham Young's words upon first seeing the Salt Lake City site; visitor center with audio presentation and murals of the Mormon migration; and **Old Deseret Pioneer Village**, a living museum that depicts the 1847–1869 era and pioneer life. (June–Sept, daily). Phone 584-8392.   ¢

18. **Hogle Zoological Garden.** 2600 E Sunnyside Ave. Wildlife exhibits; Discovery Land; animal demonstrations; miniature train (summer). Picnicking, concession. (Daily; closed Jan 1, Dec 25) Sr citizen rate. Phone 582-1631. ¢¢

19. **Raging Waters.** 1700 S 1200 West St. Water theme park with automated wave-pool, 19 water slides, water rollercoasters, other water attractions. (June–mid-Sept, daily) Phone 973-4020. ¢¢¢¢

20. **Lagoon Amusement Park, Pioneer Village and Water Park.** 17 mi N on I-15 exit 325, then N to Lagoon Dr. Rides; water slides; re-creation of 19th-century Utah town; stagecoach and steam-engine train rides. Camping. Picnicking. (Memorial Day–Aug, daily; mid-Apr–late May & Sept, Sat & Sun only). Parking (fee). Phone 451-8000. Entrance only ¢¢¢; All-day Passport ¢¢¢¢¢

21. **49th Street Galleria.** S on I-15, 53rd St S exit, W to 700 West, then N to 4998 S 360 West St, in Murray. Enclosed mall with entertainment, rides, bowling, roller skating, baseball, arcades, miniature golf; cafes. Fee for activities. (Daily exc Sun) Phone 265-3866.

22. **Wheeler Historic Farm.** 6351 S 900 East St, 15 mi SE on I-15, exit I-215. Living history farm (75 acres) depicts rural life from 1890 to 1918. Farmhouse, farm buildings; animals, crops; hay rides (fee). Tour (fee). Visitors can feed animals, gather eggs, milk cows. (Daily; no rides Sun) Phone 264-2241. ¢

23. **Fort Douglas Military Museum.** 3 mi NE, Bldg 32 Potter St. Army museum features history of military in Utah from arrival of Johnston's Army during the 1857 "Utah War" through Vietnam. Also tours of fort (self-guided or guided, by appt.) (Tues–Sat; closed most hols) Phone 588-5188. **Free.**

24. **Skiing.**

   Alta. 26 mi SE on UT 210 in Little Cottonwood Canyon in Alta (see).

   Brighton Resort. 25 mi SE via I-215, exit 6 in Big Cottonwood Canyon. Two high-speed quad, 2 triple, 3 double chairlifts; patrol, school, rentals; lodge, restaurant, cafeteria. 61 runs; longest run 3 mi, vertical drop 1,745 ft. (Mid-Nov–mid-Apr, daily) Night skiing (nightly exc Sun). Half-day rates. Cross-country skiing. Phone 800/873-5512. Sr citizen rate. ¢¢¢¢¢

   Deer Valley. 34 mi E & S via I-80, UT 224 in Park City (see).

   Park City. 32 mi E & S via I-80, UT 224 in Park City (see).

   ParkWest. 28 mi E & S via I-80, UT 224 in Park City (see).

   Snowbird. 25 mi E & S via I-215, UT 210 in Little Cottonwood Canyon (see SNOWBIRD).

   Solitude Resort. SE via I-215, in Big Cottonwood Canyon. De-tachable quad, 2 triple, 4 double chairlifts; race course, patrol, school, rentals; day lodge, cafeteria, restaurants, bar. Longest run 2½ mi, vertical drop 2,030 ft. (Thanksgiving–mid-Apr, daily) Cross-country center. Phone 534-1400. ¢¢¢¢¢

25. **Wasatch-Cache National Forest.** E via I-80; or N via US 89; Lone Peak Wilderness Area, 20 mi SE. High Uintas Wilderness Area has alpine lakes and rugged peaks; Big Cottonwood, Little Cotton-wood and Logan canyons. Forest (1 million acres) has fishing; deer and elk hunting; boating. Winter sports. Picnicking. Camping (fees). Contact the Supervisor, 8230 Federal Bldg, 125 S State St, 84138; 524-5030.

26. **Timpanogos Cave National Monument** (see). 26 mi S on I-15, then 10 mi E on UT 92.

27. **Kennecott Bingham Canyon Mine.** 25 mi SW on UT 48. Open-pit copper mine 2½ miles wide and a half-mile deep. Visitors' center, observation deck and audio presentation explain mining opera-tions, which date from 1906. (Apr–mid-Oct, daily) Phone 322-7300. Per car ¢

28. **River trips. Moki Mac River Expeditions.** Offers 1–14-day whitewa-ter trips on the Green and Colorado rivers. Phone 268-6667 or 800/284-7280. ¢¢¢¢¢

29. **Bus tours.**

   Gray Line. 553 W 100 South St, 84101; 521-7060.

   InnsBrook Tours. 1599 Stratford Ave, 84106; 466-9009.

   On the Town Tours. 150 W 500 South St, 84101; 575-6040.

   Scenic West Tours. PO Box 369, Draper 84020; 572-2717 or 800/723-6429.

Annual Events

Pageant of the Arts. Capitol Theater, 50 W 200 South. Theatrically staged pageant re-creating old and contemporary art masterpieces. Cast of 100. Phone 355-2787. Mid-June–mid-July.

Utah Arts Festival. Downtown. More than 1,000 participants, 90 performing groups; Children's Art Yard, juried show with demonstra-tions. Ethnic food. Last wk June.

"Days of '47" Celebration. Mid-July.

Utah State Fair. State FairPark. Phone 538-FAIR. Sept 8–18.

Temple Square Christmas. Includes Handel's *Messiah* sung by the Oratorio Society of Utah. Lighting ceremony Friday after Thanksgiving. Phone 240-2534. Early Dec.

Seasonal Events

Professional sports. Jazz (NBA basketball) and Golden Eagles (IHL hockey), Delta Center, 301 S West Temple; phone 325-SEAT (tickets).

Additional Visitor Information

For additional information contact the Salt Lake Convention & Visitors Bureau, 180 S West Temple, 84101-1493, phone 521-2822; or the Utah Travel Council and Visitor Information Center, Council Hall, 300 N State St, 84114, phone 538-1030.

(See Heber City, Ogden, Park City, Provo)

City Neighborhoods

Many of the restaurants, unrated dining establishments and some lodg-ings listed under Salt Lake City include neighborhoods as well as exact street addresses. Geographic descriptions of Downtown and Trolley Square are given, followed by a table of restaurants arranged by neigh-borhood.

Downtown: South of 9th Ave, west of A St and 300 East St, north of 700 South St and east of 400 West St. **East of Downtown:** East of 9th East St.

Trolley Square: South of 500 South St, west of 700 East St, north of 600 South St and east of 600 East St.

SALT LAKE CITY RESTAURANTS
BY NEIGHBORHOOD AREAS

(For full description, see alphabetical listings under Restaurants)

DOWNTOWN

Baci Trattoria. 134 W Pierpont Ave

Benihana of Tokyo. 165 S West Temple St

La Fleur de Lys. 39 Post Office Place

Litza's for Pizza. 716 E 400 South St

Market Street Grill. 48 Market St

Mikado. 67 W 100 South St

Ristorante della Fontana. 336 S 400 East St

EAST OF DOWNTOWN

Cowboy Grub. 2350½ Foothill Blvd

Log Haven. Millcreek Canyon Rd

Market Street Broiler. 258 S 1300 East St

Old Salt City Jail. 460 S 1000 East St

Rino's Italian Ristorante. 2302 Parleys Way

Note: When a listing is located in a town that does not have its own city heading, it will appear under the city nearest to its location. In these cases, the address and town appear in parenthesis immediately following the name of the establishment.

Motels

(Rates may be higher during state fair)

★★**BEST WESTERN EXECUTIVE INN.** *(280 W 7200 South St, Midvale 84047) 8 mi S on I-15, exit 301.* 801/566-4141; FAX 801/566-5142. 112 rms, 2 story. Late Dec–Mar: S $49–$59; D $59–$74; each addl $5; suites $69–$149; under 18 free; lower rates rest of yr. Crib $6. TV; cable. Heated pool; whirlpool. Complimentary coffee in lobby. Restaurant adj 6 am–midnight. Ck-out noon. Meeting rms. Downhill ski 15 mi; x-country ski 20 mi. Balconies. Cr cds: A, C, D, DS, ER, MC, V, JCB.

★**BRIGHTON LODGE.** *(Big Cottonwood Canyon, Brighton 84121) Approx 15 mi W via UT 190.* 801/532-4731; res: 800/873-5512 (exc UT); FAX 801/649-1787. 22 rms, 2 story. Mid-Nov–mid-Apr: S, D $85–$110; lower rates rest of yr. TV in game rm; cable. Heated pool; whirlpool. Restaurant adj 8 am–10 pm; Sun to 4:30 pm. Bar. Ck-out 11 am. Shopping arcade. Downhill/x-country ski on site. Game rm. Refrigerators. Picnic tables, grills. On creek. Cr cds: A, DS, MC, V.

✔★★**COMFORT INN.** *8955 S 255 West St (84070), south of downtown.* 801/255-4919; FAX 801/255-4998. 98 rms, 2 story. S $49–$59; D $55–$65; each addl $5; under 18 free. Crib free. TV; cable. In-rm movies. Indoor pool; whirlpool. Complimentary continental bkfst. Ck-out noon. Meeting rm. Valet serv. Game rm. Cr cds: A, C, D, DS, ER, MC, V, JCB.

✔★**DAYS INN AIRPORT.** *1900 W North Temple St (84116), west of downtown.* 801/539-8538; FAX 801/539-8538, ext 122. 110 rms, 2 story. S, D $47–$52; each addl $5; suites $70–$75; under 18 free. Crib free. Pet accepted; deposit required. TV; cable, in-rm movies. Complimentary continental bkfst. Restaurant nearby. Ck-out 11 am. Valet serv. Free airport, RR station, bus depot transportation. Cr cds: A, C, D, DS, MC, V.

★★**HAMPTON INN.** *(10690 S Holiday Park Dr, Sandy 84070) S via I-15, exit 10600 South St, then ½ blk E.* 801/571-0800. 131 rms, 4 story. S $59; D $65; under 18 free; wkly rates, ski plans. Crib free. TV; cable. Indoor pool; whirlpool. Complimentary continental bkfst. Restaurant adj 6 am–midnight. Ck-out noon. Coin lndry. Meeting rms. Bellhops. Valet serv. Sundries. Free RR station, bus depot transportation. Downhill ski 20 mi. Shopping center opp. Cr cds: A, C, D, DS, MC, V.

★★**LA QUINTA.** *(530 Catalpa Rd, Midvale 84047) 8 mi S on I-15, 72nd South St exit, E to Catalpa Rd.* 801/566-3291; FAX 801/562-5943. 122 rms, 2 story. S $49; D $57; each addl $5; under 18 free. Crib free. Pet accepted. TV; cable. Heated pool. Continental bkfst. Complimentary coffee in lobby. Restaurant adj open 24 hrs. Ck-out noon. Meeting rms. Downhill ski 15 mi; x-country ski 20 mi. Cr cds: A, C, D, DS, MC, V.

★★**QUALITY INN-SOUTH.** *4465 Century Dr (84123), south of downtown.* 801/268-2533; FAX 801/266-6206. 131 rms, 2 story, 27 kits.

Feb–Mar & July–Sept: S $52–$62; D $59–$69; kit. units $69–$79; under 18 free; ski plan; lower rates rest of yr. Crib free. Pet accepted; $5–$7. TV; cable. Pool; whirlpool. Complimentary continental bkfst. Restaurant adj open 24 hrs. Ck-out noon. Coin lndry. Game rm. Balconies. Cr cds: A, C, D, DS, ER, MC, V, JCB.

★★**RAMADA INN-DOWNTOWN** (formerly Holiday Inn-Downtown). *230 W 600 South St (84101), downtown.* 801/364-5200; FAX 801/364-0974. 160 rms, 2 story. S, D $66–$76; each addl $10; under 19 free. Crib free. TV; cable. Indoor pool. Restaurant 6:30 am–2 pm, 5–10 pm. Rm serv. Private club from 5 pm, closed Sun. Ck-out noon. Coin lndry. Meeting rms. Valet serv exc Sun. Free airport, RR station, bus depot transportation. Exercise equipt; weight machine, bicycles, whirlpool, sauna. Rec rm. Cr cds: A, C, D, DS, MC, V, JCB.

★★**RESIDENCE INN BY MARRIOTT.** *765 E 400 South St (84102), downtown.* 801/532-5511; FAX 801/531-0416. 128 kit. suites (1–2-bedrm), 2 story. Suites $130–$176; wkly, monthly rates; ski packages. Pet accepted, some restrictions; $10–$100. TV; cable, in-rm movies avail. Heated pool. Complimentary continental bkfst. Coin lndry. Meeting rms. Bellhops. Valet serv. Airport, RR station, bus depot transportation. Many fireplaces. Cr cds: A, C, D, DS, MC, V, JCB.

✔★**SLEEP INN.** *(10676 S 300 West St, South Jordan 84065) S on I-15, exit 10600 South St, then ½ blk W.* 801/572-2020; res: 800/221-2222; FAX 801/572-2459. 68 rms, shower only, 2 story. S $40–$50; D $45–$55; each addl $5; family rates. Crib free. TV; cable, in-rm movies. Complimentary continental bkfst. Restaurant nearby. Ck-out noon. Downhill ski 20 mi. Cr cds: A, C, D, DS, ER, MC, V, JCB.

✔★**SUPER 8.** *616 S 200 West St (84101), downtown.* 801/534-0808; FAX 801/355-7735. 123 rms, 4 story. S, D $47.88–$69.88; each addl $3–$4; under 12 free; wkend rates; higher rates special events. Crib free. TV; cable. Complimentary coffee. Restaurant opp open 24 hrs. Ck-out 11 am. Cr cds: A, C, D, DS, MC, V.

Motor Hotels

★★**COMFORT INN.** *200 N Admiral Byrd Rd (84116), in Salt Lake Intl Center, near Intl Airport, west of downtown.* 801/537-7444; FAX 801/532-4721. 154 rms, 4 story. S $69; D $79; each addl $10; suites $69–$79; under 18 free. Crib free. TV. Heated pool; whirlpool. Restaurant open 24 hrs. Rm serv. Ck-out 11 am. Meeting rms. Valet serv. Free airport transportation. Some refrigerators. Balconies. Cr cds: A, C, D, DS, MC, V.

★★★**HOLIDAY INN-DOWNTOWN** (formerly Clarion). *999 S Main St (84111), south of downtown.* 801/359-8600; FAX 801/359-7816. 263 rms, 3 story, 50 suites. S $79–$119; D $89–$129; each addl $10; suites $119–$129; under 18 free; ski plans. Crib free. Pet accepted, some restrictions; $100 refundable. TV; cable. Indoor/outdoor pool. Playground. Restaurants 6 am–10 pm. Rm serv. Bar. Ck-out noon. Coin lndry. Convention facilities. Bellhops. Gift shop. Barber, beauty shop. Free airport, RR station, bus depot transportation. Tennis. Putting green. Exercise equipt; weight machine, bicycles, whirlpool, sauna. Lawn games. Some refrigerators. Wet bar in suites. Cr cds: A, C, D, DS, ER, MC, V, JCB.

✔★★**HOWARD JOHNSON.** *122 W South Temple St (84101), downtown.* 801/521-0130; FAX 801/322-5057. 226 rms, 13 story. S $57–$90; D $62–$95; each addl $7; suites $165; under 18 free. Crib free. Pet accepted; $10. TV; cable. Heated pool; whirlpool. Restaurant 6 am–11 pm; Fri-Sun to 2 am. Rm serv. Ck-out noon. Lndry facilities. Meeting rms. Bellhops. Valet serv. Gift shop. Free airport, RR station, bus depot transportation. Some refrigerators. Cr cds: A, C, D, DS, MC, V, JCB.

[icons]

★ ★ ★ **RADISSON AIRPORT.** *2177 W N Temple St (84116), near Intl Airport, west of downtown.* 801/364-5800; FAX 801/364-5823. 127 rms, 3 story, 46 suites. S $69–$139; D $79–$149; each addl $10; suites $99–$149; under 18 free; ski, golf plans. Crib free. TV; cable, in-rm movies. Heated pool. Complimentary continental bkfst. Complimentary coffee in rms. Restaurant 6:30–11 am, 5–10 pm. Rm serv. Ck-out noon. Meeting rms. Bellhops. Free garage parking. Free airport, RR station, bus depot transportation. Exercise equipt; bicycles, stair machine. Bathrm phones, refrigerators, wet bars. Balconies. Cr cds: A, C, D, DS, ER, MC, V.

[icons]

Hotels

✔ ★ ★ **BEST WESTERN OLYMPUS.** *161 W 600 South St (84101), downtown.* 801/521-7373; FAX 801/524-0354. 393 rms, 13 story. S, D $59–$75; suites $125; under 18 free; wkend rates; ski plan. Crib free. TV; cable. Pool. Restaurant open 24 hrs. Ck-out noon. Convention facilities. Barber, beauty shop. Airport transportation. Exercise equipt; bicycles, stair machine, whirlpool. Some bathrm phones, refrigerators. Balconies. Cr cds: A, C, D, DS, ER, MC, V.

[icons]

★ ★ ★ **DOUBLETREE.** *215 W South Temple St (84101), downtown.* 801/531-7500; FAX 801/328-1289. 381 rms, 15 story. S, D $73–$148; each addl $10; suites $120–$400; under 18 free; wkend, hol rates; ski packages. Crib free. TV; cable. Indoor pool. Restaurant 6 am–11:30 pm. Bar 4 pm–midnight; entertainment. Ck-out noon. Coin lndry. Convention facilities. Concierge. Gift shop. Free covered parking. Free airport, RR station transportation. Exercise equipt; weight machines, bicycles, whirlpool, sauna. Adj to Delta Center. Cr cds: A, C, D, DS, ER, MC, V, JCB.

[icons]

★ ★ ★ **EMBASSY SUITES.** *600 S West Temple St (84101), downtown.* 801/359-7800; FAX 801/359-3753. 241 suites, 9 story. S $99–$109; D $119–$129; each addl $10; under 12 free; wkend, ski plans. Crib free. TV; cable, in-rm movies. Indoor pool. Complimentary full bkfst. Complimentary coffee in rms. Restaurant 11 am–11 pm. Private club to 1 am. Ck-out noon. Coin lndry. Meeting rms. Concierge. Gift shop. Covered parking. Free airport, RR station, bus depot transportation. Exercise equipt; bicycles, stair machine, whirlpool, sauna. Refrigerators, wet bars. Atrium lobby. Cr cds: A, C, D, DS, MC, V.

[icons]

★ ★ ★ **HILTON.** *150 W 500 South St (84101), downtown.* 801/532-3344; FAX 801/532-3344, ext 1029. 351 rms, 10 story. S, D $102–$117; each addl $12; suites $105–$350; family rates; ski plans. Crib free. Pet accepted. TV; cable. Pool; poolside serv. Restaurant 6 am–11 pm. Private clubs 11:30–1 am, Sun 5–10 pm; entertainment. Ck-out noon. Convention facilities. Barber, beauty shop. Airport transportation. Exercise equipt; weight machine, bicycles, whirlpool, sauna. Ski rentals avail. Refrigerators. Balconies. *LUXURY LEVEL:* **EXECUTIVE QUARTERS.** 39 rms, 2 floors. S, D $125–$137. Private lounge. Bathrm phones. Complimentary continental bkfst, refreshments. Cr cds: A, C, D, DS, ER, MC, V.

[icons]

★ ★ ★ **LITTLE AMERICA.** *(Box 206, 84101) 500 S Main St, downtown.* 801/363-6781; res: 800/453-9450 (exc UT), 800/662-5888 (UT); FAX 801/322-1610. 850 rms, 17 story. S $63–$118; D $73–$128; suites $450; under 13 free; wkend, ski package plans. Crib free. TV. 2 pools, 1 indoor; wading pool. Restaurant 5 am–midnight; dining rm 7–10 am, 11 am–2 pm, 5–11 pm. Bar 1 pm–1 am; entertainment. Ck-out 1 pm. Convention facilities. Shopping arcade. Barber, beauty shop. Free covered parking. Free airport, RR station, bus depot transportation. Exer-

cise equipt; weights, bicycles, whirlpool, sauna. Bathrm phones, refrigerators. Domed, stained-glass ceiling in lobby. Garden setting on 10 acres. Cr cds: A, C, D, DS, MC, V.

[icons]

★ ★ ★ **MARRIOTT.** *75 S West Temple St (84101), downtown.* 801/531-0800; FAX 801/532-4127. 515 rms, 15 story. S, D $94–$125; suites $250–$759; family rates; wkend, honeymoon, ski plans. Crib free. TV; cable. Heated indoor/outdoor pool; poolside serv. Restaurant 6:30 am–11 pm; Fri, Sat to midnight. Private club; entertainment. Ck-out 1 pm. Convention facilities. Concierge. Covered valet parking. Free airport, RR station, bus depot transportation. Tennis privileges. Exercise equipt; weights, bicycles, whirlpool, sauna. Balconies. Inside access to shopping mall. *LUXURY LEVEL:* **CONCIERGE LEVEL.** 54 rms. S, D $149–$159. Complimentary continental bkfst, refreshments, newspaper. Cr cds: A, C, D, DS, MC, V.

[icons]

★ ★ ★ **PEERY.** *110 W 300 South St (84101), downtown.* 801/521-4300; res: 800/331-0073; FAX 801/575-5014. 77 rms, 3 story. S, D $64–$109; under 16 free; wkend rates. Crib free. TV; cable. Complimentary continental bkfst. Restaurant 11 am–11 pm. Bar. Ck-out noon. Meeting rms. Concierge. Gift shop. Free airport transportation. Exercise equipt; weight machine, bicycles, whirlpool. Historic building (1910). Cr cds: A, C, D, DS, MC, V.

[icons]

★ ★ ★ **RED LION.** *255 S West Temple St (84101), downtown.* 801/328-2000; FAX 801/532-1953. 501 rms, 18 story. S, D $110–$150; each addl $15; suites $175–$1,000; under 18 free; wkend rates; ski package. Crib free. Pet accepted, some restrictions. TV. Indoor pool; poolside serv. Restaurant 6 am–11 pm. Private club; entertainment. Ck-out 1 pm. Convention facilities. Concierge. Gift shop. Free covered parking; valet. Free airport, RR station, bus depot transportation. Exercise equipt; weights, bicycles, whirlpool, sauna. Game rm. Some refrigerators. *LUXURY LEVEL:* **EXECUTIVE LEVEL.** 24 rms, 2 suites. S, D $135–$150; suites $250–$1,000. Private lounge. Minibars, full wet bars. Bathrm phones. Complimentary continental bkfst, refreshments. Cr cds: A, C, D, DS, ER, MC, V, JCB.

[icons]

✔ ★ ★ **SHILO INN.** *206 S West Temple St (84101), downtown.* 801/521-9500; FAX 801/359-6527. 200 rms, 12 story. S, D $59–$67; each addl $10; suites $135–$195; kit. units $165–$195; under 12 free. Crib free. TV; cable. Heated pool; whirlpool, sauna. Complimentary continental bkfst. Restaurant 6 am–10 pm. Bar. Ck-out noon. Coin lndry. Meeting rms. Shopping arcade. Free airport transportation. Wet bars, refrigerators; some bathrm phones. Balconies. Salt Palace opp. Cr cds: A, C, D, DS, ER, MC, V, JCB.

[icons]

★ ★ ★ **UNIVERSITY PARK.** *480 Wakara Way (84108), east of downtown.* 801/581-1000; res: 800/637-4390; FAX 801/583-7641. 220 rms, 7 story, 29 suites. S, D $140; suites $160; under 12 free; ski plans. Crib free. TV; cable. Indoor pool. Restaurant 6:30 am–10 pm. Bar 4 pm–midnight; entertainment, dancing Thurs–Sat. Ck-out noon. Meeting rms. Concierge. Gift shop. Free airport, RR station, bus depot transportation. Downhill/x-country ski 15 mi. Exercise equipt; weight machine, bicycles, whirlpool. Rec rm. Refrigerators; wet bar in suites. Cr cds: A, C, D, DS, MC, V.

[icons]

Inns

★ ★ ★ **BRIGHAM STREET INN.** *1135 E South Temple St (84102), 2 mi east of Main St, east of downtown.* 801/364-4461; FAX 801/521-3201. 9 rms, 3 story. S, D $75–$150; each addl $10. Crib free. TV. Complimentary continental bkfst, coffee. Setups. Ck-out noon, ck-in 3 pm. X-country ski 15 mi. Fireplace in 5 rms. Historic Victorian mansion;

restored. Award-winning, individually decorated rms. Cr cds: A, D, DS, MC, V.

♿ Ⓟ

★ ★ ★ INN AT TEMPLE SQUARE. 71 W S Temple St (84101), downtown. 801/531-1000; res: 800/843-4668; FAX 801/536-7272. 90 rms, 7 story, 10 suites. S, D $85–$125; each addl $10; suites $150–$220; under 18 free. Crib free. TV; cable. Pool privileges. Complimentary full bkfst. Dining rm 6:30–9:30 am, 11:30 am–2:30 pm, 5–10 pm. Rm serv. Ck-out noon, ck-in 3 pm. Bellhops. Valet serv. Concierge. Free airport, RR station, bus depot transportation. Health club privileges. Bathrm phones, refrigerators. Elegant inn built in 1929; antiques from old Hotel Utah. Antique horsedrawn carriage rides. Opp Temple Square. Totally nonsmoking. Cr cds: A, C, D, DS, MC, V.

Ⓓ Ⓢ Ⓟ sc

★ ★ SPRUCES BED & BREAKFAST. 6151 S 900 East St (84121), 15 mi S on I-15, exit 72S, south of downtown. 801/268-8762. 4 rms, 1 air-cooled, 2 story, 2 kit. units. Mid-Nov–mid-Apr: S, D $55–$100; kit. units $75–$135; under 12 free; lower rates rest of yr. Crib free. TV. Complimentary continental bkfst. Restaurant nearby. Ck-out 11 am, ck-in 2 pm. Downhill/x-country ski 15 mi. Health club privileges. Balconies. Picnic tables. Surrounded by spruce trees. Built in 1902 by a Norwegian carpenter; folk art and Southwestern decor. Totally nonsmoking. Cr cds: A, MC, V.

♿ Ⓢ Ⓟ

Restaurants

★ ★ BACI TRATTORIA. 134 W Pierpont Ave, downtown. 801/364-1500. Hrs: 11:30 am–2:30 pm, 5–10 pm; wkends to 11 pm; early-bird dinner 5–7 pm. Closed Sun; major hols; also July 24. Italian menu. Bar. A la carte entrees: lunch $4.99–$11.99, dinner $7.99–$21.99. Child's meals. Specializes in fresh pasta, rotisserie meats, fresh seafood. Parking. Large stained-glass partitions, murals. Cr cds: A, D, DS, MC, V.

 Ⓓ

✔ ★ BAJA GRILL. (1114 E Ft Union Blvd, Midvale) 3 mi E of I-15, 7200 South St exit. 801/566-3985. Hrs: 11:30 am–10 pm; Fri, Sat to 11 pm; Sun 4–9 pm. Res accepted. Mexican menu. Bar. Semi-a la carte: lunch, dinner $1.95–$9.95. Child's meals. Salsa bar. Parking. Cr cds: A, DS, MC, V.

Ⓓ

★ ★ BENIHANA OF TOKYO. 165 S West Temple St, opp Salt Palace, on Arrow Press Square, downtown. 801/322-2421. Hrs: 11:30 am–2 pm, 5:30–10 pm; Fri to 11 pm; Sat 5:30–11 pm; Sun & hols 4–9 pm. Res accepted. Japanese menu. Bar. Semi-a la carte: lunch $4.75–$12, dinner $12.50–$23. Child's meals. Specializes in seafood, steak, chicken. Tableside cooking. Japanese decor. Cr cds: A, C, D, DS, MC, V.

✔ ★ COWBOY GRUB. 2350½ Foothill Blvd, east of downtown. 801/466-8334. Hrs: 11 am–10 pm; Fri, Sat to 11 pm. Closed Sun; major hols & July 24. Res accepted. Semi-a la carte: lunch, dinner $4–$10.75. Child's meals. Specializes in barbecued ribs, Mexican dishes. Salad bar. Parking. Western decor. Cr cds: A, DS, MC, V.

★ ★ ★ LA FLEUR DE LYS. 39 Post Office Place, at 340 S 39 West, downtown. 801/359-5753. Hrs: 11:30 am–2 pm, 5:30–10 pm. Res accepted. French menu. Bar. Semi-a la carte: lunch, dinner $6–$25. Specialties: tournedos grillé, saumon sauté a la Poêle. Own baking. Pianist Fri, Sat. Tapestries. Cr cds: A, C, D, DS, MC, V.

★ ★ LOG HAVEN. On Millcreek Canyon Rd, 4 mi E of jct 3800 South St & Wasatch Blvd, east of downtown. 801/272-8255. Hrs: 5–9:30 pm; Sun brunch 10 am–2:30 pm. Closed Mon & Tues. Res accepted. Continental menu. Serv bar. Semi-a la carte: dinner $14.95–$32.95. Sun brunch $16.95. Child's meals. Specializes in seafood, steak. Patio dining. Converted mountain log mansion; fireplace. Landscaped grounds; scenic canyon view. Family-owned. Cr cds: A, DS, MC, V.

★ ★ MARKET STREET BROILER. 258 S 1300 East St, east of downtown. 801/583-8808. Hrs: 11:30 am–10 pm; Sun 4–9 pm; early-bird dinner 4–6 pm. Bar from noon. Semi-a la carte: lunch $3.99–$13.99, dinner $4.99–$24.99. Child's meals. Specializes in fresh fish, barbecued ribs. Parking. Outdoor dining. Modern decor in historic former fire station. Cr cds: A, MC, V.

★ ★ MARKET STREET GRILL. 48 Market St, downtown. 801/322-4668. Hrs: 6:30 am–3 pm, 5–10:30 pm; Fri to 11:30 pm; Sat 7 am–11:30 pm; Sun 4–9:30 pm; early-bird dinner 5–7 pm; Sun brunch 9:30 am–3 pm. Closed Labor Day, Thanksgiving, Dec 25. Bar noon–11:30 pm. Semi-a la carte: bkfst $2.99–$7.99, lunch $5.99–$10.99, dinner $10.99–$27.99. Sun brunch $4.99–$10.99. Child's meals. Specializes in steak, seafood. Parking. In renovated 1906 hotel. Cr cds: A, D, DS, MC, V.

★ ★ MIKADO. 67 W 100 South St, downtown. 801/328-0929. Hrs: 5:30–9:30 pm; Fri, Sat to 10:30 pm; summer: 6–10 pm; Fri, Sat to 11 pm. Closed Sun; major hols. Res accepted. Japanese menu. Semi-a la carte: dinner $11–$21. Child's meals. Specialties: shrimp tempura, chicken teriyaki, beef sukiyaki. Entertainment. Sushi bar. Zashiki rms. Cr cds: A, C, D, DS, MC, V, JCB.

★ ★ OLD SALT CITY JAIL. 460 S 1000 East St, east of downtown. 801/355-2422. Hrs: 5–10 pm; Fri & Sat 4–11 pm; Sun 4–9 pm; early-bird dinner 4:30–7 pm. Res accepted. Bar. Semi-a la carte: dinner $8.95–$17.95. Child's meals. Specializes in prime rib, steak, seafood. Salad bar. Cowboy singer Fri & Sat. Parking. Early brewery re-created as an old country jail. Cr cds: A, D, DS, MC, V.

Ⓓ

✔ ★ RAFAEL'S. (889 E 9400 South St, Sandy) S on I-15, exit 9000 South St, then 2 mi E, in Aspen Plaza. 801/561-4545. Hrs: 11:30 am–9 pm; Fri, Sat to 10 pm. Closed Sun; Memorial Day, Labor Day. Mexican menu. Semi-a la carte: lunch, dinner $3.50–$8. Specializes in enchiladas, fajitas. Parking. Mexican, Indian and Aztec artwork. Cr cds: DS, MC, V.

Ⓓ

★ ★ RINO'S ITALIAN RISTORANTE. 2302 Parleys Way, east of downtown. 801/484-0901. Hrs: 6–10 pm; Fri, Sat 5:30–10:30 pm; Sun 5–9 pm. Closed major hols. Res accepted. Italian, continental menu. Serv bar. Semi-a la carte: dinner $7.95–$19.95. Parking. Patio dining. Bistro-style cafe. Cr cds: A, C, D, MC, V.

✔ ★ ★ RISTORANTE DELLA FONTANA. 336 S 400 East St, downtown. 801/328-4243. Hrs: 11:30 am–10 pm. Closed Sun; Thanksgiving, Dec 25; also July 24th. Res accepted. Italian menu. Semi-a la carte: lunch $6.39–$13.99, dinner (6-course) $9.85–$17.95. Child's meals. Specializes in pasta, veal. Parking. Historic converted church, stained-glass windows, antique chandeliers. Waterfall in dining rm; decor changed seasonally. Cr cds: A, C, D, DS, MC, V.

Unrated Dining Spot

LITZA'S FOR PIZZA. 716 E 400 South St, downtown. 801/359-5352. Hrs: 11 am–11 pm; Fri, Sat to 12:30 am. Closed Sun; Thanksgiving, Dec 25. Italian menu. Semi-a la carte: lunch $5.15–$11, dinner $8–$15. Specializes in pizza. Parking. No cr cds accepted.

Snowbird (B-3)

Pop: 150 (est) **Area code:** 801 **Zip:** 84092

In 1971, a Texas oil man recognized the potential of Little Cottonwood Canyon in the Wasatch National Forest and developed the area as a ski resort. At one time home to thriving mining communities, today the resort village of Snowbird, 29 miles east of Salt Lake City, offers year-round recreational activities.

What to See and Do

Snowbird Ski and Summer Resort. On UT 210. Seven double chairlifts; 125-passenger aerial tram; patrol, school, rentals; restaurants, cafeteria, bar, children's center, 4 lodges. 7,900–11,000 ft. (Mid-Nov–May, daily) Summer activities (June–Oct, daily) include hiking, mountain biking; tram rides. Contact PO Box 929000; 742-2222 or 800/453-3000 (res). Lifts ¢¢¢¢;   Summer tram ¢¢¢

Seasonal Event

Utah Symphony. Snowbird Resort. Summer home of the orchestra. Several Sun afternoon concerts. July–Aug.

(See Alta, Park City, Salt Lake City)

Motor Hotels

★ ★ ★**THE INN.** *On UT 210, 1 blk W of Snowbird Plaza Ctr. 801/742-2222 , ext 2000 or 521-6040 (Salt Lake City); res: 800/453-3000; FAX 801/742-2211.* 41 rms, 7 story, 27 kits. No A/C. Late Dec–late Mar: S, D $157; studios $179; kit. studio lofts $336; 1-bedrm condos $493; under 12 free; ski package plans; varied lower rates late Mar–Apr, June–Sept, late Nov–late Dec. Closed rest of yr. Crib free. TV; cable. Heated pool; sauna. Playground. Supervised child's activities. Restaurant adj 7:30 am–1 pm in season. Ck-out 11 am. Coin lndry. Bellhops in winter. Valet serv in winter. Tennis privileges, pro. Downhill ski on site; x-country ski 1 mi. Fireplaces. Balconies. Cr cds: A, C, D, DS, MC, V, JCB.

★ ★ ★**IRON BLOSAM LODGE.** *On UT 210, 2 blks W of Snowbird Plaza Ctr. 801/742-2222 , ext 1000 or 521-6040 (Salt Lake City); res: 800/453-3000; FAX 801/742-3445.* 159 rms, 11 story, 125 kits. Mid-Dec–Mar: S, D $159; kit. suites $143–$489; kit. studio rms $74–$179; ski package plans; varied lower rates rest of yr. Closed 1 wk Nov, 1 wk May. Crib $9/wk. TV; cable. 2 heated pools. Supervised child's activities. Restaurant 6–10 pm. Ck-out 10 am. Coin lndry. Meeting rm. Bellhops. Valet serv. Tennis, pro (summer). Downhill ski on site; x-country ski 1 mi. Exercise equipt; weights, bicycles, whirlpool, sauna, steam rm. Rec rm. Lawn games. Fireplaces. Balconies. Scenic views. Cr cds: A, C, D, DS, MC, V, JCB.

★ ★ ★**LODGE AT SNOWBIRD.** *On UT 210, opp Snowbird Plaza Ctr. 801/742-2222 ext 3000 or 521-6040 (Salt Lake City); res: 800/453-3000; FAX 801/742-3311.* 160 rms, 7 story, 61 kits. No A/C. Late Nov–early May: S, D $157; suites $336; kit. studio rms $179; ski & half-price summer package plans; varied lower rates rest of yr. Crib $5. TV; cable, in-rm movies avail. Heated pool; whirlpool, saunas. Playground. Supervised child's activities. Restaurant 7 am–midnight (winter). Bar 3 pm–1 am. Ck-out 11 am. Coin lndry. Bellhops. Valet serv in winter. Tennis privileges, pro. Downhill ski on site; x-country ski 1 mi. Fireplaces. Balconies. Cr cds: A, C, D, DS, MC, V, JCB.

Hotel

★ ★ ★**CLIFF LODGE.** *On UT 210, just E of Snowbird Plaza Ctr. 801/742-2222 , ext 5000 or 521-6040 (Salt Lake City); res: 800/453-3000; FAX 801/742-3300.* 532 rms, 13 story. Dec–Mar: S, D $149–$199; suites $299–$735; under 12 free; ski packages; lower rates rest of yr. TV; cable. 2 heated pools, 1 rooftop; poolside serv. Supervised child's activities. Restaurant 7 am–10 pm. Private club noon–1 am; entertainment, dancing. Ck-out 11 am. Coin lndry. Convention facilities. Concierge. Gift shop. Barber, beauty shop. Free garage; valet parking. Tennis, pro. Downhill ski on site; x-country ski 1 mi. Exercise rm; instructor, weights, bicycles, whirlpool, sauna, steam rm. Game rm. Rec rm. Some

refrigerators. Some private patios, balconies. Picnic tables. Cr cds: A, C, D, DS, MC, V, JCB.

Restaurant

★ ★**STEAK PIT.** *On UT 210, in Snowbird Plaza Ctr. 801/742-2222 , ext 4060 or 521-6040 (Salt Lake City).* Hrs: 6–10 pm; Fri, Sat to 11 pm. No A/C. Serv bar. Semi-a la carte: dinner $9.95–$38. Child's meals. Specializes in steak, seafood. Parking. Mountain view. Cr cds: A, C, D, DS, MC, V, JCB.

Timpanogos Cave National Monument (B-3)

(26 mi S of Salt Lake City on I-15, then 10 mi E on UT 92)

Timpanogos (Tim-pa-NOH-gos) Cave National Monument consists of three small, beautifully decorated underground chambers within limestone beds. The cave entrance is on the northern slope of Mt Timpanogos, monarch of the Wasatch Range. Much of the cave interior is covered by a filigree of colorful crystal formations where stalactites and stalagmites are common. However, what makes Timpanogos unique is its large number of helictites—formations that appear to defy gravity as they grow outward from the walls of the cave. Temperature in Timpanogos Cave is a constant 45°F, and the interior is electrically lighted.

The cave's headquarters are located on UT 92, 8 mi E of American Fork. There is picnicking at Swinging Bridge Picnic Area, ¼ mi from the headquarters. The cave entrance is 1½ miles from headquarters via a paved trail with a vertical rise of 1,065 feet. Allow 3–5 hours for guided tour. No pets; no strollers; walking shoes advised; jackets and sweaters needed. Tours limited to 20 people (late May–early Sept, daily; hours vary spring & fall). Purchase tickets in advance from superintendent's office. Golden Age and Golden Access passports accepted (see INTRODUCTION). For information contact the Superintendent, RR 3, Box 200, American Fork 84003; 801/756-5238. Cave tours ¢¢

(For accommodations see Heber City, Park City, Provo)

Vernal (B-4)

Pop: 6,644 **Elev:** 5,336 ft **Area code:** 801 **Zip:** 84078

This is the county seat of Uintah County in northeastern Utah, which boasts oil, natural gas and many mineral deposits. A trading center for sheep and cattle, Vernal is in an area of ancient geologic interest. Nearby are beautiful canyons, striking rock formations and majestic peaks. Headquarters and a Ranger District office of the Ashley National Forest (see #2) are located here.

What to See and Do

1. **Flaming Gorge Dam and National Recreation Area.** 42 mi N on US 191, in Ashley National Forest (see #2). Area surrounds 91-mile-long Flaming Gorge Reservoir and 502-foot-high Flaming Gorge Dam. Fishing on reservoir & river (all yr); marinas, boat ramps, waterskiing; lodges; campgrounds (fee). River rafting below dam. Visitor centers at dam and Red Canyon (on secondary paved road 3 mi off UT 44). For information contact the Ranger District office, PO Box 278, Manila 84046; 784-3445.   **Free.**

2. **Ashley National Forest.** 15 mi N on US 191. The High Uinta Mountains—the only major east-west range in the US—runs through the

heart of this nearly 1.5 million-acre forest. The 1,500-foot-deep Red Canyon, the 13,528-foot Kings Peak and Sheep Creek Geological Area are also here. Swimming; fishing; boating (ramps, marinas), whitewater rafting and canoeing. Hiking and nature trails. Cross-country skiing, snowmobiling. Improved or back country campgrounds (fee). Visitors centers. For further information contact the Supervisor, 355 N Vernal Ave; 789-1181.

3. Dinosaur National Monument (see). 13 mi SE on US 40, then 7 mi N on UT 149.

4. Utah Field House of Natural History State Park. 235 Main St. Guarded outside by three life-size cement dinosaurs, this museum has exhibits of fossils, archaeology, life zones, geology and fluorescent minerals of the region. Adj Dinosaur Gardens contain 14 life-size model dinosaurs in natural surroundings. (Daily; closed Jan 1, Thanksgiving, Dec 25) Phone 789-3799. ¢

5. Daughters of Utah Pioneers Museum. 500 West & 200 South Sts. Relics and artifacts dating from before 1847, when pioneers first settled in Utah; period furniture, quilts, clothing; dolls; early doctor's, dentist's and undertaker's instruments; restored Little Rock tithing office (1887). (June–Sat before Labor Day, daily exc Sun) Donation. Phone 789-3890.

6. Thorne's Photo Studio. 18 W Main St. Museum has artifacts of ancient people of Utah; weapons. (Mon–Tues & Thur–Fri; closed hols) Phone 789-0392. **Free.**

7. Steinaker State Park. 7 mi N off US 191. Approx 2,200 acres on west shore of Steinaker Reservoir. Swimming; waterskiing; fishing; boating (ramp, dock). Picnicking. Tent & trailer sites (fee). (Apr–Nov; fishing all yr) Phone 789-4432. Per vehicle ¢¢

8. Ouray National Wildlife Refuge. 30 mi SW on UT 88. Waterfowl nesting marshes; desert scenery; self-guided auto tour (limited route during hunting season). (Daily) Phone 789-0351. **Free.**

9. River trips. Guided whitewater trips on the Green and Yampa rivers.

Adrift Adventures of Dinosaur. Phone 800/824-0150. ¢¢¢¢¢

Don Hatch River Expeditions. Phone 789-4316 or 800/342-8243. ¢¢¢¢¢

Holiday River and Bike Expeditions. Phone 266-2087 or 800/624-6323 (exc UT). ¢¢¢¢¢

(For further information contact Dinosaurland Travel Board, 235 E Main St; 789-6932 or 800/477-5558.)

Annual Events

Outlaw Trail Festival. Month-long; festivals, sporting events, entertainment, theatrical events. Mid-June–mid-July.

Dinosaur Roundup Rodeo. Early July.

Uintah County Fair. Aug.

(See Roosevelt)

Motels

✔ ★**LAMPLIGHTER.** *120 E Main St. 801/789-0312.* 167 rms, 2 story. May–Aug: S $36; D $43; each addl $8; under 12 free; varied lower rates rest of yr. TV; cable. Heated pool. Playground. Restaurant hrs vary. Ck-out 11 am. Beauty shop. Picnic tables, grills. Cr cds: A, D, MC, V.

★**WESTON PLAZA.** *1684 W US 40. 801/789-9550; FAX 801/789-4874.* 102 rms, 3 story. S, D $48–$56; each addl $8; suites $95; under 12 free; wkend rates. Pet accepted. TV; cable. Indoor pool; whirlpool. Restaurant 6 am–2 pm, 5–9 pm. Bar to 1 am; entertainment, dancing exc Sun (summer). Ck-out noon. Meeting rms. Airport, bus depot transportation. Cr cds: A, C, D, MC, V.

Wendover (B-2)

Founded: 1907 **Pop:** 1,127 **Elev:** 4,232 ft **Area code:** 801 **Zip:** 84083

Half in Utah, half in Nevada, Wendover lies on the western edge of the Great Salt Lake Desert. The town was settled to serve the Western Pacific Railroad, which cut a historic route through here across the Bonneville Salt Flats. Accommodations can be found on both sides of the state line, but gambling is allowed only in Nevada. Blue Lake, 30 miles south, provides water at a constant temperature of 75° F for scuba diving and is open to the public (no facilities).

What to See and Do

Bonneville Salt Flats. E of town. This approximately 100-square-mile area of perfectly flat salt, packed as solid as cement, is what remained after ancient Lake Bonneville, which once covered the entire area, retreated to the present-day Great Salt Lake. The area is part of the Great Salt Lake Desert.

Annual Event

Bonneville National Speed Trials. Bonneville Speedway, approx 15 mi E, then N. Held since 1914 on the Bonneville Salt Flats (see), which has been used as a track for racing the world's fastest cars. Car racing in competition and against the clock. Phone 619/274-1993. Aug or Sept.

Hotel

✔ ★★**STATE LINE.** *(Box 789) 1 mi W on I-80 Business (Wendover Blvd).* 702/664-2221; res: 800/848-7300; FAX 801/531-4090. 500 rms, 5 story. S, D $39–$54; each addl $5; suites $80–$125; under 12 free. Crib free. TV; cable. Heated pool. Restaurant open 24 hrs. Bars; entertainment. Ck-out noon. Meeting rms. Gift shop. Tennis privileges. Game rm. Casinos. Cr cds: A, C, D, DS, MC, V.

Zion National Park (E-2)

(42 mi NE of St George on UT 9)

The spectacular canyons and enormous rock formations in this 146,598-acre national park are the result of powerful upheavals of the earth and erosion by flowing water and frost. Considered the "grandfather" of Utah's national parks, Zion is one of the nation's oldest national parks and one of the state's wildest, with large sections virtually inaccessible. The Virgin River runs through the interior of the park, and Zion Canyon, with its deep, narrow chasm and multicolored, vertical walls, cuts through the middle, with smaller canyons branching from it like fingers. A paved roadway following the bottom of Zion Canyon is surrounded by massive rock formations in awe-inspiring colors that change with the light. The formations, described as temples, cathedrals and thrones, rise to great heights, the loftiest reaching 7,810 feet. The canyon road runs seven miles to the Temple of Sinawava, a natural amphitheater surrounded by cliffs. Another route, an extension of UT 9, cuts through the park in an east-west direction, taking visitors through the mile-long Zion-Mt Carmel Tunnel, then descends through a series of switchbacks with viewpoints above Pine Creek Canyon. **Note:** An escort fee is charged for large vehicles to pass through tunnel.

Zion's main visitor center is near the south entrance (daily). Check here for maps, information on the park and schedules of naturalist activities and evening programs. Each evening, spring through fall, park naturalists give illustrated talks on the natural and human history of the area. Pets must be kept on leash and are not permitted on trails. Vehicle lights should be checked; they must be in proper condition for driving through highway tunnel. The park is open year round. There is an admission fee of $5/7-day stay/car; Golden Eagle Passport is accepted (see INTRODUCTION). For further information contact Superintendent, Springdale 84767-1099; 801/772-3256.

What to See and Do

1. **Park trails** lead to otherwise inaccessible areas: the Narrows (walls of this canyon are 2,000 feet high and as little as 50 feet apart at the stream), the Hanging Gardens of Zion, Weeping Rock, the Emerald Pools. Trails range from ½-mile trips to day-long treks, some requiring tested stamina. Trails in less traveled areas should not be undertaken without first obtaining information from a park ranger. Back country permits required for travel through the Virgin River Narrows and on all overnight trips.

2. **Guided trips, hiking tours** conducted by ranger naturalists, who explain geology, plant life and history.

3. **Escorted horseback trips.** (Mar–Oct, daily) Special guide service may be obtained for other trips not regularly scheduled. Contact Bryce/Zion Trail Rides at Zion Lodge. Phone 772-3967 or 679-8665 (off-season).

4. **Bicycling** is permitted on roads in park, except through Zion-Mt Carmel Tunnel. Roads are narrow and no designated bicycle routes exist.

5. **Mountain climbing** should be undertaken with great care due to unstable sandstone. Climbers should consult with a ranger at the park Visitors Center.

6. **Camping.** At south entrance to park: South Campground provides 140 tent or trailer sites (mid-Apr–mid-Sept); Watchman Campground provides 229 tent sites and 185 trailer sites (all yr). Lava Point Campground, 26 mi N of Virgin off UT 9, provides a minimal number of tent sites (free; no facilities). South & Watchman campgrounds ¢¢¢

7. **Zion Nature Center.** Adj to South Campground. Junior Ranger program for children 6–12. (Memorial Day–Labor Day; one-time registration fee) **Free.**

8. **Kolob Canyons Visitor Center** (see CEDAR CITY).

9. **"Grand Circle: A National Park Odyssey."** O.C. Tanner Amphitheatre in Springdale. Multimedia presentation encompassing 4 states, 14 national parks and monuments and numerous state parks and historic sites, plus Glen Canyon National Recreation Area (see PAGE, AZ and LAKE POWELL, UT) and Monument Valley Navajo Tribal Park (see KAYENTA, AZ). One-hour show (Memorial Day–Labor Day). Phone 673-4811, ext 276. ¢¢

(See Cedar City, Kanab, St George)

Motels

★★**BEST WESTERN DRIFTWOOD LODGE.** *(Box 98, Springdale 84767) On UT 9, 2 mi S of park entrance.* 801/772-3262. 47 rms, 1–2 story. S $52; D $62; each addl $4. Crib $2. TV. Heated pool; whirlpool. Restaurant 7 am–10 pm. Rm serv. Ck-out 11 am. Gift shop. Private patios, balconies. Shaded grounds; good views of park. Cr cds: A, C, D, DS, MC, V.

✔★★**FLANIGAN'S INN.** *(Box 100, 428 Zion Park Blvd, Springdale 84767) On UT 9, ¼ mi S of park entrance.* 801/772-3244; res: 800/765-7787. 36 rms, 1–2 story. Mid-Mar–mid-Nov: S, D $39–$69; each addl $5; under 8 free; lower rates rest of yr. Crib free. TV; cable. Heated pool. Restaurant 8 am–8 pm. Serv bar. Ck-out 11 am. Meeting rms. Sundries. Picnic tables, grills. Local artists' gallery. Cr cds: A, C, D, DS, MC, V.

★**TERRACE BROOK LODGE.** *(Box 217, Springdale 84767) On UT 9, 2 mi S of park entrance.* 801/772-3932; res: 800/342-6779. 24 rms, 2 story. Apr–Oct: S $39; D $46–$70; each addl $4; lower rates rest of yr. Crib $4. TV; cable. Heated pool. Restaurant nearby. Ck-out 11 am. Picnic tables, grills. Cr cds: A, DS, MC, V.

★★**ZION LODGE.** *(Box 400, Cedar City 84720) On UT 9, 5 mi N of park entrance.* 801/772-3213; res: 801/586-7686. 75 rms in motel, 1–2 story, 40 cabins. S, D $62.50; each addl $5; suites $99.95; cabins $70. Crib $5. Restaurant 6:30–9:30 am, noon–2:30 pm, 5:30–9 pm. Ck-out 11 am. Bellhops. Sundries. Gift shop. Private porches. Spectacular view. Cr cds: A, C, D, DS, MC, V.

✔★**ZION PARK.** *(Box 365, Springdale 84767) On UT 9, 1 mi S of park entrance.* 801/772-3251. 21 rms. S $40–$46; D $48–$59; kit. units $95; lower rates off-season. Crib $2. TV; cable. Heated pool. Playground. Restaurant adj 7 am–10 pm. Ck-out 11 am. Sundries. Picnic tables, grill. Cr cds: A, DS, MC, V.

Index

Establishment names are listed in alphabetical order followed by a symbol identifying their classification, and then city, state and page number. Establishments affiliated with a chain appear alphabetically under their chain name, followed by the state, city and page number. The symbols for classification are: (H) for hotels; (I) for inns; (M) for motels; (L) for lodges; (MH) for motor hotels; (R) for restaurants; (RO) for resorts, guest ranches, and cottage colonies; (U) for unrated dining spots. States are arranged alphabetically as are the cities and towns within each state.

HACIENDA [M] *Alturas CA,* 90
HACIENDA RESORT [H] *Las Vegas NV,* 333
HALIOTIS [R] *Ensenada, Baja California,
    Mexico CA,* 129
HALLMARK HOTEL [M] *Hollywood (L.A.) CA,*
    144
HAMPTON INN [M]
  Arizona
        Mesa, 46; *Phoenix,* 55; *Tucson,* 77
  California
        Anaheim, 91; *Arcadia,* 94; *Buena
        Park,* 107; *Fairfield,* 131; *Los
        Angeles Intl
        Airport Area,* 175; *Oakland,* 196;
        Palm Springs, 207; *Riverside,* 226;
        San Diego, 240; *Valencia,* 309; *West
        Covina,* 314
  Utah
        Salt Lake City, 370
HANDLERY HOTEL & COUNTRY CLUB [MH]
    San Diego CA, 241
HANDLERY UNION SQUARE [H] *San
    Francisco CA,* 258
HANFORD HOUSE [I] *Jackson CA,* 149
HANSA HOUSE SMORGASBORD [R]
    Anaheim CA, 93
HAPPY LANDING [I] *Carmel CA,* 114
HARBOR COURT [H] *San Francisco CA,* 258
HARBOR HOUSE [I] *Mendocino CA,* 181
HARBOR HOUSE [R] *San Diego CA,* 245
HARBOR HOUSE INN [M] *Morro Bay CA,* 188
HARBOR LITE LODGE [M] *Fort Bragg CA,*
    133
HARBOR VIEW GROTTO [R] *Crescent City
    CA,* 123
HARBOR VILLAGE [R] *San Francisco CA,*
    265
HARD ROCK CAFE [U] *Los Angeles CA,* 174
HARDMAN HOUSE MOTOR INN [M] *Carson
    City NV,* 325
HARRAH'S [H] *Las Vegas NV,* 333
HARRAH'S [H]
  Nevada
        Reno, 339; *Stateline,* 340
HARRIS' [R] *San Francisco CA,* 265
HARRY & STEVE'S CHICAGO GRILL [U]
    Mesa AZ, 47
HARRY & STEVE'S CHICAGO GRILL [U]
    Scottsdale AZ, 67
HARVEST [I] *St Helena CA,* 231
HARVEY'S RESORT [H] *Stateline NV,* 341
HASSAYAMPA INN [H] *Prescott AZ,* 60
HAUS BAVARIA [I] *Incline Village NV,* 329
HAYDON HOUSE [I] *Healdsburg CA,* 142
HAYES STREET GRILL [R] *San Francisco CA,*
    265
HEADLANDS [I] *Mendocino CA,* 181
HEADQUARTER HOUSE [R] *Auburn CA,* 95
HEARTLINE CAFE [R] *Sedona AZ,* 68
HEMINGWAY'S [R] *Sonora CA,* 298
HENRY'S [R] *Carlsbad CA,* 112
HERITAGE INN [M] *Roseville CA,* 226
HI-HO RESORT LODGE [M] *Kernville CA,* 151
HIDEAWAY [R] *Sedona AZ,* 68
HIGHLAND DELL INN [I] *Guerneville CA,* 139
HIGHLAND SPRINGS [RO] *Beaumont CA,* 99
HIGHLANDS INN [L] *Carmel CA,* 113
HILL HOUSE [I] *Mendocino CA,* 181
HILL TOP [M] *Kingman AZ,* 43
HILTON [All H except where noted]
  Arizona
        Mesa, 46; *Phoenix,* [MH] 55, [RO], 57;
        Scottsdale, [MH] 63; *Tucson,* 78

California
        Anaheim, 92; *Beverly Hills,* 101;
        Burbank, 108; *Concord,* 119; *Del
        Mar,* 125; *Fremont,* 134; *Fresno,*
        136; *Huntington Beach,* 145; *Laguna
        Beach,* 152; *Long Beach,* 163; *Los
        Angeles,* 171; *Los Angeles Intl
        Airport Area,* 175; *Oakland,* [MH]
        196; *Ontario,* 199; *Orange,* 200;
        Oxnard, 201; *Palm Springs,* 208;
        Pasadena, 213; *Pleasanton,* 218;
        Sacramento, 229; *San Bernardino,*
        233; *San Diego,* 241, 242; *San
        Francisco,* 258; *San Francisco
        Airport Area,* 270; *Stockton,* 300;
        Sunnyvale, [MH] 301; *Valencia,* [M]
        310; *Whittier,* 316; *Woodland Hills
        (L.A.),* 317
  Nevada
        Las Vegas, 333, 334; *Laughlin,* 336;
        Reno, 339
  Utah
        Salt Lake City, 371
HOB NOB HILL [R] *San Diego CA,* 245
HOCHBURG VON GERMANIA [R] *San Jose
    CA,* 274
HoJo INN [M] *Brigham City UT,* 348
HOLIDAY HOUSE [M] *Tahoe Vista (Lake
    Tahoe Area) CA,* 303
HOLIDAY INN [All MH except where noted]
  Arizona
        Casa Grande, 35; *Flagstaff,* 38;
        Kayenta, [M] 43; *Kingman,* [M] 44;
        Lake Havasu City, 44; *Page,* 50;
        Tempe, 72; *Tucson,* [H] 78; *Yuma,*
        [M] 86
  California
        Anaheim, 91; *Chico,* 116; *Fairfield,*
        131; *Fresno,* [H] 136; *Fullerton,* 136;
        Half Moon Bay, [M] 140; *Hollywood
        (L.A.),* [M] 144; *Huntington Beach,* [H]
        146; *Irvine,* [M] 148; *Laguna Beach,*
        152; *Long Beach,* 163; *Los Angeles,*
        170, [H], 171; *Los Angeles Intl
        Airport Area,* [H] 176; *Modesto,* 183;
        Monterey, [M] 185; *Oakland,* 196;
        Palm Desert, [M] 204; *Palo Alto,* 211;
        Pasadena, 213; *Pleasanton,* [H] 218;
        Redwood Beach, [H] 224; *Sacramento,*
        [H] 229; *San Clemente,* 233; *San
        Diego,* 241, [H], 242; *San Francisco,*
        256, [H], 258; *San Francisco
        Airport Area,* [H] 270; *San Jose,* 273;
        San Juan Capistrano, [M] 276; *San
        Rafael,* 279; *Santa Cruz,* 287; *Santa
        Nella,* [M] 290; *Solvang,* [H] 295;
        Sunnyvale, [M] 301; *Van Nuys (L.A.),*
        311; *Ventura,* 312; *West Covina,* 314;
        Westwood Village (L.A.), [H] 315
  Nevada
        Battle Mountain, [M] 324; *Elko,* [M]
        326; *Las Vegas,* 332; *Reno,* 339
  Utah
        Cedar City, [M] 350; *Ogden,* 358;
        Provo, [M] 362; *Salt Lake City,* 370;
        St George, [M] 365
HOLIDAY LODGE [M] *Grass Valley CA,* 138
HOLIDAY LODGE [M] *Willits CA,* 316
HOLLIE'S FIESTA HOTEL [MH] *Calexico CA,*
    108
HOMESTEAD [RO] *Heber City UT,* 353
HORIZON INN [M] *Carmel CA,* 112
HORIZONS [R] *Sausalito CA,* 293

HORNES' EAST BAY INN [M] *Provo UT,* 362
THE HORTON GRAND [H] *San Diego CA,* 242
HOSPITALITY SUITE RESORT [M] *Scottsdale
    AZ,* 62
HOTEL CARTER [I] *Eureka CA,* 131
HOTEL CATALINA [H] *Avalon (Catalina Island)
    CA,* 96
HOTEL DE ANZA [H] *San Jose CA,* 273
HOTEL DEL CAPRI [M] *Westwood Village
    (L.A.) CA,* 315
HOTEL DEL CORONADO [RO] *Coronado CA,*
    120
HOTEL HERMOSA [M] *Redondo Beach CA,*
    224
HOTEL LA ROSE [H] *Santa Rosa CA,* 291
HOTEL LAGUNA [H] *Laguna Beach CA,* 152
HOTEL METROPOLE [H] *Avalon (Catalina
    Island) CA,* 96
HOTEL NIKKO [H] *San Francisco CA,* 258
HOTEL NIKKO AT BEVERLY HILLS [H]
    Beverly Hills CA, 101
HOTEL PACIFIC [I] *Monterey CA,* 186
HOTEL PARAISO LAS PALMAS [M]
    Ensenada, Baja California, Mexico CA, 128
HOTEL PARK TUCSON [H] *Tucson AZ,* 78
HOTEL SAINTE CLAIRE [H] *San Jose CA,*
    274
HOTEL SAN DIEGO [H] *San Diego CA,* 242
HOTEL ST HELENA [I] *St Helena CA,* 231
HOTEL ST JAMES [H] *San Diego CA,* 242
HOTEL ST LAUREN [MH] *Avalon (Catalina
    Island) CA,* 96
HOTEL ST. MAARTEN [MH] *Laguna Beach
    CA,* 152
HOTEL TRITON [H] *San Francisco CA,* 259
HOTEL UNION SQUARE [H] *San Francisco
    CA,* 259
HOTEL VENDOME [M] *Prescott AZ,* 60
HOTEL WESTCOURT [H] *Phoenix AZ,* 56
HOUSE OF CHAN [R] *Kingman AZ,* 44
HOUSE OF PRIME RIB [R] *San Francisco CA,*
    266
HOUSE OF TRICKS [R] *Tempe AZ,* 72
HOUSTON'S [R] *Phoenix AZ,* 58
HOUSTON'S TRAIL'S END [R] *Kanab UT,*
    353
HOWARD JOHNSON [All M except where
    noted]
  Arizona
        Tempe, [MH] 72
  California
        Anaheim, [MH] 91; *Barstow,* 98; *Long
        Beach,* [MH] 163; *Los Angeles,* [MH]
        170; *Mill Valley,* 183; *Redwood City,*
        225; *San Diego,* 240, [MH], 241; *San
        Francisco,* 256; *San Luis Obispo,* 277;
        Santa Clara, 284; *Santa Maria,* 288
  Nevada
        Las Vegas, [H] 334
  Utah
        Salt Lake City, [MH] 370
HUGO'S ROTISSERIE [R] *Incline Village NV,*
    329
HUMPHREY'S HALF MOON INN [M] *San
    Diego CA,* 240
HUNAN [R] *San Francisco CA,* 266
HUNGRY BEAR [R] *Needles CA,* 192
HUNGRY HUNTER [R] *Tempe AZ,* 72
HUNGRY HUNTER [R] *Yuma AZ,* 86
HUNTINGTON [H] *San Francisco CA,* 259
HYATT [All H except where noted]
  Arizona
        Phoenix, 56; *Scottsdale,* [RO] 63

OLD BATH HOUSE [R] *Pacific Grove CA*, 203
OLD MEXICO EAST [R] *Santa Rosa CA*, 291
OLD MINERS' LODGE [I] *Park City UT*, 360
OLD MONTEREY INN [I] *Monterey CA*, 186
OLD OX [R] *Pacific Beach (San Diego) CA*, 202
OLD SALT CITY JAIL [R] *Salt Lake City UT*, 372
THE OLD SAN FRANCISCO EXPRESS PASTA RESTAURANT [R] *Fairfield CA*, 131
OLD ST ANGELA [I] *Pacific Grove CA*, 203
OLD THYME INN [I] *Half Moon Bay CA*, 140
OLD TOWN BED & BREAKFAST [I] *Eureka CA*, 131
OLD TOWN MEXICAN CAFE & CANTINA [R] *San Diego CA*, 245
OLD WORLD INN [I] *Napa CA*, 191
THE OLD YACHT CLUB [I] *Santa Barbara CA*, 283
OLEANDER HOUSE [I] *Yountville CA*, 320
OLIVE TREE [R] *Tucson AZ*, 81
OLIVER HOUSE [I] *St Helena CA*, 231
OLSEN'S CABIN [R] *Quincy CA*, 219
OLYMPIA PARK HOTEL [MH] *Park City UT*, 360
OPUS [R] *Santa Monica CA*, 289
ORANGE TREE GOLF & CONFERENCE RESORT [RO] *Scottsdale AZ*, 64
ORCHARD [H] *San Francisco CA*, 260
ORGAN STOP PIZZA [U] *Mesa AZ*, 47
ORIGINAL JOE'S [R] *San Jose CA*, 275
ORLEANS [R] *Los Angeles CA*, 173
ORMACHEA'S [R] *Winnemucca NV*, 342
OSCAR TAYLOR [R] *Phoenix AZ*, 58
ÓSUMO [R] *Oakland CA*, 197
OVERLAND HOUSE GRILL [R] *Oakland CA*, 197
OWL CLUB [M] *Battle Mountain NV*, 324
OXFORD PALACE [H] *Los Angeles CA*, 172

PACIFIC BAY INN [H] *San Francisco CA*, 260
PACIFIC GRILL [R] *San Francisco CA*, 267
PACIFIC GROVE [I] *Pacific Grove CA*, 203
PACIFIC HEIGHTS BAR & GRILL [R] *San Francisco CA*, 267
PACIFIC HEIGHTS INN [M] *San Francisco CA*, 256
PACIFIC [M] *Crescent City CA*, 123
PACIFIC'S EDGE [R] *Carmel CA*, 114
PACIFIC TERRACE INN [MH] *Pacific Beach (San Diego) CA*, 202
PACIFICA DEL MAR [R] *Del Mar CA*, 126
PACIFICA GRILL & ROTISSERIE [R] *San Diego CA*, 245
PACIFICA LODGE [M] *South Lake Tahoe (Lake Tahoe Area) CA*, 298
PACK CREEK RANCH [RO] *Moab UT*, 356
PACKING HOUSE [R] *Fallbrook CA*, 132
PADRE OAKS [M] *Monterey CA*, 185
PALA MESA [RO] *Fallbrook CA*, 132
PALACE CAFE [R] *Santa Barbara CA*, 284
PALACE COURT [R] *Las Vegas NV*, 335
PALACE STATION HOTEL & CASINO [H] *Las Vegas NV*, 334
PALAZZIO [R] *Santa Barbara CA*, 284
PALIO D'ASTI [R] *San Francisco CA*, 267
THE PALM [R] *Hollywood (L.A.) CA*, 145
PALM CAFE [R] *Menlo Park CA*, 182
PALM CANYON RESORT [M] *Borrego Springs CA*, 106
PALM TEE [M] *Palm Springs CA*, 207
PALOMINO [R] *Tucson AZ*, 81

PALOS VERDES INN [MH] *Redondo Beach CA*, 224
PAN PACIFIC [H]
California
    Anaheim, 92; *San Diego*, 242; *San Francisco*, 260
PANDA INN [R] *San Diego CA*, 245
PARC FIFTY-FIVE [H] *San Francisco CA*, 260
PARC OAKLAND HOTEL [H] *Oakland CA*, 196
PARK GRILL [R] *San Francisco CA*, 267
PARK INN INTERNATIONAL [M]
Arizona
    Tucson, 77; *Yuma*, 86
PARK PLACE [I] *Bisbee AZ*, 33
PARK TERRACE INN [MH] *Redding CA*, 223
PARK VUE INN [M] *Anaheim CA*, 91
PARRY LODGE [M] *Kanab UT*, 353
PARTNERS BISTRO & TERRACE [R] *Laguna Beach CA*, 153
PASTA ITALIA [R] *Palm Desert CA*, 205
PASTA SEGIO'S [R] *Phoenix AZ*, 58
PATINA [R] *Hollywood (L.A.) CA*, 145
PATISSERIE BOISSIERE [R] *Carmel CA*, 115
PAVILION [R] *Los Angeles CA*, 173
PAVILION [R] *Newport Beach CA*, 194
PEA SOUP ANDERSEN'S [R] *Santa Nella CA*, 290
PEDRIN'S [R] *Tijuana, Baja California, Mexico CA*, 306
PEERY [H] *Salt Lake City UT*, 371
PEGASUS [R] *Las Vegas NV*, 335
PELARGONIUM [R] *Jackson CA*, 149
THE PENINSULA, BEVERLY HILLS [H] *Beverly Hills CA*, 101
PENNY SLEEPER INN [M] *Anaheim CA*, 91
PEOHE'S [R] *Coronado CA*, 120
THE PEPPERMILL [R] *Pasadena CA*, 214
PEPPERMILL HOTEL CASINO [H] *Reno NV*, 340
PEPPERS MEXICALI CAFE [R] *Pacific Grove CA*, 203
PERRINA'S [R] *Palm Springs CA*, 210
PESCATORE [R] *Oakland CA*, 197
PETERSEN VILLAGE INN [I] *Solvang CA*, 295
PETITE AUBERGE [I] *San Francisco CA*, 262
PETRELLO'S [R] *South Lake Tahoe (Lake Tahoe Area) CA*, 299
PHILIPS SUPPER HOUSE [R] *Las Vegas NV*, 335
PHILLIPE THE ORIGINAL [U] *Los Angeles CA*, 174
THE PHOENICIAN [RO] *Scottsdale AZ*, 64
PHOENIX [M] *San Francisco CA*, 256
PIATTI [R] *Sonoma CA*, 296
PIATTI RISTORANTE [R] *La Jolla (San Diego) CA*, 156
PICCADILLY INN [All M except where noted]
California
    Fresno, 135, [MH], 136
PIEMONT [R] *Mt Shasta CA*, 190
PIERO'S [R] *Las Vegas NV*, 335
PIERPONT INN [M] *Ventura CA*, 312
PILOTHOUSE [R] *Sacramento CA*, 230
PIMPAREL'S LA TABLE FRANÇAISE [R] *Reno NV*, 340
PINE BEACH INN [M] *Fort Bragg CA*, 133
PINE CONE INN [R] *Prescott AZ*, 60
PINES RESORTS [RO] *Yosemite National Park CA*, 319
THE PINK MANSION [I] *Calistoga CA*, 109
PINNACLE PEAK [R] *Tucson AZ*, 81
PIONEER HOTEL & CASINO [MH] *Laughlin NV*, 336

PISCHKE'S PARADISE [R] *Scottsdale AZ*, 66
PLAZA [MH] *Tucson AZ*, 78
PLAZA INTERNATIONAL INN [M] *El Cajon CA*, 127
PLEASANTON HOTEL [R] *Pleasanton CA*, 218
PLUMED HORSE [R] *Saratoga CA*, 292
POCO DIABLO [RO] *Sedona AZ*, 68
POINT REYES SEASHORE LODGE [I] *Inverness CA*, 147
PORT TACK [R] *Las Vegas NV*, 336
PORTOFINO BEACH HOTEL [I] *Newport Beach CA*, 193
PORTOFINO HOTEL & YACHT CLUB [MH] *Redondo Beach CA*, 224
POST RANCH INN [L] *Big Sur CA*, 104
POSTRIO [R] *San Francisco CA*, 267
THE POT STICKER [R] *San Francisco CA*, 267
PREGO [R] *Beverly Hills CA*, 102
PREGO [R] *San Francisco CA*, 267
PREMIER INN [M] *Phoenix AZ*, 55
PRESCOTT COUNTRY INN [I] *Prescott AZ*, 60
THE PRESCOTT HOTEL [I] *San Francisco CA*, 262
PRESCOTT MINING COMPANY [R] *Prescott AZ*, 61
PRIMI [R] *Los Angeles CA*, 174
PROSPECT PARK [R] *Santa Rosa CA*, 291
PROSPECT PARK INN [I] *La Jolla (San Diego) CA*, 155
PROSPECTOR SQUARE HOTEL [RO] *Park City UT*, 360
PRUNEYARD INN [MH] *San Jose CA*, 273
PUB'S PRIME RIB [R] *Salinas CA*, 232
PUDDING CREEK INN [I] *Fort Bragg CA*, 133
PUNTA MORRO [I] *Ensenada, Baja California, Mexico CA*, 128
PUNTA MORRO [R] *Ensenada, Baja California, Mexico CA*, 129
PYGMALION HOUSE [I] *Santa Rosa CA*, 291

QUAIL LODGE RESORT & GOLF CLUB [L] *Carmel CA*, 113
QUAILS INN [M] *Escondido CA*, 129
QUALITY INN [All M except where noted]
Arizona
    Cottonwood, 37; *Flagstaff*, [MH] 38;
    Kingman, 44; *Mesa*, 46; *Phoenix*,
    [MH] 55; *Sedona*, 67; *South Rim
    (Grand Canyon National Park)*, 41;
    Tucson, 77
California
    Anaheim, [MH] 92; *Bakersfield*, 97;
    Hemet, 143; *Lompoc*, [MH] 161; *Los
    Angeles Intl
    Airport Area*, [H] 176; *Mammoth
    Lakes*, 178; *Pacific Grove*, 202; *Palm
    Springs*, 207; *Petaluma*, 215;
    Rancho Cordova, [MH] 220; *San
    Francisco*, [H] 260; *San Mateo*, [MH]
    278; *San Rafael*, [MH] 279; *Santa
    Clara*, [MH] 285; *Vacaville*, 309
Utah
    Beaver, 347; *Cedar City*, 351;
    Richfield, 364; *Salt Lake City*, 370
QUALITY SUITES [All MH except where noted]
California
    Pismo Beach, 216; *San Clemente*, [H]
    234; *San Diego*, 241; *San Luis*

Mobil Travel Guide

Order Form

If you would like other editions of MOBIL TRAVEL GUIDES that might not be available at your local bookstore or Mobil dealer, please use the order form below.

Ship to:

Name _____

Address: _____

City _____ State _____ Zip _____

☐ My check is enclosed.

☐ Please charge my credit card

☐ VISA ☐ MasterCard

Credit Card # _____ Expiration _____

Signature _____

Please send me the following Mobil Travel Guides:

☐ B016 **California & the West** (Arizona, California, Nevada, Utah)
$13.95

☐ B017 **Great Lakes Area** (Illinois, Indiana, Michigan, Ohio, Wisconsin, Canada: Major Cities Ontario)
$13.95

☐ B018 **Middle Atlantic States** (Delaware, District of Columbia, Maryland, New Jersey, North Carolina, Pennsylvania, South Carolina, Virginia, West Virginia)
$13.95

☐ B019 **Northeastern States** (Connecticut, Maine, Massachusetts, New Hampshire, New York, Rhode Island, Vermont, Canada: Major Cities Atlantic Provinces, Ontario, Quebec)
$13.95

☐ B020 **Northwest & Great Plains States** (Idaho, Iowa, Minnesota, Montana, Nebraska, North Dakota, Oregon, South Dakota, Washington, Wyoming, Canada: Major Cities Alberta, British Columbia, Manitoba)
$13.95

☐ B021 **Southeastern States** (Alabama, Florida, Georgia, Kentucky, Mississippi, Tennessee)
$13.95

☐ B022 **Southwest & South Central Area** (Arkansas, Colorado, Kansas, Louisiana, Missouri, New Mexico, Oklahoma, Texas)
$13.95

☐ B023 **Frequent Traveler's Guide to Major Cities** (Detailed coverage of 46 major cities, plus airport and street maps)
$14.95

Total cost of book(s) ordered $ _____

Shipping & Handling (please add $2 for first book, $1 each additional book) $ _____

Add applicable sales tax* $ _____

TOTAL AMOUNT ENCLOSED $ _____

Please mail this form to:

Mobil Travel Guides
P.O. Box 493
Mt. Morris, IL 61054
815-734-1104

*To ensure that all orders are processed efficiently, please apply sales tax in Canada and in the following states: CA, CT, FL, IL, NJ, NY, TN and WA.

Mobil Travel Guide

California and the West

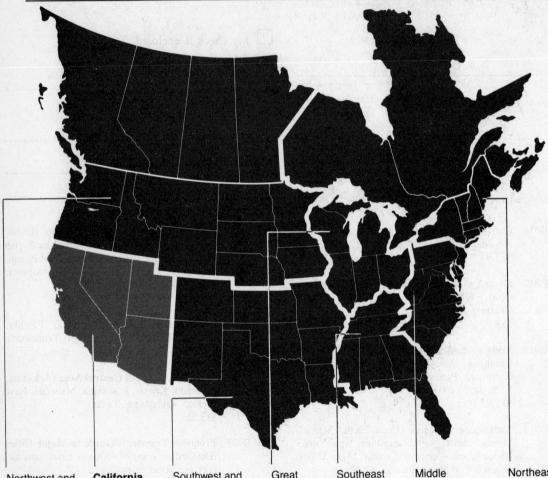

Northwest and Great Plains

Idaho
Iowa
Minnesota
Montana
Nebraska
North Dakota
Oregon
South Dakota
Washington
Wyoming

Canada:
Alberta
British Columbia
Manitoba

California and the West

Arizona
California
Nevada
Utah

Southwest and South Central

Arkansas
Colorado
Kansas
Louisiana
Missouri
New Mexico
Oklahoma
Texas

Great Lakes

Illinois
Indiana
Michigan
Ohio
Wisconsin

Canada:
Ontario

Southeast

Alabama
Florida
Georgia
Kentucky
Mississippi
Tennessee

Middle Atlantic

Delaware
District of Columbia
Maryland
New Jersey
North Carolina
Pennsylvania
South Carolina
Virginia
West Virginia

Northeast

Connecticut
Maine
Massachusetts
New Hampshire
New York
Rhode Island
Vermont

Canada:
Atlantic Provinces
Ontario
Quebec

Mobil Travel Guide.
THE GUIDE THAT SAVES YOU MONEY WHEN YOU TRAVEL.

UP TO 10% OFF

5,000 Locations Worldwide. Computerized Driving Directions.

Receive 5% off leisure daily, weekly, weekend, and monthly rates. Compact and larger cars. -OR- Receive 10% off standard daily, weekly, weekend, and monthly rates. On all car classes.

Call **(800)** 654-220 for reservations.
Request CDP **ID# 289259** Taste Publications International.

OFFER EXPIRES DECEMBER 31, 1994

CHOICE HOTELS
INTERNATIONAL

10% OFF

The next time you're traveling, call 1-800-4-CHOICE and request, "The Mobil Travel Guide Discount." You'll save 10% at thousands of participating Choice Hotels around the world!

With your 10% Traveler's Discount, the Choices - and savings- are better. So, call **1-800-4-CHOICE** today!

Advance reservations are required through 1-800-4-CHOICE. Discounts are based on availability at participating hotels and cannot be used in conjunction with any other discounts or promotions.

OFFER EXPIRES DECEMBER 31, 1994

THEATRE DISCOUNT

Please send _____ tickets at $4.00 each.
(Please add $1.00 to cover handling. Allow 2-3 weeks for delivery.)
Please fill out the form on the reverse side.

Tickets may not be used during the first two weeks of a first-run engagement or for "no-pass shows." Passes have expiration dates, generally one year from purchase.
Valid at all participating theatres. No refunds or exchanges.

OFFER EXPIRES DECEMBER 31, 1994

FREE FANNY PACK

Yours free when you join NPCA Now! Join NPCA and save our national treasures! We are offering a special one-year introductory membership for only $15! Enjoy the many benefits of an NPCA membership and receive: A free National Parks and Conservation Association Fanny Pack. A free PARK-PAK--Travel Information Kit. An annual subscription to the award-winning National Parks Magazine. Access to the NPCA"See the World, Save the Parks" rebate travel program, unforgettable naturalist-led tours, the NPCA discount photo service, car rental discounts and more.
SEE REVERSE FOR ORDER FORM.

OFFER EXPIRES DECEMBER 31, 1994

50% OFF

One Hour MotoPhoto invites you to enjoy
50% off processing and printing.

Valid at all participating locations nationally. Limit one roll per coupon, per family, per visit. Coupon must be presented at time of processing. May not be used in conjunction with any other discount or special promotion.

OFFER EXPIRES DECEMBER 31, 1994

7007 Sea World Drive
Orlando, FL 32821 • (407) 351-3600

UP TO $15 OFF

Sea World of Florida invites you to enjoy $2.50 off per person. Experience a day of real life adventures at Sea World of Florida, the world's most popular marine life park.

Limit six guests per coupon. Not valid with other discounts or on purchase of multi-park/multi-visit passes or tickets. Present coupon before bill is totaled. Redeemable only on date of attendance. Coupon has no cash value. Prices subject to change without notice.

OFFER EXPIRES DECEMBER 31, 1994 4242 / 4241

TRAVEL

5% OFF

Save at least 5% and sometimes as much as 40% off the lowest fare you can find to these destinations:
• California • Florida • New York • Europe
1-800-723-8889

SEE REVERSE FOR DETAILS.

OFFER EXPIRES DECEMBER 31, 1994

Sea World of California   Sea World of Texas

15% OFF

Sea World of California and Sea World of Texas invite you to enjoy 15% off admission.

Present this coupon at any Sea World ticket window. One coupon is good for your entire group (limit six). Not valid with any other discount, special event, special pricing, senior discount or 12- Month Pass purchase. Not for sale. An Anheuser-Busch Theme Park. ©1993 Sea World, Inc.

CA
A-3718 C-3717

TX
A-22398 C-22399

OFFER EXPIRES DECEMBER 31, 1994

Read each coupon carefully before using. Discounts only apply to the items and terms specified in the offer at participating locations. Remove the coupon you wish to use.

CHOICE HOTELS
I N T E R N A T I O N A L

Enjoy convenient, relaxing rooms at Sleep, Comfort, Quality, Clarion, Friendship, Econo Lodge and Rodeway hotels and much more! 1,400 Choice hotels will provide a free continental breakfast and children 18 and younger stay free when they share the same room as their parents.

TASTE PUBLICATIONS INTERNATIONAL

TASTE PUBLICATIONS INTERNATIONAL

❏ Yes! I want to preserve and protect our National Parks by becoming a National Parks and Conservation Association Member.
❏ I enclose a check for $15 for my one-year trial membership.
❏ Charge my $15 annual dues to my ❏ Visa ❏ MasterCard

Acct. #: _____ Exp. Date:_____

Signature: _____

Name: _____

Address: _____

City: _____ State: _____ Zip: _____

Phone: _____

Please allow 6-8 weeks for delivery of your first issue of National Parks Magazine.

TASTE PUBLICATIONS INTERNATIONAL   GA94

---

amc.

Make check payable to:
TASTE PUBLICATIONS INTERNATIONAL,
1031 Cromwell Bridge Road, Baltimore, MD 21286.
To process your order, a self-addressed, stamped envelope must be enclosed.

NAME _____

ADDRESS _____

CITY_____STATE____ZIP _____

TASTE PUBLICATIONS INTERNATIONAL

Orlando, Florida

TASTE PUBLICATIONS INTERNATIONAL

TASTE PUBLICATIONS INTERNATIONAL

Sea World of California, the world-renown marine life park, features sharks, penguins, sea lions, dolphins and of course, Shamu. Pleae call (619) 226-3901 for operating times.

Sea World of Texas is the world's largest (250 acres) marine life park and family entertainment showplace. Don't miss the all new Lost Lagoon, our 5-acre water adventure area featuring surf, sand and sun. Please call (210) 523-3000 for operating times.

TASTE PUBLICATIONS INTERNATIONAL

Just find the lowest available airlane rate for the dates and times you wish to travel, then call the travel hotline; you will be offered two options:
1. Option - will offer your exact same itinerary for 5% off the price.
2. Option - will offer you a travel alternative at a lower price.

TASTE PUBLICATIONS INTERNATIONAL

Mobil Travel Guide®

THE GUIDE THAT SAVES YOU MONEY WHEN YOU TRAVEL.

NATIONAL AMUSEMENTS

THEATRE DISCOUNT

Please send _____ tickets at $4.25 each.
(Please add $1.00 to cover handling. Allow 2-3 weeks for delivery.)
Please fill out the form on the reverse side.

Tickets may not be used during the first two weeks of a first-run engagement or for "no-pass shows." Passes have expiration dates, generally one year from purchase.
Valid at all participating theatres. No refunds or exchanges.
OFFER EXPIRES DECEMBER 31, 1994

GUEST QUARTERS® SUITE HOTELS
WEEKENDER CLUB

FREE WEEKEND NIGHT & DINING DISCOUNT

Join the Guest Quarters Weekender Club and get one free weekend night, plus a 33% dining discount.

And enjoy our special club low weekday and weekend rates.
Call **1-800-258-8826** to join.

OFFER EXPIRES DECEMBER 31, 1994

Denny's

1/2 PRICE ENTREE

Denny's invites you to enjoy any entree on our menu and get a second entree (same or lesser value) for half price.

One coupon per person per visit. No take-out orders. Not valid with any other offer or coupon. Only the lower priced entree will be discounted.

Denny's is committed to providing the best possible service to all customers regardless of race, creed or national origin.
OFFER EXPIRES DECEMBER 31, 1994

FREE CAMPING STAY

Rent a KOA Deal Motor Home from Cruise America and stay free at any participating KOA Kampground.

Call **800-327-7778** for reservations and request a KOA Deal Motor Home rental.

OFFER EXPIRES DECEMBER 31, 1994

$3 OFF

For information, call (818) 622-3794.
100 Universal City Plaza
Universal City, CA 91608

Universal Studios Hollywood invites you to enjoy $3 off the regular admission price per person. Valid for up to 4 people.

This coupon cannot be combined with any other offer or with per capita sight-seeing tours.
Not valid for separately ticketed events.

OFFER EXPIRES DECEMBER 31, 1994

5% - 25% OFF

Receive 5% off weekend, weekly and monthly rates.
or
Receive 25% off select daily business rates.
Call **1-800-CAR RENT**℠ for reservations.
Request Recap **#5708785** Taste Publications International.

Optional Loss Damage is $7.99-$13.99 per day depending on location and subject to change. Rates may include unlimited mileage or 100 miles per day with a per mile charge thereafter.

OFFER EXPIRES DECEMBER 31, 1994

CAMPING WORLD®
RV Accessories and Supplies

SPECIAL OFFER

To receive your free catalog and 10% off certificate, please fill out this form and mail to address on back or call **(800) 626-5944** and mention code number in lower right corner.

Name _____
Address _____ Apt./Lot _____
City _____ State ____ Zip _____
OFFER EXPIRES DECEMBER 31, 1994   1006

TASTEE-FREEZ.

ONE FREE SMALL CONE

Tastee Freez invites you to enjoy one free small cone when a second small cone of equal or greater value is purchased.

Valid at all participating locations nationally.

OFFER EXPIRES DECEMBER 31, 1994

TASTE PUBLICATIONS INTERNATIONAL

NATIONAL AMUSEMENTS

Make check payable to:
TASTE PUBLICATIONS INTERNATIONAL,
1031 Cromwell Bridge Road, Baltimore, MD 21286.
To process your order, a self-addressed, stamped envelope must be enclosed.

NAME _____

ADDRESS _____

CITY _____ STATE _____ ZIP _____

TASTE PUBLICATIONS INTERNATIONAL

KOA has over 600 locations
throughout the U.S. and Canada.

Cruise America and Cruise Canada
have over 100 centers.

TASTE PUBLICATIONS INTERNATIONAL

TASTE PUBLICATIONS INTERNATIONAL

National Inter rent

1. Valid at participating National locations in the U.S. Program not available on tour packages or certain other promotional rates. Subject to availability of cars and blackout dates. Time parameters, local rental and minimum rental day requirements may apply. Check at time of reservation. 2. Advance reservations are recommended. 3. Rates higher in some cities. 4. Standard rental qualifications apply. Minimum rental age at most locations is 25. 5. In addition to rental charges, renter is responsible for: • Optional Loss Damage Waiver is $7.99-$13.99 per day depending on location and subject to change; per mile charge in excess of mileage allowance. • Taxes; additional charges if car is not returned within prescribed rental period; drop charge and additional driver fee if applicable; optional refueling charge; Personal Accident Insurance/Personal Effects Coverage, Supplemental Liability Insurance (where available). 6. Program subject to change without notice and void where prohibited by law, taxed or otherwise restricted.

TASTE PUBLICATIONS INTERNATIONAL

TASTE PUBLICATIONS INTERNATIONAL

TASTE PUBLICATIONS INTERNATIONAL

RV Accessories and Supplies
Camping World
Three Springs Road
P.O. Box 90017
Bowling Green, KY 42102-9017

TASTE PUBLICATIONS INTERNATIONAL

Mobil Travel Guide®

THE GUIDE THAT SAVES YOU MONEY WHEN YOU TRAVEL.

 PREMIER'S BIG RED BOAT America's Travel Agent.

UP TO 25% OFF

The Official Cruise Line of Walt Disney World. **and International Tours & Cruises™**

Premier and IT invite you to enjoy up to 25% off a cruise or cruise & Disney resort stay.

Discount is based on two people per cabin. Choose from 3, 4 or 7 day cruise/resort vacation. Offer is not available during holiday dates. Subject to availability. May not be used in conjunction with any other special promotion or discount. For reservations, call International Tours and Cruises at **(800) BUY-TRAVEL (USA)** or **(212) 242-2277 (NYC).**

OFFER EXPIRES DECEMBER 31, 1994

 **Sheraton®**

CORPORATE RATE

Receive the guaranteed corporate rate at all participating Sheraton Hotels.

Call **(800) 325-7823** for reservations.
Request ID# **98251** Taste Publications International.

Please keep a record of your confirmation number.

OFFER EXPIRES DECEMBER 31, 1994

 **I Can't Believe It's Yogurt!** GREAT TASTE - NATURALLY

ONE FREE REGULAR OR LARGE CUP OR CONE

I Can't Believe It's Yogurt invites you to enjoy one free regular or large cup or cone when a second regular or large cup or cone of equal or greater value is purchased.

Valid at all participating full-sized stores. One coupon per customer, please. May not be used in conjunction with any other offer. Offer good for soft serve frozen yogurt only.

OFFER EXPIRES DECEMBER 31, 1994

 Alamo Rent A Car

ASSOCIATION DISCOUNT

- Guaranteed Low Flat Rate
- Unlimited Free Mileage
- Frequent Flyer Credits with Delta, Pan Am and United Airlines

Call **(800) 732-3232** for reservations.
Request ID# **BY 201598** Taste Publications International.

Advance reservations required.

OFFER EXPIRES DECEMBER 31, 1994

 **FOTOMAT**

50% OFF

Coupon valid at all Fotomat locations.
Call **1-800-568-FOTO** for a Fotomat near you.

Fotomat invites you to enjoy 50% off any Fotomat film purchase at the regular price.

Present this coupon and receive 50% off your Fotomat film purchase. Valid on Fotomat film only. Not valid with any other coupon or promotional offer.

OFFER EXPIRES DECEMBER 31, 1994

 **QUINTEX CELLULAR**

MOTOROLA DPC 500 FLIP PHONE FOR $199 (Retail value is $349).

To receive your Motorola DPC 500 flip phone for $199
Call 1-800-550-0600
Customer will recieve an information kit and credit application. Follow the directions inside and mail completed forms in envelope provided. Offer available to new activations only. Credit approval required. Minimum one year service agreement with carrier of our choice. Customer is responsible for the activation fee and shipping and handling charges. Please allow 2-3 weeks for delivery. Other restrictions apply. Limit 2 phones per customer.

OFFER EXPIRES DECEMBER 31, 1994

 **GENERAL CINEMA THEATRES**

THEATRE DISCOUNT

Please send _____ tickets at $4.50 each.
(Please add $1.00 to cover handling. Allow 2-3 weeks for delivery.)
Please fill out the form on the reverse side.

Tickets may not be used during the first two weeks of a first-run engagement or for "no-pass shows." Passes have expiration dates, generally one year from purchase.
Valid at all participating theatres. No refunds or exchanges.

OFFER EXPIRES DECEMBER 31, 1994

AMERICA at 50% Discount®

60 DAY FREE TRIAL OFFER

Enjoy 50% off at over 1,300 hotels and motels coast to coast, valid anytime. Plus 5% instant cash rebate on airline tickets, savings on car rentals, condominiums, cruises and more.

First 60 days are free, then $24.95 annually.

Satisfaction guaranteed or your current year's membership fee will be refunded in full

See reverse for order form.

OFFER EXPIRES DECEMBER 31, 1994

Sheraton

TASTE PUBLICATIONS INTERNATIONAL

PREMIER'S BIG RED BOAT

The Official Cruise Line of Walt Disney World

America's Travel Agent

and International Tours & Cruises™

TASTE PUBLICATIONS INTERNATIONAL

TASTE PUBLICATIONS INTERNATIONAL

TASTE PUBLICATIONS INTERNATIONAL

Quintex Cellular, a national cellular network, wants you to remember us as the superstore in cellular with 72 locations nationwide.
So to get in touch stay in touch with Quintex.
Certificate is valid with phone order or in store purchase.
Cellular service may not be available in all areas.

TASTE PUBLICATIONS INTERNATIONAL

TASTE PUBLICATIONS INTERNATIONAL

AMERICA at 50% Discount®
1031 Cromwell Bridge Road, Baltimore, MD 21286.

Yes, I want to start saving now with America at 50% Discount® I understand that if I do not cancel before the end of the sixty (60) day introductory period, the $24.95 annual fee will be charged to the credit card indicated below. To ensure uninterrupted service, my membership will automatically be renewed annually charged to my credit card indicated below. I understand that I am under no obligation to continue my membership beyond the sixty day trial.

Form of payment ❑ VISA ❑ MasterCard

Acct. #:_____ Exp. Date:_____

Signature:_____

Name:_____

Address:_____

City:_____ State:_____ Zip:_____

TASTE PUBLICATIONS INTERNATIONAL

GENERAL CINEMA
T HEATRES

Make check payable to:
TASTE PUBLICATIONS INTERNATIONAL,
1031 Cromwell Bridge Road, Baltimore, MD 21286.
To process your order, a self-addressed, stamped envelope must be enclosed.

NAME _____

ADDRESS _____

CITY_____ STATE_____ ZIP_____

TASTE PUBLICATIONS INTERNATIONAL

Mobil Travel Guide.
THE GUIDE THAT SAVES YOU MONEY WHEN YOU TRAVEL.

TWO FREE SHOW TICKETS

Harrah's invites you to enjoy two free show tickets at Harrah's Atlantic City, Lake Tahoe, Las Vegas or Reno locations.

For show schedule and reservations call
1-800-HARRAHS (1-800-427-7247).

Coupon redeemable Sunday thru Friday.

OFFER EXPIRES DECEMBER 31, 1994   MBL

CORPORATE RATE

Receive the guaranteed corporate rate at all participating Days Inns, Hotels and Suites.
Call **(800) 422-1115** for reservations.
Request ID# **990-000-2865** Taste Publications International.

Please keep a record of your confirmation number.

OFFER EXPIRES DECEMBER 31, 1994

AVIS.

ASSOCIATION DISCOUNT

- Full Line of Fine GM Cars
- Over 3,500 Locations
- Emergency Road Service

Call **(800) 331-1212** for reservations.
Request AWD # **A291800** Taste Publications International.
Advance reservations required.

OFFER EXPIRES DECEMBER 31, 1994

50% OFF

Sbarro invites you to enjoy 50% off one entree when a second entree of equal or greater value is purchased.

Valid at any of the 600 Sbarro locations nationwide.
This coupon may not be used in conjunction
with any other discounts or promotions.

OFFER EXPIRES DECEMBER 31, 1994

ORVIS®

15% OFF

Orvis invites you to enjoy 15% off your first order.
Call for free catalog...**1-800-815-5900**.
Ask for Key Offer **#TR101**.

Orvis Travel offers you the finest in accessories, apparel and distinctive luggage
for today's active travel lifestyle, whether by car, plane or train.
Travel in comfort and style with Orvis.

Orvis...America's Oldest Mail Order Catalog...A New England Tradition Since 1856.

OFFER EXPIRES DECEMBER 31, 1994

20-60% OFF

Save up to 60% on 5-7 day Regency Cruises* to the Caribbean, Panama Canal, Can Cun or 2 day cruises to nowhere.

Call 1-800-925-1114.

*Selected sailing dates.

OFFER EXPIRES DECEMBER 31, 1994

---

merry maids.

$10 OFF

Drop your mop! Enjoy a clean home and save $10 on your first Merry Maids visit. Bonded, trained and insured. Weekly, bi-weekly or one-time services. Satisfaction guaranteed. To arrange for a free written quote, check the Yellow Pages, or call **1-800-WE SERVE** for the Merry Maids nearest you.

Available only at participating offices. New customers only. This coupon may

Quality Service Network
ServiceMaster • Terminix • TruGreen
Merry Maids • American Home Shield

not be used in conjunction with any other discounts or promotions.

OFFER EXPIRES DECEMBER 31, 1994

UP TO $20 IN FREE CALLING CARD CALLS

When you sign up for the MCI Card®, you'll automatically receive up to $20 in free calling card calls! Just call **1-800-944-9119**. Remember, you don't have to switch your residential long distance service to take advantage of the free MCI Card!

You will receive a credit for up to $20 on your third monthly invoice.
Credit will not exceed invoice usage.

OFFER EXPIRES DECEMBER 31, 1994

TASTE PUBLICATIONS INTERNATIONAL

Harrah's
CASINOS

Terms and conditions:
- Subject to availability; headliner shows excluded.
- Reservations must be made in advance (except in Las Vegas).
- Offer is valid through December 31, 1994; some dates may be unavailable.
- Must be 21; one coupon per person.
- Offer is not valid with any other promotion.
- Program subject to change or cancellation without notice.
- The following information must be completed prior to redemption.

Name_____
Street Address_____
City_____State_____Zip_____
Date of Birth_____   Gambling Problem? Call 1-800-GAMBLER.

TASTE PUBLICATIONS INTERNATIONAL   MBL

TASTE PUBLICATIONS INTERNATIONAL

TASTE PUBLICATIONS INTERNATIONAL

TASTE PUBLICATIONS INTERNATIONAL

ORVIS

Save 15% on your first order.
Choose from any item in our award-winning travel catalog, including:
- Distinctive Sportsman's Luggage
- Travel Accessories and Gadgets
- Classic Clothing Designed Just for the Traveler
Call for your free catalog today: **1-800-815-5900.**
Ask for key offer #**TR101**.
Orvis...Serving America Since 1856

TASTE PUBLICATIONS INTERNATIONAL

THE MCI CARD IS SIMPLE TO USE.
Unlike AT&T's standard interstate Calling Card, you follow the same simple dialing method to use the MCI Card® from any phone in the U.S., anytime. Easy-to-follow voice instructions then guide you through each step of your call. And your MCI Card lets you make multiple calls without hanging up and redialing.

AND THE MCI CARD NUMBER IS EASIER TO REMEMBER.
Your MCI Card number will most likely be your own home phone number plus a 4-digit number selected by you. That's a lot easier to remember than the scrambled 14-digit authorization numbers AT&T assigns you!

TASTE PUBLICATIONS INTERNATIONAL

merry maids

TASTE PUBLICATIONS INTERNATIONAL